Simply Visual Basic® .NET 2003

Deitel Books, Cyber Classrooms, Complete Training Courses and Web-Based Training Courses
Published by Prentice Hall

Simply Series

Simply C#®: An Application-Driven Tutorial Approach

Simply Visual Basic® .NET: An Application Driven Tutorial Approach (Visual Studio .NET 2002 Edition)

Simply Java™ Programming: An Application-Driven Tutorial Approach

Simply Visual Basic® .NET: An Application Driven Tutorial Approach (Visual Studio .NET 2003 Edition)

How to Program Series

Advanced Java™ 2 Platform How to Program
C How to Program, 4/E
C++ How to Program, 4/E
C# ® How to Program
e-Business and e-Commerce How to Program
Internet and World Wide Web How to Program, 2/E
Java™ How to Program, 5/E
Perl How to Program
Python How to Program
Visual Basic® 6 How to Program
Visual Basic® .NET How to Program, 2/E
Visual C++® .NET How to Program
Wireless Internet & Mobile Business How to Program
XML How to Program

.NET How to Program Series

C#® How to Program
Visual Basic® .NET How to Program, 2/E
Visual C++® .NET How to Program

Visual Studio Series

C#® How to Program
Getting Started with Microsoft® Visual C++® 6 with an Introduction to MFC
Simply C#®: An Application-Driven Tutorial Approach
Simply Visual Basic® .NET: An Application- Driven Tutorial Approach (Visual Studio .NET 2002 Edition)
Simply Visual Basic® .NET: An Application- Driven Tutorial Approach (Visual Studio .NET 2003 Edition)
Visual Basic® 6 How to Program
Visual Basic® .NET How to Program, 2/E
Visual C++® .NET How to Program

CS1 Programming Series

Java™ Software Design

For Managers Series

e-Business and e-Commerce for Managers

DEITEL® Developer Series

Java™ Web Services for Experienced Programmers
Web Services A Technical Introduction

Multimedia Cyber Classroom Series

C++ Multimedia Cyber Classroom, 4/E
C# Multimedia Cyber Classroom
e-Business and e-Commerce Multimedia Cyber Classroom
Internet and World Wide Web Multimedia Cyber Classroom, 2/E
Java™ 2 Multimedia Cyber Classroom, 5/E
Perl Multimedia Cyber Classroom
Python Multimedia Cyber Classroom
Visual Basic® 6 Multimedia Cyber Classroom
Visual Basic® .NET Multimedia Cyber Classroom, 2/E
Wireless Internet & Mobile Business Programming Multimedia Cyber Classroom
XML Multimedia Cyber Classroom

The Complete Training Course Series

The Complete C++ Training Course, 4/E
The Complete C#® Training Course
The Complete e-Business and e-Commerce Programming Training Course
The Complete Internet and World Wide Web Programming Training Course, 2/E
The Complete Java™ 2 Training Course, 5/E
The Complete Perl Training Course
The Complete Python Training Course
The Complete Visual Basic® 6 Training Course
The Complete Visual Basic® .NET Training Course, 2/E
The Complete Wireless Internet & Mobile Business Programming Training Course
The Complete XML Programming Training Course

Computer Science Series

Operating Systems, 3/E

To communicate with the authors, send e-mail to:

deitel@deitel.com

For information on corporate on-site seminars and public seminars offered by Deitel & Associates, Inc. worldwide, visit:

www.deitel.com

For continuing updates on Prentice Hall and Deitel publications visit:

www.deitel.com,
www.prenhall.com/deitel or
www.InformIT.com/deitel

Simply Visual Basic® .NET 2003

H. M. Deitel
Deitel & Associates, Inc.

P. J. Deitel
Deitel & Associates, Inc.

C. H. Yaeger
Deitel & Associates, Inc.

Upper Saddle River, NJ 07458

Library of Congress Cataloging-in-Publication Data

On file

Vice President and Editorial Director, ECS: *Marcia J. Horton*
Senior Acquisitions Editor: *Kate Hargett*
Assistant Editor: *Sarah Parker*
Project Manager: *Carole Snyder*
Vice President and Director of Production and Manufacturing, ESM: *David W. Riccardi*
Executive Managing Editor: *Vince O'Brien*
Managing Editor: *Tom Manshreck*
Production Editor: *John F. Lovell*
Production Editor, Media: *Bob Engelhardt*
Director of Creative Services: *Paul Belfanti*
Creative Director: *Carole Anson*
Chapter Opener and Cover Designer: *Tamara L. Newnam, Dr. Harvey Deitel*
Interior Design: *Jonathan Boylan, John Root, Dr. Harvey Deitel*
Interior Design Assistance: *Geoffrey Cassar*
Manufacturing Manager: *Trudy Pisciotti*
Manufacturing Buyer: *Lisa McDowell*
Marketing Manager: *Pamela Shaffer*
Marketing Assistant: *Barrie Reinhold*

Printed in the United States of America

10 9 8 7 6 5 4 3 2 1

ISBN 0-13-142640-0

Pearson Education Ltd., *London*
Pearson Education Australia Pty. Ltd., *Sydney*
Pearson Education Singapore, Pte. Ltd.
Pearson Education North Asia Ltd., *Hong Kong*
Pearson Education Canada, Inc., *Toronto*
Pearson Educación de Mexico, S.A. de C.V.
Pearson Education–Japan, *Tokyo*
Pearson Education Malaysia, Pte. Ltd.
Pearson Education, Inc., *Upper Saddle River, New Jersey*

In memory of Phyllis Gippetti
whose smile brought joy to her family and friends.

Barbara, Harvey, Paul and Abbey Deitel

To Gabriela Toth:
I wish you the best of luck in all your endeavors.

Cheryl

Trademarks:

Brief Table of Contents

CONTENTS

PREFACE

Welcome to Visual Basic .NET and the world of Windows, Internet and World-Wide-Web programming with Visual Studio and the .NET platform! This book, which is part of our new *Simply* series, has been updated based on Visual Studio .NET 2003. Our goal was to write a book that focuses on core concepts and features of Visual Basic .NET while keeping the discussion of this highly technical subject as simple as possible.

To achieve these goals, we implemented an innovative teaching methodology. We present the core concepts of leading-edge computing technologies using the tutorial-based, APPLICATION-DRIVEN approach, combined with the DEITEL® signature LIVE-CODE approach of teaching programming using complete, working, real-world applications. We merged the notion of a lab manual with that of a conventional textbook, creating a book that works well in a traditional classroom setting or with students sitting at computers and building each example application as they read the tutorials.

As students work through the tutorials, they learn about Visual Basic .NET and its fundamental features, such as visual programming concepts, graphical-user-interface (GUI) components, multimedia (audio, images, animation and video), file processing, database processing and Internet and World-Wide-Web-based client/server networking. At the end of most sections, we provide self-review questions with answers so that students receive immediate feedback on their understanding of the material. Hundreds of additional self-review questions with answers are available on this book's Companion Web Site.

Features in Simply Visual Basic .NET 2003

This book is loaded with pedagogic features, including:

- **APPLICATION-DRIVEN *Tutorial Approach*.** Each tutorial uses a contemporary, real-world application to teach programming concepts. The examples and exercises are up-to-the-minute with Internet/Web-related examples and with popular applications, such as ATMs, game playing, graphics, multimedia and even a 3-tier Web-based bookstore. Most examples have a business focus. At the beginning of each tutorial, students "test-drive" the completed application so they can see how it works. Then they build the application by following our step-by-step instructions. The book concentrates on the principles of good software engineering and stresses program clarity.

- ***LIVE-CODE Approach.*** This book contains several LIVE-CODE examples. Each tutorial ends with the complete, working program code and the students can run the application that they just created. We call this method of teaching and writing the ***LIVE-CODE Approach***. We feel that this approach is more effective than presenting only snippets of code out of the context of a complete application.

- ***Real-World Technologies.*** This text incorporates today's technologies to develop useful applications. For example, we use the Unified Modeling Language™ (UML) to replace flowcharts—an older standard. The UML has become the preferred graphical modeling language for designing object-oriented applications. In *Simply Visual Basic .NET 2003*, we use UML to show the flow of control for several control statements, so students gain practice reading the type of diagrams that are used in industry.

■ ***Visual Programming and Graphical User Interface (GUI).*** From the first tutorial, we immerse students in visual programming techniques and modifying Visual Basic .NET GUIs. Students who learn these techniques can create graphical programs more quickly and easily. The early tutorials provide students with a foundation for designing GUIs—concepts that they will apply throughout the book as we teach core programming concepts. Many tutorials contain GUI Design Tips that are summarized at the end of the tutorials for easy reference. Appendix C compiles all the GUI Design Tips to help students as they prepare for exams.

■ ***Full-Color Presentation.*** This book is in full color so that students can see sample outputs as they would appear on a monitor. Also, we syntax color the Visual Basic .NET code, similar to the way Visual Studio .NET colors the code in its editor window. This way, students can match what they see in the book with what they see on their own screens. Our syntax-coloring conventions are as follows:

```
comments appear in green
keywords appear in dark blue
literal values appear in light blue
text, class, method, variable and property names appear in black
errors appear in red
```

■ ***Graphics and Multimedia.*** Graphics make applications fun to create and use. In our introduction to graphics, Tutorial 26, we discuss Graphical Device Interface (GDI+)—the Windows service that provides the graphical features used by .NET—to teach students to personalize a bank check. In Tutorial 27, we use a fun technology called Microsoft Agent to add interactive, animated characters to a phone book application. With Microsoft Agent, your applications can speak to users and even respond to their voice commands!

■ ***Databases.*** Databases are crucial to businesses today, and we use real-world applications to teach the fundamentals of database programming. Tutorials 25 and 30 familiarize students with databases, presented in the context of two applications—an ATM and a Web-based bookstore.

■ ***Case Study.*** This book includes a sequence of four tutorials in which the student builds a Web-based bookstore application. Tutorial 28 familiarizes readers with Microsoft's Internet Information Services (which enables Web publishing), multi-tier architecture and simple Web transactions. Tutorials 29–31 use ASP .NET and ADO .NET to build an application that retrieves information from a database and displays the information in a Web page.

■ ***Object-Oriented Programming.*** Object-oriented programming is the most widely employed technique for developing robust, reusable software, and Visual Basic .NET offers advanced object-oriented programming features. This book introduces students to defining classes and using objects, laying a solid foundation for future programming courses.

■ ***Visual Studio .NET Debugger.*** Debuggers help programmers find and correct logic errors in program code. Visual Studio .NET 2003 contains a powerful debugging tool that allows programmers to analyze their programs line-by-line as they execute. Throughout the book, we teach the Visual Studio .NET 2003 Debugger; we explain how to use its key features and offer many debugging exercises.

To the Instructor

Focus of the Book

Our goal was clear: Produce a Visual Basic .NET textbook for introductory-level courses in computer programming aimed at students with little or no programming experience. This book teaches computer programming principles and the Visual Basic .NET language, including data types, control statements, object-oriented programming, Visual Basic .NET classes, GUI concepts, event-driven programming and more. After mastering the material in this book, students will be able to program in Visual Basic .NET and to employ many key capabilities of the .NET platform.

We also wanted a textbook that was up-to-date with Microsoft's latest release of Visual Studio—Visual Studio .NET 2003, which includes an updated version of Visual Basic .NET. We have rebuilt every application in this book using the 2003 software. All applications and solutions have been fully tested and run on this new platform.

A Note Regarding Software for the Book

For the educational market only, this textbook is available in a "value pack" with the Microsoft® Visual Basic® .NET Standard Edition version 2003 integrated development environment as a free supplement. The standard edition is fully functional and is shipped on 5 CDs. There is no time limit for using the software. [*Note:* If you are a professional using this publication, you will have to purchase the necessary software to build and run the applications in this textbook.]

Lab Setup

To install some of the required software for this book, students and instructors will need Administrator-level access to the computer. For university computer labs where students do not have Administrator-level access, instructors and system administrators must ensure that the proper software is installed on the lab computers. In Tutorial 27 certain Microsoft Agent software components must be installed to execute and develop the **Phone Book** application. If students are not allowed to install software on lab computers, the Microsoft Agent components discussed in Tutorial 27 must be installed in advance. To configure and execute some of the examples and exercises, such as the **Bookstore** case study in Tutorials 28–31, students will need to have Administrator-level access. In addition, some of the examples in the book require that students have Administrator access to the computer, which is typically required to develop applications in Visual Studio .NET.

A Note Regarding Terminology Used in the Book

In Tutorial 13, we discuss methods as Sub procedures (sometimes called subroutines) and Function procedures (sometimes called functions). We use this terminology for two reasons. First, the keywords Sub and Function are used in procedure definitions, so this naming is logical for students. Second, Visual Basic professionals have used this terminology for years and will continue to do so in the future. We also use the term "function" at certain points in this text to refer to Visual Basic 6 Function procedures that remain in Visual Basic .NET 2003 (such as Val and Pmt). When we introduce object-oriented programming concepts in Tutorial 19, we discuss the difference between procedures and methods and indicate that the procedures defined throughout the text are, in fact, methods. We hope our use of terminology helps you present the material in a simple and understandable manner.

Exception Handling: Bonus Tutorial (Tutorial 32)

Exception handling is one of the most important topics in Visual Basic .NET for building mission-critical and business-critical applications. Programmers need to know how to recognize the exceptions (errors) that could occur in software components and handle those exceptions effectively, allowing programs to deal with problems and continue executing instead of "crashing." Tutorial 32 overviews the proper use of exception handling, including the termination model of exception handling, throwing exceptions and catching exceptions.

Objectives

Each tutorial begins with objectives that inform students of what to expect and give them an opportunity, after reading the tutorial, to determine whether they have met the intended goals.

Outline

The tutorial outline enables students to approach the material in top-down fashion. Along with the tutorial objectives, the outline helps students anticipate future topics and set a comfortable and effective learning pace.

Example Applications (with Outputs)

We present Visual Basic .NET features in the context of complete, working Visual Basic .NET programs. We call this our LIVE-CODE approach. All examples are available on the CD that accompanies the book or as downloads from our Web site, `www.deitel.com/books/vbnetSIMPLY1_2003/index.html`.

Illustrations/Figures

An abundance of charts, line drawings and application outputs are included. The discussion of control statements, for example, features carefully drawn UML activity diagrams. [*Note:* We do not teach UML diagramming as an application-development tool, but we do use UML diagrams to explain the precise operation of many of Visual Basic .NET's control statements.]

Programming Tips

Hundreds of programming tips help students focus on important aspects of application development. These tips and practices represent the best the authors have gleaned from a combined seven decades of programming and teaching experience.

 Good Programming Practices

Good Programming Practices highlight techniques that help students write programs that are clearer, more understandable and more maintainable.

 Common Programming Errors

Students learning a language—especially in their first programming course—frequently make errors. Pointing out these *Common Programming Errors* in the text reduces the likelihood that students will make the same mistakes.

 Error Prevention Tips

These tips describe aspects of Visual Basic .NET that prevent errors from getting into programs in the first place, which simplifies the testing and debugging process.

 Performance Tips

Teaching students to write clear and understandable programs is the most important goal for a first programming course. But students want to write programs that run the fastest, use the least memory, require the smallest number of keystrokes, etc. *Performance Tips* highlight opportunities for improving program performance.

 Portability Tips

The *Portability Tips* provide insights on how Visual Basic .NET achieves its high degree of portability among .NET platforms.

 **Software Design Tips**

The *Software Design Tips* highlight architectural and design issues that affect the construction of object-oriented software systems.

 **GUI Design Tips**

The *GUI Design Tips* highlight graphical-user-interface conventions to help students design attractive, user-friendly GUIs and use GUI features. Appendix C compiles all the GUI Design Tips to help students as they prepare for exams.

Skills Summary

Each tutorial includes a bullet-list-style summary of the new programming concepts presented. This reinforces key actions taken to build the application in each tutorial.

Key Terms

Each tutorial includes a list of important terms defined in the tutorial. These terms also appear in the index and in a book-wide glossary, so the student can locate terms and their definitions quickly.

236 Self-Review Questions and Answers

Self-review multiple-choice questions and answers are included after most sections to build students' confidence with the material and prepare them for the regular exercises. Students should be encouraged to attempt all the self-review exercises and check their answers.

850 Exercises (Solutions in Instructor's Manual)

Each tutorial concludes with exercises. Typical exercises include 10 multiple-choice questions, a "What does this code do?" exercise, a "What's wrong with this code?" exercise, three programming exercises and a programming challenge. [*Note:* In the "What does this code do?" and "What's wrong with this code?" exercises, we only show portions of the code in the text.]

The questions involve simple recall of important terminology and concepts, writing individual Visual Basic .NET statements, writing small portions of Visual Basic .NET applications and writing complete Visual Basic .NET methods, classes and applications. Every programming exercise uses a step-by-step methodology to suggest how to solve the problems. The solutions for the exercises are *available only to instructors* through their Prentice-Hall representatives. [*NOTE:* **Please do not write to us requesting the instructor's manual. Distribution of this publication is strictly limited to instructors teaching from the book. Instructors may obtain the solutions manual only from their regular Prentice Hall representatives. We regret that we cannot provide the solutions to professionals.**]

GUI Design Guidelines

Consistent and proper graphical user interface design is crucial to visual programming. In each tutorial, we summarize the GUI design guidelines that were introduced. Appendix C presents a cumulative list of these GUI design guidelines for easy reference.

Controls, Events, Properties & Methods Summaries

Each tutorial includes a summary of the controls, events, properties and methods covered in the tutorial. The summary includes a picture of each control, shows the control "in action" and lists the control's properties, events and methods that were discussed up to and including that tutorial. In addition, Appendix E groups the controls by tutorial for easy reference.

Index

The extensive index includes important terms both under main headings and as separate entries so that students can search for any term or concept by keyword. The code examples and the exercises also are included in the index. Every Visual Basic .NET 2003 source-code program in the book is indexed it under the appropriate application. We also double-indexed various features, such as controls and properties. This makes it easier to find examples using particular features.

Simply Visual Basic .NET 2003 Ancillary Package

Simply Visual Basic .NET 2003 is accompanied by extensive ancillary materials for instructors, including the following:

- *Instructor's Resource CD (IRCD)* which contains the

  - *Instructor's Manual* with solutions to the end-of-tutorial exercises and

  - *Test-Item File* of multiple-choice questions (approximately two per tutorial section).

- *Customizable PowerPoint® Slides* containing all the code and figures in the text, and bulleted items that summarize the key points in the text. The slides are downloadable from `www.deitel.com/books/vbnetSIMPLY1_2003/index.html` and are available as part of Prentice Hall's *Companion Web Site* (`www.prenhall.com/deitel`) for *Simply Visual Basic .NET 2003*, which offers resources for both instructors and students.

Companion Web Site

For instructors, the *Companion Web Site* offers a *Syllabus Manager*, which helps instructors plan courses interactively and create online syllabi. Students also benefit from the functionality of the *Companion Web Site*. Book-specific resources for students include:

- PowerPoint® slides
- Example source code
- Reference materials from the book's appendices
- Tutorial objectives
- Tutorial summaries
- Tutorial outlines
- Programming tips from each tutorial
- Online Study Guide—contains additional short-answer self-review exercises with answers
- Students can track their results and course performance on quizzes using the *Student Profile* feature, which records and manages all feedback and results from tests taken on the *Companion Web Site*. To access the *Companion Web Site* for *Simply Visual Basic .NET 2003*, visit `www.prenhall.com/deitel`.

Course Management Systems

Selected content from *Simply Visual Basic .NET 2003* and other Deitel textbooks, is available to integrate into various Course Management Systems, including CourseCompass, Blackboard and WebCT. Course Management Systems help faculty create, manage and use sophisticated Web-based educational tools and programs. Blackboard, CourseCompass and WebCT offer:

- Features to create and customize an online course
- Communication tools

- Flexible testing tools
- Support materials

In addition to the tools found in Blackboard and WebCT, CourseCompass from Prentice Hall includes:

- **CourseCompass course home page**, which makes the course as easy to navigate as a book.
- **Hosting on Prentice Hall's centralized servers**, which allows course administrators to avoid separate licensing fees or server-space issues.
- **"How Do I" online-support sections** are available for users who need help personalizing course sites.
- **Instructor Quick Start Guide**

To view free online demonstrations and learn more about Course Management Systems that support Deitel content, visit the following Web sites:

- Blackboard: www.blackboard.com and www.prenhall.com/blackboard.
- WebCT: www.webct.com and www.prenhall.com/webct.
- CourseCompass: www.coursecompass.com and www.prenhall.com/coursecompass.

Acknowledgments

One of the great pleasures of writing a textbook is acknowledging the efforts of many people whose names may not appear on the cover, but whose hard work, cooperation, friendship and understanding were crucial to the production of the book. Many people at Deitel & Associates, Inc., devoted long hours to this project.

- Abbey Deitel, President
- Christi Kelsey, Director of Business Development
- Jeff Listfield, Developer
- David Choffnes, Developer
- Barbara Deitel, Chief Financial Officer
- Christina Courtemarche, Developer
- Betsy DuWaldt, Editorial Director
- Jon Liperi, Developer
- Tem Nieto, Director of Product Development
- Laura Treibick, Director of Multimedia

We would also like to thank the participants in the Deitel & Associates, Inc., College Internship Program: Jon Henry, Emanuel Achildiev, Nicholas Cassie, Thiago Lucas da Silva, Mike Dos'Santos, Jimmy Nguyen and Ngale Truong.[1]

We are fortunate to have been able to work on this project with the talented and dedicated team of publishing professionals at Prentice Hall. We especially appreciate the extraordinary efforts of our Computer Science editor, Kate Hargett and her boss—our mentor in publishing—Marcia Horton, Editorial Director of

---

1. The Deitel & Associates, Inc. College Internship Program offers a limited number of salaried positions to college students majoring in Computer Science, Information Technology, Marketing and English. Students work at our corporate headquarters in Maynard, Massachusetts full-time in the summers and (for those attending college in the Boston area) part-time during the academic year. We also offer full-time internship positions for students interested in taking a semester off from school to gain industry experience. Regular full-time positions are available to college graduates. For more information, please contact Abbey Deitel at deitel@deitel.com, visit our Web site, www.deitel.com, and subscribe to our free e-mail newsletter at www.deitel.com/newsletter/subscribe.html.

Prentice Hall's Engineering and Computer Science Team. Tom Manshreck and Vince O'Brien did a marvelous job managing the production of the book. Chirag Thakkar and John Lovell served as production editors and Sarah Parker handled editorial responsibilities on the book's extensive ancillary package. We would like to thank the design team that created a completely new look and feel for the *Simply* series—Carole Anson, Paul Belfanti, Tom Manshreck, Jonathan Boylan, John Root and Gary Gray. We would like to thank Carol Trueheart, Editor-in-Chief of Development for Prentice Hall's Engineering, Science and Math Division, and her team of developmental editors—Laura Cheu, Deena Cloud and Susan Cohen.

We wish to acknowledge the efforts of our reviewers and to thank Carole Snyder and Jennifer Capello of Prentice Hall, who managed the review process. The 42 reviewers from colleges, industry and Microsoft helped us to get this book "right." Adhering to a tight time schedule, these reviewers scrutinized the text and the programs, providing countless suggestions for improving the accuracy and completeness of the presentation. It is a privilege to have the guidance of such talented and busy professionals.

Simply Visual Basic .NET reviewers:
Cameron McColl (Microsoft)
Colin Merry (Microsoft)
Jeffrey Welton (Microsoft)
Judith Ashworth (Orillion USA, Inc.)
James Ball (Indiana State University)
Robert Benavides (Collin County Community College)
Chadi Boudiab (Georgia Perimeter College)
Charles Cadenhead (Brookhaven College)
Kunal Cheda (DotNetExtreme.com)
Mave Coxon (Lansing Community College)
Chris Crane (Independent Consultant)
Sergio Davalos (University of Washington-Tacoma)
David Fullerton (Yeshiva University)
George Gintowt (William Rainey Harper College)
James Gips (Boston College)
Manu Gupta (Patni Computer Systems)
Richard Hewer (Ferris State University)
James Huddleston (Independent Consultant)
Terrell Hull (Sun Certified Java Architect, Rational Qualified Practitioner)
Jeff Jones (A.D.A.M. Inc.)
Faisal Kaleem (Florida International University)
Yashavant Kanetkar (KICIT Pvt. Ltd.)
Dhananjay Katre (Patni Computer Systems, Ltd.)
Kurt Kominek (Northeast State Technical CC)
Stan Kurkovsky (Columbus State University)
Brian Larson (Modesto Junior College)
Sukan Makmuri (DeVry-Fremont)
Ken McLean (Northern Virginia CC)
Gordon McNorton (Collin County Community College)
Manish Mehta (Independent Consultant)
Marilyn Meyer (Fresno City College)
John Mueller (DataCon Services)
Narayana Rao Surapaneni (Patni Computer Systems)
Michael Rudisill (Northern Michigan University)
Sara Rushinek (University of Miami)
Praveen Sadhu (Infodat Solutions, Inc.)
Kenneth Schoonover (Chubb Technical Institute)
Andrea Shelly (Florida International University)

Robert Taylor (Lansing Community College)
Yateen Thakkar (Syntel India Ltd.)
Catherine Wyman (DeVry-Phoenix)
David Zeng (DeVry-Calgary)

We would sincerely appreciate your comments, criticisms, corrections and suggestions for improving the text. Please address all correspondence to:

deitel@deitel.com

We will respond promptly.

Well, that's it for now. Welcome to the exciting world of Visual Basic .NET programming. We hope you enjoy this look at leading-edge computer applications development. Good luck!

Dr. Harvey M. Deitel
Paul J. Deitel
Cheryl H. Yaeger

About the Authors

Dr. Harvey M. Deitel, Chairman of Deitel & Associates, Inc., has 42 years experience in the computing field, including extensive industry and academic experience. Dr. Deitel earned B.S. and M.S. degrees from the Massachusetts Institute of Technology and a Ph.D. from Boston University. He worked on the pioneering virtual-memory operating-systems projects at IBM and MIT that developed techniques now widely implemented in systems such as UNIX, Linux and Windows XP. He has 20 years of college teaching experience and served as the Chairman of the Computer Science Department at Boston College before founding Deitel & Associates, Inc., with his son, Paul J. Deitel. He is the author or co-author of several dozen books and multimedia packages. With translations published in numerous foreign languages, Dr. Deitel's texts have earned international recognition. Dr. Deitel has delivered professional seminars to major corporations, government organizations and various branches of the military.

Paul J. Deitel, CEO and Chief Technical Officer of Deitel & Associates, Inc., is a graduate of the Massachusetts Institute of Technology's Sloan School of Management, where he studied information technology. Through Deitel & Associates, Inc., he has delivered professional seminars to numerous industry and government clients and has lectured on C++ and Java for the Boston Chapter of the Association for Computing Machinery. He and his father, Dr. Harvey M. Deitel, are the world's best-selling Computer Science textbook authors.

Cheryl H. Yaeger, Director of Microsoft Software Publications with Deitel & Associates, Inc., is a graduate of Boston University with a degree in Computer Science. Cheryl has co-authored various Deitel & Associates, Inc. publications, including *Simply C#, C# How to Program, C#: A Programmer's Introduction, C# for Experienced Programmers, Visual Basic .NET for Experienced Programmers* and *Simply Java™ Programming* and has contributed to several others.

About Deitel & Associates, Inc.

Deitel & Associates, Inc., is an internationally recognized corporate-training and content-creation organization specializing in computer programming languages education, object technology and Internet/World Wide Web software technology. Through its 28-year publishing partnership with Prentice Hall, Deitel & Associates, Inc. publishes leading-edge programming textbooks, professional books, interactive CD-ROM-based multimedia *Cyber Classrooms, Complete Training Courses* and course management systems e-content. To learn more about Deitel & Associates, Inc., its publications and its worldwide corporate on-site curriculum, visit:

www.deitel.com

Individuals wishing to purchase Deitel books, *Cyber Classrooms* and *Complete Training Courses* can do so through bookstores or online booksellers through:

```
www.deitel.com
www.prenhall.com/deitel
www.InformIT.com/deitel
```

Bulk orders by corporations and academic institutions should be placed directly with Prentice Hall. For ordering information, please visit:

```
www.prenhall.com/deitel
```

The Deitel® Buzz Online Newsletter

Our free e-mail newsletter includes commentary on industry trends and developments, links to articles and resources from our published books and upcoming publications, information on future publications, product-release schedules and more. For opt-in registration, visit `www.deitel.com/newsletter/subscribe.html`.

Please follow the instructions in this section to ensure that your computer is set up properly before you begin using this book.

Font and Naming Conventions

We use fonts to distinguish between IDE features (such as menu names and menu items) and other elements that appear in the IDE. Our convention is to emphasize IDE features in a sans-serif bold **Helvetica** font (for example, **Properties** window) and to emphasize program text in a sans-serif Lucida font (for example, Private Boolean x = True).

A Note Regarding Software for the Book

For the educational market only, this textbook is available in a "value pack" with the Microsoft® Visual Basic® .NET Standard Edition version 2003 integrated development environment as a free supplement. The standard edition is fully functional and is shipped on 5 CDs. There is no time limit for using the software. [*Note:* If you are a professional using this publication, you will have to purchase the necessary software to build and run the applications in this textbook.]

Hardware and Software Requirements to Run Visual Basic .NET 2003

To install and run Visual Basic .NET 2003 Standard Edition, Microsoft recommends that PCs have these minimum requirements:

- Pentium II 450 MHz processor (Pentium III 600 MHz processor recommended)

- Microsoft Windows® Server 2003, Windows XP Professional, Windows XP Home Edition, Windows 2000 Professional (with Service Pack 3 or later), or Windows 2000 Server (with Service Pack 3 or later) operating system

- 160 megabytes for a Windows Server 2003 or Windows XP Professional computer; 96 MB for a Windows XP Home Edition or Windows 2000 Professional computer; 192 MB for a Windows 2000 Server computer

- 500 megabytes of space on the system drive and 1.5 gigabytes of space on the installation drive (additional 1.9 gigabytes of available space required for optional MSDN Library documentation)

- CD-ROM or DVD-ROM drive

- Super VGA monitor (1024 x 768 or higher-resolution display) with 256 colors

- Mouse or other Microsoft-compatible pointing device

- **You must install Microsoft's Internet Information Services (IIS) before installing Visual Studio .NET.** Otherwise, the Web-based bookstore application in the case study cannot be created or executed. See Appendix G for detailed instructions on installing IIS. Note that the Web-based bookstore application cannot be created or executed on Windows XP Home Edition.

This book assumes that you are using Windows 2000 or Windows XP, plus Microsoft's Internet Information Services (IIS). Additional setup instructions for Web servers and other software are available on our Web site along with the examples. [*Note:* This is copyrighted material. Feel free to use it as you study, but you may not republish any portion of it in any form without explicit permission from Prentice Hall and the authors.]

Monitor Display Settings

Simply Visual Basic .NET 2003 includes hundreds of screenshots of applications. Your monitor-display settings may need to be adjusted so that the screenshots in the book will match what you see on your computer screen as you develop each application. [*Note:* We refer to single-clicking with the left mouse button as **selecting** or **clicking**. We refer to double clicking with the left mouse button simply as **double clicking**.] Follow these steps to set your monitor display correctly:

1. Open the **Control Panel** and double click **Display**.
2. Click the **Settings** tab.
3. Click the **Advanced...** button.
4. In the **General** tab, make sure **Small Fonts** is selected; this should indicate that **96 dpi** is now the setting. [*Note:* If you already have this setting, you do not need to do anything else.]
5. Click **Apply**.

If you choose to use different settings, the Size and Location values we provide for different GUI elements (such as Buttons and Labels) in each application might not appear correctly on your screen. If so, simply adjust Size and Location values so the GUI elements in your application appear similar to those in the screenshots in the book.

Theme Settings for Windows XP Users

If you are using Windows XP, we assume that your theme is set to Windows Classic Style. Follow these steps to set Windows XP to display the Windows Classic theme:

1. Open the **Control Panel**, then double click **Display**.
2. Click the **Themes** tab. Select **Windows Classic** from the **Theme:** drop-down list.
3. Click **OK** to save the settings.

[*Note:* Your applications may still look slightly different as screenshots for this publication were taken on a computer running Windows 2000.]

Viewing File Extensions

Several screenshots in *Simply Visual Basic .NET 2003* display file names on a user's system, including the file extension of each file. Your settings may need to be adjusted to display file extensions. Follow these steps to set your machine to display file extensions:

1. In the **Start** menu, select **Programs** (**All Programs** in Windows XP), then **Accessories**, then **Windows Explorer**.
2. In the window that appears, select **Folder Options...** from the **Tools** menu.

3. In the dialog that appears, select the **View** tab.

4. In the **Advanced settings:** pane, uncheck the box to the left of the text **Hide file extensions for known file types** (**Hide extensions for known file types** in Windows XP). [*Note*: If this item is already unchecked then no action needs to be taken.]

Copying and Organizing Files

All the examples for *Simply Visual Basic .NET 2003* are included on the CD-ROM that accompanies this textbook. Follow the steps in the next box to copy the examples directory from the CD-ROM onto your hard drive. We suggest that you work from your hard drive rather than your CD drive for two reasons:

1. You cannot save your applications to the book's CD (the CD is read-only).

2. Files can be accessed faster from a hard drive than from a CD.

The examples from the book (and our other publications) are also available on the Internet as downloads from the following Web sites:

```
www.deitel.com
www.prenhall.com/deitel
```

Screen shots in the following box might differ slightly from what you see on your computer, depending on whether you are using Windows 2000 or Windows XP. We used Windows 2000 to prepare the screenshots for this book.

Copying the Book Examples from the CD-ROM

1. **Locating the CD-ROM drive.** Insert the CD that accompanies *Simply Visual Basic .NET 2003* into your computer's CD-ROM drive. The window displayed in Fig. 1 should appear. If the page appears, proceed to *Step 3* of this box. If the page does not appear, proceed to *Step 2*.

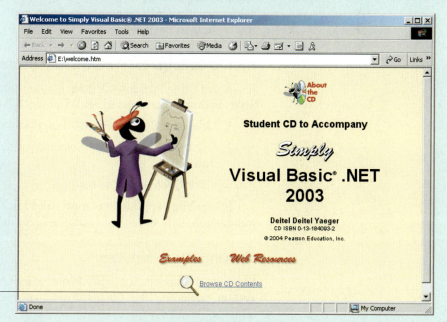

Click the **Browse CD Contents** link to access the CD's contents

Figure 1   Welcome page for *Simply Visual Basic .NET 2003* CD.

2. **Opening the CD-ROM directory using My Computer.** If the page shown in Fig. 1 does not appear, double click the **My Computer** icon on your desktop. In the **My Computer** window, double click your CD-ROM drive (Fig. 2) to access the CD's contents. Proceed to *Step 4*.

(cont.)

Selected CD-ROM drive ────────

Figure 2 Locating the CD-ROM drive.

3. ***Opening the CD-ROM directory.*** If the page in Fig. 1 does appear, click the **Browse CD Contents** link to access the CD's contents.

4. ***Copying the Examples directory.*** Right click the `Examples` directory (Fig. 3), then select **Copy**. [*Note:* A directory is also known as a folder.] Next, go to **My Computer** and double click the `C:` drive. Select the **Edit** menu and select **Paste** to copy the directory and its contents from the CD to your `C:` drive.

   [*Note:* We ask you to save the examples to the `C:` drive and we refer to this drive throughout the text. You may choose to save your files to a different disk drive based on your lab setup or personal preferences. Please see your instructor for more information if you are working in a computer lab to confirm where the examples should be saved.]

Right clicking the
`Examples` ────────
directory

Select **Copy** ────────

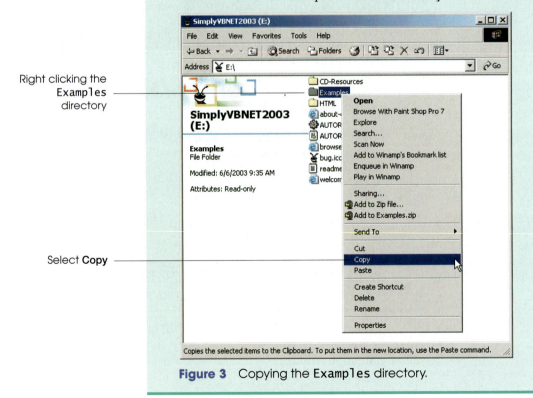

Figure 3 Copying the `Examples` directory.

By default, the book example files you copied onto your computer from the CD are read-only. To access and modify these files, you must change this property as shown in the following box.

Changing the Read-Only Property of Files

1. ***Opening the Properties dialog.*** Right click the Examples directory and select **Properties** from the menu. The **Examples Properties** dialog appears (Fig. 4).

Uncheck the
Read-only check box

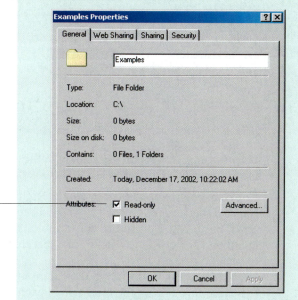

Figure 4 Viewing the properties of the **Examples** directory.

2. ***Changing the read-only property.*** In the **Attributes** section of this dialog, click the box next to **Read-only** to remove the check mark. Click **Apply** to apply the changes.

3. ***Changing the property for all files.*** Clicking **Apply** in *Step 2* will display the **Confirm Attribute Changes** window (Fig. 5). In this window, click the radio button next to **Apply changes to this folder, subfolders and files** and click **OK** to remove the read-only property for all the files and folders in the **Examples** directory.

Click this radio button to
remove the read-only
property for all the files

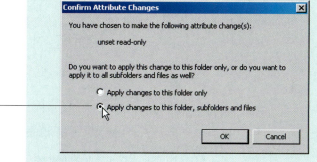

Figure 5 Removing read-only for all the files in the **Examples** directory.

As you work through this book, you will be developing your own applications. In the following box, you create a directory on your C: drive in which you will save all of your applications.

Creating a Working Directory

1. ***Selecting the drive.*** Double click the **My Computer** icon on your desktop to access a list of your computer drives (Fig. 6). Double click the C: drive. The contents of the C: drive are displayed.

(cont.)

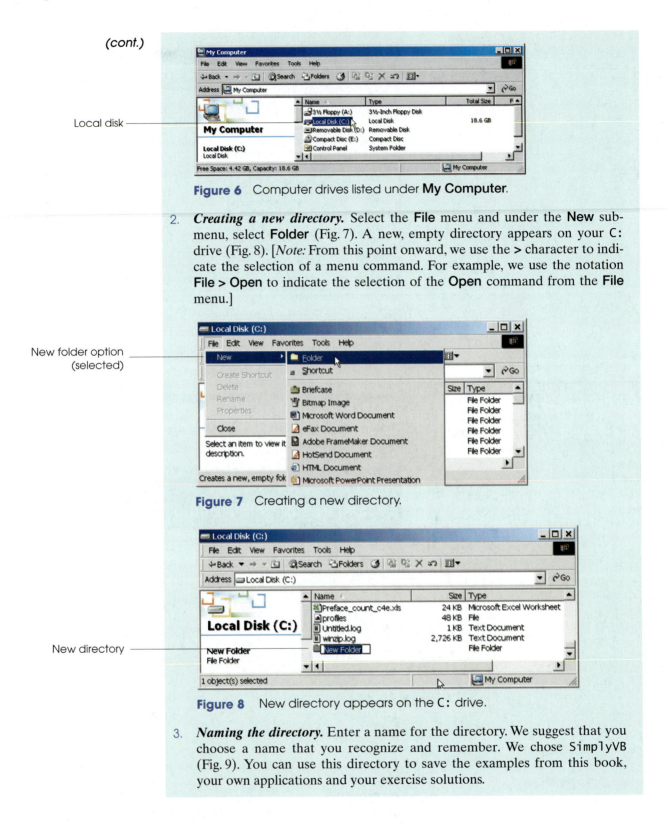

Local disk

Figure 6   Computer drives listed under **My Computer**.

2. ***Creating a new directory.*** Select the **File** menu and under the **New** sub-menu, select **Folder** (Fig. 7). A new, empty directory appears on your **C:** drive (Fig. 8). [*Note:* From this point onward, we use the **>** character to indicate the selection of a menu command. For example, we use the notation **File > Open** to indicate the selection of the **Open** command from the **File** menu.]

New folder option (selected)

Figure 7   Creating a new directory.

New directory

Figure 8   New directory appears on the **C:** drive.

3. ***Naming the directory.*** Enter a name for the directory. We suggest that you choose a name that you recognize and remember. We chose SimplyVB (Fig. 9). You can use this directory to save the examples from this book, your own applications and your exercise solutions.

(cont.)

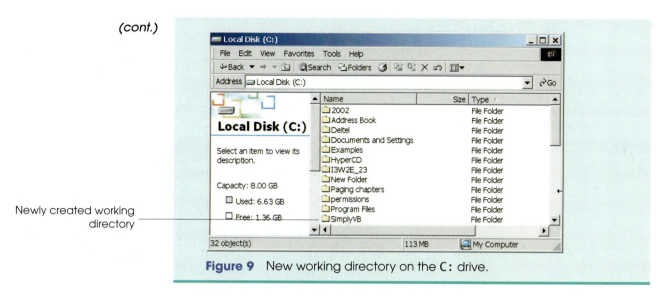

Figure 9   New working directory on the C: drive.

Newly created working directory

Before you can run the applications in *Simply Visual Basic .NET 2003* or build your own applications, you must install Visual Basic .NET Standard Edition version 2003. The following box will guide you through this process.

Installing the Visual Basic .NET Prerequisites

1. ***Launching the installer.*** Insert the light blue disc labeled **Visual Basic .NET Disc 1** into your CD-ROM drive. The installer should appear after a brief loading period (Fig. 10). If it does not appear, proceed to *Step 2* of this box. Otherwise, proceed to *Step 4.*

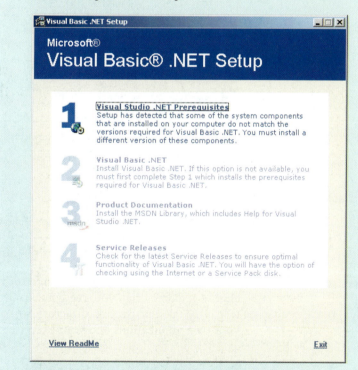

Figure 10   Setup menu for Visual Basic .NET.

2. ***Opening the CD-ROM directory using My Computer.*** If the dialog shown in Fig. 10 does not appear, double click the **My Computer** icon on your desktop. In the **My Computer** window, double click your CD-ROM drive (Fig. 11) to access the CD's contents.

(cont.)

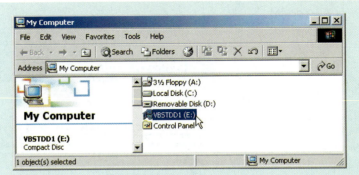

Figure 11   Opening the CD-ROM directory.

3. ***Running the installer***. Double click the `setup.exe` icon in the **VBSTDD1** window to launch the installer (Fig. 12). The dialog in Fig. 10 should appear after a brief loading period.

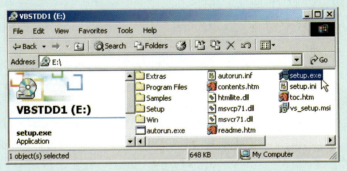

Figure 12   Running the installer.

4. ***Inserting the prerequisites disc***. Before installing Visual Basic .NET, the installer must update certain software components on your system. Click the **Visual Studio .NET Prerequisites** link to begin this process. The installer will prompt you to insert the maroon disc labeled **Visual Studio .NET Prerequisites** (Fig. 13). [*Note:* The CD-ROM drive letter shown might be different on your system]. Insert the disc, then click **OK** to continue.

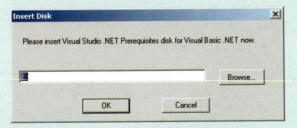

Figure 13   Inserting the prerequisites disc.

5. ***Accepting the license agreement***. After a brief loading period, the **End User License Agreement** should appear (Fig. 14). Carefully read the license agreement. Click the **I agree** radio button, then click **Continue** to agree to the terms. [*Note:* If you choose not to accept the license agreement, the software will not install and you will not be able to create or run Visual Basic .NET applications.]

(cont.)

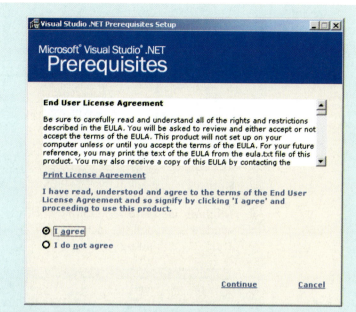

Figure 14 License agreement for the prerequisites.

6. ***Installing the prerequisites.*** At this point, the installer will inform you which software components need to be updated (Fig. 15). [*Note:* the components in the list might be different on your system]. Click **Continue** to proceed with the installation.

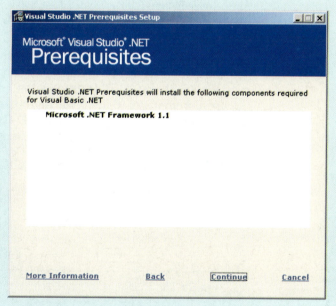

Figure 15 Listing the necessary prerequisites.

7. ***Automatic log on.*** Depending on which components require updates, your system might need to restart to complete the process. If you have access to your system's password, click the **Automatically log on** check box and enter your password twice (to ensure it is entered correctly) (Fig. 16). If you do not, you can continue installing Visual Studio .NET, but you might need to contact your system administrator if prompted for a password during the installation. Click **Install Now!** to continue.

(cont.)

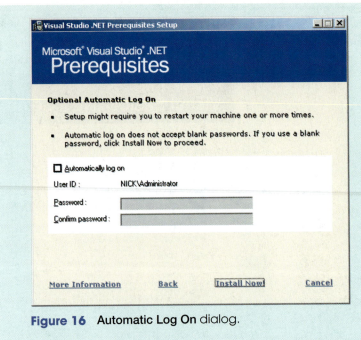

Figure 16 **Automatic Log On** dialog.

8. ***Finishing the installation.*** The installer will now update your system. When it has finished, click **Done** to return to the main menu (Fig. 17).

Directory location

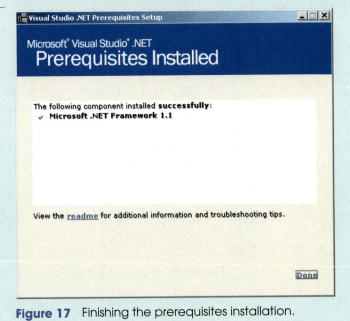

Figure 17 Finishing the prerequisites installation.

You are now ready to install Visual Basic .NET Standard Edition version 2003. The following box will guide you through the necessary steps to complete this part of the installation.

**Installing
Visual Basic .NET**

1. ***Beginning the installation.*** Click the **Visual Basic .NET** link to begin installing Visual Basic .NET (Fig. 18)

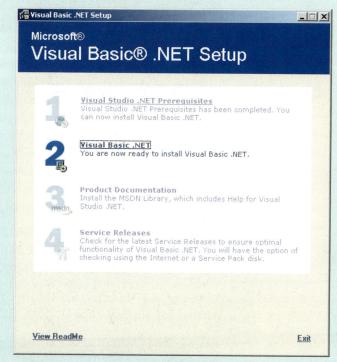

Figure 18   Visual Basic .NET installation.

2. ***Inserting the Visual Basic .NET disc.*** The installer will prompt you to insert
the light blue disc labeled **Visual Basic .NET Disc 1** (Fig. 19). [*Note:* The CD-
ROM drive letter shown might be different on your system]. Insert the disc,
then click **OK** to continue.

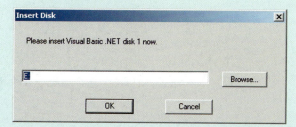

Figure 19   Inserting the Visual Basic .NET disc.

3. ***Accepting the license agreement and entering the product key.*** Carefully
read the license agreement. Click the **I agree** radio button to agree to the
terms (Fig. 20). [*Note:* If you choose not to accept the license agreement, the
software will not install and you will not be able to execute or create Visual
Basic .NET applications]. Enter your product key (located on a yellow label
on the back of your Visual Basic .NET CD case) and full name into the
boxes provided. Click **Continue** to proceed. [*Note:* If you make a mistake
when entering your product key, an error message will be displayed and you
will be asked to correct your information (Fig. 21)].

(cont.)

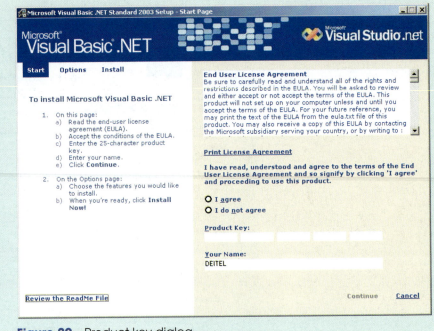

Figure 20   Product key dialog.

Figure 21   Invalid product key error message.

4. ***Selecting installation options.*** Select all the components of Visual Basic .NET Standard Edition (Fig. 22). You can also change the directory where Visual Basic .NET will be installed (we recommend using the default location). After you have selected the desired options, click **Install Now!** to proceed. [*Note:* Sometimes the checkboxes will be checked, but will have a gray background. This indicates that only a portion of the feature selected will be installed. If this is the case, uncheck and recheck the box. Now, the background of the checkbox should be white, indicating that the entire feature will be installed.]

5. ***Finishing the installation.*** The installer will now begin copying the files required by Visual Basic .NET. Depending on your system, this process can take up to an hour. When it has finished, click **Done** to return to the main menu (Fig. 23).

(cont.)

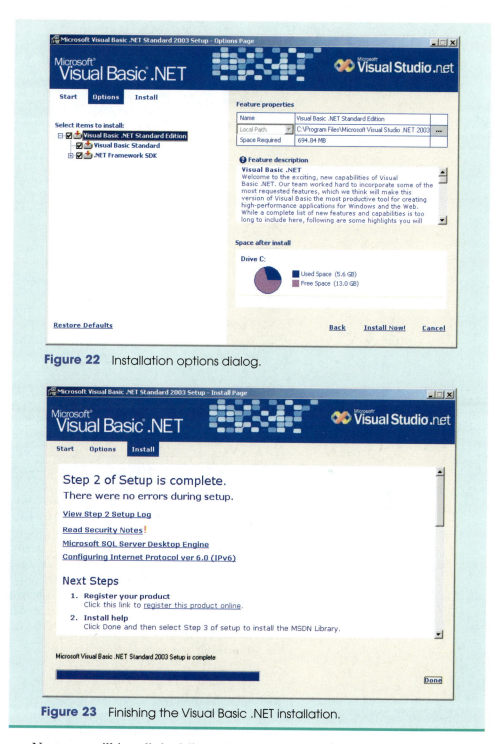

Figure 22 Installation options dialog.

Figure 23 Finishing the Visual Basic .NET installation.

Next, you will install the Microsoft Developer Network Library (MSDN). The MSDN Library contains detailed articles and tutorials on a wide range of topics, including Visual Basic .NET reference materials. The following box will guide you through this process.

**Installing the MSDN
Library**

1. *Beginning the installation.* Click the **Product Documentation** link to begin
installing the MSDN Library (Fig. 24).

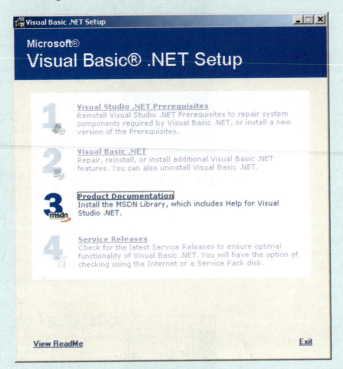

Figure 24   MSDN Library installation.

2. *Inserting MSDN Library Disc 1.* The installer will prompt you to insert the
first dark blue MSDN disc labeled **MSDN Library Disc 1** (Fig. 25). [*Note:* The
CD-ROM drive letter shown might be different on your system]. Insert the
disc, then click **OK** to continue.

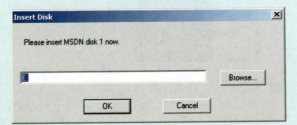

Figure 25   Inserting the first MSDN Library disc.

3. *Accepting the license agreement.* After a brief loading period, a dialog wel-
coming you to the **MSDN Library Setup Wizard** appears. Click **Next >** to
proceed to the **License Agreement** dialog. Carefully read the license agreement. Click the **I accept the terms in the license agreement** radio button,
then click **Next >** to agree to the terms (Fig. 26). [*Note:* If you choose not to
accept the license agreement, the software will not install and you will not be
able to use the online help features of Visual Basic .NET].

(cont.)

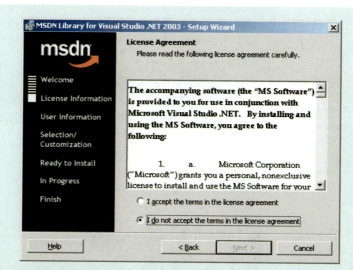

Figure 26 License agreement for the MSDN Library.

4. ***Entering your information.*** Enter your name and the name of your organization (if any) in the **Customer Information** dialog, then click **Next >** to continue (Fig. 27).

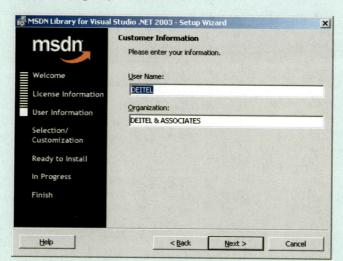

Figure 27 **Customer Information** dialog.

5. ***Selecting an installation type.*** Select an installation type from the list of available options. [*Note:* We recommend a **Full** installation if you have enough disk space, as you will be able to access all the MSDN articles without inserting the CDs in the future.] When you have made a selection, click **Next >** to continue (Fig. 28).

(cont.)

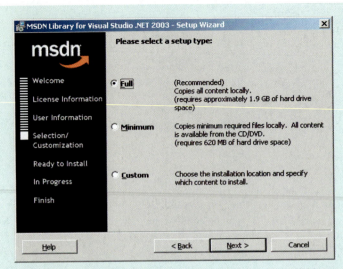

Figure 28   Selecting an installation type for the MSDN Library.

6. ***Selecting a destination directory.*** Select the directory where you would like the MSDN Library to be installed (we recommend the default location). Click **Next >** to continue (Fig. 29).

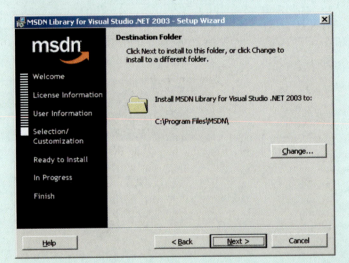

Figure 29   Selecting a destination directory for the MSDN Library.

7. ***Finishing the installation.*** A dialog informing you that the MSDN Library is ready to install will appear. Click **Install** to begin the installation process. Depending on your system, this could take up to an hour to complete. During the installation, you will be prompted twice to insert the next disc in the series, much like Fig. 25. Insert the requested disc, then click **OK** to continue. When the installation has completed, click **Finish** to return to the main menu (Fig. 30).

(cont.)

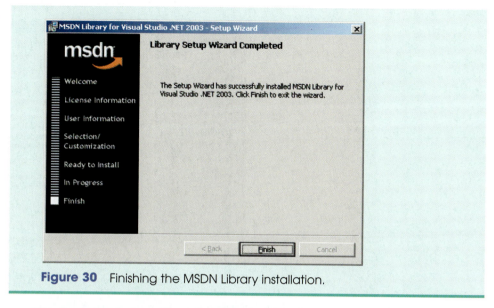

Figure 30   Finishing the MSDN Library installation.

The final step in installing Visual Basic .NET is to check for any updates (also called service releases) that Microsoft has released. The following box will guide you through this process.

Checking for Service
Releases

1. **Beginning the update check.** Click the **Service Releases** link to begin the process of checking for updates to Visual Basic .NET (Fig. 31**)**.

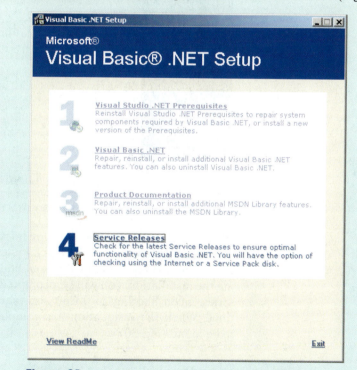

Figure 31   Update check for Visual Basic .NET.

2. **Connecting to the Internet.** Make sure your system is connected to the Internet, then click the **Check for Service Releases on the Internet** link (Fig. 32). [*Note:* If you do not have an active Internet connection, you will receive an error message (Fig. 33) repeatedly and you cannot complete this step. Click **Cancel** to return to the main menu.]

(cont.)

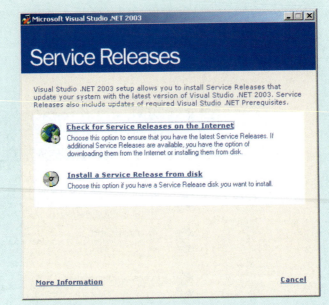

Figure 32   Connecting to the Internet to check for updates.

Figure 33   Error connecting to the Internet.

3. ***Finishing the update check.*** The installer will inform you if there are any updates to Visual Basic .NET (Fig. 34). If there are, select each item from the list to install it. [*Note:* If you are unsure how to proceed, contact your system administrator]. Once you have applied all the updates (or if there were none), click **OK** to return to the main menu.

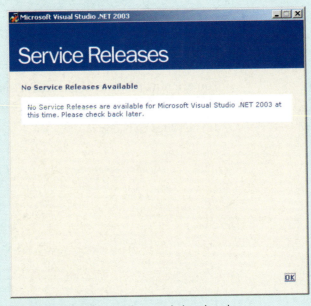

Figure 34   Finishing the update check.

(cont.)

4. ***Finishing the installation.*** The main menu should now indicate that *Steps 1–4* have been completed. Click **Exit** to close the installer (Fig. 35). If prompted to check for Windows security updates, click **No** unless you are already comfortable with this procedure and authorized to do so on your system (Fig. 36).

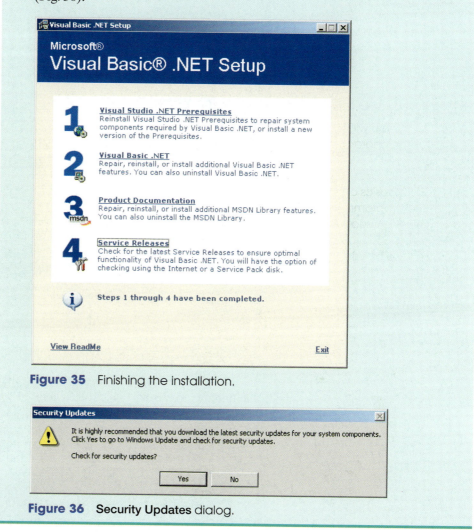

Figure 35   Finishing the installation.

Figure 36   **Security Updates** dialog.

You are now ready to begin your Visual Basic .NET studies with *Simply Visual Basic .NET 2003.* We hope you enjoy the book! You can reach us easily at:

`deitel@deitel.com`

Graphing Application

Introducing Computers, the Internet and Visual Basic .NET

Welcome to Visual Basic .NET! This book uses a straightforward, step-by-step tutorial approach to teach the fundamentals of Visual Basic .NET programming. We hope that you will be informed and entertained as you learn the basics of Visual Basic .NET programming.

The core of the book teaches Visual Basic .NET using our **application-driven approach**, which provides step-by-step instructions for creating and interacting with useful, real-world computer applications. With this approach, combined with our signature **live-code approach**, which shows dozens of complete, working Visual Basic .NET applications and depicts their outputs, you learn basic skills that underlie good programming. You will study bonus tutorials on graphics, multimedia and Web programming. All of the book's examples are available on the CD-ROM that accompanies the book and on our Web site, www.deitel.com.

Computer use is increasing in almost every field. In an era of rising costs, computing costs are actually decreasing dramatically because of rapid developments in both hardware and software technology. Silicon-chip technology has made computing so economical that hundreds of millions of general-purpose computers are in use worldwide, helping people in business, industry, government and their personal lives.

Reading this text will start you on a challenging and rewarding educational path. If you'd like to communicate with us, send an e-mail to deitel@deitel.com, and we will respond promptly. For more information, visit our Web sites at www.deitel.com, www.prenhall.com/deitel and www.InformIT.com/deitel.

1.1 What Is a Computer?

A **computer** is a device capable of performing computations and making logical decisions at speeds millions and even billions of times faster than humans can. For example, many of today's personal computers can perform billions of additions per second. A person operating a desk calculator might require a lifetime to complete the same number of calculations that a powerful personal computer can perform in one second. Today's fastest **supercomputers** can perform hundreds of billions of additions per second. Trillion-instruction-per-second computers are already functioning in research laboratories!

Computers process **data**, using sets of instructions called **computer programs**. These programs guide computers through orderly sets of actions that are specified by people known as **computer programmers**. In this book, we generally use the term "application" instead of the term "program." An application is a program that does something particularly useful. Each tutorial in this book, on average, presents five applications—one in the main example and four in the exercises—for a total of more than 100 applications in the book.

A computer is composed of various devices (such as the keyboard, screen, mouse, hard drive, memory, CD-ROM and processing units) known as **hardware**. The programs that run on a computer are referred to as **software**. Object-oriented programming (which models real-world objects with software counterparts), available in Visual Basic .NET and other programming languages, is a significant breakthrough that can greatly enhance programmers' productivity.

SELF-REVIEW   1. Computers process data, using sets of instructions called _____.

      a) hardware   b) computer programs

      c) processing units   d) programmers

    2. The devices that make up a computer are called _____.

      a) hardware   b) software

      c) programs   d) programmers

Answers: 1) b. 2) a.

1.2 Computer Organization

Computers can be thought of as being divided into six units:

1. **Input unit.** This "receiving" section of the computer obtains information (data and computer programs) from various **input devices**, such as the keyboard and the mouse. Other input devices include microphones (for recording speech to the computer), scanners (for scanning images) and digital cameras (for taking photographs and making videos).

2. **Output unit.** This "shipping" section of the computer takes information that the computer has processed and places it on various **output devices**, making the information available for use outside the computer. Output can be displayed on screens, played on audio/video devices, printed on paper, etc. Output also can be used to control other devices, such as robots used in manufacturing.

3. **Memory unit.** This rapid-access, relatively low-capacity "warehouse" section of the computer stores data temporarily while an application is running. The memory unit retains information that has been entered through input devices, so that information is immediately available for processing. To be executed, computer programs must be in memory. The memory unit also retains processed information until that information can be sent to output devices on which it is made available to users. Often, the memory unit is called either **memory** or **primary memory**. **Random-access memory (RAM)** is an example of primary memory. Primary memory is usually **volatile**, which means that it is erased when the machine is powered off.

4. **Arithmetic and logic unit (ALU).** The ALU is the "manufacturing" section of the computer. It performs calculations such as addition, subtraction, multiplication and division. It also makes decisions, allowing the computer to perform such tasks as determining whether two items stored in memory are equal.

5. **Central processing unit (CPU).** The CPU serves as the "administrative" section of the computer, supervising the operation of the other sections. The CPU alerts the input unit when information should be read into the memory unit, instructs the ALU when to use information from the memory unit in calculations and tells the output unit when to send information from the memory unit to certain output devices.

6. **Secondary storage unit.** This unit is the long-term, high-capacity "warehousing" section of the computer. Secondary storage devices, such as hard drives, CD-ROM drives, zip drives and floppy disk drives, normally hold programs or data that other units are not actively using; the computer then can retrieve this information when it is needed—hours, days, months or even years later. Information in secondary storage takes much longer to access than information in primary memory. However, secondary storage is much less expensive than primary memory. Secondary storage is nonvolatile, retaining information even when the computer is powered off.

SELF-REVIEW

1. The _____ is responsible for performing calculations, and contains decision-making mechanisms.

   a) central processing unit   b) memory unit
   c) arithmetic and logic unit   d) output unit

2. Information stored in _____ is normally erased when the computer is turned off.

   a) primary memory   b) secondary storage
   c) CD-ROM drives   d) hard drives

Answers: 1) c. 2) a.

1.3 Machine Languages, Assembly Languages and High-Level Languages

Programmers write instructions in various programming languages, some of which are directly understandable by computers and others of which require intermediate translation steps. Although hundreds of computer languages are in use today, the diverse offerings can be divided into three general types:

1. Machine languages

2. Assembly languages

3. High-level languages

A computer can directly understand only its own **machine language**. As the "natural language" of a particular computer, machine language is defined by the computer's hardware design. Machine languages generally consist of streams of numbers (ultimately reduced to 1s and 0s) that instruct computers how to perform their most elementary operations. Machine languages are **machine dependent**, which means that a particular machine language can be used on only one type of computer. The following section of a machine-language program, which adds *overtime pay* to *base pay* and stores the result in *gross pay*, demonstrates the incomprehensibility of machine language to humans:

```
+1300042774
+1400593419
+1200274027
```

As the popularity of computers increased, machine-language programming proved to be slow and error prone. Instead of using the strings of numbers that computers could directly understand, programmers began using English-like abbreviations to represent the basic operations of the computer. These abbreviations formed the basis of **assembly languages. Translator programs** called **assemblers** convert assembly-language programs to machine language at computer speeds. The following section of an assembly-language program also adds *overtime pay* to *base pay* and stores the result in *gross pay*, but presents the steps somewhat more clearly to human readers than the machine-language example:

```
LOAD    BASEPAY
ADD     OVERPAY
STORE   GROSSPAY
```

This assembly-language code is clearer to humans, but computers cannot understand it until it is translated into machine language by an assembler program.

Although the speed at which programmers could write programs increased rapidly with the creation of assembly languages, these languages still require many instructions to accomplish even the simplest tasks. To speed up the programming process, **high-level languages**, in which single program statements accomplish more substantial tasks, were developed. Translator programs called **compilers** convert high-level-language programs into machine language. High-level languages enable programmers to write instructions that look almost like everyday English and that contain common mathematical notations. For example, a payroll application written in a high-level language might contain a statement such as

```
grossPay = basePay + overTimePay
```

From these examples, it is clear why programmers prefer high-level languages to either machine languages or assembly languages. Visual Basic is the most popular high-level programming language in the world. In the next section, you will learn about Microsoft's latest version of this language, called Visual Basic .NET.

SELF-REVIEW

1. The only programming language that a computer can directly understand is its own _____.

   a) high-level language   b) assembly language
   c) machine language   d) English

2. Programs that translate high-level language programs into machine language are called _____.

   a) assemblers   b) compilers
   c) programmers   d) converters

Answers: 1) c. 2) b.

1.4 Visual Basic .NET

Visual Basic .NET evolved from **BASIC** (Beginner's All-Purpose Symbolic Instruction Code), developed in the mid-1960s by Professors John Kemeny and Thomas Kurtz of Dartmouth College as a language for writing simple programs quickly and easily. BASIC's primary purpose was to teach novices fundamental programming techniques.

When Bill Gates founded Microsoft Corporation in the 1970s, he implemented BASIC on several early personal computers. In the late 1980s and the early 1990s, Microsoft developed the Microsoft Windows **graphical user interface (GUI)**—the visual part of the application with which users interact. With the creation of the Windows GUI, the natural evolution of BASIC was to **Visual Basic**, introduced by Microsoft in 1991 to make programming Windows applications easier.

Until Visual Basic appeared, developing Microsoft Windows-based applications was a difficult process. Visual Basic .NET is a so-called object-oriented, event-driven (OOED) visual programming language in which programs are created with the use of a software tool called an **Integrated Development Environment (IDE)**. With Microsoft's **Visual Studio .NET** IDE, a programmer can write, run, test and debug Visual Basic .NET programs quickly and conveniently.

Visual Basic .NET is fully **object oriented**—you will learn some basics of object technology shortly and will study a rich treatment in the remainder of the book. Visual Basic .NET is **event driven**—you will write programs that respond to user-initiated **events** such as mouse clicks and keystrokes. It is a **visual programming** language—instead of writing detailed program statements to build your applications, you will use Visual Studio .NET's graphical user interface in which you conveniently drag and drop predefined objects into place and label and resize them. Visual Studio .NET will write much of the program for you.

Microsoft introduced its **.NET** (pronounced "dot-net") strategy in 2000. The **.NET platform**—the set of software components that enables .NET programs to run—allows Web-based applications to be distributed to a variety of devices (such as cell phones) as well as to desktop computers. The .NET platform offers a new programming model that allows programs created in different programming languages to communicate with each other, whether they reside on the same or on different computers connected to a network such as the Internet.

SELF-REVIEW

1. Microsoft created _____ in 1991 to make it easier to program Windows applications.

   a) Windows   b) BASIC
   c) Visual Basic   d) Visual Basic .NET

2. Visual Basic evolved from _____ , which was created as a language for writing simple programs quickly and easily.

   a) .NET   b) Windows
   c) Visual Basic .NET   d) BASIC

Answers: 1) c. 2) d.

1.5 Other High-Level Languages

Although hundreds of high-level languages have been developed, only a few have achieved broad acceptance. IBM Corporation developed **Fortran** in the mid-1950s to create scientific and engineering applications that require complex mathematical computations. Fortran is still widely used.

COBOL was developed in the late 1950s by a group of computer manufacturers in conjunction with government and industrial computer users. COBOL is used primarily for business applications that require the manipulation of large amounts of data. A considerable portion of today's business software is still programmed in COBOL.

The C language, which Dennis Ritchie developed at Bell Laboratories in the early 1970s, gained widespread recognition as a development language of the UNIX operating system. C++, an extension of C, was developed by Bjarne Stroustrup in the early 1980s at Bell Laboratories. C++ provides capabilities for **object-oriented programming (OOP)**. Many of today's major operating systems are written in C or C++.

Objects are reusable software **components** that model items in the real world. Object-oriented programs are often easier to understand, correct and modify than programs developed with previous techniques. Visual Basic .NET provides full object-oriented programming capabilities.

In the early 1990s, many organizations, including Sun Microsystems, predicted that intelligent consumer-electronic devices would be the next major market in which **microprocessors**—the chips that make computers work—would have a profound impact. But the marketplace for intelligent consumer-electronic devices did not develop as quickly as Sun had anticipated. By sheer good fortune, the World Wide Web exploded in popularity in 1993, and Sun saw an immediate potential for using its new **Java** programming language to create **dynamic content** (animated and interactive content) for Web pages. Sun announced Java to the public in 1995, grabbing the immediate attention of the business community because of the widespread interest in the Web. Developers now use Java to create Web pages with dynamic content, to build large-scale enterprise applications, to enhance the functionality of Web servers (the computers that provide the content that is distributed to your Web browser when you browse Web sites), to provide applications for consumer devices (for example, cell phones, pagers and PDAs) and for many other purposes.

In 2000, Microsoft announced **C#** (pronounced "C-Sharp") at the same time the company announced its .NET strategy. The C# programming language was designed specifically for the .NET platform. It has roots in C, C++ and Java, adapting the best features of each. Like Visual Basic .NET, C# is object oriented and has access to .NET's powerful library of prebuilt components, enabling programmers to develop applications quickly. C#, Java and Visual Basic .NET have comparable capabilities, so learning Visual Basic .NET may create many opportunities for you.

SELF-REVIEW

1. _____ is an extension of C and offers object-oriented capabilities.
   a) Visual Basic   b) C++
   c) assembly language   d) Windows

2. _____ is a programming language originally developed for Microsoft's .NET platform.
   a) C#   b) Java
   c) C++   d) Visual Basic

3. _____, developed in the late 1950s, is still used to produce a considerable portion of today's business software.
   a) COBOL   b) Fortran
   c) Java   d) C

4. _____, developed in the 1950s, is still used to create scientific and engineering applications that require complex mathematical computations.
   a) Visual Basic   b) Fortran
   c) COBOL   d) C#

Answers: 1) b. 2) a. 3) a. 4) b.

1.6 Structured Programming

During the 1960s, software-development efforts often ran behind schedule, costs greatly exceeded budgets and the finished products were unreliable. People began to realize that software development was a far more complex activity than they had imagined. Research activity intended to address these issues resulted in the evolution of **structured programming**—a disciplined approach to the creation of programs that are clear, correct and easy to modify.

One of the results of this research was the development of the **Pascal** programming language in 1971. Pascal, named after the 17th-century mathematician and philosopher Blaise Pascal, was designed for teaching structured programming and rapidly became the preferred introductory programming language in most colleges. Unfortunately, the language lacked many features needed to make it useful in commercial, industrial and government applications. By contrast, C, which also arose from research on structured programming, did not have the limitations of Pascal, and professional programmers quickly adopted it.

The **Ada** programming language was developed under the sponsorship of the U.S. Department of Defense (DOD) during the 1970s and early 1980s. The language was named after **Ada Byron, Lady Lovelace**, daughter of the poet Lord Byron. Lady Lovelace is generally credited as being the world's first computer programmer because of an application she wrote in the early 1800s for the Analytical Engine mechanical computing device designed by Charles Babbage.

1.7 Key Software Trend: Object Technology

As the benefits of structured programming were realized in the 1970s, improved software technology began to appear. However, it was not until object-oriented programming became widely used in the 1980s and 1990s that software developers finally felt they had the necessary tools to improve the software-development process dramatically.

What are objects, and why are they special? **Object technology** is a packaging scheme for creating meaningful software units. There are date objects, time objects, paycheck objects, invoice objects, automobile objects, people objects, audio objects, video objects, file objects, record objects and so on. In fact, almost any noun can be reasonably represented as a software object. Objects have **properties** (also called **attributes**), such as color, size and weight; and perform **actions** (also called **behaviors** or **methods**), such as moving, sleeping or drawing. **Classes** are types of related objects. For example, all cars belong to the "car" class, even though individual cars vary in make, model, color and options packages. A class specifies the general format of its objects, and the properties and actions available to an object depend on its class. An object is related to its class in much the same way as a building is related to its blueprint.

Before object-oriented languages appeared, **procedural programming languages** (such as Fortran, Pascal, BASIC and C) focused on actions (verbs) rather than things or objects (nouns). This made programming a bit awkward. However, using today's popular object-oriented languages, such as Visual Basic .NET, C++, Java and C#, programmers can program in an object-oriented manner that more naturally reflects the way in which they perceive the world. This has resulted in significant productivity gains.

With object technology, properly designed classes can be reused on future projects. Using libraries of classes can greatly reduce the amount of effort required to implement new systems. Some organizations report that such software reusability is not, in fact, the key benefit that they get from object-oriented programming. Rather, they indicate that object-oriented programming tends to produce software that is more understandable because it is better organized and has fewer maintenance requirements.

Object orientation allows the programmer to focus on the "big picture." Instead of worrying about the minute details of how reusable objects are implemented, the programmer can focus on the behaviors and interactions of objects. A road map that showed every tree, house and driveway would be difficult, if not impossible, to read. When such details are removed and only the essential information (roads) remains, the map becomes easier to understand. In the same way, an application that is divided into objects is easy to understand, modify and update because it hides much of the detail. It is clear that object-oriented programming will be the key programming methodology for at least the next decade. Visual Basic .NET is one of the world's most widely used fully object-oriented languages.

1. _____ focuses on actions (verbs) rather than things (nouns).
   - a) C#
   - c) Visual Basic .NET
   - b) Object-oriented programming
   - d) Procedural programming

2. In object-oriented programming, _____, which are in a sense like blueprints, are types of related objects.
   - a) classes
   - c) behaviors
   - b) attributes
   - d) properties

Answers: 1) d. 2) a.

1.8 The Internet and the World Wide Web

In the late 1960s, ARPA—the Advanced Research Projects Agency of the Department of Defense—rolled out the blueprints for networking the main computer systems of approximately a dozen ARPA-funded universities and research institutions. The computers were to be connected with communications lines operating at a then-stunning 56 Kbps (1 Kbps is equal to 1,024 bits per second), at a time when most people (of the few who even had networking access) were connecting over telephone lines to computers at a rate of 110 bits per second. Academic research was about to take a giant leap forward. ARPA proceeded to implement what quickly became called the **ARPAnet**, the grandparent of today's **Internet**.

Things worked out differently from the original plan. Although the ARPAnet enabled researchers to network their computers, its main benefit proved to be the capability for quick and easy communication via what came to be known as **electronic mail (e-mail)**. This is true even on today's Internet, with e-mail, instant messaging and file transfer allowing hundreds of millions of people worldwide to communicate with each other.

The protocol (in other words, the set of rules) for communicating over the ARPAnet became known as the **Transmission Control Protocol (TCP)**. TCP ensured that messages, consisting of pieces called "packets," were properly routed from sender to receiver and that those messages arrived intact.

In parallel with the early evolution of the Internet, organizations worldwide were implementing their own networks for both intraorganization (that is, within an organization) and interorganization (that is, between organizations) communication. A huge variety of networking hardware and software appeared. One challenge was to enable these different networks to communicate with each other. ARPA accomplished this by developing the **Internet Protocol (IP)**, which created a true "network of networks," the current architecture of the Internet. The combined set of protocols is now commonly called **TCP/IP**.

Businesses rapidly realized that, by using the Internet, they could improve their operations and offer new and better services to their clients. Companies started spending large amounts of money to develop and enhance their Internet presence. This generated fierce competition among communications carriers and hardware and software suppliers to meet the increased infrastructure demand. As a result, **bandwidth**—the information-carrying capacity of communications lines—on the Internet has increased tremendously, while hardware costs have plummeted.

The **World Wide Web** is a collection of hardware and software associated with the Internet that allows computer users to locate and view multimedia-based documents (documents with various combinations of text, graphics, animations, audios and videos) on almost any subject. Even though the Internet was developed more than three decades ago, the introduction of the World Wide Web (WWW) was a relatively recent event. In 1989, Tim Berners-Lee of CERN (the European Organization for Nuclear Research) began to develop a technology for sharing information via "hyperlinked" text documents. Berners-Lee called his invention the **HyperText Markup Language (HTML)**. He also wrote communication protocols to form the backbone of his new hypertext information system, which he referred to as the World Wide Web.

In October 1994, Berners-Lee founded an organization, called the **World Wide Web Consortium (W3C, www.w3.org)**, that is devoted to developing technologies for the World Wide Web. One of the W3C's primary goals is to make the Web universally accessible—regardless of a person's disabilities, language or culture.

The Internet and the World Wide Web will surely be listed among the most important creations of humankind. In the past, most computer applications ran on "stand-alone" computers (computers that were not connected to one another). Today's applications can be written with the aim of communicating among the world's hundreds of millions of computers. In fact, this is, as you will see, the focus of Microsoft's .NET strategy. The Internet and World Wide Web make information instantly and conveniently accessible to large numbers of people. They enable even individuals and small businesses to achieve worldwide exposure. They are profoundly changing the way we do business and conduct our personal lives. To highlight the importance of Internet and Web programming, we include four tutorials at the end of the book in which you will actually build and run a Web-based bookstore application.

SELF-REVIEW

1. Today's Internet evolved from the _____, which was a Department of Defense project.

   a) ARPAnet   b) HTML
   c) CERN   d) WWW

2. The combined set of protocols for communicating over the Internet is now commonly called _____.

   a) HTML   b) TCP/IP
   c) ARPA   d) TCP

Answers: 1) a. 2) b.

1.9 Introduction to Microsoft .NET

In June 2000, Microsoft announced its **.NET initiative**, a broad new vision for using the Internet and the Web in the development, engineering, distribution and use of software. Rather than forcing developers to use a single programming language, the .NET initiative permits developers to create .NET applications in any .NET-compatible language (such as Visual Basic .NET, Visual C++ .NET, C# and others). Part of the initiative includes Microsoft's **Active Server Pages (ASP) .NET** technology, which allows programmers to create applications for the Web. You will be introduced to ASP .NET as you build the Web-based bookstore application later in the book.

The .NET strategy extends the idea of software reuse to the Internet, by allowing programmers to concentrate on their specialties without having to implement every component of every application. Instead, companies can buy **Web services**, which are Web-based programs that organizations can incorporate into their systems to speed the Web-application-development process. Visual programming (which you will learn throughout this book) has become popular, because it enables programmers to create applications easily, using such prepackaged graphical components as **buttons**, **textboxes** and **scrollbars** that are so popular today in Windows applications.

The Microsoft **.NET Framework** is at the heart of the .NET strategy. This framework executes applications and Web services, contains a class library (called the **Framework Class Library** or **FCL**) and provides many other programming capabilities that you use to build Visual Basic .NET applications. In this book, you will learn how to develop .NET software with Visual Basic .NET. Steve Ballmer, Microsoft's CEO, stated in May 2001 that Microsoft was "betting the company" on .NET. Such a dramatic commitment surely indicates a bright future for Visual Basic .NET programmers.

SELF-REVIEW

1. _____ is a technology specifically designed for the .NET platform and intended for programmers to create Web-based applications.

    a) Visual Basic   b) C++
    c) HTML   d) Active Server Pages .NET

2. _____ are existing Web-based programs that can be incorporated into other applications.

    a) Web services   b) Wire services
    c) Attributes   d) Properties

3. Programmers use the _____, a part of the .NET Framework, to build Visual Basic .NET applications.

    a) Visual Basic Library (VBL)   b) Framework Class Library (FCL)
    c) Microsoft Class Library (MCL)   d) Visual Basic Framework (VBF)

Answers: 1) d. 2) a. 3) b.

1.10 Test-Driving the Visual Basic .NET Graphing Application

In this section, you will be introduced to a Visual Basic .NET application, using our application-driven approach. In each tutorial, you are given a chance to "test-drive" the application. You actually run and interact with the completed application. Then you will learn the Visual Basic .NET features you need to build the application. Finally, you will "put it all together" and actually create your own working version of the application. You begin here in Tutorial 1 simply by running a business application that graphs a fictional company's steel production for each state in which the company has a steel factory. You will actually build a similar application in Tutorial 18.

We created the steel production application because it is often helpful for business managers to view information, such as production data, in the form of a chart rather than a screen full of numbers. The following box will show you how the application graphs the production quantities from factories in four different states, so that a manager can visually compare the amounts of steel produced in each state. The elements and functionality you see in this application are typical of what you will learn to program in this text. [*Note*: We use fonts to distinguish between IDE features (such as menu names and menu items) and other elements that appear in the IDE. Our convention is to emphasize IDE features (such as the **File** menu) in a semibold **sans-serif Helvetica** font and to emphasize other elements, such as file names (for example, `Form1.vb`) in a `sans-serif Lucida` font. As you have already noticed, each term that is being defined is set in heavy bold.]

Test-Driving the Visual Basic .NET Graphing Application

1. ***Checking your setup.*** Confirm that you have set up your computer properly by reading the *For Students and Instructors: Important Information before You Begin* section in the Preface.

2. ***Locating the application directory.*** Open Windows Explorer and navigate to the `C:\Examples\Tutorial01` directory (Fig. 1.1).

(cont.)

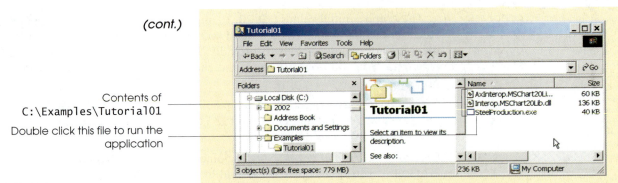

Figure 1.1   Contents of `C:\Examples\Tutorial01`.

Contents of
`C:\Examples\Tutorial01`

Double click this file to run the
application

3. ***Running the Graphing application.*** Now that you are in the directory that contains the application, double click the file name `SteelProduction.exe` to run the application (Fig. 1.2).

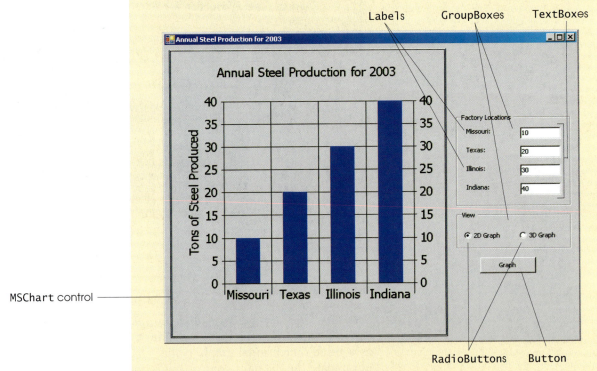

Figure 1.2   A Visual Basic .NET graphing application.

MSChart control

In Fig. 1.2, several graphical elements—called **controls**—are labelled. The controls include `GroupBoxes`, `RadioButtons`, `Buttons`, `Labels` and an `MSChart` control. You can use this application to produce an attractive business graph of the values that the user inputs into the `TextBoxes`. The application allows you to create either a two-dimensional or three-dimensional graph. You will create both in this test-drive.

Because you can use existing controls—which are objects—you can get powerful applications running in Visual Basic .NET much faster than if you had to write all the code yourself. In this text, you will learn how to use many preexisting controls, as well as how to write your own program code to customize your applications.

(cont.)

The graph's initial values (10, 20, 30 and 40) in the TextBoxes are **default** values, the initial values you see when you first run the application. Programmers include default values to provide visual cues for users to enter their own data. You will now customize the chart by entering your own production values.

4. ***Changing the sales data.*** Type 65 in the TextBox labelled **Missouri:**, 35 in the TextBox labelled **Texas:**, 53 in the TextBox labelled **Illinois:** and 46 in the TextBox labelled **Indiana:**.

5. ***Changing the type of graph.*** Note the black dot in the RadioButton labelled **2D Graph**. This means that you would like to see a two-dimensional graph. Click the **Graph** Button toward the bottom right of the screen to update the MSChart control as shown in Fig. 1.3.

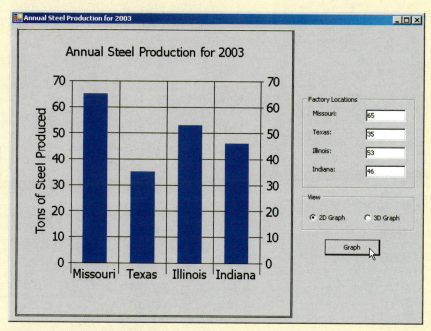

Figure 1.3   New values create a new graph.

6. ***Selecting the three-dimensional graph option.*** Click the **3D Graph** RadioButton to specify that the MSChart control should now display its data as a three-dimensional graph. Notice that clicking this RadioButton does not update the MSChart control, but it does cause the **2D Graph** RadioButton to become white and the **3D** Button to become black. Only one RadioButton in a group can be selected (black)—all the others automatically will be unselected (white).

7. ***Viewing the three-dimensional graph.*** Click the **Graph** Button to present the data in a three-dimensional graph (Fig. 1.4).

8. ***Closing the application.*** Close your running application by clicking its **close** box, ⊠.

9. ***Closing the IDE.*** Close Visual Studio .NET by clicking its close box.

(cont.)

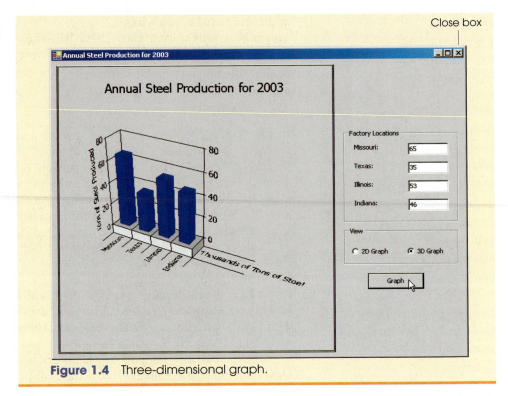

Close box

Figure 1.4   Three-dimensional graph.

Note that the MSChart control does most of the work for you. You just type in the numbers, and the control displays a professional-quality bar chart. This is an excellent example of **software reuse**. Microsoft provides this control—which the company no doubt spent a considerable amount of time and money creating—so millions of users worldwide can use the control to prepare professional quality charts without having to do much programming at all!

1.11 Internet and Web Resources

The Internet and Web are extraordinary resources. This section includes links to interesting and informative Web sites. Hot links to all these sites are included on the CD and at www.deitel.com to save you time. Reference sections like this one are included throughout the book where appropriate.

www.deitel.com
Visit this site for updates, corrections and additional resources for Deitel & Associates publications, including *Simply Visual Basic .NET* 2003 errata, Frequently Asked Questions (FAQs), hot links, code downloads and PowerPoint® slide downloads.

www.prenhall.com/deitel
The Deitel & Associates page on the Prentice Hall Web site contains information about our publications, code downloads and PowerPoint slides for this book.

www.softlord.com/comp
Visit this site to learn more about the history of computers.

www.elsop.com/wrc/h_comput.htm
This site presents the history of computing. It includes content about famous people in the computer field, the evolution of programming languages and the development of operating systems.

www.w3.org/History.html
Visit this site for the history of the World Wide Web.

www.netvalley.com/intval.html
This site presents the history of the Internet.

`msdn.microsoft.com/vbasic`
This is Microsoft's Visual Basic .NET Web site.

`www.GotDotNet.com`
A site with abundant .NET resources.

1.12 Wrap-Up

In this tutorial, you learned about how computers are organized. You studied the levels of programming languages and which kinds of languages, including Visual Basic .NET, require translators. You became familiar with some of the most popular programming languages. You learned the importance of structured programming and object-oriented programming. You studied a brief history of the Internet and the World Wide Web, were introduced to Microsoft's .NET initiative and learned some key aspects of .NET.

You took a working .NET application out for a "test-drive." In the process of doing this, you learned that .NET provides lots of prebuilt controls that perform useful functions and that, by familiarizing yourself with the capabilities of these controls, you can develop powerful applications much faster than if you tried to build them completely yourself. You were encouraged to explore several Web sites with additional information on this book, computers, the Internet, the Web, .NET and Visual Basic .NET.

In the next tutorial, you will learn about the Visual Studio .NET Integrated Development Environment (IDE). This will help you prepare to create your own Visual Basic .NET applications. You will continue to learn with our application-driven approach, in which you will see all Visual Basic .NET features in useful applications and in which you will

1. Study the user requirements for an application.

2. Test-drive a working version of the application.

3. Learn the technologies you'll need to build the application yourself.

4. Build your own version of the application.

As you work through the book, if you have any questions about Visual Basic .NET, just send an e-mail to `deitel@deitel.com`, and we will respond promptly. We sincerely hope you enjoy learning the latest version of Microsoft's powerful Visual Basic language—the most widely used programming language in the world—with *Simply Visual Basic .NET 2003*. Good luck!

KEY TERMS

Active Server Pages .NET (ASP .NET)—.NET software that helps programmers create applications for the Web.

Ada—A programming language, named after Lady Ada Lovelace, that was developed under the sponsorship of the U.S. Department of Defense (DOD) in the 1970s and early 1980s.

arithmetic and logic unit (ALU)—The "manufacturing" section of the computer. The ALU performs calculations and makes decisions.

assembly language—A type of programming language that uses English-like abbreviations to represent the fundamental operations on the computer.

attribute—Another name for a property of an object.

bandwidth—The information-carrying capacity of communications lines.

BASIC (Beginner's All-Purpose Symbolic Instruction Code)—A programming language that was developed in the mid-1960s by Professors John Kemeny and Thomas Kurtz of Dartmouth College as a language for writing simple programs and its primary purpose was to familiarize novices with programming techniques.

central processing unit (CPU)—The part of the computer's hardware that is responsible for supervising the operation of the other sections of the computer.

class—The type of a group of related objects. A class specifies the general format of its objects; the properties and actions available to an object depend on its class. An object is to its class much as a house is to its blueprint.

COBOL (COmmon Business Oriented Language)—A programming language that was developed in the late 1950s by a group of computer manufacturers in conjunction with government and industrial computer users. This language is used primarily for business applications that manipulate large amounts of data.

compiler—A translator program that converts high-level-language programs into machine language.

computer—A device capable of performing computations and making logical decisions at speeds millions and even billions of times faster than the speeds at which human beings carry out those same tasks.

computer program—A set of instructions that guides a computer through an orderly series of actions.

computer programmer—A person who writes computer programs in programming languages.

control—A reusable component, such as a GroupBox, RadioButton, Button, Label and an MSChart control.

dynamic content—A type of content that is animated or interactive.

event-driven program—A program that responds to user-initiated events such as mouse clicks and keystrokes.

Fortran (Formula Translator)—A programming language developed by IBM Corporation in the mid-1950s to create scientific and engineering applications that require complex mathematical computations.

Framework Class Library (FCL)—.NET's collection of "prepackaged" classes and methods for performing common mathematical calculations, string manipulations, character manipulations, input/output operations, error checking and many other useful operations.

graphical user interface (GUI)—The visual part of an application with which users interact.

hardware—The various devices that make up a computer, including the keyboard, screen, mouse, hard drive, memory, CD-ROM and processing units.

high-level language—A type of programming language in which a single program statement accomplishes a substantial task. High-level languages use instructions that look almost like everyday English and that contain common mathematical notations.

HyperText Markup Language (HTML)—A language for marking up information to share over the World Wide Web via hyperlinked text documents.

input unit—The "receiving" section of the computer that obtains information (data and computer programs) from various input devices, such as the keyboard and the mouse.

integrated Development Environment (IDE)—A software tool that enables programmers to write, run, test and debug programs quickly and conveniently.

Internet—A worldwide computer network. Most people today access the Internet through the World Wide Web.

machine dependent—Only one computer platform supports a machine-dependent technology.

machine language—A computer's natural language, generally consisting of streams of numbers that instruct the computer how to perform its most elementary operations.

memory unit—The rapid-access, relatively low-capacity "warehouse" section of the computer, which stores data temporarily while an application is running.

method—A portion of a Java class that performs a task and possibly returns information when it completes that task.

microprocessor—The chip that makes a computer work (that is, the "brain" of the computer).

Microsoft .NET—Microsoft's vision for using the Internet and the Web in the development, engineering and use of software. .NET includes tools such as Visual Studio .NET and programming languages such as Visual Basic .NET.

.NET Framework—Microsoft-provided software that executes applications, provides the Framework Class Library (FCL) and supplies many other programming capabilities.

objects—Reusable software components that model items in the real world.

object technology—A packaging scheme for creating meaningful software units. The units are large and are focused on particular application areas. There are date objects, time objects, paycheck objects, file objects and the like.

output device—A device to which information that is processed by the computer can be sent.

output unit—The section of the computer that takes information the computer has processed and places it on various output devices, making the information available for use outside the computer.

Pascal—A programming language named after the 17th-century mathematician and philosopher Blaise Pascal. This language was designed for teaching structured programming.

procedural programming language—A programming language (such as Fortran, Pascal, BASIC and C) that focuses on actions (verbs) rather than things or objects (nouns).

properties—Object attributes, such as size, color and weight.

secondary storage unit—The long-term, high-capacity "warehouse" section of the computer.

software—The set of applications that run on computers.

software reuse—The reuse of existing pieces of software, an approach that enables programmers to avoid "reinventing the wheel," helping them develop new applications faster.

structured programming—A disciplined approach to creating programs that are clear, correct and easy to modify.

Transmission Control Protocol/Internet Protocol (TCP/IP)—The combined set of communications protocols for the Internet.

visual programming with Visual Basic .NET—Instead of writing detailed program statements, the programmer uses Visual Studio .NET's graphical user interface to conveniently drag and drop predefined objects into place, and to label and resize them. Visual Studio .NET writes much of the Visual Basic .NET program, saving the programmer considerable effort.

World Wide Web (WWW)—A communications system that allows computer users to locate and view multimedia documents (such as documents with text, graphics, animations, audios and videos).

World Wide Web Consortium (W3C)—A forum through which qualified individuals and companies cooperate to develop and standardize technologies for the World Wide Web.

MULTIPLE-CHOICE QUESTIONS

1.1 The World Wide Web was developed _____.

a) by ARPA
b) at CERN by Tim Berners-Lee
c) before the Internet
d) as a replacement for the Internet

1.2 Microsoft's _____ initiative integrates the Internet and the Web into software development.

a) .NET
b) BASIC
c) Windows
d) W3C

1.3 TextBoxes, Buttons and RadioButtons are examples of _____.

a) platforms
b) high-level languages
c) IDEs
d) controls

1.4 _____ is an example of primary memory.

a) TCP
b) RAM
c) ALU
d) CD-ROM

1.5 Visual Basic .NET is an example of a(n) _____ language, in which single program statements accomplish more substantial tasks.

a) machine
b) intermediate-level
c) high-level
d) assembly

1.6 Which protocol is primarily intended to create a "network of networks?"

    a) TCP   b) IP

    c) OOP   d) FCL

1.7 A major benefit of _____ programming is that it produces software that is more understandable and better organized than software produced with previously used techniques.

    a) object-oriented   b) centralized

    c) procedural   d) HTML

1.8 .NET's collection of prepackaged classes and methods is called the _____.

    a) NCL   b) WCL

    c) FCL   d) PPCM

1.9 The information-carrying capacity of communications lines is called _____.

    a) networking   b) secondary storage

    c) traffic   d) bandwidth

1.10 Which of these programming languages was specifically created for .NET?

    a) C#   b) C++

    c) BASIC   d) Visual Basic

EXERCISES   **1.11** Categorize each of the following items as either hardware or software:

    a) CPU   b) Compiler

    c) Input unit   d) A word-processor program

    e) A Visual Basic .NET program

1.12 Translator programs, such as assemblers and compilers, convert programs from one language (referred to as the source language) to another language (referred to as the target language). Determine which of the following statements are *true* and which are *false*:

    a) A compiler translates high-level-language programs into target-language programs.

    b) An assembler translates source-language programs into machine-language programs.

    c) A compiler translates source-language programs into target-language programs.

    d) High-level languages are generally machine dependent.

    e) A machine-language program requires translation before it can be run on a computer.

1.13 Computers can be thought of as being divided into six units.

    a) Which unit can be thought of as "the boss" of the other units?

    b) Which unit is the high-capacity "warehouse" and retains information even when the computer is powered off?

    c) Which unit might determine whether two items stored in memory are identical?

    d) Which unit obtains information from devices like the keyboard and mouse?

1.14 Expand each of the following acronyms:

    a) W3C   b) TCP/IP

    c) OOP   d) FCL

    e) HTML

1.15 What are the advantages to using object-oriented programming techniques?

TUTORIAL

Welcome Application

Introducing the Visual Studio® .NET 2003 IDE

Visual Studio® .NET is Microsoft's **Integrated Development Environment (IDE)** for creating and running applications written in .NET programming languages, such as Visual Basic .NET. The IDE allows you to create applications by dragging and dropping existing building blocks into place—a technique, called visual programming—greatly simplifying application development. In this tutorial, you will learn the Visual Studio .NET IDE features that you will need to create Visual Basic .NET applications.

2.1 Test-Driving the Welcome Application

In this section, you continue learning with our APPLICATION-DRIVEN™ approach as you prepare to build an application that displays a welcome message and a picture. This application must meet the following requirements:

> **Application Requirements**
>
> *A software company (Deitel & Associates) has asked you to develop a Visual Basic .NET application that will display the message "Welcome to Visual Basic .NET!" and a picture of the company's bug mascot. To build this application, you must first familiarize yourself with the Visual Studio .NET IDE.*

In this tutorial, you will begin to develop the **Welcome** application. Then, in Tutorial 3, you will "put it all together" and create the **Welcome** application by following our step-by-step boxes. [*Note*: Our convention is to display application names in the **Helvetica** font.] You begin by test-driving the completed application. Then, you will learn the additional Visual Basic .NET technologies that you will need to create your own version of this application.

Test-Driving the
Welcome Application

1. ***Checking your setup.*** Confirm that you have set up your computer properly by reading the *For Students and Instructors: Important Information before You Begin* section in the Preface.

2. ***Locating the application directory.*** Open Windows Explorer and navigate to the C:\Examples\Tutorial02 directory (Fig. 2.1).

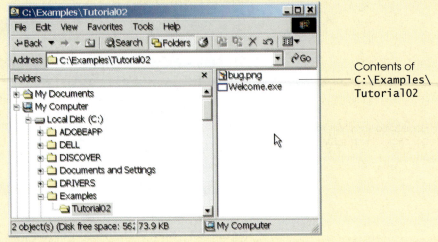

Contents of
C:\Examples\
Tutorial02

Figure 2.1   Contents of C:\Examples\Tutorial02.

3. ***Running the Welcome application.*** Double click Welcome.exe (Fig. 2.1) to run the application (Fig. 2.2).

Close
box

Figure 2.2   **Welcome** application executing.

4. ***Closing the application.*** Close your running application by clicking its close box, **x**.

5. ***Closing the IDE.*** Close Visual Studio .NET by clicking its close box.

2.2 Overview of the Visual Studio .NET 2003 IDE

This section introduces you to the Visual Studio .NET 2003 IDE. To begin, be certain that you have Visual Studio .NET 2003 installed on your computer. Then, find

Visual Studio .NET 2003, and open it; the **Start Page** displays. This page contains three tabs. Select the **Projects** tab (Fig. 2.3).

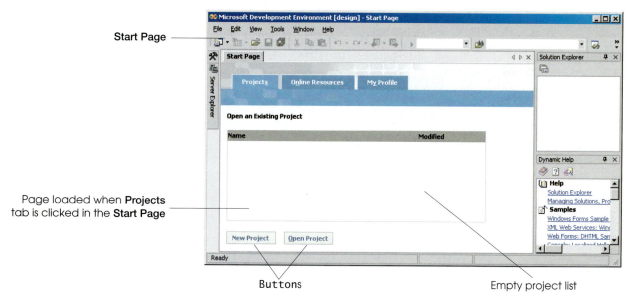

Figure 2.3 **Start Page** in Visual Studio .NET 2003 with an empty project list.

Depending upon your version of Visual Studio .NET, the **Start Page** might look different from the image in Fig. 2.3. Clicking the **Projects** tab loads a page that contains a table listing the names of recent projects (such as **WageCalculator** and **SecurityPanel** in Fig. 2.4), along with the dates on which these projects were last changed (modified). A **project** is a group of related files and images that make up an application. When you load Visual Studio .NET for the first time, the list of recent projects is empty. There are two **Button**s on the page— **New Project** and **Open Project**, which are used to open existing projects (such as the ones in the table of recent projects) and to create new projects, respectively.

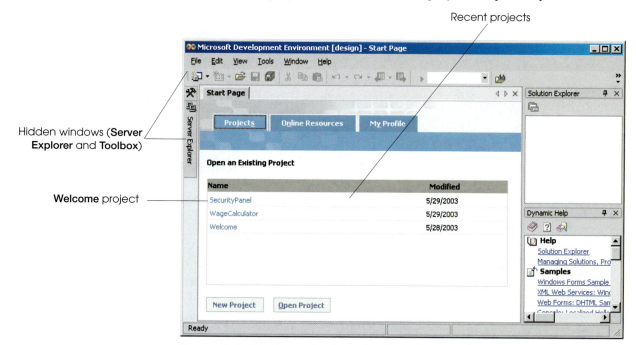

Figure 2.4 **Start Page** in Visual Studio .NET 2003 with recent projects listed.

Click the **Online Resources** tab (Fig. 2.5). The left side of the **Start Page** contains some helpful links, such as **Get Started**, **What's New** and **Online Community**. When you click a link, your computer will display information related to that link. The vast majority of the topics in these links will be more useful to you once you have gained some programming experience. Many of the **Start Page** links require that your computer be connected to the Internet. The following items describe each of the links on the **Start Page**:

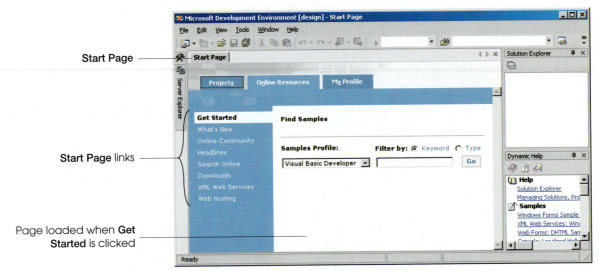

Figure 2.5   **Start Page** in Visual Studio .NET with **Online Resources** tab selected.

- Clicking the **Get Started** link loads a page that enables the user to search for sample code based on topic. For instance, when you type `Label` into the TextBox provided and click the `Go` Button, links to code samples will be provided for you.

- Clicking the **What's New** link displays a page that lists new features and updates for Visual Studio .NET, including downloads for Visual Basic .NET samples and programming tools. Information is updated frequently on this page.

- **Online Community** links to online resources for contacting other software developers through **newsgroups** (organized message boards on the Internet), user groups and Web sites.

- Clicking **Headlines** displays a page for browsing articles, news and tips for developing applications using Microsoft technologies.

- To access more extensive information, you can select **Search Online** and begin browsing through the **Microsoft Developer Network (MSDN)** online library, which contains articles and tutorials on technologies of interest to Visual Basic .NET programmers.

- When clicked, **Downloads** displays a page that provides you with access to product updates, code samples and reference materials.

- The **XML Web Services** page provides you with information about **Web services**, which are reusable pieces of Web-based software available on the Internet.

- The **Web Hosting** page allows you to post software (such as Web services) online for public use.

Clicking the final tab, **My Profile**, loads a page where you can adjust and customize various Visual Studio .NET settings, such as the location where various windows should appear in the IDE.

You also can browse the Web from Visual Studio .NET by using Microsoft's Internet Explorer (also called the **internal Web browser** in Visual Studio .NET). Select **View > Web Browser > Show Browser**. Several navigation buttons will be displayed by the top of the IDE (Fig. 2.6). By default, the site msdn.microsoft.com will be displayed for you. Enter www.deitel.com into the **location bar** (Fig. 2.6), then press the *Enter* key. This causes the DEITEL® home page to be displayed within the Visual Studio .NET IDE. Click the left-arrow Button (in the set of navigation Buttons) to return to msdn.microsoft.com. Other windows appear in the IDE in addition to the **Start Page** and the internal Web browser; we discuss several of them later in this tutorial.

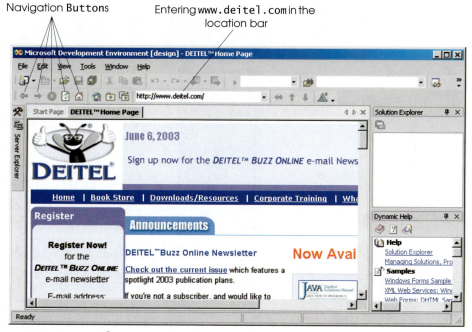

Figure 2.6   DEITEL® home page displayed in the Visual Studio .NET IDE. (Courtesy of Deitel & Associates, Inc.)

SELF-REVIEW   1. When you first open Visual Studio .NET, the _____ displays.

a) **What's New Page**   b) **Start Page**

c) **Welcome Page**   d) None of the above.

2. Clicking the _____ tab in the Visual Studio .NET **Start Page** loads a page that contains a table listing the names of recent projects.

a) **My Profile**   b) **Get Started**

c) **Projects**   d) **Online Resources**

Answers: 1) b. 2) c.

2.3 Creating a Project for the Welcome Application

In this section, you will create a simple Visual Basic .NET **Windows application**. The Visual Studio .NET IDE organizes applications into projects and **solutions**, which contain one or more projects. Every application always contains exactly one solution. Large-scale applications can contain many projects, in which each project performs a single, well-defined task (Fig. 2.7). In this book, each solution you build will contain only one project.

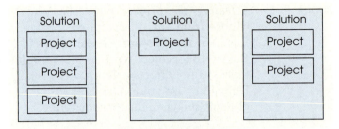

Figure 2.7 Solutions can contain one or more projects.

Creating a Project for the Welcome Application

1. *Creating a new project.* If you have not already done so, start Visual Studio .NET. In the **Projects** tab of the **Start Page**, click the **New Project** Button (Fig. 2.8), causing the **New Project** dialog to display (Fig. 2.9). **Dialogs** are windows that can display information for, and gather information from, the application's user. Like other windows, dialogs are identified by the text in their **title bar**.

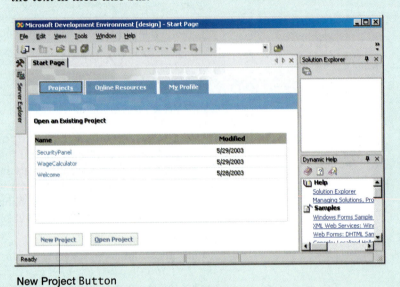

New Project Button

Figure 2.8 **New Project** Button.

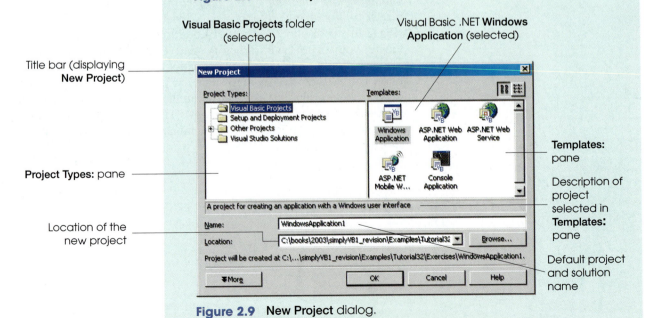

Visual Basic **Projects** folder (selected)

Visual Basic .NET **Windows Application** (selected)

Title bar (displaying **New Project**)

Project Types: pane

Location of the new project

Templates: pane

Description of project selected in **Templates:** pane

Default project and solution name

Figure 2.9 **New Project** dialog.

(cont.)

2. ***Selecting the project type.*** The Visual Studio .NET IDE allows you to choose from one of several project types. Click the **Visual Basic Projects** folder in the **Project Types:** pane (Fig. 2.10) to display the list of Visual Basic .NET project types in the **Templates:** pane. (**Templates** are building blocks for different types of Visual Basic .NET applications.) [*Note:* Depending on your version of Visual Studio .NET, the names and number of items shown in the **Project Types:** and **Templates:** panes could differ.]

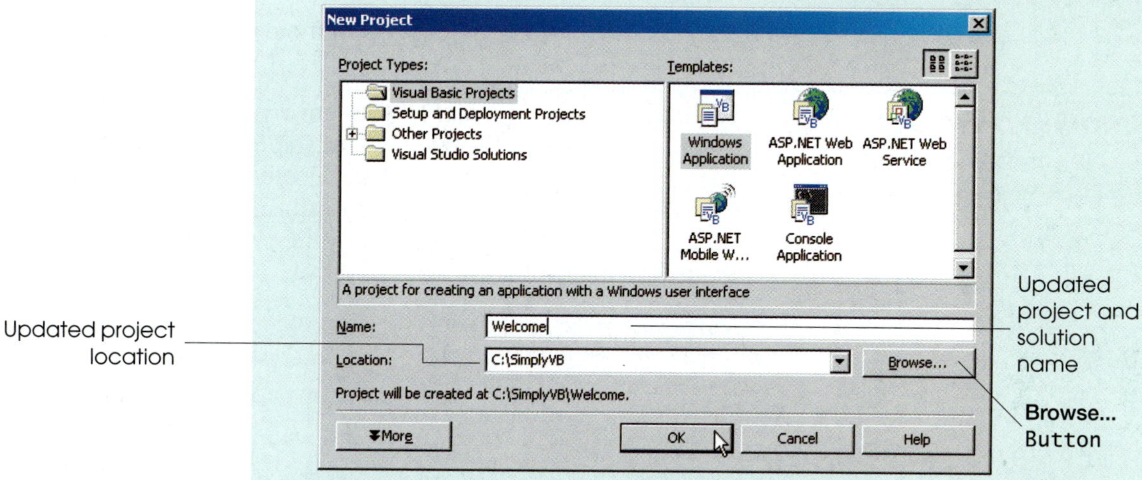

Updated project location

Updated project and solution name

Browse... Button

Figure 2.10 **New Project** dialog with updated project information.

3. ***Selecting the template.*** Select **Windows Application**, which is a template for an application that executes on machines running Microsoft® Windows. Examples of Windows applications include computer games and software products like Microsoft Word, Internet Explorer and Visual Studio .NET. In this book, you concentrate on **Windows Application**s. In the last tutorials, you will also build **ASP .NET Web Application**s.

4. ***Changing the name of the project.*** By default, the Visual Studio .NET IDE assigns the name `WindowsApplication1` to the project and solution (Fig. 2.9) and places these files in a directory named `WindowsApplication1`. To rename the project, type `Welcome` in the **Name:** TextBox (Fig. 2.10).

5. ***Changing the location of the project.*** Save this project in your `SimplyVB` directory. To change the project's location, click the **Browse...** Button (Fig. 2.10) to display the **Project Location** dialog (Fig. 2.11). In this dialog, locate your `SimplyVB` directory, and click **Open**. After providing the project's name and location in the **New Project** dialog, click **OK**. This displays the IDE in **design view** (Fig. 2.12), which contains the features you need to begin creating a Windows application. Note that your screen may look slightly different—some windows, such as the **Solution Explorer**, may not immediately appear. We will demonstrate how to open these windows shortly.

(cont.)

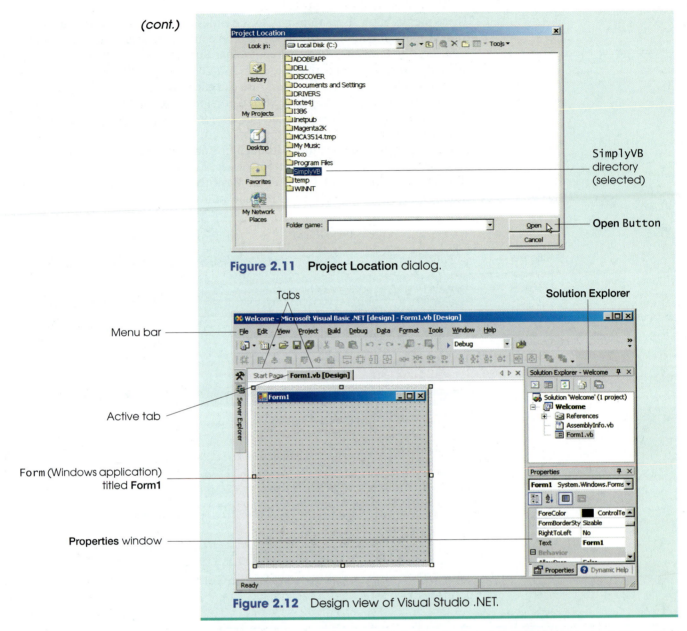

Figure 2.11   **Project Location** dialog.

Figure 2.12   Design view of Visual Studio .NET.

The name of each open file is listed on a **tab** (**Start Page** and **Form1.vb [Design]** in Fig. 2.12). To view a file, click its tab. Tabs provide easy access to multiple files. The **active tab** is displayed in bold text (**Form1.vb [Design]** in Fig. 2.12).

The contents of the **Form1.vb [Design]** tab, which includes the gray rectangle (called a **Form**), is the **Windows Form Designer**. The Form (titled **Form1**) represents the Windows application that you are creating. Forms can be enhanced by adding controls such as Buttons. Together, the Form and controls make up the application's **graphical user interface** (**GUI**), which is the visual part of the application. Users enter data (**inputs**) into the application by typing at the keyboard, by clicking the mouse buttons and in a variety of other ways. Applications display instructions and other information (**outputs**) for users to read in the GUI. For example, the **New Project** dialog in Fig. 2.9 is a GUI in which users click with the mouse to select project types and input project names and locations from the keyboard.

GUI controls (such as Buttons) aid both (1) in data entry by users and (2) in formatting and presenting data outputs to users. For example, Internet Explorer (Fig. 2.13) displays Web pages requested by users. Internet Explorer's GUI has a menu bar that contains six menus: **File**, **Edit**, **View**, **Favorites**, **Tools** and **Help**.

These menus allow users to print files, save files and more. Below the menu bar is a **toolbar** that contains Buttons. Each Button contains an image (called an **icon)** that identifies the Button. When clicked, toolbar Buttons execute tasks (such as printing and searching). Beneath the toolbar is a ComboBox in which users can type the locations of Web sites to visit. Users also can click the ComboBox's drop-down arrow to select Web sites that they have visited previously. To the left of the ComboBox is a Label (**Address**) that identifies the purpose of the ComboBox. The menus, Buttons and Label are part of Internet Explorer's GUI; they allow users to interact with the Internet Explorer application. Although not part of Internet Explorer's GUI, the Web page's TextBox at the bottom of Fig. 2.13 displays the text **<e-mail>** and allows users to input data. Using Visual Basic .NET, you can create your own applications that have all the GUI controls shown in Fig. 2.13 and many more.

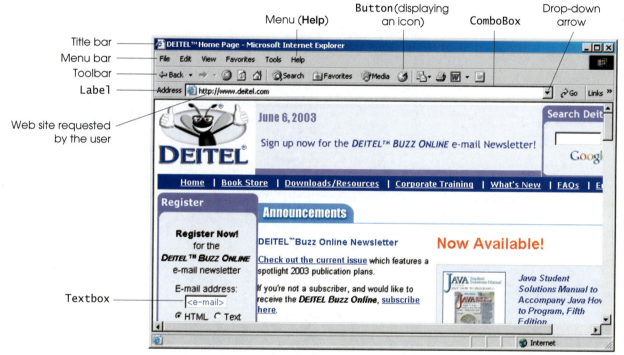

Figure 2.13 Internet Explorer window with GUI controls labelled. (Web site content courtesy of Deitel & Associates, Inc.)

SELF-REVIEW

1. The visual part of the application with which users interact is the application's _____.

   a) graphical user interface   b) project

   c) solution   d) title bar

2. A _____ contains one or more projects that collectively form a Visual Basic .NET application.

   a) dialog   b) Form

   c) solution   d) GUI

Answers: 1) a. 2) c.

2.4 Menu Bar and Toolbar

Visual Basic .NET programmers use **menus** (located on the Visual Studio .NET IDE menu bar shown in Fig. 2.14) that contain commands for managing the IDE and for developing and executing applications. Each menu has a group of related **commands** (also called **menu items**) that, when selected, cause the IDE to perform specific actions such as opening windows, saving files, printing files and executing applications. For example, to display the **Toolbox** window, select **View > Toolbox**. The menus in Fig. 2.14 are summarized in Fig. 2.15—you will learn to use many of these menus throughout the book. In Tutorial 22, **Typing** Application (Introducing Keyboard Events, Menus and Dialogs), you learn how to create and add your own menus and menu items to your applications.

| File | Edit | View | Project | Build | Debug | Data | Format | Tools | Window | Help |

Figure 2.14   Visual Studio .NET IDE menu bar.

Menu	Description
File	Contains commands for opening and closing projects, printing project data, etc.
Edit	Contains commands such as **Cut**, **Paste**, **Undo**, etc.
View	Contains commands for displaying IDE windows and toolbars.
Project	Contains commands for managing a solution's projects and their files.
Build	Contains commands for compiling a Visual Basic .NET application.
Debug	Contains commands for identifying and correcting problems in applications. Also contains commands for running applications.
Data	Contains commands for interacting with **databases**, which store the data that an application processes. [*Note:* You will learn database concepts in Tutorial 25, **ATM** Application.]
Format	Contains commands for aligning and spacing a Form's controls.
Tools	Contains commands for accessing additional IDE tools and options that enable customization of the IDE.
Window	Contains commands for hiding, opening, closing and displaying IDE windows.
Help	Contains commands for accessing the IDE's help features.

Figure 2.15   Visual Studio .NET IDE menu summary.

Rather than navigating the menus for certain commonly used commands, you can access those same commands from the IDE toolbar (Fig. 2.16). To execute a command via the IDE toolbar, simply click its icon. Some icons have associated down arrows that, when clicked, display additional commands.

Toolbar icon indicates a command to open a project or solution

Down arrow indicates additional commands are available

— Toolbar

Figure 2.16   IDE toolbar.

Positioning the mouse pointer over an icon highlights the icon and, after a few seconds, displays a description called a **tool tip** (Fig. 2.17). Tool tips help you become familiar with the IDE's features.

Tool tip displayed when the mouse pointer has rested on the icon for a few seconds

Figure 2.17 Tool-tip demonstration.

SELF-REVIEW

1. _____ contain groups of related commands.

    a) Menu items   b) Menus

    c) Tool tips   d) None of the above

2. When the mouse pointer is positioned over an IDE toolbar icon for a few seconds, a _____ is displayed.

    a) toolbox   b) toolbar

    c) menu   d) tool tip

Answers: 1) b. 2) d.

2.5 Visual Studio .NET IDE Windows

The IDE provides windows for accessing project files and for customizing forms and controls by changing their attributes (names, colors, etc.). These windows provide visual aids for common programming tasks, such as managing files in a project. In this section, you will become familiar with several windows—**Solution Explorer**, **Properties** and **Toolbox**—that are essential for creating Visual Basic .NET applications. You can access these windows by using the IDE toolbar icons (Fig. 2.18) or by selecting the window name, using the **View** menu. Two of the windows that have icons provided (**Object Browser** and **Class View**) will not be used in this text. [*Note*: These icons may not appear if the IDE window has been minimized. If you cannot view the icons of Fig. 2.18, maximize the IDE window.]

Properties icon

Toolbox icon

Solution Explorer icon

Object Browser icon

Class View icon

Figure 2.18 Toolbar icons for five Visual Studio .NET IDE windows.

Solution Explorer

The **Solution Explorer** window (located on the right side of the IDE as shown in Fig. 2.12) provides access to solution files. This window allows you to manage files visually. The **Solution Explorer** window displays a list of all the files in a project and all projects in a solution. (Remember that a Visual Basic .NET solution can contain one or more projects.) When the Visual Studio .NET IDE is first loaded, the **Solution Explorer** window is empty; there are no files to display. Once a solution is open, the **Solution Explorer** window displays that solution's contents. Figure 2.19 displays the solution contents for the **Welcome** application.

Figure 2.19 **Solution Explorer** with an open solution.

For your single-project solution, **Welcome** is the only project. The file, which corresponds to the Form shown in Fig. 2.12, is named `Form1.vb`. (Visual Basic .NET Form files use the `.vb` file name extension, which is short for "Visual Basic.")

The **plus** and **minus** boxes to the left of both the project name and the **References** folder are called **nodes**. The plus and minus boxes expand and collapse information, respectively.

Navigating a Project with the Solution Explorer

1. **Collapsing a node.** Click the minus box to the left of the project name to collapse the node (Fig. 2.20). The minus box now becomes a plus box (Fig. 2.21).

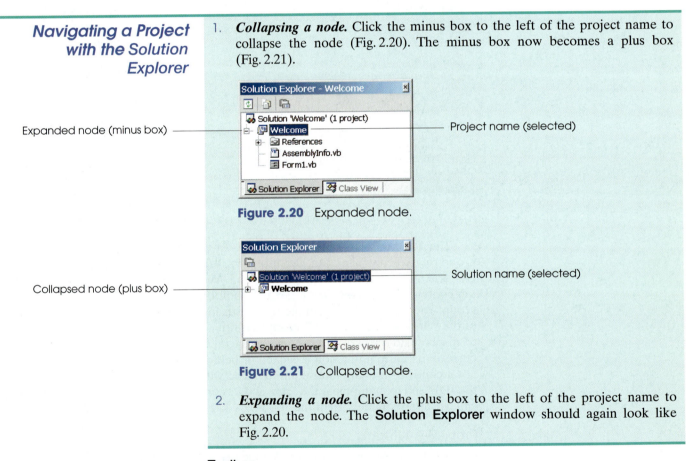

Figure 2.20 Expanded node.

Figure 2.21 Collapsed node.

2. **Expanding a node.** Click the plus box to the left of the project name to expand the node. The **Solution Explorer** window should again look like Fig. 2.20.

Toolbox

Using visual programming, you can "drag and drop" controls onto the Form quickly and easily instead of building them from "scratch," which is a slow and complex process. Just as you do not need to know how to build an engine to drive a car, you do not need to know how to build controls to create effective GUIs. The **Toolbox** (Fig. 2.22) contains a wide variety of controls for building GUIs. You will use the **Toolbox** as you finish creating the **Welcome** application in Tutorial 3. If the **Toolbox** is not visible, select **View > Toolbox**.

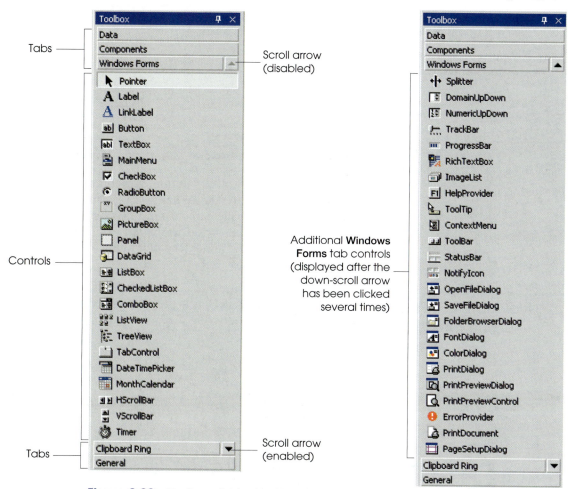

Figure 2.22 **Toolbox** displaying the contents of the **Windows Forms** tab.

The **Toolbox** contains five tabs (three at the top and two at the bottom) that group related controls: **Data**, **Components**, **Windows Forms**, **Clipboard Ring** and **General**. In this book, you will use only the **Windows Forms** tab controls and **Data** tab controls. When you click a tab, the **Toolbox** displays all of the controls in that group. You can scroll through the controls using the black **scroll arrows** to the right of the **Windows Forms** and **Clipboard Ring** tabs. When there are no more controls to display, the scroll arrow becomes gray, meaning that it is **disabled**. (It will not perform its normal function if clicked or held down.) The first item in the group is not a control—it is the **mouse pointer**. You will use the mouse pointer to navigate the IDE and to manipulate the Form and its controls. In the remaining tutorials, you will use approximately 20 of the **Toolbox**'s 47 controls.

Properties **Window**

One of the windows you will use frequently is the **Properties** window, which displays the **properties** for Form and control objects. Properties specify an object's attributes, such as the size, color and position of a control object.

The **Properties** window allows you to set object properties visually, without writing code. Setting properties visually provides a number of benefits:

- You can see which properties can be modified and, in many cases, you can learn the acceptable values for a given property.

- You do not have to remember or search the Visual Studio .NET documentation (see Section 2.7) for a property's settings.

■ This window displays a brief description of the selected property, so you can understand the property's purpose.

■ A property can be set quickly.

All of these features are designed to help you ensure that settings are correct and consistent throughout the project. If the **Properties** window is not visible, select **View > Properties Window**. Figure 2.23 shows a Form's **Properties** window:

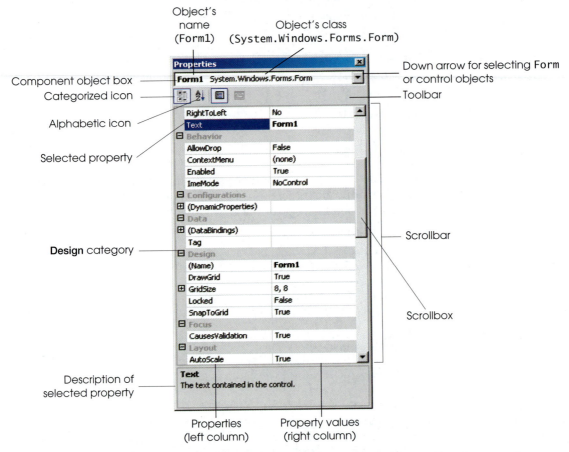

Figure 2.23 **Properties** window displaying a Form's properties.

■ Each Form or control object has its own set of properties. At the top of the **Properties** window is the **component object box**, which allows you to select the object whose properties you wish to display in the **Properties** window.

■ You can confirm that you are manipulating the correct object's properties because the object's name and class type are displayed in the component object box. Form objects have class type System.Windows.Forms.Form and are assigned generic names (such as Form1) by Visual Studio .NET. You will learn about the class types for controls in the next tutorial. Icons on the toolbar sort the properties either alphabetically (if you click the **alphabetic icon**) or categorically (if you click the **categorized icon**). Figure 2.23 shows the **Properties** window with its properties sorted categorically. Each gray horizontal bar to the left of the scrollbar is a category that groups related properties. For example, the **Design** category groups five related properties. The categories visible in Fig. 2.23 are **Behavior**, **Configurations**, **Data**, **Design**, **Focus** and **Layout**. Notice that each category is a node.

■ The left column of the **Properties** window lists the object's property names; the right column displays each property's value. In the next tutorial, you will learn how to set properties for objects.

- You can scroll through the list of properties by dragging the scrollbar's scrollbox up or down.

- Whenever you select a property, a description of the property displays at the bottom of the **Properties** window.

SELF-REVIEW

1. The _____ allows you to add controls to the Form in a visual manner.

   a) **Solution Explorer**   b) **Properties** window

   c) **Toolbox**   d) **Dynamic Help** window

2. The _____ window allows you to view a solution's files.

   a) **Properties**   b) **Solution Explorer**

   c) **Toolbox**   d) None of the above.

Answers: 1) c. 2) b.

2.6 Auto Hide

Visual Studio .NET provides a space-saving feature used for the **Toolbox**, **Properties** and **Dynamic Help** (Section 2.7) windows, called **Auto Hide**. When Auto Hide is enabled for one or more of these windows, a toolbar appears along one of the edges of the IDE.

Using Auto Hide

1. ***Displaying a hidden window.*** When Auto Hide is enabled, the toolbar along one of the edges of the IDE contains one or more tabs, each of which identifies a hidden window (Fig. 2.24). Place the mouse pointer over the **Toolbox** tab to display the **Toolbox** (Fig. 2.25).

Tabs for hidden windows

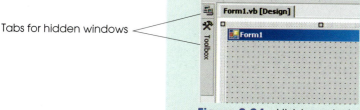

Figure 2.24   Hidden-window tabs.

Title bar

Mouse pointer over the tab for the **Toolbox**

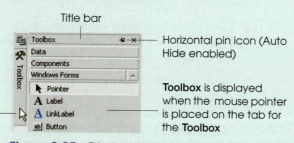

Horizontal pin icon (Auto Hide enabled)

Toolbox is displayed when the mouse pointer is placed on the tab for the **Toolbox**

Figure 2.25   Displaying a hidden window with Auto Hide enabled.

2. ***Hiding a window.*** Move the mouse pointer outside the **Toolbox** window's area to hide the **Toolbox** (Fig. 2.26).

3. ***Disabling Auto Hide.*** To keep the **Toolbox** window open and to disable Auto Hide (called "pinning down" a window), click the **pin** icon (also called the **pushpin** icon) in Fig. 2.25's title bar. Notice that, when a window is "pinned down," the pin icon is vertical (Fig. 2.27), whereas, when Auto Hide is enabled, the pin icon is horizontal.

(cont.)

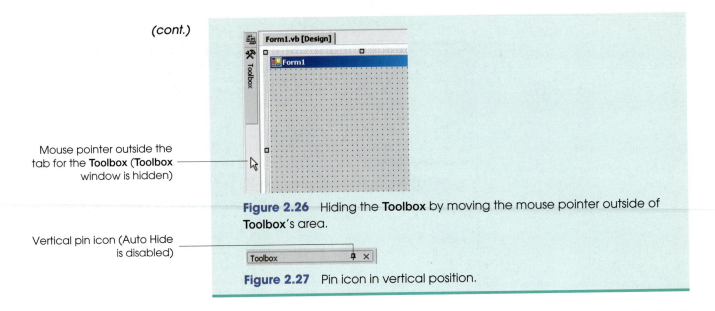

Mouse pointer outside the tab for the **Toolbox** (**Toolbox** window is hidden)

Figure 2.26   Hiding the **Toolbox** by moving the mouse pointer outside of **Toolbox**'s area.

Vertical pin icon (Auto Hide is disabled)

Figure 2.27   Pin icon in vertical position.

SELF-REVIEW

1. Visual Studio .NET provides a space-saving feature used for the _____ window(s).

   a) **Toolbox**   b) **Properties**

   c) **Dynamic Help**   d) All of the above.

2. When Auto Hide is enabled its pin icon is _____.

   a) horizontal   b) vertical

   c) down   d) diagonal

Answers: 1) d. 2) a.

2.7 Using Help

The Visual Studio .NET IDE provides extensive help features. The **Help** menu commands are summarized in Fig. 2.28. **Dynamic help** (Fig. 2.29) provides links to articles that apply to the current content (that is, the item selected with the mouse pointer). For example, if you have the **Start Page** open, **Dynamic Help** provides links to articles about the **Start Page**, customizing **Dynamic Help** and many other topics. To open the **Dynamic Help** window, select **Help > Dynamic Help**. Then, when you click a word or object (such as a Form or a control), links to relevant help articles appear in the **Dynamic Help** window. The window lists help topics, samples and "Getting Started" information. When you click a link, the help topic appears in a new window. This new window also contains a toolbar that provides access to the **Contents...**, **Index...** and **Search...** help features.

Command	Description
Contents...	Displays a categorized table of contents in which help articles are organized by topic.
Index...	Displays an alphabetized list of topics through which you can browse.
Search...	Allows you to find help articles based on search keywords.

Figure 2.28   **Help** menu commands.

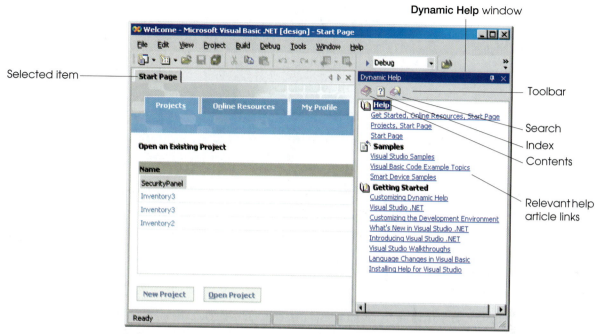

Figure 2.29 **Dynamic Help** window.

SELF-REVIEW

1. _____ displays relevant help articles, based on the selected object.

   a) Internal help
   b) Dynamic help
   c) External help
   d) Context-driven help

2. **Help** command _____ displays an alphabetized list of topics through which you can browse.

   a) **Search...**
   b) **Browse...**
   c) **Contents...**
   d) **Index...**

Answers: 1) b. 2) d.

2.8 Saving and Closing Solutions in Visual Studio .NET

Once you are finished with a solution, you will want to save the solution's files and close the solution.

Closing the Solution for the Welcome Application

1. *Saving the solution files.* Before closing the solution for the **Welcome** application, you will want to save the solution's files, ensuring that any changes made to the solution's files are not lost. Although you did not make any changes to the solution's files for this particular tutorial, you will be making such changes in most of the tutorials so, for practice, save your solution files by selecting **File > Save All**.

2. *Closing the solution.* Select **File > Close Solution**.

2.9 Internet and Web Resources

Please take a moment to visit each of these sites briefly. To save typing time, use the hot links on the enclosed CD or at www.deitel.com.

www.msdn.microsoft.com/vstudio
This site is the home page for Microsoft Visual Studio .NET. This site includes news, documentation, downloads and other resources.

`www.worldofdotnet.net`

This site offers a wide variety of information on .NET, including articles, news and links to newsgroups and other resources.

`www.vbi.org`

This site has Visual Basic articles, reviews of books and software, documentation, downloads, links and more.

`www.msdn.microsoft.com/library/default.asp?url=/library/en-us/` `vbcon/html/vbconselectingwfcclientcontrol.asp`

This Microsoft site summarizes **Toolbox** controls by function. Each control has a link to a page that contains additional resources for that control.

2.10 Wrap-Up

In this tutorial, you were introduced to the Visual Studio .NET 2003 integrated development environment (IDE). You learned key features, including tabs, menus, menu bars, toolbars, icons, Auto Hide and much more.

You created a Visual Basic .NET Windows application. The application contained one Form object named Form1. Form objects represent the application's graphical user interface (GUI).

You worked with the **Solution Explorer**, **Toolbox** and **Properties** windows that are essential to developing Visual Basic .NET applications. The **Solution Explorer** window allows you to manage your solution's files visually. The **Toolbox** window contains a rich collection of controls (organized on tabs) that allow you to create GUIs. The **Properties** window allows you to set the attributes of the Form and controls.

You explored Visual Studio .NET's help features, including the **Dynamic Help** window and the **Help** menu. The **Dynamic Help** window displays links related to the item you select with the mouse pointer. You learned about Web sites that provide additional Visual Basic .NET information.

In the next tutorial, you will begin creating Visual Basic .NET applications. You will follow step-by-step instructions for completing the **Welcome** application by using visual programming and the IDE features you learned in this tutorial.

SKILLS SUMMARY

Viewing a Page that Contains a Table Listing Names of Recent Projects
- Click the **Start Page**'s **Get Started** link.

Viewing a Page that Lists New Features and Updates for Visual Studio .NET
- Click the **Start Page**'s **What's New** link.

Viewing a Page that Lists Online Resources for Contacting Other Software Developers
- Click the **Start Page**'s **Online Community** link.

Viewing a Page that Lists News, Articles and Tips for Developing Microsoft Applications
- Click the **Start Page**'s **Headlines** link.

Viewing a Page that Allows Browsing of the Microsoft Developer Network (MSDN) Web Site
- Click the **Start Page**'s **Search Online** link.

Viewing a Page that Lists Product Updates, Code Samples and Reference Materials
- Click the **Start Page**'s **Downloads** link.

Viewing a Page that Allows You to Customize Visual Studio .NET Settings
- Click the **Start Page**'s **My Profile** link.

Creating a New Project

- Click the **Start Page**'s **New Project** Button to display the New Project dialog.
- Select **Visual Basic Projects** in the **Project Types:** pane.
- Select **Windows Application** in the **Templates:** pane.
- Provide the project's name in the **Name:** TextBox.
- Provide the project's directory information in the **Location:** TextBox.
- Click the **OK** Button.

Saving a Project

- Select **File > Save All**.

Viewing a Tool Tip for a Visual Studio .NET Icon

- Place the mouse pointer on the icon, and keep it there until the tool tip appears.

Collapsing a Node in the Solution Explorer

- Click the node's minus box.

Expanding a Node in the Solution Explorer

- Click the node's plus box.

Scrolling Through the List of Windows Forms Controls in the Toolbox

- Click the scroll arrows.

Viewing the Properties Window

- Select **View > Properties Window**.

Displaying a Hidden Window

- Place the mouse pointer over the hidden window's tab.

Disabling Auto Hide and "Pinning Down" a Window

- Click the window's horizontal pin icon to change it to a vertical pin icon.

Enabling Auto Hide

- Click the window's vertical pin icon to change it to a horizontal pin icon.

Opening the Dynamic Help Window

- Select **Help > Dynamic Help**.

KEY TERMS

active tab—The tab of the document displayed in the IDE.

alphabetic icon—The icon in the **Properties** window that, when clicked, sorts properties alphabetically.

Auto Hide—A space-saving IDE feature used for windows such as **Toolbox**, **Properties** and **Dynamic Help** that hides a window until the mouse pointer is placed on the hidden window's tab.

categorized icon—The icon in the **Properties** window that, when clicked, sorts properties categorically.

component object box—The ComboBox at the top of the **Properties** window that allows you to select the Form or control object whose properties you want set.

Contents... command—The command that displays a categorized table of contents in which help articles are organized by topic.

Data menu—The menu that contains commands for interacting with databases.

Debug menu—The menu that contains commands for debugging and running an application.

design view—The Visual Studio .NET view that contains the features necessary to begin creating Windows applications.

dialog—A window that can display and gather information.

dynamic help—A help option that provides links to articles that apply to the current content (that is, the item selected with the mouse pointer).

Form—The object that represents the Windows application's graphical user interface (GUI).

graphical user interface (GUI)—The visual components through which users interact with applications.

icon—The graphical representation of commands in the Visual Studio .NET IDE.

Integrated Development Environment (IDE)—The software used to create, document, run and debug applications.

internal Web browser—Web browser (Internet Explorer) included in Visual Studio .NET, with which you can browse the Web.

location bar—The ComboBox in Visual Studio .NET where you can enter the name of a Web site to visit.

menu—A group of related commands.

menu item—A command located in a menu that, when selected, causes an application to perform a specific action.

Microsoft Developer Network (MSDN)—An online library that contains articles, downloads and tutorials on technologies of interest to Visual Studio .NET developers.

minus box—The icon that, when clicked, collapses a node.

New Project dialog—A dialog that allows you to choose which type of application you wish to create.

pin icon—An icon that enables or disables the Auto Hide feature.

plus box—An icon that, when clicked, expands a node.

project—A group of related files that compose an application.

Properties window—The window that displays the properties for a Form or control object.

property—Specifies a control or Form object's attributes, such as size, color and position.

solution—Contains one or more projects.

Solution Explorer—A window that provides access to all the files in a solution.

Start Page—The initial page displayed when Visual Studio .NET is opened.

tool tip—The description of an icon that appears when the mouse pointer is held over that icon for a few seconds.

toolbar—A bar that contains Buttons that execute commands.

toolbar icon—A picture on a toolbar Button.

Toolbox—A window that contains controls used to customize Forms.

Tools menu—A menu that contains commands for accessing additional IDE tools and options that enable customization of the IDE.

Visual Studio .NET—Microsoft's integrated development environment (IDE), which allows developers to create applications in a variety of .NET programming languages.

Windows application—An application that executes on a Windows operating system.

MULTIPLE-CHOICE QUESTIONS

2.1 The _____ integrated development environment is used for creating applications written in .NET programming languages such as Visual Basic.NET.

a) **Solution Explorer**
b) Gates
c) Visual Studio .NET
d) Microsoft

2.2 The .vb file name extension indicates a _____.

a) Visual Basic file
b) dynamic help file
c) help file
d) very big file

2.3 The pictures on toolbar Buttons are called _____.

a) prototypes
b) icons
c) tool tips
d) tabs

2.4 The _____ allows programmers to modify controls visually, without writing code.

a) **Properties** window
b) **Solution Explorer**
c) menu bar
d) **Toolbox**

2.5 The _____ hides the **Toolbox** when the mouse pointer is moved outside the **Toolbox**'s area.

    a) component-selection feature   b) Auto Hide feature

    c) pinned command   d) minimize command

2.6 A _____ appears when the mouse pointer is positioned over an IDE toolbar icon for a few seconds.

    a) drop-down list   b) menu

    c) tool tip   d) down arrow

2.7 The Visual Studio .NET IDE provides _____.

    a) help documentation   b) a toolbar

    c) windows for accessing project files   d) All of the above.

2.8 The _____ contains a list of helpful links, such as **Get Started** and **Online Community**.

    a) **Solution Explorer** window   b) **Properties** window

    c) **Start Page**   d) **Toolbox** link

2.9 The **Properties** window contains _____.

    a) the component object box   b) a **Solution Explorer**

    c) menus   d) a menu bar

2.10 A _____ can be enhanced by adding reusable components such as `Buttons`.

    a) control   b) `Form`

    c) tab   d) property

2.11 For Web browsing, Visual Studio .NET includes _____.

    a) Web View   b) Excel

    c) a **Web** tab   d) Internet Explorer

2.12 An application's GUI can include _____.

    a) toolbars   b) icons

    c) menus   d) All of the above.

2.13 The _____ does not contain a pin icon.

    a) **Dynamic Help** window   b) **Solution Explorer** window

    c) **Toolbox** window   d) active tab

2.14 When clicked, _____ in the **Solution Explorer** window will expand nodes and _____ will collapse nodes.

    a) minus boxes; plus boxes   b) plus boxes; minus boxes

    c) up arrows; down arrows   d) left arrows; right arrows

2.15 Form _____ specify attributes such as size and position.

    a) nodes   b) inputs

    c) properties   d) title bars

EXERCISES

2.16 (*Closing and Opening the Start Page*) In this exercise, you will learn how to close and reopen the **Start Page**. To accomplish this task, perform the following steps:

    a) Close Visual Studio .NET if it is open by selecting **File > Exit** or by clicking its close box.

    b) Start Visual Studio .NET.

    c) Close the **Start Page** by clicking its close box (Fig. 2.30).

    d) Select **Help > Show Start Page** to display the **Start Page**.

Figure 2.30   Closing the **Start Page**.

2.17 (*Enabling Auto Hide for the Solution Explorer Window*) In this exercise, you will learn how to use the **Solution Explorer** window's Auto Hide feature by performing the following steps:

a) Open the **Start Page**.

b) In the **Start** page (displayed by default), click the **Open Project** Button to display the **Open Project** dialog. You can skip to step e) if the **Welcome** application is already open.

c) In the **Open Project** dialog, navigate to C:\SimplyVB\Welcome, and click **Open**.

d) In the **Open Project** dialog, select Welcome.sln, and click **Open**.

e) Position the mouse pointer on the vertical pin icon in the **Solution Explorer** window's title bar. After a few seconds, a tool tip appears displaying the words **Auto Hide** (Fig. 2.31).

Figure 2.31   Enabling Auto Hide.

f) Click the vertical pin icon. This action causes a **Solution Explorer** tab to appear on the right side of the IDE. The vertical pin icon changes to a horizontal pin icon (Fig. 2.32). Auto Hide has now been enabled for the **Solution Explorer** window.

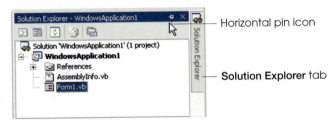

Figure 2.32   **Solution Explorer** window with Auto Hide enabled.

g) Position the mouse pointer outside the **Solution Explorer** window to hide the window.

h) Position the mouse pointer on the **Solution Explorer** tab to view the **Solution Explorer** window.

2.18 (*Sorting Properties Alphabetically in the Properties Window*) In this exercise, you will learn how to sort the **Properties** window's properties alphabetically by performing the following steps:

a) Open the **Welcome** application by performing steps a) through d) of Exercise 2.17. If the **Welcome** application is already open, you can skip this step.

b) Locate the **Properties** window. If it is not visible, select **View > Properties Window** to display the **Properties** window.

c) To sort properties alphabetically, click the **Properties** window's alphabetic icon (Fig. 2.33). The properties will display in alphabetic order.

Alphabetic icon ———

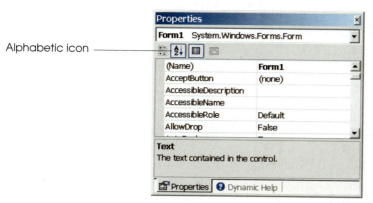

Figure 2.33   Sorting properties alphabetically.

Objectives

In this tutorial, you will learn to:
- Set the text in the **Form**'s title bar.
- Change the **Form**'s background color.
- Place a **Label** control on the **Form**.
- Display text in a **Label** control.
- Place a **PictureBox** control on the **Form**.
- Display an image in a **PictureBox** control.
- Execute an application.

Outline

3.1 Test-Driving the Welcome Application

3.2 Constructing the Welcome Application

3.3 Objects Used in the Welcome Application

3.4 Wrap-Up

Welcome Application

Introduction to Visual Programming

Today, users prefer software with interactive graphical user interfaces (GUIs) that respond to actions such as **Button** clicks, data input and much more. As a result, the vast majority of Windows applications, such as Microsoft Word and Internet Explorer, are GUI based. With Visual Basic .NET, you can create Windows applications that input and output information in a variety of ways, which you will learn throughout the book.

In this tutorial, you use visual programming to complete the **Welcome** application you began creating in Tutorial 2. You will build the application's GUI by placing two controls—a **Label** and a **PictureBox**—on the **Form**. You will use the **Label** control to display text and the **PictureBox** control to display an image. You will customize the appearance of the **Form**, **Label** and **PictureBox** objects by setting their values in the **Properties** window. You will set many property values including the **Form**'s background color, the **PictureBox**'s image and the **Label**'s text. You also will learn how to execute your application from within the Visual Studio .NET IDE.

3.1 Test-Driving the Welcome Application

The last tutorial introduced you to the Visual Studio .NET IDE. In this tutorial, you will use Visual Studio .NET to build the **Welcome** application mentioned in Tutorial 2. This application must meet the following requirements:

> **Application Requirements**
>
> *Recall that a software company (Deitel & Associates) has asked you to develop a simple **Welcome** application that includes the greeting "Welcome to Visual Basic .NET!" and a picture of the company's bug mascot. Now that you are familiar with the Visual Studio .NET IDE, your task is to develop this application to satisfy the company's request.*

You begin by test-driving the completed application. Then, you will learn the additional Visual Basic .NET technologies that you will need to create your own version of this application.

Test-Driving the Welcome Application

1. ***Opening the completed application.*** Start Visual Studio .NET and select **File > Open Solution...** (Fig. 3.1) to display the **Open Solution** dialog (Fig. 3.2). Select the `C:\Examples\Tutorial03\CompletedApplica-tion\Welcome` directory from the **Look in:** ComboBox. Select the **Welcome** solution file and click the **Open** Button.

Open Solution command (selected) opens an existing solution

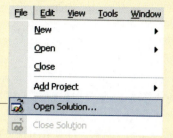

Figure 3.1 Opening an existing solution with the **File** menu's **Open Solution...** command.

Open Solution dialog

Look in: ComboBox

Welcome solution file

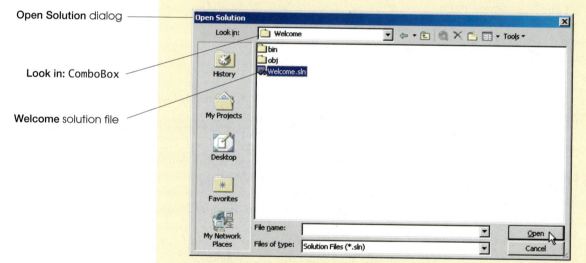

Figure 3.2 **Open Solution** dialog displaying the contents of the **Welcome** solution.

2. ***Opening the Form in design view.*** Double click on `Welcome.vb` in the **Solution Explorer** to open the **Welcome** application's Form in design view (Figure 3.3).

(cont.)

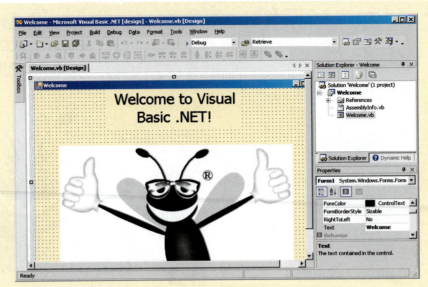

Figure 3.3   Welcome application's Form in design view.

3. ***Running the Welcome application.*** Select **Debug > Start** (Fig. 3.4). The **Start** command runs the application. The **Welcome** Form shown in Fig. 3.5 will appear.

Start command (selected) runs the application

Figure 3.4   Running the **Welcome** application using the **Debug** menu's **Start** command.

4. ***Closing the application.*** Close the running application by clicking its close box, ✕.

5. ***Closing the IDE.*** Close Visual Studio .NET by clicking its close box.

(cont.)

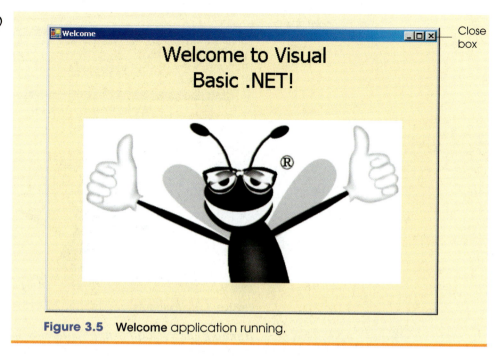

Figure 3.5 **Welcome** application running.

3.2 Constructing the Welcome Application

In this section, you perform the steps necessary to develop the **Welcome** application. The application consists of a single Form that uses a Label control and a PictureBox control. A **Label** control displays text that the user cannot change. A **PictureBox** control displays an image that the user cannot change. You will not write a single line of code to create this application. Instead, you will use the technique called **visual programming**, in which Visual Studio .NET processes your programming actions (such as clicking, dragging and dropping controls) and actually writes the program for you! The following box shows you how to begin constructing the **Welcome** application, using the solution you created in Tutorial 2 as a starting point.

Changing the Form's File Name and Title Bar Text

1. *Opening the Welcome application's solution.* Double click the C:\SimplyVB\Welcome\Welcome.sln file to open your application. Double click Form1.vb in the **Solution Explorer** window to display the blank Form. Figure 3.6 shows the **Welcome** application solution open in Visual Studio .NET.

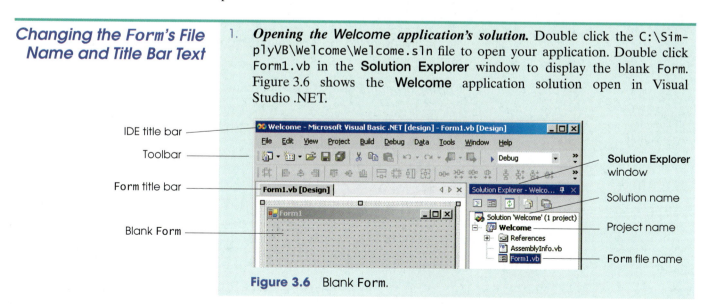

Figure 3.6 Blank Form.

(cont.)

2. ***Changing the Form's file name.*** When a Windows application is created, Visual Studio .NET names the Form file Form1.vb. Select Form1.vb in the **Solution Explorer** window (Fig. 3.6) to display the file's properties in the **Properties** window (the window on the left in Fig. 3.7). If either window is not visible, you can select **View > Properties Window** or **View > Solution Explorer** to display the appropriate window. Double click the field to the right of the File Name property's box, and type Welcome.vb (Fig. 3.7). Press the *Enter* key to update the Form's file name. Notice that the file name changes in the **Solution Explorer** window (the window on the right in Fig. 3.7) and in the **Properties** window.

Good Programming Practice

Change your application's Form file name (Form1.vb) to a name that describes the application's purpose.

File properties

Selected property

Selected property description

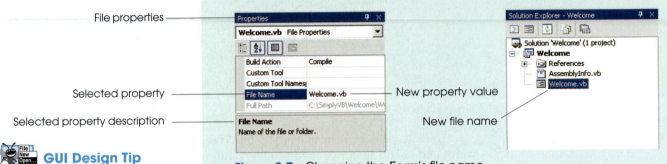

New property value

New file name

Figure 3.7   Changing the Form's file name.

GUI Design Tip

Choose short and descriptive Form titles. Capitalize words that are not articles, prepositions or conjunctions. Do not use punctuation.

3. ***Setting the text in the Form's title bar.*** The title bar is the top portion of the window that contains the window's title. To change the text in the Form's title bar from **Form1** to **Welcome**, use the **Properties** window (Fig. 3.8). Click the Form. As in Fig. 3.7, double click the field to the right of the **Text** property in the **Properties** window, and type Welcome. Press the *Enter* key to update the Form's title bar (Fig. 3.9).

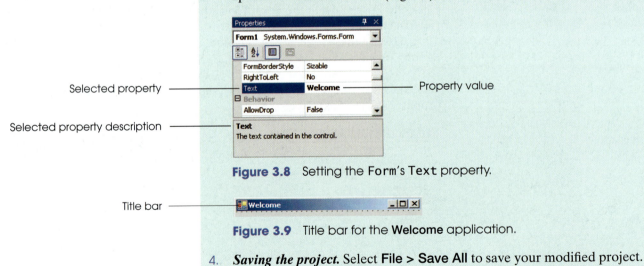

Selected property

Property value

Selected property description

Figure 3.8   Setting the Form's **Text** property.

Title bar

Figure 3.9   Title bar for the **Welcome** application.

4. ***Saving the project.*** Select **File > Save All** to save your modified project.

There are several ways to resize the Form. If the resizing does not have to be precise, you can click and drag one of the Form's enabled **sizing handles** (the small white squares that appear along the Form's edges, as shown in Fig. 3.10). The appearance of the mouse pointer changes (that is, it becomes a pointer with one or more arrows) when it is over an enabled sizing handle. The new pointer indicates the direction(s) in which resizing is allowed. Disabled sizing handles appear in gray and cannot be used to resize the Form.

The dots on the background of the Form are called a **grid**. You use the grid to align controls that you place on the Form. The grid is not visible when the application is running (Fig. 3.5).

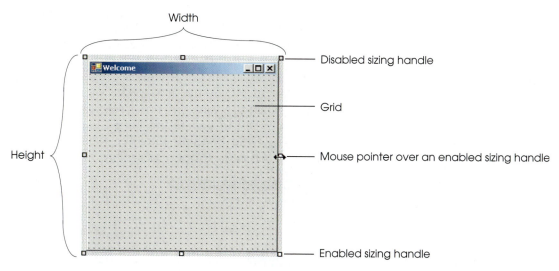

Figure 3.10 Form with sizing handles.

Forms also can be resized by using the **Size** property, which specifies the Form's width and height in units called **pixels** (*pic*ture *el*ements). A pixel is a tiny point on your computer screen that displays a color. The Size property has two members—the **Width** and the **Height** properties. The Width property indicates the width of the Form in pixels, and the Height property specifies the height in pixels. Next, you learn how to set the Form's width and height.

Setting the Form's Size Property

1. ***Setting the Form's width and height.*** For your **Welcome** application GUI to look exactly like Fig. 3.5, you will need to resize the Form and its controls. Click the Form. Locate the Form's Size property in the **Properties** window (Fig. 3.11). Click the plus box, ⊞, next to this property to expand the node. Type 616 for the Width property value, and press *Enter*. Type 440 for the Height property value and press *Enter*. Note that the Size property value (616, 440) updated when either the Width or the Height is changed. You also can enter the width and height (separated by a comma) in the Size property's value field.

Size property values

Figure 3.11 Size property values for the Form.

2. ***Saving the project.*** Select **File > Save All** to save your modified project.

Now that you have set the Form's size, you will customize the Form further by changing its background color from gray to yellow.

**Setting the Form's
Background Color**

1. ***Exploring the available colors.*** Click the Form to display its properties in the **Properties** window. The **BackColor** property specifies an object's background color. When you click the **BackColor** property's value in the **Properties** window, a down-arrow (⏷) Button appears (Fig. 3.12). When clicked, the down-arrow Button displays three tabs: **System** (the default), **Web** and **Custom**. Each tab offers a series of colors called a **palette**. The **System** tab displays a palette containing the colors used in the Microsoft Windows GUI. This palette includes the colors for Windows controls and the Windows desktop. The **System** tab's colors are based on the Windows 2000/XP settings in the **Display Properties** dialog. To access this dialog in Windows 2000, right click the desktop and select **Properties**. Click the **Appearance** tab to view the colors used by Windows. The **Web** tab displays a palette of **Web-safe colors**—colors that display the same on different computers. The **Custom** tab palette allows you to choose from a series of predefined colors or to create your own color. Click the **Custom** tab to display its palette as shown in Fig. 3.12.

Tabs ——————

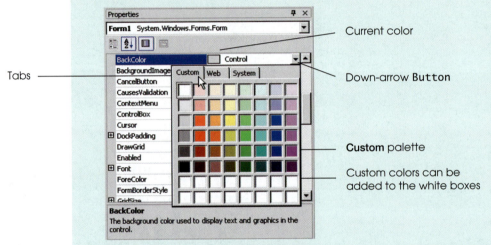

Current color

Down-arrow **Button**

Custom palette

Custom colors can be
added to the white boxes

Figure 3.12 Viewing the **Custom** palette in the Form's BackColor property value field.

2. ***Changing the Form's background color.*** Right click any one of the 16 white boxes at the bottom of the **Custom** palette to display the **Define Color** dialog (Fig. 3.13). Colors can be created either by entering three values in the **Hue:**, **Sat:** and **Lum:** TextBoxes or by providing values for the **Red:**, **Green:** and **Blue:** TextBoxes. The values for the **Red:**, **Green:** and **Blue:** TextBoxes describe the amount of red, green and blue needed to create the custom color and are commonly called **RGB values**. Each red, green and blue value is in the range 0–255, inclusive. We use RGB values in this book. Set the **Red:** value to 255, the **Green:** value to 237 and the **Blue:** value to 169. Clicking the **Add Color** Button closes the dialog, changes the Form's background color and adds the color to the **Custom** palette (Fig. 3.14).

GUI Design Tip

Use colors in your applications, but not to the point of distracting the user.

(cont.)

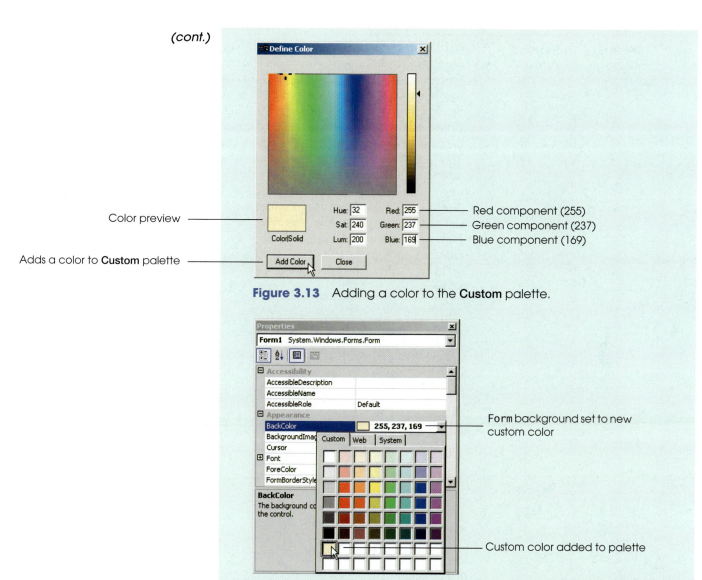

Color preview

Adds a color to **Custom** palette

Red component (255)
Green component (237)
Blue component (169)

Figure 3.13 Adding a color to the **Custom** palette.

Form background set to new custom color

Custom color added to palette

Figure 3.14 **Properties** window after the new custom color has been added.

3. *Saving the project.* Select **File > Save All** to save your modified project.

Now that you have finished customizing the Form, you can add a control to the Form. Next, you will add and customize a Label that displays a greeting.

Adding a Label to the Form

GUI Design Tip

Use Labels to display text that users cannot change.

1. *Adding a Label control to the Form.* Click the **Windows Forms** tab in the **Toolbox** (Fig. 3.15). If the **Toolbox** is not visible, select **View > Toolbox**. Double click the Label control in the **Toolbox**. A Label will appear in the upper-left corner of the Form (Fig. 3.16). You also can "drag" the Label from the **Toolbox** and drop it on the Form. You will use this Label control to display the welcome message. The Label displays the text **Label1** by default.

Notice that the Label's background color is the same as the Form's background color. When a control is added to the Form, the control's BackColor property value initially is set to the Form's BackColor property value by the Visual Studio .NET IDE.

(cont.)

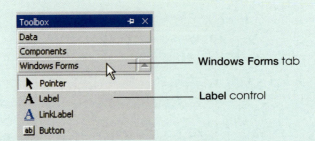

Figure 3.15   Clicking the **Windows Forms** tab in the **Toolbox**.

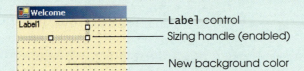

Figure 3.16   Adding a `Label` to the `Form`.

2. ***Customizing the Label's appearance.*** Click the `Label` to select it. You will notice that the `Label`'s properties now appear in the **Properties** window. The `Label`'s **Text** property specifies the text (**Label1**) that the `Label` displays. Type `Welcome to Visual Basic .NET!` for the `Label`'s **Text** property value and press *Enter*. Notice that this text does not fit in the `Label` (Fig. 3.17). Enlarge the `Label` (by using the sizing handles) until all the text is displayed (Fig. 3.18).

Figure 3.17   `Label` after updating its **Text** property.

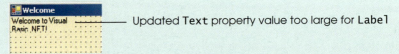

Figure 3.18   `Label` after it has been resized.

3. ***Aligning the Label.*** Drag the `Label` to the top center of the `Form`. You also can center the `Label` by clicking the `Label` and selecting **Format > Center In Form > Horizontally**. After centering the `Label`, the `Form` should look like Fig. 3.19.

Centered `Label` ————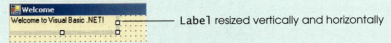

Figure 3.19   Centered `Label`.

4. ***Setting the Label's font.*** Click the value of the **Font** property to cause an **ellipsis** `Button` to appear (Fig. 3.20). Click the ellipsis `Button` to display the **Font** dialog (Fig. 3.21). In this dialog, you can select the font name (**Tahoma**, **Times New Roman**, etc.), font style (**Regular**, *Italic*, etc.) and font size (**16**, **18**, etc.) in points (one point equals 1/72 of an inch). The text in the **Sample** `Label` displays the selected font. Under the **Size:** category, select **24** points. Under the **Font** category, select **Tahoma**, and click **OK**. If the `Label`'s text does not fit on a single line, it wraps to the next line. Use the sizing handles to enlarge the `Label` vertically so that the text appears on two lines.

(cont.)

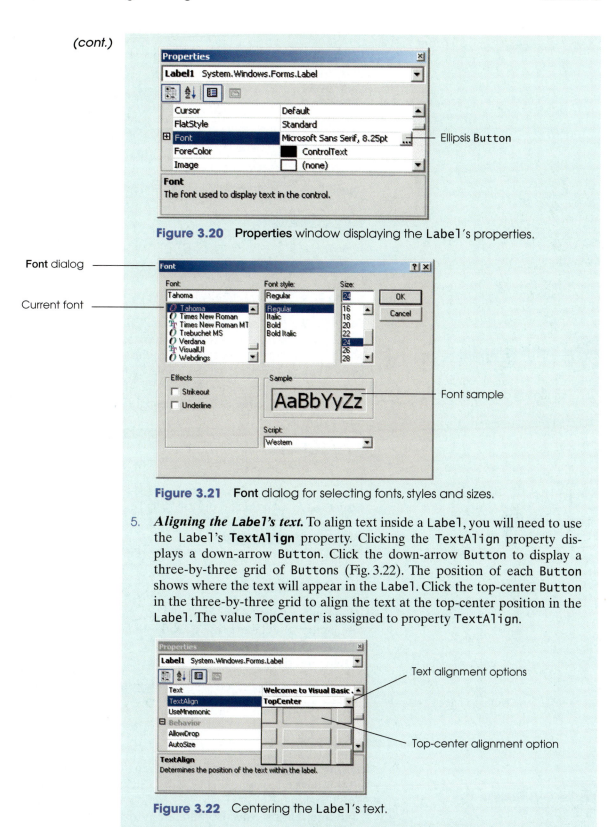

Figure 3.20 **Properties** window displaying the `Label`'s properties.

Figure 3.21 **Font** dialog for selecting fonts, styles and sizes.

5. *Aligning the Label's text.* To align text inside a `Label`, you will need to use the `Label`'s **TextAlign** property. Clicking the `TextAlign` property displays a down-arrow `Button`. Click the down-arrow `Button` to display a three-by-three grid of `Buttons` (Fig. 3.22). The position of each `Button` shows where the text will appear in the `Label`. Click the top-center `Button` in the three-by-three grid to align the text at the top-center position in the `Label`. The value `TopCenter` is assigned to property `TextAlign`.

Figure 3.22 Centering the `Label`'s text.

6. *Saving the project.* Select **File > Save All** to save your modified project.

To finish this first Visual Basic .NET Windows application, you need to insert an image and execute the application. We use a `PictureBox` control to add an image to the `Form` before running the application. The following box guides you step-by-step through the process of adding an image to your `Form`.

Inserting an Image and Running the Welcome Application

GUI Design Tip

Use PictureBoxes to enhance GUIs with graphics that users cannot change.

PictureBox

1. ***Adding a PictureBox control to the Form.*** The PictureBox allows you to display an image. To add a PictureBox control to the Form, double click the PictureBox control icon

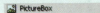

in the ToolBox. When the PictureBox appears, click and drag it to a position centered below the Label (Fig. 3.23).

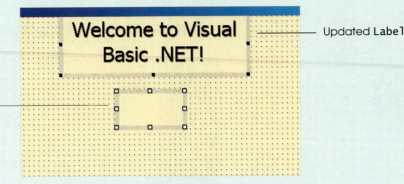

Updated Label

Figure 3.23 Inserting and aligning the PictureBox.

2. ***Setting the Image property.*** Click the PictureBox to display its properties in the **Properties** window. Locate the **Image** property, which displays a preview of the image (if one exists). No picture has yet been assigned to the Image property, so its value is (none) (Fig. 3.24). You can use any of several popular image formats, including

- *PNG* (*Portable Network Graphics*)
- *GIF* (*Graphic Interchange Format*)
- *JPEG* (*Joint Photographic Experts Group*)
- *BMP* (*Windows Bitmap*)

For this application, you will use a PNG-format image. Creating new images requires image-editing software, such as Jasc® Paint Shop Pro™ (www.jasc.com), Adobe® Photoshop™ (www.adobe.com), Microsoft Picture It!® (photos.msn.com) or Microsoft Paint (provided with Windows). You will not create images in this book; instead, you will be provided with the images used in the tutorials.

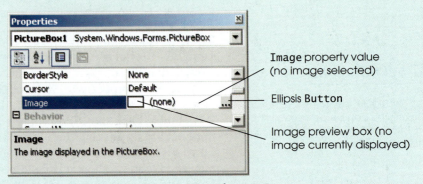

Image property value (no image selected)

Ellipsis Button

Image preview box (no image currently displayed)

Figure 3.24 Image property of the PictureBox.

(cont.)

3. ***Displaying an image.*** In the **Properties** window, click the value of the `Pic-tureBox`'s Image property to display an ellipsis `Button` (Fig. 3.24). Click the ellipsis `Button` to display the **Open** dialog (Fig. 3.25). Navigate to the `C:\Examples\Tutorial03\CompletedApplication\Welcome` directory. Click `bug.png` and click the **Open** `Button`. Once the image has been selected, the `PictureBox` displays the image (Fig. 3.26), and the Image property displays a preview of the image (Fig. 3.27). Notice that the `PictureBox` does not display the entire image (Fig. 3.26). You will solve this problem in the next step.

`bug.png` file (may
display **bug** depending
on your settings)

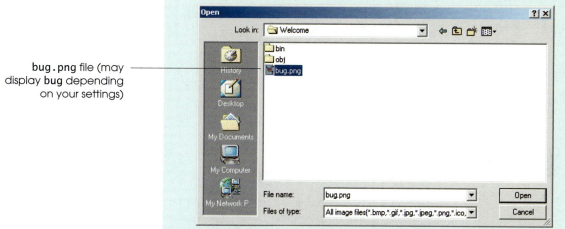

Figure 3.25   **Open** dialog used to browse for a `PictureBox` image.

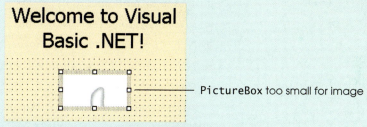

`PictureBox` too small for image

Figure 3.26   Newly inserted image.

Previewed image

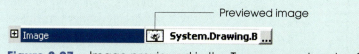

Figure 3.27   Image previewed in the Image property value field.

4. ***Sizing the image to fit the PictureBox.*** We want the image to fit in the `Pic-tureBox`. `PictureBox` property **SizeMode** specifies how an image is displayed in a `PictureBox`. To size the image to fit in the `PictureBox`, change the `SizeMode` property to **StretchImage**, which **scales** the image (changes its width and height) to the size of the `PictureBox`. To resize the `Picture-Box`, double click the `Size` property and enter 500, 250. Center the image horizontally by clicking the `PictureBox` and selecting **Format > Center in Form > Horizontally**. The `Form` should now look like Fig. 3.28. [*Note:* You may need to move the `PictureBox` up or down to at this point to make your `Form` appear as it does in Fig. 3.28. To do this, you can simply click on the `PictureBox` and then use the up and down arrow keys.]

GUI Design Tip

Images should fit inside their Pic-tureBoxes. This can be achieved by setting PictureBox property Size-Mode to StretchImage.

(cont.)

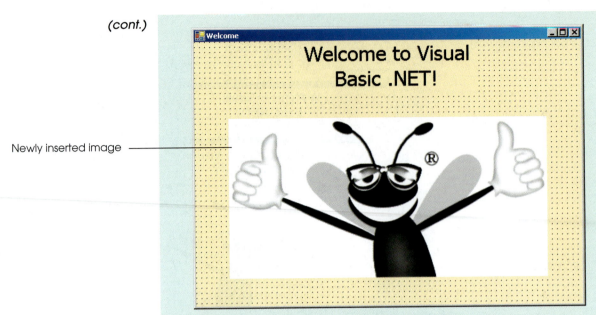

Newly inserted image ——

Figure 3.28 `PictureBox` displaying an image.

5. ***Locking the Form controls.*** Often, programmers accidentally alter the size and location of controls on the Form. To ensure that the controls remain in position, use the **Lock Controls** feature. First, select all the controls by using the **Edit > Select All** command. Next, select **Format > Lock Controls** (Fig. 3.29).

Lock Controls option

Figure 3.29 Locking controls by using the **Format** menu.

6. ***Saving the project.*** Select **File > Save All** to save your modified project. The solution file (`.sln`) contains the name(s) and location(s) of its project(s); the project file (`.vbproj`) contains the names and locations of all the files in the project. You should save your files to your `C:\SimplyVB` directory frequently. Note, however, that it is not necessary to save project files if you are about to run the application. When a Visual Basic .NET application is run in Visual Studio .NET, the project files are automatically saved for you.

7. ***Running the application.*** The text **Microsoft Visual Basic .NET [design]** in the IDE's title bar (Fig. 3.6) indicates that we have been working in the IDE **design mode**. (That is, the application being created is not executing.) While in design mode, programmers have access to all the IDE windows (for example, **Toolbox**, **Properties**, etc.), menus and toolbars. In **run mode**, the application is running, and programmers can interact with fewer IDE features. Features that are not available are disabled ("grayed out"). Select **Debug > Start** to run the application. Figure 3.30 shows the IDE in run mode. Note that many toolbar icons and menus are disabled.

(cont.)

IDE title bar displaying **[run]**

Form (with grid)

Running application

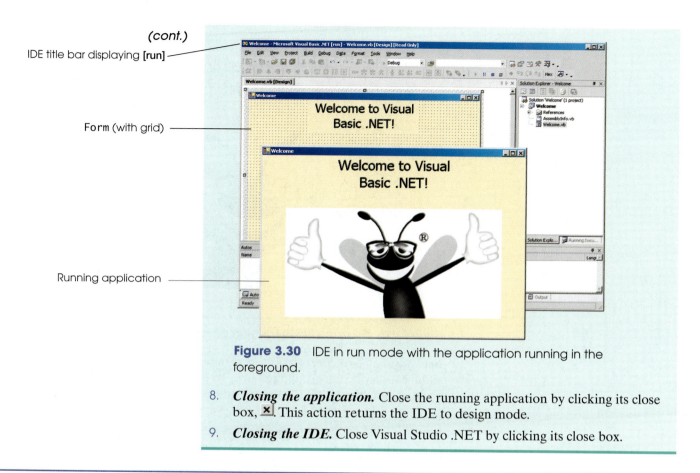

Figure 3.30   IDE in run mode with the application running in the foreground.

8. ***Closing the application.*** Close the running application by clicking its close box, ⊠. This action returns the IDE to design mode.

9. ***Closing the IDE.*** Close Visual Studio .NET by clicking its close box.

SELF-REVIEW

1. The Form's _____ property specifies the text that is displayed in the Form's title bar.
   a) `Title`   b) `Text`
   c) `(Name)`   d) `Name`

2. Property _____ specifies how text is aligned within a `Label`'s boundaries.
   a) `Alignment`   b) `AlignText`
   c) `Align`   d) `TextAlign`

Answers: 1) b. 2) d.

3.3 Objects Used in the Welcome Application

In Tutorials 1 and 2, you learned that controls are reusable software components called objects. The **Welcome** application used a `Form` object, a `Label` object and a `PictureBox` object to create a GUI that displayed text and an image. Each of these objects is an instance of a class defined in the .NET Framework Class Library (FCL). The `Form` object was created by the Visual Studio .NET IDE. The `Label` and `PictureBox` objects were created when you double clicked their respective icons in the **Toolbox**.

We used the **Properties** window to set the properties (attributes) for each object. Recall that the `ComboBox`—also called the component object box—at the top of the **Properties** window displays the names and class types of `Form` and control objects (Fig. 3.31). In Fig. 3.32, the component object box displays the name (`Form1`) and class type (`Form`) of the `Form` object. In the FCL, classes are organized by functionality into directory-like entities called **namespaces**. The class types used in this application have namespace `System.Windows.Forms`. This namespace contains control classes and the `Form` class. You will be introduced to additional namespaces in later tutorials. Close the solution by selecting **File > Close Solution**.

Welcome application GUI objects

Figure 3.31   Component object box expanded to show the **Welcome** application's objects.

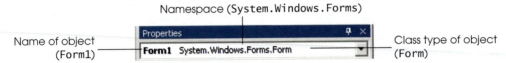

Namespace (System.Windows.Forms)

Name of object (Form1)

Class type of object (Form)

Figure 3.32   The name and class type of an object are displayed in the **Properties** window's component object box.

3.4 Wrap-Up

This tutorial introduced you to visual programming in Visual Basic .NET. You learned that visual programming helps you to design and create the graphical user interface portions of applications quickly and easily, by dragging and dropping controls onto Forms.

In creating your **Welcome** application, you used the **Properties** window to set the Form's title-bar text, size (width and height) and background color using properties Text, Size and BackColor, respectively. You learned that Labels are controls that display text and that PictureBoxes are controls that display images. You displayed text in a Label by setting its Text and TextAlign properties, and you displayed an image by setting a PictureBox control's Image and SizeMode properties.

You also examined the relationship between controls and classes. You learned that FCL classes are grouped into directory-like entities called namespaces and that controls are instances (objects) of FCL classes. The FCL classes used in this tutorial (Form, Label and PictureBox) belong to namespace System.Windows.Forms. You used the **Properties** window's component object box to view an object's name, namespace and class type.

In the next tutorial, you continue learning visual programming. In particular, you will create an application with controls that are designed to accept user input.

SKILLS SUMMARY   **Creating GUIs Quickly and Efficiently**

  ■ Use visual programming techniques.

Placing a Control on the Form

  ■ Double click the control in the **Toolbox** to place the control in the upper-left corner of the Form, or drag the control from the **Toolbox** onto the Form.

Aligning Controls

■ Use the Form's background grid for alignment. You also can use the **Format** menu's commands.

Resizing the Form or Control with Sizing Handles

■ Click and drag one of the object's enabled sizing handles.

Setting the Dimensions of the Form or Control by Using Property Size

■ Enter the height and width of the Form or control in the Size field.

Setting the Width and Height of the Form or Control

■ Enter values in the Width and Height property fields (or use the Size property field).

Setting the Form's Background Color

■ Set the Form's BackColor property.

Adding a Label Control to the Form

■ Double click the Label control in the **Toolbox** to place the control in the upper-left corner of the Form.

Setting a Label's Text Property

■ Set the Label's Text property.

Setting a Label's Font Property

■ Click the value of the Font property, which causes an ellipsis Button to appear next to the value. When the ellipsis Button is clicked, the **Font** dialog is displayed; it allows programmers to change the font name, style and size of the Label's text.

Aligning Text in a Label

■ Use the Label's TextAlign property.

Adding an Image to the Form

■ Use a PictureBox control to display the image. Click the ellipsis Button next to the PictureBox Image property's value to browse for an image to insert.

■ Scale the image to the size of the PictureBox by setting property SizeMode to value StretchImage.

Displaying a Form or Control's Properties in the Properties Window

■ Click the Form or a control on the Form.

KEY TERMS

BackColor property—Specifies its background color of the Form or a control.

design mode—IDE mode that allows you to create applications using Visual Studio .NET's windows, toolbars and menu bar.

Font property—Specifies the font name, style and size of any displayed text in the Form or one of its controls.

Height property—This property, a member of property Size, indicates the height of the Form or one of its controls in pixels.

Image property—Indicates the file name of the image displayed in a PictureBox.

Label—Control that displays text the user cannot modify.

namespace—Classes in the FCL are organized by functionality into these directory-like entities.

palette—A set of colors.

PictureBox—Control that displays an image.

pixel—A tiny point on your computer screen that displays a color.

RGB value—The amount of red, green and blue needed to create a color.

run mode—IDE mode indicating that the application is executing.

Size property—Property that specifies the height and width, in pixels, of the Form or one of its controls.

SizeMode property—Property that specifies how an image is displayed in a PictureBox.

sizing handle—Square that, when enabled, can be used to resize the Form or one of its controls.
`StretchImage`—Value of `PictureBox` property `SizeMode` that scales an image to fill the `PictureBox`.
Text property—Specifies the text displayed by the Form or a Label.
`TextAlign` **property**—Specifies how text is aligned within a Label.
Web-safe colors—Colors that display the same on different computers.
`Width` **property**—This setting, a member of property `Size`, indicates the width of the Form or one of its controls, in pixels.

GUI DESIGN GUIDELINES

Overall Design
■ Use colors in your applications, but not to the point of distracting the user.

Forms
■ Choose short and descriptive Form titles. Capitalize words that are not articles, prepositions or conjunctions. Do not use punctuation.
■ Use **Tahoma** font to improve readability for controls that display text.

Labels
■ Use Labels to display text that users cannot change.
■ Ensure that all Label controls are large enough to display their text.

PictureBoxes
■ Use PictureBoxes to enhance GUIs with graphics that users cannot change.
■ Images should fit inside their PictureBoxes. This can be achieved by setting PictureBox property SizeMode to StretchImage.

CONTROLS, EVENTS, PROPERTIES & METHODS

Label   `A Label`   This control displays on the Form text that the user cannot modify.

■ *In action*

Welcome to Visual Basic .NET!

■ *Properties*
`Text`—Specifies the text displayed on the Label.
`Font`—Specifies the font name, style and size of the text displayed in the Label.
`TextAlign`—Determines how the text is aligned within the Label.

PictureBox   `PictureBox`   This control displays an image on the Form.

■ *In action*

■ *Properties*
`Image`—Specifies the file path of the image.
`SizeMode`—Specifies the image that is displayed in the PictureBox.
`Size`—Specifies the height and width (in pixels) of the PictureBox.

MULTIPLE-CHOICE QUESTIONS

3.1 Property _____ determines the Form's background color.
  a) `BackColor`   b) `BackgroundColor`
  c) `RGB`   d) `Color`

3.2 To save all the solution's files, select _____.

   a) **Save > Solution > Save Files**   b) **File > Save**

   c) **File > Save All**   d) **File > Save As...**

3.3 When the ellipsis **Button** to the right of the **Font** property value is clicked, the _____ is displayed.

   a) **Font Property** dialog   b) **New Font** dialog

   c) **Font Settings** dialog   d) **Font** dialog

3.4 `PictureBox` property _____ contains a preview of the image displayed in the `PictureBox`.

   a) `Picture`   b) `ImageName`

   c) `Image`   d) `PictureName`

3.5 The _____ tab allows you to create your own color.

   a) **Custom**   b) **Web**

   c) **System**   d) **User**

3.6 The `PictureBox` class has namespace _____.

   a) `System.Windows.Forms`   b) `System.Form.Form`

   c) `System.Form.Font`   d) `System.Form.Control`

3.7 A `Label` control displays the text specified by property _____.

   a) `Caption`   b) `Data`

   c) `Text`   d) `Name`

3.8 In _____ mode, the application is executing.

   a) start   b) run

   c) break   d) design

3.9 The _____ command prevents programmers from accidentally altering the size and location of the `Form`'s controls.

   a) **Lock Controls**   b) **Anchor Controls**

   c) **Lock**   d) **Bind Controls**

3.10 Pixels are _____.

   a) picture elements   b) controls in the **Toolbox**

   c) a set of fonts   d) a set of colors on the **Web** tab

EXERCISES   *For Exercises 3.11–3.16, you are asked to create the GUI shown in each exercise. You will use the visual programming techniques presented in this tutorial to create a variety of GUIs. Because you are creating only GUIs, your applications will not be fully operational. For example, the* **Calculator** *GUI in Exercise 3.11 will not behave like a calculator when its* **Buttons** *are clicked. You will learn how to make your applications fully operational in later tutorials. Create each application as a separate project.*

3.11 *(Calculator GUI)* Create the GUI for the calculator shown in Fig. 3.33.

   a) *Creating a new project.* Create a new **Windows Application** named `Calculator`.

   b) *Renaming the Form file.* Name the Form file `Calculator.vb`.

   c) *Manipulating the Form's properties.* Change the `Size` property of the Form to 272, 192. Change the `Text` property of the Form to `Calculator`. Change the `Font` property to `Tahoma`.

   d) *Adding a TextBox to the Form.* Add a TextBox control by double clicking it in the **Toolbox**. A TextBox control is used to enter input into applications. Set the TextBox's `Text` property in the **Properties** window to 0. Change the `Size` property to 240, 21. Set the `TextAlign` property to `Right`; this right aligns text displayed in the TextBox. Finally, set the TextBox's `Location` property to 8, 16.

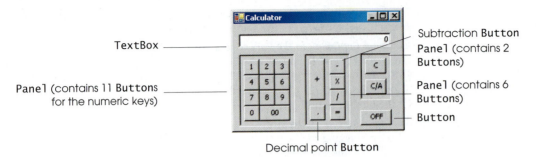

TextBox ─────────────

Panel (contains 11 Buttons
for the numeric keys) ─────

Subtraction Button
Panel (contains 2
Buttons)

Panel (contains 6
Buttons)

Button

Decimal point Button

Figure 3.33   Calculator GUI.

e) **Adding the first Panel to the Form.** Panel controls are used to group other controls. Double click the Panel icon (▢ Panel) in the **Toolbox** to add a Panel to the Form. Change the Panel's BorderStyle property to Fixed3D to make the inside of the Panel appear recessed. Change the Size property to 88, 112. Finally, set the Location property to 8, 48. This Panel contains the calculator's numeric keys.

f) **Adding the second Panel to the Form.** Click the Form. Double click the Panel icon in the **Toolbox** to add another Panel to the Form. Change the Panel's BorderStyle property to Fixed3D. Change the Size property to 72, 112. Finally, set the Location property to 112, 48. This Panel contains the calculator's operator keys.

g) **Adding the third (and last) Panel to the Form.** Click the Form. Double click the Panel icon in the **Toolbox** to add another Panel to the Form. Change the Panel's BorderStyle property to Fixed3D. Change the Size property to 48, 72. Finally, set the Location property to 200, 48. This Panel contains the calculator's **C** (clear) and **C/A** (clear all) keys.

h) **Adding Buttons to the Form.** There are 20 Buttons on the calculator. To add a Button to a Panel, double click the Button control (▣ Button) in the **Toolbox**. Then add the Button to the Panel by dragging and dropping it on the Panel. Change the Text property of each Button to the calculator key it represents. The value you enter in the Text property will appear on the face of the Button. Finally, resize the Buttons, using their Size properties. Each Button labelled 0–9, x, /, -, = and . should have a size of 24, 24. The **00** and **OFF** Buttons have size 48, 24. The **+** Button is sized 24, 64. The **C** (clear) and **C/A** (clear all) Buttons are sized 32, 24.

i) **Saving the project.** Select **File > Save All** to save your changes.

3.12 **(Alarm Clock GUI)** Create the GUI for the alarm clock in Fig. 3.34.

RadioButton ─────────

GroupBox ─────────

Buttons

Label

Figure 3.34   Alarm Clock GUI.

a) **Creating a new project.** Create a new **Windows Application** named AlarmClock.

b) **Renaming the Form file.** Name the Form file AlarmClock.vb.

c) **Manipulating the Form's properties.** Change the Size property of the Form to 256, 176. Change the Text property of the Form to Alarm Clock. Change the Font property to Tahoma.

d) **Adding Buttons to the Form.** Add six Buttons to the Form. Change the Text property of each Button to the appropriate text. Change the Size properties of the **Hour**, **Minute** and **Second** Buttons to 56, 23. The **ON** and **OFF** Buttons get size 40, 23. The **Timer** Button gets size 48, 32. Align the Buttons as shown in Fig. 3.34.

e) **Adding a Label to the Form.** Add a Label to the Form. Change the Text property to **Snooze**. Set its Size to 248, 23. Set the Label's TextAlign property to Middle-

Center. Finally, to draw a border around the edge of the **Snooze** Label, change the BorderStyle property of the **Snooze** Label to FixedSingle.

f) *Adding a GroupBox to the Form.* GroupBoxes are like Panels, except that GroupBoxes can display a title. To add a GroupBox to the Form, double click the GroupBox control (`GroupBox`) in the **Toolbox**. Change the Text property to **AM/PM**, and set the Size property to 72, 72. To place the GroupBox in the correct location on the Form, set the Location property to 104, 38.

g) *Adding AM/PM RadioButtons to the GroupBox.* Add two RadioButtons to the Form by dragging the RadioButton control (`RadioButton`) in the **Toolbox** and dropping it onto the GroupBox twice. Change the Text property of one RadioButton to AM and the other to PM. Then place the RadioButtons as shown in Fig. 3.34 by setting the Location of the **AM** RadioButton to 16, 16 and that of the **PM** RadioButton to 16, 40. Set their Size properties to 48, 24.

h) *Adding the time Label to the Form.* Add a Label to the Form and change its Text property to 00:00:00. Change the BorderStyle property to Fixed3D and the Back-Color to Black. Set the Size property to 64, 23. Use the Font property to make the time bold. Change the ForeColor to Silver (located in the **Web** tab) to make the time stand out against the black background. Set TextAlign to MiddleCenter to center the text in the Label. Position the Label as shown in Fig. 3.34.

i) *Saving the project.* Select **File > Save All** to save your changes.

3.13 *(Microwave Oven GUI)* Create the GUI for the microwave oven shown in Fig. 3.35.

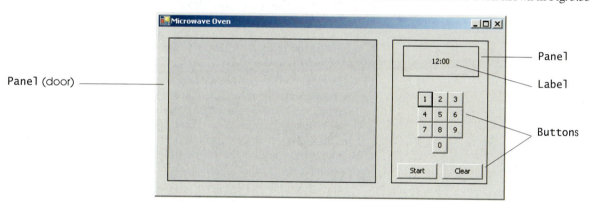

Figure 3.35 Microwave Oven GUI.

a) *Creating a new project.* Create a new **Windows Application** named Microwave.

b) *Renaming the Form file.* Name the Form file Microwave.vb.

c) *Manipulating the Form's properties.* Change the Size property of the Form to 552, 288. Change the Text property of the Form to Microwave Oven. Change the Font property to Tahoma.

d) *Adding the microwave oven door.* Add a Panel to the Form by double clicking the Panel (`Panel`) in the **Toolbox**. Select the Panel and change the BackColor property to Silver (located in the **Web** tab) in the **Properties** window. Then change the Size to 328, 224. Next, change the BorderStyle property to FixedSingle.

e) *Adding another Panel.* Add another Panel and change its Size to 152, 224 and its BorderStyle to FixedSingle. Place the Panel to the right of the door Panel, as shown in Fig. 3.35.

f) *Adding the microwave oven clock.* Add a Label to the right Panel by clicking the Label in the **Toolbox** once, then clicking once inside the right Panel. Change the Label's Text to 12:00, BorderStyle to FixedSingle and Size to 120, 48. Change TextAlign to MiddleCenter. Place the clock as shown in Fig. 3.35.

g) *Adding a keypad to the microwave oven.* Place a Button in the right Panel by clicking the Button control in the Toolbox once, then clicking inside the Panel. Change the Text to 1 and the Size to 24, 24. Repeat this process for nine more Buttons, changing the Text property in each to the next number in the keypad. Then add the **Start** and **Clear** Buttons, each of Size 64, 24. Do not forget to set the Text properties for each of these Buttons. Finally, arrange the Buttons as shown in Fig. 3.35. The **1** Button is located at 40, 80 and the **Start** Button is located at 8, 192.

h) *Saving the project.* Select **File > Save All** to save your changes.

3.14 *(Cell Phone GUI)* Create the GUI for the cell phone shown in Fig. 3.36.

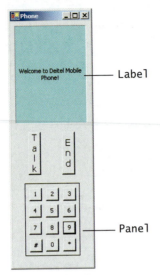

Label

Panel

Figure 3.36 Cell Phone GUI.

a) *Creating a new project.* Create a new **Windows Application** named Phone.

b) *Renaming the Form file.* Name the Form file Phone.vb.

c) *Manipulating the Form's properties.* Change the Form's Text property to Phone and the Size to 160, 488. Change the Font property to Tahoma.

d) *Adding the display Label.* Add a Label to the Form. Change its BackColor to Aqua (in the **Web** tab palette), the Text to Welcome to Deitel Mobile Phone! and the Size to 136, 184. Change the TextAlign property to MiddleCenter. Then place the Label as shown in Fig. 3.36.

e) *Adding the keypad Panel.* Add a Panel to the Form. Change its BorderStyle property to FixedSingle and its Size to 104, 136.

f) *Adding the keypad Buttons.* Add the keypad Buttons to the Form (12 Buttons in all). Each Button on the number pad should be of Size 24, 24 and should be placed in the Panel. Change the Text property of each Button such that numbers 0–9, the pound (#) and the star (*) keys are represented. Then add the final two Buttons such that the Text property for one is Talk and the other is End. Change the Size of each Button to 24, 80, and notice how the small Size causes the Text to align vertically. Also change each Button's Font size to 12 points.

g) *Placing the controls.* Arrange all the controls so that your GUI looks like Fig. 3.36.

h) *Saving the project.* Select **File > Save All** to save your changes.

3.15 *(Vending Machine GUI)* Create the GUI for the vending machine in Fig. 3.37.

a) *Creating a new project.* Create a new **Windows Application** named Vending-Machine.

b) *Renaming the Form file.* Name the Form file VendingMachine.vb.

c) *Manipulating the Form's properties.* Set the Text property of the Form to Vending Machine and the Size to 560, 488. Change the Font property to Tahoma.

d) *Adding the food selection Panel.* Add a Panel to the Form, and change its Size to 312, 344 and BorderStyle to Fixed3D. Add a PictureBox to the Panel, and change its Size to 50, 50. Then set the Image property by clicking the ellipsis Button and choosing a file from the C:\Examples\Tutorial03\ExerciseImages\VendingMachine directory. Repeat this process for 11 more PictureBoxes.

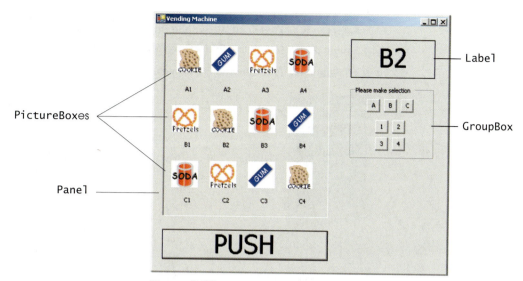

Figure 3.37   Vending Machine GUI.

e) *Adding Labels for each vending item.* Add a Label under each PictureBox. Change the Text property of the Label to A1, the TextAlign property to TopCenter and the Size to 56, 16. Place the Label so that it is located as in Fig. 3.37. Repeat this process for A2 through C4 (11 Labels).

f) *Creating the vending machine door (as a Button).* Add a Button to the Form by dragging the Button control in the **Toolbox** and dropping it below the Panel. Change the Button's Text property to PUSH, its Font Size to 36 and its Size to 312, 56. Then place the Button on the Form as shown in Fig. 3.37.

g) *Adding the selection display Label.* Add a Label to the Form, and change the Text property to B2, BorderStyle to FixedSingle, Font Size to 36, TextAlign to MiddleCenter and Size to 160, 72.

h) *Grouping the input Buttons.* Add a GroupBox below the Label, and change the Text property to Please make selection and the Size to 160, 136.

i) *Adding the input Buttons.* Finally, add Buttons to the GroupBox. For the seven Buttons, change the Size property to 24, 24. Then change the Text property of the Buttons such that each Button has one of the values A, B, C, 1, 2, 3 or 4, as shown in Fig. 3.37. When you are done, move the controls on the Form so that they are aligned as shown in the figure.

j) *Saving the project.* Select **File > Save All** to save your changes.

Programming Challenge ▶

3.16 *(Radio GUI)* Create the GUI for the radio in Fig. 3.38. [*Note:* All colors used in this exercises are from the **Web** palette.]

In this exercise, you will create this GUI on your own. Feel free to experiment with different control properties. For the image in the PictureBox, use the file (MusicNote.gif) found in the C:\Examples\Tutorial03\ExerciseImages\Radio directory.

a) *Creating a new project.* Create a new **Windows Application** named Radio.

b) *Renaming the Form file.* Name the Form file Radio.vb.

c) *Manipulating the Form's properties.* Change the Form's Text property to Radio and the Size to 576, 240. Change the Font property to Tahoma. Set BackColor to Peach-Puff.

d) *Adding the Pre-set Stations GroupBox and Buttons.* Add a GroupBox to the Form. Set its Size to 232, 64, its Text to Pre-set Stations, its ForeColor to Black and its BackColor to RosyBrown. Change its Font to bold. Finally, set its Location to 24, 16. Add six Buttons to the GroupBox. Set each BackColor to PeachPuff and each Size to 24, 23. Change the Buttons' Text properties to 1, 2, 3, 4, 5, 6, respectively.

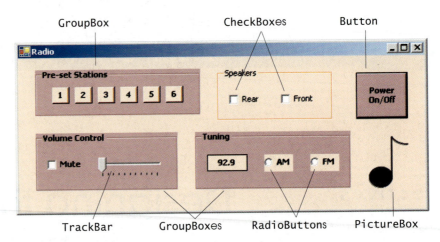

Figure 3.38 Radio GUI.

e) ***Adding the Speakers GroupBox and CheckBoxes.*** Add a GroupBox to the Form. Set its Size to 160, 72, its Text to Speakers and its ForeColor to Black. Set its Location to 280, 16. Add two CheckBoxes to the Form. Set each CheckBox's Size to 56, 24. Set the Text properties for the CheckBoxes to Rear and Front.

f) ***Adding the Power On/Off Button.*** Add a Button to the Form. Set its Text to Power On/Off, its BackColor to RosyBrown, its ForeColor to Black and its Size to 72, 64. Change its Font style to Bold.

g) ***Adding the Volume Control GroupBox, the Mute CheckBox and the Volume Track-Bar.*** Add a GroupBox to the Form. Set its Text to Volume Control, its BackColor to RosyBrown, its ForeColor to Black and its Size to 200, 80. Set its Font style to Bold. Add a CheckBox to the GroupBox. Set its Text to Mute and its Size to 56, 24. Add a TrackBar to the GroupBox.

h) ***Adding the Tuning GroupBox, the radio station Label and the AM/FM RadioButtons.*** Add a GroupBox to the Form. Set its Text to Tuning, its ForeColor to Black and its BackColor to RosyBrown. Set its Font style to Bold and its Size to 216, 80. Add a Label to the Form. Set its BackColor to PeachPuff, its ForeColor to Black, its BorderStyle to FixedSingle, its Font style to Bold, its TextAlign to Middle-Center and its Size to 56, 23. Set its Text to 92.9. Place the Label as shown in the figure. Add two RadioButtons to the GroupBox. Change the BackColor to Peach-Puff and change the Size to 40, 24. Set one's Text to AM and the other's Text to FM.

i) ***Adding the image.*** Add a PictureBox to the Form. Set its BackColor to Transparent, its SizeMode to StretchImage and its Size to 56, 72. Set its Image property to C:\Examples\Tutorial03\ExerciseImages\Radio\MusicNote.gif.

j) ***Saving the project.*** Select **File > Save All** to save your changes.

T U T O R I A L

Designing the Inventory Application

Introducing TextBoxes and Buttons

This tutorial introduces you to the fundamentals of visual programming. You will design the graphical user interface for a simple inventory application. Through each set of steps, you will enhance the application's user interface by adding controls. You will design a **Form** on which you place **Label**s, **Text-Box**es and a **Button**. You will learn new properties for **Label**s and **TextBox**es, and you will learn how to add a **Button** to the **Form**. At the end of the tutorial, you will find a list of new GUI design guidelines to help you create appealing and easy-to-use graphical user interfaces.

4.1 Test-Driving the Inventory Application

In this tutorial, you will create an inventory application that calculates the number of textbooks received by a college bookstore. This application must meet the following requirements:

Application Requirements

A college bookstore receives cartons of textbooks. In each shipment, each carton contains the same number of textbooks. The inventory manager wants to use a computer to calculate the total number of textbooks arriving at the bookstore for each shipment, from the number of cartons and the number of textbooks in each carton. The inventory manager will enter the number of cartons received and the fixed number of textbooks in each carton for each shipment; then the application will calculate the total number of textbooks in a shipment.

This application performs a simple calculation. The user (the inventory manager) inputs into **TextBox**es the number of cartons and number of items in each carton. The user then clicks a **Button**, which causes the application to multiply the two numbers and display the result—the total number of textbooks received. You begin by test-driving the completed application. Then, you will learn the additional Visual Basic .NET technologies that you will need to create your own version of this application.

Test-Driving the
Inventory Application

1. *Opening the completed application.* Open the directory C:\Examples\ Tutorial04\CompletedApplication\Inventory to locate the **Inventory** application. Double click Inventory.sln to open the application in Visual Studio .NET. Depending on your system configuration, you may not see the .sln file name extension. In this case, double click the file named Inventory that contains a solution file icon, 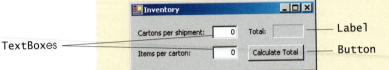.

2. *Running the Inventory application.* Select **Debug > Start** to run the application. The **Inventory** Form shown in Fig. 4.1 will appear.

TextBoxes

Label

Button

Figure 4.1   **Inventory** application Form with default data displayed by the application.

Notice that there are two controls that you did not use in the **Welcome** application—the TextBox and Button controls. A **TextBox** is a control that the user can enter data into from the keyboard and that can display data to the user. A **Button** is a control that allows the application to perform an action when clicked.

3. *Entering quantities in the application.* Some controls (such as TextBoxes) are not used to display descriptive text for other controls; therefore, we refer to these controls by using the Labels that identify them. For example, we will refer to the TextBox to the right of the **Cartons per shipment:** Label as the **Cartons per shipment:** TextBox. Enter 3 in the **Cartons per shipment:** TextBox. Enter 15 in the **Items per carton:** TextBox. Figure 4.2 shows the Form after these values have been entered.

Figure 4.2   **Inventory** application with new quantities entered.

4. *Calculating the total number of items received.* Click the **Calculate Total** Button. This causes the application to multiply the two numbers you entered and to display the result (45) in the Label to the right of **Total:** (Fig. 4.3).

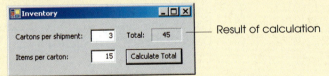

Result of calculation

Figure 4.3   Result of clicking the **Calculate Total** Button in the **Inventory** application.

5. *Closing the application.* Close your running application by clicking its close box.

6. *Closing the solution.* Select **File > Close Solution.**

4.2 Constructing the Inventory Application

Now that you have test-driven the completed application, you will begin creating your own version of the application. You will create a new project that contains the Form on which you will place the controls required for the **Inventory** application. Then, you will save the solution containing the Form to your work directory, C:\SimplyVB (ensuring that you will know which directory contains your solution if you take a break from building the application). Finally, the initial steps conclude with instructions for renaming the Form.

Creating a New Application

1. ***Creating the new project.*** To create a Windows application, select **File > New > Project...,** to display the **New Project** dialog (Fig. 4.4). Click the **Visual Basic Projects** folder in the **Project Types:** pane to retrieve the list of Visual Basic .NET project types in the **Templates:** pane. From this list, select **Windows Application**. Type Inventory in the **Name:** Textbox, and leave the dialog open.

Project Types: pane with **Visual Basic Projects** folder selected (your folder list might differ)

Name: TextBox

Location: TextBox

Templates: pane with **Windows Application** selected

Browse... Button

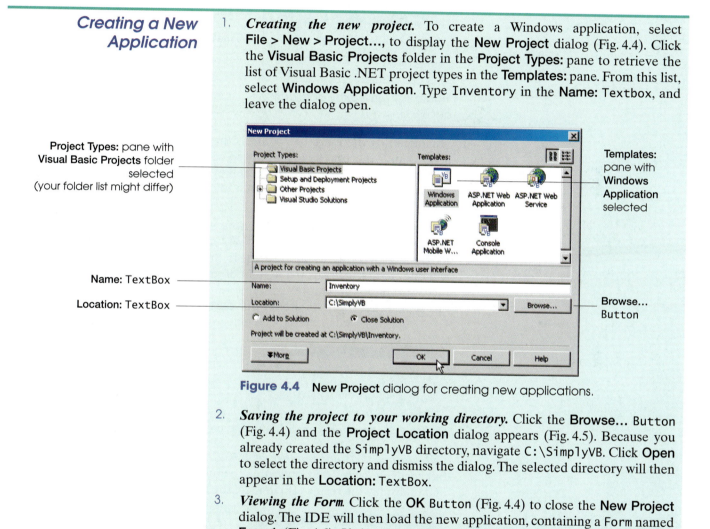

Figure 4.4 New Project dialog for creating new applications.

2. ***Saving the project to your working directory.*** Click the **Browse...** Button (Fig. 4.4) and the **Project Location** dialog appears (Fig. 4.5). Because you already created the SimplyVB directory, navigate C:\SimplyVB. Click **Open** to select the directory and dismiss the dialog. The selected directory will then appear in the **Location:** TextBox.

3. ***Viewing the Form.*** Click the **OK** Button (Fig. 4.4) to close the **New Project** dialog. The IDE will then load the new application, containing a Form named **Form1** (Fig. 4.6). If the Form does not appear as in Fig. 4.6, select **View > Designer.** Then, click the Form in the IDE to select it.

(cont.)

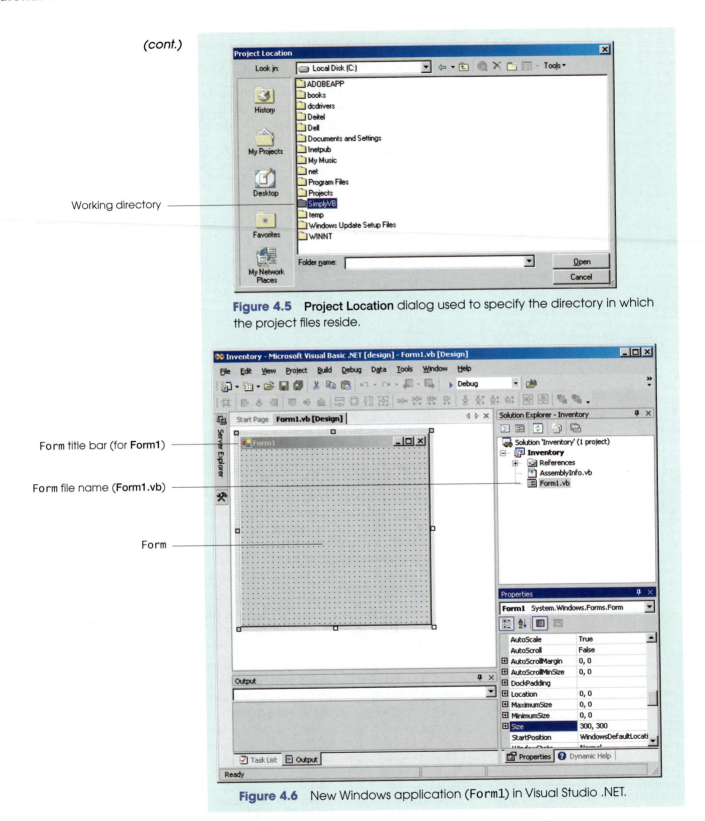

Working directory

Figure 4.5   **Project Location** dialog used to specify the directory in which the project files reside.

Form title bar (for **Form1**)

Form file name (**Form1.vb**)

Form

Figure 4.6   New Windows application (**Form1**) in Visual Studio .NET.

(cont.)

4. **Renaming the Form file.** It is a good practice to change the Form file name to a name more meaningful for your application. To change the Form file name (Fig. 4.7), click its name (Form1.vb) in the **Solution Explorer**. Then select File Name in the **Properties** window, and type Inventory.vb in the field to the right. Press *Enter* to update the file name. Unless otherwise noted, you need to press *Enter* for changes to take effect.

Form's file name after property change ⎯⎯⎯⎯

File Name property ⎯⎯⎯⎯

Type new Form file name here ⎯⎯⎯⎯

Figure 4.7 Renaming a file in the **Solution Explorer** and **Properties** windows.

5. **Renaming the Form object.** Each Form object needs a unique and meaningful name for easy identification. In Visual Studio .NET, you set the Form's name by using the **Name** property. By default, the Visual Studio .NET IDE names the Form **Form1**. Click the Form in the **Windows Form Designer**. In the **Properties** window, double click the field to the right of the Name property, listed as (Name). Type FrmInventory, then press *Enter* to update the name.

6. **Saving the project.** Select **File > Save All** to save your changes. Saving your work often will prevent losing changes to the application.

Good Programming Practice

Change the Form name to a unique and meaningful name for easy identification.

Good Programming Practice

Use standard prefixes for names of objects (controls and Forms) so that you can easily tell them apart. Prefix Form names with Frm. Capitalize the first letter of the Form name because Form is a class. Objects (such as controls) should be prefixed with lowercase letters.

When the application executes, it should begin by displaying the FrmInventory Form. For this to happen, you must set FrmInventory as the **startup object**. The startup object defines which object (in this case, the Form) loads when the program begins to run. Normally, the startup object is set as Form1, the default name for a new Form. (In the last tutorial, you did not rename the Form, so the startup object did not need to be changed.) Because you have renamed your Form, use the following box to set the startup object to the Form's new name.

Setting the Form as the Startup Object

1. **Selecting the project name in the Solution Explorer.** Right click the project name (**Inventory**) in the **Solution Explorer**, causing a **context menu** (Fig. 4.8) to appear.

2. **Selecting Properties from the context menu.** Select the **Properties** menu item (Fig. 4.8).

(cont.)

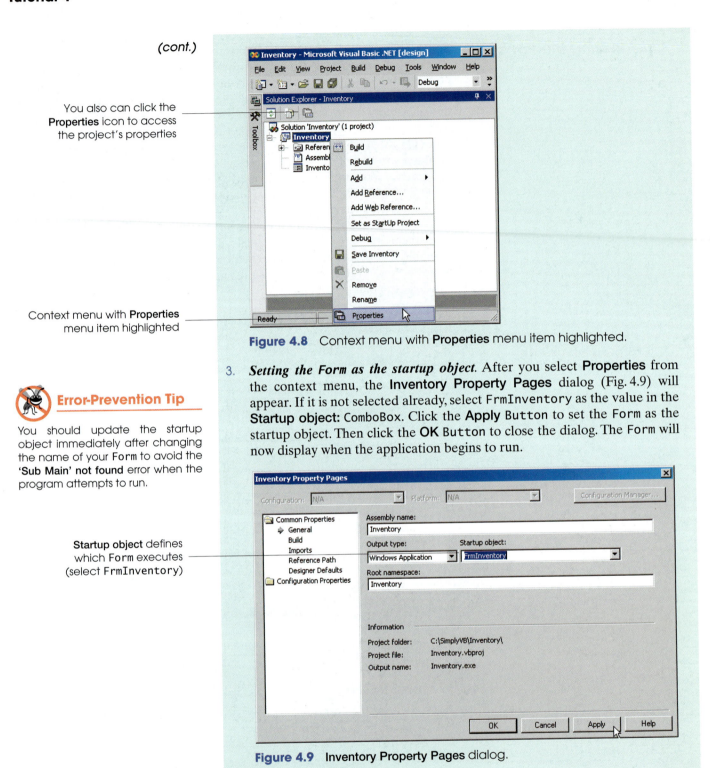

You also can click the Properties icon to access the project's properties

Context menu with Properties menu item highlighted

Figure 4.8   Context menu with **Properties** menu item highlighted.

3. ***Setting the Form as the startup object.*** After you select **Properties** from the context menu, the **Inventory Property Pages** dialog (Fig. 4.9) will appear. If it is not selected already, select FrmInventory as the value in the **Startup object:** ComboBox. Click the **Apply** Button to set the Form as the startup object. Then click the **OK** Button to close the dialog. The Form will now display when the application begins to run.

Error-Prevention Tip

You should update the startup object immediately after changing the name of your **Form** to avoid the **'Sub Main' not found** error when the program attempts to run.

Startup object defines which **Form** executes (select FrmInventory)

Figure 4.9   Inventory Property Pages dialog.

4. ***Saving the project.*** Select **File > Save All** to save your changes.

Next, you will learn how to modify your Form by setting its font. As in all our examples, you should set the Form's font to **Tahoma**, the Microsoft-recommended font for GUIs. Changing the Form's font to Tahoma ensures that controls added to the Form use the Tahoma font. You will also learn how to change the Form's title and size. Although you already changed the file name to Inventory.vb, you still need to change the title bar text to help users identify the Form's purpose. Changing the Form's size to be more appropriate for its content improves its appearance.

GUI Design Tip

Change the **Form**'s font to Tahoma to be consistent with Microsoft's recommended font for Windows.

Customizing the Form

1. **Setting the Form's font.** In the previous tutorial, you used the **Font** dialog to change the font. You will now use the **Properties** window to change the Form's font. Select the Form in the Windows Form Designer. If the **Properties** window is not already open, click the properties icon in the IDE toolbar or select **View > Properties Window**. To change the Form's font to Tahoma, click the plus box ⊞ to the left of the **Font** property in the **Properties** window (Fig. 4.10). This causes other properties related to the Form's **Font** to be displayed. In the list that appears, select the font's **Name** property, then click the down arrow to the right of property value. In the list that appears, select **Tahoma**. [*Note:* This list may appear slightly different, based on the fonts that are installed on your system.]

You will notice that several properties, such as **Font**, have a plus box ⊞ next to the property name to indicate that there are additional properties available for this node. For example, the **Font Name**, **Size** and **Bold** properties of a **Font** each have their own listings in the **Properties** window when you click the plus box.

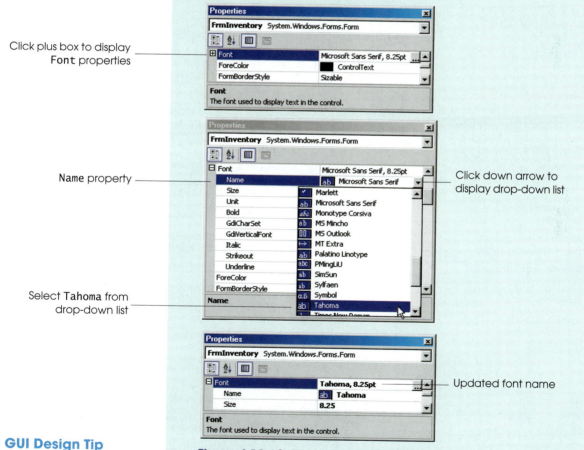

Click plus box to display **Font** properties

Name property

Click down arrow to display drop-down list

Select Tahoma from drop-down list

Updated font name

Figure 4.10 Setting a Form's font to Tahoma.

GUI Design Tip

Changing the Form's title allows users to identify the application's purpose.

GUI Design Tip

Form titles should use book-title capitalization.

2. **Setting the text in the Form's title bar.** The text in the Form's title bar is determined by the Form's **Text** property. To display the Form's properties in the **Properties** window, click the Form in the Windows Form Designer. Double click the field to the right of the **Text** property in the **Properties** window, type **Inventory** and press *Enter* (Fig. 4.11). Form titles should use book-title capitalization. **Book-title capitalization** is a style that capitalizes the first letter of each significant word in the text and does not end with any punctuation (for example, *Capitalization in a Book Title*). The updated title bar is shown in Fig. 4.12.

(cont.)

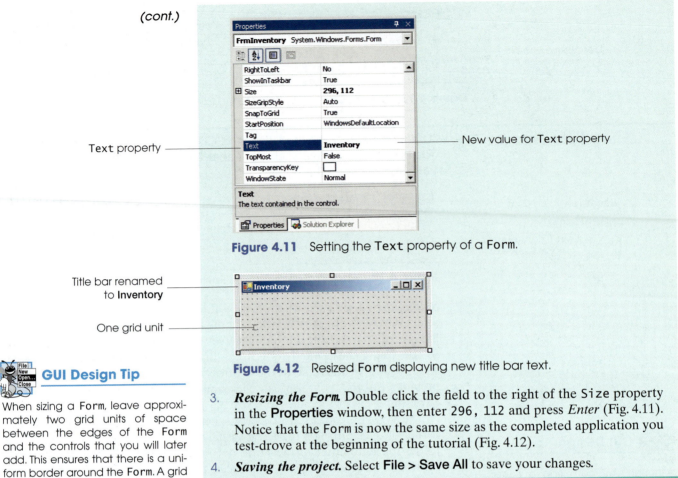

Figure 4.11 Setting the **Text** property of a **Form**.

Title bar renamed to **Inventory**

One grid unit

Figure 4.12 Resized **Form** displaying new title bar text.

GUI Design Tip

When sizing a **Form**, leave approximately two grid units of space between the edges of the **Form** and the controls that you will later add. This ensures that there is a uniform border around the **Form**. A grid unit is the distance between two adjacent dots on the **Form** in design view.

3. *Resizing the Form.* Double click the field to the right of the Size property in the **Properties** window, then enter 296, 112 and press *Enter* (Fig. 4.11). Notice that the Form is now the same size as the completed application you test-drove at the beginning of the tutorial (Fig. 4.12).

4. *Saving the project.* Select **File > Save All** to save your changes.

Now that you have created and modified the Form, you will add controls to the GUI. Labels describe the purpose of controls on the Form and can be used to display results of calculations. In the next box, you learn how to add Label controls and set each Label's name, text and position on the Form.

4.3 Adding Labels to the Inventory Application

Although you might not have noticed it, there are four Labels in this application. You can easily recognize three of the Labels from the application you designed in Tutorial 3. The fourth Label, however, has a border and contains no text until the user clicks the **Calculate Total** Button (Fig. 4.13). As the control's name indicates, Labels are often used to identify other controls on the Form. **Descriptive Labels** help the user understand each control's purpose and **output Labels** are used to display program output.

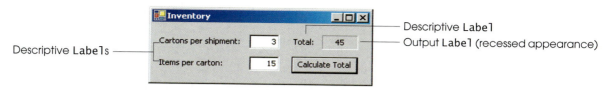

Descriptive Labels

Descriptive Label

Output Label (recessed appearance)

Figure 4.13 Labels used in the **Inventory** application.

Adding Labels to the Form

Location value 0, 0

Label control

GUI Design Tip

Although you can drag a Label control to a location on the Form, the Location property can be used to specify a precise position.

Good Programming Practice

Prefix all Label control names with lbl.

GUI Design Tip

A Label used to describe the purpose of a control should use sentence-style capitalization and end with a colon. These types of Labels are called descriptive Labels.

GUI Design Tip

The TextAlign property of a descriptive Label should be set to MiddleLeft. This ensures that text within groups of Labels align.

1. ***Adding a Label control to the Form.*** Click the **Windows Forms** tab in the **Toolbox**. Then, double click the **Label** control in the **Toolbox** to place a **Label** on the Form (Fig. 4.14).

Figure 4.14 Adding a Label to the Form.

2. ***Setting the Label's size and location.*** If the **Properties** window is not open, select **View > Properties Window**. In the **Properties** window, set the Label's Size property to 120, 21. Similarly, set the Label's Location property to 8, 16. Using these numbers ensures that the controls will align properly when you have added all of the controls to the Form. As you learned in the previous tutorial, you also can click and drag a control to place it on the Form and use sizing handles to resize it.

   The Label's **Location** property specifies the position of the upper-left corner of the control on the Form. Visual Studio .NET assigns the value 0, 0 to the top-left corner of the Form, not including the title bar (Fig. 4.14). A control's Location property is set according to its distance from that point on the Form. As the first number of the Location property increases, the control moves to the right. As the second number of the Location property increases, the control moves toward the bottom of the Form. In this case, the value of 8, 16 indicates that the Label is placed 8 pixels to the right of the top-left corner of the Form and 16 pixels down from the top-left corner of the Form (Fig. 4.16). A Location value of 16, 48 would indicate that the Label is placed 16 pixels to the right of the top-left corner of the Form and 48 pixels down from the top-left corner of the Form.

3. ***Setting the Label's Name and Text properties.*** In the **Properties** window, double click the field to the right of the Text property, then type Cartons per shipment:. Set the Name property to lblCartons.

   When entering values for a Label's Text property, you should use sentence-style capitalization. **Sentence-style capitalization** means that you capitalize the first letter of the first word in the text. Every other letter in the text is lowercase unless it is the first letter of a proper noun (for example, *Deitel*).

4. ***Modifying the Label's text alignment.*** Select the TextAlign property in the **Properties** window; then, in the field to the right, click the down arrow (Fig. 4.15). Property **TextAlign** sets the alignment of text within a control such as a Label. Clicking the down arrow opens a window in which you can select the alignment of the text in the Label (Fig. 4.15). In this window, select the middle-left rectangle, which indicates that the Label's text aligns to the middle, vertically, and to the left, horizontally in the control. The value of the property changes to MiddleLeft. Figure 4.16 displays the Label after you set its properties.

(cont.)

5. ***Modifying the Label's text alignment.*** Select the TextAlign property in the **Properties** window; then, in the field to the right, click the down arrow (Fig. 4.15). Property **TextAlign** sets the alignment of text within a control such as a Label. Clicking the down arrow opens a window in which you can select the alignment of the text in the Label (Fig. 4.15). In this window, select the middle-left rectangle, which indicates that the Label's text aligns to the middle, vertically, and to the left, horizontally in the control. The value of the property changes to MiddleLeft. Figure 4.16 displays the Label after you set its properties.

TextAlign property ———

MiddleLeft TextAlign property value

Value of TextAlign property (MiddleLeft)

Down arrow

Window displayed when down arrow is clicked

Figure 4.15   Changing the TextAlign property of a Label.

Location 8, 16 ———

Figure 4.16   GUI after the Label has been customized.

6. ***Saving the project.*** Select **File > Save All** to save your changes.

Now you will add the remaining Labels to the Form. They will help the user understand what inputs to provide and interpret the application's output. These Labels will identify the controls that you will add to the Form later.

Placing Additional Labels on the Form

1. ***Adding a second descriptive Label.*** Double click the Label control on the **Toolbox** to add a second Label. Set the Label's Size property to 104, 21 and the Label's Location property to 8, 48. Set the Label's Text property to Items per carton:, and change the Name property of this Label to lblItems. Then set the Label's TextAlign property to MiddleLeft.

2. ***Adding a third descriptive Label.*** Double click the Label control on the **Toolbox** to add a third Label. Set the Label's Size property to 40, 21 and the Label's Location property to 184, 16. Set the Label's Text property to Total: and change the Name property of this Label to lblTotal. Then set the Label's TextAlign property to MiddleLeft.

(cont.)

3. **Adding an output Label.** To add the fourth Label, double click the Label control on the **Toolbox**. Set the Label's Size property to 48, 21 and the Label's Location property to 224, 16. Then name this Label lblTotalResult. Set the Label's TextAlign property to MiddleCenter. For the previous Labels, you set this property to MiddleLeft. To select value MiddleCenter, follow the same actions as in *Step 2*, but select the center rectangle shown in Fig. 4.17. You should use MiddleCenter text alignment to display results of calculations because it distinguishes the value in the output Label from the values in the descriptive Labels (whose TextAlign property is set to MiddleLeft).

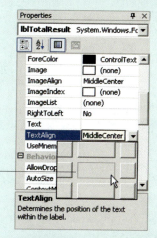

MiddleCenter TextAlign property value

Figure 4.17 Setting the TextAlign property to MiddleCenter.

4. **Changing a Label's BorderStyle property.** Label lblTotalResult displays the result of the application's calculation; therefore, you should make this Label appear different from the other Labels. To do this, you will change the appearance of the Label's border by changing the value of the **BorderStyle** property. Assign the value Fixed3D (Fig. 4.18) to lblTotalResult's BorderStyle property to make the Label seem as if it is three dimensional (Fig. 4.19). [*Note*: If selected, FixedSingle displays a single dark line as a border.]

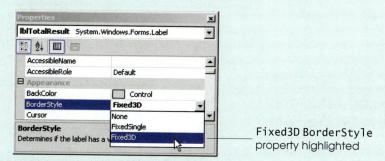

Fixed3D BorderStyle property highlighted

Figure 4.18 Changing a Label's BorderStyle property to Fixed3D.

5. **Clearing a Label's Text property.** When a Label is added to a Form, the Text property is assigned the default name of the Label. In this case, you should clear the text of the Label because you will not be adding meaningful text to Label lblTotalResult until later. To do this, delete the text to the right of the Text property in the **Properties** window and press *Enter*. Figure 4.19 displays the GUI with all Labels added.

(cont.)

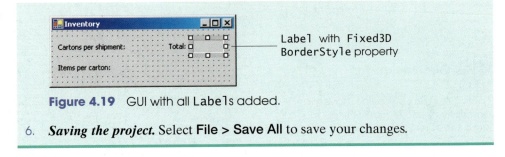

Figure 4.19 GUI with all **Labels** added.

6. *Saving the project.* Select **File > Save All** to save your changes.

SELF-REVIEW

1. The value _____ for the `Location` property indicates the top-left corner (not including the title bar) of the `Form`.

   a) `1, 1`   b) `0, 0`
   c) `1, 0`   d) `0, 1`

2. An output `Label` should _____.
   a) be distinguishable from other `Labels`   b) initially have an empty `Text` property
   c) use `Fixed3D` for the `BorderStyle` property
   d) All of the above.

Answers: 1) b. 2) d.

4.4 Adding TextBoxes and a Button to the Form

The **Inventory** application requires user input to calculate the total number of textbooks that have arrived per shipment. Specifically, the user types in the number of cartons and the fixed number of books per carton. Because this type of data is entered from the keyboard, you use a `TextBox` control. Next, you will learn how to add `TextBoxes` to your `Form` and set their properties. Then, you will add a `Button` control to complete your GUI.

Adding TextBoxes to the Form

Good Programming Practice

Prefix `TextBox` control names with `txt`.

GUI Design Tip

Use `TextBoxes` to input data from the keyboard.

1. *Adding a TextBox to the Form.* Double click the `TextBox` control,

   in the **Toolbox** to add a `TextBox` to the Form. Setting properties for a `TextBox` is similar to setting the properties for a `Label`. To name a `TextBox`, select the Name property in the **Properties** window, and enter `txtCartons` in the field to the right of the property (Fig. 4.20). Set the `TextBox`'s `Size` property to `40, 21` and `Location` property to `128, 16`. These size and location properties will cause the top of the `TextBox` to align with the top of the `Label` that describes it. Set the `TextBox`'s `Text` property to `0` (Fig. 4.21). This will cause the value for your `TextBox` to be initially 0 when the application runs.

2. *Changing the TextAlign property of a TextBox.* Change `txtCartons`'s `TextAlign` property to `Right`. Notice that, when you click the down arrow to the right of this property, the window in Fig. 4.15 does not appear. This is because `TextBoxes` have fewer `TextAlign` options, which are displayed simply as a list. Select `Right` from this list (Fig. 4.21).

(cont.)

GUI Design Tip

Each **TextBox** should have a descriptive **Label** indicating the input expected from the user.

GUI Design Tip

Place each descriptive **Label** either above or to the left of the control (for instance, a **TextBox**) that it identifies.

GUI Design Tip

Make **TextBoxes** wide enough for their expected inputs.

GUI Design Tip

A descriptive **Label** and the control it identifies should be aligned on the left if they are arranged vertically.

GUI Design Tip

A descriptive **Label** should have the same height as the **TextBox** it describes if the controls are arranged horizontally.

GUI Design Tip

A descriptive **Label** and the control it identifies should be aligned on the top if they are arranged horizontally.

GUI Design Tip

Leave at least two grid units between each group of controls on the **Form**.

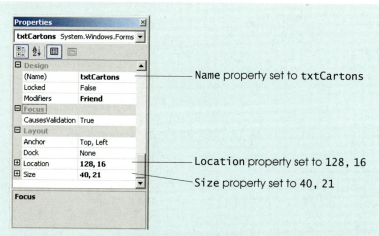

Name property set to `txtCartons`

Location property set to `128, 16`

Size property set to `40, 21`

Figure 4.20 Properties window for the `txtCartons` **TextBox**.

Figure 4.21 Selecting value `Right` of the `TextAlign` property of a **TextBox** control.

3. *Adding a second TextBox to the Form.* Double click the **TextBox** control in the **Toolbox**. Name the **TextBox** `txtItems`. Set the `Size` property to `40, 21` and the `Location` property to `128, 48`. These settings ensure that the left sides of the two **TextBoxes** align. The settings also align the top of the **TextBox** and the top of the **Label** that describes it. Set the `Text` property to `0` and the `TextAlign` property to `Right`. Figure 4.22 shows the **Form** after the **TextBoxes** have been added and their properties have been set.

Figure 4.22 GUI after **TextBoxes** have been added and modified.

4. *Saving the project.* Select **File > Save All** to save your changes.

Notice that your controls are aligning horizontally and vertically. In general, you should place each descriptive **Label** above or to the left of the control it describes (for instance, a **TextBox**). If you are arranging your controls on the same line, the descriptive **Label** and the control it describes should be the same height. However, if you arrange your controls vertically, the **Label** should be placed above the control it describes and the left sides of the controls should align. Also, leave at least two grid units between each group of controls on your **Form**. A **grid unit** is the space between two adjacent horizontal (or two adjacent vertical) dots on the **Form** in design view (Fig. 4.12). Following these simple guidelines will make your applications more appealing visually and easier to use by making the controls on the application less crowded.

Now that the user can enter data using a TextBox, you need a way for the user to command the application to perform the multiplication calculation and display the result. The most common way for a user to do this is by clicking a Button. The following box explains how to add a Button to the **Inventory** application.

<table>
<tr>
<td valign="top">

Adding a Button to the Form

GUI Design Tip

Buttons should be stacked downward from the top right of a Form or arranged on the same line starting from the bottom right of a Form.

Good Programming Practice

Prefix Button control names with btn.

GUI Design Tip

Buttons are labelled using their Text property. These labels should use book-title capitalization and be as short as possible while still being meaningful to the user.

</td>
<td valign="top">

1. ***Adding a Button to the Form.*** Add a Button to the Form by double clicking the Button control,

   in the **Toolbox**. Setting the properties for a Button is similar to setting the properties for a Label or a TextBox. Enter btnCalculate in the Button's Name property. For clarity, you should use btn (short for Button) as the prefix for Buttons.

   Set the Button's Size to 88, 24 and Location to 184, 48. Notice that these settings cause the left and right sides of the Button to align with the Labels above it (Fig. 4.23). Enter Calculate Total in the Button's Text property. A Button's Text property displays its value on the face of the Button. You should use book-title capitalization in a Button's Text property. When labelling Buttons, keep the Text as short as possible while still clearly indicating the Button's function.

2. ***Running the application.*** Select **Debug > Start** to run the application (Fig. 4.23). Notice that no action occurs if you click the **Calculate Total** Button. This is because you have not written code that tells the application how to respond to your click. In Tutorial 5, you will write code to display (in lblTotalResult) the total number of books in the shipment when you click the Button.

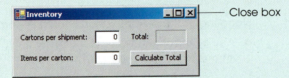

Close box

Figure 4.23   Running the application after completing its design.

3. ***Closing the application.*** Close your running application by clicking its close box.

4. ***Closing the IDE.*** Close Visual Studio .NET by clicking its close box.

</td>
</tr>
</table>

SELF-REVIEW

1. A Button's _____ property sets the value on the face of the Button.

   a) Name   b) Text
   c) Title   d) Face

2. Buttons should be _____ of the Form.

   a) on the same line, from the bottom right   b) stacked from the top left
   c) aligned with the title bar text   d) Either a or c.

Answers: 1) b. 2) a.

4.5 Wrap-Up

In this tutorial, you began constructing your **Inventory** application by designing its graphical user interface. You learned how to use Labels to describe controls and how to set a Label's TextAlign and BorderStyle properties. You used these properties to distinguish between descriptive and output Labels.

After labelling your Form, you added TextBoxes to allow users to input data from the keyboard. Finally, you added a Button to the **Inventory** application, allowing a user to signal the application to perform an action (in this case, to multiply two numbers and display the result). While you added controls to the Form, you also learned some GUI design tips to help you create appealing and intuitive graphical user interfaces.

The next tutorial teaches you to program code in Visual Basic .NET that will run when the user clicks the **Calculate Total** Button. When the Button is clicked, the application receives a signal called an event. You will learn how to program your application to respond to that event by performing the multiplication calculation and displaying the result.

SKILLS SUMMARY

Creating a New Project

- Select **File > New > Project...** to create a project
- Save a project to your working directory (C:\SimplyVB) by selecting it from the **Project Location** dialog.

Setting the Application's Font to Tahoma

- Select Tahoma from the Font Name property ComboBox in the Form's **Properties** window.

Creating a Descriptive Label

- Add a Label to your Form, then change the TextAlign property to MiddleLeft.

Creating an Output Label

- Add a Label to your Form, and change the BorderStyle property to Fixed3D and the TextAlign property to MiddleCenter.

Enabling User Input from the Keyboard

- Add a TextBox control to your Form.

Signaling that the Application Should Perform an Action

- Add a Button to the Form, and write program code to perform that action. (You learn how to add program code in Tutorial 5.)

KEY TERMS

book-title capitalization—A style that capitalizes the first letter of the each word in the text (for example, **Calculate Total**).

BorderStyle property—Specifies the appearance of a Label's border, which allows you to distinguish one control from another visually. The BorderStyle property can be set to None (no border), FixedSingle (a single dark line as a border), or Fixed3D (giving the Label a "sunken" appearance).

Button control—Commands the application to perform an action.

context menu—Appears when you right click an object.

descriptive Label—A Label used to describe another control on the Form. This helps users understand a control's purpose.

Font property—Determines the font used to display text on a Form or control.

grid unit—The space between two adjacent horizontal (or two adjacent vertical) dots on the Form in design view.

Location property—Specifies the location of the upper-left corner of a control. This property is used to place a control on the Form precisely.

Name property—Assigns a unique and meaningful name to a control for easy identification.

output Label—A Label used to display calculation results.

sentence-style capitalization—A style that capitalizes the first letter of the first word in the text. Every other letter in the text is lowercase, unless it is the first letter of a proper noun (for example, **Cartons per shipment**).

startup object—The object (for example, a Form) displayed when the application executes.

Tahoma font—The Microsoft-recommended font for use in Windows applications.

Text property—Sets the text displayed on a control.

TextAlign property—Specifies how text is aligned in the control.

TextBox control—Retrieves user input from the keyboard.

GUI DESIGN GUIDELINES	**Overall Design**

■ Leave at least two grid units between each group of controls on the Form.

■ When sizing a Form, leave approximately two grid units of space between the edges of the Form and the controls that you will later add. This ensures that there is a uniform border around the Form. A grid unit is the distance between two adjacent dots on the Form in design view.

■ Although you can drag a Label control to a location on the Form, the Location property can be used to specify a precise position.

■ Place an application's output below and/or to the right of the Form's input controls.

Buttons

■ Buttons are labelled using their Text property. These labels should use book-title capitalization and be as short as possible while still being meaningful to the user.

■ Buttons should be stacked downward from the top right of a Form or arranged on the same line starting from the bottom right of a Form.

Forms

■ Changing the Form's title allows users to identify the application's purpose.

■ Form titles should use book-title capitalization.

■ Change the Form font to Tahoma to be consistent with Microsoft's recommended font for Windows.

Labels

■ The TextAlign property of a descriptive Label should be set to MiddleLeft. This ensures that text within groups of Labels align.

■ A Label used to describe the purpose of a control should use sentence-style capitalization and end with a colon. These types of Labels are called descriptive Labels.

■ Place each descriptive Label above or to the left of the control that it identifies.

■ A descriptive Label should have the same height as the TextBox it describes if the controls are arranged horizontally.

■ A descriptive Label and the control it identifies should be aligned on the left if they are arranged vertically.

■ Align the left sides of a group of descriptive Labels if the Labels are arranged vertically.

■ Use a descriptive Label to identify an output Label.

■ Output Labels should be distinguishable from descriptive Labels. This can be done by setting the BorderStyle property to of an output Label to Fixed3D.

■ If several output Labels are arranged vertically to display numbers used in a mathematical calculation (such as in an invoice), use the MiddleRight TextAlign property.

■ A descriptive Label and the control it identifies should be aligned on the top if they are arranged horizontally.

TextBoxes

■ Use TextBoxes to input data from the keyboard.

■ Each TextBox should have a descriptive Label indicating the input expected from the user.

■ Make TextBoxes wide enough for their expected inputs. |

CONTROLS, EVENTS, PROPERTIES & METHODS

Button   `ab| Button`   This control allows the user to raise an action or event.

- *In action*

    `Calculate Total`

- *Properties*

    Name—Specifies the name used to access the Button programmatically. The name should be prefixed with btn.

    Size—Specifies the height and width (in pixels) of the Button.

    Text—Specifies the text displayed on the Button.

Label   `A Label`   This control displays text that the user cannot modify.

- *In action*

    `Total:`

- *Properties*

    BorderStyle—Specifies the appearance of the Label's border.

    Font—Specifies the font name, style and size of the text displayed in the Label.

    Location—Specifies the location of the Label on the Form relative to the Form's top-left corner.

    Name—Specifies the name used to access the Label programmatically. The name should be prefixed with lbl.

    Size—Specifies the height and width (in pixels) of the Label.

    Text—Specifies the text displayed in the Label.

    TextAlign—Determines how the text is aligned within the Label.

TextBox   `abl TextBox`   This control allows user to input data from the keyboard.

- *In action*

    `0`

- *Properties*

    Name—Specifies the name used to access the TextBox programmatically. The name should be prefixed with txt.

    Size—Specifies the height and width (in pixels) of the TextBox.

    Text—Specifies the text displayed in the TextBox.

    TextAlign—Specifies how the text is aligned within the TextBox.

MULTIPLE-CHOICE QUESTIONS

4.1 A new Windows application is created by selecting _____ from the **File** menu.

a) **New > Program**   b) **New > File...**

c) **New > Project...**   d) **New > Application**

4.2 A Label's BorderStyle property can be set to _____.

a) Fixed3D   b) Single

c) 3D   d) All of the above.

4.3 When creating a Label, you can specify the _____ of that Label.

a) alignment of the text   b) border style

c) size   d) All of the above.

4.4 Changing the value stored in the _____ property will change the name of the `Form` file.

    a) `Name`   b) `File`

    c) `File Name`   d) `Full Path`

4.5 _____ should be used to prefix all `TextBox` names.

    a) `txt`   b) `tbx`

    c) `Frm`   d) `tbn`

4.6 A(n) _____ helps the user understand a control's purpose.

    a) `Button`   b) descriptive `Label`

    c) output `Label`   d) title bar

4.7 A _____ is a control in which the user can enter data from a keyboard.

    a) `Button`   b) `TextBox`

    c) `Label`   d) `PictureBox`

4.8 A descriptive `Label` uses _____.

    a) sentence-style capitalization   b) book-title capitalization

    c) a colon at the end of its text   d) Both a and c.

4.9 You should use the _____ font in your Windows applications.

    a) Tahoma   b) MS Sans Serif

    c) Times   d) Palatino

4.10 _____ should be used to prefix all `Button` names.

    a) `but`   b) `lbl`

    c) `Frm`   d) `btn`

EXERCISES

At the end of each tutorial, you will find a summary of new GUI design tips listed in the GUI Design Guidelines section. A cumulative list of GUI design guidelines, organized by control, appears in Appendix C. In these exercises, you will find Visual Basic .NET Forms that do not follow the GUI design guidelines presented in this tutorial. For each exercise, you must modify control properties so that your end result is consistent with the guidelines presented in the tutorial. Note that these applications do not provide any functionality.

4.11 *(Address Book GUI)* In this exercise, you apply the GUI design guidelines you have learned to a graphical user interface for an address book (Fig. 4.24).

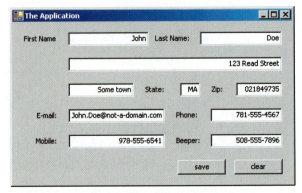

Figure 4.24 **Address Book** application without GUI design guidelines applied.

    a) ***Copying the template to your working directory.*** Copy the directory `C:\Examples\Tutorial04\Exercises\AddressBook` to your `C:\SimplyVB` directory.

    b) ***Opening the application's template file.*** Double click `AddressBook.sln` in the `AddressBook` directory to open the application.

c) *Applying GUI design guidelines.* Rearrange the controls and modify properties so that the GUI conforms to the design guidelines you have learned.

d) *Saving the project.* Select **File > Save All** to save your changes.

4.12 *(Mortgage Calculator GUI)* In this exercise, you apply the GUI design guidelines you have learned to a graphical user interface for a mortgage calculator (Fig. 4.25).

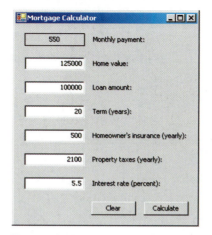

Figure 4.25 **Mortgage Calculator** application without GUI design guidelines applied.

a) *Copying the template to your working directory.* Copy the directory `C:\Examples\Tutorial04\Exercises\MortgageCalculator` to your `C:\SimplyVB` directory.

b) *Opening the application's template file.* Double click `MortgageCalculator.sln` in the `MortgageCalculator` directory to open the application.

c) *Applying GUI design guidelines.* Rearrange the controls and modify properties so that the GUI conforms to the design guidelines you have learned.

d) *Saving the project.* Select **File > Save All** to save your changes.

4.13 *(Password GUI)* In this exercise, you apply the GUI design guidelines you have learned to a graphical user interface for a password-protected message application (Fig. 4.26).

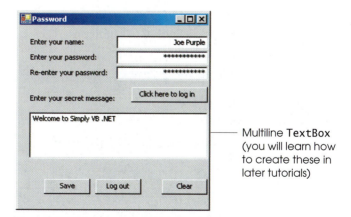

Multiline **TextBox** (you will learn how to create these in later tutorials)

Figure 4.26 **Password** application without GUI design guidelines applied.

a) *Copying the template to your working directory.* Copy the directory `C:\Examples\Tutorial04\Exercises\Password` to your `C:\SimplyVB` directory.

b) *Opening the application's template file.* Double click `Password.sln` in the `Password` directory to open the application.

c) *Applying GUI design guidelines.* Rearrange the controls and modify properties so that the GUI conforms to the design guidelines you have learned.

d) *Saving the project.* Select **File > Save All** to save your changes.

Programming Challenge ▶   **4.14** *(Monitor Invoice GUI)* In this exercise, you apply the GUI design guidelines you have
learned to a graphical user interface for an invoice application (Fig. 4.27).

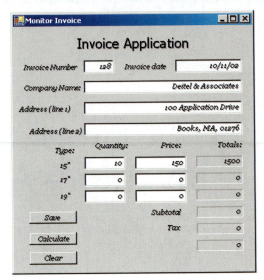

Figure 4.27   **Invoice** application without GUI design guidelines applied.

a) *Copying the template to your working directory.* Copy the directory `C:\Examples\`
   `Tutorial04\Exercises\MonitorInvoice` to your `C:\SimplyVB` directory.

b) *Opening the application's template file.* Double click the `MonitorInvoice.sln` file
   to open the application.

c) *Applying GUI design guidelines.* Rearrange the controls and modify properties so
   that the GUI conforms to the design guidelines you have learned.

d) *Saving the project.* Select **File > Save All** to save your changes.

TUTORIAL 5

Completing the Inventory Application

Introducing Programming

Objectives

In this tutorial, you will learn to:
- Add an event handler for a **Button** control.
- Insert code into an event handler.
- Access a property's value by using Visual Basic .NET code.
- Use the assignment and multiplication operators.

Outline

5.1 Test-Driving the Inventory Application

5.2 Introduction to Visual Basic .NET Code

5.3 Inserting an Event Handler

5.4 Performing a Calculation and Displaying the Result

5.5 Using the Debugger: Syntax Errors

5.6 Wrap-Up

This tutorial introduces fundamentals of nonvisual programming to create an application with which users can interact. You will learn these concepts as you add functionality (with Visual Basic .NET code) to the **Inventory** application you designed in Tutorial 4. The term **functionality** describes the actions an application can execute. In this tutorial, you will examine **events**, which represent user actions, such as clicking a **Button** or altering a value in a **TextBox**, and **event handlers**, which are pieces of code that are executed (called) when such events occur (that is, when the events are **raised**). You will learn why events and event handlers are crucial to programming Windows applications.

5.1 Test-Driving the Inventory Application

In this tutorial, you will complete the **Inventory** application you designed in Tutorial 4. Recall that the application must meet the following requirements:

> **Application Requirements**
>
> *A college bookstore receives cartons of textbooks. In each shipment, each carton contains the same number of textbooks. The inventory manager wants to use a computer to calculate the total number of textbooks arriving at the bookstore for each shipment, from the number of cartons and the number of textbooks in each carton. The inventory manager will enter the number of cartons received and the fixed number of textbooks in each carton for each shipment; then the application will calculate the total number of textbooks in a shipment.*

The inventory manager has reviewed and approved your design. Now you must add code that, when the user clicks a **Button**, will make the application multiply the number of cartons by the number of textbooks per carton and display the result—the total number of textbooks received. You begin by test-driving the completed application. Then, you will learn the additional Visual Basic .NET technologies you will need to create your own version of this application.

Test-Driving the
Inventory Application

1. ***Opening the completed application.*** Open the directory `C:\Examples\`
`Tutorial05\CompletedApplication\Inventory2` to locate the **Inventory**
application. Double click `Inventory2.sln` to open the application in Visual
Studio .NET.

2. ***Running the Inventory application.*** Select **Debug > Start** to run the application (Fig. 5.1). Enter 3 in the **Cartons per shipment:** TextBox. Enter 15 in
the **Items per carton:** TextBox. Figure 5.1 shows the Form after these values
have been entered.

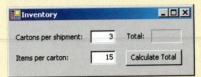

Figure 5.1   **Inventory** application with quantities entered.

3. ***Calculating the total number of items received.*** Click the **Calculate Total**
Button. The application multiplies the two numbers you entered and displays the result (45) in the **Label** to the right of **Total:** (Fig. 5.2).

Result of calculation

Figure 5.2   Result of clicking the **Calculate Total** **Button** in the **Inventory**
application.

4. ***Closing the application.*** Close your running application by clicking its close
box.

5. ***Closing the IDE.*** Close Visual Studio .NET by clicking its close box.

5.2 Introduction to Visual Basic .NET Code

In Tutorial 3 and Tutorial 4, you were introduced to a concept called visual programming, which allows you to create GUIs without writing any program code. In
this section, you will combine visual programming with conventional programming
techniques to enhance the **Inventory** application.

Before you begin to view and edit code, you should customize the way Visual
Studio .NET displays and formats your code. In the following box, you open the
template application and change display and format settings to make it easy for you
to work with code and follow our discussions. Adding line numbers, adjusting tab
sizes and setting fonts and colors help you to navigate your code more easily.

Customizing the IDE

1. ***Copying the template to your working directory.*** Copy the `C:\Examples\`
`Tutorial05\TemplateApplication\Inventory2` directory to your
`C:\SimplyVB` directory. This directory contains the application created by
following the steps in Tutorial 4.

2. ***Opening the Inventory application's template file.*** Double click
`Inventory2.sln` in the Inventory2 directory to open the application in
Visual Studio .NET.

(cont.)

This is the first tutorial in which you will use our template applications. If an error occurs when you try to copy or modify the template, please consult your system administrator to ensure that you have proper privileges to edit these applications.

3. ***Displaying line numbers.*** In all of our programming discussions, we refer to specific code elements by line number. To help you locate where you will insert code in the examples, you need to enable Visual Studio .NET's capability to show line numbers in your code.

Select **Tools > Options…**, and, in the **Options** dialog that appears (Fig. 5.3), click the **Text Editor** folder icon. Then click the **Basic** folder icon (Fig. 5.4) to expand the options for Visual Basic .NET. If the arrow is not pointing to the **General** option after you click the **Basic** folder, click **General** to display the page in Fig. 5.4. Locate the **Display** header. If the Checkbox next to **Line numbers** is not checked, click inside the box to add a checkmark. If the box is already checked, you need not do anything; however, do not close the dialog.

Text Editor
folder icon

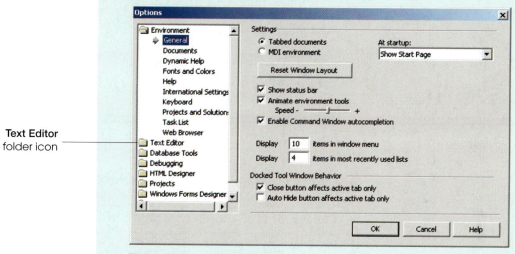

Figure 5.3 **Options** dialog.

Basic folder
General item

Line numbers
CheckBox (checked)

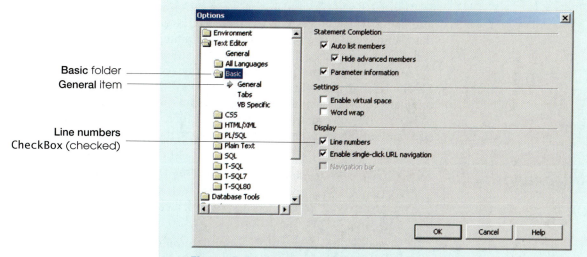

Figure 5.4 **General** settings page for Visual Basic .NET text editor.

(cont.)

4. ***Setting the tab size.*** Just as you indent the first line of each paragraph when writing a letter, it is important to use proper spacing when writing code. Indenting code improves program readability. You can control indents with tabs. Click the **Tabs** item under the **Basic** folder (Fig. 5.5). The **Smart** RadioButton, under the **Indenting** header, should be selected by default. If it is not, select the **Smart** RadioButton by clicking inside the white circle. Using this setting, Visual Studio .NET will indent code for you.

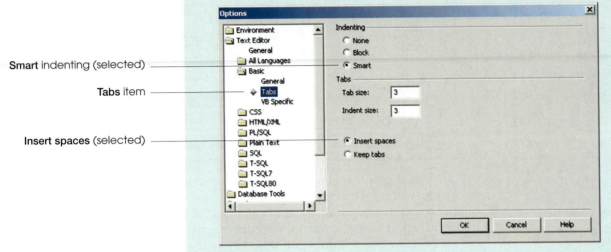

Smart indenting (selected) ─────

Tabs item ─────

Insert spaces (selected) ─────

Figure 5.5 Setting the **Tabs** options.

Set **Tab size:** to 3 and **Indent size:** to 3. The **Tab size:** setting indicates the number of spaces each tab character (inserted when you press the *Tab* key) represents. The **Indent size:** setting determines the number of spaces each indent inserted by Visual Studio .NET represents. Visual Studio .NET will now insert 3 spaces for you if you are using the **Smart** indenting feature; you can insert them yourself with one keystroke by pressing the *Tab* key.

Then make sure the **Insert spaces** RadioButton is selected (Fig. 5.5), so Visual Studio .NET will insert three one-character spaces (instead of one tab character) to indent lines. If you select the **Keep tabs** RadioButton, each tab or indent will be represented by one tab character. We suggest you select the **Insert spaces** RadioButton.

5. ***Exploring fonts and colors.*** Click the **Environment** folder icon; then click the **Fonts and Colors** item. The screen that appears allows you to customize fonts and colors used to display code. Visual Studio .NET can apply colors and fonts to make it easier for you to read and edit code. Note that, if your settings are not consistent with the default settings, what you see on your screen will appear different from what is presented in this book. If you need to reset your settings to the default for fonts and colors, click the **Use Defaults** Button (Fig. 5.6).

In the book's examples, you will see code with the **Selected Text** background set to yellow for emphasis. The default setting for **Selected Text** is a blue background. You should use the default settings on your machine.

6. ***Applying your changes.*** Click the **OK** Button to apply your changes and dismiss the **Options** dialog.

Good Programming Practice

You can change the font and color settings if you prefer a different appearance for your code. To remain consistent with this book, however, we recommend that you not change the default font and color settings.

(cont.)

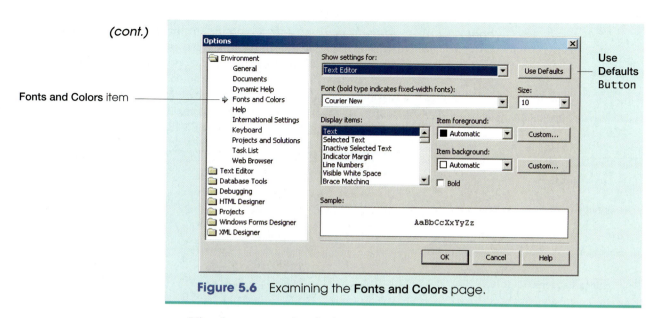

Figure 5.6 Examining the **Fonts and Colors** page.

Visual programming is fun and saves time, but it is insufficient for the vast majority of applications. While you've been programming in a completely visual environment when adding `Labels` and `TextBoxes`, Visual Studio .NET has actually been writing code for you in the background. Behind the scenes, everything that your application will do is performed by code written either by you or by the IDE. The key is to develop the right mix of visual programming with code writing ("non-visual" programming) for each application. Next, you will take your first peek at Visual Basic .NET code.

Introducing Visual Basic .NET Code

1. *Viewing application code.* If the Windows Form Designer is not open, double click the `Inventory.vb` file in the **Solutions Explorer** window. Then switch to **code view** (where the application's code is displayed in an editor window), by selecting **View > Code**. The tabbed window (`Inventory.vb`) in Fig. 5.7, also called a **code editor**, appears. Note that when you are asked to select **View > Code**, the `Inventory.vb` file must be selected in the **Solutions Explorer**.

   You will notice that the IDE through which we present code to you may appear different than your IDE. To improve readability, we have hidden the **Toolbox** and closed any extra windows, such as the **Solutions Explorer**, **Properties** and **Task List** windows.

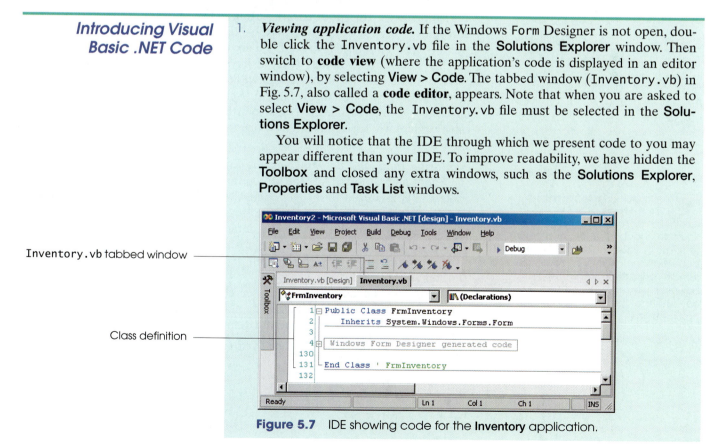

Figure 5.7 IDE showing code for the **Inventory** application.

(cont.)

Most Visual Basic .NET programs consist of pieces called classes, which simplify application organization. Recall from Tutorial 1 that classes contain groups of code statements that perform tasks and return information when the tasks are completed. The code in this application defines your **Inventory** application class. (These lines collectively are called a **class definition**.) Most Visual Basic .NET applications consist of a combination of code written by programmers (like you) and preexisting classes written and provided by Microsoft in the Framework Class Library (FCL). Again, the key to successful Visual Basic .NET application development is achieving the right mix of the two. You will learn how to use both techniques in your programs.

2. *Examining class definitions.* Line 1 (Fig. 5.7) begins the class definition. The **Class keyword** introduces a class definition in Visual Basic .NET and is immediately followed by the **class name** (FrmInventory in this application, the value you entered in the Form's Name property).

The name of the class is an **identifier**, which is a series of characters consisting of letters, digits and underscores (_). Identifiers cannot begin with a digit and cannot contain spaces. Examples of valid identifiers are intValue1, intLabel_Value and btnExit. The name 7welcome is not a valid identifier, because it begins with a digit, and the name input field is not a valid identifier, because it contains a space. The class definition ends on line 131 with the keywords **End Class**. **Keywords** (or **reserved words**) are reserved for use by Visual Basic .NET (you will learn the various keywords throughout the text). Notice that keywords appear in blue by default in the IDE. A complete list of Visual Basic .NET keywords can be found in Appendix F, Keyword Chart.

The Class keyword is preceded by the Public keyword. The code for every Form you design in Visual Studio .NET begins with the Public keyword. You will learn about this keyword in Tutorial 19.

Visual Basic .NET keywords and identifiers are not **case sensitive**. This means that uppercase and lowercase letters are considered to be identical; that practice causes FrmInventory and frminventory to be understood by Visual Basic .NET as the same identifier. Although the first letter of every keyword is capitalized, keywords are nevertheless not case sensitive. Visual Studio .NET applies the correct case to each letter of a keyword and identifier, so, when you type clasS, it is changed to Class when the *Enter* key is pressed.

3. *Understanding inheriting from class Form.* Every visual Windows application consists of at least one class that Inherits from class Form (Fig. 5.7, line 2) in the FCL. The keyword **Inherits** indicates that the class FrmInventory inherits members from another class. By inheriting from System.Windows.Forms.Form, your application uses class Form as a "template." A key benefit of inheriting from class Form is that the FCL previously has defined "what it means to be a Form." The Windows operating system expects every window (for example, a Form) to have certain capabilities. However, because class Form already provides those capabilities, programmers do not need to "reinvent the wheel" by defining all those capabilities themselves. The use of Inherits to derive from class Form enables programmers to create Forms quickly and easily.

Good Programming Practice

Capitalize the first letter of each class identifier, such as the Form name.

Good Programming Practice

Always type a keyword with the correct capitalization, even though Visual Studio .NET will correct any capitalization errors.

In the editor window (Fig. 5.7), notice the text Windows Form Designer generated code on line 4, which is surrounded by a gray rectangle and has a plus box ⊞ next to it. The plus box indicates that this section of code, called a **region**, is collapsed, as discussed in Tutorial 2. Notice that the line numbers in Fig. 5.7 jump from 4 to 130. The missing line numbers correspond to code hidden from you by Visual Studio .NET. Although collapsed code is not visible, it is still part of the application.

Code collapsing allows you to hide code in the editor, so that you can focus on key code segments. Notice that the entire class definition also can be collapsed by clicking the minus box ⊟ to the left of `Public`. In Fig. 5.7, the description to the right of the plus box indicates that the collapsed code was created by the Windows Form Designer. This collapsed code contains the code, inserted by the IDE, that creates the `Form` and its controls. In the following box, you explore the code generated by the IDE.

Examining Windows Form Designer Generated Code

1. **Viewing the generated code.** In this step, you will view other code that is part of your application. You will not be expected to understand the code. Visual programming saves development time by allowing you to build applications without needing to know how every component works "under the hood," just as you don't need to know how an engine works in order to drive a car.

   Click the plus box on line 4 to view the generated code. The **expanded code** (Fig. 5.8) certainly appears to be complex. The vast majority of the code shown has not been introduced yet. Again, you are not expected to understand how it works.

   This code is created by the IDE and normally is not edited by the programmer. This is Microsoft's intent—you can develop powerful applications without having to worry about the IDE-generated code. This type of code is present in *every* Windows application developed with Visual Studio .NET, saving you a considerable amount of development time. As you read this book, the purpose of much of this code will become clearer.

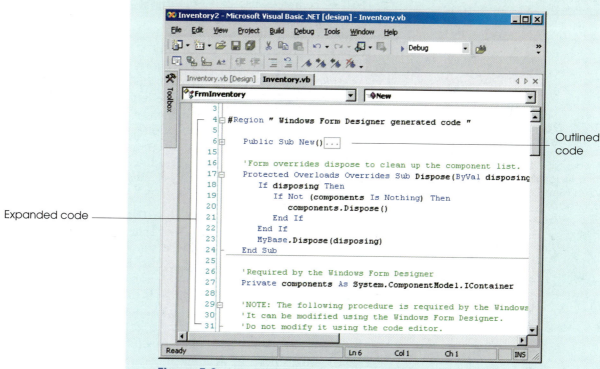

Figure 5.8 Windows `Form` Designer generated code, when expanded.

Collapse the code by clicking the node at line 6. Your code should now appear exactly as in Fig. 5.8. A box containing an ellipses appears in place of the code in that region. This area is called **outlined code**. Placing the cursor over the outlined code displays a portion of the collapsed code.

(cont.)

2. ***Viewing the generated code for a specific control.*** Click and drag the scrollbar downward until you reach the code in Fig. 5.9. This region contains code generated by the IDE for setting Label lblCarton's properties, including the Label's Location, Name, Size, Text and TextAlign properties.

When you designed this application in Tutorial 4, you used the **Properties** window to set properties for the Form, Labels, TextBoxes and Buttons. Once a property was set, the object was updated immediately. Objects (Forms and controls) have **default properties**, which are displayed initially in the **Properties** window when an object is created. These default properties provide the initial characteristics of an object. When a control, such as a Label, is placed on the Form, the IDE adds code to the class (in this case, FrmInventory) that creates the control and sets some of the control's property values, such as the name of the control and its location on the Form.

Property values for lblCartons

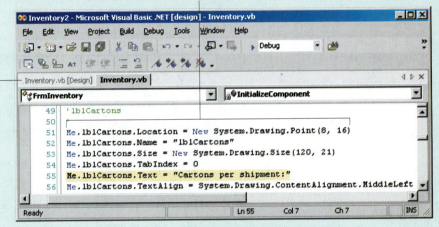

Figure 5.9 Code generated by the IDE for lblCartons (with the code setting the Text property highlighted).

The values in the code in Fig. 5.9 correspond to what you entered in the **Properties** window in the Windows Form Designer in Tutorial 4. Notice that the Label's Text property is assigned the text that you entered in the **Properties** window (line 55). When you change a property in design view, the Windows Form Designer updates the appropriate line of code in the class to reflect the new value.

3. ***Collapsing code.*** Collapse this application's generated code by clicking the node at line 4.

SELF-REVIEW

1. Identifiers _____.

   a) can begin with any character, but cannot contain spaces

   b) must begin with a digit, but cannot contain spaces

   c) cannot begin with a digit or contain spaces

   d) cannot begin with a digit, but can contain spaces

2. In code view, the plus box shown to the left of a line of code indicates that this region is _____.

   a) positive   b) closed

   c) expanded   d) collapsed

Answers: 1) c. 2) d.

5.3 Inserting an Event Handler

Now that you have finalized the GUI, you are ready to modify your application so it will respond to user input. You will do this by inserting code manually. Most of the Visual Basic .NET applications in this book provide functionality in the form of event handlers. Recall that an event handler is executed when an event occurs, such as the clicking of a `Button`. The next box shows you how to add an event handler to your application.

Adding a Button's
Click Event Handler

1. ***Adding an event handler for the Button.*** In this step, you use the Windows Form Designer to create an event handler and enter code view. Begin by clicking the `Inventory.vb [Design]` tab to enter the Windows Form Designer. Then double click the Form's **Calculate Total** `Button` to enter code view. Notice that the code for the application, which now includes the new event handler on lines 131–133 of Fig. 5.10, is displayed. Notice that we have added a blank line after the event handler by placing the cursor at the end of line 133, then pressing *Enter*.

Asterisks indicate unsaved changes to application

Empty event handler

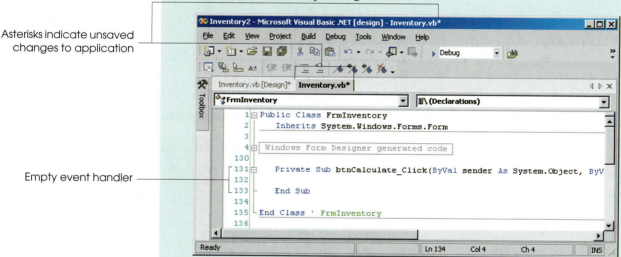

Figure 5.10 Event handler `btnCalculate_Click` before you add your program code.

Double clicking the **Calculate Total** `Button` in design view caused Visual Studio .NET to generate the `Button`'s `Click` event handler—the code that will execute when the user clicks the **Calculate Total** `Button`. When any control is double clicked in design view, Visual Studio .NET inserts an event handler for that control. The event that the handler is associated with may differ based on the control that is double clicked. For instance, double clicking `Button` controls causes `Click` event handlers to be created. Double clicking other types of controls will cause other types of event handlers to be generated. Each control has a default type of event handler that is generated when that control is clicked in design view.

In Visual Basic .NET, event handlers by convention follow the naming scheme *controlName_eventName*. The word *controlName* refers to the name of the control provided in its `Name` property (in this case, `btnCalculate`). The word *eventName* represents the name of the event (in this case, `Click`) raised by the control. When event *eventName* occurs, event handler *controlName_eventName* executes. In this application, `btnCalculate_Click` handles the **Calculate Total** `Button`'s `Click` events—in other words, the code in `btnCalculate_Click` executes when the user clicks the **Calculate Total** `Button`.

(cont.)   2. ***Running the application.*** Select **Debug > Start** to run the application (Fig. 5.11). Click the **Calculate Total** Button.

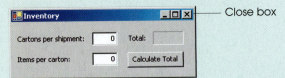

Close box

Figure 5.11   Running application without functionality.

Notice that, although you have added an event handler for the Button's Click event, no action occurs when you click the Button because you haven't added any code to the event handler yet. In the next box, you add code to the event handler so that, when a user clicks the Button, text displays in the output Label (lblTotalResult).

3. ***Closing the application.*** Close the running application by clicking its close box.

Now that you have created an event handler for the **Calculate Total** Button, you need to insert code to perform an action. Specifically, you need to make the application multiply the number of cartons in a shipment by the fixed number of items per carton when a user clicks the **Calculate Total** Button. You write your first Visual Basic .NET statement in the following box.

Adding Code to an Empty Event Handler

1. ***Changing to code view.*** If you are not already in code view, select **View > Code** to view the application's code.

2. ***Adding code to the event handler.*** In the body of the event handler, insert lines 133–134 of Fig. 5.12 by typing the text on the screen.

Event handler

Type this code

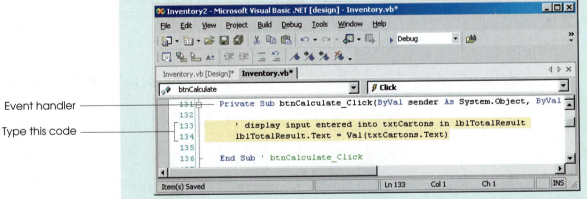

Figure 5.12   Code added to the **Calculate Total** Button's event handler.

Line 133 of Fig. 5.12 begins with a **single-quote character** (`'`), which indicates that the remainder of the line is a **comment**. Programmers insert comments in programs to improve the readability of their code. These comments explain the code so that other programmers who need to work with the application can understand it more easily.

Comments also help you read your own code, especially when you haven't looked at it for a while. Comments can be placed either on their own lines (these are called "full-line comments") or at the end of a line of Visual Basic .NET code (these are called "end-of-line comments").

Good Programming Practice

Comments written at the end of a line should be preceded by one or more spaces, to enhance program readability.

(cont.)

The Visual Basic .NET compiler ignores comments, which means that comments do not cause the computer to perform any actions when your applications run. The comment used in line 133 simply indicates that the next line displays the value entered into the **Cartons per shipment:** Text-Box in the **Total:** Label. Comments appear in green when displayed in the code editor of Visual Studio .NET.

Line 134 of Fig. 5.12 presents your first executable Visual Basic .NET **statement**, which performs an action. By default, statements end when the current line ends. Later in this tutorial, you will see how to continue a statement past one line. This statement (line 134) accesses the Text properties of txtCartons and lblTotalResult. In Visual Basic .NET, properties are accessed in code by placing a period between the control name (for example, lblTotalResult) and property name (for example, Text). This period, which is placed to the right of the control name, is called the **member access operator** (.), or the **dot operator**. Notice that, when the control name and member access operator are typed, a window appears listing that object's members (Fig. 5.13). This is known as Visual Studio .NET's **IntelliSense** feature, which displays all the members in a class for your convenience. You scroll to the member you are interested in and select it. Click the member name once to display a description of that member; double click it to add the name of the member to your application. *IntelliSense* can be useful in discovering a class's members and their purpose.

Good Programming Practice

Precede every full-line comment or group of full-line comments with a blank line. The blank line makes the comments stand out and improves program readability.

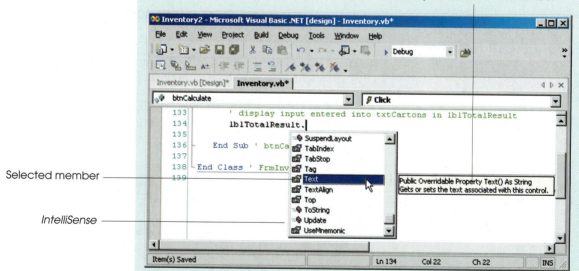

Figure 5.13   *IntelliSense* activating while entering code.

Let's examine line 134 of Fig. 5.12 more closely. Reading the line from left to right, we see lblTotalResult's Text property, followed by an "equals" sign (=), followed by txtCartons' Text property value. The "=" symbol, as used here, is known as the **assignment operator**. The expressions on either side of the assignment operator are referred to as its **operands**. This assignment operator assigns the value on the right of the operator (the **right operand**) to the variable on the left of the operator (the **left operand**). The assignment operator is known as a **binary operator**, because it has two operands—lblTotalResult.Text and txtCartons.Text.

(cont.)

The entire statement is called an **assignment statement**, because it assigns a value to the left operand. In this example, you are assigning the value of txtCartons' Text property to lblTotalResult's Text property. The statement is read as, "The Text property of lblTotalResult *gets* the value of txtCarton's Text property." Note that the right operand is unchanged by the assignment statement.

When the user clicks the **Calculate Total** Button, the event handler will execute, displaying the value the user entered in the **Cartons per shipment:** TextBox in the output Label lblTotalResult. Clearly, this is not the correct result—the correct result is the number of items per carton times the number of cartons per shipment. In the box, *Completing the Inventory Application*, you correct this error. Notice that we have added a comment on line 136 of Fig. 5.12, indicating the end of our event handler.

3. ***Running the application.*** Select **Debug > Start** to run the application (Fig. 5.14). Type 5 into the **Cartons per shipment:** TextBox and 10 into the **Items per carton:** TextBox, then click the **Calculate Total** Button. Notice that the text of lblTotalResult now incorrectly displays the data, 5, that was entered into the **Cartons per shipment:** TextBox, rather than displaying the correct result, 50.

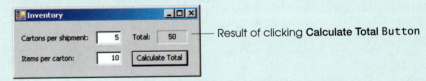
— Result of clicking **Calculate Total** Button

Figure 5.14   Running the application with event handler.

4. ***Closing the application.*** Close the running application by clicking its close box.

SELF-REVIEW

1. Event handlers generated by Visual Studio .NET follow the naming convention _____ .

    a) *controlName_eventName*   b) *eventName_controlName*
    c) *eventNameControlName*   d) *controlNameEventName*

2. The expressions on either side of the assignment operator are referred to as its _____ .

    a) operator values   b) results
    c) operands   d) arguments

Answers: 1) a. 2) c.

5.4 Performing a Calculation and Displaying the Result

Now that you are familiar with displaying output in a Label, you will complete the **Inventory** application by displaying the product of the number of cartons per shipment and the number of items per carton. In the following box, you will learn how to perform mathematical operations in Visual Basic .NET.

Completing the Inventory Application

1. ***Changing the event handler.*** If you are not already in code view, select **View > Code** or click the Inventory.vb tab. Insert underscore (_) characters as shown at the right of lines 131–132. Indent lines 132–133 as shown in Fig. 5.15 by placing the cursor at the beginning of each line's text and pressing the *Tab* key. Then replace the body of btnCalculate_Click with the code in lines 135–137 of Fig. 5.15.

(cont.)

Common Programming Error

Placing anything, including comments, to the right of a line-continuation character is a syntax error. Syntax errors are introduced in the box, *Using the Debugger: Syntax Errors.*

Modified **Inventory** application code

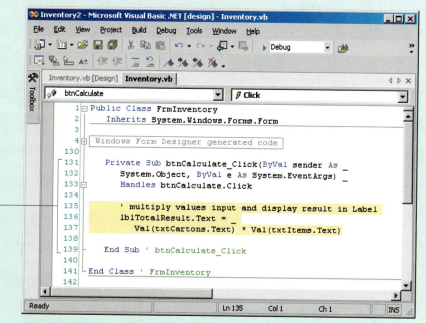

Figure 5.15 Using multiplication in the **Inventory** application.

The comment in line 135 indicates that you will be multiplying the two values input by the user and displaying the result in a Label.

Good Programming Practice

A lengthy statement may be spread over several lines. If a single statement must be split across lines, choose breaking points that make sense, such as after an operator. If a statement is split across two or more lines, indent all subsequent lines with one "level" of indentation.

2. *Adding multiline code.* Lines 135–137 perform the multiplication and assignment. You again use the assignment operator to assign a value to lblTotalResult.Text in line 136. To the right of the assignment operator is a space followed by an underscore (_), known as the **line-continuation character**. This character indicates that the next line is a continuation of the previous line. A single statement can contain as many line-continuation characters as necessary. However, at least one whitespace character must precede each line-continuation character. A **whitespace character** is a space, tab or newline (the character inserted by pressing the *Enter* key). Because this statement has been continued past the current line, look to the next line for the assignment operator's right operand. We have also used the line-continuation character on lines 131–132 to split the first line of the event handler into three lines; this enables all the program code to fit in the window. The line-continuation character has no effect when placed at the end of a comment.

Common Programming Error

Splitting a statement over several lines without including the line-continuation character is a syntax error.

The assignment operator in line 136 assigns the result of multiplying the numbers input by the user to lblTotalResult.Text. On line 137, Val(txtCartons.Text) is followed by an asterisk (*) and then Val(txtItems.Text). The asterisk is known as the **multiplication operator**—the operator's left and right operands are multiplied together.

(cont.)

Your **Inventory** application cannot prevent users from accidentally entering nonnumeric input such as letters and special characters like $ and @. Line 137 uses the **Val function** to prevent inputs like this from terminating the application. A function is a portion of code that performs a task when **called** (executed) and sends, or **returns**, a value to the location from which it was called. In this case, the values returned by Val become the values used to perform multiplication (line 137). We call functions (as in line 137) by typing their name followed by parentheses. Any values inside the parentheses (for example, `txtCartons.Text`) are known as function **arguments**. Arguments are inputs to the function that provide information that the function needs to perform its task. In this case, the argument specifies which value you want to send to function Val. You will learn how to create your own functions (called procedures) in Tutorial 13.

Function Val can be used to obtain a value from a string of characters (keyboard input) that is guaranteed to be a number. We use Val because this application is not intended to perform arithmetic calculations with characters that are not numbers. Val reads its argument one character at a time until it encounters a character that is not a number. Once a nonnumeric character is read, Val returns the number it has read up to that point. Val ignores whitespace characters (for example, "33 5" will be converted to 335). Figure 5.16 presents samples of Val calls and their results. Val recognizes the decimal point as a numeric character, and the plus and minus signs when they appear at the beginning of the string (to indicate that a number is positive or negative). Val does not recognize such symbols as commas and dollar signs. If function Val receives an argument that cannot be converted to a number (for example, "b35", which begins with a nonnumeric character), it returns 0. The result is assigned to `lblTotalResult.Text` (line 136), to display the result to the user.

You should be careful when using Val, however. Though the value returned is a number, it is not always the value the user intended (see Fig. 5.16). If incorrect data is entered from the user, Val makes no indication of the error. The function returns a value (usually not the value intended by the user) and the application continues, possibly using the incorrect input in calculations. For example, someone entering a monetary amount may enter the text $10.23, which Val will evaluate to 0. Notice how a common mistake causes an application to execute incorrectly. Visual Basic .NET provides two ways to handle invalid input. One way is to use Visual Basic .NET's string processing capabilities to examine input. You will learn about such capabilities as you read this book. The other form of handling invalid input is called exception handling, where you write code to handle errors that may be raised as the application executes. You will learn about exception handling in Tutorial 32.

3. ***Running the application.*** Select **Debug > Start** to run your application. Now the user can enter data in both TextBoxes. When the **Calculate Total Button** is clicked, the application will multiply the two numbers entered and display the result in `lblTotalResult`.

4. ***Closing the application.*** Close the running application by clicking its close box.

5. ***Closing the IDE.*** Close Visual Studio .NET by clicking its close box.

Val Function Call Samples	Results
Val("16")	16
Val("-3")	-3
Val("1.5")	1.5
Val("67a4")	67
Val("8+5")	8
Val("14 Main St.")	14
Val("+1 2 3 4 5")	12345
Val("hello")	0

Figure 5.16   Val function call examples.

Figure 5.17 presents the applications code. [*Note*: In code listings such as Fig. 5.17, we don't display the Visual Studio .NET generated code. We simply provide a comment (line 4) as a place holder. The line numbers shown in these figures are not intended to match those shown in the IDE.]

```
1   Public Class FrmInventory
2       Inherits System.Windows.Forms.Form
3
4       ' Windows Form Designer generated code
5
6       Private Sub btnCalculate_Click(ByVal sender As _
7           System.Object, ByVal e As System.EventArgs) _
8           Handles btnCalculate.Click
9
10          ' multiply values input and display result in Label
11          lblTotalResult.Text = _
12              Val(txtCartons.Text) * Val(txtItems.Text)
13
14      End Sub ' btnCalculate_Click
15
16  End Class ' FrmInventory
```

Figure 5.17   **Inventory** application code.

SELF-REVIEW

1. _____ provide information that functions need to perform their tasks.

   a) Inputs
   b) Arguments
   c) Outputs
   d) Both a and b.

2. What is the result of Val("%5")?

   a) 5
   b) 0
   c) 500
   d) 0.05

Answers: 1) d. 2) b.

5.5 Using the Debugger: Syntax Errors

So far in this book, you have executed the applications by selecting **Debug > Start**. This compiles and runs the application. If you do not write your code correctly, errors appear in a window known as the **Task List** when the application is compiled. **Debugging** is the process of fixing errors in an application. There are two types of errors: syntax errors and logic errors.

Syntax errors (or compilation errors) occur when code statements violate the grammatical rules of the programming language. Examples of syntax errors include misspellings of keywords or identifiers and failure to use the line-continuation character when splitting a statement across multiple lines. An application cannot be executed until all of its syntax errors are corrected.

Logic errors do not prevent the application from compiling successfully, but do cause the application to produce erroneous results. Visual Studio .NET contains software called a **debugger**, which allows you to analyze the behavior of your application to determine that it is executing correctly.

You can compile an application without executing it by selecting **Build > Build Solution**. Programmers frequently do this when they wish to determine whether there are any syntax errors in their code. Using either **Debug > Start** or **Build > Build Solution** will display any syntax errors in the **Task List** window. The **Output** window will display the result of the compilation. Figure 5.18 displays the output window for an application with no errors.

Figure 5.18   Results of successful build in the **Output** window.

In Visual Studio .NET, syntax errors appear in the **Task List** window along with a description of each error. Figure 5.19 displays the error that appears when the line-continuation character is left out of a multiple-line statement. For additional information on a syntax error, right click the error statement in the **Task List** window, and select **Show Task Help**. This displays a help page explaining the error message and suggests corrections.

Figure 5.19   **Task List** lists syntax errors.

Next, you will create syntax errors, view the results and fix the errors.

Using the Debugger:
Syntax Errors

1. ***Opening the completed application.*** If the **Inventory** application is not currently open, locate the `Inventory2.sln` file, then double click it to load your application in the IDE.

2. ***Creating your own syntax errors.*** You will now create your own syntax errors, for demonstration purposes. If you are not in code view, select **View > Code**. Open the Task List window by selecting **View > Other Windows > Task List**. Add an additional character (s) to Label `lblTotalResult` on line 136 and delete the right parenthesis at the end of the assignment statement on line 137. Notice the changes to the IDE (Fig. 5.20).

(cont.)

The Visual Studio .NET IDE provides **real-time error checking**. While you were manipulating the code in the code editor, you might have noticed that violations of Visual Basic .NET syntax are immediately reported in the **Task List**. The precise location of the syntax error in your code is also emphasized by a blue jagged line. Unrecognized identifier `lblTotalResults` and the missing parenthesis are reported in the **Task List** (Fig. 5.21).

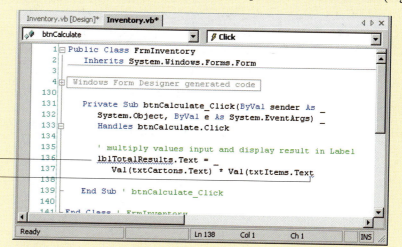

Jagged blue underline indicates syntax error

Figure 5.20 IDE with syntax errors.

These features notify you of possible errors and give you the chance to fix the error before compiling the application. The IDE will refuse to run your modified application until *all* syntax errors have been corrected.

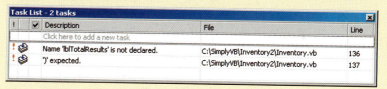

Figure 5.21 **Task List** displaying the syntax errors.

3. ***Locating the syntax errors.*** Double clicking an error in the **Task List** window selects the code containing that error. Double click the **')' expected.** error to highlight the error on line 137 (Fig. 5.22).

4. ***Getting additional help.*** Additional help regarding the syntax error is also available through the **Task List** item's context menu, which you can access by right clicking an item. Right click the **Name 'lblTotalResults' is not declared** error message from the **Task List**, and select **Show Task Help** (Fig. 5.23). This displays a reference page with information regarding the general form of the syntax error, possible solutions and links to other documentation (Fig. 5.24).

(cont.)

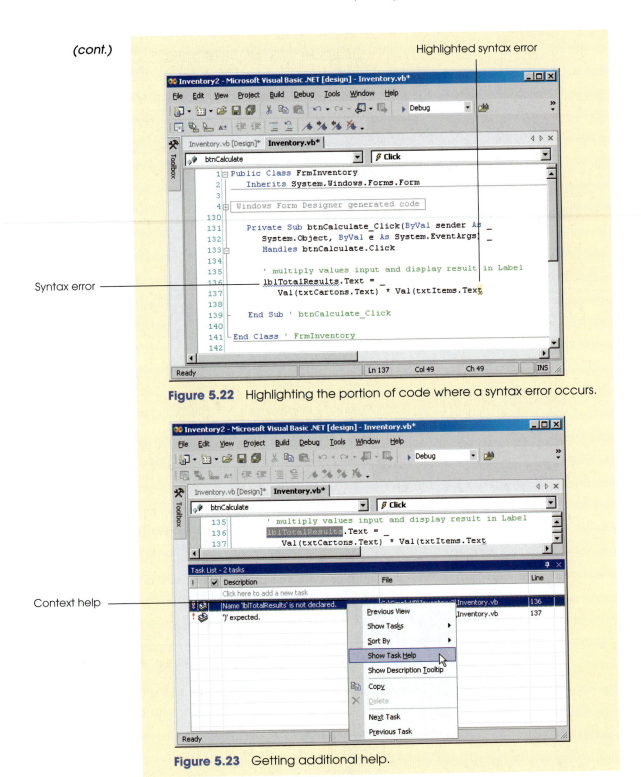

Figure 5.22   Highlighting the portion of code where a syntax error occurs.

Figure 5.23   Getting additional help.

(cont.)

Suggested solution to
misspelled keyword
(Note that the debugger
interprets the misspelling as a
new, undeclared identifier)

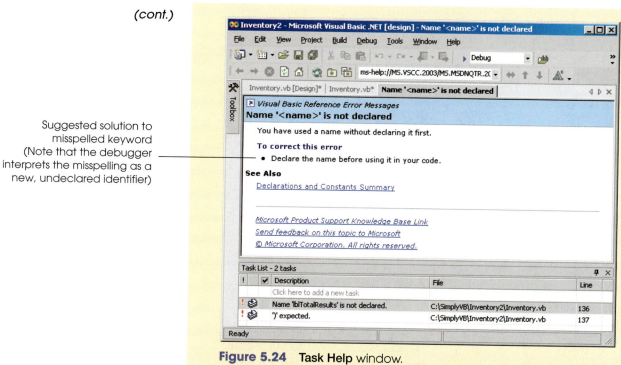

Figure 5.24   **Task Help** window.

5.   ***Fixing the syntax error.*** Now that you know how to locate and fix the syntax error, go back to code view and correct the two errors you created in *Step 2*. Note, when you correct the errors, that the jagged lines do not disappear immediately. However, when you move the cursor to another line, the debugger rechecks the code for errors and removes the jagged underline for each corrected syntax error.

6.   ***Saving the project.*** Select **File > Save All** to save your modified code. Notice that the error will be removed from the **Task List** window. The application is now ready to be compiled and executed.

In this section, you learned about syntax errors and how to find and correct them. In later tutorials, you will learn to detect and remove logic errors by using the Visual Studio .NET run-time debugger.

SELF-REVIEW

1.   If there are syntax errors in an application, they will appear in a window known as the _____ when the application is compiled.

a) **Task List**   b) **Output**

c) **Properties**   d) **Error List**

2.   A syntax error occurs when _____.

a) the application terminates unexpectedly   b) a statement breaks over several lines

c) a parenthesis is omitted   d) All of the above.

Answers: 1) a. 2) c.

5.6 Wrap-Up

In this tutorial, you were introduced to Visual Basic .NET programming. You learned how to use a `TextBox` control to allow users to input data and how to use a `Button` control to signal to your running application that it should perform a particular action. You were introduced to the code generated by Visual Studio .NET that creates an application's GUI. Though you are not yet expected to understand the meaning of the Windows Form Designer generated code, you learned that the key to good programming is to achieve the right balance between employing visual programming (in which Visual Studio .NET writes code for you) and writing your own code (nonvisual programming).

After learning about operators in Visual Basic .NET, you wrote a few lines of code as you added an event handler to your application to perform a simple multiplication calculation and display the result to the user. You also used comments to improve the readability of your code. You learned that placing code in an event handler allows an application to respond to that type of event, such as a click of a Button.

Finally, you learned about syntax errors and how to use the Visual Studio .NET debugger to reduce the number of errors you see when you try to run an application. In the next tutorial, you continue the developing of your **Inventory** application by using identifiers to create variables. You will also enhance your **Inventory** application by using the TextChanged event, which is raised when the user changes the value in a TextBox. After applying your knowledge of variables, you will use the debugger while an application runs to remove a logic error from that application.

SKILLS SUMMARY

Accessing a Property's Value by Using Visual Basic .NET Code

■ Place the property name after the control name and the member access operator (.). For example, to access the Text property of a TextBox named txtCartons, use txtCartons.Text.

Inserting Visual Basic .NET Comments in Code

■ Begin the comment with a single-quote character ('). A comment can be placed either on its own line (full-line comment) or at the end of a line of code (end-of-line comment).

Continuing a Code Statement Over More Than One Line

■ Insert a line-continuation character (_), preceded by one or more whitespace characters, to indicate that the next line is a continuation of the previous line. Only whitespace characters may follow a line-continuation character.

Naming an Event Handler

■ Use the format for an event handler, *controlName_eventName*, where *controlName* is the name of the control that the event is related to and *eventName* is the name of the event. When event *eventName* is raised on control *controlName*, event handler *controlName_eventName* executes.

Inserting an Event Handler for a Button Control's Click Event

■ Double click the Button in design view to create an empty event handler; then, insert the code that will execute when the event occurs.

Using an Assignment Statement

■ Use the = ("equals" sign) to assign the value of its right operand to its left operand. The entire statement is called an assignment statement, because it assigns a value to the left operand (for example, a property).

Using the Multiplication Operator

■ Use an asterisk (*) between the two expressions to be multiplied. The multiplication operator multiplies the right and left operands if both operands contain numeric values or variables of numeric data types. It is a syntax error to use the multiplication operator on values of nonnumeric data types.

Obtaining a Numeric Value from a TextBox

■ Access the TextBox's Text property from within a call to function Val.

Finding a Syntax Error

■ Double click the error message in the **Task List** window, or locate the jagged blue underlined text in your code.

Obtaining Help for a Syntax Error

■ Right click the error message in the **Task List** window, and select **Show Task Help** from the context menu.

KEY TERMS

argument—Inputs to a function that provide information that a function needs to perform its task.

assignment operator—The "=" symbol used to assign values in an assignment statement.

assignment statement—A statement that copies one value to another. An assignment statement contains an "equals"-sign (=) operator that causes the value of its right operand to be copied to its left operand.

binary operator—Requires two operands.

case sensitive—The instance where two words that are spelled identically are treated differently if the capitalization of the two words differs.

class definition—The code that belongs to a class, beginning with keyword Class and ending with keywords End Class.

class name—The identifier used to identify the name of a class in code.

Class keyword—Begins a class definition.

Click event—An event raised when a user clicks a control.

code editor—A window where a user can create, view or edit an application's code.

code view—A mode of Visual Studio .NET where the application's code is displayed in an editor window.

comment—A line of code that follows a single-quote character (') and is inserted to improve an application's readability.

debugging—The process of fixing errors in an application.

default property—The value of a property that provide the initial characteristics of an object when it is first created.

dot operator—See member access operator.

End Class keywords—Marks the end of a class definition.

event—A user action that can trigger an event handler.

event handler—A section of code that is executed (called) when a certain event is raised (occurs).

functionality—The actions an application can execute.

identifier—A series of characters consisting of letters, digits and underscores used to name program units such as classes, controls and variables.

Inherits keyword—Indicates that the class inherits members from another class.

***IntelliSense* feature**—Visual Studio .NET feature that aids the programmer during development by providing windows listing available class members and pop-up descriptions for those members.

keyword—A word in code reserved for a specific purpose. These words appear in blue in the IDE and cannot be used as identifiers.

line-continuation character—An underscore character (_) preceded by one or more spaces, used to continue a statement to the next line of code.

logic error—An error that does not prevent the application from compiling successfully, but does cause the application to produce erroneous results.

member access operator—Also known as the dot operator (.). Allows programmers to access a control's properties using code.

multiplication operator—The asterisk (*) used to multiply its two operands, producing their product as a result.

operand—An expression subject to an operator.

outlined code—An area of collapsed code in Visual Studio .NET that is noted by a box containing an ellipses. Placing the cursor over the outlined code displays a portion of the collapsed code.

real-time error checking—Feature of Visual Studio .NET that provides immediate notification of possible errors in your code.

region—A portion of code that can be collapsed or expanded.

single-quote character(')—Indicates the beginning of a code comment.

statement—A unit of code that, when compiled and executed, performs an action.

syntax error—An error that occurs when program statements violate the grammatical rules of a programming language.

Val function—Filters a number from its argument if possible. This avoids errors introduced by the entering of nonnumeric data when only numbers are expected. However, the result of the Val function is not always what the programmer intended.

whitespace character—A space, tab or newline character.

CONTROLS, EVENTS, PROPERTIES & METHODS

Button   `ab| Button`   This control allows user to raise an action or event.

■ *In action*

     `Calculate Total`

■ *Events*

Click—Raised when the user clicks the Button.

■ *Properties*

Location—Specifies the location of the Button on the Form relative to the top-left corner.

Name—Specifies the name used to access the Button programmatically. The name should be prefixed with btn.

Size—Specifies the height and width (in pixels) of the Button.

Text—Specifies the text displayed on the Button.

MULTIPLE-CHOICE QUESTIONS

5.1 A(n) _____ represents a user action, such as clicking a Button.

   a) statement   b) event

   c) application   d) function

5.2 To switch to code view, select _____.

   a) **Code > View**   b) **Design > Code**

   c) **View > Code**   d) **View > File Code**

5.3 Code that performs the functionality of an application _____.

   a) normally is provided by the programmer

   b) can never be in the form of an event handler

   c) always creates a graphical user interface

   d) is always generated by the IDE

5.4 Comments _____.

   a) help improve program readability

   b) are preceded by the single-quote character

   c) are ignored by the compiler   d) All of the above.

5.5 The _____ allows a statement to continue past one line (when that character is preceded by one or more whitespace characters).

   a) single-quote (') character   b) hyphen (–) character

   c) underscore (_) character   d) plus (+) character

5.6 A(n) _____ causes an application to produce erroneous results.

   a) logic error   b) event

   c) assignment statement   d) syntax error

5.7 A portion of code that performs a specific task and returns a value is known as a(n) _____.

    a) variable   b) function

    c) operand   d) identifier

5.8 Visual Basic .NET keywords are _____.

    a) identifiers   b) reserved words

    c) case sensitive   d) properties

5.9 Visual Studio .NET allows you to organize code into _____, which you can expand or collapse to facilitate code editing.

    a) statements   b) operators

    c) regions   d) keywords

5.10 An example of a whitespace character is a _____ character.

    a) space   b) tab

    c) newline   d) All of the above.

EXERCISES   **5.11** *(Inventory Enhancement)* Extend the **Inventory** application to include a TextBox in which the user can enter the number of shipments received in a week. Assume every shipment has the same number of cartons (each of which has the same number of items). Then modify the code so that the **Inventory** application uses that value in its calculation.

Figure 5.25   Enhanced **Inventory** application GUI.

a) *Copying the template application to your working directory.* Copy the directory `C:\Examples\Tutorial05\Exercises\InventoryEnhancement` to your `C:\SimplyVB` directory.

b) *Opening the application's template file.* Double click `InventoryEnhancment.sln` in the `InventoryEnhancement` directory to open the application.

c) *Resizing the Form.* Resize the Form you used in this tutorial by setting the Size property to `296, 144`. Move the Button toward the bottom of the Form, as shown in Fig. 5.25. Its new location should be `184, 78`.

d) *Adding a Label.* Add a Label to the Form and change the Text property to `Shipments this week:`. Set the Location property to `16, 80`. Resize the Label so that the entire text displays. Set the Label's Name property to `lblShipments`.

e) *Adding a TextBox.* Add a TextBox to the right of the Label. Set its Text property to `0` and the Location property to `128, 80`. Set the TextAlign and Size properties to the same values as for the other TextBoxes in this tutorial's example. Set the TextBox's Name property to `txtShipments`.

f) *Modifying the code.* Modify the **Calculate Total** Click event handler so that it multiplies the number of shipments per week with the product of the number of cartons in a shipment and the number of items in a carton.

g) *Running the application.* Select **Debug > Start** to run your application. Enter values for the number of cartons per shipment, items per carton and shipments in the current week. Click the **Calculate** Button and verify that the total displayed is equal to the result when the three values entered are multiplied together. Enter a few sets of input and verify the total each time.

h) *Closing the application.* Close your running application by clicking its close box.

i) *Closing the IDE.* Close Visual Studio .NET by clicking its close box.

5.12 *(Counter Application)* Create a counter application. Your counter application will consist of a `Label` and `Button` on the `Form`. The `Label` initially displays 0, but, each time a user clicks the `Button`, the value in the `Label` is increased by 1. When incrementing the `Label`, you will need to write a statement such as `lblTotal.Text = Val(lblTotal.Text) + 1`.

Label ——————

Button ——————

Figure 5.26   Counter GUI.

a) *Creating the application.* Create a new project named `Counter`.

b) *Changing the name of the Form file.* Change the name of `Form1.vb` to `Counter.vb`.

c) *Modifying a new Form.* Change your `Form`'s `Size` property to `168, 144`. Modify the `Form` so that the title reads **Counter**. Change the name of the `Form` to `FrmCounter`.

d) *Changing the startup object.* Change the startup object of your application to the form you modified in *Step c*.

e) *Adding a Label.* Add a `Label` to the `Form`, and place it as shown in Fig. 5.26. Make sure that the `Label`'s `Text` property is set to 0 and that `TextAlign` property is set so that any text will appear in the middle (both horizontally and vertically) of the `Label`. This can be done by using the `MiddleCenter` `TextAlign` property. Also set the `BorderStyle` property to `Fixed3D`. Set the `Label`'s `Name` property to `lblCountTotal`.

f) *Adding a Button.* Add a `Button` to the `Form` so that it appears as shown in Fig. 5.26. Set the `Button`'s `Text` property to contain the text **Count**. Set the `Button`'s `Name` property to `btnCount`.

g) *Creating an event handler.* Add an event handler to the **Count** `Button` such that the value in the `Label` increases by 1 each time the user clicks the **Count** `Button`.

h) *Running the application.* Select **Debug > Start** to run your application. Click the **Count** `Button` several times and verify that the output value is incremented each time.

i) *Closing the application.* Close your running application by clicking its close box.

j) *Closing the IDE.* Close Visual Studio .NET by clicking its close box.

5.13 *(Account Information Application)* Create an application that allows a user to input a name, account number and deposit amount. The user then clicks the **Enter** `Button`, which causes the name and account number to be copied and displayed in two output `Label`s. The deposit amount entered will be added to the deposit amount displayed in another output `Label`. The result is displayed in the same output `Label`. Every time the **Enter** `Button` is clicked, the deposit amount entered is added to the deposit amount displayed in the output `Label`, keeping a cumulative total. When updating the `Label`, you will need to write a statement such as `lblDeposits.Text = Val(lblDeposits.Text) + Val(txtDepositAmount)`.

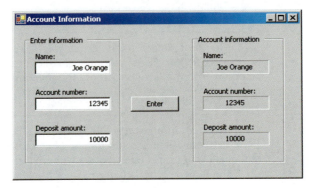

Figure 5.27   Account Information GUI.

a) *Copying the template application to your working directory.* Copy the directory C:\Examples\Tutorial05\Exercises\AccountInformation to your C:\SimplyVB directory.

b) *Opening the application's template file.* Double click AccountInformation.sln in the AccountInformation directory to open the application.

c) *Creating an event handler.* Add an event handler for the **Enter** Button's Click event.

d) *Coding the event handler.* Code the event handler to copy information from the **Name:** and **Account number:** TextBoxes to their corresponding output Labels. Then add the value in the **Deposit amount:** TextBox to the **Deposit amount:** output Label, and display the result in the **Deposit amount:** output Label.

e) *Running the application.* Select **Debug > Start** to run your application. Enter the values in Fig. 5.27 and click the **Enter** Button. Verify that the account information is displayed in the Labels on the right. Enter varying deposit amounts and click the **Enter** Button after each. Verify that the deposit amount on the right has the new values added.

f) *Closing the application.* Close your running application by clicking its close box.

g) *Closing the IDE.* Close Visual Studio .NET by clicking its close box.

What does this code do? ▶ **5.14** After entering 10 in the txtPrice TextBox and 1.05 in the txtTax TextBox, a user clicks the Button named btnEnter. What is the result of the click, given the following code?

```
1  Private Sub btnEnter_Click(ByVal sender As _
2     System.Object, ByVal e As System.EventArgs) _
3     Handles btnCalculate.Click
4
5     lblOutput.Text = Val(txtPrice.Text) * Val(txtTax.Text)
6
7  End Sub ' btnEnter_Click
```

What's wrong with this code? ▶ **5.15** The following event handler should execute when the user clicks a **Calculate** Button. Identify the error(s) in its code.

```
1  Private Sub btnCalculate_Click(ByVal sender As
2     System.Object, ByVal e As System.EventArgs) _ ' second line
3     Handles btnCalculate.Click
4
5     lblResult.Text = txtPrice.Text * txtTax.Text
6  End Sub ' btnCalculate_Click
```

Using the Debugger ▶ **5.16** *(Account Information Debugging Exercise)* Copy the directory C:\Examples\Tutorial05\Exercises\DebuggingExercise to your C:\SimplyVB directory, then run the **Account Information** application. Remove any syntax errors, so that the application runs correctly.

Programming Challenge ▶ **5.17** *(Account Information Enhancement)* Modify Exercise 5.13 so that it no longer asks for the user's name and account number, but rather asks the user for a withdrawal or deposit amount. The user can enter both a withdrawal and deposit amount at the same time. When the **Enter** Button is clicked, the balance is updated appropriately.

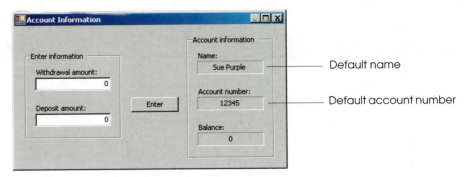

Figure 5.28   Enhanced **Account Information** GUI.

a) *Copying the template application to your working directory.* If you have not already done so, copy the C:\Examples\Tutorial05\Exercises\AccountInformation directory to your C:\SimplyVB directory.

b) *Opening the application's template file.* Double click AccountInformation.sln in the AccountInformation directory to open the application.

c) *Modifying the GUI.* Modify the GUI so that it appears as in Fig. 5.28.

d) *Setting the default values.* Set the default name and account number to the values shown in Fig. 5.28 using the **Properties** window.

e) *Writing code to add functionality.* Update the account balance for every withdrawal (which decreases the balance) and every deposit (which increases the balance). When the balance is updated, reset the TextBoxes to zero.

f) *Running the application.* Select **Debug > Start** to run your application. Enter various withdrawal and deposit amounts, click the **Enter** Button after each. Verify that after each time the **Enter** Button is clicked, the balance on the right of the application is updated appropriately.

g) *Closing the application.* Close your running application by clicking its close box.

h) *Closing the IDE.* Close Visual Studio .NET by clicking its close box.

6

Objectives

In this tutorial, you will learn to:
- Create variables.
- Handle the **TextChanged** event.
- Apply basic memory concepts using variables.
- Use the precedence rules of arithmetic operators.
- Set breakpoints to debug applications.

Outline

Enhancing the Inventory Application

Introducing Variables, Memory Concepts and Arithmetic

In the previous tutorial, you developed an **Inventory** application that performed a multiplication calculation to calculate the number of items received into inventory. You learned how to create **TextBoxes** to read user input from the keyboard. You also added a **Button** to a **Form** and programmed that **Button** to respond to a user's click. In this tutorial, you will enhance your **Inventory** application using additional programming concepts, including variables, events and arithmetic.

6.1 Test-Driving the Enhanced Inventory Application

In this tutorial, you will enhance the previous tutorial's **Inventory** application by inserting code rather than dragging and dropping Visual Basic .NET controls. You will use variables to perform arithmetic in Visual Basic .NET and you will study memory concepts, to help you understand how applications run on computers. Recall that your **Inventory** application from Tutorial 5 calculated the number of items received from information supplied by the user—the number of cartons and the number of textbooks per carton. The enhanced application must meet the following requirements:

> **Application Requirements**
>
> *The inventory manager notices a flaw in your **Inventory** application. Although the application calculates the correct result, that result continues to display even after new data is entered. The only time the output changes is when the inventory manager clicks the **Calculate Button** again. You need to alter the **Inventory** application to clear the result as soon as the user enters new information into either of the **TextBoxes**, to avoid any confusion over the accuracy of your calculated result.*

You begin by test-driving the completed application. Then, you will learn the additional Visual Basic .NET technologies that you will need to create your own version of this application. At first glance, the application does not seem to operate any differently from the application in the previous tutorial. However, you should notice that the **Total:** Label clears when you enter new data into either of the TextBoxes.

<table>
<tr>
<td valign="top">

</td>
<td valign="top">

1. *Opening the completed application.* Open the C:\Examples\Tutorial06\ CompletedApplication\Inventory3 directory to locate the enhanced **Inventory** application. Double click Inventory3.sln to open the application in Visual Studio .NET. If the Form does not appear in design view, double click Inventory.vb in the **Solutions Explorer** window. In general, if Visual Studio .NET does not open the Form in design view, you will need to double click the Form's file name in the **Solution Explorer** window.

2. *Running the Inventory application.* Select **Debug > Start** to run the application (Fig. 6.1).

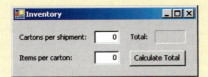

Figure 6.1   **Inventory** application GUI displayed when the application is running.

3. *Calculating the number of items in the shipment.* Enter 5 in the **Cartons per shipment:** TextBox and 6 in the **Items per carton:** TextBox. Click the **Calculate Total** Button. The result will be displayed in the **Total:** output Label (Fig. 6.2).

Figure 6.2   Running the **Inventory** application.

4. *Entering new quantities.* After you modify the application, the result displayed in the **Total:** Label will be removed when the user enters a new quantity in either TextBox. Enter 13 as the new number of cartons—the last calculation's result is cleared (Fig. 6.3). This will be explained later in this tutorial.

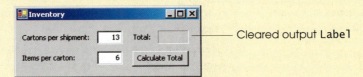

Figure 6.3   Enhanced **Inventory** application clears output Label after new input.

5. *Closing the application.* Close your running application by clicking its close box.

6. *Closing the IDE.* Close Visual Studio .NET by clicking its close box.

</td>
</tr>
</table>

6.2 Variables

Good Programming Practice

Typically, variable-name identifiers begin with a lowercase letter. Every word in the name after the first word should begin with a capital letter, for example, `intFirstNumber`.

Good Programming Practice

Use only letters and digits as characters for your variable names.

A **variable** holds data for your application, much as the `Text` property of a `Label` holds the text to be displayed to the user. Unlike the `Text` property of a `Label`, however, variable values are not shown to the user by default. Using variables in an application allows you to store and manipulate data without necessarily showing the data to the user and to store data without adding or using controls. Variables store such data as numbers, the date, the time and so on. However, each variable used in Visual Basic .NET corresponds to exactly one type of information. For example, a variable that stores a number cannot be used to store text.

In Visual Basic .NET, all variables must be **declared**, or reported, to the compiler by using program code. All **declarations** that you will make within event handlers begin with the keyword **Dim**. Recall that keywords are reserved for use by Visual Basic .NET. (A complete list of Visual Basic .NET keywords is presented in Appendix F.)

The following box introduces programming with variables. A variable name can be any valid identifier, which, as you learned in Tutorial 5, is a name that the compiler will recognize (and is not a keyword). As you also learned in the last tutorial, there are many valid characters for identifiers.

Using Variables in the Inventory Application

1. *Copying the template to your working directory.* Copy the `C:\Examples\Tutorial06\TemplateApplication\Inventory3` directory to your `C:\SimplyVB` directory.

2. *Opening the Inventory application's template file.* Double click `Inventory3.sln` in the `Inventory3` directory to open the application in Visual Studio .NET.

3. *Adding variable declarations to event handler btnCalculate_Click.* If you are in design view, enter code view by selecting **View > Code**. Add lines 136–139 of Fig. 6.4 to event handler `btnCalculate_Click`. Lines 137–139 are declarations, which begin with keyword `Dim`. Notice that, when you type the word `Dim`, as with all keywords, Visual Studio .NET colors it blue by default. The words `intCartons`, `intItems` and `intResult` are the names of variables. Lines 137–139 declare that variables `intCartons`, `intItems` and `intResult` store data of type **Integer**, using the **As** keyword. The As keyword indicates that the following word (in this case `Integer`) is the variable type. `Integer` variables store integer values (whole numbers such as 919, 0 and –11). Data types already defined in Visual Basic .NET, such as `Integer`, are known as **built-in data types** or **primitive data types**. Primitive data type names are also keywords. The 10 primitive data types are listed in Fig. 6.6. You will use some of these data types throughout the book.

Good Programming Practice

Prefix all `Integer` variable names with `int`. Using prefixes that indicate a variable's data type makes your code clearer, especially when you are first learning to program.

4. *Retrieving input from TextBoxes.* Skip one line after the variable declarations, and add lines 141–143 of Fig. 6.5 in event handler `btnCalculate_Click`. Once the user enters numbers and clicks **Calculate Total**, the values found in the `Text` property of the `TextBox` controls are converted to numerical values by the `Val` function. Then the numbers are assigned to variables `intCartons` (line 142) and `intItems` (line 143) with the assignment operator, `=`. Line 142 is read as "`intCartons` *gets* the result of the `Val` function applied to `txtCartons.Text`."

(cont.)

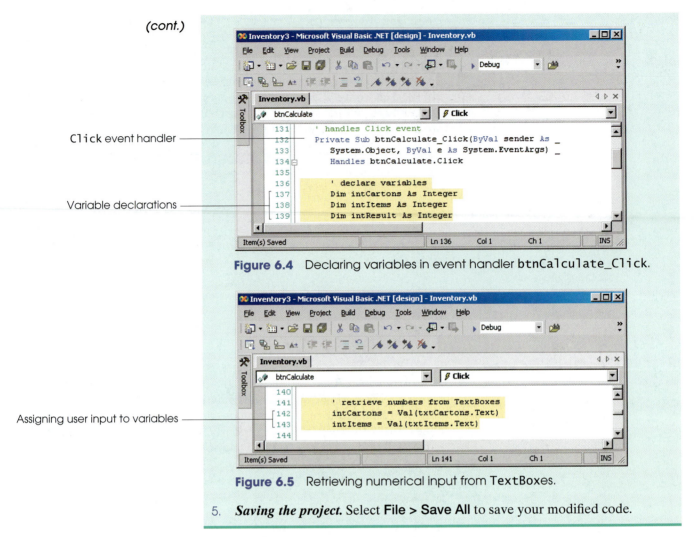

Click event handler

Variable declarations

Figure 6.4   Declaring variables in event handler `btnCalculate_Click`.

Assigning user input to variables

Figure 6.5   Retrieving numerical input from `TextBoxes`.

5. ***Saving the project.*** Select **File > Save All** to save your modified code.

The `Val` function returns a numerical value as data type **Double** when converting a value retrieved from a `TextBox`'s `Text` property. Data type `Double` is used to store both whole and fractional numbers. Normally, `Doubles` store floating-point numbers, which are numbers with decimal points such as 2.3456 and –845.4680. Variables of data type `Double` can hold values that are much larger than variables of data type `Integer`.

After `Val` converts the two values typed by the user to `Doubles`, lines 142–143 implicitly convert the `Doubles` to `Integer` values. Likewise, the integer value obtained by converting the `Double` in line 143 is assigned to variable `intItems`. Because `Doubles` and `Integers` are different types of variables, Visual Basic .NET performs a conversion from one type to the other. This process is called **implicit conversion** because the conversion takes place without any additional code. Now that you have assigned values to your new variables, you use the variables to calculate the number of textbooks received.

Built-in (primitive) data types				
Boolean	Date	Integer	Short	Char
Byte	Decimal	Long	Single	Double

Figure 6.6   Visual Basic .NET built-in data types.

Using Variables in a Calculation

1. ***Performing the multiplication operation.*** Skip one line from the end of the last statement you inserted and insert lines 145–146 in event handler `btnCalculate_Click` (Fig. 6.7). The statement on line 146 will multiply the `Integer` variable `intCartons` by `intItems` and assign the result to variable `intResult`, using the assignment operator `=`. The statement is read as, "`intResult` *gets* the value of `intCartons * intItems`." (Most calculations are performed in assignment statements.)

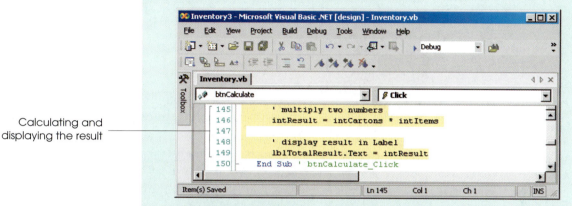

Calculating and displaying the result

Figure 6.7   Multiplication, using variables in `btnCalculate_Click`.

2. ***Displaying the result.*** Add lines 148–149 of Fig. 6.7 to event handler `btnCalculate_Click`. After the calculation is completed, line 149 will display the result of the multiplication operation. The number sets the value of `Label lblTotalResult`'s `Text` property. Once the property is updated, the `Label` will display the result of the multiplication operation (Fig. 6.8).

Result of calculation

Figure 6.8   Displaying the multiplication result using variables.

3. ***Running the application.*** Select **Debug > Start** to run your application. Enter 5 in the **Cartons per shipment:** TextBox and 6 in the **Items per carton:** TextBox. Then, click the **Calculate Total** Button to test your application.

4. ***Closing the application.*** Close your running application by clicking its close box.

SELF-REVIEW

1. When Visual Basic .NET converts a `Double` to an `Integer` without requiring any code, this is referred to as a(n) _____.

   a) explicit conversion   b) implicit conversion
   c) data-type change   d) transformation

2. Data types already defined in Visual Basic .NET, such as `Integer`, are known as _____ data types.

   a) provided   b) existing
   c) defined   d) built-in

Answers: 1) b. 2) d.

6.3 Handling the TextChanged Event

You might have noticed that the flaw, or **bug**, mentioned in the application require-ments at the beginning of this tutorial remains in your application. Although the Label lblTotalResult displays the current result, once you enter a new number into a TextBox, that result is no longer valid. However, the result displayed does not change again until you click the **Calculate Total** Button, potentially confusing anyone using the application. Visual Studio .NET provides a convenient way to deal with this problem. In the next box, you will add event handlers to clear the out-put whenever new data is entered.

Handling the TextChanged Event

1. ***Adding an event handler for txtCartons's TextChanged event.*** Double click the **Cartons per shipment:** TextBox, txtCartons to generate an event handler for the **TextChanged** event, which is raised when the TextBox's text changes. Visual Studio .NET will then generate an event handler with an empty body (no additional code) and place the cursor in the body. Insert line 157 of Fig. 6.9 into your code. Note that we have added line-continuation characters (_) at the ends of lines 153 and 154 of this code, as well as a com-ment on line 152, before the event handler. Recall from Tutorial 5 that using line-continuation characters increases code readability by avoiding long lines that don't fit in the window.

TextChanged event handler ———

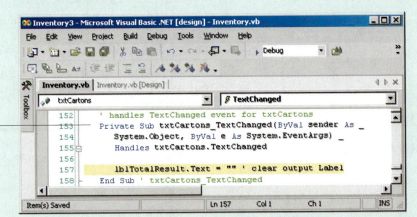

Figure 6.9 TextChanged event handler for **Cartons per shipment:** TextBox.

According to the application requirements for this tutorial, the applica-tion should clear the value in lblTotalResult every time users change the text in either TextBox. Line 157 clears the value in lblTotalResult. The notation "" (side-by-side double quotes) in line 157 is called an **empty string**, which is a value that does not contain any characters. This empty string replaces whatever is stored in lblTotalResult.Text.

2. ***Adding an event handler for txtItems's TextChanged event.*** We want the result cleared regardless of which TextBox changes value first. Return to design view by clicking the **Inventory.vb [Design]** tab. Then, double click the **Items per carton:** TextBox, and insert line 165 from Fig. 6.10 into the new event handler. Notice that these lines perform the same task as line 157—we want the same action, namely the clearing of a TextBox, to occur.

Good Programming Practice

If a statement is wider than the code editor window, use the line-continuation character within the statement to continue it on the next line.

(cont.)

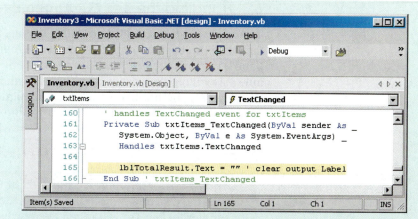

Figure 6.10 TextChanged event handler for **Items per carton:** TextBox.

3. *Running the application.* Select **Debug > Start** to run your application. To test the application, enter 8 in the **Cartons per shipment:** TextBox and 7 in the **Items per carton:** TextBox. When you click the **Calculate Total** Button, the number 56 should appear in the output Label. Then enter 9 in the **Items per carton:** TextBox to ensure that the TextChanged event handler clears the output Label.

4. *Closing the application.* Close your running application by clicking its close box.

Figure 6.11 presents the source code for the enhanced **Inventory** application. The lines of code that contain new programming concepts that you learned in this tutorial are highlighted.

```
1   Public Class FrmInventory
2       Inherits System.Windows.Forms.Form
3
4       ' Windows Form Designer generated code
5
6       ' handles Click event
7       Private Sub btnCalculate_Click(ByVal sender As _
8           System.Object, ByVal e As System.EventArgs) _
9           Handles btnCalculate.Click
10
11          ' declare variables
12          Dim intCartons As Integer
13          Dim intItems As Integer
14          Dim intResult As Integer
15
16          ' retrieve numbers from TextBoxes
17          intCartons = Val(txtCartons.Text)
18          intItems = Val(txtItems.Text)
19
20          ' multiply two numbers
21          intResult = intCartons * intItems
22
23          ' display result in Label
24          lblTotalResult.Text = intResult
25      End Sub ' btnCalculate_Click
26
```

Use keyword **Dim** to declare variables inside an event handler

Assigning a property's value to a variable

Assigning a variable to a property

Figure 6.11 **Inventory** application code. (Part 1 of 2.)

```
27        ' handles TextChanged event for txtCartons
28        Private Sub txtCartons_TextChanged(ByVal sender As _
29           System.Object, ByVal e As System.EventArgs) _
30           Handles txtCartons.TextChanged
31
32           lblTotalResult.Text = ""    ' clear output Label
33        End Sub ' txtCartons_TextChanged
34
35        ' handles TextChanged event for txtItems
36        Private Sub txtItems_TextChanged(ByVal sender As _
37           System.Object, ByVal e As System.EventArgs) _
38           Handles txtItems.TextChanged
39
40              lblTotalResult.Text = ""    ' clear output Label
41        End Sub ' txtItems_TextChanged
42
43    End Class ' FrmInventory
```

Setting a TextBox's Text property to an empty string

Figure 6.11   **Inventory** application code. (Part 2 of 2.)

SELF-REVIEW   1. The _____ is represented by "" in Visual Basic .NET.

   a) empty character   b) empty string
   c) empty value   d) None of the above.

2. Use property _____ to remove any text displayed in a TextBox.

   a) ClearText   b) Remove
   c) Display   d) Text

Answers: 1) b. 2) d.

6.4 Memory Concepts

Variable names—such as `intCartons`, `intItems` and `intResult`—correspond to actual **locations** in the computer's memory. Every variable has a **name**, **type**, **size** and **value**. In the **Inventory** application code listing in Fig. 6.11, when the assignment statement (line 17)

```
intCartons = Val(txtCartons.Text)
```

executes, the user input stored in `txtCartons.Text` is converted to an `Integer`. This `Integer` is placed into the memory location to which the name `intCartons` has been assigned by the compiler. Suppose that the user enters the characters 12 in the **Cartons per shipment:** TextBox. This input is stored in `txtCartons.Text`. When the user clicks **Calculate Total**, Visual Basic .NET then converts the user input to an `Integer` and places the `Integer` value 12 into location `intCartons`, as shown in Fig. 6.12.

intCartons   12

Figure 6.12   Memory location showing name and value of variable `intCartons`.

Whenever a value is placed in a memory location, this value replaces the value previously stored in that location. The previous value is overwritten (lost).

Suppose that the user then enters the characters 10 in the **Items per carton:** TextBox and clicks **Calculate Total**. Line 18 of Fig. 6.11

```
intItems = Val(txtItems.Text)
```

converts `txtItems.Text` to an `Integer`, placing the `Integer` value 10 into location `intItems`, and memory appears as shown in Fig. 6.13.

Figure 6.13 Memory locations after values for variables `intCartons` and `intItems` have been input.

Once the **Calculate Total** `Button` is clicked, line 21 multiplies these values and places their total into variable `intResult`. The statement

    intResult = intCartons * intItems

performs the multiplication and replaces (that is, overwrites) `intResult`'s previous value. After `intResult` is calculated, the memory appears as shown in Fig. 6.14. Note that the values of `intCartons` and `intItems` appear exactly as they did before they were used in the calculation of `intResult`. Although these values were used when the computer performed the calculation, they were not destroyed. This illustrates that, when a value is read from a memory location, the process is **non-destructive** (meaning that the value is not overwritten).

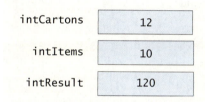

Figure 6.14 Memory locations after a multiplication operation.

SELF-REVIEW   1. When a value is placed into a memory location, the value _____ the previous value into that location.

a) copies   b) replaces

c) adds itself to   d) moves

2. When a value is read from memory, that value is _____.

a) overwritten   b) replaced with a new value

c) moved to a new location in memory   d) not overwritten

Answers: 1) b. 2) d.

6.5 Arithmetic

Most programs perform arithmetic calculations. In the last tutorial, you performed the arithmetic operation multiplication by using the multiplication operator (*). The **arithmetic operators** are summarized in Fig. 6.15. Note the use of various special symbols not used in algebra. For example, the **asterisk** (*) indicates multiplication, the keyword **Mod** represents the **modulus operator**, the **backslash** (\\) represents integer division and the **caret** (^) represents exponentiation. The majority of arithmetic operators in Fig. 6.15 are binary operators, each requiring two operands.

Visual Basic .NET operation	Arithmetic operator	Algebraic expression	Visual Basic .NET expression
Addition	+	$f + 7$	f + 7
Subtraction	–	$p - c$	p - c
Multiplication	*	bm	b * m
Division (float)	/	x / y or $\frac{x}{y}$ or $x \div y$	x / y
Division (integer)	\	none	v \ u
Modulus	Mod	r modulo s	r Mod s
Exponentiation	^	q^p	q ^ p
Unary Negative	–	$-e$	-e
Unary Positive	+	$+g$	+g

Figure 6.15   Arithmetic operators.

For example, the expression intSum + intValue contains the binary operator + and the two operands intSum and intValue. Visual Basic .NET also provides **unary operators**, which are operators that take only one operand. For example, unary versions of plus (+) and minus (–) are provided so that programmers can write expressions such as +9 (a positive number) and –19 (a negative number).

Visual Basic .NET has separate operators for **integer division** (the backslash, \) and **floating-point division** (the forward slash, /). Floating-point division divides two numbers (whole or fractional) and returns a floating-point number (a number with a decimal point). The operator for integer division treats its operands as integers and returns an integer result. Integer division takes two Integer operands and yields an Integer result; for example, the expression 7 \ 4 evaluates to 1, and the expression 17 \ 5 evaluates to 3. Note that any fractional part in the Integer division result simply is discarded (also called truncated)—no rounding occurs. When floating-point numbers (numbers with decimal points) are used with the integer-division operator, the numbers are first rounded to the nearest whole number, then divided. This means that, although 7.1 \ 4 evaluates to 1 as expected, the statement 7.7 \ 4 evaluates to 2, because 7.7 is rounded to 8 before the division occurs. Neither division operator allows division by zero. If your code divides by zero, a run-time error occurs. By default, this error will terminate the application.

The modulus operator, Mod, yields the remainder after division. The expression x Mod y yields the remainder after x is divided by y. Thus, 7 Mod 4 yields 3, and 17 Mod 5 yields 2. This operator is used most commonly with Integer operands, but also can be used with other types. The modulus operator can be applied to several interesting problems, such as discovering whether one number is a multiple of another. If a and b are numbers, a Mod b yields 0 if a is a multiple of b. 8 Mod 3 yields 2, so 8 is not a multiple of 3. But 8 Mod 2 and 8 Mod 4 each yield 0, because 8 is a multiple both of 2 and of 4.

Arithmetic expressions in Visual Basic .NET must be written in **straight-line form** so that you can type them into a computer. For example, the division of 7.1 by 4.3 cannot be written

$$\frac{7.1}{4.3}$$

but is written in straight-line form as 7.1 / 4.3. Raising 3 to the 2nd power cannot be written as 3^2, but is written in straight line form as 3 ^ 2.

Parentheses are used in Visual Basic .NET expressions in the same manner as in algebraic expressions. For example, to multiply a times the quantity b + c, you write

a * (b + c)

Common Programming Error

Attempting to divide by zero is a **run-time error** (that is, an error that has its effect while the application executes). Dividing by zero terminates an application.

Visual Basic .NET applies the operators in arithmetic expressions in a precise sequence, determined by the **rules of operator precedence,** which are generally the same as those followed in algebra. These rules enable Visual Basic .NET to apply operators in the correct order.

Rules of Operator Precedence

1. ***Operators in expressions contained within a pair of parentheses are evaluated first.*** Thus, *parentheses can be used to force the order of evaluation to occur in any sequence desired by the programmer.* Parentheses are at the highest level of precedence. With **nested** (or **embedded**) parentheses, the operators contained in the innermost pair of parentheses are applied first.

2. ***Exponentiation is applied next.*** If an expression contains several exponentiation operations, operators are applied from left to right.

3. ***Unary positive and negative, + and -, are applied next.*** If an expression contains several sign operations, operators are applied from left to right.

4. ***Multiplication and floating-point division operations are applied next.*** If an expression contains several multiplication and floating-point division operations, operators are applied from left to right.

5. ***Integer division is applied next.*** If an expression contains several `Integer` division operations, operators are applied from left to right.

6. ***Modulus operations are applied next.*** If an expression contains several modulus operations, operators are applied from left to right.

7. ***Addition and subtraction operations are applied last.*** If an expression contains several addition and subtraction operations, operators are applied from left to right.

Notice that we mention nested parentheses. Not all expressions with several pairs of parentheses contain nested parentheses. For example, although the expression

```
a * ( b + c ) + c * ( d + e )
```

contains multiple pairs of parentheses, none of the parentheses are nested. Rather, these sets are referred to as being "on the same level" and are evaluated from left to right.

Let's consider several expressions in light of the rules of operator precedence. Each example lists an algebraic expression and its Visual Basic .NET equivalent.

The following calculates the average of three numbers:

Algebra: $m = \dfrac{(a + b + c)}{3}$

Visual Basic .NET: `m = ( a + b + c ) / 3`

The parentheses are required, because floating-point division has higher precedence than addition. The entire quantity (a + b + c) is to be divided by 3. If the parentheses are omitted, erroneously, we obtain a + b + c / 3, which evaluates as

$$a + b + \frac{c}{3}$$

The following is the equation of a straight line:

Algebra: $y = mx + b$

Visual Basic .NET: `y = m * x + b`

No parentheses are required. The multiplication is applied first, because multiplication has a higher precedence than addition. The assignment occurs last because it has a lower precedence than multiplication and addition.

To develop a better understanding of the rules of operator precedence, consider how the expression $y = ax^2 + bx + c$ is evaluated:

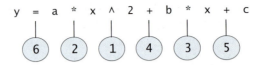

The circled numbers under the statement indicate the order in which Visual Basic .NET applies the operators. Remember that, in Visual Basic .NET, x^2 is represented as x ^ 2. Also, note that the assignment operator is applied last because it has a lower precedence than any of the arithmetic operators.

Good Programming Practice

The use of redundant parentheses in complex arithmetic expressions can make the expressions easier to read.

As in algebra, it is acceptable to place unnecessary parentheses in an expression to make the expression easier to read—these parentheses are called **redundant parentheses**. For example, the preceding assignment statement might use redundant parentheses to emphasize terms:

y = (a * x ^ 2) + (b * x) + c

SELF-REVIEW

1. Arithmetic expressions in Visual Basic .NET must be written _____ to facilitate entering applications into the computer.

    a) using parentheses   b) on multiple lines

    c) in straight-line form   d) None of the above.

2. The expression to the right of the assignment operator (=) is always evaluated _____ the assignment occurs.

    a) before   b) after

    c) at the same time   d) None of the above.

Answers: 1) c. 2) a.

6.6 Using the Debugger: Breakpoints

The debugger will be one of your most important tools in developing applications, once you become familiar with its features. You were introduced to the debugger in Tutorial 5, where you used it to locate and eliminate syntax errors. In this tutorial, you continue your study of the debugger, learning about breakpoints, which allow you to examine what your application is doing while it is running. A **breakpoint** is a marker that can be set at any executable line of code. When application execution reaches a breakpoint, execution pauses, allowing you to peek inside your application and ensure that there are no logic errors, such as an incorrect calculation. In the box, *Using the Debugger: Breakpoints*, you learn how to use breakpoints in the Visual Studio .NET debugger.

Using the Debugger: Breakpoints

1. ***Enabling the debugger.*** The debugger is enabled by default. If it is not enabled, you have to change the Solution Configuration ComboBox to **Debug**. To do this, click the ComboBox's down arrow (Fig. 6.16) to access the Solution Configuration ComboBox, and select **Debug**. The IDE toolbar will then display **Debug** in the Solution Configuration ComboBox.

(cont.)

Solution Configuration **ComboBox** ——

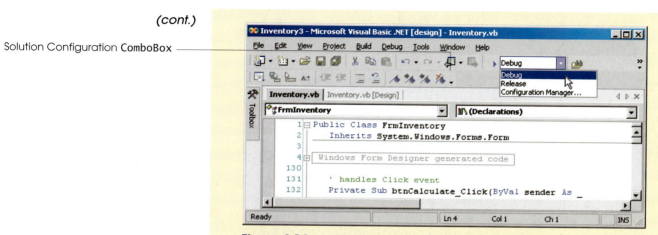

Figure 6.16 Setting Solution Configuration to **Debug**.

2. *Inserting breakpoints in Visual Studio .NET.* To insert a breakpoint in Visual Studio .NET, either click inside the **margin indicator bar** (the gray margin indicator at the left of the code window, Fig. 6.17) next to the line of code at which you wish to break, or right click that line of code and select **Insert Breakpoint.** You can set as many breakpoints as necessary. Set breakpoints at lines 146 and 149 of your code. A solid maroon circle appears where you clicked, indicating that a breakpoint has been set (Fig. 6.17). When the application runs, it suspends execution at any line that contains a breakpoint. The application is said to be in **break mode** when the debugger pauses the application's execution. Breakpoints can be set during design mode, break mode and run mode.

Margin indicator bar ——

Breakpoints ——

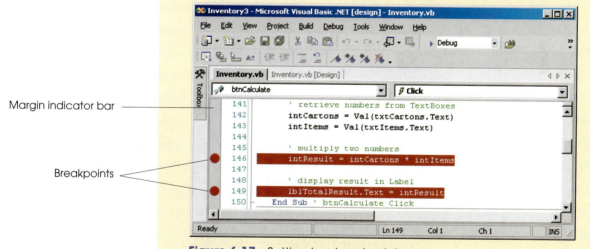

Figure 6.17 Setting two breakpoints.

3. *Beginning the debugging process.* After setting breakpoints in the code editor, select **Debug > Start** to begin the debugging process. During debugging of a Windows application, the application window appears (Fig. 6.18), allowing application interaction (input and output). Enter 10 and 7 into the Textboxes and click **Calculate Total** to continue. The title bar of the IDE will now display **[break]** (Fig. 6.19), indicating that the IDE is in break mode.

4. *Examining application execution.* Application execution suspends at the first breakpoint, and the IDE becomes the active window (Fig. 6.20). The **yellow arrow** to the left of line 146 indicates that this line contains the next statement to execute.

(cont.)

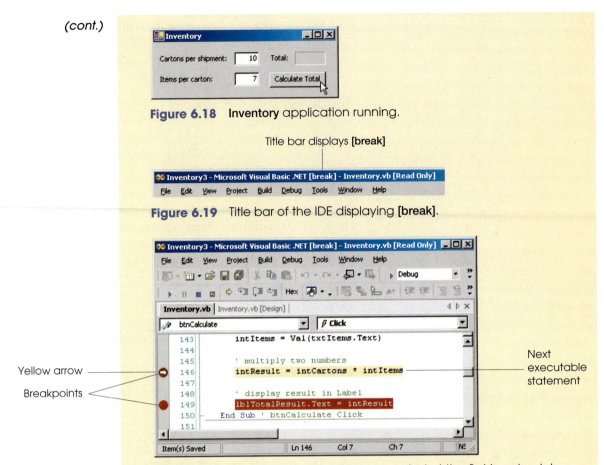

Figure 6.18　*Inventory* application running.

Figure 6.19　Title bar of the IDE displaying [break].

Figure 6.20　Application execution suspended at the first breakpoint.

5. ***Using the Continue command to resume execution.*** To resume execution, select **Debug > Continue**. The application executes until it stops at the next breakpoint on line 149. Notice that, when you place your mouse pointer over the variable name `intResult`, the value that the variable stores is displayed in a ***Quick Info*** box (Fig. 6.21). In a sense, you are peeking inside the computer at the value of one of your variables. As you'll see, this can help you spot logic errors in your applications.

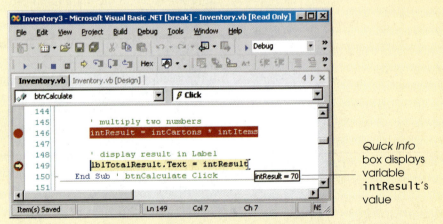

Figure 6.21　Displaying a variable value by placing the mouse pointer over a variable name.

(cont.)

6. ***Finishing application execution.*** Use the **Debug > Continue** command to complete the application execution. When there are no more breakpoints at which to suspend execution, the application will execute to completion and the output will appear in the **Total:** Label (Fig. 6.22).

Figure 6.22 Application output.

7. ***Disabling a breakpoint.*** To **disable a breakpoint**, right click a line of code on which a breakpoint has been set, and select **Disable Breakpoint**. The disabled breakpoint is indicated by a hollow maroon circle (Fig. 6.23). Disabling rather than removing a breakpoint allows you to re-enable the breakpoint (by clicking inside the hollow circle) in an application. This also can be done by right clicking the line marked by the hollow maroon circle and selecting **Enable Breakpoint**.

Disabled breakpoint ⎯⎯⎯⎯⎯⎯⎯⎯⎯

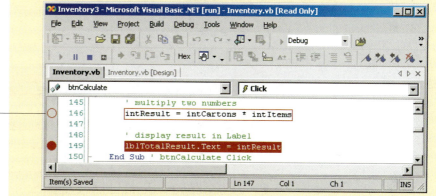

Figure 6.23 Disabled breakpoint.

8. ***Removing a breakpoint.*** To remove a breakpoint that you no longer need, right click a line of code on which a breakpoint has been set and select **Remove Breakpoint**. You also can remove a breakpoint by clicking the maroon circle in the margin indicator bar.

9. ***Saving the project.*** Select **File > Save All** to save your modified code.

10. ***Closing the IDE.*** Close Visual Studio .NET by clicking its close box.

In this section, you learned how to enable the debugger and set breakpoints so that you can examine the results of code while an application is running. You also learned how to continue execution after an application suspends execution at a breakpoint and how to disable and remove breakpoints.

SELF-REVIEW

1. A breakpoint cannot be set at a(n) _____.

    a) comment   b) executable line of code

    c) assignment statement   d) arithmetic statement

2. When application execution suspends at a breakpoint, the next statement to be executed is the statement _____ the breakpoint.

    a) before   b) after

    c) at   d) None of the above.

Answers: 1) a. 2) c.

6.7 Internet and Web Resources

Please take a moment to visit each of these sites briefly. To save typing time, use the hot links on the enclosed CD or at www.deitel.com.

www.devx.com/dotnet
This Web site contains information about the .NET platform, which includes Visual Basic .NET. The site includes links to articles, books and news.

www.vbcity.com
This site lists numerous links to articles, books and tutorials on Visual Basic .NET. The site allows programmers to submit code and have it rated by other developers. This site also polls visitors on a variety of Visual Basic .NET topics and provides access to archives, which include code listings and news.

www.cyber-matrix.com/vb.htm
This site links to Visual Basic .NET tutorials, books, tips and tricks, controls, programming tools, magazines, newsgroups and more.

searchvb.techtarget.com
This site offers a search engine designed specifically to discover Visual Basic .NET Web sites.

www.aewnet.com/root/dotnet/vbnet
The site links to demonstrations, articles, tutorials and Visual Basic .NET sites in German and Spanish.

6.8 Wrap-Up

You have now added variables to your **Inventory** application. You began by using variables to produce the same results as your previous **Inventory** application. Then you enhanced the **Inventory** application, using the TextChanged event, which allowed you to execute code that cleared the value in the output Label when the user changed a value in either TextBox.

You learned about memory concepts, including how variables are read and written. You will apply these concepts to the applications that you will build in later tutorials, which rely heavily on the use of variables. You learned how to perform arithmetic in Visual Basic .NET and you studied the rules of operator precedence to evaluate mathematical expressions correctly. Finally, you learned how to insert breakpoints in the debugger. Breakpoints allow you to pause application execution and examine variable values. This capability will prove useful to you in finding and fixing logic errors.

In the next tutorial, you will design a graphical user interface and write code to create a wage calculator. You will use pseudocode, an informal language that will help you design the application. You will learn to use to the debugger's **Watch** window, another useful tool that will help you remove logic errors.

SKILLS SUMMARY   **Declaring a Variable**

- Use the keyword Dim.
- Use a valid identifier as a variable name.
- Use the keyword As to indicate that the following word specifies the variable's data type.
- Specify a type such as Integer or Double.

Handling a TextBox's TextChanged Event

- Double click a TextBox on a Form to generate an empty event handler.
- Insert code into the event handler, which executes when the text in a TextBox changes.

Reading a Value from a Memory Location

- ■ Use the variable's name (as declared in the variable's Dim statement) on the right side of an assignment statement.

Replacing a Value in a Memory Location

- ■ Use the variable name, followed by the assignment operator (=), followed by an expression giving the new value.

Representing Positive and Negative Numbers

- ■ Use the unary versions of plus (+) and minus (-).

Performing Arithmetic Operations

- ■ Write arithmetic expressions in Visual Basic .NET in straight-line form.
- ■ Use the rules of operator precedence to determine the order in which operators will be applied.
- ■ Use operator + to perform addition.
- ■ Use operator - to perform subtraction.
- ■ Use operator * to perform multiplication.
- ■ Use operator / to perform floating-point division.
- ■ Use operator \ (backslash) to perform Integer division, which treats the operands as Integers and returns an Integer result.
- ■ Use operator ^ to perform exponentiation.
- ■ Use the modulus operator, Mod, to report the remainder after division.

Setting a Breakpoint

- ■ Click the margin indicator bar (the gray margin indicator at the left of the code window) next to the line at which you wish to break, or right click a line of code and select **Insert Breakpoint**.

Resuming Application Execution after Entering Break Mode

- ■ Select **Debug > Continue**.

Disabling a Breakpoint

- ■ Right click a line of code containing a breakpoint, and select **Disable Breakpoint**.

Removing a Breakpoint

- ■ Right click a line of code containing a breakpoint, and select **Remove Breakpoint**.
- ■ You also can remove a breakpoint by clicking the maroon circle in the margin indicator bar.

Enabling a Breakpoint

- ■ Enable a disabled breakpoint by clicking inside the hollow circle in the margin indicator bar.
- ■ You also can enable a disabled breakpoint by right clicking the line marked by the hollow maroon circle and selecting **Enable Breakpoint**.

KEY TERMS

active window—The front-most window on your screen.

arithmetic operators—The operators +, -, *, /, \, ^ and Mod.

As keyword—Used in variable declarations. Indicates that the following word (such as Integer) is the variable type.

asterisk(*)—Multiplication operator. The operator's left and right operands are multiplied together.

backslash(\)—Integer division operator. The operator divides its left operand by its right.

break mode—The IDE mode when application execution is suspended. This mode is entered through the debugger.

breakpoint—A statement where execution is to suspend, indicated by a solid maroon circle.

built-in data type—A data type already defined in Visual Basic .NET, such as an Integer (also known as a primitive data type).

caret(^)—Exponentiation operator. This operator raises its left operand to a power specified by the right operand.

Dim keyword—Indicates the declaration of a variable.

Double data type—Stores both whole and fractional numbers. Normally, `Double`s store floating-point numbers.

embedded parentheses—Another word for nested parentheses.

empty string—A string that does not contain any characters.

floating-point division—Divides two numbers (whole or fractional) and returns a floating-point number.

implicit conversion—A conversion from one data type to another performed by Visual Basic .NET.

integer—A whole number, such as 919, –11, 0 and 138624.

Integer data type—Stores integer values.

Integer division—`Integer` division takes two `Integer` operands and yields an `Integer` result. The fractional portion of the result is discarded.

margin indicator bar—A margin in the IDE where breakpoints are displayed.

Mod (modulus operator)—The modulus operator yields the remainder after division.

name of a variable—The identifier used in an application to access or modify a variable's value.

nested parentheses—When an expression in parentheses is found within another expression surrounded by parentheses. With nested parentheses, the operators contained in the innermost pair of parentheses are applied first.

nondestructive memory operation—A process that does not overwrite a value in memory.

primitive data type—A data type already defined in Visual Basic .NET, such as `Integer` (also known as a built-in data type).

rules of operator precedence—Rules that determine the precise order in which operators are applied in an expression.

run-time error—An error that has its effect at execution time.

size of a variable—The number of bytes required to store a value of the variable's type. **straight-line form**—The manner in which arithmetic expressions must be written so they can be represented in Visual Basic .NET code.

TextChanged event—Occurs when the text in a `TextBox` changes.

type of a variable—Specifies the kind of data that can be stored in a variable and the range of values that can be stored.

value of a variable—The piece of data that is stored in a variable's location in memory.

variable—A location in the computer's memory where a value can be stored.

variable declaration—The reporting of a new variable to the compiler. The variable can then be used in the Visual Basic .NET code.

CONTROLS, EVENTS, PROPERTIES & METHODS

TextBox   `abl TextBox`   This control allows the user to input data from the keyboard.

■ *In action*

`0`

■ *Events*

`TextChanged`—Raised when the text in the `TextBox` is changed.

■ *Properties*

`Location`—Specifies the location of the `Label` on the `Form` relative to the top-left corner.

`Name`—Specifies the name used to access the `TextBox` programmatically. The name should be prefixed with `txt`.

`Size`—Specifies the height and width (in pixels) of the `TextBox`.

`Text`—Specifies the text displayed in the `TextBox`.

`TextAlign`—Specifies how the text is aligned within the `TextBox`.

MULTIPLE-CHOICE QUESTIONS

6.1 Parentheses that are added to an expression simply to make it easier to read are known as _____ parentheses.

a) necessary
b) redundant
c) embedded
d) nested

6.2 The _____ operator performs `Integer` division.

a) \
b) +
c) `Mod`
d) ^

6.3 Every variable has a _____.

a) name
b) value
c) type
d) All of the above.

6.4 In Visual Basic .NET, arithmetic expressions must be written in _____ form.

a) straight-line
b) top-bottom
c) left-right
d) right-left

6.5 Arithmetic expressions are evaluated _____.

a) from right to left
b) from left to right
c) according to the rules of operator precedence
d) from the lowest level of precedence to the highest level of precedence

6.6 Variable declarations in event handlers begin with the keyword _____.

a) `Declare`
b) `Dim`
c) `Sub`
d) `Integer`

6.7 Entering a value in a `TextBox` raises the _____ event.

a) `TextAltered`
b) `ValueChanged`
c) `ValueEntered`
d) `TextChanged`

6.8 The _____ function converts user input from a `TextBox` to a variable of type `Double`.

a) `Convert`
b) `MakeDouble`
c) `Val`
d) `WriteDouble`

6.9 Variables to store integer values should be declared with keyword _____.

a) `Integer`
b) `Int`
c) `IntVariable`
d) None of the above.

6.10 Keyword _____ in a variable declaration indicates that the data type is the next word.

a) `IsA`
b) `Type`
c) `Dim`
d) `As`

EXERCISES

6.11 *(Simple Encryption Application)* This application uses a simple technique to encrypt a number. Encryption is the process of modifying data so that only those intended to receive the data can undo the changes and view the original data. The user enters the data to be encrypted via a `TextBox`. The application then multiplies the number by 7 and adds 5. The application displays the encrypted number in a `Label` as shown in Fig. 6.24.

Figure 6.24 Result of completed **Simple Encryption** application.

a) ***Copying the template to your working directory.*** Copy the directory `C:\Examples\Tutorial06\Exercises\SimpleEncryption` to your `C:\SimplyVB` directory.

b) ***Opening the application's template file.*** Double click `SimpleEncryption.sln` in the `SimpleEncryption` directory to open the application.

c) ***Coding the Click event handler.*** Encrypt the number in the `Click` event handler by using the preceding technique. The user input should be stored in an `Integer` variable (`intNumber`) before it is encrypted. The event handler then should display the encrypted number.

d) ***Clearing the result.*** Add an event handler for the **Enter number to encrypt:** Text-Box's `TextChanged` event. This event handler should clear the **Encrypted number:** TextBox whenever the user enters new input.

e) ***Running the application.*** Select **Debug > Start** to run your application. Enter the value 25 into the **Enter number to encrypt:** TextBox and click the **Encrypt** Button. Verify that the value 180 is displayed in the **Encrypted number:** output Label. Enter other values and click the **Encrypt** Button after each. Verify that the appropriate encrypted value is displayed each time.

f) ***Closing the application.*** Close your running application by clicking its close box.

g) ***Closing the IDE.*** Close Visual Studio .NET by clicking its close box.

6.12 *(Temperature Converter Application)* Write an application that converts a Celsius temperature, *C*, to its equivalent Fahrenheit temperature, *F*. Figure 6.25 displays the completed application. Use the following formula:

$$F = \frac{9}{5}C + 32$$

Figure 6.25   Completed **Temperature Converter**.

a) ***Copying the template to your working directory.*** Copy the directory `C:\Examples\Tutorial06\Exercises\TemperatureConversion` to your `C:\SimplyVB` directory.

b) ***Opening the application's template file.*** Double click `TemperatureConversion.sln` in the `TemperatureConversion` directory to open the application.

c) ***Coding the Click event handler.*** Perform the conversion in the **Convert** Button's `Click` event handler. Define `Integer` variables to store the user-input Celsius temperature and the result of the conversion. Display the Fahrenheit equivalent of the temperature conversion.

d) ***Clearing user input.*** Clear the result in the **Enter a Celsius temperature:** TextBox's `TextChanged` event.

e) ***Running the application.*** Select **Debug > Start** to run your application. Enter the value 20 into the **Enter a Celsius temperature:** TextBox and click the **Convert** Button. Verify that the value 68 is displayed in the output Label. Enter other Celsius temperatures, click the **Convert** Button after each. Use the formula provided above to verify that the proper Fahrenheit equivalent is displayed each time.

f) ***Closing the application.*** Close your running application by clicking its close box.

g) ***Closing the IDE.*** Close Visual Studio .NET by clicking its close box.

6.13 *(Simple Calculator Application)* In this exercise, you will add functionality to a simple calculator application. The calculator will allow a user to enter two numbers in the Text-Boxes. There will be four Buttons labeled +, -, / and *. When the user clicks the Button labeled as addition, subtraction, multiplication or division, the application will perform that operation on the numbers in the TextBoxes and displays the result. The calculator also should clear the calculation result when the user enters new input. Figure 6.26 displays the completed calculator.

a) *Copying the template to your working directory.* Copy the directory C:\Examples\Tutorial06\Exercises\SimpleCalculator to your C:\SimplyVB directory.

b) *Opening the application's template file.* Double click SimpleCalculator.sln in the SimpleCalculator directory to open the application.

Figure 6.26 Result of **Calculator** application.

c) *Coding the addition Click event handler.* This event handler should add the two numbers and display the result.

d) *Coding the subtraction Click event handler.* This event handler should subtract the second number from the first number and display the result.

e) *Coding the multiplication Click event handler.* This event handler should multiply the two numbers and display the result.

f) *Coding the division Click event handler.* This event handler should divide the first number by the second number and display the result.

g) *Clearing the result.* Write event handlers for the TextBoxes' TextChanged events. Write code to clear the result Label (lblResult) after the user enters new input into either TextBox.

h) *Running the application.* Select **Debug > Start** to run your application. Enter a first number and a second number, then verify that each of the Buttons works by clicking each, and viewing the output. Repeat this process with two new values and again verify that the proper output is displayed based on which Button is clicked.

i) *Closing the application.* Close your running application by clicking its close box.

j) *Closing the IDE.* Close Visual Studio .NET by clicking its close box.

What does this code do? ▶ **6.14** This code modifies values intNumber1, intNumber2 and intResult. What are the final values of these variables?

```
1   Dim intNumber1 As Integer
2   Dim intNumber2 As Integer
3   Dim intResult As Integer
4
5   intNumber1 = 5 * (4 + 6)
6   intNumber2 = 2 ^ 2
7   intResult = intNumber1 \ intNumber2
```

What's wrong with this code? ▶ **6.15** Find the error(s) in the following code, which uses variables to perform a calculation.

```
1   Dim intNumber1 As Integer
2   Dim intNumber2 As Integer
3   Dim intResult As Integer
4
5   intNumber1 = (4 * 6 ^ 4) / (10 Mod 4 - 2)
6   intNumber2 = (16 \ 3) ^ 2 * 6 + 1
7   intResult = intNumber1 - intNumber2
```

Using the Debugger ▶ **6.16** *(Average Three Numbers)* You have just written an application that takes three numbers as input in TextBoxes, stores the three numbers in variables, then finds the average of the numbers (note that the average is rounded to the nearest integer value). The output is displayed in a Label (Fig. 6.27, which displays the incorrect output). You soon realize, however, that the number displayed in the Label is not the average, but rather a number that does not make sense given the input. Use the debugger to help locate and remove this error.

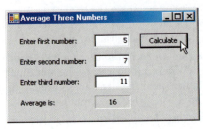

Figure 6.27   **Average Three Numbers** application.

a) *Copying the template to your working directory.* Copy the directory C:\Examples\ Tutorial06\Exercises\AverageDebugging to your C:\SimplyVB directory.

b) *Opening the application's template file.* Double click AverageDebugging.sln in the AverageDebugging directory to open the application.

c) *Running the application.* Select **Debug > Start** to run your application. View the output to observe that the output is incorrect.

d) *Closing the application.* Close the application, and view the Average.vb file in code view.

e) *Setting breakpoints.* Set a breakpoint in the btnCalculate_Click event handler. Run the application again, and use the debugger to help find the error(s).

f) *Finding and correcting the error(s).* Once you have found the error(s), modify the application so that it correctly calculates the average of three numbers.

g) *Running the application.* Select **Debug > Start** to run your application. Enter the three values from Fig. 6.27 into the input TextBoxes provided and click the **Calculate Button**. Verify that the output now accurately reflects the average of these values, which is 8.

h) *Closing the application.* Close your running application by clicking its close box.

i) *Closing the IDE.* Close Visual Studio .NET by clicking its close box.

Programming Challenge ▶   **6.17** *(Digit Extraction)* Write an application that allows the user to enter a five-digit number into a TextBox. The application then separates the number into its individual digits and displays each digit in a Label. The application should look and behave similarly to Fig. 6.28. [*Hint:* You can use the Mod operator to extract the ones digit from a number. For instance, 12345 Mod 10 is 5. You can use integer division (\) to "peel off" digits from a number. For instance, 12345 \ 100 is 123. This allows you to treat the 3 in 12345 as a ones digit. Now you can isolate the 3 by using the Mod operator. Apply this technique to the rest of the digits.]

Figure 6.28   **Digit Extractor** application GUI.

a) *Creating the application.* Create a new project named DigitExtractor. Rename the Form1.vb file DigitExtractor.vb. Change the name of the Form to FrmDigit-Extractor and set the startup object to FrmDigitExtractor. Add Labels, a Text-

Box and a Button to the application's Form. Name the TextBox txtInput and name the Button btnEnter. Name the other controls logically based on the tips provided in earlier tutorials.

b) *Adding an event handler for btnEnter's Click event.* In design view, double click btnEnter to create the btnEnter_Click event handler. In this event handler, create five variables of type Integer. Use the Mod operator to extract each digit. Store the digits in the five variables created.

c) *Adding an event handler for txtInput's TextChanged event.* In design view, double click txtInput to create the txtInput_TextChanged event handler. In this event handler, clear the five Labels used to display each digit. This event handler clears the output whenever new input is entered.

d) *Running the application.* Select **Debug > Start** to run your application. Enter a five-digit number and click the **Enter** Button. Enter a new five-digit number and verify that the previous output is cleared.

e) *Closing the application.* Close your running application by clicking its close box.

f) *Closing the IDE.* Close Visual Studio .NET by clicking its close box.

Wage Calculator Application

Introducing Algorithms, Pseudocode and Program Control

Objectives

In this tutorial, you will learn to:
- Understand basic problem-solving techniques.
- Understand control structures.
- Understand and create pseudocode.
- Use the If...Then and If...Then...Else selection statements to choose among alternative actions.
- Use the assignment operators.
- Use the debugger's **Watch** window.

Outline

Before writing an application, it is essential to have a thorough understanding of the problem you need to solve. This will allow you to design a carefully planned approach to solving the problem. When writing an application, it is equally important to recognize the types of building blocks that are available and to use proven application-construction principles. In this tutorial, you will learn the theory and principles of **structured programming**. Structured programming is a technique for organizing program control that will help you develop applications that are clear and easier to debug and modify. The techniques presented are applicable to most high-level languages, including Visual Basic .NET.

7.1 Test-Driving the Wage Calculator Application

In this section, we preview this tutorial's **Wage Calculator** application. This application must meet the following requirements:

> **Application Requirements**
>
> *A payroll company calculates the gross earnings per week of employees. Employees' weekly salaries are based on the number of hours they worked and their hourly wages. Create an application that accepts this information and calculates the employee's total (gross) earnings. The application assumes a standard work week of 40 hours. The wages for forty or fewer hours are calculated by multiplying the employee's hourly salary by the number of hours worked. Any time worked over 40 hours in a week is considered "overtime" and earns time and a half. Salary for time and a half is calculated by multiplying the employee's hourly wage by 1.5 and multiplying the result of that calculation by the number of overtime hours worked. The total overtime earned is added to the user's gross earnings for the regular 40 hours of work to calculate the total earnings for that week.*

This application calculates wages from hourly salary and hours worked per week. Normally, if an employee has worked 40 or fewer hours, the employee is paid regular wages. The calculation differs if the employee has worked more than the standard 40-hour work week. In this tutorial, we introduce a programming tool known as a **control structure** that allows us to make this distinction and perform different calculations based on different user inputs. You begin by test-driving the completed application. Then, you will learn the additional Visual Basic .NET technologies that you will need to create you own version of this application.

Test-Driving the Wage Calculator Application

1. ***Opening the completed application.*** Open the directory `C:\Examples\Tutorial07\CompletedApplication\WageCalculator` to locate the **Wage Calculator** application. Double click `WageCalculator.sln` to open the application in Visual Studio .NET.

2. ***Running the application.*** Select **Debug > Start** to run the application (Fig. 7.1). Notice that we have placed the TextBoxes vertically, rather than horizontally, in this application. To make our GUI well-organized, we have aligned the right sides of each TextBox and made the TextBoxes the same size. We have also left aligned the TextBoxes' descriptive Labels.

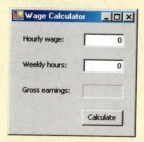

Figure 7.1 **Wage Calculator** application.

3. ***Enter the employee's hourly wage.*** Enter **10** in the **Hourly wage:** TextBox.

4. ***Enter the number of hours the employee worked.*** Enter **45** in the **Weekly hours:** TextBox.

5. ***Calculate the employee's gross earnings.*** Click the **Calculate** Button. The result (**$475.00**) is displayed in the **Gross earnings:** TextBox (Fig. 7.2). Notice that the employee's salary is the sum of the wages for the standard 40-hour work week (40 * 10) and the overtime pay (5 * 10 * 1.5).

Figure 7.2 Calculating wages by clicking the **Calculate** Button.

6. ***Closing the application.*** Close your running application by clicking its close box.

7. ***Closing the IDE.*** Close Visual Studio .NET by clicking its close box.

GUI Design Tip

When using multiple TextBoxes vertically, align the TextBoxes on their right sides, and where possible make the TextBoxes the same size. Left-align the descriptive Labels for such TextBoxes.

7.2 Algorithms

Computing problems can be solved by executing a series of actions in a specific order. A procedure for solving a problem, in terms of:

1. the **actions** to be executed and

2. the **order** in which these actions are to be executed

is called an **algorithm**. The following example demonstrates the importance of correctly specifying the order in which the actions are to be executed. Consider the "rise-and-shine algorithm" followed by one junior executive for getting out of bed and going to work: (1) get out of bed, (2) take off pajamas, (3) take a shower, (4) get dressed, (5) eat breakfast and (6) carpool to work. This routine prepares the executive for a productive day at the office.

However, suppose that the same steps are performed in a slightly different order: (1) get out of bed, (2) take off pajamas, (3) get dressed, (4) take a shower, (5) eat breakfast, (6) carpool to work. In this case, our junior executive shows up for work soaking wet.

Indicating the appropriate sequence in which to execute actions is equally crucial in computer programs. **Program control** refers to the task of ordering an application's statements correctly. In this tutorial, you will begin to investigate the program-control capabilities of Visual Basic .NET.

SELF-REVIEW

1. _____ refer(s) to the task of ordering an application's statements correctly.

   a) Actions   b) Program control

   c) Control structures   d) Visual programming

2. A(n) _____ is a plan for solving a problem in terms of the actions to be executed and the order in which these actions are to be executed.

   a) chart   b) control structure

   c) algorithm   d) ordered list

   Answers: 1) b. 2) c.

7.3 Pseudocode

Pseudocode is an informal language that helps programmers develop algorithms. The pseudocode we present is particularly useful in the development of algorithms that will be converted to structured portions of Visual Basic .NET applications. Pseudocode resembles everyday English; it is convenient and user-friendly, but it is not an actual computer-programming language.

Pseudocode statements are not executed on computers. Rather, pseudocode helps you "think out" an application before attempting to write it in a programming language, such as Visual Basic .NET. In this tutorial, we provide several examples of pseudocode.

The style of pseudocode that we present consists solely of characters, so that you can create and modify pseudocode by using editor programs, such as the Visual Studio .NET code editor or Notepad. A carefully prepared pseudocode program can be converted easily to a corresponding Visual Basic .NET application. Much of this conversion is as simple as replacing pseudocode statements with their Visual Basic .NET equivalents. Let us look at an example of a pseudocode statement:

Assign 0 to the counter

This pseudocode statement provides an easy-to-understand task. You can put several such statements together to form an algorithm that can be used to meet application requirements. When the pseudocode algorithm has been completed, the programmer can then convert pseudocode statements to their equivalent Visual Basic .NET statements. The pseudocode statement above, for instance, can be converted to the following Visual Basic .NET statement:

```
intCounter = 0
```

Pseudocode normally describes only **executable statements**, which are the actions that are performed when the corresponding Visual Basic .NET application

Software Design Tip

Pseudocode helps the programmer conceptualize an application during the application-design process. The pseudocode statements can be converted to Visual Basic .NET at a later point.

is run. An example of a programming statement that is not executed is a declaration. The declaration

```
Dim intNumber As Integer
```

informs the compiler of `intNumber`'s type and instructs the compiler to reserve space in memory for this variable. The declaration does not cause any action, such as input, output or a calculation, to occur when the application executes, so we would not include this information in the pseudocode.

SELF-REVIEW

1. _____ is an artificial and informal language that helps programmers develop algorithms.

   a) Pseudocode
   c) Notation

   b) VB-Speak
   d) None of the above.

2. Pseudocode _____.

   a) usually describes only declarations
   b) is executed on computers
   c) usually describes only executable lines of code
   d) usually describes declarations and executable lines of code

Answers: 1) a. 2) c.

7.4 Control Structures

Normally, statements in an application are executed one after another in the order in which they are written. This is called **sequential execution**. However, Visual Basic .NET allows you to specify that the next statement to be executed might not be the next one in sequence. A **transfer of control** occurs when an executed statement does not directly follow the previously executed statement in the written application. This is common in computer programs.

All programs can be written in terms of only three control structures: the **sequence structure**, the selection structure and the repetition structure. The sequence structure is built into Visual Basic .NET—unless directed to act otherwise, the computer executes Visual Basic .NET statements sequentially—that is, one after the other in the order in which they appear in the application. The **activity diagram** in Fig. 7.3 illustrates a typical sequence structure, in which two calculations are performed in order. We discuss activity diagrams in detail following Fig. 7.3.

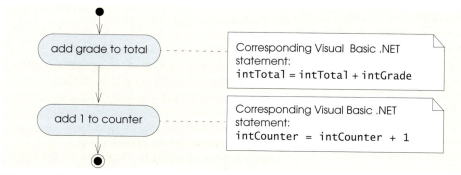

Figure 7.3 Sequence structure activity diagram.

Activity diagrams are part of the **Unified Modeling Language (UML)**—an industry standard for modeling software systems. An activity diagram models the **activity** (also called the **workflow**) of a portion of a software system. Such activities may include a portion of an algorithm, such as the sequence structure in Fig. 7.3. Activity diagrams are composed of special-purpose symbols, such as **action-state symbols** (a rectangle with its left and right sides replaced with arcs curving outward), **diamonds** and **small circles**; these symbols are connected by **transition**

arrows, which represent the flow of the activity. Figure 7.3 does not include any diamond symbols—these will be used in later activity diagrams, beginning with Fig. 7.6.

Like pseudocode, activity diagrams help programmers develop and represent algorithms, although many programmers prefer pseudocode. Activity diagrams clearly show how control structures operate.

Consider the activity diagram for the sequence structure in Fig. 7.3. The activity diagram contains two **action states** that represent actions to perform. Each action state contains an **action expression**—for example, "add grade to total" or "add 1 to counter"—that specifies a particular action to perform. Other actions might include calculations or input/output operations. The arrows in the activity diagram are called transition arrows. These arrows represent **transitions**, which indicate the order in which the actions represented by the action states occur—the application that implements the activities illustrated by the activity diagram in Fig. 7.3 first adds intGrade to intTotal, then adds 1 to intCounter.

The **solid circle** located at the top of the activity diagram represents the activity's **initial state**—the beginning of the workflow before the application performs the modeled activities. The solid circle surrounded by a hollow circle that appears at the bottom of the activity diagram represents the **final state**—the end of the workflow after the application performs its activities.

Notice, in Fig. 7.3, the rectangles with the upper-right corners folded over. These look like sheets of paper and are called **notes** in the UML. Notes are like comments in Visual Basic .NET applications—they are explanatory remarks that describe the purpose of symbols in the diagram. Figure 7.3 uses UML notes to show the Visual Basic .NET code that the programmer might associate with each action state in the activity diagram. A **dotted line** connects each note with the element that the note describes. Activity diagrams normally do not show the Visual Basic .NET code that implements the activity, but we use notes here to show you how the diagram relates to Visual Basic .NET code.

Visual Basic .NET provides three types of **selection structures**, which we discuss in this tutorial and in Tutorial 11. The **If...Then** selection structure performs (selects) an action (or sequence of actions) based on a condition. A **condition** is an expression with a **true** or **false** value that is used to make a decision. Conditions are **evaluated** (that is, tested) to determine whether their value is true or false. These values are of data type **Boolean** and are specified in Visual Basic .NET code by using the keywords **True** and **False**. Sometimes we refer to a condition as a Boolean expression.

If the condition evaluates to true, the actions specified by the If...Then structure will execute. If the condition evaluates to false, the actions specified by the If...Then structure will be skipped. The **If...Then...Else** selection structure performs an action (or sequence of actions) if a condition is true and performs a different action (or sequence of actions) if the condition is false. The Select Case structure, discussed in Tutorial 11, performs one of many actions (or sequences of actions), depending on the value of an expression.

The If...Then structure is called a **single-selection structure** because it selects or ignores a single action (or a sequence of actions). The If...Then...Else structure is called a **double-selection structure** because it selects between two different actions (or sequences of actions). The Select Case structure is called a **multiple-selection structure** because it selects among many different actions or sequences of actions.

Visual Basic .NET provides seven types of **repetition structures**—While...End While, Do While...Loop, Do...Loop While, Do Until...Loop, Do...Loop Until, For...Next and For Each...Next. Repetition structures Do While...Loop and Do Until...Loop are covered in Tutorial 8; Do...Loop While and Do...Loop Until are covered in Tutorial 9; For...Next is covered in Tutorial 10; and For Each...Next is covered in Tutorial 20.[1] The words If, Then, Else, End, Select, Case, While, Do,

Until, Loop, For, Next and Each are all Visual Basic .NET keywords—Appendix F includes a complete list of Visual Basic .NET keywords. We discuss many of Visual Basic .NET's keywords and their respective purposes throughout this book. Visual Basic .NET has a much larger set of keywords than most other popular programming languages.

Visual Basic .NET has 11 control structures—the sequence structure, three types of selection structures and seven types of repetition structures. Each Visual Basic .NET application is formed by combining as many of each type of control structure as is necessary. As with the sequence structure in Fig. 7.3, each control structure is drawn with two small circle symbols—a solid black one to represent the entry point to the control structure, and a solid black one surrounded by a hollow circle to represent the exit point.

All Visual Basic .NET control structures are **single-entry/single-exit control structures**—each has exactly one entry point and one exit point. Such control structures make it easy to build applications—the control structures are attached to one another by connecting the exit point of one control structure to the entry point of the next. This is similar to stacking building blocks, so, we call it **control-structure stacking**. The only other way to connect control structures is through **control-structure nesting**, whereby one control structure can be placed inside another. Thus, algorithms in Visual Basic .NET applications are constructed from only 11 different types of control structures combined in only two ways—this is a model of simplicity. Control structures in Visual Basic .NET are implemented as statements, so, from this point forward (after the following exercises), we use the term "statement" in preference to the term "structure."

SELF-REVIEW

1. All Visual Basic .NET applications can be written in terms of _____ types of control structures.

   a) one
   b) two
   c) three
   d) four

2. The process of application statements executing one after another in the order in which they are written is called _____.

   a) transfer of control
   b) sequential execution
   c) workflow
   d) None of the above.

Answers: 1) c. 2) b.

7.5 If...Then Selection Statement

A selection statement chooses among alternative courses of action in an application. For example, suppose that the passing grade on a test is 60 (out of 100). The pseudocode statement

> If student's grade is greater than or equal to 60
>   Display "Passed"

Common Programming Error

Omission of the Then keyword in an If...Then statement is a syntax error.

determines whether the condition "student's grade is greater than or equal to 60" is true or false. If the condition is true, then "Passed" is displayed, and the next pseudocode statement in order is "performed." (Remember that pseudocode is not a real programming language.) If the condition is false, the display statement is ignored, and the next pseudocode statement in order is performed.

---

1. We do not discuss the While...End While loop in this book. This repetition structure behaves identically to the Do While...Loop and is provided for programmers familiar with previous versions of Visual Basic.

The preceding pseudocode *If* statement may be written in Visual Basic .NET as

```
If intStudentGrade >= 60 Then
    lblGradeDisplay.Text = "Passed"
End If
```

Good Programming Practice

Indent the statements inside If...Then statements to improve readability.

Common Programming Error

It is a syntax error to add spaces between the symbols in the operators <>, >= and <= (as in < >, > =, < =).

Common Programming Error

Reversal of the operators <>, >= and <= (as in ><, =>, =<) is a syntax error.

Notice that the Visual Basic .NET code corresponds closely to the pseudocode, demonstrating the usefulness of pseudocode as an application-development tool. The body (sometimes called a **block**) of the If...Then statement displays the string "Passed" in a Label. The keywords End If close an If...Then statement.

Notice the indentation in the If...Then statement. Such indentation enhances application readability. The Visual Basic .NET compiler ignores whitespace characters, such as spaces, tabs and newlines used for indentation and vertical spacing, unless the whitespace characters are contained in strings.

The condition between keywords If and Then determines whether the statement(s) within the If...Then statement will execute. If the condition is true, the body of the If...Then statement executes. If the condition is false, the body is not executed. Conditions in If...Then statements can be formed by using the **equality operators** and **relational operators** (also called **comparison operators**), which are summarized in Fig. 7.4. The relational and equality operators all have the same level of precedence.

Algebraic equality or relational operators	Visual Basic .NET equality or relational operator	Example of Visual Basic .NET condition	Meaning of Visual Basic .NET condition
Relational operators			
>	>	intX > intY	intX is greater than intY
<	<	intX < intY	intX is less than intY
≥	>=	intX >= intY	intx is greater than or equal to intY
≤	<=	intX <= intY	intX is less than or equal to intY
Equality operators			
=	=	intX = intY	intX is equal to intY
≠	<>	intX <> intY	intX is not equal to intY

Figure 7.4 Equality and relational operators.

Figure 7.5 shows the **syntax** of the If...Then statement. A statement's syntax specifies how the statement must be formed to execute without syntax errors. Let's look closely at the syntax of an If...Then statement. The first line of Fig. 7.5 specifies that the statement must begin with the keyword If and be followed by a condition and the keyword Then. Notice that we have italicized *condition*. This indicates that, when creating your own If...Then statement, you should replace the text *condition* with the actual condition that you would like evaluated. The second line indicates that you should replace *statements* with the actual statements that you want to be included in the body of the If...Then statement. These statements make up the body of the If...Then statement. Notice that the text *statements* is placed within square brackets. These brackets do not appear in the actual If...Then statement. Instead, the square brackets indicate that certain portions of the statement are optional. In this example, the square brackets indicate that all statements in the If...Then statement's body are optional. Of course, if there are no statements in the body of the If...Then statement, then no actions will occur as part of that statement, regardless of the condition's value. The final line indicates that the statement ends with the End If keywords.

Syntax
If *condition* Then
[*statements*]
End If

Figure 7.5 If...Then statement syntax.

Figure 7.6 illustrates the single-selection If...Then statement. This activity diagram contains what is perhaps the most important symbol in an activity diagram—the diamond, or **decision symbol**, which indicates that a decision is to be made. Note the two sets of square brackets above or next to the arrows leading from the decision symbol; these are called **guard conditions**. A decision symbol indicates that the workflow will continue along a path determined by the symbol's associated guard conditions, which can be true or false. Each transition arrow emerging from a decision symbol has a guard condition (specified in square brackets above or next to the transition arrow). If a particular guard condition is true, the workflow enters the action state to which that transition arrow points. For example, in Fig. 7.6, if the grade is greater than or equal to 60, the application displays "Passed," then transitions to the final state of this activity. If the grade is less than 60, the application immediately transitions to the final state without displaying a message. Only one guard condition associated with a particular decision symbol can be true at once.

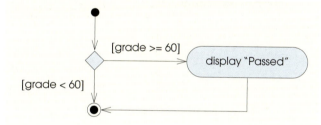

Figure 7.6 If...Then single-selection statement activity diagram.

Note that the If...Then statement (Fig. 7.6), is a single-entry/single-exit statement. The activity diagrams for the remaining control structures also contain (aside from small circle symbols and flowlines called transitions) only action-state symbols, indicating actions to be performed, and diamond symbols, indicating decisions to be made. Representing control structures in this way emphasizes the **action/decision model of programming**. To understand the process of structured programming better, we can envision 11 bins, each containing a different type of the 11 possible control structures. The control structures in each bin are empty, meaning that nothing is written in the action-state symbols and no guard conditions are written next to the decision symbols. The programmer's task is to assemble an application, using as many control structures as the algorithm demands, combining those control statements in only two possible ways (stacking or nesting) and filling in the actions and decisions (with the decisions' guard conditions) in a manner appropriate to the algorithm. Again, each of these control structures is implemented in Visual Basic .NET as a statement.

1. Which of the following `If...Then` statements correctly displays that a student received an A on an exam if the score was 90 or above?

   a) ```
      If intStudentGrade <> 90 Then
          lblDisplay.Text = "Student received an A"
      End If
      ```

   b) ```
      If intStudentGrade > 90 Then
          lblDisplay.Text = "Student received an A"
      End If
      ```

   c) ```
      If intStudentGrade = 90 Then
          lblDisplay.Text = "Student received an A"
      End If
      ```

   d) ```
      If intStudentGrade >= 90 Then
          lblDisplay.Text = "Student received an A"
      End If
      ```

2. The symbol _____ is not a Visual Basic .NET operator.

   a) *   b) ^

   c) %   d) <>

Answers: 1) d. 2) c.

7.6 If...Then...Else Selection Statement

As you have learned, the `If...Then` selection statement performs an indicated action (or sequence of actions) only when the condition evaluates to true; otherwise, the action (or sequence of actions) is skipped. The `If...Then...Else` selection statement allows the programmer to specify that a different action (or sequence of actions) be performed when the condition is true from when the condition is false. For example, the pseudocode statement

> *If student's grade is greater than or equal to 60*
> > *Display "Passed"*
>
> *Else*
> > *Display "Failed"*

displays "Passed" if the student's grade is greater than or equal to 60, but displays "Failed" if the student's grade is less than 60. In either case, after output occurs, the next pseudocode statement in sequence is "performed."

The preceding pseudocode *If...Else* statement may be written in Visual Basic .NET as

```
If intStudentGrade >= 60 Then
    lblDisplay.Text = "Passed"
Else
    lblDisplay.Text = "Failed"
End If
```

Good Programming Practice

Apply a standard indentation convention consistently throughout your applications to enhance readability.

Note that the body of the **Else** clause is indented so that it lines up with the indented body of the `If` clause. A standard indentation convention should be applied consistently throughout your applications. It is difficult to read programs that do not use uniform spacing conventions. The `If...Then...Else` selection statement follows the same general syntax as the `If...Then` statement. The `Else` keyword and any related statements are placed between the `If...Then` and closing `End If` statements as in Fig. 7.7.

Syntax
If *condition* Then
[*statements*]
Else
[*statements*]
End If

Figure 7.7 If...Then...Else statement syntax.

Figure 7.8 illustrates the flow of control in the If...Then...Else double-selection statement. Once again, note that (besides the initial state, transition arrows and final state) the only other symbols in the activity diagram represent action states and decisions. In this example, the grade is either less than 60 or greater than or equal to 60. If the grade is less than 60, the application displays "Failed". If the grade is equal to or greater than 60, the application displays "Passed". We continue to emphasize this action/decision model of computing. Imagine again a deep bin containing as many empty double-selection statements as might be needed to build any Visual Basic .NET application. Your job as a programmer is to assemble these selection statements (by stacking and nesting) with any other control statements required by the algorithm. You fill in the action states and decision symbols with action expressions and guard conditions appropriate to the algorithm.

Good Programming Practice

Indent both body statements of an If...Then...Else statement to improve readability.

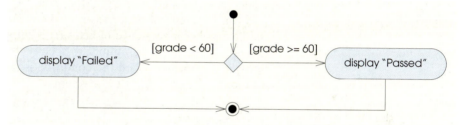

Figure 7.8 If...Then...Else double-selection statement activity diagram.

Nested If...Then...Else statements test for multiple conditions by placing If...Then...Else statements inside other If...Then...Else statements. For example, the following pseudocode (Fig. 7.9) will display "A" for exam grades greater than or equal to 90, "B" for grades in the range 80–89, "C" for grades in the range 70–79, "D" for grades in the range 60–69 and "F" for all other grades:

```
If student's grade is greater than or equal to 90
    Display "A"
Else
    If student's grade is greater than or equal to 80
        Display "B"
    Else
        If student's grade is greater than or equal to 70
            Display "C"
        Else
            If student's grade is greater than or equal to 60
                Display "D"
            Else
                Display "F"
```

Figure 7.9 Pseudocode for an application that displays a student's grades.

Good Programming Practice

If there are several levels of indentation, each level should be indented further to the right by the same amount of space.

The pseudocode in Fig. 7.9 may be written in Visual Basic .NET as shown in Fig. 7.10.

```
If intStudentGrade >= 90 Then
    lblDisplay.Text = "A"
Else
    If intStudentGrade >= 80 Then
        lblDisplay.Text = "B"
    Else
        If intStudentGrade >= 70 Then
            lblDisplay.Text = "C"
        Else
            If intStudentGrade >= 60 Then
                lblDisplay.Text = "D"
            Else
                lblDisplay.Text = "F"
            End If
        End If
    End If
End If
```

Figure 7.10   Visual Basic .NET code converted from the pseudocode in Fig. 7.9.

If `intStudentGrade` is greater than or equal to 90, the first condition evaluates to `True` and the statement `lblDisplay.Text = "A"` is executed. Notice that, with a value for `intStudentGrade` greater than or equal to 90, the remaining three conditions will evaluate to `True`. These conditions, however, are never evaluated, because they are placed within the `Else` portion of the outer `If...Then...Else` statement. Because the first condition is `True`, all statements within the `Else` clause are skipped. Let's now assume `intStudentGrade` contains the value 75. The first condition is `False`, so the application will execute the statements within the `Else` clause of this statement. This `Else` clause also contains an `If...Then...Else` statement, with the condition `intStudentGrade >= 80`. This condition evaluates to `False`, causing the statements in this `If...Then...Else` statement's `Else` clause to execute. This `Else` clause contains yet another `If...Then...Else` statement, with the condition `intStudentGrade >= 70`. This condition is `True`, causing the statement `lblDisplay.Text = "C"` to execute. The `Else` clause of this `If...Then...Else` statement is then skipped.

Most Visual Basic .NET programmers prefer to write the preceding `If...Then...Else` statement, using the **ElseIf keyword**, as

```
If intStudentGrade >= 90 Then
    lblDisplay.Text = "A"
ElseIf intStudentGrade >= 80 Then
    lblDisplay.Text = "B"
ElseIf intStudentGrade >= 70 Then
    lblDisplay.Text = "C"
ElseIf intStudentGrade >= 60 Then
    lblDisplay.Text = "D"
Else
    lblDisplay.Text = "F"
End If
```

Figure 7.11   If...Then...Else statement using the ElseIf keyword.

The two statements are equivalent, but the latter statement is popular because it avoids deep indentation of the code. Such deep indentation often leaves little room on a line, forcing lines to be split and decreasing code readability. Notice that the final portion of the `If...Then...Else` statement uses the `Else` keyword to handle all remaining possibilities. The `Else` clause must always be last in an `If...Then...Else` statement—following an `Else` clause with another `Else` or `ElseIf` clause is a syntax error. You should also note that the latter statement requires only one `End If`.

1. If...Then...Else is a _____-selection statement.

   a) single   b) double

   c) triple   d) nested

2. Placing an If...Then...Else statement inside another If...Then...Else statement is an example of _____.

   a) nesting If...Then...Else statements   b) stacking If...Then...Else statements

   c) creating sequential If...Then...Else statements   d) None of the above.

Answers: 1) b. 2) a.

7.7 Constructing the Wage Calculator Application

The following section teaches you how to build the **Wage Calculator** by using the If...Then...Else statement. The If...Then...Else statement allows you to select between calculating regular wages and including overtime pay based on the number of hours worked. The following pseudocode describes the basic operation of the **Wage Calculator** application, which runs when the user clicks **Calculate:**

> **When the user clicks the Calculate Button**
>> **Retrieve the number of hours worked and hourly wage from the TextBoxes**
>>
>> **If the number of hours worked is less than or equal to 40 hours**
>>> **Gross earnings equals hours worked times hourly wage**
>>
>> **Else**
>>> **Gross earnings equals 40 times hourly wage plus hours above 40 times wage and a half**
>>
>> **Display gross earnings**

Visual Studio .NET provides many programming tools to aid you in creating powerful and effective applications. Because there are so many tools available, it is often helpful to create a table to organize and choose the best GUI elements. Like pseudocode, these tables simplify the task of creating the application by outlining the application's actions. In addition to listing the application's actions, the table assigns controls and events to the actions described in the pseudocode.

Now that you have test-driven the **Wage Calculator** application and studied its pseudocode representation, you will use an Action/Control/Event (ACE) table to help you convert the pseudocode to Visual Basic .NET. Figure 7.12 lists the actions, controls and events that will help you complete your own version of this application.

The Labels in the first row display information about the application to the user. These Labels help guide the user through the application. The Button control, btnCalculate, is used to calculate the employee's wages. Notice that the third column of the table specifies that we will be using this control's Click event to perform any calculations. The TextBoxes will contain input from the user. The final control, lblEarningsResult, is a Label that displays the application's output.

Action/Control/Event (ACE) Table for the Wage Calculator Application

Action	Control	Event
Label the application's controls	lblWage, lblHours, lblEarnings	Application is run

Figure 7.12 Action/Control/Event table for the **Wage Calculator** application. (Part 1 of 2.)

Action	Control	Event
	`btnCalculate`	`Click`
Retrieve the number of hours worked and hourly wage from the TextBoxes	`txtWage,` `txtHours`	
If the number of hours worked is less than or equal to 40 hours Gross earnings equals hours worked times hourly wage		
Else Gross earnings equals 40 times hourly wage plus hours above 40 times wage and a half		
Display gross earnings	`lblEarningsResult`	

Figure 7.12   Action/Control/Event table for the **Wage Calculator** application. (Part 2 of 2.)

We now apply our pseudocode and the ACE table to complete the **Wage Calculator** application. The following box will guide you through the process of adding a `Click` event to the **Calculate** Button and declaring the variables you'll need to calculate the employee's wages. If you forget to add code to this `Click` event, the application will not respond when the user clicks the **Calculate** Button.

Declaring Variables in the Calculate Button's Click Event Handler	1. ***Copying the template to your working directory.*** Copy the `C:\Examples\Tutorial07\TemplateApplication\WageCalculator` directory to your `C:\SimplyVB` directory.

2. ***Opening the Wage Calculator application's template file.*** Double click `WageCalculator.sln` in the `WageCalculator` directory to open the application in Visual Studio .NET. If the application does not open in design view, double click the **WageCalculator.vb** file in the **Solution Explorer**. If the **Solution Explorer** is not open, select **View > Solution Explorer**.

3. ***Adding the Calculate Button Click event handler.*** In this example, the event handler calculates the gross wages when the **Calculate** Button's `Click` event occurs. Double click the **Calculate** Button. An event handler will be generated, and you will be switched to code view. Lines 132–135 of Fig. 7.13 display the generated event handler. Be sure to add the comments and line-continuation characters as shown in Fig. 7.13 so that the line numbers in your code match those presented in this tutorial.

    On line 135, the `End Sub` keywords indicate the end of event handler `btnCalculate_Click`. On line 137, the `End Class` keywords indicate the end of class `FrmWageCalculator`. We often add such comments so that the reader can easily determine which event handler or class is being closed without having to search for the beginning of that event handler or class in the file.

Good Programming Practice

Prefix **Double** variable names with `dbl`.

4. ***Declaring variables.*** This application uses the primitive data types `Double` and **Decimal**. A Double holds numbers with decimal points. Because hours and wages are often fractional numbers, `Integers` are not appropriate for this application. Add lines 135–138 of Fig. 7.14 into the body of event handler `btnCalculate_Click`. Line 136 contains a variable declaration for `Double dblHours`, which holds the number of hours input by the user. Notice that the variable names for `Doubles` are prefixed with `dbl`.

(cont.)

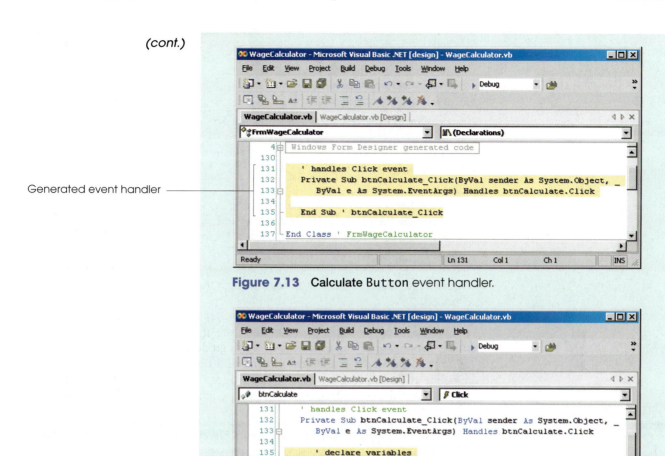

Figure 7.13 Calculate `Button` event handler.

Generated event handler

Variable declarations

Figure 7.14 Declaring variables of type `Double` and `Decimal`.

Type `Decimal` is used to store monetary amounts because this data type ensures rounding accuracy in arithmetic calculations involving monetary amounts. Lines 137–138 declare `decWage`, which stores the hourly wage input by the user, and `decEarnings`, which stores the total amount of earnings for the week. Notice that `Decimal` variable names are prefixed with `dec`.

5. **Declaring a constant.** Add line 140 of Fig. 7.15 to the end of event handler `btnCalculate_Click`. Line 140 contains a **constant**, a variable whose value cannot be changed after its initial declaration. Constants are declared with keyword **Const**. In this case, we assign to the constant `intHOUR_LIMIT` the maximum number of hours worked before mandatory overtime pay (40). Notice that we prefix this `Integer` constant with `int` and capitalize the rest of the constant's name to emphasize that it is a constant.

6. **Saving the project.** Select **File > Save All** to save your modified code.

Good Programming Practice

Prefix `Decimal` variable names with `dec`.

Good Programming Practice

Capitalize the name of a constant, leaving the prefix indicating the constant's type in lowercase. Separate each word in the name of a constant with an underscore.

(cont.)

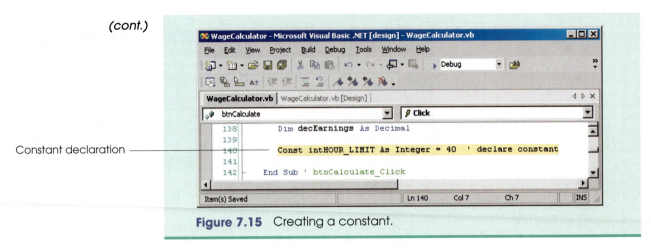

Constant declaration

Figure 7.15 Creating a constant.

Now that you have declared variables, you can use them to receive input from the user, then use that input to compute and display the user's wages. The following box walks you through using the If...Then...Else statement to determine the user's wages.

Determining the User's Wages

1. ***Obtaining inputs from the TextBoxes.*** Add lines 142–144 of Fig. 7.16 to the end of event handler btnCalculate_Click. Lines 143–144 assign values to dblHours and decWage from the TextBoxes into which the user enters data. The Val function returns the user input as Doubles (lines 143–144). Visual Basic .NET implicitly converts the Double result of Val to data type Decimal to assign the result to decWage (line 144).

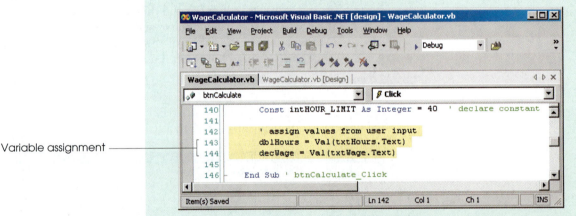

Variable assignment

Figure 7.16 Assigning data to variables.

2. ***Determining wages based on hours worked.*** Begin to add the If...Then...Else statement shown in lines 146–159 of Fig. 7.17 to the end of event handler btnCalculate_Click. First type lines 146–147, then press *Enter*. Notice that the keywords End If are added for you by Visual Studio .NET. Continue by adding lines 149–158 to the If...Then...Else statement. You might need to indent as you go. This If...Then...Else statement determines whether employees earn overtime in addition to their usual wages. Line 147 determines whether the value stored in dblHours is less than or equal to intHOUR_LIMIT. If it is, then line 150 assigns the value of the product of hours and wage to decEarnings. When you multiply a variable of data type Double by a variable of data type Decimal, Visual Basic .NET implicitly converts the Decimal variable to a Double. The Double result is implicitly converted to a Decimal when it is assigned to decEarnings.

Error-Prevention Tip

To reduce errors, the IDE sometimes adds keywords for you. One example is the adding of the keywords End If when an If...Then or an If...Then...Else statement is created. This eliminates the possibility that such keywords will be forgotten or misspelled.

(cont.)

Added
If...Then...Else
statement

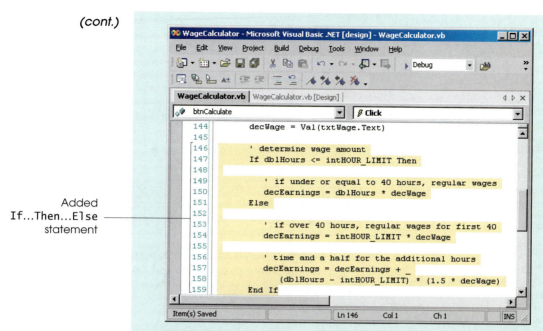

Figure 7.17 If...Then...Else statement to determine wages.

If, on the other hand, dblHours is not less than or equal to intHOUR_LIMIT, then the application proceeds to the Else keyword on line 151. Line 154 computes the wage for the hours worked up to the limit set by intHOUR_LIMIT and assigns it to decEarnings. Lines 157–158 determine how many hours over intHOUR_LIMIT there are (by using the expression dblHours - intHOUR_LIMIT) and then multiplies that by 1.5 and the user's hourly wages. This calculation results in the user's time-and-a-half pay for overtime hours. The value of this statement is then added to the value of decEarnings, and the result is assigned to decEarnings.

3. *Displaying the result.* Add lines 161–162 of Fig. 7.18 to the end of event handler btnCalculate_Click. Line 162 assigns the value in decEarnings to the Text property of the Label lblEarningsResult, implicitly converting decEarnings from a Decimal to a string.

Displaying output

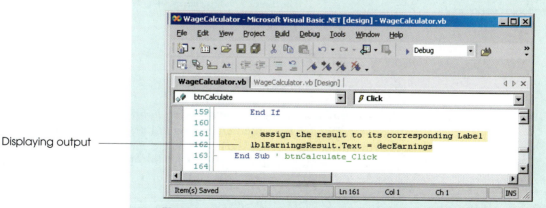

Figure 7.18 Assigning the result to lblEarningsResult.

4. *Running the application.* Select **Debug > Start** to run your application. Notice that the output is not yet formatted as it should be in the completed application. Your will learn how to add this functionality in Section 7.9.

5. *Closing the application.* Close your running application by clicking its close box.

SELF-REVIEW

1. The Decimal data type is used to store _____.

   a) letters and digits   b) integers

   c) strings   d) monetary amounts

2. Constants are declared with keyword _____.

   a) Fixed   b) Constant

   c) Final   d) Const

Answers: 1) d. 2) d.

7.8 Assignment Operators

Visual Basic .NET provides several assignment operators for abbreviating assignment statements. For example, the statement

```
intValue = intValue + 3
```

which adds 3 to the value in intValue, can be abbreviated with the addition assignment operator += as

```
intValue += 3
```

The += operator adds the value of the right operand to the value of the left operand and stores the result in the left operand. Visual Basic .NET provides assignment operators for several binary operators, including +, -, *, ^, / or \. When an assignment statement is evaluated, the expression to the right of the operator is always evaluated first, then assigned to the variable on the left. Figure 7.19 includes the assignment operators, sample expressions using these operators and explanations.

Assignment operators	Sample expression	Explanation	Assigns
Assume: intC = 4			
+=	intC += 7	intC = intC + 7	11 to intC
-=	intC -= 3	intC = intC - 3	1 to intC
*=	intC *= 4	intC = intC * 4	16 to intC
/=	intC /= 2	intC = intC / 2	2 to intC
\=	intC \= 3	intC = intC \ 3	1 to intC
^=	intC ^= 2	intC = intC ^ 2	16 to intC

Figure 7.19 Assignment operators.

The following box demonstrates abbreviating our time-and-a-half calculation with the += operator. When you run the application again, you will notice that the application runs the same as before—all that has changed is that one of the longer statements was made shorter.

Using the Addition Assignment Operator

1. *Adding the addition assignment operator.* Replace lines 157–158 of Fig. 7.17 with line 157 of Fig. 7.20.

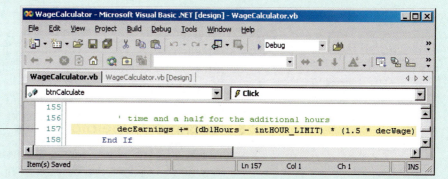

Addition assignment operator shortens statement

```
155
156                  ' time and a half for the additional hours
157             decEarnings += (dblHours - intHOUR_LIMIT) * (1.5 * decWage)
158        End If
```

Figure 7.20 Using the addition assignment operator in a calculation.

In this step, we have used the addition assignment operator to make our statement shorter. Notice that the statement still performs the same action—the time-and-a-half pay for the user is calculated and added to the regular wages earned.

2. *Running the application.* Select **Debug > Start** to run your application. Notice that the application still does not format the output properly. The functionality of the application is the same as it was in the last box—we are now only using the += operator to abbreviate a statement.

3. *Closing the application.* Close your running application by clicking its close box.

SELF-REVIEW

1. The *= operator _____.

   a) squares the value of the right operand and stores the result in the left operand

   b) adds the value of the right operand to the value of the left operand and stores the result in the left operand

   c) creates a new variable and assigns the value of the right operand to that variable

   d) multiplies the value of the left operand by the value of the right operand and stores the result in the left operand

2. If intX is initialized with the value 5, what value will intX contain after the expression intX -= 3 is executed?

   a) 3   b) 5

   c) 7   d) 2

Answers: 1) d. 2) d.

7.9 Formatting Text

There are several ways to format output in Visual Basic .NET. In this section, we introduce method **String.Format** to control how text displays. Modifying the appearance of text for display purposes is known as text **formatting**. This method takes as an argument a **format control string**, followed by arguments that indicate the values to be formatted. The format control string argument specifies how the remaining arguments are to be formatted.

Recall that your **Wage Calculator** does not display the result of its calculation with the appropriate decimal and dollar sign that you saw when test-driving the application. Next, you learn how to apply currency formatting to the value in the **Gross earnings:** TextBox.

Formatting the Gross Earnings

GUI Design Tip

Format all monetary amounts using the C (currency) format specifier.

1. ***Modifying the Calculate Button's Click event.*** If Visual Studio .NET is not already in code view, select **View > Code**. Replace line 162 of Fig. 7.18 with line 161 of Fig. 7.21. Line 161 sends the format control string, "{0:C}", and the value to be formatted, decEarnings, to the String.Format method. The number zero indicates that argument 0 (decEarnings—the first argument after the format control string) should take the format specified by the letter after the colon; this letter is called the **format specifier**. In this case, we use the format defined by the uppercase letter C, which represents the **currency format**, used to display values as monetary amounts. The effect of the C format specifier varies, depending on the locale setting of your computer. In our case, the result is preceded with a dollar sign ($) and displayed with two decimal places (representing cents) because we are in the United States.

Formatting output as currency ———

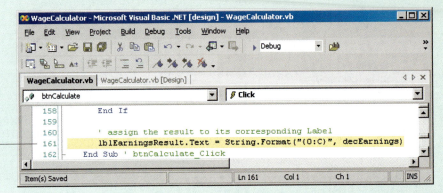

Figure 7.21   Using the Format method to display the result as currency.

2. ***Running the application.*** Select **Debug > Start** to run your application. The application should now output gross earnings as currency.

3. ***Closing the application.*** Close your running application by clicking its close box.

4. ***Closing the IDE.*** Close Visual Studio .NET by clicking its close box.

Figure 7.22 shows several format specifiers. All format specifiers are case insensitive, so the uppercase letters may be used interchangeably with their lowercase equivalents. Note that format code D must be used only with Integers.

Format Specifier	Description
C	Currency. Formats the currency based on the computer's locale setting. For U.S. currency, precedes the number with $, separates every three digits with commas and sets the number of decimal places to two.
E	Scientific notation. Displays one digit to the left of the decimal point and six digits to the right of the decimal point, followed by the character E and a three-digit integer representing the exponent of a power of 10. For example, 956.2 is formatted as 9.562000E+002.
F	Fixed point. Sets the number of decimal places to two.
G	General. Visual Basic .NET chooses either E or F for you, depending on which representation generates a shorter string.
D	Decimal integer. Displays an integer as a whole number in standard base-10 format.
N	Number. Separates every three digits with a comma and sets the number of decimal places to two.

Figure 7.22   Format specifiers for strings.

Figure 7.23 presents the source code for the **Wage Calculator** application. The lines of code that contain new programming concepts that you learned in this tutorial are highlighted.

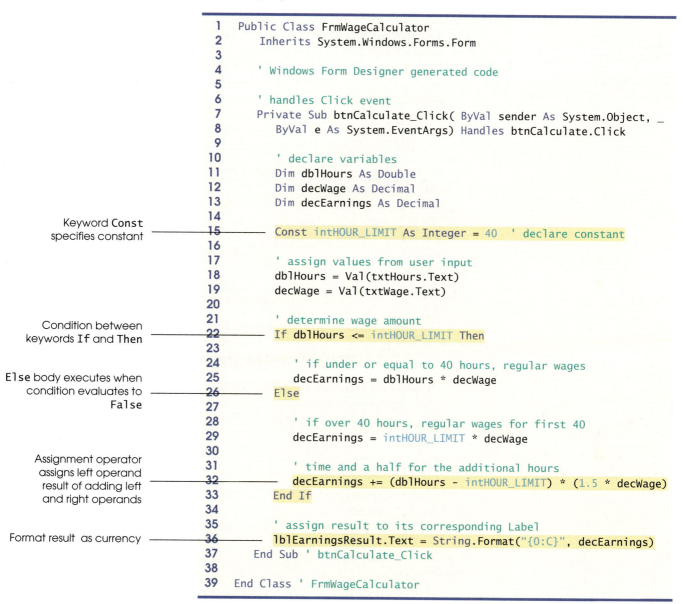

```vb
1  Public Class FrmWageCalculator
2      Inherits System.Windows.Forms.Form
3
4      ' Windows Form Designer generated code
5
6      ' handles Click event
7      Private Sub btnCalculate_Click( ByVal sender As System.Object, _
8          ByVal e As System.EventArgs) Handles btnCalculate.Click
9
10         ' declare variables
11         Dim dblHours As Double
12         Dim decWage As Decimal
13         Dim decEarnings As Decimal
14
15         Const intHOUR_LIMIT As Integer = 40  ' declare constant
16
17         ' assign values from user input
18         dblHours = Val(txtHours.Text)
19         decWage = Val(txtWage.Text)
20
21         ' determine wage amount
22         If dblHours <= intHOUR_LIMIT Then
23
24             ' if under or equal to 40 hours, regular wages
25             decEarnings = dblHours * decWage
26         Else
27
28             ' if over 40 hours, regular wages for first 40
29             decEarnings = intHOUR_LIMIT * decWage
30
31             ' time and a half for the additional hours
32             decEarnings += (dblHours - intHOUR_LIMIT) * (1.5 * decWage)
33         End If
34
35         ' assign result to its corresponding Label
36         lblEarningsResult.Text = String.Format("{0:C}", decEarnings)
37     End Sub ' btnCalculate_Click
38
39  End Class ' FrmWageCalculator
```

Keyword **Const** specifies constant — 15

Condition between keywords **If** and **Then** — 22

Else body executes when condition evaluates to **False** — 26

Assignment operator assigns left operand result of adding left and right operands — 32

Format result as currency — 36

Figure 7.23   **Wage Calculator** application code.

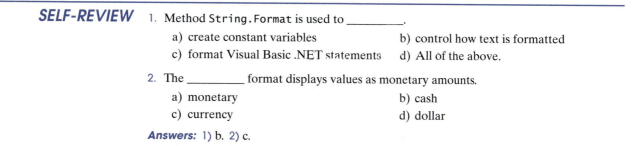

SELF-REVIEW

1. Method `String.Format` is used to _____.

    a) create constant variables   b) control how text is formatted

    c) format Visual Basic .NET statements   d) All of the above.

2. The _____ format displays values as monetary amounts.

    a) monetary   b) cash

    c) currency   d) dollar

Answers: 1) b. 2) c.

7.10 Using the Debugger: The Watch Window

Visual Studio .NET includes several debugging windows that are accessible from the **Debug > Windows** submenu. The **Watch window**, which is available only in break mode, allows the programmer to examine the value of a variable or expression. You can use the **Watch** window to view changes in a variable's value as the application executes, or you can change a variable's value yourself by entering the new value directly into the **Watch** window. Each expression or variable that is added to the **Watch** window is called a **watch**. In the following box, we demonstrate how to add, remove and manipulate watches by using the **Watch** window.

Using the Debugger: The Watch Window

1. ***Starting debugging.*** If the IDE is not in code view, switch to code view now. Set breakpoints on lines 144 and 150 (Fig. 7.24). Select **Debug > Start** to run the application. The **Wage Calculator** Form appears. Enter 12 into the **Hourly wage:** TextBox and 40 into the **Weekly hours:** TextBox (Fig. 7.25). Click the **Calculate** Button.

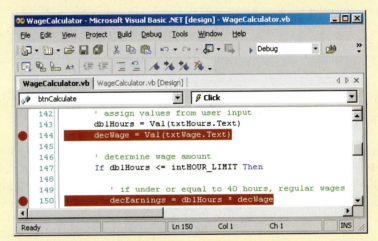

Figure 7.24 Breakpoints added to **Wage Calculator** application.

Figure 7.25 **Wage Calculator** application.

2. ***Suspending application execution.*** Clicking the **Calculate** Button will cause event handler btnCalculate_Click to execute until the breakpoint is reached. When the breakpoint is reached, application execution is paused, and the IDE switches into break mode. Notice that the **active window** has been changed from the running application to the IDE. The active window is the window that is currently being used and is sometimes referred to as the window that has the **focus**. The **Wage Calculator** application is still running, but it is hidden behind the IDE.

(cont.)

3. ***Examining data.*** Once the application has entered break mode, you are free to explore the values of various variables, using the debugger's **Watch** window. To display the **Watch** window, select **Debug > Windows > Watch > Watch 1**. Notice that there are actually four options in the **Debug > Windows > Watch** menu—**Watch 1**, **Watch 2**, **Watch 3** and **Watch 4**. Each window provides the same functionality. The four options simply allow you to have several **Watch** windows open at once. This enables you to display data side by side or to set the different **Watch** windows to display data in different formats. The **Watch** window (Fig. 7.26) is initially empty. To add a watch, you can type an expression into the **Name** column. Single click in the first field of the **Name** column. Type dblHours, then press *Enter*. The value and type will be added by the IDE (Fig. 7.26). Notice that this value is 40.0—the value assigned to dblHours on line 143. Type decWage in the next row, then press *Enter*. The value displayed for decWage is 0D. The D indicates that the number stored in decWage is of type `Decimal`.

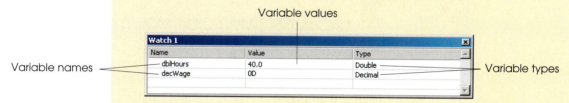

Figure 7.26 **Watch** window.

4. ***Examining different expressions.*** Add the expression (decWage + 3) * 5 into the **Watch 1** window. Notice that the **Watch** window can evaluate arithmetic expressions, returning the value **15D**. Add the expression decWage = 3 into the **Watch 1** window. Expressions containing the = symbol are treated as `Boolean` expressions instead of assignment statements. The value returned is **False**, because decWage does not currently contain the value 3. Add the expression intVariableThatDoesNotExist into the **Watch 1** window. This identifier does not exist in the current application, and therefore cannot be evaluated. An appropriate message is displayed in the **Value** field. Your **Watch** window should look similar to Fig. 7.27.

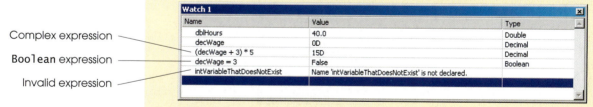

Figure 7.27 Examining expressions.

5. ***Removing an expression from the Watch window.*** At this point, we would like to clear the final expressions from the **Watch** window. To remove an expression, simply right click the expression in the **Watch** window and select **Delete Watch** (Fig. 7.28). Remove all the expressions that you added in *Step 4*.

(cont.)

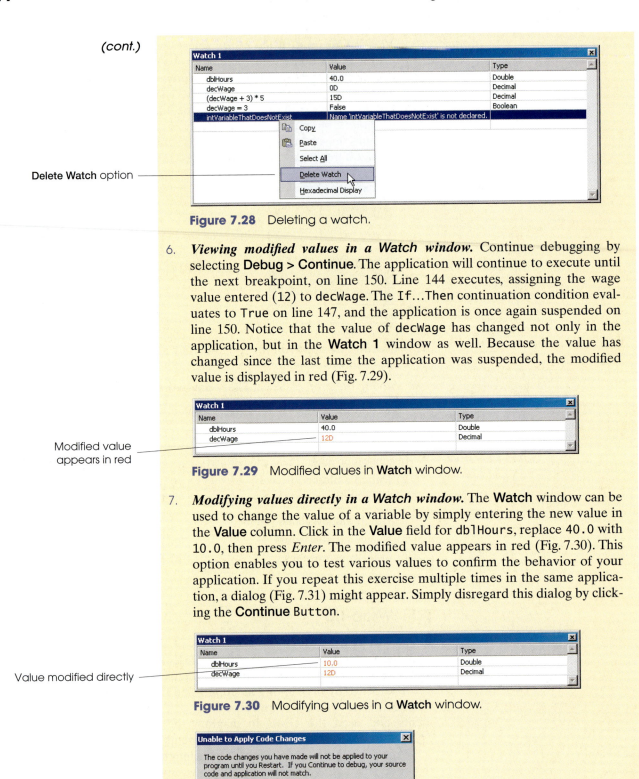

Delete Watch option —

Figure 7.28 Deleting a watch.

6. *Viewing modified values in a Watch window.* Continue debugging by selecting **Debug > Continue.** The application will continue to execute until the next breakpoint, on line 150. Line 144 executes, assigning the wage value entered (12) to decWage. The If...Then continuation condition evaluates to True on line 147, and the application is once again suspended on line 150. Notice that the value of decWage has changed not only in the application, but in the **Watch 1** window as well. Because the value has changed since the last time the application was suspended, the modified value is displayed in red (Fig. 7.29).

Modified value appears in red

Figure 7.29 Modified values in **Watch** window.

7. *Modifying values directly in a Watch window.* The **Watch** window can be used to change the value of a variable by simply entering the new value in the **Value** column. Click in the **Value** field for dblHours, replace 40.0 with 10.0, then press *Enter*. The modified value appears in red (Fig. 7.30). This option enables you to test various values to confirm the behavior of your application. If you repeat this exercise multiple times in the same application, a dialog (Fig. 7.31) might appear. Simply disregard this dialog by clicking the **Continue** Button.

Value modified directly —

Figure 7.30 Modifying values in a **Watch** window.

Figure 7.31 Dialog to continue running application after changing values in the **Watch** window.

(cont.)

8. ***Viewing the application result.*** Select **Debug > Continue** to continue application execution. Event handler btnCalculate_Click finishes execution and displays the result in a Label. Notice that the result is $120.00, because we changed dblHours to 10.0 in the last step. The TextBox to the right of **Weekly hours:** still displays the value 40, because we changed the value of dblHours, but not the Text property of either TextBoxes. Once the application has finished running, the focus is returned to the **Wage Calculator** window, and the final results are displayed (Fig. 7.32).

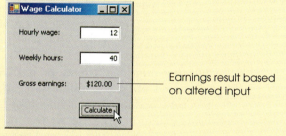

Earnings result based on altered input

Figure 7.32 Output displayed after the debugging process.

9. ***Closing the application.*** To close your application, either click the running application's close box or select **Debug > Stop Debugging**.

10. ***Saving the project.*** Select **File > Save All** to save your modified code.

11. ***Closing the IDE.*** Close Visual Studio .NET by clicking its close box.

SELF-REVIEW

1. An application enters break mode when _____.
   a) **Debug > Start** is selected
   b) a breakpoint is reached
   c) the **Watch** window is used
   d) there is a syntax error

2. The **Watch** window allows you to _____.
   a) change variable values
   b) view variable type information
   c) evaluate expressions
   d) All of the above.

Answers: 1) b. 2) d.

7.11 Wrap-Up

In this tutorial, we discussed techniques of solving programming problems. We introduced algorithms, pseudocode, the UML and control structures. We discussed different types of control structures and when each might be used.

You began by test-driving an application that used the If...Then...Else statement to determine an employee's weekly pay. You studied different control statements and used the UML to diagram the decision-making processes of the If...Then and the If...Then...Else statements.

You learned how to format text by using the method String.Format and how to abbreviate mathematical statements by using the assignment operators.

In the *Using the Debugger* section, you learned how to use the **Watch** window to view an application's data. You learned how to add watches, remove watches and change variable values.

In the next tutorial you will learn how to display message dialogs based on user input. You will study the logical operators, which give you more expressive power for forming the conditions in your control statements. You will use the CheckBox control to allow the user to select from various options in an application.

SKILLS SUMMARY

Choosing Among Alternate Courses of Action
- Use the `If...Then` or `If...Then...Else` control statements.

Conceptualizing the Application Before Using Visual Studio .NET
- Use pseudocode.
- Create an Action/Control/Event (ACE) table.

Understanding Control Statements
- View the control statement's corresponding UML diagram.

Performing Comparisons
- Use the equality and relational operators.

Creating a Constant
- Use the `Const` keyword.
- Assign a value to the constant in the declaration.

Abbreviating Assignment Expressions
- Use the assignment operators.

Formatting a Value As a Monetary Amount
- Use the format code `C` in method `String.Format`.

Examining Data During Application Execution
- Use the debugger to set a breakpoint, and examine the **Watch** window.

KEY TERMS

action/decision model of programming—Representing control statements as UML activity diagrams with rounded rectangles indicating *actions* to be performed and diamond symbols indicating *decisions* to be made.

action expression (in the UML)—Used in an action state within a UML activity diagram to specify a particular action to perform.

action state—An action to perform in a UML activity diagram that is represented by an action-state symbol.

action-state symbol—A rectangle with its left and right sides replaced with arcs curving outward that represents an action to perform in a UML activity diagram.

active window—The window that is currently being used—sometimes referred to as the window that has the focus.

activity diagram—A UML diagram that models the activity (also called the workflow) of a portion of a software system.

algorithm—A procedure for solving a problem, specifying the actions to be executed and the order in which these actions are to be executed.

block—A group of code statements.

Boolean data type—A data type that has the value `True` or `False`.

condition— An expression with a true or false value that is used to make a decision.

control structure (control statement)—An application component that specifies the order in which statements execute (also known as the flow of control).

control structure (statement) nesting—Placing one control statement in the body of another control statement.

control structure (statement) stacking—A set of control statements in sequence. The exit point of one control statement is connected to the entry point of the next control statement in sequence.

constant—A variable whose value cannot be changed after its initial declaration.

currency format—Used to display values as monetary amounts.

Decimal data type—Used to store monetary amounts.

decision symbol—The diamond-shaped symbol in a UML activity diagram that indicates that a decision is to be made.

diamond—A symbol (also known as the decision symbol) in a UML activity diagram; this symbol indicates that a decision is to be made.

dotted line—A UML activity diagram symbol that connects each UML-style note with the element that the note describes.

double-selection statement—A statement, such as If...Then...Else, that selects between two different actions or sequences of actions.

ElseIf keyword—Keyword used for the nested conditions in nested If...Then...Else statements.

equality operators—Operators = (is equal to) and <> (is not equal to) that compare two values.

executable statement—Actions that are performed when the corresponding Visual Basic .NET application is run.

fatal logic error—An error that causes an application to fail and terminate prematurely.

focus—Designates the window currently in use.

format control string—A string that specifies how data should be formatted.

format specifier—Code that specifies the type of format that should be applied to a string for output.

formatting—Modifying the appearance of text for display purposes.

final state—Represented by a solid circle surrounded by a hollow circle in a UML activity diagram; the end of the workflow after an application performs its activities.

guard condition—An expression contained in square brackets above or next to the arrows leading from a decision symbol in a UML activity diagram that determines whether workflow continues along a path.

If...Then—Selection statement that performs an action (or sequence of actions) based on a condition. This is also called the single-selection statement.

If...Then...Else—Selection statement that performs an action (or sequence of actions) if a condition is true and performs a different action (or sequence of actions) if the condition is false. This is also called the double-selection statement.

initial state—The beginning of the workflow in a UML activity diagram before the application performs the modeled activities.

multiple-selection statement—A statement that selects from among many different actions or sequences of actions.

nested statement—A statement that is placed inside another control statement.

nonfatal logic error—An error that does not terminate an application's execution but causes an application to produce incorrect results.

note—An explanatory remark (represented by a rectangle with a folded upper-right corner) describing the purpose of a symbol in a UML activity diagram.

program control—The task of ordering an application's statements in the correct order.

pseudocode—An informal language that helps programmers develop algorithms.

relational operators—Operators < (less than), > (greater than), <= (less than or equal to) and >= (greater than or eqaul to) that compare two values.

repetition structure (or repetition statement)—Allows the programmer to specify that an action or actions should be repeated, depending on the value of a condition.

selection structure (or selection statement)—Selects among alternative courses of action.

sequential execution—Statements in an application are executed one after another in the order in which they are written.

sequence structure (or sequence statement)—Built into Visual Basic .NET—unless directed to act otherwise, the computer executes Visual Basic .NET statements sequentially.

single-entry/single-exit control structure (or statement)—A control statement that has one entry point and one exit point. All Visual Basic .NET control statements are single-entry/single-exit control statements.

single-selection statement—The If...Then statement, which selects or ignores a single action or sequence of actions.

small circles (in the UML)—The solid circle in an activity diagram represents the activity's initial state and the solid circle surrounded by a hollow circle represents the activity's final state.

solid circle (in the UML)—A UML activity diagram symbol that represents the activity's initial state.

String.Format method—Formats a string.

structured programming—A technique for organizing program control to help you develop applications that are easy to understand, debug and modify.

transfer of control—Occurs when an executed statement does not directly follow the previously executed statement in the written application.

transition—A change from one action state to another that is represented by transition arrows in a UML activity diagram.

UML (Unified Modeling Language)—An industry standard for modeling software systems graphically.

Watch window—A Visual Studio .NET window that allows you to view variable values as an application is being debugged.

workflow—The activity of a portion of a software system.

GUI DESIGN GUIDELINES

Overall Design
■ Format all monetary amounts using the C (currency) format specifier.

TextBox
■ When using multiple TextBoxes vertically, align the TextBoxes on their right sides, and where possible make the TextBoxes the same size. Left-align the descriptive Labels for such TextBoxes.

CONTROLS, EVENTS, PROPERTIES & METHODS

String This control allows the user to input data from the keyboard.

■ *Methods*

Format—Arranges the String in a specified format.

MULTIPLE-CHOICE QUESTIONS

7.1 The _____ operator returns False if the left operand is larger than the right operand.

a) =   b) <
c) <=   d) All of the above.

7.2 A _____ occurs when an executed statement does not directly follow the previously executed statement in the written application.

a) transition   b) flow
c) logical error   d) transfer of control

7.3 A variable or an expression that is added to the **Watch** window is known as a _____.

a) watched variable   b) watched expression
c) watch   d) watched value

7.4 The If...Then statement is called a _____ statement because it selects or ignores one action.

a) single-selection   b) multiple-selection
c) double-selection   d) repetition

7.5 The three types of control statements are the sequence statement, the selection statement and the _____ statement.

a) repeat   b) looping
c) redo   d) repetition

7.6 In an activity diagram, a rectangle with curved sides represents _____.

a) a complete algorithm   b) a comment
c) an action   d) the termination of the application

7.7 The If...Then...Else selection statement ends with the keywords _____.

a) End If Then Else

b) End If Else

c) End Else

d) End If

7.8 A variable of data type Boolean can be assigned keyword _____ or keyword _____.

a) True, False

b) Off, On

c) True, NotTrue

d) Yes, No

7.9 A variable whose value cannot be changed after its initial declaration is called a _____.

a) Double

b) constant

c) standard

d) Boolean

7.10 The _____ operator assigns the result of adding the left and right operands to the left operand.

a) +

b) =+

c) +=

d) + =

EXERCISES

7.11 *(Currency Converter Application)* Develop an application that functions as a currency converter as shown in Fig. 7.33. Users must provide a number in the **Dollars:** TextBox and a currency name (as text) in the **Convert from Dollars to:** TextBox. Clicking the **Convert** Button will convert the specified amount into the indicated currency and display it in a Label. Limit yourself to the following currencies as user input: Dollars, Euros, Yen and Pesos. Use the following exchange rates: **1 Dollar = 1.02 Euros, 120 Yen** and **10 Pesos.**

Figure 7.33   **Currency Converter** GUI.

a) *Copying the template to your working directory.* Copy the directory C:\Examples\ Tutorial07\Exercises\CurrencyConverter to your C:\SimplyVB directory.

b) *Opening the application's template file.* Double click CurrencyConverter.sln in the CurrencyConverter directory to open the application.

c) *Add an event handler for the Convert Button's Click event.* Double click the **Convert** Button to generate an empty event handler for the Button's Click event. The code for *Steps d–f* belongs in this event handler.

d) *Obtaining the user input.* Use the Val function to convert the user input from the **Dollars:** TextBox to a Double. Assign the Double to a Decimal variable decAmount. Visual Basic .NET implicitly performs this conversion from Double to Decimal.

e) *Performing the conversion.* Use an If...ElseIf...ElseIf statement to determine which currency the user entered. Assign the result of the conversion to decAmount.

f) *Displaying the result.* Display the result using method String.Format with format specifier F.

g) *Running the application.* Select **Debug > Start** to run your application. Enter a value in dollars to be converted and the name of the currency you wish to convert to. Click the **Convert** Button and, using the exchange rates above, verify that the correct output is displays.

h) *Closing the application.* Close your running application by clicking its close box.

i) *Closing the IDE.* Close Visual Studio .NET by clicking its close box.

7.12 *(Wage Calculator that Performs Tax Calculations)* Develop an application that calcu-lates an employee's wages as shown in Fig. 7.34. The user should provide the hourly wage and number of hours worked per week. When the **Calculate** Button is clicked, the gross earnings of the user should display in the **Gross earnings:** TextBox. The **Less FWT:** TextBox should display the amount deducted for Federal taxes and the **Net earnings:** TextBox displays the difference between the gross earnings and the Federal tax amount. Assume overtime wages are 1.5 times the hourly wage and Federal taxes are 15% of gross earnings. The **Clear** But-ton should clear all fields.

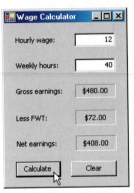

Figure 7.34 Wage Calculator GUI.

a) *Copying the template to your working directory.* Copy the directory C:\Examples\ Tutorial07\Exercises\ExpandedWageCalculator to your C:\SimplyVB directory.

b) *Opening the application's template file.* Double click WageCalculator.sln in the ExpandedWageCalculator directory to open the application.

c) *Modifying the Calculate Button's Click event handler.* Add the code for *Steps d–f* to btnCalculate_Click.

d) *Adding a new variable.* Declare decFederalTaxes to store the amount deducted for Federal taxes.

e) *Calculating and displaying the Federal taxes deducted.* Multiply the total earnings (decEarnings) by 0.15 (that is, 15%) to determine the amount to be removed for taxes. Assign the result to decFederalTaxes. Display this value using method String.Format with format specifier C.

f) *Calculating and displaying the employee's net pay.* Subtract decFederalTaxes from decEarnings to calculate the employee's net earnings. Display this value using method String.Format with format specifier C.

g) *Creating an event handler for the Clear Button.* Double click the **Clear** Button to generate an empty event handler for the Click event. This event handler should clear user input from the two TextBoxes and the results from the three Labels.

h) *Running the application.* Select **Debug > Start** to run your application. Enter an hourly wage and the number of hours worked. Click the **Calculate** Button and verify that the appropriate output is displayed for gross earnings, amount taken out for fed-eral taxes and the net earnings. Click the **Clear** Button and check that all fields are cleared.

i) *Closing the application.* Close your running application by clicking its close box.

j) *Closing the IDE.* Close Visual Studio .NET by clicking its close box.

7.13 *(Customer Charge Account Analyzer Application)* Develop an application (as shown in Fig. 7.35) that determines whether a department-store customer has exceeded the credit limit on a charge account. Each customer enters an account number (an Integer), a balance at the beginning of the month (a Decimal), the total of all items charged this month (a Deci-mal), the total of all credits applied to the customer's account this month (a Decimal), and the customer's allowed credit limit (a Decimal). The application should input each of these facts, calculate the new balance (= *beginning balance – credits + charges*), display the new bal-ance and determine whether the new balance exceeds the customer's credit limit. If the cus-tomer's credit limit is exceeded, the application should display a message (in a Label at the bottom of the Form) informing the customer of this fact.

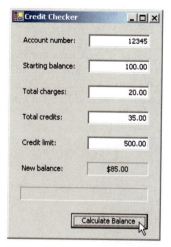

Figure 7.35 Credit Checker GUI.

a) *Copying the template application to your working directory.* Copy the directory C:\Examples\Tutorial07\Exercises\CreditChecker to C:\SimplyVB.

b) *Opening the application's template file.* Double click Credit Checker.sln in the CreditChecker directory to open the application.

c) *Adding the Calculate Button's Click event handler.* Double click the **Calculate Balance** Button to generate the empty event handler for the Click event. The code for *Steps d–g* is added to this event handler.

d) *Declaring variables.* Declare an Integer variable to store the account number. Declare four Decimal variables to store the starting balance, charges, credits and credit limit. Declare a fifth Decimal variable to store the new balance in the account after the credits and charges have been applied.

e) *Obtaining user input.* Obtain the user input from the TextBoxes' Text properties.

f) *Calculating and displaying the new balance.* Calculate the new balance by adding the total credits to the starting balance and subtracting the charges. Assign the result to a variable. Display the result formatted as currency.

g) *Determining if the credit limit has been exceeded.* If the new balance exceeds the specified credit limit, a message should be displayed in lblError.

h) *Handling the Account number: TextBox's TextChanged event.* Double click the **Account number:** TextBox to generate its TextChanged event handler. This event handler should clear the other TextBoxes, the error message Label and the result Label.

i) *Running the application.* Select **Debug > Start** to run your application. Enter an account number, your starting balance, the amount charged to your account, the amount credited to your account and your credit limit. Click the **Calculate Balance** Button and verify that the new balance displayed is correct. Enter an amount charged that exceeds your credit limit. Click the **Calculate Balance** Button and ensure that a message is displayed in the lower Label.

j) *Closing the application.* Close your running application by clicking its close box.

k) *Closing the IDE.* Close Visual Studio .NET by clicking its close box.

What does this code do? ▶

7.14 Assume that txtAge is a TextBox control and that the user has entered the value 27 into this TextBox. Determine the action performed by the following code:

```
1  Dim intAge As Integer
2
3  intAge = Val(txtAge.Text)
4
5  If intAge < 0 Then
6      txtAge.Text = "Enter a value greater than or equal to zero."
7  ElseIf intAge < 13 Then
8      txtAge.Text = "Child"
9  ElseIf intAge < 20 Then
10     txtAge.Text = "Teenager"
11 ElseIf intAge < 30 Then
12     txtAge.Text = "Young Adult"
13 ElseIf intAge < 65 Then
14     txtAge.Text = "Adult"
15 Else
16     txtAge.Text = "Senior Citizen"
17 End If
```

What's wrong with this code? ▶

7.15 Assume that lblAMPM is a Label control. Find the error(s) in the following code:

```
1  Dim intHour As Integer
2
3  intHour = 14
4
5  If intHour < 11 Then
6      If intHour > 0 Then
7          lblAMPM.Text = "AM"
8      End If
9  Else
10     lblAMPM.Text = "PM"
11 ElseIf intHour > 23 Then
12     lblAMPM.Text = "Time Error."
13 End If
```

Using the Debugger ▶

7.16 *(Grade Calculator Application)* Copy the C:\Examples\Tutorial07\Debugger directory to your working directory. This directory contains the Grades application, which takes a number from the user and displays the corresponding letter grade. For values 90–100 it should display **A**; for 80–89, **B**, for 70–79, **C**, for 60–69, **D** and for anything lower, an **F**. Run the application. Enter the value 85 in the TextBox and click **Calculate**. Notice that the application displays **D** when it ought to display **B**. Select **View > Code** to enter the code editor and set as many breakpoints as you feel necessary. Select **Debug > Start** to use the debugger to help you find the error(s). Figure 7.36 shows the incorrect output when the value 85 is input.

Figure 7.36 Incorrect output for **Grade** application.

Programming Challenge ▶

7.17 *(Encryption Application)* A company transmits data over the telephone, but it is concerned that its phones could be tapped. All its data is transmitted as four-digit Integers. The company has asked you to write an application that encrypts its data so that it may be transmitted more securely. Encryption is the process of transforming data for security reasons. Create a Form similar to Fig. 7.37. Your application should read four-digits entered by the user and encrypt the information as follows:

a) Replace each digit by *(the sum of that digit plus 7)* Mod *10.*

b) Swap the first digit with the third, and swap the second digit with the fourth.

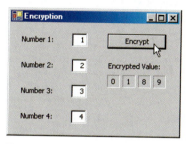

Figure 7.37 **Encryption** application.

Dental Payment Application

Introducing CheckBoxes and Message Dialogs

Objectives

In this tutorial, you will learn to:

■ Use **CheckBox**es to allow users to select options.
■ Use dialogs to display messages.
■ Use logical operators to form more powerful conditions.

Outline

8.1 Test-Driving the Dental Payment Application

8.2 Designing the Dental Payment Application

8.3 Using **CheckBoxes**

8.4 Using a Dialog to Display a Message

8.5 Logical Operators

8.6 Wrap-Up

Many Visual Basic .NET applications use **dialogs** (also called **message dialogs**), which are windows that display messages to users. You encounter many dialogs while using a computer, from those that instruct you to select files or enter passwords to others that notify you of problems while using an application. In this tutorial, you will learn how to use message dialogs to inform users of input problems.

You may have noticed that TextBoxes allow users to enter nearly any value as input. In some cases, you may want to use controls that provide users with pre-defined options. One way to do this is by providing CheckBoxes in your application. You also will learn about logical operators, which you can use in your applications to make more involved decisions based on user input.

8.1 Test-Driving the Dental Payment Application

When you visit the dentist, there are many procedures that the dentist can perform. The office assistant may present you with a bill generated by a computer. In this tutorial, you will program an application that prepares a bill for some basic dental procedures. This application must meet the following requirements:

Application Requirements

A dentist's office administrator wishes to create an application that employees can use to bill patients. The application must allow users to enter the patient's name and specify which services were performed during the visit. The application will then calculate the total charges. If a user attempts to calculate a bill before any services are specified, or before the patient's name is entered, a message will be displayed.

In the **Dental Payment** application, you will use CheckBox controls and a message dialog to assist the user in entering data. You begin by test-driving the completed application. Then, you will learn the additional Visual Basic .NET technologies that you will need to create your own version of this application.

Test-Driving the Dental Payment Application

1. ***Opening the completed application.*** Open the directory `C:\Examples\Tutorial08\CompletedApplication\DentalPayment` to locate the **Dental Payment** application. Double click `DentalPayment.sln` to open the application in Visual Studio .NET.

2. ***Running the Dental Payment application.*** Select **Debug > Start** to run the application (Fig. 8.1).

   Notice that there are three square-shaped controls in the left column of the **Form**. These are known as **CheckBox** controls. A CheckBox is a small white square that either is blank or contains a check mark. When a CheckBox is selected, a black check mark appears in the box (☑). A CheckBox can be selected by simply clicking within the CheckBox's small white square or by clicking on the text of the CheckBox. A selected CheckBox can be unchecked in the same way. You will learn how to add CheckBox controls to a Form shortly.

CheckBox controls (unchecked)

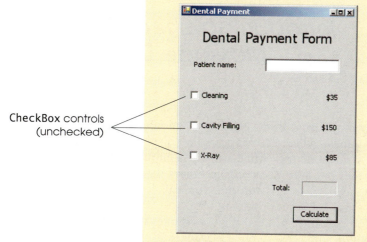

Figure 8.1   Running the completed **Dental Payment** application.

3. ***Attempting to calculate a total without entering input.*** Leave the **Patient name** field blank, and deselect any CheckBoxes that you have selected. Click the **Calculate** Button. Notice that a message dialog appears indicating that you must enter data (Fig. 8.2). Close this dialog by clicking its **OK** Button.

Figure 8.2   Message dialog appears when no name is entered and/or no CheckBoxes are selected.

4. ***Entering quantities in the application.*** The **Dental Payment** Form is still displayed. Type Bob Jones in the **Patient name** field. Check all three CheckBoxes by clicking each one. Notice that a check mark appears in each CheckBox.

5. ***Unchecking the Cavity Filling CheckBox.*** Click the **Cavity Filling** CheckBox to remove its check mark. Only the **Cleaning** and **X-Ray** CheckBoxes should now be selected (Fig. 8.3).

(cont.)

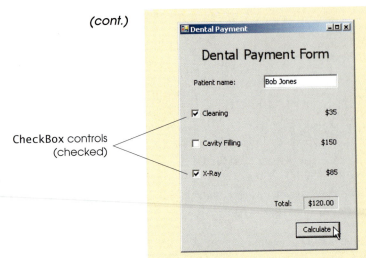

Figure 8.3 Dental Payment application with input entered.

6. ***Determining the bill.*** Click the **Calculate** Button. This causes the application to total the price of the services performed during the dentist visit. The result is displayed in the **Total:** field.

7. ***Closing the application.*** Close your running application by clicking its close box.

8. ***Closing the IDE.*** Close Visual Studio .NET by clicking its close box.

8.2 Designing the Dental Payment Application

Recall that pseudocode is an informal language that helps programmers develop algorithms. The following pseudocode describes the basic operation of the **Dental Payment** application, which runs when the user clicks **Calculate**:

When the user clicks the Calculate Button

   Clear previous total

   If user has not entered a patient name or has not selected any CheckBoxes
      Display message in dialog
   Else
      Initialize the total to zero

      If "Cleaning" CheckBox is selected
         Add cost of a cleaning to the total

      If "Cavity Filling" CheckBox is selected
         Add cost of receiving a cavity filling to the total

      If "X-Ray" CheckBox is selected
         Add cost of receiving an x-ray to the total

      Format total to be displayed as currency
      Display total

Now that you have test-driven the **Dental Payment** application and studied its pseudocode representation, you will use an ACE table to help you convert the pseudocode to Visual Basic .NET. Figure 8.4 lists the actions, controls and events that will help you complete your own version of this application. Data is input using a TextBox (txtName) and CheckBoxes (chkClean, chkCavity and chkXRay). Output is displayed in Label lblTotalResult when a Button (btnCalculate) is clicked. Field names are displayed in the Form's other Labels.

Action/Control/Event (ACE) Table for the Dental Payment Application

Action	Control/Class/Object	Event
Label all the application's controls	lblTitle, lblName, lblTotal, lblCleanCost, lblFillingCost, lblXRayCost	Application is run
	btnCalculate	Click
Clear previous tutorial	lblTotalResult	
If user has not entered a patient name or has not selected any CheckBoxes	chkClean, chkCavity, chkXRay	
Display message in dialog	MessageBox	
Else Initialize the total to zero		
If "Cleaning" CheckBox is selected Add cost of a cleaning to the total	chkClean	
If "Cavity Filling" CheckBox is selected Add cost of receiving a cavity filling to the total	chkCavity	
If "X-Ray" CheckBox is selected Add cost of receiving an x-ray to the total	chkXRay	
Format total to be displayed as currency	String	
Display total	lblTotalResult	

Figure 8.4 Action/Control/Event table for **Dental Payment** application.

8.3 Using CheckBoxes

As mentioned earlier, a CheckBox is a small white square that either is blank or contains a check mark. (A CheckBox is known as a **state button**, because it can be in the on/off [true/false] state.) When a CheckBox is selected, a black check mark appears in the box. Any number of CheckBoxes can be selected at a time, including none at all. The text that appears alongside a CheckBox is called the **CheckBox label**.

    You can determine whether a CheckBox is on (that is, checked) by using the **Checked property**. If the CheckBox is checked, the Checked property returns the Boolean value True when accessed. If the CheckBox is not checked, the Checked property returns False when accessed.

    You will now create the **Dental Payment** application from the template provided. The following box demonstrates how to add the CheckBoxes to your application. The application you will build in the next two boxes will not display a dialog if the TextBox is empty and/or all the CheckBoxes are unchecked when the **Calculate Button** is clicked. You will learn how to display that dialog in Section 8.4.

GUI Design Tip

A CheckBox's label should be descriptive and as short as possible. When a CheckBox label contains more than one word, use book-title capitalization.

Adding CheckBoxes to the Form

1. ***Copying the template application to your working directory.*** Copy the C:\Examples\Tutorial08\TemplateApplication\DentalPayment directory to your C:\SimplyVB directory.

2. ***Opening the Dental Payment application's template file.*** Double click DentalPayment.sln in the DentalPayment directory to open the application in Visual Studio .NET.

(cont.)

3. ***Adding CheckBox controls to the Form.*** Add a CheckBox to the Form by double clicking the

☑ CheckBox

icon in the **Toolbox**. Repeat this process until three CheckBoxes have been added to the Form.

4. ***Customizing the CheckBoxes.*** For this application, you will be modifying the Location, Text, Size and Name properties of each CheckBox. Change the Size property of all three CheckBoxes to 122, 24. Change the Name property of the first CheckBox to chkClean and set its Location property to 16, 112 and its Text property to Cleaning. Change the Name property of the second CheckBox to chkCavity, its Location property to 16, 159 and its Text property to Cavity Filling. Change the Name property of the final CheckBox to chkXRay, its Location property to 16, 206 and its Text property to X-Ray.

5. ***Saving the project.*** Select **File > Save All** to save your changes.

GUI Design Tip

Align groups of CheckBoxes either horizontally or vertically.

After placing the CheckBoxes on the Form and setting their properties, you need to code an event handler to enhance the application's functionality when users select CheckBoxes and click **Calculate**.

Adding the Calculate Button's Event Handler

1. ***Adding an event handler for btnCalculate's Click event.*** Double click the **Calculate** Button on the Form to create an event handler for that control's Click event.

2. ***Adding If...Then statements to calculate the patient's bill.*** Add lines 191–213 of Fig. 8.5 to your application. Be sure to include all blank lines and line-continuation characters shown in Fig. 8.5 to improve code readability and to ensure that your line numbers correspond to the figure's.

   Line 192 clears any text in the output Label that may be present from a previous calculation. Line 195 declares variable intTotal, which stores the total charges for the patient as an Integer. This variable is initialized to 0. Lines 197–210 define three If...Then statements that determine whether the user has checked any of the Form's CheckBoxes. Each If...Then statement's condition compares a CheckBox's Checked property to True. For each If...Then statement, the dollar value of the service is added to intTotal if the current CheckBox is checked. The first If...Then statement, for example, adds 35 to intTotal on line 199 if CheckBox chkClean is selected (line 198). Notice that the numeric values added to intTotal correspond to the monetary values indicated on the GUI, to the right of each service. Line 213 displays the total (formatted as a currency amount) in lblTotalResult.

3. ***Running the application.*** Select **Debug > Start** to run your application. Notice that the user is not required to enter a name or select any Check-Boxes before clicking the **Calculate** Button. If no CheckBoxes are selected, the bill displays the value **$0.00** (Fig. 8.6).

4. ***Selecting a CheckBox.*** Select the **Cleaning** CheckBox, and click the **Calculate** Button. Notice that the **Total:** field now displays **$35.00**.

5. ***Closing the application.*** Close your running application by clicking its close box.

(cont.)

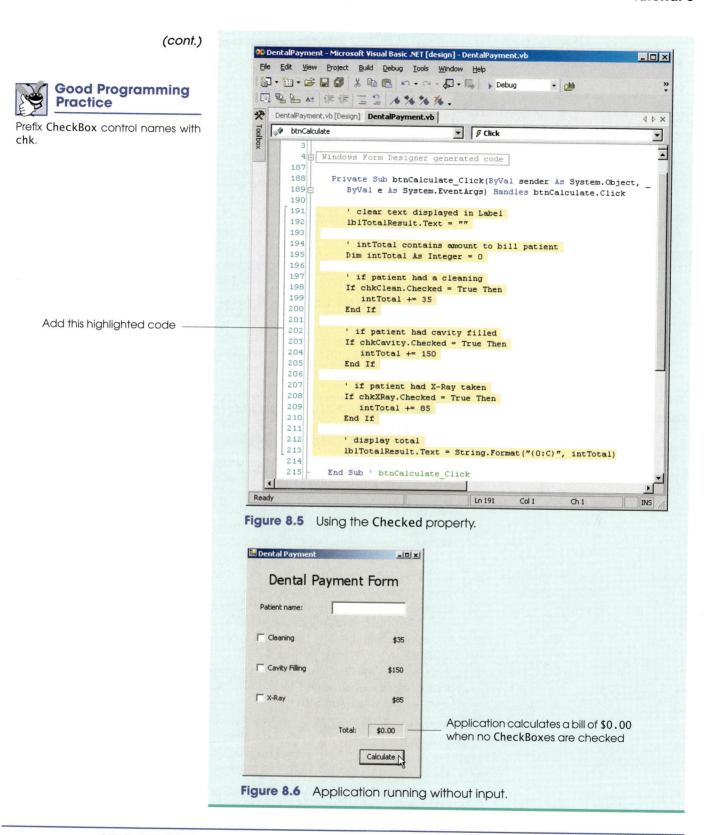

Good Programming Practice

Prefix **CheckBox** control names with chk.

Add this highlighted code ──────

Figure 8.5 Using the **Checked** property.

Application calculates a bill of $0.00 when no **CheckBoxes** are checked

Figure 8.6 Application running without input.

SELF-REVIEW 1. The _____ property sets a CheckBox's text.

    a) `Text`   b) `Value`

    c) `Label`   d) `Checked`

2. Which property determines whether a CheckBox is selected?

   a) Selected   b) Checked

   c) Clicked   d) Check

Answers: 1.) a. 2.) b.

8.4 Using a Dialog to Display a Message

In the completed application, a message is displayed in a dialog if the user attempts to calculate the total charges without specifying which services were performed and/or without entering a name. In this section, you will learn how to display a dialog when a patient name is not input. In Section 8.5, Logical Operators, you will learn how to write code to determine if at least one CheckBox is checked. When the dialog is closed, control is returned to the application's Form. The message dialog used in your application is displayed in Fig. 8.7.

Title bar — Icon indicates the tone of the message — OK Button allows the user to close the dialog

Close box — Dialog sized to accommodate contents

Figure 8.7 Dialog displayed by the application.

Notice that the message dialog contains a title bar and a close box. This dialog also contains a message (Please enter a name and check at least one item), an OK Button that allows the user to **dismiss** (close) the dialog (which the user must do to proceed) and an icon that indicates the tone of the message. (In this case, ⚠ indicates that a problem has occurred.)

Message dialogs are defined by class **MessageBox** and can be displayed by using method **MessageBox.Show**. The message dialog is customized by the arguments passed to method MessageBox.Show. The following box demonstrates displaying a message dialog based on a condition.

GUI Design Tip

Text displayed in a dialog should be descriptive and as short as possible.

Displaying a Message Dialog Using MessageBox.Show

1. ***Adding an If...Then statement to the event handler for btnCalculate's Click event.*** The message should display only if the user does not enter the patient's name. Place the cursor on line 193 and press *Enter*. Then insert lines 194–197 of Fig. 8.8 into your event handler. Be sure to include a blank line after the End If statement.

Add this highlighted code —

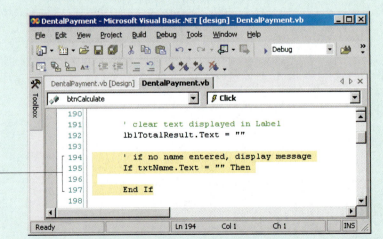

Figure 8.8 Adding an If...Then statement to the btnCalculate Click event handler to display a message dialog.

(cont.)

Line 195 tests whether data was entered in the **Patient name:** TextBox. If no data has been entered, the expression `txtName.Text = ""` evaluates to `True`. You will add the body of this `If...Then` statement in *Step 2*.

2. *Adding code to display a message dialog.* Insert lines 197–201 from Fig. 8.9 into the body of the `If...Then` statement you created in the previous step. Change the `End If` (line 197 of Fig. 8.8) to `Else` (line 203 of Fig. 8.9). Notice that the code you added to the `Click` event earlier (Fig. 8.5) now composes the body of the `Else` portion of your `If...Else` statement. The `Else` is marked as a syntax error because the `If...Else` statement is now missing an `End If` statement. You will add this statement in *Step 3*.

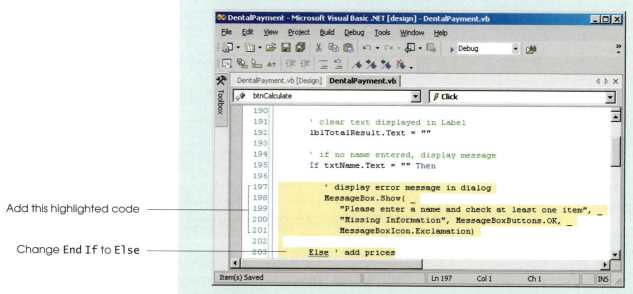

Add this highlighted code ⎯⎯⎯⎯⎯

Change `End If` to `Else` ⎯⎯⎯⎯⎯

Figure 8.9 Message dialog code that displays a message to users.

Lines 198–201 call method `MessageBox.Show` using four arguments, separated by commas. The first argument specifies the text that displays in the dialog, the second argument specifies the text that appears in its title bar, the third argument indicates which `Button`(s) to display at the bottom of the dialog and the fourth argument indicates which icon appears at the left of the dialog. We discuss the final two arguments in more detail shortly.

3. *Closing the If...Then statement.* Scroll to the end of your event handler code. Be sure to close the `If...Else` statement by inserting the keywords `End If` before the end of the event handler (line 226 of Fig. 8.10). Figure 8.11 displays the entire method `btnCalculate_Click` after the new code has been added. Compare this code to your own to ensure that you have added the new code correctly.

(cont.)

Add this highlighted code ——————

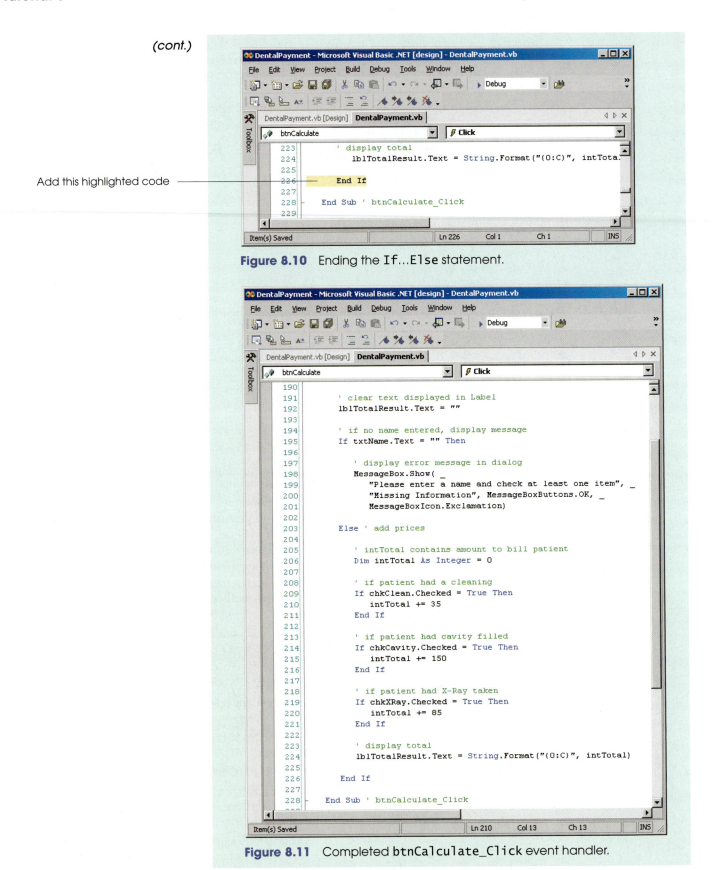

Figure 8.10 Ending the If...Else statement.

Figure 8.11 Completed btnCalculate_Click event handler.

(cont.)

4. ***Running the application.*** Select **Debug > Start** to run your application. Notice that the user does not have to select any **CheckBoxes** before clicking the **Calculate** Button, but the user must enter a name in the **Patient name:** TextBox. If none of the **CheckBoxes** is selected, the bill will contain the value **$0.00** (Fig. 8.12). In the next section, you will modify the code to test whether the user has selected any **CheckBoxes**.

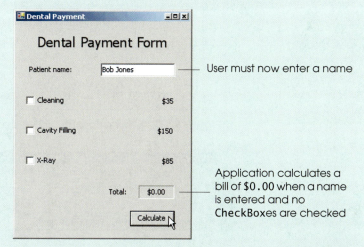

Figure 8.12   Application running without any **CheckBoxes** selected.

5. ***Closing the application.*** Close your running application by clicking its close box.

In this example, you passed four arguments to method **MessageBox.Show**. The first two arguments indicate the text of the dialog's message and the text of the dialog's title bar, respectively. The third argument specifies the **Button** that displays in the dialog. To accomplish this task, you passed one of the FCL's **MessageBoxButtons** constants to method **MessageBox.Show**. You will use only the **MessageBoxButtons.OK** constant in this book. Figure 8.13 lists the available **Button** constants. Note that several **Buttons** can be displayed at once. The fourth argument specifies the icon that displays in the dialog. To set the icon to display, you passed one of .NET's **MessageBoxIcon** constants to method **MessageBox.Show**. The available icon constants are shown in Fig. 8.14.

MessageBoxButtons Constants	Description
MessageBoxButtons.OK	**OK** Button. Allows the user to acknowledge a message.
MessageBoxButtons.OKCancel	**OK** and **Cancel** Buttons. Allow the user to either continue or cancel an operation.
MessageBoxButtons.YesNo	**Yes** and **No** Buttons. Allow the user to respond to a question.
MessageBoxButtons.YesNoCancel	**Yes**, **No** and **Cancel** Buttons. Allow the user to respond to a question or cancel an operation.
MessageBoxButtons.RetryCancel	**Retry** and **Cancel** Buttons. Allow the user either to retry or to cancel an operation that has failed.
MessageBoxButtons.AbortRetryIgnore	**Abort**, **Retry** and **Ignore** Buttons. When one of a series of operations has failed, these **Buttons** allow the user to abort the entire sequence, retry the failed operation or ignore the failed operation and continue.

Figure 8.13   Message dialog **Button** constants.

MessageBoxIcon Constants	Icon	Description
MessageBox-Icon.Exclamation	⚠	Icon containing an exclamation point. Typically used to caution the user against potential problems.
MessageBox-Icon.Information	ⓘ	Icon containing the letter "i." Typically used to display information about the state of the application.
MessageBox-Icon.Question	?	Icon containing a question mark. Typically used to ask the user a question.
MessageBox-Icon.Error	✖	Icon containing an ∞ in a red circle. Typically used to alert the user of errors or critical situations.

Figure 8.14   Message dialog icon constants.

SELF-REVIEW

1. Which constant, when passed to method `MessageBox.Show`, indicates that a question is being asked?

   a) `MessageBox.Question`   b) `MessageBoxIcon.QuestionMark`

   c) `MessageBox.QuestionMark`   d) `MessageBoxIcon.Question`

2. What is the message dialog icon containing the letter "i" typically used for?

   a) To display information about the state of the application

   b) To caution the user against potential problems

   c) To ask the user a question   d) To alert the user to critical situations

Answers: 1.) d. 2.) a.

8.5 Logical Operators

So far, you have studied only **simple conditions**, such as `intCount <= 10`, `intTotal > 1000`, and `intNumber <> intValue`. Each selection statement that you used evaluated only one condition with one of the operators >, <, >=, <=, = or <>.

To handle multiple conditions more efficiently, Visual Basic .NET provides **logical operators** that can be used to form complex conditions by combining simple ones. The logical operators are **AndAlso**, **OrElse**, **Xor** and **Not**. We will consider examples that use each of these operators. After you learn about logical operators, you will use them to create a complex condition in your **Dental Payment** application to confirm CheckBox entries.

Using AndAlso

Error-Prevention Tip

Always write the simplest condition possible by limiting the number of logical operators used. Conditions with many logical operators can be hard to read and can introduce subtle bugs into your applications.

Suppose that you wish to ensure that two conditions are *both* true in an application before choosing a certain path of execution. In that case, you can use the logical AndAlso operator as follows:

```
If txtGender.Text = "Female" AndAlso intAge >= 65 Then
   intSeniorFemales += 1
End If
```

This If...Then statement contains two simple conditions. The condition `txtGender.Text = "Female"` determines whether a person is female, and the condition `intAge >= 65` determines whether a person is a senior citizen. The = and >= operators are always evaluated before the operator AndAlso because the = and >= operators have a higher precedence than operator AndAlso. In this case, the two simple conditions are evaluated first, then the AndAlso operator is evaluated using their result. The If...Then statement then considers the combined condition

```
txtGender.Text = "Female" AndAlso intAge >= 65
```

This condition evaluates to true *if and only if* both of the simple conditions are true, meaning that `txtGender.Text` contains the value "Female" and `intAge` contains a value greater than or equal to 65. When this combined condition is true, the count of `intSeniorFemales` is incremented by 1. However, if either or both of the simple conditions are false, the application skips the increment and proceeds to the statement following the `If...Then` statement. The readability of the preceding combined condition can be improved by adding redundant (that is, unnecessary) parentheses:

```
(txtGender.Text = "Female") AndAlso (intAge >= 65)
```

Figure 8.15 illustrates the outcome of using the `AndAlso` operator with two expressions. The table lists all four possible combinations of `True` and `False` values for *expression1* and *expression2*, which represent the left operand and the right operand, respectively. Such tables are called **truth tables**. Visual Basic .NET evaluates to `True` or `False` expressions that include relational operators, equality operators and logical operators.

expression1	expression2	expression1 AndAlso expression2
False	False	False
False	True	False
True	False	False
True	True	True

Figure 8.15   Truth table for the `AndAlso` operator.

Using `OrElse`

Now let's consider the `OrElse` operator. Suppose that you wish to ensure that either *or* both of two conditions are true before you choose a certain path of execution. You would use the `OrElse` operator as in the following application segment:

```
If (intSemesterAverage >= 90 OrElse intFinalExam >= 90) Then
   MessageBox.Show("Student grade is A", "Student Grade", _
      MessageBoxButtons.OK, MessageBoxIcon.Information)
End If
```

This statement also contains two simple conditions. The condition `intSemesterAverage >= 90` is evaluated to determine whether the student deserves an "A" in the course because of an outstanding performance throughout the semester. The condition `intFinalExam >= 90` is evaluated to determine whether the student deserves an "A" in the course because of an outstanding performance on the final exam. The `If...Then` statement then considers the combined condition

```
(intSemesterAverage >= 90 OrElse intFinalExam >= 90)
```

and awards the student an "A" if either or both of the conditions are true, meaning that the student performed well during the semester, performed well on the final exam or both. Note that the text `"Student grade is A"` is displayed unless both of the conditions are false. Figure 8.16 provides a truth table for the `OrElse` operator. Note that the `AndAlso` operator has a higher precedence than the `OrElse` operator. See Appendix A for a complete listing of operator precedence in Visual Basic .NET.

Error-Prevention Tip

When writing conditions that contain combinations of **AndAlso** and **OrElse** operators, use parentheses to ensure that the conditions evaluate properly. Otherwise, logic errors could occur because **AndAlso** has higher precedence than **OrElse**.

expression1	expression2	expression1 OrElse expression2
False	False	False
False	True	True
True	False	True
True	True	True

Figure 8.16   Truth table for the `OrElse` operator.

An expression containing operator AndAlso is evaluated only until truth or falsity is known. For example, evaluation of the expression

```
(txtGender.Text = "Female" AndAlso intAge >= 65)
```

stops immediately if txtGender.Text is not equal to "Female" (which would mean the entire expression is false). In this case, the evaluation of the second expression is irrelevant; once the first expression is known to be false, the whole expression must be false. Evaluation of the second expression occurs if and only if txtGender.Text is equal to "Female" (which would mean that the entire expression could still be true if the condition intAge >= 65 is true).

Similarly, an expression containing OrElse is evaluated only until truth or falsity is known. For example, evaluation of the expression

```
If (intSemesterAverage >= 90 OrElse intFinalExam >= 90) Then
```

stops immediately if intSemesterAverage is greater than or equal to 90 (which would mean the entire expression is True). In this case, the evaluation of the second expression is irrelevant; once the first expression is known to be true, the whole expression must be true.

This way of evaluating logical expressions can require fewer operations, therefore taking less time. This performance feature for the evaluation of AndAlso and OrElse expressions is called **short-circuit evaluation**.[1]

Using Xor

A condition containing the **logical exclusive OR (Xor)** operator is True *if and only if one of its operands results in a True value and the other results in a False value*. If both operands are True or both are False, the entire condition is False. Figure 8.17 presents a truth table for the logical exclusive OR operator (Xor). This operator always evaluates both of its operands (that is, there is no short-circuit evaluation).

expression1	expression2	expression1 Xor expression2
False	False	False
False	True	True
True	False	True
True	True	False

Figure 8.17   Truth table for the logical exclusive OR (Xor) operator.

Using Not

Visual Basic .NET's **Not** (logical negation) operator enables a programmer to "reverse" the meaning of a condition. Unlike the logical operators AndAlso, OrElse and Xor, each of which combines two expressions (that is, these are all binary operators), the logical negation operator is a unary operator, requiring only one operand. The logical negation operator is placed before a condition to choose a path of execution if the original condition (without the logical negation operator) is False. The logical negation operator is demonstrated by the following application segment:

---

1. Visual Basic .NET also provides the And and Or operators, which do not short-circuit. (They always evaluate their right operand regardless of whether or not the condition's truth or falsity is already known.) In Visual Basic .NET applications, the performance benefit of using AndAlso and OrElse is negligible. One potential problem of using AndAlso/OrElse instead of And/Or is when the right operand contains a **side effect**, such as a function call that modifies a variable. Because such side effects might not occur when using short-circuit evaluation, subtle logic errors could occur. As a good programming practice, most Visual Basic .NET programmers, who prefer to use operators AndAlso and OrElse, avoid writing conditions that contain side effects.

```
If Not (intGrade = intValue) Then
   lblDisplay.Text = "They are not equal!"
End If
```

The parentheses around the condition `intGrade = intValue` are necessary, because the logical negation operator (`Not`) has a higher precedence than the equality operator. Most programmers prefer to write

```
Not (intGrade = intValue)
```

as

```
(intGrade <> intValue)
```

Figure 8.18 provides a truth table for the logical negation operator. The following box provides an example of using complex expressions. You will modify your **Dental Payment** application to use a complex expression.

expression	Not expression
False	True
True	False

Figure 8.18   Truth table for the **Not** operator (logical NOT).

Using Logical Operators in Complex Expressions

1. **Inserting a complex expression into the `Click` event handler.** Double click the **Calculate** Button on the Form. Replace lines 194–195 of Fig. 8.8 with lines 194–198 of Fig. 8.19.

Add the highlighted code ⟶

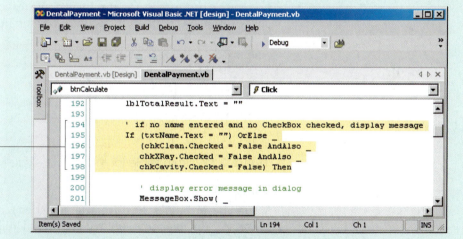

Figure 8.19   Using the `AndAlso` and `OrElse` logical operators.

Lines 195–198 define a more sophisticated logical expression than others we have used in this book. Notice the use of `OrElse` and `AndAlso`. If the name is blank or if no CheckBox is checked, a dialog should appear. After the original expression (`txtName.Text = ""`), you use `OrElse` to indicate that either the expression on the left (`txtName.Text = ""`) or the expression "on the right" (which determines if no CheckBox has been checked) needs to be `True` for the entire expression to evaluate to `True` to execute the body of the `If...Then` statement. The complex expression "on the right" uses `AndAlso` twice to determine if all of the CheckBoxes are unchecked. Note that because `AndAlso` has a higher precedence than `OrElse`, the parentheses on lines 196 and 198 are redundant (unnecessary).

(cont.)   2. ***Running the application.*** Select **Debug > Start** to run your application. Notice that users must enter a name and select at least one **CheckBox** before they click the **Calculate** Button. The application appears the same as in Figs. 8.1 and 8.3. (You have finally corrected the weakness from your earlier implementation of the **Dental Payment** application.)

3. ***Closing the application.*** Close your running application by clicking its close box.

4. ***Closing the IDE.*** Close Visual Studio .NET by clicking its close box.

Figure 8.20 presents the source code for the **Dental Payment** application. The lines of code that contain new programming concepts that you learned in this tutorial are highlighted.

```
1   Public Class FrmDentalPayment
2      Inherits System.Windows.Forms.Form
3
4      Private Sub btnCalculate_Click(ByVal sender As System.Object, _
5         ByVal e As System.EventArgs) Handles btnCalculate.Click
6
7         ' clear text displayed in Label
8         lblTotalResult.Text = ""
9
10        ' if no name entered and no CheckBox checked, display message
11        If (txtName.Text = "") OrElse _
12           (chkClean.Checked = False AndAlso _
13           chkXRay.Checked = False AndAlso _
14           chkCavity.Checked = False) Then
15
16           ' display message in dialog
17           MessageBox.Show( _
18              "Please enter your name and check at least one item", _
19              "Missing Information", MessageBoxButtons.OK, _
20              MessageBoxIcon.Exclamation)
21
22        Else ' add prices
23
24           ' intTotal contains amount to bill patient
25           Dim intTotal As Integer
26
27           ' if patient had a cleaning
28           If chkClean.Checked = True Then
29              intTotal += 35
30           End If
31
32           ' if patient had cavity filled
33           If chkCavity.Checked = True Then
34              intTotal += 150
35           End If
36
37           ' if patient had X-Ray taken
38           If chkXRay.Checked = True Then
39              intTotal += 85
40           End If
41
```

Using logical operators and the **Checked** property of a **CheckBox** ⟶ (lines 11–14)

Displaying a **MessageBox** ⟶ (lines 17–20)

Figure 8.20   Code for the **Dental Payment** application. (Part 1 of 2.)

```
42                    ' display total
43                    lblTotalResult.Text = String.Format("{0:C}", intTotal)
44
45            End If
46
47        End Sub ' btnCalculate_Click
48
49    End Class ' FrmDentalPayment
```

Figure 8.20   Code for the **Dental Payment** application. (Part 2 of 2.)

1. A unary operator _____.

   a) requires exactly one operand   b) requires two operands

   c) must use the AndAlso keyword   d) can have no operands

2. The _____ operator is used to ensure that two conditions are both true.

   a) Xor   b) AndAlso

   c) Also   d) OrElse

Answers: 1.) a. 2.) b.

8.6 Wrap-Up

In this tutorial, you used CheckBox controls to provide a series of choices to users in the **Dental Payment** application. CheckBoxes provide options that can be selected by clicking them. When a CheckBox is selected, its white square contains a check mark. You can determine whether a CheckBox is selected in your code by accessing its Checked property.

Your **Dental Payment** application also used message dialogs to display messages to the user when information was not entered appropriately. To implement dialogs in your application, you used the MessageBox class, which provides methods and constants necessary to display a dialog containing Buttons and an icon. You used an If...Then...Else statement to calculate the cost of the dental visit or display a message dialog if the user was missing input. Later in this book you will learn to avoid checking for invalid user input by disabling a control (such as a Button) when its events should not cause any action to occur.

You learned to use the logical AndAlso operator when both conditions must be true for the overall condition to be true—if either condition is false, the overall condition is false. You also learned that the logical OrElse operator requires at least one of its conditions to be true for the overall condition to be true—if both conditions are false, the overall condition is false. The logical Xor operator requires that exactly one of its conditions be true for the overall condition to be true—if both conditions are false or if both conditions are true, the overall condition is false. The logical Not operator reverses the Boolean result of a condition—True becomes False, and False becomes True. You then used the AndAlso and OrElse operators to form a complex expression.

In the next tutorial, you will learn more about Visual Basic .NET's control structures. Specifically, you will use **repetition statements**, which allow the programmer to specify that an action or a group of actions should be performed many times.

SKILLS SUMMARY

Adding a CheckBox to a Form

- Double click the CheckBox in the **ToolBox**.

Selecting a CheckBox

- Click the CheckBox, and a check mark will appear in the white box.

Deselecting a CheckBox
- Click a checked CheckBox to remove its check mark.

Determining Whether a CheckBox is Selected
- Access the CheckBox's Checked property.

Displaying a Dialog
- Use method MessageBox.Show.

Combining Multiple Conditions
- Use the logical operators to form complex conditions by combining simple ones.

KEY TERMS

AndAlso operator—A logical operator used to ensure that two conditions are *both* true before choosing a certain path of execution. Performs short-circuit evaluation.

CheckBox control—A small white square GUI element that either is blank or contains a check mark.

CheckBox label—The text that appears alongside a CheckBox.

Checked property of the CheckBox control—Specifies whether the CheckBox is checked (True) or unchecked (False).

dialog (message dialog)—A window that displays messages to users and gathers input from users.

dismiss—Synonym for close.

logical exclusive OR (Xor) operator—A logical operator that is True if and only if one of its operands results in True and the other results in False.

logical operators—The operators (for example, AndAlso, OrElse, Xor and Not) that can be used to form complex conditions by combining simple ones.

MessageBox class—Provides a method for displaying message dialogs.

MessageBoxButtons constants—The identifiers that specify Buttons that can be displayed in a MessageBox dialog.

MessageBoxIcon constants—Identifiers that specify icons that can be displayed in a MessageBox dialog.

MessageBox.show method—Displays a message dialog.

Not (logical negation) operator—A logical operator that enables a programmer to reverse the meaning of a condition: A True condition, when logically negated, becomes False and a False condition, when logically negated, becomes True.

OrElse operator—A logical operator used to ensure that either *or* both of two conditions are True in an application before a certain path of execution is chosen.

short-circuit evaluation—The evaluation of the right operand in AndAlso and OrElse expressions occurs only if the first condition meets the criteria for the condition.

simple condition—Contains one expression.

state button—A button that can be in the on/off (true/false) state.

truth table—A table that displays the boolean result of a logical operator for all possible combinations of True and False values for its operands.

GUI DESIGN GUIDELINES

CheckBoxes
- A CheckBox's label should be descriptive and as short as possible. When a CheckBox label contains more than one word, use book-title capitalization.
- Align groups of CheckBoxes either horizontally or vertically.

Message Dialogs
- Text displayed in a dialog should be descriptive and as short as possible.

CONTROLS, EVENTS, PROPERTIES & METHODS

CheckBox   ☑ CheckBox   This control allows user to select an option.

- ■ *In action*

  ☑ Cleaning
  ☐ Cavity Filling

- ■ *Properties*

  Checked—Specifies whether the CheckBox is checked (True) or unchecked (False).

  Location—Specifies the location of the CheckBox on the Form.

  Name—Specifies the name used to access the CheckBox control programmatically. The name should be prefixed with chk.

  Text—Specifies the text displayed next to the CheckBox.

MULTIPLE-CHOICE QUESTIONS

8.1 How many CheckBoxes in a GUI can be selected at once?

    a) 0   b) 1

    c) 4   d) any number

8.2 The text that appears alongside a CheckBox is referred to as the _____.

    a) CheckBox label   b) CheckBox name

    c) CheckBox value   d) CheckBox data

8.3 The first argument passed to method MessageBox.Show is _____.

    a) the text displayed in the dialog's title bar

    b) a constant representing the Buttons displayed in the dialog

    c) the text displayed inside the dialog

    d) a constant representing the icon that appears in the dialog

8.4 You can specify the Button(s) and icon to be displayed in a message dialog by using the MessageBoxButtons and _____ constants.

    a) MessageIcon   b) MessageBoxImages

    c) MessageBoxPicture   d) MessageBoxIcon

8.5 _____ are used to create complex conditions.

    a) Assignment operators   b) Activity diagrams

    c) Logical operators   d) Formatting codes

8.6 Operator AndAlso _____.

    a) performs short-circuit evaluation   b) is not a keyword

    c) is a comparison operator

    d) evaluates to false if both operands are true

8.7 A CheckBox is selected when its Checked property is set to _____.

    a) On   b) True

    c) Selected   d) Checked

8.8 The condition *expression1* AndAlso *expression2* evaluates to True when _____.

    a) *expression1* is True and *expression2* is False

    b) *expression1* is False and *expression2* is True

    c) both *expression1* and *expression2* are True

    d) both *expression1* and *expression2* are False

8.9 The condition *expression1* OrElse *expression2* evaluates to False when _____.

    a) *expression1* is True and *expression2* is False

    b) *expression1* is False and *expression2* is True

c) both *expression1* and *expression2* are True

d) both *expression1* and *expression2* are False

8.10 The condition *expression1* Xor *expression2* evaluates to True when _____.

a) *expression1* is True and *expression2* is False

b) *expression1* is False and *expression2* is True

c) both *expression1* and *expression2* are True

d) Both a and b.

EXERCISES

8.11 (*Enhanced Dental Payment Application*) Modify the **Dental Payment** application from this tutorial to include additional services, as shown in Fig. 8.21. Add the proper functionality (using If...Then structures) to determine whether any of the new CheckBoxes are selected and, if so, add the price of the service to the total bill.

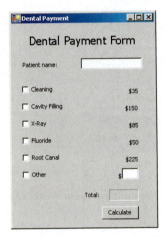

Figure 8.21   Enhanced **Dental Payment** application.

a) *Copying the template to your working directory.* Copy the directory C:\Examples\ Tutorial08\Exercises\DentalPaymentEnhanced to your C:\SimplyVB directory.

b) *Opening the application's template file.* Double click DentalPaymentEnhanced.sln in the DentalPaymentEnhanced directory to open the application.

c) *Adding CheckBoxes and Labels and a TextBox.* Add two CheckBoxes and two Labels to the Form. The new CheckBoxes should be labelled **Fluoride** and **Root Canal**, respectively. Add these CheckBoxes and Labels beneath the X-Ray CheckBox and its price Label. The price for a Fluoride treatment is $50; the price for a root canal is $225. Add a CheckBox labelled **Other** and a Label containing a dollar sign ($) to the Form, as shown in Fig. 8.21. Then add a TextBox to the right of the $ Label in which the user can enter the cost of the service performed.

d) *Modifying the Click event handler code.* Add code to the btnCalculate_Click event handler that determines whether the new CheckBoxes have been selected. This can be done using If...Then statements that are similar to the ones already in the event handler. Use the If...Then statements to update the bill amount.

e) *Running the application.* Select **Debug > Start** to run your application. Test your application by checking one or more of the new services. Click the **Calculate** Button and verify that the proper total is displayed. Test the application again by checking some of the services, then checking the Other CheckBox and entering a dollar value for this service. Click the **Calculate** Button and verify that the proper total is displayed, and that it includes the price for the "other" service.

f) *Closing the application.* Close your running application by clicking its close box.

g) *Closing the IDE.* Close Visual Studio .NET by clicking its close box.

8.12 (*Fuzzy Dice Order Form Application*) Write an application that allows users to process orders for fuzzy dice as shown in Fig. 8.22. The application should calculate the total price of the order, including tax and shipping. TextBoxes for inputting the order number, the customer name and the shipping address are provided. Initially, these fields contain text that describes their purpose. Provide CheckBoxes for selecting the fuzzy-dice color and TextBoxes for inputting the quantities of fuzzy dice to order. The application should also contain a Button that, when clicked, calculates the subtotals for each type of fuzzy dice ordered and the total of the entire order (including tax and shipping). Use 5% for the tax rate. Shipping charges are $1.50 for up to 20 pairs of dice. If more than 20 pairs of dice are ordered, shipping is free.

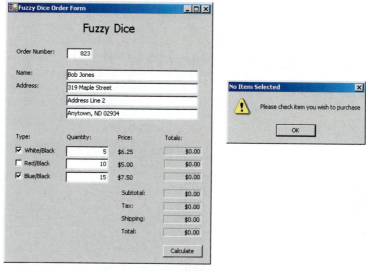

Figure 8.22 Fuzzy Dice Order Form application.

a) *Copying the template to your working directory.* Copy the directory C:\Examples\ Tutorial08\Exercises\FuzzyDiceOrderForm to your C:\SimplyVB directory.

b) *Opening the application's template file.* Double click FuzzyDiceOrderForm.sln in the FuzzyDiceOrderForm directory to open the application.

c) *Adding CheckBoxes to the Form.* Add three CheckBoxes to the Form. Label the first CheckBox **White/Black**, the second one **Red/Black** and the third **Blue/Black**.

d) *Adding a Click event handler and its code.* Create the Click event handler for the **Calculate** Button. For this application, users should not be allowed to specify an item's quantity unless the item's corresponding CheckBox is checked. For the total to be calculated, the user must enter an order number, a name and a shipping address. Use logical operators to ensure that these terms are met. If they are not, display a message in a dialog.

e) *Calculating the total cost.* Calculate the subtotal, tax, shipping and total, and display the results in their corresponding Labels.

f) *Running the application.* Select **Debug > Start** to run your application. Test the application by providing quantities for checked items. For instance, ensure that your application is calculating 5% sales tax. If more than 20 pairs of dice are ordered, verify that shipping is free. Also, determine whether your code containing the logical operators works correctly by specifying a quantity for an item that is not checked. For instance, in Fig. 8.22, a quantity is specified for **Red/Black** dice, but the corresponding Check-Box is not selected. This should cause the message dialog in Fig. 8.22 to appear.

g) *Closing the application.* Close your running application by clicking its close box.

h) *Closing the IDE.* Close Visual Studio .NET by clicking its close box.

8.13 (*Modified Fuzzy Dice Order Form Application*) Modify the **Fuzzy Dice Order Form** application from Exercise 8.12 to determine whether customers should receive a 7% discount off their purchase. Customers ordering more than $500 (before tax and shipping) in fuzzy dice are eligible for this discount.

a) *Opening the application.* Open the application you created in Exercise 8.12.

b) *Determining whether the total cost is over $500.* Use an If...Then statement to determine if the amount ordered is greater than $500.

Figure 8.23   Modified **Fuzzy Dice Order Form** application.

c) *Displaying the discount and subtracting the discount from the total*. If a customer orders more than $500, display a message dialog as shown in Fig. 8.23 that informs the user that the customer is entitled to a 7% discount. The message dialog should contain an Information icon and an **OK** Button. Calculate 7% of the total amount, and display the discount amount in the **Discount:** field. Subtract this amount from the total, and update the **Total:** field.

d) *Running the application*. Select **Debug > Start** to run your application. Confirm that your application calculates and displays the discount properly.

e) *Closing the application*. Close your running application by clicking its close box.

f) *Closing the IDE*. Close Visual Studio .NET by clicking its close box.

What does this code do? **8.14** Assume that txtName is a TextBox and that chkOther is a CheckBox next to which is a TextBox txtOther, in which the user should specify a value. What does this code segment do?

```
1   If (txtName.Text = "" OrElse _
2      (chkOther.Checked = True AndAlso _
3      txtOther.Text = "")) Then
4
5      MessageBox.Show("Please enter a name or value", _
6         "Input Error", MessageBoxButtons.OK, _
7         MessageBoxIcon.Exclamation)
8
9   End If
```

What's wrong with this code? **8.15** Assume that txtName is a TextBox. Find the error(s) in the following code:

```
1   If txtName.Text = "John Doe" Then
2
3      MessageBox.Show("Welcome, John!", _
4         MessageBoxIcon.Exclamation)
5
6   End If
```

Using the Debugger ▶

8.16 (*Sibling Survey Application*) The **Sibling Survey** application displays the siblings selected by the user in a dialog. If the user checks either the **Brother(s)** or **Sister(s)** Check-Box, and the **No Siblings** CheckBox, the user is asked to verify the selection. Otherwise, the user's selection is displayed in a MessageBox. While testing this application, you noticed that it does not execute properly. Use the debugger to find and correct the logic error(s) in the code. This exercise is located in the C:\Examples\Tutorial08\Debugger\SiblingSurvey directory. Figure 8.24 shows the correct output for the application.

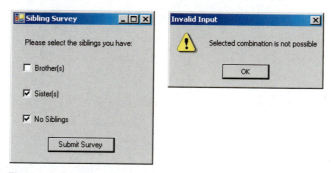

Figure 8.24 Correct output for the **Sibling Survey** application.

Programming Challenge ▶

8.17 (*Enhanced Fuzzy Dice Order Form Application*) Enhance the **Fuzzy Dice Order Form** application from Exercise 8.12 by replacing the **Calculate** Button with a **Clear** Button. The application should update the total cost, tax and shipping when the user changes any one of the three **Quantity** field's values (Fig. 8.25). The **Clear** Button should return all fields to their original values. [*Hint*: You will need to use the CheckBox **CheckedChanged** event for each CheckBox. This event is raised when the state of a CheckBox changes. Double click a CheckBox in design view to create an event handler for that CheckBox's CheckedChanged event. You also will need to assign Boolean values to the CheckBoxes' Checked properties to control their states.]

Figure 8.25 Enhanced **Fuzzy Dice Order Form** application.

Objectives

In this tutorial, you will learn to:

- Use the Do While...Loop and Do Until...Loop repetition statements to execute statements in an application repeatedly.
- Use counter-controlled repetition.
- Display information in ListBoxes.

Outline

Car Payment Calculator Application

Introducing the Do While...Loop and Do Until...Loop Repetition Statements

This tutorial continues the discussion of structured programming that we began in Tutorial 7. We introduce repetition statements, which are control statements that can repeat actions on the basis of a condition's value. You perform many repetitive tasks based on conditions. For example, each time you turn a page in this book (while there are more pages to read), you are repeating a simple task, namely turning a page, based on a condition, namely that there are more pages to read.

The ability to perform tasks repeatedly is an important part of structured programming. Repetition statements are used in many types of applications. In this tutorial, you will learn to use the Do While...Loop and the Do Until...Loop repetition statements. You will include a repetition statement in the **Car Payment Calculator** application that you build. Later tutorials will introduce additional repetition statements.

9.1 Test-Driving the Car Payment Calculator Application

The following problem statement requires an application that repeats a calculation four times—you will use a repetition statement to solve this problem. This application must meet the following requirements:

Application Requirements

Typically, banks offer car loans for periods ranging from two to five years (24 to 60 months). Borrowers repay the loans in monthly installments. The amount of each monthly payment is based on the length of the loan, the amount borrowed and the interest rate. Create an application that allows the customer to enter the price of a car, the down-payment amount and the annual interest rate of the loan. The application should display the loan's duration in months and the monthly payments for two-, three-, four- and five-year loans. The variety of options allows the user to easily compare their options and choose the payment plan that is most convenient for them.

You begin by test-driving the completed application. Then, you will learn the additional Visual Basic .NET technologies that you will need to create your own version of this application.

Test-Driving the Car Payment Calculator Application

1. *Opening the completed application.* Open the directory C:\Examples\ Tutorial09\CompletedApplication\CarPaymentCalculator to locate the **Car Payment Calculator** application. Double click CarPayment-Calculator.sln to open the application in Visual Studio .NET.

2. *Running the application.* Select **Debug > Start** to run the application (Fig. 9.1). Notice a new GUI control—the **ListBox** control, which allows users to view and select from multiple items in a list. Users cannot add items to, or remove items from, a ListBox by interacting directly with the List-Box. The ListBox does not accept keyboard input; users cannot add or delete selected items. You need to add code to your application to add or remove items from a ListBox.

ListBox control ——

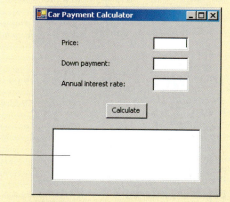

Figure 9.1 **Car Payment Calculator** application before data has been entered.

3. *Entering quantities in the application.* Enter 16900 in the **Price:** TextBox. Enter 6000 in the **Down payment:** TextBox. Enter 7.5 in the **Annual interest rate:** TextBox. The Form appears as in Fig. 9.2.

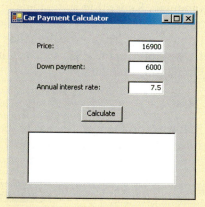

Figure 9.2 **Car Payment Calculator** application after data has been entered.

4. *Calculating the monthly payment amounts.* Click the **Calculate** Button. The application displays the monthly payment amounts in the ListBox (Fig. 4). The information is organized in tabular format.

5. *Closing the application.* Close your running application by clicking its close box.

6. *Closing the IDE.* Close Visual Studio .NET by clicking its close box.

(cont.)

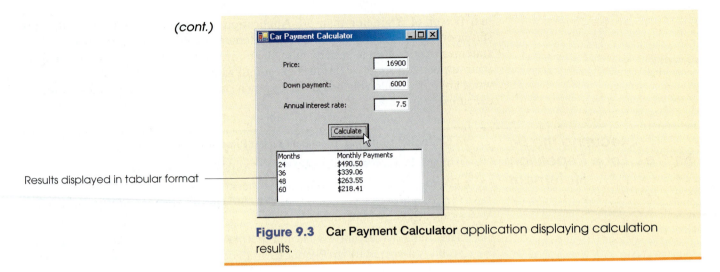

Results displayed in tabular format ————

Figure 9.3   Car Payment Calculator application displaying calculation results.

9.2 Do While…Loop Repetition Statement

A **repetition statement** can repeat actions, depending on the value of a condition (which can be either true or false). For example, if you go to the grocery store with a list of items to purchase, you go through the list until you have each item. This process is described by the following pseudocode statements:

> *Do while there are more items on my shopping list*
> *   Purchase next item*
> *   Cross it off my list*

These statements describe the repetitive actions that occur during a shopping trip. The condition, "there are more items on my shopping list" can be true or false. If it is true, then the actions, "Purchase next item" and "Cross it off my list" are performed in sequence. In an application, these actions execute repeatedly while the condition remains true. The statement(s) indented in this repetition statement constitute its **body**. When the last item on the shopping list has been purchased and crossed off the list, the condition becomes false. At this point, the repetition terminates, and the first statement after the repetition statement executes. In the shopping example, you would proceed to the checkout station.

As an example of a Do While…Loop statement, let's look at an application segment designed to find the first power of 3 greater than 50.

Common Programming Error

Provide in the body of every Do While…Loop statement an action that eventually causes the condition to become false. If you do not, the repetition statement never terminates, causing an error called an **infinite loop**. When an infinite loop occurs in an application, right click the application in the task bar and select **Close**. In the dialog box that pops up, click **End Now**.

```
Dim intProduct As Integer = 3

Do While intProduct <= 50
    intProduct *= 3
Loop
```

The application segment initializes variable intProduct to 3, taking advantage of a Visual Basic .NET feature that allows variable initialization to be incorporated into a declaration. The condition in the Do While…Loop statement, intProduct <= 50, is referred to as the **loop-continuation condition**. While the loop-continuation condition remains true, the Do While…Loop statement executes its body repeatedly. When the loop-continuation condition becomes false, the Do While…Loop statement finishes executing, and intProduct contains the first power of 3 larger than 50. Let's examine the execution of the preceding code in detail.

When the Do While…Loop statement is entered, the value of intProduct is 3. Each time the loop executes, the variable intProduct is multiplied by 3, taking on the values 3, 9, 27 and 81, successively. When intProduct becomes 81, the condition in the Do While…Loop statement, intProduct <= 50, is evaluated to false. When the repetition ends, the final value of intProduct is 81, which is, indeed, the first power of 3 greater than 50. Application execution continues with the next statement after the Do While...Loop statement. Note that, if a Do While...Loop statement's condition is initially false, the body statement(s) are not performed and your application simply continues executing with the next statement after the keyword Loop. The following box describes each step as the above repetition statement executes.

Executing the Do While...Loop Repetition Statement

1. The application declares variable intProduct and sets its value to 3.

2. The application enters the Do While...Loop repetition statement.

3. The loop-continuation condition is checked. The condition evaluates to True (intProduct is less than or equal to 50), so the application resumes execution at the next statement.

4. The number (currently 3) stored in intProduct is multiplied by 3 and the result is assigned to intProduct; intProduct now contains the number 9.

5. The loop-continuation condition is checked. The condition evaluates to True (intProduct is less than or equal to 50), so the application resumes execution at the next statement.

6. The number (currently 9) stored in intProduct is multiplied by 3 and the result is assigned to intProduct; intProduct now contains the number 27.

7. The loop-continuation condition is checked. The condition evaluates to True (intProduct is less than or equal to 50), so the application resumes execution at the next statement.

8. The number (currently 27) stored in intProduct is multiplied by 3 and the result is assigned to intProduct; intProduct now contains the number 81.

9. The loop-continuation condition is checked. The condition evaluates to False (intProduct is not less than or equal to 50), so the application exits the Do While...Loop repetition statement and the application resumes execution at the first statement after the Loop statement.

Let's use a UML activity diagram to illustrate the flow of control in the preceding Do While...Loop repetition statement. The UML activity diagram in Fig. 9.4 contains an initial state, transition arrows, a merge, a decision, two guard conditions, three notes and a final state. The oval represents the action state in which the value of intProduct is multiplied by 3.

The activity diagram clearly shows the repetition. The transition arrow emerging from the action state wraps back to the merge, creating a **loop**. The guard conditions are tested each time the loop iterates until the guard condition intProduct > 50 eventually becomes true. At this point, the Do While...Loop statement is exited, and control passes to the next statement in the application following the loop.

Figure 9.4 introduces the UML's **merge symbol**. The UML represents both the merge symbol and the decision symbol as diamonds. The merge symbol joins two flows of activity into one flow of activity. In this diagram, the merge symbol joins the transitions from the initial state and from the action state, so they both flow into the loop-continuation guard decision, which is the decision that determines whether the loop body statement should begin executing (or continue executing). In this case, the UML diagram enters its action state when the loop-continuation guard condition intProduct <= 50 is true.

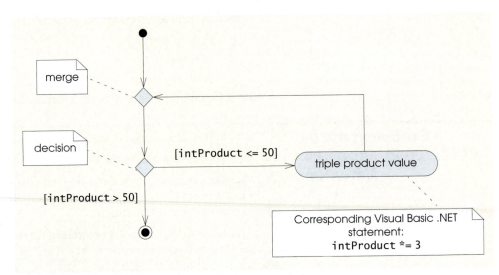

Figure 9.4 Do While...Loop repetition statement UML activity diagram.

Although the UML represents both the decision and the merge symbols with the diamond shape, the symbols can be distinguished by the number of "incoming" and "outgoing" transition arrows. A decision symbol has one transition arrow pointing to the diamond and two (or more) transition arrows pointing out from the diamond to indicate possible transitions from that point. In addition, each transition arrow pointing out of a decision symbol has a guard condition next to it. A merge symbol has two (or more) transition arrows pointing to the diamond and only one transition arrow pointing from the diamond, to indicate multiple activity flows merging to continue the activity.

SELF-REVIEW

1. The body of a Do While...Loop statement executes _____.
   a) at least once   b) never
   c) if its condition is true   d) if its condition is false

2. The UML represents both the merge symbol and the decision symbol as _____.
   a) rectangles with rounded sides   b) diamonds
   c) small black circles   d) ovals

Answers: 1) c. 2) b.

9.3 Do Until...Loop Repetition Statement

Common Programming Error

Failure to provide the body of a Do Until...Loop statement with an action that eventually causes the condition in the Do Until...Loop to become true creates an infinite loop.

Unlike the Do While...Loop repetition statement, the **Do Until...Loop** repetition statement tests the loop-termination condition for falsity before repetition can continue. For example, you can think of grocery shopping as looping through the list of items until there aren't any left on the list. Note that the condition "there are no more items on my shopping list" must be false for the loop to continue. This process is described by the following pseudocode statements:

> Do until there are no more items on my shopping list
> > Purchase next item
> > Cross it off my list

These statements describe the repetitive actions that occur during a shopping trip. Statements in the body of a Do Until...Loop are executed repeatedly for as long as the loop-termination condition remains False. As an example of a Do Until...Loop repetition statement, let's look again at an application segment designed to find the first power of 3 larger than 50:

```
Dim intProduct As Integer = 3

Do Until intProduct > 50
    intProduct *= 3
Loop
```

The following box describes each step as the repetition statement executes.

Executing the Do Until...Loop Repetition Statement	1. The application declares variable `intProduct` and sets its value to 3.
	2. The application enters the Do Until...Loop repetition statement.
	3. The loop-termination condition is checked. The condition evaluates to `False` (`intProduct` is not greater than 50), so the application resumes execution at the next statement.
	4. The number (currently 3) stored in `intProduct` is multiplied by 3 and the result is assigned to `intProduct`; `intProduct` now contains the number 9.
	5. The loop-termination condition is checked. The condition evaluates to `False` (`intProduct` is not greater than 50), so the application resumes execution at the next statement.
	6. The number (currently 9) stored in `intProduct` is multiplied by 3 and the result is assigned to `intProduct`; `intProduct` now contains the number 27.
	7. The loop-termination condition is checked. The condition evaluates to `False` (`intProduct` is not greater than 50), so the application resumes execution at the next statement.
	8. The number (currently 27) stored in `intProduct` is multiplied by 3 and the result is assigned to `intProduct`; `intProduct` now contains the number 81.
	9. The loop-termination condition is checked. The condition now evaluates to `True` (`intProduct` is greater than 50), so the application exits the Do Until...Loop repetition statement and the application resumes execution at the first statement after the Loop statement.

The UML activity diagram in Fig. 9.5 illustrates the flow of control for the Do Until...Loop repetition statement. Once again, note that (besides the initial state, transition arrows, a final state and two notes) the only other symbols in the diagram represent an action state, a decision and a merge.

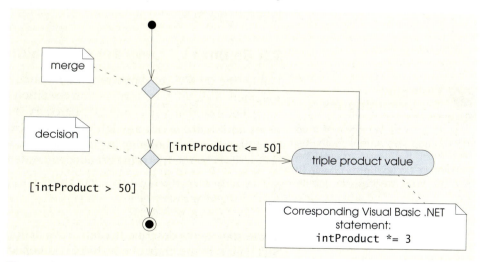

Figure 9.5 Do Until...Loop repetition statement UML activity diagram.

1. A Do Until...Loop repetition statement differs from a Do While...Loop repetition statement in _____.

   a) that a Do While...Loop repetition statement loops as long as the loop-continuation condition remains False, whereas a Do Until...Loop repetition statement loops as long as the loop-continuation condition remains True

   b) that a Do Until...Loop repetition statement loops as long as the loop-continuation condition remains False, whereas a Do While...Loop repetition statement loops as long as the loop-continuation condition remains True

   c) that a Do Until...Loop repetition statement always executes at least once

   d) no way. There is no difference between the Do Until...Loop and Do While...Loop repetition statements

   2. Statements in the body of a Do Until...Loop are executed repeatedly for as long as the _____ remains False.

   a) loop-continuation condition   b) do-loop condition

   c) loop-termination condition   d) until-loop condition

Answer: 1) b. 2) c.

9.4 Constructing the Car Payment Calculator Application

Now that you have learned the Do While...Loop and Do Until...Loop repetition statements, you are ready to construct the **Car Payment Calculator** application.

The following pseudocode describes the basic operation of the **Car Payment Calculator** application that occurs when a user enters information and clicks the **Calculate** Button:

```
When the user clicks the Calculate Button
    Initialize loan length to two years
    Clear the ListBox of any previous calculation results
    Add a header to the ListBox

    Get down payment from a TextBox
    Get sticker price from a TextBox
    Get interest rate from a TextBox

    Calculate loan amount (sticker price – down payment)
    Calculate monthly interest rate (interest rate / 12)

    Do while loan length is less than or equal to five years
        Convert the loan length in years to number of months

        Calculate monthly payment based on loan amount, monthly interest rate
        and loan length in months

        Insert result into ListBox
        Increment loan length in years by one year
```

Now that you have test-driven the **Car Payment Calculator** application and studied its pseudocode representation, you will use an Action/Control/Event (ACE) table to help you convert the pseudocode to Visual Basic .NET. Figure 9.6 lists the actions, controls and events that will help you complete your own version of this application.

Action	Control	Event
Label all the application's controls	`lblStickerPrice,` `lblDownPayment,` `lblInterest`	Application is run
	`btnCalculate`	`Click`
Initialize loan length to two years		
Clear the ListBox of any previous calculation results	`lstPayments`	
Add a header to the ListBox	`lstPayments`	
Get down payment from a TextBox	`txtDownPayment`	
Get sticker price from a TextBox	`txtStickerPrice`	
Get interest rate from a TextBox	`txtInterest`	
Calculate loan amount		
Calculate monthly interest rate		
Do while loan length is less than or equal to five years		
Convert the loan length in years to number of months		
Calculate monthly payment based on loan amount, monthly interest rate and loan length in months		
Insert result into ListBox	`lstPayments`	
Increment loan length in years by one year		

Figure 9.6 **Car Payment Calculator** application ACE table.

Notice in the pseudocode that the retrieval of the user input and the calculations of the loan amount and the monthly interest rate occur before the repetition statement because they need to be performed only once. The statements that have different results in each iteration are included in the repetition statement. The repetition statement's body includes: converting loan length in years to loan length in months, calculating the monthly payment amount, displaying the calculation's result and incrementing the loan length in years.

The application displays the calculation results in a `ListBox`. Next, you will add and customize the `ListBox` that displays the results.

*Adding a ListBox to
the Car Payment
Calculator Application*

1. *Copying the template to your working directory.* Copy the `C:\Examples\Tutorial09\TemplateApplication\CarPaymentCalculator` directory to your `C:\SimplyVB` directory.

2. *Opening the Car Payment Calculator application's template file.* Double click `CarPaymentCalculator.sln` in the `CarPaymentCalculator` directory to open the application in Visual Studio .NET (Fig. 9.7). Notice that the TextBoxes for user input and the **Calculate** Button are provided to you.

(cont.)

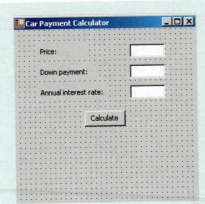

Figure 9.7 **Car Payment Calculator** application's **Form** in design mode.

3. ***Adding a ListBox control to the Form.*** Double click the ListBox control,

   in the **Toolbox.** Change the Name property of the ListBox to lstPayments. Set the Location property to 28, 168 and the Size property to 232, 82. Figure 9.8 shows the Form with the ListBox control. In design view, the ListBox control displays the value of its Name property. This text will not appear when the application executes.

Good Programming Practice

Prefix ListBox control names with lst.

ListBox's control name displayed in design view

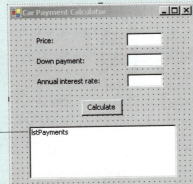

Figure 9.8 ListBox added to **Car Payment Calculator** application's **Form**.

4. ***Saving the project.*** Select **File > Save All** to save your changes.

GUI Design Tip

A ListBox should be large enough to display all of its contents or large enough that scrollbars can be used easily.

After adding the ListBox, you must add an event handler to the application so that the application can respond to the user's clicking the **Calculate** Button. Event handler btnCalculate_Click updates the ListBox's contents. The following box describes how to add items to a ListBox and how to clear a ListBox.

Using Code to Change a ListBox's Contents

1. ***Adding the Calculate Button's event handler.*** Double click the **Calculate** Button to generate the empty event handler btnCalculate_Click.

2. ***Clearing the ListBox control.*** Add lines 145–146 of Fig. 9.9 to btnCalculate_Click. Each time users click the **Calculate** Button, any content previously displayed in the ListBox is removed. To remove all content from the ListBox, call method **Clear** on property **Items** (line 146). Content can be added and deleted from the ListBox by using its Items property. The Items property returns an object that contains a list of items displayed in the ListBox. Notice that we have added comments on lines 141 and 148, and broken the first line of btnCalculate_Click into two lines for readability.

(cont.)

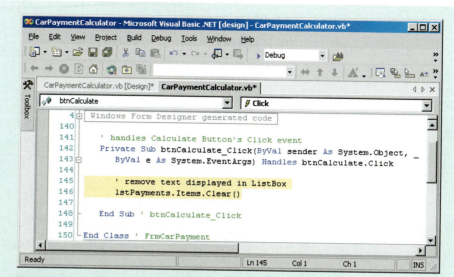

Figure 9.9 Clearing the contents of a `ListBox`.

3. *Adding content to the ListBox control.* Add lines 148–150 of Fig. 9.10 to `btnCalculate_Click`. The `ListBox` displays the number of monthly payments and the amount per payment. To clarify what information is being displayed, a line of text—called a **header**—needs to be added to the `ListBox`. Method **Add** (lines 149–150 of Fig. 9.10) adds the header—the column headings `"Months"` and `"Monthly Payment"` separated by two tab characters—to the `ListBox`'s `Items` property.

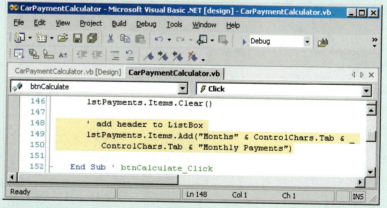

Figure 9.10 Adding a header to a `ListBox`.

GUI Design Tip

Use headers in a `ListBox` when you are displaying tabular data. Adding headers improves readability by indicating the information that will be displayed in the `ListBox`.

The ampersand symbol (&) is called the **string-concatenation operator**. This operator combines (or concatenates) its two operands into one value. In lines 149–150, the header is created by joining the values `"Months"` and `"Monthly Payments"` with two `ControlChars.Tab` constants. The constant `ControlChars.Tab` inserts a tab character into the string. The application uses two tab characters of separation between the columns (Fig. 9.3).

4. *Saving the project.* Select **File > Save All** to save your modified code.

Now that you have learned how to change a `ListBox`'s contents, you need to declare variables and obtain user input for the calculation. The following box shows you how to initialize the **Car Payment Calculator** application's variables. The box also guides you through converting the annual interest to the monthly interest rate and shows you how to calculate the amount of the loan.

Declaring Variables and Receiving User Input

1. *Declaring variables.* Place the cursor in the blank line immediately preceding the code you added in the box, *Using Code to Change a ListBox's Contents*. Add lines 145–152 of Fig. 9.11 to the application above the code you added in the previous box. Variables intYears and intMonths store the length of the loan in years and months. The calculation requires the length in months, but the loop-continuation condition will use the number of years. Variables intPrice, intDownPayment and dblInterest store the user input from the TextBoxes. Normally intPrice and intDownPayment would be represented as type Decimal, because they represent monetary values. For simplicity in this application, we have used Integers. Variables intLoanAmount and dblMonthlyInterest store calculation results.

2. *Retrieving user input needed for the calculation*. Add lines 161–165 of Fig. 9.12 below the code you added in the previous box. Lines 163–165 receive the down payment (intDownPayment), the price (intPrice) and the annual interest rate (dblInterest) provided by the user. Notice that line 165 divides the interest rate by 100 to obtain the decimal equivalent (for example, 5% becomes .05).

Variables to store the length of the loan

Variables to store user input

Variables to store calculation results

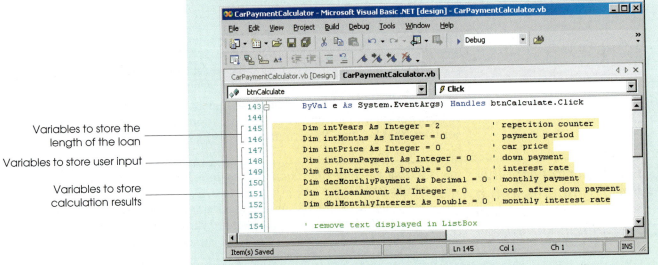

Figure 9.11   Variables for the **Car Payment Calculator** application.

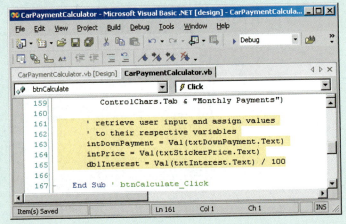

Figure 9.12   Retrieving input in the **Car Payment Calculator** application.

(cont.)

3. **Calculating values used in the calculation.** The application computes the amount of the loan by subtracting the down payment from the price. Add lines 167–169 of Fig. 9.13 to calculate the amount borrowed (line 168) and the monthly interest rate (line 169). Because these calculations need to occur only once, they are placed before the Do While...Loop. Variables intLoanAmount and dblMonthlyInterest will be used in the calculation of monthly payments, which will be added to your application shortly.

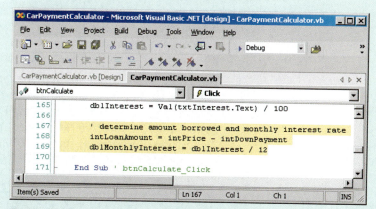

Figure 9.13 Determining amount borrowed and monthly interest rate.

4. **Saving the project.** Select **File > Save All** to save your modified code.

Next, you will add a repetition statement to the application to calculate the monthly payment for four loans. The repetition statement performs this calculation for loans that last two, three, four and five years.

Calculating the Monthly Payment Amounts with a Do While...Loop Repetition Statement

1. **Setting the loop-continuation condition.** Place the cursor after the code you entered in the previous box. Add lines 171–172 of Fig. 9.14 to the application below the lines that calculate the amount of the loan (intLoanAmount) and the monthly interest rate (dblMonthlyInterest). After you type line 172 and press *Enter*, Visual Studio .NET closes the repetition statement by adding the keyword Loop on line 174.

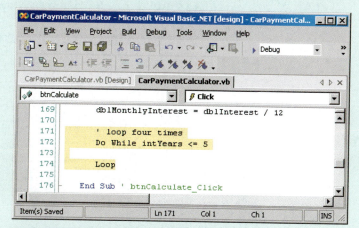

Figure 9.14 Loop-continuation condition.

(cont.)

Recall that the shortest loan in this application lasts 2 years, so you initialized `intYears` to 2 of line 145 (Fig. 9.11). The loop-continuation condition (`intYears <= 5`) in Fig. 9.14 specifies that the `Do While...Loop` statement executes while `intYears` remains less than or equal to 5. This loop is an example of **counter-controlled repetition**. This technique uses a variable called a **counter** (`intYears`) to control the number of times that a set of statements will execute. Counter-controlled repetition also is called **definite repetition**, because the number of repetitions is known before the loop begins executing. In this example, repetition terminates when the counter (`intYears`) exceeds 5.

2. *Calculating the payment period.* Add lines 174–175 of Fig. 9.15 to the `Do While...Loop` repetition statement to calculate the number of payments (that is, the length of the loan in months). The number of months changes with each iteration of the loop, and the calculation result changes as the length of the payment period changes. Variable `intMonths` will have the values 24, 36, 48 and 60, on successive iterations of the loop.

3. *Computing the monthly payment.* Add lines 177–179 of Fig. 9.16 to the `Do While...Loop` repetition statement immediately after the code you just entered. Lines 178–179 (Fig. 9.16) use the `Pmt` function to calculate the user's monthly payment. The **Pmt** function returns a `Double` value that specifies the monthly payment amount on a loan for a constant interest rate (`dblMonthlyInterest`) and a given time period (`intMonths`).

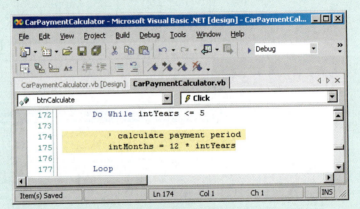

Figure 9.15 Converting the loan duration from years to months.

Line 179 passes to `Pmt` the interest rate, the total number of payments (equal to the number of months in the payment period) and the amount borrowed. Borrowed amounts are represented by negative values, because they represent a removal of cash from the person or organization that is lending money. Monetary amounts are stored in variables of type `Decimal`. Method **Convert.ToDecimal** converts the return value of `Pmt` to type `Decimal` and assigns this value to `decMonthlyPayment`.

(cont.)

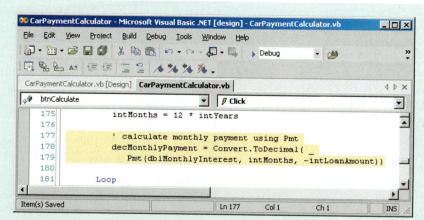

Figure 9.16 Pmt function returns monthly payment.

4. ***Displaying the monthly payment amount.*** Add lines 181–184 of Fig. 9.17 to the application. The number of monthly payments and the monthly payment amounts are displayed beneath the header. To add this content to the ListBox, call method Add (lines 182–184 of Fig. 9.17). Lines 183–184 use method String.Format to display decMonthlyPayment in currency format. Notice that the two tab characters ensure that the monthly payment amount is placed in the second column. The space provided by the extra tab character makes the application output more readable.

5. ***Incrementing the counter variable.*** Add line 186 of Fig. 9.18 before the closing statement of the repetition statement. Line 186 increments the counter variable (intYears). Variable intYears will be incremented until it equals 6. Then the loop-continuation condition (intYears <= 5) will evaluate to False and the repetition will end.

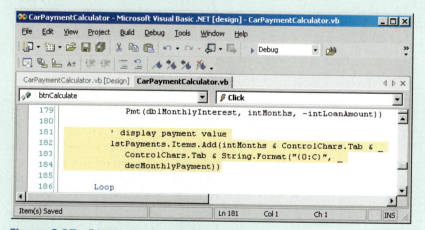

Figure 9.17 Displaying the number of months and the amount of each monthly payment.

(cont.)

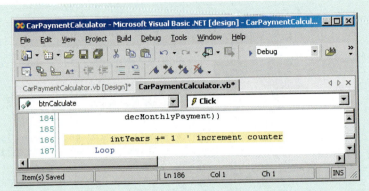

Figure 9.18 Incrementing the counter.

6. *Running the application.* Select **Debug > Start** to run your application. The application should calculate and display monthly payments. Enter values for a car's price, down payment and annual interest rate and click the **Calculate** Button to verify that the application is working correctly.

7. *Closing the application.* Close your running application by clicking its close box.

8. *Closing the IDE.* Close Visual Studio .NET by clicking its close box.

Figure 9.19 presents the source code for the **Car Payment Calculator** application. The lines of code that contain new programming concepts that you learned in this tutorial are highlighted.

```
1    Public Class FrmCarPayment
2       Inherits System.Windows.Forms.Form
3
4       ' Windows Form Designer generated code
5
6       ' handles Calculate Button's Click event
7       Private Sub btnCalculate_Click(ByVal sender As System.Object, _
8          ByVal e As System.EventArgs) Handles btnCalculate.Click
9
10         Dim intYears As Integer = 2           ' repetition counter
11         Dim intMonths As Integer = 0          ' payment period
12         Dim intPrice As Integer = 0           ' car price
13         Dim intDownPayment As Integer = 0     ' down payment
14         Dim dblInterest As Double = 0         ' interest rate
15         Dim decMonthlyPayment As Decimal = 0  ' monthly payment
16         Dim intLoanAmount As Integer = 0      ' cost after down payment
17         Dim dblMonthlyInterest As Double = 0  ' monthly interest rate
18
19         ' remove text displayed in ListBox
20         lstPayments.Items.Clear()
21
22         ' add header to ListBox
23         lstPayments.Items.Add("Months" & ControlChars.Tab & _
24            ControlChars.Tab & "Monthly Payments")
25
26         ' retrieve user input and assign values
27         ' to their respective variables
28         intDownPayment = Val(txtDownPayment.Text)
29         intPrice = Val(txtStickerPrice.Text)
30         dblInterest = Val(txtInterest.Text) / 100
```

Figure 9.19 **Car Payment Calculator** application code. (Part 1 of 2.)

```
31
32        ' determine amount borrowed and monthly interest rate
33        intLoanAmount = intPrice - intDownPayment
34        dblMonthlyInterest = dblInterest / 12
35
36        ' loop four times
37        Do While intYears <= 5
38
39            ' calculate payment period
40            intMonths = 12 * intYears
41
42            ' calculate monthly payment using Pmt
43            decMonthlyPayment = Convert.ToDecimal( _
44                Pmt(dblMonthlyInterest, intMonths, -intLoanAmount))
45
46            ' display payment value
47            lstPayments.Items.Add(intMonths & ControlChars.Tab & _
48                ControlChars.Tab & String.Format("{0:C}", _
49                decMonthlyPayment))
50
51            intYears += 1  ' increment counter
52        Loop
53
54    End Sub ' btnCalculate_Click
55
56  End Class ' FrmCarPayment
```

Figure 9.19   Car Payment Calculator application code. (Part 2 of 2.)

SELF-REVIEW

1. Counter-controlled repetition is also called _____ because the number of repetitions is known before the loop begins executing.

   a) definite repetition   b) known repetition

   c) sequential repetition   d) counter repetition

2. The line of text that is added to a ListBox to clarify the information that will be displayed is called a _____.

   a) title   b) starter

   c) header   d) clarifier

Answers: 1) a. 2) c.

9.5 Wrap-Up

In this tutorial, you began using repetition statements. You used the Do While...Loop and the Do Until...Loop statements to repeat actions in an application, depending on a loop-continuation condition or a loop-termination condition, respectively.

The Do While...Loop repetition statement executes as long as its loop-continuation condition is True. When the loop-continuation condition becomes False, the repetition terminates. An infinite loop occurs if this condition never becomes False.

The Do Until...Loop repetition statement executes as long as its loop-termination condition is False. The repetition terminates when the loop-termination condition becomes True. An infinite loop occurs if this condition never becomes True.

You learned about counter-controlled repetition, in which a repetition statement "knows" the number of times it will iterate because a variable known as a counter precisely counts the number of iterations. You used a repetition statement to develop a **Car Payment Calculator** application in which you calculated the monthly payments for a given loan amount and a given interest rate for loan durations of two, three, four and five years.

In the **Car Payment Calculator** application, you used the ListBox control to display several payment options on a car loan. You learned about the ListBox control, which is used to maintain a list of items. Items can be added and removed from the ListBox programmatically. Values are added to a ListBox control by invoking method Add on the ListBox control's Items property. The Items property returns an object that contains all the values displayed in the ListBox.

In the next tutorial, you will learn two other Do repetition statements and you will continue exploring counter-controlled repetition. The **Car Payment Calculator** application demonstrated one common use of repetition statements—performing a calculation for several different values. The next application introduces another common application of repetition statements—summing a series of numbers.

SKILLS SUMMARY

Displaying Values in a ListBox

- Property Items of the ListBox control returns an object that contains the values to be displayed in a ListBox.
- Invoke method Add to add values to the Items property.

Clearing a ListBox's Contents

- Method Clear of the Items's property deletes (clears) all the values in the ListBox.

Repeating Actions in an Application

- Use a repetition statement that depends on the true or false value of a loop-continuation condition or a loop-termination condition.

Executing a Repetition Statement for a Known Number of Repetitions

- Use counter-controlled repetition with a counter variable to determine the number of times that a set of statements will execute.

Using the Do While...Loop Repetition Statement

- This repetition statement executes while the loop-continuation condition is True.
- An infinite loop occurs if the condition never becomes False.

Using the Do Until...Loop Repetition Statement

- This repetition statement executes while the loop-termination condition is False.
- An infinite loop occurs if the condition never becomes True.

KEY TERMS

Add method of Items—Adds an item to a ListBox control.

Clear method of Items—Deletes all the values in a ListBox's control.

ControlChars.Tab constant—Represents a tab character.

Convert.ToDecimal method—Converts a value to type Decimal, which is appropriate for monetary calculations.

counter—A variable often used to determine the number of times a block of statements in a loop will execute.

counter-controlled repetition—A technique that uses a counter variable to determine the number of times that a block of statements will execute. Also called definite repetition.

definite repetition—See counter-controlled repetition.

diamond symbol (in the UML)—In the UML, represents the decision symbol and the merge symbol, depending on how it is used.

Do Until...Loop repetition statement—A control statement that executes a set of body statements until its loop-termination condition becomes True.

Do While...Loop repetition statement—A control statement that executes a set of body statements while its loop-continuation condition is True.

header—A line of text at the top of a ListBox that clarifies the information being displayed.

infinite loop—An error in which a repetition statement never terminates.

Items property of the ListBox control—Returns an object containing all the values in the ListBox.

ListBox control—Allows the user to view items in a list. Items can be added to or removed from the list programmatically.

loop—Another name for a repetition statement.

loop-continuation condition—The condition used in a repetition statement (such as a Do While...Loop) that enables repetition to continue while the condition is True and that causes repetition to terminate when the condition becomes False.

loop-termination condition—The condition used in a repetition statement (such as a Do Until...Loop) that enables repetition to continue while the condition is False and that causes repetition to terminate when the condition becomes True.

merge symbol (in the UML)—A symbol in the UML that joins two flows of activity into one flow of activity.

Pmt function—A function that, given an interest rate, a time period and a monetary loan amount, returns a Double value specifying the payment amount per specified time period.

repetition statement—Allows the programmer to specify that an action or actions should be repeated, depending on the value of a condition.

GUI DESIGN GUIDELINES

ListBox

- A ListBox should be large enough to display all of its content or large enough that scrollbars may be used easily.
- Use headers in a ListBox when you are displaying tabular data. Adding headers improves readability by indicating the information that will be displayed in the ListBox.

CONTROLS, EVENTS, PROPERTIES & METHODS

Convert The Convert class converts the value of a data type to another data type.

- *Methods*

  ToDecimal—Converts its argument to a Decimal value.

ListBox 　　 ListBox   This control allows the user to view and select from items in a list.

- *In action*

Months	Monthly Payments
24	$490.50
36	$339.06
48	$263.55
60	$218.41

- *Properties*

  Items—Returns an object that contains the items displayed in the ListBox.

  Location—Specifies the location of the ListBox on the Form.

  Name—Specifies the name used to access the properties of the ListBox programatically. The name should be prefixed with lst.

  Size—Specifies the height and width (in pixels) of the ListBox.

- *Methods*

  Items.Add—Adds an item to the Items property.

  Items.Clear—Deletes all the values in the ListBox's Items property.

MULTIPLE-CHOICE QUESTIONS

9.1 The _____ statement executes until its loop-continuation condition becomes True.

a) Do While...Loop   b) Do Until...Loop

c) Do   d) Loop

9.2 The _____ statement executes until its loop-continuation condition becomes `False`.

a) `Do While...Loop`

b) `Do Until...Loop`

c) `Do`

d) `Do While`

9.3 A(n) _____ loop occurs when a condition in a `Do While...Loop` never becomes `False`.

a) infinite

b) undefined

c) nested

d) indefinite

9.4 A _____ is a variable that helps control the number of times that a set of statements will execute.

a) repeater

b) counter

c) loop

d) repetition control statement

9.5 The _____ control allows users to add and view items in a list.

a) `ListItems`

b) `SelectBox`

c) `ListBox`

d) `ViewBox`

9.6 In a UML activity diagram, a(n) _____ symbol joins two flows of activity into one flow of activity.

a) merge

b) combine

c) action state

d) decision

9.7 Property _____ returns an object containing all the values in a `ListBox`.

a) `All`

b) `List`

c) `ListItemValues`

d) `Items`

9.8 Method _____ deletes all the values in a `ListBox`.

a) `Remove`

b) `Delete`

c) `Clear`

d) `Del`

9.9 `Items`'s method _____ adds an item to a `ListBox`.

a) `Include`

b) `Append`

c) `Add`

d) `Insert`

9.10 Method _____ calculates monthly payments on a loan based on a fixed interest rate.

a) `MonPmt`

b) `Payment`

c) `MonthlyPayment`

d) `Pmt`

EXERCISES

9.11 *(Table of Powers Application)* Write an application that displays a table of numbers from 1 to an upper limit, along with each number's squared value (for example, the number *n* to the power 2, or *n* ^ 2) and cubed value (the number *n* to the power 3, or *n* ^ 3). The users should specify the upper limit, and the results should be displayed in a `ListBox`, as in Fig. 9.20.

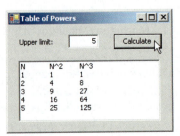

Figure 9.20   **Table of Powers** application's Form.

a) *Copying the template to your working directory.* Copy the directory `C:\Examples\Tutorial09\Exercises\TableOfPowers` to your `C:\SimplyVB` directory.

b) *Opening the application's template file.* Double click TableOfPowers.sln in the TableOfPowers directory to open the application.

c) *Adding a ListBox.* Add a ListBox to the application, as shown in Fig. 9.20. Name the ListBox lstResults.

d) *Adding the Upper limit: TextBox event handler.* Double click the **Upper limit:** TextBox to generate an event handler for this TextBox's TextChanged event. In this event handler, clear the ListBox.

e) *Adding the Calculate Button event handler.* Double click the **Calculate** Button to generate the empty event handler btnCalculate_Click. Add the code specified by the remaining steps to this event handler.

f) *Clearing the ListBox.* Use method Clear on the Items property to clear the List-Box from any previous data.

g) *Obtaining the upper limit supplied by the user.* Assign the value entered by the user in the **Upper limit:** TextBox to a variable. Note that the TextBox's Name property is set to txtInput.

h) *Adding a header.* Use method Add on the Items property to insert a header in the ListBox. The header should label three columns—N, N^2 and N^3. Column headings should be separated by tab characters.

i) *Calculating the powers from 1 to the specified upper limit.* Use a Do Until…Loop to calculate the squared value and the cubed value of each number from 1 to the upper limit, inclusive. Add an item to the ListBox containing the current number being analyzed, its squared value and its cubed value.

j) *Incrementing the counter.* Remember to increment the counter appropriately each time through the loop.

k) *Running the application.* Select **Debug > Start** to run your application. Enter an upper limit and click the Calculate Button. Verify that the table of powers displayed contains the correct values.

l) *Closing the application.* Close your running application by clicking its close box.

m) *Closing the IDE.* Close Visual Studio .NET by clicking its close box.

9.12 *(Mortgage Calculator Application)* A bank offers mortgages that can be repaid in 5, 10, 15, 20, 25 or 30 years. Write an application that allows a user to enter the price of a house (the amount of the mortgage) and the annual interest rate. When the user clicks a Button, the application displays a table of the mortgage length in years together with the monthly payment, as shown in Fig. 9.21.

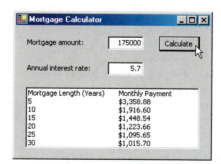

Figure 9.21   **Mortgage Calculator** application's Form.

a) *Copying the template to your working directory.* Copy the directory C:\Examples\Tutorial09\Exercises\MortgageCalculator to your C:\SimplyVB directory.

b) *Opening the application's template file.* Double click MortgageCalculator.sln in the MortgageCalculator directory to open the application.

c) *Adding a ListBox to display the results.* Add a ListBox as shown in Fig. 9.21. Name the ListBox lstResults.

d) *Adding a Calculate Button event handler.* Double click the **Calculate** Button to generate the empty event handler btnCalculate_Click. Add the code specified in the remaining steps to your event handler.

e) *Converting the annual interest rate to the monthly interest rate.* To convert the annual interest rate from a percent value into its Double equivalent, divide the annual rate by 100. Then divide the Double annual rate by 12 to obtain the monthly rate.

f) *Clearing the ListBox.* Use method Clear on the Items property to clear the List-Box from any previous data.

g) *Displaying a header.* Use method Add to display a header in the ListBox. The header should be the column headers "Mortgage Length (Years)" and "Monthly Payment", separated by a tab character.

h) *Using a repetition statement.* Add a Do While…Loop repetition statement to calculate six monthly payment options for the user's mortgage. Each option has a different number of years that the mortgage can last. For this exercise, use the following number of years: 5, 10, 15, 20, 25 and 30.

i) *Converting the length of the mortgage from years to months.* Convert the number of years to months.

j) *Calculating the monthly payments for six different mortgages.* Use the Pmt function to compute the monthly payments. Pass to the function the monthly interest rate, the number of months in the mortgage and the mortgage amount. Remember that the mortgage amount must be negative, as it represents an amount of money being paid out by the lender.

k) *Displaying the results.* Use method Add on the Items property to display the length of the mortgage in years and the monthly payment in the ListBox. You will need to use three tab characters to ensure that the monthly payment appears in the second column.

l) *Running the application.* Select **Debug > Start** to run your application. Enter a mortgage amount and annual interest rate, then click the **Calculate** Button. Verify that the monthly payments displayed contain the correct values.

m) *Closing the application.* Close your running application by clicking its close box.

n) *Closing the IDE.* Close Visual Studio .NET by clicking its close box.

9.13 *(Office Supplies Application)* Create an application that allows a user to make a list of office supplies to buy, as shown in Fig. 9.22. The user should enter the supply in a TextBox and click the **Buy** Button to add it to the ListBox. The **Clear** Button removes all the items from the ListBox.

Figure 9.22 **Office Supplies** application's Form.

a) *Copying the template to your working directory.* Copy the directory C:\Examples\ Tutorial09\Exercises\OfficeSupplies directory to your C:\SimplyVB directory.

b) *Opening the application's template file.* Double click OfficeSupplies.sln in OfficeSupplies directory to open the application.

c) *Adding a ListBox.* Add a ListBox to the Form. Name the ListBox lstSupplies. Place and size it as shown in Fig. 9.22.

d) *Adding an event handler for the Buy Button.* Double click the **Buy** Button to generate the event handler btnBuy_Click. The event handler should obtain the user input from the TextBox. The user input is then added as an item into the ListBox. After the input is added to the ListBox, clear the **Supply:** TextBox.

e) *Adding an event handler for the Clear Button.* Double click the **Clear** Button to generate the event handler btnClear_Click. The event handler should use the Clear method on the Items property to clear the ListBox.

f) *Running the application.* Select **Debug > Start** to run your application. Enter several items into the **Supply:** TextBox and click the **Buy** Button after entering each item. Verify that each item is added to the ListBox. Click the **Clear** Button and verify that all items are removed from the ListBox.

g) *Closing the application.* Close your running application by clicking its close box.

h) *Closing the IDE.* Close Visual Studio .NET by clicking its close box.

What does this code do? 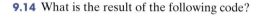   **9.14** What is the result of the following code?

```
1   Dim intX As Integer = 1
2   Dim intMysteryValue As Integer = 1
3
4   Do While intX < 6
5
6       intMysteryValue *= intX
7       intX += 1
8   Loop
9
10  lblDisplay.Text = intMysteryValue
```

What's wrong with this code?   **9.15** Find the error(s) in the following code:

a) Assume that the variable intX is declared and initialized to 1. The loop should total the numbers from 1 to 10.

```
1   Dim intTotal As Integer = 0
2
3   Do Until intX <= 10
4
5       intTotal += intX
6       intX += 1
7   Loop
```

b) Assume that the variable intCounter is declared and initialized to 1. The loop should sum the numbers from 1 to 100.

```
1   Do While intCounter <= 100
2
3       intTotal += intCounter
4   Loop
5
6   intCounter += 1
```

c) Assume that the variable intCounter is declared and initialized to 1000. The loop should iterate from 1000 to 1.

```
1   Do While intCounter > 0
2
3       lblDisplay.Text = intCounter
4       intCounter += 1
5   Loop
```

d) Assume that the variable intCounter is declared and initialized to 1. The loop should execute five times, adding the numbers 1–5 to a ListBox.

```
1    Do While intCounter < 5
2
3        lstNumbers.Items.Add(intCounter)
4        intCounter += 1
5    Loop
```

Using the Debugger ▶ **9.16** (*Odd Numbers Application*) The **Odd Numbers** application should display all of the odd integers between one and the number input by the user. Copy the **Odd Numbers** application from C:/Examples/Tutorial09/Debugger to your working directory. Run the application. Notice that, after you enter a value into the **Upper limit:** TextBox and click the **View** Button, an infinite loop occurs. Use the debugger to find and fix the error(s) in the application. Figure 9.23 displays the correct output for the application.

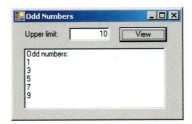

Figure 9.23　Correct output for the **Odd Numbers** application.

Programming Challenge ▶ **9.17** *(To Do List Application)* Use a ListBox as a to do list. Enter each item in a TextBox, and add it to the ListBox by clicking a Button. The item should be displayed in a numbered list as in Fig. 9.24. To do this, we introduce property Count, which returns the number of items in a ListBox's Items property. The following is a sample call to assign the number of items displayed in the lstSample ListBox to an Integer variable:

```
intCount = lstSample.Items.Count
```

Figure 9.24　**To Do List** application's Form.

T U T O R I A L

Class Average Application

Introducing the Do...Loop While and Do...Loop Until Repetition Statements

This tutorial continues our discussion of repetition statements that we began in Tutorial 9. In the previous tutorial, we examined Do While...Loop and Do Until...Loop repetition statements, which test their loop-continuation and loop-termination conditions before an iteration. This tutorial introduces two additional repetition statements, Do...Loop While and Do...Loop Until, which perform their tests after each iteration. As a result, the body statements contained in either of these repetition statements are performed at least once.

You will also learn how to disable and enable controls on a Form. When a control, such as a Button, is disabled, it will no longer respond to the user. You will use this feature to prevent the user from causing errors in your applications. This tutorial also introduces the concept of transferring the focus of the application to a control. Proper use of the focus makes an application easier to use.

10.1 Test-Driving the Class Average Application

This application must meet the following requirements:

Application Requirements

A teacher regularly issues quizzes to a class of ten students. The grades on these quizzes are integers in the range from 0 to 100 (0 and 100 are each valid grades). The teacher would like you to develop an application that computes the class average for a quiz.

The class average is equal to the sum of the grades divided by the number of students who took the quiz. The algorithm for solving this problem on a computer must input each of the grades, total the grades, perform the averaging calculation and display the result. You begin by test-driving the completed application. Then, you will learn the additional Visual Basic .NET technologies that you will need to create your own version of this application.

Test-Driving the Class Average Application

1. ***Opening the completed application.*** Open the directory `C:\Examples\Tutorial10\CompletedApplication\ClassAverage` to locate the **Class Average** application. Double click `ClassAverage.sln` to open the application in Visual Studio .NET.

2. ***Running the Class Average application.*** Select **Debug > Start** to run the application (Fig. 10.1).

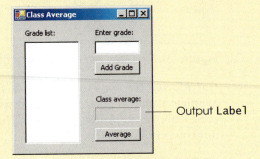

Output **Label**

Figure 10.1 **Class Average** application's **Form** in run mode.

3. ***Entering quiz grades.*** Enter 85 as the first quiz grade in the **Enter grade:** TextBox, and click the **Add Grade** Button. The grade entered will display in the ListBox as in Fig. 10.2. Notice that, after you click the **Add Grade** Button, the cursor appears in the **Enter grade:** TextBox. When a control is selected (for example, the **Enter grade:** TextBox), it is said to have the **focus** of the application. You will learn to set the focus to a control as you build this tutorial's application. As a result of the application's focus being transferred to the **Enter grade:** TextBox, you can type another grade without navigating to the TextBox with the mouse or the *Tab* key. Transferring the focus to a particular control tells the user what information the application expects next. [*Note:* If you click the **Average** Button before 10 grades have been input, an error occurs. In the dialog that displays, click **Continue** to return to design mode. Repeat *Step 2.* You will fix this problem in the exercises.]

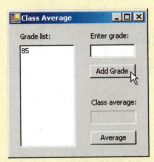

Figure 10.2 Entering grades in the **Class Average** application.

4. ***Repeat* Step 3 *nine times.*** Enter nine other grades between 0 and 100, and click the **Add Grade** Button after each entry. After 10 grades are displayed in the **Grade list:** ListBox, the Form will look similar to Fig. 10.3. Notice that, once you have entered 10 grades, the **Add Grade** Button is disabled. That is, its color is gray, and clicking the Button does not invoke its event handler.

(cont.)

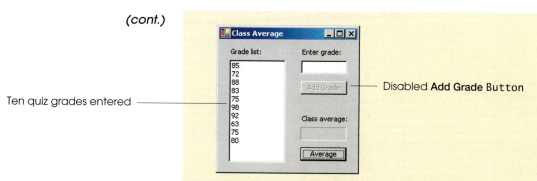

Ten quiz grades entered —————

Disabled **Add Grade** Button

Figure 10.3 **Class Average** application after 10 grades have been input.

5. ***Calculating the class average.*** Click the **Average** Button to calculate the average of the 10 quizzes. The class average will be displayed in an output Label above the **Average** Button (Fig. 10.4). Notice that the **Add Grade** Button is now enabled.

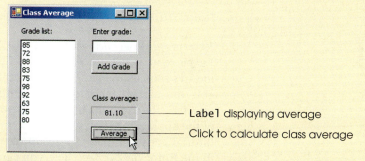

Label displaying average

Click to calculate class average

Figure 10.4 Displaying the class average.

6. ***Entering another set of grades.*** You can calculate the class average for another set of 10 grades without restarting the application. Enter a grade in the TextBox, and click the **Add Grade** Button. Notice that the **Grade list:** ListBox and the **Class average:** field are cleared when you start entering another set of grades (Fig. 10.5).

Figure 10.5 Entering a new set of grades.

7. ***Closing the application.*** Close your running application by clicking its close box.

8. ***Closing the IDE.*** Close Visual Studio .NET by clicking its close box.

10.2 Do...Loop While Repetition Statement

The **Do...Loop While** repetition statement is similar to the Do While...Loop statement; both statements iterate while their loop-continuation conditions are True. In the Do While...Loop statement, the loop-continuation condition is tested at the beginning of the loop, before the body of the loop is performed. The Do...Loop While statement performs the loop-continuation condition *after* the loop body is performed. Therefore, in a Do...Loop While statement, the loop body always executes at least once. Recall that a Do While...Loop executes only if its loop-continuation condition evaluates to true. When a Do...Loop While statement terminates, execution continues with the statement after the Loop While clause.

Common Programming Error

An infinite loop occurs when the loop-continuation condition in a Do...Loop While statement never becomes False.

To illustrate the Do...Loop While repetition style, consider the example of packing a suitcase: Before you begin packing, the suitcase is empty. You place an item in the suitcase, then determine whether the suitcase is full. As long as the suitcase is not full, you continue to put items in the suitcase. As an example of a Do...Loop While statement, let's look at the following application segment designed to display the numbers 1 through 3 in a ListBox:

```
Dim intCounter As Integer = 1

Do
    lstDisplay.Items.Add(intCounter)
    intCounter += 1
Loop While intCounter <= 3
```

The application segment initializes the counter intCounter to 1. The loop-continuation condition in the Do...Loop While statement is intCounter <= 3. While the loop-continuation condition is True, the Do...Loop While statement executes. When the loop-continuation condition becomes False (that is, when intCounter is greater than 3), the Do...Loop While statement finishes executing and lstDisplay contains the numbers 1 through 3. The following box describes each step as the above repetition statement executes.

Executing the Do...Loop While Repetition Statement

1. The application declares variable intCounter and sets its value to 1.

2. The application enters the Do...Loop While repetition statement.

3. The number (currently 1) stored in intCounter is Added to the lstDisplay ListBox's Items property.

4. The value of intCounter is increased by 1; intCounter now contains the number 2.

5. The loop-continuation condition is checked. The condition evaluates to True (intCounter is less than or equal to 3), so the application resumes execution at the first statement after the Do statement.

6. The number (currently 2) stored in intCounter is Added to the lstDisplay ListBox's Items property.

7. The value of intCounter is increased by 1; intCounter now contains the number 3.

8. The loop-continuation condition is checked. The condition evaluates to True (intCounter is less than or equal to 3), so the application resumes execution at the first statement after the Do statement.

9. The number (currently 3) stored in intCounter is Added to the lstDisplay ListBox's Items property.

10. The value of intCounter is increased by 1; intCounter now contains the number 4.

11. The loop-continuation condition is checked. The condition evaluates to False (intCounter is not less than or equal to 3), so the application exits the Do...Loop While repetition statement.

Notice that, if you mistyped the loop-continuation condition as intCounter < 3 or intCounter <= 2, the ListBox would display only 1 and 2. Including an incorrect

Error-Prevention Tip

Including a final value in the condition of a repetition statement (and choosing the appropriate relational operator) can reduce the occurrence of off-by-one errors. For example, in a Do While...Loop statement used to print the values 1–10, the loop-continuation condition should be intCounter <= 10, rather than intCounter < 10 (which is an off-by-one error) or intCounter < 11 (which is correct, but less clear).

relational operator (such as the less than sign in intCounter < 3) or an incorrect final value for a loop counter (such as the 2 in intCounter <= 2) in the condition of any repetition statement can cause **off-by-one errors**, which occur when a loop executes for one more or one fewer iterations than is necessary.

Figure 10.6 illustrates the UML activity diagram for the general Do...Loop While statement. This diagram makes it clear that the loop-continuation guard condition ([intCounter <= 3]) does not evaluate until after the loop performs the action state at least once. Recall that action states can include one or more Visual Basic .NET statements executed one after the other (sequentially) as in the preceding example. When you use a Do...Loop While repetition statement in building an application, you would provide the appropriate action state and the guard conditions for your application.

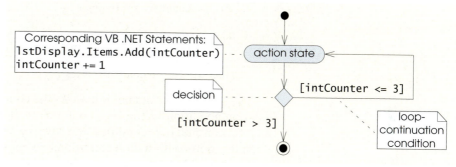

Figure 10.6   Do...Loop While repetition statement UML activity diagram.

---

1. The Do...Loop While statement tests the loop-continuation condition _____.

   a) for False after the loop body executes   b) for False before the loop body executes

   c) for True after the loop body executes   d) for True before the loop body executes

2. An infinite loop occurs when the loop-continuation condition in a Do While...Loop or Do...Loop While statement _____.

   a) never becomes True   b) never becomes False

   c) is False   d) is tested repeatedly

Answers: 1) c. 2) b.

10.3 Do...Loop Until Repetition Statement

The **Do...Loop Until** statement is similar to the Do Until...Loop statement, except that in the Do...Loop Until statement the loop-termination condition is tested after the loop body is performed. Therefore, the loop body executes at least once. When a Do...Loop Until terminates, execution continues with the statement after the Loop Until clause.

Error-Prevention Tip

An infinite loop occurs when the loop-termination condition in a Do...Loop Until statement never becomes True.

Again, consider the suitcase-packing example. Before you begin packing, the suitcase is empty. You place an item in the suitcase, then determine whether the suitcase is still empty. As long as the condition "the suitcase is full" is False, you continue to put items into the suitcase.

As an example of a Do...Loop Until statement, let's look at another application segment designed to display the numbers 1 through 3 in a ListBox:

```
Dim intCounter As Integer = 1

Do
    lstDisplay.Items.Add(intCounter)
    intCounter += 1
Loop Until intCounter > 3
```

The application segment initializes the counter `intCounter` to 1, and the loop-termination condition in the Do...Loop Until statement is `intCounter > 3`. While the loop-termination condition is `False`, the Do...Loop Until statement executes. When the loop-termination condition becomes `True`, the Do...Loop Until statement finishes executing and `lstDisplay` contains the numbers 1 through 3. The following box describes each step as the repetition statement executes.

Executing the Do...Loop Until Repetition Statement	1. The application declares variable `intCounter` and sets its value to 1.
	2. The application enters the Do...Loop Until repetition statement.
	3. The number (1) stored in `intCounter` is Added to the `lstDisplay` List-Box's `Items` property.
	4. The value of `intCounter` is increased by 1; `intCounter` now contains the number 2.
	5. The loop-termination condition is checked. The condition evaluates to `False` (`intCounter` is not greater than 3), so the application resumes execution at the first statement after the Do statement.
	6. The number (2) stored in `intCounter` is Added to the `lstDisplay` List-Box's `Items` property.
	7. The value of `intCounter` is increased by 1; `intCounter` now contains the number 3.
	8. The loop-termination condition is checked. The condition evaluates to `False` (`intCounter` is not greater than 3), so the application resumes execution at the first statement after the Do statement.
	9. The number (3) stored in `intCounter` is Added to the `lstDisplay` List-Box's `Items` property.
	10. The value of `intCounter` is increased by 1; `intCounter` now contains the number 4.
	11. The loop-termination condition is checked. The condition now evaluates to `True` (`intCounter` is greater than 3), so the application exits the Do...Loop Until repetition statement.

The Do...Loop Until UML activity diagram (Fig. 10.7) makes it clear that the loop-termination guard condition is not evaluated until after the body is executed at least once. This UML diagram indicates the exact same guard conditions as detailed in Fig. 10.6. The only difference for a Do...Loop Until repetition statement is that it continues to execute when the loop-termination guard condition is `False`. When the guard condition evaluates to `True`, the repetition ends and program control moves to the next statement following the Loop Until clause.

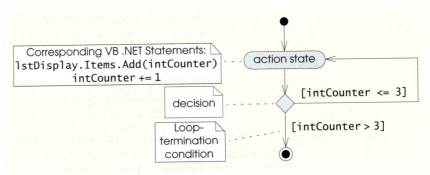

Figure 10.7   Do...Loop Until repetition statement activity diagram.

1. The Do...Loop Until statement checks the loop-termination condition _____.
   a) for False after the loop body executes
   b) for False before the loop body executes
   c) for True after the loop body executes
   d) for True before the loop body executes

2. When a Do...Loop Until terminates, execution continues with the _____.
   a) Loop Until clause
   b) statement after the Loop Until clause
   c) statements inside Do and Loop Until
   d) Do clause

Answers: 1) c. 2) b.

10.4 Creating the Class Average Application

Now that you have learned the Do...Loop While and Do...Loop Until repetition statements, you can begin to develop the **Class Average** application. First, you will use pseudocode to list the actions to be executed and to specify the order of execution. You will use counter-controlled repetition to input the grades one at a time. Recall that this technique uses a variable called a counter to determine the number of times that a set of statements executes. In this example, repetition terminates when the counter exceeds 10 because we are assuming, for simplicity, that the user will only enter 10 grades. The following pseudocode describes the basic operation of the **Class Average** application when the **Add Grade** Button is clicked:

> When the user clicks the Add Grade Button
>
> If an average has already been calculated for a set of grades
>   Clear the output Label and the ListBox
>
> Retrieve grade entered by user in the Enter grade: TextBox
> Display the grade in the ListBox
> Clear the Enter grade: TextBox
> Transfer focus to the Enter grade: TextBox
>
> If the user has entered more than 10 grades
>   Disable the Add Grade Button
>   Transfer focus to the Average Button
>
> When the user clicks the Average Button
>   Set total to zero
>   Set grade counter to zero
>
> Do
>   Read the next grade in the ListBox
>   Add the grade to the total
>   Add one to the grade counter
> Loop While the grade counter is less than 10
>
> Calculate the class average by dividing the total by 10
> Display the class average
> Enable the Add Grade Button
> Transfer focus to the Enter grade: TextBox

Now that you have test-driven the **Class Average** application and studied its pseudocode representation, you will use an ACE table to help you convert the pseudocode to Visual Basic .NET. Figure 10.8 lists the actions, controls and events that will help you complete your own version of this application.

Action/Control/Event Table for the Class Average Application

Event	Control	Event
Label all the application's controls	lblPrompt, lblGradeList, lblDescribeOutput	
	btnAdd	Click
If an average has already been calculated for a set of grades	lblOutput	
Clear the output Label and the ListBox	lblOutput, lstGrades	
Retrieve grade entered by user in the Enter grade: TextBox	txtInput	
Display the grade in the ListBox	lstGrades	
Clear the Enter grade: TextBox	txtInput	
Transfer focus to the Enter grade: TextBox	txtInput	
If the user has entered more than 10 grades	lstGrades	
Disable the Add Grade Button	btnAdd	
Transfer focus to the Average Button	btnAverage	
	btnAverage	Click
Set total to zero		
Set grade counter to zero		
Do		
Read the next grade in the ListBox	lstGrades	
Add the grade to the total		
Add one to the grade counter		
Loop While the grade counter is less than 10		
Calculate the class average by dividing the total by 10		
Display the class average	lblOutput	
Enable the Add Grade Button	btnAdd	
Transfer focus to the Enter grade: TextBox	txtInput	

Figure 10.8   ACE table for the **Class Average** application.

We label the application's GUI, using Labels lblPrompt, lblDescribeOutput and lblGradeList. The user enters grades in the txtInput TextBox and clicks the btnAdd Button. The Click event then Adds the value that the user entered in the txtInput TextBox to the ListBox, using method lstGrades.Items.Add(). When the user has entered 10 grades and clicked the btnAverage Button, the application will retrieve each value from the ListBox, add it to the total and compute the class average by dividing by 10. The class average then will be displayed in the lblOutput Label.

Now that we have formulated an algorithm for solving the **Class Average** problem, we can begin adding functionality to the template application. To display in the **Grade list:** ListBox a grade entered in the **Enter grade:** TextBox, the user clicks the **Add Grade** Button. If the application is already displaying grades in the **Grade list:** ListBox and the class average in the **Class average:** Label, the values are first cleared. The following box guides you through adding this functionality to the **Add Grade** Button's event handler.

Entering Grades in the Class Average Application

1. *Copying the template to your working directory.* Copy the C:\Examples\ Tutorial10\TemplateApplication\ClassAverage directory to your C:\SimplyVB directory.

2. *Opening the Class Average application's template file.* Double click ClassAverage.sln in the ClassAverage directory to open the application in Visual Studio .NET. Double click ClassAverage.vb in the **Solution Explorer** to display the Form (Fig. 10.9).

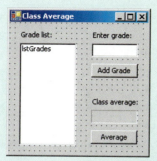

Figure 10.9 **Class Average** application's Form in design view.

3. *Adding an event handler for the Add Grade Button.* Each time users enter grades in the **Class Average** application, they must click the **Add Grade** Button. Double click the Button labelled **Add Grade** to create event handler btnAdd_Click.

4. *Clearing the ListBox and the Class average: Label of any output from a previous calculation.* Add lines 144–148 (Fig. 10.10) to event handler btnAdd_Click. Remember that you should place a comment before each event handler (line 140) and recall that we use the line-continuation character to split long lines (lines 141–142). To determine whether there was a previous calculation, test whether lblOutput displays any text by comparing the Text property's value to the empty string (line 145). If the lblOutput Label displays the result of a previous calculation, set its Text property to the empty string (line 146). Line 147 clears the grades from the ListBox.

5. *Displaying each grade in the ListBox control.* Add lines 150–152 of Fig. 10.11 to event handler btnAdd_Click below the If...Then statement. Line 151 Adds the grade entered in txtInput to ListBox lstGrades's Items property. The grade is displayed in the ListBox.

6. *Preparing for the next grade to be entered.* Method Clear (line 152 of Fig. 10.11) deletes the grade from the TextBox to prepare the application for the next grade to be entered.

(cont.)

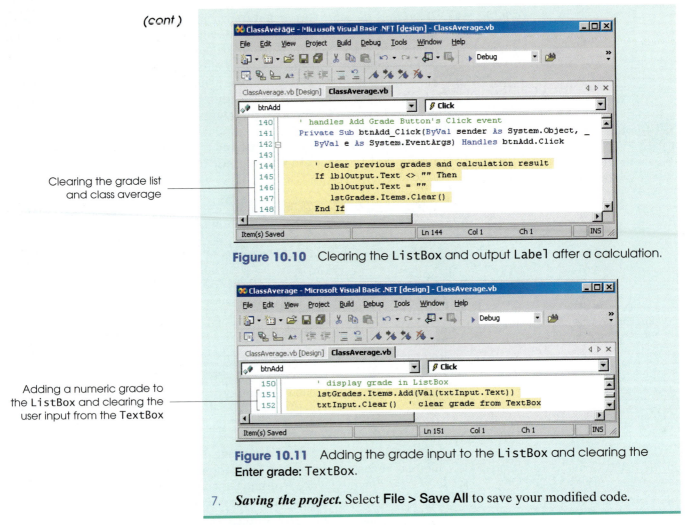

Clearing the grade list and class average

Figure 10.10   Clearing the `ListBox` and output `Label` after a calculation.

Adding a numeric grade to the `ListBox` and clearing the user input from the `TextBox`

Figure 10.11   Adding the grade input to the `ListBox` and clearing the **Enter grade:** `TextBox`.

7. **Saving the project.** Select **File > Save All** to save your modified code.

You have added the code to display the grade entered in the **Enter grade:** `TextBox` in the `ListBox` when the user clicks the **Add Grade** Button. Next, you learn how to transfer the focus to the `TextBox` for the next grade entry after the user clicks the **Add Grade** Button. The following box also shows you how to disable the **Add Grade** Button after 10 grades have been entered, because its functionality is no longer needed.

Transferring the Focus to a Control and Disabling a Button

1. **Transferring the focus to a control.** Add line 153 (Fig. 10.12) to event handler `btnAdd_Click`. Line 153 calls `txtInput`'s **Focus** method to place the cursor in the TextBox for the next grade input. This process is called **transferring the focus**. Here the focus is transferred from the Button to the TextBox.

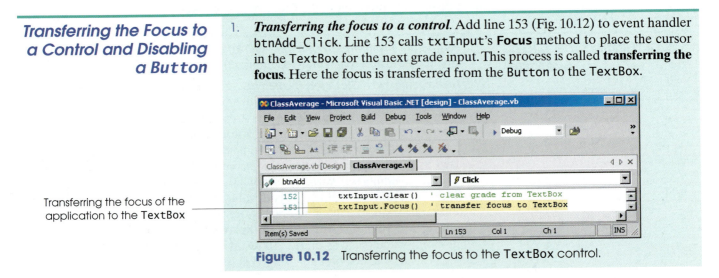

Transferring the focus of the application to the TextBox

Figure 10.12   Transferring the focus to the `TextBox` control.

(cont.)

2. ***Disabling the Add Grade Button to prohibit users from entering more than 10 grades.*** Your application should accept exactly 10 grades. If the number of grades already entered by the user is equal to 10, then the application should prevent the user from entering more grades. Add lines 155–159 of Fig. 10.13 to event handler btnAdd_Click. Line 156 determines whether 10 or more grades have been entered, using the >= comparison operator. Items's **Count** property returns the number of items displayed in the **Grade list:** ListBox. If 10 grades have been entered, line 157 disables Button btnAdd by setting its **Enabled** property to **False**. Clicking the disabled **Add Grade** Button will not cause the btnAdd_Click event handler to execute.

GUI Design Tip

Disable **Button**s when their function should not be available to users.

Disabling the **Add grade** **Button** and transferring the focus to the **Average Button**

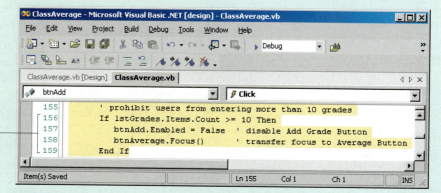

Figure 10.13   Application accepts only 10 grades.

3. ***Transferring the focus to the Average Button after 10 grades have been entered.*** After 10 grades have been entered, it does not make sense for the application to transfer the focus to the TextBox. Instead, line 158 invokes method Focus to transfer the focus to the **Average** Button. This way, you can press *Enter* to invoke **Average** Button's event handler, without navigating to the Button or using the mouse pointer.

4. ***Saving the project.*** Select **File > Save All** to save your modified code.

After 10 grades have been entered and displayed in the ListBox, the **Add Grade** Button's event handler transfers the focus to the **Average** Button. When the user clicks the **Average** Button, the application calculates and displays the average of the 10 grades. The following box shows you how to sum the grades with a Do...Loop Until repetition statement before the average calculation. The box also covers displaying the result in the **Class average:** Label.

Calculating the Class Average

1. ***Adding an event handler for the Average Button.*** Double click the Button labelled **Average** to generate event handler btnAverage_Click.

2. ***Initializing variables used in the class-average calculation.*** Add lines 167–171 of Fig. 10.14 to event handler btnAverage_Click. Line 168 declares Integer intTotal. You will use intTotal to calculate the sum of 10 grades (you will need this sum later when you calculate the average grade). Line 169 declares the counter (intGradeCounter). It is important that variables used as totals and counters have appropriate initial values before they are used. If a numerical variable is not initialized before its first use, Visual Basic .NET initializes it to a default value of 0. Variable intGrade (line 170) temporarily stores each grade read from the ListBox. Although the grades entered are Integers, the result of the averaging calculation can be a floating-point value (such as the 81.10 result in Fig. 10.4); therefore, you declare Double variable dblAverage (line 171) to store the class average.

(cont.)

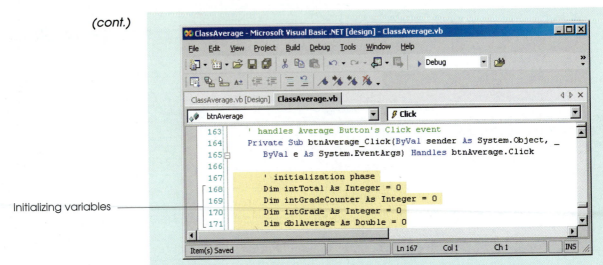

Figure 10.14   Initialization phase of class-average calculation.

Initializing variables

3. ***Summing the grades displayed in the ListBox.*** Add lines 173–180 of
    Fig. 10.15 to event handler btnAverage_Click. The Do...Loop Until state-
    ment (lines 174–180) sums the grades that it reads from the ListBox. Line
    180 indicates that the statement should iterate until the value of int-
    GradeCounter is greater than or equal to 10. Line 177 reads the current
    value from the ListBox, using property **Item** and stores that value in int-
    Grade. Line 178 adds intGrade to the previous value of intTotal and
    assigns the result to intTotal, using the += assignment operator. Variable
    intGradeCounter is incremented (line 179) to indicate that another grade
    has been processed. (Incrementing the counter ensures that the condition
    on line 180 eventually becomes True, terminating the loop.)

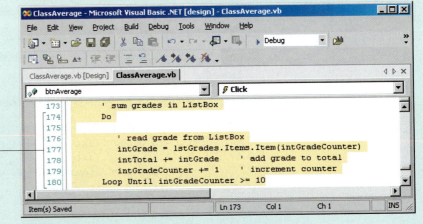

Using the Do...Loop Until
repetition statement to
sum grades in the ListBox

Figure 10.15   Do...Loop Until summing grades.

4. ***Calculating and displaying the average.*** Add lines 182–185 of Fig. 10.16 to
    event handler btnAverage_Click. Line 182 assigns the result of the aver-
    age calculation to variable dblAverage. Line 183 displays the value of vari-
    able dblAverage. After the average is displayed, another set of 10 grades
    can be entered. To allow this, you need to enable the **Add Grade** Button,
    by setting property Enabled to True (line 184). Line 185 transfers the focus
    to the **Enter grade:** TextBox.

GUI Design Tip

Enable a disabled **Button** when its
function should be available to the
user once again.

(cont.)

Calculating the class average, enabling the **Add Grade** Button and transferring the focus to the **Enter Grade:** TextBox

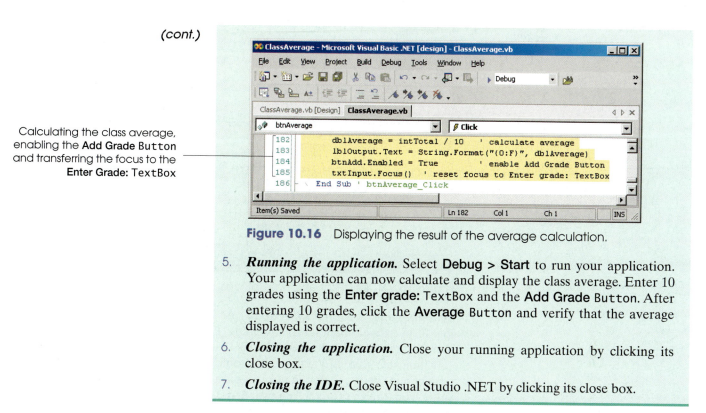

Figure 10.16 Displaying the result of the average calculation.

5. ***Running the application.*** Select **Debug > Start** to run your application. Your application can now calculate and display the class average. Enter 10 grades using the **Enter grade:** TextBox and the **Add Grade** Button. After entering 10 grades, click the **Average** Button and verify that the average displayed is correct.

6. ***Closing the application.*** Close your running application by clicking its close box.

7. ***Closing the IDE.*** Close Visual Studio .NET by clicking its close box.

Figure 10.17 presents the source code for the **Class Average** application. The lines of code that contain new programming concepts that you learned in this tutorial are highlighted.

```
1   Public Class FrmClassAverage
2      Inherits System.Windows.Forms.Form
3
4      ' Windows Form Designer generated code
5
6      ' handles Add Grade Button's Click event
7      Private Sub btnAdd_Click(ByVal sender As System.Object, _
8         ByVal e As System.EventArgs) Handles btnAdd.Click
9
10        ' clear previous grades and calculation result
11        If lblOutput.Text <> "" Then
12           lblOutput.Text = ""
13           lstGrades.Items.Clear()
14        End If
15
16        ' display grade in ListBox
17        lstGrades.Items.Add(Val(txtInput.Text))
18        txtInput.Clear()  ' clear grade from TextBox
19        txtInput.Focus()  ' transfer focus to TextBox
20
21        ' prohibit users from entering more than 10 grades
22        If lstGrades.Items.Count >= 10 Then
23           btnAdd.Enabled = False  ' disable Add Grade Button
24           btnAverage.Focus()       ' transfer focus to Average Button
25        End If
26
27     End Sub ' btnAdd_Click
28
```

Disabling the **Add Grade** Button and transferring the focus to the **Average** Button

Figure 10.17 **Class Average** application code. (Part 1 of 2.)

```
29    ' handles Average Button's Click event
30    Private Sub btnAverage_Click(ByVal sender As System.Object, _
31       ByVal e As System.EventArgs) Handles btnAverage.Click
32
33       ' initialization phase
34       Dim intTotal As Integer = 0
35       Dim intGradeCounter As Integer = 0
36       Dim intGrade As Integer = 0
37       Dim dblAverage As Double = 0
38
39       ' sum grades in ListBox
40       Do
41
42          ' read grade from ListBox
43          intGrade = lstGrades.Items.Item(intGradeCounter)
44          intTotal += intGrade      ' add grade to total
45          intGradeCounter += 1      ' increment counter
46       Loop Until intGradeCounter >= 10
47
48       dblAverage = intTotal / 10    ' calculate average
49       lblOutput.Text = String.Format("{0:F}", dblAverage)
50       btnAdd.Enabled = True         ' enable Add Grade Button
51       txtInput.Focus()   ' reset focus to Enter grade: TextBox
52    End Sub ' btnAverage_Click
53
54 End Class ' FrmClassAverage
```

Using a Do...Loop Until statement to calculate the class average

Enabling the **Add Grade** Button and transferring the focus to the **Enter grade:** TextBox

Figure 10.17   Class Average application code. (Part 2 of 2.)

SELF-REVIEW

1. If you do not want a Button to call its event handler method when the Button is clicked, set property _____ to _____.

   a) `Enabled, False`   b) `Enabled, True`

   c) `Disabled, True`   d) `Disabled, False`

2. _____ a TextBox selects that TextBox to receive user input.

   a) Enabling   b) Clearing

   c) Transferring the focus to   d) Disabling

Answers: 1) a. 2) c.

10.5 Wrap-Up

In this tutorial, you learned how to use the `Do...Loop While` and the `Do...Loop Until` repetition statements. We provided the syntax and included UML activity diagrams that explained how each statement executes. You used the `Do...Loop Until` statement in the **Class Average** application that you developed.

The `Do...Loop While` repetition statement executes as long as its loop-continuation condition is `True`. This repetition statement always executes at least once. When the loop-continuation condition becomes `False`, the repetition terminates. This repetition statement enters an infinite loop if the loop-continuation condition never becomes `False`.

The `Do...Loop Until` repetition statement also executes at least once. It executes as long as its loop-termination condition is `False`. When the loop-termination condition becomes `True`, the repetition terminates. The `Do...Loop Until` statement enters an infinite loop if the loop-termination condition never becomes `True`.

You also learned more sophisticated techniques for creating more polished graphical user interfaces for your applications. You now know how to invoke method Focus to transfer the focus in an application, indicating that the next action the user takes should involve this control. You also learned how to disable Buttons that should not be available to a user at certain times during an application's execution and you learned how to enable those Buttons again.

In the next tutorial, you will continue studying repetition statements. You will learn how to use the For...Next repetition statement, which is particularly useful for counter-controlled repetition.

SKILLS SUMMARY

Do...Loop While Repetition Statement

- Iterates while its loop-continuation condition is True.
- Tests the loop-continuation condition after the loop body is performed.
- Always executes the loop at least once.
- Becomes an infinite loop if the loop-continuation condition can never become False.

Do...Loop Until Repetition Statement

- Iterates until its loop-termination condition becomes True.
- Tests the loop-termination condition after the loop body is performed.
- Always executes the loop at least once.
- Becomes an infinite loop if the loop-termination condition can never become True.

Disabling a Button

- Set Button property Enabled to False.

Enabling a Button

- Set Button property Enabled to True.

Transferring the Focus to a Control

- Call method Focus.

KEY TERMS

Count property of Items—Returns the number of ListBox items.

Do...Loop Until repetition statement—A control statement that executes a set of statements until the loop-termination condition becomes True after the loop executes.

Do...Loop While repetition statement—A control statement that executes a set of statements while the loop-continuation condition is True; the condition is tested after the loop executes.

Enabled property—Specifies whether a control such as a Button appears enabled (True) or disabled (False).

Focus method—Transfers the focus of the application to the control, on which the method is called.

Item property of Items—Returns the value stored in the ListBox at the specified index.

off-by-one error—The kind of logic error that occurs when a loop executes for one more or one fewer iterations than is intended.

transferring the focus—Selecting a control in an application.

GUI DESIGN GUIDELINES

Button

- Disable a Button when its function should not be available to users.
- Enable a disabled Button when its function once again should be available to users.

CONTROLS, EVENTS, PROPERTIES & METHODS

Button   This control allows the user to raise an action or event.

■ *In action*

> Calculate Total

■ *Events*

Click—Raised when the user clicks the Button.

■ *Properties*

Enabled—Determines whether the Buttons event handler executes when the Button is clicked.

Location—Specifies the location of the Button on the Form relative to the top-left corner.

Name—Specifies the name used to access the Button programmatically. The name should be prefixed with btn.

Size—Specifies the height and width (in pixels) of the Button.

Text—Specifies the text displayed on the Button.

■ *Methods*

Focus—Transfers the focus of the application to the Button that calls it.

ListBox   ListBox   This control allows the user to view and select from items in a list.

■ *In action*

Months	Monthly Payments
24	$490.50
36	$339.06
48	$263.55
60	$218.41

■ *Properties*

Items—Returns an object that contains the items displayed in the ListBox.

Items.Count—Returns the number of items in the ListBox.

Items.Item—Returns the values at the specified index in the ListBox.

Location—Specifies the location of the ListBox on the Form relative to the top-left corner.

Name—Specifies the name used to access the ListBox programmatically. The name should be prefixed with lst.

Size—Specifies the height and width (in pixels) of the ListBox.

■ *Methods*

Items.Add—Adds an item to the Items property.

Items.Clear—Deletes all the values in the ListBox's Items property.

TextBox   abl TextBox   This control allows the user to input data from the keyboard.

■ *In action*

■ *Event*

TextChanged—Raised when the text in the TextBox is changed.

■ *Properties*

Location—Specifies the location of the TextBox on the Form relative to the top-left corner.

Name—Specifies the name used to access the TextBox programmatically. The name should be prefixed with txt.

Size—Specifies the height and width (in pixels) of the TextBox.

Text — Specifies the text displayed in the TextBox.

TextAlign—Specifies how the text is aligned within the TextBox.

■ *Methods*

Focus—Transfers the focus of the application to the TextBox that calls it.

MULTIPLE-CHOICE QUESTIONS

10.1 A(n) _____ occurs when a loop-continuation condition in a Do...Loop While never becomes False.

a) infinite loop

b) counter-controlled loop

c) control statement

d) nested control statement

10.2 Set property _____ to True to enable a Button.

a) Disabled

b) Focus

c) Enabled

d) ButtonEnabled

10.3 The _____ statement executes at least once and continues executing until its loop-termination condition becomes True.

a) Do While...Loop

b) Do...Loop Until

c) Do...Loop While

d) Do Until...Loop

10.4 The _____ statement executes at least once and continues executing until its loop-continuation condition becomes False.

a) Do...Loop Until

b) Do Until...Loop

c) Do While...Loop

d) Do...Loop While

10.5 Method _____ transfers the focus to a control.

a) GetFocus

b) Focus

c) Transfer

d) Activate

10.6 A _____ contains the sum of a series of values.

a) total

b) counter

c) condition

d) loop

10.7 Property _____ of _____ contains the number of items in a ListBox.

a) Count, ListBox

b) ListCount, Items

c) ListCount, ListBox

d) Count, Items

10.8 A(n) _____ occurs when a loop executes for one more or one less iteration than is necessary.

a) infinite loop

b) counter-controlled loop

c) off-by-one error

d) nested control statement

10.9 A Do...Loop Until repetition statement's loop-termination condition is evaluated _____.

a) only the first time the body executes

b) before the body executes

c) after the body executes

d) None of the above.

10.10 If its continuation condition is initially False, a Do...Loop While repetition statement _____.

a) never executes

b) executes while the condition is False

c) executes until the condition becomes True

d) executes only once

EXERCISES

10.11 (*Modified Class Average Application*) Modify the **Class Average** application, as in Fig. 10.18, so that **Average** Button is disabled until 10 grades have been entered.

Figure 10.18   Modified **Class Average** application.

a) *Copying the template to your working directory.* Copy the directory `C:\Examples\Tutorial10\Exercises\ModifiedClassAverage` to your `C:\SimplyVB` directory.

b) *Opening the application's template file.* Double click `ClassAverage.sln` in the `ModifiedClassAverage` directory to open the application.

c) *Initially disabling the Average Button.* Use the **Properties** window to modify the **Average** Button in the Form so that it is disabled when the application first executes by initially setting its `Enabled` property to `False`.

d) *Enabling the Average Button after 10 grades have been entered.* Add code to the `btnAdd_Click` event handler so that the **Average** Button becomes enabled when 10 grades have been entered.

e) *Disabling the Average Button after the calculation has been performed.* Add code to the `btnAverage_Click` event handler so that the **Average** Button is disabled once the calculation result has been displayed.

f) *Running the application.* Select **Debug > Start** to run your application. Enter 10 grades and ensure that the **Average** Button is disabled until all 10 grades are entered. Verify that the **Add Grade** Button is disabled after 10 grades are entered. Once the **Average** Button is enabled, click it and verify that the average displayed is correct. The **Average** Button should then become disabled again, and the **Add Grade** Button should be enabled.

g) *Closing the application.* Close your running application by clicking its close box.

h) *Closing the IDE.* Close Visual Studio .NET by clicking its close box.

10.12 *(Class Average Application That Handles Any Number of Grades)* Rewrite the **Class Average** application to handle any number of grades, as in Fig. 10.19. Note that, because the application does not know how many grades the user will enter, the Buttons must be enabled at all times.

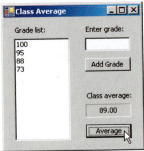

Figure 10.19   Modified **Class Average** application handling an unspecified number of grades.

a) *Copying the template to your working directory.* Copy the directory `C:\Examples\Tutorial10\Exercises\UndeterminedClassAverage` to your `C:\SimplyVB` directory.

b) *Opening the application's template file.* Double click `ClassAverage.sln` in the `UndeterminedClassAverage` directory to open the application.

c) *Never disabling the Add Grade Button.* Remove code from the `btnAdd_Click` event handler so that the **Add Grade** Button is not disabled after entering 10 grades.

d) *Summing the grades in the ListBox.* Modify code in the `btnAverage_Click` event handler so that `intGradeCounter` is incremented until it is equal to the number of grades entered. Use `lstGrades.Items.Count` to determine the number of items in the `ListBox`. The number returned by the `Count` property will be zero if there are no grades entered. Use an `If...Then` selection statement to avoid division by zero and display a message dialog to the user if there are no grades entered when the user clicks the **Average** Button.

e) *Calculating the class average.* Modify the code in the `btnAverage_Click` event handler so that `dblAverage` is computed by using `intGradeCounter` rather than the value 10.

f) *Running the application.* Select **Debug > Start** to run your application. Enter 10 grades and click the Average Button. Verify that the average displayed is correct. Follow the same actions but this time for 15 grades, then for 5 grades. Each time, verify that the appropriate average is displayed.

g) *Closing the application.* Close your running application by clicking its close box.

h) *Closing the IDE.* Close Visual Studio .NET by clicking its close box.

10.13 *(Arithmetic Calculator Application)* Write an application that allows users to enter a series of numbers and manipulate them. The application should provide users with the option of adding or multiplying the numbers. Users should enter each number in a TextBox. After entering each number, users should click a Button and the number should be inserted in a ListBox. The GUI should behave as in Fig. 10.20.

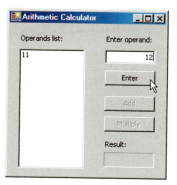
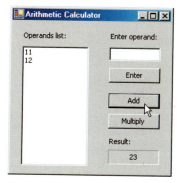

Figure 10.20 Arithmetic Calculator application.

a) *Copying the template to your working directory.* Copy the directory `C:\Examples\Tutorial10\Exercises\ArithmeticCalculator` to your `C:\SimplyVB` directory.

b) *Opening the application's template file.* Double click `ArithmeticCalculator.sln` in the `ArithmeticCalculator` directory to open the application.

c) *Add a ListBox to display the entered numbers.* Add a ListBox. Place and size it as in Fig. 10.20.

d) *Creating an event handler for the Enter Button.* Create the Click event handler for the **Enter** Button. If the result of a previous calculation is displayed, this event handler should clear the result and disable the addition and multiplication Buttons. It should then insert the current number in the **Operands list:** ListBox. When the ListBox contains at least two numbers, the event handler should then enable the addition and multiplication Buttons.

e) *Summing the grades in the ListBox.* Define the Click event handler for the **Add** Button. This event handler should compute the sum of all of the values in the **Operands list:** ListBox and display the result in a Label lblResult.

f) *Define the Click event handler for the Multiply Button.* This event handler should compute the product of all of the values in the **Operands list:** ListBox and display the result in the Label lblResult.

g) *Running the application.* Select **Debug > Start** to run your application. Enter two values, then click the **Add** and **Multiply** Buttons. Verify that the results displayed are correct. Also, make sure that the **Add** and **Multiply** Buttons are not enabled until two values have been entered.

h) *Closing the application.* Close your running application by clicking its close box.

i) *Closing the IDE.* Close Visual Studio .NET by clicking its close box.

What does this code do? ▶ **10.14** What is the result of the following code?

```
1   Dim intY As Integer
2   Dim intX As Integer
3   Dim intMysteryValue As Integer
4
5   intX = 1
6   intMysteryValue = 0
7
8   Do
9       intY = intX ^ 2
10      lstDisplay.Items.Add(intY)
11      intMysteryValue += 1
12      intX += 1
13  Loop While intX <= 10
14
15  lblResult.Text = intMysteryValue
```

What's wrong with this code? ▶ **10.15** Find the error(s) in the following code. This code should add 10 to the value in intY and store it in intZ. It then should reduce the value of intY by one and repeat until intY is less than 10. The output Label lblResult should display the final value of intZ.

```
1   Dim intY As Integer = 10
2   Dim intZ As Integer = 2
3
4   Do
5       intZ = intY + 10
6   Loop Until intY < 10
7
8   intY -= 1
9
10  lblResult.Text = intZ
```

Using the Debugger

10.16 (*Factorial Application*) The **Factorial** application calculates the factorial of an integer input by the user. The factorial of an integer is the product of the integers from one to that number. For example, the factorial of 3 is 6 ($1 \times 2 \times 3$). While testing the application you noticed that it does not execute correctly. Use the debugger to find and correct the logic error(s) in the application. Figure 10.21 displays the correct output for the **Factorial** application.

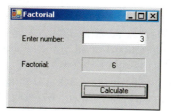

Figure 10.21 Correct output for the **Factorial** application.

Programming Challenge

10.17 (*Restaurant Bill Application*) Develop an application that calculates a restaurant bill. The user should be able to enter the item ordered, the quantity of the item ordered and the price per item. When the user clicks the **Add Item** `Button`, your application should display the number ordered, the item ordered and the price per unit in three `ListBoxes` as shown in Fig. 10.22. When the user clicks the **Total Bill** `Button`, the application should calculate the total cost. For each entry in the `ListBox`, multiply the cost of each item by the number of items ordered.

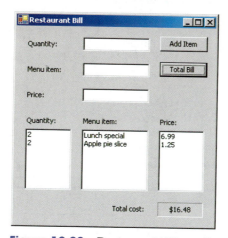

Figure 10.22 **Restaurant Bill** application's `Form`.

Interest Calculator Application

Introducing the For...Next Repetition Statement

As you learned in Tutorial 9 and Tutorial 10, applications are often required to repeat actions. Using a **Do** repetition statement allowed you to specify a condition and test that condition either before entering the loop or after execution of the body of the loop. In the **Car Payment Calculator** application and the **Class Average** application, a counter was used to determine the number of times the loop should iterate. In fact, the use of counters in repetition statement is so common in applications that Visual Basic .NET provides an additional control statement specially designed for such cases: the **For...Next** repetition statement. In this tutorial, you will use the **For...Next** repetition statement to create an **Interest Calculator** application.

11.1 Test-Driving the **Interest Calculator** Application

The **Interest Calculator** application calculates the amount of money in your savings account after you begin with a certain amount of money and are paid a certain interest rate for a certain amount of time. Users specify the principal amount (the initial amount of money in the account), the interest rate and the number of years for which interest will be calculated. The application then displays the results. This application must meet the following requirements:

Application Requirements

You are considering investing $1000.00 in a savings account that yields 5% interest and you want to forecast how your investment will grow. Assuming that you will leave all interest on deposit, calculate and print the amount of money in the account at the end of each year over a period of n years. To compute these amounts, use the following formula:

$$a = p (1 + r)^n$$

where

p is the original amount of money invested (the principal)
r is the annual interest rate (for example, .05 is equivalent to 5%)
n is the number of years
a is the amount on deposit at the end of the nth year.

You begin by test-driving the completed application. Then, you will learn the additional Visual Basic .NET technologies that you will need to create your own version of this application.

Test-Driving the Interest Calculator Application

1. **Opening the completed application.** Open the directory C:\Examples\ Tutorial11\CompletedApplication\InterestCalculator to locate the **Interest Calculator** application. Double click InterestCalculator.sln to open the application in Visual Studio .NET.

2. **Running the Interest Calculator application.** Select **Debug > Start** to run the application (Fig. 11.1).

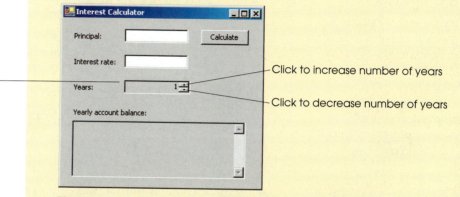

NumericUpDown control

Click to increase number of years

Click to decrease number of years

Figure 11.1 Completed **Interest Calculator** application.

3. **Providing a principal value.** Once the application is running, provide a value in the **Principal:** TextBox. Input 1000, as specified in the problem statement.

4. **Providing an interest-rate value.** Next, type a value in the **Interest Rate:** TextBox. We specified the interest rate 5% in the problem statement, so enter 5 in the **Interest Rate:** TextBox.

5. **Providing the duration of the investment.** Now, you should choose the number of years for which you want to calculate the amount in the savings account. In this case, select 10 by clicking the up arrow in the **Years:** NumericUpDown control repeatedly until the value reads 10.

6. **Calculating the amount.** After you input the necessary information, click the **Calculate** Button. The amount of money in your account at the end of each year during a period of 10 years displays in the multiline TextBox. The application should look similar to Fig. 11.2.

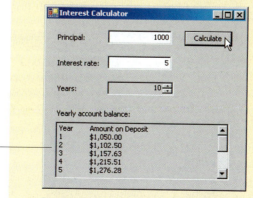

Multiline TextBox displays application results

Figure 11.2 Output of completed **Interest Calculator** application.

(cont.)

7. ***Closing the application.*** Close your running application by clicking its close box.

8. ***Closing the IDE.*** Close Visual Studio .NET by clicking its close box.

11.2 Essentials of Counter-Controlled Repetition

In Tutorial 10, you were introduced to counter-controlled repetition. The four essential elements of counter-controlled repetition are:

1. the *name* of a *control variable* (or loop counter) that is used to determine whether the loop continues to iterate

2. the *initial value* of the control variable

3. the *increment* (or *decrement*) by which the control variable is modified during each iteration of the loop (that is, each time the loop is performed)

4. the condition that tests for the *final value* of the control variable (to determine whether looping should continue).

The example of Fig. 11.3 uses the four elements of counter-controlled repetition. This Do While...Loop is similar to the **Car Payment Calculator** application's loop in Tutorial 9.

```
1    Dim intCounter As Integer = 1 ' repetition counter
2
3    Do While intCounter <= 5
4        intMonths = 12 * (intCounter + 1) ' calculate payment period
5
6        ' calculate payment value
7        decValue = Convert.ToDecimal( _
8            Pmt(dblMonthlyInterest, intMonths, -intLoanAmount))
9
10       ' display payment value
11       lstPayments.Items.Add(intMonths & ControlChars.Tab & _
12           ControlChars.Tab & String.Format("{0:C}", decValue))
13
14       intCounter += 1 ' increment counter
15   Loop
```

Figure 11.3 Counter-controlled repetition example.

Recall that the **Car Payment Calculator** application calculates and displays monthly car payments over periods of 2 to 5 years. The declaration in line 1 *names* the control variable (intCounter), indicating that it is of data type Integer. This declaration includes an initialization, which sets the variable to an *initial value* of 1.

Consider the Do While...Loop statement (lines 3–15). Line 4 uses the intCounter variable to calculate the number of months over which car payments are to be made. Lines 7–8 use the Pmt function to determine the monthly payment for the car. This value depends on the car's price, the interest rate, the duration of the loan in months and the down-payment amount. Lines 11–12 display the amount in a ListBox. Line 14 increments the control variable intCounter by 1 for each iteration of the loop. The condition in the Do While...Loop statement (line 3) tests for whether the value of the control variable is less than or equal to 5, meaning that 5 is the *final value* for which the condition is true. The body of this Do While...Loop is performed even when the control variable is 5. The loop terminates when the control variable exceeds 5 (that is, when intCounter has a value of 6).

1. The control variable's _____ is not one of the four essential elements of counter-controlled repetition.

   a) name   b) initial value

   c) type   d) final value

2. What aspect of the control variable determines whether looping should continue?

   a) name   b) initial value

   c) type   d) final value

Answers: 1) c. 2) d.

11.3 Introducing the For...Next Repetition Statement

The **For...Next** repetition statement makes it easier for you to write code to perform counter-controlled repetition. This statement specifies all four elements essential to counter-controlled repetition. The For...Next statement takes less time to code and is easier to read than an equivalent Do repetition statement.

Let's examine the first line of the For...Next repetition statement (Fig. 11.4), which we call the **For...Next header**. The For...Next header specifies all four essential elements for counter-controlled repetition. The line should be read "*for each value of intCounter starting at 2 and ending at 10, do the following statements, then add (step) two to intCounter.*"

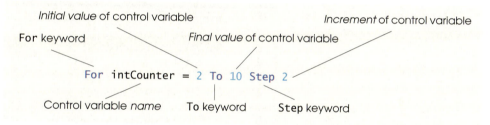

Figure 11.4 For...Next header components.

Each For...Next statement begins with the keyword **For**. Then, the statement names and initializes a control variable (in this case, intCounter is set to 2). [*Note:* We suggest you declare (using the Dim keyword) the counter variable before the For statement.] Following the initial value of the control variable is the keyword **To**, followed by the final value of the control variable to be used in the loop. You can then use the **Step** keyword to specify the amount by which to increase (or decrease) the control variable each time the loop body completes execution. If you wish to decrease the value of the control variable each time through the loop, simply use a negative number after the Step keyword. The following box describes each step as the above repetition statement executes.

Executing the For...Next Repetition Statement

1. The application sets variable intCounter's value to 2.

2. The application enters the For...Next repetition statement.

3. The value of intCounter is increased by 2; intCounter now contains the number 4.

4. The implied loop-continuation condition is checked. The implied condition evaluates to True (intCounter is less than or equal to 10), so the application resumes execution at the first statement after the For statement.

5. The value of intCounter is increased by 2; intCounter now contains the number 6.

(cont.)

6. The implied loop-continuation condition is checked. The implied condition evaluates to `True` (`intCounter` is less than or equal to 10), so the application enters the `For...Next` repetition statement.

7. The value of `intCounter` is increased by 2; `intCounter` now contains the number 8.

8. The implied loop-continuation condition is checked. The implied condition evaluates to `True` (`intCounter` is less than or equal to 10), so the application resumes execution at the first statement after the `For` statement.

9. The value of `intCounter` is increased by 2; `intCounter` now contains the number 10.

10. The implied loop-continuation condition is checked. The implied condition evaluates to `True` (`intCounter` is less than or equal to 10), so the application resumes execution at the first statement after the `For` statement.

11. The value of `intCounter` is increased by 2; `intCounter` now contains the number 12.

12. The implied loop-continuation condition is checked. The condition evaluates to `False` (`intCounter` is not less than or equal to 10), so the application exits the `For...Next` repetition statement.

Good Programming Practice

Place a blank line before and after each control statement to make it stand out in the code.

Using the keyword `Step` is optional. If you omit the `Step` keyword, the control variable is incremented by one after each repetition, by default.

In many cases, the `For...Next` statement can be represented by another repetition statement. For example, an equivalent `Do While...Loop` statement for Fig. 11.4 is

```
intCounter = 2

Do While intCounter <= 10
    body statement(s)
    intCounter += 2
Loop
```

Notice that the `For...Next` statement's header (Fig. 11.4) implies the loop-continuation condition (`intCounter <= 10`), which is shown explicitly in the preceding `Do While...Loop` statement. The starting value, ending value and increment portions of a `For...Next` statement can contain arithmetic expressions. The expressions are evaluated once (when the `For...Next` statement begins executing) and then used as the starting value, ending value and increment of the `For...Next` header. For example, assume that `intA = 2` and `intB = 10`. The header

```
For intI = intA To (4 * intA * intB) Step (intB \ intA)
```

is equivalent to the header

```
For intI = 2 To 80 Step 5
```

If the implied loop-continuation condition is initially `False` (for example, if the starting value is greater than the ending value and the increment value is positive), the `For...Next`'s body is not performed. Instead, execution proceeds with the statement after the `For...Next` statement.

The control variable frequently is displayed or used in calculations in the `For...Next` body, but it does not have to be. It is common to use the control variable only to control repetition and not use it in the `For...Next` body.

The UML activity diagram for the `For...Next` statement is similar to that of the `Do While...Loop` statement. For example, the UML activity diagram of the `For...Next` statement

Error-Prevention Tip

Although the value of the control variable can be changed in the body of a `For...Next` loop, avoid doing so, because this practice can lead to subtle errors.

```
For intCounter = 1 To 10
    lstDisplay.Items.Add(intCounter * 10)
Next
```

is shown in Fig. 11.5. This activity diagram shows that the initialization occurs only once and that incrementing occurs *after* each execution of the body statement. Note that, besides small circles and flowlines, the activity diagram contains only rounded rectangle symbols and small diamond symbols. The rounded rectangle symbols are filled with the actions, and the flowlines coming out of the small diamond symbols are labeled with the appropriate guard conditions for this algorithm.

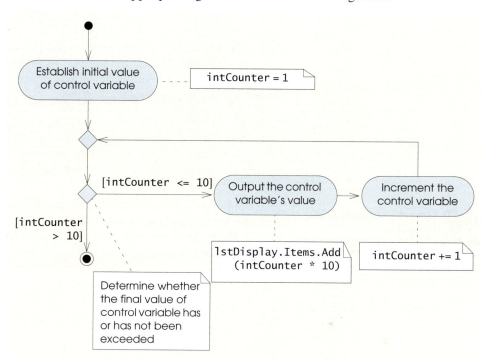

Figure 11.5 For...Next repetition statement UML activity diagram.

Notice that the For...Next header indicates each item needed to conduct counter-controlled repetition with a control variable. To help solidify your understanding of this new repetition statement, you will now learn how the Do While...Loop statement of Fig. 11.3 can be replaced by a For...Next statement.

The converted code is shown in Fig. 11.6. When the For...Next statement begins execution, line 3 of Fig. 11.6 initializes control variable intCounter to 1.

The implied loop-continuation condition intCounter <= 5 (which depends on the counter's final value) is tested in line 3. Keyword To is required in the For...Next statement. The value before this keyword specifies the initial value of intCounter; the value that follows it specifies the value tested for loop continuation (in this case, 5). Keyword Step is optional and is not used here. Step specifies the increment (the amount that is added to intCounter each time the For...Next body is executed.) If Step is not included, then the increment is 1, by default.

The initial value of intCounter is 1, so the implied loop-continuation condition is satisfied and the payment calculations within the For...Next body are executed.

After executing the For...Next body, the Next keyword is reached (line 13). This keyword marks the end of the For...Next repetition statement. When Next is reached, intCounter is incremented by 1 (the default increment amount), and the loop begins again with the implied loop-continuation condition test.

This process repeats until the implied loop-continuation condition becomes False as intCounter becomes greater than 5, then repetition terminates.

```
1   Dim intCounter As Integer
2
3   For intCounter = 1 To 5
4      intMonths = 12 * (intCounter + 1) ' calculate payment period
5
6      ' calculate payment value
7      decValue = Convert.ToDecimal( _
8         Pmt(dblMonthlyRate, intMonths, -intLoanAmount))
9
10     ' display payment value
11     lstPayments.Items.Add(intMonths & ControlChars.Tab & _
12        ControlChars.Tab & String.Format("{0:C}", decValue))
13  Next
```

Common Programming Error

Counter-controlled loops should not be controlled with floating-point variables. These are represented only approximately in the computer's memory, possibly resulting in imprecise counter values and inaccurate tests for termination that could lead to logic errors.

Figure 11.6 Code segment for the **Car Payment Calculator** application that demonstrates the For...Next statement.

SELF-REVIEW

1. If the Step clause is omitted, the increment of a For...Next statement defaults to _____.

   a) 2   b) 1

   c) 0   d) –1

2. The value before the To keyword in a For...Next statement specifies the _____.

   a) initial value of the counter variable   b) final value of the counter variable

   c) increment   d) number of times the statement iterates

   Answers: 1) b. 2) a.

11.4 Examples Using the For...Next Statement

The following examples demonstrate different ways of varying the control variable in a For...Next statement. In each case, we write the appropriate For...Next header:

a) Vary the control variable from 1 to 100 in increments of 1.

```
For intI = 1 To 100
   or
For intI = 1 To 100 Step 1
```

b) Vary the control variable from 100 to 1 in increments of –1 (decrements of 1).

```
For intI = 100 To 1 Step -1
```

c) Vary the control variable from 7 to 77 in increments of 7.

```
For intI = 7 To 77 Step 7
```

d) Vary the control variable from 20 to 2 in increments of –2 (decrements of 2).

```
For intI = 20 To 2 Step -2
```

e) Vary the control variable over the sequence of the following values: 2, 5, 8, 11, 14, 17, 20.

```
For intI = 2 To 20 Step 3
```

f) Vary the control variable over the sequence of the following values: 99, 88, 77, 66, 55, 44, 33, 22, 11, 0.

```
For intI = 99 To 0 Step -11
```

SELF-REVIEW

1. Which of the following is the appropriate For...Next header for varying the control variable over the following sequence of values: 25, 20, 15, 10, 5?

   a) For intI = 5 To 25 Step 5   b) For intI = 25 To 5 Step -5

   c) For intI = 5 To 25 Step -5   d) For intI = 25 To 5 Step 5

2. Which of the following statements describes the For...Next header

   ```
   For intI = 81 To 102?
   ```

   a) Vary the control variable from 81 to 102 in increments of 1.
   b) Vary the control variable from 81 to 102 in increments of 0.
   c) Vary the control variable from 102 to 81 in increments of -1.
   d) Vary the control variable from 81 to 102 in increments of 2.

Answers: 1) b. 2) a.

11.5 Constructing the Interest Calculator Application

Our solution to this tutorial's problem statement computes interest over a given number of years, by using the For...Next statement. This repetition statement will perform the calculation for every year that the money remains on deposit.

The following pseudocode describes the basic operation of the **Interest Calculator** application when the **Calculate** Button is clicked:

> **When the user clicks the Calculate Button**
>> Get the values for the principal, interest rate and years entered by the user
>> Store a header to be added to the output TextBox
>>
>> For each year (starting at 1 and ending with the number of years entered)
>>> Calculate the current value of the investment
>>> Display the year and the current value of the investment

The template application we provide for this tutorial contains the **Calculate** Button, plus two Labels and their corresponding TextBoxes: for **Principal:** and for **Interest Rate:**. The Form has a **Years:** Label, but you will insert the NumericUpDown control for this input. The **NumericUpDown** control limits a user's choices for the number of years to a specific range. You will then create a multiline TextBox with a scrollbar and add it to the application's GUI. Finally, you will add functionality with a For...Next statement. Now that you have test-driven the **Interest Calculator** application and studied its pseudocode representation, you will use an ACE table to help you convert the pseudocode to Visual Basic .NET. Figure 11.7 lists the actions, controls and events that will help you complete your own version of this application.

Action/Control/Event (ACE) Table for the Interest Calculator Application

Action	Control	Event
Label the application's fields	lblPrincipal, lblRate, lblYears, lblYearlyAccount	Application is run
	btnCalculate	Click
Get the values for the principal, interest rate and years entered by user	txtPrincipal, txtRate, updYear	
Store a header to be added to the output TextBox		
For each year (starting at 1 and ending with the number of years entered) Calculate the current value of the investment		
Display the year and the current value of the investment	txtResult	

Figure 11.7 ACE table for **Interest Calculator** application.

In the following box, you will begin building the **Interest Calculator** application. First, you will add a NumericUpDown control to allow the user to specify the number of years. This control provides up and down arrows that allow the user to scroll through the control's range of values. The following box shows you how to set the limits of the range (maximum and minimum values). We will use 10 as the maximum value and 1 as the minimum value for this control. The **Increment** property specifies by how much the current number in the NumericUpDown control changes when the user clicks the control's up (for incrementing) or down (for decrementing) arrow. This application uses the Increment property's default value, 1.

Adding and Customizing a NumericUpDown Control

1. **Copying the template to your working directory.** Copy the C:\Examples\Tutorial11\TemplateApplication\InterestCalculator directory to your C:\SimplyVB directory.

2. **Opening the Interest Calculator application's template file.** Double click InterestCalculator.sln in the InterestCalculator directory to open the application in Visual Studio .NET (Fig. 11.8).

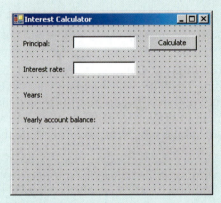

Figure 11.8 Template **Interest Calculator** application **Form** in design view.

3. **Adding a NumericUpDown control.** Double click the NumericUpDown control,

in the **Toolbox** to add it to the Form (Fig. 11.9). Change the control's Name property to updYear. To improve code readability, you should prefix NumericUpDown control names with upd which is short for up-down.

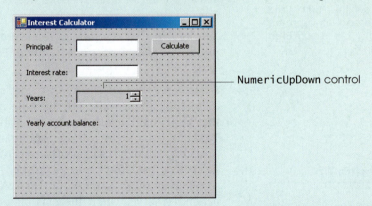

NumericUpDown control

Figure 11.9 NumericUpDown control added to **Interest Calculator** application.

GUI Design Tip

A NumericUpDown control should follow the same GUI Design Guidelines as a TextBox. (See Appendix C.)

(cont.)

4. ***Setting the NumericUpDown control's location and size.*** Set updYear's Location property to 96, 96 and its Size property to 104, 21, so that it aligns horizontally and vertically with the TextBoxes above it.

5. ***Setting property TextAlign.*** Set property TextAlign to Right. The number now appears right-aligned in the control.

6. ***Setting property ReadOnly.*** To ensure that the user cannot enter invalid values in the **Years:** NumericUpDown control, set the **ReadOnly** property to True. The ReadOnly property changes the background color of the control to gray, indicating that the user can change its value only by using the up and down arrows.

7. ***Setting range limits for the NumericUpDown control.*** By default, this control sets 0 as the minimum and 100 as the maximum. You will change these values. Set the **Maximum** property of the **Years:** NumericUpDown control to 10. Then set its **Minimum** property to 1. This (combined with setting its ReadOnly property to True) limits users to selecting values between 1 and 10 for the number of years. Notice that the NumericUpDown control displays 1, the value of its Minimum property. Your Form should now look like Fig. 11.9.

8. ***Saving the project.*** Select **File > Save All** to save your modified code.

The **Interest Calculator** application displays the results of its calculations in a multiline TextBox, which is simply a TextBox that can display more than one line of text. You can configure the TextBox to have a scrollbar, so that, if the TextBox is too small to display its contents, the user can scroll up and down to view the entire contents of the box. Next, you will create this TextBox.

Adding and Customizing a Multiline TextBox with a Scrollbar

1. ***Adding a TextBox to the Form.*** Double click the TextBox control in the **Toolbox** to add a TextBox to the Form. Name the TextBox txtResult.

2. ***Creating a multiline TextBox.*** Select the TextBox's **Multiline** property, and change its value from False to True. Doing so allows the TextBox to contain multiple lines.

3. ***Setting the size and location of the TextBox.*** Set the TextBox's Location property to 16, 160 and the Size property to 272, 88, so that it aligns horizontally with the controls above it.

4. ***Setting text appearance in the TextBox.*** Initially, txtResult should not display any text. Clear the Text property. Then, set property TextAlign to Left (if it is not already set to this value). This left-aligns text in the TextBox.

5. ***Setting property ReadOnly.*** To ensure that the user cannot change the output in the **Yearly account balance:** TextBox, set the ReadOnly property to True.

6. ***Inserting a vertical scrollbar.*** Using scrollbars allows you to keep the size of a TextBox small while still allowing the user to view all the information in that TextBox. Because the length of the text could exceed the height of the TextBox, enable the vertical scrollbar by setting txtResult's **ScrollBars** property to **Vertical**. A vertical scrollbar appears on the right side of the TextBox. By default, property ScrollBars is set to None. Note that the scrollbar is disabled on your Form. A scrollbar is enabled only when it is needed (that is, when there is enough text in the TextBox). Your Form should look like Fig. 11.10.

(cont.)

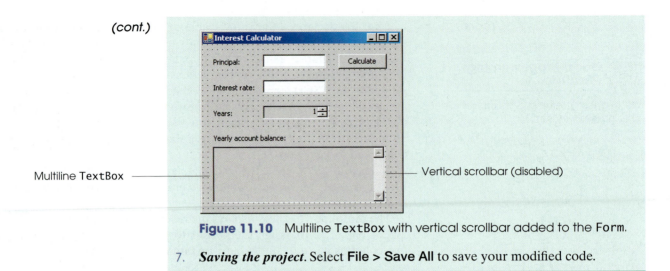

Figure 11.10 Multiline **TextBox** with vertical scrollbar added to the **Form**.

7. *Saving the project.* Select **File > Save All** to save your modified code.

Now that you have finished designing the GUI, you will add functionality to your application. When the user clicks the **Calculate** Button, you want the application to retrieve the input and then output a table containing the amount on deposit at the end of each year. You will do this by adding code to the Button's Click event handler.

Adding a Click Event Handler

1. *Creating the event handler.* Double click the **Calculate** Button. The **Calculate** Button Click event handler appears in the application's code.

2. *Adding code to event handler btnCalculate_Click.* Add lines 163–174 of Fig. 11.11 to the btnCalculate_Click event handler. Lines 163–169 declare the variables needed to store user inputs, calculation results and the output. Variable decPrincipal stores the amount of the principal as entered by the user, dblRate stores the interest rate and intYear stores the number of years the user selected in the NumericUpDown control. Variable decAmount stores the result of the interest calculation.

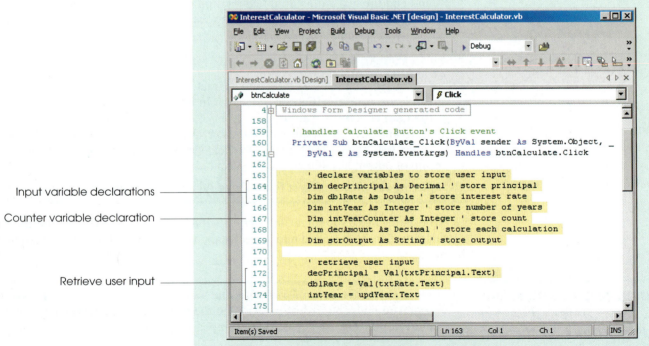

Figure 11.11 Application code for retrieving and storing user input.

(cont.)

Good Programming Practice

We suggest prefixing `String` variable names with `str`.

Line 169 declares a `String` variable `strOutput`. **String variables** store a series of characters. The most commonly used characters are letters and numbers, though characters also include many special characters such as $, *, ^, tabs and newlines. A list of characters you are likely to use is found in Appendix B, ASCII Character Set. You actually have been using `String`s all along—`Label`s and `TextBox`es both store values in the `Text` property as values of type `String`. In fact, when you assign a numeric data type, such as an `Integer`, to the `Text` property of a `Label`, the `Integer` value is implicitly converted to a `String`.

Lines 172–173 retrieve the principal and the interest rate from `TextBox`es. Line 174 uses the `NumericUpDown` control's `Text` property to obtain the user's selection.

The multiline `TextBox` displays the results in two columns. Add lines 176–178 of Fig. 11.12 to assign the header to `strOutput`. The header labels the two columns, as `Year` and `Amount on Deposit`, respectively.

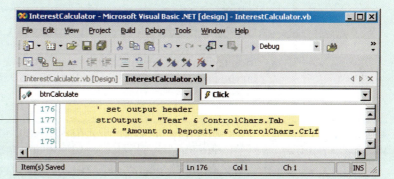

Appending header text to the output `String`

Figure 11.12 Application code for displaying a header in a multiline `TextBox`.

Recall that you cleared values in a `Label` in Tutorial 6 by setting the `Text` property to the empty string (`""`), which represents a `String` value with no characters. When assigning new text to a `String` variable, you must begin and end the text with a double quotation mark (`"`). For example, if you want to store the word `Year` in the `String` variable `strYear`, you would use the following statement:

```
strYear = "Year"
```

You can append a `String` or a character to the end of another `String` by using the concatenation operator (`&`). In lines 177–178 of Fig. 11.12, we use the `ControlChars.Tab` constant to insert a tab character between the word `Year` and the text `Amount on Deposit`. We then insert a newline character (`ControlChars.CrLf`), so that the next series of text will appear on the next line of output.

3. ***Saving the project.*** Select **File > Save All** to save your modified code.

The `For...Next` statement in lines 181–188 of Fig. 11.13 performs the interest calculations for the specified number of years. You create the `For...Next` statement in the next box.

Calculating Cumulative Interest with a For...Next Statement

1. ***Initializing the control variable and establishing the loop-continuation test.*** Add lines 180–181 of Fig. 11.13 to the `btnCalculate_Click` event handler. Notice that the keyword `Next` appears.

(cont.)

Line 181 is the For...Next header which initializes control variable intYearCounter to 1. The value after the keyword To sets the implied loop-continuation condition. This loop continues until the control variable is less than or equal to the number of years specified by the user.

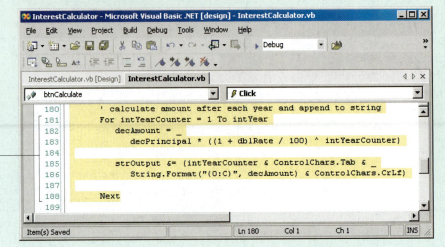

Using the For...Next statement to format and append text to the output String

```
180        ' calculate amount after each year and append to string
181        For intYearCounter = 1 To intYear
182           decAmount = _
183              decPrincipal * ((1 + dblRate / 100) ^ intYearCounter)
184
185           strOutput &= (intYearCounter & ControlChars.Tab & _
186              String.Format("{0:C}", decAmount) & ControlChars.CrLf)
187
188        Next
189
```

Figure 11.13　Application code for For...Next statement.

2. *Performing the interest calculation.* The For...Next statement executes its body once for each year up to the value of intYear, varying control variable intYearCounter from 1 to intYear in increments of 1. Add lines 182–183 of Fig. 11.13 to perform the calculation from the formula

$$a = p \ (1 + r) \ ^n$$

where *a* is decAmount, *p* is decPrincipal, *r* is dblRate and *n* is intYearCounter.

Notice that the calculation in line 183 also divides the rate, dblRate, by 100. This implies that the user must enter an interest rate value in percentage format (for example, the user should enter the number 5.5 to represent 5.5%).

3. *Appending the calculation to the output string.* Add lines 185–186 of Fig. 11.13. These lines append additional text to the end of strOutput, using the &= operator. The &= operator (which behaves much like the += operator) appends the right operand to the text in the left operand. That new value is then assigned to the variable in the left operand. The text includes the current intYearCounter value, a tab character (ControlChars.Tab) to position to the second column, the result of the call String.Format("{0:C}", decAmount) and, finally, a newline character (ControlChars.CrLf) to start the next output on the next line. Recall that the C (for "currency") formatting code indicates that its corresponding argument (decAmount) should be displayed in monetary format.

4. *Reaching the Next keyword.* After the body of the loop is performed, application execution reaches keyword Next which is now on line 188. The counter (intYearCounter) is incremented by 1, and the loop begins again with the implied loop-continuation test.

5. *Terminating the For...Next statement.* The For...Next statement executes until the control variable exceeds the number of years specified by the user.

6. *Displaying the result of the calculations.* After exiting the For...Next statement, strOutput is ready to be displayed to the user in the txtResult TextBox. Add line 190 of Fig. 11.14 to display the header and the results in the multiline TextBox.

(cont.)

Displaying in the multiline TextBox the result of the calculations performed in the For…Next statement

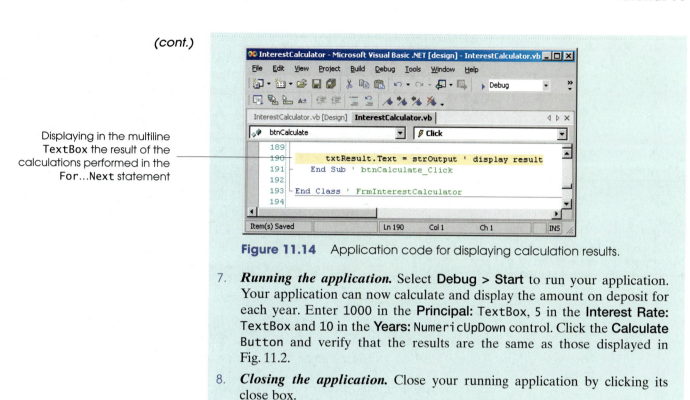

Figure 11.14 Application code for displaying calculation results.

7. *Running the application.* Select **Debug > Start** to run your application. Your application can now calculate and display the amount on deposit for each year. Enter 1000 in the **Principal:** TextBox, 5 in the **Interest Rate:** TextBox and 10 in the **Years:** NumericUpDown control. Click the **Calculate** Button and verify that the results are the same as those displayed in Fig. 11.2.

8. *Closing the application.* Close your running application by clicking its close box.

9. *Closing the IDE.* Close Visual Studio .NET by clicking its close box.

Figure 11.15 presents the source code for the **Interest Calculator** application. The lines of code that contain new programming concepts that you learned in this tutorial are highlighted.

```
1   Public Class FrmInterestCalculator
2      Inherits System.Windows.Forms.Form
3
4      ' Windows Form Designer generated code
5
6      ' handles Calculate Button's Click event
7      Private Sub btnCalculate_Click(ByVal sender As System.Object, _
8         ByVal e As System.EventArgs) Handles btnCalculate.Click
9
10        ' declare variables to store user input
11        Dim decPrincipal As Decimal ' store principal
12        Dim dblRate As Double ' store interest rate
13        Dim intYear As Integer ' store number of years
14        Dim intYearCounter As Integer ' store count
15        Dim decAmount As Decimal ' store each calculation
16        Dim strOutput As String ' store output
17
18        ' retrieve user input
19        decPrincipal = Val(txtPrincipal.Text)
20        dblRate = Val(txtRate.Text)
21        intYear = updYear.Text
22
23        ' set output header
24        strOutput = "Year" & ControlChars.Tab _
25           & "Amount on Deposit" & ControlChars.CrLf
26
```

Figure 11.15 Interest Calculator application. (Part 1 of 2.)

Using a For...Next statement
to calculate amount on
deposit

```
27        ' calculate amount after each year and append to string
28        For intYearCounter = 1 To intYear
29           decAmount = _
30              decPrincipal * ((1 + dblRate / 100) ^ intYearCounter)
31
32           strOutput &= (intYearCounter & ControlChars.Tab & _
33              String.Format("{0:C}", decAmount) & ControlChars.CrLf)
34
35        Next
36
37        txtResult.Text = strOutput ' display result
38     End Sub ' btnCalculate_Click
39
40  End Class ' FrmInterestCalculator
```

Figure 11.15   Interest Calculator application. (Part 2 of 2.)

11.6   Wrap-Up

In this tutorial, you learned that the essential elements of counter-controlled repetition are the name of a control variable, the initial value of the control variable, the increment (or decrement) by which the control variable is modified each time through the loop and the condition that tests the final value of the control variable. We then explored the For...Next repetition statement, which combines these essentials of counter-controlled repetition in its header.

After becoming familiar with the For...Next repetition statement, you changed the **Car Payment Calculator** application's Do While...Loop statement into a For...Next statement. You then built an **Interest Calculator**, after analyzing the pseudocode and ACE table for this application. In the **Interest Calculator**'s GUI, you added new design elements, including a NumericUpDown control and a multi-line TextBox that contained a scrollbar.

In the next tutorial, you will learn to use the Select Case multiple-selection statement. You have learned that the If...Then...Else selection statement can be used in code to select between multiple courses of action on the value of a condition. You will see that a Select Case multiple selection statement can save development time and improve code readability if the number of conditions is large. You will then use a Select Case multiple selection statement to build a **Security Panel** application.

SKILLS SUMMARY   **Using the For...Next Repetition Statement**

- Specify the initial value of the control variable before keyword To.
- Specify the value tested for loop continuation after keyword To.
- Use optional keyword Step to specify the increment (or decrement).
- Use keyword Next to mark the end of the repetition statement.

■ Using the For...Next statement helps eliminate off-by-one errors.

Creating a Multiline TextBox With a Vertical Scrollbar

■ Insert a TextBox onto the Form.

■ Set TextBox property Multiline to True.

■ Set TextBox property ScrollBar to Vertical.

Specifying a NumericUpDown Control's Maximum Value

■ Use NumericUpDown property Maximum.

Specifying a NumericUpDown Control's Minimum Value

■ Use NumericUpDown property Minimum.

Changing the Current Number in a NumericUpDown Control

■ Click the NumericUpDown control's up or down arrow.

Specifying By How Much The Current Number in a NumericUpDown Control Changes When the User Clicks an Arrow

■ Use NumericUpDown property Increment.

KEY TERMS

For...Next header—The first line of a For...Next repetition statement. The For...Next header specifies all four essential elements for the counter-controlled repetition of a For...Next repetition statement.

For...Next repetition statement—Repetition statement that handles the details of counter-controlled repetition. The For...Next statement uses all four elements essential to counter-controlled repetition in one line of code (the name of a control variable, the initial value, the increment or decrement value and the final value).

For keyword—Begins the For...Next statement.

Increment property of a NumericUpDown control—Specifies by how much the current number in the NumericUpDown control changes when the user clicks the control's up (for incrementing) or down (for decrementing) arrow.

Maximum property of a NumericUpDown control—Determines the maximum input value in a particular NumericUpDown control.

Minimum property of a NumericUpDown control—Determines the minimum input value in a particular NumericUpDown control.

Multiline TextBox control—Provides the ability to enter or display multiple lines of text. If the text exceeds the size of the TextBox, the control can be set to display a scrollbar.

Multiline property of a TextBox control—Specifies whether the TextBox is capable of displaying multiple lines of text. If the property value is True, the TextBox may contain multiple lines of text; if the value of the property is False, the TextBox can contain only one line of text.

NumericUpDown control—Allows you to specify maximum and minimum numeric input values. Also allows you to specify an increment (or decrement) when the user clicks the up (or down) arrow.

ReadOnly property of a NumericUpDown control—Determines whether the input value can be typed by the user.

ScrollBars property of a TextBox control—Specifies whether a TextBox has a scrollbar and, if so, of what type. By default, property ScrollBars is set to None. Setting the value to Vertical places a scrollbar along the right side of the TextBox.

Step keyword—Optional component of the For...Next header that specifies the increment (that is, the amount added to the control variable each time the loop is executed).

String variable—A variable that stores a series of characters.

To keyword—Used to specify a range of values. Commonly used in For...Next headers to specify the initial and final values of the statement's control variable.

Vertical value of ScrollBars property—Used to display a vertical scrollbar on the right side of a TextBox.

<table>
<tr><td>

GUI DESIGN
GUIDELINES

</td><td>

TextBox

- If a TextBox will display multiple lines of output, set the Multiline property to True and left-align the output by setting the TextAlign property to Left.
- If a multiline TextBox will display many lines of output, limit the TextBox height and use a vertical scrollbar to allow users to view additional lines of output.

NumericUpDown

- A NumericUpDown control should follow the same GUI Design Guidelines as a TextBox.
- Use a NumericUpDown control to limit the range of user input.

</td></tr>
</table>

<table>
<tr><td>

CONTROLS, EVENTS,
PROPERTIES &
METHODS

</td><td>

NumericUpDown   This control allows you to specify maximum and minimum numeric input values.

- ***In action***

      [6 ÷]

- ***Properties***

    Increment—Specifies by how much the current number in the NumericUpDown control changes when the user clicks the control's up (for incrementing) or down (for decrementing) arrow.

    Location—Specifies the location of the NumericUpDown control on the Form relative to the top-left corner.

    Maximum—Determines the maximum input value in a particular NumericUpDown control.

    Minimum—Determines the minimum input value in a particular NumericUpDown control.

    Name—Specifies the name used to access the NumericUpDown control programmatically. The name should be prefixed with upd.

    ReadOnly—Determines whether the input value can be typed by the user.

    Size—Specifies the height and width (in pixels) of the NumericUpDown control.

    TextAlign—Specifies how the text is aligned within the NumericUpDown control.

TextBox [abl TextBox]   This control allows the user to input data from the keyboard.

- ***In action***

      [0]

- ***Events***

    TextChanged—Raised when the text in the TextBox is changed.

- ***Properties***

    Location—Specifies the location of the TextBox on the Form relative to the top-left corner.

    Multiline—Specifies whether the TextBox is capable of displaying multiple lines of text.

    Name—Specifies the name used to access the TextBox programmatically. The name should be prefixed with txt.

    ReadOnly—Determines whether the value of a TextBox can be changed.

    ScrollBars—Specifies whether the TextBox contains a scrollbar.

    Size—Specifies the height and width (in pixels) of the TextBox.

    Text—Specifies the text displayed in the TextBox.

    TextAlign—Specifies how the text is aligned within the TextBox.

- ***Methods***

    Focus—Transfers the focus of the application to the TextBox that calls it.

</td></tr>
</table>

MULTIPLE-CHOICE QUESTIONS

11.1 "Hello" has data type _____.

a) String

b) StringLiteral

c) Character

d) StringText

11.2 A _____ provides the ability to enter or display multiple lines of text in the same control.

a) TextBox

b) NumericUpDown

c) MultilineTextBox

d) multiline NumericUpDown

11.3 The NumericUpDown control allows you to specify _____.

a) a maximum value the user can select

b) a minimum value the user can select

c) an increment for the values presented to the user

d) All of the above.

11.4 _____ is optional in a For...Next header when the control variable's increment is 1.

a) Keyword To

b) The initial value of the control variable

c) Keyword Step

d) The final value of the control variable

11.5 Setting TextBox property ScrollBars to _____ creates a vertical scrollbar.

a) True

b) Vertical

c) Up

d) Both

11.6 _____ is used to determine whether a For...Next loop continues to iterate.

a) The initial value of the control variable

b) Keyword For

c) Keyword Step

d) The control variable

11.7 In a For...Next loop, the control variable is incremented (or decremented) _____.

a) after the body of the loop executes

b) when keyword To is reached

c) while the loop-continuation condition is False

d) while the body of the loop executes

11.8 Setting a NumericUpDown control's _____ property to True ensures that the user cannot enter invalid values in the control.

a) Increment

b) ScrollBars

c) ReadOnly

d) InValid

11.9 The _____ and _____ properties limit the values users can select in the NumericUpDown control.

a) Maximum, Minimum

b) Top, Bottom

c) High, Low

d) Max, Min

11.10 For...Next header _____ can be used to vary the control variable over the odd numbers between 1 and 10.

a) For intI = 1 To 10 Step 1

b) For intI = 1 To 10 Step 2

c) For intI = 1 To 10 Step -1

d) For intI = 1 To 10 Step -2

EXERCISES

11.11 (*Present Value Calculator Application*) A bank wants to show its customers how much they would need to invest to achieve a specified financial goal (future value) in 5, 10, 15, 20, 25 or 30 years. Users must provide their financial goal (the amount of money desired after the specified number of years has elapsed), an interest rate and the length of the investment in years. Create an application that calculates and displays the principal (initial amount to invest) needed to achieve the user's financial goal. Your application should allow the user to invest money for 5, 10, 15, 20, 25 or 30 years. For example, if a customer wants to reach the financial goal of $15,000 over a period of 5 years when the interest rate is 6.6%, the customer would need to invest $10,896.96 as shown in Fig. 11.16.

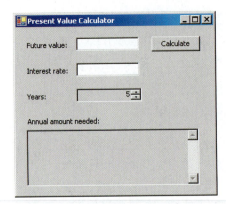 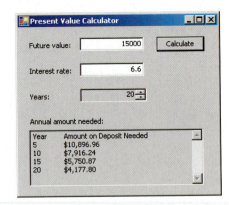

Figure 11.16   Present Value Calculator GUI

a) *Copying the template to your working directory.* Copy the directory C:\Examples\ Tutorial11\Exercises\PresentValue to your C:\SimplyVB directory.

b) *Opening the application's template file.* Double click PresentValue.sln in the PresentValue directory to open the application.

c) *Adding the NumericUpDown control.* Place and size the NumericUpDown so that it follows the GUI Design Guidelines. Set the NumericUpDown control's Name property to updYear. Set the NumericUpDown control to allow only multiples of five for the number of years. Also, allow the user to select only a duration that is in the specified range of values.

d) *Adding a multiline TextBox.* Add a TextBox to the Form below the NumericUpDown control. Change the size to 272, 88, and position the TextBox on the Form so that it follows the GUI Design Guidelines. Then set that TextBox to display multiple lines and a vertical scrollbar. Also ensure that the user cannot modify the text in the TextBox.

e) *Adding a Click event handler and adding code.* Add a Click event handler for the **Calculate** Button. Once in code view, add code to the application such that, when the **Calculate** Button is clicked, the multiline TextBox displays the necessary principal for each five-year interval. Use the following version of the present-value calculation formula:

$$p = a / (1 + r)^{n}$$

where
p is the amount needed to achieve the future value
r is the annual interest rate (for example, .05 is equivalent to 5%)
n is the number of years
a is the future-value amount.

f) *Running the application.* Select **Debug > Start** to run your application. Enter amounts for the future value, interest rate and number of years. Click the **Calculate** Button and verify that the year intervals and the amount on deposit needed for each is correct. Test the application again, this time entering 30 for the number of years. Verify that the vertical scrollbar appears to display all of the output.

g) *Closing the application.* Close your running application by clicking its close box.

h) *Closing the IDE.* Close Visual Studio .NET by clicking its close box.

11.12 *(Compound Interest: Comparing Rates Application)* Write an application that calculates the amount of money in an account after 10 years for interest rate amounts of 5–10%. For this application, users must provide the initial principal.

a) *Copying the template to your working directory.* Copy the directory C:\Examples\ Tutorial11\Exercises\ComparingRates to your C:\SimplyVB directory.

b) *Opening the application's template file.* Double click ComparingRates.sln in the ComparingRates directory to open the application.

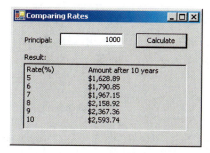

Figure 11.17   **Comparing Rates** GUI.

c) *Adding a multiline TextBox.* Add a TextBox to the Form below the **Result:** Label control. Change the size to 256, 104, and position the TextBox on the Form so that it follows the GUI Design Guidelines (Fig. 11.17). Then set that TextBox to display multiple lines. Also ensure that the user cannot modify the text in the TextBox.

d) *Adding a Click event handler and adding code.* Add a Click event handler for the **Calculate** Button. Once in code view, add code to the application such that, when the **Calculate** Button is clicked, the multiline TextBox displays the amount in the account after 10 years for interest rates of 5, 6, 7, 8, 9 and 10 percent. Use the following version of the interest-calculation formula:

$$a = p\,(1 + r)^{\,n}$$

where
p is the original amount invested (the principal)
r is the annual interest rate (for example, .05 is equivalent to 5%)
n is the number of years
a is the investment's value at the end of the nth year.

e) *Running the application.* Select **Debug > Start** to run your application. Enter the principal amount for an account and click the **Calculate** Button. Verify that the correct amounts after 10 years are then displayed, based on interest rate amounts of 5–10%.

f) *Closing the application.* Close your running application by clicking its close box.

g) *Closing the IDE.* Close Visual Studio .NET by clicking its close box.

11.13 *(Validating Input to the Interest Calculator Application)* Enhance the **Interest Calculator** application with error checking. Test for whether the user has entered valid values for the principal and interest rate. If the user enters an invalid value, display a message in the multiline TextBox. Figure 11.18 demonstrates the application handling an invalid input.

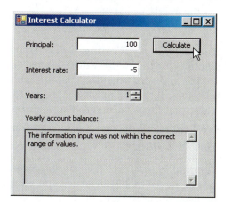

Figure 11.18   **Interest Calculator** application with error checking.

a) *Copying the template to your working directory.* Copy the directory C:\Examples\ Tutorial11\Exercises\InterestCalculatorEnhancement to your C:\SimplyVB directory.

b) ***Opening the application's template file.*** Double click `InterestCalculator.sln` in the `InterestCalculatorEnhancement` directory to open the application.

c) ***Adding a Click event handler and adding code.*** Add a `Click` event handler for the **Calculate** Button. Once in code view, modify the code to validate the input. The principal should be a positive amount greater than 0. Also, the interest rate should be greater than 0, but less than 100.

d) ***Displaying the error message.*** Display the text `"The information was not within the correct range of values."` in `txtResult` if the values are not valid.

e) ***Running the application.*** Select **Debug > Start** to run your application. Enter invalid data for the principal and interest rate. The invalid data can include negative numbers and letters. Verify that entering invalid data and clicking the **Calculate** Button results in the error message displayed in Fig. 11.18.

f) ***Closing the application.*** Close your running application by clicking its close box.

g) ***Closing the IDE.*** Close Visual Studio .NET by clicking its close box.

What does this code do? ▶ **11.14** What is the value of `intResult` after the following code executes? Assume that `intPower`, `intI`, `intResult` and `intNumber` are all declared as `Integers`.

```
1   intPower = 5
2   intNumber = 10
3   intResult = intNumber
4
5   For intI = 1 To (intPower - 1)
6       intResult *= intNumber
7   Next
```

What's wrong with this code? ▶ **11.15** Assume that the variable `intCounter` is declared as an `Integer` for both a and b. Identify and correct the error(s) in each of the following:

a) This statement should display in a `ListBox` all numbers from 100 to 1 in decreasing order.

```
1   For intCounter = 100 To 1
2       lstDisplay.Items.Add(intCounter)
3   Next
```

b) The following code should display in a `ListBox` the odd `Integers` from 19 to 1 in decreasing order.

```
1   For intCounter = 19 To 1 By -1
2       lstDisplay.Add(intCounter)
3   Next
```

Using the Debugger **11.16** (*Savings Calculator Application*) The **Savings Calculator** application calculates the amount that the user will have on deposit after one year. The application gets the initial amount on deposit from the user, and assumes that the user will add $100 dollars to the account every month for the entire year. No interest is added to the account. While testing the application, you noticed that the amount calculated by the application was incorrect. Use the debugger to locate and correct any logic error(s). Figure 11.19 displays the correct output for this application.

Figure 11.19   Correct output for the **Savings Calculator** application.

Programming Challenge ▶

11.17 (*Pay Raise Calculator Application*) Develop an application that computes the amount of money an employee makes each year over a user-specified number of years. The employee receives an hourly wage and a pay raise once every year. The user specifies the hourly wage and the amount of the raise (in percentages per year) in the application.

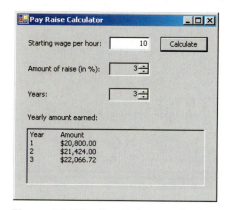

Figure 11.20   **Pay Raise** application's GUI.

a) *Copying the template to your working directory.* Copy the directory C:\Examples\Tutorial11\Exercises\PayRaise to your C:\SimplyVB directory.

b) *Opening the application's template file.* Double click PayRaise.sln in the PayRaise directory to open the application.

c) *Adding controls to the Form.* Add two NumericUpDown controls to the Form. The first NumericUpDown control should be provided to allow the user to specify the pay raise percentage. The user should only be able to specify percentages in the range of 3–8 percent. Create the second NumericUpDown control for users to select the number of years in the range 1–50. Then add a multiline TextBox control to the application. Ensure that the user cannot modify the text in the NumericUpDown and TextBox controls. Resize and move the controls you created so that they follow the GUI Design Guidelines as in Fig. 11.20.

d) *Adding a Click event handler and adding code.* Add a Click event handler for the **Calculate** Button. Once in code view, add code to use the For...Next statement to compute the yearly salary amounts, based on the yearly pay raise.

e) *Running the application.* Select **Debug > Start** to run your application. Enter a starting wage per hour, the size of the yearly raise and the number of years worked. Click the **Calculate** Button and verify that the correct amount after each year is displayed in the **Yearly amount earned:** TextBox.

f) *Closing the application.* Close your running application by clicking its close box.

g) *Closing the IDE.* Close Visual Studio .NET by clicking its close box.

Objectives

In this tutorial, you will learn to:

- Use the **Select Case** multiple-selection statement.
- Use **Case** statements.
- Use the **Is** keyword.
- Display a date and time.
- Use **TextBox** property **PasswordChar**.

Outline

Security Panel Application

Introducing the *Select Case Multiple-Selection Statement*

In the last tutorial, you learned how to use the For...Next statement, which is the most concise statement for performing counter-controlled repetition. In this tutorial, you will learn about the Select Case multiple-selection statement. The Select Case statement is used to simplify code that uses several ElseIf statements sequentially when an application must choose among many possible actions to perform.

12.1 Test-Driving the Security Panel Application

In this tutorial, you will use the Select Case multiple-selection statement to construct a **Security Panel** application. This application must meet the following requirements:

Application Requirements

A lab wants to install a security panel outside a laboratory room. Only authorized personnel may enter the lab, using their security codes. The following are valid security codes (also called access codes) and the groups of employees they represent:

Values	Groups
1645–1689	Technicians
8345	Custodians
9998, 1006–1008	Scientists

Once a security code is entered, access is either granted or denied. All access attempts are written to a window below the keypad. If access is granted, the date, time and group (scientists, custodians, etc.) are written to the window. If access is denied, the date, the time and a message, "Access Denied," are written to the window. Furthermore, the user can enter any one-digit access code to summon a security guard for assistance. The date, the time and a message, "Restricted Access," are then written to the window to indicate that the request has been received.

You begin by test-driving the completed application. Then, you will learn the additional Visual Basic .NET technologies that you will need to create your own version of this application.

Test-Driving the Security Panel Application

1. **Opening the completed application.** Open the directory `C:\Examples\ Tutorial12\CompletedApplication\SecurityPanel` to locate the **Security Panel** application. Double click `SecurityPanel.sln` to open the application in Visual Studio .NET

2. **Running the Security Panel application.** Select **Debug > Start** to run the application (Fig. 12.1). At the top of the `Form`, you are provided with a `Text-Box` that displays an asterisk for each digit in the security code entered using the GUI keypad. Notice that the GUI keypad looks much like a real-world keypad. (We will mimic real-world conditions when possible.) The **C** `Button` clears your current input, and the **#** `Button` causes the application to process the security code entered. Results are displayed in the `ListBox` at the bottom of the `Form`.

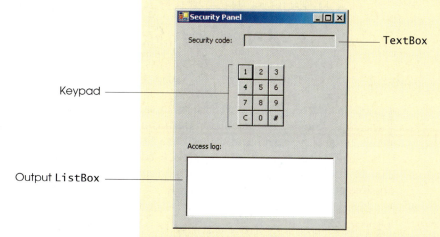

Keypad

TextBox

Output `ListBox`

Figure 12.1   **Security Panel** application executing.

3. **Entering an invalid security code.** Use the keypad to enter the invalid security code 1212. Notice that an asterisk (*) is displayed in the `TextBox` (Fig. 12.2) for each numeric key pressed (by clicking its `Button` on the `Form`). These characters do not allow other people to see the code entered. When finished, click the **#** `Button`. A message indicating that access is denied will appear in the `ListBox`, as in Fig. 12.3. Notice that the `TextBox` is cleared when the **#** `Button` is pressed.

GUI Design Tip

If your GUI is modeling a real-world object, your GUI design should mimic the physical appearance of the object.

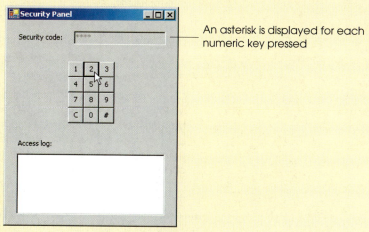

An asterisk is displayed for each numeric key pressed

Figure 12.2   Asterisks displayed in **Security code:** field.

(cont.)

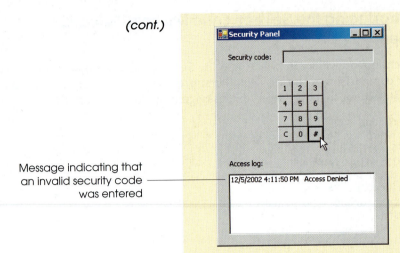

Message indicating that an invalid security code was entered

Figure 12.3   **Security Panel** displaying **Access Denied** message.

4.   ***Using the C Button.*** Press a few numeric keys, then click the **C** Button. Notice that all the asterisks displayed in the TextBox disappear. Users often make mistakes when keystroking or when clicking Buttons, so the **C** Button allows users to make a "fresh start."

5.   ***Entering a valid security code.*** Use the keypad to enter 1006, then click the # Button. Notice that a second message appears in the ListBox, as in Fig. 12.4.

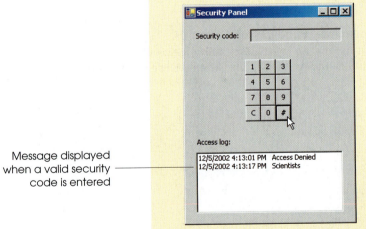

Message displayed when a valid security code is entered

Figure 12.4   **Security Panel** application confirming a valid security-code entry.

6.   ***Closing the application.*** Close your running by clicking its close box.

7.   ***Closing the IDE.*** Close Visual Studio .NET by clicking its close box.

12.2 Introducing the Select Case Multiple-Selection Statement

In this section, you will learn how to use the **Select Case multiple-selection statement**. For comparison purposes, we will first provide an If...Then...Else multiple-selection statement that displays a text message based on a student's grade:

```
If strGrade = "A" Then
    lblDisplay.Text = "Excellent!"
ElseIf strGrade = "B" Then
    lblDisplay.Text = "Very good!"
ElseIf strGrade = "C" Then
    lblDisplay.Text = "Good."
ElseIf strGrade = "D" Then
    lblDisplay.Text = "Poor."
ElseIf strGrade = "F" Then
    lblDisplay.Text = "Failure."
Else
    lblDisplay.Text = "Invalid grade."
End If
```

This statement can be used to produce the correct output when selecting among multiple values of strGrade. However, by using the Select Case statement, you can simplify every instance like

```
If strGrade = "A" Then
```

to one like

```
Case "A"
```

and eliminate the If and ElseIf keywords.

The following Select Case multiple-selection statement performs the same functionality as the preceding If...Then...Else statement:

```
Select Case strGrade

    Case "A"
        lblDisplay.Text = "Excellent!"

    Case "B"
        lblDisplay.Text = "Very good!"

    Case "C"
        lblDisplay.Text = "Good."

    Case "D"
        lblDisplay.Text = "Poor."

    Case "F"
        lblDisplay.Text = "Failure."

    Case Else
        lblDisplay.Text = "Invalid grade."

End Select
```

The Select Case statement begins with the keywords Select Case followed by a **test expression** (also called a **controlling expression**) and terminates with keywords **End Select**. The preceding Select Case statement contains five **Case statement**s and the optional **Case Else statement**. Each Case contains the keyword Case followed by an **expression list**. The expression list can contain strings such as "A" and numeric values such as 707 and 9.9. Although a Select Case statement can have any number of Cases, it must have at most one Case Else.

Good Programming Practice

Placing a blank line before and after each Case in a Select Case statement improves readability.

Good Programming Practice

Indenting the statements in the body of a Case improves readability.

Common Programming Error

When using the optional Case Else statement in a Select Case statement, failing to place the Case Else as the last Case is a syntax error.

Common Programming Error

Case statements whose controlling expressions result in the same value are logic errors. At run time, only the body of the first matching Case is executed.

Figure 12.5 shows the UML activity diagram for this Select Case multiple-selection statement. The first condition to be evaluated is strGrade = "A". If this condition is True, the text "Excellent!" is displayed, and control proceeds to the first statement after the Select Case statement. If the condition is False (that is, strGrade <> "A"), the statement continues by testing the next condition, strGrade = "B". If this condition is True, the text "Very good!" is displayed, and control proceeds to the first statement after the Select Case statement. If the condition is False (that is, strGrade <> "B"), the statement continues to test the next condition. This process continues until a matching Case is found or until the final condition evaluates to False (strGrade <> "F"). If the latter occurs, the Case Else's body is executed, and the text "Invalid grade." is displayed. The application then continues with the first statement after the Select Case statement.

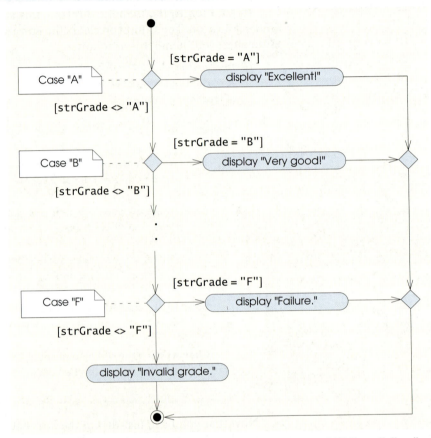

Figure 12.5 Select Case multiple-selection statement UML activity diagram.

SELF-REVIEW   1. Select Case is a _____-selection statement.

   a) multiple   b) double

   c) single   d) None of the above.

   2. When does the Case Else body execute?

   a) Every time a Select Case statement executes

   b) When more than one Case is matched

   c) When all Cases are matching Case statements in a Select Case statement

   d) None of the above.

   Answers: 1) a. 2) d.

12.3 Constructing the Security Panel Application

The **Security Panel** application contains 10 Buttons that display digits. (We call these numeric Buttons.) You will create an event handler for each Button's `Click` event. These Buttons make up the GUI keypad. The following pseudocode describes the `Click` event handler for each of these numeric Buttons:

> *If a numeric Button is clicked*
> > *Concatenate Button's digit to the TextBox's Text property value*

Later in this tutorial, you will convert this pseudocode into the Visual Basic .NET code and create the `Click` event handlers for each numeric Button. The user then will be able to use the numeric Buttons to enter digits and have those digits concatenated to the text in a TextBox.

In addition to the numeric Buttons, this application also contains a **C** Button and a **#** Button. The **C** Button clears the Form's TextBox. The pseudocode for the **#** Button's event handler is as follows:

> *When the user clicks the # Button:*
> > *Retrieve security code input by user*
> > *Clear input TextBox*
> >
> > *Select correct Case based on access code*
> >
> > > *Case where access code is less than 10*
> > > > *Store text "Restricted Access" to String variable*
> > >
> > > *Case where access code is in the range 1645 to 1689*
> > > > *Store text "Technicians" to String variable*
> > >
> > > *Case where access code equals 8345*
> > > > *Store text "Custodians" to String variable*
> > >
> > > *Case where access code equals 9998 or is in the range 1006 to 1008*
> > > > *Store text "Scientists" to String variable*
> > >
> > > *Case where none of the preceding Cases match*
> > > > *Store text "Access Denied" to String variable*
> >
> > *Display message in ListBox with current time and String variable's contents*

Now that you have test-driven the **Interest Calculator** application and studied its pseudocode representation, you will use an ACE table to help you convert the pseudocode to Visual Basic .NET. Figure 12.6 lists the actions, controls and events that will help you complete your own version of this application. The first row specifies that you will be using Labels to identify the TextBox and ListBox controls. The second row introduces the Buttons for the numeric keypad. When these Buttons are clicked, their values are concatenated to the text in the TextBox's Text property. The next row indicates that TextBox txtSecurityCode will store the security code that is input by the user. The next two rows specify Buttons that the user can click to clear the TextBox (btnClear) and enter the security code (btnEnter). The last row indicates the ListBox will be used to display a message to the user.

Action/Control/Event (ACE) Table for the Interest Calculator Application

Action	Control	Event
Label the application's fields	lblSecurityCode, lblAccessLog	
	btnEnter	Click
Retrieve security code input by user	txtSecurityCode	
Clear input TextBox	txtSecurityCode	
Select correct Case based on access code		
Case where access code is less than 10 Store text "Restricted Access"		
Case where access code is in the range 1645 to 1689 Store text "Technicians"		
Case where access code equals 8345 Store text "Scientists"		
Case where access code equals 9998 or is in the range 1006 to 1008 Store text "Scientists"		
Case where none of preceding Cases match Store text "Access Denied"		
Display message in ListBox with current time and String variable's contents	lstLogEntry	

Figure 12.6   ACE table for **Security Panel** application.

Now that you are familiar with the Select Case multiple-selection statement, you will use it to build the **Security Panel** application.

Using the PasswordChar Property

GUI Design Tip

Mask passwords or other sensitive pieces of information in TextBoxes.

1. ***Copying the template to your working directory.*** Copy the C:\Examples\ Tutorial12\TemplateApplication\SecurityPanel directory to your C:\SimplyVB directory.

2. ***Opening the Security Panel application's template file.*** Double click SecurityPanel.sln in the SecurityPanel directory.

3. ***Displaying the * character in the TextBox.*** Select the **Security code:** TextBox at the top of the Form, and set this TextBox's PasswordChar property to * in the **Properties** window. Text displayed in a TextBox can be hidden or **masked** with the character specified in property **PasswordChar**. Rather than displaying the actual TextBox text that the user types, **masking characters** are displayed. However, the TextBox's Text property does contain the text the user typed. For example, if a user enters 5469, the TextBox displays ****, yet stores "5469" in its Text property. Now any character displayed in your interface's TextBox displays as the * character.

4. ***Disabling the TextBox.*** The primary reason for using a TextBox instead of a Label to display the access code is to use the PasswordChar property. To prevent users from modifying the text in the TextBox, set its **Enabled** property to False.

5. ***Create the btnEnter_Click event handler.*** Double click the # Button to create the btnEnter_Click event handler.

(cont.)

6. ***Declaring and initializing variables.*** Add lines 230–234 of Fig. 12.7 to the `btnEnter_Click` event handler. Lines 230–231 declare variables `intAccessCode` and `strMessage`. Variable `intAccessCode` will be used to store the user's security code (access code), and variable `strMessage` will store the message that will be displayed to the user, based on the access code entered. Line 233 sets the `intAccessCode` variable to the security code input by the user. Line 234 clears the **Security code:** TextBox.

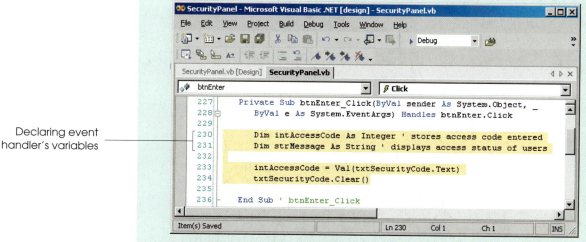

Declaring event handler's variables

Figure 12.7 Variable declarations for `btnEnter_Click`.

7. ***Saving the project.*** Select **File > Save All** to save your modified code.

Now that you have designed the GUI for your application and initialized the variables for your event handler, let's continue by creating your `Select Case` statement, as shown in the following box. This statement will determine the user's access level based on the code input.

Adding a Select Case Statement to the Application

1. ***Adding a Select Case statement to btnEnter_Click.*** Press *Enter* twice and add line 236 from Fig. 12.8 to the `btnEnter_Click` event handler, and press *Enter*. Keywords End `Select` (line 223) immediately appear below the `Select Case` line that you just added. Line 236 begins the `Select Case` statement, which contains the controlling expression `intAccessCode`—the access code entered by the user. Remember that this expression (the value `intAccessCode`) is compared sequentially with each `Case` until either a match occurs or the End `Select` statement is reached. If a matching `Case` is found, the body of that `Case` executes and program control proceeds to the first statement after the End `Select` statement.

2. ***Adding a Case to the Select Case statement.*** Press *Enter* and add lines 238–240 from Fig. 12.9 to the `Select Case` statement. [*Note:* The indentation on your machine may not appear exactly as shown in Fig. 12.9. This is because we turned off **Smart** indenting to display code in our own style. Indentation does not program execution, so you do not need to turn off **Smart** indenting.] The first `Case` statement tests whether `intAccessCode` is less than 10. Keyword **Is** along with the comparison operator < specify a range of values to test. You can use the `Is` keyword followed by a comparison operator to perform that comparison between the controlling expression and the value to the left of the operator. In this case, if the value in `intAccessCode` is less than 10, the code in the body of that `Case` statement will execute and `strMessage` will be assigned the string `"Restricted Access"`, which will be displayed after the body of the `Select Case` statement completes.

(cont.)

Creating a `Select` `Case` statement

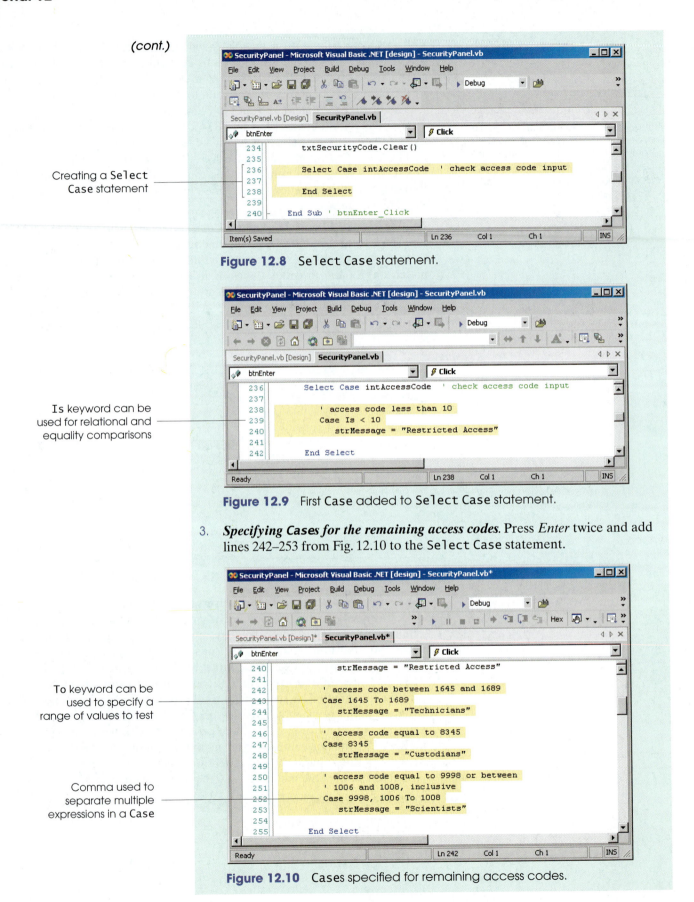

Figure 12.8 `Select Case` statement.

Is keyword can be used for relational and equality comparisons

Figure 12.9 First `Case` added to `Select Case` statement.

3. **Specifying Cases *for the remaining access codes*.** Press *Enter* twice and add lines 242–253 from Fig. 12.10 to the `Select Case` statement.

To keyword can be used to specify a range of values to test

Comma used to separate multiple expressions in a `Case`

Figure 12.10 `Cases` specified for remaining access codes.

(cont.)

Common Programming Error

If the value on the left side of the To keyword in a Case statement is larger than the value on the right side, the Case is ignored during application execution, potentially causing a logic error.

The Case statement on lines 243–244 determines whether the value of intAccessCode is in the range 1645 to 1689, inclusive. Keyword **To** is used to specify the range. If the user enters an access code in this range, the body of the Case statement sets strMessage to "Technicians".

The next Case statement (lines 247–248) checks for a specific number. If intAccessCode matches the value 8345, then the statement in that Case is executed. Specifying a single value in a Case statement is common.

The next Case statement (lines 252–253) determines whether intAccessCode is 9998 or a number in the range 1006 to 1008, inclusive. Notice that, when multiple values are provided in a Case statement, they are separated by commas.

4. ***Adding a Case Else to the Select Case statement***. Add lines 255–257 from Fig. 12.11 to the Select Case statement. These lines contain the optional **Case Else**, which is executed when the controlling expression does not match any of the previous Cases. If used, the Case Else must follow all other Case statements. In your application, the body of the Case Else statement sets variable strMessage to "Access Denied". The required keywords End Select (line 259 of Fig. 12.11) terminate the Select Case statement.

Case Else statement executes when no other Case matches

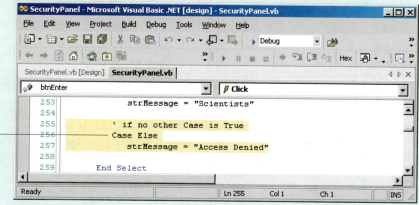

Figure 12.11 Case Else of the Select Case statement.

5. ***Displaying results in the ListBox***. Insert lines 261–262 of Fig. 12.12 after the Select Case statement. The statement on line 262 displays a String in lstLogEntry consisting of the current system date and time, followed by three spaces and the value assigned to strMessage. The first part of method Add's argument contains the expression **Date.Now**. The Framework Class Library (FCL) provides a **Date** structure that can be used to store and display date and time information. A structure is similar to a class. Like objects that you have used in this book, structure members such as properties are accessed by using the dot operator (.). The Date property Now returns the system time and date. Passing this value as a String in the argument to method Add (line 262) causes this value to be converted and displayed as a String. You will learn about how a date is stored using the Date structure in Tutorial 14.

6. ***Saving the project***. Select **File > Save All** to save your modified code.

(cont.)

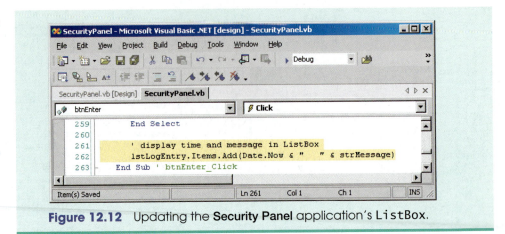

Figure 12.12   Updating the **Security Panel** application's ListBox.

Now that you have defined the btnEnter_Click event handler, you will focus on the numeric Buttons. You will create event handlers for each numbered Button and for the **C** Button.

Programming the Remaining Event Handlers

1. ***Create the btnZero_Click event handler.*** In design view, double click the **0** Button (btnZero) to create the btnZero_Click event handler.

2. ***Coding the btnZero_Click event handler.*** Insert line 268 of Fig. 12.13 to the event handler. Line 268 appends the String "0" to the end of txtSecurity-Code's Text property value. You do this to append the numeric Button's value to the access code in the TextBox.

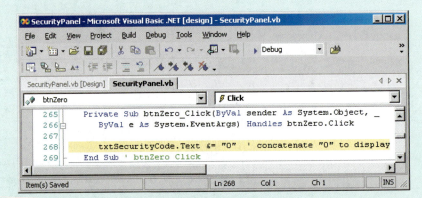

Figure 12.13   Event handler btnZero_Click.

3. ***Define the other numeric Buttons' event handlers.*** Repeat *Steps 1–2* for the remaining numeric Buttons (**1** through **9**). Be sure to substitute the Button's number for the value between the quotes (for example, btnOne_Click sets txtSecurityCode's number as &= "1"). Figure 12.14 shows the event handlers for Buttons btnOne and btnTwo.

(cont.)

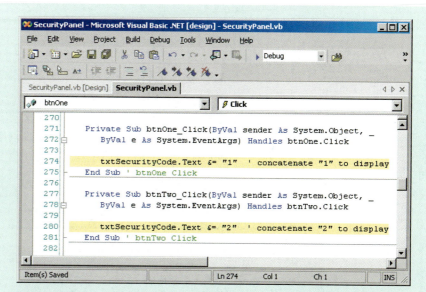

Figure 12.14 Event handlers btnOne_Click and btnTwo_Click.

4. **Define the btnClear_Click event handler.** Double click the **C** Button, and add line 328 as shown in Fig. 12.15. Line 328 clears the **Security code:** TextBox.

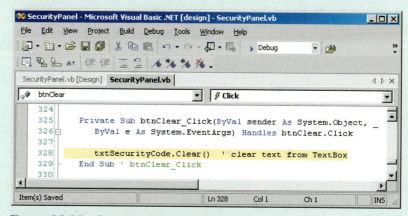

Figure 12.15 Event handler btnClear_Click defined.

5. **Running the application.** Select **Debug > Start** to run your application.

6. **Closing the application.** Close your running application by clicking its close box.

7. **Closing the IDE.** Close Visual Studio .NET by clicking its close box.

Figure 12.16 presents the source code for the **Security Panel** application. The lines of code that contain new programming concepts that you learned in this tutorial are highlighted. Look over the code carefully to make sure that you have added all of the event handlers correctly.

```
1  Public Class FrmSecurityPanel
2     Inherits System.Windows.Forms.Form
3
4     ' Windows Form Designer generated code
5
```

Figure 12.16 **Security Panel** application. (Part 1 of 3.)

```
 6      Private Sub btnEnter_Click(ByVal sender As System.Object, _
 7          ByVal e As System.EventArgs) Handles btnEnter.Click
 8
 9          Dim intAccessCode As Integer ' stores access code entered
10          Dim strMessage As String ' displays access status of users
11
12          intAccessCode = Val(txtSecurityCode.Text)
13          txtSecurityCode.Clear()
14
15          Select Case intAccessCode  ' check access code input
16
17              ' access code less than 10
18              Case Is < 10
19                  strMessage = "Restricted Access"
20
21              ' access code between 1645 and 1689
22              Case 1645 To 1689
23                  strMessage = "Technicians"
24
25              ' access code equal to 8345
26              Case 8345
27                  strMessage = "Custodians"
28
29              ' access code equal to 9998 or between
30              ' 1006 and 1008, inclusive
31              Case 9998, 1006 To 1008
32                  strMessage = "Scientists"
33
34              ' if no other Case is True
35              Case Else
36                  strMessage = "Access Denied"
37
38          End Select
39
40          ' display time and message in ListBox
41          lstLogEntry.Items.Add(Date.Now & "    " & strMessage)
42      End Sub ' btnEnter_Click
43
44      Private Sub btnZero_Click(ByVal sender As System.Object, _
45          ByVal e As System.EventArgs) Handles btnZero.Click
46
47          txtSecurityCode.Text &= "0"  ' concatenate "0" to display
48      End Sub ' btnZero_Click
49
50      Private Sub btnOne_Click(ByVal sender As System.Object, _
51          ByVal e As System.EventArgs) Handles btnOne.Click
52
53          txtSecurityCode.Text &= "1"  ' concatenate "1" to display
54      End Sub ' btnOne_Click
55
56      Private Sub btnTwo_Click(ByVal sender As System.Object, _
57          ByVal e As System.EventArgs) Handles btnTwo.Click
58
59          txtSecurityCode.Text &= "2"  ' concatenate "2" to display
60      End Sub ' btnTwo_Click
61
62      Private Sub btnThree_Click(ByVal sender As System.Object, _
63          ByVal e As System.EventArgs) Handles btnThree.Click
```

Annotations (left margin):
- Declaring variables → lines 9–10
- Retrieving access code and clearing TextBox → lines 12–13
- Using a **Select Case** statement to determine user access level → line 15
- Appending the numeric **Button** value to the text stored in the TextBox → line 46

Figure 12.16 **Security Panel** application. (Part 2 of 3.)

```
64
65            txtSecurityCode.Text &= "3"  ' concatenate "3" to display
66      End Sub ' btnThree_Click
67
68      Private Sub btnFour_Click(ByVal sender As System.Object, _
69         ByVal e As System.EventArgs) Handles btnFour.Click
70
71            txtSecurityCode.Text &= "4"  ' concatenate "4" to display
72      End Sub ' btnFour_Click
73
74      Private Sub btnFive_Click(ByVal sender As System.Object, _
75         ByVal e As System.EventArgs) Handles btnFive.Click
76
77            txtSecurityCode.Text &= "5"  ' concatenate "5" to display
78      End Sub ' btnFive_Click
79
80      Private Sub btnSix_Click(ByVal sender As System.Object, _
81         ByVal e As System.EventArgs) Handles btnSix.Click
82
83            txtSecurityCode.Text &= "6"  ' concatenate "6" to display
84      End Sub ' btnSix_Click
85
86      Private Sub btnSeven_Click(ByVal sender As System.Object, _
87         ByVal e As System.EventArgs) Handles btnSeven.Click
88
89            txtSecurityCode.Text &= "7"  ' concatenate "7" to display
90      End Sub ' btnSeven_Click
91
92      Private Sub btnEight_Click(ByVal sender As System.Object, _
93         ByVal e As System.EventArgs) Handles btnEight.Click
94
95            txtSecurityCode.Text &= "8"  ' concatenate "8" to display
96      End Sub ' btnEight_Click
97
98      Private Sub btnNine_Click(ByVal sender As System.Object, _
99         ByVal e As System.EventArgs) Handles btnNine.Click
100
101           txtSecurityCode.Text &= "9"  ' concatenate "9" to display
102     End Sub ' btnNine_Click
103
104     Private Sub btnClear_Click(ByVal sender As System.Object, _
105        ByVal e As System.EventArgs) Handles btnClear.Click
106
107        txtSecurityCode.Clear()  ' clear text from TextBox
108     End Sub ' btnClear_Click
109
110 End Class ' FrmSecurityPanel
```

Clearing the TextBox ——— 107

Figure 12.16 Security Panel application. (Part 3 of 3.)

SELF-REVIEW

1. A Case that handles all values larger than a specified value must precede the > operator with keyword _____.

   a) Select   b) Is
   c) Case   d) All

2. Use a(n) _____ to separate multiple conditions in a Case statement.

   a) period   b) asterisk
   c) comma   d) colon

Answers: 1) b. 2) c.

12.4 Wrap-Up

In this tutorial, you learned how to use the `Select Case` multiple-selection statement and discovered its similarities to the `If...Then...Else` statement. You studied a UML activity diagram that illustrates the flow of control in `Select Case` statements.

You then applied what you learned to create your **Security Panel** application. You used a `Select Case` statement to determine whether the user inputted a correct security code. You also defined several `Cases` and included a `Case Else` statement, which executes if a valid security code is not provided.

In the next tutorial, you will learn how to construct applications from small, manageable pieces of reusable code called procedures. You will use this capability to enhance an example you created earlier in the book.

SKILLS SUMMARY

Creating a `Select Case` Statement

- Use the keywords `Select Case` followed by a controlling expression.
- Use the keyword `Case` followed by an expression to compare with the controlling expression.
- Define the statements that execute if the `Case`'s expression matches the controlling expression.
- Use the keywords `Case Else` followed by statements to execute if the controlling expression does not match any of the provided `Cases`. `Case Else`, if used, must be the last `Case` statement.

Masking User Input in a TextBox

- Set the TextBox's `PasswordChar` property to the desired character, typically the asterisk (*), to mask the user input.
- Retrieve the value typed by the user in the `Text` property.

Retrieving the Current Date and Time

- Use property `Now` of structure `Date`, which, when converted to a `String`, displays the current date in the format 12/31/2002 11:59:59 P.M.

KEY TERMS

Case Else statement—Optional statement whose body executes if the `Select Case`'s test expression does not match any of the `Cases`' expressions.

Case statement—Statement whose body executes if the `Select Case`'s test expression matches any of the `Cases`' expressions.

controlling expression—Value compared sequentially with each `Case` until either a match occurs or the `End Select` statement is reached. Also known as a test expression.

Date.Now—Returns the current system time and date.

Date structure—A structure whose properties can be used to store and display date and time information.

Enabled property of a TextBox—Determines whether the TextBox will respond to user input.

End Select keywords—Terminates the `Select Case` statement.

expression list—Multiple expressions separated by commas. Used for `Cases` in `Select Case` statements, when certain statements should execute based on more than one condition.

Is keyword—A keyword that when followed by a comparison operator, can be used to perform a comparison between the controlling expression of a `Select Case` statement and a value.

masking—Hiding text such as passwords or other sensitive pieces of information that should not be observed by other people as they are typed. Masking is achieved by using the `PasswordChar` property of the `TextBox` for which you would like to hide data. The actual data entered is retained in the TextBox's `Text` property.

masking character—Used to replace each character displayed in a `TextBox` when the TextBox's data is masked for privacy.

multiple-selection statement—Performs one of many actions (or sequences of actions) depending on the value of the controlling expression.

PasswordChar property of a TextBox—Specifies the masking character for a TextBox.

Select Case statement—The multiple-selection statement used to make a decision by comparing an expression to a series of conditions. The algorithm then takes different actions based on those values.

GUI DESIGN GUIDELINES

Overall Design

■ If your GUI is modeling a real-world object, your GUI design should mimic the physical appearance of the object.

TextBox

■ Mask passwords or other sensitive pieces of information in TextBoxes.

CONTROLS, EVENTS, PROPERTIES & METHODS

TextBox   [abl TextBox]   This control allows the user to input data from the keyboard.

■ *In action*

[0]

■ *Events*

TextChanged—Raised when the text in the TextBox is changed.

■ *Properties*

Enabled—Determines whether the user can enter data (True) in the TextBox or not (False).

Location—Specifies the location of the TextBox on the Form relative to the top-left corner.

Multiline—Specifies whether the TextBox is capable of displaying multiple lines of text.

Name—Specifies the name used to access the TextBox programmatically. The name should be prefixed with txt.

PasswordChar—Specifies the masking character to be used when displaying data in the TextBox.

ReadOnly—Determines whether the value of a TextBox can be changed.

ScrollBars—Specifies whether the TextBox contains a scrollbar.

Size—Specifies the height and width (in pixels) of the TextBox.

Text—Specifies the text displayed in the TextBox.

TextAlign—Specifies how the text is aligned within the TextBox.

■ *Methods*

Focus—Transfers the focus of the application to the TextBox that calls it.

MULTIPLE-CHOICE QUESTIONS

12.1 The _____ keywords signify the end of a Select Case statement.

   a) End Case   b) End Select

   c) End Select Case   d) Case End

12.2 The expression _____ returns the current system time and date.

   a) Date.DateTime   b) Date.SystemDateTime

   c) Date.Now   d) Date.SystemTimeDate

12.3 You can hide information entered into a TextBox by setting that TextBox's _____ property to a character; that character will be displayed for every character entered by the user.

   a) PrivateChar   b) Mask

   c) MaskingChar   d) PasswordChar

12.4 Which of the following is a syntax error?

a) Having duplicate Case statements in the same Select Case statement

b) Having a Case statement in which the value to the left of a To keyword is larger than the value to the right

c) Preceding a Case statement with the Case Else statement in a Select Case statement

d) Using keyword Is in a Select Case statement

12.5 Keyword _____ is used to specify a range in a Case statement.

a) Also   b) Between

c) To   d) From

12.6 _____ separates multiple values tested in a Case statement.

a) A comma   b) An underscore

c) Keyword Also   d) A semicolon

12.7 The _____ method inserts a value in a ListBox.

a) Append   b) Items.Insert

c) Insert   d) Items.Add

12.8 If the value on the left of the To keyword in a Case statement is larger than the value on the right, _____.

a) a syntax error occurs   b) the body of the Case statement executes

c) the body of the Case statement never executes

d) the statement causes a runtime error

12.9 The expression following the keywords Select Case is called a _____.

a) guard condition   b) controlling expression

c) selection expression   d) case expression

12.10 To prevent a user from modifying text in a TextBox, set its _____ property to False.

a) Enabled   b) Text

c) TextChange   d) Editable

EXERCISES

12.11 *(Sales Commission Calculator Application)* Develop an application that calculates a salesperson's commission from the number of items sold (Fig. 12.17). Assume that all items have a fixed price of 10 dollars per unit. Use a Select Case statement to implement the following sales commission schedule:

Fewer than 10 items sold = 1% commission
Between 10 and 40 items sold = 2% commission
Between 41 and 100 items sold = 4% commission
More than 100 items sold = 8% commission

Figure 12.17   **Sales Commission Calculator** GUI.

a) *Copying the template to your working directory.* Copy the directory C:\Examples\ Tutorial12\Exercises\SalesCommissionCalculator to your C:\SimplyVB directory.

b) *Opening the application's template file.* Double click SalesCommissionCalculator.sln in the SalesCommissionCalculator directory to open the application.

c) *Defining an event handler for the Button's Click event.* Create an event handler for the **Calculate** Button's Click event.

d) *Display the salesperson's gross sales.* In your new event handler, multiply the number of items that the salesperson has sold by 10, and display the resulting gross sales as a monetary amount.

e) *Calculate the salesperson's commission percentage.* Use a Select Case statement to compute the salesperson's commission percentage, from the number of items sold. The rate that is selected is applied to all the items the salesperson sold.

f) *Display the salesperson's earnings.* Multiply the salesperson's gross sales by the commission percentage determined in the previous step to calculate the salesperson's earnings. Remember to divide by 100 to obtain the percentage.

g) *Running the application.* Select **Debug > Start** to run your application. Enter a value for the number of items sold and click the **Calculate** Button. Verify that the gross sales displayed is correct, that the percentage of commission is correct and that the earnings displayed is correct based on the commission assigned.

h) *Closing the application.* Close your running application by clicking its close box.

i) *Closing the IDE.* Close Visual Studio .NET by clicking its close box.

12.12 *(Cash Register Application)* Use the numeric keypad from the **Security Panel** application to build a **Cash Register** application (Fig. 12.18). In addition to numbers, the cash register should include a decimal point Button. Apart from this numeric operation, there should be **Enter, Delete, Clear** and **Total** Buttons. Sales tax should be calculated on the amount purchased. Use a Select Case statement to compute sales tax. Add the tax amount to the subtotal to calculate the total. Display the tax and total for the user. Use the following sales-tax percentages, which are based on the amount of money spent:

Amounts under $100 = 5% (.05) sales tax
Amounts between $100 and $500 = 7.5% (.075) sales tax
Amounts above $500 = 10% (.10) sales tax

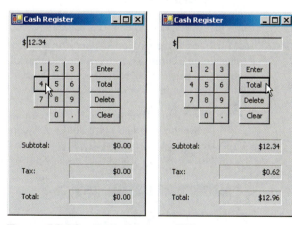

Figure 12.18   Cash Register GUI.

a) *Copying the template to your working directory.* Copy the directory C:\Examples\ Tutorial12\Exercises\CashRegister to your C:\SimplyVB directory.

b) *Opening the application's template file.* Double click CashRegister.sln in the CashRegister directory to open the application.

c) *Define event handlers for the numeric Buttons and decimal point in the keypad.* Create event handlers for each of these Button's Click events. Have each event handler concatenate the proper value to the TextBox at the top of the Form.

d) *Define an event handler for the Enter Button's Click event.* Create an event handler for this Button's Click event. Have this event handler add the current amount to the subtotal and display the new subtotal.

e) *Define an event handler for the Total Button's Click event.* Create an event handler for this Button's Click event. Have this event handler use the subtotal to compute the tax amount.

f) *Define an event handler for the Clear Button's Click event.* Create an event handler for this Button's Click event. Have this event handler clear the user input and display the value $0.00 for the subtotal, sales tax and total.

g) *Define an event handler for the Delete Button's Click event.* Create an event handler for this Button's Click event. Have this event handler clear only the data in the TextBox.

h) *Running the application.* Select **Debug > Start** to run your application. Use the keypad to enter various dollar amounts, clicking the **Enter** Button after each. After several amounts have been entered, click the **Total** Button and verify that the appropriate sales tax and total are displayed. Enter several values again and click the **Delete** Button to clear the current input. Click the **Clear** Button to clear all the output values.

i) *Closing the application.* Close your running application by clicking its close box.

j) *Closing the IDE.* Close Visual Studio .NET by clicking its close box.

12.13 (*Income Tax Calculator Application*) Create an application that computes the amount of income tax that a person must pay, depending upon that person's salary. Your application should perform as shown in Fig. 12.19. Use the following income ranges and corresponding tax rates:

Under $20,000 = 2% income tax
$20,000 – 50,000 = 5% income tax
$50,001 – 75,000 = 10% income tax
$75,001 – 100,000= 15% income tax
Over $100,000 = 20% income tax

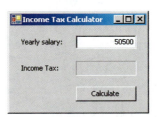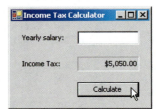

Figure 12.19 Income Tax Calculator GUI.

a) *Copying the template to your working directory.* Copy the directory C:\Examples\Tutorial12\Exercises\IncomeTaxCalculator to your C:\SimplyVB directory.

b) *Opening the application's template file.* Double click IncomeTaxCalculator.sln in the IncomeTaxCalculator directory to open the application.

c) *Define an event handler for the Calculate Button's Click event.* Use the designer to create an event handler for this Button's Click event. Have this event handler use a Select Case statement to determine the user's income-tax percentage. For simplicity, this value should then be multiplied by the user's salary and displayed in the output Label.

d) *Running the application.* Select **Debug > Start** to run your application. Enter a yearly salary and click the **Calculate** Button. Verify that the appropriate income tax is displayed, based on the ranges listed in the exercise description.

e) *Closing the application.* Close your running application by clicking its close box.

f) *Closing the IDE.* Close Visual Studio .NET by clicking its close box.

What does this code do? ▶ **12.14** What is output by the following code? Assume that btnDonation is a Button, txt-Donation is a TextBox and lblMessage is an output Label.

```
 1   Private Sub btnDonation_Click(ByVal sender As _
 2      System.Object, ByVal e As System.EventArgs) _
 3      Handles btnDonation.Click
 4
 5      Select Case Val(txtDonationAmount.Text)
 6
 7         Case 0
 8            lblMessage.Text = "Please consider donating to our cause."
 9
10         Case 1 To 100
11            lblMessage.Text = "Thank you for your donation."
12
13         Case Is > 100
14            lblMessage.Text = "Thank you very much for your donation!"
15
16         Case Else
17            lblMessage.Text = "Please enter a valid amount."
18
19      End Select
20
21   End Sub
```

What's wrong with this code? ▶ **12.15** This Select Case statement should determine whether an Integer is even or odd. Find the error(s) in the following code:

```
1   Select Case intValue Mod 2
2
3      Case 0
4         lblOutput.Text = "Odd Integer"
5
6      Case 1
7         lblOutput.Text = "Even Integer"
8
9   End Select
```

Using the Debugger ▶ **12.16** (*Discount Calculator Application*) The **Discount Calculator** application determines the discount the user will receive, based on how much money the user spends. A 15% discount is received for purchases over $200, a 10% discount is received for purchases between $150 and $199, a 5% discount is received for purchases between $100 and $149 and a 2% discount is received for purchases between $50 and $99. While testing your application, you notice that the application is not calculating the discount properly for some values. Use the debugger to find and fix the logic error(s) in the application. Figure 12.20 displays the correct output for the application.

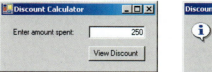

Figure 12.20   Correct output for the **Discount Calculator** application.

Programming Challenge

12.17 *(Enhanced Cash Register Application)* Modify the **Cash Register** application (Exercise 12.12) to include the operations addition, subtraction and multiplication. Remove the **Enter** Button, and replace it with the addition (**+**), subtraction (**−**) and multiplication (*) Buttons. These Buttons should take the value displayed in the **Subtotal:** field and the value displayed in the upper Label and perform the operation of the clicked Button. The result should be displayed in the **Subtotal:** field. Fig. 12.21 displays the enhanced **Cash Register** application GUI.

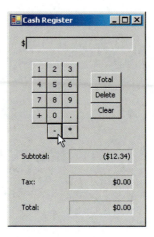

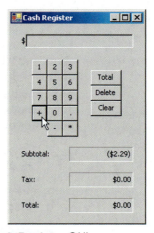

Figure 12.21   Enhanced Cash Register GUI.

13

Objectives

In this tutorial, you will learn to:
- Construct applications modularly from pieces called procedures.
- Work with "built-in" procedures.
- Distinguish between Function procedures and Sub procedures, and determine when each should be used.
- Create your own Function procedures and Sub procedures.

Outline

Enhancing the Wage Calculator Application

Introducing *Function Procedures and Sub Procedures*

Most software applications that solve real-world problems are much larger than the applications presented in the first few tutorials of this text. Experience has shown that the best way to develop and maintain a large application is to construct it from smaller, more manageable pieces. This technique is known as **divide and conquer**. These manageable pieces include program components, known as **procedures**, that simplify the design, implementation and maintenance of large applications. In this tutorial, you will learn how to create two kinds of procedures—namely, Function procedures and Sub procedures.

13.1 Test-Driving the Enhanced Wage Calculator Application

Next, you will use procedures to enhance the **Wage Calculator** application that you created in Tutorial 7. This application must meet the following requirements:

Application Requirements

Recall the problem statement from Tutorial 7: A payroll company calculates the gross earnings per week of employees. Employees' weekly salaries are based on the number of hours they worked and their hourly wages. Create an application that accepts this information and calculates the employee's total (gross) earnings. The application assumes a standard work week of 40 hours. The wages for forty or fewer hours are calculated by multiplying the employee's hourly salary by the number of hours worked. Any time worked over 40 hours in a week is considered "overtime" and earns time and a half. Salary for time and a half is calculated by multiplying the employee's hourly wage by 1.5 and multiplying the result of that calculation by the number of overtime hours worked. The total overtime earned is added to the user's gross earnings for the regular 40 hours of work to calculate the total earnings for that week.

The completed application has the same functionality as that of the application in Tutorial 7, but uses procedures to better organize the code. This application calculates wages that are based on an employee's hourly salary and the number of hours worked per week. Normally, an employee who works 40 or fewer hours earns the hourly wage multiplied by the number of hours worked. The calculation differs if the employee has worked more than the standard 40-hour work week. In this tutorial, you learn about procedures that perform calculations based on input values that may differ with each execution of the application. You begin by test-driving the completed application. Then, you will learn the additional Visual Basic .NET technologies that you will need to create your own version of this application.

Test-Driving the Wage Calculator Application

1. ***Opening the completed application.*** Open the directory C:\Examples\ Tutorial13\CompletedApplication\WageCalculator2 to locate the **Wage Calculator** application. Double click WageCalculator2.sln to open the application in Visual Studio .NET.

2. ***Running the Wage Calculator application.*** Select **Debug > Start** to run the application.

3. ***Entering the employee's hourly wage.*** Enter 10 in the **Hourly wage:** Text-Box (Fig. 13.1).

Figure 13.1 **Wage Calculator** running.

4. ***Entering the number of hours the employee worked.*** Enter 45 in the **Weekly hours:** TextBox.

5. ***Calculating wages earned.*** Click the **Calculate** Button. The result ($475.00) is displayed in the **Gross earnings:** Label.

6. ***Closing the application.*** Close the running application by clicking its close box.

7. ***Closing the IDE.*** Close Visual Studio .NET by clicking its close box.

13.2 Classes and Procedures

The key to creating large applications is to break the applications into smaller pieces. In object-oriented programming, these pieces consist primarily of classes, which can be further broken down into methods. In Visual Basic .NET programming, methods are implemented (created) by writing procedures.

Programmers typically combine **programmer-defined** classes and methods with preexisting (also predefined) code available in the FCL. Using preexisting code saves time, effort and money. This concept of **reusing code** increases efficiency for application developers. Figure 13.2 explains and demonstrates several preexisting Visual Basic .NET procedures.

You have already used several preexisting classes and methods in the FCL. For example, all of the GUI controls you have used in your applications are defined in the FCL as classes. You have also used FCL class methods, such as method Format of class String, to display output properly in your applications. Without method String.Format, you would have needed to code this functionality yourself—a task that would have included many lines of code and programming techniques that have not been introduced yet. You will learn many more FCL classes and methods in this book.

Procedure	Description	Example
Math.Max(x, y)	Returns the larger value of x and y	Math.Max(2.3, 12.7) is 12.7 Math.Max(-2.3, -12.7) is -2.3
Math.Min(x, y)	Returns the smaller value of x and y	Math.Min(2.3, 12.7) is 2.3 Math.Min(-2.3, -12.7) is -12.7
Math.Sqrt(x)	Returns the square root of x	Math.Sqrt(9) is 3.0 Math.Sqrt(2) is 1.4142135623731
Pmt(x, y, z)	Calculates loan payments where x specifies the interest rate, y specifies the number of payment periods and z specifies the principal value of the loan	Pmt(0.05, 12, -4000) is 451.301640083261
Val(x)	Returns a numeric value for x	Val("5") is 5 Val("5a8") is 5 Val("a5") is 0
String.Format(x, y)	Returns String values where x is a format string, and y is a value to be formatted as a String	String.Format("{0:C}", 1.23) is "$1.23"

Figure 13.2 Some predefined Visual Basic .NET procedures.

However, the FCL cannot provide every conceivable feature that you might want, so Visual Basic .NET allows you to create your own programmer-defined procedures to meet the unique requirements of your particular applications. Two types of procedures exist: **Function procedures** and **Sub procedures**. In the next section, you will learn about Function procedures; in Section 13.4, you will learn about Sub procedures. Throughout this tutorial, the term "procedure" refers to both Function procedures and Sub procedures, unless otherwise noted.

SELF-REVIEW

1. _____ provides the programmer with preexisting classes that perform common tasks.

   a) The Framework Class Library   b) The PreExisting keyword
   c) The Framework Code Library   d) The Library keyword

2. Programmers normally use _____.

   a) programmer-defined procedures   b) preexisting procedures
   c) both programmer-defined and preexisting procedures
   d) neither programmer-defined nor preexisting procedures

Answers: 1) a. 2) c.

13.3 Function Procedures

The applications presented earlier in this book have called FCL methods (such as String.Format) to help accomplish the applications' tasks. You will now learn how to write your own programmer-defined procedures. You will first learn how to create procedures in the context of two small applications, before you create the enhanced **Wage Calculator** application. The first application uses the Pythagorean Theorem to calculate the length of the hypotenuse of a right triangle, and the second application determines the maximum of three numbers. Let us begin by reviewing the Pythagorean Theorem. A right triangle (which is a triangle with a 90-degree angle) always satisfies the following relationship—the sum of the squares of the two smaller sides of the triangle equal the square of the largest side of the triangle, which is known as the hypotenuse. In this application, the two smaller sides are called sides A and B, and their lengths are used to calculate the length of the hypotenuse. Follow the steps in the next box to create the application.

Creating the Hypotenuse Calculator Application

1. ***Copying the template to your working directory.*** Copy the `C:\Examples\Tutorial13\TemplateApplication\HypotenuseCalculator` directory to your `C:\SimplyVB` directory.

2. ***Opening the Hypotenuse Calculator application's template file.*** Double click `HypotenuseCalculator.sln` in the `HypotenuseCalculator` directory to open the application in Visual Studio .NET. You will see the GUI shown in Fig. 13.3. When this application is running, the user enters the lengths of a triangle's two shorter sides into the **Length of side A:** and **Length of side B:** TextBoxes, then clicks the **Calculate Hypotenuse** Button. The completed application will calculate the length of the hypotenuse at this time and display the result in the **Length of hypotenuse:** output Label.

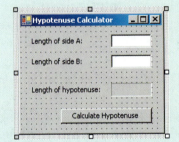

Figure 13.3   Hypotenuse Calculator GUI.

Software Design Tip

Use procedures to increase the clarity and organization of your applications. This not only helps others understand your applications, but it also helps you develop, test and debug your applications.

3. ***Viewing the template application code.*** Switch to code view, and examine the code provided in the template, shown in Fig. 13.4. We have provided an incomplete event handler for the **Calculate Hypotenuse** Button. This event handler contains six declarations (lines 135–140). Variables `dblSideA` and `dblSideB` will contain the lengths of sides A and B, entered by the user. Variable `dblHypotenuse` will contain the length of the hypotenuse, which will be calculated shortly. Variable `dblSquareSideA` will be used to store the length of side A, squared. Similarly, variables `dblSquareSideB` and `dblSquareHypotenuse` will be used to store the squares of the lengths of sides B and the hypotenuse, respectively. Lines 142–143 store the user input for the lengths of sides A and B. Lines 146–152 contain an `If...Then...Else` statement. The `If` statement's body displays a message dialog if a negative value (or zero) is input as the length of side A or side B, or both. The `Else`'s body, which will execute if values greater than zero are entered, will be used to calculate the length of the hypotenuse.

4. ***Creating an empty `Function` procedure.*** Add lines 156–158 of Fig. 13.5 after event handler `btnCalculate_Click`. The keywords `End Function` will appear (line 160). You will learn about these keywords shortly. Notice that we have added a comment on line 160 to identify the procedure being terminated.

(cont.)

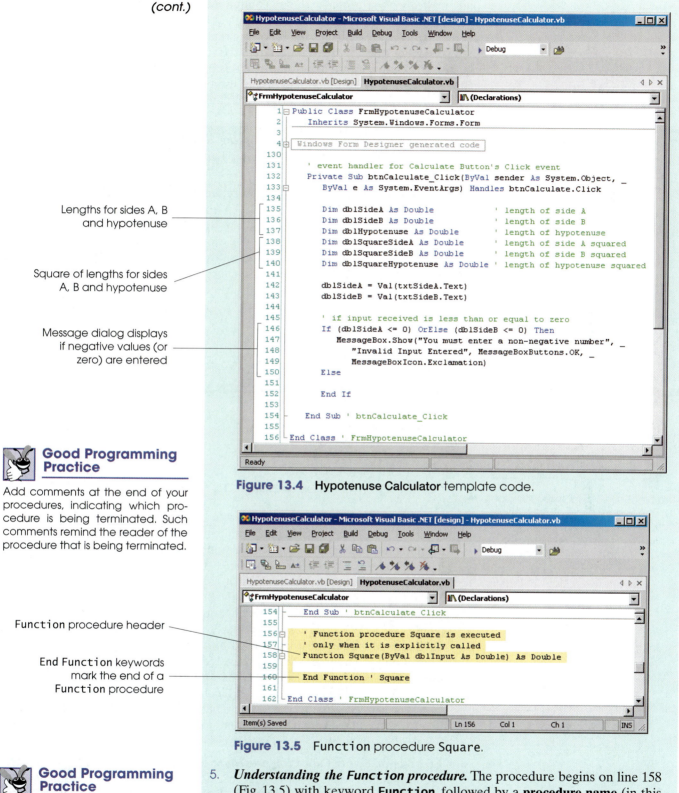

Lengths for sides A, B and hypotenuse

Square of lengths for sides A, B and hypotenuse

Message dialog displays if negative values (or zero) are entered

Figure 13.4 **Hypotenuse Calculator** template code.

Function procedure header

End Function keywords mark the end of a Function procedure

Figure 13.5 **Function** procedure Square.

5. ***Understanding the Function procedure.*** The procedure begins on line 158 (Fig. 13.5) with keyword **Function**, followed by a **procedure name** (in this case, Square). The procedure name can be any valid identifier. The procedure name is followed by a set of parentheses containing a variable declaration.

(cont.)

The declaration within the parentheses is known as the **parameter list**, where variables (called **parameters**) are declared. Although this parameter list contains only one declaration, the parameter list can contain multiple declarations separated by commas. This parameter list declares each parameter's name and type. Notice that the declarations of parameter variables here use the keyword ByVal instead of keyword Dim. We will discuss keyword ByVal shortly. Parameter variables are used in the Function procedure body.

The parameter list is followed by the keyword As, which is in turn followed by the data type Double. The type that follows As is known as the **return type**, which indicates the type of the result returned from the Function (in this case, Double). The first line of a procedure (including the keyword Function, the procedure name, the parameter list and the return type) is often called the **procedure header**. The procedure header for Square declares one parameter variable, dblInput, to be of type Double and sets the return type of Square to be Double.

The Function procedure of Fig. 13.5 ends on line 160 with the keywords **End Function**. The declarations and statements that appear after the procedure header but before the keywords End Function form the **procedure body**. The procedure body contains Visual Basic .NET code that performs actions, generally by manipulating or interacting with the parameters from the parameter list. In the next step, you will add statements to the body of procedure Square. The procedure header, the body and the keywords End Function collectively make up the **procedure definition**.

6. ***Adding code to the body of a Function procedure.*** You want your Function procedure to perform the squaring functionality needed in this application. Add lines 160–161 of Fig. 13.6 to Square's body.

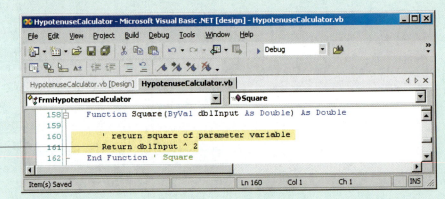

Calculating squares by using the ^ operator

Figure 13.6 Square procedure definition.

Line 161 uses the ^ operator to calculate the square of dblInput—the parameter of this procedure. Line 161 uses a **Return statement** to return this value. This statement begins with the keyword **Return**, followed by an expression. The Return statement returns the result of the expression following keyword Return, in this case dblInput ^ 2, and terminates execution of the procedure. This value is returned to the point at which the procedure was called. You will write the code to call the procedure in the next step.

7. ***Calling procedure Square.*** Now that you have created your procedure, you will need to call it from your event handler. Add lines 152–154 of Fig. 13.7 to your application, in the Else block of the If...Then...Else statement. These lines call Square by using the procedure name followed by a set of parentheses that contain the procedure's argument. In this case, the arguments are the result of Val(txtSideA.Text) and Val(txtSideB.Text).

Software Design Tip

To promote reusability, each procedure should perform a single, well-defined task, and the procedure name should express that task effectively.

Good Programming Practice

Procedure names should be verbs and should begin with an uppercase first letter. Each subsequent word in the name should begin with an uppercase first letter.

Good Programming Practice

Placing a blank line between procedure definitions enhances application readability.

(cont.)

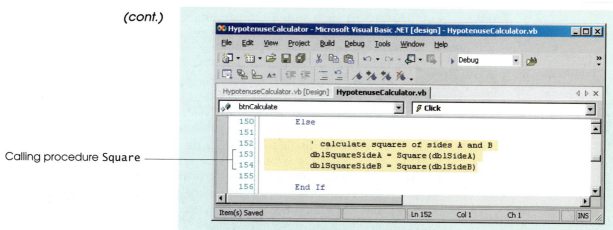

Calling procedure `Square`

Figure 13.7 Invoking procedure `Square`.

Notice that typing the opening parenthesis after a procedure name causes Visual Studio .NET to display a window containing the procedure's argument names and types (Fig. 13.8). This is the ***Parameter Info*** feature of the IDE, which provides you with information about procedures and their arguments. The *Parameter Info* feature displays information for programmer-defined procedures as well as for FCL methods. If the *Parameter Info* window does not appear, it may have been disabled. You can enable *Parameter Info* by selecting **Tools > Options**. In the dialog that appears, select the **Text Editor** option in the left pane, and then select the **Basic** option. In the right portion of the dialog, check the **Parameter information** CheckBox.

Good Programming Practice

Selecting descriptive parameter names makes the information provided by the *Parameter Info* feature more meaningful.

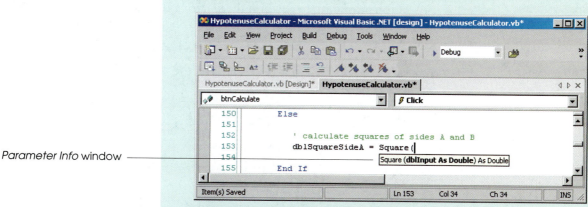

Parameter Info window

Figure 13.8 *Parameter Info* window.

A procedure is **invoked** (that is, made to perform its designated task) by a **procedure call**. The procedure call specifies the procedure name and provides information (**arguments**) that the **callee** (the procedure being called) requires to do its job. When the called procedure completes its task, it returns control to the **caller** (the **calling procedure**). For example, we have typically called function `Val` as follows:

```
intResult = Val(txtInput.Text)
```

where `Val` is the name of the function, and `txtInput.Text`'s value is the argument passed to this function. The procedure uses this value to perform its defined task (returning the value of `txtInput.Text` as a number).

When program control reaches line 153 of Fig. 13.7, the application calls **Function** procedure `Square`. At this point, the application makes a copy of the value entered into the **Length of side A:** TextBox (after this value has been passed to function `Val`), and program control transfers to the first line of `Square`.

(cont.)

Keyword **ByVal**, specified in the header of procedure Square, indicates that a copy of the argument's value (the length of side A) should be passed to Square. Square receives the copy of the value input by the user and stores it in the parameter dblInput. When the Return statement in Square is reached, the value to the right of keyword Return is returned to the point on line 153 where Square was called, and the procedure's execution completes (any remaining statements of the procedure's body will not be executed). Program control will also be transferred to this point, and the application will continue by assigning the return value of Square to variable dblSquareSideA. These same actions will occur again when program control reaches the second call to Square on line 154. With this call, the value passed to Square is the value entered into the **Length of side B:** TextBox (after this value has been passed to function Val), and the value returned is assigned to variable dblSquareSideB.

8. ***Calling a preexisting method of the FCL.*** Add lines 156–164 of Fig. 13.9 to the Else's body of the If...Then...Else statement in your application. Line 158 adds the square of side A and the square of side B, resulting in the square of the hypotenuse, which is assigned to variable dblSquareHypotenuse. Line 162 then calls FCL method **Sqrt** of class Math (by using the dot operator). This method will calculate the square root of the square of the hypotenuse to find the length of the hypotenuse.

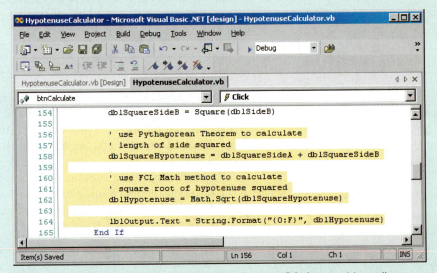

Figure 13.9   Completing the btnCalculate_Click event handler.

9. ***Running the application.*** Select **Debug > Start** to run your application. Enter 3 into the **Length of side A:** TextBox and 4 into the **Length of side B:** TextBox. Click the **Calculate Hypotenuse** Button. The output is shown in Fig. 13.10.

Error-Prevention Tip

Small procedures are easier to test, debug and understand than are large ones.

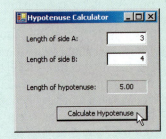

Figure 13.10   **Hypotenuse Calculator** application running.

(cont.)

10. ***Closing the application***. Close your running application by clicking its close box.

11. ***Closing the IDE***. Close Visual Studio .NET by clicking its close box.

You have now successfully created a **Function** procedure. You have also tested this **Function** procedure (by running the application) to confirm that it works correctly. This **Function** procedure can now be used in any Visual Basic .NET application where you wish to calculate the square of a **Double**. All you need to do is include the procedure definition in your application. This is an example of code reuse, which helps programmers create application's faster.

As demonstrated in the **Hypotenuse Calculator** application, the procedure call used to call a **Function** procedure follows the format

name(*argument list*)

There must be one argument in the argument list of the procedure call for each parameter in the parameter list of the procedure header. The arguments also must be compatible with the parameters' types (that is, Visual Basic .NET must be able to assign the value of the argument to its corresponding parameter variable). For example, a parameter of type **Double** could receive the value of 53547.350009, 22 or −.03546, but not "hello", because a **Double** variable cannot contain a **String**. If a procedure does not receive any values, the parameter list is empty (that is, the procedure name is followed by an empty set of parentheses). You will study procedure parameters in detail in Tutorial 15.

As you saw in the previous example, the statement

Return *expression*

can occur anywhere in a **Function** procedure body and returns the value of *expression* to the caller. If necessary, Visual Basic .NET attempts to convert the value of *expression* to the **Function** procedure's return type. **Functions Return** exactly one value. When a **Return** statement is executed, control returns immediately to the point at which that **Function** procedure was called.

You will now create another **Function** procedure. This procedure, which is part of the **Maximum** application, returns the largest of three numbers input by the user. In the following box, you will create the **Maximum** application.

Creating a Function Procedure That Returns the Largest of Three Numbers

1. ***Copying the template to your working directory***. Copy the C:\Examples\Tutorial13\TemplateApplication\Maximum directory to your C:\SimplyVB directory.

2. ***Opening the Maximum application's template file***. Double click Maximum.sln in the Maximum directory to open the application in Visual Studio .NET. Switch to design view (Fig. 13.11).

3. ***Creating an event handler for the Maximum Button***. Double click the **Maximum** Button to create an event handler for this Button's **Click** event. Add a comment on line 155 of Fig. 13.12 and split the header over two lines, as shown on lines 156–157. Add lines 159-160 to the event handler. Lines 159–160 call **Function** procedure Maximum and pass it the three values the user has input into the application's TextBoxes. Notice that Maximum has been underlined in blue, indicating a syntax error. This occurs because **Function** procedure Maximum has not yet been defined. You will define Maximum in the next step. This syntax error will occur whenever you call a procedure that is not recognized by Visual Studio .NET. Misspelling the name of a procedure in a procedure call will likewise cause a syntax error. Finally, add the comment after keywords End Sub on line 161.

Common Programming Error

Calling a procedure that does not yet exist, or misspelling the procedure name in a procedure call results in a syntax error.

(cont.)

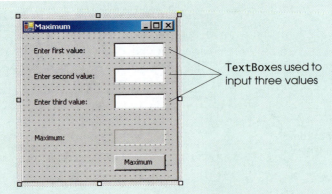

Figure 13.11   **Maximum** application in design view.

TextBoxes used to input three values

4. *Creating an event handler for the Maximum Button.* Double click the **Maximum** Button to create an event handler for this Button's Click event. Add a comment on line 155 of Fig. 13.12 and split the header over two lines, as shown on lines 156–157. Add lines 159–160 to the event handler. Lines 159–160 call Function procedure Maximum and pass it the three values the user has input into the application's TextBoxes. Notice that Maximum has been underlined in blue, indicating a syntax error. This occurs because Function procedure Maximum has not yet been defined. You will define Maximum in the next step. This syntax error will occur whenever you call a procedure that is not recognized by Visual Studio .NET. Misspelling the name of a procedure in a procedure call will likewise cause a syntax error. Finally, add the comment after keywords End Sub on line 161.

Common Programming Error

Calling a procedure that does not yet exist, or misspelling the procedure name in a procedure call results in a syntax error.

Calling a procedure that has not yet been defined is an error

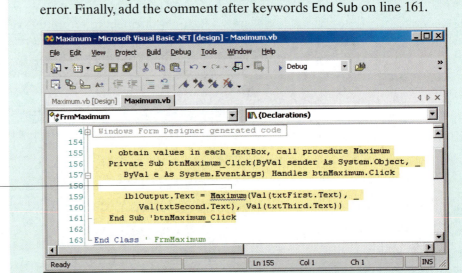

Figure 13.12   Invoking Function procedure Maximum.

5. *Creating Function procedure Maximum.* Add lines 163–165 of Fig. 13.13 after event handler btnMaximum_Click, then press *Enter*. Notice that the keywords End Function will be added for you by the IDE. The parameter list specifies that the values of the three arguments passed to Maximum will be stored in parameters dblOne, dblTwo and dblThree. The parameter list is followed by the keyword As and the return type Double.

(cont.)

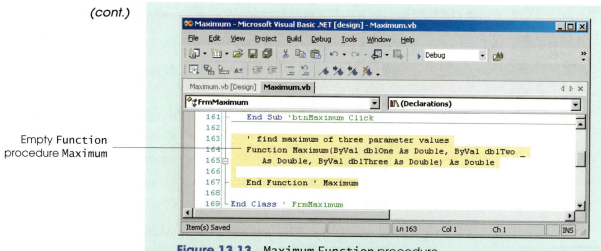

Figure 13.13 Maximum **Function** procedure.

Empty **Function** procedure **Maximum**

6. ***Adding functionality to Function procedure Maximum.*** Add lines 167–173 of Fig. 13.14 to the body of **Maximum**. Line 167 creates a variable that will contain the maximum of the first two numbers passed to this procedure. This maximum is determined on line 170 by using the **Max** method of FCL class **Math**. This method takes two **Doubles** and returns the maximum of those two values. The value returned is assigned to variable **dblTemporaryMaximum** on line 170. You then compare that value to **Function** procedure **Maximum**'s third parameter, **dblThree**, on line 171. The maximum determined on this line, **dblFinalMaximum**, is the maximum of the three values. Line 173 uses a **Return** statement to return this value. The **Return** statement terminates execution of the procedure and returns the result of **dblFinalMaximum** to the calling procedure. The result is returned to the point (line 159 of Fig. 13.12) where **Maximum** was called and is assigned to **lblOutput**'s **Text** property.

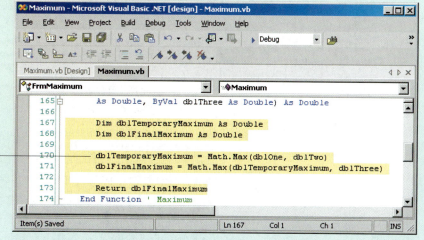

Calling **Math.Max** to determine the maximum of two values

Figure 13.14 **Math.Max** returns the larger of its two arguments.

7. ***Running the application.*** Select **Debug > Start** to run your application (Fig. 13.15). Enter a numeric value into each **TextBox**, and click the **Maximum** **Button**. Notice that the largest of the three values is displayed in the output **Label**.

(cont.)

Figure 13.15 **Maximum** application running.

8. ***Closing the application.*** Close your running application by clicking its close box.

9. ***Closing the IDE.*** Close Visual Studio .NET by clicking its close box.

SELF-REVIEW

1. A procedure is invoked by a(n) _____.

   a) callee   b) caller

   c) argument   d) parameter

2. The _____ statement in a Function procedure sends a value back to the calling procedure.

   a) Return   b) Back

   c) End   d) None of the above.

Answers: 1) b. 2) a.

13.4 Using Sub Procedures in the Wage Calculator Application

The **Calculate** Button's Click event handler in the original version of the **Wage Calculator** application (Tutorial 7) calculated the wages and displayed the result in a Label. In the following box, you will write Sub procedure DisplayPay to perform these tasks. **Sub procedures** are similar to Function procedures, with one important difference: Sub procedures do not return a value to the caller. When the user clicks the **Calculate** Button, event handler btnCalculate_Click calls Sub procedure DisplayPay.

Creating a Sub Procedure within the Wage Calculator Application

1. ***Copying the template to your working directory.*** Copy the C:\Examples\Tutorial13\TemplateApplication\WageCalculator2 directory to your C:\SimplyVB directory.

2. ***Opening the Wage Calculator application's template file.*** Double click WageCalculator2.sln in the WageCalculator2 directory to open the application in Visual Studio .NET.

3. ***Creating the btnCalculate_Click event handler.*** View the application's Form in design view. Double click the **Calculate** Button to generate the Click event handler.

(cont.)

4. ***Entering functionality to btnCalculate_Click.*** Add lines 135–144 of Fig. 13.16 to the empty event handler. This code calls procedure `DisplayPay` to calculate and display the wages. Lines 140–141 retrieve the user input from the `TextBoxes` and assign the values to variables declared in lines 136–137. Line 144 calls procedure `DisplayPay`, which you will define shortly. This procedure call takes two arguments: the hours worked (`dblUserHours`) and the hourly wage (`decWage`). Notice that the call to `DisplayPay` is underlined in blue, as the procedure has not yet been defined; for the moment, this is a syntax error. Also notice that the procedure's arguments in this example are variables. Arguments also can be constants or expressions.

Call to `DisplayPay` ———————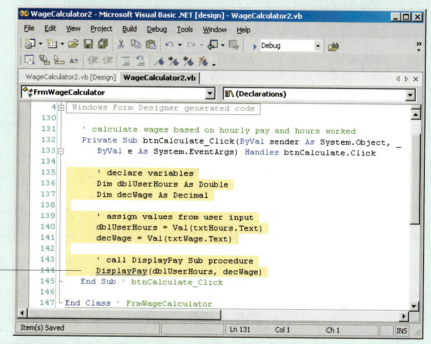

Figure 13.16   `btnCalculate_Click` calls `DisplayPay`.

5. ***Creating a Sub procedure.*** After event handler `btnCalculate_Click`, add Sub procedure `DisplayPay` to your application (lines 147–172 of Fig. 13.17).

Procedure `DisplayPay` receives the argument values and stores them in the parameters `dblHours` and `decRate`. Notice that the syntax of a Sub procedure is the same as the syntax of a `Function` procedure, with a few small changes. One change is that the `Function` keywords are replaced with **Sub** keywords (lines 148 and 172 of Fig. 13.17). Another difference is that there is no return type, because Sub procedures do not return a value.

Note that the variable `decEarnings` and the constant `intHOUR_LIMIT` have been moved to the `DisplayPay` procedure. (In Fig. 7.14 and Fig. 7.15 of Tutorial 7, they were located within the `btnCalculate_Click` event handler.) Because they are no longer needed in `btnCalculate_Click`, they should be removed from that event handler.

Lines 156–168 define the `If...Then...Else` statement that determines whether overtime must be calculated. The condition for this statement determines whether `dblHours` is less than or equal to constant `intHOUR_LIMIT`. If it is, then the employee's earnings without overtime are calculated. Otherwise, the employee's earnings including overtime are calculated. Line 171 displays the result (formatted as currency) in a `Label`.

When the `End Sub` statement on line 172 is encountered, control is returned to the calling procedure, `btnCalculate_Click` (line 144 of Fig. 13.16).

Software Design Tip

The procedure header and procedure calls all must agree with regard to the number, types and order of parameters.

Common Programming Error

Declaring a variable in the procedure's body with the same name as a parameter variable in the procedure header is a syntax error.

(cont.)

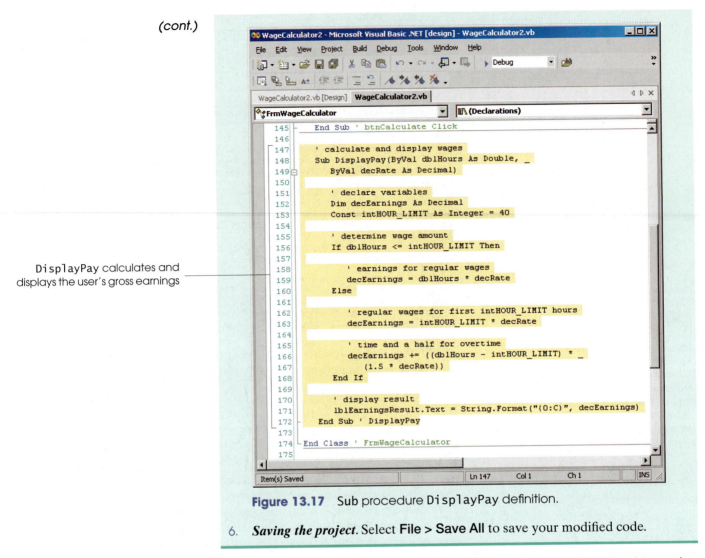

DisplayPay calculates and
displays the user's gross earnings

Figure 13.17 Sub procedure `DisplayPay` definition.

6. ***Saving the project.*** Select **File > Save All** to save your modified code.

The following box shows you how to add `Function` procedure `CheckOvertime` to the **Wage Calculator** application. `CheckOvertime` will be used to determine whether an employee has worked overtime.

Creating a Function Procedure within the Wage Calculator Application	1. ***Creating a Function procedure header.*** Add `Function` procedure `Check-Overtime` (lines 174–184 of Fig. 13.18) to your application, after the `DisplayPay` procedure definition. Notice that the return type of the procedure is `Boolean`. This indicates that the value returned by the procedure must be a `Boolean` (that is constants, variables or expressions that evaluate to `True` or `False`).
	When `CheckOvertime` is called, program control is transferred to the beginning of this procedure at line 175. The arguments passed to this procedure (passed in the procedure call, which you will write in the next step) are stored in the parameter variables `dblTotal` and `intLimit`. Line 179 returns the `Boolean` value `True`, to indicate that the employee has worked overtime; line 181 returns the `Boolean` value `False`, to indicate that the employee has not worked any overtime. Program control and the value (either `True` or `False`) are returned to the line where `CheckOvertime` was initially called.

(cont.)

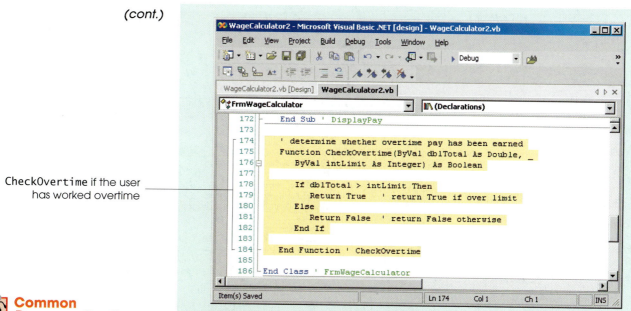

CheckOvertime if the user has worked overtime

Figure 13.18 Function procedure CheckOverTime definition.

2. ***Modifying Sub procedure DisplayPay.*** In Sub procedure DisplayPay, replace the statement (line 156 of Fig. 13.17)

```
If dblHours <= intHOUR_LIMIT Then
```

with line 156 of Fig. 13.19. We modify DisplayPay so that it now calls Function procedure CheckOvertime to determine whether the employee qualifies for overtime pay.

Function procedure CheckOvertime is called (line 156) with the procedure call CheckOvertime(dblHours, intHOUR_LIMIT). When program control reaches this expression, the application calls Function procedure CheckOvertime. At this point, the application makes a copy of the value of dblHours and intHOUR_LIMIT (the arguments in the procedure call), and control transfers to the header of Function procedure CheckOvertime.

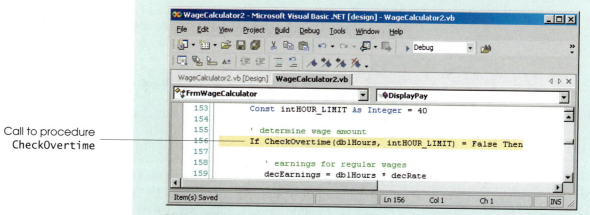

Call to procedure CheckOvertime

Figure 13.19 DisplayPay calls Function procedure CheckOvertime.

The parameter variables in CheckOvertime's header are initialized to copies of dblHours's value and intHOUR_LIMIT's value. The value returned from CheckOvertime is compared to the value False on line 156.

Now when the **Calculate** Button is clicked, DisplayPay is called and executed. Recall that Function procedure CheckOvertime is called by the DisplayPay Sub procedure. This sequence of calls is repeated every time the user clicks the **Calculate** Button.

(cont.)

3. ***Running the application.*** Select **Debug > Start** to run your application. Enter an hourly wage and number of hours worked (under 40), then click the **Calculate** Button. Verify that the appropriate earnings are displayed. Change the number of hours worked to a value over 40 and click the **Calculate** Button again. Verify that the appropriate output is displayed.

4. ***Closing the application.*** Close your running application by clicking its close box.

5. ***Closing the IDE.*** Close Visual Studio .NET by clicking its close box.

Figure 13.20 presents the source code for the **Wage Calculator** application. The lines of code that contain new programming concepts that you learned in this tutorial are highlighted.

```
1   Public Class FrmWageCalculator
2       Inherits System.Windows.Forms.Form
3
4       ' Windows Forms Designer generated code
5
6       ' calculate wages based on hourly pay and hours worked
7       Private Sub btnCalculate_Click(ByVal sender As System.Object, _
8           ByVal e As System.EventArgs) Handles btnCalculate.Click
9
10          ' declare variables
11          Dim dblUserHours As Double
12          Dim decWage As Decimal
13
14          ' assign values from user input
15          dblUserHours = Val(txtHours.Text)
16          decWage = Val(txtWage.Text)
17
18          ' call DisplayPay Sub procedure
19          DisplayPay(dblUserHours, decWage)
20      End Sub ' btnCalculate_Click
21
22      ' calculate and display wages
23      Sub DisplayPay(ByVal dblHours As Double, _
24          ByVal decRate As Decimal)
25
26          ' declare variables
27          Dim decEarnings As Decimal
28          Const intHOUR_LIMIT As Integer = 40
29
30          ' determine wage amount
31          If CheckOvertime(dblHours, intHOUR_LIMIT) = False Then
32
33              ' earnings for regular wages
34              decEarnings = dblHours * decRate
35          Else
36
37              ' regular wages for first intHOUR_LIMIT hours
38              decEarnings = intHOUR_LIMIT * decRate
39
40              ' time and a half for overtime
41              decEarnings += ((dblHours - intHOUR_LIMIT) * _
42                  (1.5 * decRate))
43          End If
```

Call to **Sub** procedure that calculates and displays wages — line 19

Sub procedure header specifies parameter names and types — lines 23–24

Call to **Function** procedure that determines if user has worked overtime — line 31

Figure 13.20   Code for **Wage Calculator** application. (Part 1 of 2.)

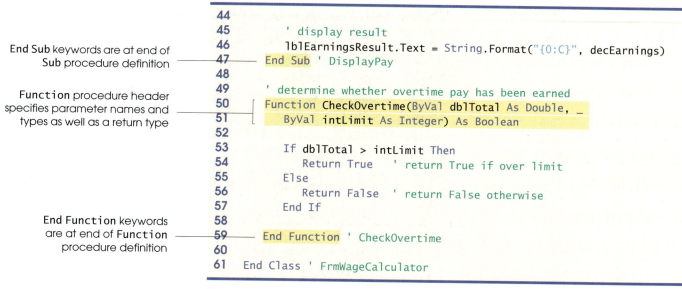

End Sub keywords are at end of Sub procedure definition

Function procedure header specifies parameter names and types as well as a return type

End Function keywords are at end of Function procedure definition

```
44
45          ' display result
46          lblEarningsResult.Text = String.Format("{0:C}", decEarnings)
47       End Sub ' DisplayPay
48
49       ' determine whether overtime pay has been earned
50       Function CheckOvertime(ByVal dblTotal As Double, _
51          ByVal intLimit As Integer) As Boolean
52
53          If dblTotal > intLimit Then
54             Return True    ' return True if over limit
55          Else
56             Return False   ' return False otherwise
57          End If
58
59       End Function ' CheckOvertime
60
61    End Class ' FrmWageCalculator
```

Figure 13.20   Code for **Wage Calculator** application. (Part 2 of 2.)

SELF-REVIEW

1. Arguments to a procedure can be _____.

   a) constants   b) expressions
   c) variables   d) All of the above.

2. The _____ is a comma-separated list of declarations in a procedure header.

   a) argument list   b) parameter list
   c) value list   d) variable list

Answers: 1) d. 2) b.

13.5 Using the Debugger: Debug Toolbar

Now, you continue your study of the debugger by learning about the debug toolbar, which contains Buttons for controlling the debugging process. These Buttons provide convenient access to actions in the **Debug** menu. In this section, you will learn how to use the debug toolbar's Buttons to verify that a procedure's code is executing correctly. In the following box, we use the debug toolbar Buttons to examine the **Wage Calculator** application.

Using the Debugger: Debug Toolbar

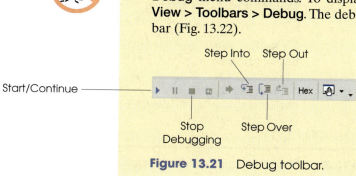

1. **Opening the completed application.** Open the **Wage Calculator** application.

2. **Opening the debug toolbar.** The debug toolbar contains Buttons for controlling the debugging process. These Buttons provide easy access to the **Debug** menu commands. To display the debug toolbar (Fig. 13.21), select **View > Toolbars > Debug**. The debug toolbar appears below the IDE menu bar (Fig. 13.22).

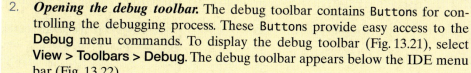

Step Into   Step Out

Start/Continue

Stop Debugging   Step Over

Figure 13.21   Debug toolbar.

(cont.)

3. ***Setting a breakpoint***. Set a breakpoint on line 144 by clicking in the margin indicator bar (Fig. 13.22).

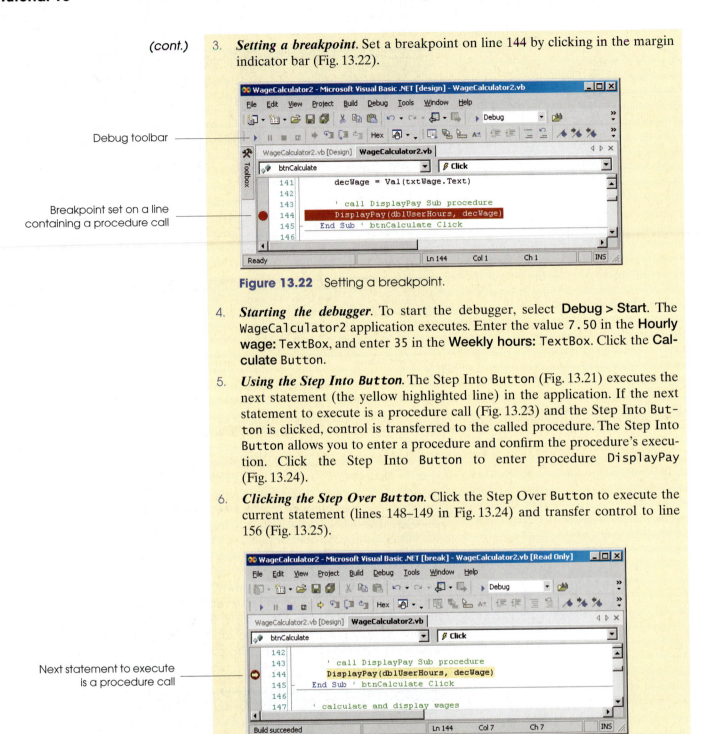

Figure 13.22   Setting a breakpoint.

4. ***Starting the debugger***. To start the debugger, select **Debug > Start**. The WageCalculator2 application executes. Enter the value 7.50 in the **Hourly wage:** TextBox, and enter 35 in the **Weekly hours:** TextBox. Click the **Calculate** Button.

5. ***Using the Step Into Button***. The Step Into Button (Fig. 13.21) executes the next statement (the yellow highlighted line) in the application. If the next statement to execute is a procedure call (Fig. 13.23) and the Step Into Button is clicked, control is transferred to the called procedure. The Step Into Button allows you to enter a procedure and confirm the procedure's execution. Click the Step Into Button to enter procedure DisplayPay (Fig. 13.24).

6. ***Clicking the Step Over Button***. Click the Step Over Button to execute the current statement (lines 148–149 in Fig. 13.24) and transfer control to line 156 (Fig. 13.25).

Figure 13.23   Statement calls procedure DisplayPay.

(cont.)

Control is transferred to the procedure definition

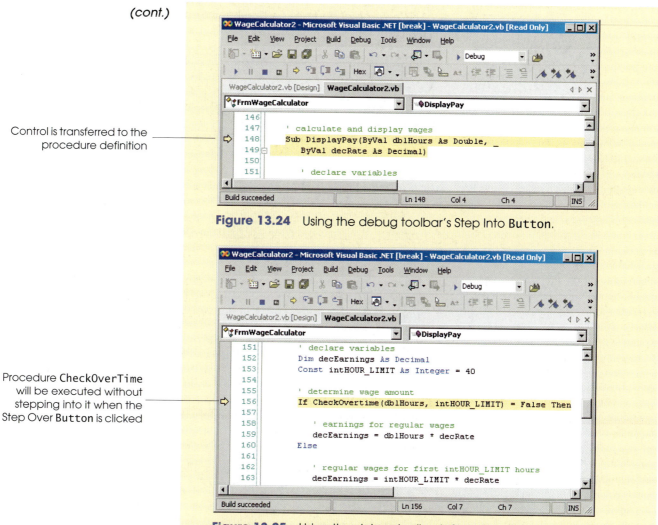

Figure 13.24   Using the debug toolbar's Step Into **Button**.

Procedure `CheckOverTime` will be executed without stepping into it when the Step Over **Button** is clicked

Figure 13.25   Using the debug toolbar's Step Over **Button**.

7. ***Clicking the Step Over Button again.*** Click the Step Over **Button**. This **Button** behaves like the Step Into **Button** when the next statement to execute does not contain a procedure call. If the next statement to execute contains a procedure call, the called procedure executes in its entirety (without transferring control and entering the procedure), and the yellow arrow advances to the next executable line in the current procedure (Fig. 13.26).

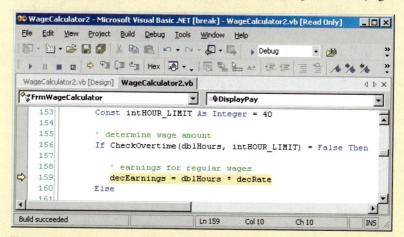

Figure 13.26   Using the debug toolbar's Step Over **Button** again.

(cont.)

8. **Setting a breakpoint.** Set a breakpoint at the end of procedure `DisplayPay` on line 172 (End Sub) of Fig. 13.27. You will make use of this breakpoint in the next step.

9. **Using the Continue Button.** Clicking the Continue `Button` will execute any statements between the next executable statement and the next breakpoint or the end of the current event handler, whichever comes first. Notice that there is one executable statement (line 172) before the breakpoint that was set in Step 8. Click the Continue `Button`. The next executable statement is now line 172 (Fig. 13.27). This feature is particularly useful when you have many lines of code before the next breakpoint that you do not want to step through line by line.

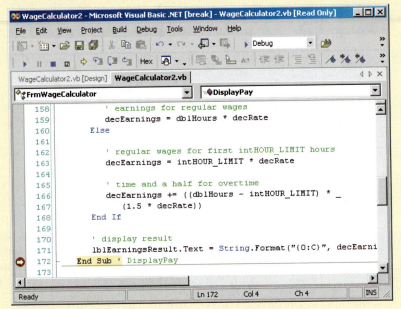

Figure 13.27   Using the debug toolbar's Continue `Button`.

10. **Using the Stop Debugging Button.** Click the Stop Debugging `Button` to end the debugging session and return the IDE to design mode.

11. **Starting the debugger.** We have one last feature we wish to present that will require you to start the debugger again. Start the debugger, as you did in *Step 4*, entering the same values as input.

12. **Using the Step Into Button.** Keep the breakpoint on line 144 (Fig. 13.22) and remove the breakpoint from line 172. Repeat *Step 5*.

13. **Clicking the Step Out Button.** After you have stepped into the `DisplayPay` procedure, click the Step Out `Button` to execute the statements in the procedure and return control to line 144, which contains the procedure call. Often, in lengthy procedures, you will want to look at a few key lines of code and then continue debugging the caller's code. This feature is useful for such situations, where you do not want to continue stepping through the entire procedure line by line.

14. **Clicking the Stop Debugging Button.** Click the Stop Debugging `Button` to end the debugging session.

15. **Close the IDE.** Close Visual Studio .NET by clicking its close box.

SELF-REVIEW

1. During debugging, the _____ Button executes the remaining statements in the current procedure call and returns program control to the place where the procedure was called.

   a) Step Into
   b) Step Out
   c) Step Over
   d) Steps

2. The _____ Button behaves like the Step Into Button when the next statement to execute does not contain a procedure call.

   a) Step Into
   b) Step Out
   c) Step Over
   d) Steps

Answers: 1) b. 2) c.

13.6 Wrap-Up

In this tutorial, you learned about the difference between Function and Sub procedures, and you learned how procedures can be used to better organize an application. This tutorial introduced you to the concept called code reuse, showing how time and effort can be saved by using preexisting code. You used preexisting code provided by the FCL and learned to create your own code that can be used in other applications.

You were introduced to the syntax for creating and invoking the two types of procedures. You learned the components of a procedure, including the procedure header, parameter list and (in the case of Function procedures) the Return statement. After learning how to develop and write procedures, you learned about the order of execution that occurs from the line where a procedure is called (invoked) to the procedure definition, and returning control back to the point of invocation. In this tutorial's applications, you created three Function procedures—Square, Maximum and CheckOvertime and a Sub procedure (DisplayPay).

After creating the procedures in this tutorial, you learned how to debug the procedures in the application by using the Buttons in debug toolbar. These Buttons (including the Step Into, Step Out and Step Over Buttons) can be used to determine whether a procedure is executing correctly.

In the next tutorial, you learn about such controls as GroupBoxes and DateTime-Pickers and use them to build a **Shipping Time** application. This application controls information about a package being shipped from one location to another.

SKILLS SUMMARY

Invoking a Procedure

- Specify the procedure name and any arguments in parentheses.
- Ensure that the arguments passed match the procedure definition's parameters in number, type and order.

Using a Function Procedure

- Use a Function procedure when a value needs to be returned to the caller.
- Use keyword Function to begin the procedure.
- Specify a parameter list declaring each parameter's name and type. In the parameter list, use keyword ByVal in place of keyword Dim.
- Place the keyword As and the return type after the parenthesis that terminates the parameter list.
- Press *Enter* to generate the terminating End Function statement.
- Add code to the procedure's body to perform a specific task.
- Return a value with the Return statement.

Returning a Value From a Function Procedure

- Use the Return keyword followed by the value to be returned.

Creating a Sub Procedure

■ Start the procedure header with keyword Sub.

■ Specify a parameter list declaring each parameter's name and type. In the parameter list, use keyword ByVal in place of keyword Dim.

■ Press *Enter* to generate the terminating End Sub statement.

■ Add code to the procedure's body to perform a specific task.

KEY TERMS

argument—Information provided to a procedure call.

ByVal—The keyword specifying that the calling procedure should pass a copy of its argument's value in the procedure call to the called procedure.

callee—The procedure being called.

caller—The procedure that calls another procedure. Also known as the calling procedure.

divide-and-conquer technique—Constructing large applications from small, manageable pieces to make development and maintenance of large applications easier.

End Function Keywords—Indicates the end of a Function procedure.

End Sub Keywords—Indicates the end of a Sub procedure.

Function keyword—Begins the definition of a Function procedure.

Function procedure—A procedure similar to a Sub procedure, with one important difference: Function procedures return a value to the caller, whereas Sub procedures do not.

invoking a procedure—Causing a procedure to perform its designated task.

method—A procedure contained in a class.

Parameter Info **feature of Visual Studio .NET**—Provides the programmer with information about procedures and their arguments.

parameter list—A comma-separated list in which the procedure declares each parameter variable's name and type.

parameter variable—A variable declared in a procedure's parameter list that can be used in the body of the procedure.

procedure—A set of instructions for performing a particular task.

procedure body—The declarations and statements that appear after the procedure header but before the keywords End Sub or End Function. The procedure body contains Visual Basic .NET code that performs actions, generally by manipulating or interacting with the parameters from the parameter list.

procedure call—Invokes a procedure, and specifies the procedure name and provides arguments that the callee (the procedure being called) requires to perform its task.

procedure definition—The procedure header, body and ending statement.

procedure header—The first line of a procedure (including the keyword Sub or Function, the procedure name, the parameter list and the Function procedure return type).

procedure name—Follows the keyword Sub or Function and distinguishes one procedure from another. A procedure name can be any valid identifier.

programmer-defined procedure—A procedure created by a programmer to meet the unique needs of a particular application.

Return keyword—Signifies the return statement that sends a value back to the procedure's caller.

Return statement—Used to return a value from a procedure.

return type—Data type of the result returned from a Function procedure.

reusing code—The practice of using existing code to build new code. Reusing code saves time, effort and money.

Sqrt method of class Math—A procedure similar to a Function procedure, with one important difference: Sub procedures do not return a value to the caller, whereas Function procedures do.

Sub keyword—Begins the definition of a Sub procedure.

Sub procedure—A procedure similar to a Function procedure, with one important difference: Sub procedures do not return a value to the caller, whereas Function procedures do.

CONTROLS, EVENTS, PROPERTIES & METHODS

Math This class provides methods used to perform common arithmetic calculations.

- *Methods*

Min — Returns the smaller of two numeric values.

Max — Returns the larger of two numeric values.

Sqrt — Returns the square root of a numeric value.

MULTIPLE-CHOICE QUESTIONS

13.1 A procedure defined with keyword Sub _____.

   a) must specify a return type   b) does not accept arguments

   c) returns a value   d) does not return a value

13.2 The technique of developing large applications from small, manageable pieces is known as _____.

   a) divide and conquer   b) returning a value

   c) click and mortar   d) a building-block algorithm

13.3 What is the difference between Sub and Function procedures?

   a) Sub procedures return values, Function procedures do not.

   b) Function procedures return values, Sub procedures do not.

   c) Sub procedures accept parameters, Function procedures do not.

   d) Function procedures accept parameters, Sub procedures do not.

13.4 What occurs after a procedure call is made?

   a) Control is given to the called procedure. After the procedure is run, the application continues execution at the point where the procedure call was made.

   b) Control is given to the called procedure. After the procedure is run, the application continues execution with the statement after the called procedure's definition.

   c) The statement before the procedure call is executed.

   d) The application terminates.

13.5 Functions can return _____ value(s).

   a) zero   b) exactly one

   c) one or more   d) any number of

13.6 Which of the following must be true when making a procedure call?

   a) The number of arguments in the procedure call must match the number of parameters in the procedure header.

   b) The argument types must be compatible with their corresponding parameter types.

   c) Both a and b.   d) None of the above.

13.7 Which of the following statements correctly returns the variable intValue from a Function procedure?

   a) Return Dim intValue   b) Return intValue As Integer

   c) intValue Return   d) Return intValue

13.8 The _____ Button executes the next statement in the application. If the next statement to execute contains a procedure call, the called procedure executes in its entirety.

   a) Step Into   b) Step Out

   c) Step Over   d) Steps

13.9 The first line of a procedure (including the keyword Sub or Function, the procedure name, the parameter list and the Function procedure return type) is known as the procedure _____.

   a) body   b) title

   c) caller   d) header

13.10 Method _____ of class Math calculates the square root of the value passed as an argument.

    a) SquareRoot   b) Root

    c) Sqrt   d) Square

EXERCISES

13.11 (*Temperature Converter Application*) Write an application that performs various temperature conversions (Fig. 13.28). The application should be capable of performing two types of conversions: degrees Fahrenheit to degrees Celsius and degrees Celsius to degrees Fahrenheit.

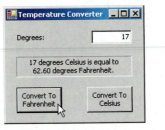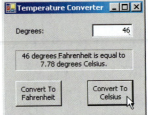

Figure 13.28 Temperature Converter GUI.

a) *Copying the template to your working directory.* Copy the directory C:\Examples\Tutorial13\Exercises\TemperatureConversion to your C:\SimplyVB directory.

b) *Opening the application's template file.* Double click TemperatureConversion.sln in the TemperatureConversion directory to open the application.

c) *Convert Fahrenheit to Celsius.* To convert degrees Fahrenheit to degrees Celsius, use this formula:

```
dblCelsius = (5 / 9) * (dblFahrenheit - 32)
```

d) *Convert Celsius to Fahrenheit.* To convert degrees Celsius to degrees Fahrenheit, use this formula:

```
dblFahrenheit = (9 / 5) * dblCelsius + 32
```

e) *Adding event handlers to your application.* Double click each Button to add the proper event handlers to your application. These event handlers will call procedures (that you will define in the next step) to convert the degrees entered to either Fahrenheit or Celsius. Each event handler will display the result in the application's output Label.

f) *Adding Function procedures to your application.* Create Function procedures to perform each conversion, using the formulas above. The user should provide the temperature to convert.

g) *Formatting the temperature output.* To format the temperature information, use the String.Format method. Use F as the formatting code to limit the temperature to two decimal places.

h) *Running the application.* Select **Debug > Start** to run your application. Enter a temperature value. Click the **Convert to Fahrenheit** Button and verify that correct output is displayed based on the formula given. Click the **Convert to Celsius** Button and again verify that the output is correct.

i) *Closing the application.* Close your running application by clicking its close box.

j) *Closing the IDE.* Close Visual Studio .NET by clicking its close box.

13.12 *(Display Square Application)* Write an application that displays a solid square composed of a character input by the user (Fig. 13.29). The user also should input the size.

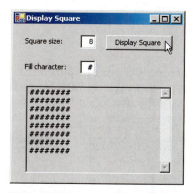

Figure 13.29   **Display Square** application.

a) *Copying the template to your working directory.* Copy the directory C:\Examples\Tutorial13\Exercises\DisplaySquare to your C:\SimplyVB directory.

b) *Opening the application's template file.* Double click DisplaySquare.sln in the DisplaySquare directory to open the application.

c) *Adding a Sub procedure.* Write a Sub procedure DisplaySquare to display the solid square. The size should be specified by the Integer parameter intSize. The character that fills the square should be specified by the String parameter strFillCharacter. You should use a For...Next statement nested within another For...Next statement to create the square. The outer For...Next specifies what row is currently being displayed. The inner For...Next appends all the characters that form the row to a display String.

d) *Adding an event handler for your Button's Click event.* Double click the **Display Square** Button to create the event handler. Program the event handler to call procedure DisplaySquare.

e) *Displaying the output.* Use the multiline TextBox provided to display the square. For example, if intSize is 8 and strFillCharacter is #, the application should look similar to Fig. 13.29.

f) *Running the application.* Select **Debug > Start** to run your application. Enter a size for the square (the length of each side) and a fill character. Click the **Display Square** Button. A square should be displayed of the size you specified, using the character you specified.

g) *Closing the application.* Close your running application by clicking its close box.

h) *Closing the IDE.* Close Visual Studio .NET by clicking its close box.

13.13 *(Miles Per Gallon Application)* Drivers often want to know the miles per gallon their cars get so they can estimate gasoline costs. Develop an application that allows the user to input the number of miles driven and the number of gallons used for a tank of gas.

Figure 13.30   **Miles Per Gallon** application.

a) *Copying the template to your working directory.* Copy the directory C:\Examples\Tutorial13\Exercises\MilesPerGallon to your C:\SimplyVB directory.

b) *Opening the application's template file.* Double click `MilesPerGallon.sln` in the `MilesPerGallon` directory to open the application.

c) *Calculating the miles per gallon.* Write a `Function` procedure `MilesPerGallon` that takes the number of miles driven and gallons used (entered by the user), calculates the amount of miles per gallon and returns the miles per gallon for a tankful of gas.

d) *Displaying the result.* Create a `Click` event handler for the **Calculate MPG** Button that invokes the `Function` procedure `MilesPerGallon` and displays the result returned from the procedure as in Fig. 13.30.

e) *Running the application.* Select **Debug > Start** to run your application. Enter a value for the number of miles driven and the amount of gallons used. Click the **Calculate MPG** Button and verify that the correct output is displayed.

f) *Closing the application.* Close your running application by clicking its close box.

g) *Closing the IDE.* Close Visual Studio .NET by clicking its close box.

What does this code do? ▶   **13.14** What does the following code do? Assume this procedure is invoked by using `Mystery(70, 80)`.

```
1   Sub Mystery(ByVal intNumber1 As Integer, ByVal _
2      intNumber2 As Integer)
3
4      Dim intX As Integer
5      Dim dblY As Double
6
7      intX = intNumber1 + intNumber2
8      dblY = intX / 2
9
10     If dblY <= 60 Then
11        lblResult.Text = "<= 60 "
12     Else
13        lblResult.Text = "Result is " & dblY
14     End If
15
16  End Sub ' Mystery
```

What's wrong with this code? ▶   **13.15** Find the error(s) in the following code, which should take an `Integer` value as an argument and return the value of that argument multiplied by two.

```
1   Function TimesTwo(ByVal intNumber As Integer) As Integer
2
3      Dim intResult As Integer
4
5      intResult = intNumber * 2
6   End Function ' CheckValue
```

Using the Debugger ▶   **13.16** (*Gas Pump Application*) The **Gas Pump** application calculates the cost of gas at a local gas station. This gas station charges `$1.41` per gallon for **Regular** grade gas, `$1.47` per gallon for **Special** grade gas and `$1.57` per gallon for **Super+** grade gas. The user enters the number of gallons to purchase and clicks the desired grade. The application calls a Sub procedure to compute the total cost from the number of gallons entered and the selected grade. While testing your application, you noticed that one of your totals was incorrect, given the input.

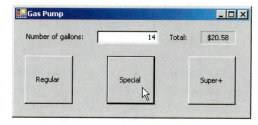

Figure 13.31 **Gas Pump** application executing correctly.

a) *Copying the template to your working directory.* Copy the directory `C:\Examples\Tutorial13\Debugger\GasPumpIncorrect` to your `C:\SimplyVB` directory.

b) *Opening the application's template file.* Double click `GasPump.sln` in the `GasPumpIncorrect` directory to open the application.

c) *Running the application.* Select **Debug > Start** to run your application. Determine which total is incorrect.

d) *Setting a breakpoint.* Set a breakpoint at the beginning of the event handler that is providing incorrect output. For instance, if the **Regular** `Button` is providing incorrect output when clicked, add a breakpoint at the beginning of that `Button`'s `Click` event handler. Use the debugger to help find any logic error(s) in the application.

e) *Modifying the application.* Once you have located the error(s), modify the application so that it behaves correctly.

f) *Running the application.* Select **Debug > Start** to run your application. Enter a number of gallons and click the **Regular, Special** and **Super+** `Buttons`. After each `Button` is clicked, verify that the total displayed is correct based on the prices given in this exercise's description.

g) *Closing the application.* Close your running application by clicking its close box.

h) *Closing the IDE.* Close Visual Studio .NET by clicking its close box.

Programming Challenge **13.17** *(Prime Numbers Application)* An `Integer` greater than 1 is said to be prime if it is divisible by only 1 and itself. For example, 2, 3, 5 and 7 are prime numbers, but 4, 6, 8 and 9 are not. Write an application that takes two numbers (representing a lower bound and an upper bound) and determines all of the prime numbers within the specified bounds, inclusive.

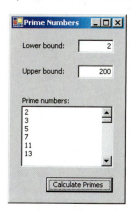 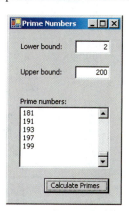

Figure 13.32 **Prime Numbers** application.

a) *Creating the application.* Create an application named `PrimeNumbers` and have its GUI appear as shown in Fig. 13.32. Add an event handler for the **Calculate Primes** `Button`'s `Click` event.

b) *Checking for prime numbers.* Write a `Function` procedure `Prime` that returns `True` if a number is prime, `False` otherwise.

c) *Limiting user input.* Allow users to enter a lower bound (`intLower`) and an upper bound (`intUpper`). Prevent the user from entering bounds less than or equal to 1, or an upper bound that is smaller than the lower bound.

d) *Displaying the prime numbers.* Call Function procedure Prime from your event handler to determine which numbers between the lower and upper bounds are prime. Then have the event handler display the prime numbers in a multiline, scrollable TextBox, as in Fig. 13.32.

e) *Running the application.* Select **Debug > Start** to run your application. Enter a lower bound and an upper bound that is smaller than the lower bound. Click the **Calculate Primes** Button. You should receive an error message. Enter negative bounds and click the **Calculate Primes** Button. Again, you should receive an error message. Enter valid bounds and click the **Calculate Primes** Button. This time, the primes within that range should be displayed.

f) *Closing the application.* Close your running application by clicking its close box.

g) *Closing the IDE.* Close Visual Studio .NET by clicking its close box.

Objectives

In this tutorial, you will learn to:
- Create and manipulate **Date** variables.
- Execute code at regular intervals using a **Timer** control.
- Retrieve **Date** input with a **DateTimePicker** control.
- Group controls using a **GroupBox** control.

Outline

Shipping Time Application

Using Dates and Timers

Many companies rely on date and time information in daily operations, from airlines to shipping companies. These companies often require applications that reliably perform date and time calculations. In this tutorial, you will create an application that performs calculations using the **Date** structure, which allows you to store and manipulate date and time information. You will also learn how to use a **DateTimePicker** control to retrieve date and time information from the user. Finally, you will learn how to use a **Timer**—a Visual Basic .NET control that allows you to execute code at specified time intervals.

14.1 Test-Driving the Shipping Time Application

In this tutorial, you will build the **Shipping Time** application. This application must meet the following requirements:

Application Requirements

A seafood distributor has asked you to create an application that will calculate the delivery time for fresh seafood shipped from Portland, Maine to its distribution center in Las Vegas, Nevada, where only the freshest seafood is accepted. The distributor has arrangements with local airlines to guarantee that seafood will ship on either flights that leave at noon or ones that leave at midnight. However, for security reasons, the airport requires the distributor to drop off the seafood at the airport at least one hour before each flight. When the distributor specifies the drop-off time, the application should display the delivery time in Las Vegas. This application should take into account the 3-hour time difference (it's 3 hours earlier in Las Vegas) and the 6-hour flight time between the two cities. The application should allow the user to select drop-off times within the current day (seafood must be shipped within a day to guarantee freshness). The application should also include a running clock that displays the current time.

This application calculates the shipment's delivery time from the user's drop-off time, taking into account factors such as transit time and time zones. You will use the `DateTimePicker` control to enable the user to enter the drop-off time. You will use the `Date` structure properties and methods to calculate the delivery time. You begin by test-driving the completed application. Then, you will learn the additional Visual Basic .NET technologies that you will need to create your own version of this application.

1. *Opening the completed application.* Open the directory C:\Examples\ Tutorial14\CompletedApplication\ShippingTime to locate the **Shipping Time** application. Double click ShippingTime.sln to open the application in Visual Studio .NET.

2. *Running the Shipping Time application.* Select **Debug > Start** to run the application (Fig. 14.1).

GroupBoxes

DateTimePicker with up-down arrows

Figure 14.1   Shipping Time application.

3. *Entering a drop-off time.* Notice that the default drop-off time is set to your computer's current time when the application is loaded (opened). When you change the drop-off time, the `Label` displaying the delivery time will display the delivery time based on the new time. Notice that if you select a time before 11:00 A.M., the shipment will arrive in Las Vegas at 3:00 P.M. If you specify a time between 11:00 A.M. and 11:00 P.M., the shipment will arrive in Las Vegas at 3:00 A.M. the following day. Finally, if you specify a time after 11:00 P.M., the shipment will not arrive until 3:00 P.M. the following day.

   The time displayed in the **Current time is:** `Label` will update to the current time once each second. However, the drop-off time displayed in the `DateTimePicker` will change only if you select different values by using the up and down arrows or by typing in a new value.

4. *Closing the application.* Close your running application by clicking its close box.

5. *Closing the IDE.* Close Visual Studio .NET by clicking its close box.

14.2 Date Variables

Choosing the correct data type in which to store information can decrease development time by simplifying code. For example, if you are counting whole numbers, variables of type `Integer` are your best choice; if you need to store monetary values, you should use variables of type `Decimal`. However, if you want to store date information (such as the day, month, year and time), there is no obvious primitive-data type. For example, if you used an `Integer` to count days, you would also need separate variables to keep track of the month, day of the week, year and other date-related information. Keeping track of all of these variables would be a complicated task and could slow the development of applications that require date and time information.

Declaring a Date Variable

The Date structure in Visual Basic .NET simplifies manipulation, storage and display of date (and time) information. A **Date** variable, which is created from the Date structure, stores information about a point in time (for example, 12:00:00 A.M. on January 1, 2003). Using code, you can access a Date's properties, including the day, the hour and the minute. Your **Shipping Time** application requires calculations involving time, so you will use Date variables to store and manipulate this information.

Because the Date type is a structure, you must use the New keyword when creating a Date value. In the code,

Date constructor ——————

Date variable ——————

```
Dim dtmDelivery As Date = New Date(2003, 1, 1, 0, 0, 0)
```

Good Programming Practice

Prefix Date variable names with dtm (short for date/time).

a new Date variable named dtmDelivery is declared. The **New** keyword calls the Date structure's constructor. A **constructor** is a procedure that initializes a class object or structure value when it is created. You will use FCL class constructors in Tutorial 16. You will also learn how to write your own constructors in Tutorial 19. Notice that this particular constructor takes six arguments: year, month, day, hour, minute and second. These values are described in Fig. 14.2.

Argument	Range	Description
Initializing a Date variable using New Date(*year*, *month*, *day*, *hour*, *minute*, *second*)		
year	Integer values 1–9999	Specifies the year.
month	Integer values 1–12	Specifies the month of the year.
day	Integer values 1–*number of days in month*	Specifies the day of the month. Each month has 28 to 31 days depending on the month and year.
hour	Integer values 0–23	Specifies the hour of the day. The value 0 represents 12:00 A.M.
minute	Integer values 0–59	Specifies the minute of the hour.
second	Integer values 0–59	Specifies the number of elapsed seconds in the current minute.

Figure 14.2 Date constructor arguments.

Using Date Members

After assigning a value to a Date variable, you can access that variable's properties using the member-access (dot) operator, as follows:

```
intYear = dtmDelivery.Year       ' retrieves Date dtmDelivery's year
intMonth = dtmDelivery.Month     ' retrieves Date dtmDelivery's month
intDay = dtmDelivery.Day         ' retrieves Date dtmDelivery's day
intHour = dtmDelivery.Hour       ' retrieves Date dtmDelivery's hour
intMinute = dtmDelivery.Minute   ' retrieves Date dtmDelivery's minute
intSecond = dtmDelivery.Second   ' retrieves Date dtmDelivery's second
```

In this tutorial, you will use several Date properties and methods that can be accessed through the member-access operator.

Values in Date variables cannot be added like numeric primitive data types such as Integers and Decimals. Instead of using arithmetic operators to add or subtract values in Date variables, you must call the correct method, using the member-access operator. Figure 14.3 demonstrates how to perform various calculations with Date variables.

Visual Basic .NET statement	Result
Assume dtmDelivery has been initialized with a Date value.	
dtmDelivery = dtmDelivery.AddHours(3)	Add 3 hours.
dtmDelivery = dtmDelivery.AddMinutes(-5)	Subtract 5 minutes.
dtmDelivery = dtmDelivery.AddDays(1)	Add 1 day.
dtmDelivery = dtmDelivery.AddMinutes(30)	Add 30 minutes.
dtmDelivery = dtmDelivery.AddHours(-12)	Subtract 12 hours.

Figure 14.3 Date methods that perform various calculations.

Note that each "add" method does not actually change the value of the Date variable on which that method is called. Instead, each "add" method returns a Date value containing the result of the calculation. To change the value of Date variable dtmDelivery, you must assign to dtmDelivery the value returned by the "add" method.

Visual Basic .NET provides a simple way to assign the current date and time to a Date variable. You can use the **Now** property to assign your computer's current date and time to a Date variable:

```
Dim dtmCurrentTime As Date = Date.Now
```

Much like methods MessageBox.Show and String.Format, you can access the Now property of the Date structure by following the name of the structure with the member-access operator and the name of the property. Notice that this assignment does not require keyword New. This is because the Date.Now property returns a Date value.

Now that you are familiar with Date variables, you will design the **Shipping Time** application by using two new controls—the GroupBox control and the DateTimePicker control. A **GroupBox** control groups related controls visually by drawing a labeled box around them. The **DateTimePicker** control allows users to enter date and time information.

SELF-REVIEW

1. The _____ property of the Date structure retrieves your computer's current date and time.

    a) Time   b) Now

    c) CurrentTime   d) DateTime

2. The fourth argument to the Date constructor specifies the variable's _____.

    a) day   b) year

    c) hour   d) minute

Answers: 1) b. 2) c.

14.3 Building the Shipping Time Application: Design Elements

You are now ready to begin analyzing the problem statement and developing pseudocode. The following pseudocode describes the basic operation of the **Shipping Time** application:

    When the Form loads:
        Set range of possible drop off times to any time in the current day
        Determine the shipment's delivery time
        Display the shipment's delivery time

When the user changes the drop-off time:
   Determine the shipment's delivery time
   Display the shipment's delivery time

After one second has elapsed:
   Update the current time displayed

When the DisplayDeliveryTime procedure gets called:
   Determine the time the shipment's flight will depart
   Add three hours to determine the delivery time (takes into account 6 hours
      for time of flight minus 3 hours for the time difference)
   Display the delivery time

When the DepartureTime procedure gets called:

   Select correct Case based on the hour the shipment was dropped off

      Case where the drop off hour is between the values 0 and 10
         Delivery set to depart on noon flight of current day

      Case where the drop off hour is 23
         Delivery set to depart on noon flight of next day

      Case where none of the preceding Cases match
         Delivery set to depart on midnight flight of current day

Now that you have test-driven the **Shipping Time** application and studied its pseudocode representation, you will use an ACE table to help you convert the pseudocode to Visual Basic .NET. Figure 14.4 lists the actions, controls and events that \will help you complete your own version of this application.

Action/Control/Event (ACE) Table for the Shipping Time Application

Action	Control	Event/Method
Label the application's controls	lblCurrentTime, lblDropOff, lblDeliveryTime	Application is run
	FrmShippingTime	Load
Set range of possible drop off times to any time in the current day	dtpDropOff	
Determine the shipment's delivery time	dtpDropOff	
Display the shipment's delivery time	lblLasVegasTime	
	dtpDropOff	ValueChanged
Determine the shipment's delivery time	dtpDropOff	
Display the shipment's delivery time	lblLasVegasTime	
	tmrClock	Tick
Update and display the current time	lblCurrentTime	
		Display-DeliveryTime
Determine the time the shipment's flight will depart	dtpDropOff	
Add three hours to determine the delivery time		
Display the delivery time	lblLasVegasTime	

Figure 14.4   ACE table for the **Shipping Time** application. (Part 1 of 2.)

Action	Control	Event/Method
		DepartureTime
Select correct Case based on the hour the shipment was dropped off	dtpDropOff	
Case where drop off hour is 0-10		
Delivery set to depart on noon flight		
Case where drop off hour is 23		
Delivery set to depart on noon flight of next day		
Case were none of the preceding Cases match		
Delivery set to depart on midnight flight		

Figure 14.4   ACE table for the **Shipping Time** application. (Part 2 of 2.)

The following box demonstrates how to insert a GroupBox control into your application.

Placing Controls in a GroupBox

1. **Copying the template to your working directory.** Copy the C:\Examples\ Tutorial14\TemplateApplication\ShippingTime to your C:\SimplyVB directory.

2. **Opening the Shipping Time application's template file.** Double click ShippingTime.sln in the ShippingTime directory to open the application in Visual Studio .NET.

3. **Displaying the template Form.** Double click ShippingTime.vb in the **Solution Explorer** window to display the Form in Visual Studio .NET.

4. **Inserting a GroupBox control in the Form.** The template includes a GroupBox that displays the seafood shipment delivery time. Add a second GroupBox to contain the drop-off time by double clicking the **GroupBox** control,

in the **Toolbox**. Change the Text property to Drop Off and the Name property to fraDropOff. Change the Location property to 16, 56 and the Size property to 328, 64. After these modifications, your Form should look like Fig. 14.5.

Newly created GroupBox displaying the text **Drop Off**

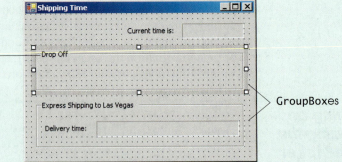

GroupBoxes

Figure 14.5   GroupBox controls on the **Shipping Time** Form.

(cont.)

5. ***Creating Labels inside the GroupBox.*** To place a Label inside the Group-Box, click the **Label** tab in the **Toolbox**, then click inside the GroupBox (Fig. 14.6). Change the Text property of the Label to Enter drop-off time: and the Name property to lblDropOff. Then change the position and size of the Label by setting its Location property to 40, 32 and the Size property to 104, 21. Change the Label's TextAlign property to MiddleLeft.

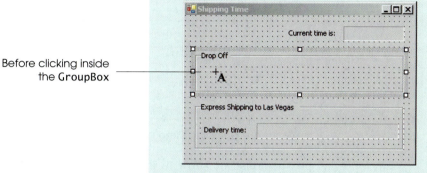

Before clicking inside the GroupBox

Figure 14.6 Adding a Label to a GroupBox.

Notice that the Location values you entered are measured from the top-left corner of the GroupBox and not from the top-left corner of the Form. Objects, such as Forms, GroupBoxes and Panels (which you'll use in Tutorial 19), that contain controls are called **containers**. Location values for controls in an application are measured from the top-left corner of the object that contains them.

If a GroupBox is placed over a control that is already on the Form, the control will be behind the GroupBox (that is, the GroupBox hides the control by covering it). To avoid this problem, remove all controls from the area in which you wish to place the GroupBox control before inserting it. You can then either drag and drop existing controls into the GroupBox or add new controls as needed by using the method described earlier.

GUI Design Tip

Use GroupBoxes to group related controls on the Form visually.

6. ***Saving the project.*** Select **File > Save All** to save your changes.

You have now added a GroupBox and a Label to the **Shipping Time** application to display the drop-off time. In the following box, you will add a DateTimePicker control to retrieve the drop-off time from the user.

Recall that the DateTimePicker retrieves date and time information from the user. The DateTimePicker allows you to select from a variety of predefined date and time formats to present to the user (for example, date formats like 12/31/02 and December 31, 2002; and time formats like 2:00 PM and 14:00) or you can create your own format. The date and time information is then stored in a variable of type Date, which you can manipulate using Date methods. Note that the format limits the date and/or time information the user can specify. However, the format used to present the date and/or time does not alter the value stored in the DateTimePicker.

Creating and Customizing the DateTimePicker

1. ***Adding the DateTimePicker.*** To add a DateTimePicker to your application, click the **DateTimePicker** control,

DateTimePicker

in the **Toolbox**, then click to the right of lblDropOff to place the DateTimePicker. Your Form should look similar to Fig. 14.7. (Your control will contain your computer's current date.)

(cont.)

2. ***Modifying the DateTimePicker.*** With the DateTimePicker selected, change the Name property of the DateTimePicker to dtpDropOff.

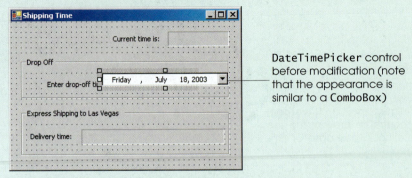

Figure 14.7   DateTimePicker control on the Form.

Align the DateTimePicker with its Label by setting its Size property to 88, 21 and its Location property to 152, 32. Next, change its **Format** property to Custom. This indicates that you will specify how the date will appear in the DateTimePicker.

3. ***Specifying a custom display format.*** When the DateTimePicker's Format property is set to Custom, it uses the custom format that you specify in the **CustomFormat** property. Notice that the DateTimePicker now displays the date in the format 1/1/2003, the default format when the CustomFormat property has not been set.

Set the value of the CustomFormat property to hh:mm tt. The "hh" displays the hour as a number from 01 to 12, the ":" inserts a colon and the "mm" indicates that the number of minutes from 00 to 59 should follow the colon. The "tt" indicates that AM or PM should appear, depending on the time of day. Note that this property eliminates the problem of a user entering a letter or symbol when the application expects a number—the DateTimePicker will not allow values in any format other than what you specify in the CustomFormat property.

4. ***Using up-down arrows in the DateTimePicker.*** Set the DateTimePicker's **ShowUpDown** property to True. This setting allows the user to select the date or time by clicking the up or down arrows that appear on the right side of the control, much like a NumericUpDown control. When the property is set to False (which is the default), a down arrow will appear on the right side of the control (Fig. 14.7), much like a ComboBox. Clicking the down arrow will cause a month calendar to appear, allowing the user to select a date (but not a time). A demonstration of the month calendar is shown in the Controls, Events, Properties & Methods section at the end of this tutorial. Because the user needs to enter only the time of day, you will use up-down arrows to display the time.

(cont.)

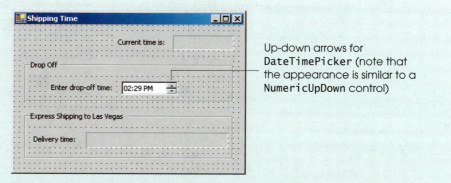

Up-down arrows for
DateTimePicker (note that
the appearance is similar to a
NumericUpDown control)

Error-Prevention Tip

If the user should specify a date and/or time, use a DateTime-Picker control to prevent the user from entering invalid date or time values.

Figure 14.8 Customized DateTimePicker control on the Form.

5. **Saving the project.** Select **File > Save All** to save your modified code.

The final control you will add to the Form is a Timer. You will use the Timer to place a clock on the Form so that users can see the current time of day while using the application.

Creating a Timer Control

1. **Adding a Timer control.** A **Timer** control is an object that can "wake up" every millisecond (1/1000 of a second) by generating a **Tick** event. By default, the Timer "wakes up" every 100 milliseconds (1/10 of a second). Each time the Tick event is generated, its event handler is executed. You can customize the "wake period" (the amount of time between each instance of the Timer's Tick event) and the code that it executes (the event handler for the Tick event) so that a certain task is performed once every "wake up" period.

Add a Timer to the Form by clicking the **Timer** control,

in the **Toolbox** and dragging and dropping it anywhere on the Form. Notice that the Timer does not actually appear on the Form; it appears below the Windows Form Designer in an area called the **component tray** (Fig. 14.9). The Timer control is placed in the component tray because it is not part of the graphical user interface—users never see the Timer control.

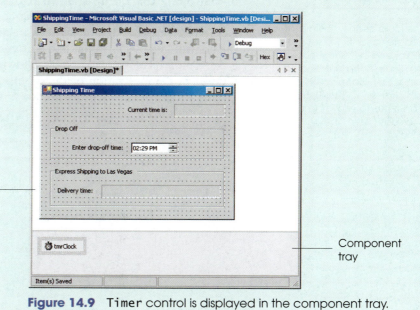

Timer control

Component tray

Figure 14.9 Timer control is displayed in the component tray.

(cont.)

Good Programming Practice

Prefix Timer control names with tmr.

2. ***Customizing the Timer control.*** Rename the Timer by setting its Name property to tmrClock. To allow the Timer's Tick event to be raised, set the Timer's Enabled property to True. Then set the Timer's **Interval** property to 1000, which specifies the number of milliseconds between Tick events (1,000 milliseconds = 1 second).

3. ***Saving the project.*** Select **File > Save All** to save your modified code.

SELF-REVIEW

1. If a GroupBox is placed over a control that is already on the Form, the control will be _____ the GroupBox.

    a) replaced by   b) inside

    c) behind   d) in front of

2. Setting the Format property of the DateTimePicker control to _____ indicates that you will specify how the date will appear in the DateTimePicker.

    a) Custom   b) Unique

    c) User   d) Other

Answers: 1) c. 2) a.

14.4 Creating the Shipping Time Application: Inserting Code

Now that you have completed the visual design of the **Shipping Time** application, you will complete the application by inserting code. You will begin coding the application's functionality by creating a clock on the application that updates the current time every second. You will then write code that displays the delivery time from Portland to Las Vegas. You will implement this feature by inserting code that is run when the Form loads or whenever the user specifies a new drop-off time. In the following box, you will write the code to create the clock.

Coding the Shipping Time Application's Clock

1. ***Inserting code to handle the Timer's Tick event.*** Double click the Timer control in the component tray to generate the empty event handler for the Tick event. (A Tick event is raised once per Interval, as set in the Timer's Interval property.) Add lines 160–162 of Fig. 14.10 to the body of the event handler. Be sure to format the event handler as shown in Fig. 14.10 to ensure that your line numbers will match those in the text.

Printing the current time

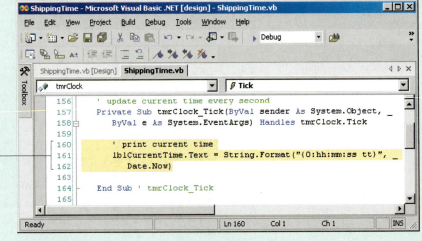

Figure 14.10 Inserting code for a Tick event.

(cont.)

Lines 157–164 display the event handler for the `Tick` event, which executes every second. `Date` property `Now` retrieves your computer's time when it is accessed. The event handler takes this information and formats it to match the format you specify, `"hh:mm:ss tt"`. The `Text` property of `lblCurrentTime` is then set to the formatted `String` for display to the user. Recall that the 0 corresponds to `Date.Now` and the text following the first colon contains your format information. You are already familiar with the purpose of `hh:mm` and `tt`. The `:ss` following `mm` indicates that a colon followed by the number of seconds (00–59) should be displayed.

2. **Saving the project.** Select **File > Save All** to save your modified code.

Now that you have coded your application's clock, using the Timer's `Tick` event handler, you will insert code to display a delivery time when the application opens. You will begin by creating a `Load` event handler for your application.

Using Code to Display a Delivery Time

1. **Adding the FrmShippingTime_Load event handler.** When an application runs, the `Form` is displayed. However, sometimes you also want a specific action to occur when the application opens but before the `Form` displays. To run code when the application first opens, create an event handler for the **Load** event. To create a `Load` event handler, return to the Windows Form Designer by clicking the **ShippingTime.vb [Design]** tab. Double click an empty area of the `Form` to generate the `Load` event handler and enter code view.

2. **Storing the current date.** Add line 171 from Fig. 14.11 into the `Load` event handler. Line 171 stores the current date in variable `dtmCurrentTime`. (You will store the date as a variable so that you can preserve information about the current date for use later in the event handler.) Be sure to add the comments and line-continuation characters as shown in Fig. 14.11 so that the line numbers in your code match those presented in this tutorial.

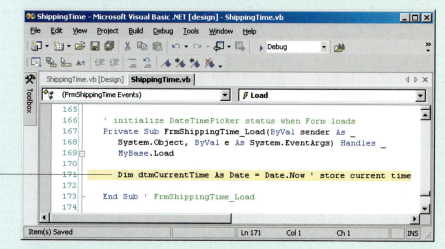

Storing the current time in `dtmCurrentTime`

Figure 14.11   Storing the current time.

3. **Setting the drop-off hours.** Add lines 173–177 of Fig. 14.12 to the `FrmShippingTime_Load` event handler. These lines set the `MinDate` and `MaxDate` properties for `dtpDropOff`. The **MinDate** property specifies the earliest value that the `DateTimePicker` will allow the user to enter. The **MaxDate** property specifies the latest value that the `DateTimePicker` will allow the user to enter. Together, these two properties set the range of drop-off times from which the user can select.

(cont.)

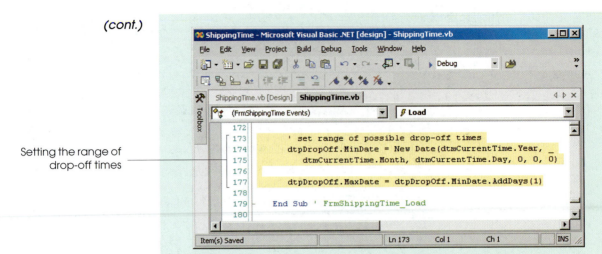

Setting the range of
drop-off times

Figure 14.12　Setting the `MinDate` and `MaxDate` properties.

To guarantee freshness, the seafood shipment should be dropped off at the airline within the current day; therefore, the earliest drop-off time (`MinDate`) is set to 12:00 A.M. of the current day (lines 174–175), and the latest drop-off time (`MaxDate`) is set to 12:00 A.M. the following day (line 177). Notice that the `MaxDate` value is calculated by adding one day to the `MinDate` value using the `AddDays` method. Recall that the `AddDays` method does not change the `Date` value on which it operates—it returns a new `Date` value. This value is assigned to the `MaxDate` property on line 177.

The `Date` constructor (called in line 174) creates a value that stores a time. Recall that the first parameter is the year, the second is the month and the third is the day. The last three parameters specify the hour, minute and number of seconds. A `Date` variable's `Year` property returns the value of its year as an `Integer` (for example, 2003). Its `Month` property returns the value of the `Date` variable's month as an `Integer` (for example, 6 for June). Finally, the `Date` variable's `Day` property returns the day of the month (an `Integer` between 1 and 31, depending on the month and year). You assigned to the `dtmCurrentTime` variable the value of the current time (using `Date.Now`); therefore, the first three arguments combine to specify the current date.

4. ***Calling the `DisplayDeliveryTime` procedure.*** Add lines 179–180 of Fig. 14.13 to call the `DisplayDeliveryTime` procedure. Notice that `DisplayDeliveryTime` is underlined in blue. This is due to the syntax error you introduce when you call a procedure that has not yet been written. You will write this procedure later in this tutorial. The `DisplayDeliveryTime` calculates the delivery time in Las Vegas and displays the result in the **Delivery time:** `Label`.

(cont.)

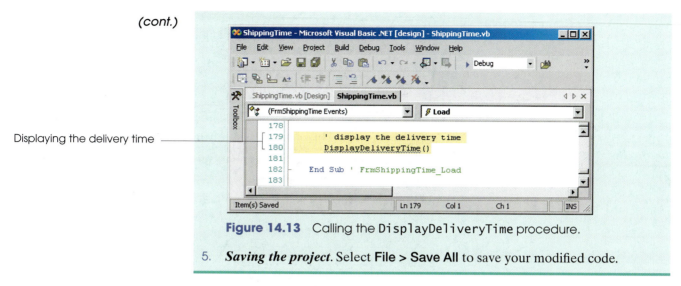

Displaying the delivery time

Figure 14.13 Calling the `DisplayDeliveryTime` procedure.

5. **Saving the project.** Select **File > Save All** to save your modified code.

So far, you have added functionality that calculates and displays the delivery time when the application runs initially. However, you should allow a user to select any drop-off time and instantly see when the seafood shipment will be delivered. In the following box, you will learn how to handle the `DateTimePicker`'s **ValueChanged** event, which is raised when the user changes the time in the `DateTimePicker`.

Coding the ValueChanged Event Handler

1. **Creating the ValueChanged event handler.** Click the **ShippingTime.vb [Design]** tab. Double click the `DateTimePicker` control `dtpDropOff` to generate the `ValueChanged` event handler.

2. **Inserting code in the event handler.** Insert lines 189–190 of Fig. 14.14 into the event handler. This code will run when the user changes the time in the `DateTimePicker`. Be sure to add the comments and line-continuation characters as shown in Fig. 14.14 so that the line numbers in your code match those presented in this tutorial.

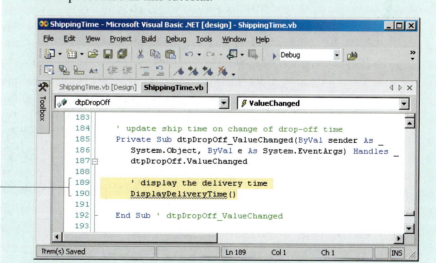

Calculating and displaying the delivery time

Figure 14.14 Inserting code in the `ValueChanged` event handler.

The `ValueChanged` event handler also uses the `DisplayDeliveryTime` procedure to calculate and display the delivery time in Las Vegas. In the next box, you will write the `DisplayDeliveryTime` procedure, after which the syntax error will no longer appear.

3. **Saving the solution.** Select **File > Save All** to save your modified code.

Though you have called the DisplayDeliveryTime procedure in two event handlers, you still need to write the procedure. Next, you will use Date methods to display the delivery time in an output Label.

Coding the DisplayDeliveryTime Procedure

1. ***Creating the DisplayDeliveryTime procedure.*** Add lines 194–205 of Fig. 14.15 below the ValueChanged event handler. Line 198 calls the DepartureTime procedure. Notice that DepartureTime is underlined in blue. This is due to the syntax error you introduce when you call a procedure that has not yet been written. You will write this procedure in the following box. The DepartureTime procedure determines which flight (midnight or noon) the seafood shipment will use. It returns a Date value representing the flight's departure time. Line 198 stores this value in the Date variable dtmDelivery.

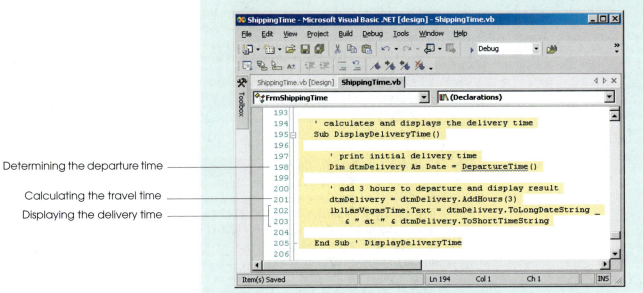

Determining the departure time

Calculating the travel time
Displaying the delivery time

```
193
194      ' calculates and displays the delivery time
195      Sub DisplayDeliveryTime()
196
197          ' print initial delivery time
198          Dim dtmDelivery As Date = DepartureTime()
199
200          ' add 3 hours to departure and display result
201          dtmDelivery = dtmDelivery.AddHours(3)
202          lblLasVegasTime.Text = dtmDelivery.ToLongDateString _
203              & " at " & dtmDelivery.ToShortTimeString
204
205      End Sub ' DisplayDeliveryTime
206
```

Figure 14.15   Calling the DepartureTime procedure.

2. ***Calculating and displaying the delivery time.*** Line 201 calculates the delivery time by adding 3 hours to the departure time (see the discussion following this box). Lines 202–203 display the Las Vegas delivery time by calling the Date structure's ToLongDateString and ToShortTimeString methods. A Date variable's **ToLongDateString** method returns the date as a String in the format "Wednesday, October 30, 2002." A Date variable's **ToShortTimeString** returns the time as a String in the format "4:00 PM."

3. ***Saving the project.*** Select **File > Save All** to save your modified code.

When calculating the shipment's delivery time, you must account for the time-zone difference and the flight time. For instance, if you send a shipment from Portland to Las Vegas, it will travel west three time zones (the time in Las Vegas is 3 hours earlier) and spend 6 hours in transit. If you drop off the shipment at 5:00 P.M. in Portland, the shipment will leave on the midnight flight and arrive in Las Vegas at

12:00 A.M. + (*time zone change* + *flight time*) = 12:00 A.M. + (-3 + 6) *hours*,

which is 3:00 A.M. Las Vegas time. Similarly, if the shipment takes the noon flight to Las Vegas, it will arrive at 3 P.M. in Las Vegas.

To complete the application, you need to code the DepartureTime procedure. You will use a Select Case statement and Date methods to return a Date containing the departure time (noon or midnight) for the seafood shipment's flight.

Coding the DepartureTime Procedure

1. *Writing the DepartureTime procedure and declaring variables.* Insert lines 207–213 of Fig. 14.16 into your code below the DisplayDeliveryTime procedure. Line 210 stores the current date in the Date variable dtmCurrentDate. Line 211 declares the Date variable dtmDepartureTime, the variable you will use to store the DepartureTime Function procedure's return value.

Declaring variables ⎯⎯⎯⎯⎯⎯

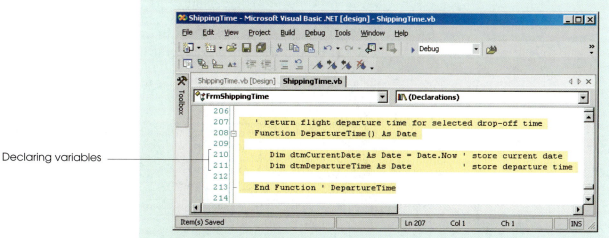

Figure 14.16 Inserting procedure DepartureTime into the application.

2. *Determining which flight the shipment uses.* Insert lines 213–233 of Fig. 14.17 after the variable declarations and before the End Function statement. The Select Case statement that begins on line 214 uses the hour specified by the user in the DateTimePicker as the controlling expression. The value selected by the user in the DateTimePicker is located in its **Value** property. The Date structure's Hour property returns the hour of the Date stored in the DateTimePicker's Value property.

The body of the first Case statement (line 217) executes if the value in the DateTimePicker is between midnight (Hour = 0) and 10:59 A.M. (Hour = 10). If the drop-off time occurs between midnight and 10:59:59 A.M., the seafood shipment takes the noon flight to Las Vegas (recall that the shipment leaves for the airport one hour before the flight leaves). The body of the first Case (lines 218–219) then stores the departure time of noon on the current day in the return variable dtmDepartureTime.

The body of the next Case statement (line 222) executes if the value in the DateTimePicker is between 11:00 P.M. and 11:59 P.M. (Hour = 23). If the drop-off time occurs between 11:00 P.M. and 11:59 P.M, the seafood shipment takes the noon flight to Las Vegas the next day. The body of this Case (lines 223–225) then stores the departure time of noon on the next day in the return variable dtmDepartureTime.

The body of the Case Else statement (line 228) executes if the controlling expression of neither of the other two Case statements evaluates to True (the value in the DateTimePicker is between 11:00 A.M. and 10:59 P.M.). In this case, the seafood shipment takes the midnight flight to Las Vegas. The body of this Case (lines 229–231) then stores the departure time of midnight in the return variable dtmDepartureTime. Note that because midnight occurs on the following day, the Date variable representing midnight should contain a Day property value corresponding to the next day. Line 229 ensures this occurs.

(cont.)

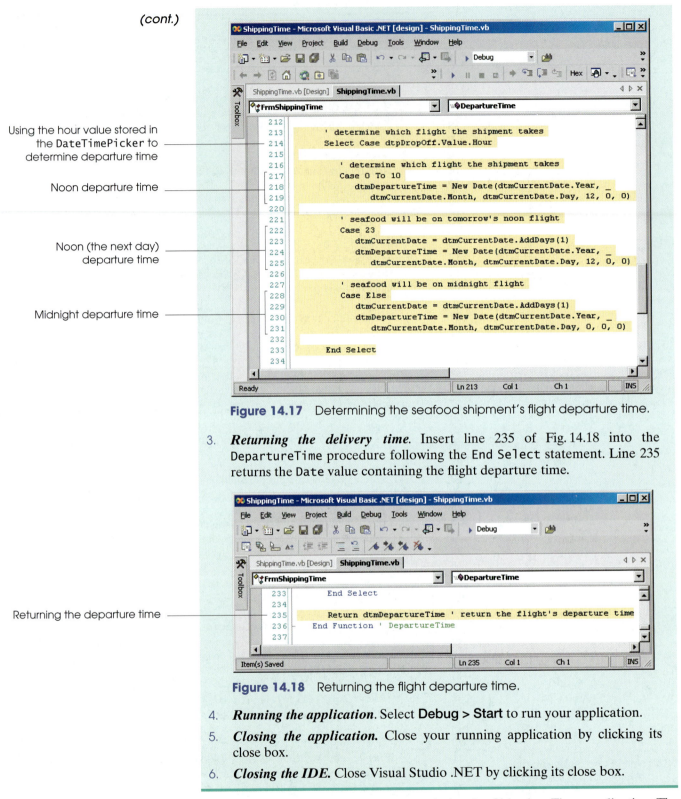

Using the hour value stored in the `DateTimePicker` to determine departure time

Noon departure time

Noon (the next day) departure time

Midnight departure time

Figure 14.17 Determining the seafood shipment's flight departure time.

3. ***Returning the delivery time.*** Insert line 235 of Fig. 14.18 into the `DepartureTime` procedure following the `End Select` statement. Line 235 returns the `Date` value containing the flight departure time.

Returning the departure time

Figure 14.18 Returning the flight departure time.

4. ***Running the application.*** Select **Debug > Start** to run your application.

5. ***Closing the application.*** Close your running application by clicking its close box.

6. ***Closing the IDE.*** Close Visual Studio .NET by clicking its close box.

Figure 14.19 presents the source code for the **Shipping Time** application. The lines of code that contain new programming concepts that you learned in this tutorial are highlighted.

```vb
1   Public Class FrmShippingTime
2       Inherits System.Windows.Forms.Form
3
4       ' Windows Form Designer generated code
5
6       ' update current time every second
7       Private Sub tmrClock_Tick(ByVal sender As System.Object, _
8          ByVal e As System.EventArgs) Handles tmrClock.Tick
9
10          ' print current time
11          lblCurrentTime.Text = String.Format("{0:hh:mm:ss tt}", _
12             Date.Now)
13
14      End Sub ' tmrClock_Tick
15
16      ' initialize DateTimePicker status when Form loads
17      Private Sub FrmShippingTime_Load(ByVal sender As _
18         System.Object, ByVal e As System.EventArgs) Handles _
19         MyBase.Load
20
21          Dim dtmCurrentTime As Date = Date.Now ' store current time
22
23          ' set range of possible drop-off times
24          dtpDropOff.MinDate = New Date(dtmCurrentTime.Year, _
25             dtmCurrentTime.Month, dtmCurrentTime.Day, 0, 0, 0)
26
27          dtpDropOff.MaxDate = dtpDropOff.MinDate.AddDays(1)
28
29          ' display the delivery time
30          DisplayDeliveryTime()
31
32      End Sub ' FrmShippingTime_Load
33
34      ' update ship time on change of drop-off time
35      Private Sub dtpDropOff_ValueChanged(ByVal sender As _
36         System.Object, ByVal e As System.EventArgs) Handles _
37         dtpDropOff.ValueChanged
38
39          ' display the delivery time
40          DisplayDeliveryTime()
41
42      End Sub ' dtpDropOff_ValueChanged
43
44      ' calculates and displays the delivery time
45      Sub DisplayDeliveryTime()
46
47          ' print initial delivery time
48          Dim dtmDelivery As Date = DepartureTime()
49
50          ' add 3 hours to departure and display result
51          dtmDelivery = dtmDelivery.AddHours(3)
52          lblLasVegasTime.Text = dtmDelivery.ToLongDateString _
53             & " at " & dtmDelivery.ToShortTimeString
54
55      End Sub ' DisplayDeliveryTime
56
```

Displaying current time — (lines 11–12)

Setting the DateTimePicker's minimum and maximum values — (lines 24–27)

Calculating and displaying the delivery time in Las Vegas — (lines 51–53)

Figure 14.19 Shipping Time application code. (Part 1 of 2.)

```
57        ' returns flight departure time for selected drop-off time
58        Function DepartureTime() As Date
59
60            Dim dtmCurrentDate As Date = Date.Now ' store current date
61            Dim dtmDepartureTime As Date          ' store departure time
62
63            ' determine which flight the shipment takes
64            Select Case dtpDropOff.Value.Hour
65
66                ' seafood will be on the noon flight
67                Case 0 To 10
68                    dtmDepartureTime = New Date(dtmCurrentDate.Year, _
69                        dtmCurrentDate.Month, dtmCurrentDate.Day, 12, 0, 0)
70
71                ' seafood will be on tomorrow's noon flight
72                Case 23
73                    dtmCurrentDate = dtmCurrentDate.AddDays(1)
74                    dtmDepartureTime = New Date(dtmCurrentDate.Year, _
75                        dtmCurrentDate.Month, dtmCurrentDate.Day, 12, 0, 0)
76
77                ' seafood will be on midnight flight
78                Case Else
79                    dtmCurrentDate = dtmCurrentDate.AddDays(1)
80                    dtmDepartureTime = New Date(dtmCurrentDate.Year, _
81                        dtmCurrentDate.Month, dtmCurrentDate.Day, 0, 0, 0)
82
83            End Select
84
85            Return dtmDepartureTime ' return the flight's departure time
86        End Function ' DepartureTime
87
88    End Class ' FrmShippingTime
```

Using a Select Case statement to determine departure time (annotation pointing to line 64)

Figure 14.19   Shipping Time application code. (Part 2 of 2.)

SELF-REVIEW

1. The ToShortTimeString method is called on a Date variable to return its value in the format _____.

   a) 11 o'clock   b) 23:00

   c) 11:00   d) 11:00 PM

2. DateTimePicker properties _____ and _____ specify the earliest and latest dates that can be selected, respectively.

   a) MinDate, MaxDate   b) Now, Later

   c) Minimum, Maximum   d) Early, Late

Answers: 1) d. 2) a.

14.5 Wrap-Up

In this tutorial, you learned how to use the Date type, a structure for manipulating time and date information. You used variables of this type to calculate and display delivery times in your **Shipping Time** application. To help users enter date and time information, you used a DateTimePicker control. You observed how a DateTime-Picker control can display custom date and time formats and limit user input. To help you group controls on the Form visually, you used the GroupBox control. You also learned how to use the Timer control on the Form, which allowed your application to execute code once every second.

You then learned how to use three new event handlers to help you complete the **Shipping Time** application. You learned that the Form's Load event handler allows your application to execute code when the application is opened initially. You used this event to set initial values in your application. You then learned how to use the `DateTimePicker` control's `ValueChanged` event handler, which allows you to execute code when the control's value changes. You used this event handler to update the delivery time each time the user entered a new time. Finally, you learned about the `Timer`'s `Tick` event handler, which you used to update and display the current time in a `Label` that serves as a clock.

In the next tutorial, you will use the **Fund Raiser** to introduce two programming concepts: arguments and scope rules. Learning these concepts will help you build more powerful and dependable applications because you will understand how Visual Basic .NET keeps track of variables throughout your application.

SKILLS SUMMARY

Storing and Manipulating Date and Time Information

- Use a `Date` variable to store and manipulate date and time information. A `Date` variable stores information about a point in time (for example, 12:00:00 A.M. on January 1, 2003). This information can be formatted for display in predefined long or short formats or in custom (programmer-defined) formats.

Using Date variables

- Use keyword `New` to declare a new `Date` value.
- Use property `Date.Now` to obtain your computer's current date and time.
- Use the member-access operator to access properties of a `Date` variable.
- Use `Date` methods, such as `AddHours` and `AddDays`, to add or subtract time from values in `Date` variables. Then assign the value returned by the method to a `Date` variable.

Using a GroupBox Control

- Use a `GroupBox` control to group related controls visually. To add a `GroupBox` to the `Form`, double click the **GroupBox** control in the **Toolbox**.

Placing Controls Inside a GroupBox

- Place a control inside the `GroupBox` by clicking the control's name in the **Toolbox** and clicking inside the `GroupBox`.

Using the DateTimePicker Control

- Use a `DateTimePicker` control to get date and time information from the user.
- Set property `Format` to `Custom` to indicate that you will specify how the date will appear in the `DateTimePicker`. The format is specified in property `CustomFormat`.
- Set property `ShowUpDown` to `True` to allow the user to select the date or time by clicking an up or down arrow. If this property's value is `False`, a monthly calendar will drop down, allowing the user to pick a date.

Using the Timer Control

- Use a `Timer` control to execute code (the `Tick` event handler) at specified intervals. To add a `Timer` control to the `Form`, click **Timer** in the **Windows Forms** tab of the **Toolbox**, and click anywhere on the `Form`. The `Timer` control will appear in the component tray.
- Customize the time between `Tick` events by using the `Interval` property, which specifies the number of milliseconds between each `Tick` event.
- Set the `Enabled` property to `True` so that the `Tick` event is raised once per `Interval`.

KEY TERMS

component tray—The area below the Windows Form Designer that contains controls, such as `Timer`s, that are not part of the graphical user interface.

constructor—A procedure that initializes a class object or structure value when it is created.

container—An object that contains controls.

CustomFormat property of a DateTimePicker control—The `DateTimePicker` property that contains the programmer-specified format string with which to display the date and/or time when `DateTimePicker` `Format` property is set to `Custom`.

Date variable—A variable of type Date, capable of storing date and time data.

DateTimePicker control—Retrieves date and time information from the user.

Format property of a DateTimePicker control—The DateTimePicker property that allows the programmer to specify a predefined or custom format with which to display the date and/or time.

GroupBox control—Groups related controls visually.

Interval property of a Timer control—The Timer property that specifies the number of milliseconds between each Tick event.

Load event of a Form—Raised when an application initially executes.

MaxDate property of a DateTimePicker control—The DateTimePicker property that specifies the latest value that the DateTimePicker will allow the user to enter.

MinDate property of a DateTimePicker control—The DateTimePicker property that specifies the earliest value that the DateTimePicker will allow the user to enter.

New keyword—Used to call a constructor when creating an object.

Now property—The property of structure Date that retrieves your computer's current time.

ShowUpDown property of a DateTimePicker control—The DateTimePicker property that, when true, allows the user to specify the time using up and down arrows.

Tick event of a Timer control—Raised after the number of milliseconds specified in the Timer control's Interval property has elapsed.

Timer control—Wakes up at specified intervals to execute code in its Tick event handler.

ToLongDateString method of type Date—Returns a String containing the date in the format "Wednesday, October 30, 2002."

ToShortTimeString method of type Date—Returns a String containing the time in the format "4:00 PM."

Value property of a DateTimePicker control—Stores the value (such as a time) in a DateTimePicker control.

ValueChanged event of a DateTimePicker control—Raised when a user selects a new day or time in the DateTimePicker control.

GUI DESIGN GUIDELINES

DateTimePicker

- Use a DateTimePicker to retrieve date and time information from the user.
- Each DateTimePicker should have a corresponding descriptive Label.
- If the user should specify a time of day or a date and time, set the DateTimePicker's ShowUpDown property to True. If the user should specify a date, set the DateTimePicker's ShowUpDown property to False to allow the user to select a day from the month calendar.

GroupBox

- GroupBox titles should be concise and should use book-title capitalization.
- Use GroupBoxes to group related controls on the Form visually.

CONTROLS, EVENTS, PROPERTIES & METHODS

Date This structure provides properties and methods to store and manipulate date and time information.

- *Properties*
  Day—Returns the day stored in a Date variable.
  Hour—Returns the hour stored in a Date variable.
  Month—Returns the month stored in a Date variable.
  Now—Returns the system's current date and time.
  Year—Returns the year stored in a Date variable.
- *Methods*
  AddDays—Creates a new Date value that is the specified number of days later (or earlier) in time.
  AddHours—Creates a new Date value that is the specified number of hours later (or earlier) in time.

AddMinutes—Creates a new Date value that is the specified number of minutes later (or earlier) in time.

ToLongDateString—Returns a String containing the date in the format "Wednesday, October 30, 2002."

ToShortTimeString—Returns a String containing the time in the format "4:00 PM."

DateTimePicker   📅 DateTimePicker   This control is used to retrieve date and time information from the user.

■ *In action*

DateTimePicker using default format

■ *Event*

ValueChanged—Raised when the Value property is changed.

■ *Properties*

CustomFormat—Sets which format string to use when displaying the date and/or time.

Format—Specifies the format in which the date and time are displayed on the control. Long specifies that the date should be displayed in the format "Monday, December 09, 2002." Short specifies that the date should be displayed in the format "12/9/2002." Time specifies that the time should be displayed in the format "8:39:53 PM." Custom allows the programmer to specify a custom format in which to display the date and/or time.

Hour—Stores the hour in the DateTimePicker control.

Location—Specifies the location of the DateTimePicker control on its container relative to the container's top-left corner.

MinDate—Specifies the minimum date and/or time that can be selected when using this control.

MaxDate—Specifies the maximum date and/or time that can be selected when using this control.

Name—Specifies the name used to access the DateTimePicker control programmatically. The name should be prefixed with dtp.

ShowUpDown—Specifies whether the up-down arrows (True) are displayed on the control for time values. If False, a down arrow is displayed for accessing a drop-down calendar.

Value—Stores the date and/or time in the DateTimePicker control.

GroupBox   🔲 GroupBox   This control groups related controls visually.

■ *In action*

■ *Properties*

Name—Specifies the name used to access the GroupBox control programmatically. The name should be prefixed with fra.

Location—Specifies the location of the GroupBox control on the Form.

Size—Specifies the height and width (in pixels) of the GroupBox control.

Text—Specifies the text displayed on the GroupBox.

Timer ⏱ Timer   This control wakes up at specified intervals of time
to execute code in its Tick event handler.

■ *Event*

   Tick—Raised after the number of milliseconds specified in the Interval property has
   elapsed.

■ *Properties*

   Enabled—Determines whether the Timer is running (True). The default is False.

   Interval—Determines the time interval between Tick events.

   Name—Specifies the name used to access the Timer control programmatically. The name
   should be prefixed with tmr.

MULTIPLE-CHOICE QUESTIONS

14.1 The _____ allows you to store and manipulate date information easily.

   a) Date structure   b) DatePicker control

   c) GroupBox control   d) Now property

14.2 You can _____ to a Date variable.

   a) add hours   b) add days

   c) subtract hours   d) All of the above.

14.3 To subtract one day from Date variable dtmDay's value, assign the value returned by
_____ to dtmDay.

   a) dtmDay.AddHours(-24)   b) dtmDay.SubtractDays(1)

   c) dtmDay.AddDays(-1)   d) Both a and c.

14.4 The time 3:45 and 35 seconds in the afternoon would be formatted as 03:45:35 PM
according to the format string _____.

   a) "hh:mm:ss"   b) "hh:mm:ss tt"

   c) "hh:mm:ss am:pm"   d) "h:m:s tt"

14.5 A(n) _____ event occurs before the Form is displayed.

   a) LoadForm   b) InitializeForm

   c) Load   d) FormLoad

14.6 Timer property Interval sets the rate at which Tick events occur in _____.

   a) nanoseconds   b) microseconds

   c) milliseconds   d) seconds

14.7 To set Date dtmNow's time five hours earlier, use _____.

   a) dtmNow = dtmNow.SubtractHours(5) b) dtmNow = dtmNow.AddHours(-5)

   c) dtmNow = dtmNow.AddHours(5)   d) dtmNow.AddHours(-5)

14.8 A _____ is a container.

   a) GroupBox   b) Form

   c) Timer   d) Both a and b.

14.9 A Date variable stores hour values in the range _____.

   a) 1 to 12   b) 0 to 12

   c) 0 to 24   d) 0 to 23

14.10 A DateTimePicker's _____ property specifies the format string with which to
display the date.

   a) CustomFormat   b) FormatString

   c) Format   d) Text

EXERCISES   **14.11** (*World Clock Application*) Create an application that displays the current time in Los Angeles, Atlanta, London and Tokyo. Use a `Timer` to update the clock every second. Assume that your local time is the time in Atlanta. Atlanta is three hours later than Los Angeles. London is five hours later than Atlanta. Tokyo is eight hours later than London. The application should look similar to Fig. 14.20.

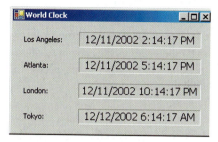

Figure 14.20   World Clock GUI.

a) *Copying the template to your working directory.* Copy the directory `C:\Examples\ Tutorial14\Exercises\WorldClock` to your `C:\SimplyVB` directory.

b) *Opening the application's template file.* Double click `WorldClock.sln` in the `WorldClock` directory to open the application.

c) *Adding a Timer to the Form.* Add a Timer control to the **World Clock** application. Set the `Timer` control's name property to `tmrClock`.

d) *Adding a Tick event handler for `tmrClock`.* Add a `Tick` event handler for Timer `tmrClock`. The event handler should calculate and display the current times for Los Angeles, Atlanta, London and Tokyo. Use the `Date` variable's `ToShortDateString` and `ToLongTimeString` methods to create the display text.

e) *Running the application.* Select **Debug > Start** to run your application. Look at the clock on your machine to verify that the time for Los Angeles is three hours earlier, the time in Atlanta is the same as what your clock says, the time in London is five hours later, and the time in Tokyo is 13 hours later (eight hours later than London).

f) *Closing the application.* Close your running application by clicking its close box.

g) *Closing the IDE.* Close Visual Studio .NET by clicking its close box.

14.12 (*Shipping Time Application Enhancement*) During the winter, a distribution center in Denver, Colorado needs to receive seafood shipments to supply the local ski resorts. Enhance the **Shipping Time** application by adding Denver, Colorado as another shipping destination. Denver is two time zones west of Portland, meaning time is two hours earlier than Portland, Maine. Because there are no direct flights to Denver, shipments from Portland will take 8 hours.

Figure 14.21   Enhanced Shipping Time GUI.

a) *Copying the template to your working directory.* Copy the directory `C:\Examples\ Tutorial14\Exercises\ShippingTimeEnhanced` to your `C:\SimplyVB` directory.

b) *Opening the application's template file.* Double click `ShippingTime.sln` in the `ShippingTimeEnhanced` directory to open the application.

c) *Inserting a GroupBox.* Resize the Form to fit the **Express Shipping to Denver** GroupBox as shown in Fig. 14.21. Add a GroupBox to the Form. Change the Text property of the GroupBox to indicate that it will contain the delivery time in Denver. Resize and move the GroupBox so that it resembles the GUI shown in Fig. 14.21.

d) *Inserting Labels.* In the GroupBox you just created, add an output Label to display the delivery time for a seafood shipment to Denver and a corresponding descriptive Label.

e) *Inserting code to the DisplayDeliveryTime procedure.* Add code to Display-DeliveryTime procedure to compute and display the delivery time in Denver.

f) *Running the application.* Select **Debug > Start** to run your application. Select various drop off times and ensure the delivery times are correct for both Las Vegas and Denver.

g) *Closing the application.* Close your running application by clicking its close box.

h) *Closing the IDE.* Close Visual Studio .NET by clicking its close box.

14.13 (*Alarm Application*) Create an application that allows the user to set an alarm clock. The application should allow the user to set the exact time of the alarm by using a `DateTimePicker`. While the alarm is set, the user should not be able to modify the `DateTimePicker`. If the alarm is set and the current time matches or exceeds the time in the `DateTimePicker`, play the computer's "beep" sound. (Your computer must have the necessary hardware for sound.) The user should be able to cancel an alarm by using a **Reset** Button. This Button is disabled when the application starts.

Figure 14.22 Alarm GUI.

a) *Copying the template to your working directory.* Copy the directory `C:\Examples\Tutorial14\Exercises\AlarmClock` to your `C:\SimplyVB` directory.

b) *Opening the application's template file.* Double click `AlarmClock.sln` in the `AlarmClock` directory to open the application.

c) *Inserting a DateTimePicker.* Add a `DateTimePicker` control to the Form. Set the `DateTimePicker` to display only the time, as is shown in Fig. 14.22. Set the `DateTimePicker` control's `Size` property to `80, 20`, and move the control so that it appears as it does in Fig. 14.22.

d) *Coding the Set Button's Click event handler.* Add a `Click` event handler for the **Set** Button. This event handler should disable the **Set** Button and the `DateTimePicker` and enable the **Reset** Button.

e) *Coding the Timer's Tick event handler.* Define the `Tick` event handler for the `Timer`. A `Tick` event should occur every 1000 milliseconds (one second). If the alarm is set and the current time matches or exceeds the time in the `DateTimePicker`, play the computer's "beep" sound by calling the `Beep` function. To call the `Beep` function, type `Beep()` on its own line in your code.

f) *Coding the Reset Button's Click event handler.* Define the `Click` event handler for the **Reset** Button. When the **Reset** Button is clicked, the GUI should be set back to its original state.

g) *Running the application.* Select **Debug > Start** to run your application. Use the `DateTimePicker` and the **Set** Button to set a time for the alarm to go off. Wait for that time to verify that the alarm will make beeping sounds. Click the **Reset** Button to set a new time for the alarm to go off.

h) ***Closing the application.*** Close your running application by clicking its close box.

i) ***Closing the IDE.*** Close Visual Studio .NET by clicking its close box.

What does this code do? ▶ **14.14** This code creates a Date variable. What date does this variable contain?

```
Dim dtmTime As Date = New Date(2003, 1, 2, 3, 4, 5)
```

What's wrong with this code? ▶ **14.15** The following lines of code are supposed to create a Date variable and increment its hour value by two. Find the error(s) in the code.

```
Dim dtmNow As Date = Date.Now
dtmNow.AddHours(2)
```

Programming Challenge ▶ **14.16** (***Parking Garage Fee Calculator***) Create an application that computes the fee for parking a car in a parking garage (Fig. 14.23). The user should provide the **Time In:** and **Time Out:** values by using DateTimePickers. The application should calculate the cost of parking in the garage for the specified amount of time. Assume that parking costs three dollars an hour. When calculating the total time spent in the garage, you can ignore the seconds value, but treat the minutes value as a fraction of an hour (1 minute is 1/60 of an hour). For simplicity, assume that no overnight parking is allowed, so each car leaves the garage on the same day in which it arrives.

Figure 14.23   Parking Garage **Fee Calculator** GUI.

a) ***Copying the template to your working directory.*** Copy the directory C:\Examples\ Tutorial14\Exercises\ParkingGarageFeeCalculator to your C:\SimplyVB directory.

b) ***Opening the application's template file.*** Double click ParkingGarageFeeCalculator.sln in the ParkingGarageFeeCalculator directory to open the application.

c) ***Inserting the DateTimePicker controls.*** Add two DateTimePicker controls to the Form. Set the DateTimePickers so that they show the time only. Set the Size property of each DateTimePicker control to 80, 20, and move the DateTimePickers so that they are positioned as in Fig. 14.23.

d) ***Writing the Function procedure Fee.*** Define a Function procedure Fee that accepts four Integers as parameters—the hour value of the **Time In:**, the hour value of the **Time Out:**, the minute value of the **Time In:** and the minute value of the **Time Out:**. Using this information, procedure Fee should calculate the fee for parking in the garage. The Function procedure should then return this value as a Decimal.

e) ***Coding the Calculate Button's Click event handler.*** Add the Click event handler for the **Calculate** Button. This event handler should call Fee to obtain the amount due. It should then display the amount (formatted as currency) in a Label.

f) ***Running the application.*** Select **Debug > Start** to run your application. Use the DateTimePickers' up and down arrows to select a time the car was placed in the garage and the time the car was taken out of the garage. Click the **Calculate** Button and verify that the correct fee is displayed.

g) ***Closing the application.*** Close your running application by clicking its close box.

h) ***Closing the IDE.*** Close Visual Studio .NET by clicking its close box.

Fund Raiser Application

Introducing Scope, Pass-by-Reference and Option Strict

Objectives

In this tutorial, you will learn to:

- Create variables that can be used in all the Form's procedures.
- Pass arguments by reference, using ByRef, so that the called procedure can modify the caller's variables.
- Eliminate subtle data-type errors by enabling Option Strict.
- Change a value from one data type to another, using methods of class Convert.

Outline

In this tutorial, you will learn several important Visual Basic .NET concepts. First, you will learn how to declare variables that can be referenced from any procedure within your Form's code. Next, you will learn another technique for passing arguments to procedures. In the procedures that you have created so far, the application has made a copy of the argument's value, and any changes the called procedure made to the copy did not affect the original variable's value. You will learn how to pass an argument to a procedure—using a technique called pass-by-reference—so that changes made to the parameter's value in the procedure are also made to the original variable in the caller. You will learn how the Visual Basic .NET compiler handles conversions between different data types and how to enable a feature called Option Strict to avoid subtle errors that can occur when a value of one type is assigned to a variable of another type. In addition, you will be introduced to methods from class Convert that allow you to convert data from one type to another.

15.1 Test-Driving the Fund Raiser Application

In this tutorial, you will create a fund raiser application that determines how much donated money is available after operating costs. This application must meet the following requirements:

Application Requirements

An organization is hosting a fund raiser to collect donations. A portion of each donation is used to cover the operating expenses of the organization; the rest of the donation goes to the charity. Create an application that allows the organization to keep track of the total amount of money raised. The application should deduct 17% of each donation for operating costs; the remaining 83% is given to the charity. The application should display the amount of each donation after the 17% operating expenses are deducted; it also should display the total amount raised for the charity (that is, the total amount donated less all operating costs) for all donations up to that point.

The user inputs the amount of a donation into a TextBox and clicks a Button to calculate the net amount of that donation the charity receives after operating expenses have been deducted. In addition, the total amount of money raised for charity is updated and displayed. You begin by test-driving the completed application. Then, you will learn the additional Visual Basic .NET technologies that you will need to create your own version of this application.

Test-Driving the Fund Raiser Application

1. **Opening the completed application.** Open the directory C:\Examples\Tutorial15\CompletedApplication\FundRaiser to locate the **Fund Raiser** application. Double click FundRaiser.sln to open the application in Visual Studio .NET.

2. **Running the Fund Raiser application.** Select **Debug > Start** to run the application (Fig. 15.1).

Figure 15.1   **Fund Raiser** application's Form.

3. **Entering a donation in the application.** Enter 1500 in the **Donation:** Text-Box. Click the **Make Donation** Button. The application calculates the amount of the donation after the operating expenses have been deducted and displays the result ($1245.00) in the **After expenses:** field. Because this is the first donation entered, this amount is repeated in the **Total raised:** field (Fig. 15.2).

Figure 15.2   **Fund Raiser** application's Form with first donation entered.

4. **Entering additional donations.** Enter more donations, and click the **Make Donation** Button. Notice that the total raised increases with each additional donation (Fig. 15.3).

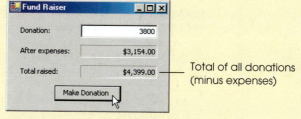

Total of all donations (minus expenses)

Figure 15.3   Making further donations.

5. **Closing the application.** Close your running application by clicking its close box.

6. **Closing the IDE.** Close Visual Studio .NET by clicking its close box.

15.2 Constructing the Fund Raiser Application

The following pseudocode statements describe the basic operation of the **Fund Raiser** application:

> *When the user changes the current donation amount in the TextBox:*
>> *Clear Label that displays amount of current donation that goes toward charity*
>
> *When the user clicks the Make Donation Button:*
>> *Obtain amount of current donation from TextBox*
>> *Calculate amount of current donation that goes toward charity (amount after operating costs)*
>> *Display amount of current donation that goes toward charity*
>> *Update total amount raised for charity (from all donations received)*
>> *Display total amount raised for charity*
>
> *When the CalculateDonation procedure gets called:*
>> *Calculate operating costs (multiply the donated amount by the operating cost percentage)*
>> *Calculate amount of donation that goes to charity (Subtract operating costs from donated amount)*

Now that you have test-driven the **Fund Raiser** application and studied its pseudocode representation, you will use an ACE table to help you convert the pseudocode to Visual Basic .NET. Figure 15.4 lists the actions, controls and events that will help you complete your own version of this application.

	Action	Control	Event/Method
Action/Control/Event Table for the Fund Raiser Application	Label all the application's controls	`lblDonations, lblDonated, lblTotal`	Application is run
		`txtDonation`	TextChanged
	Clear Label that displays amount of current donation that goes toward charity	`lblDonatedValue`	
		`btnDonate`	Click
	Obtain user donation from TextBox	`txtDonation`	
	Calculate amount of current donation that goes toward charity		
	Display amount of current donation that goes toward charity	`lblDonatedValue`	
	Update total amount raised for charity		
	Display total amount raised for charity	`lblTotalValue`	
			Calculate-Donation
	Calculate operating costs		
	Calculate amount of donation that goes to charity		

Figure 15.4 **Fund Raiser** application's ACE table.

You're now ready to begin programming the **Fund Raiser** application. First, you will declare the variables needed in the application. In this discussion, you will learn a new concept—scope. The **scope** of a variable identifier is the portion of an application in which the variable's identifier can be referenced. Some identifiers can be referenced throughout an application; others can be referenced only from limited portions of an application (such as within a single procedure). You will now add code to your application to illustrate these various scopes.

Examining Scope with the Fund Raiser Application

1. **Copying the template to your working directory.** Copy the `C:\Examples\Tutorial15\TemplateApplication\FundRaiser` directory to your `C:\SimplyVB` directory.

2. **Opening the Fund Raiser application's template file.** Double click `FundRaiser.sln` in the `FundRaiser` directory to open the application in Visual Studio .NET (Fig. 15.5).

Figure 15.5   **Fund Raiser** template application's `Form`.

3. **Placing declarations in the code file.** Select **View > Code**, and add lines 4–5 of Fig. 15.6 to `FundRaiser.vb`. In this application, you need a variable that stores the total amount of money raised for charity.

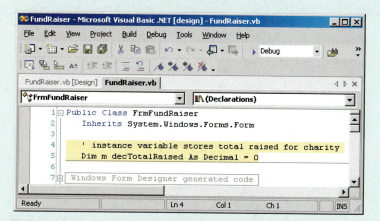

Figure 15.6   Declaring an instance variable in the application.

This variable is initialized when the application first runs and must retain its value while the application executes (that is, it cannot be created each time a procedure is invoked). Variable `m_decTotalRaised` stores the total amount of money raised. This variable is an **instance variable**—a variable declared inside a class, but outside any procedure definitions of that class. All procedures in class `FrmFundRaiser` will have access to this variable and will be able to modify its value.

Instance variables have **module scope**. Module scope begins at the identifier after keyword `Class` and terminates at the `End Class` statement. This scope enables any procedure in the same class to access all instance variables defined in that class. `Form` instance variables with module scope are created when the application begins executing.

Good Programming Practice

Prefix instance variables with m_ (for module scope) to distinguish them from other variables.

(cont.)

4. ***Creating the Click event handler for the Make Donation Button.*** Select **View > Designer** to return to design view. Double click the **Make Donation** Button to generate its Click event handler btnDonate_Click. Split the procedure header over two lines as in lines 160–161 of Fig. 15.7, and place the comments on lines 159 and 163 around the event handler.

5. ***Declaring local variables in event handler btnDonate_Click.*** Add lines 163–164 of Fig. 15.8 to event handler btnDonate_Click. Variable decDonation (line 163) stores the donation amount. Variable decAfterCosts (line 164) stores the donation amount after the operating expenses have been deducted.

   In Visual Basic. NET, identifiers, such as decDonation and decAfterCosts, that are declared inside a procedure (but outside of a control statement, such as a Do While...Loop) have **procedure scope**. Identifiers with procedure scope cannot be referenced outside of the procedure in which they are declared. Parameters to procedures are also considered to have procedure scope.

   Identifiers declared inside control statements, such as inside an If...Then statement, have **block scope**. Block scope begins at the identifier's declaration and ends at the block's final statement (for example, End If).

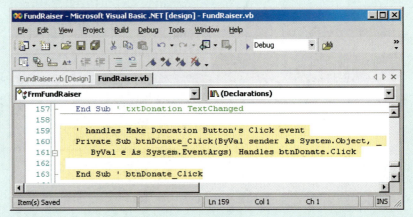

Figure 15.7   Adding a Click event handler to the application.

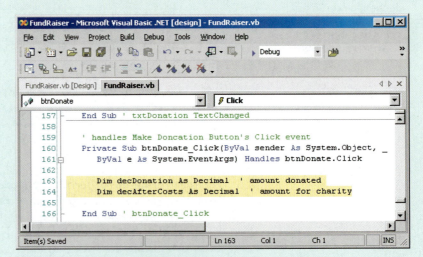

Figure 15.8   Declaring local variables in the **Fund Raiser** application.

(cont.)

Variables with either procedure scope or block scope are called **local variables**, because they cannot be referenced outside the procedure or block in which they are declared. If a local variable (that is, a variable with either block scope or procedure scope) has the same name as an instance variable (that is, a variable with module scope), the instance variable is hidden in that procedure or block. Any expression containing the variable name will use the local variable's value and not the instance variable's value. The instance variable's value is not destroyed, though—it is still available for access outside that procedure or block.

6. ***Examining the `CalculateDonation` procedure.*** The template application provides the `CalculateDonation` `Function` procedure (lines 136–149 of Fig. 15.9). Line 140 declares constant `dblCOSTS`, which stores the operating-cost percentage. This constant also is "local" to the procedure and cannot be used elsewhere. The `Function` procedure accepts one parameter value—the total donation amount (`decDonatedAmount`). The amount of the donation that goes toward operating costs is 17% of the initial donation. The net donation (the amount that goes toward charity) is calculated by multiplying local constant `dblCOSTS`, whose value is `0.17`, by the initial donation amount.

Procedure `CalculateDonation` subtracts the operating cost from the initial donation amount (`decDonatedAmount`) and assigns the result to `decNetDonation` (lines 144–145). The `Function` procedure then returns the `Decimal` result (line 147).

Error-Prevention Tip

Hidden variable names can sometimes lead to subtle logic errors. Use unique names for all variables, regardless of scope, to prevent an instance variable from becoming hidden.

Parameter
`decDonatedAmount` has procedure scope because it is declared in the procedure header

Local variable
`decNetDonation` has procedure scope because it is declared in the procedure body

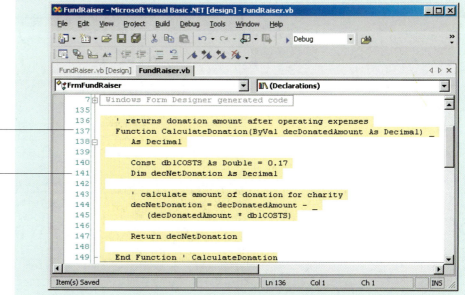

Figure 15.9 `Function` procedure `CalculateDonation` provided by the template application.

7. ***Demonstrating the difference between module scope and procedure scope.*** Now you are going to demonstrate the limits of procedure scope. Temporarily replace constant `dblCOSTS` with `decDonation`, `btnDonate_Click`'s local variable (line 145 in Fig. 15.10). Notice the jagged line under `decDonation` to indicate an error. Variables with procedure scope can be accessed and modified only in the procedure in which they are defined. The error message displayed when the mouse pointer rests on `decDonation` indicates that `decDonation` is not declared. Because this variable is "local" to `btnDonate_Click`, `Function` `CalculateDonation` cannot "see" the declaration of `decDonation`. Replace `decDonation` with `dblCOSTS`.

(cont.)

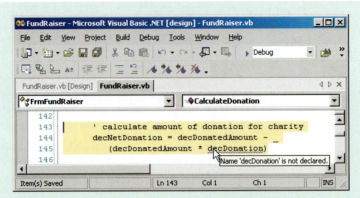

Figure 15.10 Demonstrating procedure scope.

8. ***Obtaining the donation amount.*** Add lines 166–167 of Fig. 15.11 to event handler btnDonate_Click. You obtain the total donation amount from TextBox txtDonation (line 167).

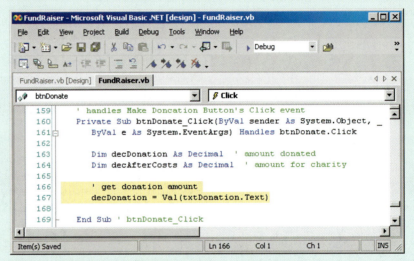

Figure 15.11 Obtaining the donation amount.

9. ***Calculating and displaying the donation amount after the operating expenses.*** Add lines 169–173 of Fig. 15.12 to the event handler. Line 170 invokes procedure CalculateDonation with the amount of the donation (decDonation). The result of this procedure—the net amount that goes to charity after the deduction for operating costs—is assigned to variable decAfterCosts. The donation amount after expenses is formatted as a currency string and displayed in the **After expenses:** field (line 173).

10. ***Updating and displaying the fund raiser total.*** Add lines 175–179 of Fig. 15.13 to the event handler. Line 176 updates instance variable m_decTotalRaised, which stores the total amount given to the charity after the operating costs have been deducted. Line 179 displays the total amount raised for charity.

    Notice that m_decTotalRaised is not declared as a local variable in this event handler and that m_decTotalRaised does not have a jagged line beneath it. Recall that m_decTotalRaised is an instance variable, declared on line 5 of Fig. 15.6. Instance variables may be used in any of the class's procedures.

(cont.)

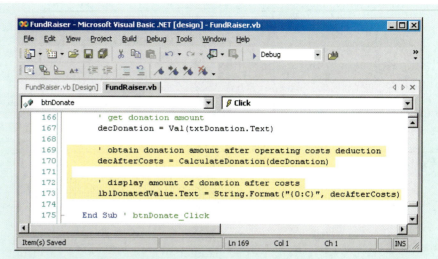

Figure 15.12 Calculating and displaying the donation amount after operating expenses.

Because `m_decTotalRaised` has module scope, it maintains its value between procedure calls. Variables with procedure scope do not retain their values between procedure calls. Variables with procedure scope, such as `decDonation`, are re-initialized each time their procedure is invoked.

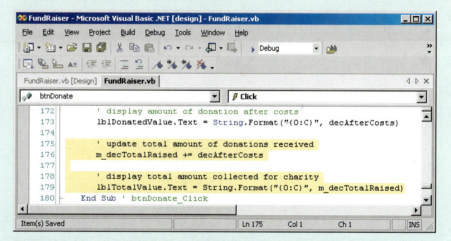

Figure 15.13 Updating and displaying the total amount raised for charity.

11. ***Clearing the After expenses: field to display the next result.*** The template application includes event handler `txtDonation_TextChanged` (lines 151–157 of Fig. 15.14) for the **Donation:** TextBox's TextChanged event. When the user enters data into the TextBox, the TextChanged event occurs and line 156 clears the donation for charity from the **After expenses:** field.

12. ***Running the application.*** Select **Debug > Start** to run your application. Enter several donation values to see that the total donation amount is added to each time the **Make Donation** Button is clicked. The application will now run and display the correct output, but we can also solve this problem using a sophisticated yet sometimes error-prone technique known as pass-by-reference. You will modify your application to use pass-by-reference in the next section.

13. ***Closing the application.*** Close your running application by clicking its close box.

(cont.)

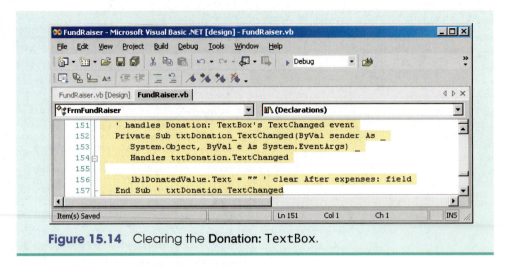

Figure 15.14 Clearing the **Donation:** TextBox.

15.3 Passing Arguments: Pass-by-Value vs. Pass-by-Reference

Arguments are passed to procedures in one of two ways: **pass-by-value** and **pass-by-reference** (also called **call-by-value** and **call-by-reference**). The keyword ByVal (which we have used in all our procedures until now, including event handlers generated by Visual Basic .NET) indicates that a variable has been passed by value. When an argument is passed by value, the application makes a copy of the argument's value and passes that copy to the called procedure. Changes made to the copy in the called procedure do not affect the original variable's value in the calling procedure.

In contrast, when an argument is passed by reference (using keyword **ByRef**), the original data can be accessed and modified directly by the called procedure. This is useful in some situations, such as when a procedure needs to produce more than one result. However, it can cause subtle errors and is used largely only by experienced programmers. In the following box, you will learn to use keyword ByRef to pass an argument by reference to the procedure that calculates the donation amount after operating costs.

Passing Arguments with ByRef in the *Fund Raiser Application*

1. ***Passing variable decAfterCosts by reference.*** Replace line 170 in event handler btnDonate_Click with line 170 of Fig. 15.15. The procedure call in line 170 of Fig. 15.15 passes two variables to procedure CalculateDonation. Notice that because procedure CalculateDonation currently only accepts one argument, the second argument (decAfterCosts) is flagged as a syntax error. In the following steps, we will rewrite procedure CalculateDonation so that it accepts two arguments, resolving the syntax error. The first argument (in this case, decDonation) will be passed by value; the second argument (in this case, decAfterCosts) will be passed by reference. When the CalculateDonation procedure returns, variable decAfterCosts will contain the portion of the donation that the charity receives.

(cont.)

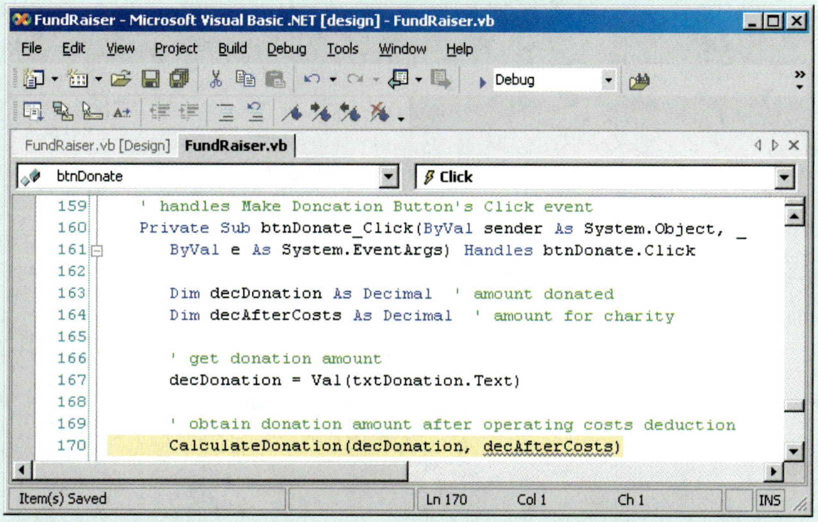

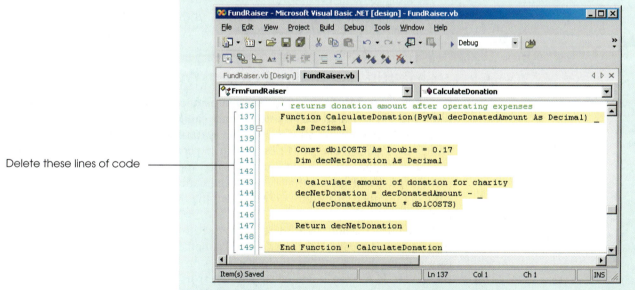

Figure 15.15 Passing variable decAfterCosts by reference.

2. ***Removing the old CalculateDonation Function procedure.*** Delete the CalculateDonation Function procedure (lines 137–149 of Fig. 15.16) from FundRaiser.vb.

Delete these lines of code ——————

Figure 15.16 Function procedure CalculateDonation to be removed.

3. ***Coding the new CalculateDonation Sub procedure.*** Add lines 137–140 of Fig. 15.17 in your code. Lines 137–138 specify procedure CalculateDonation's header. Keyword ByRef (line 138) indicates that variable decNetDonation is passed by reference. This means that any changes made to variable decNetDonation in CalculateDonation affect btnDonate_Click's local variable decAfterCosts. Because it is no longer necessary for CalculateDonation to return a value, CalculateDonation is now created as a Sub procedure, rather than a Function procedure.

(cont.)

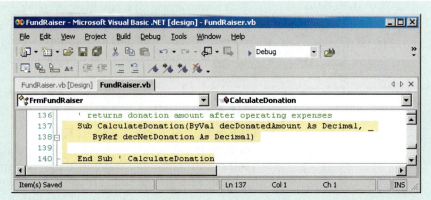

Figure 15.17 `CalculateDonation` Sub procedure.

4. ***Calculating the donation amount for charity after operating costs.*** Add lines 140–144 of Fig. 15.18 to Sub procedure `CalculateDonation`. Lines 143–144 calculate the amount of the donation that goes toward charity after operating costs have been deducted. Notice that this is the same calculation that was performed in lines 144–145 of the `Function` procedure `CalculateDonation` in Fig. 15.16. The only difference is that assigning the calculation result to variable `decNetDonation` actually assigns the value to `btnDonate_Click`'s local variable `decAfterCosts`. You do not need to return the calculation result.

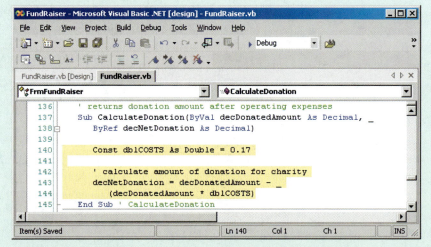

Figure 15.18 Calculating the donation that goes toward charity after operating costs have been deducted.

5. ***Running the application.*** Select **Debug > Start** to run your application. Again, the application will display the correct results, adding to the total donation amount for each input. This solution, however, uses pass-by-reference rather than pass-by-value. In the next section you will improve upon this application once more using `Option Strict`, which will help you write cleaner code.

6. ***Closing the application.*** Close your running application by clicking its close box.

---

1. Keyword _____ indicates pass-by-reference.

    a) `Reference`   b) `ByRef`

    c) `ByReference`   d) `PassByRef`

2. When an argument is passed by reference, the called procedure can access and modify _____.

   a) the caller's original data directly   b) a copy of the caller's data
   c) other procedures' local variables   d) None of the above.

Answers: 1) b. 2) a.

15.4 Option Strict

When the computer accesses data, it needs to know what type that data is for the data to make sense. Imagine you are purchasing a book from an online store that ships internationally. You notice that the price for the book is 20, but no currency is associated with the price; it could be dollars, euros, pesos, yen or some other currency. Therefore, it is important to know what type of currency is being used. If the currency is different from the one that you normally use, you will need to perform a conversion to get the price.

Similar conversions occur many times in an application. The computer determines a data type, and, with that knowledge, it adds two `Integers` or combines two `Strings` of text. Visual Basic .NET can convert one data type to another, as long as the conversion makes sense. For example, you are allowed to assign an `Integer` value to a `Decimal` variable without writing code that tells the application how to do the conversion. These types of assignments perform conversions called **implicit conversions**. When an attempted conversion doesn't make sense, such as assigning `"hello"` to an `Integer` variable, an error occurs. Figure 15.19 lists Visual Basic .NET's data types and their allowed implicit conversions. [*Note*: We do not discuss every data type in this book. Consult the Visual Basic .NET documentation to learn more about Visual Basic .NET's types.]

Data Type	Can be implicitly converted to these (larger) types
Boolean	Object
Byte	Short, Integer, Long, Decimal, Single, Double or Object
Char	String or Object
Date	Object
Decimal	Single, Double or Object
Double	Object
Integer	Long, Decimal, Single, Double or Object
Long	Decimal, Single, Double or Object
Object	none
Short	Integer, Long, Decimal, Single, Double or Object
Single	Double or Object
String	Object

Figure 15.19   Data types and their allowed conversions.

The types listed in the right column are "larger" types, in that they can store more data than the types in the left column. For example, `Integer` types (left column) can be converted to `Long` types (right column, which includes four other data types). An `Integer` variable can store values in the approximate range ±2.1 billion; a `Long` variable can store numbers in the approximate range $\pm 9 \times 10^{18}$ (9 followed by 18 zeros). This means that any `Integer` value can be assigned to a `Long` variable without losing any data. These kinds of conversions are called implicit **widening conversions**, because the value of a "smaller" type (`Integer`) is being assigned to a variable of a "larger" type (`Long`).

When a "larger" type, such as Double, is assigned to a "smaller" type, such as Integer, either a run-time error will occur because the value being assigned is too large to be stored in the "smaller" type or the assignment will be permitted. Consider the following code:

```
Dim dblValue As Double = 4.6
Dim intValue As Integer = dblValue
```

Variable intValue will be assigned 5—the result of implicitly converting the Double value 4.6 to an Integer. These types of conversions are called implicit **narrowing conversions**. These types of conversions can introduce subtle errors in applications, because the actual value being assigned could have been altered without you being aware of it—a dangerous practice. For example, if the programmer was expecting variable intValue to be assigned a value other than 5 (such as 4.6 or 4), a logic error would occur.

Visual Basic .NET provides a feature called **Option Strict** that, when set to On, disallows implicit narrowing conversions. If you attempt an implicit narrowing conversion, the compiler issues a syntax error. Later, we will show you how programmers can "override" this by performing narrowing conversions explicitly. First, however, you will learn how to enable Option Strict, which is set to Off by default. The following box demonstrates how to set Option Strict to On through the Visual Studio .NET IDE.

**Enabling Option
Strict**

1. *Activating Option Strict.* In the **Solution Explorer** window, right click the project name (FundRaiser) to display a context menu. Select **Properties** to open the **FundRaiser Property Pages** dialog (Fig. 15.20).

2. *Selecting the Build option.* In the left side of the **FundRaiser Property Pages** dialog, select **Build** from the **Common Properties** directory (Fig. 15.21). In the middle of the dialog under **Compiler Defaults** is a ComboBox labelled **Option Strict:**. By default, the option is set to Off.

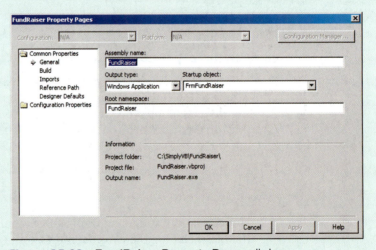

Figure 15.20 **FundRaiser Property Pages** dialog.

3. *Setting Option Strict to On.* Select On in the ComboBox labelled **Option Strict:**. Click **Apply**, then click **OK** to close the dialog. Option Strict is now set to On for this application. You will need to set Option Strict to On for each application you create.

4. *Saving the project.* Select **File > Save All** to save your modified code.

(cont.)

Build option —————

ComboBox containing value for `Option Strict`, which is set to `Off` by default

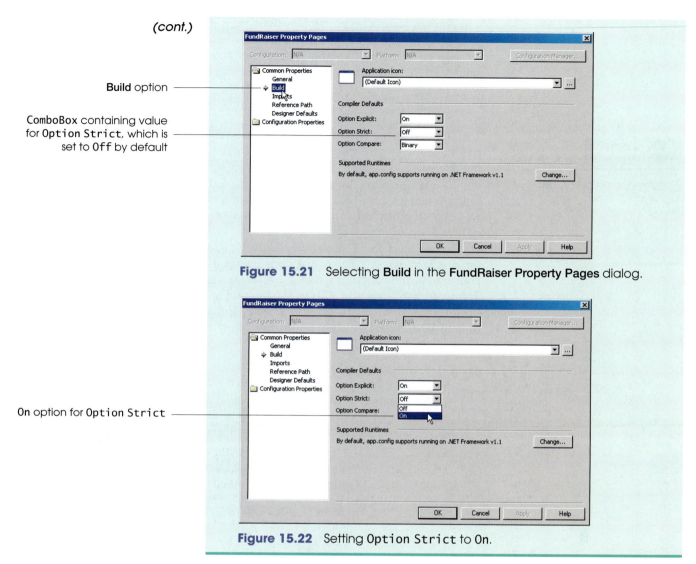

Figure 15.21 Selecting **Build** in the **FundRaiser Property Pages** dialog.

On option for `Option Strict` —————

Figure 15.22 Setting `Option Strict` to On.

As an alternative to setting `Option Strict` to On through the Visual Studio .NET IDE, you can set `Option Strict` to On programmatically by writing the statement `Option Strict On` as the first line of code. For example, to set `Option Strict` to On in FundRaiser.vb, the first three lines of the file would appear as

```
Option Strict On
```

```
Public Class FrmFundRaiser
```

Notice that the statement `Option Strict On` must appear before any other code in the file, including the class definition. From this point forward, all code examples in the remainder of this book have had `Option Strict` set to On through the Visual Studio .NET IDE.

When `Option Strict` is On, you must write code to perform narrowing conversions explicitly. At first, this may seem like a nuisance. However, it will help you create more robust applications that will avoid subtle errors that could result from implicit conversions. To help you perform conversions when `Option Strict` is On, Visual Basic .NET provides methods in class **Convert** (Fig. 15.23).

 **Error-Prevention Tip**

Set `Option Strict` to On in every application to avoid subtle errors that can be introduced by implicit narrowing conversions.

Convert To	Use Convert Method	Sample Statement
Integer	ToInt32	intValue = Convert.ToInt32(_ Val(txtInput.Text))

Decimal	ToDecimal	decValue = Convert.ToDecimal(_
		   Pmt(dblMonthlyInterest, _
		   intMonths,-intLoanAmount))

Double	ToDouble	dblRate = Convert.ToDouble(_ Val(txtRate.Text)) / 100
String	ToString	strResult = Convert.ToString(intTotal)

Figure 15.23   Four of class **Convert**'s methods.

The name of each conversion method is the word To, followed by the name of the data type to which the method converts its argument. For example, to convert a String input by the user in TextBox txtInput to an Integer (represented in Visual Basic .NET as type Int32) use the statement

```
intNumber = Convert.ToInt32(Val(txtInput.Text))
```

Conversions in statements that call Convert methods are called **explicit conversions**. In the following box, you will learn to use explicit conversions.

Using Class Convert in the Fund Raiser Application

1. ***Converting a Double donation amount to a Decimal value.*** Notice that lines 143–144 in Fig. 15.24 are underlined. Place the mouse pointer over the jagged lines. An error message now displays, indicating that Option Strict prohibits an implicit conversion from Double to Decimal. This is because converting from Double to Decimal could result in data loss.

   Replace the underlined expression with lines 143–144 of Fig. 15.25. Method Convert.ToDecimal converts the Double value to a Decimal value. When the conversion is performed explicitly with a call to method Convert.ToDecimal, the jagged lines disappear.

2. ***Converting the user input from a String to a Decimal.*** Line 163 of Fig. 15.26 is underlined. The error message that appears when the mouse pointer rests on this line indicates that Option Strict prohibits an implicit conversion from Double to Decimal.

   Replace the underlined expression with line 163 of Fig. 15.27. Method Convert.ToDecimal explicitly converts the Double to a Decimal. After this change is made, the jagged line disappears.

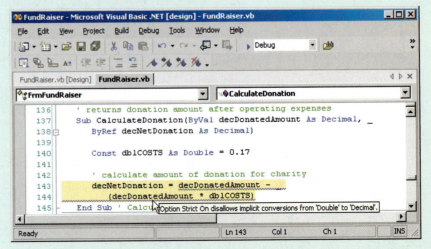

Figure 15.24   Option Strict prohibits implicit narrowing conversions.

(cont.)

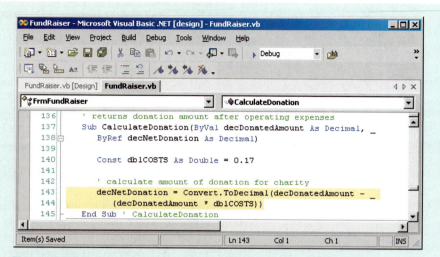

Figure 15.25 Explicitly performing a narrowing conversion with Convert.ToDecimal.

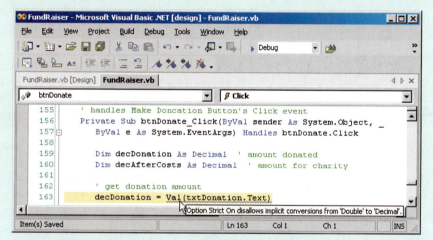

Figure 15.26 Option Strict prohibits a narrowing conversion from type Double to type Decimal.

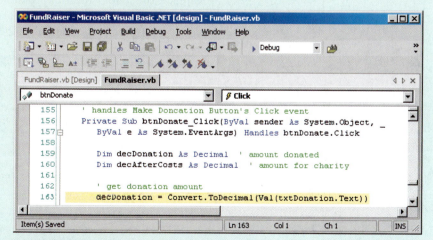

Figure 15.27 Explicitly converting a Double to type Decimal with Convert.ToDecimal.

(cont.)

3. ***Running the application.*** Select **Debug > Start** to run your application. Enter a donation amount and click the **Make Donation** Button. Verify that the total raised and the amount after expenses is correct. Enter more donations, each time verifying the output. Note that the total amount raised should also reflect previous donation amounts.

4. ***Closing the application.*** Close your running application by clicking its close box.

5. ***Closing the IDE.*** Close Visual Basic .NET by clicking its close box.

Figure 15.28 presents the source code for the **Fund Raiser** application. The lines of code that contain new programming concepts that you learned in this tutorial are highlighted.

```vb
1   Public Class FrmFundRaiser
2      Inherits System.Windows.Forms.Form
3
4      ' instance variable stores total raised for charity
5      Dim m_decTotalRaised As Decimal = 0
6
7      ' Windows Form Designer generated code
8
9      ' returns donation amount after operating expenses
10     Sub CalculateDonation(ByVal decDonatedAmount As Decimal, _
11        ByRef decNetDonation As Decimal)
12
13        Const dblCOSTS As Double = 0.17
14
15        ' calculate amount of donation for charity
16        decNetDonation = Convert.ToDecimal(decDonatedAmount - _
17           (decDonatedAmount * dblCOSTS))
18     End Sub ' CalculateDonation
19
20     ' handles Donation: TextBox's TextChanged event
21     Private Sub txtDonation_TextChanged(ByVal sender As _
22        System.Object, ByVal e As System.EventArgs) _
23        Handles txtDonation.TextChanged
24
25        lblDonatedValue.Text = "" ' clear After expenses: field
26     End Sub ' txtDonation_TextChanged
27
28     ' handles Make Donation Button's Click event
29     Private Sub btnDonate_Click(ByVal sender As System.Object, _
30        ByVal e As System.EventArgs) Handles btnDonate.Click
31
32        Dim decDonation As Decimal    ' amount donated
33        Dim decAfterCosts As Decimal  ' amount for charity
34
35        ' get donation amount
36        decDonation = Convert.ToDecimal(Val(txtDonation.Text))
37
38        ' obtain donation amount after operating costs deduction
39        CalculateDonation(decDonation, decAfterCosts)
40
41        ' display amount of donation after costs
42        lblDonatedValue.Text = String.Format("{0:C}", decAfterCosts)
43
```

Procedure `CalculateDonation` determines the amount of donation after operating costs; parameter `decNetDonation` is modified directly (using `ByRef`) — (lines 10–11)

Subtract operating costs from amount donated, assign value to `decNetDonation` — (lines 16–17)

Convert donation amount from a `String` to a `Decimal` value — (line 36)

Figure 15.28 **Fund Raiser** application's code. (Part 1 of 2.)

```
44            ' update total amount of donations received
45            m_decTotalRaised += decAfterCosts
46
47            ' display total amount collected for charity
48            lblTotalValue.Text = String.Format("{0:C}", m_decTotalRaised)
49         End Sub ' btnDonate_Click
50
51    End Class ' FrmFundRaiser
```

Figure 15.28 **Fund Raiser** application's code. (Part 2 of 2.)

---

1. When Option Strict is set to On, the programmer must explicitly perform _____.

   a) narrowing conversions   b) widening conversions

   c) all type conversions   d) no conversions

2. The methods in _____ are used to change data types explicitly.

   a) class Strict   b) class Change

   c) class Convert   d) class Conversion

Answers: 1) a. 2) c.

15.5 Wrap-Up

In this tutorial, you learned concepts about data types and variables, and you built the **Fund Raiser** application to demonstrate these concepts.

You learned how to create instance variables, which are declared inside a class, but outside any procedure definitions. Instance variables have module scope, which means that they are accessible to all procedures in the class in which they are declared. In this tutorial, you declared your instance variable in the Form class. In Tutorial 19, you will learn how to create your own classes and how to declare instance variables in them. Until now, all the variables you have declared have been local variables—that is, variables with either procedure scope or block scope. Variables with procedure scope are modifiable only within the procedure in which they are declared. Variables with block scope are modifiable only within the block (such as the body of an If...Then statement) in which they are declared.

You learned the difference between passing arguments by reference and passing arguments by value. When using pass-by-value, the calling procedure makes a copy of the argument's value and passes the copy to the called procedure. Changes to the called procedure's copy do not affect the original variable value in the calling procedure. When using pass-by-reference, the original data can be accessed and modified directly by the called procedure. You now know to use keyword ByVal to pass arguments by value and keyword ByRef to pass arguments by reference.

You also learned about data-type conversions. You learned that narrowing conversions (such as converting a Double to a Decimal) can result in data loss and that widening conversions (such as a conversion from Integer to Double) don't have this problem. You learned that setting Option Strict to On causes Visual Basic .NET to flag implicit narrowing conversions as syntax errors and forces the programmer to perform such conversions explicitly.

In the next tutorial, you will learn about random-number generation, and you will create an application that simulates the dice game called Craps.

SKILLS SUMMARY

Setting Option Strict to On

■ Right click the project in the **Solution Explorer**, and select **Properties**.

■ Select **Build** from the directory tree in the **Property Pages** dialog.

■ Set the **Option Strict:** ComboBox to **On**.

■ Click **Apply**, then click **OK**.

Passing Arguments

■ Arguments can be passed in two ways: pass-by-value (ByVal) and pass-by-reference (ByRef).

Passing Arguments by Value

■ In the procedure header, place keyword ByVal before the name of each argument that should be passed by value.

■ The application makes a copy of the argument's value and passes the copy to the called procedure.

■ Changes to the called procedure's copy do not affect the original argument value.

Passing Arguments by Reference

■ In the procedure header, place keyword ByRef before the name of each argument that should be passed by reference.

■ Called procedures can access and modify original arguments directly.

Understanding Scope

■ You have learned the differences between module scope, procedure scope and block scope.

■ Instance variables have module scope and can be accessed by all procedures in the same class.

■ Local variables have either procedure scope or block scope.

■ Variables with procedure scope cannot be referenced outside the procedure in which they are declared.

■ Variables with block scope cannot be referenced outside the block (such as the body of an If...Then statement) in which they are declared.

■ Block scope begins at the identifier's declaration and ends at the block's end statement.

KEY TERMS

block scope—Variables declared inside control statements, such as an If...Then statement, have block scope. Block scope begins at the identifier's declaration and ends at the block's final statement (for example, End If).

ByRef keyword—Used to pass an argument by reference.

call-by-reference—See *pass-by-reference*.

call-by-value—See *pass-by-value*.

Convert class—Provides methods for converting data types.

explicit conversion—An operation that converts a value of one type to another type using code to (explicitly) tell the application to do the conversion. An example of an explicit conversion is to convert a value of one type to another type using a Convert method.

implicit conversion—An operation that converts a value of one type to another type without writing code to (explicitly) tell the application to do the conversion.

instance variable—Declared inside a class but outside any procedure of that class. Instance variables have module scope.

local variable—Declared inside a procedure or block, such as the body of an If...Then statement. Local variables have either procedure scope or block scope.

module scope—Begins at the identifier after keyword Class and terminates at the End Class statement, enables all procedures in the same class to access all instance variables defined in that class.

narrowing conversion—A conversion where the value of a "larger" type is being assigned to a variable of a "smaller" type, where the "larger" type can store more data than the "smaller" type. Narrowing conversions can result in loss of data, which can cause subtle logic errors.

`Option Strict`—When set to `On`, `Option Strict` causes the compiler to check all conversions and requires the programmer to perform an explicit conversion for all narrowing conversions (for example, conversion from `Double` to `Decimal`) or application termination (conversion of a `String`, such as `"hello"`, to type `Integer`).

pass-by-reference—When an argument is passed by reference, the called procedure can access and modify the caller's original data directly. Keyword `ByRef` indicates pass-by-reference (also called call-by-reference).

pass-by-value—When an argument is passed by value, the application makes a copy of the argument's value and passes that copy to the called procedure. With pass-by-value, changes to the called procedure's copy do not affect the original variable's value. Keyword `ByVal` indicates pass-by-value (also called call-by-value).

procedure scope—Variables declared inside a procedure but outside of a control structure, have procedure scope. Variables with procedure scope cannot be referenced outside the procedure in which they are declared.

scope—The portion of an application in which an identifier (such as a variable name) can be referenced. Some identifiers can be referenced throughout an application; others can be referenced only from limited portions of an application (such as within a single procedure or block).

widening conversion—A conversion where the value of a "smaller" type is being assigned to a variable of a "larger" type, where the "larger" type can store more data than the "smaller" type.

MULTIPLE-CHOICE QUESTIONS

15.1 In the **Property Pages** dialog, _____ must be selected to access `Option Strict`.
a) **Build**
b) **Designer Defaults**
c) **General**
d) **Imports**

15.2 When `Option Strict` is set to `On`, variables _____.
a) are passed by value
b) are passed by reference
c) might need to be converted explicitly to a different type to avoid errors
d) are used only within the block in which the variables are declared

15.3 A variable declared inside a class, but outside a procedure, is called a(n) _____.
a) local variable
b) hidden variable
c) instance variable
d) constant variable

15.4 Visual Basic .NET provides methods in class _____ to convert from one data type to another.
a) `ChangeTo`
b) `Convert`
c) `ConvertTo`
d) `ChangeType`

15.5 When `Option Strict` is _____, the conversion attempt `intX = dblPercent` results in an error.
a) `On`
b) `True`
c) `Off`
d) `False`

15.6 Keyword _____ indicates pass-by-reference.
a) `ByReference`
b) `ByRef`
c) `Ref`
d) `Reference`

15.7 With _____, changes made to a parameter variable's value do not affect the value of the variable in the calling procedure.
a) `Option Strict`
b) pass-by-value
c) pass-by-reference
d) None of the above.

15.8 Instance variables _____.

a) are members of class

b) are prefixed by m_

c) can be accessed by a procedure in the same class

d) All of the above.

15.9 Assigning a "smaller" type to a "larger" type is a _____ conversion.

a) narrowing

b) shortening

c) widening

d) lengthening

15.10 A value of type Boolean can be implicitly converted to _____.

a) Integer

b) String

c) Object

d) Double

EXERCISES

15.11 (*Task List Application*) Create an application that allows users to add items to a daily task list. The application should also display the number of tasks to be performed. Use method Convert.ToString to display the number of tasks in a Label. The application should look like the GUI in Fig. 15.29.

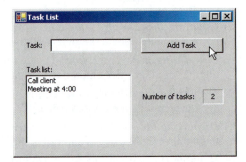

Figure 15.29 **Task List** application's GUI.

a) *Copying the template to your working directory.* Copy the directory C:\Examples\ Tutorial15\Exercises\TaskList to your C:\SimplyVB directory.

b) *Opening the application's template file.* Double click TaskList.sln in the TaskList directory to open the application.

c) *Setting Option Strict to On.* Use the directions provided in the box, *Enabling Option Strict*, to set Option Strict to On.

d) *Adding the Add Task Button's Click event handler.* Double click the **Add Task** Button to generate the empty event handler btnAdd_Click. This event handler should display the user input in the ListBox and clear the user input from the Text-Box. The event handler should also update the Label that displays the number of tasks. Use method Convert.ToString to display the number of tasks in the Label. Finally, the event handler should transfer the focus to the TextBox.

e) *Running the application.* Select **Debug > Start** to run your application. Enter several tasks, click the **Add Task** Button after each. Verify that each task is added to the **Task list:** ListBox, and that the number of tasks is incremented with each new task.

f) *Closing the application.* Close your running application by clicking its close box.

g) *Closing the IDE.* Close Visual Studio .NET by clicking its close box.

15.12 (*Quiz Average Application*) Develop an application that computes a student's average quiz score for all of the quiz scores entered. The application should look like the GUI in Fig. 15.30. Use method Convert.ToInt32 to convert the user input to an Integer. Use instance variables with module scope to keep track of the sum of all the quiz scores entered and the number of quiz scores entered.

a) *Copying the template to your working directory.* Copy the directory C:\Examples\ Tutorial15\Exercises\QuizAverage to your C:\SimplyVB directory.

b) *Opening the application's template file.* Double click QuizAverage.sln in the QuizAverage directory to open the application.

Figure 15.30 **Quiz Average** application's GUI.

c) *Setting `Option Strict` to `On`.* Use the directions provided in the box, *Enabling Option Strict*, to set `Option Strict` to `On`.

d) *Adding instance variables.* Add two instance variables—`m_intTotalScore`, which keeps track of the sum of all the quiz scores entered, and `m_intTaken`, which keeps track of the number of quiz scores entered.

e) *Adding the Grade Quiz Button's event handler.* Double click the **Submit Score** `Button` to generate the empty event handler `btnCalculate_Click`. The code required in *Steps f–k* should be placed in this event handler.

f) *Obtaining user input.* Use method `Convert.ToInt32` to convert the user input from the `TextBox` to an `Integer`.

g) *Updating the number of quiz scores entered.* Increment the number of quiz scores entered.

h) *Updating the sum of all the quiz scores entered.* Add the current quiz score to the current total to update the sum of all the quiz scores entered.

i) *Calculating the average score.* Divide the sum of all the quiz scores entered by the number of quiz scores entered to calculate the average score.

j) *Displaying the average score.* Use method `Convert.ToString` to display the average quiz grade in the **Average:** field.

k) *Displaying the number of quizzes taken.* Use method `Convert.ToString` to display the number of quiz scores entered in the **Number taken:** field.

l) *Running the application.* Select **Debug > Start** to run your application. Enter several quiz scores, clicking the **Submit Score** `Button` after each. With each new score, verify that the **Number taken:** field is incremented and that the average is updated correctly.

m) *Closing the application.* Close your running application by clicking its close box.

n) *Closing the IDE.* Close Visual Studio .NET by clicking its close box.

15.13 (*Maximum Application*) Modify the **Maximum** application from Chapter 13 (Fig. 15.31) to use keyword `ByRef` to pass a fourth argument to procedure `Maximum` by reference. Also, use methods from class `Convert` to perform any necessary type conversions.

Figure 15.31 **Maximum** application's GUI.

a) *Copying the template to your working directory.* Copy the directory `C:\Examples\Tutorial15\Exercises\Maximum` to your `C:\SimplyVB` directory.

b) *Opening the application's template file.* Double click `Maximum.sln` in the `Maximum` directory to open the application.

c) *Setting `Option Strict` to `On`.* Use the directions provided in the box, *Enabling Option Strict*, to set `Option Strict` to `On`.

d) *Adding a local variable.* Add local variable dblMaximum of type Double to event handler btnMaximum_Click. The code required in *Steps d–f* should be placed in this event handler. Variable dblMaximum will store the result of procedure Maximum.

e) *Passing four arguments to procedure Maximum.* Use method Convert.ToDouble to convert the user input from the TextBoxes to Doubles. Pass these three values as the first three arguments to procedure Maximum. Pass local variable dblMaximum as the fourth argument to procedure Maximum.

f) *Displaying the maximum value.* Use method Convert.ToString to display local variable dblMaximum in the **Maximum:** field.

g) *Changing procedure Maximum to a Sub procedure.* Change procedure Maximum to a Sub procedure. Make sure that Sub procedure Maximum no longer returns a value and does not specify a return type. The modifications required in *Steps g–h* should be performed on this Sub procedure.

h) *Adding a fourth parameter to procedure Maximum.* Add a fourth parameter dblFinalMaximum of type Double to Maximum's procedure header. Use keyword ByRef to specify that this argument will be passed by reference. Remove the declaration of variable dblFinalMaximum from the body of procedure Maximum.

i) *Running the application.* Select **Debug > Start** to run your application. Enter three different values into the input fields and click the **Maximum Button**. Verify that the largest value is displayed in the **Maximum:** field.

j) *Closing the application.* Close your running application by clicking its close box.

k) *Closing the IDE.* Close Visual Studio .NET by clicking its close box.

What does this code do? **15.14** What is displayed in Label lblDisplay when the following code is executed?

```
1   Public Class FrmScopeTest
2      Inherits System.Windows.Forms.Form
3
4      Dim intValue2 As Integer = 5
5
6      Private Sub btnEnter_Click(ByVal sender As System.Object, _
7         ByVal e As System.EventArgs) Handles btnEnter.Click
8
9         Dim intValue1 As Integer = 10
10        Dim intValue2 As Integer = 3
11
12        Test(intValue1)
13        lblDisplay.Text = Convert.ToString(intValue1)
14     End Sub ' btnEnter_Click
15
16     Sub Test(ByRef intValue1 As Integer)
17        intValue1 *= intValue2
18     End Sub ' Test
19
20  End Class ' FrmScopeTest
```

What's wrong with this code? ▶ **15.15** Find the error(s) in the following code (the procedure should assign the value 14 to variable intResult).

```
1   Sub Sum()
2      Dim strNumber As String = "4"
3      Dim intNumber As Integer = 10
4      Dim intResult As Integer
5
6      intResult = strNumber + intNumber
7   End Sub ' Sum
```

Programming Challenge **15.16** (*Schedule Book Application*) Develop an application that allows a user to enter a schedule of appointments and their respective times. Create the Form in Fig. 15.32 and name the application **Schedule Book**. Add a Function procedure called TimeTaken that returns a Boolean value. Each time a user enters a new appointment, Function procedure TimeTaken determines if the user has scheduled more than one appointment at the same time. If Time-Taken returns True, the user will be notified via a message dialog. Otherwise, the appointment should be added to the ListBoxes. Set Option Strict to On and use methods from class Convert as necessary.

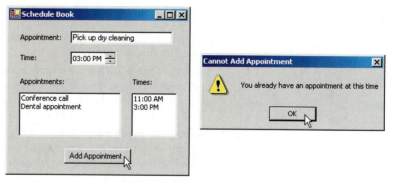

Figure 15.32 Schedule Book application's GUI.

Craps Game Application

Introducing Random-Number Generation

Y ou will now be introduced to a popular type of application—simulation and game playing. In this tutorial, you will develop a **Craps Game** application. There is something in the air of a gambling casino that invigorates each person—from the high rollers at the plush mahogany-and-felt Craps tables to the quarter-poppers at the one-armed bandits. Many of these individuals are drawn by the element of chance—the possibility that luck will convert a pocketful of money into a mountain of wealth.

The element of chance can be introduced into computer applications using random numbers. This tutorial's **Craps Game** application introduces several new concepts, including random-number generation and enumerations. It also uses important concepts that you learned earlier in this book, including instance variables, procedures and the `Select Case` multiple-selection control structure.

16.1 Test-Driving the Craps Game Application

One of the most popular games of chance is a dice game known as "Craps," played in casinos throughout the world. This application must meet the following requirements:

> **Application Requirements**
>
> *Create an application that simulates playing the game of "Craps." In this game, a player rolls two dice. Each die has six faces. Each face contains 1, 2, 3, 4, 5 or 6 spots. After the dice have come to rest, the sum of the spots on the two top faces is calculated. If the sum is 7 or 11 on the first throw, the player wins. If the sum is 2, 3 or 12 on the first throw (called "craps"), the player loses (the "house" wins). If the sum is 4, 5, 6, 8, 9 or 10 on the first throw, that sum becomes the player's "point." To win, a player must continue rolling the dice until the player rolls the point value. The player loses by rolling a 7 before rolling the point.*

Creating this application will teach you two important concepts; random-number generation and enumerations. You begin by test-driving the completed application. Then, you will learn the additional Visual Basic .NET technologies that you will need to create your own version of this application.

351

Test-Driving the Craps Game Application

1. ***Opening the completed application.*** Open the directory C:\Examples\ Tutorial16\CompletedApplication\CrapsGame to locate the **Craps Game** application. Double click CrapsGame.sln to open the application in Visual Studio .NET.

2. ***Running the Craps Game application.*** Select **Debug > Start** to run the application (Fig. 16.1).

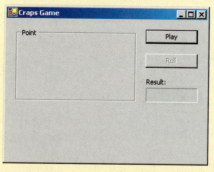

Figure 16.1 **Craps Game** application initial appearance.

3. ***Starting the game.*** Click the **Play** Button. There are three possible outcomes at this point: The player wins by rolling a 7 or an 11 (Fig. 16.2). The player loses by rolling 2, 3 or 12 (Fig. 16.3). Otherwise, the roll becomes the player's point (4, 5, 6, 8, 9 or 10), which is then displayed for the remainder of the game (Fig. 16.4). Note that unlike the real game of Craps, the value of the roll is computed using the forward-facing die faces instead of the top faces in this application.

Figure 16.2 Player wins on first roll by rolling 7 or 11.

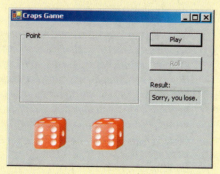

Figure 16.3 Player loses on first roll by rolling 2, 3 or 12.

(cont.)

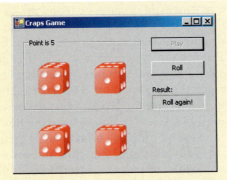

Figure 16.4   First roll sets the point that the player must match to win.

4. ***Continuing the game.*** If the application displays **Roll again!**, as in Fig. 16.4, click the **Roll** Button repeatedly until either you win—by matching your point value (Fig. 16.5)—or you lose—by rolling a 7 (Fig. 16.6). When the game ends, you can click **Play** to start over.

Figure 16.5   Winning the game by matching your point before rolling a 7.

Figure 16.6   Losing by rolling a 7 before matching your point.

5. ***Closing the application.*** Close your running application by clicking its close box.

6. ***Closing the IDE.*** Close Visual Studio .NET by clicking its close box.

16.2 Random-Number Generation

Now you will learn how to use an object of class **Random** to introduce the element of chance into your computer applications. You will learn more about working with objects of existing classes over the next few tutorials, then you will learn to create your own classes and create objects of those classes in Tutorial 19. Consider the following statements:

Good Programming Practice

Prefix references to objects, such as Random objects, with obj.

```
Dim objRandom As Random = New Random
Dim intRandomNumber As Integer = objRandom.Next()
```

The first statement declares objRandom as a reference of type Random and assigns it a Random object. A **reference** is a variable to which you assign an object. Recall that keyword New creates a new structure value or a new instance of an object in memory.

The second statement declares Integer variable intRandomNumber. It then assigns to it the value returned by calling Random's Next method on object objRandom using the dot operator. The **Next** method generates a positive Integer value between zero and the largest possible Integer, which is the constant **Int32.MaxValue** (2,147,483,647). You can use the Next method to generate random values of type Integer or use the **NextDouble** method to generate random values of type Double. The NextDouble method returns a positive Double value between 0.0 and 1.0 (not including 1.0). Class Random does not contain a Next method for any other data type.

If the Next method were to produce truly random values, then every value in this range would have an equal chance (or probability) of being chosen when Next is called. However, the values returned by Next are actually **pseudorandom numbers**, a sequence of values produced by a complex mathematical calculation. This mathematical calculation comes close, but is not exactly random in choosing numbers.

The range of values produced by Next (that is, values between 0 and 2,147,483,647) often is different from the range needed in a particular application. For example, an application that simulates coin tossing might require only 0 for "heads" and 1 for "tails." An application that simulates the rolling of a six-sided die would require random Integers from 1 to 6. Similarly, an application that randomly predicts the next type of spaceship (out of four possibilities) that flies across the horizon in a video game might require random Integers from 1 to 4.

By passing an argument to the Next method[1] as follows

```
intValue = 1 + objRandom.Next(6)
```

you can produce integers in the range from 1 to 6. When a single argument is passed to Next, the values returned by Next will be in the range from 0 to (but not including) the value of that argument (that is, 5 in the preceding statement). You can change the range of numbers produced by adding 1 to the previous result, so that the return values are between 1 and 6, rather than 0 and 5. That new range, 1 to 6, corresponds nicely with the roll of a six-sided die, for example.

Visual Basic .NET simplifies this process of setting the range of numbers by allowing the programmer to pass two arguments to Next. For example, the preceding statement also could be written as

```
intValue = objRandom.Next(1, 7)
```

Note that you must use 7 as the second argument to the Next method to produce integers in the range from 1 to 6. The first argument indicates the minimum value in the desired range; the second is equal to *one more than the maximum value desired*.

As with method Next, the range of values produced by method NextDouble (that is, values greater than or equal to 0.0 and less than 1.0) is also usually different from the range needed in a particular application. By multiplying the value returned from method NextDouble as follows

```
dblValue = 6 * objRandom.NextDouble()
```

you can produce Double values in the range from 0.0 to 6.0 (not including 6.0). Figure 16.7 shows examples of the ranges returned by calls to methods Next and NextDouble.

---

1. In Tutorial 13, you learned that the number, type and order of arguments to a procedure must exactly match the procedure definition. You may notice that the Next method of class Random is called using zero, one and two arguments. There is a sophisticated feature of Visual Basic .NET called procedure overloading that allows multiple procedure definitions of the same name but with different numbers of arguments, types, and/or order.

Method call	Resulting range
`objRandom.Next()`	0 to one less than `Int32.MaxValue`
`objRandom.Next(30)`	0 to 29
`10 + objRandom.Next(10)`	10 to 19
`objRandom.Next(10, 20)`	10 to 19
`objRandom.Next(5, 100)`	5 to 99
`objRandom.NextDouble()`	0.0 to less than 1.0
`8 * objRandom.NextDouble()`	0.0 to less than 8.0

Figure 16.7 `Next` and `NextDouble` method calls with corresponding ranges.

SELF-REVIEW

1. The statement _____ returns a number in the range from 8 to 300.

   a) `objRandom.Next(8, 300)`   b) `objRandom.Next(8, 301)`
   c) `1 + objRandom.Next(8, 300)`   d) None of the above.

2. The statement _____ returns a number in the range 15 to 35.

   a) `objRandom.Next(15, 36)`   b) `objRandom.Next(15, 35)`
   c) `10 + objRandom.Next(5, 26)`   d) Both a and c.

Answers: 1) b. 2) d.

16.3 Using Enumerations in the Craps Game Application

The following pseudocode describes the basic operation of the **Craps Game** application:

```
When the player clicks the Play Button:
     Roll the dice using random numbers
     Display images corresponding to the numbers on the rolled dice
     Calculate the sum of both dice

     Select correct case based on the sum of the two dice:

     Case where first roll is 7 or 11
          Disable the Roll Button
          Display the winning message

     Case where first roll is 2, 3 or 12
          Disable the Roll Button
          Display the losing message

     Case where none of the preceding Cases are true
          Set the value of the point to the sum of the dice
          Display point value
          Display message to roll again
          Display images for user's point
          Disable the Play Button
          Enable the Roll Button

When the player clicks the Roll Button:
     Roll the dice using random numbers
     Display images corresponding to the numbers on the rolled dice
     Calculate the sum of both dice

     If the player rolls the same value as the point
          Display the winning message
          Disable the Roll Button
          Enable the Play Button
```

> Else If the player rolls a 7
> > Display the losing message
> > Disable the Roll Button
> > Enable the Play Button

Now that you have test-driven the **Craps Game** application and studied its pseudocode representation, you will use an ACE table to help you convert the pseudocode to Visual Basic .NET. Figure 16.8 lists the actions, controls and events that will help you complete your own version of this application.

Action/Control/Event (ACE) Table for the Craps Game Application

Action	Control/Object	Event
Label the application's controls	lblResult, fraPointDiceGroup	
	btnPlay	Click
Roll the dice using random numbers	m_objRandomObject	
Display images corresponding to the numbers on the rolled dice	picDie1, picDie2	
Calculate the sum of both dice		
Select correct case based on sum:		
Case where first roll is 7 or 11 Disable the Roll Button	btnRoll,	
Display the winning message	lblStatus	
Case where first roll is 2, 3 or 1 Disable the Roll Button	btnRoll	
Display the losing message	lblStatus	

Case where none of the preceding Cases are true
        Set the value of the point to
        the sum of the dice		

Display the point value	fraPointDiceGroup	
Display message to roll again	lblStatus	
Display images for user's point	picPointDie1, picPointDie2	
Disable the Play Button	btnPlay	
Enable the Roll Button	btnRoll	
	btnRoll	Click
Roll the dice using random numbers	m_objRandomObject	
Display images corresponding to the numbers on the rolled dice	picDie1, picDie2	
Calculate the sum of both dice		
If the player rolls the same value as the point Display the winning message	lblStatus	
Disable the Roll Button	btnRoll	
Enable the Play Button	btnPlay	
If the player rolls a 7 Display the losing message	lblStatus	
Disable the Roll Button	btnRoll	
Enable the Play Button	btnPlay	

Figure 16.8 ACE table for the **Craps Game** application.

In the following boxes, you will create an application to simulate playing the game of Craps. The steps that follow show you how to add code to import the System.IO namespace. As you have already learned, Visual Basic .NET has access to the Framework Class Library (FCL), which is a rich collection of classes that can be used to enhance applications. The FCL includes classes that provide methods for using files, graphics, multimedia and more. These FCL classes are grouped (by functionality) in units called **namespaces**. The **System.IO namespace** provides classes and methods for accessing files (such as images and text) and directories (such as C:\SimplyVB). You will need to use code to access image files for the **Craps Game** application; therefore, you import the System.IO namespace. Importing a namespace (using the **Imports** statement) allows you to access its members.

Viewing the Craps Game Template Application

1. ***Copying the template to your working directory.*** Copy the C:\Examples\Tutorial16\TemplateApplication\CrapsGame directory to your C:\SimplyVB directory.

2. ***Opening the application's template file.*** Double click CrapsGame.sln in the CrapsGame directory to open the application in Visual Studio .NET. Figure 16.9 displays the Form in design view.

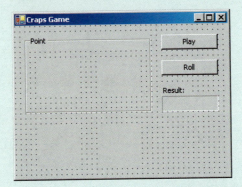

Figure 16.9   Template **Craps Game** Form in design view.

3. ***Allowing image-file access.*** The application will display images; therefore, you need to import the System.IO namespace to allow access to methods to help you read image files. Select **View > Code**. Add Imports System.IO (line 1) into your code before the class definition (Fig. 16.10).

Importing the System.IO namespace

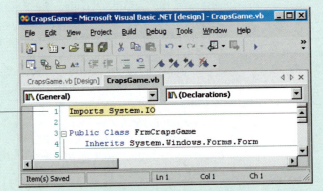

Figure 16.10   **Imports** statement added in the **Craps Game** application.

4. ***Saving the project.*** Select **File > Save All** to save your modified code.

Notice that the numbers 2, 3, 7, 11 and 12 have special meanings during a game of Craps. Throughout the course of a Craps game, you will use these numbers (as constants) quite often. In this case, it would be helpful to create a group of related constants and assign them meaningful names for use in your application. Visual Basic .NET allows you to accomplish this by using an **enumeration**. You will learn how to create constant identifiers that describe various significant dice combinations in Craps (such as SNAKE_EYES, TREY, CRAPS, LUCKY_SEVEN, YO_LEVEN and BOX_CARS). By providing descriptive identifiers for a group of related constants, enumerations enhance program readability and ensure that numbers are consistent throughout the application. Next, you will learn how to use enumerations.

Introducing Enumerations and Declaring Instance Variables

1. **Declaring an enumeration.** Add lines 153–154 of Fig. 16.11 to your application after the `Windows Form Designer generated code`, then press *Enter*. Notice that keywords End Enum appear. Enumerations begin with the keyword **Enum** (line 154), and end with the keywords **End Enum** (line 161). The name of the enumeration (`DiceNames`) follows the keyword Enum (line 154). Now add lines 155–160 of Fig. 16.11 into your application between the lines containing keywords Enum and End Enum.

Defining an enumeration ————

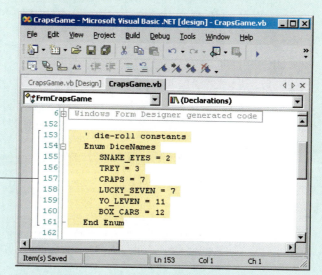

Figure 16.11 Enumeration `DiceNames` in the **Craps Game** application.

Enumerations are used in this application to make the code easier to read, especially for someone who is unfamiliar with the application. You can refer to the numbers using the enumeration constants and the member-access operator. For instance, use `DiceNames.SNAKE_EYES` for the number 2, `DiceNames.TREY` for the number 3, `DiceNames.CRAPS` and `DiceNames.LUCKY_SEVEN` for the number 7, `DiceNames.YO_LEVEN` for the number 11 and `DiceNames.BOX_CARS` for the number 12. Notice that you can assign the same value to multiple enumeration constants, as you did in lines 157 and 158.

2. **Declaring instance variables.** Several methods will require the use of the same variables throughout the lifetime of the application. You will declare instance variables for this purpose. Add lines 163–169 of Fig. 16.12 below the enumeration definition.

Good Programming Practice

Use enumerations to group related constants and enhance code readability.

Common Programming Error

An enumeration type can be specified after the enumeration name by using the keyword As followed by Byte, Integer, Long or Short. Enumerations use type Integer if no type is specified. Attempting to create enumeration values of type String, Decimal and Double results in a syntax error.

(cont.)

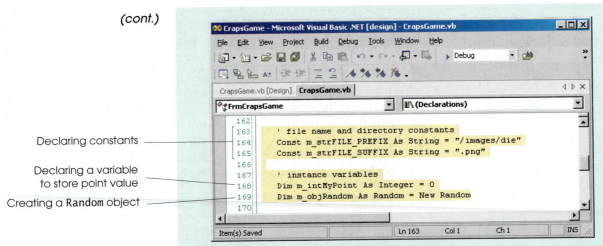

Declaring constants

Declaring a variable
to store point value

Creating a **Random** object

Figure 16.12 Instance variables added to the **Craps Game** application.

In this application, you will need to access images that display the six faces of a die. For convenience, each file has a name that differs only by one number. For example, the image for the die face displaying 1 is named `die1.png`, and the image for the die face displaying 6 is named `die6.png`. Recall that `png` is an image-file name extension that is short for Portable Network Graphic. These images are stored in the folder named `images` in your project's `bin` directory. As such, the `String` `images/die1.png` would correctly indicate the location of the die face displaying 1 relative to the `bin` directory. [*Note*: You also can indicate the location of the die face by using the `String` `images\die1.png`.] To help create a `String` representing the path to the image, `Strings` `m_strFILE_PREFIX` (`images/die`) and `m_strFILE_SUFFIX` (`.png`) are used (as constants) to store the prefix and suffix of the file name (lines 164–165).

The game of Craps requires that you store the user's point, once established on the first roll, for the duration of the game. Therefore, variable `m_intMyPoint` (line 168 of Fig. 16.12) is declared as an `Integer` to store the value of the dice on the first roll. You will use the `Random` object referenced by `m_objRandom` (line 169) to "roll" the dice and generate those values.

3. ***Saving the project.*** Select **File > Save All** to save your modified code.

SELF-REVIEW

1. Use keyword _____ to define groups of related constants.

 a) `ReadOnly`   b) `Enum`

 c) `Constants`   d) `Enumeration`

2. Namespace _____ is used to access files and directories.

 a) `System.File`   b) `System.FileDirectory`

 c) `System.FileAccess`   d) `System.IO`

Answers: 1) b. 2) d.

16.4 Using Random Numbers in the Craps Game Application

Now that you have declared an enumeration and instance variables, you will add code to execute when the user clicks the **Craps Game** application's `Buttons`. The following box explains how to add the code that executes when the user clicks the **Play** `Button`.

Coding the Play Button's Click Event Handler

1. **Creating the Play Button's Click event handler.** Return to the **Design View** to display the Form. Double click the **Play** Button to generate the **Play** Button's Click event handler and view the code file. (The **Play** Button is used to begin a new game of Craps.)

2. **Removing Images from a PictureBox and rolling dice.** Begin coding the Click event handler by adding lines 175–184 from Fig. 16.13 into the btnPlay_Click event handler. Be sure to add the comments and line-continuation characters as shown in Fig. 16.13 so the line numbers in your code match those presented in this tutorial. [*Note*: RollDice() will be underlined in blue because the procedure is not yet defined.]

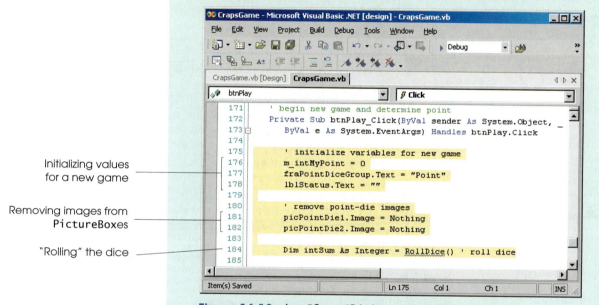

Initializing values for a new game

Removing images from PictureBoxes

"Rolling" the dice

Figure 16.13 btnPlay_Click event handler definition.

Lines 176–178 initialize variables for a new game. Line 176 sets variable m_intMyPoint, the Craps game point value, to 0. Line 177 changes the text displayed on the GroupBox to Point, using the GroupBox's Text property. As you saw in the test-drive, the GroupBox's Text property will be used to display the point value. Finally, line 178 clears the value of the output Label because the user is starting a new game.

Lines 181–182 remove any images from the PictureBoxes used to display the point die. Though there are no images when the application is first run, if the user chooses to continue playing after completing a game, the images from the previous game must be cleared. Setting the Image property to keyword Nothing indicates that there is no image to display. Keyword **Nothing** is used to clear a reference's value, much as the empty string ("") is used to clear a String's value.

Line 184 declares the variable intSum and assigns to it the value returned by rolling the dice. This is accomplished by calling the RollDice procedure, which you will define later in this tutorial. [*Note*: RollDice() will be underlined in blue because the procedure is not yet defined.] The RollDice procedure will not only roll dice and return the sum of their values, but also will display the die images in the lower two PictureBoxes.

(cont.)   3. ***Using a Select Case statement to determine the result of rolling the dice.***
            Recall that if the player rolls 7 or 11 on the first roll, the player wins. However,
            if the player rolls 2, 3 or 12 on the first roll, the player loses. Add lines 186–187
            of Fig. 16.14 to the `btnPlay_Click` event handler beneath the code you added
            in the previous step. Press *Enter*. Notice that the keywords `End Select` are
            auto-generated. Now add lines 189–200 of Fig. 16.14 into the `btnPlay_Click`
            event handler between the `Select` and `End Select` keywords.

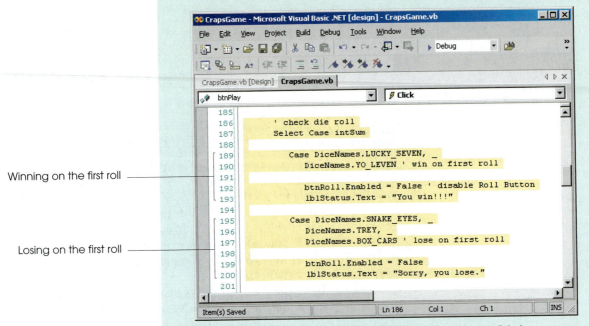

Winning on the first roll

Losing on the first roll

Figure 16.14   `Select Case` statement in `btnPlay_Click`.

The first `Case` statement (lines 189–193) selects values 7 and 11, using the
enumeration values `DiceNames.LUCKY_SEVEN` and `DiceNames.YO_LEVEN`.
Recall that several expressions can be specified in the same `Case` statement
when they are separated by commas. If the sum of the dice is 7 or 11, the
code in lines 192–193 disables the **Roll** Button and displays "`You win!!!`" in
the output Label `lblStatus`. If the dice add up to 2 (`Dice-
Names.SNAKE_EYES`), 3 (`DiceNames.TREY`) or 12 (`DiceNames.BOX_CARS`),
the code in the second `Case` statement executes (lines 195–200). This code
disables the **Roll** Button and displays a message in Label `lblStatus` indicating that the player has lost.

4. ***Using the Case Else statement to continue the game.*** If the player did not
    roll a 2, 3, 7, 11 or 12, then the value of the dice becomes the point and the
    player must roll again. Add lines 202–210 of Fig. 16.15 within the `Select
    Case` statement to implement this rule.
        The first line of the `Case Else` statement's body (line 203) sets the
    instance variable `m_intMyPoint` to the sum of the die values. Next, line 204
    changes the text in the GroupBox, using its `Text` property to display the
    value of the current point. The Label `lblStatus` is changed to notify the
    user to roll again (line 205).

(cont.)

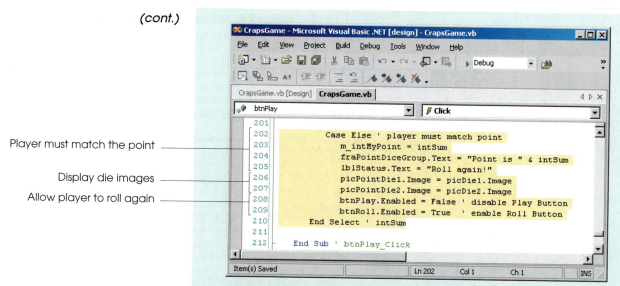

Player must match the point

Display die images

Allow player to roll again

Figure 16.15 `Case Else` statement in `btnPlay_Click`.

If the user must match the point, you display the die images corresponding to the result of the dice roll. In Tutorial 3, you learned how to insert an image into a `PictureBox` in the Windows Form Designer. To set the image for a `PictureBox`, you used its `Image` property. You can also use code to set this property as well. To display the die faces for the point in the Group-Box, you should set the `Image` property of the each `PictureBox` in the GroupBox to the same `Image` property value as its corresponding `Picture-Box` below the GroupBox (lines 206–207). Finally, the **Play** Button is disabled (line 208) and the **Roll** Button is enabled (line 209), limiting users to clicking the **Roll** Button for the rest of the game. Line 210 ends the `Select Case` statement.

5. ***Saving the project.*** Select **File > Save All** to save your modified code.

Because the **Roll** Button is enabled after the user clicks **Play**, you must code an event handler for it. You define the event handler in the following box.

Coding the Roll Button's `Click` Event Handler

1. ***Generating the Roll Button's `Click` event handler.*** Return to design view, and double click the **Roll** Button. This generates the **Roll** Button's `Click` event handler and opens the code window.

2. ***Rolling the dice.*** The user clicks the **Roll** Button to try to match the point, which requires rolling dice. Add line 218 of Fig. 16.16 which will roll the dice, display the die images and store the sum of the dice in variable `intSum`. [*Note:* `RollDice()` is underlined in blue because the procedure is not yet defined. You will define it to roll the dice and display the die images, shortly.]

3. ***Determining the output of the roll.*** If the roll matches the point, the user wins and the game ends. However, if the user rolls a 7 (`DiceNames.CRAPS`), the user loses and the game ends. Add lines 220–229 of Fig. 16.17 into the `btnRoll_Click` event handler to incorporate this processing into your **Craps Game** application.

The `If...Then` statement (lines 221–224) determines whether the sum of the dice in the current roll matches the point. If the sum and point match, the program displays a winning message in Label `lblStatus`. It then allows the user to start a new game, by disabling the **Roll** Button and enabling the **Play** Button.

(cont.)

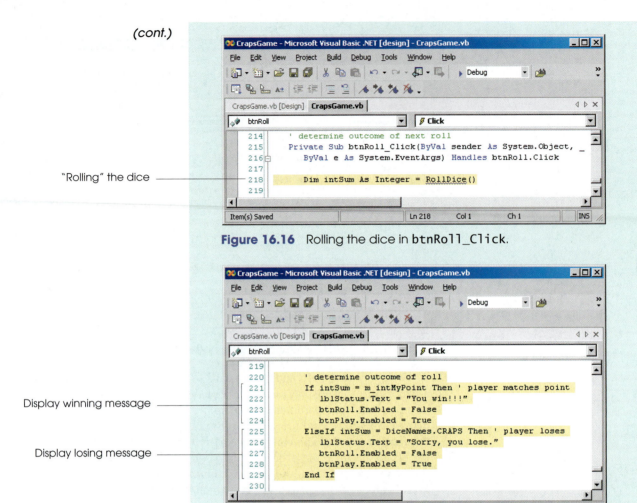

"Rolling" the dice

Figure 16.16   Rolling the dice in `btnRoll_Click`.

Display winning message

Display losing message

Figure 16.17   Determining the outcome of a roll.

The `ElseIf` statement (lines 225–228) determines whether the sum of the dice in the current roll is 7 (`DiceNames.CRAPS`). If so, the application displays a message that the user has lost (in Label `lblStatus`) and ends the game by disabling the **Roll** Button and enabling the **Play** Button. If the player neither matches the point nor rolls a 7, then the player is allowed to roll again. The player rolls the dice again by clicking the **Roll** Button.

4. ***Saving the project.*** Select **File > Save All** to save your modified code.

In the following box, you add code into the application to simulate rolling dice and use code to display the dice in the appropriate `PictureBox`es.

Using Random Numbers to Simulate Rolling Dice

1. ***Creating a Random object and simulating die rolling.*** This application will roll and display dice many times as it executes. Therefore, it is a good idea to create two procedures: one to roll the dice (`RollDice`) and one to display the dice (`DisplayDie`). Define `Function` procedure `RollDice` first, by adding lines 233–246 of Fig. 16.18. [*Note*: The calls to `DisplayDie` will be underlined in blue because the procedure is not yet defined.]

This code sets the values of `intDie1` and `intDie2` to the values returned by `m_objRandom.Next(1, 7)`, which is an `Integer` random number between the values 1 to 6 (lines 237 and 238). Remember that the number returned is always less than the second argument.

(cont.)

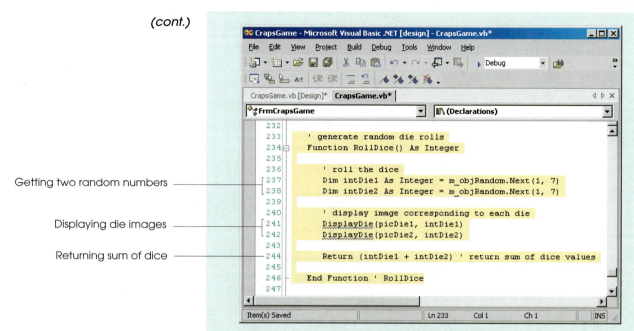

Getting two random numbers

Displaying die images

Returning sum of dice

Figure 16.18 `RollDice` procedure definition.

The procedure then makes two calls to `DisplayDie` (lines 241 and 242), a procedure that displays the image of the die face corresponding to each number. The first parameter in `DisplayDie` is the `PictureBox` that will display the image, and the second parameter is the number that appears on the face of the die. The calls to `DisplayDie` are underlined in blue as syntax errors because the procedure has not yet been defined. You will define the `DisplayDie` procedure in *Step 2*. Finally, the procedure returns the sum of the values of the dice (line 244), which the application uses to determine the outcome of the Craps game.

2. ***Displaying the dice images.*** You will now define procedure `DisplayDie` to display the die images corresponding to the random numbers generated in procedure `RollDice`. Add lines 248–257 of Fig. 16.19 (after the `RollDice` procedure) to create the `DisplayDie` procedure.

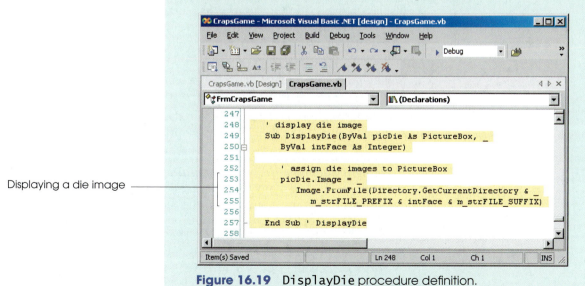

Displaying a die image

Figure 16.19 `DisplayDie` procedure definition.

(cont.)

Line 253 begins the statement that sets the Image property for the specified PictureBox. Because the Image property must be set using an object of type Image, you must create an Image object.

The Image class contains a FromFile method to help create Image objects. **Image.FromFile** returns an Image object containing the image located at the path you specify. To specify the location, use the path (as a String) as the parameter to the FromFile method. In this case, you can begin by using the Directory.GetCurrentDirectory method (line 254). The **Directory.GetCurrentDirectory** method (contained in the System.IO namespace) returns the location of the folder from which your application was loaded (the bin directory). In this case, Directory.GetCurrentDirectory will return the string C:\SimplyVB\CrapsGame\bin.

Now append m_strFILE_PREFIX & intFace & m_strFILE_SUFFIX to create the rest of the location of the file (line 255). If the value of intFace is 1, the expression would represent the string images/die1.png. This is the location of the image of a die face showing 1. If you combine the value of Directory.GetCurrentDirectory with the expression mentioned earlier, the result is C:\SimplyVB\CrapsGame\bin\images\die1.png, the location of the image on your computer. You can use Windows Explorer to verify that this is the correct location. This image is then displayed in the Picture-Box by using its Image property.

3. ***Running the application.*** Select **Debug > Start** to run your completed application and enjoy the game!

4. ***Closing the application.*** Close your running application by clicking its close box.

5. ***Closing the IDE.*** Close Visual Basic .NET by clicking its close box.

Figure 16.20 presents the source code for the **Craps Game** application. The lines of code that contain new programming concepts that you learned in this tutorial are highlighted. Note that, as part of the project settings, Option Strict is set to On (to ensure explicit narrowing conversions).

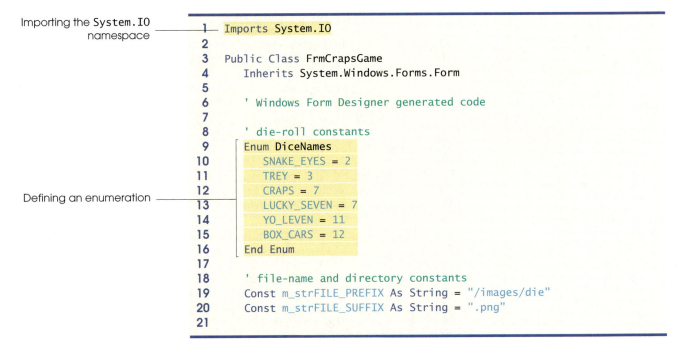

Importing the System.IO namespace

Defining an enumeration

```
1   Imports System.IO
2
3   Public Class FrmCrapsGame
4       Inherits System.Windows.Forms.Form
5
6       ' Windows Form Designer generated code
7
8       ' die-roll constants
9       Enum DiceNames
10          SNAKE_EYES = 2
11          TREY = 3
12          CRAPS = 7
13          LUCKY_SEVEN = 7
14          YO_LEVEN = 11
15          BOX_CARS = 12
16      End Enum
17
18      ' file-name and directory constants
19      Const m_strFILE_PREFIX As String = "/images/die"
20      Const m_strFILE_SUFFIX As String = ".png"
21
```

Figure 16.20   **Craps Game** application code listing. (Part 1 of 3.)

Creating a **Random** object ⎯⎯⎯⎯

```
22      ' instance variables
23      Dim m_intMyPoint As Integer = 0
24      Dim m_objRandomObject As Random = New Random
25
26      ' begin new game and determine point
27      Private Sub btnPlay_Click(ByVal sender As System.Object, _
28         ByVal e As System.EventArgs) Handles btnPlay.Click
29
30         ' initialize variables for new game
31         m_intMyPoint = 0
32         fraPointDiceGroup.Text = "Point"
33         lblStatus.Text = ""
34
35         ' remove point-die images
36         picPointDie1.Image = Nothing
37         picPointDie2.Image = Nothing
38
39         Dim intSum As Integer = RollDice() ' roll dice
40
41         ' check die roll
42         Select Case intSum
43
44            Case DiceNames.LUCKY_SEVEN, _
45               DiceNames.YO_LEVEN ' win on first roll
46
47               btnRoll.Enabled = False ' disable Roll Button
48               lblStatus.Text = "You win!!!"
49
50            Case DiceNames.SNAKE_EYES, _
51               DiceNames.TREY, _
52               DiceNames.BOX_CARS ' lose on first roll
53
54               btnRoll.Enabled = False
55               lblStatus.Text = "Sorry, you lose."
56
57            Case Else ' player must match point
58               m_intMyPoint = intSum
59               fraPointDiceGroup.Text = "Point Is " & intSum
60               lblStatus.Text = "Roll again!"
61               picPointDie1.Image = picDie1.Image
62               picPointDie2.Image = picDie2.Image
63               btnPlay.Enabled = False ' disable Play Button
64               btnRoll.Enabled = True  ' enable Roll Button
65         End Select ' intSum
66
67      End Sub ' btnPlay_Click
68
69      ' determine outcome of next roll
70      Private Sub btnRoll_Click(ByVal sender As System.Object, _
71         ByVal e As System.EventArgs) Handles btnRoll.Click
72
73         Dim intSum As Integer = RollDice()
74
75         ' determine outcome of roll
76         If intSum = m_intMyPoint Then ' player matches point
77            lblStatus.Text = "You win!!!"
78            btnRoll.Enabled = False
79            btnPlay.Enabled = True
80         ElseIf intSum = DiceNames.CRAPS Then ' player loses
```

Figure 16.20 Craps Game application code listing. (Part 2 of 3.)

```
81              lblStatus.Text = "Sorry, you lose."
82              btnRoll.Enabled = False
83              btnPlay.Enabled = True
84          End If
85
86      End Sub ' btnRoll_Click
87
88      ' generate random die rolls
89      Function RollDice() As Integer
90
91          ' roll the dice
92          Dim intDie1 As Integer = m_objRandomObject.Next(1, 7)
93          Dim intDie2 As Integer = m_objRandomObject.Next(1, 7)
94
95          ' display image corresponding to each die
96          DisplayDie(picDie1, intDie1)
97          DisplayDie(picDie2, intDie2)
98
99          Return (intDie1 + intDie2) ' return sum of dice values
100
101     End Function ' RollDice
102
103     ' display die image
104     Sub DisplayDie(ByVal picDie As PictureBox, _
105         ByVal intFace As Integer)
106
107         ' assign die images to PictureBox
108         picDie.Image = _
109             Image.FromFile(Directory.GetCurrentDirectory & _
110                 m_strFILE_PREFIX & intFace & m_strFILE_SUFFIX)
111
112     End Sub ' DisplayDie
113
114 End Class ' FrmCrapsGame
```

Generating random numbers — (lines 92–93)

Using code to display an image — (lines 108–110)

Figure 16.20   Craps Game application code listing. (Part 3 of 3.)

16.5 Wrap-Up

In this tutorial, you created the **Craps Game** application to simulate playing the popular dice game called Craps. You learned about the Random class and how it can be used to generate random numbers by creating a Random object and calling method Next on it. You then learned how to specify the range of values within which random numbers should be generated by passing various arguments to method Next. You were also introduced to enumerations, which enhance program readability by using descriptive identifiers to represent constants in an application.

Using your knowledge of random-number generation and event handlers, you wrote code that added functionality to your **Craps Game** application. You used random-number generation to simulate the element of chance. In addition to "rolling dice" in code, you learned how to use a `PictureBox` to display an image by using code. You used the `System.IO` namespace to help access images located in a file.

In the next tutorial, you will learn how to use arrays, which allow you to use one name to store many values. You will apply your knowledge of random numbers and arrays to create a **Flag Tutor** application that tests your knowledge of various nations' flags.

SKILLS SUMMARY

Generating Random Numbers

■ Create an object of class Random, and call this object's `Next` method. Use an argument to specify the maximum value for the random numbers.

Generating Random Numbers within a Specified Range

■ Call the Random class's `Next` method with two arguments. The first argument represents the minimum possible value; the second argument represents one more than the maximum possible desired value.

Declaring Enumerations

■ Begin an enumeration with keyword Enum; then use a list of descriptive names, and set each one to the value that you want it to represent. End the enumeration with keywords `End Enum`.

KEY TERMS

Directory.GetCurrentDirectory—A method of class `Directory` in the `System.IO` namespace that returns a `String` containing the path to the directory that contains the application.

End Enum keyword—Ends an enumeration.

Enum keyword—Begins an enumeration.

enumeration—A group of related, named constants.

Image.FromFile—A method of class `Image` that returns an `Image` object containing the image located at the path you specify.

Imports keyword—Used to import namespaces.

Int32.MaxValue constant—The largest possible `Integer`—more specifically, 2,147,483,647.

namespace—A group of related classes in the Framework Class Library.

Next method of class Random—A method of class `Random` that, when called with no arguments, generates a positive `Integer` value between zero and the constant `Int32.MaxValue`.

NextDouble method of class Random—A method of class `Random` that generates a positive `Double` value that is greater than or equal to 0.0 and less than 1.0.

Nothing keyword—Used to clear a reference's value.

pseudorandom numbers—A sequence of values produced by a complex mathematical calculation that simulates random-number generation.

Random class—Contains methods to generate pseudorandom numbers.

reference—A variable to which you assign an object.

System.IO namespace—Contains methods to access files and directories.

CONTROLS, EVENTS, PROPERTIES & METHODS

Directory This class provides functionality to manipulate directories such as creating, moving, and navigating through them.

■ *Method*

   `GetCurrentDirectory`—Returns the location of the folder from which the application was loaded.

Image This class provides functionality to manipulate images.

■ *Method*

   `FromFile`—Used to specify the physical location (path) of the image.

Random This class is used to generate random numbers.

- **Methods**
    Next—When called with no arguments, generates a positive Integer value between zero and the largest possible Integer, which is the constant Int32.MaxValue (2,147,483,647).
    NextDouble—Generates a positive Double value that is greater than or equal to 0.0 and less than 1.0.

MULTIPLE-CHOICE QUESTIONS

16.1 A Random object can generate pseudorandom numbers of type _____.

a) Integer   b) Single
c) Double   d) Both a and c.

16.2 A _____ is a group of related classes in the Framework Class Library.

a) classspace   b) directory
c) namespace   d) library

16.3 Object variable names should be prefixed with _____.

a) var   b) obj
c) ran   d) ojt

16.4 The Next method of class Random can be called using _____.

a) one argument   b) no arguments
c) two arguments   d) All of the above.

16.5 The statement _____ assigns intValue a random number in the range from 5 to 20.

a) intValue = objRandom.Next(5, 21)   b) intValue = objRandom.Next(4, 20)
c) intValue = objRandom.Next(5, 20)   d) intValue = objRandom.Next(4, 21)

16.6 The _____ method specifies the file from which an image is loaded.

a) Next in class Random   b) FromFile in class Image
c) GetCurrentDirectory in class   d) None of the above.
   Directory

16.7 The System.IO namespace contains classes and methods to _____.

a) access files and directories   b) display graphics in an application
c) insert multimedia into an application d) All of the above.

16.8 The values returned by the _____ method of class Random are actually pseudorandom numbers.

a) NextRandom   b) Pseudorandom
c) Next   d) Pseudo

16.9 When creating random numbers, the second argument passed to the Next method is _____.

a) equal to the maximum value you wish to be generated
b) equal to one more than the maximum value you wish to be generated
c) equal to one less than the maximum value you wish to be generated
d) equal to the minimum value you wish to be generated

16.10 A(n) _____ is a group of related, named constants.

a) namespace   b) variable
c) enumeration   d) None of the above.

EXERCISES

16.11 (*Guess the Number Application*) Develop an application that generates a random number and prompts the user to guess the number (Fig. 16.21). When the user clicks the **New Game** Button, the application chooses a number in the range 1 to 100 at random. The user enters guesses into the **Guess:** TextBox and clicks the **Enter** Button. If the guess is correct, the game ends, and the user can start a new game. If the guess is not correct, the application should indicate if the guess is higher or lower than the correct number.

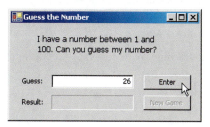 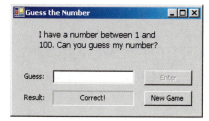

Figure 16.21 **Guess the Number** application.

a) *Copying the template to your working directory.* Copy the directory C:\Examples\ Tutorial16\Exercises\GuessNumber to your C:\SimplyVB directory.

b) *Opening the application's template file.* Double click GuessNumber.sln in the GuessNumber directory to open the application (Fig. 16.21).

c) *Creating a Random object.* Create two instance variables. The first variable should store a Random object and the second variable should store a random-generated number.

d) *Adding a Click event handler for the Enter Button.* Add a Click event handler for the **Enter** Button that retrieves the value entered by the user and compares that value to the random-generated number. If the guess is correct, display **Correct!** in the output Label. Then disable the **Enter** Button and enable the **New Game** Button. If the user's guess is higher than the correct answer, display **Too high...** in the output Label. If the user's guess is lower than the correct answer, display **Too low...** in the output Label.

e) *Adding a Click event handler for the New Game Button.* Add a Click event handler for the **New Game** Button that generates a new random number for the instance variable. The event handler should then disable the **New Game** Button, enable the **Enter** Button and clear the **Result:** TextBox.

f) *Running the application.* Select **Debug > Start** to run your application. Enter guesses (clicking the **Enter** Button after each) until you have successfully determined the answer. Click the **New Game** Button and test the application again.

g) *Closing the application.* Close your running application by clicking its close box.

h) *Closing the IDE.* Close Visual Studio .NET by clicking its close box.

16.12 (*Dice Simulator Application*) Develop an application that simulates rolling two six-sided dice. Your application should have a **Roll** Button that, when clicked, displays two dice images corresponding to random numbers. It should also display the number of times each face has appeared. Your application should appear similar to Fig. 16.22.

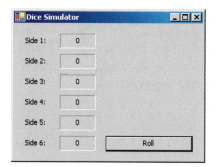 

Figure 16.22 **Dice Simulator** application.

a) *Copying the template to your working directory.* Copy the directory C:\Examples\ Tutorial16\Exercises\DiceSimulator to your C:\SimplyVB directory.

b) *Opening the application's template file.* Double click DiceSimulator.sln in the DiceSimulator directory to open the application.

c) *Displaying the die image.* Create a Sub procedure named DisplayDie that takes a PictureBox control as an argument. This method should generate a random number to simulate a die roll. Then display the die image in the corresponding PictureBox control on the Form. The die image should correspond to the random number that was generated. To set the image, refer to the code presented in Fig. 16.20.

d) *Adding a Click event handler for the Roll Button.* Add a Click event handler for the **Roll** Button. Call method DisplayDie in this event handler to display the images for both dice.

e) *Displaying the frequency.* Add a Sub procedure called DisplayFrequency that uses a Select Case statement to update the number of times each face has appeared. Create an enumeration for the dice faces which will be used in the Select Case statement.

f) *Running the application.* Select **Debug > Start** to run your application. Click the **Roll** Button several times. Each time, two die faces should be displayed at random. Verify after each roll that the appropriate face values on the left are incremented.

g) *Closing the application.* Close your running application by clicking its close box.

h) *Closing the IDE.* Close Visual Studio .NET by clicking its close box.

16.13 (*Lottery Picker Application*) A lottery commission offers four different lottery games to play: Three-number, Four-number, Five-number and Five-number + 1 lotteries. Each game has independent numbers. Develop an application that randomly picks numbers for all four games and displays the generated numbers in a GUI (Fig. 16.23). The games are played as follows:

- Three-number lotteries require players to choose three numbers in the range of 0–9.
- Four-number lotteries require players to choose four numbers, in the range of 0–9.
- Five-number lotteries require players to choose five numbers in the range of 1–39.
- Five-number + 1 lotteries require players to choose five numbers in the range of 1–49 and an additional number in the range of 1–42.

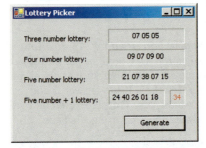

Figure 16.23 **Lottery Picker** application.

a) *Copying the template to your working directory.* Copy the directory C:\Examples\ Tutorial16\Exercises\LotteryPicker to your C:\SimplyVB directory.

b) *Opening the application's template file.* Double click LotteryPicker.sln in the LotteryPicker directory to open the application.

c) *Generating random numbers.* Create a Function procedure that will generate the random numbers for all four games.

d) *Drawing numbers for the games.* Add code into your application to generate numbers for all four games. To make the applications simple, allow repetition of numbers.

e) *Running the application.* Select **Debug > Start** to run your application. Click the **Generate** Button multiple times. Make sure the values displayed are within the ranges described in the exercise description.

f) *Closing the application.* Close your running application by clicking its close box.

g) *Closing the IDE.* Close Visual Studio .NET by clicking its close box.

What does this code do? **16.14** What does the following code do?

```
 1  Sub PickRandomNumbers()
 2
 3      Dim intNumber1 As Integer
 4      Dim dblNumber As Double
 5      Dim intNumber2 As Integer
 6      Dim objRandom As Random = New Random
 7
 8      intNumber1 = objRandom.Next()
 9      dblNumber = 5 * objRandom.NextDouble()
10      intNumber2 = objRandom.Next(1, 10)
11      lblInteger1.Text = Convert.ToString(intNumber1)
12      lblDouble1.Text = Convert.ToString(dblNumber)
13      lblInteger2.Text = Convert.ToString(intNumber2)
14  End Sub ' PickRandomNumbers
```

What's wrong with this code? **16.15** This Sub procedure should assign a random Decimal number (in the range 0 to Int32.MaxValue) to Decimal decNumber. (Assume that Option Strict is On.) Find the error(s) in the following code.

```
 1  Sub RandomDecimal()
 2
 3      Dim decNumber As Decimal
 4      Dim objRandom As Random = New Random
 5
 6      decNumber = objRandom.Next()
 7      lblDisplay.Text = Convert.ToString(decNumber)
 8
 9  End Sub ' RandomDecimal
```

Programming Challenge ▶ **16.16** (*Multiplication Teacher Application*) Develop an application that helps children learn multiplication. Use random-number generation to produce two positive one-digit integers that display in a question, such as "How much is 6 times 7?" The student should type the answer into a TextBox. If the answer is correct, then the application randomly displays one of three messages: **Very Good!**, **Excellent!** or **Great Job!** in a Label and displays the next question. If the student is wrong, the Label displays the message **No. Please try again.**

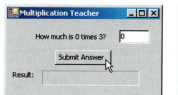 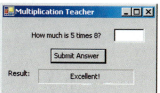

Figure 16.24 Multiplication Teacher application.

a) *Copying the template to your working directory.* Copy the directory C:\Examples\ Tutorial16\Exercises\MultiplicationTeacher to your C:\SimplyVB directory.

b) *Opening the application's template file.* Double click MultiplicationTeacher.sln in the MultiplicationTeacher directory to open the application.

c) *Generating the questions.* Add a method into your application (Fig. 16.24) to generate each new question.

d) *Determining whether the right answer was entered.* Add code into your application to call the method created in the previous step. After this method has been called, determine whether the student answered the question correctly, and display the appropriate message.

e) *Displaying a random message.* Add a procedure GenerateOutput that displays a random message congratulating the student for answering correctly. This method should be called if the student answered the question correctly.

f) *Running the application.* Select **Debug > Start** to run your application. Enter several correct answers and at least one incorrect answer. Verify that **No. Please try again** is displayed when you are incorrect, and one of the other responses is displayed at random when you are correct.

g) *Closing the application.* Close your running application by clicking its close box.

h) *Closing the IDE.* Close Visual Studio .NET by clicking its close box.

Objectives

In this tutorial, you will learn to:
- Create and initialize arrays.
- Store information in an array.
- Refer to individual elements of an array.
- Sort arrays.
- Use ComboBoxes to display options in a drop-down list.
- Determine whether a specific character is in a String.
- Remove a character from a String.
- Convert a String to lowercase characters.

Outline

Flag Quiz Application

Introducing One-Dimensional Arrays and ComboBoxes

This tutorial introduces basic concepts and features of **data structures**. Data structures group together and organize related data. **Arrays** are data structures that consist of data items of the same type. You will learn how to create arrays and how to access the information that they contain. You also will learn how to sort a String array's information alphabetically.

This tutorial's **Flag Quiz** application also includes a ComboBox control. A ComboBox presents user options in a drop-down list. This will be the first time that you will add a ComboBox to an application, but you have used them many times before in the Visual Studio .NET environment. For example, when you activated Option Strict in Tutorial 15, you selected On from a ComboBox.

17.1 Test-Driving the Flag Quiz Application

You will now create an application that tests a student's knowledge of the flags of various countries. The application will use arrays to store information, such as the country names and Boolean values that determine if a country name has been previously selected by the application as a correct answer. This application must meet the following requirements:

> ### Application Requirements
>
> *A geography teacher would like to quiz students on their knowledge of the flags of various countries. The teacher has asked you to write an application that displays a flag and allows the student to select the corresponding country from a list. The application should inform the user of whether the answer is correct and display the next flag. The application should display five flags randomly chosen from the flags of Australia, Brazil, China, Italy, Russia, South Africa, Spain and the United States. When the application is run, a given flag should be displayed only once.*

You begin by test-driving the completed application. Then, you will learn the additional Visual Basic .NET technologies that you will need to create your own version of this application.

Test-Driving the Flag Quiz Application

1. **Opening the completed application.** Open the directory C:\Examples\ Tutorial17\CompletedApplication\FlagQuiz to locate the **Flag Quiz** application. Double click FlagQuiz.sln to open the application in Visual Studio .NET.

2. **Running the Flag Quiz application.** Select **Debug > Start** to run the application (Fig. 17.1). Note that you might see a different flag when you run the application, because the application randomly selects which flag to display.

PictureBox displays flag ———

ComboBox contains answers (country names)

Figure 17.1 **Flag Quiz** application's Form.

3. **Selecting an answer.** The ComboBox contains eight country names. One country name corresponds to the displayed flag and is the correct answer. The scrollbar allows you to browse through the ComboBox's drop-down list. Select an answer from the ComboBox, as shown in Fig. 17.2.

Answer being selected ———

Scrollbar in ComboBox's drop-down list

Figure 17.2 Selecting an answer from the ComboBox.

4. **Submitting a correct answer.** Click the **Submit** Button to check your answer. If it is correct, the message "Correct!" is displayed in an output Label (Fig. 17.3). Notice that the **Submit** Button is now disabled and that the **Next Flag** Button is enabled.

Figure 17.3 Submitting the correct answer.

5. **Displaying the next flag.** Click the **Next Flag** Button to display a different flag (Fig. 17.4). Notice that the **Submit** Button is now enabled, the **Next Flag** Button is disabled, the ComboBox displays **Australia** (the first country listed in the ComboBox) and the output Label is cleared.

Figure 17.4 Displaying the next flag.

(cont.)

6. ***Submitting an incorrect answer.*** To demonstrate the application's response, select an incorrect answer and click **Submit** as in Fig. 17.5. The application displays "Sorry, incorrect." in the output Label.

Figure 17.5 Submitting an incorrect answer.

7. ***Finishing the quiz.*** After the application displays five flags and the user has submitted five answers, the quiz ends (Fig. 17.6). Notice that the two Buttons and the ComboBox are disabled.

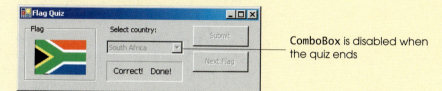

ComboBox is disabled when the quiz ends

Figure 17.6 Finishing the quiz.

8. ***Closing the application.*** Close your running application by clicking its close box.

9. ***Closing the IDE.*** Close Visual Studio .NET by clicking its close box.

17.2 Introducing Arrays

An array is a group of memory locations all containing data items of the same name and type. Array names follow the same conventions that apply to other identifiers. To refer to a particular location in an array, you specify the name of the array and the **position number** of the location, which is a value that indicates a specific location within an array. Position numbers begin at 0 (zero).

Figure 17.7 depicts an Integer array named intNetUnitsSold. This array contains 13 items, also called **elements**. Each array element represents the net number of "units sold" of a particular book in one month at a bookstore. For example, intNetUnitsSold(1) is the net sales of that book for January (month 1), intNet-UnitsSold(2) is the net sales for February, etc. In this example, you simply ignore the first element of the array, because there is no month zero.

Each array element is referred to by providing the name of the array followed by the position number of the element in parentheses (). The position numbers for the elements in an array begin with 0. Thus, the **zeroth element** of array intNet-UnitsSold is referred to as intNetUnitsSold(0), element 1 of array intNet-UnitsSold is referred to as intNetUnitsSold(1), element 6 of array intNetUnitsSold is referred to as intNetUnitsSold(6) and so on. Element *i* of array intNetUnitsSold is referred to as intNetUnitsSold(i). The position number in parentheses is called an **index** or a **subscript**. An index must be either zero, a positive integer or an integer expression that yields a positive result. If an application uses an expression as an index, the expression is evaluated first to determine the index. For example, if variable intValue1 is equal to 5, and variable intValue2 is equal to 6, then the statement

```
intNetUnitsSold(intValue1 + intValue2) += 2
```

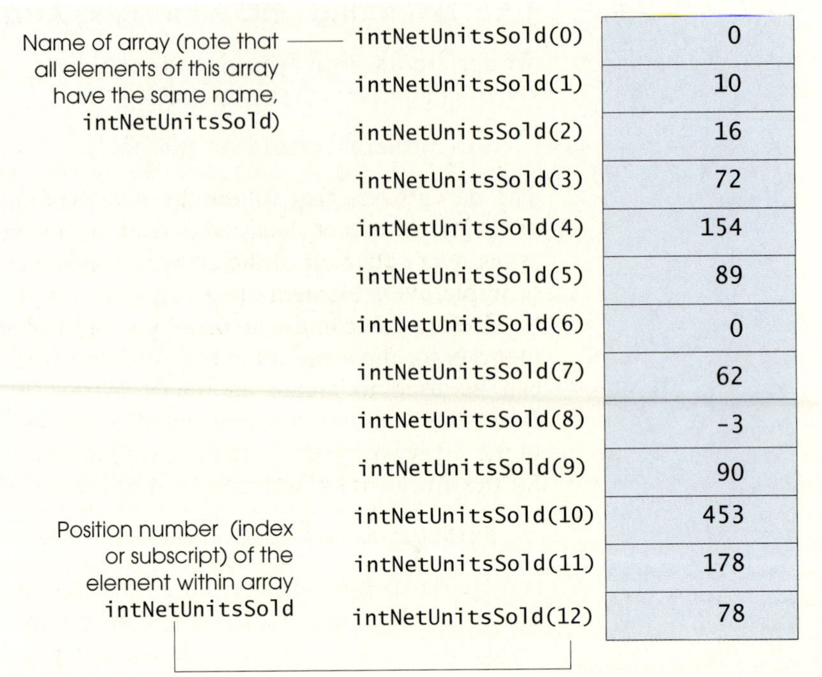

Figure 17.7   Array consisting of 13 elements.

adds 2 to array element `intNetUnitsSold(11)`. Note that an **indexed array name** (the array name followed by an index enclosed in parentheses)—like any other variable name—can be used on the left side of an assignment statement to place a new value into an array element.

Let's examine array `intNetUnitsSold` in Fig. 17.7 more closely. The **name** of the array is `intNetUnitsSold`. The 13 elements of the array are referred to as `intNetUnitsSold(0)` through `intNetUnitsSold(12)`. The **value** of `intNetUnitsSold(1)` is 10, the value of `intNetUnitsSold(2)` is 16, the value of `intNetUnitsSold(3)` is 72, the value of `intNetUnitsSold(7)` is 62 and the value of `intNetUnitsSold(11)` is 178. A positive value for an element in this array indicates that more books were sold than were returned. A negative value for an element in this array indicates that more books were returned than were sold. A value of zero indicates that the number of books sold was equal to the number of books returned.

Values stored in arrays can be used in various calculations and applications. For example, to determine the net units sold in the first three months of the year, then store the result in variable `intFirstQuarterUnits`, we would write

```
intFirstQuarterUnits = intNetUnitsSold(1) + intNetUnitsSold(2) + _
    intNetUnitsSold(3)
```

You will deal exclusively with **one-dimensional** arrays, such as `intNetUnitsSold`, in this tutorial. The indexed array names of one-dimensional arrays use only one index. In the next tutorial, you will study two-dimensional arrays; their indexed array names use two indices.

SELF-REVIEW   1. The number that refers to a particular element of an array is called its _____.

a) value   b) size

c) indexed array name   d) index (or subscript)

2. The indexed array name of one-dimensional array `decUnits`'s element 2 is _____.

a) `decUnits{2}`   b) `decUnits(2)`

c) `decUnits[0,2]`   d) `decUnits[2]`

Answers: 1) d. 2) b.

17.3 Declaring and Allocating Arrays

To declare an array, you provide the array's name and data type. The following statement declares the array in Fig. 17.7:

```
Dim intNetUnitsSold As Integer()
```

The parentheses that follow the data type indicate that `intNetUnitsSold` is an array. Arrays can be declared to contain any data type. In an array of primitive data types, every element of the array contains one value of the declared data type. For example, every element of an `Integer` array contains an `Integer` value.

Before you can use an array, you must specify the size of the array and allocate memory for the array, using keyword `New`. Recall from Tutorial 15 that keyword `New` can be used to create an object. Arrays are represented as objects in Visual Basic .NET, so they, too, must be allocated by using keyword `New`. The value stored in the array variable is actually a reference to the array object. To allocate memory for the array `intNetUnitsSold` after it has been declared, the statement

```
intNetUnitsSold = New Integer(12) {}
```

is used. **Array bounds** determine what indices can be used to access an element in the array. Here, the array bounds are 0 (which is implicit in the preceding statement) and 12 (one less than the number of elements in the array). Notice that because of array element 0, the actual number of elements in the array (13) is one larger than the upper bound specified in the allocation (12).

The required braces ({ and }) are called an **initializer list** and specify the initial values of the elements in the array. When the initializer list is empty, as it is here, the elements in the array are initialized to the default value for the array's data type. Again, these default values are 0 for numeric primitive-data-type variables (such as `Integer`), `False` for `Boolean` variables and `Nothing` for references. Recall that keyword `Nothing` denotes an empty reference (that is, a value indicating that a reference variable has not been assigned an object). The initializer list also can contain a comma-separated list specifying the initial values of the elements in the array. For example,

```
Dim intSalesPerDay As Integer()
intSalesPerDay = New Integer() {0, 2, 3, 6, 1, 4, 5, 6}
```

declares and allocates an array containing eight `Integer` values. Visual Basic .NET can determine the array bounds from the number of elements in the initializer list. Thus, it is not necessary to specify the size of the array when a nonempty initializer list is present.

You can specify both the upper bound and an initializer list, as in the following statement:

```
Dim dblTemperatures As Double() = _
    New Double(3) {23.45, 34.98, 78.98, 53.23}
```

Notice that the upper bound is one less than the number of items in the array.

Often, the elements of an array are used in a calculation. The following box demonstrates declaring and initializing an array and accessing the array's elements.

Common Programming Error

Attempting to access elements in the array by using an index outside the array bounds is a run-time error.

Common Programming Error

If you specify an upper bound when initializing an array, it is a syntax error if you provide too many or too few values.

Computing the Sum of an Array's Elements

1. ***Copying the template to your working directory.*** Copy the `C:\Examples\Tutorial17\TemplateApplication\SumArray` directory to your `C:\SimplyVB` directory.

2. ***Opening the Sum Array application's template file.*** Double click `SumArray.sln` in the `SumArray` directory to open the application in Visual Studio .NET.

(cont.)   3.   ***Adding the Button's Click event handler.*** Double click the **Sum Array** Button in design view (Fig. 17.8) to generate the empty event handler btnSum_Click (Fig. 17.8).

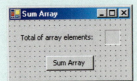

Figure 17.8   **Sum Array** application's **Form** in design view.

4.   ***Combining the declaration and allocation of an array.*** Add lines 86–91 of Fig. 17.9 to the event handler. Lines 87–88 combine the declaration and allocation of an array into one statement.

Creating an array of Integers —

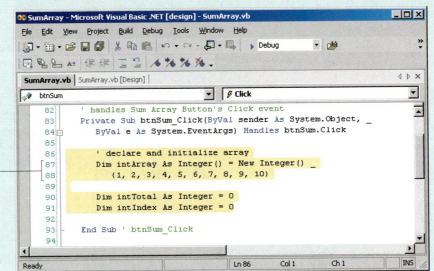

Figure 17.9   Declaring an array in the event handler.

5.   ***Calculating the sum.*** Add lines 93–100 (Fig. 17.10) to the event handler. The For...Next loop (lines 94–98) retrieves each element's value (one at a time), which is added to intTotal. Method **GetUpperBound** returns the index of the last element in the array. Method GetUpperBound takes one argument, indicating a dimension of the array. We discuss arrays with two dimensions in Tutorial 18. For one-dimensional arrays, such as intArray, the argument passed to GetUpperBound is always 0, to indicate the first (and only) dimension (or row) of the array. In this case,

```
intArray.GetUpperBound(0)
```

returns 9.

Every array in Visual Basic .NET "knows" its own length. The **length** (or the number of elements) of the array (10 in this case) is returned by the following expression:

```
intArray.Length
```

We could have set the upper bound in the For...Next loop as

```
intArray.Length - 1
```

which returns 9. The value returned by method GetUpperBound is one less than the value of the array's **Length** property.

Error-Prevention Tip

Use method GetUpperBound when you need to find the largest index in an array. Using an actual numerical value for the upper bound instead could lead to errors if you change the number of array elements.

(cont.)

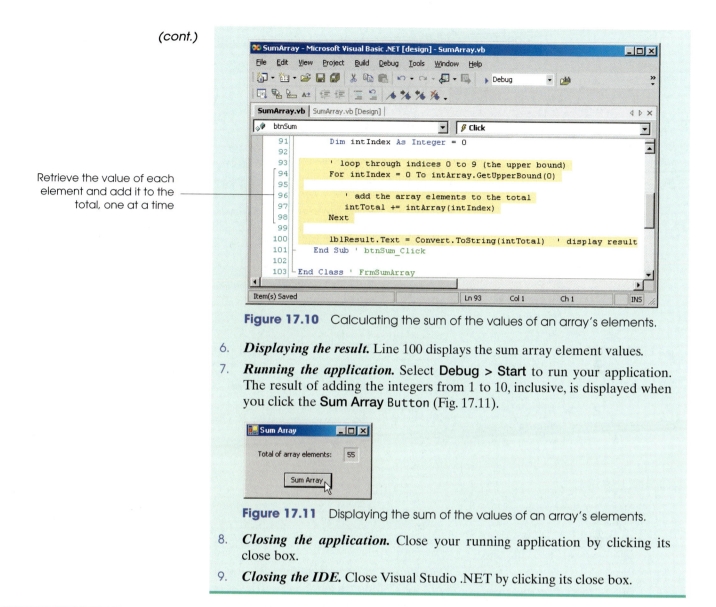

Retrieve the value of each element and add it to the total, one at a time

Figure 17.10   Calculating the sum of the values of an array's elements.

6. ***Displaying the result.*** Line 100 displays the sum array element values.

7. ***Running the application.*** Select **Debug > Start** to run your application. The result of adding the integers from 1 to 10, inclusive, is displayed when you click the **Sum Array** Button (Fig. 17.11).

Figure 17.11   Displaying the sum of the values of an array's elements.

8. ***Closing the application.*** Close your running application by clicking its close box.

9. ***Closing the IDE.*** Close Visual Studio .NET by clicking its close box.

SELF-REVIEW

1. Arrays can be allocated using keyword _____.

   a) `Declare`   b) `Create`

   c) `New`   d) `Allocate`

2. An array's length is _____.

   a) one more than the array's last index   b) one less than the array's last index

   c) the same as the array's last index   d) returned by method `GetUpperBound`

Answers: 1) c. 2) a.

17.4 Constructing the Flag Quiz Application

Before you can begin building the **Flag Quiz** application, you will need to develop the application, using pseudocode and an ACE table. The following pseudocode describes the basic operation of the **Flag Quiz** application:

    When the Form loads:
        Sort the country names alphabetically
        Place country names in the ComboBox
        Randomly select a flag
        Display the flag

When the user clicks the Submit Button:
    Retrieve the selected country name from the ComboBox

    If the selected value matches the correct answer
        Display "Correct!" in the Label
    Else
        Display "Sorry, incorrect." in the Label

    If five images have been displayed
        Append "Done!" to the Label's text
        Disable the Buttons and ComboBox
    Else
        Disable Submit Button
        Enable Next Flag Button

When the user clicks the Next Flag Button:
    Randomly select a flag that has not been chosen previously
    Display the new flag
    Clear the Label's text
    Set ComboBox to display its first item
    Update the number of flags shown
    Enable Submit Button
    Disable Next Flag Button

Now that you have test-driven the **Flag Quiz** application and studied its pseudocode representation, you will use an ACE table to help you convert the pseudocode to Visual Basic .NET. Figure 17.12 lists the actions, controls and events that will help you complete your own version of this application.

Action/Control/Event (ACE) Table for the Flag Quiz Application

Action	Control/Class/Object	Event
Label the application's controls	`fraFlagGroupBox`, `lblChoose`	
	`FrmFlagQuiz`	Load
Sort the countries alphabetically	`Array`	
Place countries in the ComboBox	`cboOptions`	
Randomly select a flag	`objRandom`	
Display the flag	`picFlag`	
	`btnSubmit`	Click
Retrieve the selected country	`cboOptions`	
If selected value matches the correct answer Display "Correct!" in the Label	`lblFeedback`	
Else Display "Sorry, incorrect." in Label	`lblFeedback`	
If five images have been displayed Append "Done!" to Label's text	`lblFeedback`	
Disable the Buttons and ComboBox	`btnNext`, `btnSubmit`, `cboOptions`	
Else Disable Submit Button	`btnSubmit`	
Enable Next Flag Button	`btnNext`	

Figure 17.12 **Flag Quiz** application's ACE table. (Part 1 of 2.)

Action	Control/Class/Object	Event
	btnNext	Click
Randomly select a flag that has not been chosen previously	objRandom	
Display the new flag	picFlag	
Clear the Label's text	lblFeedback	
Set ComboBox to display first item	cboOptions	
Update the number of flags shown		
Enable Submit Button	btnSubmit	
Disable Next Flag Button	btnNext	

Figure 17.12 **Flag Quiz** application's ACE table. (Part 2 of 2.)

The following box shows you how to initialize the variables used in the application. In particular, the application requires two one-dimensional arrays.

Initializing Important Variables

1. *Copying the template to your working directory.* Copy the C:\Examples\ Tutorial17\TemplateApplication\FlagQuiz directory to your C:\SimplyVB directory.

2. *Opening the Flag Quiz application's template file.* Double click FlagQuiz.sln in the FlagQuiz directory to open the application in Visual Studio .NET.

3. *Declaring the array of country names.* Add lines 4–7 of Fig. 17.13 to the application. Lines 5–7 declare and initialize array m_strOptions. Each element is a String containing the name of a country. These lines assign the initializer list to the array, combining the declaration and initialization into one statement. The compiler allocates the size of the array (in this case, eight elements) to suit the number of items in the initializer list.

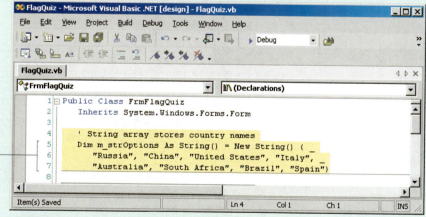

Creating an array of Strings to store country names

Figure 17.13 **String** array that stores country names.

4. *Creating a Boolean array.* The application should not display any flag more than once. The application uses random-number generation to pick a flag, so the same flag could be selected more than once—just as, when you roll a six-sided die many times, a die face could be repeated. You will use a Boolean array to keep track of which flags have been displayed. Add lines 9–11 of Fig. 17.14 to FlagQuiz.vb. Lines 10–11 declare and create Boolean array m_blnUsed.

(cont.)

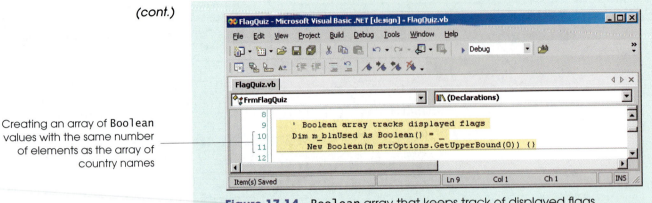

Creating an array of `Boolean` values with the same number of elements as the array of country names

Figure 17.14 `Boolean` array that keeps track of displayed flags.

Method `GetUpperBound` returns array `m_strOptions`'s largest index, which is used as the upper bound of `m_blnUsed`. Therefore, array `m_blnUsed` has the same size as `m_strOptions`. The elements of `m_blnUsed` correspond to the elements of `m_strOptions`; for example, `m_blnUsed( 0 )` specifies whether the flag corresponding to the country name of `m_strOptions( 0 )` (Russia) has been displayed. Recall that, by default, each uninitialized element in a `Boolean` array is `False`. The application will set an element of `m_blnUsed` to `True` if its corresponding flag has been displayed.

5. ***Initializing a counter and a variable to store the answer.*** Add lines 13–14 of Fig. 17.15 to `FlagQuiz.vb`. The application ensures that only five flags are displayed by incrementing counter `m_intCount`, which is initialized to 1 (line 13). The correct answer (the name of the country whose flag is displayed) will be stored in `m_strCountry` (line 14).

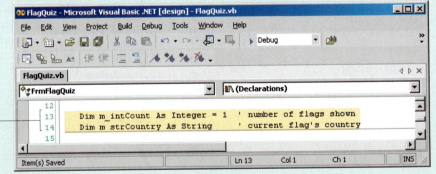

Creating instance variables

Figure 17.15 Instance variables, used throughout the application.

6. ***Saving the project.*** Select **File > Save All** to save your modified code.

GUI Design Tip

Each **ComboBox** should have a descriptive **Label** that describes the **ComboBox**'s contents.

Now you will add another control to the **Flag Quiz** application template. The **Flag Quiz** application allows students to select answers from a **ComboBox**. The ComboBox control combines a `TextBox` and a `ListBox`. A ComboBox usually appears as a `TextBox` with a down arrow to its right. The user can click the down arrow to display a list of predefined items. If a user chooses an item from this list, that item is displayed in the ComboBox. If the list contains more items than the drop-down list can display at one time, a vertical scrollbar appears. The following box shows you how to assign an array's elements to a ComboBox before the `Form` is displayed to users.

Adding and Customizing a ComboBox

1. **Adding a ComboBox to the Form.** Double click FlagQuiz.vb in the **Solution Explorer** to display the application's Form (Fig. 17.16). Add a ComboBox to the Form by double clicking the

control in the **Toolbox**.

Figure 17.16 Flag Quiz template application's Form.

2. **Customizing the ComboBox.** Change the Name property of the ComboBox to cboOptions. Clear the ComboBox's Text property, and set the Location property to 136, 32. Leave the Size property at its default setting, 121, 21. The Form should look like Fig. 17.17.

Figure 17.17 ComboBox added to **Flag Quiz** application's Form.

Good Programming Practice

Prefix ComboBox control names with cbo.

GUI Design Tip

If a ComboBox's content should not be editable, set its DropDownStyle property to DropDownList.

3. **Setting the appearance of ComboBox.** Property **DropDownStyle** determines the ComboBox's appearance. Value **DropDownList** specifies that the ComboBox is not editable (the user cannot type text in its TextBox portion). You can click the arrow button to display a drop-down list from which you can select an item. In this style of ComboBox, if you press the key that corresponds to the first letter of an item in the ComboBox, that item is selected and displayed in the ComboBox's TextBox portion. Set the DropDownStyle property of the ComboBox to DropDownList. Finally, set the **MaxDropDownItems** property of cboOptions to 4, so that the drop-down list can display a maximum of four items at one time. A vertical scrollbar will be added to the drop-down list, to allow users to select the remaining items.

4. **Generating an event handler to add items to the ComboBox during the Load event.** The ComboBox should contain a list of country names when the Form is displayed. The Form's Load event occurs before the Form is displayed; as a result, you should add the items to the ComboBox in the Form's Load event handler. Double click the Form to generate the empty event handler FrmFlagQuiz_Load.

5. **Displaying items in the ComboBox.** Add lines 148–149 of Fig. 17.18 to the FrmFlagQuiz_Load. ComboBox property **DataSource** specifies the source of the items displayed in the ComboBox. In this case, the source is array m_strOptions (discussed shortly).

6. **Saving the project.** Select **File > Save All** to save your modified code.

(cont.)

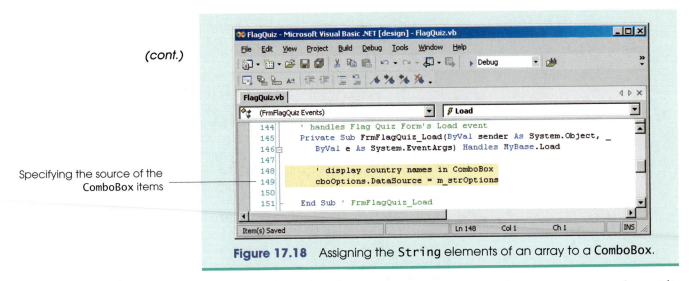

Specifying the source of the ComboBox items

Figure 17.18   Assigning the `String` elements of an array to a `ComboBox`.

Recall that, to specify the image displayed in a `PictureBox`, you need to set its `Image` property to the image's file name. The flag images are stored in `C:\SimplyVB\FlagQuiz\bin\images`. The name of each flag-image file is of the form *countryname*`.png`, where *countryname* has no whitespace. The following box shows how the application constructs the full path name needed to locate and display each flag.

Building a Flag-Image File's Path Name

1. **Creating a procedure to build the flag-image file's path name.** Add lines 153–157 of Fig. 17.19 to the **Flag Quiz** application after event handler `FrmFlagQuiz_Load`. Procedure `BuildPathName` constructs a full path name for a flag-image file, beginning with the country name. The country name is retrieved from instance variable `m_strCountry` (the correct answer) and stored in local variable `strOutput`.

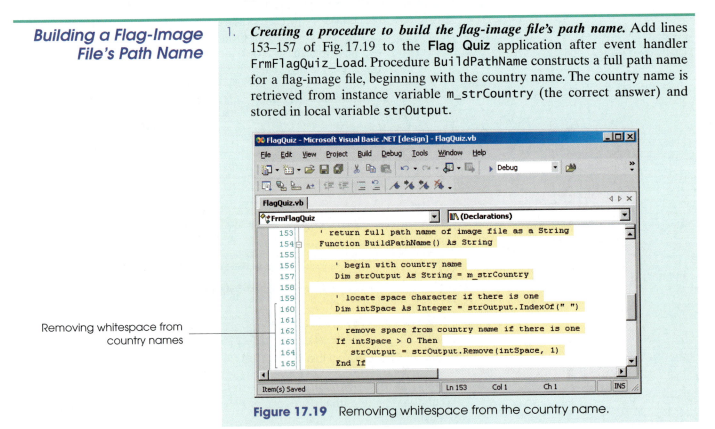

Removing whitespace from country names

Figure 17.19   Removing whitespace from the country name.

(cont.)

2. ***Removing whitespace from the country name.*** Some countries—for example, South Africa and the United States—have a space character in their names, but the flag-image file names do not allow whitespace characters. Add lines 159–165 of Fig. 17.19 to procedure BuildPathName. Line 160 uses String method **IndexOf** to assign to intSpace the index where the space character (" ") in the country name occurs. For instance, if strOutput were "South Africa", intSpace would be 5, because the space appears at index 5 of the name, counting from position zero. If the country does not have a space character, method IndexOf returns –1. Line 163 tests for whether intSpace is a positive number. In this application, method IndexOf returns a number greater than 0 if the country name is "South Africa" or "United States."

If a space is found, the **Remove** method is called to eliminate the space character (line 164). Method Remove receives an index as its first argument and the number of characters to remove as its second argument. For example, the words "South Africa" would become the word "SouthAfrica". Method Remove returns a copy of the String without the space character. The copy is assigned to variable strOutput. [*Note:* String methods, such as Remove, do not modify the String object for which they are called. The String object returned by these methods contains a copy of the modified String.]

3. ***Ensuring that all characters are lowercase.*** Add line 167 of Fig. 17.20 to procedure BuildPathName. Now that strOutput contains a country name without whitespace, line 167 invokes method **ToLower**, which returns a copy of the String with any uppercase letters in the name converted to lowercase. All the flag-image file names are in lowercase, for consistency.

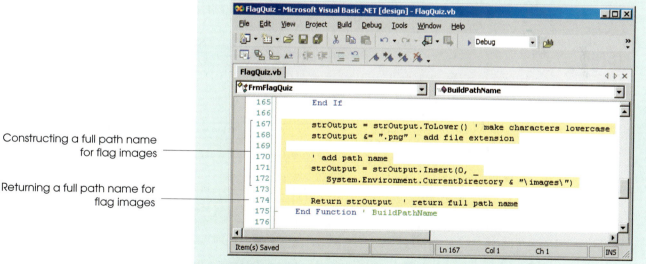

Constructing a full path name for flag images

Returning a full path name for flag images

Figure 17.20   Building the flag-image file path name.

4. ***Adding the file extension.*** Add line 168 of Fig. 17.20 to procedure Build-PathName. The flag-image files are in PNG format. Line 168 appends the file extension ".png" to strOutput.

(cont.)

5. ***Adding the fully qualified path name.*** Add lines 170–172 of Fig. 17.20 to procedure `BuildPathName`. The flag-image files are stored in an `images` directory in the directory containing the application's executable file. Property **CurrentDirectory** of class `System.Environment` (line 172) returns the directory from which the application is executing as a fully qualified path name (for example, `C:\SimplyVB\FlagQuiz\bin`). Method **Insert** combines this path name and `"\images\"` to *countryname*.png. The first argument to `Insert` specifies at what index the `String` will be added, and the second argument is the `String` to insert. Method `Insert` returns a copy of the string with the inserted characters. This copy is assigned to `strOutput`.

6. ***Returning the full path name.*** Add line 174 of Fig. 17.20 to procedure `BuildPathName`. Line 174 returns the fully qualified path name of the specified country's flag image file.

7. ***Saving the project.*** Select **File > Save All** to save your modified code.

To ensure that the user is not asked the same question twice, a flag must be displayed no more than once when running the application. The application uses `Boolean` array `m_blnUsed` to track which flags have been displayed. The following box shows you how to ensure that the application displays a flag no more than once.

Selecting a Unique Flag to Display

1. ***Creating the GetUniqueRandomNumber procedure.*** Add lines 177–178 of Fig. 17.21 to the **Flag Quiz** application after procedure `BuildPathName`. Line 178 is the header for the `GetUniqueRandomNumber` procedure. `GetUniqueRandomNumber` returns the index of a country name whose flag has not been displayed.

2. ***Generating a random index.*** Add line 180 of Fig. 17.21 to the procedure `GetUniqueRandomNumber`. To select the next flag to display, you create a reference, `objRandom` (line 180), to a `Random` object.

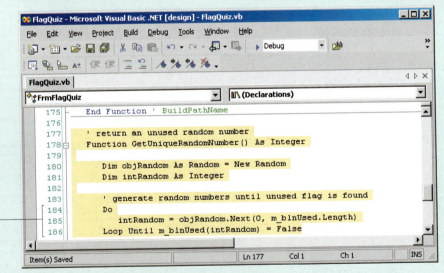

Determining if a country's flag has been displayed previously

Figure 17.21　Generating a unique index.

(cont.)

3. ***Ensuring that each flag displays only once.*** Add lines 181–186 of Fig. 17.21 to GetUniqueRandomNumber. Method Next (line 185) of class Random generates a random index between 0 and m_blnUsed.Length (the number of country names). If the index has been selected previously, the element of m_blnUsed at the generated index is True. The Do...Loop Until statement (lines 184–186) iterates until it finds a unique index (that is, until m_blnUsed(intRandom) is False).

4. ***Indicating that the index has been used.*** Add lines 188–189 of Fig. 17.22 to the GetUniqueRandomNumber procedure. Line 189 sets the element at the selected index of m_blnUsed to True. This indicates that the flag has been used. Checking the values in this array ensures that the index will not be used again in the application.

Indicating that the unused flag will be displayed and return the flag's index for use

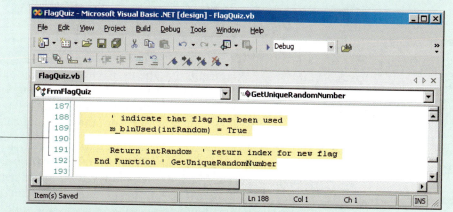

Figure 17.22 Returning the unique index.

5. ***Returning the unique random number.*** Add line 191 of Fig. 17.22 to the GetUniqueRandomNumber procedure. Line 191 returns the unique random index.

6. ***Saving the project.*** Select **File > Save All** to save your modified code.

With the full path name and a unique flag selected, the application can display that flag. The following box shows how to display the selected flag.

Displaying a Flag

1. ***Creating the DisplayFlag procedure.*** Add lines 194–195 of Fig. 17.23 to the **Flag Quiz** application after procedure GetUniqueRandomNumber. Procedure DisplayFlag selects a random country name and displays that country's flag.

Getting the index of the unused flag

Retrieving the flag's corresponding country name

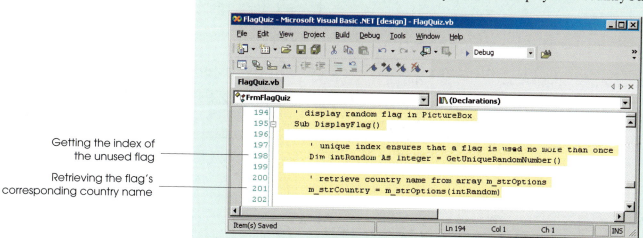

Figure 17.23 Choosing a random country name.

(cont.)

2. ***Obtaining a unique index.*** Add lines 197–198 of Fig. 17.23 to the `Display-Flag` procedure. Line 198 invokes `GetUniqueRandomNumber` to find an index of a flag that has not been displayed during the application's execution and assigns it to `intRandom`.

3. ***Retrieving a country name.*** Add lines 200–201 of Fig. 17.23 to the `Display-Flag` procedure. Line 201 assigns to `m_strCountry` the flag's corresponding country name at index `intRandom` of `String` array `m_strOptions`.

4. ***Building the flag image's path name.*** Add lines 203–204 of Fig. 17.24 to the `DisplayFlag` procedure. Line 204 invokes procedure `BuildPathName`. The procedure returns the flag image's path name, which is assigned to `strPath`.

Getting the path name of the flag and displaying the flag image

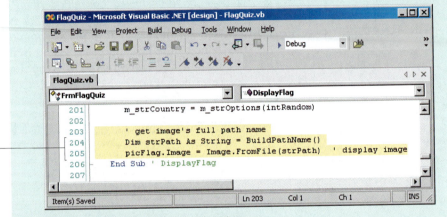

Figure 17.24   Displaying a flag image.

5. ***Displaying the flag image.*** Add line 205 of Fig. 17.24 to the `DisplayFlag` procedure. Line 205 sets `PictureBox picFlag`'s `Image` property to the `Image` object returned by method `Image.FromFile`. Recall that method `Image.FromFile` returns an `Image` object from the specified file.

6. ***Displaying a flag when the application is run.*** When the `Form` loads, the first flag image in the quiz is displayed. The `Form Load` event handler should invoke procedure `DisplayFlag`. Add line 151 of Fig. 17.25 to event handler `FrmFlagQuiz_Load`.

Displaying a flag when application is first run

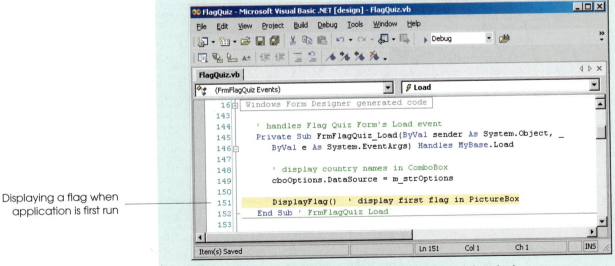

Figure 17.25   Displaying a flag when the **Form** is loaded.

7. ***Saving the project.*** Select **File > Save All** to save your modified code.

The user submits an answer by selecting a country name from the ComboBox and clicking the **Submit** Button. The application displays whether the user's answer is correct. If the application is finished (that is, five flags have been displayed), the application informs the user that the quiz is done; otherwise, the application enables the user to view the next flag. The following box implements this functionality.

Processing a User's Answer

1. *Adding the Submit Button's `Click` event handler.* Return to design view (**View > Designer**). Double click the **Submit** Button to generate the `Click` event handler btnSubmit_Click.

2. *Retrieving the selected ComboBox item.* Add lines 213–215 of Fig. 17.26 to the empty event handler. Lines 214–215 retrieve the user's answer, convert it to a String and assign it to strResponse. Property **SelectedValue** returns the value of the ComboBox's selected item. Visual Basic .NET method Convert.ToString converts the selected item to a String. Recall that we now use Option Strict, which requires explicit conversions. Variable strResponse contains the selected country's name.

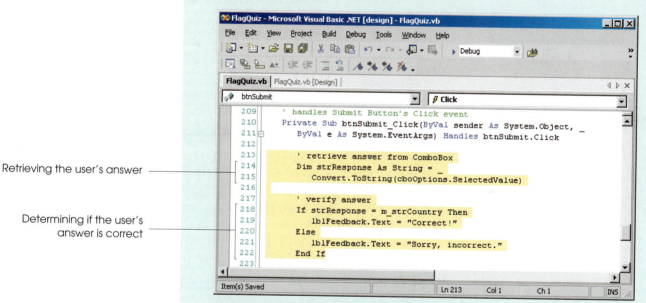

Retrieving the user's answer

Determining if the user's answer is correct

Figure 17.26 Submit Button `Click` event handler.

3. *Verifying the user's answer.* Add lines 217–222 of Fig. 17.26 to btnSubmit_Click. The If...Then...Else statement (lines 218–222) determines whether the user's response matches the correct answer. Line 219 displays "Correct!" in the Label if the user's response matches the correct answer. Otherwise, line 221 displays "Sorry, incorrect.".

4. *Informing the user that the quiz is over, when five flags have been displayed.* Add lines 224–233 of Fig. 17.27 to the btnSubmit_Click event handler. If five flags have been displayed (lines 225–229), the Label displays text informing the user that the quiz is over, and both Buttons are disabled. The ComboBox is also disabled, by setting its **Enabled** property to False.

5. *Continuing the quiz while fewer than five flags have been shown.* If the quiz is not finished (that is, m_intCount is less than 5), the application disables the **Submit** Button and enables the **Next Flag** Button (lines 231–232). The functionality of the **Next Flag** Button will be discussed shortly.

6. *Saving the project.* Select **File > Save All** to save your modified code.

(cont.)

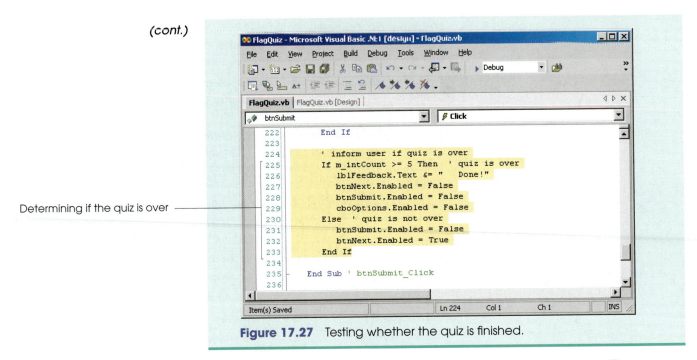

Determining if the quiz is over ——

Figure 17.27 Testing whether the quiz is finished.

The user requests the next flag in the quiz by clicking the **Next Flag** Button. The application then displays the next flag and increments the number of flags shown. In the following box, you will implement this functionality.

Displaying the Next Flag

1. ***Adding the Next Flag Button's Click event handler to the application.*** Return to design view (**View > Designer**). Double click the **Next Flag** Button to generate the Click event handler btnNext_Click.

2. ***Displaying the next flag.*** Add line 241 of Fig. 17.28 to the empty event handler. This line calls procedure DisplayFlag to place the next flag in the PictureBox.

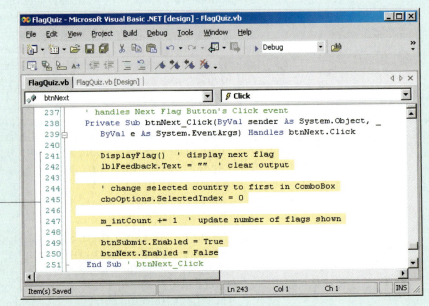

Displaying the next flag for the user to identify ——

Figure 17.28 **Next Flag** Button Click event handler.

3. ***Clearing the previous results.*** Add line 242 of Fig. 17.28 to btnNext_Click to clear the output Label, deleting the results of the previous question.

(cont.)

4. ***Resetting the ComboBox.*** Add lines 244–245 of Fig. 17.28 to btnNext_Click. Line 245 sets property **SelectedIndex** of ComboBox cboOptions to 0, the first item in the ComboBox's drop-down list.

5. ***Updating the number of flags shown.*** Add line 247 of Fig. 17.28 to btnNext_Click to update m_intCount to indicate that one more flag has been shown.

6. ***Enabling the Submit Button and disabling the Next Flag Button.*** Add lines 249–250 of Fig. 17.28 to btnNext_Click. Line 249 enables the **Submit Button**; line 250 disables the **Next Flag** Button. This is a visual reminder to the user that an answer must be submitted before another flag can be displayed.

7. ***Saving the project.*** Select **File > Save All** to save your modified code.

SELF-REVIEW

1. Property _____ specifies the source of the data displayed in the ComboBox.

   a) ComboData   b) Source

   c) DataList   d) DataSource

2. ComboBox property _____ is 0 when the first ComboBox item is selected.

   a) SelectedIndex   b) SelectedValue

   c) Index   d) SelectedNumber

   Answers: 1) d. 2) a.

17.5 Sorting Arrays

Sorting data refers to arranging the data into some particular order, such as ascending or descending order. Sorting is one of the most popular computing capabilities. For example, a bank sorts checks by account number, so that it can prepare individual bank statements at the end of each month. Telephone companies sort account information by last name and, within last-name listings, by first name, to make it easy to find phone numbers. Virtually every organization must sort some data, and often, massive amounts of it. In this section, you learn how to sort the values in an array so that you can alphabetize the list of countries in the **Flag Quiz** application.

Users are able to find a country name in the ComboBox faster if the country names are alphabetized. [*Note*: Class ComboBox contains property **Sorted**, which, when set to True, sorts the items in the ComboBox alphabetically. Because this tutorial focuses on arrays, we do not use this property.] The following box shows you how to sort an array.

Sorting an Array

1. ***Sorting the array of country names.*** Add line 148 of Fig. 17.29 to event handler FrmFlagQuiz_Load. Line 148 passes array m_strOptions to method **Array.Sort**, which sorts the values in the array into ascending alphabetical order. Note that this line is placed prior to the assigning of m_strOptions to property DataSource, so that the items in the ComboBox are displayed in alphabetical order.

2. ***Running the application.*** Select **Debug > Start** to run your application. The country names should now be alphabetized. Enter different answers and make sure that the proper message is displayed based on whether the answer is correct. Make sure that after 5 answers have been entered, the text **Done!** is appended to the current message displayed.

3. ***Closing the application.*** Close your running application by clicking its close box.

4. ***Closing the IDE.*** Close Visual Studio .NET by clicking its close box.

(cont.)

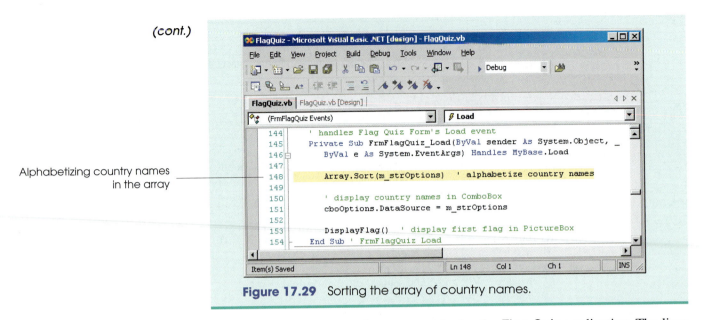

Alphabetizing country names in the array

Figure 17.29 Sorting the array of country names.

Figure 17.30 presents the source code for the **Flag Quiz** application. The lines of code that contain new programming concepts that you learned in this tutorial are highlighted.

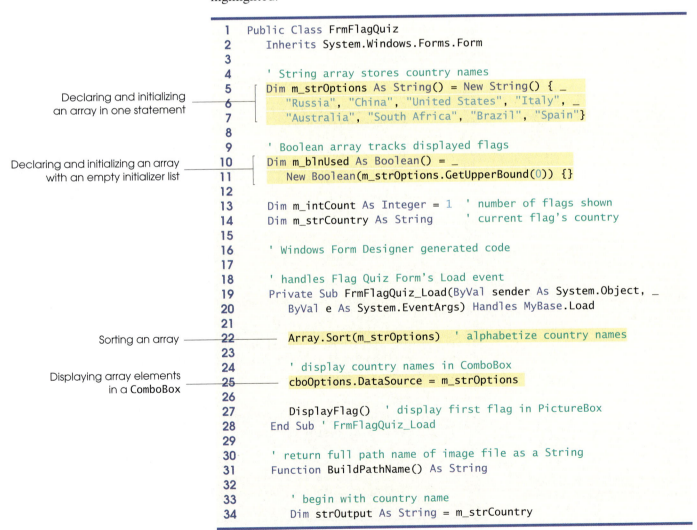

```vb
1    Public Class FrmFlagQuiz
2        Inherits System.Windows.Forms.Form
3
4        ' String array stores country names
5        Dim m_strOptions As String() = New String() { _
6            "Russia", "China", "United States", "Italy", _
7            "Australia", "South Africa", "Brazil", "Spain"}
8
9        ' Boolean array tracks displayed flags
10       Dim m_blnUsed As Boolean() = _
11           New Boolean(m_strOptions.GetUpperBound(0)) {}
12
13       Dim m_intCount As Integer = 1  ' number of flags shown
14       Dim m_strCountry As String     ' current flag's country
15
16       ' Windows Form Designer generated code
17
18       ' handles Flag Quiz Form's Load event
19       Private Sub FrmFlagQuiz_Load(ByVal sender As System.Object, _
20           ByVal e As System.EventArgs) Handles MyBase.Load
21
22           Array.Sort(m_strOptions)  ' alphabetize country names
23
24           ' display country names in ComboBox
25           cboOptions.DataSource = m_strOptions
26
27           DisplayFlag()  ' display first flag in PictureBox
28       End Sub ' FrmFlagQuiz_Load
29
30       ' return full path name of image file as a String
31       Function BuildPathName() As String
32
33           ' begin with country name
34           Dim strOutput As String = m_strCountry
```

Declaring and initializing an array in one statement

Declaring and initializing an array with an empty initializer list

Sorting an array

Displaying array elements in a ComboBox

Figure 17.30 **Flag Quiz** application's code. (Part 1 of 3.)

```
35
Locating a space          36          ' locate space character if there is one
character in a String     37          Dim intSpace As Integer = strOutput.IndexOf(" ")
                          38
                          39          ' remove space from country name if there is one
                          40          If intSpace > 0 Then
Removing a character      41              strOutput = strOutput.Remove(intSpace, 1)
from a String             42          End If
                          43
Converting a String       44          strOutput = strOutput.ToLower() ' make characters lowercase
to lowercase              45          strOutput &= ".png" ' add file extension
                          46
                          47          ' add path name
Inserting characters      48          strOutput = strOutput.Insert(0, _
into a String             49              System.Environment.CurrentDirectory & "\images\")
                          50
                          51          Return strOutput  ' return full path name
                          52      End Function ' BuildPathName
                          53
                          54      ' return an unused random number
                          55      Function GetUniqueRandomNumber() As Integer
                          56
                          57          Dim objRandom As Random = New Random
                          58          Dim intRandom As Integer
                          59
                          60          ' generate random numbers until unused flag is found
                          61          Do
                          62              intRandom = objRandom.Next(0, m_blnUsed.Length)
                          63          Loop Until m_blnUsed(intRandom) = False
                          64
                          65          ' indicate that flag has been used
Assigning a value to      66          m_blnUsed(intRandom) = True
an array element          67
                          68          Return intRandom  ' return index for new flag
                          69      End Function ' GetUniqueRandomNumber
                          70
                          71      ' display random flag in PictureBox
                          72      Sub DisplayFlag()
                          73
                          74          ' unique index ensures that a flag is used no more than once
                          75          Dim intRandom As Integer = GetUniqueRandomNumber()
                          76
                          77          ' retrieve country name from array m_strOptions
Retrieving a value from an array  78  m_strCountry = m_strOptions(intRandom)
                          79
                          80          ' get image's full path name
                          81          Dim strPath As String = BuildPathName()
                          82          picFlag.Image = Image.FromFile(strPath) ' display image
                          83      End Sub ' DisplayFlag
                          84
                          85      ' handles Submit Button's Click event
                          86      Private Sub btnSubmit_Click(ByVal sender As System.Object, _
                          87          ByVal e As System.EventArgs) Handles btnSubmit.Click
                          88
                          89          ' retrieve answer from ComboBox
                          90          Dim strResponse As String = _
Converting the selected value  91      Convert.ToString(cboOptions.SelectedValue)
from the ComboBox into a String  92
```

Figure 17.30 **Flag Quiz** application's code. (Part 2 of 3.)

```
 93          ' verify answer
 94          If strResponse = m_strCountry Then
 95             lblFeedback.Text = "Correct!"
 96          Else
 97             lblFeedback.Text = "Sorry, incorrect."
 98          End If
 99
100          ' inform user if quiz is over
101          If m_intCount >= 5 Then   ' quiz is over
102             lblFeedback.Text &= "   Done!"
103             btnNext.Enabled = False
104             btnSubmit.Enabled = False
105             cboOptions.Enabled = False
106          Else   ' quiz is not over
107             btnSubmit.Enabled = False
108             btnNext.Enabled = True
109          End If
110
111       End Sub ' btnSubmit_Click
112
113       ' handles Next Flag Button's Click event
114       Private Sub btnNext_Click(ByVal sender As System.Object, _
115          ByVal e As System.EventArgs) Handles btnNext.Click
116
117          DisplayFlag()   ' display next flag
118          lblFeedback.Text = ""   ' clear output
119
120          ' change selected country to first in ComboBox
121          cboOptions.SelectedIndex = 0
122
123          m_intCount += 1   ' update number of flags shown
124
125          btnSubmit.Enabled = True
126          btnNext.Enabled = False
127       End Sub ' btnNext_Click
128
129    End Class ' FrmFlagQuiz
```

Setting the selected ComboBox item — 121

Figure 17.30 **Flag Quiz** application's code. (Part 3 of 3.)

SELF-REVIEW

1. The process of ordering the elements of an array is called _____ the array.

   a) allocating   b) sorting

   c) declaring   d) initializing

2. Which of the following sorts array `dblAverageRainfall`?

   a) `Array(dblAverageRainfall).Sort()`   b) `Sort.Array(dblAverageRainfall)`

   c) `Sort(dblAverageRainfall)`   d) `Array.Sort(dblAverageRainfall)`

Answers: 1) b. 2) d.

17.6 Wrap-Up

In this tutorial, you learned about data structures called arrays, which contain elements of the same type. You then learned how to create, initialize and access one-dimensional arrays. You created a simple application called **SumArray**, which calculated the sum of the `Integer` values stored in an array. You studied pseudocode and an ACE table to help you begin creating the **Flag Quiz** application.

In building the **Flag Quiz** application, you were introduced to the ComboBox control. You learned how to add a ComboBox to the Form and modify the Combo-

Box's appearance. You then populated the ComboBox with data from an array. You reviewed how to display images in a PictureBox and how to generate random numbers by using an object of class Random.

　　　You were introduced to several new String methods, including method Insert (for inserting characters), method Remove (for removing characters), method ToLower (for converting uppercase letters to lowercase letters) and method IndexOf (for returning the index of a character in a String). You learned how to sort an array alphabetically by using method Array.Sort.

　　　In the next tutorial, you will learn how to create more sophisticated arrays with two dimensions, and you will use them to implement a graphing application. You will see that two-dimensional arrays are like tables organized in rows and columns.

SKILLS SUMMARY

Creating an Array
■ Declare the array using the format:

>   Dim arrayName As arrayType()

where *arrayName* is the reference name of the array and *arrayType* is the type of data that will be stored in the array.

Assigning an Object to an Array Reference
■ Use keyword New as in the statement:

>   arrayName = New arrayType() {arrayInitializerList}

where *arrayInitializerList* is a comma-separated list of the items that will initialize the elements of the array.

Referring to Element *n* of an Array
■ Use index *n*.
■ Enclose the index in parentheses after the array name.

Obtaining the Length of an Array
■ Use property Length.

Obtaining the Index of the Last Element in a One-Dimensional Array
■ Invoke method GetUpperBound with 0 as its argument.

Combining TextBox Features With ListBox Features
■ Use a ComboBox control.

Setting the Maximum Number of Drop-Down Items a ComboBox's List Displays
■ Use property MaxDropDownItems.

Specifying the Source of Data Displayed in a ComboBox
■ Use property DataSource.

Obtaining a User's Selection in a ComboBox
■ Use property SelectedValue.

Sorting an Array
■ Invoke method Array.Sort.

Determining Whether a String Contains a Specified Character
■ Method IndexOf returns the index of a specified character in a String.
■ If the character is not in the String, method IndexOf returns –1.

Converting a String to Lowercase
■ Method ToLower returns a copy of a String with all uppercase characters converted to lowercase.

Inserting Characters into a String
■ Method Insert returns a copy of a String with specified characters added at a specified index.

Removing Characters from a `String`

■ Method `Remove` returns a copy of the `String` with a specified number of characters removed.

KEY TERMS

array—A data structure containing data items of the same type.

array bounds—Integers that determine what indices can be used to access an element in the array. The lower bound is 0; the upper bound is the length of the array minus one.

`Array.Sort` method—Sorts the values of an array into ascending order.

`ComboBox` control—Combines a `TextBox` with a `ListBox`.

`CurrentDirectory` property of `System.Environment`—Returns the directory from which the application is executing as a fully qualified path name.

`DataSource` property of class `ComboBox`—Specifies the source of items listed in a `ComboBox`.

data structure—Groups and organizes related data.

`DropDownList` value of `DropDownStyle` property—Specifies that a `ComboBox` is not editable.

`DropDownStyle` property of class `ComboBox`—Property of the `ComboBox` control that specifies the appearance of the `ComboBox`.

element—An item in an array.

`Enabled` property of class `ComboBox`—Specifies whether a user can select an item from a `ComboBox`.

`GetUpperBound` method of class `Array`—Returns the largest index of an array.

index—An array element's position number, also called a subscript. An index must be zero, a positive integer or an integer expression. If an application uses an expression as an index, the expression is evaluated first, to determine the index.

indexed array name—The array name followed by an index enclosed in parentheses. The indexed array name can be used on the left side of an assignment statement to place a new value into an array element. The indexed array name can be used in the right side of an assignment to retrieve the value of that array element.

`IndexOf` method of class `String`—`String` method that accepts as an argument a character to search for in a `String`. The method returns the index of a specified character in a `String`. If the `String` does not contain the character, the method returns –1.

initializer list—The required braces ({ and }) surrounding the initial values of the elements in the array. When the initializer list is empty, the elements in the array are initialized to the default value for the array's data type.

`Insert` method of class `String`—`String` method that inserts its second argument (a `String`) at the position specified by the first argument.

length of an array—The number of elements in an array.

`Length` property of class `Array`—Contains the length (or number of elements in) an array.

`MaxDropDownItems` property of class `ComboBox`—Property of the `ComboBox` class that specifies how many items can be displayed in the drop-down list.

one-dimensional array—An array that uses only one index.

position number—A value that indicates a specific location within an array. Position numbers begin at 0 (zero).

`Remove` method of class `String`—`String` method that deletes a specified number of characters (the second argument) starting at the index specified by the first argument.

`SelectedIndex` property of class `ComboBox`—Specifies the index of the selected item. Returns –1 if no item is selected.

`SelectedValue` property of class `ComboBox`—Specifies the value of the selected item.

`Sorted` property of class `ComboBox`—When set to `True`, sorts the items in a `ComboBox` alphabetically.

subscript—See *index*.

`ToLower` method of class `String`—Returns a copy of the `String` for which it is called with any uppercase letters converted to lowercase letters.

zeroth element—The first element in an array.

GUI DESIGN GUIDELINES

ComboBoxes

- Each ComboBox should have a descriptive Label that describes the ComboBox's contents.
- If a ComboBox's content should not be editable, set its DropDownStyle property to Drop-DownList.

CONTROLS, EVENTS, PROPERTIES & METHODS

ComboBox This control allows users to select from a drop-down list of options.

- *In action*

- *Properties*

  DataSource—Specifies the source of items listed in a ComboBox.

  DropDownStyle—Specifies a ComboBox's appearance.

  Enabled—Specifies whether a user can select an item from the ComboBox.

  Location—Specifies the location of the ComboBox control on the container control relative to the top-left corner.

  MaxDropDownItems—Specifies the maximum number of items the ComboBox can display in its drop-down list.

  Name—Specifies the name used to access the ComboBox control programmatically. The name should be prefixed with cbo.

  SelectedIndex—Specifies the index of the selected item. Returns –1 if no item is selected.

  SelectedValue—Specifies the selected item.

  Size—Specifies the height and width (in pixels) of the ComboBox control.

  Sorted—When set to True, displays the ComboBox options in alphabetical order or ascending order.

Array This data structure stores a fixed number of elements of the same type.

- *Property*

  Length—Specifies the number of elements in the array.

- *Methods*

  GetUpperBound—Method returns the largest index of the array.

  Sort—Orders an array's elements. An array of numerical values would be organized in ascending order and an array of Strings would be organized in alphabetical order.

String The String class represents a series of characters treated as a single unit.

- *Methods*

  Format—Arranges the String in a specified format.

  IndexOf—Returns the index of the specified character(s) in a String.

  Insert—Returns a copy of the String for which it is called with the specified character(s) inserted.

  Remove—Returns a copy of the String for which it is called with the specified character(s) removed.

  ToLower—Returns a copy of the String for which it is called with any uppercase letters converted to lowercase letters.

MULTIPLE-CHOICE QUESTIONS

17.1 Arrays can be declared to hold values of _____.

a) type Double

b) type Integer

c) type String

d) any data type

17.2 The elements of an array are related by the fact that they have the same name and _____.

a) constant value

b) subscript

c) type

d) value

17.3 Method _____ returns the largest index in the array.

a) `GetUpperBound`

b) `GetUpperLimit`

c) `GetLargestIndex`

d) `GetUpperSubscript`

17.4 The first element in every array is the _____.

a) subscript

b) zeroth element

c) length of the array

d) smallest value in the array

17.5 Arrays _____.

a) are controls

b) always have one dimension

c) keep data in sorted order at all times

d) are objects

17.6 The initializer list can _____.

a) be used to determine the size of the array

b) contain a comma-separated list of initial values for the array elements

c) be empty

d) All of the above.

17.7 Which method call sorts array `strWords` in ascending order?

a) `Array.Sort(strWords)`

b) `strWords.SortArray()`

c) `Array.Sort(strWords, 1)`

d) `Sort(strWords)`

17.8 The ComboBox control combines a TextBox with a _____ control.

a) `DateTimePicker`

b) `ListBox`

c) `NumericUpDown`

d) `Label`

17.9 To search for a period (`.`) in a String called `strTest`, call method _____.

a) `String.Search(strTest, ".")`

b) `String.IndexOf(strTest, ".")`

c) `strTest.IndexOf(".")`

d) `strTest.Search(".")`

17.10 Property _____ contains the size of an array.

a) `Elements`

b) `ArraySize`

c) `Length`

d) `Size`

EXERCISES

17.11 (*Enhanced Flag Quiz Application*) Enhance the **Flag Quiz** application by counting the number of questions that were answered correctly (Fig. 17.31). After all the questions have been answered, display a message in a Label that describes how well the user performed. The following table shows which messages to display:

Number of correct answers	Message
5	`Excellent!`
4	`Very good`
3	`Good`
2	`Poor`
1 or 0	`Fail`

a) *Copying the template to your working directory.* Copy the directory `C:\Examples\Tutorial17\Exercises\FlagQuiz2` to your `C:\SimplyVB` directory.

b) *Opening the application's template file.* Double click `FlagQuiz.sln` in the `FlagQuiz2` directory to open the application.

Figure 17.31   Enhanced **Flag Quiz** application's GUI.

c) *Adding a variable to count the number of correct answers.* Add an instance variable `m_intNumberCorrect`, and initialize it to 0. You will use this variable to count the number of correct answers submitted by the user.

d) *Counting the correct answers.* Increment `m_intNumberCorrect` in the **Submit** Button's event handler whenever the submitted answer is correct.

e) *Displaying the message.* Write a procedure `DisplayMessage` that displays a message in `lblScore` depending on the value of `m_intNumberCorrect`. Call this procedure from the **Submit** Button's event handler when the quiz is completed.

f) *Running the application.* Select **Debug > Start** to run your application. The finished application should behave as in Fig. 17.31. Run the application a few times and enter a different number of correct answers each time to verify that the correct feedback is displayed.

g) *Closing the application.* Close your running application by clicking its close box.

h) *Closing the IDE.* Close Visual Studio .NET by clicking its close box.

17.12 (*Salary Survey Application*) Use a one-dimensional array to solve the following problem: A company pays its salespeople on a commission basis. The salespeople receive $200 per week, plus 9% of their gross sales for that week. For example, a salesperson who grosses $5000 in sales in a week receives $200 plus 9% of $5000, a total of $650. Write an application (using an array of counters) that determines how many of the salespeople earned salaries in each of the following ranges (assuming that each salesperson's salary is truncated to an integer amount): $200–299, $300–399, $400–499, $500–599, $600–699, $700–799, $800–899, $900–999 and over $999.

Allow the user to enter the sales for each employee in a TextBox. The user should click the **Calculate** Button to calculate that salesperson's salary. When the user is done entering this information, clicking the **Show Totals** Button should display how many of the salespeople earned salaries in each of the above ranges. The finished application should behave like Fig. 17.32.

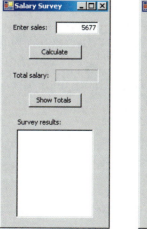
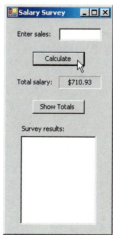
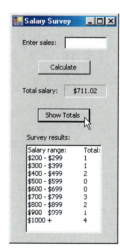

Figure 17.32   **Salary Survey** application's GUI.

a) *Copying the template to your working directory.* Copy the directory `C:\Examples\Tutorial17\Exercises\SalarySurvey` to your `C:\SimplyVB` directory.

b) *Opening the application's template file.* Double click `SalarySurvey.sln` in the `SalarySurvey` directory to open the application.

c) *Creating an array of salary ranges.* Create a `String` array, and initialize it to contain the salary ranges (the `String`s displayed in the `ListBox`'s first column).

d) *Create an array that represents the number of salaries in each range.* Create an empty `Decimal` array to store the number of employees who earn salaries in each range.

e) *Creating an event handler for the Calculate Button.* Write event handler `btnCalculate_Click`. Obtain the user input from the **Enter sales:** TextBox. Calculate the commission due to the employee and add that amount to the base salary. Increment the element in array `decSalaries` that corresponds to the employee's salary range. This event handler should also display the employee's salary in the **Total salary:** Label.

f) *Writing an event handler for the Show Totals Button.* Create event handler `btnShowTotals_Click` to display the salary distribution in the `ListBox`. Use a `For...Next` statement to display the range (an element in `strSalaryRanges`) and the number of employees whose salary falls in that range (an element in `decSalaries`).

g) *Running the application.* Select **Debug > Start** to run your application. Enter several sales amounts using the **Calculate** Button. Click the **Show Totals** Button and verify that the proper amounts are displayed for each salary range, based on the salaries calculate from your input.

h) *Closing the application.* Close your running application by clicking its close box.

i) *Closing the IDE.* Close Visual Studio .NET by clicking its close box.

17.13 (*Cafeteria Survey Application*) Twenty students were asked to rate, on the scale from 1 to 10, the quality of the food in the student cafeteria, with 1 being "awful" and 10 being "excellent." Allow the user input to be entered using a `ComboBox`. Place the 20 responses in an `Integer` array, and determine the frequency of each rating. Display the frequencies as a histogram in a multiline, scrollable `TextBox`. Figure 17.33 demonstrates the completed application.

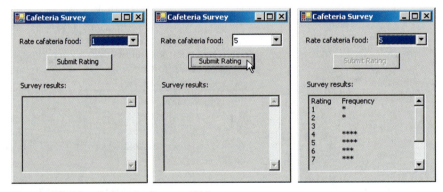

Figure 17.33   Cafeteria Survey GUI.

a) *Copying the template to your working directory.* Copy the directory `C:\Examples\Tutorial17\Exercises\CafeteriaSurvey` to your `C:\SimplyVB` directory.

b) *Opening the application's template file.* Double click `CafeteriaSurvey.sln` in the `CafeteriaSurvey` directory.

c) *Creating an array of the possible ratings.* Create an array of 10 consecutive integers, called `m_intChoices` to contain the integers in the range 1–10, inclusive.

d) *Adding a ComboBox.* Add a `ComboBox` to the GUI as in Fig. 17.33. The `ComboBox` will display the possible ratings. Set property `DropDownStyle` to `DropDownList`.

e) *Displaying the possible ratings when the application starts.* Write the event handler for the `Load` event so that the `DataSource` of the `ComboBox` is set to `intChoices` when the application starts.

f) *Creating an array to store the responses.* Create an `Integer` array of length 11 named `m_intResponses`. This will be used to store the number of responses in each of the 10 categories (element 0 will not be used).

g) *Counting the number of responses.* Create an `Integer` variable named `m_intResponseCounter` to keep track of how many responses have been input.

h) *Storing the responses.* Write the event handler btnSubmit_Click to increment m_intResponseCounter. Store the response in array m_intResponses. Call procedure DisplayHistogram to display the results.

i) *Creating procedure DisplayHistogram.* Add a header to the TextBox. Use nested For...Next loops to display the ratings in the first column. The second column uses asterisks to indicate how many students surveyed submitted the corresponding rating.

j) *Running the application.* Select **Debug > Start** to run your application. Enter 20 responses using the **Submit Rating** Button. Verify that the resulting histogram displays the responses entered.

k) *Closing the application.* Close your running application by clicking its close box.

l) *Closing the IDE.* Close Visual Studio .NET by clicking its close box.

What does this code do? ▶ **17.14** This procedure declares intNumbers as its parameter. What does it return?

```
1   Function Mystery(ByVal intNumbers As Integer()) As Integer()
2
3      Dim intI As Integer
4      Dim intLength As Integer = intNumbers.Length - 1
5      Dim intTempArray As Integer() = _
6         New Integer(intLength) {}
7
8      For intI = intLength To 0 Step -1
9         intTempArray(intLength - intI) = intNumbers(intI)
10     Next
11
12     Return intTempArray
13  End Function ' Mystery
```

What's wrong with this code? ▶ **17.15** The code that follows uses a For...Next loop to sum the elements in an array. Find the error(s) in the following code:

```
1   Sub SumArray()
2      Dim intSum As Integer
3      Dim intCounter As Integer
4      Dim intNumbers As Integer() = _
5         New Integer() {1, 2, 3, 4, 5, 6, 7, 8}
6
7      For intCounter = 0 To intNumbers.Length
8         intSum += intNumbers(intCounter)
9      Next
10
11  End Sub ' SumArray
```

Programming Challenge ▶ **17.16** (*Road Sign Test Application*) Write an application that will test the user's knowledge of road signs. Your application should display a random sign image and ask the user to select the sign name from a ComboBox. This application should look like Fig. 17.34. [*Hint*: The application is similar to the **Flag Quiz** application.] You can find the images in C:\Examples\ Tutorial17\Exercises\images. Remember to set Option Strict to On.

Figure 17.34 Road Sign Test GUI.

Sales Data Application

Introducing Two-Dimensional Arrays, RadioButtons and the MSChart Control

Objectives

In this tutorial, you will learn to:
- Understand the differences between one-dimensional and two-dimensional arrays.
- Declare and manipulate two-dimensional arrays.
- Understand the usefulness of two-dimensional arrays.
- Use `RadioButtons` to enable users to select exactly one option out of several.
- Use an `MSChart` control to graph data.

Outline

U sing graphs to display data enhances the effectiveness of business presentations. It often is easier for the audience to read and understand data from a colorful, well-organized chart than from a large table of data values. In this tutorial, you will learn to use Microsoft's `MSChart` control to create and display graphs for your **Sales Data** application. You will use the `MSChart` control's properties to customize the graph. You will also learn about two-dimensional arrays, which, like one-dimensional arrays, store multiple values. However, with two-dimensional arrays, you will learn to store multiple rows of values and display them in a graph. Finally, you will learn about the `RadioButton` control, which you will employ to enable users to customize the appearance of your application's graph.

18.1 Test-Driving the Sales Data Application

In this tutorial, you will complete the **Sales Data** application by using a two-dimensional array. This application must meet the following requirements:

Application Requirements

The CEO of a steel company is giving a presentation that details recent sales. The presentation requires a chart that displays the number of tons of steel produced by the company's factories in Missouri, Texas, Illinois and Indiana. The application should allow a user to input the annual steel production (in thousands of tons) for each factory and to view the chart produced as either a two-dimensional or a three-dimensional bar graph. The chart should display as a two-dimensional chart by default.

You begin by test-driving the completed application. Then, you will learn the additional Visual Basic .NET technologies that you will need to create your own version of this application.

Test-Driving the Sales Data Application

1. *Opening the completed application.* Open the directory C:\Examples\ Tutorial18\CompletedApplication\SalesData to locate the **Sales Data** application. Double click SalesData.sln to open the application in Visual Studio .NET.

2. *Running the Sales Data application.* Select **Debug > Start** to run the application (Fig. 18.1).

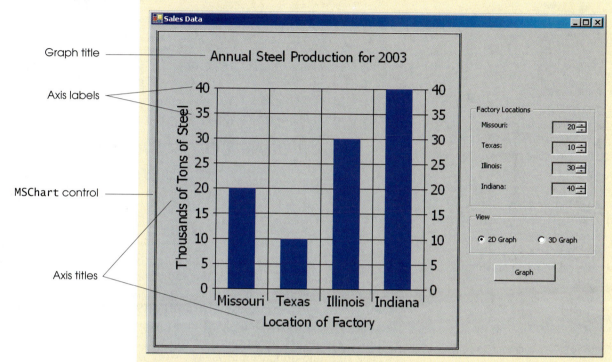

Graph title

Axis labels

MSChart control

Axis titles

Figure 18.1 Completed **Sales Data** application.

3. *Entering data.* By default, the **Sales Data** application graphs the data shown in Fig. 18.1. You will add this functionality when you create the application. Use the NumericUpDown controls' up and down arrows to set the number of thousands of tons of steel produced in each factory. Enter 30 in the **Missouri:** NumericUpDown control, 20 in the **Texas:** NumericUpDown control, 25 in the **Illinois:** NumericUpDown control and 65 in the **Indiana:** NumericUpDown control. Click the **Graph** Button to display the new data in the MSChart control (Fig. 18.2).

4. *Selecting the graph's appearance.* Change the graph's appearance by clicking the **3D Graph** RadioButton (Fig. 18.3). The graph will display the data in a 3D bar graph. Click the **2D Graph** RadioButton to once again display the graph in a 2D bar graph (Fig. 18.2).

5. *Closing the application.* Close your running application by clicking its close box.

6. *Closing the IDE.* Close Visual Studio .NET by clicking its close box.

(cont.)

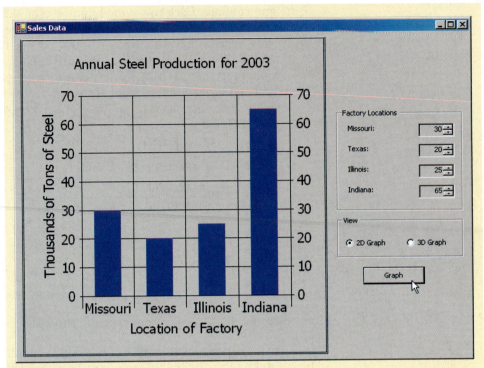

Figure 18.2   Updated graph in the **Sales Data** application.

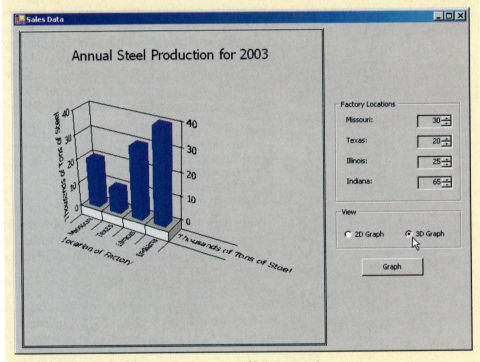

Figure 18.3   Displaying chart data as a 3D bar graph.

18.2 Two-Dimensional Rectangular Arrays

So far, you have studied one-dimensional arrays, which contain one sequence (or row) of values. In this section, we introduce **two-dimensional arrays** (often called **double-subscripted arrays**), which require two indices to identify particular elements. **Rectangular arrays** with two indices are two-dimensional arrays that are often used to represent **tables** of values consisting of information arranged in **rows** and **columns**. Each row is the same size and therefore has the same number of columns (hence, the term "rectangular"). To identify a particular table element, you must specify the two indices—by convention, the first identifies the element's row and the second identifies the element's column. Figure 18.4 illustrates a two-dimensional rectangular array, intArray, which contains three rows and four columns. A rectangular two-dimensional array with *m* rows and *n* columns is called an ***m-by-n* array**; therefore, the array in Fig. 18.4 is a 3-by-4 array.

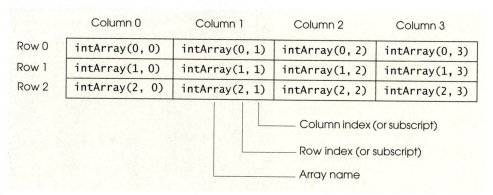

Figure 18.4   Two-dimensional rectangular array with three rows and four columns.

Every element in array intArray is identified in Fig. 18.4 by an element name of the form intArray(intI, intJ), where intArray is the name of the array and intI and intJ are the indices that uniquely identify the row and column of each element in array intArray. Notice that, because row numbers and column numbers in two-dimensional arrays each begin with zero, the names of the elements in the first row each have a first index of 0; the names of the elements in the last column each have a second index of 3 (Fig. 18.4).

Two-dimensional arrays are initialized in declarations through the same process and notations employed for one-dimensional arrays. For example, a two-dimensional rectangular array, intNumbers, with two rows and two columns, could be declared and initialized with

```
Dim intNumbers As Integer(,) = New Integer(1, 1) {}
intNumbers(0, 0) = 1
intNumbers(0, 1) = 2
intNumbers(1, 0) = 3
intNumbers(1, 1) = 4
```

Notice that the values of the arguments in the array declaration (in this case, 1) always indicate *one less than* the number of elements in the row or column. Alternatively, the preceding initialization could be written on one line:

```
Dim intNumbers As Integer(,) = New Integer(,) {{1, 2}, {3, 4}}
```

The values are grouped by row in braces, with 1 and 2 initializing intNumbers(0,0) and intNumbers(0,1), respectively, and 3 and 4 initializing intNumbers(1,0) and intNumbers(1,1), respectively.

SELF-REVIEW

1. Arrays that use two indices are referred to as _____ arrays.

   a) single-subscripted   b) two-dimensional

   c) Double   d) one-dimensional

2. _____ creates an Integer array of two rows and five columns.

   a) New Integer(2, 5){}   b) New Integer(1, 5){}

   c) New Integer(1, 4){}   d) New Integer(2, 4){}

Answers: 1) b. 2) c.

18.3 Creating and Customizing a Chart Graphic by Using the MSChart Control

The Microsoft Chart control (also known as the **MSChart** control) uses two-dimensional arrays to graph and display data on a Form. Using the MSChart control, you can create a chart on the Form and customize its appearance. Such a chart can be used to display statistical information in a visual format that is easy to read and analyze.

When you view charts, you often refer to their *x*- and *y*-axes. As in Fig. 18.5, the *y*-axis is the vertically oriented line and the *x*-axis is the horizontally oriented line.

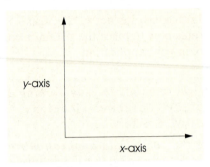

Figure 18.5   Chart axes.

The following pseudocode describes the operation of the **Sales Data** application:

When the Form loads:
    Display the chart in the MSChart control

When the user clicks the Graph Button:
    Retrieve graphing data from the NumericUpDown controls
    Display the chart in the MSChart control

When the user selects the 2D Graph RadioButton:
    Display the chart as a 2D bar graph

When the user selects the 3D Graph RadioButton:
    Display the chart as a 3D bar graph

Now that you have test-driven the **Sales Data** application and studied its pseudocode representation, you will use an ACE table to help you convert the pseudocode to Visual Basic .NET. Figure 18.6 lists the actions, controls and events that will help you complete your own version of this application.

Action/Control/Event (ACE) Table for the Sales Data Application

Action	Control/Class/Object	Event
Label the application's controls	fraLocations, fraView, lblMissouri, lblTexas, lblIllinois, lblIndiana	
	FrmSalesData	Load
Display the chart in the MSChart control	chSales	
	btnGraph	Click
Retrieve graphing data from the NumericUpDown controls	updMissouri, updTexas, updIllinois, updIndiana	
Display the chart in the MSChart control	chSales	

Figure 18.6   ACE table for the **Sales Data** application. (Part 1 of 2.)

Action	Control/Class/Object	Event
	rad2D	CheckedChanged
Display chart as a 2D bar graph	chSales	
	rad3D	CheckedChanged
Display chart as a 3D bar graph	chSales	

Figure 18.6 ACE table for the **Sales Data** application. (Part 2 of 2.)

The MSChart control is not in the Visual Studio .NET **Toolbox**. The following box demonstrates how to place the MSChart control in the **Toolbox** so that you can use the control in your application.

Adding the MSChart Control to the Toolbox

1. *Copying the template to your working directory.* Copy the `C:\Examples\Tutorial18\TemplateApplication\SalesData` directory to your `C:\SimplyVB` directory.

2. *Opening the Sales Data application's template file.* Double click `Sales-Data.sln` in the `SalesData` directory to open the application in Visual Studio .NET.

3. *Opening the Customize Toolbox dialog.* If the **Toolbox** is not currently open, go to **View > Toolbox**. Right click the **Windows Forms** tab of the **Toolbox**. Click **Add/Remove Items...** in the context menu that appears (Fig. 18.7). After a pause, the **Customize Toolbox** dialog will appear (Fig. 18.8).

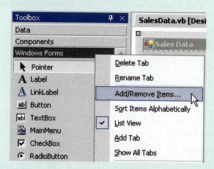

Figure 18.7 Customize Toolbox context menu.

4. *Selecting the Microsoft Chart control.* Select the **COM Components** tab in the **Customize Toolbox** dialog if it is not already selected. Scroll down until the option **Microsoft Chart Control 6.0 (SP4) (OLEDB)** appears, as shown in Fig. 18.8. Note that the text in the parentheses of the **Microsoft Chart Control** option may differ on your system. Also note that the names and number of controls listed in your **Customize Toolbox** dialog may differ from Fig. 18.8. Click that option's CheckBox to select the **Microsoft Chart Control**, and click the **OK** Button to add the MSChart control to the **Toolbox**.

5. *Viewing the Microsoft Chart control in the Toolbox.* Select the MSChart control,

> Microsoft Chart Control 6.0 (SP4) (OLEDB)

from the **Windows Forms** tab of the **Toolbox**. Note that it could be the last control in the list.

(cont.)

COM Components tab ⎯⎯⎯

Selected control ⎯⎯⎯

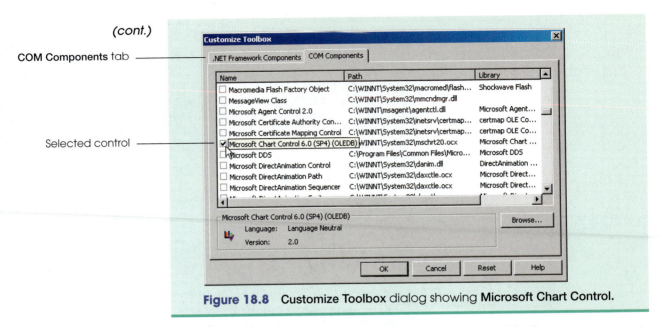

Figure 18.8 Customize Toolbox dialog showing **Microsoft Chart Control**.

Now that you have added the MSChart control to the **Toolbox**, you can create an MSChart control in the **Sales Data** application to take advantage of MSChart's many features. You will begin creating the application in the following box.

Placing the MSChart Control on the Form

GUI Design Tip

Resize an MSChart control so that all the data is clearly visible.

Good Programming Practice

Prefix MSChart control names with ch (for chart).

GUI Design Tip

Set the MSChart control's Enabled property to False to prevent users from repositioning the chart within the MSChart control.

1. ***Inserting the MSChart control.*** With the MSChart control selected in the **Toolbox**, click near the upper left corner of the Form. An MSChart control will appear (Fig. 18.9).

Figure 18.9 MSChart control placed on the Form.

2. ***Resizing and positioning the MSChart.*** In the **Properties** window, set the Location property to 8, 8. Set the Size property to 480, 495, so that the chart is large enough to display all its data clearly. The data that appears on the chart merely indicates how data will be formatted in the chart and does not represent actual values in your application. The initial values for the chart will be set when the application loads.

3. ***Renaming the chart.*** In the **Properties** window, set the Name property to chSales.

4. ***Disabling the chart.*** In the **Properties** window, set property Enabled to False, so users cannot change the size or position of the chart within the MSChart control while the application is running.

5. ***Saving the project.*** Select **File > Save All** to save your modified code.

Now that you have added an MSChart control to your Form, you will customize the control. You will change the properties and the appearance of the chart in the following box.

Customizing the MSChart Control Using the Properties Window

1. *Viewing the Properties dialog.* To display the MSChart's properties, select chSales from the **Properties** window component object box (the ComboBox at the top of the **Properties** window). Notice the hyperlink named **ActiveX - Properties** appears above the description pane of the **Properties** window (Fig. 18.10), regardless of which MSChart control property is selected. Click this hyperlink to display the **Properties** dialog (Fig. 18.11). Though you can set the MSChart control's properties via the **Properties** window, the **Properties** dialog simplifies this process by grouping related settings in a tabbed interface.

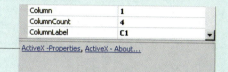

ActiveX -Properties hyperlink displays **Properties** dialog

Figure 18.10   **ActiveX -Properties** hyperlink in the **Properties** window.

2. *Creating a two-dimensional bar/pictograph.* In the **Properties** dialog (Fig. 18.11), the **Chart** tab should be selected by default. If it is not, click the **Chart** tab. In the **Chart Type** GroupBox, make sure that the **2D** RadioButton is selected and that option **Bar/Pictograph** is selected in the ListBox.

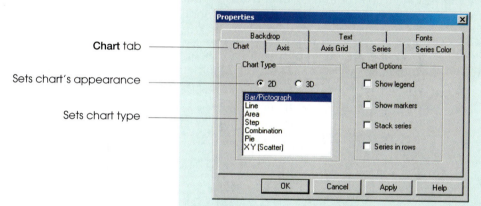

Chart tab

Sets chart's appearance

Sets chart type

Figure 18.11   **Chart** tab in MSChart control **Properties** dialog.

3. *Changing the color of the data in the graph.* The MSChart control can graph data in a variety of colors. To change the color of your bar graph, click the **Series Color** tab in the **Properties** dialog (Fig. 18.12). In the **Interior** GroupBox, click the **Color:** ComboBox to display a palette of colors. Select the blue color shown in Fig. 18.12.

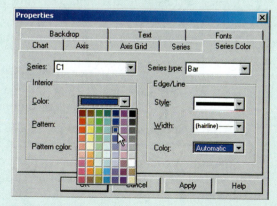

Figure 18.12   **Series Color** tab in the MSChart control's **Properties** dialog.

(cont.)

4. **Setting the MSChart control's title.** The MSChart title contains text that appears above the graph. This title, much like the Form's Text property, is used to describe the purpose of the chart. Click the **Text** tab in the **Properties** dialog (Fig. 18.13). If it is not already selected, select **Title** from the **Property Name:** ComboBox. In the **Text:** TextBox, type `Annual Steel Production for 2003`. Click the **Apply** Button to apply the new settings to the MSChart control. Note that the **Apply** Button is disabled until you change the MSChart control settings again.

Text tab ————

Property Name: ComboBox ————

Text: TextBox ————

Apply Button sets the property ————

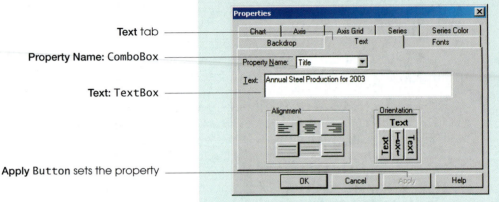

Figure 18.13 **Text** tab in MSChart control **Properties** dialog.

5. **Labelling the x- and y-axes.** In the **Text** tab of the **Properties** dialog, select **X Axis Title** from the **Property Name:** ComboBox. In the **Text:** TextBox, type `Location of Factory`. Click the **Apply** Button to set the *x*-axis label to the value you typed in the TextBox. Your *y*-axis indicates the thousands of tons of steel produced at each location. To label the *y*-axis, select **Y Axis Title** from the ComboBox and type `Thousands of Tons of Steel` in the TextBox. Click the **Apply** Button to set the *y*-axis label.

    Labelling chart axes allows users to easily interpret the data presented. As you saw in the test-drive, the *x*-axis (that is, the horizontal line) in your MSChart will be divided into four sections, one for each state. A state name (Missouri, Texas, Illinois or Indiana) is displayed below each bar in the graph. To help the user read the graph, you should include a descriptive label below the *x*-axis.

6. **Changing the font properties of the title and axis labels.** The graph's title describes the purpose of the chart, so it should be large enough to draw the user's attention. Click the **Fonts** tab in the **Properties** dialog (Fig. 18.14). The default font for the title should be Tahoma. If it is not, select **Title** from the **Property Name:** ComboBox and change the font of the chart title by selecting **Tahoma** from the **Font:** ComboBox. Then change the size of the title to 16 points by changing the value to 16 in the **Size:** ComboBox. A **point** is a measurement that determines the height of the font (1 point is 1/72 of an inch).

    The text that labels the axes is difficult to read on a graph of this size; therefore, you should also increase the text's font size. Choose **Axis Labels** in the **Property Name:** ComboBox, and make sure the **Font:** ComboBox is set to **Tahoma** and change the **Size:** to 16. **Axis labels** display the values associated with data in the graph. Finally, select **Axis Title** from the **Property Name:** ComboBox, and make sure the **Font:** ComboBox is set to **Tahoma** and change its **Size:** to 16. (**Axis titles** describe the meaning of the values on an axis.) Click **Apply** to apply the changes to the chart.

(cont.)

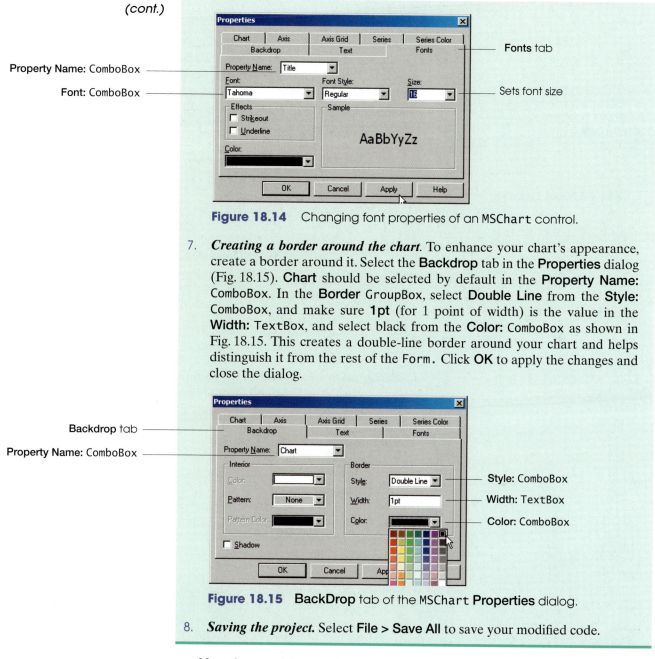

Figure 18.14 Changing font properties of an `MSChart` control.

7. *Creating a border around the chart.* To enhance your chart's appearance, create a border around it. Select the **Backdrop** tab in the **Properties** dialog (Fig. 18.15). **Chart** should be selected by default in the **Property Name: ComboBox**. In the **Border** GroupBox, select **Double Line** from the **Style: ComboBox**, and make sure **1pt** (for 1 point of width) is the value in the **Width: TextBox**, and select black from the **Color: ComboBox** as shown in Fig. 18.15. This creates a double-line border around your chart and helps distinguish it from the rest of the Form. Click **OK** to apply the changes and close the dialog.

Figure 18.15 **BackDrop** tab of the `MSChart` **Properties** dialog.

8. *Saving the project.* Select **File > Save All** to save your modified code.

Now that you have set the `MSChart` control's properties, you are ready to insert additional design elements into your application. You will use `RadioButton` controls to allow the user to change the appearance of the graph.

SELF-REVIEW

1. The *x*-axis in a chart is the _____ oriented line.

   a) vertically   b) horizontally

   c) diagonally   d) None of the above.

2. To use the `MSChart` control, it must be added to the Visual Studio .NET _____.

   a) **Toolbox**   b) **Solution Explorer**

   c) **Properties** window   d) code file

Answers: 1) b. 2) a.

18.4 Using RadioButtons

A **RadioButton** is a small white circle that either is blank or contains a smaller black dot. When a RadioButton is selected, a black dot appears in the circle. A RadioButton is known as a state button because it can be only in the "on" state or in the "off" state. (The other state button you have learned is the CheckBox, which was introduced in Tutorial 8.)

RadioButtons are similar to CheckBoxes in that they are state buttons, but RadioButtons normally appear as a group; only one RadioButton in the group can be selected at a time. Similar to car-radio preset buttons, in which only one station can be selected at a time, RadioButtons are used to represent a set of mutually exclusive options. **Mutually exclusive options** are a set of options in which only one can be selected at a time. By default, all RadioButtons added to the Form become part of the same group. To separate RadioButtons into several groups, each RadioButton group must be in a different container (such as a GroupBox).

The RadioButton control's **Checked** property indicates whether the RadioButton is checked (contains a small black dot) or unchecked (blank). If the RadioButton is checked, property Checked returns the Boolean value True. If the RadioButton is not checked, property Checked returns False.

A RadioButton also generates an event when its checked state changes. Event **CheckedChanged** is generated when a RadioButton is either selected or deselected. You now learn how to insert RadioButtons in the **Sales Data** application.

GUI Design Tip

Use RadioButtons when the user should choose only one option from a group.

GUI Design Tip

Always place each group of RadioButtons in a separate container (such as a GroupBox).

Placing RadioButtons in the GroupBox

1. **Creating RadioButtons in the GroupBox.** Create a RadioButton on the Form by clicking the **RadioButton** control,

   in the **Toolbox**, then clicking inside the **View** GroupBox located to the right of the MSChart control (Fig. 18.16). Repeat this process until two RadioButtons have been added to the GroupBox. Notice that, as with CheckBoxes, each RadioButton control contains a label.

2. **Customizing the RadioButtons.** To align the RadioButtons horizontally, set the Location property of one RadioButton to 13, 29, and set the other RadioButton's Location property to 108, 29. Then resize the RadioButton labels by setting each RadioButton's Size property to 76, 28. Rename the left RadioButton by changing its Name property to rad2D and set its Text property to 2D Graph. Then set the right RadioButton control's Name property to rad3D, and set its Text property to 3D Graph. Your GroupBox should now look similar to Fig. 18.16.

Good Programming Practice

We suggest prefixing RadioButton controls with rad.

GUI Design Tip

Align groups of RadioButtons either horizontally or vertically.

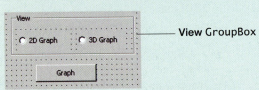
View GroupBox

Figure 18.16 RadioButtons placed in the GroupBox.

3. **Saving the project.** Select **File > Save All** to save modified code.

SELF-REVIEW   1. Which property determines whether a RadioButton is selected?

   a) Selected   b) Clicked

   c) Checked   d) Enabled

2. The _____ event is raised when a RadioButton is either selected or deselected.
   a) CheckedChanged
   b) Changed
   c) SelectedChanged
   d) None of the above.

Answers: 1) c. 2) a.

18.5 Inserting Code into the Sales Data Application

Now that you have placed the controls on the Form, you are ready to write code to display data in the chart when the application first run. You can accomplish this task by using the Form's Load event handler. Recall that the Form's Load event occurs before the application is displayed for the first time. You will write code to display data in the chart while completing the following box.

Coding the Form's Load Event Handler

1. ***Creating the Load event handler.*** Double click an empty area of the Form to enter code view and generate the event handler FrmSalesData_Load.

2. ***Inserting code into the event handler.*** Insert lines 232–241 of Fig. 18.17 in event handler FrmSalesData_Load. Be sure to add the comments and line-continuation characters as shown in Fig. 18.17 so that the line numbers in your code match those presented in this tutorial.

Setting initial data ————

Checking the **2D Graph** RadioButton ————

Graphing the data ————

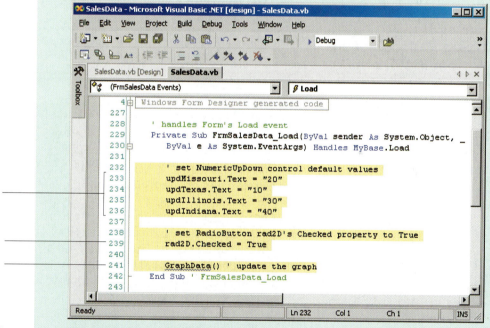

Figure 18.17 Sales Data application's Load event handler.

Lines 233–236 assign default values to the NumericUpDown controls by using their Text properties. These values will be used to draw the initial graph. Line 239 selects the **2D Graph** RadioButton, because the initial chart type will be a 2D bar graph.

Line 241 calls the GraphData procedure. The GraphData procedure will use the data in the NumericUpDown controls to create a graph. You will define the procedure in the next box.

3. ***Saving the project.*** Select **File > Save All** to save your modified code.

Error-Prevention Tip

To avoid subtle logic errors, one RadioButton in a group should be selected by default by setting its Checked property to True. This can be done using code (as shown) or by setting the value using the **Properties** window.

When the user clicks the **Graph** Button, the application should read the chart data entered by the user and update the graph.

Coding the Graph Button's Click Event Handler

1. **Switching to design view.** Click the **SalesData.vb [Design]** tab to switch to design view.

2. **Adding the Click event handler.** Double click the **Graph** Button to enter code view and generate the event handler btnGraph_Click.

3. **Inserting code in the event handler.** Insert line 248 of Fig. 18.18 into event handler btnGraph_Click.

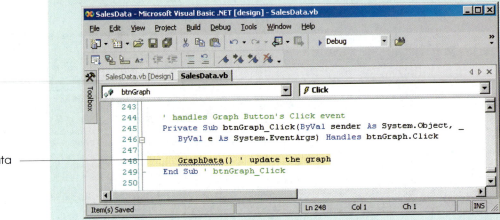

Graphing the data

Figure 18.18 Graph Button's Click event handler.

The GraphData procedure will use the data in the NumericUpDown controls to create a graph (line 248). You will define the procedure in the next box.

4. **Saving the project.** Select **File > Save All** to save your modified code.

The MSChart control uses two-dimensional arrays as input to display data. In the following box, you will write code that creates an array in which you will store user input. You will then use code to enable the MSChart control to display that data.

Coding the GraphData Procedure

1. **Writing the GraphData procedure code.** Add lines 251–270 of Fig. 18.19 below your btnGraph_Click event handler.

Lines 255–258 retrieve user input from the NumericUpDown controls by using their Text properties and store the values in String variables. Lines 262–267 create and initialize a 5-by-2 String array strSales. Array str-Sales contains the data that will be displayed in the chart.

The MSChart control does not use the first element of the array ("Location") to display data. In this case, we use the first element to label our array. The second column of the first row ("Thousands of Tons of Steel") contains a label that displays to the right of the graph in the 3D bar graph (Fig. 18.3).

The x-axis is divided into four factory locations. The first column (the first elements in the last four rows)—strSales(1,0), strSales(2,0), str-Sales(3,0) and strSales(4,0)—contains the axis labels for the x-axis categories, as seen on lines 263–267. Each label (that is, Missouri, Texas, Illinois and Indiana) appears below the values in its column.

The String variables (which represent numbers) in array strSales indicate the value associated with each state. For instance, if strMissouri contains the value "30", then line 264 indicates that the Missouri factory produced 30 thousand tons of steel. As a result, the chart displays a blue bar of height 30 above the **Missouri** label on the x-axis, as shown in Fig. 18.2.

(cont.)

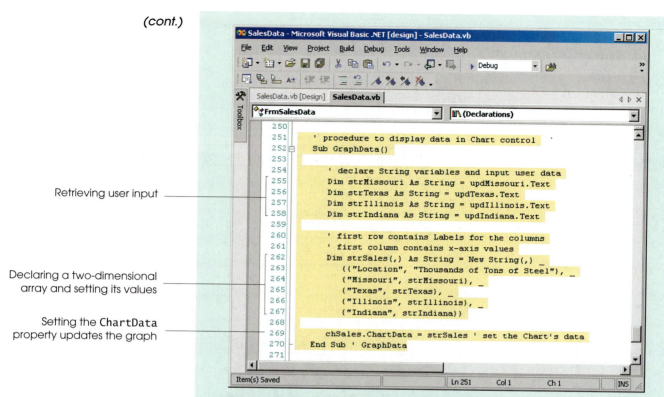

Retrieving user input

Declaring a two-dimensional array and setting its values

Setting the ChartData property updates the graph

Figure 18.19 GraphData procedure code.

Lines 263–267 follow this pattern as well. Notice that you do not have to specify the values along the *y*-axis. The MSChart control uses the data in the chart to place the values on the *y*-axis in such a way that the values fit the range of data. The *y*-axis in your chart in Fig. 18.2 extends from 0 to 70, because this includes the range of values (20–65) that you specified in the NumericUpDown controls.

Line 269 sets the data displayed in MSChart chSales to be the data contained in array strSales. Property **ChartData** stores the two-dimensional array of data displayed by an MSChart.

2. ***Running the application.*** Select **Debug > Start** to run your application. Notice that you can select new values in the NumericUpDown control and update the graph by clicking the **Graph** Button, but the RadioButtons do not change the appearance of the graph. You will add this functionality in the next box.

3. ***Closing the application.*** Close your running application by clicking its close box.

You will now code an event handler to enhance the application's functionality by allowing users to select whether they want to view the chart in two dimensions or in three dimensions. You will learn how to code this functionality in the following box.

Coding Event Handlers for the RadioButtons

1. ***Creating event handlers for RadioButtons CheckedChanged events.*** While in design mode, double click the rad2D RadioButton on the Form. This will generate an event handler for that RadioButton control's CheckedChanged event.

(cont.)

2. ***Coding the 2D Chart RadioButton's CheckedChanged event.*** Insert lines 277–279 from Fig. 18.20 into the rad2D_CheckedChanged event handler. Lines 278–279 set the chSales MSChart control's **ChartType** property to a two-dimensional bar graph. The VtChChartType2dBar value (line 279) specifies a two-dimensional bar graph.

Setting the MSChart control to display a 2D bar graph

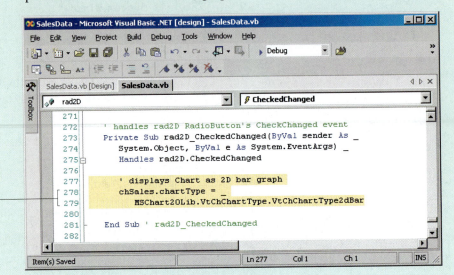

Figure 18.20 rad2D_CheckedChanged event handler.

3. ***Coding the 3D Chart RadioButton's CheckedChanged event.*** In the Windows Form Designer, double click the rad3D RadioButton to generate its CheckedChanged event handler, and enter code view. Then insert lines 288–290 of Fig. 18.21 into the event handler. This code will set the chSales control's ChartType property to a three-dimensional bar graph. Value VtChChartType3dBar (line 290) specifies a three-dimensional bar graph.

Setting the MSChart control to display a 3D bar graph

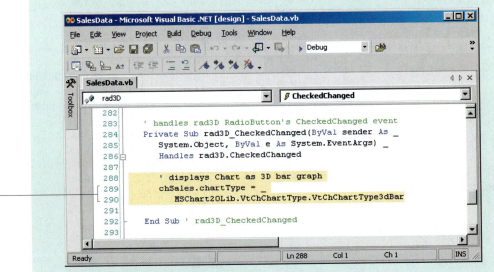

Figure 18.21 rad3D_CheckedChanged event handler.

4. ***Running the application.*** Select **Debug > Start** to run your application. Notice that the chart appearance now changes when you change the RadioButton selection.

5. ***Closing the application.*** Close your running application by clicking its close box.

6. ***Closing the IDE.*** Close Visual Studio .NET by clicking its close box.

Figure 18.22 presents the source code for the **Sales Data** application. The lines of code that contain new programming concepts that you learned in this tutorial are highlighted.

```vbnet
1  Public Class FrmSalesData
2      Inherits System.Windows.Forms.Form
3
4      ' Windows Form Designer generated code
5
6      ' handles Form's Load event
7      Private Sub FrmSalesData_Load(ByVal sender As System.Object, _
8          ByVal e As System.EventArgs) Handles MyBase.Load
9
10         ' set NumericUpDown control default values
11         updMissouri.Text = "20"
12         updTexas.Text = "10"
13         updIllinois.Text = "30"
14         updIndiana.Text = "40"
15
16         ' set RadioButton rad2D's Checked property to True
17         rad2D.Checked = True
18
19         GraphData() ' update the graph
20      End Sub ' FrmSalesData_Load
21
22      ' handles Graph Button's Click event
23      Private Sub btnGraph_Click(ByVal sender As System.Object, _
24          ByVal e As System.EventArgs) Handles btnGraph.Click
25
26         GraphData() ' update the graph
27      End Sub ' btnGraph_Click
28
29      ' procedure to display data in Chart control
30      Sub GraphData()
31
32         ' declare String variables and input user data
33         Dim strMissouri As String = updMissouri.Text
34         Dim strTexas As String = updTexas.Text
35         Dim strIllinois As String = updIllinois.Text
36         Dim strIndiana As String = updIndiana.Text
37
38         ' first row contains Labels for the columns
39         ' first column contains x-axis values
40         Dim strSales(,) As String = New String(,) _
41            {{"Location", "Thousands of Tons of Steel"}, _
42            {"Missouri", strMissouri}, _
43            {"Texas", strTexas}, _
44            {"Illinois", strIllinois}, _
45            {"Indiana", strIndiana}}
46
47         chSales.ChartData = strSales ' set the Chart's data
48      End Sub ' GraphData
49
50      ' handles rad2D RadioButton's CheckedChanged event
51      Private Sub rad2D_CheckedChanged(ByVal sender As _
52          System.Object, ByVal e As System.EventArgs) _
53          Handles rad2D.CheckedChanged
54
```

Using code to select a RadioButton control → (line 17)

Declaring a 5-by-2 String array to store values for graphing → (lines 40–45)

Sets the data for the MSChart control to graph → (line 47)

Event raised when user checks or unchecks the RadioButton → (lines 51–53)

Figure 18.22 Completed **Sales Data** application code. (Part 1 of 2.)

Using the `ChartType` property
to display a 2D bar graph

```
55            ' displays Chart as 2D bar graph
56            chSales.chartType = _
57               MSChart20Lib.VtChChartType.VtChChartType2dBar
58
59         End Sub ' rad2D_CheckedChanged
60
61         ' handles rad3D RadioButton's CheckedChanged event
62         Private Sub rad3D_CheckedChanged(ByVal sender As _
63            System.Object, ByVal e As System.EventArgs) _
64            Handles rad3D.CheckedChanged
65
66            ' displays Chart as 3D bar graph
67            chSales.chartType = _
68               MSChart20Lib.VtChChartType.VtChChartType3dBar
69
70         End Sub ' rad3D_CheckedChanged
71
72      End Class ' FrmSalesData
```

Using the `ChartType` property
to display a 3D bar graph

Figure 18.22   Completed **Sales Data** application code. (Part 2 of 2.)

SELF-REVIEW

1. The _____ of an array used to store data for an `MSChart` control contains values that will display as the *x*-axis labels.

   a) first row   b) second row

   c) first column   d) second column

2. The _____ property of an `MSChart` control stores the data values it will graph.

   a) `DataSource`   b) `ChartSource`

   c) `ChartDataSource`   d) `ChartData`

Answers: 1.) c. 2.) d.

18.6 Wrap-Up

In this tutorial, you learned how to use two-dimensional arrays to display chart data in an `MSChart` control. You studied two-dimensional arrays and learned how to declare and assign values to a rectangular array.

To help complete the **Sales Data** application, you used the `RadioButton` control and the `MSChart` control. You learned that `RadioButton`s are used to represent a set of mutually exclusive options—one `RadioButton` in a group of `RadioButton`s can be checked. You also learned that you must group related `RadioButton`s by placing them in separate containers.

The `MSChart` control is not in the **Toolbox** by default, so you learned how to place this control in the **Toolbox**. You then created an `MSChart` control on your Form and used its properties to set display options, including the graph's title, border and axes labels.

After learning about `RadioButton`s and the `MSChart` control, you used code to store user input in a two-dimensional array and you assigned that array to the `MSChart` control's `ChartData` property to graph that data. You also learned how to use the `RadioButton`'s `CheckedChanged` event handler to change a graph's appearance when the user selects a display option.

In the next tutorial, you will learn about classes. (Recall that you have been using classes all along, from the Form class that represents the application's GUI to the Random class that you use to generate random numbers.) You will learn how to create your own classes for use in your applications.

SKILLS SUMMARY

Using Two-Dimensional Arrays

■ Declare a rectangular array to create a table of values (each row will contain the same number of columns).

Adding the MSChart Control to the Visual Studio .NET Toolbox.

■ Right click the **Windows Forms** tab in the **Toolbox** and select **Customize Toolbox...** to display the **Customize Toolbox** dialog.

■ Then check the **Microsoft Chart Control 6.0 (SP4) (OLEDB)** CheckBox within the **COM Components** tab.

■ Click **OK** to add the control to the **Toolbox**.

Displaying the Properties Dialog to Customize the MSChart Control

■ Select the MSChart control on the Form, and click the **ActiveX -Properties** link at the bottom of the **Properties** window.

Setting the Title of an MSChart Control

■ Select the **Text** tab in the **Properties** dialog of the MSChart control.

■ Then select the **Title** option in the **Property Name:** ComboBox and type the desired title in the **Text:** TextBox.

Labelling the X- (or Y-) Axis of the MSChart Control

■ Select the **Text** tab in the **Properties** dialog of the MSChart control.

■ Then select the **X Axis Title** (or **Y Axis Title**) option in the **Property Name:** ComboBox, and type the desired title in the **Text:** TextBox.

Changing the Font Properties of the Text in an MSChart Control

■ Select the **Fonts** tab in the **Properties** dialog of the MSChart control.

■ Then select from the **Property Name:** ComboBox the desired option that you wish to change.

■ You can then specify a font in the **Font:** ComboBox and a font size in the **Size:** ComboBox.

Using a RadioButton

■ Use a RadioButton in an application to present the user with mutually exclusive options.

Selecting a RadioButton at Runtime

■ Click the white circle of the RadioButton. (A small black dot will appear inside the white circle.)

Determining Whether a RadioButton Is Selected

■ Access the RadioButton's Checked property.

Executing Code When a RadioButton's State Has Changed

■ Use the CheckedChanged event handler, which executes when a RadioButton is selected or deselected.

KEY TERMS

ActiveX -Properties—A hyperlink at the bottom-left of the **Properties** window for the MSChart control. When clicked, it displays a dialog with which you can set the MSChart properties.

axis label—Display the values associated with data in a graph.

axis title—Describe the meaning of the values on an axis.

ChartData property of an MSChart control—The MSChart property that stores the array containing the data to be displayed as a graph.

ChartType property of an MSChart control—The MSChart property that determines the type of graph the control uses to display its data.

Checked property of class RadioButton—The RadioButton property that, when True, displays a small black dot in the control. When False, the control displays an empty white circle.

CheckedChanged event of class RadioButton—Raised when a RadioButton's state (checked or unchecked) changes.

double-subscripted array—See *two-dimensional array*.

m-by-n array—A rectangular two-dimensional array with *m* rows and *n* columns. For instance, a 3-by-4 array has 3 rows and 4 columns.

MSChart control— Allows you to display data as a graph on the Form.

mutually exclusive option—A set of options in which only one can be selected at a time.

RadioButton control—Appears as a small white circle that is either blank (unchecked) or contains a smaller black dot (checked). Usually these controls appear in groups of two or more. Exactly one RadioButton in a group is selected at once.

rectangular array—A type of two-dimensional array that can represent tables of values consisting of information arranged in rows and columns. Each row contains the same number of columns.

two-dimensional array—A double-subscripted array that contains multiple rows of values.

GUI DESIGN GUIDELINES

MSChart Control

- Resize an MSChart control so that all the data is clearly visible.
- Set the MSChart control's Enabled property to False to prevent users from repositioning the chart within the MSChart control.
- Assign meaningful descriptions in the MSChart graph's title and axis labels. Use book-title capitalization for these descriptions.
- Increase the MSChart graph's title and axis label font sizes to enhance readability.

RadioButton

- Use RadioButtons when the user should choose only one option in a group.
- Always place each group of RadioButtons in a separate container (such as a GroupBox).
- Align groups of RadioButtons either horizontally or vertically.

CONTROLS, EVENTS, PROPERTIES & METHODS

MSChart   Microsoft Chart Control 6.0 (S   This control is used to display data in graphs.

- *In action*

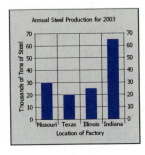

- *Properties*

ChartData—Contains the data to be graphed.

ChartType—Determines the appearance of the graph.

Location—Specifies the location of the MSChart control on the container control relative to the top-left corner.

Name—Specifies the name used to access the MSChart control programmatically. The name should be prefixed with ch.

Size—Specifies the height and width (in pixels) of the MSChart control.

RadioButton   ◉ RadioButton   This control is used to enable users to select exactly one option from several.

- *In action*

◉ 3D Graph

■ *Event*

`CheckedChanged`—Raised when the control is either selected or deselected.

■ *Properties*

`Checked`—`True` if the control is selected and `False` if it is not selected.

`Location`—Specifies the location of the `RadioButton` control on the container control relative to the top-left corner.

`Name`—Specifies the name used to access the `RadioButton` control programmatically. The name should be prefixed with `rad`.

`Size`—Specifies the height and width (in pixels) of the `RadioButton` control.

`Text`—Specifies the text displayed in the label to the right of the `RadioButton`.

MULTIPLE-CHOICE QUESTIONS

18.1 `RadioButton` controls should be prefixed with _____.

a) `rad`
b) `rbn`
c) `btn`
d) `radbtn`

18.2 A two-dimensional array in which each row contains the same number of columns is called a _____ array.

a) data
b) rectangular
c) tabular
d) All of the above.

18.3 In an *m*-by-*n* array, the *m* stands for _____.

a) the number of columns in the array
b) the total number of array elements
c) the number of rows in the array
d) the number of elements in each row

18.4 The statement _____ assigns an array of three columns and five rows to two-dimensional `Integer` array `intArray`.

a) `intArray = New Integer(5, 3)`
b) `intArray = New Integer(4, 2)`
c) `intArray = New Integer(4, 3)`
d) `intArray = New Integer(5, 2)`

18.5 To change the `MSChart` graph's title size, use the _____ tab of the `MSChart` **Properties** dialog.

a) **Size**
b) **Title**
c) **Fonts**
d) **Font Size**

18.6 Use a _____ to group `RadioButtons` on the Form.

a) `GroupBox` control
b) `ComboBox` control
c) `ListBox` control
d) None of the above.

18.7 Use the _____ tab of the `MSChart` **Properties** dialog to access properties to include a border around your chart.

a) **Border**
b) **Backdrop**
c) **BorderStyle**
d) **Background**

18.8 A point of height is approximately equal to _____.

a) 1/72"
b) 1"
c) 1/4"
d) 1/36"

18.9 The **Chart Type** `GroupBox` of the `MSChart` control's **Properties** dialog is located in the _____ tab.

a) **Chart**
b) **Graph**
c) **Series**
d) **ChartType**

18.10 The **Fonts** tab of the `MSChart` control's **Properties** dialog allows you to change the font _____.

a) **Style**
b) **Width**
c) **Color**
d) All of the above.

EXERCISES   **18.11** (*Stock Price Application*) It is often useful to track a company's stock price over time by using a line graph. You will learn to create a line graph by using an MSChart control in this exercise. Create an application that allows users to enter values for a company's stock price at the end of six consecutive quarters and graph that data, using an MSChart control (Fig. 18.23).

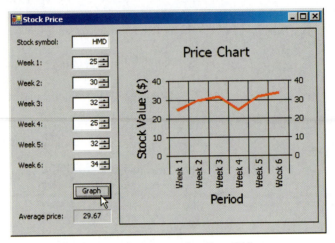

Figure 18.23   **Stock Price** application GUI.

a) *Copying the template to your working directory.* Copy the directory C:\Examples\ Tutorial18\Exercises\StockPrice to your C:\SimplyVB directory.

b) *Opening the application's template file.* Double click StockPrice.sln in the StockPrice directory to open the application.

c) *Changing the graph type and color.* To change the graph type and color, select the chart in the ComboBox at the top of the **Properties** window and select the **ActiveX - Properties** hyperlink from the **Properties** window to display the **Properties** dialog. In the **Chart** tab's **Chart Type** GroupBox, select **Line** (if it is not already selected), and make sure the RadioButton is set to **2D**. Click the **Series Color** tab, and, in the **Edge/Line** GroupBox, change the color to red (if this color is not already selected).

d) *Inserting code in the Graph Button's Click event handler.* Double click the **Graph** Button in **Design** view to generate the **Graph** Button Click event handler. Insert an If...Then statement that verifies that the user entered a stock name. If the value in the TextBox is the empty string, the application should display a message dialog.

e) *Checking the remaining NumericUpDowns.* For the chart to function properly, the user must enter values in all NumericUpDowns. Add If...ElseIf...Else statements to verify that there is a value greater than zero in each NumericUpDown (using the Value property), and display a message in a MessageBox if any values are missing (contain the zero).

f) *Calculating the average.* Calculate the average of all of the values from the Numeric-UpDowns, and output the result in the output Label lblAverage.

g) *Inserting data into an array.* Create a 6-by-2 array from the data that will display the week number on the *x*-axis and prices on the *y*-axis. (The week number should be in the first column, and the stock price should be in the second column.) Use the Numer-icUpDown's Text property to retrieve the value stored in the control as a String.

h) *Displaying the chart.* Assign the array to the ChartData property to display the data in the array. Remember to set Label lblMessage's Visible property to False and set the MSChart control's Visible property to True. A control's Visible property determines if the control is displayed on the Form (True) or hidden (False).

i) *Running the application.* Select **Debug > Start** to run your application. Enter the name of a stock, and the stock's price for each week. Click the **Graph** Button. Verify that the average displayed is correct, and that the graph displayed shows the proper data. Also, make sure your graph's labels appear as in Fig. 18.23.

j) *Closing the application.* Close your running application by clicking its close box.

k) *Closing the IDE.* Close Visual Studio .NET by clicking its close box.

18.12 *(Enhanced Lottery Picker)* A lottery commission offers four different lottery games to play: three-number, four-number, five-number and five-number + 1 lotteries. In Tutorial 16, your **Lottery Picker** application could select duplicate numbers for each lottery. In this exercise, you enhance the **Lottery Picker** to prevent duplicate numbers for the five-number and five-number + 1 lotteries (Fig. 18.24). According to this new requirement the games are now played as follows:

- Three-number lotteries require players to choose three numbers in the range of 0–9.

- Four-number lotteries require players to choose four numbers, in the range of 0–9.

- Five-number lotteries require players to choose five unique numbers in the range of 1–39.

- Five-number + 1 lotteries require players to choose five unique numbers in the range of 1–49 and an additional unique number in the range of 1–42.

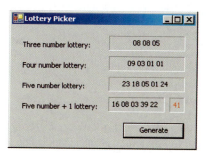

Figure 18.24 Enhanced **Lottery Numbers Picker** application.

a) *Copying the template to your working directory.* Copy the directory `C:\Examples\Tutorial18\Exercises\EnhancedLotteryPicker` to your `C:\SimplyVB` directory.

b) *Opening the application's template file.* Double click `EnhancedLotteryPicker.sln` in the `EnhancedLotteryPicker` directory to open the application.

c) *Declaring a two-dimensional array to maintain unique random numbers.* Declare an instance variable `m_blnNumbers` that stores a 2-by-50 `Boolean` array. You will use this array later in this exercise to test whether a lottery number has already been chosen.

d) *Initializing the array.* Each time the user clicks the **Generate** `Button`, the application should initialize the array by declaring its rows and setting the initial values. Write a `ClearArray` procedure that uses a `For...Next` statement to assign each value in the `m_blnNumbers` array to `False`.

e) *Modifying the `Generate Function` procedure.* You will modify the `Generate Function` procedure to use the `Boolean` array to pick unique random numbers. Begin by writing a statement that generates a random number and assigns its value to an `Integer` variable `intNumber`.

f) *Determining whether the random number has already been selected.* Use an `If...Then` statement to determine whether the maximum lottery number is less than 40. (This happens when the upper limit on the random number equals 40.) In this case, you will examine the first row of the array. To maintain unique numbers, you will set the value of the element in that row whose index equals the random number to `True` (indicating that it has been picked). For example, if the random number 34 has been picked, `blnNumbers(0)(34)` would contain the value `True`. To test whether a number has been picked, use a `Do While...Loop` statement inside the `If...Then` statement to access that element of the array. If the array element's value is `True`, use the body of the loop to assign a new random number to `intNumber`. If the value in the array is `False`, use the condition in the `Do While...Loop` header to ignore the body of the loop. Just outside the `Do While...Loop`, include a statement that modifies the array to indicate that the number has now been picked.

g) *Completing the application.* Use a second `If...Then` statement to determine whether the maximum lottery number is greater than 40. In this case, you will examine the second row of the array. Repeat the process in the previous step. Remember to return the value stored in `intNumber` at the end of the `Generate Function` procedure.

h) ***Running the application.*** Select **Debug > Start** to run your application. Click the **Generate** Button and verify that the values displayed fall into the ranges specified in the exercise's description.

i) ***Closing the application.*** Close your running application by clicking its close box.

j) ***Closing the IDE.*** Close Visual Studio .NET by clicking its close box.

18.13 (*Student Grades Application*) A teacher needs an application that computes each student's grade average (on a scale of 0 to 100 points) and the class average for ten students. The application should add a student's name and test average (separated by a tab character) to a ListBox and calculate the class grade average each time the user clicks the **Submit Grades** Button (Fig. 18.25). The **Submit Grades** Button should be disabled after ten students' grades have been entered.

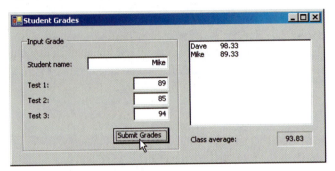

Figure 18.25 **Student Grades** application.

a) ***Copying the template to your working directory.*** Copy the directory `C:\Examples\ Tutorial18\Exercises\StudentGrades` to your `C:\SimplyVB` directory.

b) ***Opening the application's template file.*** Double click `StudentGrades.sln` in the `StudentGrades` directory to open the application.

c) ***Declare instance variables.*** Declare an `Integer` counter and a 10-by-2 `String` array as instance variables.

d) ***Coding the Submit Grades Button's Click event handler.*** Double click the **Submit Grades** Button to generate its `Click` event handler. Write code in the event handler to retrieve input from the TextBoxes. Then store the student's name in the first column of the two-dimensional `String` array and the student's test average in the second column of the array. Use a `Function` procedure to calculate the student's test average.

e) ***Computing the class average.*** Add the student's name and the student's test average (separated by a tab character) to the ListBox. Then calculate and display the class average, using a `Function` procedure. [*Hint*: You should use the two-dimensional `String` array and the `Integer` counter to calculate the class average.]

f) ***Completing the event handler.*** Increment the counter by one after calculating the class average. If ten students' grades have been entered, disable the **Submit Grades** Button.

g) ***Running the application.*** Select **Debug > Start** to run your application. Enter 10 students and their grades. Make sure that all averages are correct, and that the **Submit Grades** Button is disabled after 10 students' grades have been entered.

h) ***Closing the application.*** Close your running application by clicking its close box.

i) ***Closing the IDE.*** Close Visual Studio .NET by clicking its close box.

What does this code do? ▶   **18.14** What is returned by the following code? Assume that `GetStockPrices` is a `Function` procedure that returns a 2-by-31 array, with the first row containing the stock price at the beginning of the day and the last row containing the stock price at the end of the day, for each day of the month.

```
1    Function Mystery() As Integer()
2       Dim intPrices As Integer(,) = New Integer(1, 30) {}
3
4       intPrices = GetStockPrices()
5
6       Dim intResult As Integer() = New Integer(30) {}
7       Dim intI As Integer
8
9       For intI = 0 To 30
10          intResult(intI) = intPrices(0, intI) - intPrices(1, intI)
11      Next
12
13      Return intResult
14   End Function ' Mystery
```

What's wrong with this code? ▶   **18.15** Find the error(s) in the following code. The TwoDArrays procedure should create a two-dimensional array and initialize all its values to one.

```
1    Sub TwoDArrays()
2       Dim intArray As Integer(,)
3
4       intArray = New Integer(3, 3) {}
5
6       Dim intI As Integer
7
8       ' assign 1 to all cell values
9       For intI = 0 To 3
10          intArray(intI, intI) = 1
11      Next
12
13   End Sub ' TwoDArrays
```

Programming Challenge ▶   **18.16** (*Enhanced Student Grades Application*) Modify the application in Exercise 18.13 to include a bar graph that displays each student's grade and the class average. The chart should display only after the user enters the grades for ten students (Fig. 18.26). Until then, a Label should display the text, "Enter ten grades to display the chart." Student names and the text Class Average should display on the *x*-axis, and grades should display on the *y*-axis. Also write code that ensures that the user has entered values in each TextBox when the **Submit Grades** Button is clicked.

a) *Copying the template to your working directory.* Copy the directory C:\Examples\ Tutorial18\Exercises\EnhancedStudentGrades to your C:\SimplyVB directory.

b) *Opening the application's template file.* Double click EnhancedStudentGrades.sln in the EnhancedStudentGrades directory to open the application. If you have not completed Exercise 18.13, follow the steps in Exercise 18.13 before proceeding to the next step. If you have completed Exercise 18.13, copy the code you wrote into this application.

c) *Completing the application design.* Place a Label on the Form that reads "Enter ten grades to display the chart." Then insert an MSChart control at the bottom of the Form. Set its Visible property to False to hide the graph initially. A control's Visible property determines if the control is displayed on the Form (True) or hidden (False). Open the MSChart control's **Properties** dialog, set the **Chart Type** to a 2D Bar/PictoGraph and set the **Series Interior Color** property (under the **Series Color** tab) to yellow.

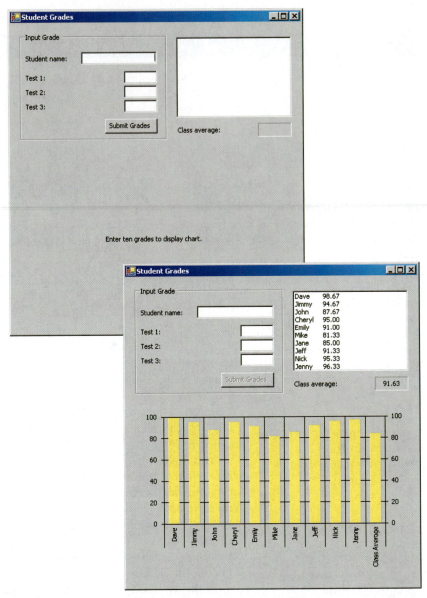

Figure 18.26 Enhanced **Student Grades** application.

d) ***Inserting code to check input.*** Write code that determines whether the user has entered values in each TextBox. If the student name is missing, display a MessageBox indicating that the user must enter a student name. If any grades are missing, display a MessageBox indicating that three grades are required.

e) ***Enhancing the user interface.*** Write code to clear each TextBox after the user clicks the **Submit Grades** Button. Then insert code to set the focus of the application to the **Student name:** TextBox.

f) ***Displaying the chart.*** Write a procedure that displays each of the ten students' test averages and the class average in the MSChart control. Recall that student names and the text Class Average should display on the *x*-axis, and grades should display on the *y*-axis. Finally, set the chart's Visible property to True, and set the Visible property of the Label you added in *Step b* to False.

g) ***Running the application.*** Select **Debug > Start** to run your application. Enter 10 sets of grades. Verify that the resulting chart displays the proper data, and that the chart is formatted as in Fig. 18.26.

h) ***Closing the application.*** Close your running application by clicking its close box.

i) ***Closing the IDE.*** Close Visual Studio .NET by clicking its close box.

Objectives

In this tutorial, you will learn to:
- Create your own classes.
- Create and use objects of your own classes.
- Control access to object instance variables.
- Use keyword `Private`.
- Create your own properties.
- Use the `Panel` control.
- Use `String` methods `PadLeft` and `Substring`.

Outline

Microwave Oven Application

Building Your Own Classes and Objects

In earlier tutorials, you used the following application-development methodology: You analyzed many typical problems that required an application to be built and determined what classes from the FCL were needed to implement each application. You then selected appropriate methods from these classes and created any necessary procedures to complete each application.

You have now seen several FCL classes. Each GUI control is defined as a class. When you add a control to your application from the **Toolbox**, an object (also known as an **instance**) of that class is created and added to your application. You have also seen FCL classes that are not GUI controls. Classes `String` and `Random`, for example, have been used to create `String` objects (for textual data) and `Random` objects (for generating random numbers), respectively. When you create and use an object of a class in an application, your application is known as a **client** of that class.

In this tutorial, you will learn to create and use your own classes (sometimes known as **programmer-defined classes**, or **programmer-defined types**). Creating your own classes is a key part of object-oriented programming (OOP). As with procedures, classes can be reused. In the world of Visual Basic .NET programming, applications are created by using a combination of FCL classes and methods and programmer-defined classes and procedures. You have already created several procedures in this book. Note that all of these procedures were created within classes, because all of your applications have been defined as classes. In this tutorial (and for the remainder of the book), you will refer to a class's procedures as methods, which is the industry-preferred term for procedures located within a class.

You will create a microwave-oven simulator where the user will enter an amount of time for the microwave to cook food. To handle the time data, you will create a class called `Time`. This class will store a number of minutes and seconds (which your **Microwave Oven** application will use to keep track of the remaining cook time) and provide properties whereby clients of this class can change the number of minutes and seconds.

19.1 Test-Driving the Microwave Oven Application

In this tutorial you will build your own class as you construct your **Microwave Oven** application. This application must meet the following requirements:

Application Requirements

*An electronics company is considering building microwave ovens. The company has asked you to develop an application that simulates a microwave oven. The oven will contain a keypad that allows the user to specify the microwave cook time, which is displayed for the user. Once a time is entered, the user clicks the **Start Button** to begin the cooking process. The microwave's glass window changes color (from gray to yellow) to simulate the oven's light that remains on while the food cooks, and a timer counts down one second at a time. Once the time expires, the color of the microwave's glass window returns to gray (indicating that the microwave's light is now off) and the microwave displays the text "Done!". The user can click the **Clear Button** at any time to stop the microwave and enter a new time. The user should be able to enter a number of minutes no larger than 59 and a number of seconds no larger than 59; otherwise, the invalid cook time will be set to zero. A beep will be sounded whenever a **Button** is clicked, and when the microwave oven has finished a countdown.*

You begin by test-driving the completed application. Then, you will learn the additional Visual Basic .NET technologies that you will need to create your own version of this application.

Test-Driving the Microwave Oven Application

1. **Opening the completed application.** Open the directory `C:\Examples\Tutorial19\CompletedApplication\MicrowaveOven` to locate the **Microwave Oven** application. Double click `MicrowaveOven.sln` to open the application in Visual Studio .NET.

2. **Running the Microwave Oven application.** Select **Debug > Start** to run the application (Fig. 19.1). The application contains a large rectangle on the left (representing the microwave oven's glass window) and a keypad on the right, including a `Label` with the text **Microwave Oven**. The numeric `Buttons` are used to enter the cook time, which will be displayed in the `Label` on the top right. Notice that the keypad `Buttons` appear flat, to give the application a more "real-world" appearance. To create this appearance, the `Buttons`' `FlatStyle` property has been set to `Flat`. Similarly, the `Label`'s `BorderStyle` property has been set to `FixedSingle`.

Microwave's glass window ——

Numeric keypad (`Buttons` appear flat)

Figure 19.1   **Microwave Oven** application's `Form`.

(cont.)   3. ***Entering a time.*** Click the following numeric Buttons in order: **1, 2, 3, 4** and **5**. Each time you click a keypad Button, you will hear a beeping sound. (If you do not hear a beeping sound, please check your computer settings to ensure that the volume of your machine's speaker has not been lowered or muted.)

Notice that you can enter no more than four digits (the first two for the minutes and the second two for the seconds)—any extra digits will not appear (Fig. 19.2). The number of minutes and the number of seconds must each be 59 or less. If the user enters an invalid number of minutes or seconds (such as 89), the invalid amount will be set to zero.

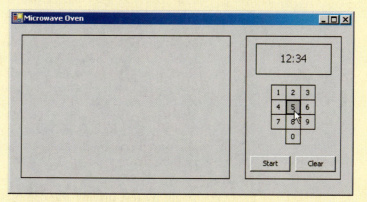

Figure 19.2 **Microwave Oven** application accepts only four digits.

4. ***Entering invalid data.*** Click the **Clear** Button to clear your input. Click the following numeric Buttons in order: **7, 2, 3** and **5** (Fig. 19.3). This input is invalid because the number of minutes, 72, is larger than the maximum allowed value, 59, so the number of minutes is reset to zero when the **Start** Button is clicked. Click the **Start** Button now. Notice that the number of minutes has been reset to **00** (Fig. 19.4). Also notice that the microwave oven's window has changed to yellow, to simulate the light that goes on inside the oven so that the user can watch the food cooking.

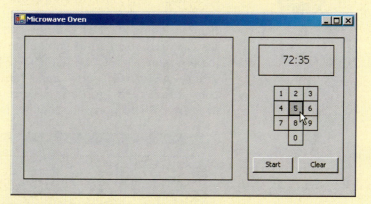

Figure 19.3 **Microwave Oven** application with invalid input.

5. ***Entering valid data.*** Click the **Clear** Button to enter a new cook time. Click Button **5** (to indicate 5 seconds); then, click **Start** (Fig. 19.5).

6. ***Viewing the application after the cooking time has expired.*** Wait five seconds. Notice that the display Label shows the time counting down by 1 each second. When the time has reached zero, the oven beeps, the display Label changes to contain the text **Done!** and the microwave oven's window changes back to the same color as the Form (Fig. 19.6).

(cont.)

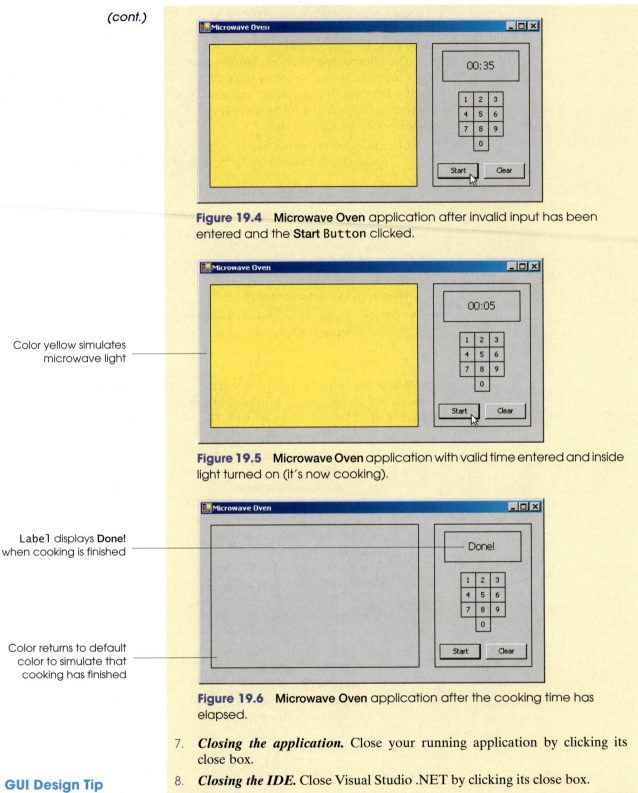

Figure 19.4　**Microwave Oven** application after invalid input has been entered and the **Start Button** clicked.

Color yellow simulates microwave light

Figure 19.5　**Microwave Oven** application with valid time entered and inside light turned on (it's now cooking).

Label displays **Done!** when cooking is finished

Color returns to default color to simulate that cooking has finished

Figure 19.6　**Microwave Oven** application after the cooking time has elapsed.

7. ***Closing the application.*** Close your running application by clicking its close box.

8. ***Closing the IDE.*** Close Visual Studio .NET by clicking its close box.

GUI Design Tip

Use **Panel**s to organize groups of related controls, where the purpose of those controls is obvious. If the purpose of the controls is not obvious, use a **GroupBox** in place of a **Panel**, because **GroupBox**es can contain captions.

19.2 Designing the Microwave Oven Application

In Tutorial 14, you learned to use **GroupBox**es to group various controls. The **Microwave Oven** application also groups controls, using a **Panel control**. The main difference between **Panel**s and **GroupBox**es is that **GroupBox**es can display a caption, and **Panel**s cannot. The **Microwave Oven** application requires two **Panel**s—one to contain the controls of the application, and the other to represent the microwave oven's glass window. The template application provided for you contains one of these `Panel`s.

The **Microwave Oven** application contains a class (called `Time`) whose objects store the cook time in minutes and seconds. All the controls you have used (including the `Form` itself) are defined as classes. You will create the `Time` class before you create the class for the **Microwave Oven**. The following pseudocode describes the basic operation of class `Time`:

> *When the time object is created:*
>> *Assign input to variables for number of minutes and number of seconds*
>
> *When setting the number of minutes:*
>
>> *If the number of minutes is less than 60*
>>> *Set the number of minutes to specified value*
>> *Else*
>>> *Set the number of minutes to 0*
>
> *When setting the number of seconds:*
>
>> *If the number of seconds is less than 60*
>>> *Set the number of seconds to specified value*
>> *Else*
>>> *Set the number of seconds to 0*

When an object of class `Time` is created, the number of minutes and number of seconds will be initialized. Invalid data will cause both the number of minutes and the number of seconds to be set to 0. The following pseudocode describes the basic operation of your **Microwave Oven** class:

> *When the user clicks a numeric Button:*
>> *Sound beep*
>> *Display the formatted time*
>
> *When the user clicks the Start Button:*
>> *Store the minutes and seconds*
>> *Display the formatted time*
>> *Begin countdown—Start timer*
>> *Turn the microwave light on*
>
> *When the timer ticks (once per second):*
>> *Decrease time by one second*
>>
>> *If new time is zero*
>>> *Stop the countdown*
>>> *Sound beep*
>>> *Display text "Done!"*
>>> *Turn the microwave light off*
>> *Else*
>>> *Display new time*
>
> *When the user clicks the Clear Button:*
>> *Display the text "Microwave Oven"*
>> *Clear input and time data*
>> *Stop the countdown*
>> *Turn the microwave light off*

The user enters input by clicking the numeric `Button`s. Each time a numeric `Button` is clicked, the number on that `Button` is appended to the end of the cook time that is displayed in the GUI's `Label`. At most, four digits can be displayed.

After entering the cook time, the user can click the **Start** Button to begin the cooking process or click the **Clear** Button and enter a new time. Each Button makes a beeping sound when clicked. If the **Start** Button is clicked, a countdown using a Timer control begins, and the microwave oven's window changes to yellow, indicating that the microwave oven's light is on (so that the user can watch the food cook). Each second, the display is updated to show the remaining cooking time. When the countdown finishes, another beep is sounded, the display Label displays the text **Done!** and the microwave oven's "light" is turned off, by changing the window's color back to its default gray.

Now that you have test-driven the **Microwave Oven** application and studied its pseudocode representation, you will use an ACE table to help you convert the pseudocode to Visual Basic .NET. Figure 19.7 lists the actions, controls and events that will help you complete your own version of this application.

Action/Control/Event (ACE) Table for the Microwave Oven Application	**Action**	**Control/Object**	**Event**
		bntOne, btnTwo, btnThree, btnFour, btnFive, btnSix, btnSeven, btnEight, btnNine, btnZero	Click
	Sound beep		
	Display the formatted time	lblDisplay	
		btnStart	Click
	Store the minutes and seconds	m_objTime	
	Display the formatted time	lblDisplay	
	Begin countdown—Start timer	tmrClock	
	Turn microwave light on	pnlWindow	
		tmrClock	Tick
	Decrease time by one second	m_objTime	
	If new time is zero	m_objTime	
	Stop the countdown	tmrClock	
	Sound beep		
	Display text "Done!"	lblDisplay	
	Turn the microwave light off	pnlWindow	
	Else	lblDisplay	
	Display new time		
		btnClear	Click
	Display the text "Microwave Oven"	lblDisplay	
	Clear input and time data	m_strTime, m_objTime	
	Stop the countdown	tmrClock	
	Turn microwave light off	pnlWindow	

Figure 19.7 ACE table for the **Microwave Oven** application.

Input is sent to the application when the user clicks one of the numeric Buttons. Values are displayed in lblDisplay as they are entered. Once all input has been entered, the user clicks the **Start** Button to begin the countdown. The pnlWindow Panel's background color is set to yellow to simulate the microwave oven's light being turned on, and Timer tmrClock will update lblDisplay each second during the countdown. To clear the input and start over, the user can click the **Clear** Button. In the following box, you begin creating your **Microwave Oven** application by adding the second Panel to the Form and viewing the template code.

Adding a Panel Control to the Microwave Oven Application

GUI Design Tip

Although it is possible to have a `Panel` without a border (by setting the `BorderStyle` property to `None`), use borders on your `Panels` to improve readability and organization.

Good Programming Practice

We recommend you use prefix `pnl` when naming your `Panel` controls.

GUI Design Tip

A `Panel` can display scrollbars for use when the `Panel` is not large enough to display all of its controls at once. To increase readability, we suggest avoiding the use of scrollbars on `Panels`. If a `Panel` is not large enough to display all of its contents, increase the size of the `Panel`.

1. *Copying the template to your working directory.* Copy the `C:\Examples\ Tutorial19\TemplateApplication\MicrowaveOven` directory to your `C:\SimplyVB` directory.

2. *Opening the Microwave Oven application's template file.* Double click `MicrowaveOven.sln` in the `MicrowaveOven` directory to open the application in Visual Studio .NET.

3. *Adding a Panel to the Form.* Add a `Panel` control to the `Form` by double clicking the **Panel** control (⬜ Panel) in the **Toolbox**. Name the control `pnlWindow` as this `Panel` will represent your microwave oven's window. Set the `Panel`'s `Size` property to `328, 224` and its `Location` property to `16, 16`. Set the `BorderStyle` property to `FixedSingle`, to display a thin black rectangle surrounding your `Panel`.

4. *Viewing the template code.* Before you add code to this application, switch to code view, and examine the code provided. Line 5 of Fig. 19.8 declares variable `m_strTime`, a `String` that will store user input.

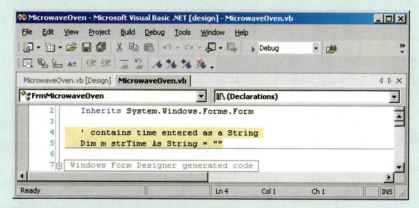

Figure 19.8 Variable `m_strTime` contains the user's input.

The template code also contains event handlers for the numeric `Buttons`' `Click` events. Each `Button` is clicked when the user wants to append the current `Button`'s digit to the amount of cooking time. Let's look at one of these event handlers closely (Fig. 19.9). Line 242 calls function **Beep**, which causes your computer to make a beep sound. Each event handler for the numeric keypad `Buttons` begins with a call to `Beep`, appends the current `Button`'s number to `m_strTime` (line 243) and calls method `DisplayTime` (line 244), which displays the remaining cook time in the application's `Label`. There are ten of these event handlers—one for each digit from 0 to 9.

`MicrowaveOven.vb` contains four more methods that you will define in this tutorial. The first is the `btnStart_Click` event handler on lines 328–332 of Fig. 19.10. This event handler will be used to start the microwave oven's cooking process, which in this simulation consists of a time countdown and a change in the window's color to yellow, simulating the oven's light being on.

Event handler `btnClear_Click` (lines 334–338) will be used to clear the time entered. The **Clear Button** is used to change the time entered or terminate cooking early. The event handler resets the time to all zeros and displays the text **Microwave Oven**. Method `DisplayTime` (lines 340–343) will be used to display the cooking time as it is being entered. Event handler `tmrClock_Tick` (lines 345–349) will be used to change the application's `Label` during the countdown.

(cont.)

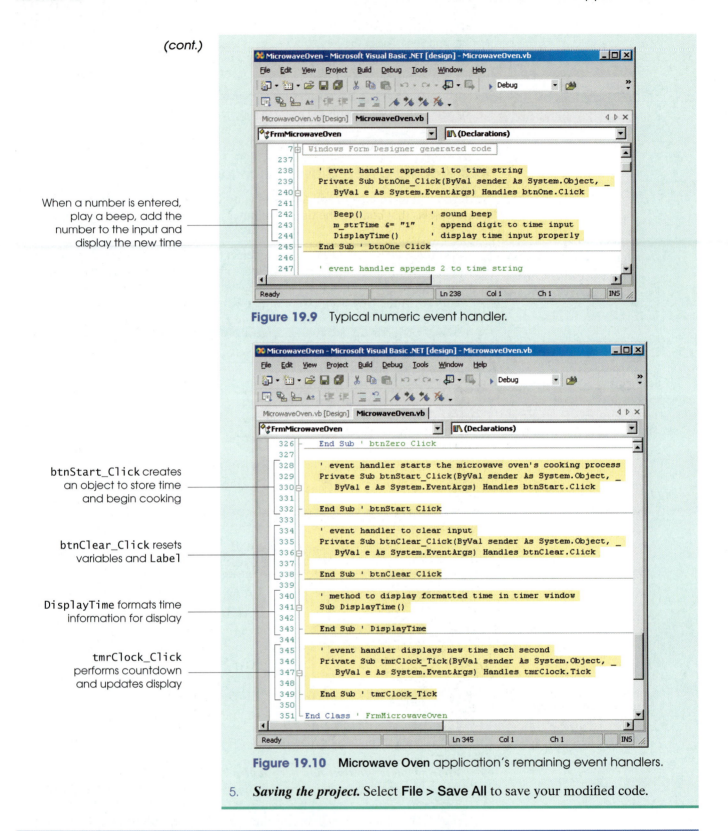

When a number is entered, play a beep, add the number to the input and display the new time

Figure 19.9 Typical numeric event handler.

btnStart_Click creates an object to store time and begin cooking

btnClear_Click resets variables and Label

DisplayTime formats time information for display

tmrClock_Click performs countdown and updates display

Figure 19.10 **Microwave Oven** application's remaining event handlers.

5. ***Saving the project.*** Select **File > Save All** to save your modified code.

SELF-REVIEW 1. A Panel is different from a GroupBox in that a _____.

   a) GroupBox can be used to organize controls, whereas a Panel cannot

   b) Panel contains a caption, whereas a GroupBox does not

   c) GroupBox contains a caption, whereas a Panel does not

   d) Panel can be used to organize controls, whereas a GroupBox cannot

2. Function Beep causes the computer to _____.
   a) make three beeping sounds in sequence
   b) make a beeping sound
   c) display a message dialog and make a beeping sound
   d) set off the system alarm and pause the application

Answers: 1) c. 2) b.

19.3 Adding a New Class to the Project

Next, you will learn how to add a class to your application. This class will be used to create objects that contain the time in minutes and seconds.

Adding a Class to the Microwave Oven Application

1. ***Adding a new class to the project.*** Select **Project > Add Class**. In the dialog that appears (Fig. 19.11), enter the class name (Time) in the **Name:** field and click **Open**. Note that the class name (ending with the .vb file extension) appears in the **Solution Explorer** below the project name (Fig. 19.12).

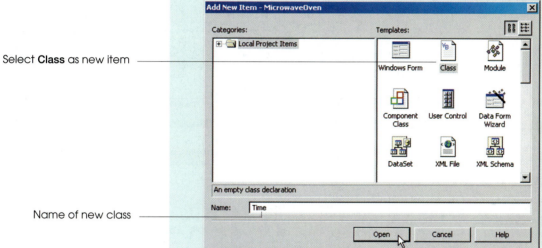

Select **Class** as new item

Name of new class

Figure 19.11 **Add New Item** dialog allows you to create a new class.

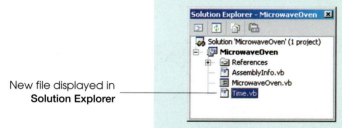

New file displayed in **Solution Explorer**

Figure 19.12 **Solution Explorer** displaying new class file.

2. ***Viewing the code that has been added to this class.*** If Time.vb does not open for you when it is created, double click the file in the **Solution Explorer**. Notice that a few lines of code have been added for you (Fig. 19.13). Line 1, which begins the Time class definition, contains the keywords Public and Class, followed by the name of the class (in this case, Time). Keyword **Class** indicates that what follows is a class definition. You will learn about keyword Public in Section 19.7. The keywords **End Class** (line 3) indicate the end of the class definition. Any code placed between these two lines form the class definition's body. Any methods or variables defined in the body of a class are considered to be **members** of that class.

(cont.)

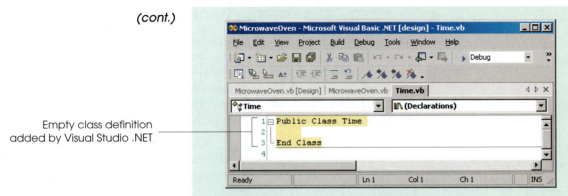

Empty class definition
added by Visual Studio .NET

Figure 19.13 Empty class definition.

3. *Adding instance variables to your application.* Add lines 1–2 of Fig. 19.14 to `Time.vb`, above the class definition. You should add comments indicating the name and purpose of your class files. Add lines 6–8 to the `Time` class definition.

   Lines 7 and 8 declare each of the two `Integer` instance variables—`m_intMinute` and `m_intSecond`. The `Time` class will store a time value containing minutes and seconds—the value for minutes is stored in `m_intMinute` and the value for seconds is stored in `m_intSecond`. Recall from Tutorial 15 that our member-naming preference is to prefix an 'm_' to each instance variable. Finally, be sure to add a comment on line 10 where the class definition is terminated.

Good Programming Practice

Add comments at the beginning of programmer-defined classes to increase readability. The comments should indicate the name of the file that contains the class and the purpose of the class being defined.

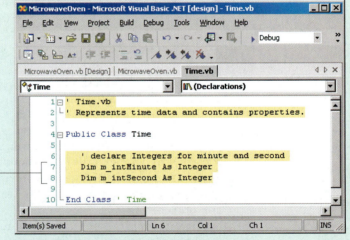

Instance variables
store minute and
second information

Figure 19.14 `Time`'s instance variables.

4. *Saving the project.* Select **File > Save All** to save your modified code.

---

1. To add a class to a project in Visual Studio .NET, select _____.

   a) **File > Add Class**   b) **File > Add File > Add Class**

   c) **Project > Add Class**   d) **Project > Add File > Add Class**

2. A class definition ends with the keyword(s) _____.

   a) `Class End`   b) `End Class`

   c) `EndClass`   d) `End`

Answers: 1) c. 2) b.

19.4 Initializing Class Objects: Constructors

A class can contain methods as well as instance variables. You have already used method `Format` from class `String` and method `Next` from class `Random`. A **constructor** is a special method within a class definition that is used to initialize a class's instance variables. In Tutorial 16, you learned how to use constructors to create objects. In the following box, you will create a constructor for your `Time` class, allowing clients to create `Time` objects and initialize those objects' data.

Defining a Constructor

1. ***Adding a constructor to a class.*** Add lines 10–12 of Fig. 19.15 to the body of class `Time`, then press *Enter*. The keywords `End Sub` will be added for you, just as with the other Sub procedures you created in this text.

    New is the constructor method. You write code for the constructor, which is invoked each time an object of that class is instantiated (created). This constructor method then performs the actions in its body, which you will add in the next few steps. A constructor's actions consist mainly of statements that initialize the class's instance variables.

New is the
constructor method ————

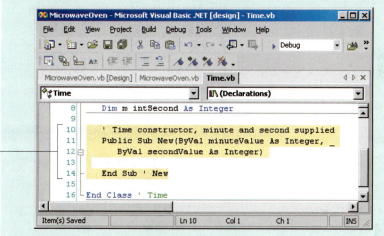

Figure 19.15   Empty constructor.

Constructors can take arguments (you'll see how to provide arguments to constructors momentarily) but cannot return values. An important difference between constructors and other methods is that constructors cannot specify a return data type—for this reason, Visual Basic .NET constructors are implemented as `Sub` procedures rather than `Function` procedures, because `Sub` procedures cannot return values. A class's instance variables can be initialized in the constructor, or when those variables are defined in the class definition. Variable `m_intSecond`, for instance, can be initialized where it is declared (line 8) or it can be initialized in `Time`'s constructor.

2. ***Initializing variables in a constructor.*** Add lines 14 and 15 of Fig. 19.16 to the constructor. These lines initialize `Time`'s instance variables to the values of the constructor's parameter variables (lines 11–12 of Fig. 19.15). When an object is created in a client of a class, values are often specified for that object. A `Time` object can now be created with the statement

    ```
    m_objTimeObject = New Time(5, 3)
    ```

This `Time` object will be created and the constructor will execute. The values 5 and 3 are assigned to the constructor's parameters, which will be used to initialize `m_intSecond` and `m_intMinute`.

Common Programming Error

Attempting to declare a constructor as a `Function` procedure instead of as a `Sub` procedure and/or attempting to `Return` a value from a constructor are both syntax errors.

Error-Prevention Tip

Providing a constructor to ensure that every object is initialized with meaningful values can help eliminate logic errors.

(cont.)

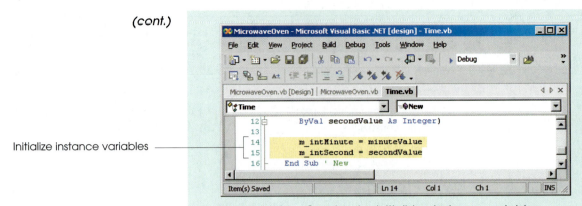

Figure 19.16 Constructor initializing instance variables.

3. **Creating a Time object.** After defining the class, you can use it as a type (just as you would use `Integer` or `Double`) in declarations. View `MicrowaveOven.vb` by selecting the **MicrowaveOven.vb** tab above the code editor. Add lines 7–8 of Fig. 19.17 to your application. Notice the use of the class name, `Time`, as a type. Just as you can create many variables from a data type, such as `Integer`, you can create many objects from class types. You can create your own class types as needed; this is one reason why Visual Basic .NET is known as an **extensible language**—the language can be "extended" with new data types. Notice that, after you type `As` in line 8, *IntelliSense* displays a window of available types. Notice that new class `Time` will be displayed in the *IntelliSense* window (Fig. 19.18).

4. **Saving the project.** Select **File > Save All** to save your modified code.

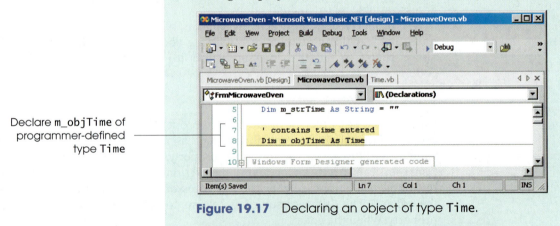

Figure 19.17 Declaring an object of type `Time`.

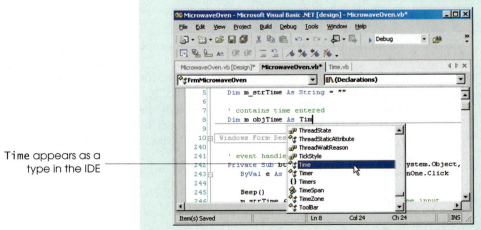

Figure 19.18 `Time` appearing as a type in an *Intellisense* window.

1. A(n) _____ language is one that can be "extended" with new data types.

    a) data   b) extensible

    c) typeable   d) extended

2. Variables can be initialized _____.

    a) when they are declared   b) to their default values

    c) in a constructor   d) All of the above.

Answers: 1) b. 2) d.

19.5 Properties

Clients of a class usually want to manipulate that class's instance variables. For example, assume a class (`Person`) that stores information about a person, including age information (stored in `Integer` instance variable `intAge`). Clients who create an object of class `Person` could want to modify `intAge`—perhaps incorrectly, by assigning a negative value to `intAge`, for example. Classes often provide **properties** to allow clients to access and modify instance variables safely. You have already seen and used several properties in previous tutorials. For instance, many GUI controls contain a `Text` property, used to retrieve or modify the text displayed by a control. When a value is to be assigned to a property, the code in that property definition is executed. The code in that property typically checks the value to be assigned and rejects invalid data. In this tutorial, you learn how to create your own properties to help clients of a class read and modify the class's instance variables. You will create two properties, `Minute` and `Second`, for your `Time` class. `Minute` allows clients to access variable `m_intMinute` safely, and `Second` allows clients to access variable `m_intSecond` safely.

A **property definition** actually consists of two **accessors**—method-like code units that handle the details of modifying and returning data. The **Set accessor** allows clients to set (that is, assign values to) properties. For example, when the code

```
objTime.Minute = 35
```

executes, the `Set` accessor of the `Minute` property executes. `Set` accessors typically provide data-validation capabilities (such as range checking) to ensure that the value of each instance variable is set properly. In your **Microwave Oven** application, users can specify an amount of minutes only in the range 0 to 59. Values not in this range will be discarded by the `Set` accessor, and `m_intMinute` will be assigned the value 0. The **Get accessor** allows clients to get (that is, obtain the value of) a property. When the code

```
intMinuteValue = objTime.Minute
```

executes, the **Get accessor** of the `Minute` property executes (and returns the value of the `m_intMinute` instance variable).

Each property is typically defined to perform validity checking—to ensure that the data assigned to the property is valid. Keeping an object's data valid is also known as keeping that data in a **consistent state**. Property `Minute` keeps instance variable `m_intMinute` in a consistent state. In the following box, you will create properties `Minute` and `Second` for your `Time` class, defining `Get` and `Set` accessors for each.

Defining Properties

1. ***Adding property Minute to class Time.*** View Time.vb by selecting the
Time.vb tab above the code editor. Add lines 18–19 of Fig. 19.19, then press
Enter to add property Minute to class Time. Lines 20–26 will be added for
you automatically by the IDE. Notice the syntax used in a property definition. You begin on line 19 with the keyword Public (which will be discussed
in Section 19.7), followed by the keyword **Property**, which indicates that
you are defining a property. The keyword Property is followed by the name
of the property (in this case, Minute) and a set of parentheses, which is similar to the way you define methods. The first line of the property then concludes with the keyword As followed by a data type (in this case, Integer),
indicating the data type of any value assigned to, or read from, this property.

Get accessor retrieves data

Set accessor stores data

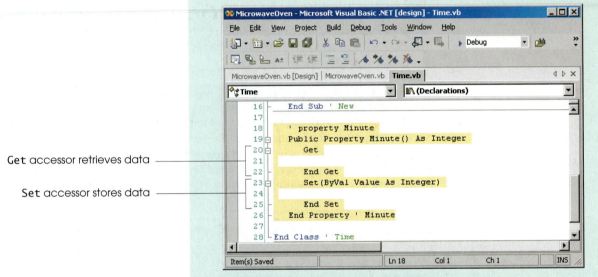

Figure 19.19 Empty Minute property.

The keyword **Get** on line 20 indicates the beginning of this property's Get
accessor. The keywords **End Get** on line 22 indicate the end of the Get accessor. Any code that you insert between these two lines will make up the Get
accessor's body and will be executed when a client of this class attempts to
read a value from the Minute property, such as with the code int-
MinuteValue = objTime.Minute.

The keyword **Set** on line 23 indicates the beginning of this property's Set
accessor. The keywords **End Set** on line 25 indicate the end of the Set accessor. Any code that you insert between these two lines will make up the Set
accessor's body and will be executed automatically (that's the beauty of
properties) when a client of this class attempts to assign a value to the
Minute property, such as with the code objTime.Minute = 35. The value
assigned is stored in the parameter specified on line 23, which by default uses
the identifier Value. This identifier is used to access the value assigned to
property Minute. The property ends on line 26 with the keywords **End Property**. Notice that we have added a comment to this line, indicating the name
of the property being terminated.

2. ***Defining the Get accessor.*** Add line 23 of Fig. 19.20 to your Get accessor.
Also add a blank line (line 20) and a comment (line 21) above the Get accessor, to increase readability. When property Minute is referenced, you want
your Get accessor to return the value of m_intMinute just as you would
return a value from a method, so you use the keyword Return on line 23,
followed by the identifier m_intMinute. Finally, you should add a comment
on line 24 to indicate the end of the Get accessor.

 **Error-Prevention Tip**

A property that sets the value of an
instance variable should verify that
the intended new value is correct. If
it is not, the Set accessor should
place the instance variable into an
appropriate consistent state.

(cont.)

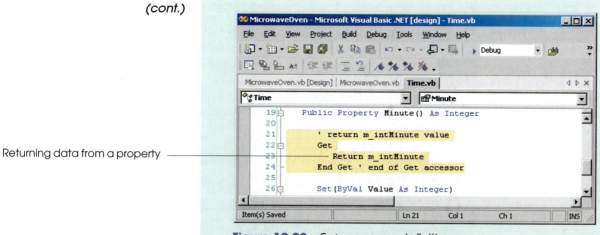

Figure 19.20 Get accessor definition.

3. **Defining the Set accessor.** Add lines 29–34 of Fig. 19.21 to your Set accessor. Also add a blank line (line 25) and a comment (line 26) above the Set accessor, to increase readability. When property Minute is assigned a value, you want to test whether the value to be assigned is valid. You do not want to accept a minutes value greater than 59, a condition that is tested on line 30. If the number of minutes is valid, it will be assigned to m_intMinute on line 31. Otherwise, the value 0 will be assigned to m_intMinute on line 33. Finally, you should add a comment on line 36 to indicate the end of the Set accessor.

(cont.)

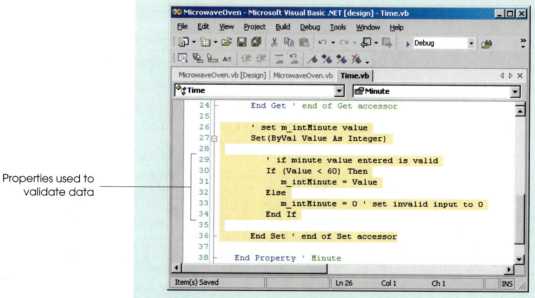

Figure 19.21 Set accessor definition.

4. **Adding property Second to class Time.** Add lines 40–41 of Fig. 19.22 to your application, then press *Enter*. Lines 42–48 are added for you automatically by the IDE. You should add the comments on lines 40 and 48 manually.

5. **Defining the Second property's accessors.** Add blank lines and comments above each accessor (lines 42–43 and 47–48 of Fig. 19.23). Add line 45 to property Second's Get accessor and lines 51–56 to property Second's Set accessor. Notice that this property is similar to Minute, except that variable m_intSecond is being modified and read, as opposed to variable m_intMinute. Finally, you should add comments at the end of each accessor (lines 46 and 58) to increase readability.

(cont.)

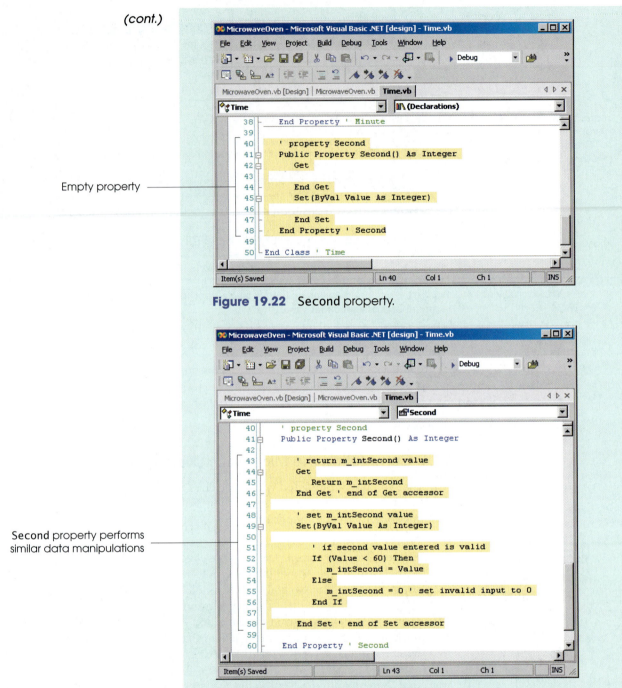

Figure 19.22   **Second** property.

Figure 19.23   **Second** property definition.

6. *Assigning values to properties.* Change lines 14–15 of Fig. 19.16 to lines 14–15 of Fig. 19.24. Now that you have defined properties to ensure that only valid data will be assigned to `m_intMinute` and `m_intSecond`, you can use these properties to safely initialize instance variables in the class's constructor.

(cont.)

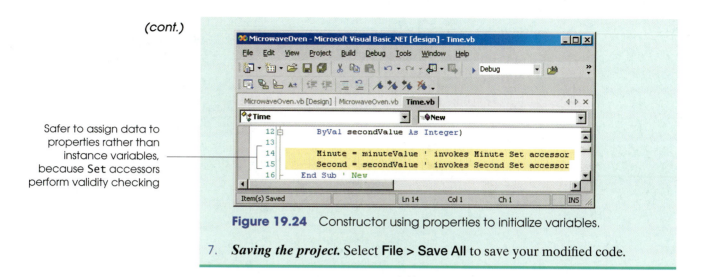

Safer to assign data to properties rather than instance variables, because **Set** accessors perform validity checking

Figure 19.24   Constructor using properties to initialize variables.

7. ***Saving the project.*** Select **File > Save All** to save your modified code.

SELF-REVIEW

1. A(n) _____ can ensure that a value is appropriate for a data member, before the data member is assigned that value.

   a) `Get` accessor   b) `Access` accessor
   c) `Modify` accessor   d) `Set` accessor

2. Properties can contain both _____ accessors.

   a) `Return` and `Value`   b) `Get` and `Value`
   c) `Get` and `Set`   d) `Return` and `Set`

Answers: 1) d. 2) c.

19.6 Completing the Microwave Oven Application

Now that you have completed your `Time` class, you will use an object of this class to maintain the cook time in your application. Follow the steps in the next box to add this functionality to your application.

Completing the Microwave Oven Application

1. ***Formatting user input.*** View `MicrowaveOven.vb` by selecting the **MicrowaveOven.vb** tab above the code editor. Add lines 335–340 of Fig. 19.25 to event handler `btnStart_Click`. Variables `intSecond` and `intMinute` (lines 335–336) will be used to store the second and minute values entered by the user. Lines 339–340 use `String` method **PadLeft**, which appends characters to the beginning of a `String` based on that `String`'s length. This method can be used to guarantee the length of a `String`—if that `String` has fewer characters than desired, method `PadLeft` will add characters to the beginning of that `String` until the `String` has the proper number of characters. You want `m_strTime` to contain 4 characters (for example, `"0325"` rather than `"325"` for a time of `"3:25"`, representing 3 minutes and 25 seconds). Having four digits makes the conversion to minutes and seconds easier. You can now simply convert the first two digits (03) to a minute value and the last two digits (25) to a second value. The first argument in the `PadLeft` call, 4, specifies the length that `m_strTime` will have after characters have been appended. If `m_strTime` already contains four or more characters, `PadLeft` will not have any effect. The second argument (the character 0) specifies the character that will be appended to the beginning of the `String`. Notice that specifying only `"0"` as the second argument will cause an error, as `"0"` is of type `String`. Method `PadLeft` expects the second argument to be a single character, which is of data type **Char**. You obtain the character 0 by calling method **Convert.ToChar**, which converts your `String` zero to a character zero.

(cont.)

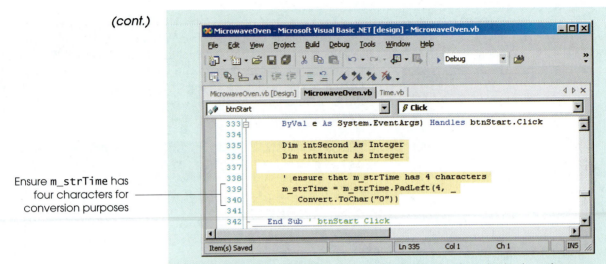

Ensure `m_strTime` has four characters for conversion purposes

Figure 19.25 Declaring variables for second and minute values.

2. *Converting user input to Integers.* Add lines 342–344 of Fig. 19.26 to event handler `btnStart_Click`. Line 343 calls method `Convert.ToInt32` to convert the last two characters of `m_strTime` to an `Integer` and assign this value to `intSecond`. The last two characters are selected from `m_strTime` by using method **Substring**. This is another `String` method, used to return only a portion of a `String` from `m_strTime`. The argument passed to `Substring`, 2, indicates that the subset of characters returned from this method should begin with the character at position 2, and continue until the end of the string. Remember that the character at position 2 is actually the third character in the `String`, because the position values of a `String` being at 0. In the example `"0325"`, calling `Substring` with the argument 2 returns `"25"`. Line 344 selects the first two characters of `m_strTime`, converts the value to an `Integer`, and assigns this value to `intMinute`. The call to `Substring` on line 344 takes two arguments. The first argument, 0, indicates that the characters returned from this method start with the first character (at position 0) of `m_strTime`. The second argument, 2, indicates that only two characters from the starting position should be returned. In the example `"0325"`, calling `Substring` with the arguments 0 and 2 returns `"03"`.

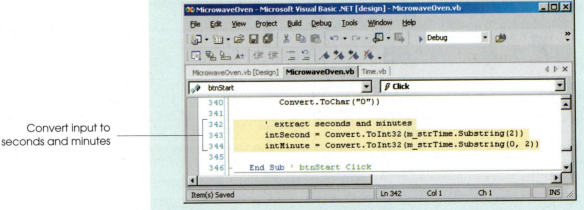

Convert input to seconds and minutes

Figure 19.26 Form minute and second values from input.

(cont.)

3. **Creating a Time object.** Add lines 346–347 of Fig. 19.27 to `btnStart_Click`. Line 347 creates an object of type `Time`. When the object is instantiated, keyword `New` allocates the memory in which the `Time` object will be stored; then, the `Time` constructor is called (with the values of `intMinute` and `intSecond`) to initialize the instance variables of the `Time` object. The constructor then returns a reference to the newly created object; this reference is assigned to `m_objTime`.

Use keyword **New** to create a new object

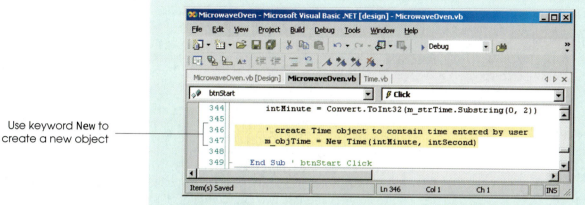

Figure 19.27 Creating a `Time` object.

4. **Accessing a Time object's properties.** Add lines 349–350 of Fig. 19.28 to `btnStart_Click`. These lines use the newly created `Time` object and method `String.Format` to display the cook time properly. You want the resulting `String` to contain two digits (for the minute), a colon (:) and finally another two digits (for the second). For example, if the time entered was 3 minutes and 20 seconds, the `String` that will display for the user is `"03:20"`. To achieve this result, you pass to the method the format control string `"{0:D2}:{1:D2}"`, which indicates that arguments 0 and 1 (the first and second arguments after the format `String` argument) should take the format D2 (base 10 decimal number format using two digits) for display purposes—thus, 8 would be converted to 08. The colon between the curly braces } and { will be included in the output, separating the minutes from the seconds. The arguments after the format-control string access `m_objTime`'s minute and second values, using the `Minute` and `Second` properties. Notice that `Time`'s properties appear in the *IntelliSense* window (Fig. 19.29) when you try to access the object's members (using the dot operator).

Display cook time

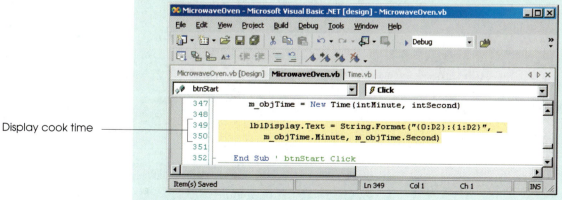

Figure 19.28 Displaying time information with separating colon.

Time's properties appear in *Intellisense*

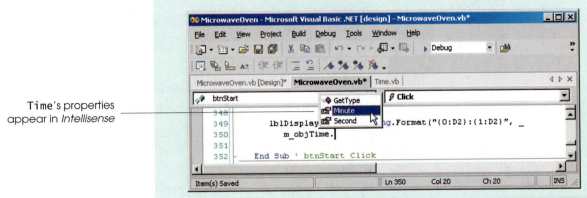

Figure 19.29   Properties of a programmer-defined type also appear in *IntelliSense*.

5. ***Starting the cooking process.*** Add lines 352–356 of Fig. 19.30 to your application. Line 352 clears the user's input, so that the user can enter new input at any time. Line 354 starts the `Timer` by setting its `Enabled` property to `True`. The `Timer`'s `Tick` event will now be raised each second. You will implement the event handler for this event shortly. Line 356 sets the `Panel`'s `BackColor` property to yellow to simulate the light inside the microwave oven. The color yellow is assigned to property `BackColor` using property `Yellow` of structure `Color`. The **Color** structure contains several predefined colors as properties.

Start timer and turn "light" on to indicate microwave oven is cooking

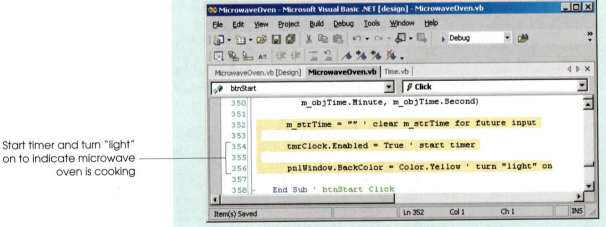

Figure 19.30   Starting the microwave oven countdown.

6. ***Clearing the cook time.*** Add lines 364–369 of Fig. 19.31 to event handler `btnClear_Click`. Line 365 sets the application's `Label` to **Microwave Oven**. Line 366 clears the input values stored in `m_strTime`, and line 367 resets the `Time` object to zero minutes and zero seconds. Line 368 disables the `Timer`, which stops the countdown. Line 369 sets the `Panel`'s background back to the `Panel`'s original color to simulate turning off the light inside the microwave oven. Notice that we set the `Panel`'s color using the **DefaultBackColor** property. This property contains the default background color for a `Panel` control. When a `Panel` is added to a `Form`, its background takes on the default background color of the `Panel`.

(cont.)

Resetting **Microwave Oven** application

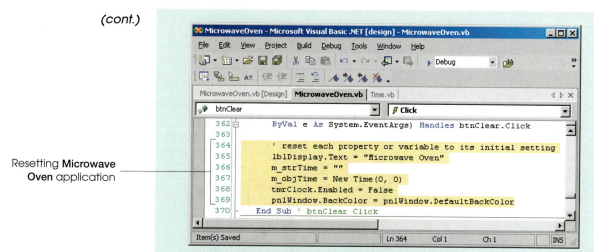

Figure 19.31 Clearing the **Microwave Oven** input.

7. ***Displaying data as it is being input.*** Add lines 375–383 of Fig. 19.32 to method `DisplayTime`. This method will be called each time the user enters another digit for the cook time. Lines 375–376 declare variables `intSecond` and `intMinute`, which will store the current number of seconds and minutes. Line 378 declares `strDisplay`, which will store the user's current input in the proper display format. Lines 381–383 remove any extra digits entered by the user. (Recall that the user may enter a maximum of four digits.) Line 381 uses `String` property **Length**, which returns the number of characters in a `String`, to determine whether `m_strTime` has more than four digits.

If it does, line 382 uses `String` method `Substring` to remove the extra digits. The arguments (0 followed by 4) indicate that the substring returned should begin with the first character in `m_strTime` and continue for four characters. The result is assigned back to `m_strTime`, ensuring that any characters appended past the first four will be removed.

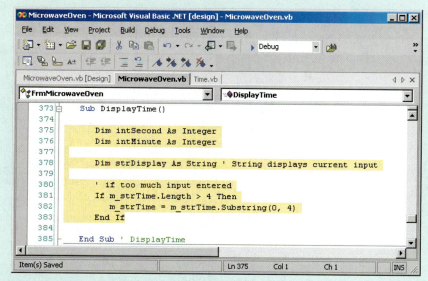

Figure 19.32 Modifying invalid user input.

(cont.)

8. ***Completing the DisplayTime method.*** Add lines 385–393 of Fig. 19.33 to method `DisplayTime`. These lines are similar to those of event handler `btnStart_Click`. Line 385 appends zeros to the front of `m_strTime` if fewer than four digits were entered. Lines 388–389 use method `Substring` to isolate the number of seconds and minutes currently entered. Lines 392–393 then use method `Format` to display the input correctly.

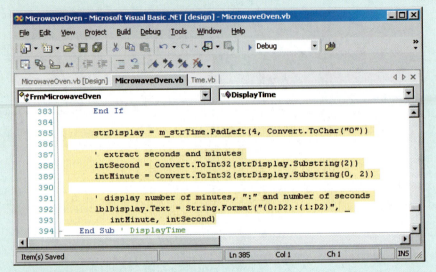

Figure 19.33   Display current input.

9. ***Performing the countdown.*** Add lines 400–416 of Fig. 19.34 to event handler `tmrTimer_Tick`. Remember that this event handler executes every second for as long as the `Timer` is enabled. Lines 401–413 modify the display `Label` once per second so that the time remaining is shown to the user.

   If the value of seconds is greater than zero (line 401), the number of seconds is decremented by one (line 402). If the value of seconds is zero but the value of minutes is greater than zero (line 403), the number of minutes is decremented by one (line 404) and the number of seconds is reset to 59 for the new minute (line 405). If the number of seconds is zero and the number of minutes is zero, the cooking process is stopped—the `Timer` is disabled (line 407), a beep is sounded (line 408), the display `Label` is set to **Done!** (line 409) and the window `Panel`'s background color is set back to its default background color (line 410).

10. ***Running the application.*** Select **Debug > Start** to run your application. Enter a cook time and click the **Start** `Button`. The application should now countdown correctly, as you have defined the `Tick` event handler for `tmr-Clock`. Click the **Clear** `Button` and verify that the input is cleared and that the countdown is stopped.

11. ***Closing the application.*** Close your running application by clicking its close box.

(cont.)

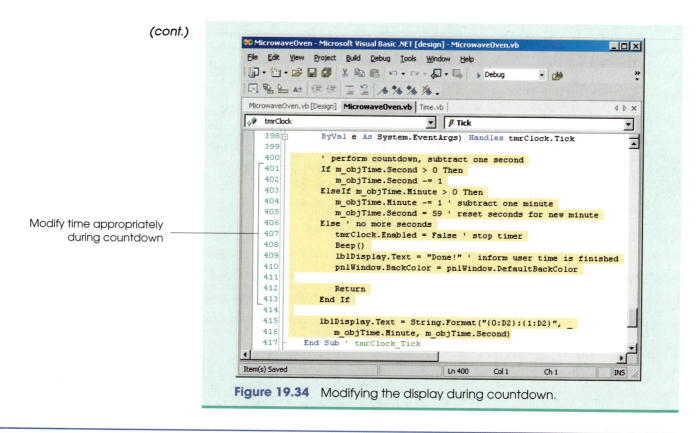

Modify time appropriately
during countdown

```
       ByVal e As System.EventArgs) Handles tmrClock.Tick
398
399
400          ' perform countdown, subtract one second
401          If m_objTime.Second > 0 Then
402              m_objTime.Second -= 1
403          ElseIf m_objTime.Minute > 0 Then
404              m_objTime.Minute -= 1 ' subtract one minute
405              m_objTime.Second = 59 ' reset seconds for new minute
406          Else ' no more seconds
407              tmrClock.Enabled = False ' stop timer
408              Beep()
409              lblDisplay.Text = "Done!" ' inform user time is finished
410              pnlWindow.BackColor = pnlWindow.DefaultBackColor
411
412              Return
413          End If
414
415          lblDisplay.Text = String.Format("{0:D2}:{1:D2}", _
416              m_objTime.Minute, m_objTime.Second)
417      End Sub ' tmrClock_Tick
```

Figure 19.34 Modifying the display during countdown.

SELF-REVIEW

1. The _____ property returns the number of characters in a `String`.
    a) `Length` b) `Size`
    c) `Char` d) `Width`

2. The expression `strExample.Substring(0, 7)` returns the character(s) _____.
    a) that begin at position seven and run backward to position zero
    b) that begin at position zero and continue for seven characters
    c) at position zero and position seven d) at position 0, repeated 7 times

Answers: 1) a. 2) b.

19.7 Controlling Access to Members

Common Programming Error

Attempting to access a `Private` class member from outside that class is a syntax error.

Keywords **Public** and **Private** are called **member-access modifiers**. You defined properties with member access modifier `Public` earlier in this tutorial. Class members that are declared with access modifier `Public` are available to any `Time` object. The declaration of instance variables or properties with member-access modifier `Private` makes them available only to methods, properties and events of the class. Attempting to access a class's `Private` data from outside the class definition is a compilation error. Normally, instance variables are declared `Private`, whereas methods and properties are declared `Public`. In the following box, you will declare this application's instance variables as `Private`.

Controlling Access to Members

1. ***Declaring Time's instance variables as Private.*** View `Time.vb` by selecting the **Time.vb** tab above the code editor. Replace keyword `Dim` on lines 7 and 8 with keyword `Private` (as in Fig. 19.35), indicating that these instance variables are accessible only to members of class `Time`. A class's `Private` instance variables may be accessed by methods, properties and events of that class.

(cont.)

Good Programming Practice

Group all `Private` class members in a class definition, followed by all `Public` class members. This helps enhance clarity and readability.

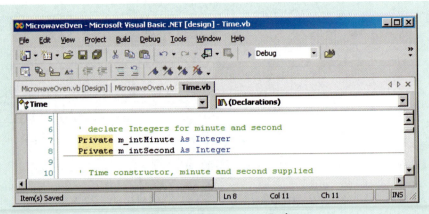

Figure 19.35 Time's instance variables are `Private`.

2. ***Declaring FrmMicrowaveOven's instance variables as Private.*** View `MicrowaveOven.vb` by selecting the **MicrowaveOven.vb** tab above the code editor. Replace keyword `Dim` in lines 5 and 8 with keyword `Private` (as in Fig. 19.36), indicating that these instance variables are accessible only to members of class `FrmMicrowaveOven`. When an object of the class contains such instance variables, only methods, properties and events of that object's class can access the variables.

Good Programming Practice

For clarity, every instance variable or property definition should be preceded by a member-access modifier.

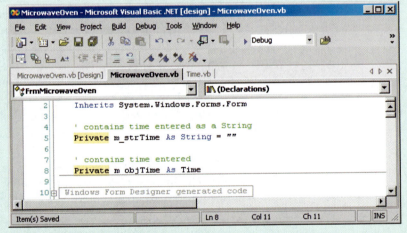

Figure 19.36 Microwave Oven's instance variables are `Private`.

3. ***Setting method DisplayTime as Private.*** Add keyword `Private` to the beginning of method `DisplayTime` (line 373 of Fig. 19.37). As with variables, methods are declared `Private` when they should only be accessible to other members of the current class. In this example only the class that defines your **Microwave Oven** uses method `DisplayTime`, so you should make this method `Private`.

Notice that the event handlers you have created throughout this book have the keyword `Private` automatically added to their headers. You now know that this occurs because event handlers are specific to the Form's class, and not the entire application, which includes class `Time`.

(cont.)

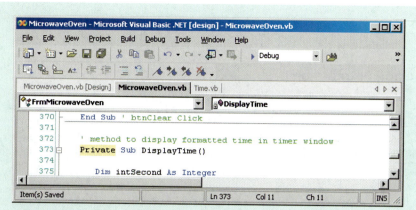

Figure 19.37 Microwave Oven's methods are `Private`.

Software Design Tip

Declare all instance variables of a class as `Private`. When necessary, provide `Public` properties to set and get the values of `Private` instance variables.

4. *Running the application.* Select **Debug > Start** to run your application. Notice that the application performs exactly as it did at the end of the last box. This occurs because when instance variables are declared by using keyword `Dim`, they are by default `Private` variables. For example, recall that the instance variables of `Time` did not appear in the *IntelliSense* window of Fig. 19.29. These variables were `Private` by default, and therefore not accessible outside of class `Time`. Inaccessible variables do not appear in the *IntelliSense* window. It is a good practice always to precede instance variables with a member-access modifier (usually `Private`). Changing `DisplayTime` to be `Private` did not affect the application either, because your code does not attempt to access this method from outside the class in which it is defined.

5. *Closing the application.* Close your running application by clicking its close box.

6. *Closing the IDE.* Close Visual Studio .NET by clicking its close box.

Figures 19.38 and 19.39 present the source code for the **Microwave Oven** application. The lines of code that contain new programming concepts that you learned in this tutorial are highlighted.

```
1   Public Class FrmMicrowaveOven
2      Inherits System.Windows.Forms.Form
3
4      ' contains time entered as a String
5      Private m_strTime As String = ""
6
7      ' contains time entered
8      Private m_objTime As Time
9
10     ' Windows Form Designer generated code
11
12     ' event handler appends 1 to time string
13     Private Sub btnOne_Click(ByVal sender As System.Object, _
14        ByVal e As System.EventArgs) Handles btnOne.Click
15
16        Beep()               ' sound beep
17        m_strTime &= "1"     ' append digit to time input
18        DisplayTime()        ' display time input properly
19     End Sub ' btnOne_Click
```

Figure 19.38 **Microwave Oven** application code. (Part 1 of 4.)

```
20
21      ' event handler appends 2 to time string
22      Private Sub btnTwo_Click(ByVal sender As System.Object, _
23         ByVal e As System.EventArgs) Handles btnTwo.Click
24
25         Beep()              ' sound beep
26         m_strTime &= "2"    ' append digit to time input
27         DisplayTime()       ' display time input properly
28      End Sub ' btnTwo_Click
29
30      ' event handler appends 3 to time string
31      Private Sub btnThree_Click(ByVal sender As System.Object, _
32         ByVal e As System.EventArgs) Handles btnThree.Click
33
34         Beep()              ' sound beep
35         m_strTime &= "3"    ' append digit to time input
36         DisplayTime()       ' display time input properly
37      End Sub ' btnThree_Click
38
39      ' event handler appends 4 to time string
40      Private Sub btnFour_Click(ByVal sender As System.Object, _
41         ByVal e As System.EventArgs) Handles btnFour.Click
42
43         Beep()              ' sound beep
44         m_strTime &= "4"    ' append digit to time input
45         DisplayTime()       ' display time input properly
46      End Sub ' btnFour_Click
47
48      ' event handler appends 5 to time string
49      Private Sub btnFive_Click(ByVal sender As System.Object, _
50         ByVal e As System.EventArgs) Handles btnFive.Click
51
52         Beep()              ' sound beep
53         m_strTime &= "5"    ' append digit to time input
54         DisplayTime()       ' display time input properly
55      End Sub ' btnFive_Click
56
57      ' event handler appends 6 to time string
58      Private Sub btnSix_Click(ByVal sender As System.Object, _
59         ByVal e As System.EventArgs) Handles btnSix.Click
60
61         Beep()              ' sound beep
62         m_strTime &= "6"    ' append digit to time input
63         DisplayTime()       ' display time input properly
64      End Sub ' btnSix_Click
65
66      ' event handler appends 7 to time string
67      Private Sub btnSeven_Click(ByVal sender As System.Object, _
68         ByVal e As System.EventArgs) Handles btnSeven.Click
69
70         Beep()              ' sound beep
71         m_strTime &= "7"    ' append digit to time input
72         DisplayTime()       ' display time input properly
73      End Sub ' btnSeven_Click
74
75      ' event handler appends 8 to time string
76      Private Sub btnEight_Click(ByVal sender As System.Object, _
77         ByVal e As System.EventArgs) Handles btnEight.Click
```

Figure 19.38 Microwave Oven application code. (Part 2 of 4.)

```
78
79          Beep()              ' sound beep
80          m_strTime &= "8"    ' append digit to time input
81          DisplayTime()       ' display time input properly
82      End Sub ' btnEight_Click
83
84      ' event handler appends 9 to time string
85      Private Sub btnNine_Click(ByVal sender As System.Object, _
86          ByVal e As System.EventArgs) Handles btnNine.Click
87
88          Beep()              ' sound beep
89          m_strTime &= "9"    ' append digit to time input
90          DisplayTime()       ' display time input properly
91      End Sub ' btnNine_Click
92
93      ' event handler appends 0 to time string
94      Private Sub btnZero_Click(ByVal sender As System.Object, _
95          ByVal e As System.EventArgs) Handles btnZero.Click
96
97          Beep()              ' sound beep
98          m_strTime &= "0"    ' append digit to time input
99          DisplayTime()       ' display time input properly
100     End Sub ' btnZero_Click
101
102     ' event handler starts the microwave oven's cooking process
103     Private Sub btnStart_Click(ByVal sender As System.Object, _
104         ByVal e As System.EventArgs) Handles btnStart.Click
105
106         Dim intSecond As Integer
107         Dim intMinute As Integer
108
109         ' ensure that m_strTime has 4 characters
110         m_strTime = m_strTime.PadLeft(4, _
111             Convert.ToChar("0"))
112
113         ' extract seconds and minutes
114         intSecond = Convert.ToInt32(m_strTime.Substring(2))
115         intMinute = Convert.ToInt32(m_strTime.Substring(0, 2))
116
117         ' create Time object to contain time entered by user
118         m_objTime = New Time(intMinute, intSecond)
119
120         lblDisplay.Text = String.Format("{0:D2}:{1:D2}", _
121             m_objTime.Minute, m_objTime.Second)
122
123         m_strTime = "" ' clear m_strTime for future input
124
125         tmrClock.Enabled = True ' start timer
126
127         pnlWindow.BackColor = Color.Yellow ' turn "light" on
128
129     End Sub ' btnStart_Click
130
131     ' event handler to clear input
132     Private Sub btnClear_Click(ByVal sender As System.Object, _
133         ByVal e As System.EventArgs) Handles btnClear.Click
134
```

Creating a new object of a programmer-defined type → (line 118)

Accessing variables of a programmer-defined type → (lines 120–121)

Start timer to begin countdown → (line 123)

Use property BackColor to change the Panel's color → (line 127)

Figure 19.38 Microwave Oven application code. (Part 3 of 4.)

```
135                ' reset each property or variable to its initial setting
136                lblDisplay.Text = "Microwave Oven"
137                m_strTime = ""
138                m_objTime = New Time(0, 0)
139                tmrClock.Enabled = False
140                pnlWindow.BackColor = pnlWindow.DefaultBackColor
141           End Sub ' btnClear_Click
142
143           ' method to display formatted time in timer window
144           Private Sub DisplayTime()
145
146                Dim intSecond As Integer
147                Dim intMinute As Integer
148
149                Dim strDisplay As String ' String displays current input
150
151                ' if too much input entered
152                If m_strTime.Length > 4 Then
153                   m_strTime = m_strTime.Substring(0, 4)
154                End If
155
156                strDisplay = m_strTime.PadLeft(4, Convert.ToChar("0"))
157
158                ' extract seconds and minutes
159                intSecond = Convert.ToInt32(strDisplay.Substring(2))
160                intMinute = Convert.ToInt32(strDisplay.Substring(0, 2))
161
162                ' display number of minutes, ":" and number of seconds
163                lblDisplay.Text = String.Format("{0:D2}:{1:D2}", _
164                   intMinute, intSecond)
165           End Sub ' DisplayTime
166
167           ' event handler displays new time each second
168           Private Sub tmrClock_Tick(ByVal sender As System.Object, _
169                ByVal e As System.EventArgs) Handles tmrClock.Tick
170
171                ' perform countdown, subtract one second
172                If m_objTime.Second > 0 Then
173                   m_objTime.Second -= 1
174                ElseIf m_objTime.Minute > 0 Then
175                   m_objTime.Minute -= 1 ' subtract one minute
176                   m_objTime.Second = 59 ' reset seconds for new minute
177                Else ' no more seconds
178                   tmrClock.Enabled = False ' stop timer
179                   Beep()
180                   lblDisplay.Text = "Done!" ' inform user time is finished
181                   pnlWindow.BackColor = pnlWindow.DefaultBackColor
182
183                   Return
184                End If
185
186                lblDisplay.Text = String.Format("{0:D2}:{1:D2}", _
187                   m_objTime.Minute, m_objTime.Second)
188           End Sub ' tmrClock_Tick
189
190      End Class ' FrmMicrowave
```

Property **Length** returns number of characters in a **String** → (line 152)

Method **Substring** returns a subset of characters in a **String** → (line 153)

Method **PadLeft** appends characters to the beginning of a **String** → (line 156)

Figure 19.38   Microwave Oven application code. (Part 4 of 4.)

Keyword **Class** used to define a class

New is the constructor

Assign data to properties, rather than to instance variables directly

End Sub keywords end the constructor definition

Keyword **Property** used to define a property

Get accessor returns data

Set accessor modifies data

```vb
1    ' Time.vb
2    ' Represents time data and contains properties.
3
4    Public Class Time
5
6        ' declare Integers for minute and second
7        Private m_intMinute As Integer
8        Private m_intSecond As Integer
9
10       ' Time constructor, minute and second supplied
11       Public Sub New(ByVal minuteValue As Integer, _
12           ByVal secondValue As Integer)
13
14           Minute = minuteValue ' invokes Minute Set accessor
15           Second = secondValue ' invokes Second Set accessor
16       End Sub ' New
17
18       ' property Minute
19       Public Property Minute() As Integer
20
21           ' return m_intMinute value
22           Get
23               Return m_intMinute
24           End Get ' end of Get accessor
25
26           ' set m_intMinute value
27           Set(ByVal Value As Integer)
28
29               ' if minute value entered is valid
30               If (Value < 60) Then
31                   m_intMinute = Value
32               Else
33                   m_intMinute = 0 ' set invalid input to 0
34               End If
35
36           End Set ' end of Set accessor
37
38       End Property ' Minute
39
40       ' property Second
41       Public Property Second() As Integer
42
43           ' return m_intSecond value
44           Get
45               Return m_intSecond
46           End Get ' end of Get accessor
47
48           ' set m_intSecond value
49           Set(ByVal Value As Integer)
50
51               ' if second value entered is valid
52               If (Value < 60) Then
53                   m_intSecond = Value
54               Else
55                   m_intSecond = 0 ' set invalid input to 0
56               End If
57
58           End Set ' end of Set accessor
```

Figure 19.39   Class Time. (Part 1 of 2.)

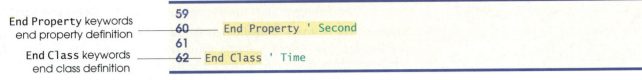

End Property keywords end property definition	59	
	60	`End Property ' Second`
	61	
End Class keywords end class definition	62	`End Class ' Time`

Figure 19.39   Class Time. (Part 2 of 2.)

19.8 Using the Debugger: The Autos and Locals Windows

Now you will enhance your knowledge of the debugger by studying the capabilities of the **Autos** and **Locals** windows. These windows allow you to view the values stored in an object's instance variables. In this section, you will learn how to view the contents of the Time object m_objTime's instance variables to verify that your application is executing correctly. In the following box, you use these windows to examine the state of the Time object in the **Microwave Oven** application.

Using the Debugger: Using the Autos and Locals Windows

1. ***Viewing the application code.*** View `MicrowaveOven.vb` by selecting the **MicrowaveOven.vb** tab above the code editor.

2. ***Setting breakpoints.*** Set breakpoints at lines 401 and 410 by clicking in the margin indicator bar (Fig. 19.40). You can set breakpoints in your application to examine an object's instance variables at certain places during execution. In the **Microwave Oven** application, the tmrClock's Tick event handler modifies the properties of m_objTime. Setting breakpoints at lines 401 and 410 allows you to suspend execution before and after certain properties have been modified, ensuring that data is being modified properly.

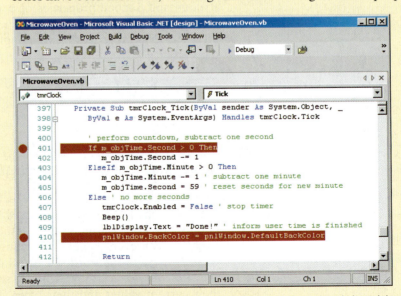

Figure 19.40   Microwave Oven application with breakpoints added.

(cont.)

3. ***Starting the debugger.*** Start the debugger by selecting **Debug > Start**.

4. ***Opening the Autos window.*** Open the **Autos** window (Fig. 19.41) by selecting **Debug > Windows > Autos** while the debugger is running. The **Autos** window allows you to view the contents of the properties used in the last statement that was executed. This allows you to verify that the previous statement executed correctly. The **Autos** window also lists the values in the next statement to be executed.

Figure 19.41 Empty **Autos** window.

5. ***Opening the Locals window.*** Open the **Locals** window (Fig. 19.42) by selecting **Debug > Windows > Locals** while the debugger is running. The **Locals** window allows you to view the state of the variables in the current scope. Recall that the scope of a variable's identifier is the portion of an application in which that identifier can be referenced. Because the Timer's Tick event is a method of the Form class, all of the instance variables and controls of the Form are viewable in the **Locals** window. This means that you will be able to view the values of the properties of m_objTime, because m_objTime is an instance variable of the Form class.

Figure 19.42 Empty **Locals** window.

6. ***Setting the time.*** Set the microwave oven's time to 1:01, and click the **Start Button**.

7. ***Using the Autos window.*** When execution halts at the breakpoint on line 401, view the **Autos** window (Fig. 19.43). If the **Autos** window is now hidden, reselect **Debug > Windows > Autos**. Notice that the **Autos** window lists the Minute and Second properties of m_objTime, their values (returned from each property's Get accessor) and their types. Viewing the values stored in an object lets you verify that your application is manipulating these variables correctly.

Properties of m_objTime ——— 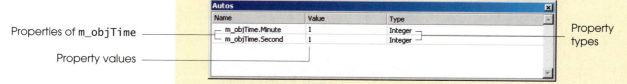 ——— Property types

Property values ———

Figure 19.43 **Autos** window displaying the state of m_objTime.

8. ***Using the Locals window.*** While execution is still halted, look at the **Locals** window. If the **Locals** window is now hidden, reselect **Debug > Windows > Locals**. The **Locals** window lists all the variables that are in the scope of the Timer's Tick event handler. To view the contents of m_objTime, click the plus box next to the word **Me**. Scroll down until you reach m_objTime, and click the plus box next to it. This will show all of the members of m_objTime, their current values and their types (Fig. 19.44). Notice that the values for minute and second are the same as they were in the **Autos** window.

(cont.)

Figure 19.44 **Locals** window displaying the state of `m_objTime`.

9. ***Continuing program execution.*** Click the debug toolbar's Continue Button, and view the values of the `m_objTime`'s members in both the **Autos** and **Locals** windows. Notice that the value for the amount of seconds (as represented by variable `m_intSecond` and property `Second`) is now shown in red, indicating that it has changed. Click the Continue Button again. Notice that both the amount of seconds and minutes have changed, so that the values of `m_intSecond`, `m_intMinute` and properties `Second` and `Minute` are shown in red (Fig. 19.45 and Fig. 19.46).

Figure 19.45 **Autos** window displaying changed variables in red.

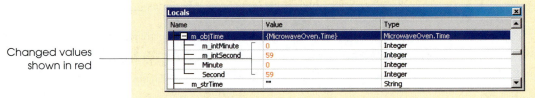

Figure 19.46 **Locals** window displaying changed variables in red.

10. ***Changing the value of a variable.*** In the **Autos** window, double click the value for property `Second`. Type 0 and press *Enter* to set the microwave oven's time to zero (Fig. 19.47). The **Autos** and **Locals** windows allow you to change the values of variables to verify that program execution is correct at certain points without having to run the program again for each value.

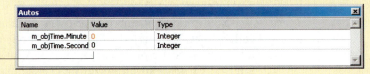

Figure 19.47 Changing the value of a variable in the **Autos** window.

11. ***Continuing execution.*** Click the Continue Button. Execution continues until the breakpoint on line 410 is reached.

12. ***Viewing the Autos and Locals window.*** View the **Autos** window, and notice that the variables listed have now changed (Fig. 19.48). This happened because execution is now at a new statement that uses new variables. View the **Locals** window. Notice that the **Locals** window still lets you view the state of `m_objTime`.

(cont.)

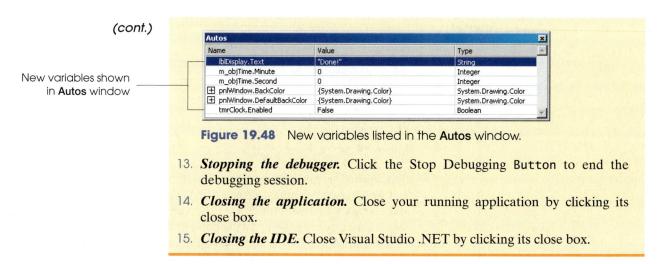

New variables shown
in **Autos** window

Figure 19.48   New variables listed in the **Autos** window.

13. *Stopping the debugger.* Click the Stop Debugging Button to end the debugging session.

14. *Closing the application.* Close your running application by clicking its close box.

15. *Closing the IDE.* Close Visual Studio .NET by clicking its close box.

In this section, you learned how to use the **Autos** and **Locals** windows to view the state of an object and verify that your application is executing correctly.

19.9 Wrap-Up

In previous tutorials, you used FCL classes and methods to add functionality to your applications. In this tutorial, you learned how to create your own classes, also known as programmer-defined classes, to provide functionality not available in the FCL. In the world of Visual Basic .NET programming, applications are created by using a combination of FCL classes and methods and programmer-defined classes and methods.

You created a microwave-oven simulator using a programmer-defined class called `Time`. You added a file to your application to create the `Time` class; then, you added a constructor, instance variables and properties to that class. You defined your constructor to initialize the class's instance variables. For each property, you defined `Get` and `Set` accessors that allow the class's instance variables to be safely accessed and modified. You then applied what you have already learned about using classes and properties to create a `Time` object. You used the properties of class `Time` to access and display the number of minutes and number of seconds that the user has specified as the microwave oven's cook time. You also learned how `Panels` can organize controls (much like `GroupBoxes`), and used a `Panel` to simulate the microwave oven's door. You concluded the tutorial by learning how to view an application's values using the debugger's **Autos** and **Locals** windows.

In the next tutorial, you will learn about collections. The FCL provides several collection classes, which enable you to store collections of data in an organized way. A collection can be thought of as a group of items. You will use collections to create a **Shipping Hub** application that stores information about several packages that are being shipped to various states. Each package will be defined by using a Package programmer-defined class. Several Package objects will be maintained by using collections.

SKILLS SUMMARY

Defining a Property

■ Use keyword Public and Property followed by the name of the property and a set of parentheses.

■ After the parentheses, specify the property's type with the As keyword.

■ Press *Enter*. Empty Get and Set accessors will be added for you by the IDE, followed by the keywords End Property. The Get accessor begins with keyword Get and ends with keywords End Get. The Set accessor begins with keyword Set and ends with keywords End Set.

■ In the Get accessor, provide code to return the requested data.

■ In the Set accessor, provide code to modify the relevant data. Be sure to do validity checking.

Adding a Class File to Your Project

■ Select **Project > Add Class**.

■ In the **Add New Item** dialog, select **Class**, and enter a name for the class.

Creating a Constructor

■ Use keywords Public Sub New, followed by a set of parentheses enclosing any parameter variables for the constructor.

■ Press *Enter*. The keywords End Sub will be provided by the IDE.

■ Add code to initialize the object's data.

Adding a Panel to Your Application

■ Double click the Panel control in the **Toolbox**, or drag the Panel control from the **Toolbox** to the Form. We recommend prefixing Panel names with pnl.

KEY TERMS

accessor—Method-like code units that handle the details of modifying and returning data.

Autos window—Allows you to view the contents of the properties used in the last statement that was executed in an application. This allows you to verify that the previous statement executed correctly and lists the values in the next statement to be executed.

Beep function—Causes your computer to make a beep sound.

client—When an application creates and uses an object of a class, that application is known as a client of that class.

Color structure—Contains several predefined colors as properties.

consistent state—A way to maintain the values of an object's instance variables such that those values are always valid.

constructor—A special class method that initializes a class's variables.

DefaultBackColor property—Contains the default background color for a Panel control.

extensible language—A language that can be "extended" with new data types. Visual Basic .NET is an extensible language.

FixedSingle property of a Label—Specifies that the Label will display a thin, black border.

Flat property of a Button—Specifies that a Button will appear flat.

FlatStyle property of a Button—Determines whether the Button will appear flat or three-dimensional.

Get accessor—Used to retrieve a value of an instance variable.

instantiate an object—Create an object of a class.

Length property of class String—Returns the number of characters in a String.

Locals window—Allows you to view the state of the variables in the current scope during debugging.

members of a class—Methods and variables declared within the body of a class.

member-access modifier—Keywords used to specify what members of a class that a client may access. Includes keywords `Public` and `Private`.

New keyword—Allocates memory in which an object will be stored.

PadLeft method of class String—Adds characters to the beginning of the string until the length of a string equals the specified length.

Panel control—Used to group controls. Unlike `GroupBoxes`, `Panels` do not have captions.

Private keyword—Member-access modifier that makes instance variables or methods accessible only to that class.

programmer-defined classes (programmer-defined types)—Defined by a programmer, as opposed to a class predefined in the Framework Class Library.

property—Contains accessors—portions of code that handle the details of modifying and returning data.

Public keyword—Member-access modifier that makes instance variables or methods accessible wherever the application has a reference to that object.

Set accessor—Provides data-validation capabilities to ensure that the value is set properly.

Substring method of class String—Returns characters from a string that correspond to the arguments passed by the user that indicate the start and the end positions within a `String`.

ToChar method of class Convert—Converts a `String` to a character.

GUI DESIGN GUIDELINES

Panel

- Use `Panels` to organize groups of related controls where the purpose of those controls is obvious. If the purpose of the controls is not obvious, use a `GroupBox` in place of a `Panel`, because `GroupBoxes` can contain captions.

- A `Panel` can display scrollbars for use when the `Panel` is not large enough to display all of its controls at once. To increase readability, we suggest avoiding the use of scrollbars on a `Panel`. If the `Panel` is not large enough to display all of its contents, increase the size of the `Panel`.

- Although it is possible to have a `Panel` without a border (by setting the `BorderStyle` property to `None`), use borders on your `Panels` to improve readability and organization.

CONTROLS, EVENTS, PROPERTIES & METHODS

Button   `abl Button`   This control allows the user to raise an action or event.

- *In action*

  `Calculate Total`

- *Event*

  `Click`—Raised when the user clicks the `Button`.

- *Properties*

  `Enabled`—Determines whether the `Button`'s event handler is executed when the `Button` is clicked.

  `FlatStyle`—Determines whether the `Button` will appear flat or three-dimensional.

  `Flat`—Specifies that a `Button` will appear flat.

  `Location`—Specifies the location of the `Button` on the `Form` relative to the top-left corner.

  `Name`—Specifies the name used to access the `Button` programmatically. The name should be prefixed with `btn`.

  `Size`—Specifies the height and width (in pixels) of the `Button`.

  `Text`—Specifies the text displayed on the `Button`.

- *Method*

  `Focus`—Transfers the focus of the application to the `Button` that calls it.

Convert The Convert class converts the value of a data type to another data type.

■ *Methods*

ToChar—Converts a value into a character (of data type Char).

ToDecimal—Converts the value from another data type to type Decimal.

Label   This control displays text on the Form that the user cannot modify.

■ *In action*

Total: [   ]

■ *Properties*

BorderStyle—Specifies the appearance of the Label's border.

FixedSingle—Specifies that the Label will display a thin, black border.

Font—Specifies the font name, style and size of the text displayed in the Label.

Location—Specifies the location of the Label on the Form relative to the top-left corner.

Name—Specifies the name used to access the Label programmatically. The name should be prefixed with lbl.

Size—Specifies the height and width (in pixels) of the Label.

Text—Specifies the text displayed on the Label.

TextAlign—Specifies how the text is aligned within the Label.

Panel   ☐ Panel   This control is used to organize various controls. Unlike a GroupBox control, the Panel control does not display a caption.

■ *In action*

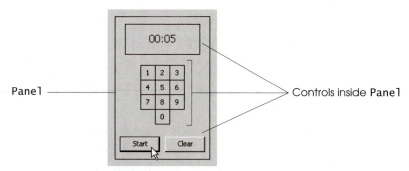

Panel — Controls inside Panel

■ *Properties*

DefaultBackColor—Returns the default background color of a Panel control.

Name—Specifies the name of the Panel.

Size—Specifies the size of the Panel.

Location—Specifies the Panel's location on the Form.

BorderStyle—Specifies the Panel's border style. Options include None (displaying no border), FixedSingle (a single-line border) and Fixed3D (a three-dimensional border).

None—Specifies that the Panel's will not display a border.

FixedSingle—Specifies that the Panel will display a thin, black border.

Fixed3D—Specifies that the Panel will display a three-dimensional border.

BackColor—Specifies the background color of the Panel.

String The String class represents a series of characters treated as a single unit.

■ *Property*

Length—Returns the number of characters in the String.

■ *Methods*

Format—Arranges the string in a specified format.

IndexOf—Returns the index of the specified character(s) in a String.

Insert—Returns a copy of the String for which it is called with the specified character(s) inserted.

PadLeft—Inserts characters at the beginning of a String.

Remove—Returns a copy of the String for which it is called with the specified character(s) removed.

Substring—Returns a substring from a String.

ToLower—Returns a copy of the String for which it is called with any uppercase letters converted to lowercase letters.

MULTIPLE-CHOICE QUESTIONS

19.1 A Button appears flat if its _____ property is set to Flat.

a) BorderStyle   b) FlatStyle

c) Style   d) BackStyle

19.2 Keyword _____ introduces a class definition.

a) NewClass   b) ClassDef

c) VBClass   d) Class

19.3 Keyword _____ is used to create an object.

a) CreateObject   b) Instantiate

c) Create   d) New

19.4 String characters are of data type _____.

a) Char   b) StringCharacter

c) Character   d) strCharacter

19.5 The _____ is used to retrieve the value of an instance variable.

a) Get accessor of a property   b) Retrieve method of a class

c) Client method of a class   d) Set accessor of a property

19.6 When you enter the header for a constructor in Visual Studio .NET then press *Enter*, the keywords _____ are created for you.

a) End Public Class   b) End Procedure

c) End Sub   d) End

19.7 An important difference between constructors and other methods is that _____.

a) constructors cannot specify a return data type

b) constructors cannot specify any parameters

c) other methods are implemented as Sub procedures

d) constructors can assign values to instance variables

19.8 A class can yield many _____, just as a primitive data type can yield many variables.

a) names   b) objects

c) values   d) types

19.9 The Set accessor enables you to _____.

a) provide range checking   b) modify data

c) provide data validation   d) All of the above.

19.10 Instance variables declared Private are not accessible _____.

a) outside the class   b) by other methods of the same class

c) by other members of the same class d) inside the same class

EXERCISES   **19.11** (*Triangle Creator Application*) Create an application that allows the user to enter the lengths for the three sides of a triangle as Integers. The application should then determine whether the triangle is a right triangle (two sides of the triangle form a 90-degree angle), an equilateral triangle (all sides of equal length) or neither. The application's GUI is completed for you (Fig. 19.49). You must create a class to represent a triangle object and define the event handler for the **Create** Button.

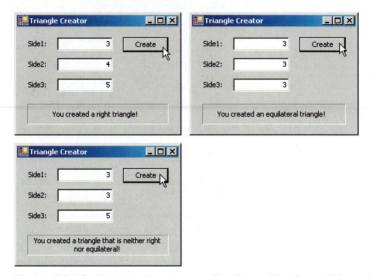

Figure 19.49   **Triangle Creator** application with all possible outputs.

a) *Copying the template to your working directory.* Copy the directory C:\Examples\ Tutorial19\Exercises\Triangle to your C:\SimplyVB directory.

b) *Opening the application's template file.* Double click Triangle.sln in the Triangle directory to open the application.

c) *Creating the Triangle class.* Add a class to the project, and name it Triangle. This is where you will define the properties of the Triangle class.

d) *Defining the necessary properties.* Define a constructor that will take the lengths of the three sides of the triangle as arguments. Create three properties that enable clients to access and modify the lengths of the three sides. If the user enters a negative value, that side should be assigned the value zero.

e) *Adding additional features.* Create two more properties in the Triangle class: One determines whether the sides form a right triangle, the other an equilateral triangle. These properties are considered **read-only**, because you would naturally define only the Get accessor. There is no simple Set accessor that can make a triangle a right triangle or an equilateral triangle without first modifying the lengths of the triangle's sides. To create a read-only property (where the Set accessor is omitted), precede keyword Property with the keyword **ReadOnly**.

f) *Adding code to event handler.* Now that you have created your Triangle class, you can use it to create objects in your application. Double click the **Create** Button in **Design View** to generate the event handler. Create new variables to store the three lengths from the TextBoxes; then, use those values to create a new Triangle object.

g) *Displaying the result.* Use an If...ElseIf statement to determine if the triangle is a right triangle, an equilateral triangle or neither. Display the result in a Label.

h) *Running the application.* Select **Debug > Start** to run your application. Create various inputs until you have create an equilateral triangle, a right triangle and a triangle that is neither right nor equilateral. Verify that the proper output is displayed for each.

i) *Closing the application.* Close your running application by clicking its close box.

j) *Closing the IDE.* Close Visual Studio .NET by clicking its close box.

19.12 (*Modified Microwave Oven Application*) Modify the tutorial's **Microwave Oven** application to include an additional digit, which would represent the hour. Allow the user to enter up to 9 hours, 59 minutes, and 59 seconds (Fig. 19.50).

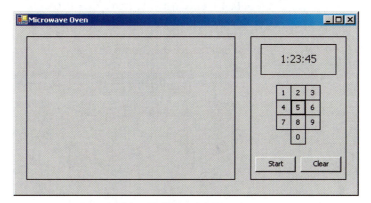

Figure 19.50   **Microwave Oven** application's GUI.

a) *Copying the template to your working directory.* Copy the directory `C:\Examples\Tutorial19\Exercises\MicrowaveOven2` to your `C:\SimplyVB` directory.

b) *Opening the application's template file.* Double click `MicrowaveOven2.sln` in the `MicrowaveOven2` directory to open the application.

c) *Adding the hour variable.* To allow cooking time that includes the hour digit, you will need to modify the `Time` class. Define a new `Private` instance variable to represent the hour. Change the `Time` constructor to take in as its first argument (now `Time` should have three arguments) the hour amount. You will also have to modify the **Start** `Button` event handler and the `DisplayTime` method to include an hour variable.

d) *Adding the Hour property.* Use the `Minute` and `Second` properties as your template to create the property for the hour. Remember, we are allowing an additional digit to represent the hour (hour < 10).

e) *Changing the padding amount.* Change the calls to the `PadLeft` method to be consistent with the new time format.

f) *Extracting the hour.* Add a call to the `Substring` method so that hour gets the first digit in the `m_strTime` String. Also, change the calls to the `Substring` method for minute and second so that they extract the proper digits from the `m_strTime` String.

g) *Accessing the first five digits.* Change the `If...Then` statement from the `DisplayTime` method to take and display the first five digits entered by the user.

h) *Edit the Timer object.* Edit the `tmrClock_Tick` event handler to provide changes to hours and its corresponding minutes and seconds.

i) *Displaying the time.* Edit the `Format` String so that the display `Label` includes the hour.

j) *Running the application.* Select **Debug > Start** to run your application. Enter various times and verify that the application counts down properly. Enter an amount of time that is 10 hours or longer, and verify that the application handles invalid input correctly.

k) *Closing the application.* Close your running application by clicking its close box.

l) *Closing the IDE.* Close Visual Studio .NET by clicking its close box.

19.13 (*Account Information Application*) The local bank wants you to create an application that will allow them to view their clients' information. The interface is created for you; you need to implement the class (Fig. 19.51). Once the application is completed, the bank manager should be able to click the **Next** or **Previous** Button to run through each client's information. The information is stored in four arrays containing first names, last names, account numbers and account balances.

Figure 19.51   Account Information application GUI.

a) *Copying the template to your working directory.* Copy the directory C:\Examples\ Tutorial19\Exercises\AccountInformation to your C:\SimplyVB directory.

b) *Opening the application's template file.* Double click AccountInformation.sln in the AccountInformation directory to open the application.

c) *Determining variables for the class.* Examine the code from AccountInformation.vb, including all the properties that the Client object uses to retrieve the information.

d) *Creating the Client class.* Create a new class, and call it Client. Add this class to the project. Define four Private instance variables to represent each property value, to ensure that each Client object contains all the required information about each client. Use those variables to define a constructor.

e) *Defining each property.* Each Private variable should have a corresponding property, allowing the user to set or get each Private variable's value.

f) *Adding more information.* In the FrmAccountInformation_Load event handler, add one more account. Include name, account number, and balance for each corresponding array.

g) *Running the application.* Select **Debug > Start** to run your application. Click the **Previous** and **Next** Buttons to ensure that each account's information is displayed properly.

h) *Closing the application.* Close your running application by clicking its close box.

i) *Closing the IDE.* Close Visual Studio .NET by clicking its close box.

What does this code do? ▶   **19.14** What does the following code do? The first code listing contains the definition of class Shape. Each Shape object represents a closed shape with a number of sides. The second code listing contains a method (Mystery) created by a client of class Shape. What does this method do?

```
1   Public Class Shape
2
3       Private m_intSides As Integer
4
5       ' constructor with number of sides
6       Public Sub New(ByVal intSides As Integer)
7          Side = intSides
8       End Sub ' New
9
10      ' set and get side value
11      Public Property Side() As Integer
12
13          ' return m_intSides
14          Get
15              Return m_intSides
16          End Get ' end of Get accessor
17
18          ' set m_intSides
19          Set(ByVal Value As Integer)
20
21              If Value > 0 Then
22                  m_intSides = Value
23              Else
24                  m_intSides = 0
25              End If
26
27          End Set ' end of Set accessor
28
29      End Property ' Side
30
31   End Class ' Shape
```

```
1   Public Function Mystery(ByVal objShape As Shape) As String
2       Dim strShape As String
3
4       ' determine case with objShape.Side
5       Select Case objShape.Side
6
7          Case Is < 3
8              strShape = "Not a Shape"
9
10         Case 3
11             strShape = "Triangle"
12
13         Case 4
14             strShape = "Square"
15
16         Case Else
17             strShape = "Polygon"
18
19      End Select
20
21      Return strShape
22   End Function ' Mystery
```

What's wrong with this code? **19.15** Find the error(s) in the following code. The following method should create a new Shape object with `intNumberSides` sides. Assume the Shape class from Exercise 19.14.

```
1   Private Sub ManipulateShape(ByVal intNumberSides As Integer)
2      Dim objShape As Shape = New Shape(3)
3
4      Shape.m_intSides = intNumberSides
5   End Sub ' ManipulateShape
```

Using the Debugger ▶ **19.16** (*View Name Application*) The **View Name** application allows the user to enter the user's first and last name. When the user clicks the **View Name** Button, a MessageBox that displays the user's first and last name appears. The application creates an instance of Class Name. This class uses its property definitions to set the first-name and last-name instance variables. Copy the Names folder from `C:\Examples\Tutorial19\Exercises\Debugger` to your Debugger folder. Open and run the application. While testing your application, you noticed that the MessageBox did not display the correct output. Use the debugger to find the logic error(s) in the application. The application with the correct output is displayed in Fig. 19.52.

Figure 19.52 **View Name** application with correct output.

Programming Challenge ▶ **19.17** (*DVD Burner Application*) Create an application that simulates a DVD burner. Users create a DVD with their choice of title and bonus materials. The GUI is provided for you (Fig. 19.53). You will create a class (DVDObject) to represent the DVD object and another class (Bonus) to represent bonus materials for a DVD object.

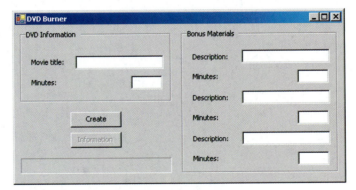

Figure 19.53 **DVD Burner** application's GUI.

a) *Copying the template to your working directory.* Copy the directory `C:\Examples\Tutorial19\Exercises\DVDBurner` to your `C:\SimplyVB` directory.

b) *Opening the application's template file.* Double click `DVDBurner.sln` in the DVD-Burner directory to open the application.

c) *Creating the bonus material object.* Create a class, and name it Bonus. The class's objects will each represent one bonus-material item on the DVD. Each Bonus object should have a name (description) and a length (in minutes). Use this tutorial's Time class as your guide in creating the properties for the name and length of each bonus material.

d) *Creating the DVD class*. Create a class, and name it DVDObject. This class contains the movie title and the length of the movie. The class should also include an array of three Bonus items.

e) *Creating the necessary variables*. Before you define the **Create** Button's event handler, create a DVDObject class instance variable. Inside the **Create** Button's event handler, create the necessary variables to store the information from the TextBoxes on the GUI. Also, this is where you need to create the array of Bonus objects to store the bonus materials.

f) *Adding bonus-material information*. Add the description and length of each bonus item to the Bonus array you created from the previous step.

g) *Creating a DVD object*. Use information about the movie, its title, length and the array of bonus materials to make your DVD object.

h) *Displaying the output*. The **Information** Button's Click event is already defined for you. Locate the event handler, add a String containing the complete information on the DVD object that you created earlier and display this String to a MessageBox.

i) *Running the application*. Select **Debug > Start** to run your application. Enter information for several DVDs. After information is entered for each, click the **Create** Button. Then, click the **Information** Button and verify that the information being displayed is correct for your newly created DVD.

j) *Closing the application*. Close your running application by clicking its close box.

k) *Closing the IDE*. Close Visual Studio .NET by clicking its close box.

Objectives

In this tutorial, you will learn to:

■ Create and manipulate an `ArrayList` object.
■ Set the `TabStop` and `TabIndex` properties of a control.
■ Create an access key for a control.
■ Use a `For Each...Next` loop to iterate through an `ArrayList`.

Outline

Shipping Hub Application

Introducing Collections, the For Each...Next Statement and Access Keys

Though most business can be conducted over phone lines and using e-mail messages, often it is necessary to send documents using a shipping company. As the pace of business increases, it is essential that shipping companies develop an efficient means to transfer packages from one location to another. To accomplish this task, many shipping companies send packages to a central location (a hub) before the packages reach their final destination. In this tutorial, you will develop a **Shipping Hub** application to simulate package processing at a shipping warehouse. You will develop the application by using collections, which provide you with a quick and easy way to organize and manipulate the data used by your application. This tutorial focuses on the `ArrayList` collection, which includes data storage capabilities of an array, but with much greater flexibility. You will also learn to use the `For Each...Next` repetition statement to iterate through the objects in a collection.

20.1 Test-Driving the Shipping Hub Application

In this section, you will test-drive the **Shipping Hub** application. This application must meet the following requirements:

Application Requirements

*A shipping company receives packages at its headquarters, which functions as its shipping hub. After receiving the packages, the company ships them to a distribution center in one of the following states: Alabama, Florida, Georgia, Kentucky, Mississippi, North Carolina, South Carolina, Tennessee, West Virginia or Virginia. The company needs an application to track the packages that pass through its shipping hub. The application generates a package ID number for each package that arrives at the shipping hub when the user clicks the application's **Scan New** Button. Once a package has been scanned, the user should be able to enter the shipping address for the package. The user should be able to navigate through the list of scanned packages by using < BACK or NEXT > Buttons and by viewing a list of all packages destined for a particular state.*

This application stores a list of packages in an `ArrayList`. You will use the `For Each...Next` repetition statement to access the objects stored in the `ArrayList`. You begin by test-driving the completed application. Then, you will learn the additional Visual Basic .NET technologies that you will need to create your own version of this application.

Test-Driving the Shipping Hub Application

1. **Opening the completed application.** Open the directory C:\Examples\ Tutorial20\CompletedApplication\ShippingHub to locate the **Shipping Hub** application. Double click ShippingHub.sln to open the application in Visual Studio .NET.

2. **Running the Shipping Hub application.** Select **Debug > Start** to run the application (Fig. 20.1).

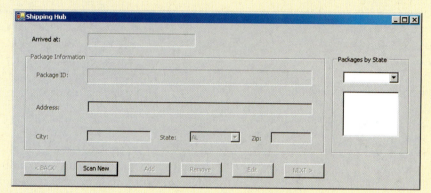

Figure 20.1   **Shipping Hub** application when first run.

3. **Scanning a new package.** Click the **Scan New** Button. The application displays a package ID number, enables the TextBoxes and allows the user to enter the package information (Fig. 20.2).

Figure 20.2   Scanning a new package.

4. **Using the Tab key.** Type 318 Some Street in the **Address:** TextBox, then press the *Tab* key. Notice that the cursor moves to the **City:** TextBox (Fig. 20.3).

5. **Adding a package to the list of packages.** Type Point Pleasant in the **City:** field, then press the *Tab* key. Select **WV** from the **State:** ComboBox, then press the *Tab* key. Type 25550 in the **Zip:** field, and click the **Add** Button to add the package to the application's `ArrayList`.

(cont.)

Cursor now appears in the **City:** TextBox

Figure 20.3 Pressing the *Tab* key moves the cursor to the next TextBox.

Note that you cannot enter more than five numbers in the **Zip:** field because the **Zip:** TextBox's MaxLength property is set to 5. The value in the **MaxLength** property determines the maximum number of characters that the user can enter into a TextBox. The values in the **State:** ComboBox were added using its **Items** property in the Windows Form Designer. When you open the template application, examine the values stored in the Items property to see how this is accomplished.

6. ***Removing***, ***editing and browsing packages***. The application's **NEXT >** and **< BACK** Buttons allow the user to navigate the list of packages. The **Remove** Button allows the user to delete packages and the **Edit** Button allows the user to update a particular package's information. Experiment with the various Buttons by adding, removing and editing packages. We suggest using the following sample data:

- 9 Some Road, Goose Creek, SC, 29445
- 234 Some Place, Tamassee, SC, 29686
- 46 Some Avenue, Mammoth Cave, KY, 42259
- 3 Some Street, Yazoo City, MS, 39194

7. ***Viewing all packages going to a state***. The ComboBox on the right side of the application allows the user to select a state. When a state is selected, all of the package ID numbers of packages destined for that state are displayed in the ListBox (Fig. 20.4). If the ListBox contains more package numbers than it can display, a vertical scrollbar will be added to the ListBox.

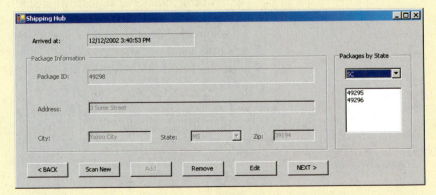

Figure 20.4 Viewing all packages going to South Carolina.

8. ***Closing the application***. Close your running application by clicking its close box.

9. ***Closing the IDE***. Close Visual Studio .NET by clicking its close box.

20.2 Package Class

Your application must store data retrieved from the packages' shipping information. Each package ships to one location with an address, city, state and zip code. However, since multiple packages can be shipped to the same location, each package will need a unique identification number to distinguish it from other packages. As you learned in Tutorial 19, a convenient way to group related information is by creating instances of a class. The `Package` class included with the template application provides the necessary properties to keep track of package information. It also provides properties that ensure that only methods of class `Package` can access the instance variables of the class. The table in Fig. 20.5 describes the properties for class `Package`.

Property	Description
Address	Provides access to instance variable m_strAddress. Represents the package's address as a String.
City	Provides access to instance variable m_strCity, which represents the package's city as a String.
State	Provides access to m_strState, which stores the package's state as a String. It uses the standard two-letter state abbreviations. For example, NC is used for North Carolina.
Zip	Provides access to m_intZip. Represents the zip code as a five-digit Integer.
PackageNumber	Provides access to m_intPackageNumber, which stores the package's identification number as a String.

Figure 20.5   Properties listing for class `Package`.

The `Package` class must be added to the **Shipping Hub** application before objects of this class can be created. You will learn how to add the `Package` class to the **Shipping Hub** application in the following box.

Adding a Class to an Application	1. ***Copying the template to your working directory.*** Copy the `C:\Examples\Tutorial20\TemplateApplication\ShippingHub` directory to your `C:\SimplyVB` directory.
	2. ***Opening the Shipping Hub application's template file.*** Double click `ShippingHub.sln` in the `ShippingHub` directory to open the application in Visual Studio .NET.
	3. ***Adding class Package.*** In the **Solution Explorer**, right click the **Shipping-Hub** project. Select **Add > Add Existing Item...** from the context menu that appears. When the **Add Existing Item** dialog appears, select the `Package.vb` file and click **Open**. The `Package` class is now included in the application and shown in the **Solution Explorer** (Fig. 20.6).

Package class added to the
ShippingHub project

Figure 20.6   **Solution Explorer** with `Package.vb` added.

20.3 Using Properties TabIndex and TabStop

Many applications require users to enter information into multiple TextBoxes. It is awkward for users to have to select each TextBox using the mouse. It is often easier to allow the user to use the *Tab* key to navigate the controls on the Form. To ensure ease of use, the focus must be transferred to the proper control when the *Tab* key is pressed. The **TabIndex** property allows you to specify the order in which focus is transferred to controls when *Tab* is pressed. However, some controls, such as a read-only TextBox, should not be selected using the *Tab* key. The **TabStop** property specifies whether the user can select the control using the *Tab* key. Setting this property to False prevents the control from being selected. You set both of these properties in the following box.

Setting Properties TabIndex and TabStop	1. **Opening *ShippingHub.vb*.** Double click ShippingHub.vb in the **Solution Explorer** to open the file in design view. The **Shipping Hub** application requires that the user enter the package information into these TextBoxes. To ensure the user can easily enter the data, you should allow the user to press the *Tab* key to access the proper control.
	2. **Setting property *TabStop*.** The TabStop property defaults to True for controls that receive user input. Ensure that this is the case by setting the Tab-Stop properties to True for the **Address:**, **City:**, and **Zip:** TextBoxes, the **State:** and **Packages by State** ComboBox and the **Scan New** Button if they are not already set to True.
 **GUI Design Tip** Set a control's TabStop property to True only if the control is used to receive user input.	3. **Disabling property *TabStop*.** If it has not already been done so, set the Tab-Stop property for the other controls on the Form to False. The user should be given access only to certain controls; therefore, you must prevent the *Tab* key from transferring the focus to an improper control, such as a disabled TextBox.
	4. **Using the *Tab Order* view in the *Windows Form Designer*.** To help visualize the tab order, Visual Studio .NET provides a view called **Tab Order**. To use the **Tab Order** view, select the Form by clicking it, then select **View > Tab Order**. White numbers indicating the TabIndex appear in blue boxes in the upper-left corner of the control (Fig. 20.7). The first time you click a control in this view, its TabIndex value will be set to zero, as displayed in the TabIndex box (Fig. 20.7). Subsequent clicks will increment the value by one.
 **GUI Design Tip** Use the TabIndex property to define the logical order in which the user should enter data. Usually the order transfers the focus of the application from top to bottom and left to right.	Begin by clicking the **Package Information** GroupBox. Notice its value becomes 0 and the background of the surrounding box changes to white (Fig. 20.7). Then click the **Address:** TextBox and notice that the value changes to 0.0. The first zero refers to the TabIndex of the container (in this case, the GroupBox) and the second zero refers to the TabIndex for that control within the container. Continue setting the tab indices by clicking the **City:** TextBox, then the **State:** ComboBox and finally the **Zip:** TextBox. Complete setting the tab indices for the GroupBox by clicking each control that has not been changed. Controls that have not been changed display a box with a blue background.
	5. **Setting the *TabIndex* properties for the rest of the application.** Continue setting the TabIndex properties by clicking the **Scan New** Button. Then click the remaining unchanged controls in the order indicated in Fig. 20.8. When all the application's controls have been ordered, the TabIndex boxes will once again display a blue background. Exit the **Tab Order** view by selecting **View > Tab Order**.
	6. **Saving the project.** Select **File > Save All** to save your modified code.

(cont.)

TabIndex box set to zero

TabIndex boxes (not modified)

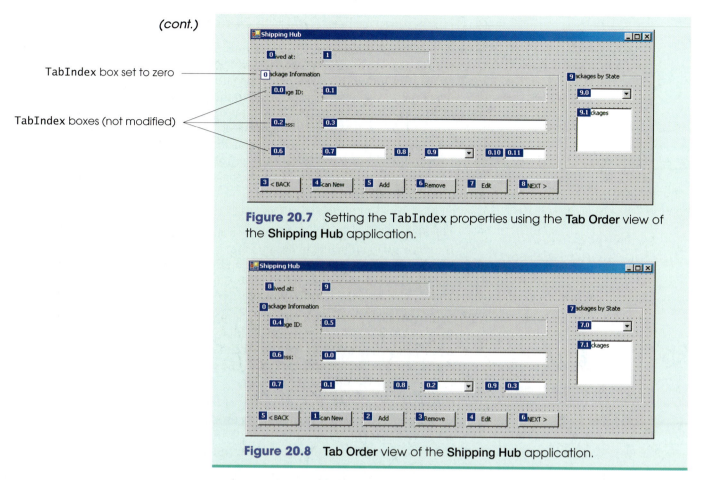

Figure 20.7 Setting the **TabIndex** properties using the **Tab Order** view of the **Shipping Hub** application.

Figure 20.8 **Tab Order** view of the **Shipping Hub** application.

Using the **TabIndex** and **TabStop** properties properly improves the speed at which the user enters data into an application. Most controls have **TabIndex** and **TabStop** properties. **TabIndex** values on a **Form** or within a **GroupBox** must be unique—two controls cannot receive the focus at the same time. By default, the first control added to the **Form** has a value of 0 for its **TabIndex** property. The second control added has a value of 1 for its **TabIndex** property. The third control has a value of 2 (one more than the last control's value) for its **TabIndex** property, etc.

SELF-REVIEW

1. Property _____ specifies the order in which controls receive the focus when *Tab* is pressed.

a) **Text**
b) **TabStop**
c) **Index**
d) **TabIndex**

2. To prevent the focus from being transferred to a control using the *Tab* key, set property _____ to _____.

a) **TabIndex, 0**
b) **TabStop, False**
c) **TabControl, True**
d) **TabIndex, Nothing**

Answers: 1) d. 2) b.

20.4 Using Access Keys

Applications that require the user to enter a great deal of text data should provide users with the ability to enter data by using only the keyboard. Setting the **TabIndex** and **TabStop** properties, for instance, helps the user enter data in a logical order. **Access keys** (or keyboard shortcuts) allow the user to perform an action on a control using the keyboard.

To specify an access key for a control, insert an & (ampersand) symbol in the Text property before the letter you wish to use as an access key. If you wish to use "s" as the access key on the **Scan New** Button, set its Text property to &Scan New. You can specify many access keys in an application, but each letter used as an access key in a container must be unique. To use the access key, you must press and hold the *Alt* key, then press the access key character on the keyboard (release both keys after pressing the access key character). In this case of the **Scan New** Button, you would press and hold the *Alt* key, then press the *S* key (also written as *Alt+S*) You would then release the *Alt* key.

Access keys are often used on Button controls and on the MainMenu control, which will be introduced in Tutorial 22. If you wish to display an ampersand character on a control, you must type && in its Text property. Follow the steps in the next box to use access keys in your **Shipping Hub** application.

Creating Access Keys

GUI Design Tip

Use access keys to allow users to "click" a control using the keyboard.

Using the & symbol to create an access key (there is no space between & and S)

1. ***Creating an access key for the Scan New Button.*** Insert an & symbol before the letter S in the Text property of the **Scan New** Button (Fig. 20.9). Press *Enter* or click outside the field to update the property. Notice that the letter S is now underlined on the Button (Fig. 20.9). If the user presses *Alt* then *S* during execution, this will have the same effect as if the user "clicks" the **Scan New** Button. (The Click event will be raised.) Note that depending on your system configuration, you may need to press the *Alt* key to display the underline under the access key character.

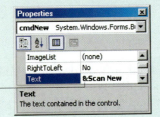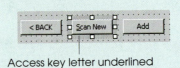

Access key letter underlined

Figure 20.9   Creating an access key.

2. ***Inserting access keys for the remaining Buttons.*** Use the Text properties of the remaining Buttons to create access keys. Precede the B on the **< BACK** Button with an ampersand. Repeat this process for the A on the **Add** Button, the R on the **Remove** Button, the E on the **Edit** Button and the N on the **NEXT >** Button.

3. ***Saving the project.*** Select **File > Save All** to save your modified code.

20.5 Collections

The .NET Framework provides several classes, called **collections**, which you can use to store groups of related objects. These classes provide methods that facilitate the storage and organization of your data without requiring any knowledge of the details of how the objects are being stored. This capability improves your application development time because you do not have to write code to organize your data efficiently—the methods in the collection classes are proven to be reliable and efficient.

In Tutorials 17 and 18, you learned how to declare and use arrays in your applications. You may have noticed a limitation to arrays—once an array is declared, its size will not change to match its data set. This poses a problem if the number of items in an array will change over time.

Class `ArrayList` (a member of the `Collections` namespace) provides a convenient solution to this problem. The **`ArrayList`** collection provides all of the capabilities of an array, but also provides dynamic resizing capabilities. **Dynamic resizing** enables the `ArrayList` object to increase its size to accommodate new elements and to decrease its size when elements are removed.

Software Design Tip

Use an `ArrayList` to store a group of values when the number of elements in the group varies during the running of an application.

SELF-REVIEW

1. Collections _____.
   a) force you to focus on how your data is stored
   b) speed up application development
   c) allow you to focus on the details of your application
   d) Both b and c.

2. One limitation of arrays is that _____.
   a) their size cannot change dynamically
   b) they can only store primitive data types
   c) `Strings` cannot be placed in them
   d) All of the above.

Answers: 1) d. 2) a.

20.6 Shipping Hub Application: Using Class `ArrayList`

By now, you are familiar with designing GUIs and writing methods and event handlers. This tutorial's template file provides much of the application's functionality so that you may concentrate on using an `ArrayList`. You are encouraged to study the full source code at the end of the tutorial to understand how the application is implemented. The following pseudocode statements describe the basic operation of your **Shipping Hub** application:

```
When the Form loads:
    Generate an initial package ID number
    Create an empty ArrayList

When the user clicks the Scan New Button:
    Generate a unique package ID number
    Enable TextBoxes, the ComboBox and the Add Button

When the user clicks the Add Button:
    Retrieve address, city, state and zip code values; and disable input controls
    Add the package to the ArrayList
    Add the package number to the ListBox
    Change the ComboBox value to the package's destination state

When the user clicks the < BACK Button:
    Display the previous package in the list

When the user clicks the NEXT > Button:
    Display the next package in the list

When the user clicks the Remove Button:
    Remove the package from the list
```

When the user clicks the Edit Button:
    Change the Button to read Update
    Allow the user to modify package address information

When the user clicks the Update Button:
    Update the package's information in the list
    Disable controls that allow user input, and change the
        Update Button to read Edit

When the user chooses a different state in the ComboBox:
    Display the package number for each package destined for that
        state in the ListBox

The **Shipping Hub** application must store a list of packages through which the user can navigate using the **NEXT >** and **< BACK** Buttons. Each time the application runs, it must allow for any number of packages to be added. Using arrays, you would be limited by the number of values that you could store in the array. The ArrayList collection solves this problem by combining the functionality of an array with dynamic resizing capabilities.

Now that you have test-driven the **Shipping Hub** application and studied its pseudocode representation, you will use an ACE table to help you convert the pseudocode to Visual Basic .NET. Figure 20.10 lists the actions, controls and events that will help you complete your own version of this application.

Action	Control/Object	Event
Action/Control/Event (ACE) Table for the Shipping Hub Application		
Label the application's controls	fraAddress, fraListByState, lblArrived, lblPackageID, lblAddress, lblCity, lblState, lblZip	Application is run
	FrmShippingHub	Load
Generate an initial package ID number	m_objRandom	
Create an empty ArrayList	m_objList	
	btnNew	Click
Generate a unique package ID number	m_objRandom	
Enable TextBoxes, the ComboBox and the Add Button	btnAdd, txtAddress, txtCity, cboState, txtZip	
	btnAdd	Click
Retrieve address, city, state and zip code values; and disable input controls	txtAddress, txtCity, cboState, txtZip	
Add the package to the ArrayList	m_objList	
Add the package number to the ListBox	lstPackages	
Change the ComboBox value to the package's destination state	cboState	
	btnBack	Click
Display the previous package in the list	m_objList	
	btnNext	Click
Display the next package in the list	m_objList	

Figure 20.10   ACE table for the **Shipping Hub** application. (Part 1 of 2.)

Action	Control/Object	Event
	btnRemove	Click
Remove the package from the list	m_objList	
	btnEditUpdate	Click
Change the Button to read Update	btnEditUpdate	
Allow the user to modify package address information	txtAddress, txtCity, cboState, txtZip	
	btnEditUpdate	Click
Update the package's information in the list	m_objList	
Disable controls that allow user input, and change the Update Button to read Edit	txtAddress, txtCity, cboState, txtZip, m_objList, btnEditUpdate	
	cboViewPackages	Selected-Index-Changed
Display the package number for each package destined for that state in the ListBox	lstPackages	

Figure 20.10   ACE table for the **Shipping Hub** application. (Part 2 of 2.)

In this tutorial, you focus on the use of an ArrayList in the **Shipping Hub** application. You begin by creating an ArrayList object.

Creating a List of Packages

1. ***Declaring an ArrayList.*** Insert line 4 of Fig. 20.11 into your application to declare ArrayList m_objList. Notice the use of the member-access operator (.) to gain access to the ArrayList class, which is located in namespace System.Collections. Alternatively, you could use the Imports statement to import the **Collections** namespace such as

   ```
   Imports System.Collections
   ```

   In this case, you would not need to use the member-access operator because the namespace has been imported. In the following discussion, we will refer to the Collections.ArrayList object as an ArrayList.

Declaring an ArrayList reference

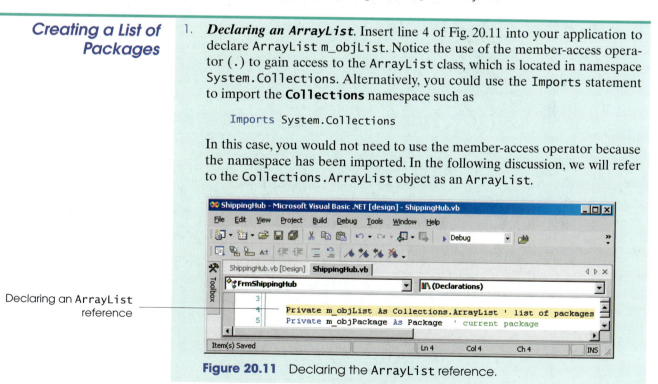

Figure 20.11   Declaring the ArrayList reference.

(cont.)   2. ***Initializing the ArrayList.*** To use the `ArrayList` instance variable declared in *Step 1*, you must create a new `ArrayList` object. You will then assign a reference to the `ArrayList` object to the instance variable. Insert line 338 (Fig. 20.12) to the Form's Load event handler. This line uses the New keyword to create an empty `ArrayList` object when the application loads. Notice that line 337 uses the ComboBox's `Items.Item` property to show the first state in the list. The **Items.Item** property retrieves the value stored in the ComboBox at the specified index.

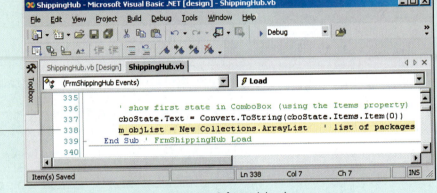

Initializing the `ArrayList` reference

Figure 20.12   Creating an `ArrayList` object.

3. ***Saving the project.*** Select **File > Save All** to save your modified code.

Now that you have created an `ArrayList` object, you will need to insert code that allows the user to add packages to the `ArrayList`. To accomplish this, you will create a reference to an object of class `Package` and use the `ArrayList`'s Add method to store the reference in the `ArrayList`. Recall that you already added the `Package` class to your application. You will now create packages and add them to your list.

Adding and Removing Packages

1. ***Creating a package.*** The user clicks the **Scan New** Button when a new package arrives at the shipping hub. When this occurs, the application should create a package number and allow the user to enter the shipping address. Insert lines 345–346 from Fig. 20.13 into the **Scan New** Button's `Click` event handler. Line 345 increments `m_intPackageID` to ensure that all packages have a unique identification number. Line 346 passes the package number as an argument to the constructor for class `Package`. The value that you pass to the `Package` constructor can then be accessed using its `PackageNumber` property. Note that line 346 uses the same reference, `m_objPackage`, many times to reference a new `Package` object. However, the previous `Package` object will not be destroyed each time the reference is changed. This is because each package reference is stored in the `ArrayList`.

2. ***Displaying the package number and arrival time.*** After the package has been "scanned," the application should display the new package's arrival time and package number to the user. Insert lines 349–352 of Fig. 20.14 into your application. Lines 349–350 display the package identification number in a `Label`. The **ToString** method, which is defined for most objects and data types, returns a value representing the object as text (of type `String`). For instance, a `Date` structure's `ToString` method returns the date as a `String`, in the format `11/11/2002 9:34:00 AM`. However, be aware that for many FCL classes, `ToString` merely returns the class name. The `ToString` method can be used as an alternative to the `Convert.ToString` method. Lines 351–352 display the arrival time (the current time) in a `Label`.

(cont.)

Create a new **Package** object with a unique ID

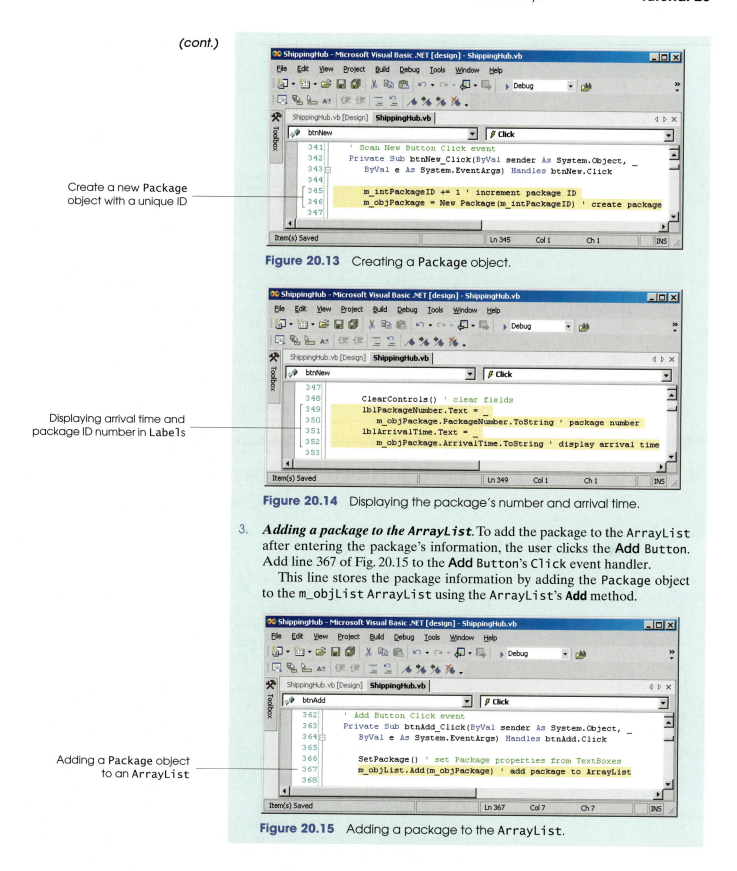

Figure 20.13   Creating a **Package** object.

Displaying arrival time and package ID number in **Label**s

Figure 20.14   Displaying the package's number and arrival time.

3. *Adding a package to the **ArrayList**.* To add the package to the **ArrayList** after entering the package's information, the user clicks the **Add** Button. Add line 367 of Fig. 20.15 to the **Add** Button's **Click** event handler.

This line stores the package information by adding the **Package** object to the m_objList **ArrayList** using the **ArrayList**'s **Add** method.

Adding a **Package** object to an **ArrayList**

Figure 20.15   Adding a package to the **ArrayList**.

(cont.)   Each time you add an object to the `ArrayList` by calling the `Add` method, the object is added to the end of the `ArrayList`. With arrays, you refer to a value's location by its index. Similarly, in an `ArrayList`, you refer to an object's location in the `ArrayList` as the object's **index**. Much like an array, the index of an object at the beginning of the `ArrayList` is zero and the index of an object at the end of the `ArrayList` is one less than the number of objects in the `ArrayList`.

4. ***Removing a package from the ArrayList.*** When the user selects a package and clicks the **Remove** Button, the application should remove the package from the `ArrayList`. The `ArrayList` class provides a simple way to remove objects from the `ArrayList`. Insert line 422 (Fig. 20.16) into the **Remove** Button's `Click` event handler. This line uses the **RemoveAt** method to remove a package from the `ArrayList`. The argument passed to the `RemoveAt` method is the index of the package in the `ArrayList`, contained in the variable `m_intPosition`. This variable keeps track of the position and is incremented or decremented each time the user clicks the **NEXT >** or **< BACK** Buttons.

Removing the current package
from the `ArrayList`

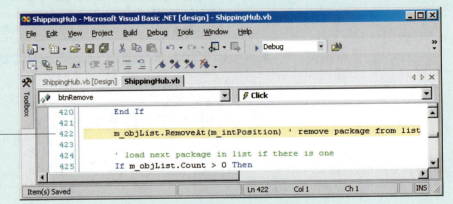

Figure 20.16   Removing a package from the `ArrayList`.

If a package at index 3 is removed from the `ArrayList`, the package that was previously at index 4 will then be located at index 3. Whenever an object is removed from an `ArrayList`, the indices update accordingly. Notice that line 425 of Fig. 20.16 uses the `Count` property of class `ArrayList`. The **Count** property returns the number of objects contained in the `ArrayList`.

5. ***Saving the project.*** Select **File > Save All** to save your modified code.

Once a package has been added to the `ArrayList`, the **Shipping Hub** application disables the `TextBox`es so that the user does not accidentally modify the package information. To allow users to modify any of the package information except for the arrival time and the package identification number, an **Edit** Button is provided. When the user clicks the **Edit** Button, its event handler should enable the controls that allow the user to modify the package data. You add functionality to accomplish this in the following box.

Updating Package
Information

1. ***Changing the Edit Button's Text property.*** Add lines 452–453 of Fig. 20.17 to your application. When the **Edit** Button is clicked, line 453 changes the text on the **Edit** Button to **&Update** (using U as the access key). This indicates that the user should click the same Button, which now is labelled **Update**, to submit changes to the package information.

(cont.)

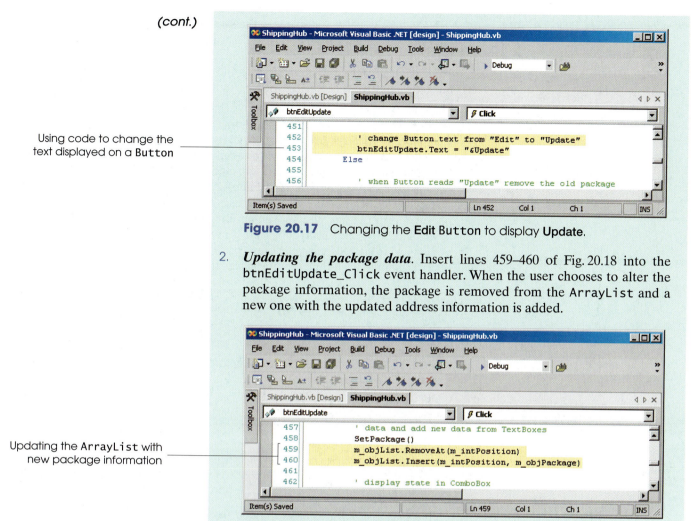

Using code to change the
text displayed on a **Button**

Figure 20.17   Changing the **Edit Button** to display **Update**.

2. *Updating the package data.* Insert lines 459–460 of Fig. 20.18 into the `btnEditUpdate_Click` event handler. When the user chooses to alter the package information, the package is removed from the `ArrayList` and a new one with the updated address information is added.

Updating the **ArrayList** with
new package information

Figure 20.18   Removing and inserting a package to update data.

Line 459 removes the old package object from the `ArrayList`. Line 460 uses class `ArrayList`'s `Insert` method to add the package to the ArrayList. The **Insert** method is like the Add method, but `Insert` allows you to specify the index in the `ArrayList` at which to insert the package. The first argument to the `Insert` method is the index at which to insert the package (in this case, `m_intPosition`), and the second argument contains the package to insert into the `ArrayList` (`m_objPackage`). Using the `Insert` method allows you to place the updated package object at the same index in the `ArrayList` as the package object you just removed.

3. *Changing the Button's Text property to Edit.* After the user clicks the **Update** Button, the TextBoxes are once again disabled. The user's changes have been applied; therefore, you should reset the text on the **Update** Button to read **Edit**. Insert line 470 of Fig. 20.19 into the event handler to reset the text on the **Button** to **Edit**. Notice once again the use of the & to enable the **Button**'s access key.

(cont.)

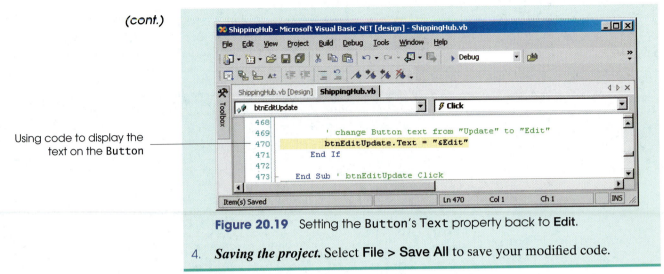

Using code to display the text on the **Button**

Figure 20.19 Setting the **Button**'s **Text** property back to **Edit**.

4. ***Saving the project.*** Select **File > Save All** to save your modified code.

The user navigates the **ArrayList** by clicking the **NEXT >** and **< BACK** Buttons. Each time the user chooses to view a different package in the **ArrayList**, the package information displayed in the **Form**'s controls must be updated. To display a package's information, you must retrieve the information from the **ArrayList** that you created. You will learn how to do this in the following box.

Displaying a Package

1. ***Retrieving package data.*** Insert lines 487–489 from Fig. 20.20 into your application's **LoadPackage** method. To display the information, you must retrieve the data from the **ArrayList** using the **Item** method. The **Item** method returns the object stored at the index specified by the method's argument. Lines 488–489 assign to **m_objPackage** the package stored at index **m_intPosition**. Function **CType** converts its first argument to the type of object specified by the second argument. In this case, it item returned is being converted to a **Package**.

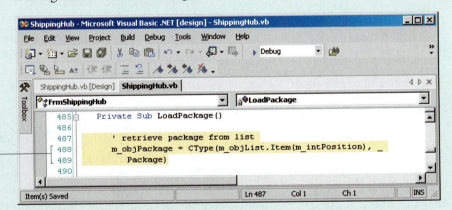

Retrieving a **Package** object from an **ArrayList**

Figure 20.20 Retrieving a package from the **ArrayList**.

Note that the code you inserted explicitly converts the object returned by the **ArrayList** to an object of type **Package**. One of the many advantages of using an **ArrayList** is that it stores references to objects of type **Object**—which means that it can store *any* object you choose, from predefined objects (like a **Random** object) to programmer-defined objects (like a **Package** object). To use and access the properties and methods of a package returned from an **ArrayList**, you must explicitly convert it to a **Package** object.

(cont.)

2. ***Displaying the package information.*** Insert lines 491–499 of Fig. 20.21 into your application. These lines retrieve the package information from `m_objPackage` and display the data in the corresponding controls on the Form, using the `ToString` method.

Displaying data stored in the Package object

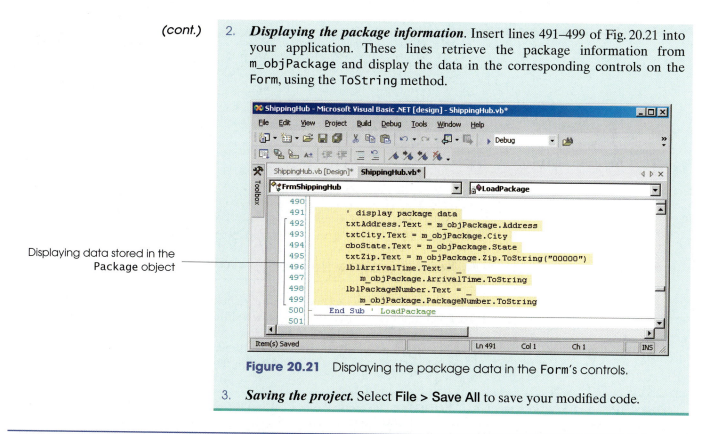

```
490
491        ' display package data
492        txtAddress.Text = m_objPackage.Address
493        txtCity.Text = m_objPackage.City
494        cboState.Text = m_objPackage.State
495        txtZip.Text = m_objPackage.Zip.ToString("00000")
496        lblArrivalTime.Text = _
497            m_objPackage.ArrivalTime.ToString
498        lblPackageNumber.Text = _
499            m_objPackage.PackageNumber.ToString
500    End Sub ' LoadPackage
501
```

Figure 20.21 Displaying the package data in the Form's controls.

3. ***Saving the project.*** Select **File > Save All** to save your modified code.

SELF-REVIEW

1. Method _____ of class `ArrayList` can be used to add an object at a specific location in the `ArrayList`.

   a) `AddAt`   b) `Insert`
   c) `AddObjectAt`   d) `Add`

2. The **Shipping Hub** application uses an `ArrayList` because class `ArrayList` _____.

   a) can store a variable number of objects
   b) allows the addition and removal of packages
   c) allows the insertion of items into any index in the `ArrayList`
   d) All of the above.

Answers: 1) b. 2) d.

20.7 For Each...Next Repetition Statement

Visual Basic .NET provides the **For Each...Next** repetition statement for iterating through the values in an array or a collection. Instead of setting initial and final values for a counter variable, the For Each...Next statement uses a control variable (a reference) that can reference each object in the collection. Assuming that you have created an `ArrayList objArrayList` that contains only `Package` objects, the code

Good Programming Practice

Use a For Each...Next repetition statement to iterate through values in an array or collection without using a counter variable.

```
Dim objPackage As Package

For Each objPackage In objArrayList
    lstPackages.Items.Add(objPackage.PackageNumber)
Next
```

adds each package's ID number to a `ListBox`. The For Each...Next statement requires both a collection type and an element. The **collection type** specifies the array or collection (in this case, the `ArrayList objArrayList`) through which you wish to iterate. The **element** is used to store a reference to a value in the collection type. If the For Each...Next statement contains an element of the same type (or one that can be converted to the same type) as the collection type, the statement assigns the collection type's object to the element (in this case, objPackage). The body of the For Each...Next statement is then executed. Notice that because the For Each...Next statement does not require you to specify initial and final counter values, it simplifies access to groups of values.

Figure 20.22 shows the UML activity diagram for the preceding For Each...Next statement. Notice that it is similar to the UML diagram for the For...Next statement in Tutorial 11. The only difference is that the For Each...Next continues to execute the body until all elements in the array (or collection) have been accessed.

Common Programming Error

If the element in a For Each...Next statement cannot be converted to the same type as the collection type's objects, a runtime error occurs. For example, if an Array-List contained only Date values, declaring a reference to a Package object as the element would cause a runtime error.

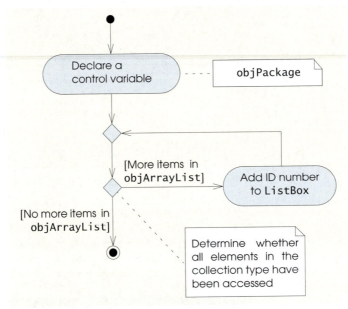

Figure 20.22   UML activity diagram for For Each...Next repetition statement.

When the user selects a state from the ComboBox, the application should display the package number for each package destined for that state. You will use the For Each...Next statement in the **Shipping Hub** application to add this functionality.

Inserting a For Each...Next Statement

1. ***Declaring a control variable (reference).*** Add line 538 of Fig. 20.23 to your application. This line declares reference objViewPackage of type Package. The reference objViewPackage will be used to reference each Package object (one at a time) in your ArrayList as you iterate through the Array-List of Package objects. Notice that you have added code to a ComboBox's SelectedIndexChanged event handler. The **SelectedIndexChanged** event is raised when the value selected in the ComboBox changes.

Declaring the control variable for the For Each...Next repetition statement

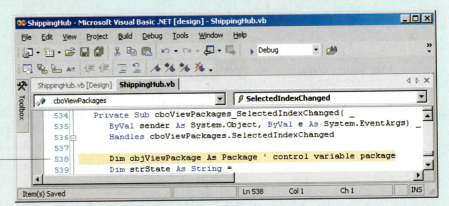

Figure 20.23   Declaring a reference for use in For Each...Next loop.

(cont.)

2. ***Inserting a For Each...Next statement.*** Add lines 544–545 of Fig. 20.24 to your application, then press *Enter*. Notice that the Next statement has been added for you on line 547. Line 545 is the header for the repetition statement. This loop will iterate through ArrayList m_objList, assigning the next element in the ArrayList (beginning with the first package object) to reference objViewPackage before executing the body of the loop. When a new package is reached, the For Each...Next body executes.

For Each...Next header

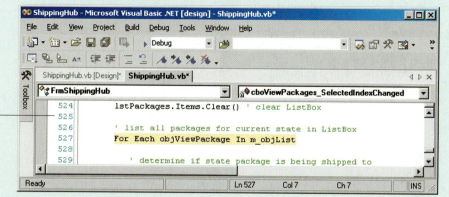

Figure 20.24 Writing a For Each...Next statement.

3. ***Determining a package's destination state.*** Insert lines 547–553 of Fig. 20.25 into your application. These lines contain an If...Then statement that tests each package's destination state against the state name displayed in the **Packages By State** ComboBox. If the two state names match, line 552 displays the package number in the ListBox.

Displaying package ID numbers only for packages destined for the specified state

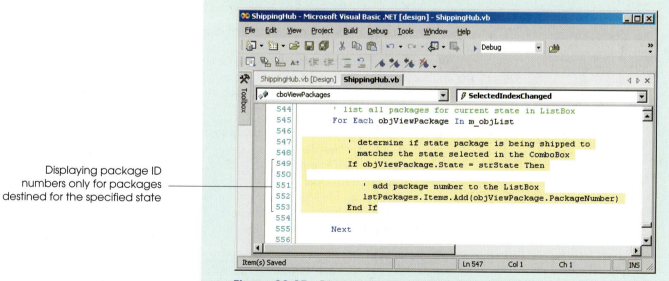

Figure 20.25 Displaying all packages going to selected state.

4. ***Running the application.*** Select **Debug > Start** to run your application. Enter information for several packages going to the same state. Select that state in the **Packages by State** GroupBox and verify that correct packages are listed. Click the application's Buttons and make sure that you can remove, cycle through or modify the packages.

5. ***Closing the application.*** Close your running application by clicking its close box.

6. ***Closing the IDE.*** Close Visual Studio .NET by clicking its close box.

Figure 20.26 presents the source code for the **Shipping Hub** application. The lines of code that contain new programming concepts that you learned in this tutorial are highlighted.

```vbnet
1    Public Class FrmShippingHub
2        Inherits System.Windows.Forms.Form
3
4        Private m_objList As Collections.ArrayList ' list of packages
5        Private m_objPackage As Package    ' current package
6        Private m_intPosition As Integer   ' position of current package
7        Private m_objRandom As Random      ' random number for package id
8        Private m_intPackageID As Integer  ' individual package number
9
10       ' Windows Form Designer generated code
11
12       ' Form Load event
13       Private Sub FrmShippingHub_Load(ByVal sender As _
14           System.Object, ByVal e As System.EventArgs) _
15           Handles MyBase.Load
16
17           m_intPosition = 0 ' set initial position to zero
18           m_objRandom = New Random ' create new Random object
19           m_intPackageID = m_objRandom.Next(1, 100000) ' new package ID
20
21           ' show first state in ComboBox (using the Items property)
22           cboState.Text = Convert.ToString(cboState.Items.Item(0))
23           m_objList = New Collections.ArrayList() ' list of packages
24       End Sub ' FrmShippingHub_Load
25
26       ' Scan New Button Click event
27       Private Sub btnNew_Click(ByVal sender As System.Object, _
28           ByVal e As System.EventArgs) Handles btnNew.Click
29
30           m_intPackageID += 1 ' increment package ID
31           m_objPackage = New Package(m_intPackageID) ' create package
32
33           ClearControls() ' clear fields
34           lblPackageNumber.Text = _
35               m_objPackage.PackageNumber.ToString ' package number
36           lblArrivalTime.Text = _
37               m_objPackage.ArrivalTime.ToString ' display arrival time
38
39           ' only allow user to add package
40           fraAddress.Enabled = True ' disable GroupBox and its controls
41           SetButtons(False) ' enable/disable Buttons
42           btnAdd.Enabled = True   ' enable Add Button
43           btnNew.Enabled = False ' disable Scan New Button
44           txtAddress.Focus() ' transfer the focus to txtAddress TextBox
45       End Sub ' btnNew_Click
46
47       ' Add Button Click event
48       Private Sub btnAdd_Click(ByVal sender As System.Object, _
49           ByVal e As System.EventArgs) Handles btnAdd.Click
50
51           SetPackage() ' set Package properties from TextBoxes
52           m_objList.Add(m_objPackage) ' add package to ArrayList
53
```

Initially, there are no objects in the ArrayList, so set the position to zero → (line 17)

Use a Random object to generate a random number for package IDs → (lines 18–19)

Figure 20.26   Complete code listing for the **Shipping Hub** application. (Part 1 of 5.)

Display package ID numbers in ListBox if the state names match

When the user clicks the < BACK Button, decrement the position. If the position was zero, set the position to the last object in the ArrayList

When the user clicks the NEXT > Button, increment the position. If the position was the last object in the array, set the position to zero

```vbnet
54        fraAddress.Enabled = False ' disable GroupBox and its controls
55        SetButtons(True) ' enable appropriate Buttons
56
57        ' package cannot be added until Scan New is clicked
58        btnAdd.Enabled = False ' disable Add Button
59
60        ' if package's state displayed, add ID to ListBox
61        If cboState.Text = cboViewPackages.Text Then
62           lstPackages.Items.Add(m_objPackage.PackageNumber)
63        End If
64
65        cboViewPackages.Text = m_objPackage.State ' list packages
66        btnNew.Enabled = True ' enable Scan New Button
67     End Sub ' btnAdd_Click
68
69     ' Back Button Click event
70     Private Sub btnBack_Click(ByVal sender As System.Object, _
71        ByVal e As System.EventArgs) Handles btnBack.Click
72
73        ' move backward one package in the list
74        If m_intPosition > 0 Then
75           m_intPosition -= 1
76        Else ' wrap to end of list
77           m_intPosition = m_objList.Count - 1
78        End If
79
80        LoadPackage() ' load package data from item in list
81     End Sub ' btnBack_Click
82
83     ' Next Button Click event
84     Private Sub btnNext_Click(ByVal sender As System.Object, _
85        ByVal e As System.EventArgs) Handles btnNext.Click
86
87        ' move forward one package in the list
88        If m_intPosition < m_objList.Count - 1 Then
89           m_intPosition += 1
90        Else
91           m_intPosition = 0 ' wrap to beginning of list
92        End If
93
94        LoadPackage() ' load package data from item in list
95     End Sub ' btnNext_Click
96
97     ' Remove Button click event
98     Private Sub btnRemove_Click(ByVal sender As _
99        System.Object, ByVal e As System.EventArgs) _
100       Handles btnRemove.Click
101
102       ' remove ID from ListBox if state displayed
103       If cboState.Text = cboViewPackages.Text Then
104          lstPackages.Items.Remove(m_objPackage.PackageNumber)
105       End If
106
107       m_objList.RemoveAt(m_intPosition) ' remove package from list
108
```

Figure 20.26   Complete code listing for the **Shipping Hub** application. (Part 2 of 5.)

```
109          ' load next package in list if there is one
110          If m_objList.Count > 0 Then
111
112             ' if not at first position, go to previous one
113             If m_intPosition > 0 Then
114                m_intPosition -= 1
115             End If
116
117             LoadPackage() ' load package data from item in list
118          Else
119             ClearControls() ' clear fields
120          End If
121
122          SetButtons(True) ' enable appropriate Buttons
123       End Sub ' btnRemove_Click
124
125       ' Edit/Update Button Click event
126       Private Sub btnEditUpdate_Click(ByVal sender As _
127          System.Object, ByVal e As System.EventArgs) _
128          Handles btnEditUpdate.Click
129
130          ' when Button reads "Edit", allow user to
131          ' edit package information only
132          If btnEditUpdate.Text = "&Edit" Then
133             fraAddress.Enabled = True
134             SetButtons(False)
135             btnEditUpdate.Enabled = True
136
137             ' change Button text from "Edit" to "Update"
138             btnEditUpdate.Text = "&Update"
139          Else
140
141             ' when Button reads "Update" remove the old package
142             ' data and add new data from TextBoxes
143             SetPackage()
144             m_objList.RemoveAt(m_intPosition)
145             m_objList.Insert(m_intPosition, m_objPackage)
146
147             ' display state in ComboBox
148             cboViewPackages.Text = m_objPackage.State
149
150             ' when done, return to normal operating state
151             fraAddress.Enabled = False  ' disable GroupBox
152             SetButtons(True) ' enable appropriate Buttons
153
154             ' change Button text from "Update" to "Edit"
155             btnEditUpdate.Text = "&Edit"
156          End If
157
158       End Sub ' btnEditUpdate_Click
159
160       ' set package properties
161       Private Sub SetPackage()
162          m_objPackage.Address = txtAddress.Text
163          m_objPackage.City = txtCity.Text
164          m_objPackage.State = _
165             Convert.ToString(cboState.SelectedItem)
166          m_objPackage.Zip = Convert.ToInt32(Val(txtZip.Text))
167       End Sub ' SetPackage
```

Set the position to the next package in the **ArrayList** → (annotation for lines 109–120)

Retrieve data from user, and store it in the **Package** object → (annotation for lines 161–167)

Figure 20.26   Complete code listing for the **Shipping Hub** application. (Part 3 of 5.)

```
168
169    ' load package information into Form
170    Private Sub LoadPackage()
171
172       ' retrieve package from list
173       m_objPackage = CType(m_objList.Item(m_intPosition), _
174          Package)
175
176       ' display package data
177       txtAddress.Text = m_objPackage.Address
178       txtCity.Text = m_objPackage.City
179       cboState.Text = m_objPackage.State
180       txtZip.Text = m_objPackage.Zip.ToString("00000")
181       lblArrivalTime.Text = _
182          m_objPackage.ArrivalTime.ToString
183       lblPackageNumber.Text = _
184          m_objPackage.PackageNumber.ToString
185    End Sub ' LoadPackage
186
187    ' clear all the input controls on the Form
188    Private Sub ClearControls()
189       txtAddress.Clear()
190       txtCity.Clear()
191       txtZip.Clear()
192       cboState.SelectedText = ""
193       lblArrivalTime.Text = ""
194       lblPackageNumber.Text = ""
195    End Sub ' ClearControls
196
197    ' enable/disable Buttons
198    Private Sub SetButtons(ByVal blnState As Boolean)
199       btnRemove.Enabled = blnState
200       btnEditUpdate.Enabled = blnState
201       btnNext.Enabled = blnState
202       btnBack.Enabled = blnState
203
204       ' disable navigation if not multiple packages
205       If m_objList.Count < 2 Then
206          btnNext.Enabled = False
207          btnBack.Enabled = False
208       End If
209
210       ' if no items, disable Remove and Edit/Update Buttons
211       If m_objList.Count = 0 Then
212          btnEditUpdate.Enabled = False
213          btnRemove.Enabled = False
214       End If
215
216    End Sub ' SetButtons
217
218    ' event raised when user selects a new state in ComboBox
219    Private Sub cboViewPackages_SelectedIndexChanged( _
220       ByVal sender As System.Object, ByVal e As System.EventArgs) _
221       Handles cboViewPackages.SelectedIndexChanged
222
223       Dim objViewPackage As Package ' control variable package
224       Dim strState As String = _
225          Convert.ToString(cboViewPackges.SelectedItem)
```

Enable or disable Buttons depending on value of blnState *(annotation pointing to lines 199–202)*

Figure 20.26   Complete code listing for the **Shipping Hub** application. (Part 4 of 5.)

```
226
227          lstPackages.Items.Clear() ' clear ListBox
228
229          ' list all packages for current state in ListBox
230          For Each objViewPackage In m_objList
231
232             ' determine if state package is being shipped to
233             ' matches the state selected in the ComboBox
234             If objViewPackage.State = strState Then
235
236                ' add package number to the ListBox
237                lstPackages.Items.Add(objViewPackage.PackageNumber)
238             End If
239
240          Next
241
242       End Sub ' cboViewPackages_SelectedIndexChanged
243
244    End Class ' FrmShippingHub
```

Figure 20.26   Complete code listing for the **Shipping Hub** application. (Part 5 of 5.)

SELF-REVIEW
1. The collection type in a For Each...Next repetition statement represents _____.

   a) the counter used for iteration   b) the reference used for iteration

   c) an array or collection   d) the guard condition

2. The _____ statement provides a convenient way to iterate through values in an array or collection.

   a) Do While...Loop   b) For...Next

   c) For Each...Next   d) None of the above.

Answers: 1) c. 2) c.

20.8 Wrap-Up

In this tutorial, you learned how to use the TabStop and TabIndex properties to enhance the **Shipping Hub** application's usability. You learned how to determine which controls receive the application's focus when the *Tab* key is pressed using the TabStop property. You then set the TabIndex property, to specify the order in which controls receive the focus of the application when the *Tab* key is pressed. To further enhance the user interface, you created access keys to allow the user to "click" Buttons in the **Shipping Hub** application by pressing the *Alt* key and then the access key for the particular Button.

You learned about using the ArrayList collection. You used ArrayList methods to add a package object to an ArrayList and delete the package from a specific index in an ArrayList. You then wrote code to insert a Package object into the ArrayList at a specific index. These methods helped you store, edit and navigate an ArrayList of packages in the **Shipping Hub** application.

Finally, you learned about the For Each...Next repetition statement. You declared a control variable for use in the loop and used that reference in the For Each...Next statement to iterate through each element in a collection type (which can be an array or a collection). Then you used the For Each...Next statement to iterate through package objects in the ArrayList in your **Shipping Hub** application.

In the next tutorial, you will learn about mouse events, which are events raised when the user moves or clicks the mouse. You will use these mouse events to allow the user to draw art on a Form.

SKILLS SUMMARY

Using the TabIndex and TabStop Properties

■ Set the TabIndex properties of controls on your Form using numbers to specify the order in which to transfer the focus of the application when the user presses the *Tab* key.

■ Set the TabStop property of a control to False if a control is not used by the user to input data. Set the TabStop property of a control to True if focus should be transferred to the control using the *Tab* key.

Creating Access Keys

■ Insert the & symbol in a control's Text property before the character you wish you use as an access key (keyboard shortcut).

Creating an ArrayList

■ Assign a reference to an ArrayList to an object of type Collections.ArrayList using keyword New.

Using an ArrayList

■ Call ArrayList method Add on an ArrayList object to add the method's argument to the ArrayList.

■ Call ArrayList method RemoveAt on an ArrayList object to remove the object from the ArrayList at the index specified by the method's argument.

■ Call ArrayList method Insert on an ArrayList object to add the object specified by the second argument to the ArrayList at the index specified by the first argument.

Using a For Each...Next Repetition Statement

■ Declare a reference of the same type as elements you wish to access in a collection type (array or collection).

■ Specify the reference as the control variable in the For Each...Next repetition statement and the array or collection through which you wish to iterate. The loop repeats and the body of the For Each...Next repetition statement executes for each element in the collection type. The value accessed at the beginning of each iteration is stored in the element reference for the body of the loop.

KEY TERMS

access key—Keyboard shortcut that allows the user to perform an action on a control using the keyboard.

Add method of class ArrayList—Adds a specified object to the end of an ArrayList.

ArrayList class—Performs the same functionality as an array, but has resizing capabilities.

collection—A class used to store groups of related objects.

collection type of a For Each...Next statement—Specifies the array or collection through which you wish to iterate.

Collections namespace—Contains collection classes such as ArrayList.

Count property of ArrayList—Returns the number of objects contained in the ArrayList.

CType function—Function that converts the type of its first argument to the type specified by the second argument.

dynamic resizing—A capability that allows certain objects (such as ArrayLists) to increase or decrease in size based on the addition or removal of elements from that object. Enables the ArrayList object to increase its size to accommodate new elements and to decrease its size when elements are removed.

element of a For Each...Next statement—Used to store a reference to the current value of the collection being iterated.

For Each...Next repetition statement—Iterates through elements in an array or collection.

index of an ArrayList—The value with which you can refer to a specific element in an ArrayList, based on the element's location in that ArrayList.

Insert method of class ArrayList—Inserts a specified object into the specified location of an ArrayList.

Items property of ComboBox—Specifies the values the user can select from the ComboBox.

Items.Item property of ComboBox—Retrieves the value at the specified index of a ComboBox.

MaxLength property of TextBox—Specifies the maximum number of characters that can be input into a TextBox.

RemoveAt method of class ArrayList—Removes the object located at a specified location of an ArrayList.

SelectedIndexChanged event of ComboBox—Raised when a new value is selected in a ComboBox.

TabIndex property—A control property that specifies the order in which focus is transferred to controls on the Form when the *Tab* key is pressed.

TabStop property—A control property that specifies whether a control can receive the focus when the *Tab* key is pressed.

ToString method—Returns a String representation of the object or data type on which the method is called.

<table>
<tr><td>

**GUI DESIGN
GUIDELINES**
</td><td>

Overall Design

- Set a control's TabStop property to True only if the control is used to receive user input.
- Use the TabIndex property to define the logical order in which the user should enter data. Usually the tab order transfers the focus of the application from top to bottom and left to right.
- Use access keys to allow users to "click" a control using the keyboard.
</td></tr>
<tr><td>

**CONTROLS, EVENTS,
PROPERTIES &
METHODS**
</td><td>

ArrayList This class is used to store a variable number of objects.

- *Property*

  Count—Returns the number of objects contained in the ArrayList.

- *Methods*

  Add—Adds an object to the ArrayList object.

  Insert—Adds an object to the ArrayList object at a specific index.

  RemoveAt—Removes an object from the ArrayList object at the specified index.

ComboBox 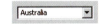 This control allows users to select options from a drop-down list.

- *In action*

  ![Australia combo box]

- *Event*

  SelectedIndexChanged—Raised when a new value is selected in the ComboBox.

- *Properties*

  DataSource—Allows you to add items to the ComboBox.

  DropDownStyle—Determines the ComboBox's style.

  Enabled—Determines whether the user can enter data (True) in the ComboBox or not (False).

  Item—Retrieves the value at the specified index.

  Items—Specifies the values the user can select from the ComboBox.

  Location—Specifies the location of the ComboBox control on its container control relative to the top-left corner.

  MaxDropDownItems—Determines the maximum number of items to be displayed when user clicks the drop-down arrow.

  Name—Specifies the name used to access the ComboBox control programmatically. The name should be prefixed with cbo.

  SelectedValue—Contains the item selected by the user.

  Text—Specifies the text displayed in the ComboBox.
</td></tr>
</table>

TextBox   [abi TextBox]   This control allows the user to input data from the keyboard.

■ *In action*

[0   ]

■ *Events*

TextChanged—Raised when the text in the TextBox is changed.

■ *Properties*

Enabled—Determines whether the user can enter data in the TextBox or not.

Location—Specifies the location of the TextBox on its container control relative to the top-left corner.

MaxLength—Specifies the maximum number of characters that can be input into the TextBox.

Multiline—Specifies whether the TextBox is capable of displaying multiple lines of text.

Name—Specifies the name used to access the TextBox programmatically. The name should be prefixed with txt.

PasswordChar—Specifies the masking character to be used when displaying data in the TextBox.

ReadOnly—Determines whether the value of a TextBox can be changed.

ScrollBars—Specifies whether a multiline TextBox contains a scrollbar.

Size—Specifies the height and width (in pixels) of the TextBox.

Text—Specifies the text displayed in the TextBox.

TextAlign—Specifies how the text is aligned within the TextBox.

■ *Method*

Focus—Transfers the focus of the application to the TextBox that calls it.

MULTIPLE-CHOICE QUESTIONS

20.1 _____ are specifically designed to store groups of values.

    a) Collections   b) Properties

    c) Accessors   d) None of the above.

20.2 The _____ key provides a quick and convenient way to navigate through controls on a Form.

    a) *Tab*   b) *Enter*

    c) *Caps Lock*   d) *Alt*

20.3 An ArrayList differs from an array in that an ArrayList can _____.

    a) store objects of any type   b) resize dynamically

    c) be accessed programmatically   d) All of the above.

20.4 The element in a For Each…Next statement _____.

    a) must be of type Integer

    b) must be of (or convertible to) the same type as the collection or array type

    c) must be of type ArrayList   d) None of the above.

20.5 The control that receives the focus the first time *Tab* is pressed has a TabIndex property set to _____.

    a) First   b) 0

    c) Next   d) 1

20.6 Users should be able to use the *Tab* key to transfer the focus to _____.

    a) only Buttons   b) only TextBoxes

    c) only controls that have an AcceptTab property

    d) only the controls that receive user input

20.7 To ensure that the proper controls obtain the focus when the *Tab* key is pressed, use the _____.

a) `TabIndex` property   b) `TabStop` and `TabIndex` properties
c) `TabStop` property   d) `Focus` property

20.8 To add a value to the end of an `ArrayList`, call the _____ method.

a) `Add`   b) `AddToEnd`
c) `AddAt`   d) `InsertAt`

20.9 To remove a value from a specific index in the `ArrayList`, use method _____.

a) `Remove`   b) `RemoveAt`
c) `Delete`   d) `DeleteAt`

20.10 To display an ampersand character on a control, type a _____ in its `Text` property.

a) `&_`   b) `&`
c) `&&`   d) `_&`

EXERCISES

20.11 (***Modified Salary Survey Application***) Modify the **Salary Survey** application you created in Exercise 17.12 by using a `For Each...Next` loop to replace the `For...Next` loop that is used in Tutorial 17 (Fig. 20.27).

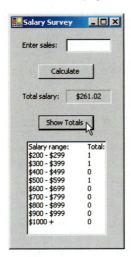

Figure 20.27   Modified **Salary Survey** GUI.

a) ***Copying the template to your working directory.*** Copy the directory `C:\Examples\Tutorial20\Exercises\SalarySurveyModified` to your `C:\SimplyVB` directory.

b) ***Opening the application's template file.*** Double click `SalarySurveyModified.sln` in the `SalarySurvey` directory to open the application.

c) ***Locating the event handler.*** In **Design View**, double click the **Show Totals** Button to bring up the event handler. The code to handle the `Click` event should include two statements, one to clear the items in the `ListBox` and the other to add a header.

d) ***Creating a counter variable.*** The `For Each...Next` loop allows you to loop through each element in a specified collection. The `For...Next` loop from Exercise 17.12 handles the `String` (`m_strSalaryRanges`) and `Integer` (`m_intSalaries`) arrays. This presents a problem. You cannot loop through both of these arrays using the same element reference. (One is an `Integer`, and the other is a `String`.) To handle this you need to create a common counter variable, one that you will use to loop through the indices of both arrays. This is possible because the lengths of both arrays are the same.

e) ***Adding an element reference.*** It does not matter which array you decide to use in this exercise, because these arrays are of the same length. Declare an element reference with the correct data type.

f) ***Create the For Each...Next loop.*** Use the new element reference that you have created along with the array of your choice to create the `For Each...Next` loop statement.

g) *Adding text to the ListBox.* Adding the statement to output to the ListBox is exactly the same as the one from Exercise 17.12. The only difference will be the name of the counter variable that you decide to use.

h) *Increment the counter variable.* To successfully loop through both arrays and output the data, you need to increment the counter variable. This ensures that the proper data is added to the ListBox through each iteration.

i) *Running the application.* Select **Debug > Start** to run your application. Enter several sales amounts using the **Calculate** Button. Click the **Show Totals** Button and verify that the proper amounts are displayed for each salary range, based on the salaries calculate from your input.

j) *Closing the application.* Close your running application by clicking its close box.

k) *Closing the IDE.* Close Visual Studio .NET by clicking its close box.

20.12 (*Modified Shipping Hub Application*) Modify the **Shipping Hub** application created in this tutorial, so that the user can double click a package in the lstPackages ListBox. When a package number is double clicked, the package's information should be displayed in a MessageBox (Fig. 20.28).

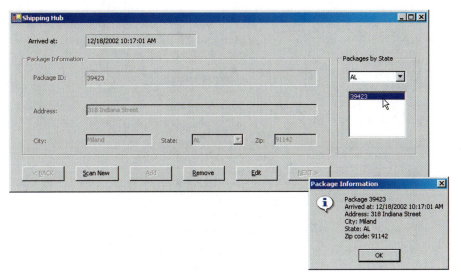

Figure 20.28 Modified **Shipping Hub** application GUI.

a) *Copying the template to your working directory.* Copy the directory C:\Examples\ Tutorial20\Exercises\ShippingHubModified to your C:\SimplyVB directory.

b) *Opening the application's template file.* Double click ShippingHubModified.sln in the ShippingHubModified directory to open the application.

c) *Viewing the event handler.* Click ShippingHub.vb in the **Solution Explorer** and select **View > Code**. Scroll to the end of code listing to locate the ListBox's Double-Click event handler.

d) *Initializing necessary variables.* To loop through the packages in the ArrayList of Packages, you need to create a reference of type Package. It is also helpful to create a String variable to store the information about the given package. Write code in the DoubleClick event handler to declare the String strPackage. A ListBox's DoubleClick event is raised when the control is double clicked.

e) *Check whether the user has selected a valid item.* To determine whether the user has selected a valid item (and not an empty element in the ListBox), write an If...Then statement to make sure that the ListBox is not empty when the user selected an item. [*Hint*: A SelectedIndex value of -1 means that no item is currently selected.]

f) *Writing a For Each...Next loop.* Use the Package reference you declared in *Step c* to create a For Each...Next loop with the m_objList collection.

g) *Determining whether the current selected package is correct.* Insert an If...Then statement to determine whether the current object that is selected from the m_objList collection matches the selected item from the ListBox. Because the packages are listed in the ListBox by their package number, use that information in your If...Then statement. Once the correct package is matched, store that package's information in the strPackage String.

h) *Inserting the Else statement.* Make sure to notify the user if an invalid item has been selected from the ListBox. If this occurs, add a message to the strPackage String that will be displayed in the MessageBox.

i) *Displaying the MessageBox.* Call the MessageBox's Show method to display the text you have added to the strPackage String. This displays either the information for the package they have selected or the message telling them they have selected an invalid package.

j) *Running the application.* Select **Debug > Start** to run your application. Add several packages. In the **Packages by State** GroupBox, select a state for which there are packages being sent. Double click one of the packages listed in the **Packages by State** ListBox, and verify that the correct information is displayed in a MessageBox.

k) *Closing the application.* Close your running application by clicking its close box.

l) *Closing the IDE.* Close Visual Studio .NET by clicking its close box.

20.13 (*Controls Collection Application*) Visual Basic .NET provides many different types of collections. One such collection is the Controls collection, which is used to provide access to all of the controls on a Form. Create an application that uses the Controls collection and a For Each...Next loop to iterate through each control on the Form. As each control is encountered, add the control's name to a ListBox, and change the control's background color (in Fig. 20.29, Color.Wheat, is used).

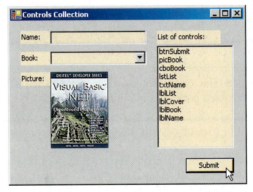

Figure 20.29   Controls Collection GUI.

a) *Copying the template to your working directory.* Copy the directory C:\Examples\ Tutorial20\Exercises\ControlsCollection to your C:\SimplyVB directory.

b) *Opening the application's template file.* Double click ControlsCollection.sln in the ControlsCollection directory to open the application.

c) *Generating an event handler.* Switch to Design view. Double click the **Submit** Button in design view to create an event handler for the click event.

d) *Declaring a control variable.* Declare a reference of type Control. This reference represents each element in the For Each...Next statement as it iterates through each Control on the Form.

e) *Clearing the ListBox.* To ensure that the information in the ListBox is updated each time the **Submit** Button is clicked, clear the ListBox of all items.

f) *Writing a For Each...Next loop.* To create the For Each...Next loop, use the control variable that you created to iterate through the Form's Controls collection.

g) *Adding each control's name to the ListBox.* Use the ListBox's Add method to insert the name of each control on the Form. Recall that a control's Name property contains the name of the control.

h) *Changing the control's background color.* Use the Control's BackColor property to change the control's background color. Set the property to a new color using a member of the Color structure. [*Hint:* Type the word Color followed by the member-access operator to display a list of predefined colors using the *IntelliSense* feature.]

Note that the color of the PictureBox does not appear to change because its image displays in the control's foreground.

i) *Running the application.* Select **Debug > Start** to run your application. Click the **Submit** Button. Verify that the controls' background colors change, and that all the controls are listed in the **List of controls:** ListBox.

j) *Closing the application.* Close your running application by clicking its close box.

k) *Closing the IDE.* Close Visual Studio .NET by clicking its close box.

What does this code do? ▶ **20.14** What is the result of the following code?

```
1   Dim intList As Collections.ArrayList
2   Dim intListItems As Integer
3   Dim strOutput As String
4
5   intList = New ArrayList
6   intList.Add(1)
7   intList.Add(3)
8   intList.Add(5)
9
10  For Each intListItems In intList
11      strOutput &= (" " & intListItems.ToString)
12  Next
13
14  MessageBox.Show(strOutput, "Mystery", _
15      MessageBoxButtons.OK, MessageBoxIcon.Information)
```

What's wrong with this code? ▶ **20.15** This code should iterate through an array of Packages in ArrayList objList and print each package's number in Label lblDisplay. Find the error(s) in the following code.

```
1   Dim objValue As Collections.ArrayList
2
3   For Each objValue In objList
4     lblDisplay.Text &= (" " & objValue.PackageNumber)
5   Next
```

Programming Challenge ▶ **20.16** (*Enhanced Shipping Hub Application*) Enhance the **Shipping Hub** application created in Exercise 20.12 to allow the user to move a maximum of five packages from the warehouse to a truck for shipping (Fig. 20.30). If you have not completed Exercise 20.12, follow the steps in Exercise 20.12 before proceeding to the next step. If you have completed Exercise 20.12, copy the code you added to the lstPackages ListBox DoubleClick event handler to the same event handler in this application before beginning the exercise.

a) *Copying the template to your working directory.* Copy the directory C:\Examples\Tutorial20\Exercises\ShippingHubEnhanced to your C:\SimplyVB directory.

b) *Opening the application's template file.* Double click ShippingHubEnhanced.sln in the ShippingHubEnhanced directory to open the application.

c) *Enabling the Ship Button.* The **Ship** Button should not be enabled until a package is selected in the lstPackage ListBox. Double click the lstPackage ListBox from design view to define the event handler. Use the Button's Enabled property to enable the Button if the SelectedIndex of the ListBox is not -1. This means that when the user selects a package from the ListBox, the user can send the package to the truck by clicking the **Ship** Button. Also, insert a line of code after the For Each...Next statement in the SelectedIndexChanged event handler to disable the **Ship** Button when a user chooses a different state.

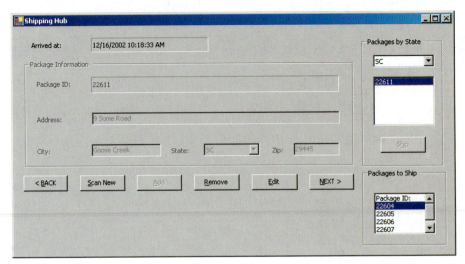

Figure 20.30   Enhanced **Shipping Hub** GUI.

d) *Defining the Ship Button's Click Event*. Double click the **Ship** Button in **Design View** to define the Click event.

e) *Incrementing the counter*. Because you are only allowing five packages to be "shipped," declare an instance variable that will track how many packages have been placed onto the truck. Increment the variable each time the **Ship** Button is clicked.

f) *Creating temporary variables*. Create two temporary Package references to store the correct package's information. Use objTempPackage as the reference to the element in the collection type of a For Each...Next statement, and the objTruckPackage as a reference to the package added to the truck.

g) *Using the If...Then...Else statement*. Use an If...Then...Else statement to allow packages to be placed onto the truck if the number of packages on the truck is less than five.

h) *Using the For Each...Next loop*. Use a For Each...Next loop to iterate through the values in m_objList. Each iteration should determine whether the current package is the one selected from the ListBox.

i) *Adding the package to the truck*. When the For Each...Next loop has located the correct package, add that package to the truck by adding the reference to objTempPackage to the truck's ArrayList, m_objTruckList. Then assign the value in objTempPackage (the package sent to the truck) to objTruckPackage.

j) *Removing the package*. When the For Each...Next loop completes, remove the package meant for the truck from m_objList and the lstPackages ListBox.

k) *Displaying the package in the ListBox*. Use a For Each...Next loop that iterates through each package in the m_objTruckList ArrayList and displays each package in the lstTruck ListBox.

l) *Refreshing the GUI*. Call the ClearControls and SetButtons methods to clear the TextBoxes and enable the appropriate Buttons. Also, set the **Ship** Button's Enabled property to False.

m) *Coding the Else statement*. Display a MessageBox that notifies the user if the number of packages on the truck is already five. Then disable the **Ship** Button.

n) *Running the application*. Select **Debug > Start** to run your application. Add several packages. In the **Packages by State** GroupBox, select several packages and add them to the **Packages to Ship** ListBox. Verify that you can add only 5 packages to this ListBox.

o) *Closing the application*. Close your running application by clicking its close box.

p) *Closing the IDE*. Close Visual Studio .NET by clicking its close box.

TUTORIAL

"Cat and Mouse" Painter Application

Introducing the *Graphics* Object and *Mouse Events*

Objectives

In this tutorial, you will learn to:
- Use mouse events to allow user interaction with an application.
- Handle MouseDown, MouseUp and MouseMove events.
- Use the Graphics object to draw circles on the Form.
- Determine which mouse button was pressed.

Outline

The computer mouse is one of the most important input devices and is essential to the GUIs of Windows applications. With the mouse, the user can point to, click and drag items in applications. Clicking and releasing a mouse button are associated with events, as is moving the mouse. Every time you move the mouse, Windows interprets that event and redraws the mouse pointer as it moves across the screen.

In this tutorial, you create a **Painter** application that handles mouse events. The user clicks the left mouse button over the Form to enable drawing. By moving the mouse pointer over the Form with the left mouse button pressed, the user can create line drawings composed of small circles. In addition to learning how to draw a shape on the Form (a circle), you will learn how to set the shape's color. You will then learn how to stop drawing when the user releases the mouse button. You will also enable the user to erase a drawing by holding down the right mouse button.

21.1 Test-Driving the Painter Application

In this tutorial, you will create a **Painter** application. This application must meet the following requirements:

Application Requirements

The principal of an elementary school wants to introduce computers to children by appealing to their creative side. Many elementary-level applications test skills in mathematics, but the principal wishes to use an application that allows children to express their artistic skills. Develop an application that allows the student to "paint" on a Form, using the mouse. The application should draw when the user moves the mouse with the left mouse button held down and stop drawing when the left mouse button is released. The application draws many small blue-violet circles side by side to trace out lines, curves and shapes. An important part of any drawing application is the ability to erase mistakes or to clear the Form for more drawing room. The user can erase portions of the drawing by moving the mouse with the right mouse button held down.

You begin by test-driving the completed application. Then, you will learn the additional Visual Basic .NET technologies that you will need to create your own version of this application.

Test-Driving the Painter Application

1. *Opening the completed application*. Open the directory `C:\Examples\Tutorial21\CompletedApplication\Painter` to locate the **Painter** application. Double click `Painter.sln` to open the application in Visual Studio .NET.

2. *Running the Painter application*. Select **Debug > Start** to run the application (Fig. 21.1).

Figure 21.1   **Painter** application before drawing.

3. *Drawing with the mouse*. To draw on the Form using the **Painter** application, press and hold down the left mouse button while the mouse pointer is anywhere over the Form (Fig. 21.2). To stop drawing, release the mouse button. Note that the application draws little blue-violet circles as you move the mouse while pressing the left mouse button. The size of these circles will vary depending on your display settings.

Drawing lines composed of small, colored circles

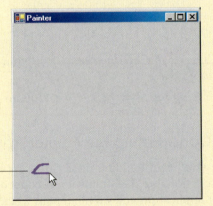

Figure 21.2   Drawing on the **Painter** application's Form.

4. *Being creative*. Draw a cat and a computer mouse, as shown in Fig. 21.3. Be creative and have fun—your drawing need not look like the image shown.

(cont.)

Figure 21.3 Drawing a cat and a computer mouse on the **Form**.

5. ***Using the eraser.*** Hold down the right mouse button and move the mouse pointer over part of your drawing. This "erases" the drawing wherever the mouse pointer comes into contact with the colored line (Fig. 21.4). You will see, when you add code to the application to erase, that you are actually drawing circles in **Form**'s background color.

Erasing by drawing circles that are the same color as the **Form**'s background

Figure 21.4 Erasing part of the drawing.

6. ***Closing the application.*** Close your running application by clicking its close box.

7. ***Closing the IDE.*** Close Visual Studio .NET by clicking its close box.

21.2 Constructing the Painter Application

Before you begin building the **Painter** application, you should review the application's functionality. The following pseudocode describes the basic operation of the **Painter** application and what happens when the user moves the mouse pointer over the application's **Form**:

When a mouse button is pressed:

    If the left mouse button is pressed
        Enable user to draw
    Else if the right mouse button is pressed
        Enable the user to erase

When a mouse button is released:
    Disable the user from drawing
    Disable the user from erasing

When the mouse is moved:

    If the user is allowed to paint
        Draw a blue-violet circle at the position of the mouse pointer
    Else If the user is allowed to erase
        "Erase" by drawing a circle at the position of the mouse pointer in the
        Form's background color

Now that you have test-driven the **Painter** application and studied its pseudocode representation, you will use an ACE table to help you convert the pseudocode to Visual Basic .NET. Figure 21.5 lists the actions, controls and events that will help you complete your own version of this application.

This tutorial starts by showing you how to use two mouse events—the event that occurs when you press a mouse button and the event that occurs when you release that mouse button. At first, your **Painter** application will draw a circle when the user presses or releases any mouse button. The circles drawn by pressing a mouse button will have a larger size than and a different color from the circles drawn by releasing the mouse button. Next, you will modify the application so that it draws when the user moves the mouse with a button pressed. If the user moves the mouse without pressing a mouse button, nothing will be drawn.

Action/Control/Event (ACE) Table for the Painter Application	Action	Control/Object/Class	Event
		FrmPainter	MouseDown
	If the left mouse button is pressed	MouseEventArgs	
	Enable user to draw		
	Else if the right mouse button is pressed	MouseEventArgs	
	Enable the user to erase		
		FrmPainter	MouseUp
	Disable the user from drawing		
	Disable the user from erasing		
		FrmPainter	MouseMove
	If the user is allowed to paint Draw blue-violet circle at position of mouse pointer	m_objGraphic	
	Else If the user is allowed to erase "Erase" by drawing a circle at the position of the mouse in the Form's background color	m_objGraphic	

Figure 21.5   **Painter** application's ACE table.

To complete the **Painter** application, you will need to add the eraser capability, which requires you to determine which mouse button the user presses. The last section of this tutorial will show you how to assign the drawing capability to the left mouse button and the eraser capability to the right mouse button.

21.3 Using a Graphics Object

Now that you have seen the pseudocode and ACE table, you are ready to begin building the **Painter** application. You will use a **Graphics** object to enable the user to draw on the Form. Class Graphics contains methods used for drawing text, lines, rectangles and other shapes. The following box shows you how to create the **Painter** application's Graphics object.

Creating a Graphics Object

1. **Copying the template to your working directory.** Copy the C:\Examples\Tutorial21\TemplateApplication\Painter directory to your C:\SimplyVB directory.

2. **Opening the Painter application's template file.** Double click Painter.sln in the Painter directory to open the application in Visual Studio .NET. Open Painter.vb in code view.

3. **Creating a Graphics object.** Add lines 7–8 of Fig. 21.6 into the **Painter** application. Line 8 declares Graphics reference m_objGraphic. The **CreateGraphics** method (which is a member of class Form) creates a Graphics object with which you will draw shapes on the Form. Note that because you are writing code in the Form's class (FrmPainter), you do not need to use the member-access operator to access the Form's CreateGraphics method. Notice that the template already contains a declaration of constant m_intDIAMETER (line 5). We will discuss this constant shortly.

Creating a **Graphics** object ——————

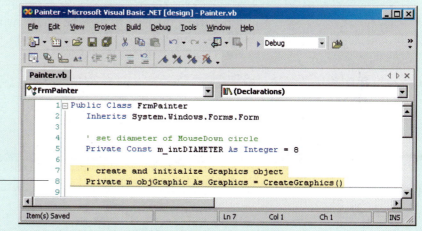

Figure 21.6   Declaring a **Graphics** reference.

4. **Saving the project.** Select **File > Save All** to save your modified code.

---

1. To draw on a Form, use an object of class _____.

    a) Graphics   b) Drawing

    c) Paint   d) Sketch

2. The _____ method creates a Graphics object.

    a) GetGraphics   b) MakeGraphics

    c) CreateGraphics   d) InitializeGraphics

Answers: 1) a. 2) c.

21.4 Handling the MouseDown Event

This section begins our discussion of handling **mouse events**, which are generated when the mouse is used to interact with the Form or controls on the Form. In the **Painter** application, the mouse interacts exclusively with the Form. (There are no controls on the Form.)

A Form's **MouseDown** event occurs when a mouse button is pressed while the mouse pointer is over the Form. You will learn how to add a MouseDown event handler to your application in the following box. You will notice that, when you run your application after following the steps in this box, you can press any mouse button to draw a circle on the Form. When you add the eraser capability to the **Painter** application in Section 21.7, you will learn how to determine which mouse button was pressed.

Handling the MouseDown Event	1. ***Generating the MouseDown event handler.*** To generate the `MouseDown` event handler, select **(FrmPainter Events)** from the Class Name ComboBox (Fig. 21.7). Then select `MouseDown` from the Method Name ComboBox.

This generates the event handler `FrmPainter_MouseDown` (Fig. 21.8). As always, you should add a comment and format your code to improve readability (lines 52–57). The application invokes `FrmPainter_MouseDown` when the user generates the Form's `MouseDown` event by pressing a mouse button when the mouse pointer is over the Form `FrmPainter`.

Notice that the second argument passed to event handler `FrmPainter_MouseDown` is a variable of type **MouseEventArgs** (line 54). This `MouseEventArgs` object (referenced by `e`) contains information about the `MouseDown` event, including the coordinates of the mouse pointer when the mouse button was pressed on the Form.

Class Name ComboBox with **(FrmPainter Events)** selected

Method Name ComboBox

Select **MouseDown**

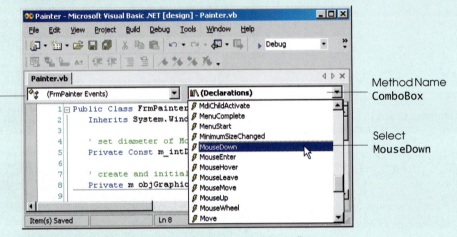

Figure 21.7   Creating a `MouseDown` event handler.

MouseEventArgs argument

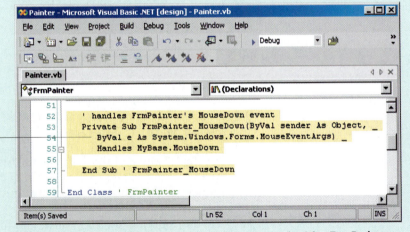

Figure 21.8   `MouseDown` event handler generated for `FrmPainter`.

Note that the *x*- and *y*-coordinates of the `MouseEventArgs` object are relative to the top-left corner Form or control that raises the event. Point *(0,0)* represents the upper-left corner of the Form. If you wish to access the *x*-coordinate of the mouse, use property **X** of reference **e**. To access the *y*-coordinate of the mouse, use property **Y** of reference **e**.

(cont.)

2. ***Drawing on the Form whenever a mouse button is clicked.*** Add lines 57–59 of Fig. 21.9 to the **MouseDown** event handler. The **FillEllipse** method of class **Graphics** draws an ellipse on the **Form**. Recall that you declared **m_objGraphic** as your **Graphics** reference earlier in this tutorial. Figure 21.10 shows a diagram of a general ellipse. The dotted rectangle is known as the ellipse's **bounding box**. The bounding box specifies an ellipse's height, width and location on the **Form**.

The first argument passed to the **FillEllipse** method is a **brush**, which can be used to fill shapes with colors. In this case, the **SolidBrush** class, which fills a shape using a single color, is specified as the brush. The color of the brush is specified in the call to the constructor. The color you select (**Color.BlueViolet**) is a member of the **Color** structure. For a complete list of predefined colors in Visual Basic .NET, simply type the word **Color** followed by a dot, and the *IntelliSense* feature will provide a drop-down list of over 100 pre-defined colors (Fig. 21.11).

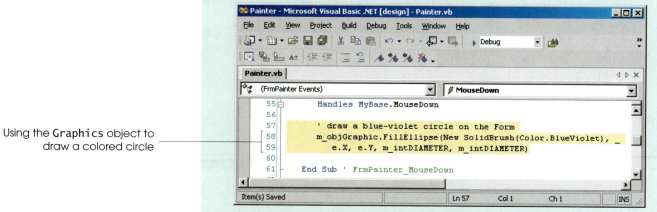

Using the **Graphics** object to draw a colored circle

Figure 21.9 Adding code to the **MouseDown** event handler.

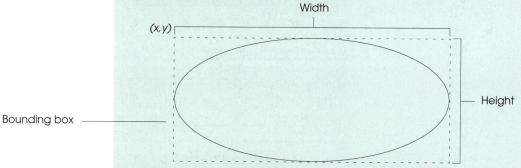

Width

(x, y)

Height

Bounding box

Figure 21.10 General ellipse.

The second and third arguments to the **FillEllipse** method specify the *x*- and *y*-coordinates of the upper-left corner of the bounding box, relative to the upper-left corner of the **Form**. In this application, you use the *x*- and *y*-coordinates of the mouse (returned by properties X and Y of **MouseEventArgs** reference **e**). The fourth and fifth arguments passed to the **FillEllipse** method (constant **m_intDIAMETER**) specify the height and width of the bounding box. An ellipse with equal width and height is a circle—this method call draws a blue-violet circle.

The **Graphics** object provides methods for drawing shapes other than ellipses. You will learn about these methods in Tutorial 26. Note that the *x*- and *y*-coordinates the **Graphics** object uses to draw a shape are relative to the control or **Form** that created it. In this case, the **Graphics** object draws shapes at positions relative to the **Form**.

(cont.)

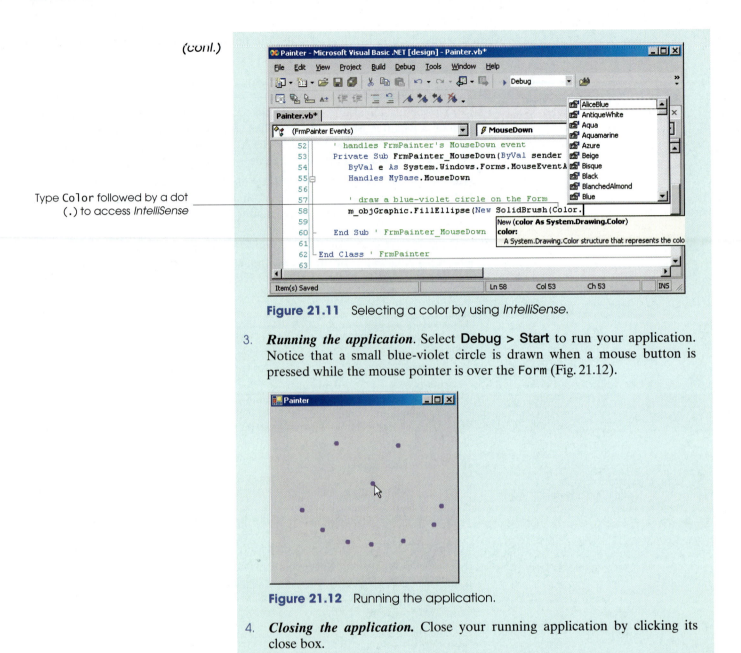

Type **Color** followed by a dot (.) to access *IntelliSense*

Figure 21.11   Selecting a color by using *IntelliSense*.

3. *Running the application.* Select **Debug > Start** to run your application. Notice that a small blue-violet circle is drawn when a mouse button is pressed while the mouse pointer is over the **Form** (Fig. 21.12).

Figure 21.12   Running the application.

4. *Closing the application.* Close your running application by clicking its close box.

---

1. To draw a solid shape, the `FillEllipse` method uses a _____.

   a) `Pencil` object   b) `Marker` object

   c) `PaintBrush` object   d) `SolidBrush` object

2. `BlueViolet` is a member of the _____ structure.

   a) `SolidColor`   b) `FillColor`

   c) `Color`   d) `SystemColor`

Answers: 1) d. 2) c.

21.5 Handling the MouseUp Event

Using the application, you can click anywhere on the **Form** and place a blue-violet circle. To enhance the application further, you will place a green circle on the **Form** when the user releases the mouse button. A **Form**'s **MouseUp** event is generated when a mouse button is released when the pointer is over the Form. You will add this functionality in the following box.

Handling the MouseUp Event

1. ***Adding a second diameter.*** Add lines 7–8 of Fig. 21.13 to your application (above the initialization of the Graphics reference and below the initialization of constant m_intDIAMETER). These lines declare a second constant that stores the diameter of a smaller circle. A circle with this diameter (in pixels) will be drawn whenever the user releases a mouse button.

2. ***Adding the MouseUp event handler.*** Select (**FrmPainter Events**) from the Class Name ComboBox, as you did in Fig. 21.7. Then select MouseUp from the Method Name ComboBox. This creates an empty event handler called FrmPainter_MouseUp (Fig. 21.14).

    Add the comments on lines 66 and 71 to your application. This header is similar to the header for the MouseDown event handler (the only difference is that the word Down is changed to Up). The MouseUp event handler executes only when a mouse button is released.

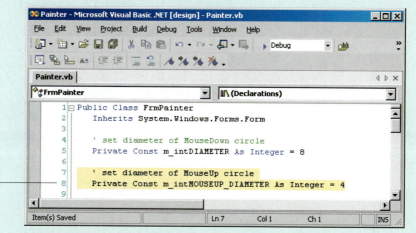

Using a constant to store a circle's diameter

Figure 21.13 Declaring a constant for use in the MouseUp event handler.

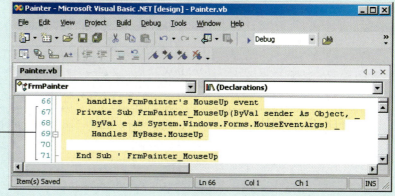

MouseUp event handler after commenting and formatting

Figure 21.14 MouseUp empty event handler.

3. ***Drawing a circle when the user releases a mouse button.*** Add lines 71–72 of Fig. 21.15 to the MouseUp event handler to draw a circle at the position of the mouse pointer on the Form whenever the user releases the mouse button. The diameter of each "mouse up" circle is only half the diameter of the BlueViolet circles drawn by the MouseDown event handler that is called when a mouse button is pressed.

(cont.)

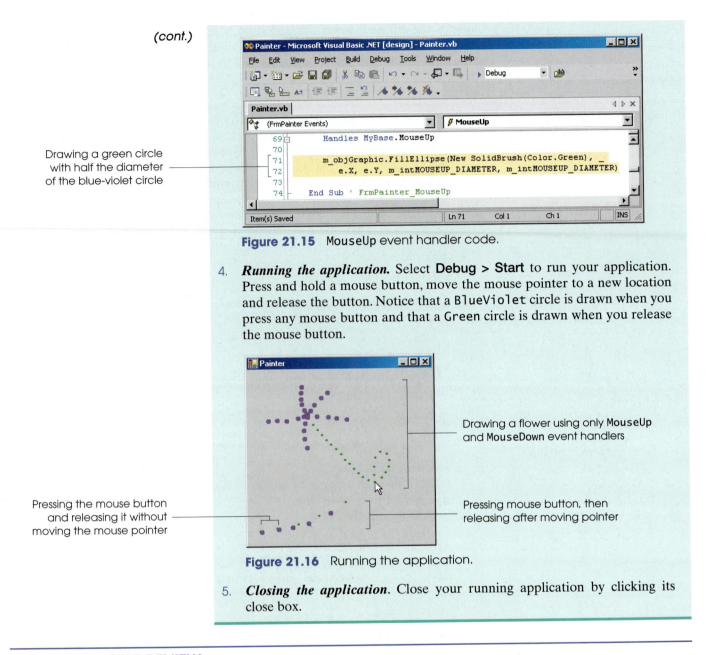

Drawing a green circle with half the diameter of the blue-violet circle

Figure 21.15   MouseUp event handler code.

4. ***Running the application.*** Select **Debug > Start** to run your application. Press and hold a mouse button, move the mouse pointer to a new location and release the button. Notice that a BlueViolet circle is drawn when you press any mouse button and that a Green circle is drawn when you release the mouse button.

Drawing a flower using only MouseUp and MouseDown event handlers

Pressing the mouse button and releasing it without moving the mouse pointer

Pressing mouse button, then releasing after moving pointer

Figure 21.16   Running the application.

5. ***Closing the application.*** Close your running application by clicking its close box.

SELF-REVIEW   1. Releasing a mouse button generates a _____ event.

a) MouseRelease

b) MouseUp

c) MouseOff

d) MouseClick

2. The second and third arguments of the FillEllipse method specify the *x*- and *y*-coordinates of the _____.

a) ellipse's center

b) bounding box's lower-left corner

c) bounding box's upper-right corner

d) bounding box's upper-left corner

Answers: 1) b. 2) d.

21.6 Handling the MouseMove Event

Currently, the application allows you to draw only isolated circles when a mouse button is pressed or released. It does not yet allow you to draw more sophisticated shapes and designs. Next, you will enhance your application to provide more drawing capabilities. The application should continuously draw BlueViolet circles as long as the mouse is being dragged (that is, moved with a button pressed). If the mouse button is not pressed, moving the mouse across the Form should not draw anything. To add this functionality, you will begin by modifying your two event handlers.

<table>
<tr>
<td valign="top">

Modifying the Painter Application

</td>
<td valign="top">

1. ***Adding a Boolean variable to specify whether a mouse button is pressed.*** Delete the constant m_intMOUSEUP_DIAMETER (lines 7–8 of Fig. 21.13) and add lines 4–5 of Fig. 21.17 to your application (above the initialization of m_intDIAMETER). This line declares and initializes the Boolean variable m_blnShouldPaint. The application must be able to determine whether a mouse button is pressed, because the application should draw on the Form only when the mouse button is held down.

   You will alter the MouseDown and MouseUp event handlers so that m_blnShouldPaint is True when any mouse button is held down and False when the mouse button is released. When the application is first loaded, it should not "paint" anything, so this instance variable is initialized to False.

</td>
</tr>
</table>

Declaring and setting an instance variable to control painting

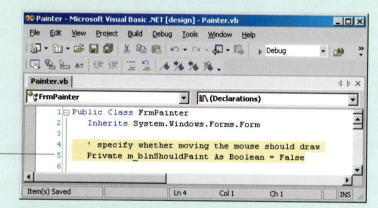

Figure 21.17 Boolean instance variable m_blnShouldPaint is declared and set to False.

2. ***Altering the MouseDown event handler.*** Remove the code inside the Mouse-Down event handler, leaving just the procedure header and the End Sub statement (as in Fig. 21.8). Add line 60 of Fig. 21.18 to the MouseDown event handler to set m_blnShouldPaint to True. This indicates that a mouse button is pressed.

Allow drawing when mouse button is pressed

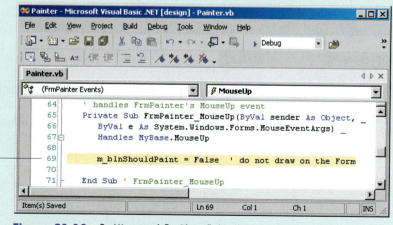

Figure 21.18 Setting m_blnShouldPaint to True.

(cont.)　　3.　***Altering the MouseUp event handler.*** Remove the code inside the MouseUp event handler, leaving just the procedure header and End Sub statement (as in Fig. 21.14). Add line 69 of Fig. 21.19 to set m_blnShouldPaint to False. This indicates that a mouse button has been released.

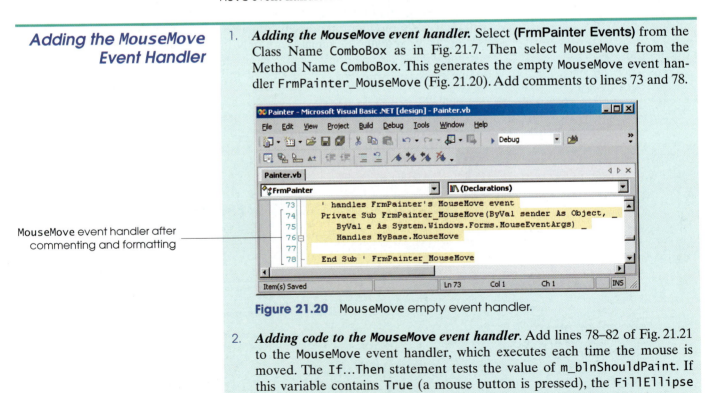

Disable drawing when mouse button is released

Figure 21.19　Setting m_blnShouldPaint to False.

4.　***Saving the project.*** Select **File > Save All** to save your modified code.

You have altered the event handlers to set the value of the m_blnShouldPaint variable to indicate whether a mouse button is pressed. Next, you will handle the **MouseMove** event, which is raised whenever the mouse moves. Whenever you move the mouse over the **Painter** application's Form, the application invokes the Mouse-Move event handler. You define the MouseMove event handler in the following box.

Adding the MouseMove Event Handler

1.　***Adding the MouseMove event handler.*** Select **(FrmPainter Events)** from the Class Name ComboBox as in Fig. 21.7. Then select MouseMove from the Method Name ComboBox. This generates the empty MouseMove event handler FrmPainter_MouseMove (Fig. 21.20). Add comments to lines 73 and 78.

MouseMove event handler after commenting and formatting

Figure 21.20　MouseMove empty event handler.

2.　***Adding code to the MouseMove event handler.*** Add lines 78–82 of Fig. 21.21 to the MouseMove event handler, which executes each time the mouse is moved. The If...Then statement tests the value of m_blnShouldPaint. If this variable contains True (a mouse button is pressed), the FillEllipse method draws a BlueViolet circle on the Form. If m_blnShouldPaint contains False (no mouse button is pressed), then nothing is drawn.

(cont.)

Drawing a circle when the mouse moves and a mouse button is pressed

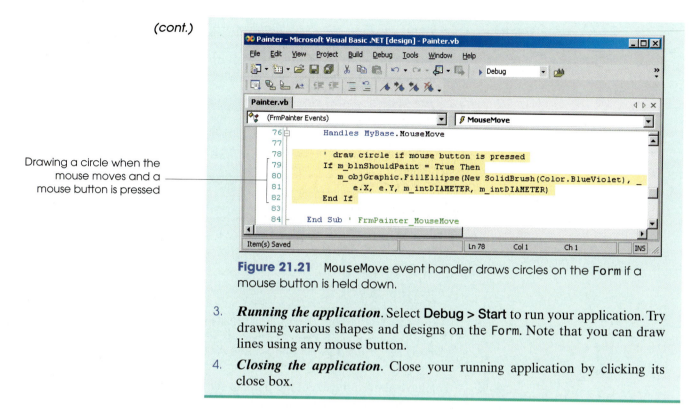

Figure 21.21   **MouseMove** event handler draws circles on the **Form** if a mouse button is held down.

3. **Running the application.** Select **Debug > Start** to run your application. Try drawing various shapes and designs on the **Form**. Note that you can draw lines using any mouse button.

4. **Closing the application.** Close your running application by clicking its close box.

21.7 Distinguishing Between Mouse Buttons

Now that your application allows the user to draw using the mouse, you are going to add the code that allows the user to "erase" by moving the mouse over the drawing with the right mouse button pressed. You also will alter the application so that the user draws by moving the mouse with only the left mouse button pressed. To do this, you will need to determine which mouse button was pressed. You learn how to do this in the following box.

Distinguishing Between Mouse Buttons

1. **Adding a Boolean variable to specify whether the application should erase while the mouse pointer is moving.** Add lines 4–5 of Fig. 21.22 to your application (above the initialization of m_blnShouldPaint). Instance variable m_blnShouldErase specifies whether moving the mouse pointer should act like an eraser.

Declaring and setting an instance variable to control erasing

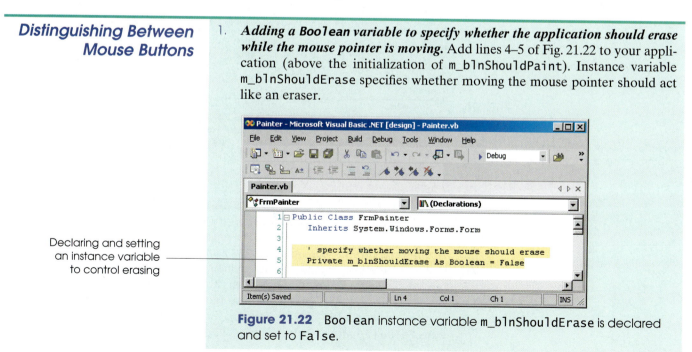

Figure 21.22   **Boolean** instance variable m_blnShouldErase is declared and set to **False**.

(cont.)

2. ***Determining which mouse button was pressed.*** Replace the code in event handler FrmPainter_MouseDown with lines 63–70 of Fig. 21.23. The **Button** property of the MouseEventArgs object (referenced by **e**) specifies which mouse button was pressed. The **MouseButtons** enumeration defines constants that represent the mouse buttons.

   The two most common mouse buttons—**Right** and **Left**—are included in MouseButtons. If the left mouse button was pressed (line 64), line 65 sets m_blnShouldPaint to True to indicate that dragging the mouse should draw. If the right mouse button was pressed (line 68), line 69 sets m_blnShouldErase to True to indicate that dragging the mouse should erase any blue-violet circles touched by the mouse pointer. Notice that only one of the variables can be True at a time. For example, if m_blnShouldPaint is True, then m_blnShouldErase is False. To ensure this, both variables are set to False when the mouse button is released. (See *Step 3*.)

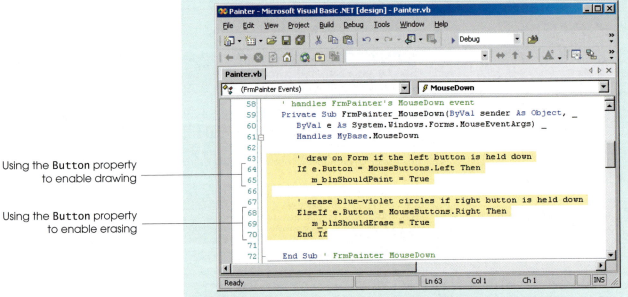

Using the **Button** property to enable drawing

Using the **Button** property to enable erasing

Figure 21.23   Determining which mouse button was pressed.

3. ***Changing the MouseUp event handler.*** Add line 80 of Fig. 21.24 to the FrmPainter_MouseUp event handler. The application should not erase or draw when no mouse buttons are pressed. Line 80 sets m_blnShouldErase to False to indicate that the mouse pointer should not act as an eraser. Note that m_blnShouldPaint is also set to False.

4. ***Drawing when the left mouse button is pressed.*** Replace the code in event handler FrmPainter_MouseMove with lines 89–99 of Fig. 21.25. If m_blnShouldPaint is True (line 90), lines 91–92 draw a BlueViolet circle. Your changes to the MouseDown event handler make m_blnShouldPaint True when the left mouse button is pressed. As a result, the application only draws BlueViolet circles when the user drags the mouse while pressing the left mouse button.

(cont.)

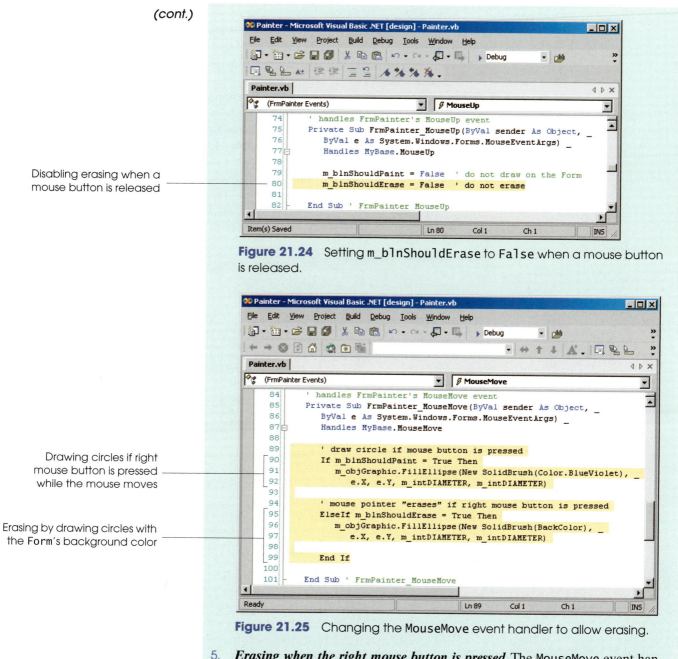

Disabling erasing when a mouse button is released

Figure 21.24   Setting `m_blnShouldErase` to `False` when a mouse button is released.

Drawing circles if right mouse button is pressed while the mouse moves

Erasing by drawing circles with the `Form`'s background color

Figure 21.25   Changing the `MouseMove` event handler to allow erasing.

5. **Erasing when the right mouse button is pressed.** The `MouseMove` event handler does not actually erase anything. Instead, when `m_blnShouldErase` is `True` (line 95 of Fig. 21.25), the `FillEllipse` method (lines 96–97) draws a circle that is the same size as the `BlueViolet` circle and has the same color as the `Form`'s background. This allows the mouse pointer to act like an eraser. Notice that the first argument to `FillEllipse` is `BackColor`. Much like the `CreateGraphics` method, the `BackColor` property of the `Form` can be accessed without the member-access operator. The **BackColor** property returns the `Form`'s background color as a `Color` value.

6. **Running the application.** Select **Debug > Start** to run your application. Try drawing various shapes and designs on the `Form`, then try to erase them.

7. **Closing the application.** Close your running application by clicking its close box.

8. **Closing the IDE.** Close Visual Studio .NET by clicking its close box.

Figure 21.26 presents the source code for the **Painter** application. The lines of code that contain new programming concepts that you learned in this tutorial are highlighted.

```vb
1    Public Class FrmPainter
2       Inherits System.Windows.Forms.Form
3
4       ' specify whether moving the mouse should erase
5       Private m_blnShouldErase As Boolean = False
6
7       ' specify whether moving the mouse should draw
8       Private m_blnShouldPaint As Boolean = False
9
10      ' set diameter of MouseDown circle
11      Private Const m_intDIAMETER As Integer = 8
12
13      ' create and initialize Graphics object
14      Private m_objGraphic As Graphics = CreateGraphics()
15
16      ' Windows Form Designer generated code
17
18      ' handles FrmPainter's MouseDown event
19      Private Sub FrmPainter_MouseDown(ByVal sender As Object, _
20         ByVal e As System.Windows.Forms.MouseEventArgs) _
21         Handles MyBase.MouseDown
22
23         ' draw on Form if the left button is held down
24         If e.Button = MouseButtons.Left Then
25            m_blnShouldPaint = True
26
27         ' erase blue-violet circles if right button is held down
28         ElseIf e.Button = MouseButtons.Right Then
29            m_blnShouldErase = True
30         End If
31
32      End Sub ' FrmPainter_MouseDown
33
34      ' handles FrmPainter's MouseUp event
35      Private Sub FrmPainter_MouseUp(ByVal sender As Object, _
36         ByVal e As System.Windows.Forms.MouseEventArgs) _
37         Handles MyBase.MouseUp
38
39         m_blnShouldPaint = False   ' do not draw on the Form
40         m_blnShouldErase = False   ' do not erase
41
42      End Sub ' FrmPainter_MouseUp
43
44      ' handles FrmPainter's MouseMove event
45      Private Sub FrmPainter_MouseMove(ByVal sender As Object, _
46         ByVal e As System.Windows.Forms.MouseEventArgs) _
47         Handles MyBase.MouseMove
48
49         ' draw circle if left mouse button is pressed
50         If m_blnShouldPaint = True Then
51            m_objGraphic.FillEllipse(New SolidBrush(Color.BlueViolet), _
52               e.X, e.Y, m_intDIAMETER, m_intDIAMETER)
53
```

Property **Button** specifies which button was pressed → (line 24)

Enumeration **MouseButtons** specifies constants for the mouse button → (line 28)

Method **FillEllipse** used to draw a **BlueViolet** ellipse → (line 51)

Figure 21.26   Painter application's code. (Part 1 of 2.)

Create a **Brush** with the Form's background color

```
54            ' mouse pointer "erases" if right mouse button is pressed
55            ElseIf m_blnShouldErase = True Then
56               m_objGraphic.FillEllipse(New SolidBrush(BackColor), _
57                  e.X, e.Y, m_intDIAMETER, m_intDIAMETER)
58
59         End If
60
61      End Sub ' FrmPainter_MouseMove
62
63   End Class ' FrmPainter
```

Figure 21.26   **Painter** application's code. (Part 2 of 2.)

SELF-REVIEW

1. Moving the mouse pointer generates a _____ event.

   a) MouseMove   b) MousePositionChanged

   c) MouseMoved   d) MouseChanged

2. The _____ enumeration specifies constants for the mouse buttons.

   a) MouseButtons   b) Buttons

   c) MouseOptions   d) ButtonOptions

Answers: 1) a. 2) a.

21.8 Wrap-Up

In this tutorial, you learned the essential elements of mouse-event handling. You handled three common mouse events—MouseMove, MouseUp and MouseDown. You learned to create mouse event handlers associated with a Form. You generated these event handlers by selecting the appropriate mouse event from the Method Name ComboBox after selecting (**FrmPainter Events**) from the Class Name ComboBox.

You used mouse events and a Graphics object in the **Painter** application. You invoked the CreateGraphics method to create a Graphics object. You used the FillEllipse method of the Graphics class to draw a solid circle on the Form. You learned how to use a SolidBrush object to draw a shape in a single, solid color. You used a member of the Color structure to specify the brush's color.

The **Painter** application uses mouse events to determine what the user wants to do. The user moves the mouse with the left mouse button held down to draw on the Form. Moving the mouse across the Form without pressing a button does not draw anything on the Form.

You learned to distinguish which mouse button was pressed. You used this to provide the **Painter** application with an eraser. When users move the mouse with the right mouse button pressed, the **Painter** application draws circles with the same background color as the Form.

To build the **Painter** application, you used MouseEventArgs objects, which are passed to mouse event handlers and provide information about mouse events. Properties X and Y of the MouseEventArgs object specify the *x*- and *y*-coordinates where the mouse event occurred. The Button property specifies which (if any) mouse button was pressed. You used constants defined by the MouseButtons enumeration to determine which button the Button property specified.

In the next tutorial, you will learn how to use event handlers that respond to user interactions with the keyboard. You will then build an application that uses keyboard events. The application will also teach you how to create menus and dialogs.

SKILLS SUMMARY

Raising Events with a Mouse

■ Pressing a mouse's buttons and moving the mouse raise events.

Handling Mouse Events

■ The MouseEventArgs class contains information about mouse events, such as the *x*- and *y*-coordinates where the mouse event occurred. Each mouse-event handler receives an object of class MouseEventArgs as an argument.

■ Moving the mouse raises event MouseMove.

■ Pressing a mouse button raises event MouseDown.

■ Releasing a mouse button raises event MouseUp.

Distinguishing Between Mouse Buttons

■ The Button property of MouseEventArgs specifies which mouse button was pressed.

■ The MouseButtons enumeration specifies the constants Left and Right for mouse buttons. These are used to determine which button was pressed.

Creating an Event Handler for a Mouse Event Associated with a Form

■ Select (*FormName* Events) from the Class Name ComboBox, where *FormName* is the name of the application's Form. Then select the appropriate event from the Method Name ComboBox.

Drawing on a Form

■ Graphics methods are used to draw shapes on a Form or a control.

■ Create a Graphics object (by invoking the Form's CreateGraphics method) to access methods for drawing shapes.

Drawing a Solid Ellipse

■ Use the Graphics method FillEllipse to draw a solid ellipse.

■ Pass a SolidBrush object to the FillEllipse method to specify the shape's interior color.

■ Specify the color, the height and width of the bounding box and the coordinates of the bounding box's upper-left corner. When the height and width of the bounding box are equal, a circle is drawn.

KEY TERMS

BackColor property of class Form—Returns the Color value used as the background color of the Form or control.

bounding box of ellipse—Specifies an ellipse's height, width and location.

brush—Used to fill shapes with colors.

Button property of class MouseEventArgs—Specifies which (if any) mouse button is pressed.

CreateGraphics method—Creates a Graphics object on a Form or control.

FillEllipse method of class Graphics—The method of the Graphics class that draws an ellipse. This method takes as arguments a brush, a Color, the coordinates of the ellipse's bounding box's upper-left corner and the width and height of the bounding box.

Graphics class—Defines methods for drawing shapes.

Left value of MouseButtons enumeration—Used to represent the left mouse button.

mouse event—Generated when a user interacts with an application using the computer's mouse.

MouseButtons enumeration—Defines constants, such as Left and Right, to specify mouse buttons.

MouseDown event—Generated when a mouse button is pressed.

MouseEventArgs class—Specifies information about a mouse event.

MouseMove event—Generated when a mouse pointer is moved.

MouseUp event—Generated when the mouse button is released.

Right value of MouseButtons enumeration—Used to represent the right mouse button.

SolidBrush class—Defines a brush that draws with a single color.

X property of class MouseEventArgs—The property of class MouseEventArgs that specifies the *x*-coordinate of the mouse event.

Y property of class MouseEventArgs—The property of class MouseEventArgs that specifies the *y*-coordinate of the mouse event.

CONTROLS, EVENTS, PROPERTIES & METHODS

Form The class that represents an application's GUI.

- *Events*

  Load—Raised when an application initially executes.
  MouseDown—Raised when a mouse button is clicked.
  MouseMove—Raised when the mouse pointer is moved.
  MouseUp—Raised when a mouse button is released.

- *Property*

  BackColor—Specifies the background color of the Form.Method
  CreateGraphics—Creates a Graphics object.

Graphics The class that contains methods used to draw text, lines and shapes.

- *Method*

  FillEllipse—Draws a solid ellipse of a specified size and color at the specified location.

MouseEventArgs The class that contains information about mouse events.

- *Properties*

  Buttons—Specifies which (if any) mouse button was pressed.
  X—Specifies the *x*-coordinate of the mouse event.
  Y—Specifies the *y*-coordinate of the mouse event.

MULTIPLE-CHOICE QUESTIONS

21.1 The *x*- and *y*-coordinates of the MouseEventArgs object are relative to _____.

   a) the screen   b) the application

   c) the Form or control that contains the control that raised the event

   d) None of the above.

21.2 The _____ method of the Graphics class draws a solid ellipse.

   a) FillEllipse   b) Ellipse

   c) SolidEllipse   d) FilledEllipse

21.3 The _____ object passed to a mouse event handler contains information about the mouse event that was raised.

   a) EventHandler   b) MouseEventHandler

   c) MouseEventArgs   d) EventArgs

21.4 The _____ event is raised when a mouse button is pressed.

   a) MousePress   b) MouseClick

   c) MouseDown   d) MouseButtonDown

21.5 A _____ is used to fill a shape with color using a Graphics object.

   a) painter   b) brush

   c) paint bucket   d) marker

21.6 A _____ event is raised every time the mouse interacts with a control.

   a) control   b) mouse pointer

   c) mouse   d) user

21.7 The _____ property of MouseEventArgs specifies which mouse button was pressed.

a) Source

b) Button

c) WhichButton

d) ButtonPressed

21.8 The _____ class contains methods for drawing text, lines, rectangles and other shapes.

a) Pictures

b) Drawings

c) Graphics

d) Illustrations

21.9 An ellipse with its _____ is a circle.

a) height twice the length of its width

b) width set to zero

c) height half the length of its width

d) height equal to its width

21.10 The _____ method creates a Graphics object.

a) NewGraphics

b) CreateGraphics

c) PaintGraphics

d) InitializeGraphics

EXERCISES

21.11 *(Line Length Application)* The **Line Length** application should draw a straight black line on the Form and calculate the length of the line (Fig. 21.27). The line should begin at the coordinates where the mouse button is pressed and should stop at the point where the mouse button is released. The application should display the line's length (that is, the distance between the two endpoints) in the Label **Length =**. Use the following formula to calculate the line's length, where (x_1, y_1) is the first endpoint (the coordinates where the mouse button is pressed) and (x_2, y_2) is the second endpoint (the coordinates where the mouse button is released). To calculate the distance (or length) between the two points, use the following equation:

$$d = \sqrt{(x_1 - x_2)^2 + (y_1 - y_2)^2}$$

To draw a straight line, you need to use the **DrawLine** method on a Graphics object. When drawing lines, you should use a **Pen** object, which is an object used to specify characteristics of lines and curves. Use the following method call to draw a black line between the two points using a Graphics object reference objGraphic:

```
objGraphic.DrawLine(New Pen(Color.Black), x1 , y1 , x2 , y2 )
```

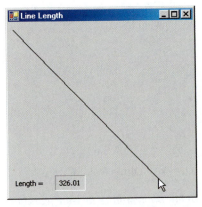

Figure 21.27 **Line Length** application's GUI.

a) *Copying the template to your working directory.* Copy the directory C:\Examples\ Tutorial21\Exercises\LineLength to your C:\SimplyVB directory.

b) *Opening the application's template file.* Double click LineLength.sln in the Line-Length directory to open the application.

c) *Declaring instance variables.* Declare and initialize a reference to a Graphics object that you will use to draw a line. Then declare four Integers in which you will store the *x*- and *y*-coordinates of the two points.

d) *Adding a MouseDown event handler.* Create a MouseDown event handler. Add code to the MouseDown event handler to store the coordinates of the first endpoint of the line.

e) *Creating the Distance method.* Define a Function procedure named Length that returns the distance between two endpoints as a Double. The Function procedure should use the following statement to perform the line length calculation, where intXDistance is the difference between the *x*-coordinates of the two points and intYDistance is the difference between the *y*-coordinates of the two points:

```
Math.Sqrt((intXDistance ^ 2) + (intYDistance ^ 2))
```

f) *Adding a MouseUp event handler.* Create a MouseUp event handler. First store the coordinates of the line's second endpoint. Then call the Length method to obtain the distance between the two endpoints (the line's length). Finally, display the line on the Form and the line's length in the **Length =** Label, as in Fig. 21.27.

g) *Running the application.* Select **Debug > Start** to run your application. Draw several lines and view their lengths. Verify that the length values are accurate.

h) *Closing the application.* Close your running application by clicking its close box.

i) *Closing the IDE.* Close Visual Studio .NET by clicking its close box.

21.12 *(Circle Painter Application)* The **Circle Painter** application should draw a blue circle with a randomly chosen size when the user presses a mouse button anywhere over the Form (Fig. 21.28). The application should randomly select a circle diameter in the range from 5 to 199, inclusive. To draw a blue circle with a given diameter (intDiameter), use the following statement:

```
objGraphic.DrawEllipse(New Pen(Color.Blue), e.X, e.Y, _
   intDiameter, intDiameter)
```

The **DrawEllipse** method, when passed a Pen (instead of a brush) as an argument, draws the outline of an ellipse. Recall that an ellipse is a circle if the height and width arguments are the same (in this case, the randomly selected intDiameter). Use the *x*- and *y*-coordinates of the MouseDown event as the *x*- and *y*-coordinates of the circle's bounding box (that is, the second and third arguments to the DrawEllipse method). Notice that the first argument to the DrawEllipse method is a Pen object. See Exercise 21.11 for a description of Pen.

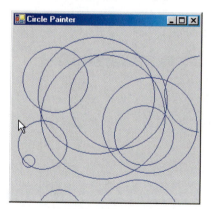

Figure 21.28   **Circle Painter** application's GUI.

a) *Copying the template to your working directory.* Copy the directory C:\Examples\Tutorial21\Exercises\CirclePainter to your C:\SimplyVB directory.

b) *Opening the application's template file.* Double click CirclePainter.sln in the CirclePainter directory to open the application.

c) *Adding a MouseDown event handler.* Create a MouseDown event handler. In the event handler, retrieve the *x*- and *y*-coordinates of the location the mouse pointer when a mouse button was pressed. Then generate a random number to use as the circle's diameter, using a Random object, and store it in a variable. Finally, call the DrawEllipse method on a reference to a Graphics object to draw a blue circle on the Form with the diameter generated by the Random object.

d) *Running the application.* Select **Debug > Start** to run your application. Draw several blue circles and make sure that they are of different sizes.

e) *Closing the application.* Close your running application by clicking its close box.

f) *Closing the IDE.* Close Visual Studio .NET by clicking its close box.

21.13 *(Advanced Circle Painter Application)* In this exercise, you will enhance the application you created in Exercise 21.12. The advanced **Circle Painter** application should draw blue circles with a randomly generated diameter when the user presses the left mouse button. When the user presses the right mouse button, the application should draw a red circle with a randomly generated diameter (Fig. 21.29).

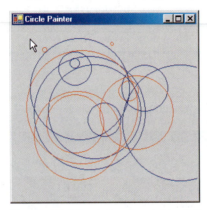

Figure 21.29   Advanced **Circle Painter** application's GUI.

a) *Copying the template to your working directory.* Make a copy of the CirclePainter directory from Exercise 21.12 in your C:\SimplyVB directory. Rename the copied directory AdvancedCirclePainter. If you have not completed Exercise 21.12, follow the steps in Exercise 21.12 to complete the application.

b) *Opening the application's template file.* Double click CirclePainter.sln file in the AdvancedCirclePainter directory to open the application.

c) *Drawing the appropriate circle.* Use the Button property of the MouseEventArgs reference, e, to determine which mouse button was pressed. Finally, call the DrawEllipse method on a reference to a Graphics object to draw a blue circle on the Form if the left mouse button was clicked, or a red circle if the right mouse button was clicked.

d) *Running the application.* Select **Debug > Start** to run your application. Draw several blue circles of different sizes using the left mouse button, then draw several red circles of different sizes using the right mouse button.

e) *Closing the application.* Close your running application by clicking its close box.

f) *Closing the IDE.* Close Visual Studio .NET by clicking its close box.

What does this code do? ▶   **21.14** Consider the code in Fig. 21.26. Suppose we change the MouseMove event handler to the code below. What happens when the user moves the mouse? Assume that a Label lblDisplay has been placed on the Form.

```
1   Private Sub FrmPainter_MouseMove(ByVal sender As Object, _
2      ByVal e As System.Windows.Forms.MouseEventArgs)
3      Handles MyBase.MouseMove
4
5      lblDisplay.Text = "I'm at " & e.X & ", " & e.Y & "."
6   End Sub ' FrmPainter_MouseMove
```

What's wrong with this code? ▶ 21.15 The following code should draw a `BlueViolet` circle of diameter 4 that corresponds to the movement of the mouse. Find the error(s) in the following code:

```
1   Private Sub FrmPainter_MouseMove(ByVal sender As Object, _
2      ByVal e As System.Windows.Forms.MouseEventArgs) _
3      Handles MyBase.MouseMove
4
5      If m_blnshouldPaint = True Then
6         Dim objGraphic As Graphics = Graphics()
7
8         objGraphic.FillEllipse = ( _
9            New SolidBrush(Color.BlueViolet), e.Y, e.X, 5, 4)
10     End If
11  End Sub ' FrmPainter_MouseMove
```

Programming Challenge ▶ 21.16 *(Advanced Painter Application)* Extend the `Painter` application to enable a user to change the size and color of the circles drawn.

Figure 21.30 **Advanced Painter** application's GUI.

a) *Copying the template to your working directory.* Copy the directory `C:\Examples\Tutorial21\Exercises\AdvancedPainter` to your `C:\SimplyVB` directory.

b) *Opening the application's template file.* Double click `AdvancedPainter.sln` in the `AdvancedPainter` directory to open the application (Fig. 21.30).

c) *Understanding the provided instance variables.* The template already provides you with four instance variables. Variable `m_objBrushColor` is a `Color` value that specifies the color of the brush used in the **Advanced Painter** application. The `m_blnShouldPaint` and `m_blnShouldErase` variable perform the same functions as in this tutorial's **Painter** application. The `m_intDiameter` variable stores the diameter of the circle to be drawn.

d) *Declaring an enumeration to store the circle diameter sizes.* Declare an enumeration `Sizes` to store the possible values of `m_intDiameter`. Set constant `SMALL` to 4, `MEDIUM` to 8 and `LARGE` to 10.

e) *Adding event handlers for the Color RadioButtons.* The **Color** `RadioButton`'s event handlers should set `m_objBrushColor` to their specified colors (`Color.Red`, `Color.Blue`, `Color.Green` or `Color.Black`).

f) *Adding event handlers for the Size RadioButtons.* The **Size** `RadioButton`'s event handlers should set `m_intDiameter` to `Sizes.SMALL` (for the **Small** `RadioButton`), `Sizes.MEDIUM` (for the **Medium** `RadioButton`) or `Sizes.LARGE` (for the **Large** `RadioButton`).

g) *Adding a mouse event handler to a Panel.* To associate mouse events with the Panel, select pnlPainter from the Class Name ComboBox. Then select the appropriate mouse event from the Method Name ComboBox.

h) *Coding the MouseDown and MouseUp event handlers.* The MouseUp and MouseDown event handlers behave exactly as they do in the **Painter** application.

i) *Coding the MouseMove event handler.* The MouseMove event handler behaves as the one in **Painter** application does. The color of the brush that draws the circle when m_blnShouldPaint is True is specified by m_objBrushColor. The eraser color is specified by the Panel's BackColor property.

j) *Running the application.* Select **Debug > Start** to run your application. Start drawing on the Panel using different brush sizes and colors. Use the right mouse button to erase part of your drawing.

k) *Closing the application.* Close your running application by clicking its close box.

l) *Closing the IDE.* Close Visual Studio .NET by clicking its close box.

22

T U T O R I A L

Objectives

In this tutorial, you will learn to:
- Handle keyboard events.
- Create menus for your Windows applications.
- Use dialogs to display messages.
- Use the ShowDialog method of the **Font** and **Color** dialogs.
- Display the **Font** dialog to enable users to choose fonts.
- Display the **Color** dialog to enable users to choose colors.

Outline

Typing Application

Introducing Keyboard Events, Menus and Dialogs

Text editor applications enable you to perform a wide variety of tasks, from writing e-mails to creating business proposals. These applications often use menus and dialogs to help you customize the appearance of your document. They also respond to keys pressed on the keyboard either by displaying characters or performing actions (such as accessing menus or dialogs). In this tutorial, you will learn how to handle **keyboard events**, which occur when keys on the keyboard are pressed and released. Handling keyboard events allows you to specify the action that the application should take when a key is pressed. You will then learn how to add menus to your application. By now, you are familiar with using various menus and dialogs provided by Windows applications. You will learn to create menus, which group related commands and can allow the user to select various actions the application should take. Finally, you will learn about the **Font** and **Color** dialogs, which you will use to allow the user to change the appearance of text in the application.

22.1 Test-Driving the Typing Application

In this tutorial, you will create a **Typing** Application to help students learn how to type. This application must meet the following requirements:

Application Requirements

A high-school course teaches students how to type. The instructor would like to use a Windows application that allows students to watch what they are typing on the screen without looking at the keyboard. You have been asked to create an application that displays what the student types. The application should display a virtual keyboard that highlights any key the student presses on the real keyboard. This application should also contain menu commands for selecting the font style and color of the text displayed, clearing the text displayed and inverting the background and foreground colors of the display.

This application allows the user to type text. As the user presses each key, the application highlights the corresponding key on the GUI and adds the character to a TextBox. The user can select the color and style of the characters the user types, invert the background and foreground colors and clear the TextBox. You will begin by test-driving the completed application. Then, you will learn the additional Visual Basic .NET technologies that you will need to create your own version of this application.

Test-Driving the Typing Application

1. ***Opening the completed application.*** Open the directory C:\Examples\ Tutorial22\CompletedApplication\Typing to locate the **Typing** Application. Double click Typing.sln to open the application in Visual Studio .NET.

2. ***Running the Typing application.*** Select **Debug > Start** to run the application. Once the application has loaded, type the sentence "Programming in Visual Basic .NET is simple." Notice that as you are typing, the corresponding keys light up on the Form's virtual keyboard, and the text is displayed in the TextBox (Fig. 22.1).

Display menu ——

Virtual keyboard ——

Highlighted key ——

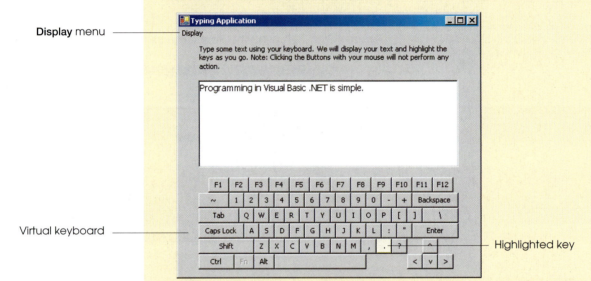

Figure 22.1   **Typing** Application with key pressed.

3. ***Changing the font.*** Select **Display > Text > Font...** (Fig. 22.2) to open the **Font** dialog shown in Fig. 22.3. The **Font** dialog allows you to choose the font style that should be used to display the application's output. Select Tahoma from the **Font:** ComboBox, select Bold from the **Font style:** ComboBox and select 11 from the **Size:** ComboBox. Click the **OK** Button. Notice that the text you typed in *Step 2* is now bold.

(cont.)

Menu item ——————

Submenu ——————

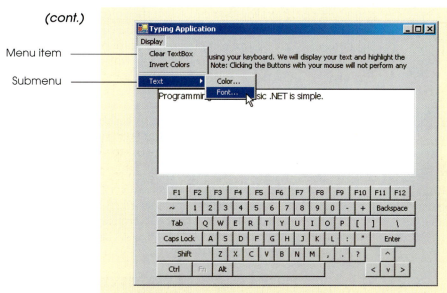

Figure 22.2 Selecting the **Font...** menu item.

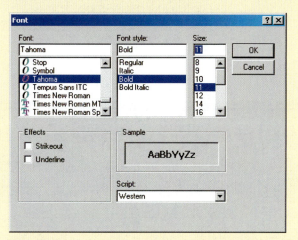

Figure 22.3 **Font** dialog displayed when **Display > Text > Font...** is selected.

4. ***Changing the color of the font.*** Select **Display > Text > Color...** to display the **Color** dialog (Fig. 22.4). This dialog is similar to the **Font** dialog, except that it allows you to choose the color of the text displayed. Select a color, and click **OK**.

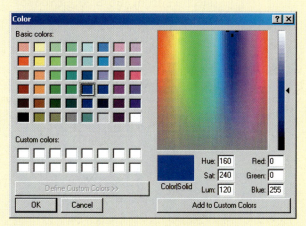

Figure 22.4 **Color** dialog displayed when **Display > Text > Color...** is selected.

(cont.)   5.   ***Inverting the background and foreground colors.*** Select **Display > Invert Colors** (Fig. 22.5). This option allows you to swap the background and foreground colors. The result is shown in Fig. 22.6.

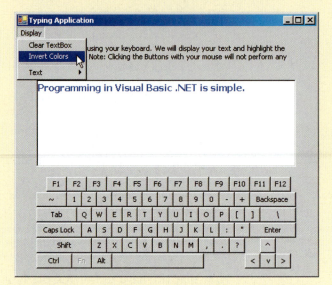

Figure 22.5   Selecting the **Invert Colors** menu item.

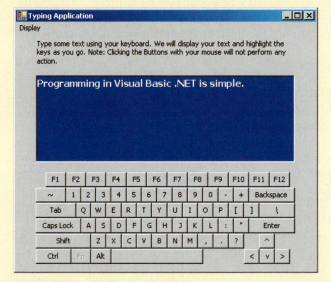

Figure 22.6   Output with colors inverted.

6.   ***Clearing the TextBox.*** Select **Display > Clear TextBox** to remove all the text from the TextBox.

7.   ***Closing the application.*** Close your running application by clicking its close box.

8.   ***Closing the IDE.*** Close Visual Studio .NET by clicking its close box.

22.2 Analyzing the Typing Application

Before you begin building the **Typing Application**, you should analyze the application's components. The following pseudocode describes the basic operation of the **Typing Application**:

When the user presses a key:
    Highlight the corresponding Button on the GUI
    Display the key's value in the TextBox

When the user releases a key:
    Reset the corresponding Button's color to the Button's default color

When the user selects the Color... menu item:
    Display the Color dialog
    Update the TextBox text's color

When the user selects the Font... menu item:
    Display the Font dialog
    Update the TextBox text's font

When the user selects the Clear TextBox menu item:
    Clear the TextBox

When the user selects the Invert Colors menu item:
    Swap the TextBox's background and foreground colors

Now that you have test-driven the **Typing Application** application and studied its pseudocode representation, you will use an ACE table to help you convert the pseudocode to Visual Basic .NET. Figure 22.7 lists the actions, controls and events that will help you complete your own version of this application. [*Note*: The number of Buttons is large and no Button events are used; therefore, the Buttons in the virtual keyboard are not included in the ACE table.]

Action/Control/Event (ACE) Table for the Typing Application

Action	Control	Event
Label the application's controls	lblPrompt	Application is run
	txtOutput	KeyPress, KeyDown
Highlight the corresponding Button on the GUI	keyboard Buttons	
Display the key's value in the TextBox	txtOutput	
	txtOutput	KeyUp
Reset the corresponding Button's color to the Button's default color	keyboard Buttons	
	mnuitmColor	Click
Display the Color dialog	dlgColorDialog	
Update the TextBox text's color	txtOutput	
	mnuitmFont	Click
Display the Font dialog	dlgFontDialog	
Update the TextBox text's font	txtOutput	
	mnuitmClear	Click
Clear the TextBox	txtOutput	
	mnuitmInvert	Click
Swap the TextBox's background and foreground colors	txtOutput	

Figure 22.7   ACE table for the **Typing Application**.

22.3 Keyboard Events

This section introduces how to handle keyboard events, which are generated when keys on the keyboard are pressed and released. All keyboard events are raised using the control that currently has the focus. In the **Typing Application**, these events are raised on the TextBox control. The first kind of keyboard event you will learn about is the **KeyDown** event, which is raised when a key is pressed. Since there are many keys on the keyboard, you will find that the template application provides much of the required code. In the following box, you will insert the remaining code to handle the event when the user presses a key.

Coding the KeyDown Event Handler

1. *Copying the template to your working directory.* Copy the C:\Examples\ Tutorial22\TemplateApplication\Typing directory to your C:\SimplyVB directory.

2. *Opening the Typing application's template file.* Double click Typing.sln in the Typing directory to open the application in Visual Studio .NET.

3. *Adding the Backspace key case.* Add lines 880–888 of Fig. 22.8 to your code. These lines remove a character from the TextBox and highlight the **Back-Space** Button when the *Backspace* key is pressed.

Testing whether key pressed was the *Backspace* key

Highlighting the *Backspace* key

Removing the last character in the TextBox

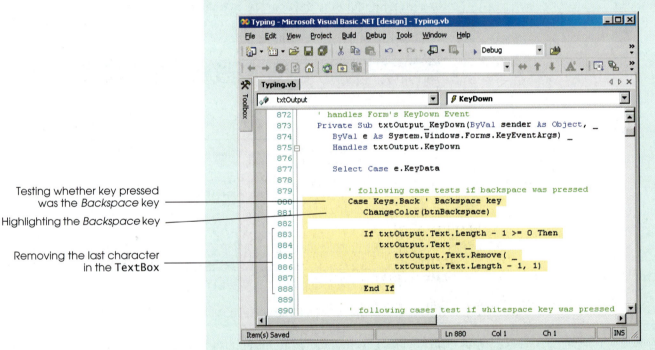

Figure 22.8 Removing a character when *Backspace* is pressed.

When a key is pressed, the KeyDown event is raised. As you have seen in previous tutorials, many event handlers are passed two arguments: **sender** and e. The **sender** Object is the GUI component that raised the event (this is also known as the source of the event) and **e** contains data for the event. In this case, e (of type **KeyEventArgs**) contains data about which key was pressed. The **KeyData** property of e (line 877) contains a value that represents which key was pressed.

(cont.) Visual Basic .NET provides the **Keys enumeration** to represent keyboard keys using meaningful names. Recall that enumerations are used to assign meaningful names to constant values. In this case, each value in the Keys enumeration is an Integer that represents a key. Keys.Back (line 880) is the Keys enumeration's representation of the *Backspace* key. Line 881 calls method ChangeColor to highlight the **Backspace** Button. The Change-Color method is provided for you in the template. The If...Then statement on lines 883–888 tests whether there is text in the TextBox. If the TextBox contains text, lines 884–886 remove the last character from the TextBox. If the TextBox is empty, no action is performed.

When invoked, String method **Remove** deletes characters from a String. The first argument contains the index in the String at which to begin removing characters, and the second argument specifies the number of characters to remove. The String property Length returns the number of characters in the String. The position of the first character in a String is zero; therefore, you must subtract 1 from the value returned by the Length property to indicate the position of the last character. Use 1 as the second argument to indicate that you want to remove only one character.

4. ***Adding the* Enter *key case*.** Add lines 891–893 of Fig. 22.9 to the Select Case statement in the KeyDown event handler. Keys.Enter (line 891) represents the *Enter* key. Line 892 changes the color of the **Enter** key on the GUI, and line 893 inserts a new line in the TextBox.

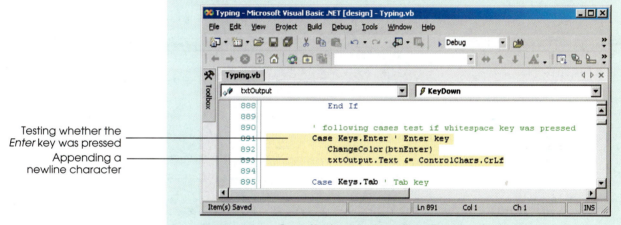

Testing whether the *Enter* key was pressed

Appending a newline character

Figure 22.9 Case that executes when *Enter* key is pressed.

5. ***Saving the project.*** Select **File > Save All** to save your modified code.

The KeyDown event handler in this application does not test whether any of the letter keys were pressed. It is often inconvenient to use the KeyDown event handler to detect keyboard events because the KeyEventArgs object's KeyData property is case insensitive. If you try to handle letters in the KeyDown event handler, only uppercase letters will be recognized. This is not appropriate for the **Typing Application** because the user should be able to type uppercase and lowercase letters. Visual Basic .NET provides the **KeyPress** event handler, which can be used to recognize both uppercase and lowercase letters. You will learn how to use the KeyPress event handler in the following box.

Adding Code to the KeyPress Event Handler

1. ***Writing the* Select Case *statement*.** Add lines 1062 of Fig. 22.10 to the Key-Press event handler. Line 1062 begins a Select Case statement that uses the uppercase equivalent of the pressed key for the controlling expression.

(cont.)

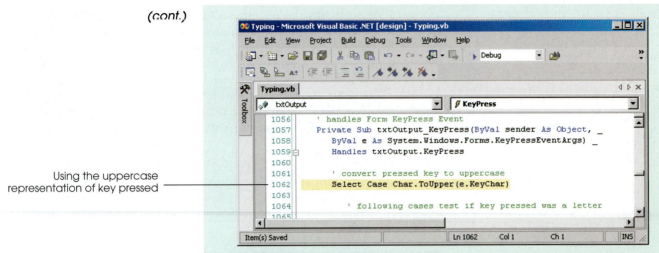

Using the uppercase
representation of key pressed

Figure 22.10   Converting the pressed key to an uppercase letter.

The key names in the Keys enumeration are in their uppercase form; therefore, the Case statement must use the uppercase representation of the key that was pressed. Structure **Char** provides methods for manipulating individual characters. Char method **ToUpper** returns the uppercase representation of its argument. Note that the value returned by the ToUpper method does not alter the data in its argument.

In this example, the argument that is passed to the ToUpper method uses the KeyChar property of e. (Type KeyPressEventArgs.) The **KeyChar** property is similar to KeyData property of the KeyEventArgs object, but contains only values representable as characters. Note that parameter e for the KeyDown and KeyPress event handlers are of different types. The KeyChar property can represent both uppercase and lowercase character values.

2. ***Inserting the* A *key case.*** Add lines 1065–1067 of Fig. 22.11 to the Select Case statement in the KeyPress event handler. These lines highlight the **A** Button in the application and display an **A** in the TextBox when the user presses the *A* key.

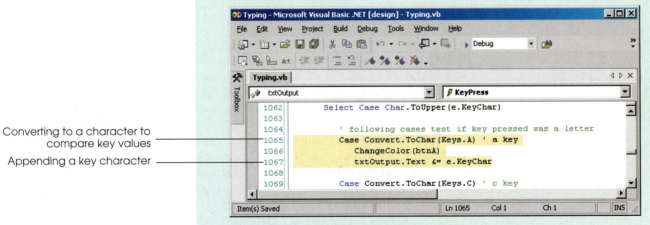

Converting to a character to
compare key values

Appending a key character

Figure 22.11   Performing actions when the *A* key is pressed.

(cont.)

Line 1065 compares the key pressed to the value `Keys.A`, which represents the *A* key. The `Keys` enumeration stores numeric values, but the key pressed by the user is passed to the `KeyPress` event handler as a character; therefore, the `Keys` enumeration value needs to be converted to a character before a comparison can be made. Line 1065 passes the enumeration value to method `Convert.ToChar` to convert that value into a character. Line 1066 changes the color of the **A** `Button` on the GUI, and line 1067 adds either the "a" or "A" character, depending on if *Shift* was pressed, to the end of the text in the `TextBox`.

3. **Inserting the B key case.** Add lines 1069–1071 of Fig. 22.12 to the `Select Case` statement. These lines will highlight the **B** `Button` and add a B to the `TextBox` when the user presses the *B* key. Notice that for each key pressed, its `Button` should be highlighted, and the correct output should be displayed in the `TextBox`.

Converting to a character to compare key values ———

Appending a key character ———

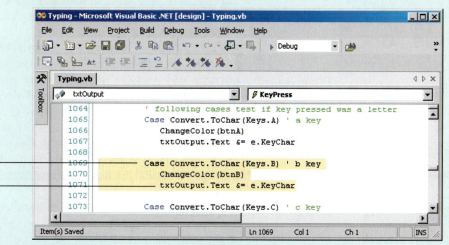

Figure 22.12 Performing actions when the *B* key is pressed.

4. **Saving the project.** Select **File > Save All** to save your modified code.

Software Design Tip

Use the `KeyPress` event handler for letter key events. Use the `KeyDown` event handler for modifier, number and symbol key events.

You may be wondering why you could not just use the `KeyPress` event handler to test for all of the keys on the keyboard. Like the `KeyDown` event handler, the `KeyPress` event handler has its limitations. The `KeyPress` event handler cannot handle the modifier keys (*Ctrl*, *Shift* and *Alt*). **Modifier keys** do not display characters on the keyboard, but can be used to modify the way that applications respond to a keyboard event. For instance, pressing the *Shift* key while pressing a letter in a text editor displays the uppercase form of the letter. You used the `KeyDown` event handler to handle the event raised when a modifier key is pressed. Another reason not to use only the `KeyPress` event handler is that the `KeyChar` property used in this event handler stores the pressed key as a character, requiring an explicit conversion of the `Keys` enumeration values before a comparison can be performed. It is more straightforward to compare the pressed key's numeric value against the numeric values stored in the `Keys` enumeration. The `KeyData` property used in the `KeyDown` event handler allows you to do this.

The **KeyUp** event is raised whenever a key is released by the user. It is raised regardless of whether the key pressed was handled by the `KeyPress` or the `KeyDown` event handler. The **Typing Application** uses the KeyUp event handler to remove the highlight color from the `Buttons` on the GUI when the user releases a key. You will learn how to add the KeyUp event handler to your application in the following box.

Creating the KeyUp Event Handler

1. *Creating the KeyUp event handler.* To maintain clarity in the template application, an empty KeyUp event handler is provided for you. However, if you want to generate KeyUp, KeyDown or KeyPress event handlers for other controls, begin by selecting the control for which you wish to add the event handler. In the **Typing Application** select txtOutput from the Class Name ComboBox. Then select the appropriate event handler from the Method Name ComboBox, as shown in Fig. 22.13. When you select an event name from the Method Name ComboBox, that event handler is generated in your code.

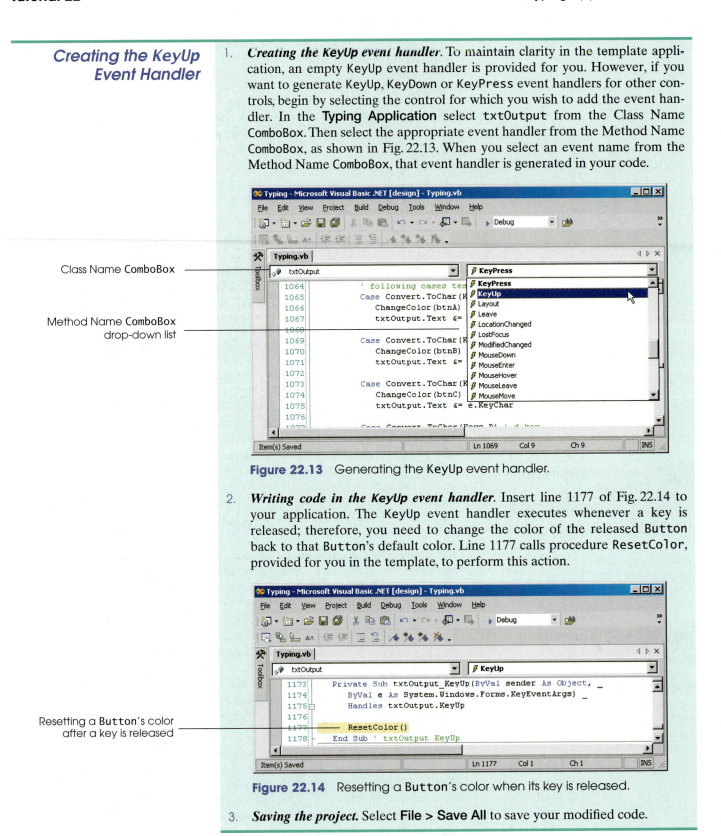

Class Name ComboBox

Method Name ComboBox drop-down list

Figure 22.13   Generating the KeyUp event handler.

2. *Writing code in the KeyUp event handler.* Insert line 1177 of Fig. 22.14 to your application. The KeyUp event handler executes whenever a key is released; therefore, you need to change the color of the released Button back to that Button's default color. Line 1177 calls procedure ResetColor, provided for you in the template, to perform this action.

Resetting a Button's color after a key is released

Figure 22.14   Resetting a Button's color when its key is released.

3. *Saving the project.* Select **File > Save All** to save your modified code.

Now that you have added code that enables the user to see what they are typing by highlighting the corresponding Buttons and displaying output in a TextBox, you must allow the user to alter the display. To do this, you will use the **MainMenu** control, which creates a menu that allows the user to select various options to format the TextBox.

1. A _____ event is raised when a key on the keyboard is pressed or released.

    a) keyboard   b) KeyDownEvent

    c) KeyChar   d) KeyUpEvent

2. The _____ event is raised when a key is released.

    a) KeyEventUp   b) KeyRelease

    c) KeyUp   d) None of the above.

Answers: 1) a. 2) c.

22.4 Menus

Menus allow you to group related commands for Windows applications. Although most menus and commands vary among applications, some—such as **Open** and **Save**—are common to many applications. Menus are an important part of GUIs because they organize commands without "cluttering" the GUI. In this section, you will learn how to enhance the **Typing Application** by adding menus that allow the user to control how to display text in the TextBox.

Creating a Menu

1. ***Creating a MainMenu control.*** Switch to Design view. Double click the Main-Menu control in the **Windows Forms** tab of the **Toolbox** to add a MainMenu to your application (Fig. 22.15). Notice that when you do this, a MainMenu control appears in the component tray. Recall that controls in the component tray are not part of the graphical user interface. Also, on the top of your Form, a box that reads **Type Here** appears. This represents a **menu item**—a cell of text that the user can select in the MainMenu control. Visual Basic .NET uses the MenuItem object to store these items. When you type text in the **Type Here** field, Visual Studio .NET creates a MenuItem. To edit the menu item, click the **MainMenu** icon in the component tray. This puts the IDE in **Menu Designer mode**, which allows you to create and edit menus. Change the Name property of the MainMenu control to mnuMainMenu.

Good Programming Practice

We suggest prefixing MainMenu controls with mnu.

2. ***Creating the first menu item.*** Click inside the **Type Here** box, type &Display and press *Enter*. This sets the text to be displayed in that menu item and indicates that the letter D is the access shortcut key. Then change the Name property of the MenuItem to mnuitmDisplay. Notice that when you clicked the **Type Here** field, two more fields appeared (Fig. 22.16). The one on the right represents a new menu item that can be created to the right of the **Display** menu item. The field below the **Display** menu item represents a menu item that will appear when the **Display** menu item is selected. You will use the **Display** menu item to display all of the options that allow the user to customize the output displayed in the TextBox.

Good Programming Practice

We suggest prefixing MenuItem controls with mnuitm.

3. ***Creating additional menu items.*** In the box that appeared below the **Display** menu, type &Clear TextBox. Name this menu item mnuitmClear by changing its Name property. Notice that once again, two more boxes appear. Every time you add an item to a menu these two boxes will appear (Fig. 22.17). Entering text in the right box turns the menu item on the left into a submenu. The right box is now a menu item of that submenu. Recall that a **submenu** is a menu within another menu. The box that appears on the bottom of the menu allows you to add another item to that menu. Type &Invert Colors in this box to add another menu item. Set the Name property of this menu item to mnuitmInvert.

(cont.)

MenuItem field ——

MainMenu control in
the component tray ——

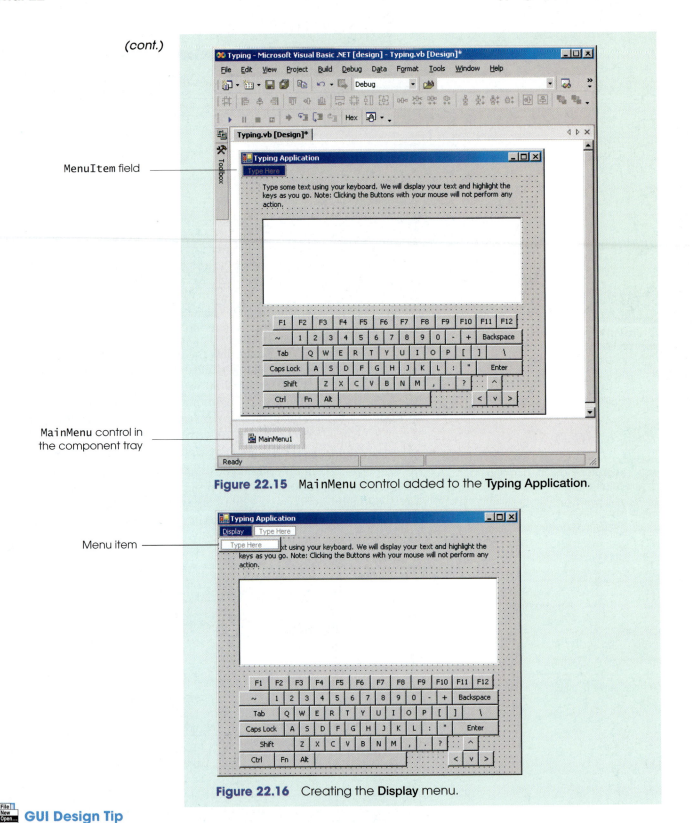

Figure 22.15 MainMenu control added to the **Typing Application**.

Menu item ——

Figure 22.16 Creating the **Display** menu.

GUI Design Tip

Use book-title capitalization in menu
item text.

(cont.)

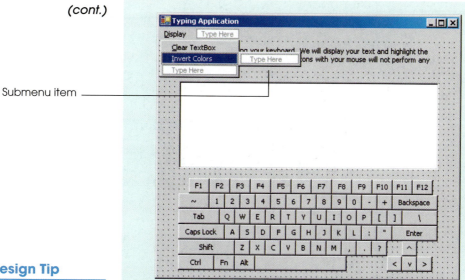

Submenu item ——

Figure 22.17   Adding items to the menu.

GUI Design Tip

If clicking a menu item opens a dialog, an ellipsis (...) should follow the the menu item's text.

GUI Design Tip

Use separator bars in a menu to group related menu items.

4. ***Inserting a separator bar***. Right click the box that appears below the **Invert Colors** menu item, and select **Insert Separator** from the context menu that appears. Notice that a **separator bar**, which is a gray, recessed horizontal rule, appears below the **Invert Colors** menu item. Separator bars are used to group submenus and menu items. A separator bar also can be created by typing a hyphen (–) in the Text property of a menu item.

5. ***Creating a submenu***. In the box under the separator bar, type &Text. This menu item will contain options to format the appearance of the text displayed in the TextBox. Set the Name property of this menu item to mnuitm-Text. All menu items can contain both menu items and submenus. Insert &Color... and &Font... as menu items in your submenu, naming them mnu-itmColor and mnuitmFont, respectively. (Fig. 22.18)

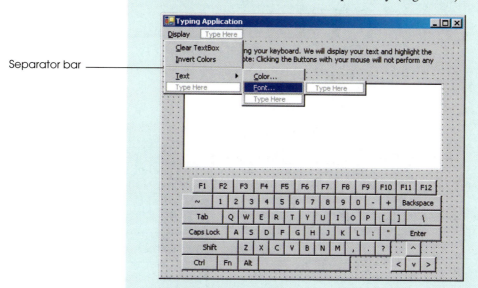

Separator bar ——

Figure 22.18   Adding a submenu to a menu item.

6. ***Running the application***. Select **Debug > Start** to run your application, and select a menu item. Notice that nothing happens because you have not created event handlers for the menu items.

7. ***Closing the application.*** Close the application by clicking its close box.

For a menu item to perform some action when it is selected, an event handler must be added for that item. The **Typing Application** introduces the **Font** dialog and the **Color** dialog to allow the user to customize the appearance of what is being typed. Dialogs allow you to receive input from and display messages to the user. You will learn how to use the **Font** dialog in the following box.

Coding the Font... Menu Item's Click Event Handler

1. ***Creating an event handler.*** In the Windows Form Designer, double click the **Font...** menu item, that you created, to generate an event handler for this menu item.

2. ***Declaring the dialog variables.*** Add lines 1262–1263 of Fig. 22.19 to your code. Line 1262 creates a new **FontDialog** object that will allow the user to select the font style to apply to the text. Line 1263 declares a variable of type **DialogResult** that will store information indicating which **Button** the user clicked to exit the dialog.

Declaration for the FontDialog and its result

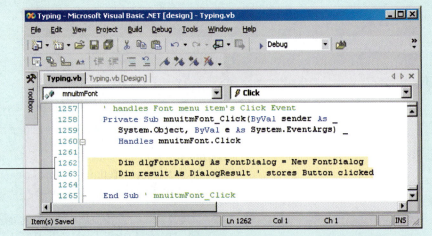

Figure 22.19 Declarations for the **FontDialog** and its **DialogResult**.

Good Programming Practice

We suggest prefixing references to dialogs with `dlg`.

3. ***Displaying the dialog.*** Add lines 1265–1266 of Fig. 22.20 to your event handler. These lines call the **ShowDialog** method to display the **Font** dialog to the user.

Showing the dialog and assigning the result

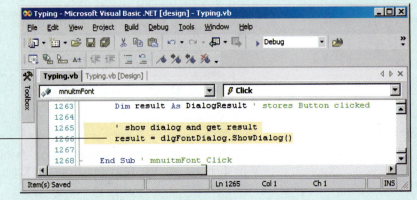

Figure 22.20 Opening the **Font** dialog.

(cont.)   4. ***Exiting the event handler if the user clicks Cancel.*** Add lines 1268–1271 of Fig. 22.21 to your application. These lines determine whether the user clicked the **Font** dialog's **Cancel** Button. Line 1269 compares the value stored in `result` with the enumeration value `DialogResult.Cancel`. `DialogResult` is an enumeration that contains values corresponding to standard dialog Button names. This provides a convenient way to determine which Button the user clicked. If the user clicks the **Cancel** Button, no action should take place and the method should exit using the `Return` statement (line 1270).

Take no action if user cancels ———

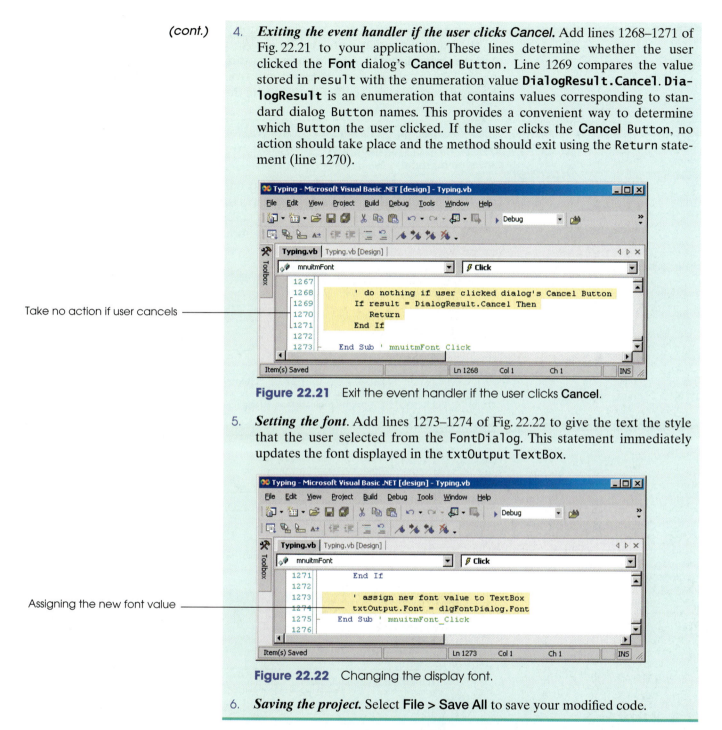

Figure 22.21   Exit the event handler if the user clicks **Cancel**.

5. ***Setting the font.*** Add lines 1273–1274 of Fig. 22.22 to give the text the style that the user selected from the `FontDialog`. This statement immediately updates the font displayed in the `txtOutput` TextBox.

Assigning the new font value ———

Figure 22.22   Changing the display font.

6. ***Saving the project.*** Select **File > Save All** to save your modified code.

The user of the **Typing Application** should also be able to select the color of the font displayed in the TextBox. You will learn how to display the **Color** dialog in the following box.

Coding the Color...
Menu Item's Click
Event Handler

1. *Creating an event handler.* In the Windows Form Designer, double click the **Color...** menu item to generate a `Click` event handler.

2. *Declaring the dialog variables.* Add lines 1282–1283 of Fig. 22.23 to your application. Line 1282 creates a new `ColorDialog` object that will allow the user to select the color of the text. Line 1283 declares a `DialogResult` variable to store the value of the `Button` clicked by the user.

Declarations for the
`ColorDialog` and its result

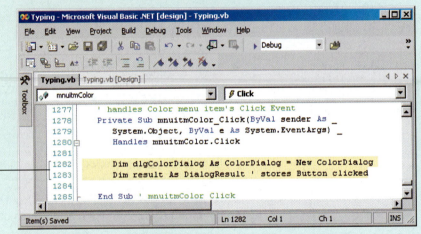

Figure 22.23   Declarations for the **Color** dialog and its `DialogResult`.

3. *Setting the ColorDialog's open property.* Add lines 1285–1286 of Fig. 22.24 to your application. The **ColorDialog** object allows you to specify which color options the dialog presents to the user of your application. To display the **Color** dialog shown in Fig. 22.4, the **FullOpen** option is set to `True` on line 1285. If this option is set to `False`, only the left half of the dialog will be displayed. Line 1286 opens the **Color** dialog using the `ShowDialog` method.

Displaying the `ColorDialog`
with a complete color
selection

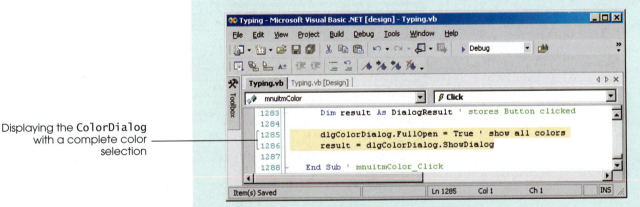

Figure 22.24   Displaying the **Color** dialog.

4. *Setting the font color.* Add lines 1288–1294 of Fig. 22.25 to your application. The `If...Then` statement on lines 1289–1291 prevents the color from being changed if the user clicks **Cancel**. Line 1294 sets the text's color to the color the user selected in the **Color** dialog.

(cont.)

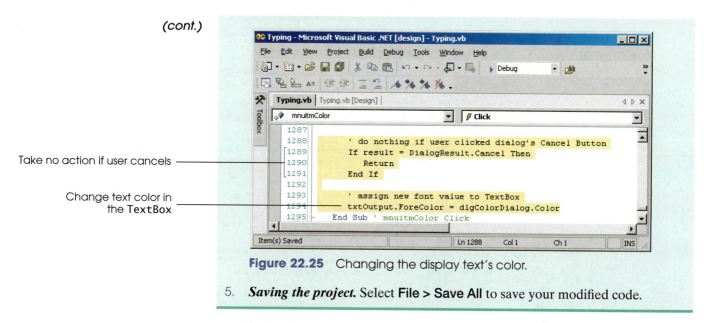

Take no action if user cancels ——————

Change text color in the TextBox ——————

Figure 22.25 Changing the display text's color.

5. *Saving the project.* Select **File > Save All** to save your modified code.

The user should be able to clear all of the text in the TextBox using the **Clear TextBox** menu item. You will learn how to do this in the following box.

Clearing the TextBox

1. *Generating an event handler.* Double click the **Clear TextBox** menu item to generate the item's Click event.

2. *Clearing the text.* Add line 1302 of Fig. 22.26 to your application. This line calls the Clear method to erase the text from the TextBox. Calling the Clear method on a TextBox has the same effect as setting its Text property to the empty string.

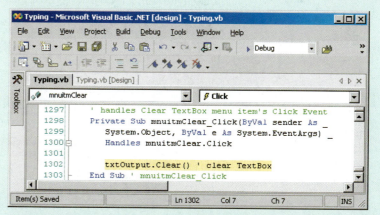

Figure 22.26 Calling the Clear method of class TextBox to erase the text.

3. *Saving the project.* Select **File > Save All** to save your modified code.

The user should be able to swap the foreground and background colors of the TextBox. You will learn how to accomplish this in the following box.

Inverting Colors

1. *Creating an event handler.* Double click the **Invert Colors** menu item in design view. This creates an empty event handler for the **Invert Colors** menu item's Click event (Fig. 22.27).

(cont.)

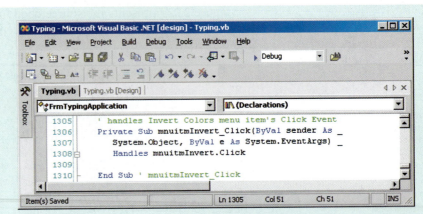

Figure 22.27 Empty event handler for **Invert Color** menu item.

2. *Inverting the colors.* Insert lines 1310–1314 of Fig. 22.28 to your application. Line 1310 declares a `Color` variable. Recall that `Color` variables store color values. To swap colors, you must use a temporary variable to hold one of the colors that you want to swap. A **temporary variable** is used to store data when swapping values. Such a variable is no longer needed after the swap occurs. Without a temporary variable, you would lose the value of one color property (by reassigning its value) before you could assign its color to the other property.

   Line 1312 assigns the `Color` variable the background color of the `Text-Box`. Line 1313 then sets the background color to the foreground color. Finally, line 1314 assigns the text color the value stored in the temporary `Color` variable, which contains the `TextBox`'s background color from before the swap.

Using a temporary variable to swap color values

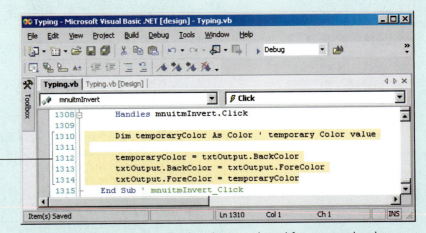

Figure 22.28 Swapping the background and foreground colors.

3. *Running the application.* Select **Debug > Start** to run your application. Enter text using your keyboard. The keys you press should be highlighted in the virtual keyboard on the `Form`. Use the menu to change the color of the text, then invert the colors of the text and the `TextBox`. Finally, use the menus to change the text's font, then clear the `TextBox`.

4. *Closing the application.* Close your running application by clicking its close box.

5. *Closing the IDE.* Close Visual Studio .NET by clicking its close box.

Figure 22.29 presents the source code for the **Typing Application**. The lines of code that contain new programming concepts that you learned in this tutorial are highlighted.

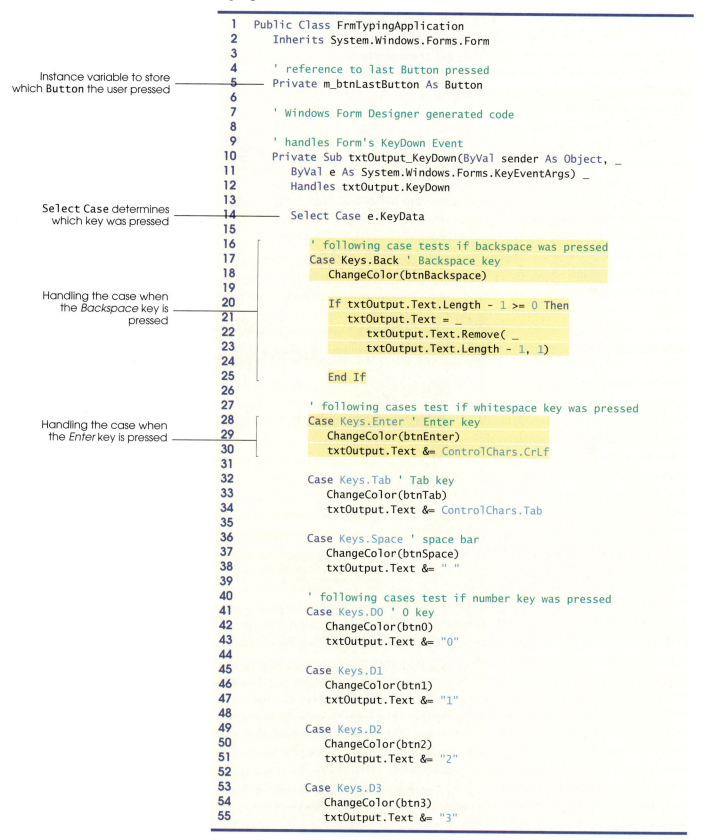

```vb
1   Public Class FrmTypingApplication
2       Inherits System.Windows.Forms.Form
3
4       ' reference to last Button pressed
5       Private m_btnLastButton As Button
6
7       ' Windows Form Designer generated code
8
9       ' handles Form's KeyDown Event
10      Private Sub txtOutput_KeyDown(ByVal sender As Object, _
11          ByVal e As System.Windows.Forms.KeyEventArgs) _
12          Handles txtOutput.KeyDown
13
14          Select Case e.KeyData
15
16              ' following case tests if backspace was pressed
17              Case Keys.Back ' Backspace key
18                  ChangeColor(btnBackspace)
19
20                  If txtOutput.Text.Length - 1 >= 0 Then
21                      txtOutput.Text = _
22                          txtOutput.Text.Remove( _
23                          txtOutput.Text.Length - 1, 1)
24
25                  End If
26
27              ' following cases test if whitespace key was pressed
28              Case Keys.Enter ' Enter key
29                  ChangeColor(btnEnter)
30                  txtOutput.Text &= ControlChars.CrLf
31
32              Case Keys.Tab ' Tab key
33                  ChangeColor(btnTab)
34                  txtOutput.Text &= ControlChars.Tab
35
36              Case Keys.Space ' space bar
37                  ChangeColor(btnSpace)
38                  txtOutput.Text &= " "
39
40              ' following cases test if number key was pressed
41              Case Keys.D0 ' 0 key
42                  ChangeColor(btn0)
43                  txtOutput.Text &= "0"
44
45              Case Keys.D1
46                  ChangeColor(btn1)
47                  txtOutput.Text &= "1"
48
49              Case Keys.D2
50                  ChangeColor(btn2)
51                  txtOutput.Text &= "2"
52
53              Case Keys.D3
54                  ChangeColor(btn3)
55                  txtOutput.Text &= "3"
```

Labels (left margin):
- Instance variable to store which **Button** the user pressed → line 5
- **Select Case** determines which key was pressed → line 14
- Handling the case when the *Backspace* key is pressed → lines 16–25
- Handling the case when the *Enter* key is pressed → lines 28–30

Figure 22.29 **Typing Application** code listing. (Part 1 of 7.)

```
56
57            Case Keys.D4
58                ChangeColor(btn4)
59                txtOutput.Text &= "4"
60
61            Case Keys.D5
62                ChangeColor(btn5)
63                txtOutput.Text &= "5"
64
65            Case Keys.D6
66                ChangeColor(btn6)
67                txtOutput.Text &= "6"
68
69            Case Keys.D7
70                ChangeColor(btn7)
71                txtOutput.Text &= "7"
72
73            Case Keys.D8
74                ChangeColor(btn8)
75                txtOutput.Text &= "8"
76
77            Case Keys.D9
78                ChangeColor(btn9)
79                txtOutput.Text &= "9"
80
81            ' following cases test if one of the F keys was pressed
82            Case Keys.F1 ' F1 key
83                ChangeColor(btnF1)
84
85            Case Keys.F2 ' F2 key
86                ChangeColor(btnF2)
87
88            Case Keys.F3 ' F3 key
89                ChangeColor(btnF3)
90
91            Case Keys.F4 ' F4 key
92                ChangeColor(btnF4)
93
94            Case Keys.F5 ' F5 key
95                ChangeColor(btnF5)
96
97            Case Keys.F6 ' F6 key
98                ChangeColor(btnF6)
99
100           Case Keys.F7 ' F7 key
101               ChangeColor(btnF7)
102
103           Case Keys.F8 ' F8 key
104               ChangeColor(btnF8)
105
106           Case Keys.F9 ' F9 key
107               ChangeColor(btnF9)
108
109           Case Keys.F10 ' F10 key
110               ChangeColor(btnF10)
111
112           Case Keys.F11 ' F11 key
113               ChangeColor(btnF11)
```

Figure 22.29   Typing Application code listing. (Part 2 of 7.)

```
114
115            Case Keys.F12 ' F12 key
116                ChangeColor(btnF12)
117
118            ' following cases test if a special character was pressed
119            Case Keys.OemOpenBrackets ' left square bracket
120                ChangeColor(btnLeftBrace)
121                txtOutput.Text &= "["
122
123            Case Keys.OemCloseBrackets ' right square bracket
124                ChangeColor(btnRightBrace)
125                txtOutput.Text &= "]"
126
127            Case Keys.Oemplus ' plus sign
128                ChangeColor(btnPlus)
129                txtOutput.Text &= "+"
130
131            Case Keys.OemMinus ' minus sign
132                ChangeColor(btnHyphen)
133                txtOutput.Text &= "-"
134
135            Case Keys.Oemtilde ' tilde (~)
136                ChangeColor(btnTilde)
137                txtOutput.Text &= "~"
138
139            Case Keys.OemPipe ' backslash
140                ChangeColor(btnSlash)
141                txtOutput.Text &= "\"
142
143            Case Keys.OemSemicolon ' colon
144                ChangeColor(btnColon)
145                txtOutput.Text &= ":"
146
147            Case Keys.OemQuotes ' quotation marks
148                ChangeColor(btnQuote)
149                txtOutput.Text &= ControlChars.Quote
150
151            Case Keys.OemPeriod ' period
152                ChangeColor(btnPeriod)
153                txtOutput.Text &= "."
154
155            Case Keys.Oemcomma ' comma
156                ChangeColor(btnComma)
157                txtOutput.Text &= ","
158
159            Case Keys.OemQuestion ' question mark
160                ChangeColor(btnQuestion)
161                txtOutput.Text &= "?"
162
163            Case Keys.CapsLock ' Caps Lock key
164                ChangeColor(btnCaps)
165
166            ' following cases test if an arrow key was pressed
167            Case Keys.Down ' down arrow
168                ChangeColor(btnDown)
169
170            Case Keys.Up ' up arrow
171                ChangeColor(btnUp)
```

Figure 22.29   **Typing Application** code listing. (Part 3 of 7.)

```
172
173            Case Keys.Left ' left arrow
174                ChangeColor(btnLeft)
175
176            Case Keys.Right ' right arrow
177                ChangeColor(btnRight)
178
179            ' following cases test if a modifier key was pressed
180            Case CType(65552, Keys) ' Shift key
181                ChangeColor(btnShiftLeft)
182
183            Case CType(131089, Keys) ' Control key
184                ChangeColor(btnCtrlLeft)
185
186            Case CType(262162, Keys) ' Alt key
187                ChangeColor(btnAltLeft)
188
189        End Select
190
191    End Sub ' txtOutput_KeyDown
192
193    ' handles Form KeyPress Event
194    Private Sub txtOutput_KeyPress(ByVal sender As Object, _
195        ByVal e As System.Windows.Forms.KeyPressEventArgs) _
196        Handles txtOutput.KeyPress
197
198        ' convert pressed key to uppercase
199        Select Case Char.ToUpper(e.KeyChar)
200
201            ' following cases test if key pressed was a letter
202            Case Convert.ToChar(Keys.A) ' a key
203                ChangeColor(btnA)
204                txtOutput.Text &= e.KeyChar
205
206            Case Convert.ToChar(Keys.B) ' b key
207                ChangeColor(btnB)
208                txtOutput.Text &= e.KeyChar
209
210            Case Convert.ToChar(Keys.C) ' c key
211                ChangeColor(btnC)
212                txtOutput.Text &= e.KeyChar
213
214            Case Convert.ToChar(Keys.D) ' d key
215                ChangeColor(btnD)
216                txtOutput.Text &= e.KeyChar
217
218            Case Convert.ToChar(Keys.E) ' e key
219                ChangeColor(btnE)
220                txtOutput.Text &= e.KeyChar
221
222            Case Convert.ToChar(Keys.F) ' f key
223                ChangeColor(btnF)
224                txtOutput.Text &= e.KeyChar
225
226            Case Convert.ToChar(Keys.G) ' g key
227                ChangeColor(btnG)
228                txtOutput.Text &= e.KeyChar
229
```

Using the **KeyChar** property to determine which letter key was pressed

Code executed when the *a* key is pressed

Code executed when the *b* key is pressed

Figure 22.29 Typing Application code listing. (Part 4 of 7.)

```
230              Case Convert.ToChar(Keys.H) ' h key
231                 ChangeColor(btnH)
232                 txtOutput.Text &= e.KeyChar
233
234              Case Convert.ToChar(Keys.I) ' i key
235                 ChangeColor(btnI)
236                 txtOutput.Text &= e.KeyChar
237
238              Case Convert.ToChar(Keys.J) ' j key
239                 ChangeColor(btnJ)
240                 txtOutput.Text &= e.KeyChar
241
242              Case Convert.ToChar(Keys.K) ' k key
243                 ChangeColor(btnK)
244                 txtOutput.Text &= e.KeyChar
245
246              Case Convert.ToChar(Keys.L) ' l key
247                 ChangeColor(btnL)
248                 txtOutput.Text &= e.KeyChar
249
250              Case Convert.ToChar(Keys.M) ' m key
251                 ChangeColor(btnM)
252                 txtOutput.Text &= e.KeyChar
253
254              Case Convert.ToChar(Keys.N) ' n key
255                 ChangeColor(btnN)
256                 txtOutput.Text &= e.KeyChar
257
258              Case Convert.ToChar(Keys.O) ' o key
259                 ChangeColor(btnO)
260                 txtOutput.Text &= e.KeyChar
261
262              Case Convert.ToChar(Keys.P) ' p key
263                 ChangeColor(btnP)
264                 txtOutput.Text &= e.KeyChar
265
266              Case Convert.ToChar(Keys.Q) ' q key
267                 ChangeColor(btnQ)
268                 txtOutput.Text &= e.KeyChar
269
270              Case Convert.ToChar(Keys.R) ' r key
271                 ChangeColor(btnR)
272                 txtOutput.Text &= e.KeyChar
273
274              Case Convert.ToChar(Keys.S) ' s key
275                 ChangeColor(btnS)
276                 txtOutput.Text &= e.KeyChar
277
278              Case Convert.ToChar(Keys.T) ' t key
279                 ChangeColor(btnT)
280                 txtOutput.Text &= e.KeyChar
281
282              Case Convert.ToChar(Keys.U) ' u key
283                 ChangeColor(btnU)
284                 txtOutput.Text &= e.KeyChar
285
286              Case Convert.ToChar(Keys.V) ' v key
287                 ChangeColor(btnV)
```

Figure 22.29 **Typing Application** code listing. (Part 5 of 7.)

```
288                  txtOutput.Text &= e.KeyChar
289
290             Case Convert.ToChar(Keys.W) ' w key
291                 ChangeColor(btnW)
292                 txtOutput.Text &= e.KeyChar
293
294             Case Convert.ToChar(Keys.X) ' x key
295                 ChangeColor(btnX)
296                 txtOutput.Text &= e.KeyChar
297
298             Case Convert.ToChar(Keys.Y) ' y key
299                 ChangeColor(btnY)
300                 txtOutput.Text &= e.KeyChar
301
302             Case Convert.ToChar(Keys.Z) ' z key
303                 ChangeColor(btnZ)
304                 txtOutput.Text &= e.KeyChar
305
306         End Select ' ends test for letters
307
308      End Sub ' txtOutput_KeyPress
309
310      Private Sub txtOutput_KeyUp(ByVal sender As Object, _
311          ByVal e As System.Windows.Forms.KeyEventArgs) _
312          Handles txtOutput.KeyUp
313
314          ResetColor()
315      End Sub ' txtOutput_KeyUp
316
317      ' highlight Button passed as argument
318      Private Sub ChangeColor(ByVal btnButton As Button)
319
320          ResetColor()
321          btnButton.BackColor = Color.LightGoldenrodYellow
322          m_btnLastButton = btnButton
323      End Sub ' ChangeColor
324
325      ' changes m_btnLastButton's color if it refers to a Button
326      Private Sub ResetColor()
327
328          If IsNothing(m_btnLastButton) = False Then
329              m_btnLastButton.BackColor = _
330                  m_btnLastButton.DefaultBackColor
331
332          End If ' m_btnLastButton is not Nothing
333
334      End Sub ' ResetColor
335
336      ' handles Font menu item's Click Event
337      Private Sub mnuitmFont_Click(ByVal sender As _
338          System.Object, ByVal e As System.EventArgs) _
339          Handles mnuitmFont.Click
340
341          Dim dlgFontDialog As FontDialog = New FontDialog
342          Dim result As DialogResult ' stores Button clicked
343
344          ' show dialog and get result
345          result = dlgFontDialog.ShowDialog()
```

Resets the **Button** background color — (line 314)

Changes the background color for the m_btnLastButton to the default color — (lines 329)

Create **FontDialog** and **DialogResult** variables — (lines 341)

Display dialog and get **Button** clicked to exit the dialog — (line 345)

Figure 22.29   Typing Application code listing. (Part 6 of 7.)

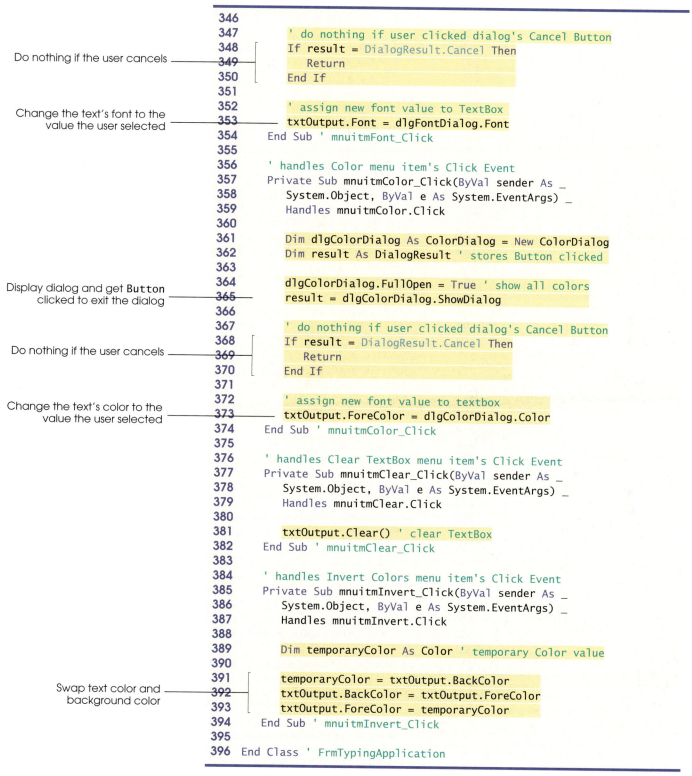

```
346
347          ' do nothing if user clicked dialog's Cancel Button
348          If result = DialogResult.Cancel Then
349            Return
350          End If
351
352          ' assign new font value to TextBox
353          txtOutput.Font = dlgFontDialog.Font
354       End Sub ' mnuitmFont_Click
355
356       ' handles Color menu item's Click Event
357       Private Sub mnuitmColor_Click(ByVal sender As _
358          System.Object, ByVal e As System.EventArgs) _
359          Handles mnuitmColor.Click
360
361          Dim dlgColorDialog As ColorDialog = New ColorDialog
362          Dim result As DialogResult ' stores Button clicked
363
364          dlgColorDialog.FullOpen = True ' show all colors
365          result = dlgColorDialog.ShowDialog
366
367          ' do nothing if user clicked dialog's Cancel Button
368          If result = DialogResult.Cancel Then
369            Return
370          End If
371
372          ' assign new font value to textbox
373          txtOutput.ForeColor = dlgColorDialog.Color
374       End Sub ' mnuitmColor_Click
375
376       ' handles Clear TextBox menu item's Click Event
377       Private Sub mnuitmClear_Click(ByVal sender As _
378          System.Object, ByVal e As System.EventArgs) _
379          Handles mnuitmClear.Click
380
381          txtOutput.Clear() ' clear TextBox
382       End Sub ' mnuitmClear_Click
383
384       ' handles Invert Colors menu item's Click Event
385       Private Sub mnuitmInvert_Click(ByVal sender As _
386          System.Object, ByVal e As System.EventArgs) _
387          Handles mnuitmInvert.Click
388
389          Dim temporaryColor As Color ' temporary Color value
390
391          temporaryColor = txtOutput.BackColor
392          txtOutput.BackColor = txtOutput.ForeColor
393          txtOutput.ForeColor = temporaryColor
394       End Sub ' mnuitmInvert_Click
395
396   End Class ' FrmTypingApplication
```

Labels in margin:
- Do nothing if the user cancels (lines 348–350)
- Change the text's font to the value the user selected (line 353)
- Display dialog and get **Button** clicked to exit the dialog (line 365)
- Do nothing if the user cancels (lines 368–370)
- Change the text's color to the value the user selected (line 373)
- Swap text color and background color (lines 391–393)

Figure 22.29 **Typing Application** code listing. (Part 7 of 7.)

SELF-REVIEW

1. Menus can contain _____.

    a) commands that the user can select   b) submenus

    c) separator bars   d) All of the above.

2. _____ allow you to receive input from and display messages to users.
   a) Dialogs   b) Menus
   c) Separator bars   d) Enumerations

Answers: 1) d. 2) a.

22.5 Wrap-Up

In this tutorial, you learned about keyboard events. You learned how to handle the event raised when the user presses a key on the keyboard by using the KeyDown and KeyPress events. You then learned how to use the KeyUp event handler to handle the event raised when the user releases a key.

You added menus to the **Typing Application**. You learned that menus allow you to add controls to your application without cluttering the GUI. You also learned how to code a menu item's Click event handler to alter the displayed text in the **Typing Application**. You learned how to display the **Color** and **Font** dialogs so the user could specify the font style and color of the text in the TextBox. You also learned how to use the DialogResult enumeration to determine which Button the user pressed to exit a dialog.

In the next tutorial, you will learn about the methods in the String class that allow you to manipulate Strings. These methods will help you build a screen scraper application that can search text for a particular value.

SKILLS SUMMARY

Adding Keyboard Event Handlers to Your Application
- Select the control for which you want to add the event handler from the Class Name ComboBox.
- Select the desired event handler from the Method Name ComboBox.

Executing Code When the User Presses a Letter Key on the Keyboard
- Use the KeyPress event handler.
- Use property KeyChar to determine which key was pressed.
- Use method ToUpper to convert the pressed key to an uppercase letter.
- Use a Select Case statement to perform an action depending on what key was pressed.
- Compare the pressed key to a Keys enumeration value in each Case.

Executing Code When the User Presses a Key that is not a Letter
- Use the KeyDown event handler.
- Use property KeyData to determine which key was pressed.

Executing Code When the User Releases a Key
- Use the KeyUp event handler.

Adding Menus to Your Application
- Select the MainMenu control from the tool bar.
- Add menu items to the menu by typing the item's name in the **Type Here** boxes that appear on the bottom of the menu.
- Add submenus by typing a menu item's name in the **Type Here** box that appears to the right of the submenu's name.
- Use a menu item's Click event handler to perform an action when that menu item is selected by the user.

Adding a Font Dialog to Your Application
- Use keyword New to create a new FontDialog object.
- Use a DialogResult variable to store the Button the user clicked to exit the dialog.
- Use method ShowDialog to display the dialog.

Adding a Color Dialog to Your Application
- Use keyword New to create a new FontDialog object.
- Use a DialogResult variable to store the Button the user clicked to exit the dialog.
- Set the FullOpen option to True to provide the user with the full range of colors and to allow custom colors.
- Use method ShowDialog to display the dialog.

KEY TERMS

Cancel value of DialogResult enumeration—Used to determine if the user clicked the Cancel Button of a dialog.

Char structure—Stores characters (such as letters and symbols).

Click event of class MenuItem—Generated when an item is clicked or a shortcut key is used.

ColorDialog class—Used to display a dialog containing color options to a use.

DialogResult enumeration—An enumeration that contains values corresponding to standard dialog Button names.

e event argument—Contains data for the event (such as KeyData).

FontDialog class—Used to display a dialog containing font options to a user and record the result.

FullOpen property of class ColorDialog—Property that, when True, enables the ColorDialog to provide a full range of color options when displayed.

keyboard event—Raised when a key on the keyboard is pressed or released.

KeyChar property of class KeyPressEventArgs—Contains data about the key that raised the KeyPress event.

KeyData property of class KeyEventArgs—Contains data about the key that raised the KeyDown event.

KeyDown event—Generated when a key is initially pressed. Use to handle the event raised when a key that is not a letter key is pressed.

KeyEventArgs class—Stores information about special modifier keys.

KeyPress event—Generated when a key is pressed. Use to handle the event raised when a letter key is pressed.

KeyPressEventArgs class—Stores information about character keys.

Keys enumeration—Contains values representing keyboard keys.

KeyUp event—Generated when key is released.

MainMenu control—Allows you to add menus to your application.

Menu Designer mode in Visual Studio .NET—Design mode in Visual Studio .NET that allows you to create and edit menus.

menu—Design element that groups related commands for Windows applications. Although these commands depend on the application, some—such as **Open** and **Save**—are common to many applications. Menus are an integral part of GUIs, because they organize commands without cluttering the GUI.

menu-access shortcut—*Alt* key shortcut that allows the user to combine the *Alt* key with another key to access a menu item.

menu item—Command located in a menu that, when selected, causes the application to perform a specific action.

modifier key—Key such as *Shift*, *Alt* or *Control* that modify the way that applications respond to a keyboard event.

Remove method of class String—Deletes characters from a String. The first argument contains the index in the String at which to begin removing characters, and the second argument specifies the number of characters to remove.

sender event argument—Event argument that contains the GUI component that raised the event (also called the source of the event).

separator bar—Bar placed in a menu to separate related menu items.

ShowDialog method of class FontDialog or ColorDialog—The method that displays the dialog on which it is called.

submenu—Menu within another menu.

temporary variable—Used to store data when swapping values.

Text property of class MenuItem—Specifies the menu item's text.

ToUpper method of structure Char—Returns the uppercase representation of the character passed as a parameter.

GUI DESIGN GUIDELINES

MainMenu

- Use book-title capitalization in menu item text.
- Use separator bars in a menu to group related menu items.
- If clicking a menu item opens a dialog, an ellipsis (…) should follow the menu item's text.

CONTROLS, EVENTS, PROPERTIES & METHODS

Char This structure represents Unicode® characters.

- *Method*

  ToUpper—Returns the uppercase equivalent of an alphabetic character.

ColorDialog　[ColorDialog]　This control allows the user to customize the color of what is being typed.

- *Properties*

  Color—Contains the color selected by the user. The default color is black.

  FullOpen—When True, displays an extended color palette. If this property is set to False, a dialog with less options is displayed.

- *Methods*

  ShowDialog—Displays the **Color** dialog to the user.

FontDialog　[FontDialog]　This control allows the user to customize the font, size and style of what is being typed.

- *Methods*

  ShowDialog—Displays the **Font** dialog to the user.

KeyEventArgs This class represents arguments passed to the KeyPress event handler.

- *Property*

  KeyData—Contains data about the key that raised the KeyDown event.

KeyPressEventArgs This class represents arguments passed to the KeyPress event handler.

- *Property*

  KeyChar—Contains data about the key that raised the KeyPress event.

MainMenu　[MainMenu]　This control allows you to group related commands for a Windows application.

- *In action*

- *Events*

  Click—Raised when the user clicks a menu item or presses a shortcut key that represents an item.

TextBox   `[abl] TextBox`   This control allows the user to input data from the keyboard.

■ *In action*

`|         0 |`

■ *Events*

KeyDown—Raised when a key is pressed. KeyDown is case insensitive. It cannot recognize lowercase letters.

KeyPress—Raised when a key is pressed. KeyPress cannot handle modifier keys.

KeyUp—Raised when a key is released by the user.

TextChanged—Raised when the text in the TextBox is changed.

■ *Properties*

Enabled—Determines whether the user can enter data (True) in the TextBox or not (False).

Location—Specifies the location of the TextBox on the container control relative to the top-left corner.

MaxLength—Specifies the maximum number of characters that can be input into the TextBox.

Multiline—Specifies whether the TextBox is capable of displaying multiple lines of text.

Name—Specifies the name used to access the TextBox programmatically. The name should be prefixed with txt.

PasswordChar—Specifies the masking character to be used when displaying data in the TextBox.

ReadOnly—Determines whether the value of a TextBox can be changed.

ScrollBars—Specifies whether the TextBox contains a scrollbar.

Size—Specifies the height and width (in pixels) of the TextBox.

Text—Specifies the text displayed in the TextBox.

TextAlign—Specifies how the text is aligned within the TextBox.

■ *Methods*

Focus—Transfers the focus of the application to the TextBox that calls it.

MULTIPLE-CHOICE QUESTIONS

22.1 When creating a menu, typing a _____ in front of a menu item name will create an access shortcut for that item.

a) &   b) !

c) $ d) #

22.2 *Alt*, *Shift* and *Control* are _____ keys.

a) modifier   b) ASCII

c) function   d) special

22.3 KeyChar is a property of _____.

a) KeyEventArgs   b) Key

c) KeyArgs   d) KeyPressEventArgs

22.4 Typing a hyphen (–) as a menu item's Text property will create a(n) _____.

a) separator bar   b) access shortcut

c) new submenu   d) keyboard shortcut

22.5 A _____ provides a group of related commands for Windows applications.

a) separator bar   b) hot key

c) menu   d) margin indicator bar

22.6 The _____ enumeration specifies key codes and modifiers.

a) Keyboard   b) Key

c) KeyboardTypes   d) Keys

22.7 The _____ event is raised when a key is pressed by the user.

a) `KeyPress`   b) `KeyHeld`

c) `KeyDown`   d) Both a and c.

22.8 Which of the following is not a keyboard event?

a) `KeyPress`   b) `KeyDown`

c) `KeyUp`   d) `KeyClicked`

22.9 Which of the following is not a structure?

a) `Char`   b) `Color`

c) `String`   d) `Date`

22.10 The _____ type allows you to determine which `Button` the user clicked to exit a dialog.

a) `DialogButtons`   b) `DialogResult`

c) `Buttons`   d) `ButtonResult`

EXERCISES

22.11 (*Inventory Application with Keyboard Events*) Enhance the **Inventory** application that you developed in Tutorial 4 to prevent the user from entering input that is not a number. Use keyboard events to allow the user to press the number keys, the left and right arrows and the *Backspace* keys. If a key other than these is pressed, display a `MessageBox` instructing the user to enter a number (Fig. 22.30).

Figure 22.30 Enhanced **Inventory** application.

a) *Copying the template to your working directory.* Copy the directory `C:\Examples\Tutorial22\Exercises\KeyEventInventory` to your `C:\SimplyVB` directory.

b) *Opening the application's template file.* Double click `KeyEventInventory.sln` in the `KeyEventInventory` directory to open the application.

c) *Adding the KeyDown event handler for the first TextBox.* Add an empty `KeyDown` event handler for the **Cartons per shipment:** `TextBox`.

d) *Adding a Select Case statement.* Add a `Select Case` statement to the `KeyDown` event handler that determines whether a number key, a left or right arrow or the *Backspace* key was pressed.

e) *Adding the Case Else statement.* Add a `Case Else` statement that will determine whether a key other than a valid one for this application was pressed. If an invalid key was pressed, display a `MessageBox` that instructs the user to enter a number.

f) *Adding the KeyDown event handler for the second TextBox.* Repeat *Steps c–e*, but this time create a `KeyDown` event handler for the **Items per carton:** `TextBox`. This event handler should perform the same functionality as the one for the **Cartons per shipment:** `TextBox`.

g) *Running the application.* Select **Debug > Start** to run your application. Try entering letters or pressing the up and down arrow keys in the `TextBoxes`. A `MessageBox` should be displayed. Enter valid input and click the **Calculate Total** `Button`. Verify that the correct output is displayed.

h) *Closing the application.* Close your running application by clicking its close box.

i) *Closing the IDE.* Close Visual Studio .NET by clicking its close box.

22.12 (*Bouncing Ball Game*) Write an application that allows the user to play a game, the goal of which is to prevent a bouncing ball from falling off the bottom of the `Form`. When the user presses the *S* key, a blue ball will bounce off the top, left and right sides (the "walls") of the `Form`. There should be a horizontal bar on the bottom of the `Form`, which serves as a paddle to prevent the ball from hitting the bottom of the `Form`. (The ball can bounce off the paddle, but not the bottom of the Form.) The user can move the paddle using the left and right arrow keys. If the ball hits the paddle, the ball should bounce up, and the game should continue. If the ball hits the bottom of the Form, the game should end. The paddle's width should decrease every 20 seconds to make the game more challenging. The GUI is provided for you (Fig. 22.31).

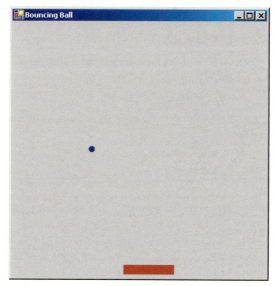

Figure 22.31 **Bouncing Ball** application.

a) *Copying the template to your working directory.* Copy the directory `C:\Examples\Tutorial22\Exercises\BouncingBall` to your `C:\SimplyVB` directory.

b) *Opening the application's template file.* Double click `BouncingBall.sln` in the `BouncingBall` directory to open the application.

c) *Creating the KeyDown event handler.* Insert a KeyDown event handler for the Form.

d) *Writing code to start the game.* Write an If...Then statement in the KeyDown event handler that tests whether the user presses the *S* key. You can use the KeyDown event handler for the *S* key in this case because you do not care whether the user presses an uppercase *S* or a lowercase *S*. If the user presses the *S* key, start the two Timers that are provided in the template.

e) *Inserting code to move the paddle left.* Write an If...Then statement that tests if the user pressed the left-arrow key and if the paddle's horizontal position is greater than zero. If the paddle's horizontal position equals zero, the left edge of the paddle is touching the left wall and the paddle should not be allowed to move farther to the left. If both the conditions in the If...Then are true, decrease the paddle's *x*-position by 10.

f) *Inserting code to move the paddle right.* Write an If...Then statement that tests if the user pressed the right-arrow key and whether the paddle's *x*-coordinate is less than the width of the Form minus the width of the paddle. If the paddle's *x*-coordinate equals the Form's width minus the width of the paddle, the paddle's right edge is touching the right wall and the paddle should not be allowed to move farther to the right. If both the conditions in the If...Then statement are true, increase the paddle's *x*-coordinate by 10.

g) *Running the application.* Select **Debug > Start** to run your application. Press the *S* key to begin the game and use the paddle to keep the bouncing ball from dropping off the Form. Continue doing this until 20 seconds have passed, and verify that the paddle is decreased in size at that time.

h) *Closing the application.* Close your running application by clicking its close box.

i) *Closing the IDE.* Close Visual Studio .NET by clicking its close box.

22.13 (*Modified Painter Application*) Modify the **Painter** application that you developed in Tutorial 21 to include menus that allow the user to select the size and color of the painted ellipses and the color of the Form (Fig. 22.32). (The menus replace the RadioButtons.) Also, add a multiline TextBox that allows the user to type text to accompany the painting. The user should be able to use menus to select the font style and color of the text and the background color of the TextBox.

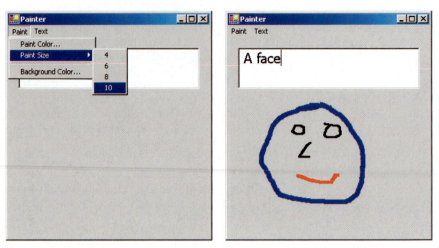

Figure 22.32   Enhanced **Painter** GUI.

a) *Copying the template to your working directory.* Copy the directory `C:\Examples\Tutorial22\Exercises\ModifiedPainter` to your `C:\SimplyVB` directory.

b) *Opening the application's template file.* Double click `ModifiedPainter.sln` in the `ModifiedPainter` directory to open the application.

c) *Creating the menus.* Create two menus. The first one should be titled **Paint** and should contain a **Paint Color...** menu item, a **Paint Size** submenu that contains menu items **4, 6, 8** and **10**, a separator bar and a **Background Color...** menu item. The second menu should be titled **Text** and have **Text Color...** and **Font...** menu items, a separator bar and a **TextBox Color...** menu item.

d) *Changing the paint color.* Add an event handler for the **Paint Color...** menu item. This event handler should display a **Color** dialog that allows the user to change the value stored in m_paintColor.

e) *Changing the paint size.* Add an event handler for each of the **Size** submenu's menu items. Each event handler should change the value stored in m_intDiamter to the value displayed on the menu (that is, clicking the **4** menu item will change the value of m_intDiameter to 4).

f) *Changing the background color.* Add an event handler for the **Background Color...** menu item. This event handler should display a **Color** dialog that allows the user to change the value stored in m_backgroundColor and also change the BackColor property of the Form. To change the background color of the Form, assign the value specifying the background color to BackColor. For instance, the statement BackColor = Color.White changes the background color of the Form to white.

g) *Changing the text color.* Add an event handler for the **Text Color...** menu item. This event handler should display a **Color** dialog that allows the user to change the color of the text displayed in the TextBox.

h) *Changing the text style.* Add an event handler for the **Font...** menu item. This event handler should display a **Font** dialog that allows the user to change the style of the text displayed in the TextBox.

i) *Changing the TextBox's background color.* Add an event handler for the **TextBox Color...** menu item. This event handler should display a **Color** dialog that allows the user to change the background color of the TextBox.

j) *Running the application.* Select **Debug > Start** to run your application. Use the menus to draw shapes of various colors and brush sizes. Enter text to describe your drawing. Use the other menu options to change the color of the Form, the TextBox and the text in the TextBox.

k) *Closing the application.* Close your running application by clicking its close box.

l) *Closing the IDE.* Close Visual Studio .NET by clicking its close box.

What does this code do? **22.14** What is the result of the following code?

```
1   Private Sub mnuitmColor_Click(ByVal sender As _
2       System.Object, ByVal e As System.EventArgs) _
3       Handles mnuitmColor.Click
4
5       Dim dlgColorDialog As ColorDialog = New ColorDialog
6       Dim result As DialogResult
7
8       dlgColorDialog.FullOpen = True
9
10      result = dlgColorDialog.ShowDialog()
11
12      If result = DialogResult.Cancel Then
13         Return
14      End If
15
16      BackColor = dlgColorDialog.Color
17   End Sub ' mnuitmColor_Click
```

What's wrong with this code? **22.15** This code should allow a user to pick a font from a **Font** dialog and set the text in txt-Display to that font. Find the error(s) in the following code, assuming that a TextBox named txtDisplay exists on a Form.

```
1   Private Sub Fonts()
2       Dim dlgFontDialog As FontDialog
3
4       dlgFontDialog = New FontDialog
5       dlgFontDialog.ShowDialog
6       txtDisplay.Font = dlgFontDialog.Font
7   End Sub
```

Programming Challenge **22.16** (*Dvorak Keyboard Application*) Create an application that simulates the letters on the Dvorak keyboard. A Dvorak keyboard allows faster typing by placing the most commonly used keys in the most accessible locations. Use keyboard events to create an application similar to the **Typing Application**, except that it simulates the Dvorak keyboard instead of the standard keyboard. The correct Dvorak key should be highlighted on the virtual keyboard and the correct character should be displayed in the TextBox. The keys and characters map as follows:

- On the top row, the *P* key of the Dvorak keyboard maps to the *R* key on a standard keyboard, and the *L* key of the Dvorak keyboard maps to the *P* key on a standard keyboard.
- On the middle row, the *A* key remains in the same position and the *S* key on the Dvorak keyboard maps to the semicolon key on the standard keyboard.
- On the bottom row, the *Q* key on the Dvorak keyboard maps to the *X* key on the standard keyboard and the *Z* key maps to the question mark key.
- All of the other keys on the Dvorak keyboard map to the location shown in Fig. 22.33.

Figure 22.33   Dvorak Keyboard GUI.

a) *Copying the template to your working directory.* Copy the directory C:\Examples\ Tutorial22\Exercises\DvorakKeyboard to your C:\SimplyVB directory.

b) *Opening the application's template file.* Double click DvorakKeyboard.sln in the DvorakKeyboard directory to open the application.

c) *Creating the KeyPress event handler.* Add a KeyPress event handler for the TextBox.

d) *Creating a Select Case statement.* Add a Select Case statement to the KeyPress event handler. The Select Case statement should test whether all of the letter keys on the Dvorak keyboard were pressed except for the *S, W, V* and *Z* keys. If a Dvorak key was pressed, highlight it on the GUI and display the character in the TextBox.

e) *Creating a KeyDown event handler.* Add a KeyDown event handler for the TextBox. The *S, W, V* and *Z* keys do not map to a letter key on the standard keyboard; therefore, a KeyDown event handler must be used to determine whether one of these keys was pressed.

f) *Adding a Select Case statement.* Add a Select Case statement to your KeyDown event handler that determines whether *S, W, V* or *Z* was pressed. If one of these keys was pressed, highlight the key, and add the character to the TextBox.

g) *Running the application.* Select **Debug > Start** to run your application. Use your keyboard to enter text. Verify that the text entered is correct based on the rules in the exercise description. Make sure the correct Buttons on the Form are highlighted as you enter text.

h) *Closing the application.* Close your running application by clicking its close box.

i) *Closing the IDE.* Close Visual Studio .NET by clicking its close box.

23

T U T O R I A L

Objectives

In this tutorial, you will learn to:
- Create and manipulate `String` objects.
- Use properties and methods of class `String`.
- Search for substrings within `Strings`.
- Extract substrings within `Strings`.
- Replace substrings within `Strings`.

Outline

Screen Scraping Application

Introducing *String* Processing

This tutorial introduces Visual Basic .NET's `String`-processing capabilities. The techniques presented in this tutorial can be used to create applications that process text. Earlier tutorials introduced class `String` from the `System` namespace and several of its methods. In this tutorial, you will learn how to search `Strings`, retrieve characters from `String` objects and replace characters in a `String`. You will create an application that uses these `String`-processing capabilities to manipulate a string containing **HTML (HyperText Markup Language)**. HTML is a technology for describing Web content. Extracting desired information from the HTML that composes a Web page is called **screen scraping**. Applications that perform screen scraping can be used to extract specific information, such as weather conditions or stock prices, from Web pages so that the information can be formatted and manipulated more easily by computer applications. In this tutorial, you will create a simple **Screen Scraping** application.

23.1 Test-Driving the Screen Scraping Application

This application must meet the following requirements:

Application Requirements

An online European auction house wants to expand its business to include bidders from the United States. However, all of the auction house's Web pages currently display their prices in Euros, not dollars. The auction house wants to generate separate Web pages for American bidders that will display the prices of auction items in dollars. These new Web pages will be generated by using screen-scraping techniques on the already existing Web pages. You have been asked to build a prototype application that will test the screen-scraping functionality. The application should search a sample string of HTML and extract information about the price of a specified auction item. For testing purposes, a ComboBox should be provided that contains auction items listed in the HTML. The selected item's amount must then be converted to dollars. For simplicity, assume that the exchange rate is one to one (that is, one Euro is equivalent to one dollar). The price (in dollars) and sample HTML are displayed in Labels.

The **Screen Scraping** application searches for the name of a specified auction item in a string of HTML. Users select the item for which to search from a ComboBox. The application then extracts and displays the price in dollars of this item. You begin by test-driving the completed application. Then, you will learn the additional Visual Basic .NET technologies that you will need to create your own version of this application.

Test-Driving the Screen Scraping Application

1. ***Opening the completed application.*** Open the directory C:\Examples\ Tutorial23\CompletedApplication\ScreenScraping to locate the **Screen Scraping** application. Double click ScreenScraping.sln to open the application in Visual Studio .NET.

2. ***Running the application.*** Select **Debug > Start** to run the application (Fig. 23.1). Notice that the HTML string is displayed in a Label at the bottom of the Form.

Label containing HTML ————

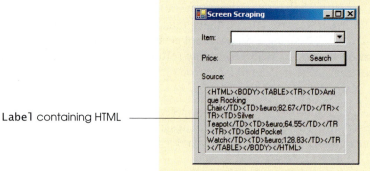

Figure 23.1 **Screen Scraping** application's Form.

3. ***Selecting an item name.*** The ComboBox contains three item names. Select an item name from the ComboBox as shown in Fig. 23.2.

ComboBox's drop-down list ————

Figure 23.2 Selecting an item name from the ComboBox.

4. ***Searching for an item's price.*** Click the **Search** Button to display the price for the selected item. The extracted price is displayed in a Label (Fig. 23.3).

5. ***Closing the application.*** Close your running application by clicking its close box.

6. ***Closing the IDE.*** Close Visual Studio .NET by clicking its close box.

(cont.)

Extracted price
(converted to dollars)

Price located in HTML string
(specified in Euros)

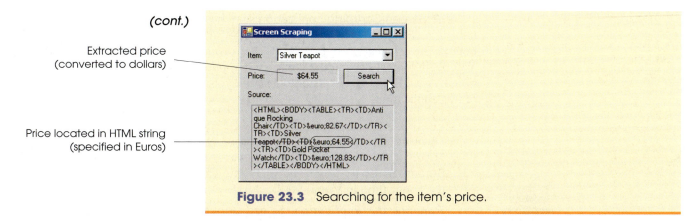

Figure 23.3   Searching for the item's price.

23.2 Fundamentals of Strings

A string is a series of characters treated as a single unit. These **characters** can be uppercase letters, lowercase letters, digits and various **special characters**, such as +, -, *, /, $ and others. A string is an object of class String in the System namespace. We write **string literals**, or **string constants** (often called **literal String objects**), as sequences of characters in double quotation marks, as follows:

```
"This is a string!"
```

You've already created and used Strings in previous tutorials. You know that a declaration can assign a String literal to a String reference. For example, the declaration

```
Dim strColor As String = "blue"
```

initializes String reference strColor to refer to the String literal object "blue".

Like arrays, Strings always know their own size. String property Length returns the length of the String (that is, the number of characters in the String). For example, the expression strColor.Length evaluates to 4 for the String "blue".

Another useful property of class String is **Chars**, which returns the character located at a specific index in a String. Property Chars takes an Integer argument specifying the index and returns the character at that index. As in arrays, the first element of a String is at index 0. For example, the following code

```
If strString1.Chars(0) = strString2.Chars(0) Then
    lblMessage.Text = "The first characters are the same."
```

compares the character at index 0 (that is, the first character) of strString1 with the character at index 0 of strString2.

In earlier tutorials, you used several methods of class String to manipulate String objects. Figure 23.4 lists some of these methods. You will be introduced to new String methods later in this tutorial.

Method	Sample Expression Method Call (assume strText = "My String")	Returns
Insert(*index, string*)	strText.Insert(9,"!")	"My String!"
Remove(*index, count*)	strText.Remove(2,1)	"MyString"
ToLower()	strText.ToLower()	"my string"
ToUpper()	strText.ToUpper()	"MY STRING"

Figure 23.4   String-class methods introduced in earlier tutorials.

Any String method that appears to modify a String actually returns a new String that contains the results. For example, String method ToUpper does not actually modify the original String, but instead returns a new String in which each lowercase letter has been converted to uppercase. This occurs because Strings are **immutable** objects—that is, characters in Strings cannot be changed after the Strings are created.

SELF-REVIEW

1. The _____ property of the class String returns the number of characters in the String.

   a) MaxChars   b) Length

   c) CharacterCount   d) TotalLength

2. A String can be composed of _____.

   a) digits   b) lowercase letters

   c) special characters   d) All of the above.

Answers: 1) b. 2) d.

23.3 Analyzing the Screen Scraping Application

Before building the **Screen Scraping** application, you must analyze its components. The following pseudocode describes the basic operation of the **Screen Scraping** application.

> When the Form loads:
>   Display the HTML that contains the items' prices in a Label
>
> When the user clicks the Search Button:
>   Search the HTML for the item the user selected from the ComboBox
>   Extract the item's price
>   Convert the item's price from Euros to dollars
>   Display the item's price in a Label

Now that you have test-driven the **Screen Scraping** application and studied its pseudocode representation, you will use an ACE table to help you convert the pseudocode to Visual Basic .NET. Figure 23.5 lists the actions, controls and events that will help you complete your own version of this application.

Action/Control/Event (ACE) Table for the Screen Scraping Application

Action	Control/Object	Event
Label the application's controls	lblItem lblPrice lblSource	Application is run
	FrmScreenScraping	Load
Display the HTML that contains the items' prices in a Label	lblHTML	
	btnSearch	Click
Search the HTML for the item the user selected from the ComboBox	strHTML, cboItems	
Extract the item's price	strHTML	
Convert the item's price from Euros to dollars	strPrice	
Display the item's price in a Label	lblResult	

Figure 23.5 ACE table for **Screen Scraping** application.

Now that you've analyzed the **Screen Scraping** application's components, you will learn about the `String` methods that you will use to construct the application.

23.4 Locating Substrings in `Strings`

In many applications, it is necessary to search for a character or set of characters in a `String`. For example, a programmer creating a word-processing application would want to provide capabilities that allow users to search their documents. Class `String` provides methods that make it possible to search for specified **substrings** (or sequences of characters) in a `String`. In the following box, you begin building the **Screen Scraping** application.

Locating the Selected Item's Price

1. ***Copying the template to your working directory.*** Copy the `C:\Examples\Tutorial23\TemplateApplication\ScreenScraping` directory to your `C:\SimplyVB` directory.

2. ***Opening the Screen Scraping application's template file.*** Double click `ScreenScraping.sln` in the `ScreenScraping` directory to open the application in Visual Studio .NET. Double click `ScreenScraping.vb` in the **Solution Explorer** to display the application's Form in Design view.

3. ***Creating a `Click` event handler for the Search `Button`.*** Double click the **Search** `Button` on the application's Form to generate the event handler `btnSearch_Click`.

4. ***Formatting the `Click` event handler.*** Add the comments on lines 140 and 144 of Fig. 23.6 around event handler `btnSearch_Click`. Also, split the procedure header over two lines using a line-continuation character (that is, underscore) as in lines 141–142 of Fig. 23.6 to improve its readability.

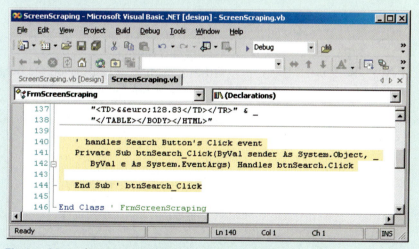

Figure 23.6 `btnSearch_Click` event handler.

5. ***Declaring three Integer variables and a String reference.*** Add lines 144–147 of Fig. 23.7 to the `btnSearch_Click` event handler. These lines declare variables `intItemLocation`, `intPriceBegin` and `intPriceEnd` and `String` reference `strPrice`.

(cont.)

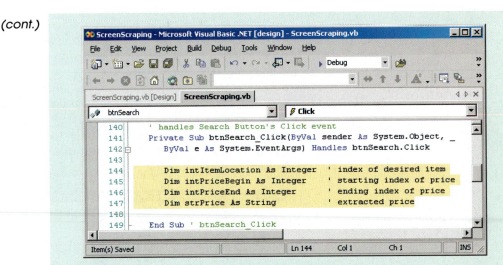

Figure 23.7 btnSearch_Click *event-handler declarations.*

6. ***Locating the specified item name.*** Add lines 149–151 of Fig. 23.8 to event handler btnSearch_Click. Lines 150–151 call String method **IndexOf** to locate the first occurrence of the specified item name in the HTML string (strHTML). There are three versions of IndexOf that search for substrings in a String. Lines 150–151 use the version of IndexOf that takes a single argument—the substring for which to search. (The specified item name is the SelectedItem of ComboBox, cboItems.)

Because Option Strict is set to On, we must first convert SelectedItem to a String, by using method ToString, before passing the selected item to method IndexOf. If IndexOf finds the specified substring (in this case, the item name), IndexOf returns the index at which the substring begins in the String. For example, the return value 0 means that the substring begins at the first element of the String. If IndexOf does not find the specified substring, IndexOf returns –1. The result is stored in intItemLocation.

Search for the
SelectedItem in the
String strHTML

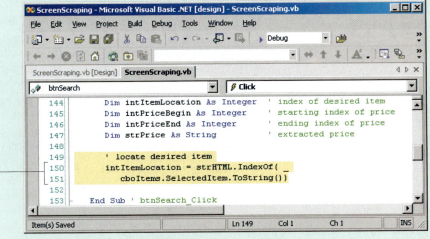

Figure 23.8 *Locating the desired item name.*

(cont.)

7. ***Locating the start of the price.*** Add lines 153–155 of Fig. 23.9 to event handler `btnSearch_Click`. Lines 154–155 locate the index at which the item's price begins. Lines 154–155 use a version of method `IndexOf` that takes two arguments—the substring to search for and the starting index in the `String` at which the search should begin. The method does not examine any characters that occur prior to the starting index (specified by `intItemLocation`). The third version of method `IndexOf` takes three arguments—the substring for which to search, the index at which to start searching and the number of characters to search. We do not use this version of `IndexOf` in the **Screen Scraping** application.

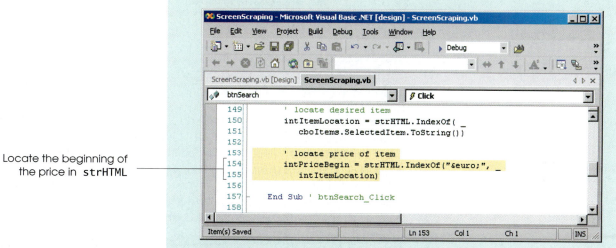

Locate the beginning of the price in `strHTML`

Figure 23.9 Locating the desired item price.

We know that the first price that follows the specified item name will be the desired price, therefore, we can begin our search at `intItemLocation`. The substring we search for is `"&euro;"`. This is the HTML representation of the Euro symbol, which appears before every price value in the HTML string in this application. The index returned from method `IndexOf` is stored in variable `intPriceBegin`.

8. ***Locating the end of the price.*** Add line 156 of Fig. 23.10 to event handler `btnSearch_Click`. Line 156 finds the index at which the desired price ends. Line 156 calls method `IndexOf` with the substring `"</TD>"` and the starting index `intPriceBegin`. A `</TD>` tag directly follows every price (excluding any spaces) in the HTML string, so the index of the first `</TD>` tag after `intPriceBegin` marks the end of the current price.

The index returned from method `IndexOf` is stored in variable `intPriceEnd`. In the next box, we will use `intPriceBegin` and `intPriceEnd` to obtain the price from the string `strHTML`.

9. ***Saving the project.*** Select **File > Save All** to save your modified code.

(cont.)

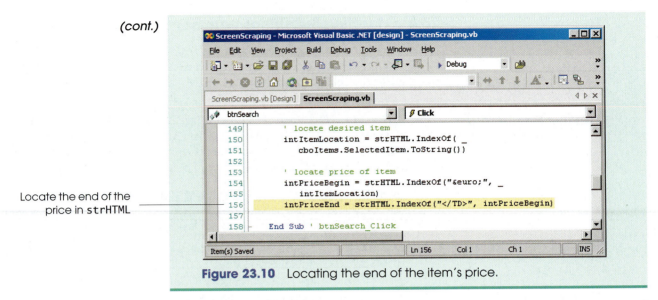

Locate the end of the price in strHTML

Figure 23.10   Locating the end of the item's price.

Another method that is similar to method IndexOf is the **LastIndexOf** method. Method LastIndexOf locates the last occurrence of a substring in a String; it performs the search starting from the end of the String and searches toward the beginning of the String. If method LastIndexOf finds the substring, LastIndexOf returns the starting index of the specified substring in the String; otherwise, LastIndexOf returns –1.

There are three versions of LastIndexOf that search for substrings in a String. The first version takes a single argument—the substring for which to search. The second version takes two arguments—the substring for which to search and the highest index from which to begin searching backward for the substring. The third version of method LastIndexOf takes three arguments—the substring for which to search, the starting index from which to start searching backward and the number of characters to search. Figure 23.11 demonstrates the use of the three versions of LastIndexOf.

Method	Example Expression (assume strText = " My String")	Returns
LastIndexOf(*string*)	strText.LastIndexOf("n")	8
LastIndexOf(*string, integer*)	strText.LastIndexOf("n", 6)	-1
LastIndexOf(*string, integer, integer*)	strText.LastIndexOf("m", 7, 3)	-1

Figure 23.11   Demonstration of LastIndexOf methods.

SELF-REVIEW

1. Method _____ locates the first occurrence of a substring.

   a) IndexOf   b) FirstIndexOf
   c) FindFirst   d) Locate

2. The third argument passed to the LastIndexOf method is _____.

   a) the starting index from which to start searching backward
   b) the starting index from which to start searching forward
   c) the length of the substring to locate
   d) the number of characters to search

Answers: 1) a. 2) d.

23.5 Extracting Substrings from Strings

Once you've located a substring in a String, you might want to retrieve the substring from the String. The following box uses the Substring method to retrieve the price of the selected item from the HTML string.

Retrieving the Desired Item's Price

1. **Extracting the price.** Add lines 158–160 of Fig. 23.12 to the btnSearch_Click event handler. Class String provides two versions of the **Substring** method, each of which returns a new String object that contains a copy of a part of an existing String object.

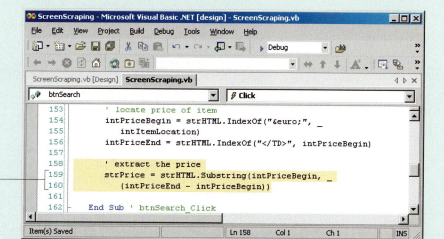

Extract price from strHTML

```
153          ' locate price of item
154          intPriceBegin = strHTML.IndexOf("&euro;", _
155             intItemLocation)
156          intPriceEnd = strHTML.IndexOf("</TD>", intPriceBegin)
157
158          ' extract the price
159          strPrice = strHTML.Substring(intPriceBegin, _
160             (intPriceEnd - intPriceBegin))
161
162       End Sub ' btnSearch_Click
```

Figure 23.12 Retrieving the desired price.

Lines 159–160 extract the price, using the version of the Substring method that takes two Integer arguments. The first argument (intPriceBegin), specifies the starting index from which the method copies characters from the original String.

The second argument (intPriceEnd - intPriceBegin) specifies the length of the substring to be copied. The substring returned (strPrice) contains a copy of the specified characters from the original String. In this case, the substring returned is the item's price (in Euros).

The other version of method Substring takes one Integer argument. The argument specifies the starting index from which the method copies characters in the original String.

The substring returned contains a copy of the characters from the starting index to the end of the String. We do not use this version of Substring in the **Screen Scraping** application.

2. **Saving the project.** Select **File > Save All** to save your modified code.

SELF-REVIEW

1. The Substring method _____.

   a) accepts either one or two arguments

   b) returns a new String object

   c) creates a String object by copying part of an existing String object

   d) All of the above.

2. The second argument passed to method Substring specifies _____.

   a) the last index of the String to copy   b) the length of the substring to copy

   c) the index from which to begin copying backwards

   d) a character which, when reached, signifies that copying should stop

Answers: 1) d. 2) b.

23.6 Replacing Substrings in `Strings`

You might want to replace certain characters in `Strings`. Class `String` provides the **Replace** method to replace occurrences of one substring with a different substring. The `Replace` method takes two arguments—a `String` to replace in the original `String` and a `String` with which to replace all occurrences of the first argument. Method `Replace` returns a new `String` with the specified replacements. The original `String` remains unchanged. If there are no occurrences of the first argument in the `String`, the method returns the original `String`. The following box uses method `Replace` to convert the extracted price from Euros to dollars.

Converting the Price to Dollars

1. *Converting the price.* Add lines 162–163 of Fig. 23.13 to `btnSearch_Click`. Line 163 converts the extracted price from Euros to dollars. For simplicity, we assume that dollars are equal to Euros.

   Therefore, to perform the conversion, we need change only the name of the currency. Line 163 uses `String` method `Replace` to return a new `String` object, replacing every occurrence (one in this example) in `strPrice` of substring `"&euro;"` with substring `"$"`. Notice that we assign the value returned from method `Replace` to `lblResult.Text` to display the text in dollars.

Replace `"&euro;"` with `"$"` ———

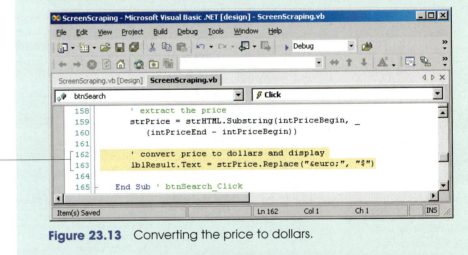

Figure 23.13 Converting the price to dollars.

2. *Saving the project.* Select **File > Save All** to save your modified code.

Method `Replace` also is used when the `Form` for the **Screen Scraping** application first loads. The following box uses method `Replace` to ensure that the HTML string displays correctly in a `Label`.

Displaying the HTML String

1. *Creating a Load event handler for the Form.* In **Design** view (**View > Designer**), double click the `Form` to generate an empty `Load` event handler. This event handler will execute when the application runs.

2. *Formatting the Load event handler.* Add the comments on lines 167 and 172 of Fig. 23.14 around event handler `FrmScreenScraping_Load`. Also, split the procedure header over three lines using line-continuation characters (that is, an underscores) as in lines 168–170 of Fig. 23.14 to improve its readability.

(cont.)

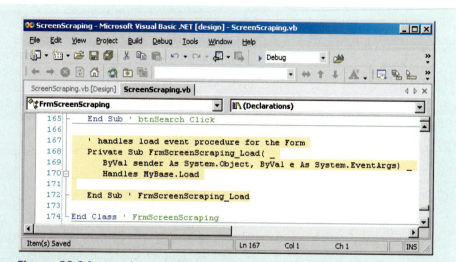

Figure 23.14   `Load` event for the `Form`.

3. **Displaying the HTML string in a Label.** Add lines 172–173 of Fig. 23.15 to event handler `FrmScreenScraping_Load`. Line 173 calls `String` method `Replace` to replace every occurrence of `"&euro;"` in the HTML string with `"&&euro;"`. As explained previously, the substring `"&euro;"` is the HTML for the Euro symbol. However, for this text to display in a `Label` correctly, we must prefix it with an additional ampersand (&) so the `"e"` in `"euro"` is not confused with an access shortcut. The value returned from method `Replace` is displayed in the `lblHTML` `Label`.

Replace all occurrences of "&euro" with "&&euro"

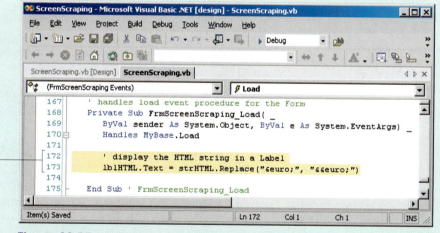

Figure 23.15   Displaying the HTML string in a `Label`.

4. **Running the application.** Select **Debug > Start** to run your application. Select the different items from the **Item** ComboBox, clicking the **Search** Button after each selection. Make sure that in each case, the proper price is extracted and displayed in dollar amounts.

5. **Closing the application.** Close your running application by clicking its close box.

6. **Closing the IDE.** Close Visual Studio .NET by clicking its close box.

1. If there are no occurrences of the substring in the `String`, method `Replace` returns
_____.

a) 0	b) -1
c) Nothing	d) the original `String`

Answer: 1) d.

23.7 Other String Methods

Class `String` provides several additional methods that allow you to manipulate `Strings`. Figure 23.16 lists some of these methods and provides a description of what each method does.

Method	Description	Sample Expression (assume `strText = " My String"`)
`EndsWith(`*string*`)`	Returns True if a String ends with the argument *string*; otherwise, returns `False`.	`strText.EndsWith("ing")` Returns: `True`

`Join(`*separator, array*`)`	Concatenates the elements in a String array, separated by the first argument. A new String containing the concatenated elements is returned.	`Dim strArray As String() = _`
		　`New String() {"a", "b", "c"}`
		
		 `String.Join(";", strArray)`
		
		 Returns: `"a;b;c"`

`Split()`	Splits the words in a String whenever a space is reached.	`Dim strArray As String() = _`
		　`strText.Split()`
		
		 Returns: `"My"` and `"String"` in an array of Strings

`StartsWith(`*string*`)`	Returns True if a String starts with argument *string*; otherwise, returns `False`.	`strText.StartsWith("Your")` Returns: `False`
`Trim()`	Removes any whitespace (that is, blank lines, spaces and tabs) from the beginning and end of a String.	`strText.Trim()` Returns: `"My String"`

Figure 23.16　Description of other `String` methods.

Figure 23.17 presents the source code for the **Screen Scraping** application. The lines of code that contain new programming concepts that you learned in this tutorial are highlighted.

```
1   Public Class FrmScreenScraping
2      Inherits System.Windows.Forms.Form
3
```

Figure 23.17　**Screen Scraping** application. (Part 1 of 2.)

```
4          ' Windows Form Designer generated code
5
6          ' String of HTML to extract prices from
7          Dim strHTML As String = "<HTML><BODY><TABLE>" & _
8             "<TR><TD>Antique Rocking Chair</TD>" & _
9             "<TD>&&euro;82.67</TD></TR>" & _
10            "<TR><TD>Silver Teapot</TD>" & _
11            "<TD>&&euro;64.55</TD></TR>" & _
12            "<TR><TD>Gold Pocket Watch</TD>" & _
13            "<TD>&&euro;128.83</TD></TR>" & _
14            "</TABLE></BODY></HTML>"
15
16         ' handles Search Button's Click event
17         Private Sub btnSearch_Click(ByVal sender As System.Object, _
18            ByVal e As System.EventArgs) Handles btnSearch.Click
19
20            Dim intItemLocation As Integer   ' index of desired item
21            Dim intPriceBegin As Integer     ' starting index of price
22            Dim intPriceEnd As Integer       ' ending index of price
23            Dim strPrice As String           ' extracted price
24
25            ' locate desired item
26            intItemLocation = strHTML.IndexOf( _
27               cboItems.SelectedItem.ToString())
28
29            ' locate price of item
30            intPriceBegin = strHTML.IndexOf("&euro;", _
31               intItemLocation)
32            intPriceEnd = strHTML.IndexOf("</TD>", intPriceBegin)
33
34            ' extract the price
35            strPrice = strHTML.Substring(intPriceBegin, _
36               (intPriceEnd - intPriceBegin))
37
38            ' convert price to dollars and display
39            lblResult.Text = strPrice.Replace("&euro;", "$")
40
41         End Sub ' btnSearch_Click
42
43         ' handles load event procedure for the Form
44         Private Sub FrmScreenScraping_Load( _
45            ByVal sender As System.Object, ByVal e As System.EventArgs) _
46            Handles MyBase.Load
47
48            ' display the HTML string in a Label
49            lblHTML.Text = strHTML.Replace("&euro;", "&&euro;")
50
51         End Sub ' FrmScreenScraping_Load
52
53      End Class ' FrmScreenScraping
```

Side annotations: Search for the SelectedItem in the String strHTML; Locate the beginning of the price in strHTML; Locate the end of the price in strHTML; Extract the price from strHTML; Replace "€" with "$"; Replace all occurrences of "&euro" with "&&euro"

Figure 23.17   Screen Scraping application. (Part 2 of 2.)

SELF-REVIEW   1. The _____ method removes all whitespace characters that appear at the beginning and end of a String.

a) RemoveSpaces
b) NoSpaces
c) Trim
d) Truncate

2. The StartsWith method returns _____ if a String begins with the String text passed to StartsWith as an argument.

   a) True   b) False

   c) 1   d) the index of the substring

Answers: 1) c. 2) a.

23.8 Wrap-Up

In this tutorial, we introduced you to class String from the System namespace. You learned how to create and manipulate String objects. You learned how to locate, retrieve and replace substrings in Strings. You reviewed several methods from class String and also learned additional methods. You applied your knowledge of Strings in Visual Basic .NET to create a simple **Screen Scraping** application that retrieved the price of an item from an HTML String.

    In the next tutorial, you will learn how data is represented in a computer. You will be introduced to the concepts of files and streams. You will learn how to store data in sequential-access files.

SKILLS SUMMARY

Determining the Size of a String
- Use String property Length.

Locating Substrings in Strings
- Use String method IndexOf to locate the first occurrence of a substring.
- Use String method LastIndexOf to locate the last occurrence of a substring.

Retrieving Substrings from Strings
- Use String method Substring with one argument to obtain a substring that begins at the specified starting index and contains the remainder of the original String.
- Use String method Substring with two arguments to specify the starting index and the length of the substring.

Replacing Substrings in Strings
- Use String method Replace to replace occurrences of one substring with another substring.
- Method Replace returns a new String containing the replacements.

Comparing Substrings to the Beginning or End of a String
- Use String method StartsWith to determine whether a String starts with a particular substring.
- Use String method EndsWith to determine whether a String ends with a particular substring.

Removing Whitespace from a String
- Use String method Trim to remove all whitespace characters that appear at the beginning and end of a String.

KEY TERMS

characters—Digits, letters and special symbols.

Chars property of class String—Returns the character located at a specific index in a String.

EndsWith method of class String—Determines if a String ends with a particular substring.

HTML (HyperText Markup Language)—A technology for describing Web content.

immutable—An object that cannot be changed after it is created. In Visual Basic .NET, Strings are immutable.

IndexOf method of class String—Returns the index of the first occurrence of a substring in a String. Returns -1 if the substring is not found.

Join method of class `String`—Concatenates the elements in a `String` array, separated by the first argument. A new `String` containing the concatenated elements is returned.

LastIndexOf method of class `String`—Returns the index of the last occurrence of a substring in a `String`. It returns -1 if the substring is not found.

literal `String` objects—A `String` constant written as a sequence of characters in double quotation marks (also called a string literal).

Replace method of class `String`—Returns a new `String` object in which every occurrence of a substring is replaced with a different substring.

screen scraping—The process of extracting desired information from the HTML that composes a Web page.

special characters—Characters that are neither digits or letters.

Split method of class `String`—Splits the words in a `String` whenever a space is reached.

StartsWith method of class `String`—Determines if a `String` starts with a particular substring.

string constant—A `String` constant written as a sequence of characters in double quotation marks (also called a string literal).

string literal—A `String` constant written as a sequence of characters in double quotation marks (also called a literal `String` object).

substring—A sequence of characters in a `String`.

Substring method of class `String`—Creates a new `String` object by copying part of an existing `String` object.

ToLower method of class `String`—Creates a new `String` object that replaces every uppercase letter in a `String` with its lowercase equivalent.

ToUpper method of class `String`—Creates a new `String` object that replaces every lowercase letter in a `String` with its uppercase equivalent.

Trim method of class `String`—Removes all whitespace characters from the beginning and end of a `String`.

CONTROLS, EVENTS, PROPERTIES & METHODS

String The `String` class represents a series of characters treated as a single unit.

■ *Property*

`Length`—Returns the number of characters in the `String`.

■ *Methods*

`EndsWith`—Determines if a `String` ends with a particular substring.

`Format`—Arranges the string in a specified format.

`IndexOf`—Returns the index of the specified character(s) in a `String`.

`Insert`—Returns a copy of the `String` for which it is called with the specified character(s) inserted.

`LastIndexOf`—Returns the index of the last occurrence of a substring in a `String`. It returns -1 if the substring is not found.

`PadLeft`—Inserts characters at the beginning of a `String`.

`Remove`—Returns a copy of the `String` for which it is called with the specified character(s) removed.

`Replace`—Returns a new `String` object in which every occurrence of a substring is replaced with a different substring.

`StartsWith`—Determines if a `String` starts with a particular substring.

`Substring`—Returns a substring from a `String`.

`ToLower`—Returns a copy of the `String` for which it is called with any uppercase letters converted to lowercase letters.

`ToUpper`—Creates a new `String` object that replaces every lowercase letter in a `String` with its uppercase equivalent.

`Trim`—Removes all whitespace characters from the beginning and end of a `String`.

MULTIPLE-CHOICE QUESTIONS

23.1 Extracting desired information from Web pages is called _____.

a) Web crawling

b) screen scraping

c) querying

d) redirection

23.2 If `IndexOf` method does not find the specified substring, it returns _____.

a) `False`

b) `0`

c) `-1`

d) None of the above.

23.3 The `String` class allows you to _____ `String`s.

a) search

b) retrieve characters from

c) replace characters in

d) All of the above.

23.4 _____ is a technology for describing Web content.

a) Class `String`

b) A `String` literal

c) HTML

d) A screen scraper

23.5 The `String` class is located in the _____ namespace.

a) `String`

b) `System.Strings`

c) `System.IO`

d) `System`

23.6 The _____ method creates a new `String` object by copying part of an existing `String` object.

a) `StringCopy`

b) `Substring`

c) `CopyString`

d) `CopySubString`

23.7 All `String` objects are _____.

a) the same size

b) always equal to each other

c) preceded by at least one whitespace character

d) immutable

23.8 The `IndexOf` method does not examine any characters that occur prior to the _____.

a) starting index

b) first match

c) last character of the `String`

d) None of the above.

23.9 The _____ method determines whether a `String` ends with a particular substring.

a) `CheckEnd`

b) `StringEnd`

c) `EndsWith`

d) `EndIs`

23.10 The `Trim` method removes all whitespace characters that appear _____ a `String`.

a) in

b) at the beginning of

c) at the end of

d) at the beginning and end of

EXERCISES

23.11 (*Supply Cost Calculator Application*) Write an application that calculates the cost of all the supplies added to the user's shopping list (Fig. 23.18). The application should contain two `ListBox`es. The first `ListBox` contains all the supplies offered and their respective prices. Users should be able to select the desired supplies from the first `ListBox` and add them to the second `ListBox`. Provide a **Calculate** `Button` that displays the total price for the user's shopping list (the contents of the second `ListBox`).

a) *Copying the template to your working directory.* Copy the directory `C:\Examples\Tutorial23\Exercises\SupplyCalculator` to your `C:\SimplyVB` directory.

b) *Opening the application's template file.* Double click `SupplyCalculator.sln` in the `SupplyCalculator` directory to open the application.

c) *Adding code to the Add >> Button.* Double click the **Add >>** `Button` to create an empty event handler. Add code to the event handler that adds the selected item from the first `ListBox` to the `lstStock` `ListBox`. Make sure to check that at least one item is selected in the first `ListBox` before attempting to add an item to the `lstStock` `ListBox`.

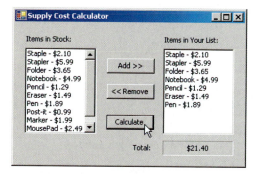

Figure 23.18 **Supply Cost Calculator** application's GUI.

d) *Enabling the Buttons.* Once the user adds something to the 1stStock ListBox, set the Enabled properties of the **<< Remove** and **Calculate** Buttons to True.

e) *Deselecting the items.* Once the items are added to the 1stStock ListBox, make sure that those items are deselected in the 1stSupply ListBox. Also, clear the **Total:** Label to indicate to the user that a new total price must be calculated.

f) *Adding code to the << Remove Button.* Double click the **<< Remove** Button to create an empty event handler. Use a Do While loop to remove any selected items in the 1stStock ListBox. Make sure to check that at least one item is selected before attempting to remove an item. [*Hint:* Method 1stStock.Items.RemoveAt(intIndex) will remove the item located at intIndex from the 1stStock ListBox.]

g) *Adding code to the Calculate Button.* Double click the **Calculate** Button to create an empty event handler. Use a For...Next statement to loop through all the items in the 1stStock ListBox. Convert each item from the ListBox into a String. Then use the String method Substring to extract the price of each item.

h) *Displaying the total.* Convert the String representing each item's price to a Decimal, and add this to the overall total (of type Decimal). Remember to output the value in currency format.

i) *Running the application.* Select **Debug > Start** to run your application. Use the **Add >>** and **<< Remove** Buttons to add and remove items from the **Items in Your List:** ListBox. Click the **Calculate** Button and verify that the total price displayed is correct.

j) *Closing the application.* Close your running application by clicking its close box.

k) *Closing the IDE.* Close Visual Studio .NET by clicking its close box.

23.12 (*Encryption Application*) Write an application that encrypts a message from the user (Fig. 23.19). The application should be able to encrypt the message in two different ways: substitution cipher and transposition cipher (both described below). The user should be able to enter the message in a TextBox and select the desired method of encryption. Display the encrypted message in a Label.

In a substitution cipher, every character in the English alphabet is represented by a different character in the substitution alphabet. Every time a letter occurs in the English sentence, it is replaced by the letter in the corresponding index of the substitution string. In a transposition cipher, two Strings are created. The first new String contains all the characters at the even indices of the input String. The second new String contains all of the characters at the odd indices. The new Strings are the encrypted text. For example a transposition cipher for the word "code" would be: "cd oe."

a) *Copying the template to your working directory.* Copy the directory C:\Examples\Tutorial23\Exercises\Encryption to your C:\SimplyVB directory.

b) *Opening the application's template file.* Double click Encryption.sln in the Encryption directory to open the application.

c) *Adding code to the Encrypt Button.* Double click the **Encrypt** Button to create an empty event handler.

d) *Determine the cipher method.* Use If...Then...Else statements to determine which method of encryption the user has selected and call the appropriate procedure.

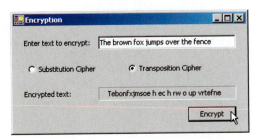

Figure 23.19 Encryption application's GUI.

e) *Locating the SubstitutionCipher method.* Locate the SubstitutionCipher procedure. The English and substitution alphabet Strings have been defined for you in this procedure.

f) *Converting the text input to lowercase.* Add code to the SubstitutionCipher method that uses the ToLower method of class String to make all the characters in the input string (txtPlainText.Text) lowercase.

g) *Performing the substitution encryption.* Use nested For...Next loops to iterate through each character of the input String. When each character from the input String is found in the String holding the English alphabet, replace the character in the input String with the character located at the same index in the substitution String.

h) *Display the String.* Now that the String has been substituted with all the corresponding cipher characters, assign the cipher String to the lblCipherText Label.

i) *Locating the TranspositionCipher method.* Locate the TranspositionCipher method. Define three variables—a counter variable and two Strings (each representing a word).

j) *Extracting the first word.* Use a Do While...Loop to retrieve all the "even" indices (starting from 0) from the input String. Increment the counter variable by 2 each time, and add the characters located at even indices to the first String created in *Step h*.

k) *Extracting the second word.* Use another Do While...Loop to retrieve all the "odd" indices (starting from 1) from the same input String. Increment the counter variable by 2, and add the characters at odd indices to the second String that you created in *Step h*.

l) *Output the result.* Add the two Strings together with a space in between, and output the result to the lblCipherText Label.

m) *Running the application.* Select **Debug > Start** to run your application. Enter text into the **Enter text to encrypt:** TextBox. Select the **Substitution Cipher** RadioButton and click the **Encrypt** Button. Verify that the output is the properly encrypted text using the substitution cipher. Select the **Transposition Cipher** RadioButton and click the **Encrypt** Button. Verify that the output is the properly encrypted text using the transposition cipher.

n) *Closing the application.* Close your running application by clicking its close box.

o) *Closing the IDE.* Close Visual Studio .NET by clicking its close box.

23.13 (*Anagram Game Application*) Write an **Anagram Game** that contains an array of pre-set words (Fig. 23.20). The game should randomly select a word and scramble its letters. A Label displays the scrambled word for the user to guess. If the user guesses correctly, display a message, and repeat the process with a different word. If the guess is incorrect, display a message, and let the user try again.

a) *Copying the template to your working directory.* Copy the directory C:\Examples\ Tutorial23\Exercises\Anagram to your C:\SimplyVB directory.

b) *Opening the application's template file.* Double click Anagram.sln in the Anagram directory to open the application.

c) *Locating the GenerateAnagram method.* Locate the GenerateAnagram method. It is the first method after the FrmAnagram_Load event handler.

Figure 23.20 **Anagram Game** application's GUI.

d) *Picking a random word.* Generate a random number to use as the index of the word in the m_strAnagram array. Retrieve word from the m_strAnagram array, using the first random number as an index. Store the word in another String variable. Generate a second random number to store the index of a character to be moved.

e) *Generate the scrambled word.* Use a For...Next statement to iterate through the word 20 times. Each time the loop executes, pass the second random number created in *Step c* to the Chars property of class String. Append the character returned by Chars to the end of the String, and remove it from its original position. Next, generate a new random number to move a different character during the next iteration of the loop. Remember to output the final word to the lblAnagram Label.

f) *Defining the Submit Button.* Double click the **Submit** Button to generate an empty event handler.

g) *Testing the user's input.* Use an If...Then...Else statement to determine whether the user's input matches the actual word. If the user is correct, clear and place the focus on the TextBox and generate a new word. Otherwise, select the user's text and place focus on the TextBox.

h) *Running the application.* Select **Debug > Start** to run your application. Submit correct answers and incorrect answers, and verify that the appropriate message is displayed each time.

i) *Closing the application.* Close your running application by clicking its close box.

j) *Closing the IDE.* Close Visual Studio .NET by clicking its close box.

What does this code do? **23.14** What is assigned to strResult when the following code executes?

```
1   Dim strWord1 As String = "CHORUS"
2   Dim strWord2 As String = "d i n o s a u r"
3   Dim strWord3 As String = "The theme is string."
4   Dim strResult As String
5
6   strResult = strWord1.ToLower()
7   strResult = strResult.Substring(4)
8   strWord2 = strWord2.Replace(" ", "")
9   strWord2 = strWord2.Substring(4, 4)
10  strResult = strWord2 & strResult
11
12  strWord3 = strWord3.Substring(strWord3.IndexOf(" ") + 1, 3)
13
14  strResult = strWord3.Insert(3, strResult)
```

What's wrong with this code? ▶ **23.15** This code should remove all commas from `strTest` and convert all lowercase letters to uppercase letters. Find the error(s) in the following code.

```
1   Dim strTest As String = "Bug,2,Bug"
2
3   strTest = strTest.ToUpper()
4   strTest = strTest.Replace("")
```

Programming Challenge ▶ **23.16** (*Pig Latin Application*) Write an application that encodes English language phrases into pig Latin (Fig. 23.21). Pig Latin is a form of coded language often used for amusement. Many variations exist in the methods used to form pig Latin phrases. For simplicity, use the following method to form the pig Latin words:

> *To form a pig Latin word from an English-language phrase, the translation proceeds one word at a time. To translate an English word into a pig Latin word, place the first letter of the English word (if it is not a vowel) at the end of the English word and add the letters "ay." If the first letter of the English word is a vowel, place it at the end of the word and add "y." Using this method, the word "jump" becomes "umpjay," the word "the" becomes "hetay" and the word "ace" becomes "ceay." Blanks between words remain blanks.*

Assume the following: The English phrase consists of words separated by blanks, there are no punctuation marks and all words have two or more letters. Enable the user to input a sentence. The `TranslateToPigLatin` method should translate the sentence into pig Latin, word by word. [*Hint*: You will need to use the `Join` and `Split` methods of class `String` demonstrated in Fig. 23.16 to form the pig Latin phrases].

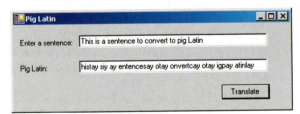

Figure 23.21   Pig Latin application.

a) *Copying the template to your working directory.* Copy the `C:\Examples\Tutorial23\Exercises\PigLatin` directory to your `C:\SimplyVB` directory.

b) *Opening the application's template file.* Double click `PigLatin.sln` in the `PigLatin` directory to open the application.

c) *Splitting the sentence.* Use method `Split` on the `String` passed to the `TranslateToPigLatin` method. Assign the result of this operation to `strWords`.

d) *Retrieving the word's first letter.* Declare a `For...Next` loop that iterates through your array of words. As you iterate through the array, store each word's first letter in `strTemporary`.

e) *Determining the suffix.* Use `If...Then...Else` statements to determine the suffix for each word. Store this suffix in `strSuffix`.

f) *Generating new words.* Generate the new words by arranging each word's pieces in the proper order.

g) *Returning the new sentence.* When the `For...Next` loop finishes, use method `Join` to combine all of the elements in `strWords`, and `Return` the new pig Latin sentence.

h) *Running the application.* Select **Debug > Start** to run your application. Enter a sentence and click the **Translate** Button. Verify that the sentence is correctly converted into pig Latin.

i) *Closing the application.* Close your running application by clicking its close box.

j) *Closing the IDE.* Close Visual Studio .NET by clicking its close box.

Ticket Information Application

Introducing Sequential-Access Files

Y ou have used variables and arrays to store data temporarily—the data is lost when a method or application terminates. When you want to store data for a longer period of time, you can use **files**, which are collections of data that are given a name such as data.txt or Welcome.sln. Data in files exists even after the application that created the data terminates. Such data often is called **persistent data**. Computers store these files on **secondary storage media**, including magnetic disks (for example, the hard drive of your computer), optical disks (for instance, CD-ROMs or DVDs) and magnetic tapes (which are similar to music cassette tapes).

File processing, which includes creating, reading from, writing to and updating files, is an important capability of Visual Basic .NET. It enables Visual Basic .NET to support commercial applications that typically process massive amounts of persistent data. In this tutorial, you will learn about **sequential-access files**, which contain information that is read from a file in the order that it was originally written to the file. You will learn how to create, open and write to a sequential-access file by building a **Write Event** application. This application allows the user to create or open a **text file** (a file containing human-readable characters) and to input the date, time and description of a community event (such as a concert or a sporting match).

You will then learn how to read data from a file by building the **Ticket Information** application. This application displays data from a file called calendar.txt created by the **Write Event** application.

24.1 Test-Driving the Ticket Information Application

Many communities and businesses use computer applications to allow their members and customers to view information about upcoming events, such as movies, concerts, sports and other activities. The **Write Event** application that you build in Section 24.4 writes the community event information to a sequential-access file. The **Ticket Information** application that you build in this tutorial displays the data stored in the file generated by the **Write Event** application. This application must meet the following requirements:

Application Requirements

A local town has asked you to write an application that allows its residents to view community events for the current month. Events taking place in the town include concerts, sporting events, movies and other forms of entertainment. When the user selects a date, the application must indicate whether there are events scheduled for that day. The application must list the scheduled events and allow the user to select a listed event. When the user selects an event, the application must display the time and price of the event and a brief description of the event. The community event information is stored in a sequential-access file named calendar.txt.

Your application will allow a user to select a date from a **MonthCalendar** control. Then the application will open the `calendar.txt` file and read its contents to display information about events scheduled for the selected date. You begin by test-driving the completed application. Then, you will learn the additional Visual Basic .NET technologies that you will need to create your own version of this application.

Test-Driving the Ticket Information Application	1. ***Opening the completed application.*** Open the directory `C:\Examples\Tutorial24\CompletedApplication\TicketInformation` to location the **Ticket Information** application. Double click `TicketInformation.sln` to open the application in Visual Studio .NET.

2. ***Running the Ticket Information application.*** Select **Debug > Start** to run the application (Fig. 24.1). The calendar will look different, depending on the date that you test-drive this application. The calendar should reflect the day and month on which you actually run the application. The **MonthCalendar** control is similar to the **DateTimePicker** control (Tutorial 14), except that **MonthCalendar** allows you to select a range of dates, whereas the **DateTimePicker** allows you to select the time, but no more than one date. For simplicity, users of this application should select only one date. In addition, the application deals only with the current month, but the **MonthCalendar** control does allow the user to view calendars of previous or future months by using the arrow buttons.

Arrow buttons allow user to scroll through months

MonthCalendar control

ComboBox lists any events

TextBox displays event details

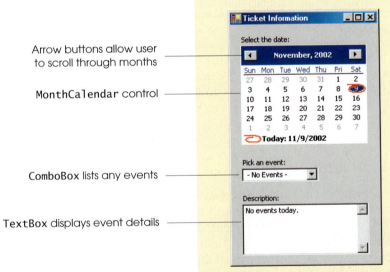

Figure 24.1 **Ticket Information** application's GUI.

(cont.)

3. **Getting event information.** Select the 18th day of the current month in the MonthCalendar. Notice that the ComboBox displays the message "- No Events -" (Fig. 24.2). This is because there are no events scheduled for the 18th. Select the 19th day of the month. Notice that the ComboBox now displays "- Events -". Click the ComboBox to view the scheduled events and select **Comedy club**. The time, price and description of the event appear in the **Description:** TextBox (Fig. 24.2).

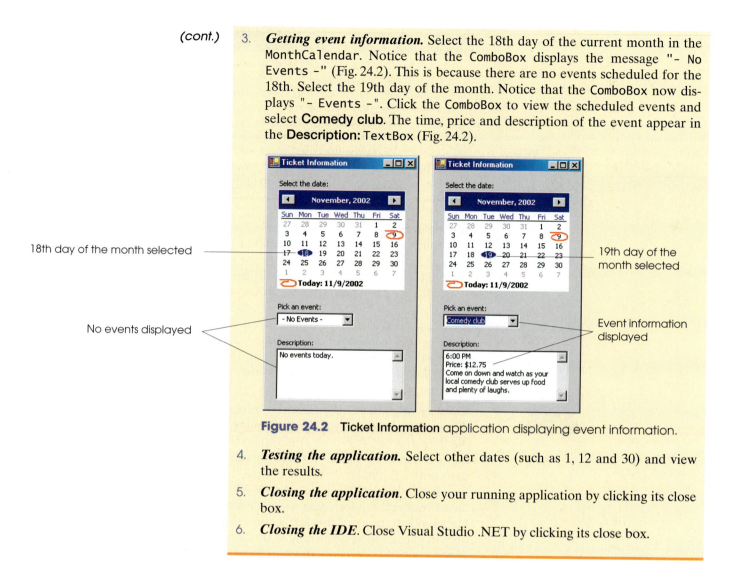

18th day of the month selected

No events displayed

19th day of the month selected

Event information displayed

Figure 24.2 **Ticket Information** application displaying event information.

4. **Testing the application.** Select other dates (such as 1, 12 and 30) and view the results.

5. **Closing the application.** Close your running application by clicking its close box.

6. **Closing the IDE.** Close Visual Studio .NET by clicking its close box.

SELF-REVIEW

1. The _____ control allows a user to select a range of dates.
   a) DateTimePicker
   b) MonthCalender
   c) ComboBox
   d) TextBox

2. The MonthCalendar control is similar to the _____ control.
   a) DateTimePicker
   b) ComboBox
   c) TextBox
   d) Timer

Answers: 1) b. 2) a.

24.2 Data Hierarchy

Data items processed by computers form a **data hierarchy** (Fig. 24.3) in which data items become larger and more complex in structure as they progress from bits, to characters, to fields and to larger data structures.

Throughout this book, you have been manipulating data in your applications. The data has been in several forms: **decimal digits** (0, 1, 2, 3, 4, 5, 6, 7, 8 and 9), **letters** (A–Z and a–z) and **special symbols** ($, @, %, &, *, (,), -, +, ", :, ?, / and many others). Digits, letters and special symbols are referred to as **characters**. The set of all characters used to write applications and represent data items on a particular computer is called that computer's **character set**.

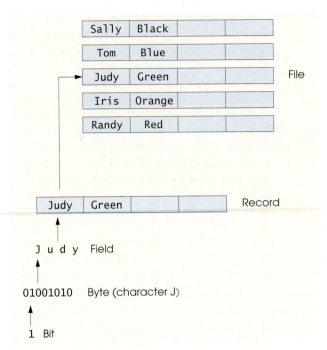

Figure 24.3 Data hierarchy.

The computer's character set is readable and understandable by humans. Ultimately, however, all data items processed by a computer are reduced to combinations of zeros and ones. The smallest data item that computers support is called a **bit**. "Bit" is short for "**binary digit**"—a digit that can be one of two values. Each data item, or bit, can be set only to the value 0 or the value 1. Computer circuitry performs various simple bit manipulations, such as examining the value of a bit, setting the value of a bit and reversing the value of a bit (from 1 to 0 or from 0 to 1). This approach has been adopted because it is simple and economical to build electronic devices that can assume two stable states—0 representing one state and 1 representing the other. It is remarkable that the extensive functions performed by computers involve only the most fundamental manipulations of 0s and 1s.

Because computers can process only 0s and 1s, every character in a computer's character set is represented as a pattern of 0s and 1s. **Bytes** are composed of 8 bits. Characters in Visual Basic .NET are **Unicode** characters, which are composed of 2 bytes. Programming with data in the low-level form of bits is difficult, so programmers create applications and data items with characters, and computers manipulate and process these characters as patterns of bits.

Just as characters are composed of bits, **fields** are composed of characters. A field is a group of characters that conveys some meaning. For example, a field consisting of uppercase and lowercase letters can represent a person's name.

Typically, a **record** (which usually is represented as a Class in Visual Basic .NET) is a collection of several related fields (called member variables in Visual Basic .NET). In a payroll system, for example, a record for a particular employee might include the following fields:

1. Employee identification number
2. Name
3. Address
4. Hourly pay rate
5. Number of exemptions claimed
6. Year-to-date earnings
7. Amount of taxes withheld

Thus, a record is a group of related fields. In the preceding example, each field is associated with the same employee. A **file** is a group of related records. A company's payroll file normally contains one record for each employee. Hence, a payroll file for a small company might contain only 22 records, whereas a payroll file for a large company might contain 100,000 records. It is not unusual for a company to have many files, some containing millions, billions or even trillions of characters of information.

To facilitate the retrieval of specific records from a file, at least one field in each record is chosen as a **record key**. A record key identifies a record as belonging to a particular person or entity and distinguishes that record from all other records. Therefore, the record key must be unique. In the payroll record just described, the employee identification number normally would be chosen as the record key because each employee's identification number is different.

There are many ways to organize records in a file. The most common type of organization is called a sequential file, in which records typically are stored in order by a record-key field. In a payroll file, records usually are placed in order by employee identification number. The first employee record in the file contains the lowest employee identification number, and subsequent records contain increasingly higher employee identification numbers.

Most businesses use many different files to store data. For example, a company might have payroll files, accounts receivable files (listing money due from clients), accounts payable files (listing money due to suppliers), inventory files (listing facts about all the items handled by the business) and many other types of files. Sometimes, a group of related files is called a **database**. A collection of programs designed to create and manage databases is called a **database management system** (DBMS). You will learn about databases in Tutorial 25.

SELF-REVIEW

1. The smallest data item a computer can process is called a _____.

   a) database   b) byte

   c) file   d) bit

2. A _____ is a group of related records.

   a) file   b) field

   c) bit   d) byte

Answers: 1) d. 2) a.

24.3 Files and Streams

Visual Basic .NET actually views each file as a sequential **stream** of bytes (Fig. 24.4). When a file is opened, Visual Basic .NET creates an object and associates a stream with that object.

Figure 24.4   Visual Basic .NET's conceptual view of an *n*-byte file.

Common Programming Error

Having a `StreamReader` and `StreamWriter` object open for the same file at the same time causes an error because both objects are attempting to access the same file at the same time.

To perform file processing in Visual Basic .NET, namespace `System.IO` must be imported. This namespace includes definitions of stream classes such as **Stream-Reader** (for text input from a file) and **StreamWriter** (for text output to a file).

24.4 Writing to a File: Creating the Write Event Application

An important aspect of the **Ticket Information** application is its ability to read data sequentially from a file. You will need to create the file from which the **Ticket Infor-**

mation application will read its data. Therefore, before you create the **Ticket Information** application, you must learn how to write to a file sequentially.

The **Write Event** application should enable the user to create a new file or open an existing file. The user might want to create a new file for events or update an existing file by adding more event information. You will add this functionality in the following box.

Adding a Dialog to Open or Create a File	1. ***Copying the template to your working directory.*** Copy the `C:\Examples\Tutorial24\TemplateApplication\WriteEvent` directory to your `C:\SimplyVB` directory.

2. ***Opening the Write Event application's template file.*** Double click `WriteEvent.sln` in the `WriteEvent` directory to open the application in Visual Studio .NET.

3. ***Adding a dialog to the Form.*** The application uses the **OpenFileDialog** control to customize the **Open** dialog. To add an `OpenFileDialog` component to the application, double click the `OpenFileDialog` control

    ![OpenFileDialog icon]

    in the **Windows Forms** tab of the **Toolbox**. Change the control's Name property to `objOpenFileDialog`. Change its **FileName** property to `calendar.txt`, which will be the default file name displayed in the **Open** dialog. [*Note:* This is the name of the file from which the **Ticket Information** application retrieves information.] The **Open** dialog normally allows the user to open only existing files, but you also want the user to be able to create a file. For this reason, set property **CheckFileExists** to `False` so that the **Open** dialog allows the user to specify a new file name. If the user specifies a file that does not exist, the file is created and opened. Figure 24.5 shows the application in design view after the `OpenFileDialog` control has been added and renamed. |

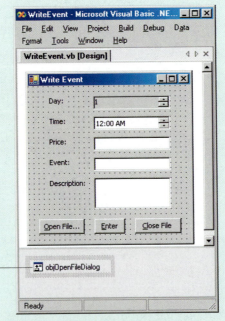

OpenFileDialog control

Figure 24.5 `OpenFileDialog` added and renamed.

4. ***Saving the project.*** Select **File > Save All** to save your modified code.

The **Write Event** application stores the user-input information in a text file. It expects the user to open or create a file with the extension .txt. If the user does not do so, the application displays an error message. The following box guides you through adding this functionality.

Determining Whether a File Name Is Valid

1. ***Adding the header for method CheckValidity.*** Add lines 213–217 of Fig. 24.6 to the application. Method CheckValidity receives a file name as a String and returns a Boolean value. If the file name is valid, the Function returns True. Otherwise, the Function returns False.

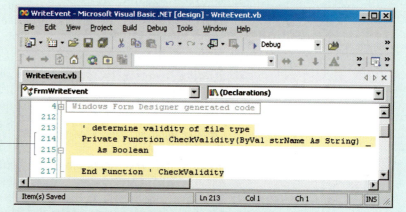

CheckValidity Function procedure header

Figure 24.6   Method CheckValidity header.

2. ***Displaying a MessageBox to indicate an invalid file name.*** Add lines 217–224 of Fig. 24.7 to method CheckValidity. String method EndsWith (line 218) returns False if strName does not end with .txt, the extension that indicates a text file. Lines 219–221 display a MessageBox informing the user that the application expects a text file.

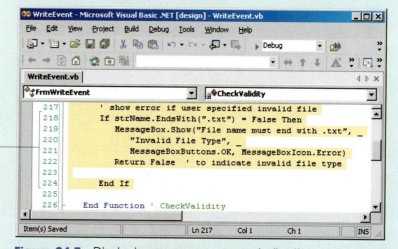

Displaying error message if incorrect file type is provided

Figure 24.7   Displaying an error message indicating an invalid file name.

3. ***Receiving a valid file name.*** Add lines 224–229 of Fig. 24.8 to the If...Then statement. If a valid file name is entered, method CheckValidity should return True. The GUI should indicate that the user cannot create or open another file, but the user may enter data into the file or close the file. For this reason, line 226 disables the **Open File...** Button, while lines 227–228 enable the **Enter** and **Close File** Buttons, respectively. The method returns True (line 229) to indicate that the user entered a valid file name.

(cont.)

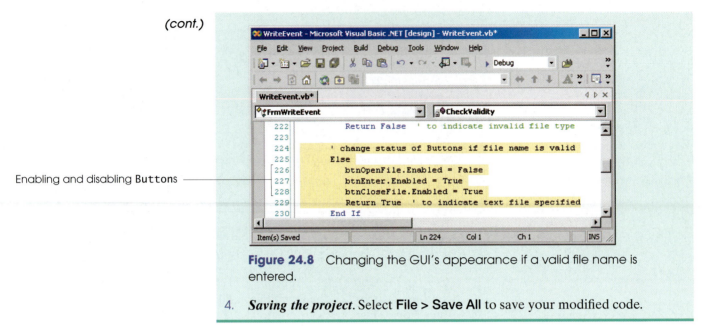

Enabling and disabling Buttons ⟶

Figure 24.8   Changing the GUI's appearance if a valid file name is entered.

4. *Saving the project.* Select **File > Save All** to save your modified code.

You have added the OpenFileDialog control to allow users to open a file and a method that determines whether the user has entered a valid file name. Now you will add code that associates the specified file with a stream.

Creating a StreamWriter Object

1. *Importing namespace System.IO to enable file processing.* To access the classes and methods that will enable you to perform file processing with sequential-access files, you must import namespace System.IO. Accordingly, add line 1 of Fig. 24.9.

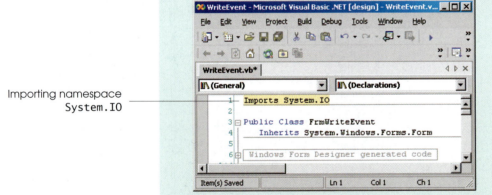

Importing namespace System.IO ⟶

Figure 24.9   System.IO namespace imported into FrmWriteEvent class.

2. *Declaring a StreamWriter variable.* Namespace System.IO includes class StreamWriter, which is used to create objects for writing text to a file. You will use a StreamWriter to write data into the file created or opened by the user. Add line 6 of Fig. 24.10 to the FrmWriteEvent class definition to declare the variable that will be assigned a StreamWriter object.

(cont.)

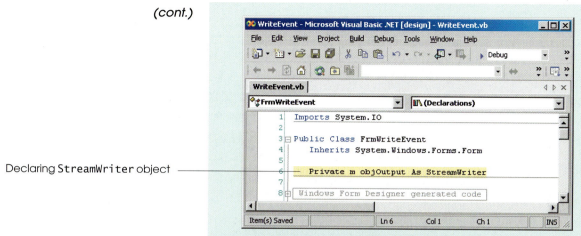

Figure 24.10 Declaring a StreamWriter object.

Declaring StreamWriter object

3. ***Creating the Open File... Button's Click event handler.*** Switch to Design view and double click the **Open File...** Button on the **Write Event** application's Form (Fig. 24.11) to create the empty btnOpenFile_Click event handler.

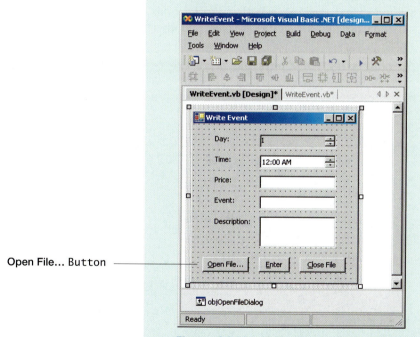

Open File... Button

Figure 24.11 **Write Event** application Form in design view.

4. ***Displaying the Open dialog.*** Add lines 242–251 of Fig. 24.12 to the event handler. When the user clicks the **Open File...** Button, the **ShowDialog** method of the OpenFileDialog control displays the **Open** dialog to allow the user to open a file (line 243). If the user specifies a file that does not exist, it will be created. The user can use the default file name (calendar.txt) or specify another file name. Line 243 assigns the return value of method ShowDialog to a DialogResult variable named result. Be sure to add the comments and line-continuation characters as shown in Fig. 24.12 so that the line numbers in your code match those presented in this tutorial.

(cont.)

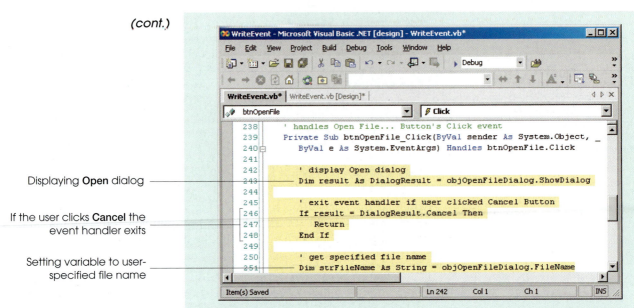

Displaying **Open** dialog

If the user clicks **Cancel** the event handler exits

Setting variable to user-specified file name

Figure 24.12   Displaying the **Open** dialog and retrieving the result.

5. *Exiting event handler if the user clicks the Cancel Button*. Consider Fig. 24.12. The value of the `DialogResult` variable specifies whether the user clicked the **Cancel** Button in the **Open** dialog. If the user did so, the event handler exits (line 247). At this point, the user can still open or create a file by clicking the enabled **Open File...** Button again.

6. *Retrieving the file name*. Property `FileName` of `OpenFileDialog` specifies the file name that the user selected (line 251 of Fig. 24.12). The application stores the path and file name in `strFileName`. The file name will be tested to determine whether it is valid and then used to initialize the Stream-Writer object.

7. *Checking for a valid file type*. Add lines 253–258 of Fig. 24.13 to the event handler. Line 254 invokes method `CheckValidity` (which you defined in earlier in this tutorial) to determine whether the specified file is a text file (that is, the file name ends with ".txt").

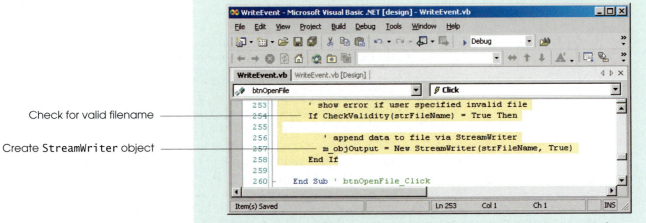

Check for valid filename

Create `StreamWriter` object

Figure 24.13   Validating the filename and initializing a `StreamWriter` object.

(cont.)

Common Programming Error

When you open an existing file by invoking the StreamWriter constructor with a False second argument, data previously contained in the file will be lost.

8. *Initializing a StreamWriter object.* The call to the StreamWriter constructor (line 257) initializes StreamWriter object m_objOutput, which will be used to write to the new file specified by the user. Notice that the StreamWriter constructor takes two arguments. The first indicates the name of the file (specified by variable strFileName) to which you will write information. The second is a Boolean value that determines whether the StreamWriter will append information to the end of the file. You pass value True, so that any information written to the file will be appended to the end of the file.

9. *Saving the project.* Select **File > Save All** to save your modified code.

Now that the application can open a file, the user can input information that will be written to that file. In the following box, you will add code that makes the **Enter** Button's Click event handler write the data to the text file.

Writing Information to a Sequential-Access File

1. *Clearing user input from the TextBoxes and resetting the NumericUpDown control.* Add lines 262–268 of Fig. 24.14 to the application below the btnOpenFile_Click event handler. After the user's input is processed, the **Enter** Button's event handler will invoke method ClearUserInput to clear the TextBoxes and to reset the NumericUpDown control's value to 1 (the first day of the month).

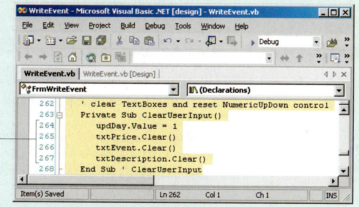

Clearing user input

Figure 24.14 Clearing user input.

2. *Creating the btnEnter_Click event handler.* In design view, double click the **Enter** Button to add the btnEnter_Click event handler.

3. *Defining the btnEnter_Click event handler.* Add lines 274–280 of Fig. 24.15 to the event handler. Lines 275–279 write the user input line by line to the file by using the StreamWriter's **WriteLine** method. The WriteLine method writes its argument to the file, followed by a newline character. The information is written to the file in the following order: day of the event, time, price, event name and description. Each piece of information is written on a separate line of the file. Line 280 invokes the ClearUserInput procedure that you defined in *Step 1* of this box. Be sure to add the comments and line-continuation characters as shown in Fig. 24.15 so that the line numbers in your code match those presented in this tutorial.

(cont.)

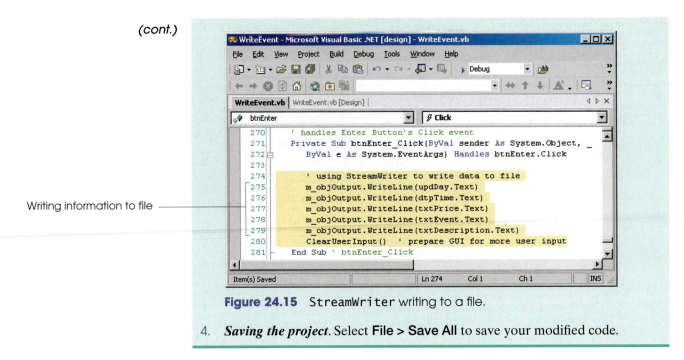

Figure 24.15 StreamWriter writing to a file.

4. *Saving the project.* Select **File > Save All** to save your modified code.

You should close the connection to the file after you have finished processing it. You will add this capability to the **Close File** Button's Click event handler in the following box.

Closing the StreamWriter

1. *Create the btnClose_Click event handler.* In Design view, double click the **Close File** Button of the **Write Event** application's Form. The btnClose_Click event handler appears in the WriteEvent.vb file.

2. *Defining the btnClose_Click event handler.* Add lines 287–292 of Fig. 24.16 to the event handler. Line 287 uses the StreamWriter's **Close** method to close the stream. Line 290 reenables the **Open File...** Button in case the user would like to create or update another sequential-access file. Lines 291–292 disable the **Enter** and **Close File** Buttons because users should not be able to click these Buttons when a file is not open.

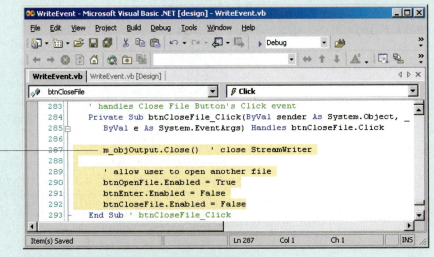

Figure 24.16 Closing the StreamWriter.

3. *Saving the project.* Select **File > Save All** to save your modified code.

You have now successfully created the **Write Event** application. You will test this application to see how it works and will view the file contents in the following box.

---

1. ***Running the Write Event application.*** Select **Debug > Start** to run your application (Fig. 24.17).

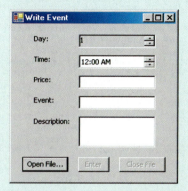

Figure 24.17 **Write Event** application running.

2. ***Creating a file.*** Click the **Open File...** Button to create the file to which you will write. The **Open** dialog appears. Browse to the directory C:\Examples\ Tutorial24\TemplateApplication\TicketInformation\bin (Fig. 24.18). [*Note:* An existing calendar.txt file should appear in the **Open** dialog.] The file name calendar.txt should be displayed in the **File name:** field, as in Fig. 24.18. The **File name:** field may not display the extension (.txt), or calendar may be displayed with a capital "C" based on your computer's settings. Click the **Open** Button. This will open the existing calendar.txt file.

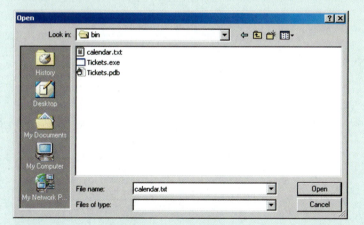

Figure 24.18 **Open** dialog displaying contents of the template **Ticket Information** application's bin folder.

3. ***Inputting event information.*** In the **Day:** NumericUpDown control, select 4 to indicate that the event is scheduled on the fourth day of the month. Enter 2:30 PM in the **Time:** DateTimePicker. Type 12.50 in the **Price:** TextBox. Enter Arts and Crafts Fair in the **Event:** TextBox. In the **Description:** TextBox, enter the information Take part in creating various types of arts and crafts at this fair. Click the **Enter** Button to add this event's information to the calendar.txt file.

4. ***Inputting more event information.*** Write more event information to the file by repeating *Step 3* with your own set of events.

(cont.)

5. ***Closing the file.*** When you have entered all the events you wish, click the **Close File** Button. This closes the `calendar.txt` file and prevents any more events from being written.

6. ***Closing the application.*** Close your running application by clicking its close box.

7. ***Opening and closing the sequential-access file.*** Use Visual Studio .NET to open `calendar.txt`. Select **File > Open > File...** to display the **Open** dialog. Select the `calendar.txt` file that you created and click **Open**. Scroll down towards the bottom of the file. The information you entered in *Step* 3 should appear in the file, similar to Fig. 24.19. Close the `calendar.txt` file.

Day and time of event, ticket price, event name and description ——

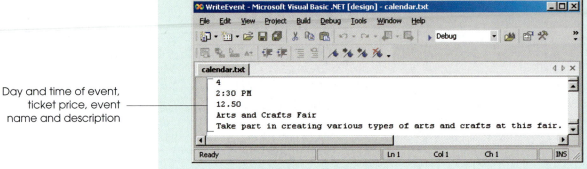

Figure 24.19   Sequential-access file generated by **Write Event** application.

8. ***Closing the IDE.*** Close Visual Studio .NET by clicking its close box.

Figure 24.20 presents the source code for the **Write Event** application. The lines of code that contain new programming concepts that you have learned so far in this tutorial are highlighted.

Importing a namespace System.IO ——

StreamWriter that will write text to a file ——

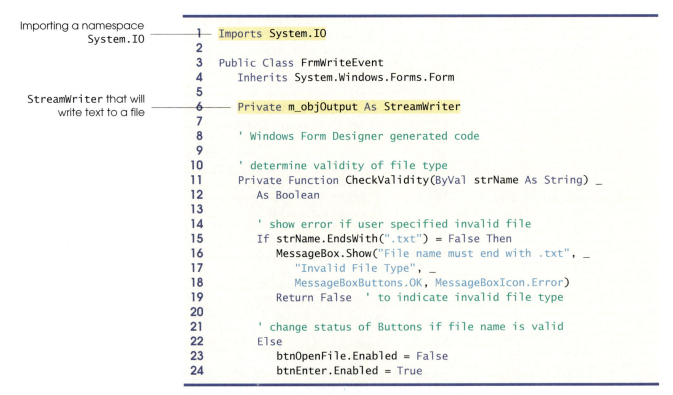

```
1   Imports System.IO
2
3   Public Class FrmWriteEvent
4       Inherits System.Windows.Forms.Form
5
6       Private m_objOutput As StreamWriter
7
8       ' Windows Form Designer generated code
9
10      ' determine validity of file type
11      Private Function CheckValidity(ByVal strName As String) _
12          As Boolean
13
14          ' show error if user specified invalid file
15          If strName.EndsWith(".txt") = False Then
16              MessageBox.Show("File name must end with .txt", _
17                  "Invalid File Type", _
18                  MessageBoxButtons.OK, MessageBoxIcon.Error)
19              Return False  ' to indicate invalid file type
20
21          ' change status of Buttons if file name is valid
22          Else
23              btnOpenFile.Enabled = False
24              btnEnter.Enabled = True
```

Figure 24.20   **Write Event** application's code. (Part 1 of 3.)

```
25              btnCloseFile.Enabled = True
26              Return True   ' to indicate text file specified
27           End If
28
29        End Function ' CheckValidity
30
31        ' handles Open File... Button's Click event
32        Private Sub btnOpenFile_Click(ByVal sender As System.Object, _
33           ByVal e As System.EventArgs) Handles btnOpenFile.Click
34
35           ' display Open dialog
36           Dim result As DialogResult = objOpenFileDialog.ShowDialog
37
38           ' exit event handler if user clicked Cancel Button
39           If result = DialogResult.Cancel Then
40              Return
41           End If
42
43           ' get specified filename
44           Dim strFileName As String = objOpenFileDialog.FileName
45
46           ' show error if user specified invalid file
47           If CheckValidity(strFileName) = True Then
48
49              ' append data to file via StreamWriter
50              m_objOutput = New StreamWriter(strFileName, True)
51           End If
52
53        End Sub ' btnOpenFile_Click
54
55        ' clear TextBoxes and reset NumericUpDown control
56        Private Sub ClearUserInput()
57           updDay.Value = 1
58           txtPrice.Clear()
59           txtEvent.Clear()
60           txtDescription.Clear()
61        End Sub ' ClearUserInput
62
63        ' handles Enter Button's Click event
64        Private Sub btnEnter_Click(ByVal sender As System.Object, _
65           ByVal e As System.EventArgs) Handles btnEnter.Click
66
67           ' using StreamWriter to write data to file
68           m_objOutput.WriteLine(updDay.Text)
69           m_objOutput.WriteLine(dtpTime.Text)
70           m_objOutput.WriteLine(txtPrice.Text)
71           m_objOutput.WriteLine(txtEvent.Text)
72           m_objOutput.WriteLine(txtDescription.Text)
73           ClearUserInput()   ' prepare GUI for more user input
74        End Sub ' btnEnter_Click
75
76        ' handles Close File Button's Click event
77        Private Sub btnCloseFile_Click(ByVal sender As System.Object, _
78           ByVal e As System.EventArgs) Handles btnCloseFile.Click
79
80           m_objOutput.Close()   ' close StreamWrit
81
```

Annotations (left margin):
- Retrieve user input from **Open** dialog → line 36
- Storing filename entered by user → line 44
- Create StreamWriter object to associate a stream with the user-specified text file → line 50
- Append data to end of file → lines 68–72
- Closing the file's associated stream → line 80

Figure 24.20   **Write Event** application's code. (Part 2 of 3.)

```
82            ' allow user to open another file
83            btnOpenFile.Enabled = True
84            btnEnter.Enabled = False
85            btnCloseFile.Enabled = False
86         End Sub ' btnCloseFile_Click
87
88   End Class ' FrmWriteEvent
```

Figure 24.20 **Write Event** application's code. (Part 3 of 3.)

24.5 Building the Ticket Information Application

Now that you have created the **Write Event** application to enable a user to write community-event information to a sequential-access text file, you will create the **Ticket Information** application you test-drove at the beginning of the tutorial. First you need to analyze the application. The following pseudocode describes the basic operation of the **Ticket Information** application:

```
When the Form loads:
    Display the current day's events

When the user selects a date on the calendar:
    Display the selected day's events

When the user selects an event from the Pick an event: ComboBox:
    Retrieve index of selected item in the Pick an event: ComboBox
    Display event information in the Description: TextBox

When procedure CreateEventList is called:
    Extract data for the current day from calendar.txt
    Clear the Pick an event: ComboBox

    If events are scheduled for that day
        Add each event to the Pick an event: ComboBox
        DIsplay "- Events -" in the Pick an event: ComboBox
        Display "Pick an event." in the Description: TextBox
    Else
        DIsplay "- No Events -" in the Pick an event: ComboBox
        Display "No events today." in the Description: TextBox

When procedure ExtractData is called:
    Retrieve the selected date from the calendar
    Open calendar.txt file for reading
    Read the first line of the file

    While there are events left in the file and the number of events is less than 10

        If the current event is for the day selected by the user
            Store the event information
            Increment the number of events for the selected day
        Else
            Move to the beginning of the next record in the file
        Read the next line of the file
```

Now that you have test-driven the **Ticket Information** application and studied its pseudocode representation, you will use an ACE table to help you convert the pseudocode to Visual Basic .NET. Figure 24.21 lists the actions, controls and events that will help you complete your own version of this application.

Action/Control/Event (ACE) Table for the Ticket Information Application

Action	Control	Event/Method
Label the application's controls	lblDay, lblTime, lblPrice, lblEvent, lblDescription	Application is run
	FrmEvents	Load
Display the current day's events		
	mvwDate	DateChanged
Display the selected day's events		
	cboEvent	Selected-IndexChanged
Retrieve index of selected item in the Pick an event: ComboBox	cboEvent	
Display event information in the Description: TextBox	txtDescription	
		Create-EventList
Extract data for the current day		
Clear the Pick an event: ComboBox	cboEvent	
If events are scheduled for that day Add each event to the Pick an event: ComboBox	cboEvent, m_strData	
DIsplay "- Events -" in the Pick an event: ComboBox	cboEvent	
Display "No events today." in the Description: TextBox	txtDescription	
Else DIsplay "- No Events -" in the Pick an event: ComboBox	cboEvent	
Display "No events today." in the Description: TextBox	txtDescription	
		ExtractData
Retrieve the selected date from the calendar	mvwDate	
Open calendar.txt file for reading	objInput	
Read the first line of the file	objInput	
While there are events left in the file and the number of events is less than 10	objInput	
If the current event is for the day selected by the user Store the event information	m_strData, strLine, objInput	
Increment the number of events for the selected day		
Else Move to the beginning of the next record in the file	objInput	
Read the next line of the file	objInput	

Figure 24.21 ACE table for the **Ticket Information** application.

The **Ticket Information** application allows the user to view the information for a specific date by selecting the date from a MonthCalendar control. The following box guides you through configuring the MonthCalendar control.

Adding a *MonthCalendar Control*	1. ***Copying the template to your working directory.*** Copy the C:\Examples\ Tutorial24\TemplateApplication\TicketInformation directory to your C:\SimplyVB directory.
	2. ***Opening the Ticket Information template application.*** Double click TicketInformation.sln in the TicketInformation directory to open the application in Visual Studio .NET (Fig. 24.22). The template provides the empty methods CreateEventList and ExtractData. You will add code to these methods later.

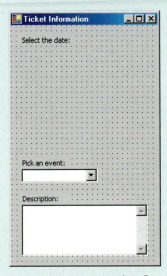

Figure 24.22 MonthCalendar template application's Form.

3. ***Add a MonthCalendar control to the Form.*** Double click the MonthCalendar control

in the **Windows Form** tab of the **Toolbox**. The **Properties** window should display the control's properties. Change the Name property to mvwDate. Set the Location of the MonthCalendar control to 16, 32.

4. ***Saving the project.*** Select **File > Save All** to save your modified code.

![icon] **Good Programming Practice**

Prefix the names of MonthCalendar controls with mvw.

Now that you have added the MonthCalendar control, you can begin writing code for the **Ticket Information** application. For this application, you will define two Sub procedures named CreateEventList and ExtractData. Before adding any functionality to the application, you will import System.IO and create two instance variables in the next box.

Beginning to Build the *Ticket Information* *Application*	1. ***Importing namespace System.IO.*** Switch to Code view. You must import namespace System.IO to allow the application to use class StreamReader to read information from a sequential-access file. Accordingly, add line 1 of Fig. 24.23 before the class definition.

(cont.)

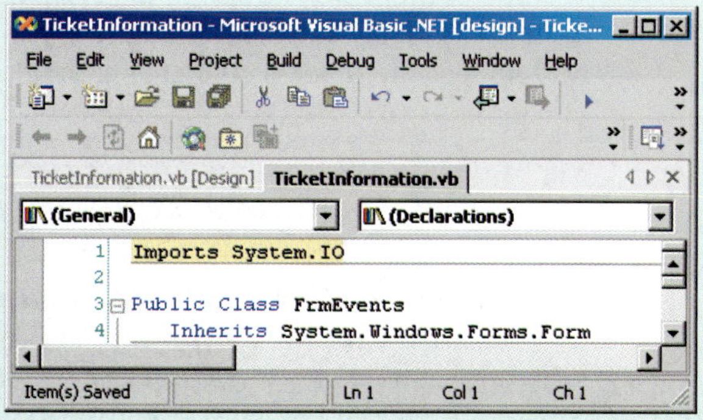

Figure 24.23   `System.IO` namespace imported to `FrmEvents`.

2. *Adding instance variables.* Add lines 6–10 of Fig. 24.24 to the application. To keep track of information, you will store the event information read from the file in array `m_strData` (line 7) and the number of events for a specified day in `m_intNumberOfEvents` (line 10). For simplicity, the array `m_strData` is initialized with ten rows of five items each (allowing up to ten total events per day).

Creating an array of `Strings`

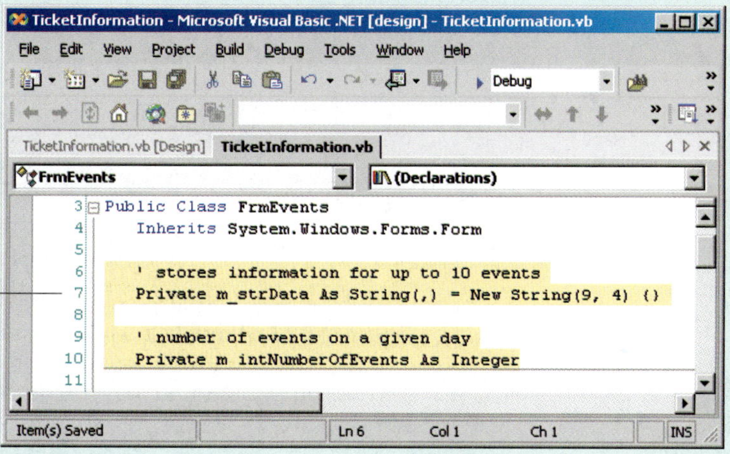

Figure 24.24   Instance variables declared in the **Ticket Information** application.

3. *Saving the project.* Select **File > Save All** to save your modified code.

When you run the **Ticket Information** application, by default, the current day should be selected in the `MonthCalendar` control. The application should show the list of the day's events in the ComboBox. Recall that, if there are no events for the day, the ComboBox displays `"- No Events -"`. In the following box, you will invoke a method from the Form's Load event handler to set the display in the ComboBox appropriately.

Handling the Form's Load Event

1. *Defining the Form's Load event.* Double click the Form in design view to generate the event handler `FrmEvents_Load`. Add lines 135–136 of Fig. 24.25 to the Load event handler. Line 136 invokes method `CreateEventList`. You will soon add code to `CreateEventList` to populate the ComboBox with any events scheduled for the current day.

(cont.)

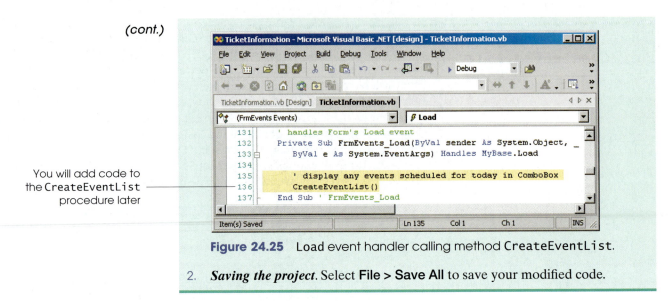

You will add code to the `CreateEventList` procedure later

Figure 24.25 Load event handler calling method `CreateEventList`.

2. *Saving the project.* Select **File > Save All** to save your modified code.

When the user selects a date in the `MonthCalendar` control, the **DateChanged** event is raised. You add code to the event handler that invokes the `CreateEventList` method in the following box.

Handling the MonthCalendar's DateChanged Event

1. *Creating the MonthCalendar's DateChanged event handler.* In design view, double click the `MonthCalendar` to generate the empty event handler `mvwDate_DateChanged`.

2. *Invoking the CreateEventList method.* Add lines 144–145 of Fig. 24.26 to the `mvwDate_DateChanged` event handler. Line 145 invokes method `CreateEventList`, which you will define in the next box.

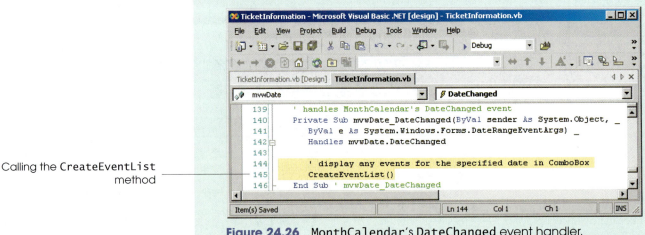

Calling the `CreateEventList` method

Figure 24.26 `MonthCalendar`'s `DateChanged` event handler.

3. *Saving the project.* Select **File > Save All** to save your modified code.

The application invokes method `CreateEventList` during the Form's Load event and the `MonthCalendar`'s `DateChanged` event. The `CreateEventList` method will populate the ComboBox with event names if there are any events for the date the user chooses, or it will indicate that the event list is empty if there are no events for that day. You define this functionality in the following box.

Defining the CreateEventList Method

1. *Setting variables and clearing the ComboBox in the CreateEventList method.* Add lines 123–130 of Fig. 24.27 to the CreateEventList method. The CreateEventList method first declares a counter, intCount (line 123) that will be used to iterate through the events. Line 127 invokes the Extract-Data method defined in the next box, passing the Date that is currently selected in the MonthCalendar. The ExtractData method will store event information in array m_strData and assign the number of events scheduled for the specified date to m_intNumberOfEvents. This date is specified by the MonthCalendar control's **SelectionStart** property. The Items.Clear method removes any events currently displayed in the ComboBox (line 130).

You will add code to the ExtractData procedure in the next box

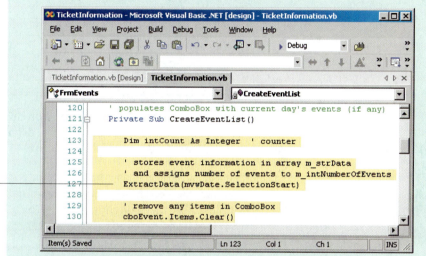

Figure 24.27 CreateEventList modified to call method ExtractData and clear the ComboBox.

2. *Setting events displayed in the ComboBox.* Add lines 132–149 of Fig. 24.28 to the CreateEventList method.

Extracting event name from array and displaying it in the ComboBox

Indicating that events are scheduled for the day

Indicating that no events are scheduled for the day

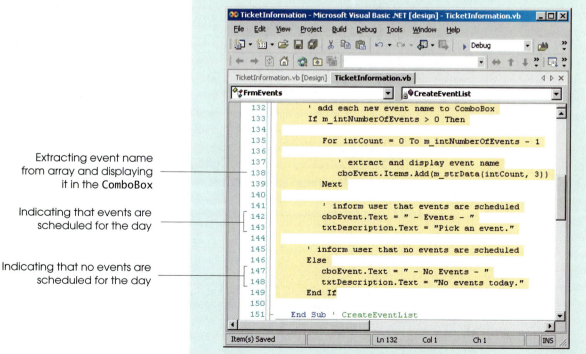

Figure 24.28 Displaying the events scheduled for the specified day.

(cont.)   If there are events scheduled for the chosen day (line 133), then the For...Next statement iterates through array m_strData and adds the name of each event to the ComboBox (lines 135–139). The CreateEventList method informs the user that there are events scheduled for the specified day by using the Text properties of the ComboBox and TextBox (lines 142–143). If there are events for the chosen day, then the ComboBox displays "- Events -" and the Textbox displays "Pick an event.". If there are no events for the chosen day, the ComboBox displays "- No events -" and the Textbox displays "No events today." (lines 147–148).

3. **Saving the project.** Select **File > Save All** to save your modified code.

As described in *Step 1* of the previous box, the ExtractData method uses a variable of type Date (dtmDay) as its only parameter. The ExtractData method assigns the information about any events scheduled for that day to the m_strData array and assigns the number of events for that day to the m_intNumberOfEvents variable. You define the ExtractData method in the following box.

Reading a Sequential-Access File

1. **Adding variables to the ExtractData method.** Add lines 157–162 of Fig. 24.29 to the ExtractData method. The Date selected in the MonthCalendar control is passed to the ExtractData method as the parameter dtmDay. Variable intChosenDay (line 158) stores the day selected using the Day property of the Date variable dtmDay. The intFileDay variable (line 159) will store the day of the event read from the file. The intLineNumbers variable (line 160) will store the number of lines to skip between events in the file. The ExtractData method will assign the number of events scheduled for the specified date to the variable m_intNumberOfEvents, which is initialized to 0 in line 162.

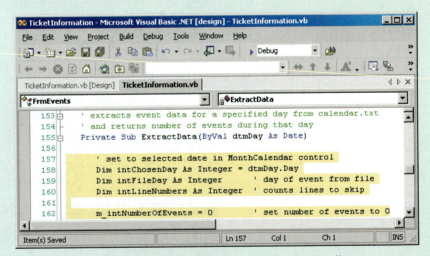

Figure 24.29 ExtractData method's variable declarations.

2. **Using a StreamReader to read from the file.** Add lines 164–168 of Fig. 24.30 to the method. To read from the file, ExtractData creates a new Stream-Reader object (line 165), passing the name of the file to be read ("calendar.txt"). Recall that you wrote information to this file using the **Write Event** application earlier in this tutorial. [*Note*: Because the data file is in the same directory as the application's executable (C:\SimplyVB\TicketIn-formation\bin), you do not need to use the full path name.]

(cont.)   The **ReadLine** method (line 168) of the `StreamReader` reads a line of characters up to and including a newline character from the specified stream (`objInput`) and returns the characters as a `String`. Line 168 assigns the first line of the file to `strLine`.

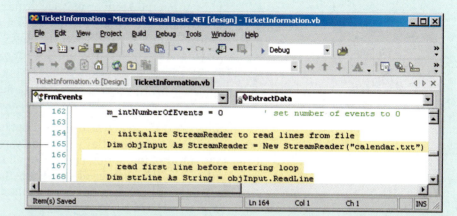

Creating a `StreamReader` object to read the `calendar.txt` file

Figure 24.30   Using `StreamReader` to read data from a sequential-access file.

3. *Extracting the day from an event in the file.* Add lines 170–175 of Fig. 24.31 to the `ExtractData` method. The `Do While...Loop` determines whether there is more information to read in the file. This condition ensures that the end of the file has not been reached, at which point looping should stop. This is done by using the `StreamReader` object's **Peek** method, which returns the next character to be read or `-1` if there are no more characters to read in the file (that is, the end of the file has been reached). The condition also ensures that no more than 10 events for the specified day are read from the file (that is, `m_intNumberOfEvents` is less than 10). This constraint is necessary due to the fixed size of the array `m_strData`. If these conditions are met, the body of the `Do While...Loop` executes. Line 173 converts the line read from the file (that is, the day of the event) to an `Integer` and assigns that value to `intFileDay`. The first time the loop executes, `strLine` contains the first line in the file.

4. *Reading event information from the sequential-access file.* Add lines 175–193 of Fig. 24.32 to the `ExtractData` method's `Do While...Loop`. The loop reads each event sequentially from the file. If the day of the event read from the file (`intFileDay`) and the specified day (`intChosenDay`) are the same (line 176), then the event information (day, time, ticket price, name and description) is read from the file and is stored in array `m_strData` (lines 177–181).

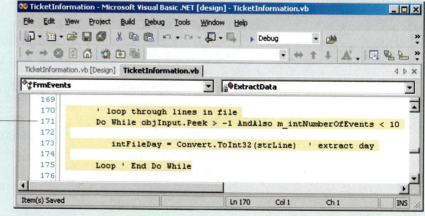

Verify that end of file has not been reached and less than 10 events are stored in the array

Figure 24.31   Extracting the day from an event entry in the file.

(cont.)

Recall that when you created the **Write Event** application, each piece of data (day, time, price, event and description) was written to `calendar.txt` on a separate line, so the event data is retrieved using the `ReadLine` method. Each event for the chosen day is placed in its own row of the array (indicated by `m_intNumberOfEvents`), and each piece of event information is placed in its own column of the array. Line 182 increments `m_intNumberOfEvents` to indicate that an event has been scheduled for that date.

If `intFileDay` and the selected day do not match, then the `StreamReader` skips to the next event, using a For...Next loop (lines 186–188). Line 193 then reads the next line in the file that contains an event's date. This entire process is repeated until the end of the file is reached or until 10 events have been added to the `m_strData` array.

Store event information in a row of the array

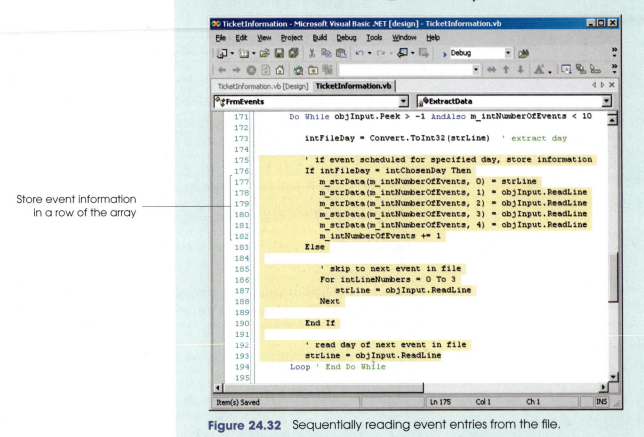

```
171    Do While objInput.Peek > -1 AndAlso m_intNumberOfEvents < 10
172
173       intFileDay = Convert.ToInt32(strLine)  ' extract day
174
175       ' if event scheduled for specified day, store information
176       If intFileDay = intChosenDay Then
177          m_strData(m_intNumberOfEvents, 0) = strLine
178          m_strData(m_intNumberOfEvents, 1) = objInput.ReadLine
179          m_strData(m_intNumberOfEvents, 2) = objInput.ReadLine
180          m_strData(m_intNumberOfEvents, 3) = objInput.ReadLine
181          m_strData(m_intNumberOfEvents, 4) = objInput.ReadLine
182          m_intNumberOfEvents += 1
183       Else
184
185          ' skip to next event in file
186          For intLineNumbers = 0 To 3
187             strLine = objInput.ReadLine
188          Next
189
190       End If
191
192       ' read day of next event in file
193       strLine = objInput.ReadLine
194    Loop ' End Do While
195
```

Figure 24.32 Sequentially reading event entries from the file.

5. *Saving the project.* Select **File > Save All** to save your modified code.

The ComboBox displays the names of any events scheduled for the date specified in the `MonthCalendar` control. When the user selects the community event from the ComboBox, the `SelectedIndexChanged` event is raised and the description of the community event is displayed in the TextBox. The next box explains how to add this functionality.

Handling the
SelectedIndexChanged
Event

1. *Creating the ComboBox's SelectedIndexChanged event handler.* Double click the **Pick an Event** ComboBox in design view to generate the empty event handler cboEvent_SelectedIndexChanged.

(cont.)

2. ***Displaying event information.*** Add lines 220–226 of Fig. 24.33 to the event handler. When the user selects an event in the ComboBox, the cboEvent_SelectedIndexChanged event handler displays information about the event in the TextBox txtDescription. The SelectedIndex property of the ComboBox returns the index number of the selected event, which is equivalent to the row number of the event in the m_strData array. The event handler appends descriptive text, newline characters, the time that the event starts (line 221), the ticket price (lines 223–224) and the event's description (line 226) to the TextBox's Text property.

Displaying event information
in the TextBox

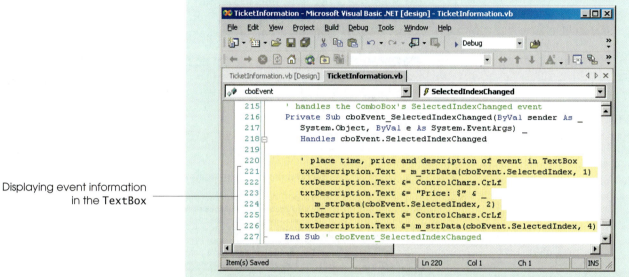

Figure 24.33   cboEvent_SelectedIndexChanged defined to display event information.

3. ***Running the application.*** Select **Debug > Start** to run your application. Select various dates and view the event information. Select the 4th day of the current month. You should be able to view the arts and crafts fair event added earlier in the tutorial.

4. ***Closing the application.*** Close your running application by clicking its close box.

5. ***Closing the IDE.*** Close Visual Studio .NET by clicking its close box.

Figure 24.34 presents the source code for the **Ticket Information** application. The lines of code that contain new programming concepts that you have learned so far in this tutorial are highlighted.

Importing namespace
System.IO

```
1   Imports System.IO
2
3   Public Class FrmEvents
4      Inherits System.Windows.Forms.Form
5
6      ' stores information for up to 10 events
7      Private m_strData As String(,) = New String(9, 4) {}
8
9      ' number of events on a given day
10     Private m_intNumberOfEvents As Integer
11
```

Figure 24.34   **Ticket Information** application's code. (Part 1 of 3.)

```
12        ' Windows Form Designer generated code
13
14        ' populates ComboBox with current day's events (if any)
15        Private Sub CreateEventList()
16
17            Dim intCount As Integer  ' counter
18
19            ' stores event information in array m_strData
20            ' and assigns number of events to m_intNumberOfEvents
21            ExtractData(mvwDate.SelectionStart)
22
23            ' remove any items in ComboBox
24            cboEvent.Items.Clear()
25
26            ' add each new event name to ComboBox
27            If m_intNumberOfEvents > 0 Then
28
29                For intCount = 0 To m_intNumberOfEvents - 1
30
31                    ' extract and display event name
32                    cboEvent.Items.Add(m_strData(intCount, 3))
33                Next
34
35                ' inform user that events are scheduled
36                cboEvent.Text = " - Events - "
37                txtDescription.Text = "Pick an event."
38
39            ' inform user that no events are scheduled
40            Else
41                cboEvent.Text = " - No Events - "
42                txtDescription.Text = "No events today."
43            End If
44
45        End Sub ' CreateEventList
46
47        ' extracts event data for a specified day from calendar.txt
48        ' and returns number of events during that day
49        Private Sub ExtractData(ByVal dtmDay As Date)
50
51            ' set to selected date in MonthCalendar control
52            Dim intChosenDay As Integer = dtmDay.Day
53            Dim intFileDay As Integer      ' day of event from file
54            Dim intLineNumbers As Integer  ' counts lines to skip
55
56            m_intNumberOfEvents = 0          ' set number of events to 0
57
58            ' initialize StreamReader to read lines from file
59            Dim objInput As StreamReader = New StreamReader("calendar.txt")
60
61            ' read first line before entering loop
62            Dim strLine As String = objInput.ReadLine
63
64            ' loop through lines in file
65            Do While objInput.Peek > -1 AndAlso m_intNumberOfEvents < 10
66
67                intFileDay = Convert.ToInt32(strLine)  ' extract day
68
```

Creating `StreamReader` object —— (line 59)

Using method `ReadLine` to read the first line of the file —— (line 62)

Ensuring that the end of the file has not been reached —— (line 65)

Figure 24.34 Ticket Information application's code. (Part 2 of 3.)

Reading information from a file
and storing the data in an array

Using method ReadLine to skip
to the next event in the file

Using method ReadLine to
read the day of the next event

```
69              ' if event scheduled for specified day, store information
70              If intFileDay = intChosenDay Then
71                  m_strData(m_intNumberOfEvents, 0) = strLine
72                  m_strData(m_intNumberOfEvents, 1) = objInput.ReadLine
73                  m_strData(m_intNumberOfEvents, 2) = objInput.ReadLine
74                  m_strData(m_intNumberOfEvents, 3) = objInput.ReadLine
75                  m_strData(m_intNumberOfEvents, 4) = objInput.ReadLine
76                  m_intNumberOfEvents += 1
77              Else
78
79                  ' skip to next event in file
80                  For intLineNumbers = 0 To 3
81                      strLine = objInput.ReadLine
82                  Next
83
84              End If
85
86              ' read day of next event in file
87              strLine = objInput.ReadLine
88          Loop ' End Do While
89
90      End Sub ' ExtractData
91
92      ' handles Form's Load event
93      Private Sub FrmEvents_Load(ByVal sender As System.Object, _
94          ByVal e As System.EventArgs) Handles MyBase.Load
95
96          ' display any events scheduled for today in ComboBox
97          CreateEventList()
98      End Sub ' FrmEvents_Load
99
100     ' handles MonthCalendar's DateChanged event
101     Private Sub mvwDate_DateChanged(ByVal sender As System.Object, _
102         ByVal e As System.Windows.Forms.DateRangeEventArgs) _
103         Handles mvwDate.DateChanged
104
105         ' display any events for the specified date in ComboBox
106         CreateEventList()
107     End Sub ' mvwDate_DateChanged
108
109     ' handles ComboBox's SelectedIndexChanged event
110     Private Sub cboEvent_SelectedIndexChanged(ByVal sender As _
111         System.Object, ByVal e As System.EventArgs) _
112         Handles cboEvent.SelectedIndexChanged
113
114         ' place time, price and description of event in TextBox
115         txtDescription.Text = m_strData(cboEvent.SelectedIndex, 1)
116         txtDescription.Text &= ControlChars.CrLf
117         txtDescription.Text &= "Price: $" & _
118             m_strData(cboEvent.SelectedIndex, 2)
119         txtDescription.Text &= ControlChars.CrLf
120         txtDescription.Text &= m_strData(cboEvent.SelectedIndex, 4)
121     End Sub ' cboEvent_SelectedIndexChanged
122
123 End Class ' FrmEvents
```

Figure 24.34   **Ticket Information** application's code. (Part 3 of 3.)

24.6 Wrap-Up

In this tutorial, you learned how to store data in sequential-access files. Data in files is called persistent data because the data is maintained after the application that generates the data terminates. Computers store files on secondary storage devices.

Sequential-access files store data items in the order that they are written to the file. They are part of the data hierarchy in which computers process data items. These files are composed of records, which are collections of related fields. Fields are made up of characters, which are composed of bytes. Bytes are composed of the smallest data items that computers can support—bits.

You learned how Visual Basic .NET views each file as a sequential stream of bytes with an end-of-file marker. You learned how to create a sequential-access file in the **Write Event** application by associating a `StreamWriter` object with a specified file name. You used `StreamWriter` to add information to that file. After creating a file of community events with the **Write Event** application, you developed the **Ticket Information** application, which uses a `StreamReader` object to read information from that file sequentially. The user selects a date in the **Ticket Information** application's `MonthCalendar` control and extracts event information from a sequential-access file about any events scheduled for the specified date.

In the next tutorial, you will be introduced to databases, which were briefly mentioned earlier in this tutorial. Databases provide another common mechanism for maintaining persistent data.

SKILLS SUMMARY

Displaying the Open Dialog

- Add an `OpenFileDialog` object to your application by double clicking the `OpenFileDialog` tab in the **ToolBox**.
- Invoke the `OpenFileDialog`'s `ShowDialog` method.

Retrieving the Filename From the Open Dialog

- Use the `Filename` property of the `OpenFileDialog` object.

Writing to a Sequential-Access File

- Import namespace `System.IO`.
- Create a `StreamWriter` object by passing two arguments to the constructor: the name of the file to open for writing and a `Boolean` value that determines whether information will be appended to the file.
- Use the `WriteLine` method of `StreamWriter` to write information to the file.

Reading from a Sequential-Access File

- Import namespace `System.IO`.
- Create a `StreamReader` object by passing the name of the file to open for reading to the constructor.
- Use the `ReadLine` method of `StreamReader` to read information from the file.

Adding a MonthCalendar Control

- Double click the `MonthCalendar` control's tab in the **ToolBox** to add a `MonthCalendar` to the application.

Handling a MonthCalendar Control's DateChanged Event

- Double click the `MonthCalendar` control to generate the `DateChanged` event handler.
- Property `SelectionStart` returns the first (or only) date selected.

Handling a ComboBox Control's SelectedIndexChanged Event

- Double click the `ComboBox` control to generate the `SelectedIndexChanged` event handler.

KEY TERMS

binary digit—A digit that can assume one of two values.

bit—Short for "binary digit." A digit that can assume one of two values.

byte—Eight bits.

character—A digit, letter or special symbol (characters in Visual Basic .NET are Unicode characters, which are composed of 2 bytes).

character set—The set of all characters used to write applications and represent data items on a particular computer. Visual Basic .NET uses the Unicode character set.

CheckFileExists property of class OpenFileDialog—Enables the user to display a warning if a specified file does not exist.

Close method of class StreamWriter or StreamReader—Used to close the stream.

database—Can be a group of related files.

database management system (DBMS)—Collection of programs designed to create and manage databases.

data hierarchy—Collection of data items processed by computers that become larger and more complex in structure as you progress from bits, to characters, to fields and up to larger data structures.

DateChanged event of MonthCalendar control—Raised when a new date (or a range of dates) is selected.

decimal digits—The digits 0, 1, 2, 3, 4, 5, 6, 7, 8 and 9.

field—Group of characters that conveys some meaning. For example, a field consisting of uppercase and lowercase letters can represent a person's name.

file—Collection of data that is assigned a name. Used for long-term persistence of large amounts of data, even after the application that created the data terminates.

FileName property of class OpenFileDialog—Specifies the file name displayed in the dialog.

MonthCalendar control—Displays a calendar from which a user can select a range of dates.

OpenFileDialog control—Enables an application to use the **Open** dialog, which allows users to specify a file to be opened

Peek method of class StreamReader—Returns the next character to be read or –1 if there are no more characters to read in the file (that is, the end of the file has been reached).

persistent data—Data maintained in files.

ReadLine method of class StreamReader—Method of class StreamReader that reads a line from a file and returns it as a String.

record—A collection of related fields. Usually a Class in Visual Basic .NET composed of several fields (called member variables in Visual Basic .NET).

record key—Identifies a record and distinguishes that record from all other records.

secondary storage media—Devices such as magnetic disks, optical disks and magnetic tapes on which computers store files.

SelectionStart property of MonthCalendar control—Returns the first (or only) date selected.

sequential-access file—File which contains data that is read in the order that it was written to the file.

ShowDialog method of class OpenFileDialog—Displays the **Open** dialog and returns the result of the user interaction with the dialog.

special symbols—$, @, %, &, *, ( ), -, +, ", :, ?, / and the like.

stream—Object that has access to a sequence of characters.

StreamReader class—Provides methods for reading information from a file.

StreamWriter class—Provides methods for writing information to a file.

text file—A file containing human-readable characters.

Unicode—A character set containing characters that are composed of 2 bytes. Characters are represented in Visual Basic .NET using the Unicode character set.

WriteLine method of class StreamWriter—Method of class StreamWriter that writes a String and a line terminator to a file.

CONTROLS, EVENTS, PROPERTIES & METHODS

ComboBox This control allows users to select options from a drop-down list.

- **In action**

  Australia ▼

- **Events**

  SelectedIndexChanged—Raised when a new value is selected in the ComobBox.

- **Properties**

  DataSource—Allows you to add items to the ComboBox.

  DropDownStyle—Determines the ComboBox's style.

  Enabled—Determines whether the user can enter data (True) in the ComboBox or not (False).

  Items—Specifies the values the user can select from the ComboBox.

  Item—Retrieves the value at the specified index.

  Location—Specifies the location of the ComboBox control on its container control relative to the top-left corner.

  MaxDropDownItems—Determines the maximum number of items to be displayed when user clicks the drop-down arrow.

  Name—Specifies the name used to access the ComboBox control programmatically. The name should be prefixed with cbo.

  SelectedIndex—Specifies the index of the item selected.

  SelectedValue—Contains the item selected by the user.

  Text—Specifies the text displayed in the ComboBox.

- **Methods**

  Items.Add—Adds an item to the ComboBox.

  Items.Clear—Deletes all the values in the ComboBox.

MonthCalendar MonthCalendar This control displays a calendar from which the user can select a date or a range of dates.

- **In action**

- **Events**

  DateChanged—Raised when a new date (or a range of dates) is selected.

- **Properties**

  Location—Specifies the location of the MonthCalendar control on the Form.

  Name—Specifies the name used to access the properties of the MonthCalendar control in application code. The name should be prefixed with mvw.

  SelectionStart—Returns the first (or only) date selected.

OpenFileDialog OpenFileDialog This object enables an application to use the **Open** dialog.

- **Properties**

  CheckFileExists—Enables the user to display a warning if a specified file does not exist.

`FileName`—Sets the default file name displayed in the dialog. It can also be used to retrieve the name of the user-entered file.

`Name`—Specifies the name that will be used to reference the control's properties and methods.

■ *Method*

`ShowDialog`—Displays the **Open** dialog and returns the result of the user interaction with the dialog.

StreamWriter This class is used to write data to a file.

■ *Methods*

`Close`—Used to close the stream.

`WriteLine`—Writes the data specified in its argument, followed by a new line character.

StreamReader This class is used to read data from a file.

■ *Methods*

`Close`—Closes the stream.

`ReadLine`—Reads a line of data from a particular file.

MULTIPLE-CHOICE QUESTIONS

24.1 Data maintained in a file is called _____.

a) persistent data   b) bits

c) secondary data   d) databases

24.2 Methods from the _____ class can be used to write data to a file.

a) `StreamReader`   b) `FileWriter`

c) `StreamWriter`   d) `WriteFile`

24.3 Namespace _____ provides the classes and methods that you need to use to perform file processing.

a) `System.IO`   b) `System.Files`

c) `System.Stream`   d) `System.Windows.Forms`

24.4 Sometimes a group of related files is called a _____.

a) field   b) database

c) collection   d) byte

24.5 A(n) _____ allows the user to select a file to open.

a) `CreateFileDialog`   b) `OpenFileDialog`

c) `MessageBox`   d) None of the above.

24.6 Digits, letters and special symbols are referred to as _____.

a) constants   b) `Integers`

c) `Strings`   d) characters

24.7 The _____ method reads a line from a file.

a) `ReadLine`   b) `Read`

c) `ReadAll`   d) `ReadToNewline`

24.8 A _____ contains information that is read in the order that it was written to the file.

a) sequential-access file   b) text file

c) `StreamReader`   d) `StreamWriter`

24.9 The smallest data item that a computer can support is called a _____.

a) character set   b) character

c) special symbol   d) bit

24.10 Methods from the _____ class can be used to read data from a file.

a) StreamWriter

b) FileReader

c) StreamReader

d) ReadFile

EXERCISES   **24.11** (*Birthday Saver Application*) Create an application that stores people's names and birthdays in a file (Fig. 24.35). The user creates a file and inputs each person's first name, last name and birthday on the Form. The information is then written to the file.

Figure 24.35   **Birthday Saver** application's GUI.

a) *Copying the template to your working directory.* Copy the directory C:\Examples\ Tutorial24\Exercises\BirthdaySaver to your C:\SimplyVB directory.

b) *Opening the application's template file.* Double click BirthdaySaver.sln in the BirthdaySaver directory to open the application (Fig. 24.35).

c) *Adding and customizing an OpenFileDialog component.* Add an OpenFileDialog component to the Form. Change its Name property to objOpenFileDialog. Set the CheckFileExists property to False.

d) *Importing namespace System.IO.* Import System.IO to allow file processing.

e) *Declaring a StreamWriter object.* Declare a StreamWriter object that can be used throughout the entire class.

f) *Defining the Open File... Button's Click event handler.* Double click the **Open File...** Button to create the btnOpen_Click event handler. Write code to display the **Open** dialog. If the user clicks the **Cancel** Button in the dialog, then the event handler should perform no further actions. Otherwise, determine whether the user provided a file name that has the .txt extension (indicating a text file). If the user did not, display a MessageBox asking the user to select an appropriate file. If the user specified a valid file name, perform *Step f*.

g) *Initializing the StreamWriter.* Initialize the StreamWriter in the event handler btnOpenFile_Click, passing the user-input file name as an argument. Allow the user to append information to the file by passing the Boolean value True as the second argument to the StreamWriter.

h) *Defining the Enter Button's Click event handler.* Double click the **Enter** Button to create the event handler btnEnter_Click. This event handler should write the entire name of the person on one line in the file. Then the person's birthday should be written on the next line in the file. Finally, the TextBoxes on the Form should be cleared, and the DateTimePicker's value should be set back to the current date.

i) *Defining the Close File Button's Click event handler.* Double click the **Close File** Button to create the btnClose_Click event handler. Close the StreamWriter connection in this event handler.

j) *Running the application.* Select **Debug > Start** to run your application. Open a file by clicking **Open File...** Button. After a file has been opened, use the input fields provided to enter birthday information. After each person's name and birthday are typed in, click the **Enter** Button. When you are finished, close the file by clicking the **Close File** Button. Browse to the file and ensure that its contents contain the birthday information that you entered.

k) *Closing the application.* Close your running application by clicking its close box.

l) *Closing the IDE.* Close Visual Studio .NET by clicking its close box.

24.12 (*Photo Album Application*) Create an application that displays images for the user, as shown in Fig. 24.36. This application should display the current image in a large Picture-Box and display the previous and next images in smaller PictureBoxes. A description of the book represented by the large image should be displayed in a multiline TextBox. The application should use the Directory class's methods to facilitate the displaying of the images.

Figure 24.36   **Photo Album** application GUI.

a) *Copying the template to your working directory.* Copy the directory C:\Examples\ Tutorial24\Exercises\PhotoAlbum to your C:\SimplyVB directory.

b) *Opening the application's template file.* Double click PhotoAlbum.sln in the PhotoAlbum directory to open the application.

c) *Creating instance variables.* Create instance variable m_intCurrent to represent the current image that is displayed, and set it to 0. Create the m_strLargeImage array (to store the path names of five large images), the m_strSmallImage array (to store the path names of five small images) and the m_strDescriptions array (to store the descriptions of the five books represented by the images).

d) *Defining the RetrieveData procedure.* Create a Sub procedure named RetrieveData to store the path names of the larger images in m_strLargeImages and the path names of the smaller images in m_strSmallImage. Use the Directory class's GetCurrentDirectory method to determine the directory path for the images\large and images\small folders. Sequential-access file books.txt stores the file name of each image. The file is organized such that the file name of the small and large images are on the first line. These files have similar names. The small image's file name ends with _thumb.jpg (that is, *filename*_thumb.jpg) while the large image's file name ends with _large.jpg (that is, *filename*_large.jpg). The description of the book, which should be stored in array m_strDescriptions, follows the file name.

e) *Defining the DisplayPicture procedure.* Create a Sub procedure named DisplayPicture to display the current image in the large PictureBox and to display the previous and next images in the smaller PictureBoxes.

f) *Using If...Then...Else in the DisplayPicture procedure.* Use an If...Then...Else statement to display the images on the Form. If the Integer instance variable is 0, display the image of the first book. Also, display the next book's image in the next image PictureBox. However, because there is no previous image, nothing should be displayed in the previous image PictureBox, and the **Previous Image** Button should be disabled. If the last image is displayed in the large PictureBox, then disable the **Next Image** Button, and do not display anything in the next image PictureBox. Otherwise, all three PictureBoxes should display their corresponding images, and the **Previous Image** and **Next Image** Buttons should be enabled.

g) *Defining the FrmPhotoAlbum_Load event handler.* Double click the Form to create the FrmPhotoAlbum_Load event handler. Invoke methods RetrieveData and DisplayPicture in this event handler.

h) *Defining the btnPrevious_Click event handler.* Double click the **Previous Image** Button to create the btnPrevious_Click event handler. In this event handler, decrease the Integer instance variable by 1 and invoke procedure DisplayPicture.

i) *Defining the btnNext_Click event handler.* Double click the **Next Image** Button to create the btnNext_Click event handler. In this event handler, increment the Integer instance variable by 1 and invoke the DisplayPicture procedure.

j) *Running the application.* Select **Debug > Start** to run your application. Click the **Previous Image** and **Next Image** Buttons to ensure that the proper images and descriptions are displayed.

k) *Closing the application.* Close your running application by clicking its close box.

l) *Closing the IDE.* Close Visual Studio .NET by clicking its close box.

24.13 (*Car Reservation Application*) Create an application that allows a user to reserve a car for the specified day (Fig. 24.37). The small car reservation company can rent out only four cars per day. Let the application allow the user to specify a certain day. If four cars have already been reserved for that day, then indicate to the user that no vehicles are available.

Figure 24.37   Car Reservation application GUI.

a) *Copying the template to your working directory.* Copy the directory C:\Examples\Tutorial24\Exercises\CarReservation to your C:\SimplyVB directory.

b) *Opening the application's template file.* Double click CarReservation.sln in the CarReservation directory to open the application.

c) *Adding a MonthCalendar control to the Form.* Drag and drop a MonthCalendar control on the Form. Set the Location property of the control to 16, 32.

d) *Importing System.IO namespace.* Import namespace System.IO to allow file processing.

e) *Defining the FrmReserve_Load event handler.* Double click the Form to create the FrmReserve_Load event handler.

f) *Defining a method.* Create a method named NumberOfReservations that takes one argument of type Date. The procedure should create a StreamReader that reads from the reservations.txt file. Use a Do While Loop to allow the StreamReader to search through the entire reservations.txt file to see how many cars have been rented for the day selected by the user. The procedure should close the StreamReader connection and return the number of cars rented for the day selected.

g) *Defining a Sub procedure.* Create a Sub procedure named CheckReservations. This procedure should invoke the NumberOfReservations method, passing in the user-selected day as an argument. The CheckReservations method should then retrieve the number returned by NumberOfReservations and determine if four cars have been rented for that day. If four cars have been rented, then display a message dialog to the user stating that no cars are available that day for rental. If fewer than four cars have been rented for that day, create a StreamWriter object, passing reservations.txt as the first argument True as the second argument. Write the day and the user's name to the reservations.txt file and display a message dialog to the user stating that a car has been reserved.

[handwritten marginal note: reservations.txt is a file that has dates — each date is one car reservation]

h) *Defining the btnReserve_Click event handler.* Double click the **Reserve Car** Button to create the btnReserve_Click event handler. In this event handler, invoke the CheckReservations procedure and clear the **Name:** TextBox.

i) *Running the application.* Select **Debug > Start** to run your application. Enter several reservations, including four reservations for the same day. Enter a reservation for a day that already has four reservations to ensure that a message dialog will be displayed.

j) *Closing the application.* Close your running application by clicking its close box. Open reservations.txt to ensure that the proper data has been stored (based on the reservations entered in *Step i*).

k) *Closing the IDE.* Close Visual Studio .NET by clicking its close box.

What does this code do? ▶   **24.14** What is the result of the following code?

```
1   Dim strPath1 As String = "oldfile.txt"
2   Dim strPath2 As String = "newfile.txt"
3   Dim strLine As String
4
5   Dim objStreamWriter As StreamWriter
6   objStreamWriter = New StreamWriter(strPath2)
7
8   Dim objStreamReader As StreamReader
9   objStreamReader = New StreamReader(strPath1)
10
11  strLine = objStreamReader.ReadLine()
12
13  Do While strLine <> ""
14     objStreamWriter.WriteLine(strLine)
15     strLine = objStreamReader.ReadLine()
16  Loop
17
18  objStreamWriter.Close()
19  objStreamReader.Close()
```

What's wrong with this code? ▶   **24.15** Find the error(s) in the following code, which is supposed to read a line from somefile.txt, convert the line to uppercase and then append it to somefile.txt.

```
1   Dim strPath As String = "somefile.txt"
2   Dim strContents As String
3
4   Dim objStreamWriter As StreamWriter
5   objStreamWriter = New StreamWriter(strPath, True)
6
7   Dim objStreamReader As StreamReader
8   objStreamReader = New StreamReader(strPath)
9
10  strContents = objStreamReader.ReadLine()
11
12  strContents = strContents.ToUpper()
13
14  objStreamWriter.Write(strContents)
15
16  objStreamWriter.Close()
17  objStreamReader.Close()
```

Programming Challenge

24.16 (*File Scrape Application*) Create an application similar to the screen scraping application of Tutorial 23, that opens a user-specified file and searches the file for the price of a book, returning it to the user (Fig. 24.38). [*Hint:* You will need to use the ReadToEnd method of class StreamReader to retrieve the entire contents of the files. The book price appears, for example, in the sample booklist.htm file as Our Price: $59.99.]

Figure 24.38   **File Scrape** application GUI.

a) *Copying the template to your working directory.* Copy the directory C:\Examples\ Tutorial24\Exercises\FileScrape to your C:\SimplyVB directory. Notice that two HTML files—booklist.htm and bookpool.htm—are provided for you.

b) *Opening the application's template file.* Double click FileScrape.sln in the File-Scrape directory to open the application.

c) *Creating an event handler.* Create an event handler for the **Open...** Button that allows the user to select a file to search for prices.

d) *Creating a second event handler.* Create an event handler for the **Search** Button. This event handler should search the specified HTML file for the book price. When the price is found, display it in the output Label.

e) *Running the application.* Select **Debug > Start** to run your application. Click the **Open...** Button and select one of the .htm files provided in the FileScrape directory. Click the **Search** Button and view the price of the book. For booklist.htm, the price should be $59.99 and bookpool.htm the price should be $39.50.

f) *Closing the application.* Close your running application by clicking its close box.

g) *Closing the IDE.* Close Visual Studio .NET by clicking its close box.

TUTORIAL

Objectives

In this tutorial, you will learn to:
- Connect to databases.
- View the contents of an Access database.
- Add database controls to Windows Forms.
- Use the **Server Explorer** window.
- Use the **Query Builder** dialog.
- Read information from and update information in databases.

Outline

ATM Application

Introducing Database Programming

In the last tutorial, you learned how to create sequential-access files and how to search through such files to locate information. Sequential-access files are inappropriate for so-called **instant-access applications**, in which information must be located immediately. Popular instant-access applications include airline-reservation systems, banking systems, point-of-sale systems, automated teller machines (ATMs) and other transaction-processing systems that require rapid access to specific data. The bank at which an individual has an account might have hundreds of thousands or even millions of other customers; however, when that individual uses an ATM, the appropriate account is checked for sufficient funds in seconds. This type of instant access is made possible by databases. Individual database records can be accessed directly (and quickly) without sequentially searching through large numbers of other records, as is required with sequential-access files. In this tutorial, you will be introduced to databases and the part of Microsoft .NET—called **ADO .NET**—used for interacting with databases. You will learn about databases and ADO .NET as you create this tutorial's **ATM** application.

25.1 Test-Driving the ATM Application

Many banks offer ATMs to provide their customers with quick and easy access to their bank accounts. When customers use these machines, their account information is updated immediately to reflect the actions they perform (for example, withdrawals). This application must meet the following requirements:

> **Application Requirements**
>
> *A local bank has asked you to create a prototype automated teller machine (ATM) application to access a database that contains fictitious customer records. Each record consists of an account number, Personal Identification Number (PIN), first name and balance amount. For testing purposes, valid account numbers will be provided in a ComboBox. The ATM application should allow the user to log in to an account by providing a valid PIN. Once logged in, the user can view the account balance and withdraw money from the account (if the account contains sufficient funds). If money is withdrawn, the application should update the database.*

Your **ATM** application will allow the user to enter a PIN number. If the user provides a correct PIN number, then the ATM will retrieve information about the requested account, such as the account holder's name and balance, from the database. If the PIN number entered is invalid, a message is displayed asking the user to reenter the PIN number. You begin by test-driving the completed application. Then, you will learn the additional Visual Basic .NET technologies that you will need to create your own version of this application.

Test-Driving the ATM Application

1. ***Opening the completed application.*** Open the directory `C:\Examples\Tutorial25\CompletedApplication\ATM` to locate the **ATM** application. Double click `ATM.sln` to open the application in Visual Studio .NET.

2. ***Running the application.*** Select **Debug > Start** to run the application (Fig. 25.1). The `Form` will appear with the **OK**, **Balance**, **Withdraw** and **Done** Buttons disabled.

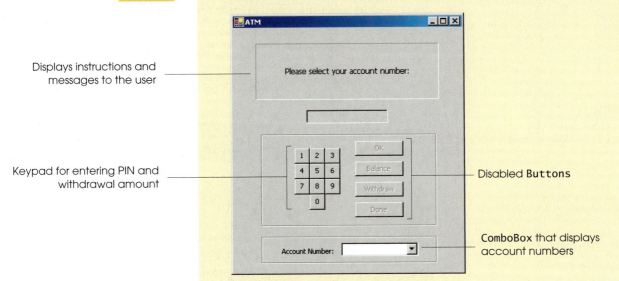

Displays instructions and messages to the user

Keypad for entering PIN and withdrawal amount

Disabled **Buttons**

ComboBox that displays account numbers

Figure 25.1 **ATM** application `Form`.

3. ***Selecting an account number.*** The `Label` at the top of the ATM displays a message informing the user to select an account number. Use the `ComboBox` at the bottom of the `Form` to choose an account number. Select account number 12548693. Notice that the `Label` now prompts the user to provide a PIN number (Fig. 25.2). The **Done** Button has also been enabled allowing the user to restart the ATM transaction.

4. ***Entering a PIN number.*** Use the keypad to input the PIN number 1234. As you enter the PIN number, your entry is displayed as an *, to conceal the input. The **OK** Button should be enabled now. Click **OK**. The `Label` at the top of the ATM displays a welcome message telling the user to select a transaction (Fig. 25.3). Notice that the **Balance** and **Withdraw** Buttons have been enabled, allowing the user to perform these types of transactions.

5. ***Viewing balance information.*** Click the **Balance** Button to view the account balance. The amount displays in the `Label` at the top of the `Form`.

6. ***Withdrawing money from the account.*** Click the **Withdraw** Button to perform a withdrawal. The `Label` at the top of the `Form` asks you to input the amount you want to withdraw. Use the keypad to input 20 for the amount. Click **OK**. The `Label` displays your new account balance after deducting the 20 dollars (Fig. 25.4).

(cont.)

Asterisk is displayed here for
each keypad **Button** pressed
for the PIN numbers

Account number
selected

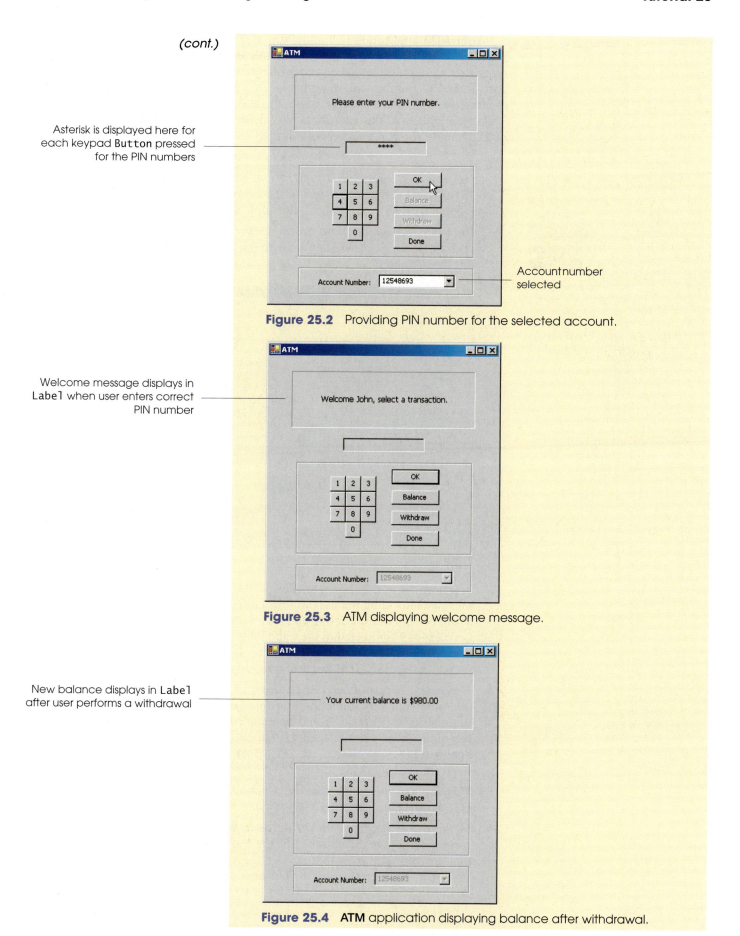

Figure 25.2 Providing PIN number for the selected account.

Welcome message displays in
Label when user enters correct
PIN number

Figure 25.3 ATM displaying welcome message.

New balance displays in **Label**
after user performs a withdrawal

Figure 25.4 **ATM** application displaying balance after withdrawal.

(cont.)

7. ***Ending the transaction.*** Click the **Done** Button to complete the ATM transaction. The transaction ends, and the Label prompts for the ncxt customer's account number. The **Balance**, **Withdraw** and **OK** Buttons are disabled.

8. ***Checking on whether the account information has been updated.*** Click the running application's close box to terminate the application. Repeat *Steps 2–5* to check the balance of the same account. Notice that the balance amount reflects the withdrawal you performed in *Step 7*. This shows that the account's new balance has been retained.

9. ***Closing the application.*** Close your running application by clicking its close box.

10. ***Closing the IDE.*** Close Visual Studio .NET by clicking its close box.

25.2 Planning the ATM Application

Now that you have test-driven the **ATM** application, you will begin by analyzing the application. The following pseudocode describes the basic operation of the **ATM** application.

```
When the user selects an account number from the ComboBox:
    Prompt the user to enter a PIN
    Enable the Done Button
    Clear the TextBox for the PIN

When the user enters the PIN:
    Append the number to the PIN

When the text in the TextBox changes:
    Enable the OK Button

When the user clicks the OK Button to submit the PIN:

Search the database for the account number's corresponding account
    information

    If the user provided a correct PIN
        Enable the Balance and Withdraw Buttons
        Disable the ComboBox
        Display the user's name and prompt the user to select a transaction
    Else
        Prompt the user to enter a valid PIN

    Clear the TextBox

When the user clicks the Balance Button:
    Display the balance

When the user clicks the Withdraw Button:
    Prompt the user to enter the withdrawal amount

When the user clicks the OK Button to submit the withdrawal amount:

    If the withdrawal amount is less than the balance
        Calculate the new balance and update the database
    Else
        Indicate that the amount is too large

    Clear the withdrawal amount

When the user clicks the Done Button:
    Disable the OK, Balance, Withdraw and Done Buttons
    Enable the ComboBox
    Display instructions for the next customer
```

Now that you have test-driven the **ATM** application and studied its pseudocode representation, you will use an ACE table to help you convert the pseudocode to Visual Basic .NET. Figure 25.5 lists the actions, controls and events that you will help complete your own version of this application.

Action/Control/Event (ACE) Table for the ATM Application

Action	Control	Event
Display account numbers	cboAccountNumber	
	cboAccountNumber	SelectedIndex-Changed
Prompt the user to enter a PIN	lblDisplay	
Enable the Done Button	btnDone	
Clear the TextBox for the PIN	txtInput	
	btnOne, btnTwo, btnThree, btnFour, btnFive, btnSix, btnSeven, btnEight, btnNine	Click
Append the number to the PIN		
	txtInput	TextChanged
Enable the OK Button	btnOK	
	btnOK	Click
Search the database for the account number's corresponding account information	objOleDbConnection, objSelectAccount-Data	

If the user provided a correct PIN
  Enable the Balance and
  Withdraw Buttons
	btnBalance, btnWithdraw	

Disable the ComboBox	cboAccountNumber	
Display the user's name and prompt the user to select a transaction	lblDisplay	
Else Prompt the user to enter a valid PIN	lblDisplay	
Clear the TextBox	txtInput	
	btnBalance	Click
Display the balance	lblDisplay	
	btnWithdraw	Click
Prompt the user to enter the withdrawal amount	lblDisplay	
	btnOK	Click
If the withdrawal amount is less than the balance Calculate the new balance and update the database	objOleDbConnection, objUpdateBalance, lblDisplay	
Else Indicate that the amount is too large	lblDisplay	
Clear the withdrawal amount	txtInput	

Figure 25.5 ACE table for the **ATM** application. (Part 1 of 2.)

Action	Control	Event
	`btnDone`	`Click`

Disable the OK, Balance, Withdraw and Done Buttons	`btnOk,`
	`btnBalance,`
	`btnWithdraw,`
	`btnDone`	

Enable the ComboBox	`cboAccountNumber`	
Display instructions for the next customer	`lblDisplay`	

Figure 25.5   ACE table for the **ATM** application. (Part 2 of 2.)

25.3 Creating Database Connections

In this tutorial, you use Visual Studio .NET's **Server Explorer** window to connect to a database. A **database** is an organized collection of data. Many different strategies exist for organizing data in databases to allow easy access to and manipulation of the data. A **database management system** (**DBMS**) enables you to access and store data without worrying about how the data is organized. In this tutorial, you use a Microsoft Access database. You connect to the database in the following box.

Adding a Database Connection to the ATM Application

1. ***Copying the template to your working directory.*** Copy the C:\Examples\ Tutorial25\TemplateApplication\ATM directory to your C:\SimplyVB directory.

2. ***Opening the ATM application's template file.*** Double click ATM.sln in the ATM directory to open the application in Visual Studio .NET.

3. ***Displaying the Server Explorer window.*** Select **View > Server Explorer** to display the **Server Explorer** window.

4. ***Adding a database connection.*** To access and manipulate data in a database, you must first establish a connection to the database. Click the **Server Explorer** window's Connect to Database Button (Fig. 25.6) to display the **Data Link Properties** dialog (Fig. 25.7). [*Note*: The contents of your **Server Explorer** window will differ.]

Click the Connect to Database Button

Figure 25.6   **Server Explorer** window.

5. ***Selecting the type of database to access.*** Click the **Provider** tab in the **Data Link Properties** dialog, and select the **Microsoft Jet 4.0 OLE DB Provider** item in the **OLE DB Provider(s)** box as in Fig. 25.7. This selection corresponds to a Microsoft Access database. Click **Next >>**. [*Note*: The number of items displayed in Fig. 25.7 might vary on your system.]

(cont.)

Provider tab ——————

Select this provider ——————

Click **Next >>** to continue ——————

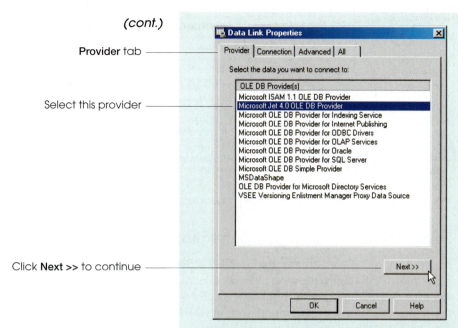

Figure 25.7 **Provider** tab in the **Data Link Properties** dialog.

6. ***Specifying the database connection.*** Before you can manipulate the database, you must first use Visual Studio .NET to connect to the database. After clicking **Next >>**, you are brought to the **Connection** tab of the **Data Link Properties** dialog (Fig. 25.8). Here, you create a **connection object** for the Visual Studio .NET IDE. A connection object maintains a connection to a database. Click the ellipsis (**...**) Button to the right of the **Select or enter a database name:** field, shown in Fig. 25.8, to display the **Select Access Database** dialog (Fig. 25.9).

Connection tab ——————

Click ellipsis **Button** to select a database

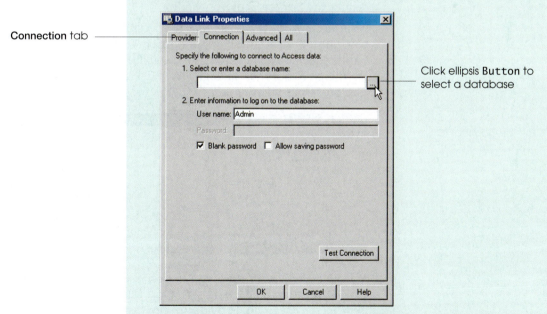

Figure 25.8 **Connection** tab of the **Data Link Properties** dialog.

7. ***Using the Select Access Database dialog.*** In the **Select Access Database** dialog, select the db_ATM.mdb database in C:\SimplyVB\ATM directory as in Fig. 25.9. Click **Open**. You will be directed back to the **Connection** tab of the **Data Link Properties** dialog.

(cont.)

Select the db_ATM.mdb file ⎯⎯⎯⎯⎯⎯

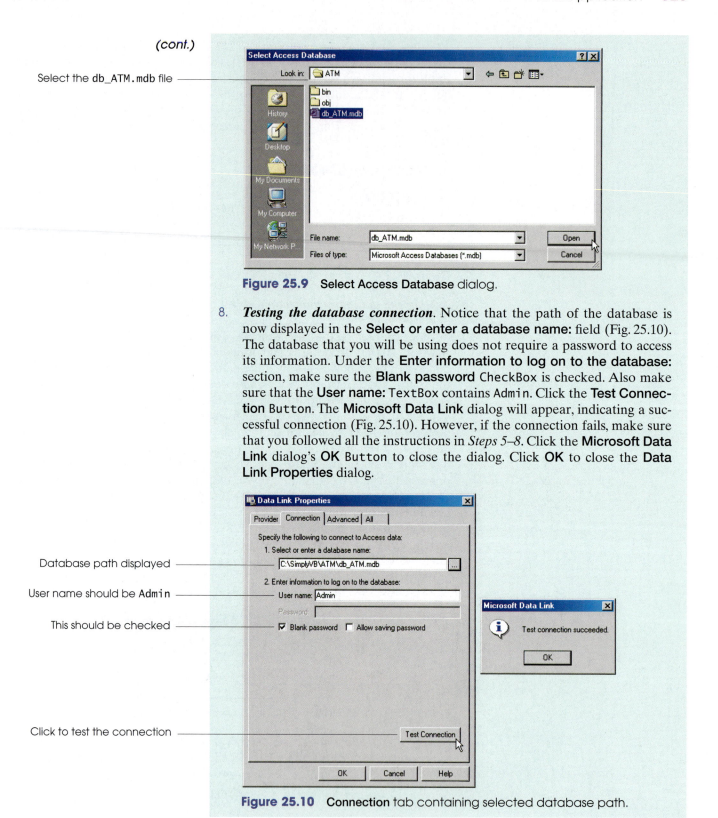

Figure 25.9   Select Access Database dialog.

8. *Testing the database connection*. Notice that the path of the database is now displayed in the **Select or enter a database name:** field (Fig. 25.10). The database that you will be using does not require a password to access its information. Under the **Enter information to log on to the database:** section, make sure the **Blank password** CheckBox is checked. Also make sure that the **User name:** TextBox contains Admin. Click the **Test Connection** Button. The **Microsoft Data Link** dialog will appear, indicating a successful connection (Fig. 25.10). However, if the connection fails, make sure that you followed all the instructions in *Steps 5–8*. Click the **Microsoft Data Link** dialog's **OK** Button to close the dialog. Click **OK** to close the **Data Link Properties** dialog.

Database path displayed ⎯⎯⎯⎯⎯⎯

User name should be Admin ⎯⎯⎯⎯⎯⎯

This should be checked ⎯⎯⎯⎯⎯⎯

Click to test the connection ⎯⎯⎯⎯⎯⎯

Figure 25.10   Connection tab containing selected database path.

(cont.)   9. ***Viewing the database connection in the Server Explorer window.*** Notice that a data connection to the db_ATM.mdb database appears in the **Server Explorer** window (Fig. 25.11). You will use the **Server Explorer**'s data connection to add a data connection to the **ATM** application in the next step. [*Note*: As well as displaying the connection to db_ATM.mdb, your system may display data from previous connections or data about your network connection.]

Click to expand ——————— Data connection
———— Drag-and-drop the data connecton onto the **Form** to create an OleDbConnection object

Figure 25.11   Database connection shown in the **Server Explorer** window.

10. ***Adding the database-connection object to the Form.*** If you are not already in design view, switch to design view at this time. Select the data connection in the **Server Explorer** window (listed as **ACCESS.C:\SimplyVB\ATM\db_ATM.mdb.Admin**), and drag-and-drop it onto the Form. A message dialog will be displayed asking if the database's password should included in the source code. Because this database does not include a password, click the **Don't include password** Button. An ADO .NET **OleDbConnection** object appears in the component tray. You now have established a connection between the **ATM** application and the db_ATM.mdb database. The OleDbConnection object maintains a connection to the database. Class OleDbConnection provides methods, such as Open and Close, which allow you to open and close the connection to the database. You will use these methods shortly. Notice that the data connection (Fig. 25.11) displays the exact, or absolute, path of the database. In this case, the database connection references a database in the C:\SimplyVB\ATM directory. This is known as an absolute path. If the database is moved, the application will not run. If the database is moved, you can reset the connection by selecting the ConnectionString property of the OleDbConnection object, selecting **<New Connection...>** and specifying the new directory in the dialog that appears.

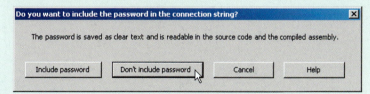

Figure 25.12   Storing the database's password.

11. ***Setting the OleDbConnection object's properties.*** Click the OleDbConnection object to view its properties in the **Properties** window. Change the name to objOleDbConnection. The object appears as in Fig. 25.13.

12. ***Saving the project.*** Select **File > Save All** to save your modified code.

(cont.)

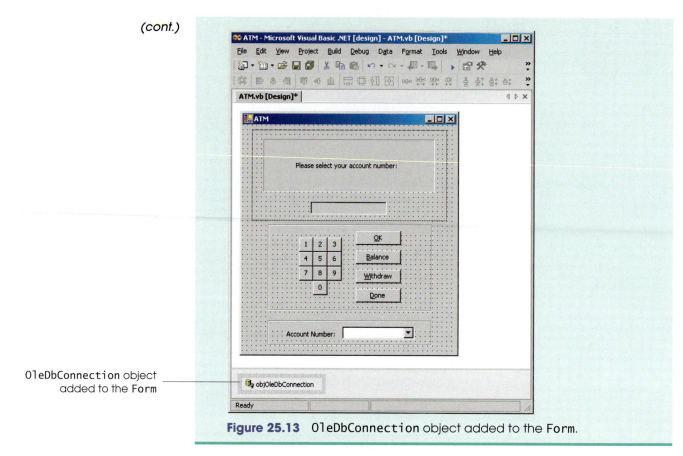

Figure 25.13 OleDbConnection object added to the Form.

OleDbConnection object
added to the Form

Now that you have established a connection to the database by using the **Server Explorer** window, you will need to understand how the db_ATM.mdb database organizes its data. You will use the **Server Explorer** window to view the database information in the Visual Studio .NET IDE. You will learn about the database in the following box.

Understanding the
db_ATM.mdb Database
Structure

1. ***Viewing the*** AccountInformation ***table of the*** db_ATM.mdb ***database.*** Expand the **Access.C:\SimplyVB\ATM\db_ATM.mdb.Admin** node in the **Server Explorer**, then expand the **Tables** node to display the **AccountInformation** node (Fig. 25.14). AccountInformation is a table in the db_ATM.mdb database. A **table** is used to store related information in rows and columns. Relational databases, such as Microsoft Access, are composed of one or more tables. Right click **AccountInformation**, and select **Retrieve Data from Table** (Fig. 25.14). The contents of the AccountInformation table display in Visual Studio .NET (Fig. 25.15).

Click to display the **Tables** node

Right click the
AccountInformation node

Select to view the table's
contents

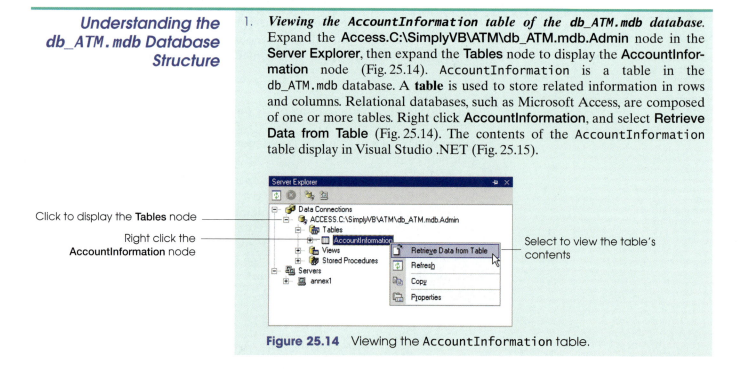

Figure 25.14 Viewing the AccountInformation table.

(cont.)

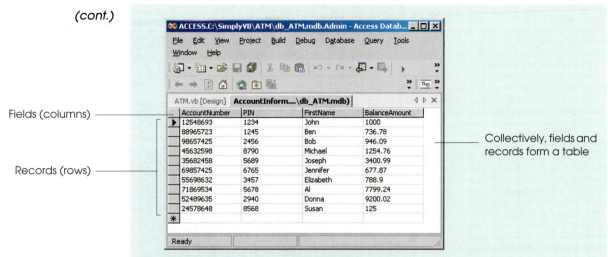

Fields (columns)

Records (rows)

Collectively, fields and records form a table

Figure 25.15 AccountInformation table's content.

2. *Understanding the database*. Figure 25.15 displays the entire database (because it consists of one table) used in the **ATM** application. This table contains ten **records** and four **fields**. A record is a table row, and a field is a table column. For example, in this table, the row containing the 12548693, 1234, John and 1000 is considered a single record, and the AccountNumber, PIN, FirstName and BalanceAmount columns are fields that represent the data in each record.

In addition to records and fields, a table should contain a **primary key**, which is a field (or combination of fields) that contains unique values that are used to distinguish records from one another. In this table, the AccountNumber field is the primary key for referencing the data. Because no two account number values are the same, the AccountNumber field can act as the primary key.

3. *Closing the AccountInformation window*. Right click the **AccountInformation** tab and select **Close**.

Now that you have established a connection to the database and examined the contents of the database, you will add three **data command objects** to the Form. These objects will be used to retrieve information from and update information in the database.

Adding Data Command Objects to the Form

1. *Adding a data command object to the Form*. Select the **Data** tab in the **Toolbox**. Drag-and-drop an ADO .NET **OleDbCommand** control from the **Data** tab onto the Form to create a data command object. You will use this particular data command object to retrieve information from the database.

2. *Setting the Name and Connection properties of the data command object*. Set the Name property of the OleDbCommand object to objSelectAccount. Because the OleDbCommand object will interact with the database, it must be provided with an existing data connection. Select the OleDbCommand's Connection property. Click the down-arrow Button that appears next to the Connection property field. Expand the **Existing** node and select the connection object (objOleDbConnection) you created earlier in this tutorial (Fig. 25.16).

(cont.)

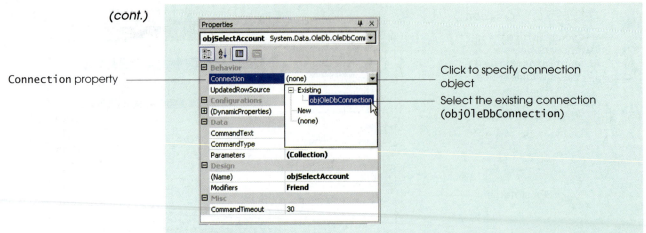

Connection property

Click to specify connection object

Select the existing connection (objOleDbConnection)

Figure 25.16 Properties of objSelectAccount.

3. *Setting the CommandText property of the data command object.* Select the CommandText property of the data command object in the **Properties** window. Click the ellipsis (**...**) Button that appears next to the CommandText property field. The **Query Builder** and **Add Table** dialogs appear (Fig. 25.17). **Query Builder** is a Visual Studio .NET tool that allows you to specify the commands that retrieve information from and modify information in databases.

4. *Adding a table to the Query Builder.* Notice that the AccountInformation table name appears in the **Add Table** dialog. The **Add Table** dialog displays all of the database's tables. This table appears in the dialog because you set the OleDbConnection object's Connection property, which connects to the db_ATM.mdb database. Select AccountInformation in the **Tables** tab of the **Add Table** dialog and click the **Add** Button. Notice that a window containing the AccountInformation table's fields now appears in the **Query Builder** dialog (Fig. 25.18). Click the **Close** Button in the **Add Table** dialog.

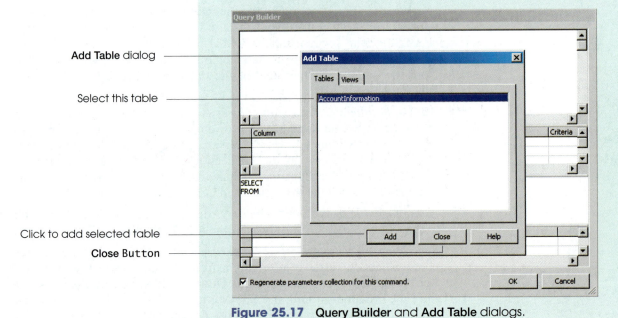

Add Table dialog

Select this table

Click to add selected table

Close Button

Figure 25.17 Query Builder and Add Table dialogs.

(cont.)

AccountInformation window appears once AccountInformation is added in the **Add Table** dialog

Primary-key-field name displayed in bold

Partial SQL statement

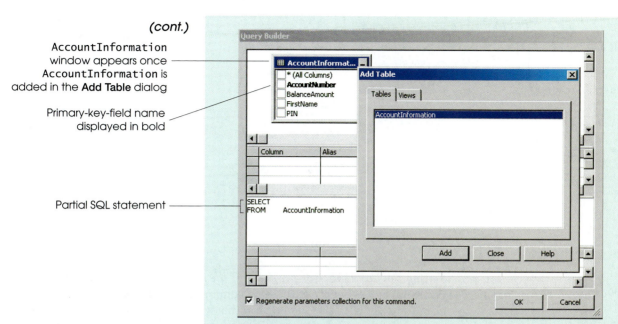

Figure 25.18 AccountInformation table added to the **Query Builder** dialog.

5. ***Specifying the fields from which to retrieve data.*** You want this data command object to retrieve information from the database. Notice that the lower portion of the **Query Builder** dialog contains the words SELECT, FROM and AccountInformation. This represents the **Structured Query Language (SQL)** statement that will be used to select information from the database. SQL is a language often used to perform database queries (requests for specified information) and to manipulate data. The FROM AccountInformation portion of the SQL statement indicates that the information you will select will be from the database's AccountInformation table.

   In the **AccountInformation** window of the **Query Builder**, place a checkmark in the **AccountNumber** CheckBox. Notice that AccountNumber appears in the table beneath the **AccountInformation** window (Fig. 25.19). The AccountNumber field also appears next to the SELECT keyword. This indicates that the data command object will retrieve the data from the AccountNumber field in the database. Click **OK** in the **Query Builder** dialog.

6. ***Adding another data command object.*** Add another OleDbCommand object to the Form. Set its Name property to objSelectAccountData. Click the field next to the Connection property, click the down arrow and expand the **Existing** node to set the connection object objOleDbConnection. Click the ellipsis (...) Button that appears next to the CommandText property field to display the **Add Table** and **Query Builder** dialogs.

7. ***Adding a table to the Query Builder.*** Add the AccountInformation table to the **Query Builder** dialog and click the **Add Table** dialog's **Close** Button.

8. ***Specifying the fields from which to retrieve data.*** You want this data command object to retrieve information from the database, as well. In the **AccountInformation** window of the **Query Builder**, place a checkmark in the **PIN**, **BalanceAmount** and **FirstName** CheckBoxes (Fig. 25.20). These names appear in the table beneath the **AccountInformation** window. The names PIN, BalanceAmount and FirstName fields also should appear next to the SELECT keyword to indicate that the data command object will retrieve the data from these three fields in the database.

(cont.)

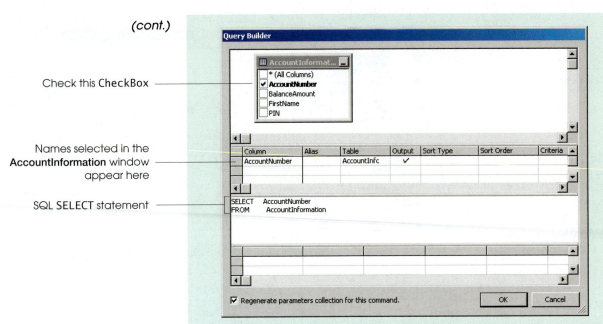

Check this **CheckBox**

Names selected in the **AccountInformation** window appear here

SQL SELECT statement

Figure 25.19 Selecting fields in the **Query Builder** dialog.

9. *Specifying where to retrieve the information.* Check the **AccountNumber** CheckBox in the **AccountInformation** window of the **Query Builder** dialog. AccountNumber appears in the table below the **AccountInformation** window and the word AccountNumber has been added to the SELECT portion of the SQL statement. In the **Criteria** column of the AccountNumber row, type =? and press *Enter* (Fig. 25.20). Notice that the words WHERE (AccountNumber=?) have been added to the end of the SQL statement (Fig. 25.20). The **WHERE** clause specifies the selection criteria for the statement (in this case, the AccountNumber field having a specific value). The **criteria** of the statement indicates from which specific record data will be retrieved or manipulated. The (AccountNumber=?) portion of the statement indicates that the application will search for the AccountNumber value (which you do not yet know, because the user provides it when the application runs) in the database.

   Also notice that a funnel icon appears to the right of the **AccountNumber** CheckBox in the **AccountInformation** window. This funnel icon indicates that you have specified a value in the **Criteria** column of the AccountNumber row. In the **Output** column, uncheck the **AccountNumber**'s CheckBox to remove AccountNumber from the SELECT portion of the statement. This means the result of the SELECT statement should not contain the AccountNumber field. Notice that the **AccountNumber** CheckBox in the **AccountInformation** window has been unchecked as well. The SQL statement should now look like the statement in Fig. 25.21. This SQL statement will retrieve the PIN, BalanceAmount and FirstName values from the AccountInformation table, where the AccountNumber value equals a value that you will specify shortly. Click the **OK** Button to accept the SQL statement, and close the **Query Builder** dialog.

(cont.)

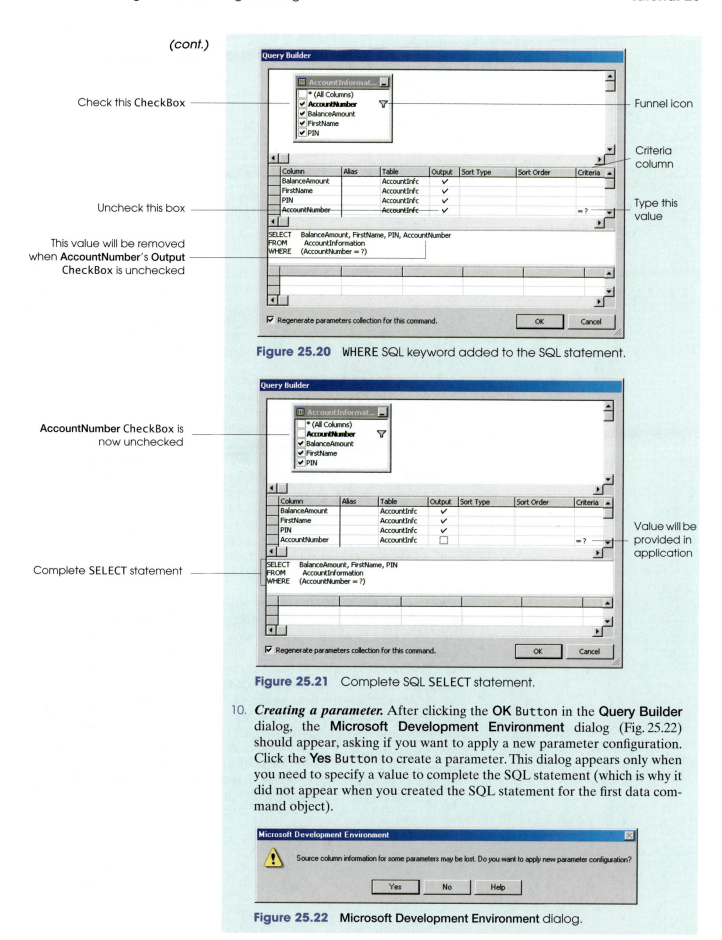

Check this **CheckBox**

Funnel icon

Criteria column

Uncheck this box

Type this value

This value will be removed when **AccountNumber**'s **Output CheckBox** is unchecked

Figure 25.20 WHERE SQL keyword added to the SQL statement.

AccountNumber CheckBox is now unchecked

Value will be provided in application

Complete **SELECT** statement

Figure 25.21 Complete SQL SELECT statement.

10. *Creating a parameter.* After clicking the **OK** Button in the **Query Builder** dialog, the **Microsoft Development Environment** dialog (Fig. 25.22) should appear, asking if you want to apply a new parameter configuration. Click the **Yes** Button to create a parameter. This dialog appears only when you need to specify a value to complete the SQL statement (which is why it did not appear when you created the SQL statement for the first data command object).

Figure 25.22 **Microsoft Development Environment** dialog.

(cont.)   11. ***Viewing the Parameters property of the data command object.*** Select the
data command object's `Parameters` property in the **Properties** window, and
click the ellipsis (...) Button that appears in the **Parameters** property field
(Fig. 25.23). The **OleDbParameter Collection Editor** dialog appears
(Fig. 25.24). Notice that an `AccountNumber` parameter appears in the collection. Although you do not need to change any settings in this dialog, you will
use the `AccountNumber` parameter in the code file to specify the value that
will replace the ? in the SQL statement (created in *Step 9*). You will write
Visual Basic .NET code to specify the value for this parameter, because you
will not know the `AccountNumber` value until the user selects it from the
ComboBox in the application's GUI. Click **OK** to close the dialog.

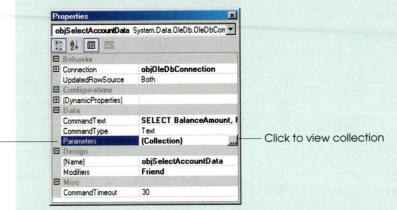

Parameters property ——————— Click to view collection

Figure 25.23   **Parameters** property of a data command object.

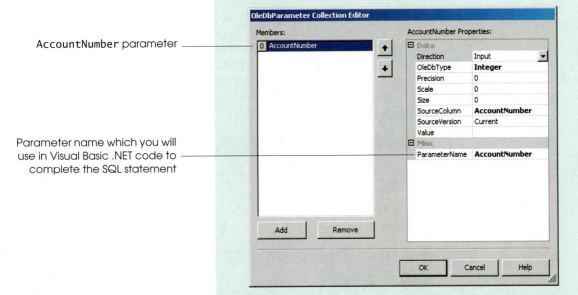

AccountNumber parameter ———————

Parameter name which you will
use in Visual Basic .NET code to ———————
complete the SQL statement

Figure 25.24   **OleDbParameter Collection Editor** dialog.

12. ***Adding a third data command object.*** Drag and drop another `OleDbCom-`
`mand` object on the Form. Name the object `objUpdateBalance` and set the
`Connection` property to `objOleDbConnection`. The command objects
should appear in the component tray as in Fig. 25.25. Repeat *Steps 3–4* in this
box to display the **Query Builder** dialog.

(cont.)

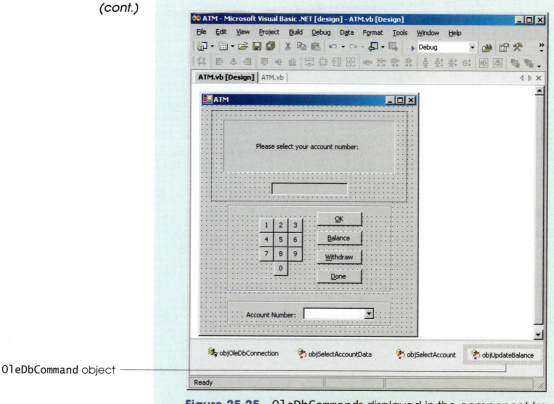

OleDbCommand object

Figure 25.25 OleDbCommands displayed in the component tray.

13. ***Changing the statement to update the database.*** After you have added the
AccountInformation table to the **Query Builder** dialog, right click the
Column column in the table beneath the **AccountInformation** window
(Fig. 25.26). Select **Change Type > Update**. Notice that the SELECT statement in the lower portion of the **Query Builder** dialog has been changed to
an UPDATE statement. You will use this UPDATE statement to modify (that is,
update) data in the database.

Right click the **Column**

Select this to create an
UPDATE statement

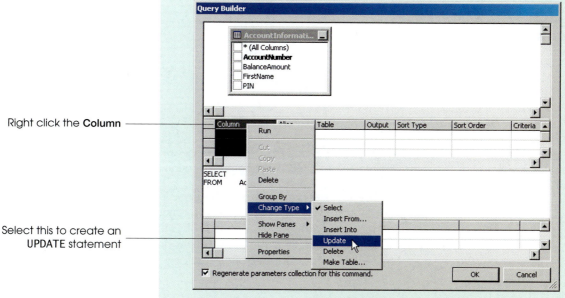

Figure 25.26 Specifying an **UPDATE** statement.

(cont.)

14. ***Specifying a value to update.*** Check the **BalanceAmount** CheckBox in the **AccountInformation** window. Notice that the `BalanceAmount` field name appears in the UPDATE statement after the SQL keyword SET. In the **New Value** column of the table beneath the **AccountInformation** window, type ? to indicate that the new value is not yet known. Press *Enter*. The SQL statement in the **Query Builder** dialog now appears as Fig. 25.27. This indicates that the `BalanceAmount` field in the `AccountInformation` table will be updated to a new value that you will specify when the application runs.

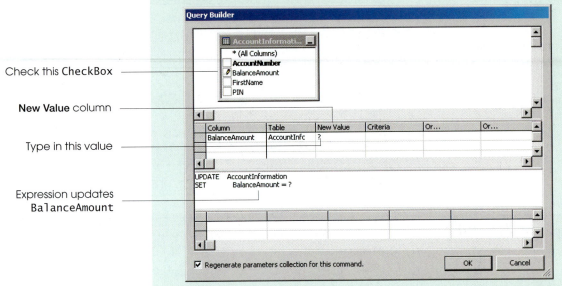

Check this **CheckBox**

New Value column

Type in this value

Expression updates `BalanceAmount`

Figure 25.27   Specifying the `BalanceAmount` field in the UPDATE statement.

15. ***Specifying which account to update.*** Specify which account to update by checking the **AccountNumber** CheckBox in the **AccountInformation** window. In the table beneath the **AccountInformation** window, type =? in the **Criteria** field of the `AccountNumber` row to indicate that the account number to update is not yet known. Press *Enter*. Now uncheck the **AccountNumber** CheckBox in the **AccountInformation** window to remove the `AccountNumber` value from the SET clause of the SQL statement. The UPDATE statement should now appear as shown in Fig. 25.28. This SQL statement will update the `BalanceAmount` to a value that you will specify by writing Visual Basic .NET code. Click the **OK** Button to dismiss the **Query Builder** dialog and click **Yes** in the **Microsoft Development Environment** dialog to create parameters.

16. ***Viewing the Parameters property.*** View the parameters created for this data command as you did in *Step 11*. Notice that there are two parameters: `BalanceAmount` and `Original_AccountNumber`. The parameter name `Original_AccountNumber` was created by Visual Studio .NET. This value will represent the `AccountNumber` value that will be specified when the user selects an account number from the ComboBox. You will use both these parameters in the code file shortly.

17. ***Saving the project.*** Select **File > Save All** to save your modified code.

(cont.)

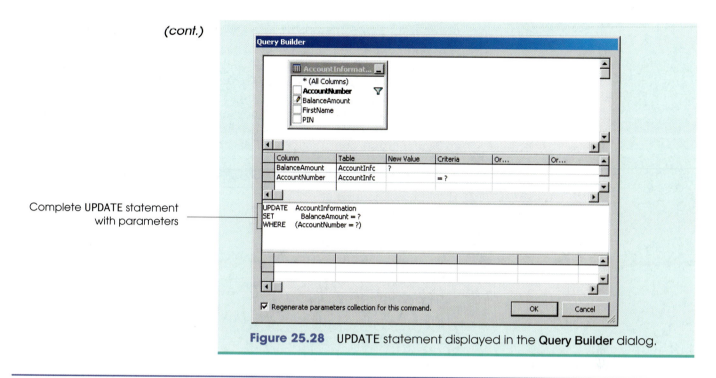

Complete UPDATE statement with parameters

Figure 25.28   UPDATE statement displayed in the **Query Builder** dialog.

SELF-REVIEW

1. The _____ object maintains a connection to the database.

   a) OleDbCommand
   b) OleDbAdapter
   c) OleDbConnection
   d) None of the above.

2. You can specify the value of a parameter by using the Parameters property of an _____ object.

   a) OleDbCommand
   b) OleDbConnection
   c) OleDbParameter
   d) None of the above.

Answers: 1) c. 2) a.

25.4 Programming the ATM Application

When you view the code file (ATM.vb), you will notice that code has been provided for you. This code defines the basic functionality of the ATM; however, you will be defining the FrmATM_Load event handler and the RetrieveAccountInformation and UpdateBalance methods that will access the database. The empty FrmATM_Load event handler and method headers for these have been provided for you. Your task will be to code their functionality. Now that you have established a connection to the db_ATM.mdb database and have created data commands, you will write the necessary code to complete the application. You import an ADO .NET namespace into the application in the following box to provide access to the OleDb database objects.

Importing Namespace System.Data.OleDb

1. *Viewing the application code.* Select **View > Code** to display the **ATM** application code file.

2. *Importing namespace System.Data.OleDb.* Add line 1 of Fig. 25.29 to import System.Data.OleDb. Importing this namespace will allow you to perform database processing and omit typing System.Data.OleDb when referring to the classes in this namespace.

3. *Saving the project.* Select **File > Save All** to save your modified code.

(cont.)

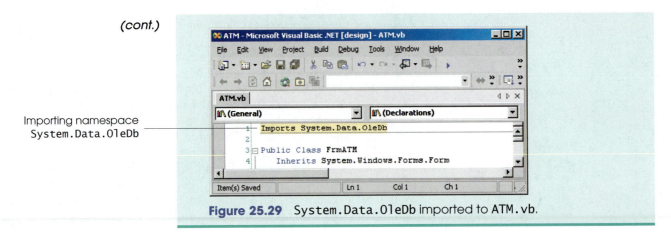

Importing namespace
System.Data.OleDb

Figure 25.29 System.Data.OleDb imported to ATM.vb.

Now you will define the FrmATM_Load event handler to fill the ComboBox with a list of account numbers from the database. This will allow the user to select an existing account number when the **ATM** application is executed. You do this in the next box.

Displaying Existing Account Numbers in the ComboBox

1. ***Connecting to the database.*** Locate the FrmATM_Load event handler (lines 563–567). Add lines 567–571 of Fig. 25.30 to the FrmATM_Load event handler. Because the OleDbConnection object's connection to the database is not open by default, you must open it. Line 567 opens the connection to the database by invoking the Open method of the OleDbConnection object. Lines 570–571 create an **OleDbDataReader** object (called a **data reader** object) and assign it to reference objReader. Data readers are used to read data from a database. These objects only retrieve data and cannot modify data. The data reader is created by invoking method **ExecuteReader** for the object referenced by objSelectAccount (an OleDbCommand object). This method executes the SQL statement and makes the result of the query available in the data reader.

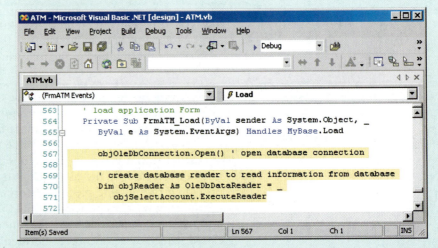

Figure 25.30 Opening the connection to the database and creating a data reader.

(cont.)

2. ***Filling the ComboBox with account numbers.*** Add lines 573–578 of Fig. 25.31 to the FrmATM_Load event handler. Lines 574–576 are a Do While...Loop that fills the ComboBox with account numbers.

Line 574 invokes the data reader object's **Read** method to begin reading information from the database. You must call method Read to position the data reader to the table's first record. Line 575 retrieves the value stored in the AccountNumber field and adds it to the ComboBox. To retrieve the data from the database, you simply provide the name of the field (in double-quotes) in parentheses after the reference name of the data reader. Thus, the objReader("AccountNumber") expression retrieves the value stored in the AccountNumber field. The Do While...Loop will continue to execute as long as the data reader has information to read. Line 578 invokes the Close method of OleDbConnection to close the database connection.

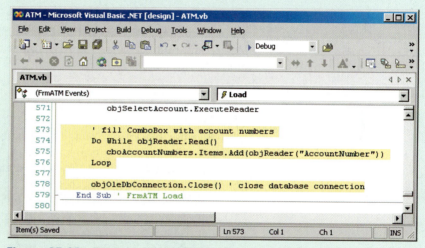

Figure 25.31   Filling the **ComboBox** with account numbers.

3. ***Saving the project.*** Select **File > Save All** to save your modified code.

Now you are ready to define the RetrieveAccountInformation method, which will be used to determine whether the PIN number provided by the user is valid. You create this method in the following box.

Retrieving Account Information from the Database

1. ***Connecting to the database.*** Locate the method header for RetrieveAccountInformation near the bottom of the code file. Add lines 584–589 of Fig. 25.32 to the RetrieveAccountInformation method. Lines 586–587 set the AccountNumber parameter value of the objSelectAccountData data command to the value of cboAccountNumber.SelectedItem (the account number selected by the user). This statement completes the SQL query by providing the missing piece of information—the account number. This will set the command to perform a SELECT query on the AccountInformation table of the database. The PIN, BalanceAmount and FirstName values associated with the provided account number (specified through the ComboBox) are selected from the database. Line 589 opens a connection to the database by invoking the Open method of the OleDbConnection object.

(cont.)

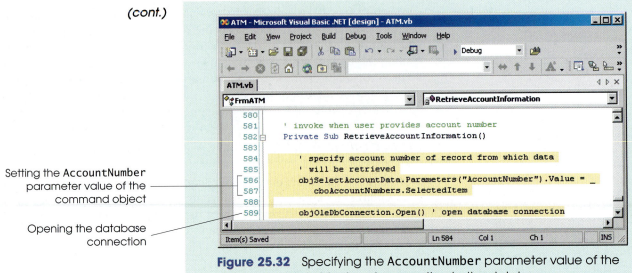

Setting the **AccountNumber** parameter value of the command object

Opening the database connection

Figure 25.32   Specifying the **AccountNumber** parameter value of the data command object and connecting to the database.

2.   ***Creating and using a data reader.*** You are now ready to read information from the database. Add lines 591–604 of Fig. 25.33 to the **Retrieve-AccountInformation** method. Lines 592–593 create an **OleDbDataReader** object and assign it to reference **objReader**.

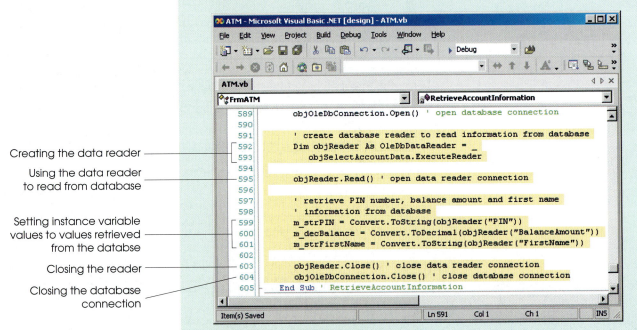

Creating the data reader

Using the data reader to read from database

Setting instance variable values to values retrieved from the databse

Closing the reader

Closing the database connection

Figure 25.33   **OleDbDataReader** for reading a record's data.

Line 595 invokes the data reader object's **Read** method to begin reading information from the database. Recall that the **Read** method must be called to position the data reader to the table's first record. Lines 599–601 set the instance variables **m_strPIN**, **m_decBalance** and **m_strFirstName** to the PIN number, balance amount and first name stored in the database for the requested account, respectively. Each account number is unique, so we know there is only one record from which this information is being read. The data reader returns items as **Objects**, so conversions are needed before the assignment in lines 599–601 can be performed. **Convert** methods **ToDecimal** and **ToString** are used to convert the information retrieved from the database to a **Decimal** and a **String**, respectively.

(cont.)

Line 603 invokes the reader's `Close` method to close the data-reader connection. While the data reader is being used, the connection object is busy and cannot be used for any other actions, besides closing the connection. Calling the `Close` method of the data reader allows the data connection to be used for other operations. You did not need to call this method when you filled the `ComboBox` because you used the `Do While...Loop` which kept the data reader open until no more data could be read. Line 604 uses the `Close` method of `OleDbConnection` to close the database connection.

3. **Saving the project.** Select **File > Save All** to save your modified code.

After defining the `RetrieveAccountInformation` method, you will need to create the `UpdateBalance` method. This method is invoked if the user-requested withdrawal amount can be deducted from the account balance. The `UpdateBalance` method updates the account balance in the database by writing to the database. You define this method in the following box.

Updating the Balance Amount in the Database

1. **Connecting to the database and creating an update statement.** Locate the `UpdateBalance` method. Add lines 610–616 of Fig. 25.34 to the `UpdateBalance` method. Lines 611–612 set a value for the `BalanceAmount` parameter of the `objUpdateBalance` data command object equal to the value of the variable `m_decBalance`. The value stored in this variable reflects any withdrawals made by the user. Lines 615–616 set the `Original_AccountNumber` parameter value of the `objUpdateBalance` data command object equal to the value of the selected account number from the `ComboBox`. Now the `UPDATE` statement you created for the `objUpdateBalance` data command object is complete. The SQL statement will update the `BalanceAmount` field for the record containing the `AccountNumber` field value of the selected account. The new value of the `BalanceAmount` for that record will be set to the value of `m_decBalance`.

Specifying `objUpdateBalance`'s `BalanceAmount` parameter value

Specifying `objUpdateBalance`'s `Original_AccountNumber` parameter value

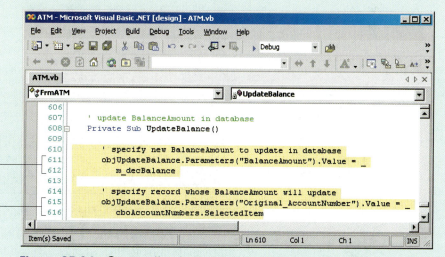

Figure 25.34 Connecting to the database to update a field.

2. **Executing the update statement.** Add lines 618–623 of Fig. 25.35 to the `UpdateBalance` method. Line 618 opens the connection to the database. Line 621 executes the update statement by using the **ExecuteNonQuery** method of the `objUpdateBalance` data command object. This method executes an SQL statement and returns the number of rows modified. The database has now been updated. Line 623 closes the database connection by using the `Close` method.

(cont.)

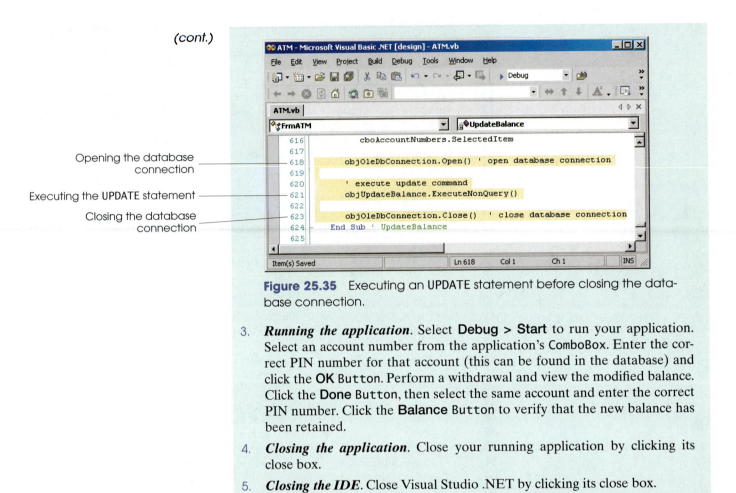

Opening the database connection

Executing the UPDATE statement

Closing the database connection

Figure 25.35 Executing an UPDATE statement before closing the database connection.

3. *Running the application.* Select **Debug > Start** to run your application. Select an account number from the application's ComboBox. Enter the correct PIN number for that account (this can be found in the database) and click the **OK** Button. Perform a withdrawal and view the modified balance. Click the **Done** Button, then select the same account and enter the correct PIN number. Click the **Balance** Button to verify that the new balance has been retained.

4. *Closing the application.* Close your running application by clicking its close box.

5. *Closing the IDE.* Close Visual Studio .NET by clicking its close box.

Figure 25.36 presents the source code for the **ATM** application. The lines of code that contain new programming concepts that you learned in this tutorial are highlighted.

```
1    Imports System.Data.OleDb
2
3    Public Class FrmATM
4        Inherits System.Windows.Forms.Form
5
6        ' variables to store user-entered PIN number
7        Private m_strUserPIN As String
8
9        ' variables to store account balance and user's first name
10       Private m_decBalance As Decimal
11       Private m_strFirstName As String
12       Private m_strPIN As String
13
14       ' variable to indicate action being performed
15       Private m_strAction As String = "Account"
16
17       ' Windows Form Designer generated code
18
19       ' invoke when 0 Button is clicked
20       Private Sub btnZero_Click(ByVal sender As System.Object, _
21           ByVal e As System.EventArgs) Handles btnZero.Click
```

Figure 25.36 **ATM** application code. (Part 1 of 6.)

```
22
23          InputNumber("0") ' invoke method with argument 0
24       End Sub ' btnZero_Click
25
26       ' invoke when 1 Button is clicked
27       Private Sub btnOne_Click(ByVal sender As System.Object, _
28          ByVal e As System.EventArgs) Handles btnOne.Click
29
30          InputNumber("1") ' invoke method with argument 1
31       End Sub ' btnOne_Click
32
33       ' invoke when 2 Button is clicked
34       Private Sub btnTwo_Click(ByVal sender As System.Object, _
35          ByVal e As System.EventArgs) Handles btnTwo.Click
36
37          InputNumber("2") ' invoke method with argument 2
38       End Sub ' btnTwo_Click
39
40       ' invoke when 3 Button is clicked
41       Private Sub btnThree_Click(ByVal sender As System.Object, _
42          ByVal e As System.EventArgs) Handles btnThree.Click
43
44          InputNumber("3") ' invoke method with argument 3
45       End Sub ' btnThree_Click
46
47       ' invoke when 4 Button is clicked
48       Private Sub btnFour_Click(ByVal sender As System.Object, _
49          ByVal e As System.EventArgs) Handles btnFour.Click
50
51          InputNumber("4") ' invoke method with argument 4
52       End Sub ' btnFour_Click
53
54       ' invoke when 5 Button is clicked
55       Private Sub btnFive_Click(ByVal sender As System.Object, _
56          ByVal e As System.EventArgs) Handles btnFive.Click
57
58          InputNumber("5") ' invoke method with argument 5
59       End Sub ' btnFive_Click
60
61       ' invoke when 6 Button is clicked
62       Private Sub btnSix_Click(ByVal sender As System.Object, _
63          ByVal e As System.EventArgs) Handles btnSix.Click
64
65          InputNumber("6") ' invoke method with argument 6
66       End Sub ' btnSix_Click
67
68       ' invoke when 7 Button is clicked
69       Private Sub btnSeven_Click(ByVal sender As System.Object, _
70          ByVal e As System.EventArgs) Handles btnSeven.Click
71
72          InputNumber("7") ' invoke method with argument 7
73       End Sub ' btnSeven_Click
74
75       ' invoke when 8 Button is clicked
76       Private Sub btnEight_Click(ByVal sender As System.Object, _
77          ByVal e As System.EventArgs) Handles btnEight.Click
78
79          InputNumber("8") ' invoke method with argument 8
80       End Sub ' btnEight_Click
```

Figure 25.36 **ATM** application code. (Part 2 of 6.)

```
81
82     ' invoke when 9 Button is clicked
83     Private Sub btnNine_Click(ByVal sender As System.Object, _
84         ByVal e As System.EventArgs) Handles btnNine.Click
85
86         InputNumber("9") ' invoke method with argument 9
87     End Sub ' btnNine_Click
88
89     ' determines what text will display in TextBox
90     Private Sub InputNumber(ByVal strNumber As String)
91
92         ' if user is entering PIN number display * to
93         ' conceal PIN entry; store entered PIN in variable
94         If m_strAction = "PIN" Then
95            txtInput.Text &= "*"
96            m_strUserPIN &= strNumber
97
98         Else ' otherwise display number
99            txtInput.Text &= strNumber
100        End If
101
102    End Sub ' InputNumber
103
104    ' invoke when OK Button is clicked
105    Private Sub btnOK_Click(ByVal sender As System.Object, _
106        ByVal e As System.EventArgs) Handles btnOK.Click
107
108        ' determine what action to perform
109        Select Case m_strAction
110
111           ' if user provided PIN number
112           Case "PIN"
113
114              RetrieveAccountInformation() ' invoke method
115
116              ' determine if PIN number is within valid range
117              If m_strUserPIN = m_strPIN Then
118
119                 ' enable Buttons and disable ComboBox
120                 btnBalance.Enabled = True
121                 btnWithdraw.Enabled = True
122                 cboAccountNumber.Enabled = False
123
124                 ' display status to user
125                 lblDisplay.Text = "Welcome " & m_strFirstName & _
126                    ", select a transaction."
127
128                 ' change action to indicate that no user-action
129                 ' is expected
130                 m_strAction = "NoAction"
131              Else
132
133                 ' indicate that incorrect PIN was provided
134                 lblDisplay.Text = "Sorry, PIN number is incorrect." _
135                    & "Please re-enter the PIN number."
136
```

Figure 25.36 **ATM** application code. (Part 3 of 6.)

```
137                              ' clear user's previous PIN entry
138                              m_strUserPIN = ""
139
140                         End If
141
142                         txtInput.Clear() ' clear TextBox
143
144                      ' if user provided withdrawal amount
145                      Case "Withdrawal"
146
147                         ' invoke Withdrawal method with decimal argument
148                         Withdrawal(Convert.ToDecimal(txtInput.Text))
149                         txtInput.Clear()
150                         m_strAction = "NoAction"
151                   End Select
152
153             End Sub ' btnOK_Click
154
155             ' invoke when Withdraw Button is clicked
156             Private Sub btnWithdraw_Click(ByVal sender As System.Object, _
157                ByVal e As System.EventArgs) Handles btnWithdraw.Click
158
159                ' display message to user
160                lblDisplay.Text = _
161                   "Enter the amount you would like to withdraw."
162
163                ' change action to indicate user will
164                ' provide withdrawal amount
165                m_strAction = "Withdrawal"
166             End Sub ' btnWithdraw_Click
167
168             ' determine new balance amount
169             Private Sub Withdrawal(ByVal decWithdrawAmount As Decimal)
170
171                ' determine if amount can be withdrawn
172                If decWithdrawAmount <= m_decBalance Then
173
174                   ' determine new balance amount after withdrawal
175                   m_decBalance -= decWithdrawAmount
176
177                   UpdateBalance() ' invoke method to update database
178
179                   ' display balance information to user
180                   lblDisplay.Text = "Your current balance is " & _
181                         String.Format("{0:C}", m_decBalance)
182                Else
183
184                   ' indicate amount cannot be withdrawn
185                   lblDisplay.Text = "The withdrawal amount is too large." & _
186                      " Select Withdraw and enter a different amount."
187
188                End If
189
190             End Sub ' Withdrawal
191
192             ' invoke when Balance Button is clicked
193             Private Sub btnBalance_Click(ByVal sender As System.Object, _
194                ByVal e As System.EventArgs) Handles btnBalance.Click
```

Figure 25.36   **ATM** application code. (Part 4 of 6.)

```
195
196          ' display user's balance
197          lblDisplay.Text = "Your current balance is " & _
198             String.Format("{0:C}", m_decBalance)
199
200       End Sub ' btnBalance_Click
201
202       ' invoke when Cancel Button is clicked
203       Private Sub btnDone_Click(ByVal sender As System.Object, _
204          ByVal e As System.EventArgs) Handles btnDone.Click
205
206          lblDisplay.Text = "Please select your account number."
207
208          ' change action to indicate that user will
209          ' provide account number
210          m_strAction = "Account"
211          m_strUserPIN = ""
212
213          txtInput.Clear() ' clear TextBox
214          btnOK.Enabled = False ' disable OK Button
215          btnBalance.Enabled = False ' disable Balance Button
216          btnWithdraw.Enabled = False ' disable Withdraw Button
217          btnDone.Enabled = False ' disable Done Button
218          cboAccountNumber.Enabled = True ' enable ComboBox
219          cboAccountNumber.Text = "" ' clear selected account
220       End Sub ' btnDone_Click
221
222       ' invoke when user inputs information in TextBox
223       Private Sub txtInput_TextChanged(ByVal sender As _
224          System.Object, ByVal e As System.EventArgs) _
225          Handles txtInput.TextChanged
226
227          btnOK.Enabled = True ' enable OK Button
228       End Sub ' txtInput_TextChanged
229
230       ' invoke when selection is made in ComboBox
231       Private Sub cboAccountNumber_SelectedIndexChanged(ByVal _
232          sender As System.Object, ByVal e As System.EventArgs) _
233          Handles cboAccountNumber.SelectedIndexChanged
234
235          ' change action to indicate that user will
236          ' provide account number
237          m_strAction = "PIN"
238
239          ' prompt user to enter PIN number
240          lblDisplay.Text = "Please enter your PIN number."
241          btnDone.Enabled = True ' enable Done Button
242          txtInput.Clear() ' clear TextBox
243       End Sub ' cboAccountNumber_SelectedIndexChanged
244
245       ' load application Form
246       Private Sub FrmATM_Load(ByVal sender As System.Object, _
247          ByVal e As System.EventArgs) Handles MyBase.Load
248
249          objOleDbConnection.Open() ' open database connection
250
```

Opens database connection ————— 249

Figure 25.36 **ATM** application code. (Part 5 of 6.)

Creates data reader

```
251         ' create database reader to read information from database
252     [ Dim objReader As OleDbDataReader = _
253           objSelectAccount.ExecuteReader
254
```

Fills **ComboBox** with account numbers

```
255         ' fill ComboBox with account numbers
256     [ Do While objReader.Read()
257           cboAccountNumbers.Items.Add(objReader("AccountNumber"))
258     [ Loop
259
```

Closes database connection

```
260         objOleDbConnection.Close() ' close database connection
261     End Sub ' FrmATM_Load
262
263     ' invoke when user provides account number
264     Private Sub RetrieveAccountInformation()
265
266         ' specify account number of record from which data
267         ' will be retrieved
```

Sets the **AccountNumber** parameter of **objSelectAccountData**

```
268     [ objSelectAccountData.Parameters("AccountNumber").Value = _
269           cboAccountNumbers.SelectedItem
270
```

Opens database connection

```
271         objOleDbConnection.Open() ' open database connection
272
273         ' create database reader to read information from database
```

Creates data reader

```
274     [ Dim objReader As OleDbDataReader = _
275           objSelectAccountData.ExecuteReader
276
```

Reads with data reader

```
277         objReader.Read() ' open data reader connection
278
279         ' retrieve PIN number, balance amount and first name
280         ' information from database
```

Sets instance variables to data read from database

```
281     [ m_strPIN = Convert.ToString(objReader("PIN"))
282       m_decBalance = Convert.ToDecimal(objReader("BalanceAmount"))
283     [ m_strFirstName = Convert.ToString(objReader("FirstName"))
284
```

Closes data reader

```
285         objReader.Close() ' close data reader connection
```

Closes database connection

```
286         objOleDbConnection.Close() ' close database connection
287     End Sub ' RetrieveAccountInformation
288
289     ' update BalanceAmount in database
290     Private Sub UpdateBalance()
291
292         ' specify new BalanceAmount to update in database
```

Sets **BalanceAmount** parameter of **objUpdateBalance**

```
293     [ objUpdateBalance.Parameters("BalanceAmount").Value = _
294           m_decBalance
295
296         ' specify record whose BalanceAmount will update
```

Sets parameter of **objUpdateBalance**

```
297     [ objUpdateBalance.Parameters("Original_AccountNumber").Value= _
298           cboAccountNumbers.SelectedItem
299
```

Opens database connection

```
300         objOleDbConnection.Open() ' open database connection
301
302         ' execute update statement
```

Executes UPDATE statement

```
303         objUpdateBalance.ExecuteNonQuery()
304
```

Closes database connection

```
305         objOleDbConnection.Close()  ' close database connection
306     End Sub ' UpdateBalance
307
308 End Class ' FrmATM
```

Figure 25.36 **ATM** application code. (Part 6 of 6.)

1. The _____ method opens the connection to the database.
  a) Open   b) Start
  c) Connect   d) None of the above.

2. While a _____ is being used, the connection object is busy and cannot be used for any other actions, besides closing the connection to the database.
  a) data command object   b) connection object
  c) database   d) data reader

Answers: 1) a. 2) d.

25.5 Wrap-Up

In this tutorial, you learned that a database is an organized collection of data and that database management systems provide mechanisms for storing and organizing data in a format consistent with that of a database. You then examined the contents of the Microsoft Access database that was used in the **ATM** application. While examining the db_ATM.mdb database, you learned that a field in a database table is a column and that a record is an entire table row. You also learned that each record must contain a primary key, which is used to distinguish one record from another.

After learning about the Access database, you used ADO .NET objects to communicate with the database. You learned how to create a connection to the database by using the **Server Explorer** and also how to create data command objects by using the **Toolbox**. You then were introduced to the database objects that you used in the **ATM** application. You learned about connection objects that are used to establish connections to databases, and about data command objects that allow you to access and manipulate database data. By creating the data command objects, you learned how to use Visual Studio .NET's **Query Builder** tool to build Structured Query Language (SQL) statements. These statements allowed you to retrieve and update information in the database. Using **Query Builder**, you created SELECT and UPDATE statements. You also learned about data readers that allowed you to retrieve information from a database.

In the next tutorial, you will learn about graphics. In particular, you will learn about coordinate systems and how to create colors and draw shapes. You will then use the concepts and techniques presented in the tutorial to create an application that can draw and print payroll checks.

SKILLS SUMMARY

Adding a Database Connection by Using the Server Explorer Window

- Click the Connect to Database Button to display the **Data Link Properties** dialog.
- Click the **Provider** tab in the **Data Link Properties** dialog.
- Select **Microsoft Jet 4.0 OLE DB Provider** in the **OLE DB Provider(s)** box.
- Click **Next**; then, click the ellipsis (...) Button next to the **Select or enter a database name:** field.
- Choose the desired database, and click **Open**.
- Click the **Test Connection** Button. Click **OK** in the dialog that appears; then, click **OK** in the **Data Link Properties** dialog.

Adding a Connection Object to the Form

- Select the desired database connection in the **Server Explorer** window.
- Drag-and-drop the connection on the Form.

Adding a Data Command Object to the Form

- Select the OleDbCommand icon from the **Data** tab in the **Toolbox**.
- Drag-and-drop the icon on the Form.

- Select the Connection property in the **Properties** window, and specify the name of the connection object created for the Form previously.
- Select the CommandText property, and click the ellipsis Button to display the **Add Table** and **Query Builder** dialogs.
- Add a table to the **Query Builder** dialog by using the **Add Table** dialog.
- Set the desired statement type by right clicking the **Column** field and selecting **Change Type**.
- Check desired field CheckBoxes, and use the **Criteria** column if necessary.

Opening the Database Connection

- Use the Open method of the connection object.

Closing the Database Connection

- Use the Close method of the connection object.

Using a Data Reader

- Invoke the ExecuteReader method of the data command object to create the data reader object.
- Invoke the data reader object's Read method.
- Retrieve the necessary information.
- Invoke the data reader object's Close method to close the data reader.

KEY TERMS

ADO .NET—Part of Microsoft .NET that is used to interact with databases.

connection object—Used to establish a connection to a database.

criteria of WHERE clause—Indicates from which specific record data will be retrieved or manipulated.

data command object—Executes commands that retrieve or modify data in a database.

data reader—Reads data from a database.

database—Organized collection of data.

database management system (DBMS)—Provides mechanisms for storing and organizing data in a manner that is consistent with the database's format.

ExecuteReader method of OleDbCommand object—Executes an SQL statement and makes the result of the query available in the data reader.

ExecuteNonQuery method of OleDbCommand object—Executes an SQL statement and returns the number of rows modified.

field—Column in a table of a database.

FROM SQL keyword—Specifies table from which to get data.

instant-access application—Application that immediately locates a particular record of information.

OleDbCommand object—Used to execute an SQL statement on a database.

OleDbDataReader object—Used to read data from a database. Also known as a data reader object.

primary key—Field (or combination of fields) in a database table that contains unique values used to distinguish records from one another.

Query Builder—Visual Studio .NET tool that allows you to specify the statements that retrieve information from and modify information in databases.

Read method of OleDbDataReader object—Retrieves information from a database.

record—An entire table row in a database.

SELECT SQL keyword—Used to request specified information from a database.

Structured Query Language (SQL)—Language often used by relational databases to perform queries and manipulate data in relational databases.

table—Used to store related information in rows and columns.

UPDATE SQL keyword—Used to modify data in a database table.

WHERE SQL keyword—Specifies criteria that determine the rows to retrieve.

CONTROLS, EVENTS, PROPERTIES & METHODS

OleDbConnection   `OleDbConnection`   This object establishes connection to a database.

- **Property**

  ConnectionString—Specifies to which database to connect.

- **Methods**

  Close—Closes the connection to the database.

  Open—Opens the connection to the database.

OleDbCommand   `OleDbCommand`   This object is used to execute a statement on a database.

- **Properties**

  CommandText—Specifies an SQL statement.

  Connection—Specifies the connection to a database.

  Parameters—Specifies an unknown value for the SQL statement.

- **Methods**

  ExecuteNonQuery—Executes an SQL statement and returns the number of rows modified.

  ExecuteReader—Creates a data reader by executing a database query.

OleDbDataReader This object is used to read data from a database.

- **Methods**

  Read—Retrieves information from the data reader.

  Close—Closes the data reader.

MULTIPLE-CHOICE QUESTIONS

25.1 A _____ provides mechanisms for storing and organizing data in a manner that is consistent with a database's format.

a) relational database

b) connection object

c) data command

d) database management system

25.2 An entire row in a database table is known as a _____.

a) record

b) field

c) column

d) primary key

25.3 A primary key is used to _____.

a) create rows in a database

b) identify fields in a database

c) distinguish between records in a table

d) read information from a database

25.4 A data command object allows you to _____.

a) connect to a database

b) read information from a database

c) execute a statement to retrieve or modify a database

d) create a database

25.5 A data reader can _____.

a) retrieve information from a database

b) modify information stored in a database

c) establish a connection to a database

d) close a connection to a database

25.6 In a SELECT statement, what follows the SELECT keyword?

a) the name of the table

b) the name of the field

c) the name of the database

d) the criteria that the record must meet

25.7 What does the following SELECT statement do?

```
SELECT Age FROM People WHERE LastName = 'Purple'
```

a) It selects the age of the person (or people) with the last name Purple from the People table.

b) It selects the value Purple from the Age table of the People database.

c) It selects the age of the person with the last name Purple from the People database.

d) It selects the People field from the Age table with the LastName value Purple.

25.8 The SQL _____ modifies information in a database.

  a) SELECT statement   b) MODIFY statement

  c) CHANGE statement   d) UPDATE statement

25.9 Assuming the account number is 2, which of the following statements modifies the PIN field in the Accounts table?

a) SELECT PIN FROM Accounts WHERE AccountNumber = 2

b) SELECT Accounts FROM AccountNumber = 2 WHERE PIN

c) UPDATE Accounts SET PIN=1243 WHERE AccountNumber = 2

d) UPDATE PIN=1243 SET AccountNumber = 2 WHERE Accounts

25.10 A _____ is an organized collection of data.

  a) record   b) database

  c) data reader   d) primary key

EXERCISES

25.11 *(Stock Portfolio Application)* A stock broker wants an application that will display a client's stock portfolio (Fig. 25.37). All the companies that the user holds stock in should be displayed in a ComboBox when the application is loaded. When the user selects a company from the ComboBox and clicks the **Stock Information** Button, the stock information for that company should be displayed in Labels.

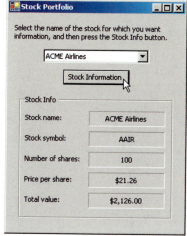

Figure 25.37 **Stock Portfolio** application.

a) *Copying the template to your working directory.* Copy the directory C:\Examples\Tutorial25\Exercises\StockPortfolio to your C:\SimplyVB directory.

b) *Opening the application's template file.* Double click StockPortfolio.sln in the StockPortfolio directory to open the application.

c) *Copying the database to your working directory.* Copy the stocks.mdb database from your C:\Examples\Tutorial25\Exercises\Databases directory to your C:\SimplyVB\StockPortfolio directory.

d) *Adding a data connection to the Server Explorer.* Click the Connect to Database icon in the **Server Explorer**, and add a data connection to the `stock.mdb` database. Add an `OleDbConnection` object to the Form.

e) *Adding command objects to the Form.* Add two command objects to the Form, and set both their `Connection` properties to the database connection object. Name the command objects `objSelectStockNameCommand` and `objSelectStockInformationCommand`. The first object will be used to retrieve the name of a stock and the second item will be used to retrieve all of a stock's information, based on the name of the stock.

f) *Setting the command objects' CommandText properties.* Select the `objSelectStockNameCommand` object and click the ellipses `Button` that appears to the right of the `CommandText` property in the **Properties** window. In the **Query Builder**, select **stockName** from the **stocks** table and click **OK**. Select the `objSelectStockInformationCommand` and open the **Query Builder** as you did for `objSelectStockNameCommand`. This time, select the **stockSymbol**, **shares** and **price** items from the **stocks** table. Then, select the **stockName** item and provide it with the `=?` criteria value. Finally, uncheck the **stockName** item from the **stocks** table. Click **OK** to dismiss the **Query Builder**.

g) *Adding a Load event to the Form.* Add a Load event handler for the Form. Add code to this event handler that opens a connection to the database. Use the `objSelectStockNameCommand` to retrieve the `StockNames`, and add them to the ComboBox.

h) *Adding a Click event handler for the btnStockInformation Button.* Add a Click event handler for the **Stock Information** `Button`. Add code to the event handler that passes the `SelectedItem` to the `StockData` method as a `String`. Then close the connection.

i) *Defining the StockData method.* Create a `StockData` method that takes a `String` representing the name of the stock as an argument. Connect to the database, and retrieve the information for the stock passed as an argument (using `objSelectStockInformationCommand`). Display the information in the corresponding `Labels` and close the connection to the database. Call the `ComputeTotalValueString` method, which you define in the next step, to calculate the total value.

j) *Defining the ComputeTotalValueString method.* Create the `ComputeTotalValueString` method to compute the total value by multiplying the number of shares by the price per share.

k) *Running the application.* Select **Debug > Start** to run your application. Select a company from the ComboBox and click the **Stock Information** `Button`. Verify that the information displayed in the **Stock Info** GroupBox is correct, based on the information stored in `stock.mdb`. Repeat this process for the other companies.

l) *Closing the application.* Close your running application by clicking its close box.

m) *Closing the IDE.* Close Visual Studio .NET by clicking its close box.

25.12 *(Restaurant Bill Calculator Application)* A restaurant wants you to develop an application that calculates a table's bill (Fig. 25.38). The application should display all the menu items from the restaurant's database in four ComboBoxes. Each ComboBox should contain a category of food offered by the restaurant (**Beverage, Appetizer, Main course** and **Dessert**). The user can choose from one of these ComboBoxes to add an item to a table's bill. When the table is finished ordering, the user can click the **Calculate Bill** Button to display the **Subtotal:, Tax:** and **Total:** for the table.

a) *Copying the template to your working directory.* Copy the directory `C:\Examples\Tutorial25\Exercises\RestaurantBillCalculator` to your `C:\SimplyVB` directory.

b) *Opening the application's template file.* Double click `RestaurantBillCalculator.sln` in the `RestaurantBillCalculator` directory to open the application.

c) *Copying the database to your working directory.* Copy the `menu.mdb` database from `C:\Examples\Tutorial25\Exercises\Databases` to your `C:\SimplyVB\RestaurantBillCalculator` directory.

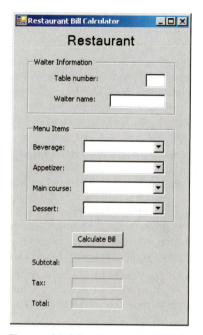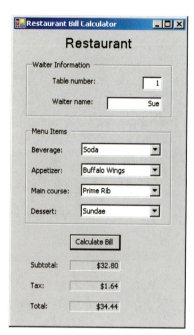

Figure 25.38 **Restaurant Bill Calculator** application.

d) *Adding a data connection to the Server Explorer.* Click the Connect to Database icon in the **Server Explorer**, and add a data connection to the menu.mdb database. Add an OleDbConnection object to the Form.

e) *Adding command objects to the Form.* Add two command objects to the Form, and set both their Connection properties to the database connection object. Name the command objects objSelectNameCommand and objSelectPriceCommand. The first object will be used to retrieve the name of a menu item, based on category (for example, appetizer). The second command object will be used to retrieve a menu item's price, based on the item's name.

f) *Setting the command objects' CommandText properties.* Select the objSelectNameCommand object and open the **Query Builder**. Add the **menu** table and select the **name** and **category** items. Provide the **category** item with the =? criteria value, then deselect **category** in the **menu** table. Click **OK**. Select the objSelectPriceCommand and open the **Query Builder**. This time, select the items marked **price** and **name** from the **menu** table. Provide the **name** item with the =? criteria value. Finally, uncheck the **name** item in the **menu** table. Click **OK** to dismiss the **Query Builder**.

g) *Adding a Load event to the Form.* Create the Load event handler for the Form. Add code to the event handler that opens a connection to the database. Call the LoadCategory method four times, each time passing a different category and ComboBox as arguments. Close the connection to the database.

h) *Coding the LoadCategory method.* Create a method LoadCategory that takes a String representing the Category to load and the name of the ComboBox to add items to as arguments. Because the Form's Load event handler is calling this method before it closes the connection to the database, the connection should still be open. Create a data reader to read all the items from the database for the specified Category, using objSelectNameCommand. Close the reader before exiting the method, so that a new reader can be created when the method is invoked again.

i) *Adding SelectedIndexChanged event handler for the ComboBoxes.* Add a SelectedIndexChanged event handler for all the ComboBoxes. Add code to the event handler that adds the String representation of the SelectedItem to the ArrayList.

j) *Adding a Click event handler for the btnCalculateBill Button.* Add a Click event handler for the **Calculate Bill** Button. Add code to the event handler that ensures that a table number and waiter name have been entered. If one of these fields is empty, display a MessageBox informing the user that both fields must contain information. The event handler should then call the CalculateSubtotal method to calculate the subtotal of the bill. Display the subtotal, tax and total of the bill in the appropriate `Label`s.

k) *Coding the `CalculateSubtotal` method*. The `CalculateSubtotal` method should open a connection to the database and retrieve the `Price` field for all the menu items in the `m_objBillItems` `ArrayList` (using `objSelectPriceCommand`). This method should then calculate the total price of all the items in the `ArrayList` and return this value as a `Decimal`. Remember to close the connection to the database.

l) *Running the application.* Select **Debug > Start** to run your application. Enter a table number and waiter name, and select different menu items from the ComboBoxes. Click the **Calculate Bill** `Button` and verify that the subtotal, tax and total values are correct. Select more items from the ComboBoxes and again click the **Calculate** `Button`. Verify that the price of the new items has been added to the bill.

m) *Closing the application.* Close your running application by clicking its close box.

n) *Closing the IDE.* Close Visual Studio .NET by clicking its close box.

25.13 *(Airline Reservation Application)* An airline company wants you to develop an application that displays flight information (Fig. 25.39). The database contains two tables, one containing information about the flights, the other containing passenger information. The user should be able to choose a flight number from a ComboBox. When the **View Flight Information** `Button` is clicked, the application should display the date of the flight, the flight's departure and arrival cities and the names of the passengers schedule to take the flight.

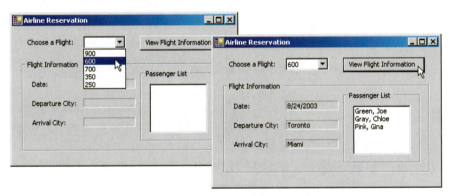

Figure 25.39   **Airline Reservation** application.

a) *Copying the template to your working directory.* Copy the `C:\Examples\Tutorial25\Exercises\AirlineReservation` directory to your `C:\SimplyVB` directory.

b) *Opening the application's template file.* Double click `AirlineReservation.sln` in the `AirlineReservation` directory to open the application.

c) *Copying the database to your working directory.* Copy the `reservations.mdb` database from `C:\Examples\Tutorial25\Exercises\Databases` to your `C:\SimplyVB\AirlineReservation` directory.

d) *Adding a data connection to the Server Explorer.* Click the Connect to Database icon in the **Server Explorer**, and add a data connection to the `reservations.mdb` database. Add an `OleDbConnection` object to the Form.

e) *Adding command objects to the Form.* Add three command objects to the Form, and set all their `Connection` properties to the database connection object. Name the command objects `objSelectFlightNumberCommand` (used to retrieve flight numbers), `objSelectFlightInformationCommand` (used to retrieve information about a flight based on the flight's number) and `objSelectPassengerInformationCommand` (used to retrieve information about a flight's passengers based on the flight's number).

f) *Setting the command objects' `CommandText` properties.* Select the `objSelectFlightNumberCommand` object and open the **Query Builder**. Select **FlightNumber** from the **flights** table and click **OK**. Select the `objSelectFlightInformationCommand` and open the **Query Builder**. This time, select the **Date**, **DepartureCity** and **ArrivalCity** items from the **flights** table. This action causes all items from the table to be returned. Then, select the **FlightNumber** item and provide it with the **=?** criteria value. Finally, uncheck the **FlightNumber** item from the **flights** table. Click **OK** to dismiss the **Query Builder**. Select the objSelectPassengerInformationCommand and open the **Query Builder**. Select the **LastName** and **FirstName** items from the **reservations** table. Then, select the **FlightNumber** item and provide it with the **=?** criteria value. Finally, uncheck the **FlightNumber** item from the **reservations** table. Click **OK** to dismiss the **Query Builder**.

g) *Adding a Load event to the Form.* Create a Load event handler for the Form that opens a connection to the database. Retrieve all the FlightNumbers from the Flights table in the reservations.mdb database (using objSelectFlightNumberCommand), and add those FlightNumbers to the ComboBox.

h) *Adding a Click event handler for the btnViewFlightInformation Button.* Add a Click event handler for the **View Flight Information** Button. Add code to the event handler to pass the SelectedItem to the DisplayFlightInformation method.

i) *Defining the DisplayFlightInformation method.* The DisplayFlightInformation method should take as an argument a String representing the flight number chosen. You will need to define two readers in this method, to read from the two tables in the database. Once you open the connection to the database, create a reader that reads the specified flight information from the flights table (using objSelectFlightInformationCommand). Display the flight information in the correct Label. Close this reader, and create a second reader that reads passenger information from the reservations table (using objPassengerInformationCommand). Retrieve from the table all the passengers scheduled to take the specified flight. Clear any old items from the ListBox, and display passengers' names in the ListBox.

j) *Running the application.* Select **Debug > Start** to run your application. Select a flight and click the **View Flight Information** Button. Verify that the flight information is correct. Repeat this process for the other flights.

k) *Closing the application.* Close your running application by clicking its close box.

l) *Closing the IDE.* Close Visual Studio .NET by clicking its close box.

What does this code do? **25.14** What is the result of executing the following code?

```
1  objSelectAgeData.Parameters("Name").Value = "Bob"
2
3  objOleDbConnection.Open()
4
5  Dim objReader As OleDbDataReader = _
6      objSelectAgeData.ExecuteReader
7
8  objReader.Read()
9
10 m_intAge = Convert.ToInt32(objReader("Age"))
11
12 objReader.Close()
13 objOleDbConnection.Close()
```

What's wrong with this code? **25.15** Find the error(s) in the following code. This method should modify the Age field of strUserName.

```
1  objUpdateAge("Age").Value = _
2      intAge
3
4  objUpdateBalance.Parameters("Original_NAME").Value = _
5      strUserName
6
7  objUpdateAge.ExecuteNonQuery()
```

```
8
9   objOleDbConnection.Close()
```

Programming Challenge ▶ **25.16** *(Enhanced Restaurant Bill Calculator Application)* Modify the application you developed in Exercise 25.12 to keep track of multiple table bills at the same time. The user should be able to calculate a bill for a table and save that table's subtotal and waiter's name. The user should also be able to retrieve that information at a later time. [*Hint:* This database contains two tables, one for the menu items, as before, and another for all the tables in the restaurant.] Sample outputs are shown in Fig. 25.40.

Figure 25.40 Enhanced **Restaurant Bill Calculator** application's GUI.

a) *Copying the template to your working directory.* Copy the directory C:\Examples\ Tutorial25\Exercises\RestaurantBillCalculatorEnhanced to your C:\SimplyVB directory.

b) *Opening the application's template file.* Double click RestaurantBillCalculator.sln in the RestaurantBillCalculatorEnhanced directory to open the application.

c) *Copying the database to your working directory.* Copy the menu2.mdb database from C:\Examples\Tutorial25\Exercises\Databases to your C:\SimplyVB\ RestaurantBillCalculatorEnhanced directory.

d) *Adding a data connection to the Server Explorer.* Click the Connect to Database icon in the **Server Explorer**, and add a data connection to the menu2.mdb database. Add an OleDbConnection object to the Form.

e) *Adding command objects to the Form.* Add five command objects to the Form, and set their Connection properties to the database connection object. Name the command objects objSelectNameCommand, objSelectPriceCommand, objSelectTableNumberCommand, objSelectTableInfoCommand and objUpdateSubtotal-Command.

f) *Setting the command objects' CommandText properties.* Set the CommandText properties of objSelectNameCommand and objSelectPriceCommand as you did in Exercise 25.12. Set objSelectTableNumberCommand to retrieve table numbers from the **tables** table. Set objSelectTableInfoCommand to retrieve the name of the waiter and the subtotal of a table, based on that table's number. Set objUpdateSubtotalCommand to modify the subtotal for a table, also based on that table's number. [*Note*: For the last command object, you will need to change the type of query in the **Query Builder**, as you did earlier in this tutorial.]

g) *Copying your existing code.* Copy the code for the application you created in Exercise 25.12 into the template application for this exercise. Place this code before method ResetForm. Disregard any syntax errors that may appear in the **Task List** at this point.

h) *Adding an instance variable.* Add an instance variable (after the declaration of m_objBillItems) called m_decSubtotal, that will hold the subtotal for each table when it is loaded in the application.

i) *Modifying methods btnCalculateBill_Click and CalculateSubtotal.* Remove the portion of the btnCalculateBill_Click event handler that checked for a table number and waiter name—this information will be displayed shortly. Modify the CalculateSubtotal method to update the table's subtotal based on the table's previous subtotal and any new items selected.

j) *Creating a method.* Create method LoadTables that reads the table numbers from the database and adds them to the **Table number:** ComboBox. This method should be called in FrmRestaurantBillCalculator_Load directly after the connection to the database is opened.

k) *Adding an event handler.* Add an event handler for the **Table number:** ComboBox. When a table is selected from the ComboBox, that table's data should be loaded from the database.

l) *Creating an event handler for the Save Table Button.* Create an event handler for the **Save Table** Button. This event handler should calculate the subtotal for the selected table. The event handler should then call method UpdateTable, passing the subtotal and table number as arguments. Finally, call the ResetForm method to reset the data displayed in the GUI.

m) *Creating an event handler for the Pay Bill Button.* Create an event handler for the **Pay Bill** Button. This event handler should retrieve the current table number then call method UpdateTable, passing a subtotal of 0 (for new customers) and table number as arguments. Finally, call the ResetForm method to reset the data displayed in the GUI.

n) *Creating method UpdateTable.* Create a method UpdateTable that takes the subtotal and table number as arguments. This method should save the table data in the database.

o) *Running the application.* Select **Debug > Start** to run your application. Select a table number and various menu items from the ComboBoxes. Click the **Calculate Bill** Button and verify that the subtotal, tax and total values are correct. Select more items from the ComboBoxes and again click the **Calculate Bill** Button. Verify that the price of the new items has been added to the bill. Click the **Save Table** Button. Select a different table and various menu items. Click the **Calculate Bill** Button and verify that the price of the new items has been added to the bill. Click the **Save Table** Button. Select the first table and verify that the subtotal is the same as it was when the table was saved. Select various menu items and Click the **Calculate Bill** Button. Verify that the subtotal, tax and total values are correct (and now include prices of the new menu items). Click the **Pay Bill** Button and verify that the subtotal is not reset to **$0.00**.

p) *Closing the application.* Close your running application by clicking its close box.

q) *Closing the IDE.* Close Visual Studio .NET by clicking its close box.

T U T O R I A L 26

Objectives

In this tutorial, you will learn to:
- Draw two-dimensional shapes.
- Control the colors and patterns of filled shapes.
- Use **Graphics** objects.
- Draw shapes on an object.
- Create an application to write checks.

Outline

CheckWriter Application

Introducing Graphics and Printing

In this tutorial, you will learn about Visual Basic .NET's tools for drawing two-dimensional shapes and for controlling colors and fonts. Visual Basic .NET supports graphics that allow you to visually enhance Windows applications. To build the **CheckWriter** application, you will take advantage of the GDI+ Application Programming Interface (API). An **API** is the interface used by an application to access the operating system and various services on the computer. **GDI+** is a graphics API that provides classes for creating and manipulating two-dimensional vector graphics, fonts and images. A **vector graphic** is not represented as a grid of pixels, but is instead represented by a set of mathematical properties called vectors, which describe a graphic's dimensions, attributes and position. Using the GDI+ API, you can create robust graphics without worrying about the specific details of graphics hardware.

The Framework Class Library contains many sophisticated drawing capabilities as part of the **System.Drawing** namespace and the other namespaces that comprise GDI+. The **System.Drawing.Printing** namespace will be used in the **CheckWriter** application to specify how the check will be printed on the page.

As you will see, GDI+ graphics capabilities will help you preview and print a check using the **CheckWriter** application. To complete the application, you will learn some more powerful drawing capabilities, such as changing the styles of lines used to draw shapes and controlling the colors of filled shapes. You will also learn how to specify a text style using fonts.

26.1 Test-Driving the CheckWriter Application

Before test-driving the completed **CheckWriter** application, you should understand the purpose of the application. This application must meet the following requirements:

> ### Application Requirements
>
> *A local business is responsible for distributing paychecks to its employees. The human-resources department needs a way to generate and print the paychecks. You have been asked to create an application that allows the human-resources department to input all information necessary for a valid check, which includes the employee's name, the date, the amount that the employee should be paid and the company's address information. Your application should graphically draw the check so that it can be printed.*

This application prints a paycheck. The user inputs the check number, the date, the numeric amount of the check, the employee's name, the amount of the check written in words and the company's address information. The user can press the **Preview** Button, which displays the format of the check. The user can then press the **Print** Button if the format is acceptable, causing the check to print from the printer. You begin by test-driving the completed application. Then, you will learn the additional Visual Basic .NET technologies that you will need to create your own version of this application.

Test-Driving the CheckWriter Application

1. ***Opening the completed application.*** Open the directory C:\Examples\ Tutorial26\CompletedApplication\CheckWriter to locate the **Check-Writer** application. Double click CheckWriter.sln to open the application in Visual Studio .NET.

2. ***Running the CheckWriter application.*** Select **Debug > Start** to run the application (Fig. 26.1).

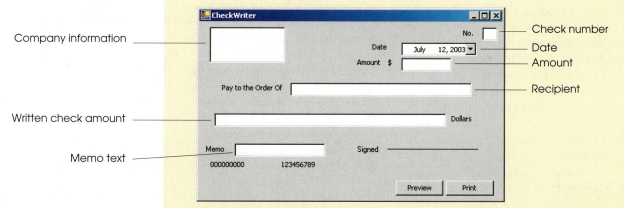

Figure 26.1 **CheckWriter** application displaying an empty check.

3. ***Providing inputs for the company information.*** In the company information TextBox, type The Company, then press *Enter* to proceed to the next line of the TextBox. Type 123 Fake Street. Press *Enter* to proceed to the third line of the TextBox. Type Any Town, MA 11111.

4. ***Providing values for the remaining information.*** For the **No.** field, input the check number 100. Leave the **Date** field (represented by a DateTimePicker control) as today's date, which is the default. Input 1,000.00 as the check amount. Enter John Smith as the recipient, and type One Thousand and 00/ 100 in the TextBox to the left of **Dollars**. In the **Memo** field, type Paycheck. The check should appear as shown in Fig. 26.2.

(cont.)

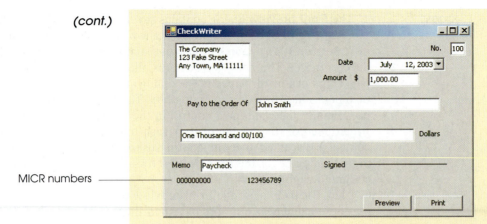

Figure 26.2   CheckWriter application displaying a completed check.

MICR numbers

You may have noticed that at the bottom left side of all bank checks is a string of numbers and symbols. These are called Magnetic Ink Character Recognition (MICR) numbers. MICR numbers are broken into three components. The first nine digits are the bank's routing number, followed by the account number and then the check number. Banks have special machines that read these numbers and route the check to the appropriate account. Using the MICR font, you can create MICR numbers in your check-writing application. To download the MICR font, visit `newfreeware.com/publishers/1561/`.

5. ***Previewing the check.*** Click the **Preview** Button. A **Print preview** dialog appears, displaying the completed check as shown in Fig. 26.3. This dialog is actually a control of type `PrintPreviewDialog`, which is used to display how a document appears before it is printed.

Print

Zoom

Displays three pages

Page to view

Close

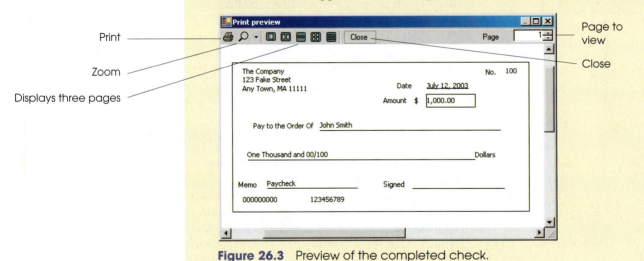

Figure 26.3   Preview of the completed check.

(cont.)

The **Print preview** dialog contains several toolbar Buttons. The first Button is the print Button (🖨), which allows users to print the document. The next Button (🔍) zooms in and out, allowing users view the document at different sizes. The next five Buttons allow users to specify the number of pages that can be displayed in the dialog at one time. Users can view 1, 2, 3, 4 or 6 pages at a time in the dialog box. The **Close** Button closes the dialog box. Finally, the right-most control in the dialog box allows users to specify which page of the document they wish to view. The PrintPreviewDialog control is discussed in detail later in this tutorial. The document that displays in this dialog box is the PrintDocument, an object that you will create when coding the application.

Click **Close** to close the **Print preview** dialog. [*Note:* Printing or previewing the document is not possible when there is no printer installed on your computer.]

6. ***Printing the check.*** To print the check, your computer must be connected to a printer. Click the **Print** Button. The check prints from the default printer of your computer.

7. ***Closing the application.*** Close your running application by clicking its close box.

8. ***Closing the IDE.*** Close Visual Studio .NET by clicking its close box.

26.2 GDI+ Introduction

This section introduces the graphics classes and structures used in this tutorial and discusses GDI+ graphics programming. Graphics typically consist of lines, shapes, colors and text drawn on the background of a control.

Objects of the Pen and Brush classes affect the appearances of the lines and shapes you draw. A **Pen** specifies the line style used to draw a shape (for example, line thickness, solid lines, dashed lines, etc.). A **Brush** specifies how to fill a shape (for example, solid color or pattern). As you learned in Tutorial 21, the Graphics class contains methods used for drawing. The drawing methods of the Graphics class usually require a Pen or Brush object to render a specified shape.

The Color structure contains predefined colors that can be used for the graphics in an application. The Color structure also contains methods that allow users to create new colors.

Objects of the Font class affect the appearance of text. The **Font** class contains properties (such as **Bold**, **Italic** and **Size**) that describe font characteristics. The **FontFamily** class contains methods for obtaining font information (such as **Get-Name** and **GetType**).

GDI+ uses a **coordinate system** (Fig. 26.4) to identify every point on the screen. A coordinate pair has both an *x*-**coordinate** (the **horizontal coordinate**) and a *y*-**coordinate** (the **vertical coordinate**). The *x*-coordinate is the horizontal distance from zero at the left of the drawing area, which increases as you move to the right. The *y*-coordinate is the vertical distance from zero at the top of the drawing area, which increases as you move down.

Portability Tip

Different computer monitors have different resolutions, so the density of pixels on various monitors will vary. This may cause graphics to appear in different sizes on different monitors.

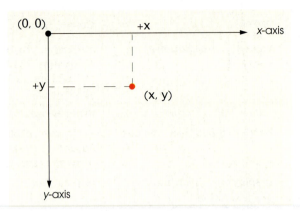

Figure 26.4 GDI+ coordinate system.

The *x-axis* defines every horizontal coordinate, and the *y-axis* defines every vertical coordinate. Programmers position text and shapes on the screen by specifying their (x, y) coordinates. The upper left corner of a GUI component (such as a `Panel` or the `Form`) has the coordinates $(0, 0)$. In the diagram in Fig. 26.4, the red point at position (x, y) is x pixels from the left of position $(0, 0)$ along the x-axis and y pixels from the top of position $(0, 0)$ along the y-axis. Coordinate units are measured in pixels, which are the smallest units of resolution on a computer monitor.

SELF-REVIEW

1. The _____ class contains properties that describe font characteristics.

    a) `Font`   b) `GDIFont`

    c) `SystemFont`   d) `FontStyle`

2. The _____ corner of a GUI component has the coordinate $(0, 0)$.

    a) lower left   b) upper right

    c) upper left   d) lower right

Answers: 1) a. 2) c.

26.3 Constructing the CheckWriter Application

Now that you have learned about the features that you will use in your **Check-Writer** application, you need to analyze the application. The following pseudocode describes the basic operation of the **CheckWriter** application:

> When the user clicks the Preview Button
> > Retrieve input from the user
> > Display the check in a Print preview dialog
>
> When the user clicks the Print Button
> > Retrieve input from the user
> > Print the check on the printer

Now that you have test-driven the **CheckWriter** application and studied its pseudocode representation, you will use an ACE table to help you convert the pseudocode to Visual Basic .NET. Figure 26.5 lists the actions, controls and events that will help you complete your own version of this application.

Action/Control/Event (ACE) Table for the CheckWriter Application

Action	Control/Object	Event
Label the application's controls	lblNumber, lblDate, lblAmount, lblPayee, lblDollars, lblMemo, lblSigned	
	btnPreview	Click
Retrieve input from the user	txtNumber, dtpDate, txtAmount, txtPayee, txtPayment, txtMemo, txtPayer	
Display the check in a Print preview dialog	objPreview	
	btnPrint	Click
Retrieve input from the user	txtNumber, dtpDate, txtAmount, txtPayee, txtPayment, txtMemo, txtPayer	
Print the check on the printer	objPrintDocument	

Figure 26.5   ACE table for the **CheckWriter** application.

Now that you have an understanding of the **CheckWriter** application, you can begin to create it. A template application is provided that contains many of the GUI's controls. You might notice that the application does not follow some GUI design guidelines. This is because the controls must be placed near or sometimes overlapping one another for the printed check to appear correctly. You begin writing code for this application by creating a `PrintPreviewDialog` object in the following box.

Adding a PrintPreviewDialog in the CheckWriter Application

1. **Copying the template to your working directory.** Copy the `C:\Examples\Tutorial26\TemplateApplication\CheckWriter` directory to your `C:\SimplyVB` directory.

2. **Opening the CheckWriter application's template file.** Double click `CheckWriter.sln` in the `CheckWriter` directory to open the application in Visual Studio .NET.

3. **Adding the `PrintPreviewDialog`.** In the **Toolbox**, locate the **PrintPreviewDialog** control

    > 🖾 PrintPreviewDialog

    in the **Windows Forms** group, and drag and drop it onto the Form. The control should appear in the component tray as shown in Fig. 26.6.

    The **PrintPreviewDialog** control uses a dialog to allow users to view a document of different sizes, print a document and display multiple pages of a document before printing. Make sure the `PrintPreviewDialog` object that you just created is selected and change its Name property to `objPreview`. This object has a Document property that specifies the document to preview. The document must be a `PrintDocument` object, which will be discussed later in the tutorial. For now, do not specify the document.

(cont.)

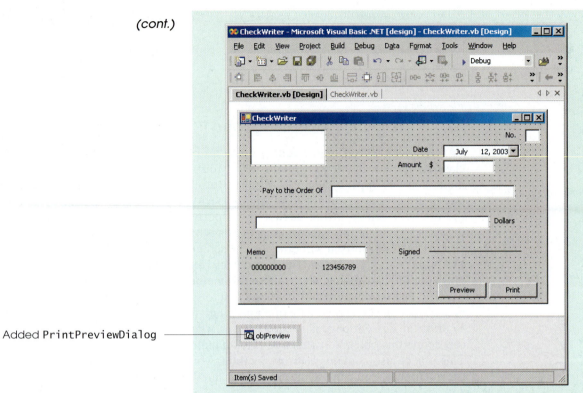

Added `PrintPreviewDialog` ——

Figure 26.6   **CheckWriter** application in **Design** view with `PrintPreview-Dialog`.

4. *Running the application.* Select **Debug > Start** to run your application (Fig. 26.7). Click the **Preview** Button, then click the **Print** Button. Currently, the application does nothing because you have not yet added event handlers for the Buttons. You will add functionality to the application in the next series of boxes.

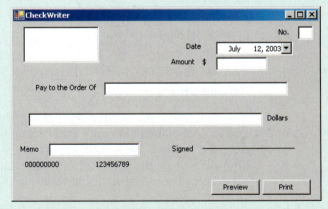

Figure 26.7   Running template application.

5. *Closing the application.* Close your running application by clicking its close box.

---

1. Use a _____ control to preview a document before it is printed.

    a) `PrintDialog`   b) `PrintPreviewDialog`

    c) `PrintPreviewControl`   d) `PrintDocument`

2. A `PrintPreviewDialog` object has a _____ property that specifies the document to preview.

   a) `Preview`   b) `PreviewDocument`

   c) `View`   d) `Document`

Answers: 1) b. 2) d.

26.4 PrintPreviewDialogs and PrintDocuments

In the **CheckWriter** application, you use an object of the `PrintPreviewDialog` class. As previously mentioned, this object displays a dialog that will show a document as it will appear when it is printed. Recall that the dialog object contains the **Document** property, which allows you to specify the document to preview and that the object specified in the `Document` property must be of type `PrintDocument`. `PrintPreviewDialog` also contains the **UseAntiAlias** property, which makes the text in the dialog appear smoother on the screen. To accomplish this, set the `UseAntiAlias` property to `True`. The `PrintPreviewDialog`'s `ShowDialog` method displays the preview dialog. You will use this method later in the application.

The **PrintDocument** object allows you to specify how to print a specified document. The object can raise a **PrintPage** event, which occurs when the data required to print the current page is needed (that is, when the `Print` method is called). You can define this object's `PrintPage` event handler to specify what you want to print. This object also contains a **Print** method, which uses a `Graphics` object to print the document. You will use method `Print` later in the application.

SELF-REVIEW

1. The object in the `Document` property must be of type _____.

   a) `PrintPreviewDialog`   b) `PrintDocument`

   c) `PrintPreviewControl`   d) `PrintDialog`

2. The _____ method of object `PrintDocument` uses a graphics object to print the document.

   a) `Graphics`   b) `Document`

   c) `Print`   d) None of the above.

Answers: 1) b. 2) c.

26.5 Creating an Event Handler for the CheckWriter Application

Now that you have created the `PrintPreviewDialog` object in the **CheckWriter** application, you can begin to add functionality to the application. Before you can use print features, you must import the `System.Drawing.Printing` namespace. You will also create an instance variable that will be used by several different methods. You will implement these features in the following box.

Importing a Namespace and Declaring an Instance Variable

1. ***Switching to code view.*** Select **View > Code** to view the `CheckWriter.vb` code.

2. ***Importing namespaces.*** Add line 1 before the class `FrmCheckWriter` definition, as shown in Fig. 26.8 to import the **System.Drawing.Printing** namespace. This statement allows your applications to access all services related to printing. After you import the namespace, the application can use `PrintDocument` objects. The namespace also enables access to the **PrintPageEventArgs.Graphics** property, which you will use to draw the graphics that will appear on the printed page.

(cont.)

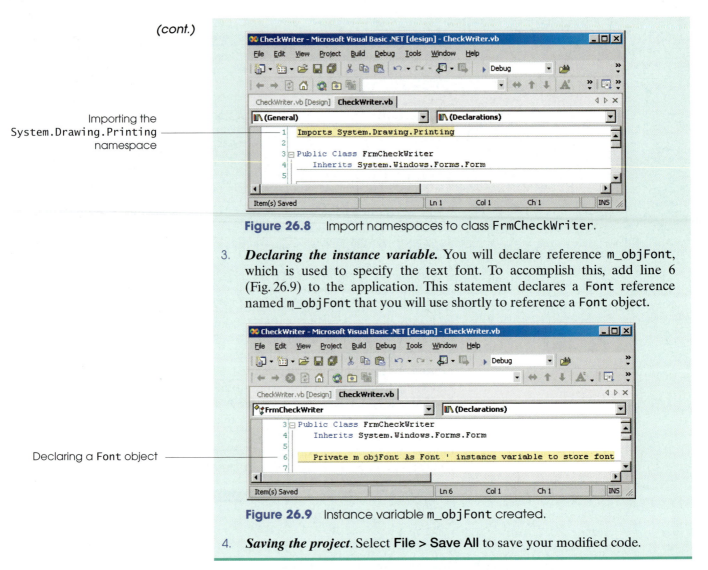

Figure 26.8   Import namespaces to class `FrmCheckWriter`.

3. ***Declaring the instance variable.*** You will declare reference `m_objFont`, which is used to specify the text font. To accomplish this, add line 6 (Fig. 26.9) to the application. This statement declares a `Font` reference named `m_objFont` that you will use shortly to reference a `Font` object.

Importing the
`System.Drawing.Printing`
namespace

Declaring a **Font** object

Figure 26.9   Instance variable `m_objFont` created.

4. ***Saving the project.*** Select **File > Save All** to save your modified code.

Now that you have imported a namespace for the **CheckWriter** application and declared the `Font` reference, you can write code to enable printing and previewing. You will begin by defining the `objPrintDocument_PrintPage` method, which will specify what to print. When printing the check, you want the printed document to resemble the application's `Form`. This can be completed using a `For Each...Next` statement that draws the contents of each control in a `Graphics` object. You can then print the check using this `Graphics` object. You will begin writing code to perform these actions in the following box.

Defining an Event Handler to Print Pages

1. ***Creating the objPrintDocument_PrintPage method.*** Add lines 279–283 into the application code below the `Windows Form Designer generated code` as in Fig. 26.10. These lines create the event handler for the `PrintPage` event. You need to type these lines to create the event handler because the `PrintDocument` object has not yet been created. You will create this object later in this tutorial.

(cont.)

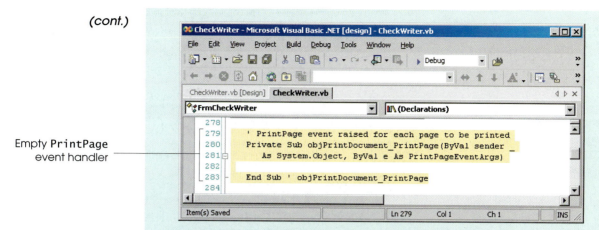

Figure 26.10 objPrintDocument_PrintPage event handler.

2. *Declaring the variables.* Add lines 283–292 of Fig. 26.11 to the event handler. Lines 283–284 declare Single variables that represent the *x*- and *y*-coordinates where controls appear on the Form. **Single** is a data type that stores floating-point values. Single is similar to Double, but is less precise and requires less memory. Lines 287 and 290 declare Single variables, which specify the coordinates of the left and top margins of the page to be printed. These values are determined by using the **MarginBounds.Left** and **MarginBounds.Top** properties of the PrintPageEventArgs object (e from line 281) that is passed when the PrintPage event is raised.

Line 291 declares the String variable strLine, which will be used to store text from the controls. Line 292 declares a **Control** reference (an object that represents a control on the Form), which you will use as the control variable in your For Each...Next statement.

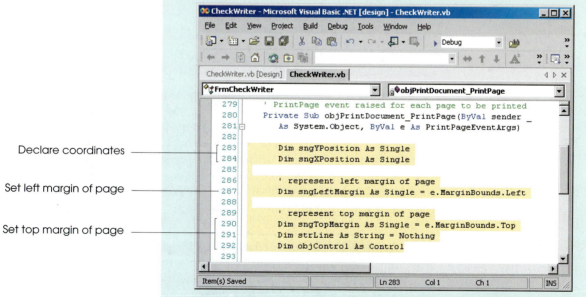

Figure 26.11 Variables created for objPrintDocument_PrintPage.

3. *Iterating through the controls on the Form.* Add lines 294–297 of Fig. 26.12 to the method. This For Each...Next statement iterates through each control on the Form to print the check. You will define the body of this statement in the next box.

(cont.)

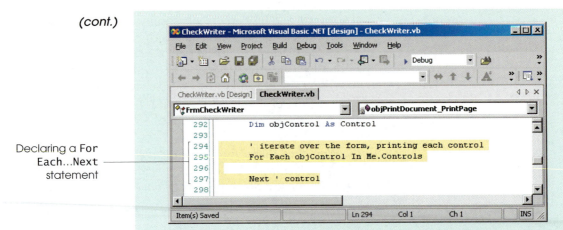

Declaring a For
Each...Next
statement

Figure 26.12 For Each...Next statement used for iteration.

4. ***Drawing the check's border.*** Add lines 299–301 of Fig. 26.13 into the event handler. The Form's border is not contained in a control; therefore, you must use a Graphics object to draw a rectangle around the check to be printed. These lines of code draw the rectangle.

To draw the rectangle around the check, use the PrintPageEventArgs object (e from line 281) that is passed when the PrintPage event is raised. The Graphics property of this object allows you to specify what you want to print. By calling the **DrawRectangle** method on the Graphics object, you can specify the properties of the rectangle to draw.

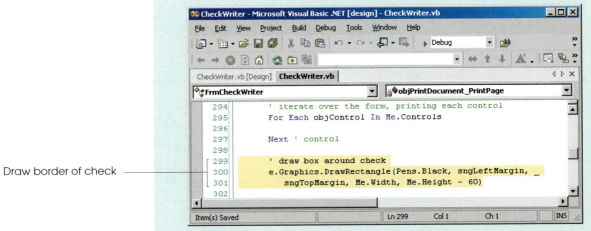

Draw border of check

Figure 26.13 Event handler objPrintDocument_PrintPage modified to draw border of check.

The first argument you pass to the method is the Pens.Black object. This is a Pen object that uses a black color to draw the rectangle's border. The second argument specifies the *x*-coordinate that defines the left side of the rectangle you wish to draw. Use the sngLeftMargin variable that you created in *Step 2* to represent the position of the left margin of the page on which the check will print. This value ensures that the rectangle will align with the left margin. The third argument in the method specifies the *y*-coordinate that defines the top of the rectangle. Use the sngTopMargin variable that you created in *Step 2* to represent the position of the top margin of the page on which the check will print. Together, the *x*- and *y*-coordinates in the second and third arguments define the upper left corner of the rectangle.

(cont.)   The fourth and fifth arguments specify the width and height of the rectangle. The width is set to `Me.Width`, which returns the width of the `Form`. Keyword **Me** references the current object—in this case, the `Form`. The height, on the other hand, is set to `Me.Height - 60`. This value is the height of the `Form` minus 60 pixels. You subtract 60 pixels because you do not want to print the `Buttons` on the bottom of the `Form`. These `Buttons` were created to allow users to print and preview the checks. (They were not intended to be printed on the checks.)

5. *Indicating that there are no more pages to print.* Add lines 303–304 of Fig. 26.14 to the method. Line 304 indicates that there are no more pages to print by setting the event argument's **HasMorePages** property to `False`.

Indicate no more pages to print ⎯⎯⎯⎯⎯

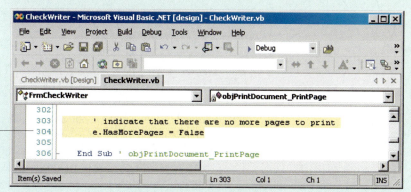

Figure 26.14   Event handler `objPrintDocument_PrintPage` modified to indicate that there are no more pages to print.

6. *Saving the project.* Select **File > Save All** to save your modified code.

SELF-REVIEW

1. Importing the `System._____` namespace gives you access to print-related functions.
   a) `Windows`   b) `Printing`
   c) `Drawing.Printing`   d) `Drawing`

2. The _____ keyword references the current object.
   a) `Me`   b) `Current`
   c) `Form`   d) None of the above.

Answers: 1) c. 2) a.

26.6 Graphics Objects: Colors, Lines and Shapes

A **Graphics** object controls how information is drawn. In addition to providing methods for drawing various shapes, `Graphics` objects contain methods for font manipulation, color manipulation and other graphics-related actions. You can draw on many controls, such as `Labels` and `Buttons`, which have their own drawing areas. To draw on a control, first obtain a `Graphics` object for that control by invoking the control's `CreateGraphics` method as in

```
Dim objGraphics As Graphics = pnlDisplay.CreateGraphics()
```

Now you can use the methods provided in class `Graphics` to draw on the `pnlDisplay` `Panel`. You will see many `Graphics` methods throughout this tutorial.

Good Programming Practice

When working with color, keep in mind that many people are color blind or have varying difficulties perceiving and distinguishing colors. So, use colors that can be distinguished easily.

Colors

Colors can enhance an application's appearance and help convey meaning. For example, a red traffic light indicates stop, yellow indicates caution and green indicates go. The `Color` structure defines methods and constants used to manipulate colors.

Every color can be created from a combination of alpha, red, green and blue components. The alpha value determines the **opacity** (amount of transparency) of the color. For example, the alpha value 0 specifies a transparent color, and the value 255 specifies an opaque color. Alpha values between 0 and 255 (inclusive) result in a blending of the color's RGB value with that of any background color, causing a semitransparent effect. All three RGB components are Bytes that represent integer values in the range 0–255. The first number in the RGB value defines the amount of red in the color, the second defines the amount of green and the third defines the amount of blue. The larger the value for a particular color, the greater the amount of that particular color. Visual Basic .NET enables you to choose from almost 17 million colors. If a particular computer monitor cannot display all of these colors, it displays the color closest to the one specified, or the computer attempts to imitate it using **dithering** (using small dots of existing colors to form a pattern that simulates the desired color). Figure 26.15 summarizes some predefined Color constants. You can also find a list of various RGB values and their corresponding colors at http:/ /www.pitt.edu/~nisg/cis/web/cgi/rgb.html.

Constant	RGB value	Constant	RGB value
Color.Orange	255, 200, 0	Color.White	255, 255, 255
Color.Pink	255, 175, 175	Color.Gray	128, 128, 128
Color.Cyan	0, 255, 255	Color.DarkGray	64, 64, 64
Color.Magenta	255, 0, 255	Color.Red	255, 0, 0
Color.Yellow	255, 255, 0	Color.Green	0, 255, 0
Color.Black	0, 0, 0	Color.Blue	0, 0, 255

Figure 26.15 Color structure constants and their RGB values.

You can use pre-existing colors, or you can create your own by using the **FromArgb** method. The following demonstrates how to create a color:

```
Dim colorSilver As Color
colorSilver = Color.FromArgb(192, 192, 192)
```

These statements create a silver color and assign it to variable colorSilver. Now you can use colorSilver whenever you need a silver color. The Color method FromArgb is used to create this color and other colors by specifying the RGB values as arguments. The method sets the alpha value to 255 (that is, opaque) by default.

Drawing Lines, Rectangles and Ovals

This section presents several Graphics methods for drawing lines, rectangles and ovals. To draw shapes and Strings, you must specify the type of Brushes and Pens to use. A Pen, which functions much like an ordinary pen, is used to specify characteristics such as the color and width of the shape's lines. Most drawing methods require a Pen object. To fill the interior of objects, you must specify a Brush. All classes derived from the abstract class Brush define objects that fill the interiors of shapes with color patterns or images. For example, a SolidBrush specifies the Color that fills the interior of a shape. The following statement creates a Solid-Brush with the color orange:

```
Dim objBrush As SolidBrush = New SolidBrush(Color.Orange)
```

Many drawing methods have multiple versions. When employing methods that draw outlined hollow shapes, use versions that take a Pen argument. When employing methods that draw shapes filled with colors, patterns or images, use versions that take a Brush argument. Many of these methods require x, y, width and height arguments. The x and y arguments represent the shape's upper-left corner coordinate. The width and height arguments represent the width and height of the shape in pixels, respectively. Figure 26.16 summarizes several `Graphics` methods and their parameters.

Graphics Drawing Methods and Descriptions

Note: Many of these methods have multiple versions.

```
DrawLine(ByVal p As Pen, ByVal x1 As Single, ByVal y1 As Single,
    ByVal x2 As Single, ByVal y2 As Single)
```
Draws a line from the point (x1, y1) to the point (x2, y2). The `Pen` determines the color, style and width of the line.

```
DrawRectangle(ByVal p As Pen, ByVal x As Single, ByVal y As Single,
    ByVal width As Single, ByVal height As Single)
```
Draws a rectangle of the specified width and height. The top-left corner of the rectangle is at the point (x, y). The `Pen` determines the rectangle's color, style and border width.

```
FillRectangle(ByVal b As Brush, ByVal x As Single, ByVal y As Single,
    ByVal width As Single, ByVal height As Single)
```
Draws a solid rectangle of the specified width and height. The top-left corner of the rectangle is at the point (x, y). The `Brush` determines the fill pattern inside the rectangle.

```
DrawEllipse(ByVal p As Pen, ByVal x As Single, ByVal y As Single,
    ByVal width As Single, ByVal height As Single)
```
Draws an ellipse inside a rectangular area of the specified width and height. The top-left corner of the rectangular area is at the point (x, y) and the `Pen` determines the color, style and border width of the ellipse.

```
FillEllipse(ByVal b As Brush, ByVal x As Single, ByVal y As Single,
    ByVal width As Single, ByVal height As Single)
```
Draws a filled ellipse inside a rectangular area of the specified width and height. The top-left corner of the rectangular area is at the point (x, y) and the `Brush` determines the pattern inside the ellipse.

Figure 26.16 `Graphics` methods that draw lines, rectangles and ovals.

SELF-REVIEW

1. The RGB value of a `Color` represents _____.
   a) the index number of a color
   b) the amount of red, green and blue in a color
   c) the thickness of the drawing object   d) the type of shape to draw

2. The _____ method is used to draw solid rectangles.
   a) `DrawRectangle`   b) `FillRectangle`
   c) `SolidRectangle`   d) `OpaqueRectangle`

Answers: 1) b. 2) b.

26.7 Printing Each Control of the CheckWriter Application

Recall earlier that you created the empty For Each...Next statement to iterate through all the controls on the Form. Now you will write code for the body of the For Each...Next statement to print all controls on the Form, except for the Buttons.

Iterating through All the Objects of the Form to Print Each Control

1. ***Checking for Buttons.*** In the body of the For Each...Next statement of objPrintDocument_PrintPage, add lines 297–300 of Fig. 26.17. Adding this If...Then statement determines whether the current control is a Button. If the control is not a Button, then the body of the If...Then statement executes. However, if the control is a Button, the For Each...Next statement continues to the next control on the Form.

(cont.)

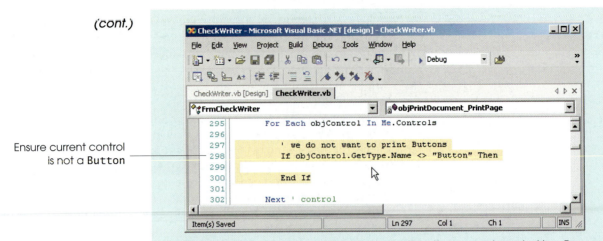

Ensure current control is not a `Button`

Figure 26.17 Code to determine whether the current control is a `Button`.

2. ***Defining the body of the If...Then statement.*** Now you must add code that properly prints the value that appears in each control on the check. Add lines 299–320 of Fig. 26.18 into the body of the `If...Then` statement.

Line 299 sets the `strLine` variable that you created earlier to `objControl.Text`. This property contains the value contained in the control's `Text` property (text displayed to the user or entered by the user). The `Select Case` statement (lines 301–320) specifies how each control prints. The controlling expression is set to the value `objControl.Name`. This is the `Name` property of the control. You can use the `Name` property to select specific controls that need to be treated differently when printed.

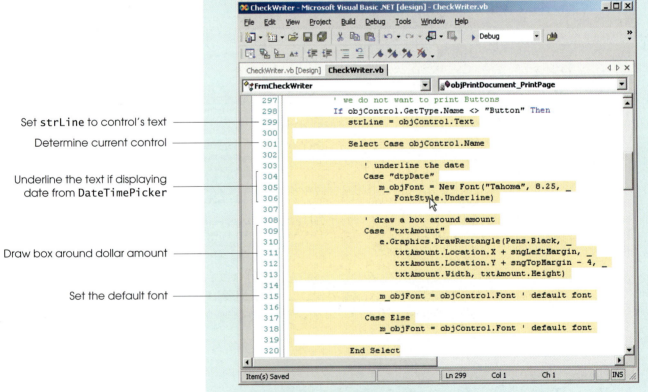

Set `strLine` to control's text

Determine current control

Underline the text if displaying date from `DateTimePicker`

Draw box around dollar amount

Set the default font

Figure 26.18 `Select Case` statement to print controls.

(cont.)

The first Case (lines 304–306) determines what happens when the current control is the dtpDate DateTimePicker. This Case sets the m_objFont reference to the font style of the date—an underlined Tahoma font, with a size of 8.25 (the same size as the text in the control). So, the date on the check will be underlined and will appear in 8.25 points in Tahoma font. Fonts are discussed in detail later in this tutorial.

The second Case (lines 309–315) executes if the control is the txtAmount TextBox. This Case draws the box that surrounds the decimal amount of the check. DrawRectangle (a Graphics method) is invoked by using the e.Graphics property. The outline of the rectangle prints in black, indicated by Pens.Black. The *x*- and *y*-coordinates are specified by adding the Text-Box's *x-y* location on the Form to the sngLeftMargin and sngTopMargin variables, respectively. Recall that we begin printing the check at the corner of the top and left margins. Adding the margin values to the Location properties ensures that the txtAmount TextBox prints in the same position as it appears on the Form. (Line 312 subtracts four points of space to center the box on the text.) Line 315 sets the font of the text to draw to the same value as the font used to display text in the control.

The third Case (lines 317–318) executes for all the other controls. This Case sets the m_objFont font style to the same value as the font used to display text in the control. Line 320 ends the Select Case statement.

3. ***Setting the positions of the text of each control.*** Add lines 322–331 of Fig. 26.19 to the body of the If...Then statement. Lines 323–324 set the sngXPosition variable to sngLeftMargin + objControl.Location.X. By adding the *x*-coordinate of the current control (represented by objControl.Location.X) to the left margin, you ensure that the check will not draw outside the margins of the page.

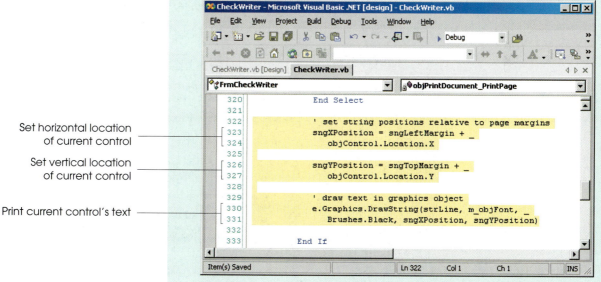

Figure 26.19 Code to set String positions of the controls.

(cont.)

Lines 326–327 perform a similar operation, setting `sngYPosition` to the sum of the top margin and *y*-coordinate of the control's location. Lines 330–331 call the `DrawString` method on the `e.Graphics` property. The **Draw-String** method draws the specified `String` of text in the `Graphics` object. The first argument is the `String` to draw, in this case `strLine`. Recall earlier that you set `strLine` to the `Text` property of the current control. The second argument is the font, which is specified by `m_objFont`. The third argument specifies a `Brush`. You pass the value `Brushes.Black`, which creates a black brush object to draw the text. The fourth and fifth arguments are the *x*- and *y*-coordinates where the first character of the `String` prints. Use the `sngX-Position` and `sngYPosition` variables that you set in lines 323–327 to print the text at the correct location on the page.

4. ***Saving the project.*** Select **File > Save All** to save your modified code.

---

1. The _____ method draws a specified `String` of text.

   a) `String`   b) `PrintString`
   c) `DrawString`   d) `Draw`

2. Typing `Brushes.Black` _____.

   a) obtains a black `Brush` object   b) retrieves the color of a brush
   c) paints the screen black   d) creates a `Pen` object

Answers: 1) c. 2) a.

26.8 Font Class

In the **CheckWriter** application, you used a `Font` object to specify the style of the text printed on a page. This section introduces the methods and constants contained in the `Font` class. Note that once a `Font` has been created, its properties cannot be modified. That means that if you require a different `Font`, you must create a new `Font` object with the appropriate settings. There are many versions of the `Font` constructor for creating custom `Fonts` to help you do this. Some properties of the `Font` class are summarized in Fig. 26.20.

Property	Description
`Bold`	Sets a font to a bold font style if value is set to `True`.
`FontFamily`	Represents the `FontFamily` of the `Font` (a grouping structure to organize fonts with similar properties).
`Height`	Represents the height of the font.
`Italic`	Sets a font to an italic font style if value is set to `True`.
`Name`	Sets the font's name to the specified `String`.
`Size`	Represents a `Single` value indicating the current font size measured in design units. (Design units are any specified units of measurement for the font.)
`SizeInPoints`	Represents a `Single` value indicating the current font size measured in points.
`Strikeout`	Sets a font to the strikeout font style if value is set to `True` (for example, ~~Deitel~~).
`Underline`	Sets a font to the underline font style if the value is set to `True`.

Figure 26.20   `Font` class read-only properties.

Common Programming Error

Specifying a font that is not available on a system is a logic error. If this occurs, that system's default font will be used instead.

Note that the `Size` property returns the font size as measured in **design units**, whereas `SizeInPoints` returns the font size as measured in points (a more common measurement). The `Size` property can be specified in a variety of ways, such as inches or millimeters. Some versions of the Font constructor accept a `Graphics-Unit` argument—an enumeration that allows users to specify the unit of measurement used to describe the font size. Members of the `GraphicsUnit` enumeration include `Point` (1/72 inch), `Display` (1/75 inch), `Document` (1/300 inch), `Millimeter`, `Inch` and `Pixel`. If this argument is provided, the `Size` property contains the size of the font as measured in the specified design unit, and the `SizeInPoints` property contains the size of the font in points. For example, if you create a `Font` having size 1 and specify that `GraphicsUnit.Inch` will be used to measure the font, the `Size` property will be 1, and the `SizeInPoints` property will be 72 because there are 72 points in an inch. If you create a new `Font` object without specifying a `GraphicsUnit`, the default measurement for the font size is `Graphics-Unit.Point` (thus, the `Size` and `SizeInPoints` properties will be equal). [*Note*: There is no way to change the properties of a `Font` object—to use a different font, you must create a new `Font` object.]

The `Font` class has a number of constructors. Most require a **font name**, which is a `String` representing a font currently supported by the system. Common fonts include *SansSerif* and *Serif*. Constructors also require the **font size** as an argument. Lastly, Font constructors usually require a **font style**, specified by an element of the **FontStyle** enumeration: `Fontstyle.Bold`, `Fontstyle.Italic`, `Fontstyle.Regular`, `Fontstyle.Strikeout` and `Fontstyle.Underline`.

SELF-REVIEW

1. The most common measurement of font size is _____.

   a) points   b) inches

   c) pixels   d) millimeters

2. _____ is an example of a font style.

   a) `Bold`   b) `Italic`

   c) `StrikeOut`   d) All of the above.

Answers: 1) a. 2) d.

26.9 Previewing and Printing the Check

After defining how objects are printed in the `objPrintDocument_PrintPage` event handler, you must define what occurs when each `Button` is clicked. You begin with the `btnPrint_Click` event handler to specify the functionality when clicking the **Print** `Button`. You will write this event handler in the following box.

Defining the btnPrint_Click Event Handler

1. **Creating the btnPrint_Click event handler.** In the Windows Form Designer, double click the **Print** Button. The `btnPrint_Click` event handler appears in the `CheckWriter.vb` file.

2. **Creating a PrintDocument object.** Add lines 351–352 of Fig. 26.21 into the event handler. The `PrintDocument` object is used to help print the check. Be sure to add the comments and line-continuation characters as shown in Fig. 26.21 so that the line numbers in your code match those presented in this tutorial.

(cont.)

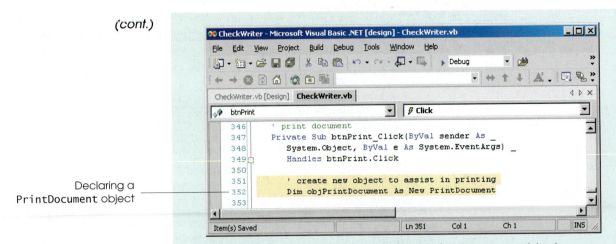

Declaring a
PrintDocument object

Figure 26.21   Code that creates the `PrintDocument` object.

3. ***Specifying the PrintPage event handler.*** Add lines 354–356 of Fig. 26.22 into the event handler. These lines specify the event handler called when the `PrintPage` event is raised. Lines 355-356 use the **AddHandler** statement to associate the `PrintPage` event of the `objPrintDocument` object with the event handler specified after the **AddressOf** operator (the `objPrintDocument_PrintPage` event handler that you created earlier in this tutorial). To execute the code in the event handler, you must provide the name of the event handler you created to handle the event after operator `AddressOf`.

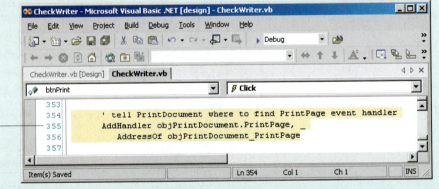

Adding an event handler for
the PrintDocument object

Figure 26.22   Code that adds an event handler to the `PrintDocument` object.

4. ***Verifying that the user has a printer.*** Add lines 358–362 of Fig. 26.23 to the `btnPrint_Click` event handler. Line 359 uses the property **PrinterSettings.InstalledPrinters.Count** to determine how many printers the user has installed on the computer. If there are no printers installed (that is, if the `Count` property returns 0), the user cannot print or preview the document. Line 360 in the body of the `If...Then` statement displays an error message by calling procedure `ErrorMessage`, which you will define in the next box. Line 361 exits the event handler using the `Return` keyword.

(cont.)

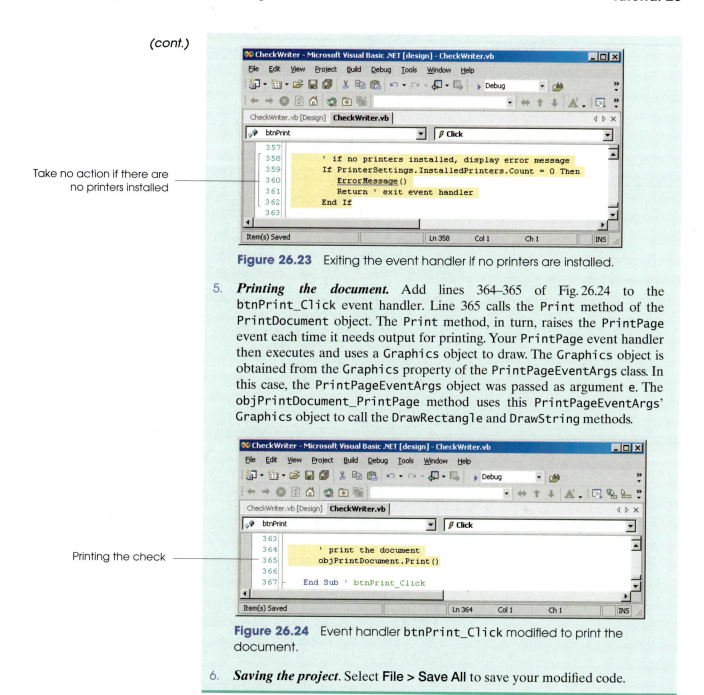

Take no action if there are no printers installed

Figure 26.23   Exiting the event handler if no printers are installed.

5. ***Printing the document.*** Add lines 364–365 of Fig. 26.24 to the `btnPrint_Click` event handler. Line 365 calls the `Print` method of the `PrintDocument` object. The `Print` method, in turn, raises the `PrintPage` event each time it needs output for printing. Your `PrintPage` event handler then executes and uses a `Graphics` object to draw. The `Graphics` object is obtained from the `Graphics` property of the `PrintPageEventArgs` class. In this case, the `PrintPageEventArgs` object was passed as argument `e`. The `objPrintDocument_PrintPage` method uses this `PrintPageEventArgs'` `Graphics` object to call the `DrawRectangle` and `DrawString` methods.

Printing the check

Figure 26.24   Event handler `btnPrint_Click` modified to print the document.

6. ***Saving the project.*** Select **File > Save All** to save your modified code.

Now that you have defined the `btnPrint_Click` method, you will complete the application by coding the `Click` event handler for the **Preview** Button. When this Button is clicked, a dialog appears allowing users to preview the check before printing it. You will create the `btnPreview_Click` event handler to enable this feature in the following box.

***Defining the
btnPreview_Click
Event Handler***

1. ***Creating the btnPreview_Click event handler.*** In the Windows Form Designer, double click the **Preview** Button. The btnPreview_Click event handler appears in the CheckWriter.vb file.

2. ***Creating the PrintDocument object and adding the PrintPage handler.*** Add lines 374–379 of Fig. 26.25 into the event handler. As in the btnPrint_Click event handler, line 375 creates a new PrintDocument object named objPrintDocument. Lines 378–379 specify that the PrintDocument object's PrintPage event handler is method objPrintDocument_PrintPage.

Creating a
PrintDocument object

Adding an event handler
for the PrintDocument

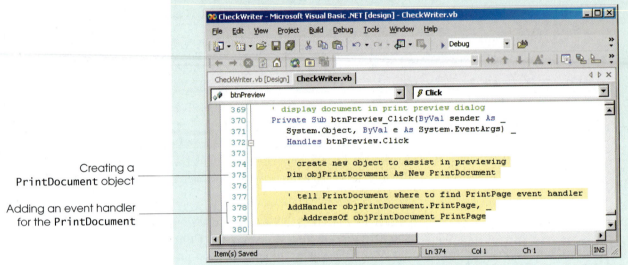

Figure 26.25 Event handler btnPreview_Click modified to create PrintDocument and add PrintPage event handler.

3. ***Verifying that the user has a printer.*** Add lines 381–385 of Fig. 26.26 to the btnPrint_Click event handler. These lines of code are exactly the same as the code from *Step 4* of the previous box. An error message is displayed if there are no installed printers.

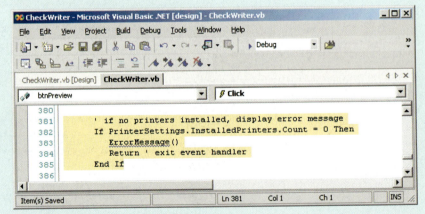

Figure 26.26 Exiting the print preview event handler if no printers are installed.

(cont.)

4. ***Specifying the PrintPreviewDialog object's Document property.*** Add line 387 of Fig. 26.27 into the event handler. Recall earlier when you created the PrintPreviewDialog object, that you learned that its Document property specifies the document to preview. This property requires that its value be of type PrintDocument, the same class you use to print the check. This line sets objPreview's Document property to objPrintDocument (the PrintDocument you created on line 375).

Setting the document to preview

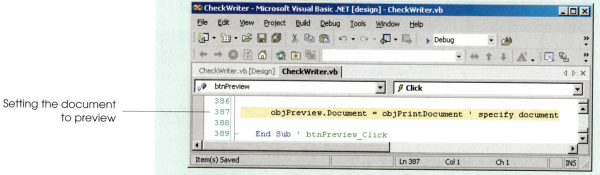

Figure 26.27 Event handler btnPreview_Click modified to set the PrintPreviewDialog object's Document property.

5. ***Showing the Print preview dialog.*** Add line 388 into the event handler, as shown in Fig. 26.28. This line invokes the PrintPreviewDialog object's ShowDialog method to display the **Print preview** dialog that displays how the PrintDocument will appear when printed. To display the document, the PrintPreviewControl of the PrintPreviewDialog raises the PrintPage event. Rather than using the Graphics object to print a page using your printer, the PrintPreviewDialog uses the Graphics object to display the page on the screen.

Displaying the preview dialog

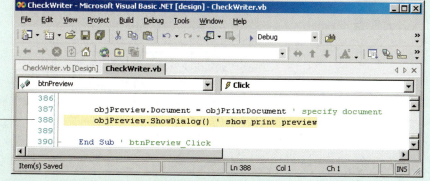

Figure 26.28 Event handler btnPreview_Click modified to show preview dialog.

6. ***Defining the ErrorMessage procedure.*** Add lines 392–400 of Fig. 26.29 into your application. Lines 395–398 display an error message to the user indicating that printing and print previewing the check is not possible if there are no printers installed on the computer.

(cont.)

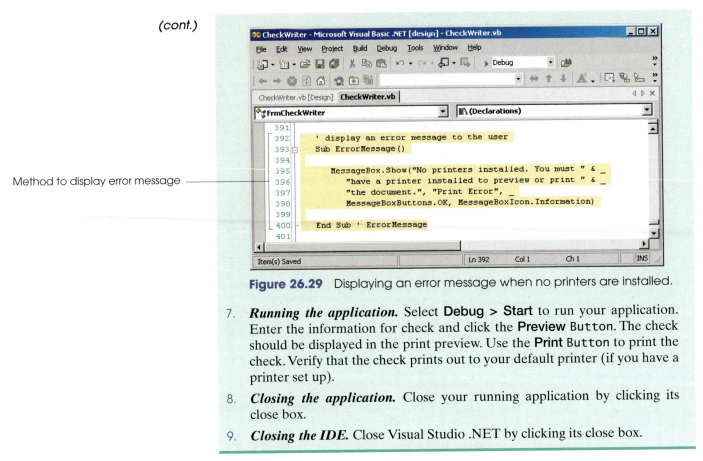

Method to display error message

Figure 26.29 Displaying an error message when no printers are installed.

7. *Running the application.* Select **Debug > Start** to run your application. Enter the information for check and click the **Preview** Button. The check should be displayed in the print preview. Use the **Print** Button to print the check. Verify that the check prints out to your default printer (if you have a printer set up).

8. *Closing the application.* Close your running application by clicking its close box.

9. *Closing the IDE.* Close Visual Studio .NET by clicking its close box.

Figure 26.30 presents the source code for the **CheckWriter** application. The lines of code that contain new programming concepts that you learned in this tutorial are highlighted.

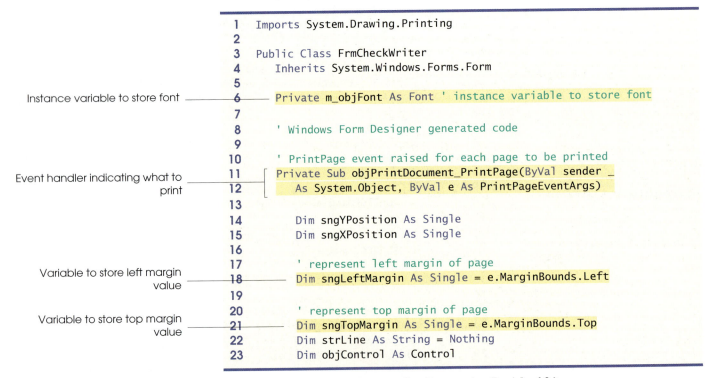

```vb
1    Imports System.Drawing.Printing
2
3    Public Class FrmCheckWriter
4        Inherits System.Windows.Forms.Form
5
6        Private m_objFont As Font ' instance variable to store font
7
8        ' Windows Form Designer generated code
9
10       ' PrintPage event raised for each page to be printed
11       Private Sub objPrintDocument_PrintPage(ByVal sender _
12           As System.Object, ByVal e As PrintPageEventArgs)
13
14           Dim sngYPosition As Single
15           Dim sngXPosition As Single
16
17           ' represent left margin of page
18           Dim sngLeftMargin As Single = e.MarginBounds.Left
19
20           ' represent top margin of page
21           Dim sngTopMargin As Single = e.MarginBounds.Top
22           Dim strLine As String = Nothing
23           Dim objControl As Control
```

Instance variable to store font — 6

Event handler indicating what to print — 11, 12

Variable to store left margin value — 18

Variable to store top margin value — 21

Figure 26.30 **CheckWriter** application code. (Part 1 of 3.)

```
24
25              ' iterate over the form, printing each control
26              For Each objControl In Me.Controls
27
28                  ' we do not want to print Buttons
29                  If objControl.GetType.Name <> "Button" Then
30                      strLine = objControl.Text
31
32                      Select Case objControl.Name
33
34                          ' underline the date
35                          Case "dtpDate"
36                              m_objFont = New Font("Tahoma", 8.25, _
37                                  FontStyle.Underline)
38
39                          ' draw a box around amount
40                          Case "txtAmount"
41                              e.Graphics.DrawRectangle(Pens.Black, _
42                                  txtAmount.Location.X + sngLeftMargin, _
43                                  txtAmount.Location.Y + sngTopMargin - 4, _
44                                  txtAmount.Width, txtAmount.Height)
45
46                              m_objFont = objControl.Font ' default font
47
48                          Case Else
49                              m_objFont = objControl.Font ' default font
50
51                      End Select
52
53                      ' set string positions relative to page margins
54                      sngXPosition = sngLeftMargin + _
55                          objControl.Location.X
56
57                      sngYPosition = sngTopMargin + _
58                          objControl.Location.Y
59
60                      ' draw text in graphics object
61                      e.Graphics.DrawString(strLine, m_objFont, _
62                          Brushes.Black, sngXPosition, sngYPosition)
63
64                  End If
65
66              Next ' control
67
68              ' draw box around check
69              e.Graphics.DrawRectangle(Pens.Black, sngLeftMargin, _
70                  sngTopMargin, Me.Width, Me.Height - 60)
71
72              ' indicate that there are no more pages to print
73              e.HasMorePages = False
74
75          End Sub ' objPrintDocument_PrintPage
76
77          ' print document
78          Private Sub btnPrint_Click(ByVal sender As _
79              System.Object, ByVal e As System.EventArgs) _
80              Handles btnPrint.Click
```

Labels (left margin):
- Looping through each control on the **Form** → line 26
- Underlining text → lines 36–37
- Drawing a box around text → lines 41–44
- Using the control's font → line 46
- Printing text → lines 61–62
- Drawing a box around the check → lines 69–70
- Indicate that there are no more pages → line 73

Figure 26.30 CheckWriter application code. (Part 2 of 3.)

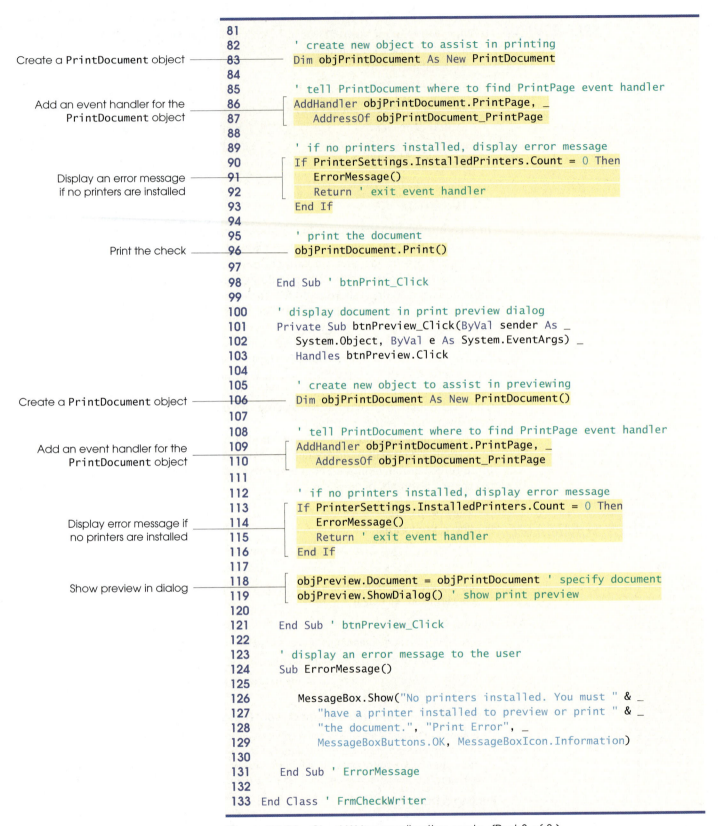

Create a `PrintDocument` object ────
```
81
82          ' create new object to assist in printing
83          Dim objPrintDocument As New PrintDocument
84
85          ' tell PrintDocument where to find PrintPage event handler
86          AddHandler objPrintDocument.PrintPage, _
87             AddressOf objPrintDocument_PrintPage
88
89          ' if no printers installed, display error message
90          If PrinterSettings.InstalledPrinters.Count = 0 Then
91             ErrorMessage()
92             Return ' exit event handler
93          End If
94
95          ' print the document
96          objPrintDocument.Print()
97
98       End Sub ' btnPrint_Click
99
100      ' display document in print preview dialog
101      Private Sub btnPreview_Click(ByVal sender As _
102         System.Object, ByVal e As System.EventArgs) _
103         Handles btnPreview.Click
104
105         ' create new object to assist in previewing
106         Dim objPrintDocument As New PrintDocument()
107
108         ' tell PrintDocument where to find PrintPage event handler
109         AddHandler objPrintDocument.PrintPage, _
110            AddressOf objPrintDocument_PrintPage
111
112         ' if no printers installed, display error message
113         If PrinterSettings.InstalledPrinters.Count = 0 Then
114            ErrorMessage()
115            Return ' exit event handler
116         End If
117
118         objPreview.Document = objPrintDocument ' specify document
119         objPreview.ShowDialog() ' show print preview
120
121      End Sub ' btnPreview_Click
122
123      ' display an error message to the user
124      Sub ErrorMessage()
125
126         MessageBox.Show("No printers installed. You must " & _
127            "have a printer installed to preview or print " & _
128            "the document.", "Print Error", _
129            MessageBoxButtons.OK, MessageBoxIcon.Information)
130
131      End Sub ' ErrorMessage
132
133   End Class ' FrmCheckWriter
```

Figure 26.30 CheckWriter application code. (Part 3 of 3.)

1. When you associate an event with an event handler, keyword _____ is used to specify the location of the event handler.

    a) `AddHandler`   b) `AddressOf`

    c) `HandlerEvent`   d) Both a and b.

2. The _____ object contains the `PrintPage` event.

    a) `PrintDocument`   b) `PrintPreviewDialog`

    c) `PrintPreviewControl`   d) `PrintDialog`

Answers: 1) b. 2) a.

26.10 Wrap-Up

In this tutorial, you were introduced to the topic of graphics and printing. You created a **CheckWriter** application, which allows you to enter data in a check and print it using the printer installed on your computer. You learned how to use the `Graphics` object and its members. While building the **CheckWriter** application, you used these concepts to draw shapes and `String`s using graphics objects such as `Pen`s and `Brush`es. You also learned how to use code to create fonts to apply to text you wish to display or print.

    You also learned about several new classes, which included `PrintPreviewDialog`, `PrintPreviewControl` and `PrintDocument`. You used the `PrintDocument` class to create a `PrintDocument` object. You then used its `PrintPage` event to execute code that draws and prints the check when the user clicks the **Print** Button. You also added a `PrintPreviewDialog` in your application, allowing the user to preview a check before printing it.

    In the next tutorial, you will learn how to use multimedia in your applications. In particular, you will be introduced to Microsoft Agent, a technology used to add three-dimensional, animated characters to a program. You will use this technology to create a phone book application.

SKILLS SUMMARY

Printing a Rectangle

- Use the `PrintPageEventArgs` object's `Graphics` property.
- Use the `Graphics` property to invoke the `DrawRectangle` method.
- Specify the five parameters: A `Brush` (or `Pen`) object, the *x*-coordinate, the *y*-coordinate, the width and the height.

Printing a `String`

- Use the `PrintPageEventArgs` object's `Graphics` property.
- Use the `Graphics` property to invoke the `DrawString` method.
- Specify the five parameters: the string to print, the font style, the `Brush` object, the *x*-coordinate and the *y*-coordinate.

Associating an Event with a Defined Event Handler

- Follow the format `AddHandler` *objectName*.*eventName*, `AddressOf` *eventHandlerName* where *objectName* represents the name of the object with which the event will be associated, *eventName* represents the name of a valid event and *eventHandlerName* represents the name of the defined event handler to be associated with the specified event.

Printing a Document

- Create a new `PrintDocument` object.
- Define the `PrintDocument`'s `PrintPage` event handler to specify what to print.
- Use the `PrintDocument` to invoke the `Print` method.

Displaying a Print Preview Dialog

- Create a `PrintPreviewDialog` object.

■ Specify the `PrintDocument` to preview in the `PrintPreviewDialog`'s `Document` property.

■ Invoke the `PrintPreviewDialog`'s `ShowDialog` method.

KEY TERMS

`AddHandler` statement—Adds an event handler for a specific event.

`AddressOf` operator—Specifies the location of an event handler associated with an event.

API (application programming interface)—The interface used by a program to access the operating system and various services on the computer.

ARGB values—A combination of alpha, red, green and blue components from which every color is created.

Brush object—An object used to specify drawing parameters when drawing solid shapes.

`Control` reference—An object that represents a control on the `Form`.

coordinate system—A scheme for identifying every possible point on the computer screen.

design units—Any specified units of measurement for the font.

dithering—Process that uses small dots of existing colors to form a pattern that simulates a desired color.

`Document` property—Property of the `PrintPreviewDialog` that allows you to specify the document that will be displayed in the dialog.

`DrawRectangle` method of the `Graphics` class—Draws the outline of a rectangle of a specified size and color at a specified location.

`DrawString` method—`Graphics` method that draws the specified `String`.

`Font` class—Contains properties that define unique fonts.

`FontFamily` class—Contains methods for obtaining font information, such as `GetName` and `GetType`.

`FromArgb` method of the `Color` class—Creates a new `Color` object from RGB values.

GDI+—An application programming interface (API) that provides classes for creating two-dimensional vector graphics.

`GetName` method of the `Font` class—Returns the name of the `Font` object.

`GetType` method of the `Font` class—Returns the type of the `Font` object.

`Graphics` object—Draws two-dimensional images.

`HasMorePages` property of the `PrintPageEventArgs` class—Specifies if there are more pages to print. When `False`, the `PrintPage` event is no longer raised.

`Image` class—Stores and manipulate images from various file formats.

`MarginBounds.Left` property of the `PrintPageEventArgs` class—Specifies the left margin of a printed page.

`MarginBounds.Top` property of the `PrintPageEventArgs` class—Specifies the top margin of a printed page.

`Me` keyword—References the current object.

opacity—Amount of transparency) of the color.

`Pen` object—Specifies drawing parameters when drawing shape outlines.

`Print` method—`PrintDocument` method used to print a document.

`PrintDocument` class—Allows users to describe how to print a document.

`PrintPage` event—Occurs when the data required to print the current page is needed.

`PrintPageEventArgs` class—Contains data passed to a `PrintPage` event.

`PrintPreviewDialog` class—Previews a document before it prints in a dialog box.

`PrinterSettings.InstalledPrinters.Count` property—Determines how many printers the user has installed on the computer.

`Rectangle` structure—Enables you to define rectangular shapes and their dimensions.

`Single` data type—Stores floating-point values. `Single` is similar to `Double`, but is less precise and requires less memory.

`System.Drawing.Printing` namespace—Allows your applications to access all services related to printing.

UseAntiAlias property—Property of class `PrintPreviewDialog` that makes the text in the `PrintPreviewDialog` appear smoother on the screen.

vector graphics—Graphics created by a set of mathematical properties called vectors, which include the graphics' dimensions, attributes and positions.

x-**axis**—Describes every horizontal coordinate.

x-**coordinate**—Horizontal distance (increasing to the right) from the left of the drawing area.

y-**axis**—Describes every vertical coordinate.

y-**coordinate**—Vertical distance (increasing downward) from the top of the drawing area.

CONTROLS, EVENTS, PROPERTIES & METHODS

Font This class is used to define the font face, size and style of text throughout an application.

■ *Properties*

`Bold`—Sets the weight of the text.

`Italic`—Sets the angle of the text.

`Size`—Sets the size of the text.

`FontFamily`—Contains a `FontFamily` object, which is used to store font face information.

`FontStyle`—Specifies the style applied to a `Font` object.

Graphics The class that contains methods used to draw text, lines and shapes.

■ *Methods*

`DrawLine`—Draws a line of a specified size and color.

`DrawEllipse`—Draws the outline of an ellipse of a specified size and color at a specified location.

`DrawRectangle`—Draws the outline of a rectangle of a specified size and color at a specified location.

`DrawEllipse`—Draws a `String` in a specified font and color at a specified position.

`FillEllipse`—Draws a solid ellipse of a specified size and color at the specified location.

`FillRectangle`—Draws a solid rectangle of a specified size and color at the specified location.

PrintDocument This class allows you to specify how to print a document.

■ *Event*

`PrintPage`—Raised when data required to print a page is needed.

■ *Method*

`Print`—Uses a `Graphics` object to print a page.

PrinterSettings This class stores information about the system's printer settings.

■ *Property*

`Count`—Returns the number of printers installed on the system.

PrintPageEventArgs This class contains data passed to a `PrintPage` event.

■ *Properties*

`HasMorePages`—Specifies if there are more pages to print. When `False`, the `PrintPage` event is no longer raised.

`MarginBounds`—Specifies the margin of the printed page.

    `Left`—Specifies the left margin of the page.

    `Top`—Specifies the top margin of the page.

PrintPreviewDialog PrintPreviewDialog This control is used to display how a document will look when it is printed.

■ *Properties*

Document—Specifies the document that the control will preview. The document must be of type PrintDocument.

Name—Specifies the name used to access the PrintPreviewDialog control programmatically. The name should be prefixed with obj.

UseAntiAlias—Specifies whether the dialog will display a smoothed image.

■ *Method*

ShowDialog—Used to display the PrintPreviewDialog to the user.

MULTIPLE-CHOICE QUESTIONS

26.1 The RGB value $(0, 0, 255)$ represents _____.

   a) Color.Red   b) Color.Green

   c) Color.Blue   d) Color.Yellow

26.2 The _____ property of the PrintPreviewDialog object makes text appear smoother.

   a) AntiAlias   b) UseAntiAlias

   c) Alias   d) UseAlias

26.3 Use a _____ object to allow the users to preview a document before it is printed.

   a) PrintPreviewDialog   b) PrintDocument

   c) Print   d) PrintPreviewControl

26.4 The _____ event handler specifies what will be printed.

   a) OnPaint   b) Print

   c) Document   d) PrintPage

26.5 To display the preview dialog of the _____ object, call method ShowDialog.

   a) PrintPreviewDialog   b) PrintDocument

   c) PrintDialog   d) Both a and b.

26.6 Set the _____ property to False to indicate that there are no more pages to print.

   a) Document   b) HasMorePages

   c) TerminatePrint   d) Both a and b.

26.7 The Print method sends a _____ object to the printer for printing.

   a) Graphics   b) PrintDocument

   c) PrintPreviewDialog   d) Brush

26.8 Keyword _____ references the current object.

   a) This   b) Class

   c) Me   d) Property

26.9 Opacity is the _____ value of a color.

   a) red   b) transparency

   c) dithering   d) blue

26.10 Design units are used to specify the _____ of a Font.

   a) Size   b) Name

   c) FontFamily   d) Style

EXERCISES

26.11 (*CheckWriter Modified to Print Background Images*) Modify the **CheckWriter** application to display and print a background for the check. The GUI should look similar to Fig. 26.31. Users can select a background image. The image should appear in the **Print preview** dialog box and also should print as a background to the check.

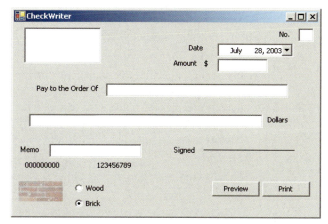

Figure 26.31 Modified **CheckWriter** GUI.

a) *Copying the template to your working directory.* Copy the directory `C:\Examples\Tutorial26\Exercises\ModifiedCheckWriter` to your `C:\SimplyVB` directory.

b) *Opening the application's template file.* Double click `CheckWriter.sln` in the CheckWriter directory to open the application.

c) *Create the CheckedChanged event handler.* Double click the **Wood** RadioButton to create its CheckedChanged event handler.

d) *Defining the CheckedChanged event handler.* Define the RadioButton's CheckedChanged event handler to notify the application when users have made a background selection. If the **Wood** RadioButton is selected, then a preview of the wooden background should display in the `picPreview` PictureBox. Otherwise, if the **Brick** RadioButton is selected, then a preview of the brick background should display in the `picPreview` PictureBox.

e) *Modifying the objPrintDocument_PrintPage event handler.* Modify event handler `objPrintDocument_PrintPage` to print the background image. [*Hint*: Use the DrawImage method to display the background image to print. DrawImage takes five arguments: The image file, the *x*-coordinate, the *y*-coordinate, the width and the height.] To print the image in the background, the DrawImage method must be the first method called on the Graphics object.

f) *Running the application.* Select **Debug > Start** to run your application. Enter data into the input fields and select either the **Wood** or **Brick** RadioButton. Verify that the appropriate image is displayed to the left of the RadioButtons. Click the **Preview** Button and verify that the check is displayed with the proper background. Close the preview and repeat this process selecting the background you had not selected before.

g) *Closing the application.* Close your running application by clicking its close box.

h) *Closing the IDE.* Close Visual Studio .NET by clicking its close box.

26.12 (*Company Logo Designer Application*) Develop a **Company Logo** application that allows users to design a company logo (Fig. 26.32). The application should provide the user with RadioButtons to allow the selection of the next shape to draw. TextBoxes should be provided to allow the user to enter the dimensions of the shapes.

a) *Copying the template to your working directory.* Copy the directory `C:\Examples\Tutorial26\Exercises\CompanyLogo` to your `C:\SimplyVB` directory.

b) *Opening the application's template file.* Double click `CompanyLogo.sln` in the CompanyLogo directory to open the application.

c) *Defining the Add Button's Click event handler.* Create the **Add** Button's Click event handler. Define the event handler so that the shape that users specify is drawn on the PictureBox. Use the CreateGraphics method on the PictureBox to retrieve the Graphics object used to draw on the PictureBox. [*Note:* The TextBoxes labeled **X1:, Y1:, X2:** and **Y2:** must contain integers to draw a line. Also, the TextBoxes labeled **X:, Y:, Width:** and **Height:** must contain integers to draw any other shape.]

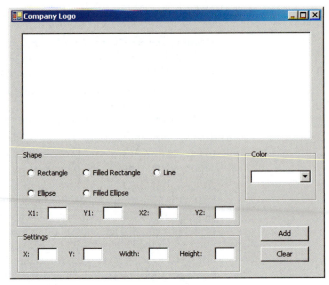

Figure 26.32   Company Logo GUI.

d) *Defining the Clear Button's Click event handler.* Create the **Clear** Button's Click event handler, and define it so that the PictureBox is cleared. [*Hint*: To clear the entire PictureBox, use the PictureBox's Invalidate method. The Invalidate method is often used to refresh (update) graphics of a control. By using the Invalidate method without specifying a graphic to draw, the PictureBox clears.] Also ensure that all TextBoxes are cleared when the **Clear** Button is clicked.

e) *Running the application.* Select **Debug > Start** to run your application. Use the RadioButtons and TextBoxes to display at least one of each type of shape. Use different colors for the different shapes. Click the **Clear** Button to clear the shapes.

f) *Closing the application.* Close your running application by clicking its close box.

g) *Closing the IDE.* Close Visual Studio .NET by clicking its close box.

26.13 (*Letter Head Designer Application*) Create a **Letter Head** application that allows users to design stationery for company documents (Fig. 26.33). Allow users to specify the image that will serve as the letterhead.

PictureBox displays image —

User enters contact
information here —

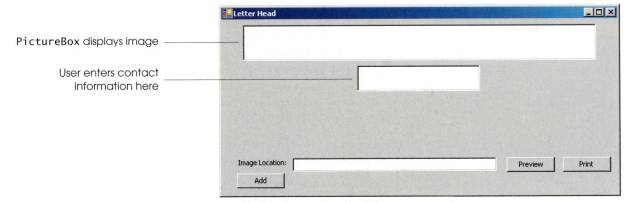

Figure 26.33   Letter Head GUI.

a) *Copying the template to your working directory.* Copy the directory C:\Examples\Tutorial26\Exercises\LetterHead to your C:\SimplyVB directory.

b) *Opening the application's template file.* Double click LetterHead.sln in the LetterHead directory to open the application.

c) *Creating a PrintPreviewDialog control.* Add a PrintPreviewDialog control to allow users to preview the letterhead before it is printed.

d) **Defining the PrintPage event handler.** Allow users to print the document by defining the PrintPage event handler as you did in the **CheckWriter** application.

e) **Defining the btnPrint_Click event handler.** The btnPrint_Click event handler should tell the PrintDocument where to find the PrintPage event handler, as in the **CheckWriter** application, and print the document.

f) **Defining the btnPreview_Click event handler.** The btnPreview_Click event handler should tell the PrintDocument where to find the PrintPage event handler, as in the **CheckWriter** application, and then show the preview dialog.

g) **Testing the application.** The Letterhead.png image file, located in C:\Examples\Tutorial26\Exercises\Images has been provided for you to test the application's letter head image capability.

h) **Running the application.** Select **Debug > Start** to run your application. Enter your contact information and specify the location of an image. [*Note:* An image has been supplied in an Images directory, located in your C:\Examples\Tutorial26\Exercises directory.] The image should be displayed in the PictureBox at the top of the Form. Click the **Preview** Button and verify that the image and contact information is displayed in the preview. Finally, click the **Print** Button to verify that the letterhead prints with the appropriate image and contact information.

i) **Closing the application.** Close your running application by clicking its close box.

j) **Closing the IDE.** Close Visual Studio .NET by clicking its close box.

What does this code do? **26.14** What is the result of the following code? Assume that objOutput_PrintPage is defined.

```
1  Private Sub btnPrint_Click(ByVal sender As System.Object, _
2     ByVal e As System.EventArgs) Handles btnPrint.Click
3
4     Dim objOutput As New PrintDocument()
5
6     AddHandler objOutput.PrintPage, _
7        AddressOf objOutput_PrintPage
8
9     objPrintOutput.Print()
10
11  End Sub ' btnPrint_Click
```

What's wrong with this code? ▶ **26.15** Find the error(s) in the following code. This is the definition for a Click event handler for a Button. This event handler should draw a rectangle on a PictureBox control.

```
1  Private Sub btnDrawImage_Click(ByVal sender As System.Object, _
2     ByVal e As System.EventArgs) Handles btnDrawImage.Click
3
4     ' create an orange colored brush
5     Dim objBrush As SolidBrush = New SolidBrush(Orange)
6
7     ' create a Graphics object to draw on the PictureBox
8     Dim objGraphics As Graphics = picPictureBox.AcquireGraphics
9
10    ' draw a filled rectangle
11    objGraphics.FillRectangle(objBrush, 2, 3, 40, 30)
12
13  End Sub ' btnDrawImage_Click
```

Programming Challenge

26.16 (*Screen Saver Simulator Application*) Develop an application that simulates a screen saver. This application should add random-colored, random-sized, solid and hollow shapes at different positions of the screen (Fig. 26.34). Copy the `C:\Exercises\Tutorial26\ScreenSaver` directory, and place it in your `C:\SimplyVB` directory. The design of the Form has been created, which consists of a black Form and a Timer control. In the `ScreenSaver.vb` code view, the `DisplayShape` method has been provided and the Timer's tick event handler has already been defined for you.

You must write the rest of the `DisplayShape` method code. Create the `Graphics` object from the Form using the Form's `CreateGraphics` method, and specify random colors, sizes and positions for the filled and hollow shapes that will be displayed on the screen. The width and height of the shapes should be no larger than 100 pixels.

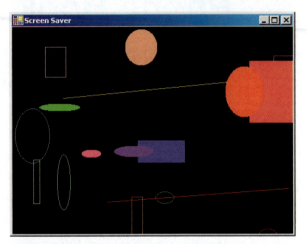

Figure 26.34   Screen Saver running.

26.17 (*Screen Saver Simulator Enhancement Application*) Enhance the **Screen Saver Simulator** application from Exercise 26.16 by modifying the Timer control's Tick event handler. Add code to this event handler so that after a specified amount of time, the screen should clear the displayed shapes. After the screen clears, random shapes should continue to display. Also, use the `FromArgb` method so that you can specify random opacity (alpha values) for the colors. You should pass four arguments to this method. The first argument is the alpha value, the second is the red value, the third is the green value and the fourth is the blue value.

27

T U T O R I A L

Phone Book Application

Introducing Multimedia Using Microsoft Agent

When computers were first introduced, they were large and expensive and were used primarily to perform arithmetic calculations. **Multimedia** applications, which use a variety of media including graphics, animation, video and sound, were made impractical by the high cost and slow speed of computers. However, today's affordable, ultrafast processors are making multimedia-based applications commonplace. As the market for multimedia explodes, users are purchasing computers with faster processors, larger amounts of memory and wider communications bandwidths needed to support multimedia applications.

Users are seeing exciting new three-dimensional multimedia applications that interact with the user by means of animation, audio and video. Multimedia programming is an entertaining and innovative field, but one that presents many challenges. Visual Basic .NET enables you to include such multimedia presentations in your applications.

In this tutorial, you will explore the **Microsoft Agent** technology, which uses entertaining, animated three-dimensional cartoon characters to interact with the application user. You will create a phone book application that uses one of the predefined Agent characters.

27.1 Microsoft Agent

In this tutorial, you will create a phone book application that displays people's phone numbers, using Microsoft Agent to interact with users and enhance the application. This application must meet the following requirements:

> ### Application Requirements
>
> *A software company's customer-service department is responsible for calling clients. They need a quick way to access their clients' phone numbers and have asked you to develop an application that stores and retrieves the names and numbers of their clients. The service-department employees want an application that employs multimedia (using the Microsoft Agent character, Peedy the Parrot) to allow them to retrieve the phone numbers by speaking the clients' names and also by selecting clients' names with the mouse.*

Microsoft Agent is a technology used to add **interactive animated characters** to Windows applications or Web pages. Microsoft Agent characters can speak (by using voice synthesis) and respond to user input (by using speech recognition). Microsoft employs its Agent technology in such applications as Word, Excel and PowerPoint, where they help users understand how to use the application.

The Microsoft Agent control provides you with access to four predefined characters—*Genie* (a genie), *Merlin* (a wizard), *Peedy* (a parrot) and *Robby* (a robot). Each character contains unique animations that you can use in their applications to illustrate different instructions and actions. For instance, the Peedy character-animation set includes several flying animations which you can use to move Peedy across the screen. Microsoft provides basic information on Agent technology at:

www.microsoft.com/msagent

Microsoft Agent technology enables users to interact with applications and Web pages by using speech. When the user speaks into a microphone, the control uses a **speech-recognition engine**, an application that translates vocal sound input from a microphone into a language that the computer understands. The Microsoft Agent control also uses a text-to-speech engine, which allows the Microsoft Agent characters to speak lines of text. A **text-to-speech engine** is an application that translates typed words into sound that users hear through headphones or speakers connected to a computer. Microsoft provides speech recognition and text-to-speech engines for several languages at

www.microsoft.com/products/msagent/downloads.htm

SELF-REVIEW

1. A _____ translates typed words into sound.
   a) speech-recognition engine   b) text-to-speech engine
   c) character-animation set   d) All of the above.

2. The application that translates vocal sound input from a microphone to a language understood by the computer is called the _____.
   a) speech-recognition engine   b) text-to-speech engine
   c) character-animation set   d) All of the above.

Answers: 1) b. 2) a.

27.2 Downloading Microsoft Agent Components

Microsoft Agent characters can be used as visual aids for applications. These Agents also allow users to speak to, listen to and interact with the characters. This tutorial demonstrates how to use the Microsoft Agent characters to build the **Phone Book** application. To run this tutorial's application, you must download and install the Agent control, speech-recognition engine, text-to-speech engine and Peedy character definition from the Microsoft Agent Web site. Begin by visiting:

www.microsoft.com/products/msagent/downloads.htm

This page (Fig. 27.1) displays a list of Microsoft Agent downloads. The first component you need to download is the Agent character file. Click the **Microsoft Agent character files** link (Fig. 27.1).

Clicking this link directs users to the location where the Microsoft Agent character files can be downloaded (Fig. 27.2). Select the Peedy character from the drop-down list and click the **Download selected character** link. Save the file Peedy.exe to your computer, and install the Peedy character files by double clicking this file.

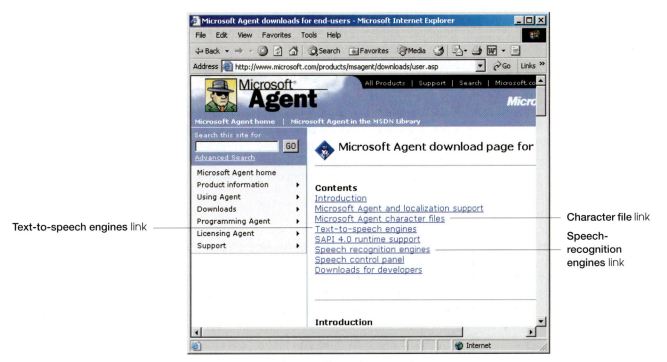

Text-to-speech engines link

Character file link

Speech-recognition engines link

Figure 27.1 Microsoft Web page containing Agent-related downloads.

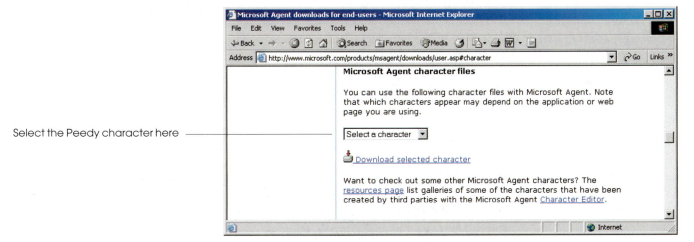

Select the Peedy character here

Figure 27.2 Location for downloading the Microsoft Agent character.

Next, you should download the text-to-speech engine. Return to the **Microsoft Agent Downloads Contents** list by scrolling to the top of the current page, and click the **Text-to-speech engines** link. Click the ComboBox to display the drop-down list, and select the engine that supports American English. Click the **Download selected engine** link to save the file `tv_enua.exe`. Double click this file once it has been downloaded to install the text-to-speech engine. You may need to restart your machine after this installation.

You must also download the speech-recognition engine. Return to the **Microsoft Agent Downloads Contents** list by scrolling to the top of the current page, and click the **Speech recognition engines** link. Click the **Download Microsoft Speech Recognition Engine** link to save the file `actcnc.exe`. Double click this file once it has been downloaded to install the speech-recognition engine. The installation process will walk you through the configuration of your microphone. Once you have downloaded and installed all of the components, you are ready to use Microsoft Agent.

27.3 Test-Driving the Phone Book Application

Recall that you will be creating the **Phone Book** application to allow users to search for a phone number using an interactive Microsoft Agent character. Your **Phone Book** application, which you build in the next section, will contain people's names and phone numbers for the customer-service department. You begin by test-driving the completed application. Then, you will learn the additional Visual Basic .NET technologies that you will need to create your own version of this application.

Test-Driving the Phone Book Application

1. *Opening the completed application.* Open the directory C:\Examples\ Tutorial27\CompletedApplication\PhoneBook to locate the **Phone Book** application. Double click PhoneBook.sln to open the application in Visual Studio .NET.

2. *Running the Phone Book application.* Select **Debug > Start** to run the application (Fig. 27.3).

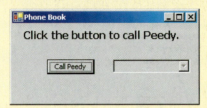

Figure 27.3   **Phone Book** application Form.

3. *Calling Peedy.* Click the **Call Peedy** Button to display Peedy. Peedy flies onto the screen into a position beneath the Form, waves and speaks the instructions shown in Fig. 27.4. When he is finished speaking, Peedy goes into a resting position (Fig. 27.5).

ComboBox disabled until Peedy arrives

Figure 27.4   Peedy appears after **Call Peedy** button is clicked.

Figure 27.5   Peedy in a resting pose.

4. *Using the ComboBox to select a name.* After Peedy appears on the screen, the ComboBox is enabled. Select the name Howard from the list (Fig. 27.6). Notice that the **Call Peedy** Button is disabled, as Peedy is already on the screen. After Howard is selected, Peedy executes several animations. He first appears to be thinking (Fig. 27.7), tells you Howard's number (Fig. 27.8), then smiles for the user (Fig. 27.9).

(cont.)

Disabled **Call Peedy** Button —————

Figure 27.6 Selecting a name from the ComboBox.

Figure 27.7 Peedy thinking.

Figure 27.8 Peedy communicates Howard's phone number.

Figure 27.9 Peedy smiles after speaking phone number.

5. ***Providing a voice command.*** Press the *Scroll Lock* key. A box appears beneath Peedy (called a **status box**) that displays information about Peedy's actions. The status box states that Peedy is listening for your command, as in Fig. 27.10. Speak the name John into your microphone.

Figure 27.10 Peedy listening for a voice command.

If Peedy hears and understands your command, the status box displays the command he heard, as in Fig. 27.11. Otherwise, you must repeat the command clearly, so that Peedy can understand. When Peedy successfully hears your command, he gestures as if he is thinking about your request. He then displays John's phone number, as in Fig. 27.12. You will have noticed that Peedy performs several gestures during this application. You will learn how to control these gestures later in the tutorial.

(cont.)

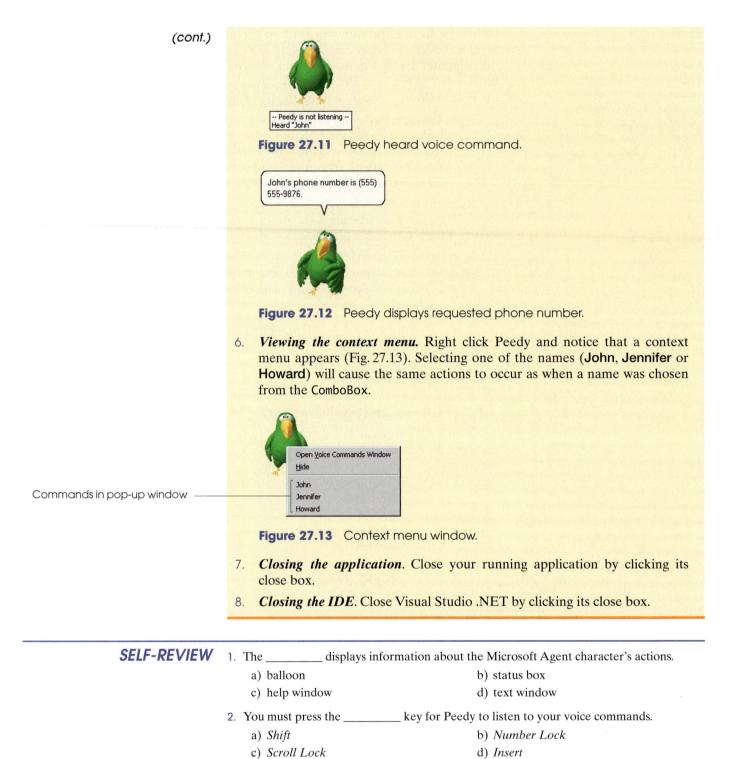

Figure 27.11 Peedy heard voice command.

Figure 27.12 Peedy displays requested phone number.

6. ***Viewing the context menu.*** Right click Peedy and notice that a context menu appears (Fig. 27.13). Selecting one of the names (**John**, **Jennifer** or **Howard**) will cause the same actions to occur as when a name was chosen from the ComboBox.

Commands in pop-up window

Figure 27.13 Context menu window.

7. ***Closing the application.*** Close your running application by clicking its close box.

8. ***Closing the IDE.*** Close Visual Studio .NET by clicking its close box.

SELF-REVIEW

1. The _____ displays information about the Microsoft Agent character's actions.

   a) balloon   b) status box

   c) help window   d) text window

2. You must press the _____ key for Peedy to listen to your voice commands.

   a) *Shift*   b) *Number Lock*

   c) *Scroll Lock*   d) *Insert*

Answers: 1) b. 2) c.

27.4 Constructing the Phone Book Application

Now that you have test-driven the **Phone Book** application, you need to analyze the application, using pseudocode. The Microsoft Agent character, Peedy, helps users search for a specific telephone number. The user can click the ComboBox to select a name and retrieve the specified telephone numbers. However, thanks to the enhancement of the Microsoft Agent character, the user also can communicate verbally with Peedy. The user can retrieve a phone number simply by pressing the *Scroll Lock* key and speaking the name of a person into a microphone connected to the computer. Peedy listens for a name, and, if he recognizes it, displays and speaks the number to the user. The following pseudocode describes the basic operation of the **Phone Book** application when the **Call Peedy** Button is clicked.

When the Form loads
        Display names in the ComboBox
        Load Peedy the Parrot character into the Agent control
        Obtain Peedy the Parrot from the Agent control's Characters property
        Add names as commands for Peedy the Parrot

When the user clicks the Call Peedy Button:
        Display Peedy the Parrot and have the parrot speak the instructions
        Enable ComboBox containing people's names
        Disable the Call Peedy Button

When the user selects a name from the ComboBox:
        Have Peedy the Parrot speak the name and phone number of the person
        selected by the user

When the user speaks a name to Peedy the Parrot:
        Have Peedy the Parrot speak the name and phone number of the person
        selected by the user

When Peedy the Parrot hides:
        Disable ComboBox containing people's names
        Enable the Call Peedy Button

Now that you have test-driven the **Phone Book** application and studied its pseudocode representation, you will use an ACE table to help you convert the pseudocode to Visual Basic .NET. Figure 27.14 lists the actions, controls and events that will help you complete your own version of this application.

Action/Control/Event (ACE) Table for the Phone Book Application

Action	Control/Object	Event
Label the application's controls	lblInformation	
	FrmPhoneBook	Load
Display names in the ComboBox	cboName, m_strNameList	
Load Peedy the Parrot character into the Microsoft Agent control	objMainAgent	
Obtain Peedy the Parrot from the Agent control's Characters property	objMainAgent, m_objMSpeaker	
Add names as commands for Peedy the Parrot	m_objMSpeaker, m_strNameList	
	btnCall	Click
Display Peedy the Parrot and have the parrot speak the instructions	m_objMSpeaker	
Enable ComboBox containing people's names	cboName	
Disable the Call Peedy Button	btnCall	
	cboName	Selected-IndexChanged
Have Peedy the Parrot speak the name and phone number of the person selected by the user	cboName, m_strNameList, m_strNumberList, m_objSpeaker	

Figure 27.14   ACE table for the **Phone Book** application. (Part 1 of 2.)

Action	Control/Object	Event
	objMainAgent	Command
Have Peedy the Parrot speak the name and phone number of the person selected by the user	cboName, m_strNameList, m_strNumberList, m_objSpeaker	
	objMainAgent	HideEvent
Enable ComboBox containing people's names	cboName	
Disable the Call Peedy Button	btnCall	

Figure 27.14   ACE table for the **Phone Book** application. (Part 2 of 2.)

Now that you understand the purpose of the **Phone Book** application, you will begin to create it. In the next box, you follow the instructions for adding the Microsoft Agent control to your **Toolbox**.

Customizing the Toolbox for the *Phone Book* Application

1. *Copying the template to your working directory.* Copy the C:\Examples\ Tutorial27\TemplateApplication\PhoneBook directory to your C:\ SimplyVB directory.

2. *Opening the application's template file.* Double click PhoneBook.sln in the PhoneBook directory to open the application in Visual Studio .NET. If the project does not open in design view, switch to design view at this time.

3. *Adding the Microsoft Agent to the Toolbox.* Before you begin designing the Form, you must make the Microsoft Agent accessible. To do this, you must add the Microsoft Agent control to the **Toolbox** window. Right-click the **Windows Forms** tab in the **Toolbox** then select **Add/Remove Items...** as in Fig. 27.15. The **Customize Toolbox** dialog appears (Fig. 27.16). Select the **COM Components** tab and search for the **Microsoft Agent Control 2.0** item. Then, click its CheckBox to select the control as in Fig. 27.16. Click the **OK** Button. The Agent control now appears in the **Windows Forms** group in the **Toolbox**, as in Fig. 27.17.

Figure 27.15   **Tools** menu.

4. *Saving the project.* Select **File > Save All** to save your modified code.

(cont.)

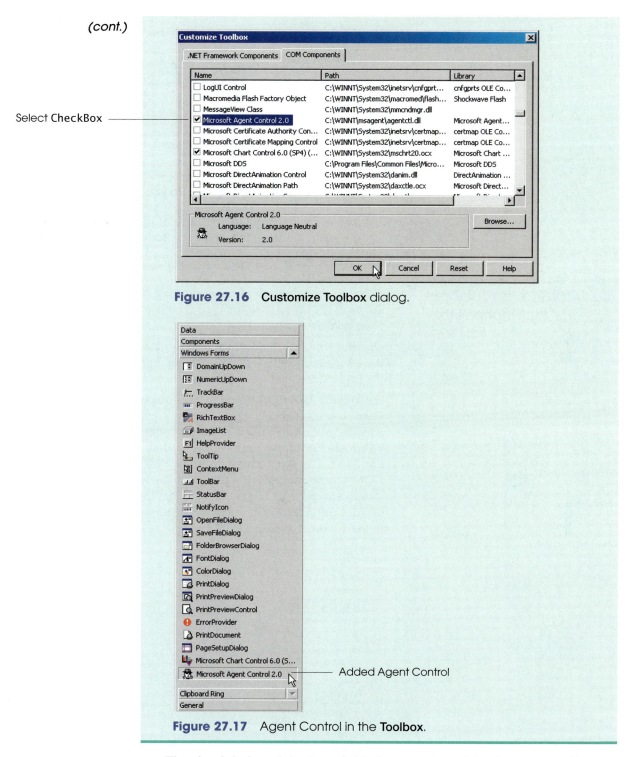

Select CheckBox

Added Agent Control

Figure 27.16   **Customize Toolbox** dialog.

Figure 27.17   Agent Control in the **Toolbox**.

The visual design of the Form (with the exception of the Agent control) is provided in the template application. The next step after adding the Microsoft Agent control to the **Toolbox** is to place a Microsoft Agent control on the Form.

Adding the Microsoft Agent Control to the Application

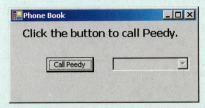

Good Programming Practice

Controls in a container should not overlap. Place your controls so that they are clearly separated from one another, making the design of your application a clean one.

1. **Placing the Microsoft Agent control on the Form.** To meet the application requirements, you must add a Microsoft Agent control to your Form, which will be used to display and manage the actions of the Microsoft Agent characters in your application. Drag and drop the Microsoft Agent control from the **Toolbox** onto the Form. Change the Microsoft Agent control's Name property from the default (AxAgent1) to objMainAgent. Change the Microsoft Agent control's Location property to 16, 48 (Fig. 27.18). Because the control icon is not visible when the application runs, the location on the Form does not affect the application's appearance. However, it is good practice to place the control so that it is not overlapping another control on the Form. Though you set the Agent control's Location property in this step, you will write code later that will determine where the Agent character appears when the application is running. As you saw in the test drive, the Microsoft Agent character can be displayed outside the application's Form.

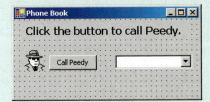

Figure 27.18 Form format of **Phone Book**.

2. **Running the application.** Select **Debug > Start** to run your application (Fig. 27.19). The **Call Peedy** Button will be used to make the Agent (in this case, Peedy) appear on the screen. However, clicking the Button does not cause any action to take place yet, because the Button's Click event handler has not been defined. Notice that the ComboBox next to the **Call Peedy** Button is disabled. You will use code to enable and fill the ComboBox with names shortly.

Figure 27.19 **Phone Book** Form with no functionality.

3. **Closing the application.** Close the application by clicking its close box.

Now that you have placed the Agent control on the application's Form, you will define the event handlers for the **Phone Book** application. These event handlers will define how the Agent responds to user actions. You begin writing code in the following box.

Using Code to Display the Peedy Agent Character

1. **Declaring instance variables.** To view the code file, select **View > Code**. Declare the instance variables you will use in several event handlers by inserting lines 4–12 of Fig. 27.20 within this Form's class definition. In addition to the Microsoft Agent object, objMainAgent, that manages all the application's characters, you also need an object to represent the current character (sometimes referred to as the speaker). In this example, the current character will always be Peedy the Parrot. Line 4 creates a variable to represent this Agent character. The m_objMSpeaker variable is declared as an **AgentObjects.IAgentCtlCharacter** object.

(cont.)

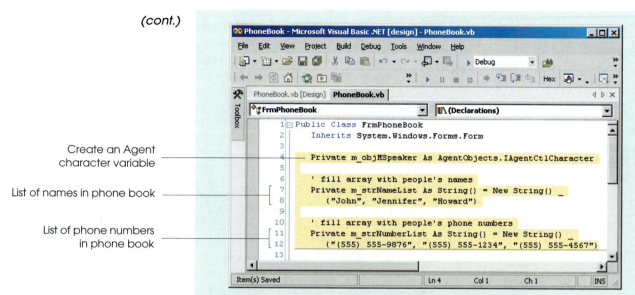

Figure 27.20   Declaring and creating arrays in **Phone Book**.

The arrays m_strNameList and m_strNumberList are then declared and filled. The m_strNameList array (lines 7–8) stores the names of people in the phone book (John, Jennifer and Howard), and the m_strNumberList array (lines 11–12) stores the corresponding phone number for each person ((555) 555-9876, (555) 555-1234 and (555) 555-4567).

2. ***Writing code that executes when the application loads.*** The next step in creating the **Phone Book** application is to use the Form's Load event to execute code before the application becomes available to the user. Double click the Form in the Windows Form Designer to generate the Load event handler, and enter code view. Add lines 110–115 of Fig. 27.21 into the Load event handler. The intCounter variable (line 111) is used to iterate through the m_strNameList array in the For...Next statement (lines 113–115). This statement fills the ComboBox with the contact names that are stored in the m_strNameList array. This allows the user to select names by using the ComboBox instead of speaking the name to Peedy. Be sure to add the comments and line-continuation characters as shown in Fig. 27.21 so that the line numbers in your code match those presented in this tutorial.

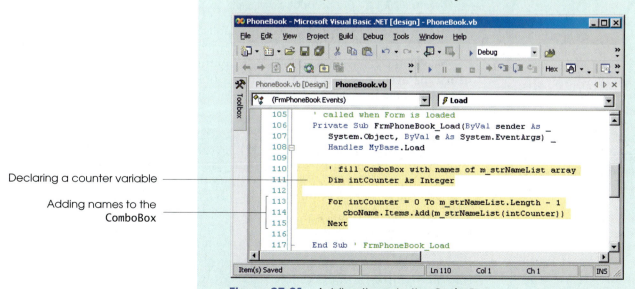

Figure 27.21   Adding items to the **ComboBox**.

(cont.)

3. ***Initializing the Peedy Agent character.*** Insert lines 117–121 of Fig. 27.22 into the event handler. Lines 118–119 load the Peedy character into objMain-Agent. The first argument of the Load method is a String used to represent the Agent character being loaded. In this case, use the String "Peedy". The second argument is a String representing the file where the character is defined ("Peedy.acs").

Several characters can be loaded into a Microsoft Agent control. In this example, however, we will only be using Peedy the Parrot, so no more characters will be loaded. Line 121 assigns the loaded character to m_objMSpeaker. The character is accessed using the **Characters** property of our Microsoft Agent control. The variable m_objMSpeaker can now be used to represent the Peedy Agent character. It is not necessary to create a separate object of type AgentObjects.IAgentCtlCharacter—the Peedy character can be accessed with the expression objMainAgent.Characters("Peedy"). We have created m_objMSpeaker to increase application clarity.

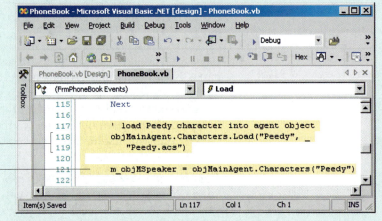

Loading the Peedy character

Assigning Peedy to the Agent character variable

Figure 27.22 Loading the Microsoft Agent character.

4. ***Inserting commands in the Agent Commands context menu.*** Insert lines 123–129 of Fig. 27.23 to your event handler. This code uses the same counter from the previous step in its For...Next statement (lines 124–129). The header of the For...Next statement resets the counter variable's value to 0. Then, the For...Next statement adds names from the m_strNameList to the Peedy character as voice-enabled commands. The list of valid commands for a character is stored in the **Commands** property of AgentObjects.IAgentCtl-Character objects.

Method **Add** of the Commands property adds a new command to the command list. The Add method takes five arguments. The first three arguments are Strings and the last two are Boolean values. The first argument identifies the command name. This value enables access to the command from your application. The second argument is a String that appears in a context menu when the user right clicks Peedy. The third String represents the word(s) for which Peedy listens when users make a verbal request. The fourth argument indicates whether the command is enabled. If so, the Agent character will respond to the spoken command. The final argument specifies whether the command is visible in the Commands context menu, which you have already seen in Fig. 27.13.

Good Programming Practice

Use a variable to represent an object when the full reference to the object is long. This improves code readability.

(cont.)

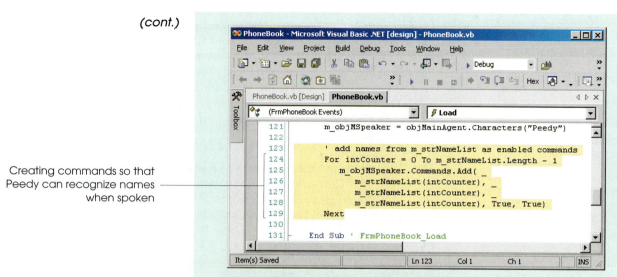

Creating commands so that Peedy can recognize names when spoken

Figure 27.23 Adding commands to Peedy's context menu.

In this example, you set the first three arguments to the same value in the m_strNameList array and set the last two arguments to True for each name. Now Peedy understands users if they speak any of the names found in the m_strNameList array—John, Jennifer or Howard.

A **Command** event is raised when the user selects the command from the Commands pop-up window or speaks the command into a microphone. Command events are handled by the Command event handler of the Microsoft Agent control (objMainAgent, in this example).

5. *Defining the btnCall_Click event handler.* After defining the Form's Load event, you must create an event handler for the **Call Peedy** Button. When this Button is clicked, Peedy should appear and interact with the user. To create the **Call Peedy** Button's Click event handler, double click the **Call Peedy** Button in the Windows Form Designer. Insert lines 137–142 of Fig. 27.24. Be sure to add the comments and line-continuation characters as shown in Fig. 27.24 so that the line numbers in your code match those presented in this tutorial.

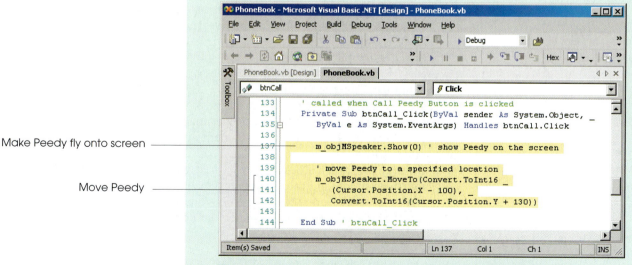

Make Peedy fly onto screen

Move Peedy

Figure 27.24 Displaying the Microsoft Agent character.

(cont.)

Line 137 uses the **Show** method to display Peedy on the screen. Specifying 0 as the argument makes Peedy fly onto the screen and land at his default location. However, if 1 is passed to the method, Peedy's image pops onto the screen at his default location (without the flying animation).

After the Show method is called, Peedy appears at (or flies to) the default position on the screen. The command in lines 140–142 causes Peedy to move to a new location. These lines use the **MoveTo** method of the m_objMSpeaker Agent object. Method MoveTo takes two arguments: an *x*-coordinate and a *y*-coordinate, both of type **Short**. The Short data type is similar to the Integer data type, but Short variables occupy less space in memory and therefore cannot hold larger Integer values. **Convert.ToInt16** converts the value of Cursor.Position.X – 100 to a Short value, where **Cursor.Position.X** contains the current position of the mouse pointer. We have subtracted 100 to specify a position that is 100 pixels to the left of the mouse pointer. The same was done for the *y*-coordinate. In this case, the method moves the Agent character 100 pixels to the left and 130 pixels below the mouse pointer at the time the **Call Peedy** Button is clicked. This keeps Peedy near the application Form.

GUI Design Tip

Locate the Microsoft Agent character near the application Form.

6. ***Coding Peedy's greeting.*** Insert lines 144–154 of Fig. 27.25 into your Click event handler. Line 144 uses the **Play** method to command Peedy to perform an action. This method plays the character animation specified by the String argument that is passed. In this line, Peedy's Wave animation is played—he waves hello to the user. [*Note*: We use only a few of the Peedy character's available animations. To see a listing of the available animations, please visit msdn.microsoft.com/library/default.asp?url=/library/en-us/msagent/peedylst_53xw.asp.]

Lines 147–152 call method Speak twice to specify what Peedy says. The argument passed to the Speak method contains the String that Peedy speaks by using the computer's speakers. This String also appears in a conversation bubble above his head. You have already seen an example of this in Fig. 27.4. In this example, you provide the instructions for using the **Phone Book** application. After Peedy displays the instructions, he is positioned in his rest pose (Fig. 27.5) by passing String RestPose (line 154) to the Play method.

GUI Design Tip

Use Microsoft Agent character gestures to indicate actions the user should take, or a response to an action the user has already taken.

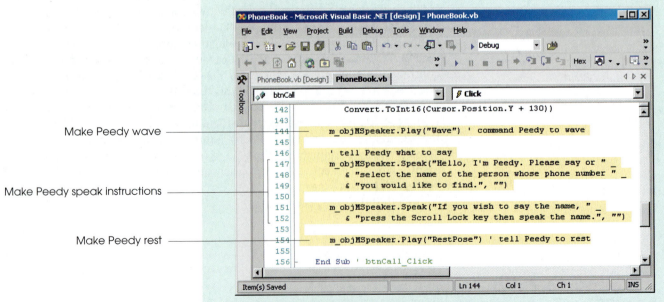

Make Peedy wave — line 144

Make Peedy speak instructions — lines 147–152

Make Peedy rest — line 154

```
142                  Convert.ToInt16(Cursor.Position.Y + 130))
143
144          m_objMSpeaker.Play("Wave") ' command Peedy to wave
145
146          ' tell Peedy what to say
147          m_objMSpeaker.Speak("Hello, I'm Peedy. Please say or " _
148              & "select the name of the person whose phone number " _
149              & "you would like to find.", "")
150
151          m_objMSpeaker.Speak("If you wish to say the name, " _
152              & "press the Scroll Lock key then speak the name.", "")
153
154          m_objMSpeaker.Play("RestPose") ' tell Peedy to rest
155
156      End Sub ' btnCall_Click
```

Figure 27.25 Code that defines Microsoft Agent's actions when Peedy first appears on the screen.

(cont.)

7. ***Enabling and disabling controls.*** Now that you have made the Agent character available by clicking the **Call Peedy** Button, you should disable the Button and allow the ComboBox to be used. Insert lines 156–157 of Fig. 27.26 into your Click event handler. These lines set the **Call Peedy** Button's Enabled property to False and cboName's Enabled property to True while the Agent character is shown. Recall that the ComboBox is disabled by default. You disable the **Call Peedy** Button because Peedy is on the screen at this point.

Enable the ComboBox and disable the **Call Peedy** Button

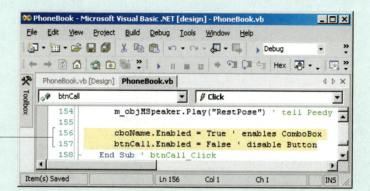

Figure 27.26   Disable btnCall after Peedy has appeared on the screen.

8. ***Saving the project.*** Select **File > Save All** to save your modified code.

Now that you have written code to display Peedy on the screen and have him speak to the user, you must insert code that allows Peedy to respond to user input. Peedy needs to display and read a phone number when the user selects a valid name, either by speaking, by using the context menu or by using the ComboBox. You will enable these features in the following box.

Completing the Phone Book Application

1. ***Defining the objMainAgent_Command event handler.*** Event handler objMainAgent_Command runs when the Command event is raised. Recall that this happens when a user speaks a command to the Agent character by using the microphone (while pressing the *Scroll Lock* key). The event is also raised if the user selects a command from Peedy's context menu. You can generate the event handler by selecting objMainAgent from the Class Name ComboBox and Command from the Method Name ComboBox. Insert lines 165–167 of Fig. 27.27 into this event handler. Be sure to add the comments and line-continuation characters as shown in Fig. 27.27 so that the line numbers in your code match those presented in this tutorial.

Lines 166–167 declare the objCommand variable, which stores values of type **AgentObjects.IAgentCtlUserInput**. This object is used to retrieve the commands that users give Peedy. Notice that you use function CType to convert the first argument to the type of object specified by the second argument. This line converts the user input to be of type AgentObjects.IAgentCtlUserInput. You do this to access the name of the command the Agent received.

(cont.)

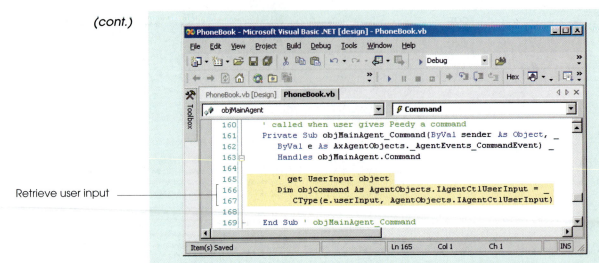

Retrieve user input

Figure 27.27 Event handler `objMainAgent_Command` defined.

2. *Interpreting user input and displaying a phone number.* Insert lines 169–185 of Fig. 27.28 into your code. Line 169 creates a counter variable that is used in a For...Next statement (lines 174–185). The body of this statement contains an If...Then statement (lines 176–183). The code inside the If...Then statement executes if the user's command matches one of the voice-enabled commands you added earlier by using the `m_strNameList` array. Using the counter variable, the For...Next statement iterates through each index of the array, comparing the command name (for example, `John`) to the name in the array. If the names match, the body of the If...Then statement plays Peedy's Think animation (line 177) and uses Peedy to speak and display the requested phone number (lines 178–180). After speaking the phone number, Peedy smiles (the Pleased animation played at line 182).

3. *Creating the cboName_SelectedIndexChanged event handler.* You must now write code to display a phone number if the user chooses a name from the cboName ComboBox. Double click the cboName ComboBox in the Windows Form Designer to generate the `cboName_SelectedIndexChanged` event handler, and enter code view. Insert lines 194–211 of Fig. 27.29 into the event handler. Be sure to add the comments and line-continuation characters as shown in Fig. 27.29 so that the line numbers in your code match those presented in this tutorial.

   This ComboBox allows users who are unable to access the voice-recognition engines to use the application. Much as in the Command event handler, lines 198–211 search the array for a String that matches the selected item in the ComboBox. If a match is found, then Peedy's Think animation plays (Fig. 27.7), and the phone number is provided. After Peedy states the number, his Pleased animation plays, indicating that he is content with his ability to provide the user with the correct phone number (Fig. 27.9).

   The `cboName_SelectedIndexChanged` method executes code similar to the `objMainAgent_Command` event handler. The only difference is that the Command method is invoked by verbal requests, whereas this method is invoked by selecting items in the cboName.

4. *Resetting the application's controls when Peedy is hidden.* You might have noticed that you can choose **Hide** from Peedy's context menu (when you right click Peedy). When the user hides the Peedy character, you should enable the **Call Peedy** Button to allow the user to make Peedy reappear. Also, to prevent the user from selecting a name from the ComboBox while Peedy is hidden, you should disable the ComboBox.

(cont.)

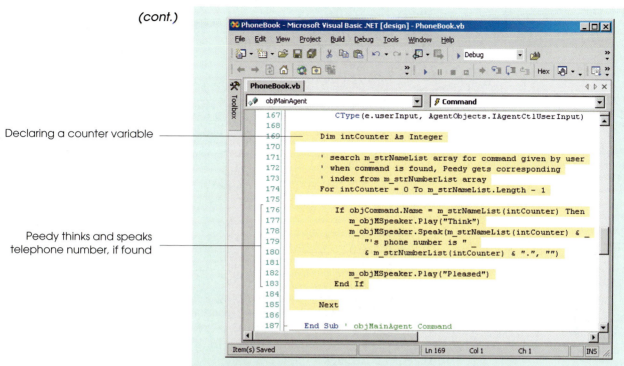

Figure 27.28 Finding the spoken or selected name.

When the user selects **Hide**, a **HideEvent** is raised. To generate the HideEvent event handler, select objMainAgent from the Class Name ComboBox and HideEvent from the Method Name ComboBox. Then, insert lines 220–221 of Fig. 27.30 into the event handler. These lines enable the **Call Peedy** Button and disable the ComboBox.

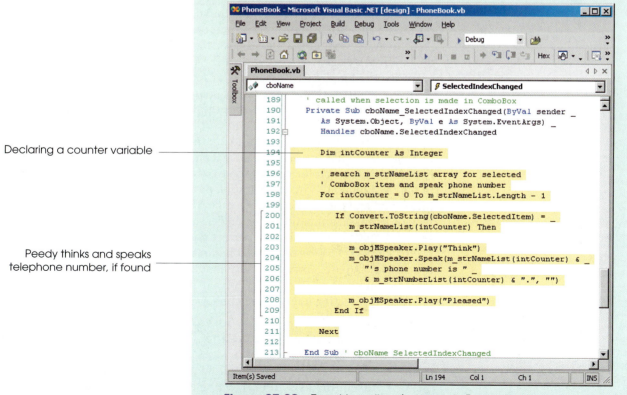

Figure 27.29 Event handler cboName_SelectedIndexChanged defined.

(cont.)

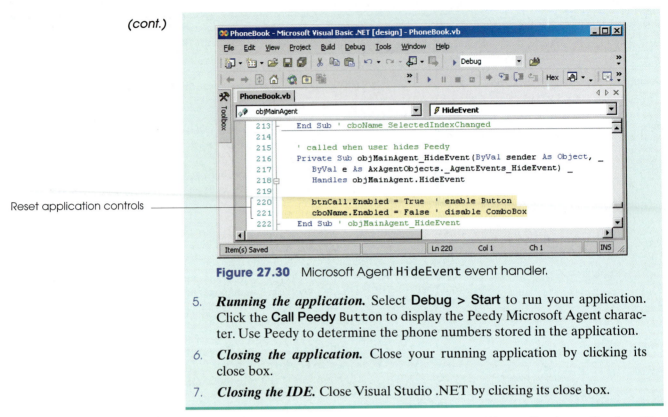

Figure 27.30 Microsoft Agent `HideEvent` event handler.

Reset application controls

5. *Running the application.* Select **Debug > Start** to run your application. Click the **Call Peedy** Button to display the Peedy Microsoft Agent character. Use Peedy to determine the phone numbers stored in the application.

6. *Closing the application.* Close your running application by clicking its close box.

7. *Closing the IDE.* Close Visual Studio .NET by clicking its close box.

Figure 27.31 presents the source code for the **Phone Book** application. The lines of code that contain new programming concepts that you learned in this tutorial are highlighted.

```
 1   Public Class FrmPhoneBook
 2       Inherits System.Windows.Forms.Form
 3
 4       Private m_objMSpeaker As AgentObjects.IAgentCtlCharacter
 5
 6       ' fill array with people's names
 7       Private m_strNameList As String() = New String() _
 8          {"John", "Jennifer", "Howard"}
 9
10       ' fill array with people's phone numbers
11       Private m_strNumberList As String() = New String() _
12          {"(555) 555-9876", "(555) 555-1234", "(555) 555-4567"}
13
14       ' called when Form is loaded
15       Private Sub FrmPhoneBook_Load(ByVal sender As _
16          System.Object, ByVal e As System.EventArgs) _
17          Handles MyBase.Load
18
19          ' fill ComboBox with names from m_strNameList array
20          Dim intCounter As Integer
21
22          For intCounter = 0 To m_strNameList.Length - 1
23             cboName.Items.Add(m_strNameList(intCounter))
24          Next
25
```

Variable to hold Microsoft Agent character

Figure 27.31 **Phone Book** application code. (Part 1 of 3.)

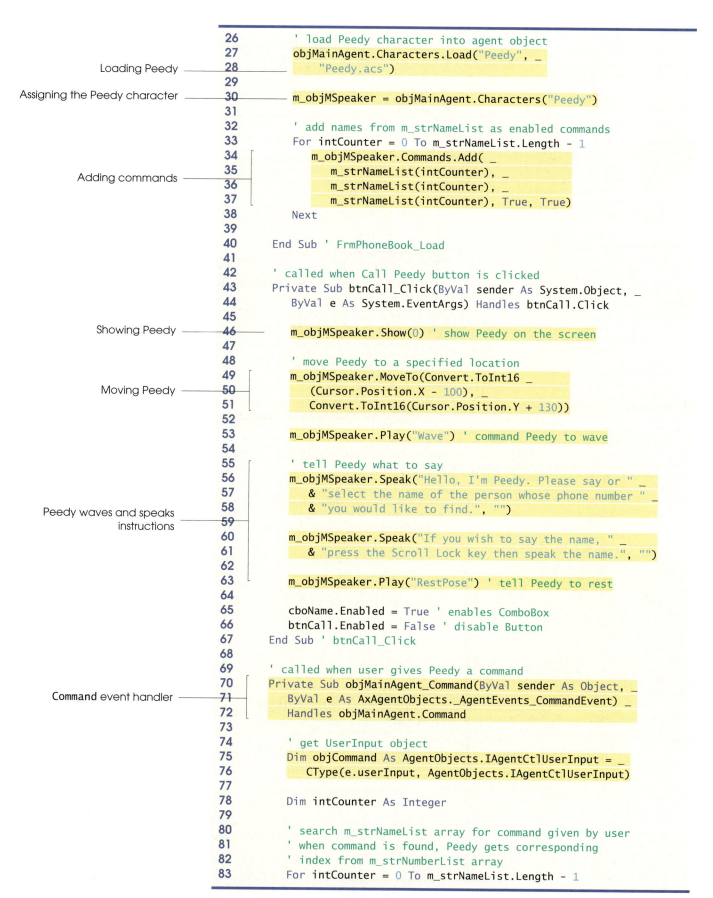

```
26          ' load Peedy character into agent object
27          objMainAgent.Characters.Load("Peedy", _
28              "Peedy.acs")
29
30          m_objMSpeaker = objMainAgent.Characters("Peedy")
31
32          ' add names from m_strNameList as enabled commands
33          For intCounter = 0 To m_strNameList.Length - 1
34              m_objMSpeaker.Commands.Add( _
35                  m_strNameList(intCounter), _
36                  m_strNameList(intCounter), _
37                  m_strNameList(intCounter), True, True)
38          Next
39
40      End Sub ' FrmPhoneBook_Load
41
42      ' called when Call Peedy button is clicked
43      Private Sub btnCall_Click(ByVal sender As System.Object, _
44          ByVal e As System.EventArgs) Handles btnCall.Click
45
46          m_objMSpeaker.Show(0) ' show Peedy on the screen
47
48          ' move Peedy to a specified location
49          m_objMSpeaker.MoveTo(Convert.ToInt16 _
50              (Cursor.Position.X - 100), _
51              Convert.ToInt16(Cursor.Position.Y + 130))
52
53          m_objMSpeaker.Play("Wave") ' command Peedy to wave
54
55          ' tell Peedy what to say
56          m_objMSpeaker.Speak("Hello, I'm Peedy. Please say or " _
57              & "select the name of the person whose phone number " _
58              & "you would like to find.", "")
59
60          m_objMSpeaker.Speak("If you wish to say the name, " _
61              & "press the Scroll Lock key then speak the name.", "")
62
63          m_objMSpeaker.Play("RestPose") ' tell Peedy to rest
64
65          cboName.Enabled = True ' enables ComboBox
66          btnCall.Enabled = False ' disable Button
67      End Sub ' btnCall_Click
68
69      ' called when user gives Peedy a command
70      Private Sub objMainAgent_Command(ByVal sender As Object, _
71          ByVal e As AxAgentObjects._AgentEvents_CommandEvent) _
72          Handles objMainAgent.Command
73
74          ' get UserInput object
75          Dim objCommand As AgentObjects.IAgentCtlUserInput = _
76              CType(e.userInput, AgentObjects.IAgentCtlUserInput)
77
78          Dim intCounter As Integer
79
80          ' search m_strNameList array for command given by user
81          ' when command is found, Peedy gets corresponding
82          ' index from m_strNumberList array
83          For intCounter = 0 To m_strNameList.Length - 1
```

Figure 27.31 Phone Book application code. (Part 2 of 3.)

```
84
85            If objCommand.Name = m_strNameList(intCounter) Then
86               m_objMSpeaker.Play("Think")
87               m_objMSpeaker.Speak(m_strNameList(intCounter) & _
88                 "'s phone number is " _
89                 & m_strNumberList(intCounter) & ".", "")
90
91               m_objMSpeaker.Play("Pleased")
92            End If
93
94         Next
95
96      End Sub ' objMainAgent_Command
97
98      ' called when selection is made in ComboBox
99      Private Sub cboName_SelectedIndexChanged(ByVal sender _
100        As System.Object, ByVal e As System.EventArgs) _
101        Handles cboName.SelectedIndexChanged
102
103        Dim intCounter As Integer
104
105        ' search m_strNameList array for selected
106        ' ComboBox item and speak phone number
107        For intCounter = 0 To m_strNameList.Length - 1
108
109           If Convert.ToString(cboName.SelectedItem) = _
110              m_strNameList(intCounter) Then
111
112              m_objMSpeaker.Play("Think")
113              m_objMSpeaker.Speak(m_strNameList(intCounter) & _
114                 "'s phone number is " _
115                 & m_strNumberList(intCounter) & ".", "")
116
117              m_objMSpeaker.Play("Pleased")
118           End If
119
120        Next
121
122     End Sub ' cboName_SelectedIndexChanged
123
124     ' called when user hides Peedy
125     Private Sub objMainAgent_HideEvent(ByVal sender As Object, _
126        ByVal e As AxAgentObjects._AgentEvents_HideEvent) _
127        Handles objMainAgent.HideEvent
128
129        btnCall.Enabled = True  ' enable Button
130        cboName.Enabled = False ' disable ComboBox
131     End Sub ' objMainAgent_HideEvent
132
133 End Class ' FrmPhoneBook
```

HideEvent event handler —— (lines 125–127)

Figure 27.31   Phone Book application code. (Part 3 of 3.)

SELF-REVIEW 1. When Peedy is hidden, you can show him by _____.

a) using method Show

b) selecting **Show** from Peedy's tray icon context menu

c) double clicking Peedy's tray icon   d) All of the above.

2. Method _____ used to relocate the Microsoft Agent character on the screen.
   a) `Move`   b) `Relocate`
   c) `MoveTo`   d) `Place`

Answers: 1) d. 2) c.

27.5 Wrap-Up

In this tutorial, you were introduced to Microsoft Agent and learned how it can be used to enhance software applications. You learned what Microsoft Agent is used for and how to download all the necessary components. You then wrote code to use a Microsoft Agent character, Peedy the Parrot.

Using Peedy, you created an application that interacts with the user by listening to the user's commands and by answering using speech. You used the `Show` and `MoveTo` methods to show Peedy and move him on the screen. You also used Peedy's `Speak` method to speak instructions and phone numbers to the user. You then learned how to control Peedy's gestures, such as `Wave` and `Think`, not only to entertain the user but also to signal visually what the application is doing.

Tutorials 28–31 present you with a Web-based bookstore application case study. You will learn how to build an application that can be accessed by using a Web browser. In Tutorial 28, You will be introduced to the concept of a multi-tier application and you will take your first steps toward building a three-tier application, which you will complete in the subsequent tutorials.

SKILLS SUMMARY

Displaying The Microsoft Agent to Users
- Load the desired Microsoft Agent, using the `Characters.Load` method.
- Call the Microsoft Agent object's `Show` method.

Allowing Verbal Communication With The Agent
- Add voice-enabled commands, using the Microsoft Agent's `Commands.Add` method.
- Define the `Commands` event handler.

Causing The Agent to Speak
- Call the Microsoft Agent's `Speak` method.
- Specify the `String` that Microsoft Agent should speak.

Causing Agent to Perform Actions
- Call the Microsoft Agent character's `Play` method.
- Specify the animation that Microsoft Agent should display.

KEY TERMS

Add method of the Commands property—Adds a command to a Microsoft Agent character.

AgentObject.IAgentCtlCharacter object—References a Microsoft Agent character.

AgentObject.IAgentCtlUserInput object—Stores the user input retrieved from a Microsoft Agent character.

Characters property of MSAgent control—Used to access a specific Microsoft Agent character.

Command event—Raised when a user speaks a command to a Microsoft Agent character or selects a command from a character's context menu.

Commands property—Sets which commands the Microsoft Agent character can understand as input from the user.

Convert.ToInt16 method—Converts data to type `Short`.

Cursor.Position property—Contains the *x*- and *y*-coordinates of the mouse cursor on the screen (in pixels).

HideEvent event—Raised when a Microsoft Agent character is hidden.

interactive animated characters—The Microsoft Agent technology adds such characters to Windows applications and Web pages. These characters can interact with the user through mouse clicks and microphone input.

Microsoft Agent—A technology used to add interactive animated characters to Windows applications and Web pages.

MoveTo method—Relocates the Microsoft Agent character on the screen.

multimedia—The use of various media, such as sound, video and animation, to create content in an application.

Play method—Plays a Microsoft Agent character animation.

Short data type—Holds small Integers.

Show method—Displays a Microsoft Agent character on the screen.

Speak method—Used to have the Microsoft Agent character speak text to the user.

speech-recognition engine—Application that translates vocal sound input from a microphone into a language that the computer understands.

speech synthesis—The process by which a computer converts text to spoken words.

status box—A box that appears below a Microsoft agent character that displays information about the character's actions.

text-to-speech engine—Application that translates typed words into spoken sound that users hear through headphones or speakers connected to a computer.

GUI DESIGN GUIDELINES

Microsoft Agent Control

- Locate the Microsoft Agent character near the application Form.
- Use Microsoft Agent character gestures to indicate actions the user should take, or a response to an action the user has already taken.

CONTROLS, EVENTS, PROPERTIES & METHODS

Convert The Convert class converts the value of a data type to another data type.

- *Methods*

  ToChar—Converts a value into a character (of data type Char).

  ToDecimal—Converts the value from another data type to type Decimal.

  ToInt16—Converts the value from another data type to type Short.

IAgentCtlCharacter This class is used to represent the Agent character that is used in the application.

- *Property*

  Commands—Contains the commands the character will recognize.

- *Methods*

  Show—Displays the character on the screen.

  MoveTo—Moves the character to a specified location on the screen.

  Play—Plays character animations.

  Speak—Specifies the text to be spoken by the character.

  Commands.Add—Adds a new command to the command list for the Agent object.

IAgentCtlUserInput This class is used to retrieve commands from users.

- *Property*

  Name—Retrieves the name of the command given by the user.

Microsoft Agent Control   Control   This control is used to create and manipulate the multimedia features of a Microsoft Agent character.

- ◼ *In action*

- ◼ *Events*

    Command—Raised when a user gives the Microsoft Agent character a verbal command or selects an option from the character's context menu.

    HideEvent—Raised when a user hides the Microsoft Agent character.

- ◼ *Property*

    Location—Specifies the location of the Microsoft Agent control on the Form.

- ◼ *Method*

    Characters.Load—Loads a character into the Microsoft Agent control.

MULTIPLE-CHOICE QUESTIONS

27.1 The _____ method is used to specify what the Microsoft Agent will say.

a) Speak
b) Say
c) Command
d) Voice

27.2 The _____ method is used to activate a Microsoft Agent character's animation.

a) Show
b) Play
c) Speak
d) Appear

27.3 Method MoveTo takes two arguments. What do these arguments represent?

a) The direction in which the Agent should move (left, right, up, down).
b) The name of the character and its position.
c) The *x*-coordinate and *y*-coordinate of the location to which the Agent should move.
d) The name of the character and the direction of movement.

27.4 Which method of IAgentCtlCharacter displays the Microsoft Agent character on the screen?

a) Play
b) Show
c) Speak
d) Appear

27.5 Use the _____ event handler to execute code when users click **Hide** the Agent character context menu.

a) Hide
b) HideEvent
c) Command
d) Disappear

27.6 The Add method of the Commands property _____.

a) adds a new command to the command list
b) joins two commands together
c) displays the Commands pop-up window
d) Both a and c.

27.7 The _____ event handler controls what occurs when users speak to the Agent.

a) Command
b) ClickEvent
c) Click
d) SelectedIndexChanged

27.8 _____ specifies the *x*-coordinate of the mouse cursor on the screen.

a) `Cursor.Location.X`   b) `Cursor.Position.X`

c) `Mouse.Location.X`   d) `Mouse.Position.X`

27.9 Specifying _____ as a parameter to Peedy's `Play` method causes him to smile.

a) `"Think"`   b) `"Smile"`

c) `"Pleased"`   d) `"Happy"`

27.10 Specifying _____ as a parameter to Peedy's `Play` method causes him to rest.

a) `"RestPose"`   b) `"Rest"`

c) `"Think"`   d) `"Pose"`

EXERCISES   **27.11** (***Appointment Book Application Using Microsoft Agent***) Write an application that allows users to add appointments to an appointment book that uses Microsoft Agent. When users speak a person's name, Merlin returns the time and date of the appointment that users have with that person. If users say "Today," Merlin returns a list of the users' appointments for the day.

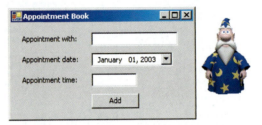

Figure 27.32   Appointment Book GUI.

a) ***Downloading the Merlin Microsoft Agent.*** Download the `Merlin.acs` character file from the Microsoft Web site.

b) ***Copying the template to your working directory.*** Copy the directory `C:\Examples\Tutorial27\Exercises\AppointmentBook` to your `C:\SimplyVB` directory.

c) ***Opening the application's template file.*** Double click `AppointmentBook.sln` in the `AppointmentBook` directory to open the application.

d) ***Adding the Agent Control to the Form.*** Add the Microsoft Agent control to the `Form`.

e) ***Creating module-level variables.*** Create three module-level variables of type `Array-List` to store the date, time and person with which the user has an appointment. Create a module-level variable of type `AgentObjects.IAgentCtlCharacter` (as you did in the **Phone Book** application).

f) ***Defining the FrmAppointments_Load event handler.*** Load Merlin's character file, display him on the screen and add the "Today" command to the command list.

g) ***Defining the btnAdd_Click event handler.*** Define this event handler so that the information provided by the user is added to its corresponding `ArrayList`. The **Appointment With:** TextBox input should be added to the `ArrayList` containing the names of people with whom the user has an appointment. The input for the appointment date and time should also be added to their respective `ArrayLists`. Display an error message if the user leaves the **Appointment With:** or the **Appointment Time:** TextBox empty.

h) ***Adding voice-enabled commands.*** Within the `btnAdd_Click` event handler, add a voice-enabled command that allows a user to speak the name of the person with whom the user has an appointment to the command list. This allows a user to check for whether there is an appointment with someone by speaking the person's name. The command should also appear in the Commands context menu.

i) ***Defining the Agent's Command event handler.*** As you did in the **Phone Book** application, define what occurs when a user speaks or selects a command. If the user specifies the Today command, Merlin should tell the user the names of all the people with whom the user has an appointment today. If the user specifies a specific name, Merlin should state the time and date at which the user has an appointment with this person. If the user did not schedule any appointments, then Merlin should inform the user that no appointments were scheduled.

j) *Running the application.* Select **Debug > Start** to run your application. Enter various appointments, where at least two of the appointments are scheduled for the current day. Input the name of the person you are meeting at one of the appointments by either speaking the name into your microphone, or right-clicking the agent and selecting that person's name. Verify that the agent repeats back correct information about that appointment. Input the value "Today" by either speaking it into the microphone or right-clicking the agent and selecting **Today**. Verify that the agent repeats back all the appointments for the current day.

k) *Closing the application.* Close your running application by clicking its close box.

l) *Closing the IDE.* Close Visual Studio .NET by clicking its close box.

27.12 (*Craps Game Application Using Microsoft Agent*) Modify the **Craps Game** application from Tutorial 16 to include a Microsoft Agent character.

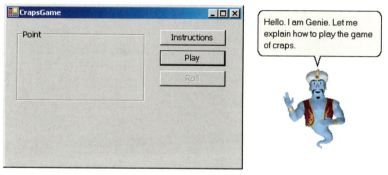

Figure 27.33 Modified **Craps Game** GUI.

a) *Downloading the Genie Microsoft Agent.* Download the Genie.acs character file from the Microsoft Web site.

b) *Copying the template to your working directory.* Copy the directory C:\Examples\ Tutorial27\Exercises\CrapsGameEnhancement to your C:\SimplyVB directory.

c) *Opening the application's template file.* Double click CrapsGame.sln in the Craps-GameEnhancement directory to open the application.

d) *Adding the Agent control to the Form.* Add the Microsoft Agent control to the Form.

e) *Creating a module-level variable.* Create a module-level variable of type AgentObjects.IAgentCtlCharacter (as you did in the **Phone Book** application).

f) *Defining the FrmCrapsGame_Load event handler.* Load Genie's character file, and display him on the screen.

g) *Modifying the btnPlay_Click event handler.* Add code to the btnPlay_Click event handler to control the Agent. When the user wins the game, Genie should play his Pleased animation and congratulate the user. If the user loses, Genie should play his Confused animation and say that the user lost. If the user neither wins nor loses, Genie should tell the user to roll again. Make sure to reset him to his RestPose after he plays any animation.

h) *Defining the btnRoll_Click event handler.* Add code to the btnRoll_Click event handler to control the Agent. If users "make their point," Genie should play his Pleased animation and state that the user won. If the user rolls a 7, Genie should play his Confused animation and say that the user lost. Otherwise, Genie should tell the user to roll again.

i) *Defining the btnInstructions_Click event handler.* Define event handler btnInstructions_Click to make Genie introduce himself to the user. Genie should then explain the rules to the game of craps.

j) *Running the application.* Select **Debug > Start** to run your application. Click the **Instructions** Button and allow the agent character to tell you the rules of the game. Use the **Play** and **Roll** Buttons to play a few games of craps. When you need to roll again, verify that the agent tells you to roll again. Also, verify that the agents informs you whether you won or lost at the end of each game.

k) *Closing the application.* Close your running application by clicking its close box.

l) *Closing the IDE.* Close Visual Studio .NET by clicking its close box.

27.13 (*Security Panel Application Using Microsoft Agent*) Modify the **Security Panel** application from Tutorial 12 to include Microsoft Agent.

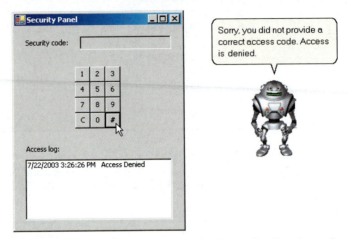

Figure 27.34   Robby from modified **Security Panel** application.

a) *Downloading the Robby Microsoft Agent.* Download the Robby.acs character file from the Microsoft Web site.

b) *Copying the template to your working directory.* Copy the directory C:\Examples\ Tutorial27\Exercises\SecurityPanelEnhancement to your C:\SimplyVB directory.

c) *Opening the application's template file.* Double click SecurityPanel.sln in the SecurityPanelEnhancement directory to open the application.

d) *Adding the Agent control to the Form.* Add the Microsoft Agent control to the Form.

e) *Creating a module-level variable.* Create a module-level variable of type AgentObjects.IAgentCtlCharacter (as you did in the **Phone Book** application).

f) *Defining the FrmSecurityPanel_Load event handler.* Load Robby's character file, and display him on the screen. Command Robby to tell users to input their access codes.

g) *Modifying the btnEnter_Click event handler.* Add code to the btnEnter_Click event handler to use the Microsoft Agent. If the user enters a valid access code, Robby should welcome the user and state the type of employee that the access code represents. If the access code is invalid, then Robby should state that an invalid code was provided and that access is denied.

h) *Running the application.* Select **Debug > Start** to run your application. Enter various access codes. For correct access codes, verify that the agent tells you what type of employee the access code represents. For incorrect access codes, verify that the agents tells you that access is denied.

i) *Closing the application.* Close your running application by clicking its close box.

j) *Closing the IDE.* Close Visual Studio .NET by clicking its close box.

What does this code do? ▶ **27.14** After the user clicks the **Call** Button, what does the following event handler do?

```
 1  Private Sub btnCall_Click(ByVal sender As System.Object, _
 2     ByVal e As System.EventArgs) Handles btnCall.Click
 3
 4     objMainAgent.Characters.Load("Genie", "Genie.acs")
 5
 6     objMSpeaker = objMainAgent.Characters("Genie")
 7
 8     objMSpeaker.Show(0)
 9
10     objMSpeaker.Speak("Hello, I'm Genie the special agent!")
11
12  End Sub
```

What's wrong with this code? ▶ **27.15** Find the error(s) in the following code. The event handler should have an agent object appear and say, "Hello, my name is Merlin." This should happen when the user clicks the **Call** Button.

```
 1  Private Sub btnCall_Click(ByVal sender As System.Object, _
 2     ByVal e As System.EventArgs) Handles btnCall.Click
 3
 4     objMainAgent.Characters.Load("Merlin", "Merlin.acs")
 5
 6     objMSpeaker = objMainAgent.Characters("Merlin")
 7
 8     Dim intNumber As Integer = 10
 9
10     objMSpeaker.Show(intNumber)
11
12     objMSpeaker.Play("Hello, my name is Merlin")
13
14  End Sub
```

Programming Challenge ▶ **27.16** (*Car Payment Application Using Microsoft Agent*) Enhance the **Car Payment Calculator** application from Tutorial 9 to use the Microsoft Agent, Robby. When the application is executed, Robby should appear on the screen and wave to users. He should then explain the purpose of the application. After the user enters information into each field of the **Car Payment Calculator** and clicks the **Calculate** Button, Robby should speak the calculated payment amounts and the period (number of months) over which they were calculated. The C:\Examples\Tutorial27\Exercises\CarPaymentCalculatorEnhancement directory contains the template application for this exercise. Copy it to your working directory and open the application to begin the exercise.

Bookstore Application: Web Applications

Introducing Internet Information Services

Objectives

In this tutorial, you will learn to:
- Use Internet Information Services to serve Web content to Web browser clients.
- Request documents from a Web server.
- Execute an ASP .NET Web application.

Outline

In previous tutorials, you used Visual Basic .NET to develop Windows applications. These applications contained a GUI with which the user interacted. You can also use Visual Studio .NET to create **Web applications**. These applications, also known as Web-based applications, use Visual Basic .NET in combination with Microsoft's **ASP .NET technology** to create Web content (data that can be viewed in a Web browser such as Internet Explorer). This Web content includes HTML (HyperText Markup Language) documents and images.

In this tutorial, you will learn important Web-development concepts in the context of the **Bookstore** application. This application consists of two Web pages. The first page displays a list of books. After selecting a book, the user clicks a `Button`, which directs the browser to a second Web page. Information about the selected book is then retrieved from a database and displayed for the user. The second Web page also contains a `Button` that, when clicked, directs the Web browser back to the first Web page, allowing the user to select a different book. Before you create this application, you will be introduced to fundamental Web development concepts that are required to understand the **Bookstore** application. You will then test-drive the **Bookstore** application. In Tutorials 28–31, you will analyze the pseudocode and ACE table and develop the **Bookstore** application.

28.1 Multi-Tier Architecture

Web applications are **multi-tier applications**, sometimes referred to as *n-tier applications*. Multi-tier applications divide functionality into separate **tiers** (that is, logical groupings of functionality). The separate tiers of an application can be located on the same computer or on separate computers distributed across any computer network, including the Internet. Figure 28.1 illustrates the basic structure of a multi-tier application.

The **information tier** (also called the **data tier** or the **bottom tier**) maintains data for the application. The information tier for the **Bookstore** application is represented by a database that contains product information, such as book titles, author names, publication dates and edition numbers. The database also contains ISBN numbers, book descriptions and prices.

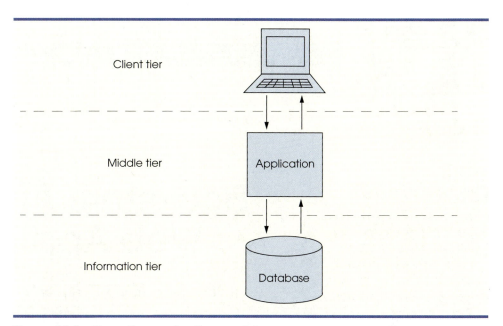

Figure 28.1 Three-tier application model.

The **middle tier** controls interactions between application clients (such as Web browsers) and application data in the information tier. In the **Bookstore** application, the middle-tier code determines which book was selected and which book's information is retrieved from the database. The middle-tier code also determines how the selected book's data will be displayed. The middle tier processes client requests (for example, a request to view a book's information) from the top tier, which we define shortly, and retrieves data from the database (author names, prices, descriptions, etc.) in the information tier. The middle tier then processes data and presents the content to the client. In other words, the middle tier represents the functionality of the Web application.

The **client tier**, or **top tier**, is the application's user interface, which is typically a Web browser. In the **Bookstore** application, the client tier is represented by the pages displayed in the Web browser. The user interacts directly with this application through the client tier (browser) by entering text, selecting from a list, clicking But-tons, etc. The browser reports the user's actions to the middle tier which processes the information. The middle tier can also make requests to and retrieve data from the information tier. The client then displays to the user the data retrieved by the middle tier from the information tier.

SELF-REVIEW

1. A database is located in the _____ tier.
   a) top
   b) middle
   c) bottom
   d) client

2. The role of the middle tier is to _____.
   a) display the application's user interface   b) provide a database for the application
   c) control the interaction between the client and information tiers
   d) control the interaction between the client and the user interface

Answers: 1) c. 2) c.

28.2 Web Servers

A **Web server** is specialized software that responds to client (Web browser) requests by providing requested resources (such as HTML documents). To request documents from Web servers, users must know the locations at which those documents reside. A **URL** (**Uniform Resource Locator**) can be thought of as an address that directs a browser to a resource on the Web. A URL contains a computer name (called a **host name**) or an IP address (we will discuss IP addresses shortly) that identifies the computer on which the Web server resides.

Once the **Bookstore** application is properly set up, users can run the application by typing its URL into a Web browser. This action is translated into a request to the Web server where the **Bookstore** application resides. The Web server sends back Web content created by the **Bookstore** application. This content is displayed in the Web browser for the user.

When you access the **Bookstore** application, you provide a URL in a browser to locate the Web pages of the application. In this tutorial, you will use `localhost` in the URL, which is a special host name that identifies the local computer. You also can use your machine's name. [*Note*: Your computer's name can be determined by right clicking **My Computer** and selecting **Properties** from the context menu to display the **System Properties** dialog. If your operating system is Windows 2000, click the **Network Identification** tab. The **Full computer name:** field in the **System Properties** window displays the computer's name. If your operating system is Windows XP, select the **Computer Name** tab. The **Full computer name:** field in the **Computer Name** tab displays the computer name.]

A **host** is a computer that stores and maintains resources, such as Web pages, databases, multimedia files, etc. In the case of the **Bookstore** application, the host is your computer. A **domain** represents a group of hosts on the Internet; it combines with a host name (for example, www for World Wide Web) and a **top-level domain** *(TLD)* to form a **fully qualified domain name** (**FQDN**), which provides a user-friendly way to identify a site on the Internet. In a fully qualified domain name, the TLD often describes the type of organization that owns the domain. For example, the com TLD usually refers to a commercial business, the org TLD usually refers to a nonprofit organization and edu usually refers to an educational institution. In addition, each country has its own TLD, such as cn for China, et for Ethiopia, om for Oman and us for the United States.

Each fully qualified domain name corresponds to a numeric address called an **IP** (**Internet Protocol**) **address**, which is much like the street address of a house. Just as people use street addresses to locate houses or businesses in a city, computers use IP addresses to locate other computers on the Internet. A **domain name system** *(DNS) server* is a computer that maintains a database of host names and their corresponding IP addresses. The process of translating fully qualified domain names to IP addresses is called a **DNS lookup**. For example, to access the Deitel Web site, type the fully qualified domain name www.deitel.com into a Web browser. The DNS lookup translates www.deitel.com into the IP address of the Deitel Web server (that is, 63.110.43.82). The IP address of `localhost` is always 127.0.0.1.

SELF-REVIEW

1. A _____ is a computer that stores and maintains resources.

    a) host   b) IP address

    c) domain name   d) domain name system

2. A DNS lookup is a _____.

    a) translation of an IP address to a domain name

    b) translation of a fully qualified domain name to an IP address

    c) translation of a fully qualified domain name to a host name

    d) search for a domain name

Answers: 1) a. 2) b.

28.3 Internet Information Services (IIS)

Microsoft **Internet Information Services (IIS)** is the Web server you will use to respond to client requests. IIS must be installed on your machine before you can create Web applications using Visual Studio .NET. To determine if IIS is installed you should read Appendix G. [*Note*: If you encounter problems setting up IIS, please visit www.deitel.com/books/vbnetSIMPLY1_2003/index.html. This site contains frequently asked questions (FAQs) from our readers and an errata list. If you cannot find the solution to your problem there, please email us at deitel@deitel.com and we will respond promptly.]

Before you can test-drive the completed application you must specify initial settings for the **Bookstore** application.

Specifying Initial Settings for the Bookstore Application

1. *Copying the Bookstore application files to IIS's root directory.* Copy the C:\Examples\Tutorial28\CompletedApplication\Bookstore directory to IIS's root directory. This directory is usually C:\Inetpub\wwwroot (Fig. 28.2). [*Note*: The directory names and file names in the wwwroot directory may be different on your computer.]

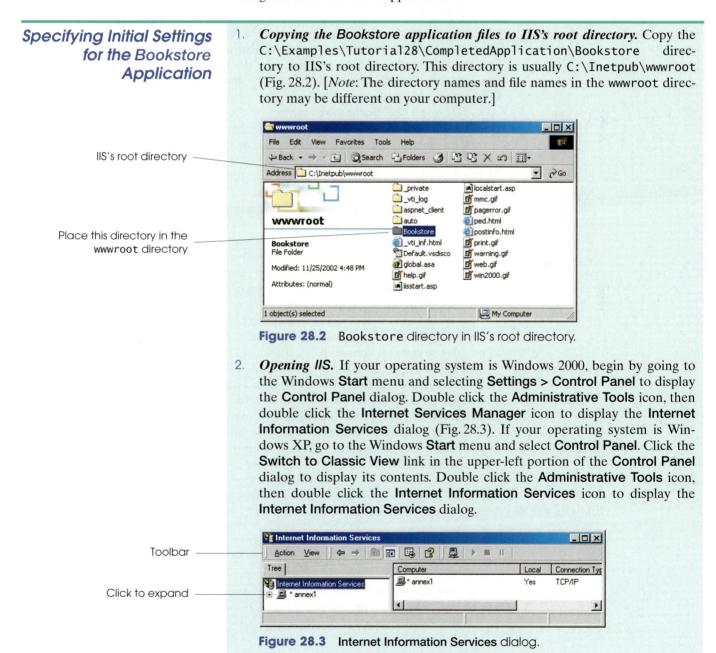

IIS's root directory

Place this directory in the wwwroot directory

Figure 28.2 Bookstore directory in IIS's root directory.

2. *Opening IIS.* If your operating system is Windows 2000, begin by going to the Windows **Start** menu and selecting **Settings > Control Panel** to display the **Control Panel** dialog. Double click the **Administrative Tools** icon, then double click the **Internet Services Manager** icon to display the **Internet Information Services** dialog (Fig. 28.3). If your operating system is Windows XP, go to the Windows **Start** menu and select **Control Panel**. Click the **Switch to Classic View** link in the upper-left portion of the **Control Panel** dialog to display its contents. Double click the **Administrative Tools** icon, then double click the **Internet Information Services** icon to display the **Internet Information Services** dialog.

Toolbar

Click to expand

Figure 28.3 **Internet Information Services** dialog.

(cont.)

3. ***Viewing the Default Web Site.*** Beneath the name **Internet Information Services** (on the **Tree** tab in Windows 2000) is the name of your computer (on which IIS has been installed). Our computer's name is **annex1**. Your computer's name will be different. Expand this node by clicking the plus box. The default sites (Windows 2000 only) set up by IIS should be displayed (Fig. 28.4). The default sites that display in the left pane may differ on your screen. In Windows XP, a node named **Web Sites** appears (Fig. 28.5). Recall that the theme used for the appearance of windows and dialogs is set to **Windows Classic**. The appearance of your windows and dialogs may be different. Expand the **Web Sites** node to display the **Default Web Site** node.

In both Windows 2000 and Windows XP, you will be using only the **Default Web Site**. If no text appears next to **Default Web Site**, then this means that IIS is started and you can proceed to *Step 4*. However, if the text **(Stopped)** appears (Fig. 28.4) then you need to start IIS. To start IIS in either Windows 2000 or Windows XP, select the **Default Web Site** entry and click the Start Item **Button** in the toolbar. IIS will then start, allowing IIS to respond to client requests. [*Note*: The contents of the right pane may be different on your system.]

Click Start Item **Button** to start IIS

Tree tab

Default Web site node; **(Stopped)** indicates that the IIS Web server is not running

Click to stop IIS

Right pane

Figure 28.4 Starting IIS on a computer running Windows 2000.

Click Stop Item **Button** to stop IIS
Click Start Item **Button** to start IIS

Click to display **Default Web Site** in Windows XP

Figure 28.5 Location of **Default Web Site** on a Windows XP computer.

4. ***Opening the Bookstore Properties dialog.*** Click **Default Web Site**, in the left pane, to display the contents of your Web site in the right pane. Right click **Bookstore** in the right pane, then select **Properties** (Fig. 28.6). This option opens the **Bookstore Properties** dialog (Fig. 28.7).

5. ***Setting IIS to recognize the Bookstore application.*** To successfully run the application, IIS must recognize the **Bookstore** as a Web application. In the **Directory** tab, click the **Create** Button (Fig. 28.7). The dialog should now look like Fig. 28.8. Click the **OK** Button. This directory is now recognized by IIS as a Web application with the name **Bookstore**. Close the **Internet Information Services** dialog.

Common Programming Error

Failure to configure IIS to recognize a directory as an application results in an error that prevents the Web application's start page from loading in a Web browser.

(cont.)

Click **Default Web Site** to display the Web site's contents in the right pane

Right click this directory

Contents of **Default Web Site**

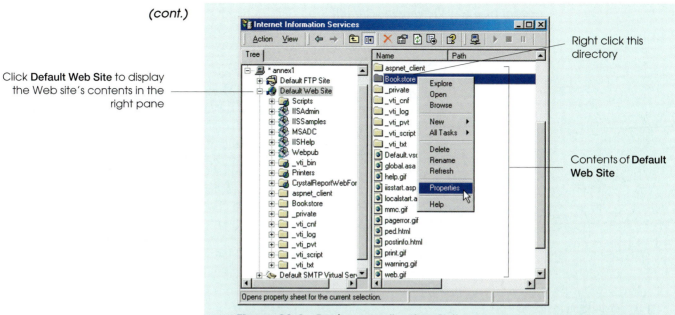

Figure 28.6 `Bookstore` directory in the **Internet Information Services** dialog.

Directory tab

Click to create application

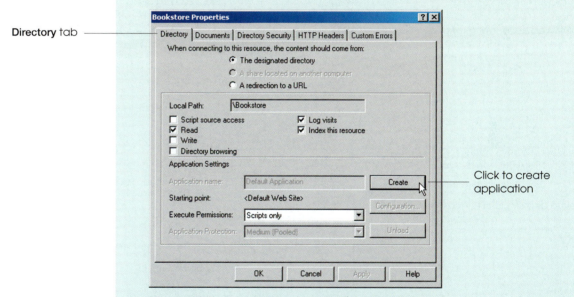

Figure 28.7 **Properties** of the `Bookstore` directory.

6. ***Adding the Databases directory to the wwwroot directory.*** Open a Windows Explorer window, and navigate to the wwwroot directory. Copy the `C:\Examples\Tutorial28\Databases` directory to the wwwroot directory. This directory contains the database that will be used for the application. This database contains information about various books.

7. ***Changing the settings of the Databases directory.*** Your application will need to open and retrieve information from the database stored in the `Databases` directory. You must change some settings of this directory. If your operating system is Windows 2000, complete all the instructions presented in *Step 8* and move on to the next section. (The remaining steps in this box do not apply to Windows 2000.) If your operating system is Windows XP skip *Step 8* and complete the remaining steps (9–12) of this box.

(cont.)

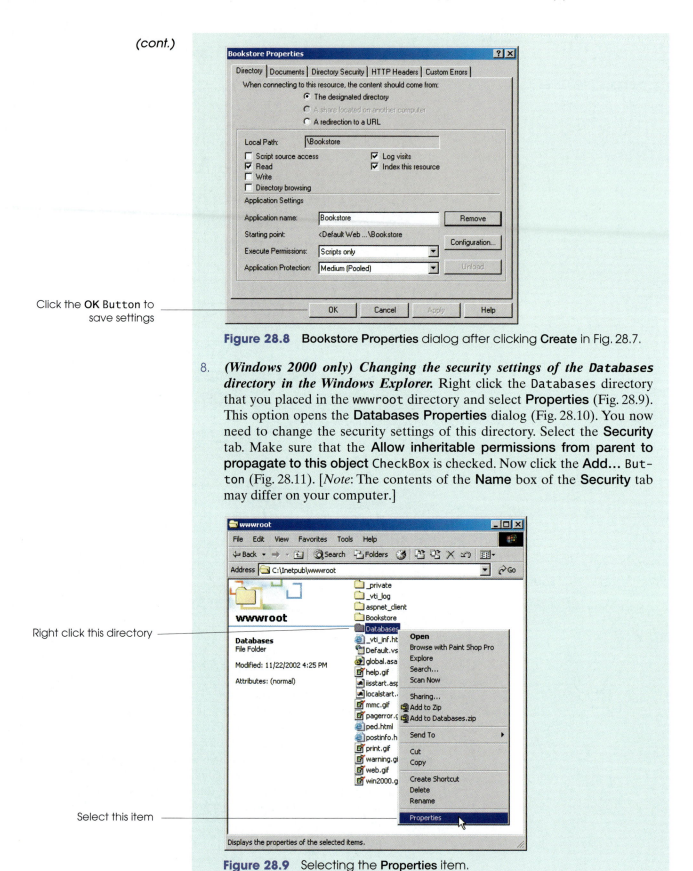

Click the **OK Button** to save settings

Figure 28.8 **Bookstore Properties** dialog after clicking **Create** in Fig. 28.7.

8. ***(Windows 2000 only) Changing the security settings of the Databases directory in the Windows Explorer.*** Right click the Databases directory that you placed in the wwwroot directory and select **Properties** (Fig. 28.9). This option opens the **Databases Properties** dialog (Fig. 28.10). You now need to change the security settings of this directory. Select the **Security** tab. Make sure that the **Allow inheritable permissions from parent to propagate to this object** CheckBox is checked. Now click the **Add...** Button (Fig. 28.11). [*Note*: The contents of the **Name** box of the **Security** tab may differ on your computer.]

Right click this directory

Select this item

Figure 28.9 Selecting the **Properties** item.

(cont.)

Databases Properties dialog

Security tab

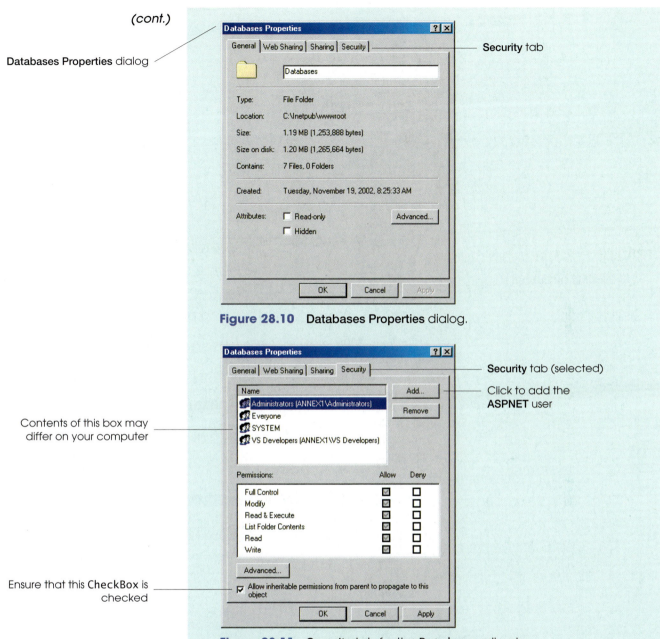

Figure 28.10   **Databases Properties** dialog.

Contents of this box may differ on your computer

Security tab (selected)

Click to add the **ASPNET** user

Ensure that this **CheckBox** is checked

Figure 28.11   **Security** tab for the `Databases` directory.

A **Select Users or Groups** dialog (Fig. 28.12) appears, where you can specify the users or groups of users who can access the directory. Make sure that the **Look in:** drop-down list at the top of the dialog displays your computer name. If it does not, search for your computer name in the drop-down list and select it. Locate the **ASPNET** user in the **Name** box. Double click the **ASPNET** user so that it is added to the bottom half of the dialog. The **ASPNET** user represents a user that is configured to run ASP .NET Web applications with the minimum amount of access privileges. Click the **OK** Button.

(cont.)

Make sure your computer name displays here

Name box

Double click the **ASPNET** user

ASPNET user has been added for **ANNEX1**

Click to add user

Click this to select your computer name

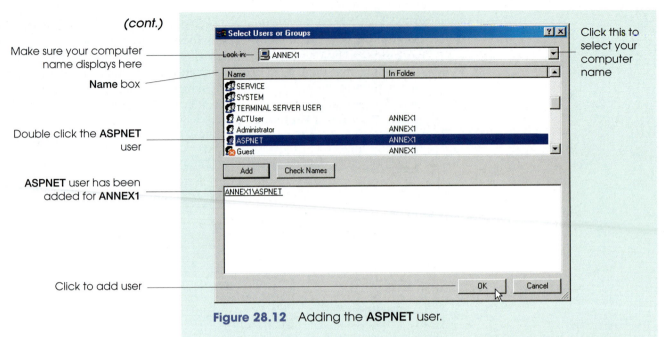

Figure 28.12 Adding the **ASPNET** user.

You are then returned to the **Databases Properties** dialog (Fig. 28.13). Select the **ASPNET** user you added from the **Name** box, and check the **Write** CheckBox in the **Permissions:** box to give the **ASPNET** user permission to write to the Databases directory (Fig. 28.13). Any application that opens an Access database writes a **lock file** in the directory to indicate that the database is in use. Only one lock file can be written at a time. Therefore, only one application can modify the database at a time. Giving the **ASPNET** user write permission enables the ASP .NET application to write a lock file in this directory when the application opens the database. Click the **OK** Button to close the **Databases Properties** dialog.

Common Programming Error

Failure to give the **ASPNET** user write permission to the directory containing the database will cause an error when the application executes. The application will not be able to open the database.

ASPNET user added

Permissions: box

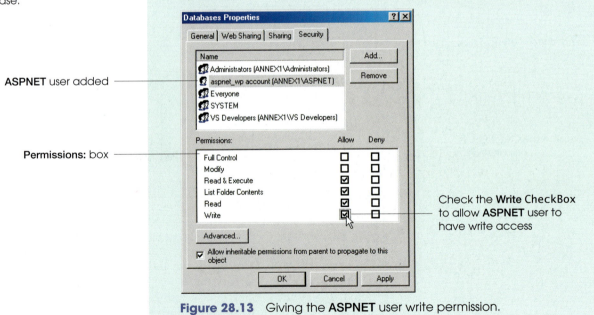

Check the **Write CheckBox** to allow **ASPNET** user to have write access

Figure 28.13 Giving the **ASPNET** user write permission.

(cont.)   9. **(Windows XP Only) Displaying the Security tab of the Databases directory.** In the wwwroot directory, select **Tools > Folder Options...** (Fig. 28.14) to open the **Folder Options** dialog (Fig. 28.15). Select the **View** tab, and make sure that the **Use simple file sharing (Recommended)** CheckBox at the bottom of the **Advanced settings:** box is unchecked. You need to make sure this box is unchecked to ensure that the **Security** tab will be displayed in the **Databases Properties** dialog, which you access in the next step. If you changed any of the settings, click **Apply**, then **OK** to save the changes.

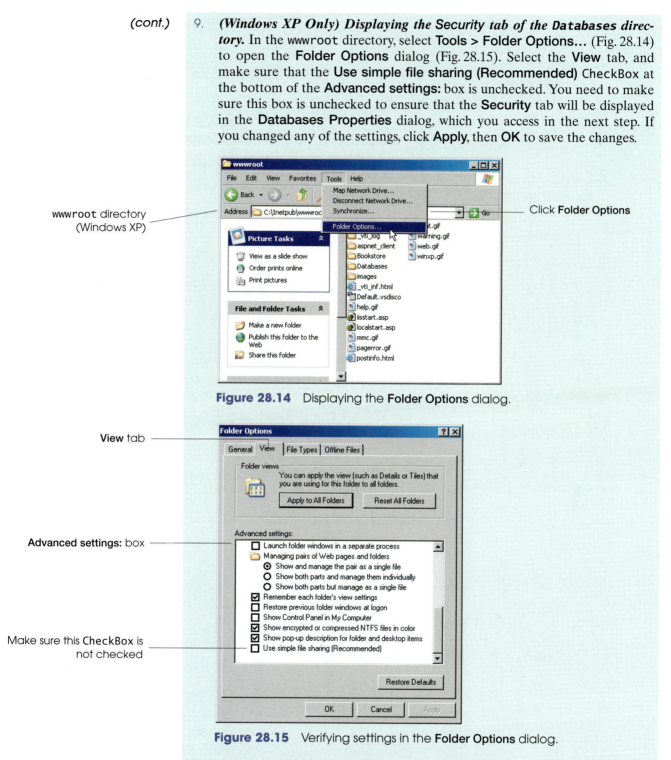

Figure 28.14   Displaying the **Folder Options** dialog.

Figure 28.15   Verifying settings in the **Folder Options** dialog.

10. **(Windows XP Only) Displaying the Databases Properties dialog.** Right click the Databases directory, and select **Properties**. The **Databases Properties** dialog appears. Click the **Security** tab; then click the **Advanced** Button to display the **Advanced Security Settings for Databases** dialog. Make sure that the **Inherit from parent the permission entries that apply to child objects. Include these with entries explicitly defined here.** CheckBox contains a checkmark. Click the **OK** Button to return to the **Database Properties** dialog. Click the **Add...** Button to add a user to the directory (Fig. 28.16). The **Select Users or Groups** dialog appears (Fig. 28.17).

(cont.)

Security tab

TEST is the name of the
computer running
Windows XP

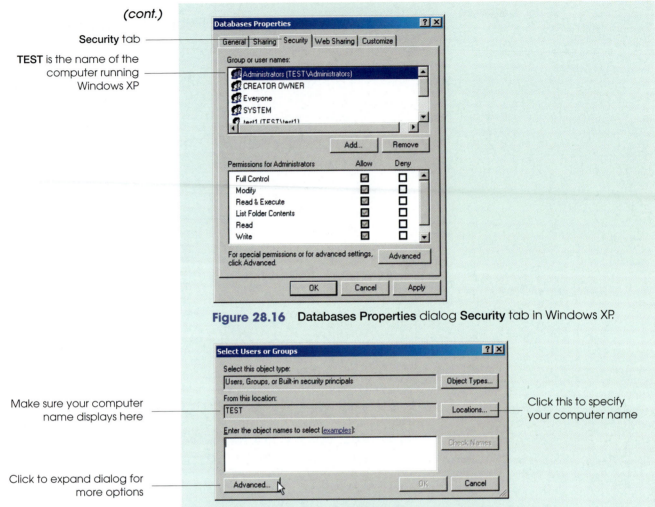

Figure 28.16   **Databases Properties** dialog **Security** tab in Windows XP.

Make sure your computer
name displays here

Click this to specify
your computer name

Click to expand dialog for
more options

Figure 28.17   **Select Users or Groups** dialog in Windows XP.

11. *(Windows XP Only) Adding a new user to the Databases directory.* In the
    Select Users or Groups dialog, make sure that the **From this location:**
    field contains your computer name. If it does not, click the **Locations...**
    Button, select your computer name from the **Location:** box and click the
    OK Button to accept the changes. In the **Select Users or Groups** dialog,
    click the **Advanced...** Button. This dialog expands to provide more
    options (Fig. 28.18). Click the **Find Now** Button, select the **ASPNET** user
    name and click **OK** (Fig. 28.19). The **ASPNET** user represents a user that is
    configured to run ASP .NET Web applications with the minimum amount
    of access privileges. User **ASPNET** should now be displayed in the **Select
    Users or Groups** dialog (Fig. 28.20). Click **OK**.

12. *(Windows XP Only) Giving the ASPNET user write permissions.* The
    ASPNET user should appear in the **Security** tab of the **Databases Proper-
    ties** dialog. Select the **ASPNET** user and check the **Write** CheckBox to give
    the user write permission (Fig. 28.21). Any application that opens an
    Access database writes a lock file in the directory to indicate that the data-
    base is in use. Only one lock file can be written at a time. Therefore, only
    one application can modify the database at a time. Giving the **ASPNET**
    user write permission enables the ASP .NET application to write a lock file
    in this directory when the application opens the database. Click the **OK**
    Button to close the **Databases Properties** dialog.

(cont.)

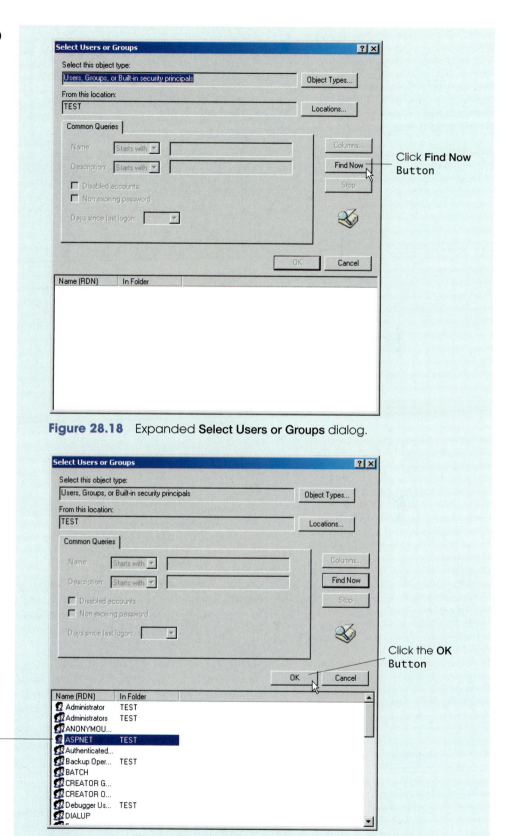

Figure 28.18   Expanded **Select Users or Groups** dialog.

Figure 28.19   Adding the **ASPNET** user to the **Databases** directory.

(cont.)

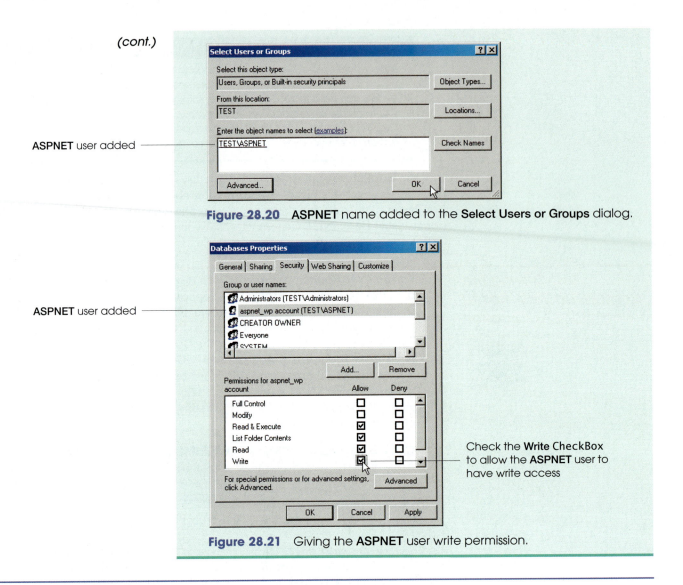

ASPNET user added

Figure 28.20 **ASPNET** name added to the **Select Users or Groups** dialog.

ASPNET user added

Check the **Write CheckBox** to allow the **ASPNET** user to have write access

Figure 28.21 Giving the **ASPNET** user write permission.

SELF-REVIEW

1. The _____ user represents a user that is configured to run ASP .NET Web applications with the minimum amount of access privileges.

   a) **TEST**

   b) **WEB**

   c) **ASPNET**

   d) **ASPX**

2. To start IIS in the **Internet Information Services** dialog, you must select _____ and click the Start Item `Button`.

   a) the Web application's directory

   b) **Default Web Site**

   c) Both a and b.

   d) None of the above.

Answers: 1) c. 2) b.

28.4 Test-Driving the Bookstore Application

In the next three tutorials, you will build an application that displays book information to users upon request. Your **Bookstore** application must meet the following requirements:

> ### Application Requirements
>
> *A bookstore employee receives e-mails from customers asking for information pertaining to the books the store provides online. Responding to the numerous e-mails can be a tedious and time-consuming task. The employee has asked you to create a Web application that allows users to view information about various books online. This information includes the author, price, ISBN number, edition number, copyright date and a brief description of the book.*

The **Bookstore** application you create uses ASP .NET and is designed to allow users to view various pieces of information about the books offered by the store. You begin by test-driving the completed application. Then, you will learn the additional Visual Basic .NET technologies that you will need to create your own version of this application.

Test-Driving the Completed Web-Based Bookstore Application

1. **Opening the Bookstore project.** Open the `C:\InetPub\wwwroot\Bookstore` directory to locate the **Bookstore** application. Double click `Bookstore.sln` to open the application in Visual Studio .NET.

   When you open the application, you may receive the error message in Fig. 28.22. If this is this occurs, open the **Command Prompt** window by selecting **Start > Programs > Accessories > Command Prompt**. Change directories to the .NET Framework directory by typing `cd C:\`*windowsDirectory*`\ Microsoft.NET\Framework\v1.1.4322` where *windowsDirectory* is normally `WINDOWS` or `WINNT`. Then type `aspnet_regiis /i` and press *Enter* to set up ASP .NET version 1.1.

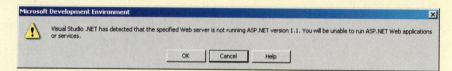

Figure 28.22   Error message for ASP .NET version 1.1.

2. **Setting the start page.** The start page is the first page that loads when the application is run. To specify the start page, right click the `Books.aspx` file in the **Solution Explorer**, and select **Set As Start Page** (Fig. 28.23). Files with the extension `.aspx` (usually referred to as **Web Forms**, **Web Form Pages** or **ASPX pages**) contain the Web page's GUI. The Web Form file represents the Web page that is sent to the client browser. [*Note*: From this point onward, we refer to Web Form files as ASPX pages.] A Web application can contain several ASPX pages. In this example, `Books.aspx` displays the available books to the user. The `BookInformation.aspx` page displays information about the book selected. You must set `Books.aspx` to appear first because you do not know in which book the user is interested until the user makes a selection from the `Books.aspx` page.

3. **Running the application.** Select **Debug > Start** to run your application. The `Books.aspx` page appears in Internet Explorer, as shown in Fig. 28.24. [*Note*: If you are unable to run the project, make sure that you have followed all of the instructions for copying files, starting IIS and setting the `Database` directory's properties.] This page displays a `ListBox` containing the available books. Although this `ListBox` looks similar to the `ListBox` control you have used in Windows applications, this `ListBox` is actually a **Web control** (also called an **ASP .NET server control**). Programmers customize ASPX pages by adding Web controls, such as `Labels`, `TextBoxes`, `Buttons` and other GUI components. As you will learn, Web controls look similar to their Windows application counterparts.

(cont.)

Right click the `Books.aspx` page

Select this option to set the start page

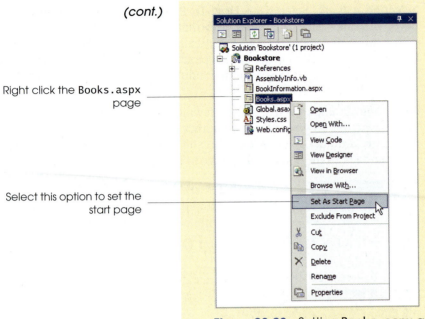

Figure 28.23 Setting `Books.aspx` as the Web application's start page.

Location of `Books.aspx` page

`Label` controls

`ListBox` control containing available books

`Button` control

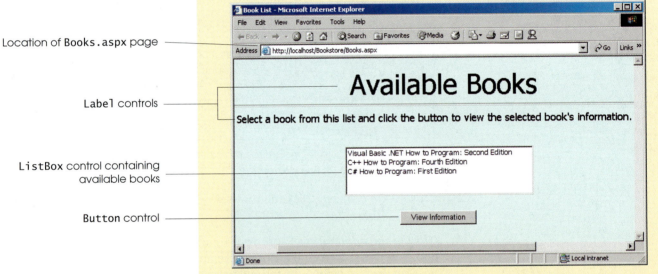

Figure 28.24 Page that displays a list of available books.

Internet Explorer and its HTML content represent the client tier. In Tutorial 29, you will add Web controls, such as `Label`s to display text, a `ListBox` to display the list of available books, `Button`s to load a different page and a `Table` to display information on a particular book.

The books displayed in the `ListBox` are retrieved from a database. The database, named db_bookstore.mdb, is the information tier of this three-tier application. Although only the book titles are displayed in the `List-Box`, the database includes other information, such as the authors and prices of the books. In Tutorial 30, you will examine the application's information tier and learn how to connect to the database to access the data.

(cont.)

4. ***Selecting a book.*** Select **C++ How To Program: Fourth Edition** from the book list, and click the **View Information** Button. The BookInformation.aspx page appears (Fig. 28.25). This page displays the title, author and an image of the selected book. This page also contains a table that lists the selected book's price, ISBN number, edition number and copyright date as well as a description of the book.

5. ***Returning to Books.aspx.*** After viewing a book's information, users can decide whether they wish to view another book's information. The bottom of this page contains a **Book List** Button that, when clicked, redirects the browser back to the Books.aspx page to redisplay the list of book titles.

Location of BookInformation.aspx page

Table Web control

When clicked, this Button returns user to Books.aspx

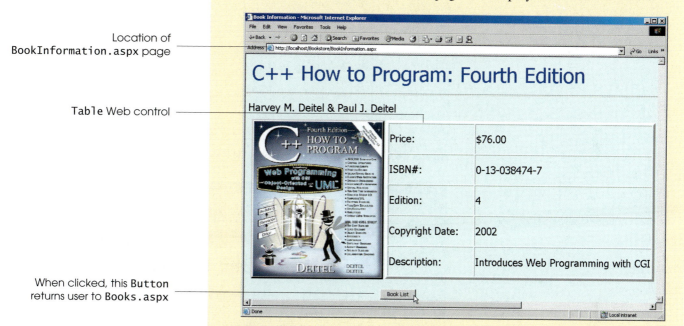

Figure 28.25   Page that displays the selected book's information. (Image courtesy of Deitel & Associates, Inc.)

6. ***Closing the browser.*** Click the browser's close box to close the browser window.

7. ***Closing the application.*** Close your running application by clicking its close box. You have now run the **Bookstore** application from Visual Studio .NET on your local machine. In the next step, you will request the Books.aspx Web page, using only Internet Explorer. With real-world ASP .NET applications, clients are browsers that request ASPX pages that reside on remote Web servers.

8. ***Closing the IDE.*** Close Visual Studio .NET by clicking its close box.

9. ***Requesting the Books.aspx page from Internet Explorer.*** Open Internet Explorer, type in the URL http://localhost/Bookstore/Books.aspx, then press *Enter*. The URL is the location of the Books.aspx page of the **Bookstore** application on your computer. The Books.aspx page should load in the browser. Select a book and click the Button to verify that the **Bookstore** application behaves properly.

10. ***Closing the browser.*** Click the browser's close box.

(cont.)

11. ***Removing the completed application from the IIS's root directory.*** Now you will need to remove the completed application from IIS's root directory before you begin developing the application. You cannot have two applications with the same name in the wwwroot directory. Therefore, you must delete the completed application so that you can create the **Bookstore** application from scratch over the next three tutorials. Stop IIS by clicking the Stop Item Button (the filled square next to the Start Item Button) in the **Internet Information Services** dialog. Right click Bookstore in the right pane and select **Delete** to remove the completed **Bookstore** application from IIS's root directory (Fig. 28.26).

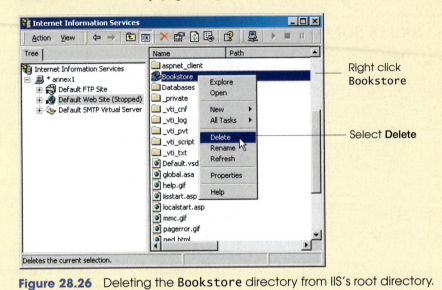

Figure 28.26   Deleting the Bookstore directory from IIS's root directory.

Notice that this example uses all three tiers of a three-tier application. The information tier is the database from which the application retrieves information. The middle tier is the code that controls what occurs when users interact with the Web pages. The client tier is represented by the Web pages from which the user views and selects books.

28.5 Wrap-Up

In this tutorial, you learned about the components of a three-tier application. You were introduced to the information tier, which maintains the data for the application. You then learned about the client tier, which displays the application's user interface, and the middle tier, which provides the communication between the information and client tiers. Next, you were introduced to Microsoft Internet Information Services (IIS), which is used for serving Web content such as ASP .NET Web pages. You then test-drove the three-tier **Bookstore** application. In doing this, you learned how to start and stop IIS and how to run ASP .NET Web-based applications. You were also introduced to ASPX pages, and you learned that Web controls are used to customize these pages.

In the next tutorial, you will create the user interface for this application. You will design the Web pages that display the book list and book information. You will then proceed to Tutorial 30, **Bookstore** Application: Information Tier. This tutorial describes the database used in the application and provides a step-by-step discussion of how the application connects to the database. Discussion of the **Bookstore** application will conclude with Tutorial 31, **Bookstore** Application: Middle Tier. In this tutorial, you will write the functionality for the entire **Bookstore** application.

SKILLS SUMMARY

Starting IIS in Windows 2000

- Go to the Windows **Start** menu, and select **Settings > Control Panel**.
- Double click **Administrative Tools**, then double click **Internet Services Manager** to display the **Internet Information Services** dialog.
- Click the plus box next to your computer name's node to display the sites set up by IIS.
- Click **Default Web Site** in the left pane.
- Click the Start Item `Button` in the toolbar (if the **Default Web Site** is stopped).

Starting IIS in Windows XP

- Go to the Windows **Start** menu, and select **Control Panel**.
- In the **Control Panel** dialog, click the **Switch to Classic View** link.
- Double click **Administrative Tools**, then double click **Internet Information Services** to display the **Internet Information Services** dialog.
- Click the plus box next to your computer name's node to display the **Web Sites** node.
- Click the **Web Sites** node to display the **Default Web Site** node.
- Click **Default Web Site** in the left pane.
- Click the Start Item `Button` in the toolbar (if the **Default Web Site** is stopped).

Stopping IIS in Windows 2000

- Go to the Windows **Start** menu, and select **Settings > Control Panel**.
- Double click **Administrative Tools**, then double click **Internet Services Manager** to display the **Internet Information Services** dialog.
- Click the plus box next to your computer name's node to display the sites set up by IIS.
- Click **Default Web Site** in the left pane.
- Click the Stop Item `Button` in the toolbar.

Stopping IIS in Windows XP

- Go to the Windows **Start** menu, and select **Control Panel**.
- In the **Control Panel** dialog, click the **Switch to Classic View** link.
- Double click **Administrative Tools**, then double click **Internet Information Services** to display the **Internet Information Services** dialog.
- Click the plus box next to your computer name's node to display the **Web Sites** node.
- Click the **Web Sites** node to display the **Default Web Site** node.
- Click **Default Web Site** in the left pane.
- Click the Stop Item `Button` in the toolbar.

Setting up a Web Application on Your Machine

- Place the Web application's project directory in your Web server's root directory (usually `C:\Inetpub\wwwroot`).
- Start IIS.
- Click **Default Web Site** in **Internet Information Services** dialog to display the contents of the directory in the right pane.
- Right click the desired project's directory, and select **Properties**.

- Click the **Create** Button; then click **OK**.
- Open the application, and right click the start page in the **Solution Explorer** window.
- Select **Set As Start Page**.

Enabling Web Applications to use Access Databases in Windows 2000

- Search for the directory containing the database in the wwwroot directory; right click the name of the directory, and select **Properties**.
- Select the **Security** tab.
- Make sure that the **Allow inheritable permissions from parent to propagate to this object** CheckBox is checked, and click the **Add** Button.
- Double click the **ASPNET** user, and click the **OK** Button.
- Give the **ASPNET** user write permission by selecting the **ASPNET** user and checking the **Write** CheckBox.
- Click **OK** to accept the settings.

Enabling Web Applications to use Access Databases in Windows XP

- Select **Tools > Folder Options...** in the wwwroot directory.
- Click the **View** tab; then make sure that the **Use simple file sharing (Recommended)** CheckBox in the **Advanced settings:** tab of the **Folder Options** dialog is unchecked.
- If you changed any settings, click **OK** to accept the changes.
- Search for the directory containing the database in the wwwroot directory; right click the name of the directory, and select **Properties**.
- Select the **Security** tab, and click the **Add** Button.
- Click **Advanced...** to display more options in the **Select Users or Groups** dialog.
- Click the **Find Now** Button.
- Double click the **ASPNET** user, and click the **OK** Button.
- Click the **OK** Button again to add **ASPNET** as a user.
- Give the **ASPNET** user write permission by selecting the **ASPNET** user and checking the **Write** CheckBox.
- Click **OK** to accept the settings.

Testing the Web Application on localhost, Using Visual Studio .NET

- Open the application in Visual Studio .NET.
- Select **Debug > Start** to run the application.

Testing the Web Application on localhost, Using Internet Explorer

- Open an Internet Explorer browser.
- Type the URL http://localhost/*nameOfProject*/*nameOfStartPage*, where *nameOf-Project* is the name of the project directory and *nameOfStartPage* is the name of the first ASPX page that loads when the application is run.
- Press *Enter* to run the application.

KEY TERMS

ASP .NET technology—Can be combined with Visual Basic .NET to create web applications.

ASPX page—File that specifies the GUI of a Web page using Web controls. Also called Web Forms or Web Form Pages.

bottom tier—The tier (also known as the information tier, or the data tier) containing the application data of a multi-tier application—typically implemented as a database.

client tier—The user interface of a multi-tier application (also called the top tier).

data tier—The tier (also known as the information tier, or the bottom tier) containing the application data of a multi-tier application—typically implemented as a database.

DNS lookup—Process that translates domain names to IP addresses.

domain—Represents a group of hosts on the Internet.

domain name system (DNS) server—Computer that maintains a database of host names and their corresponding IP addresses.

fully qualified domain name (FQDN)—Host name combined with a domain and top-level domain that provides a user-friendly way to identify a site on the Internet.

host—A computer that stores and maintains resources, such as Web pages, databases and multimedia files.

host name—Name of a computer where resources reside.

information tier—Tier containing the application data; typically implemented as a database. Also called the bottom tier or data tier.

Internet Information Services (IIS)—A Microsoft Web server.

IP address—Unique address used to locate a computer on the Internet.

localhost—Host name that identifies the local computer.

middle tier—Tier that controls interaction between the client and information tiers.

multi-tier application—Application (sometimes referred to as an *n*-tier application) whose functionality is divided into separate tiers, which can be on the same machine or can be distributed to separate machines across a network.

top-level domain (TLD)—Describes the type of organization that owns the domain name.

top tier—Tier containing the application's user interface. Also called the client tier.

uniform resource locator (URL)—Address that can be used to direct a browser to a resource on the Web.

Web applications—Applications that create web content.

Web controls—Controls, such as TextBoxes and Buttons, that are used to customize ASPX pages.

Web server—Specialized software that responds to client requests by providing resources.

MULTIPLE-CHOICE QUESTIONS

28.1 ASPX pages have the _____ extension.

   a) .html   b) .wbform

   c) .vbaspx   d) .aspx

28.2 _____ applications divide functionality into separate tiers.

   a) *n*-tier   b) Multi-tier

   c) Both a and b.   d) None of the above.

28.3 All tiers of a multi-tier application _____.

   a) must be located on the same computer

   b) must be located on different computers

   c) can be located on the same computer or on different computers

   d) must be arranged so that the client and middle tier are on the same computer and the information tier is on a different computer

28.4 The client tier interacts with the _____ tier to access information from the _____ tier.

   a) middle; information   b) information; middle

   c) information; bottom   d) bottom; information

28.5 A _____ is software that responds to client requests by providing resources.

   a) host   b) host name

   c) DNS server   d) Web server

28.6 A(n) _____ can be thought of as an address that is used to direct a browser to a resource on the Web.

   a) middle tier   b) ASPX page

   c) URL   d) query string

28.7 A _____ represents a group of _____ on the Internet.

   a) domain; hosts   b) host; domain names

   c) host name; hosts   d) None of the above.

28.8 _____ is a Web server.

a) IIS

b) `localhost`

c) Visual Studio .NET

d) `wwwroot`

28.9 A _____ is a Web server that is located on a computer across a network such as the Internet.

a) `localhost`

b) local Web server

c) remote Web server

d) None of the above.

28.10 The _____ tier is the application's user interface.

a) middle

b) client

c) bottom

d) information

EXERCISES

28.11 (_Phone Book Application_) Over the next three tutorials, you will create a **Phone-Book** application. This phone book should be a Web-based version of the **PhoneBook** application created in Tutorial 27. [_Note_: This Web application will not use Microsoft Agent.] The **PhoneBook** application should consist of two ASPX pages, which will be named PhoneBook and PhoneNumber. The PhoneBook page displays a `DropDownList` (a Web control similar to a `ComboBox` Windows Form control) that contains the names of several people. The names are retrieved from the db_Phone.mdb database. When a name is selected and the **Get Number** `Button` is clicked, the client browser is redirected to the PhoneNumber page. The telephone number of the selected name should be retrieved from a database and displayed in a `Label` on the PhoneNumber page. For this exercise, you need only organize the components (Phone-Book and PhoneNumber ASPX pages, db_Phone.mdb database and the code that performs the specified functionality) of this Web application into separate tiers. Decide which components belong in which tiers. You will begin building the solution, using Visual Studio .NET, in the next tutorial.

28.12 (_US State Facts Application_) Over the next three tutorials, you will create a **USStateFacts** application. This application is designed to allow users to review their knowledge about specific U.S. states. This application should consist of two ASPX pages. The first page (named States) should display a `ListBox` containing 10 different state names. These state names are stored in the db_StateFacts.mdb database. The user should be allowed to select a state name and click a `Button` to retrieve information about the selected state from the database. The information should be displayed on a different ASPX page (named State-Facts). The StateFacts page should display an image of the state flag and list the state capital, state flower, state tree and state bird (retrieved from the database) in a `Table`. You will be provided with images of the state flags. For this exercise, you need only organize the components (States and StateFacts ASPX pages, db_StateFacts.mdb database and the code that performs the specified functionality) of this Web application into separate tiers. Decide which components belong in which tiers. You will begin building the solution, using Visual Studio .NET, in the next tutorial.

28.13 (_Road Sign Review Application_) Over the next three tutorials, you will create a **RoadSignReview** application. The **RoadSignReview** application should consist of two ASPX pages. This application displays road signs for users to review and allows them to schedule a driving test. The first page (named RoadSigns) should display 15 road signs in a `Table`. You will be provided images of the road signs. When the mouse pointer is moved over a sign, the name of the sign will appear in a tooltip in the Web browser window. The table should display the images by retrieving their information from the db_RoadSigns.mdb database. This page also will contain two `TextBoxes` and a `Button` that allow users to provide their information to register for a driving test. When users click the **Register** `Button`, the second page (RoadTestRegistered) displays confirmation information that the user has registered for a driving test. For this exercise, you need only organize the components (RoadSigns and RoadTestRegistered ASPX pages, db_RoadSigns.mdb database and the code that performs the specified functionality) of this Web application into separate tiers. Decide which components belong in which tiers. You will begin building the solution, using Visual Studio .NET, in the next tutorial.

T U T O R I A L

29

Bookstore Application: Client Tier

Introducing Web Controls

In this tutorial, you will create the client tier (user interface) of your three-tier **Bookstore** application, using visual-programming techniques. You will begin by creating the application's project—an ASP .NET Web application project. You then will learn about Web controls by creating the application's GUI.

29.1 Analyzing the Bookstore Application

Now that you have taken the three-tier **Bookstore** application (in Tutorial 28) for a test-drive, you need to analyze the application components. The following pseudocode describes the basic operation of the **Bookstore** application:

> *When the Books page is requested*
>> *Retrieve the book titles from the database*
>> *Display book titles in a ListBox*
>
> *When the user selects a book title from the ListBox and clicks the View Information Button*
>> *Store the selected book in a variable*
>> *Redirect the user to the BookInformation page*
>
> *When the BookInformation page is requested*
>> *Retrieve the selected book's information from a database*
>> *Display the book title in a Label*
>> *Display the authors in a Label*
>> *Display the cover art in an image*
>> *Display the remaining information in a Table*
>
> *When the user presses the Book List Button on the BookInformation page*
>> *Redirect the client browser back to the Books page*

736

The ACE table in Fig. 29.1 lists the actions, controls and events that will help you complete your own version of this application.

Action	Control/Object	Event
Label the Books page	`lblAvailable`, `lblInstructions`	
	`Page`	`Load` (for `Books.aspx`)
Retrieve the book titles from the database	`objOleDbConnection`, `objSelectTitles`	
Display book titles in a ListBox	`lstBookTitles`	
	`btnInformation`	`Click`
Store the selected book in a variable	`Session`	
Redirect the user to the BookInformation page	`Response`	
	`Page`	`Load` (for `Book-Information.aspx`)
Retrieve the selected book's information from a database	`objOleDbConnection`, `objSelectBookData`	
Display the book title in a Label	`lblBookTitle`	
Display the authors in a Label	`lblAuthors`	
Display the cover art in an image	`imgBook`	
Display the remaining information in a Table	`tblBook`	
	`btnBookList`	`Click`
Redirect the client browser back to the Books page	`Response`	

Figure 29.1   ACE table for the Web-based **Bookstore** application.

29.2 Creating ASPX Pages

Now that you have been introduced to IIS and three-tier, Web-based application concepts, you will begin creating the **Bookstore** application that you test-drove in the last tutorial. Before you begin to create the GUI for the **Bookstore** application, you need to set Visual Studio .NET to display line numbers for the ASPX page.

1. ***Opening the* Options *dialog.*** Open Visual Studio .NET. Select **Tools > Options...** to display the **Options** dialog.

2. ***Enabling line numbers to be displayed.*** Click **Text Editor** in the left pane of the **Options** dialog; then click **HTML/XML**. Click **General**, and check the **Line Numbers** CheckBox (Fig. 29.2). Click the **OK** Button to save the settings and close the **Options** dialog.

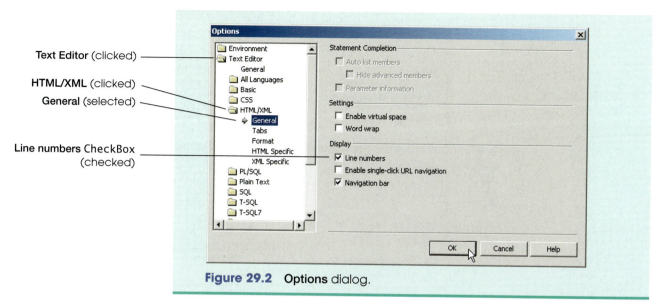

Text Editor (clicked)
HTML/XML (clicked)
General (selected)
Line numbers CheckBox (checked)

Figure 29.2   **Options** dialog.

Now that you have configured Visual Studio .NET to display line numbers for the ASPX page, you can begin creating the **Bookstore** application. This Web-based application allows users to view information about books they select. After viewing a book's information, users can return to the page containing the list of books and select another book. You will create the ASP .NET Web application project for the **Bookstore** in the following box.

Creating an ASP .NET Web Application

1. **Starting IIS.** IIS must be running on the server machine (localhost, in this case) for you to be able to create ASP .NET Web applications in Visual Studio .NET. Start IIS as demonstrated in *Step 3* of the box, *Specifying Initial Settings for the Bookstore Application* in Tutorial 28.

2. **Creating the project.** In Visual Studio .NET, select **File > New > Project...** to display the **New Project** dialog (Fig. 29.3). In this dialog, select **Visual Basic Projects** in the **Project Types:** pane and **ASP .NET Web Application** in the **Templates:** pane. Notice that the **Name:** TextBox for the project name is disabled. Specify the name and location of the project in the **Location:** TextBox. The default value in this TextBox is http://localhost/ WebApplication1. The files for this application will be stored in a directory called WebApplication1, located at http://localhost. Recall that this location is really IIS's root directory (usually C:\Inetpub\wwwroot).

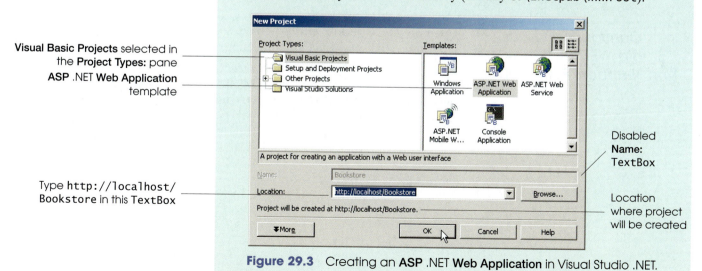

Visual Basic Projects selected in the **Project Types:** pane
ASP .NET Web Application template
Type http://localhost/ Bookstore in this TextBox
Disabled **Name:** TextBox
Location where project will be created

Figure 29.3   Creating an **ASP .NET Web Application** in Visual Studio .NET.

(cont.)   Change `WebApplication1` to `Bookstore`. If the `Bookstore` directory does not yet exist at `http://localhost`, it will be created for you. Below the **Location:** TextBox, the text "**Project will be created at http://local-host/Bookstore.**" appears. When you click **OK**, the project is created. The **Create New Web** dialog displays next, while Visual Studio .NET creates the Web site on the server (Fig. 29.4).

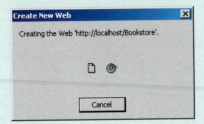

Figure 29.4   Visual Studio .NET creating the **Bookstore** application.

3. ***Examining the project files.*** The **Solution Explorer** window for the **Book-store** application is shown in Fig. 29.5. As with Windows applications, Visual Studio .NET creates several files for each new **ASP .NET Web Application** project. `WebForm1.aspx` is the default name for the ASPX page.

Project name —————

Default ASPX page name —————

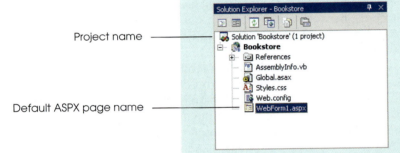

Figure 29.5   **Solution Explorer** window for the **Bookstore** project.

4. ***Setting Option Strict to On.*** Right click the `Bookstore` project name in the **Solution Explorer**, and select **Properties**. In the **Bookstore Property Pages** dialog, select **Build** under **Common Properties**, and set `Option Strict` to `On`. Recall that we use Option Strict to avoid subtle errors that may occur in implicit conversions. Click the **OK** Button to close the dialog.

5. ***Viewing the Toolbox.*** ASPX pages can be customized by using Web controls. These types of controls are used for ASPX pages in a manner similar to how Windows controls are used for Windows Forms. You will be using these controls to create the user interface of your **Bookstore** application. Web controls are located in the **Web Forms** tab of the **Toolbox**. Select **View > Toolbox**, and click the **Web Forms** tab. Figure 29.6 shows the **Web Forms** controls listed in the **Toolbox**. The left part of the figure displays the beginning of the **Web Forms** controls list, and the right part of the figure displays the remaining **Web Forms** controls. Notice that some of the control icons, such as `Label`, `TextBox` and `Button`, are the same as the Windows controls presented earlier in the book. Although some of these control names appear the same, the functionality provided by **Web Forms** controls is different and they can be used only with ASPX pages.

(cont.)

Web Forms tab ——

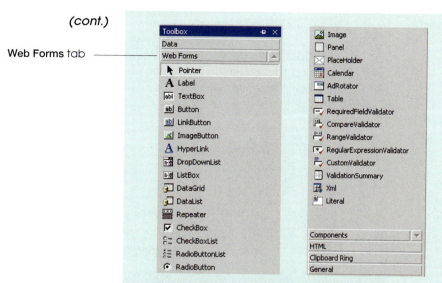

Figure 29.6   Web Forms tab in **Toolbox.**

6. ***Viewing the ASPX page in Design mode.*** When you create a Web application, an ASPX page will be displayed in the **Web Form Designer** (Fig. 29.7). [*Note:* We do not apply a Lucida font to the word "Form" (in "Web Form Designer"), because Web Forms are not instances of class Form.] Unlike the Windows Form Designer, the Web Form Designer contains two different viewing modes. The first mode is the **Design mode.** Figure 29.7 shows the ASPX page displayed in **Design** mode for WebForm1.aspx. It consists of a grid on which you drag and drop components, such as Buttons and Labels, from the **Toolbox.** If the **Design** mode for the ASPX page does not display, click the **Design** Button, in the lower left corner of the Web Form Designer. **Design** mode should be used when you want to visually create the ASPX page's GUI by dragging and dropping Web controls onto the ASPX page.

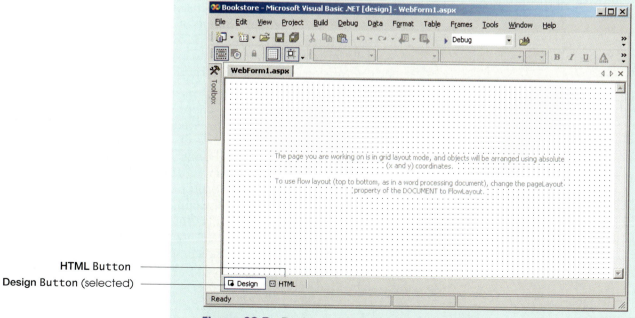

HTML Button ——
Design Button (selected) ——

Figure 29.7   Design mode of Web Form Designer.

(cont.)   7. ***Switching to HTML mode.*** The Web Form Designer also can display the ASPX page in **HTML** mode (Fig. 29.8). Click the **HTML** Button. ASPX pages are defined using a combination of HTML and ASP .NET markup. ASP .NET markup is the set of instructions processed on the Web server's machine. ASP .NET markup is often converted into HTML and sent to a browser client as part of a response to a client request. When you click the **HTML** Button in the Web Form Designer, the Web Form Designer switches to **HTML** mode. You use **HTML mode** when you wish to view your ASPX page's markup. You also can use this mode to edit the markup. When you click the **Design** Button, the Web Form Designer switches to **Design** mode. Although you will not be writing markup to create Web controls for this ASPX page, you will be using it to set the locations of the Web controls.

[*Note*: Your markup may look different from that in Fig. 29.8—we have modified the code slightly for presentation purposes.]

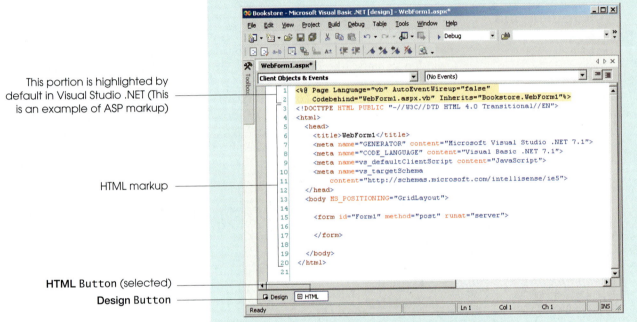

This portion is highlighted by default in Visual Studio .NET (This is an example of ASP markup)

HTML markup

HTML Button (selected)

Design Button

Figure 29.8 **HTML** mode of Web Form Designer.

8. ***Saving the project to your Bookstore directory.*** By default, Visual Studio .NET saves project files for ASP .NET Web applications in a separate directory. For easy access, you will save the project in your `Bookstore` directory located in the `wwwroot` directory. Click on **Solution 'Bookstore' (1 project)** in the **Solution Explorer**, and then select **File > Save Bookstore.sln As...** to display the **Save File As** dialog.

[*Note*: A **Microsoft Development Environment** dialog may appear first asking if you would like to save your changes. No changes should have been made so far, so if this dialog appears we suggest you click the **No** Button and undo any of your changes. If you would instead like to save the changes you've made, click the **Yes** Button to dismiss this dialog.] In this dialog, navigate to the `wwwroot` directory, and save the project in the `Bookstore` directory.

SELF-REVIEW   1. _____ mode allows you to view the ASPX page's markup.

a) **HTML**   b) **Design**

c) Web control   d) Markup

2. Some Web control names are the same as Windows control names, _____.
   a) because their functionality is the same
   b) but the functionality provided by Web controls is different
   c) because both Web controls and Windows controls can be used in Web applications
   d) None of the above.

Answers: 1) a. 2) b.

29.3 Designing the Books.aspx Page

This **Bookstore** application consists of two ASPX pages, which you create one at a time. The first page of the **Bookstore** application will be named Books.aspx. This page will display the list of available books. You design the first ASPX page in the following box.

Creating the
Books.aspx Page

1. **Renaming the ASPX page.** After you have viewed the contents of the default ASPX page (WebForm1.aspx), you will want to give this ASPX page a meaningful name. Select the WebForm1.aspx file in the **Solution Explorer** window. Change the **File Name** property in the **Properties** window from WebForm1.aspx to Books.aspx (Fig. 29.9).

   Now click the Web Form Designer. The properties of the ASPX page should display in the **Properties** window. Notice that ASPX pages are listed with the identifier **DOCUMENT** in the Component Object Box (Fig. 29.10), because they do not have individual names. Select the **title** property, and change WebForm1 to Book List. This step sets the text that is displayed in the requesting browser's title bar.

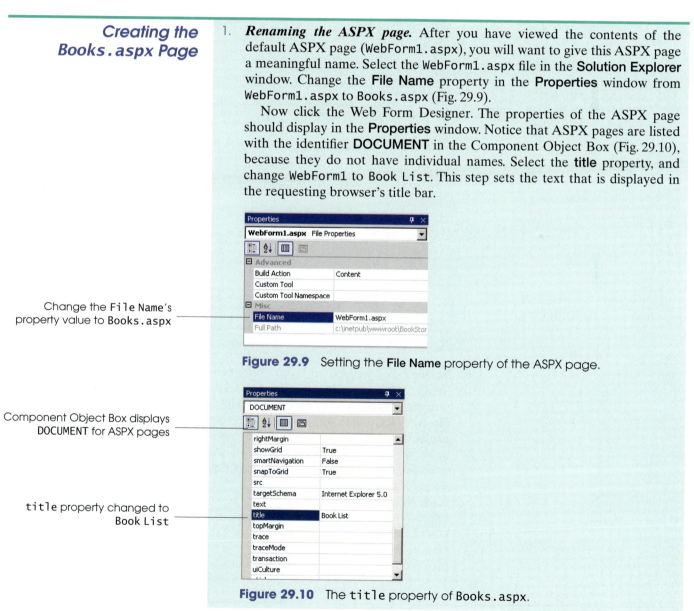

Change the File Name's property value to Books.aspx

Figure 29.9 Setting the **File Name** property of the ASPX page.

Component Object Box displays DOCUMENT for ASPX pages

title property changed to Book List

Figure 29.10 The title property of Books.aspx.

(cont.)

2. ***Changing the background color of the ASPX page.*** Now you are ready to begin creating the GUI. Make sure you are in **Design** mode of the designer. First change the **bgColor** property of the Books.aspx page so that the background color of Books.aspx is set to light blue. Select bgColor in the **Properties** window, and click the ellipsis (...) Button to display the **Color Picker** dialog (Fig. 29.11). Click the **Web Palette** tab, and select light blue, as shown in Fig. 29.11. Click the **OK** Button. The background color of the Books.aspx page is now light blue.

3. ***Creating a Label.*** Next, click the Label Web control from the **Web Forms** tab of the **Toolbox**. Drag and drop the control

> **A** Label

onto the Books.aspx page. The Label should appear on the ASPX page (Fig. 29.12). View its properties in the **Properties** window. Select the ID property, and change Label1 to lblAvailable. The **ID property** is used to identify controls, much like the Name property in Windows controls. Now change the Label's Text property from Label to Available Books. Set the Label's font size by setting Size, under the Font property to XX-Large (Fig. 29.13). Set the Label's font to Tahoma by clicking the down arrow next to property Name (also under the Font property) and selecting **Tahoma** from the list that appears. To display the words correctly in the Label, you will need to set the height and width of the control. Set the **Height** property of the Label to 56px, and set the **Width** to 335px.

Web Palette tab

Light-blue color box (selected)

Color: #ccffff

Figure 29.11 Light blue selected in the **Color Picker** dialog.

Label Web control ——

Label

Figure 29.12 Label control displayed in the ASPX page.

(cont.)

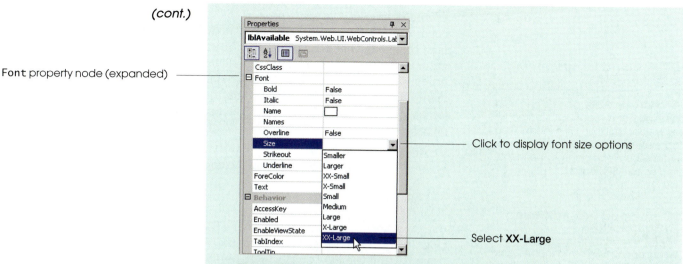

Font property node (expanded) ————

———— Click to display font size options

———— Select **XX-Large**

Figure 29.13 Setting the font size of the Label control.

4. **Positioning the Label.** Place the Label in the top center of the page. To set the exact location of the Label, switch to **HTML** mode. Notice that lines 15–20 of Fig. 29.14 (`<asp:label id="lblAvailable"...>`) have been added to the markup. Line 16 contains the `style` attribute, as shown in Fig. 29.14. Set the LEFT: portion of the `style` attribute value to 295px and the TOP: portion of the attribute value to 16px. The **px** portion of these values specify that the Label will be positioned 295 pixels from the left side of the page and 16 pixels down from the upper left corner of the ASPX page.

Switch back into **Design** mode. The Label should now be repositioned on the page (Fig. 29.15).

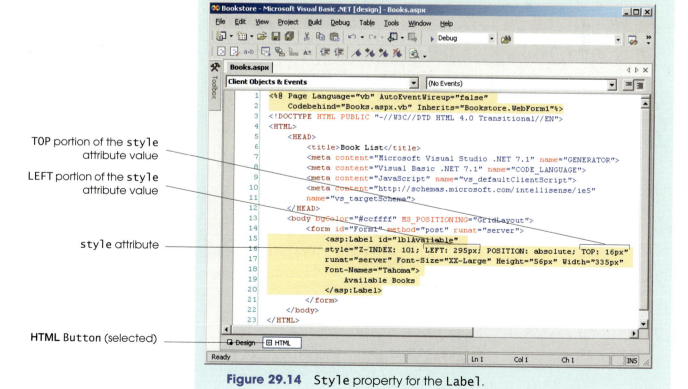

TOP portion of the `style` attribute value

LEFT portion of the `style` attribute value

`style` attribute

HTML Button (selected)

Figure 29.14 Style property for the Label.

(cont.)

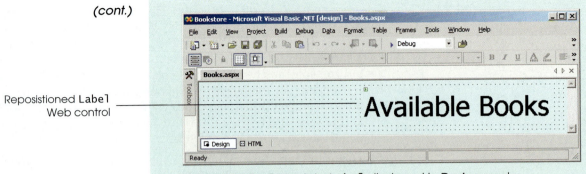

Figure 29.15   Complete **Label** displayed in **Design** mode.

5. *Creating a Horizontal Rule.* Drag and drop the Horizontal Rule control (found in the **HTML** tab in the **Toolbox**),

 Horizontal Rule

and place it beneath the `lblAvailable` Label. A **Horizontal Rule** provides a horizontal line on a Web page. You use it to separate content on your ASPX page. Horizontal Rules are types of **HTML controls**, which correspond to standard HTML elements. In this case study, we ask you to assume that a control is a Web control, unless we explicitly tell you that it is an HTML control.

In the **Properties** window, set the `id` property of the Horizontal Rule to `hrzBooks`. Next, click the `style` property value in the **Properties** window. Click the ellipsis (**...**) Button that appears in the `style` field. The **Style Builder** dialog appears (Fig. 29.16). Click the **Position** Tab in the left pane of the dialog. Set the **Top:** value to 80px, the **Left:** value to 8px, the **Height:** value to 4px and the **Width:** value to 150%. Click **OK**. These settings position the Horizontal Rule 80 pixels from the upper left corner of the page and 8 pixels from the left side of the page. The height of the control is now 4 pixels. Setting the width to 150% ensures that the Horizontal Rule extends to the entire width of the page.

Good Programming Practice

When naming a Horizontal Rule control, use the prefix `hrz` followed by a word that describes the control's use.

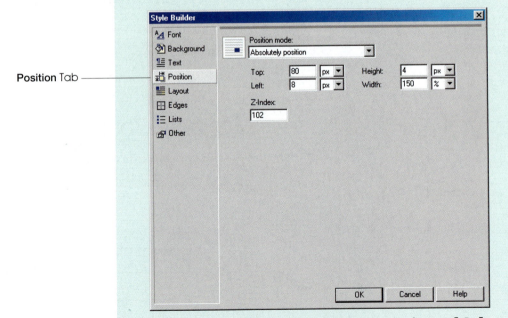

Figure 29.16   **Style Builder** dialog for the **Horizontal Rule** control.

(cont.)

6. ***Creating another Label.*** After the Horizontal Rule is in place, create another Label control (found in the **Web Forms** tab in the **Toolbox**). Change the ID of the Label to lblInstructions. In the **Properties** window, change the Text property to Select a book from this list and click the button to view the selected book's information. Then, set the font size to Medium. Set the height to 18px and the width to 699px. Switch to **HTML** mode and reposition the Label control as you did in *Step 4*. However, set the LEFT: portion of the style attribute value to 152px and the TOP: portion of the attribute value to 95px.

7. ***Creating a ListBox.*** Switch to **Design** mode. The next control you will place on this page is a ListBox. The **ListBox** will contain a list of the available books offered by the bookstore. In the next two tutorials, you will retrieve information from the database to populate the ListBox with book titles. Drag and drop the ListBox control,

> ⊞ ListBox

and place it below lblInstructions. Change the ID property of the ListBox to lstBookTitles. In the **Properties** window, set the Height to 100 pixels and the Width to 330 pixels. In **HTML** mode, set the LEFT: portion of the style attribute value of the ListBox to 286px and the TOP: portion of the attribute value to 155px.

8. ***Adding a Button control.*** The final control you will add to the page is a Button (found in the **Web Forms** tab in the **Toolbox**). Switch to **Design** mode. Drag and drop the Button control,

> ab| Button

onto the ASPX page. Change the Button's ID to btnInformation, and change its Text property to View Information. Set its Width to 130 pixels in the **Properties** window. Then switch to **HTML** mode. Change the LEFT: portion of the style attribute value to 380px and the TOP: portion of the attribute value to 270px. The Books.aspx page should look like Fig. 29.17. [*Note*: Unbound appears in the ListBox because no items have been added to it.]

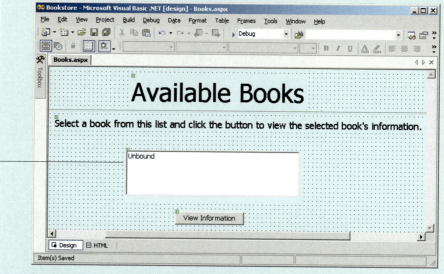

ListBox control

Figure 29.17 **Design** mode of Books.aspx.

9. ***Saving the project.*** Select **File > Save All** to save your modified code.

1. Use the _____ property to change the name of a **Web Forms** control.

    a) Text   b) Name

    c) ID   d) Value

2. The Horizontal Rule is a(n) _____ control.

    a) **Web Forms**   b) **HTML**

    c) **Data**   d) **Windows Forms**

Answers: 1) c. 2) b.

29.4 Designing the BookInformation Page

Now that you have designed the Books.aspx page, you will design the BookInformation.aspx page, which displays the information about the book that was selected from the ListBox.

Creating the BookInformation Page

1. *Creating a new ASPX page.* Select **File > Add New Item...**, to display the **Add New Item - Bookstore** dialog (Fig. 29.18). Select **Web Form** in the **Templates:** pane, and rename the ASPX page to BookInformation.aspx, using the **Name:** TextBox. Click the **Open** Button. A new ASPX page named BookInformation.aspx appears in the **Solution Explorer** window.

Web Form template ——

Change this to BookInformation.aspx ——

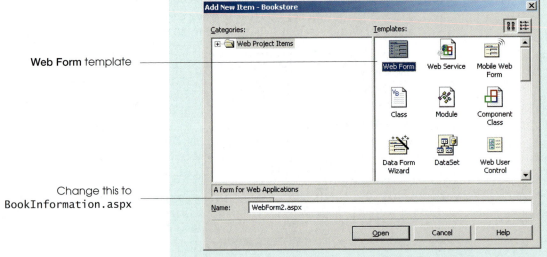

Figure 29.18 Add New Item - Bookstore dialog.

2. *Changing the background color.* If the file does not open in **Design** mode, switch to **Design** mode at this time. Change the background color of this page to light blue as you did in *Step 2* of the box, *Creating the Books.aspx Page*.

(cont.)

3. ***Creating the `lblBookTitle` Label.*** Create a new `Label` by double clicking the `Label` tab in the **Web Forms** tab of the **Toolbox**. This `Label` will display the title of the book selected by the user. Because you do not yet know what book title will be selected, clear the `Text` property of this `Label`. The `Text` property will be set in Tutorial 31. Change the `ID` property of the `Label` to `lblBookTitle`, set the font size to XX-Large and set the `ForeColor` to `Blue`. The **ForeColor** property specifies the color of the text that displays on the `Label`. To set the `ForeColor`, select the `ForeColor` property in the **Properties** window, and click the down arrow that appears in the `ForeColor` field. Click the **Web** tab and select `Blue` to set the forecolor (Fig. 29.19). Set the height to 60px and the width to 1100px. In **HTML** mode, set the `LEFT:` portion of the `style` attribute value of the `Label` to 20px and the `TOP:` portion of the attribute value to 15px.

4. ***Creating the Horizontal Rule.*** Switch to **Design** mode. Drag and drop a Horizontal Rule beneath the `lblBookTitle` `Label`. Set the `id` property to `hrzBookInformation`; then change the `style` property, setting the **Top:** value to 90px, the **Left:** value to 0px, the **Height:** value to 4px and the **Width:** value to 150%.

5. ***Creating the `lblAuthors` Label.*** After adding the Horizontal Rule, create another `Label`. Name the `Label` `lblAuthors`, and change its `Font` property's `Size` to Large. Set the height of the `Label` to 34px and the width to 989px. Clear the text for this `Label`, because you do not know which book will be selected. You will set this text in Tutorial 31. In **HTML** mode, set the `LEFT:` portion of the `style` attribute value to 20 and the `TOP:` portion to 110.

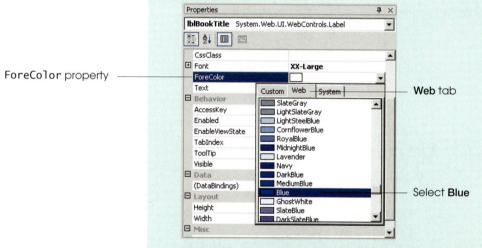

ForeColor property

Web tab

Select **Blue**

Figure 29.19 Setting a `Label`'s `ForeColor` property.

6. ***Creating the Image control.*** Switch to **Design** mode. Now you must add the **Image control** that displays the cover of the selected book. Drag and drop the `Image` control,

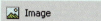

from the **Web Forms** tab in the **Toolbox** window. Change the `Image` control's `ID` property to `imgBook`. Set the `Height` and `Width` properties to 360 and 300 pixels, respectively. Specify the **BorderStyle** as `Outset` and set the **BorderWidth** to 5 pixels.

Good Programming Practice

When naming an `Image` Web control, use the prefix `img` followed by a word that describes what the `Image` will display.

(cont.)

The BorderStyle property specifies the type of border that displays around the Image. Setting BorderStyle to Outset gives the Image a raised-control appearance. Property BorderWidth specifies the width of the border of the Image control. Setting BorderWidth to 5 causes the border to be 5 pixels thick. Switch to **HTML** mode. Set the LEFT: portion of the style attribute value of the Image to 20px and the TOP: portion to 150px. In Tutorial 31, you will specify the image that will be displayed.

7. *Creating the btnBookList Button.* Switch to **Design** mode. Add a Button to the page. Set the Button's ID to btnBookList, and set its Text to Book List. In the **Properties** window, set the Width property to 80 pixels. Switch to **HTML** mode, then change the LEFT: portion of the style attribute value of the Button to 325px and the TOP: portion to 550px. Switch to **Design** mode. The design of the BookInformation.aspx page should look like Fig. 29.20.

8. *Saving the project.* Select **File > Save All** to save your modified code.

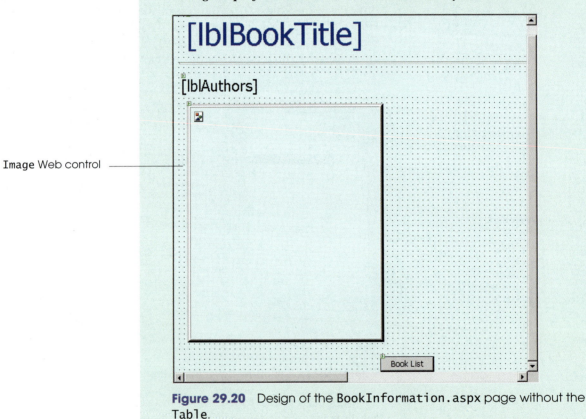

Image Web control

Figure 29.20   Design of the BookInformation.aspx page without the Table.

You are now ready to add the Table control to the page. The Table is perhaps the most significant control on this page, because it will display the book information in a structured manner. You add the Table in the following box.

Adding the Table Control

(cont.)

Five TableRows added by the user

Members: pane

Click to add rows to the table

1. ***Creating the Table control.*** From the **Web Forms** tab of the **Toolbox**, drag and drop the Table control,

    🔲 Table

    onto the page. In the **Properties** window, change the ID of the Table to tblBook, set the BorderStyle to OutSet and change the BorderWidth to 5 pixels. Also, change the **Gridlines** property to value Both. The Gridlines property displays separators between the cells (known as **cell borders**) in the Table. Setting Gridlines to Both displays both horizontal and vertical separators between each cell. In **HTML** mode, set the LEFT: portion of the style attribute value of the Table to 335px and change the TOP: portion to 150px.

2. ***Creating rows in the Table.*** Switch to **Design** mode. You now must create rows for the Table. To do so, select the Rows property in the **Properties** window. Click the ellipsis (...) Button to the right of property Rows. A **TableRow Collection Editor** dialog appears. Add five rows to the table by clicking the **Add** Button five times (Fig. 29.21). Leave the dialog open so you can customize the Table's rows in the next few steps.

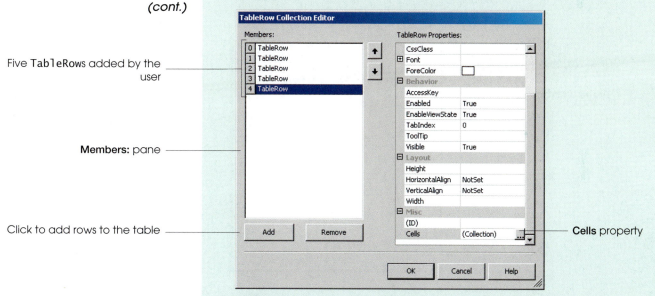

Cells property

Figure 29.21 TableRow Collection Editor dialog for the Table control.

3. ***Creating cells in the Table.*** Table rows contain cells that display data. You will now create each individual cell in each table row. Select TableRow 0 in the **Members:** pane. Go to the **TableRow Properties** pane, and click the ellipsis (...) Button to the right of the **Cells** property to display the **TableCell Collection Editor** dialog (Fig. 29.22). Add two cells to the row by clicking **Add** twice. Select **TableCell** 0, and set the Font property's Size to Large. Change the TableCell's Height property to 70 pixels, Width property to 200 pixels and specify the Text property as Price:. Select the TableCell 1 in the **Members:** box, and set the Font property's Size to Large. Click **OK** in the **TableCell Collection Editor** to accept the settings.

(cont.)

Two `TableCell`s added by
the user

Add `TableCell`s by clicking **Add**

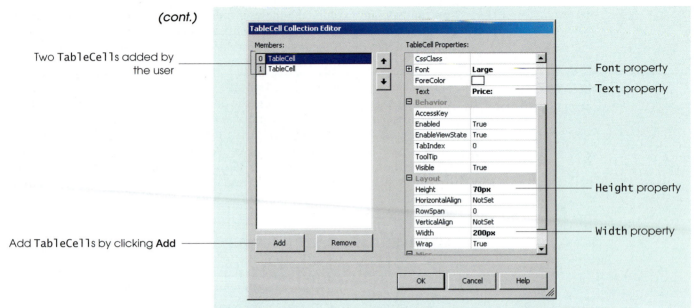

Figure 29.22   **TableCell Collection Editor** dialog of the `Table` control.

4. ***Placing text into Table cells.*** Notice that you set only the font size for the second `TableCell`. We have not yet set the `Text` property of the second `TableCell` because the information that will be displayed in this `Table-Cell` is currently unknown. You will specify the information that will be displayed in this `TableCell` in Tutorial 31. Perform *Step 3* on the rest of the `TableRow`s and `TableCell`s, changing the text in the first cells of each row to `ISBN#:`, `Edition:`, `Copyright Date:` and `Description:`, respectively. Click **OK** in the **TableRow Collection Editor** when you are finished. Your `BookInformation.aspx` page will look like Fig. 29.23.

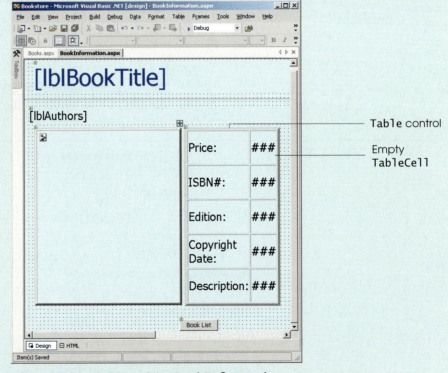

Figure 29.23   Design of the `BookInformation.aspx` page.

5. ***Saving the project.*** Select **File > Save All** to save your modified code.

Now that you have completed the user interface design, you will run the application. You have specified only the **Bookstore** application's user interface; therefore, it does not have any functionality. Test the application in the following box.

Running the Bookstore Application

1. **Testing the application.** Select **Debug > Start** to run your application. The `Books.aspx` page appears, because the first page you create in an ASP .NET application (in this case, `Books.aspx`) will be automatically set as the start page (Fig. 29.24). Notice that the `ListBox` does not yet contain any book titles. This is because you have not yet set up the database connections to retrieve the information. Click the **View Information** Button. Notice that nothing happens. Currently, you have specified only the visual aspects of the page. Thus, users are not forwarded to `BookInformation.aspx` when the **View Information** Button is clicked.

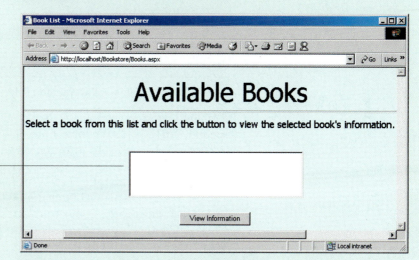

Empty `ListBox` control

Figure 29.24 Empty `ListBox` of the `Books.aspx` page.

2. **Closing the application.** Close your running application by clicking the browser's close box.

3. **Stopping IIS.** Open the **Internet Information Services** dialog. Select **Default Web Site**, and click the stop Button in the toolbar to stop IIS.

4. **Closing the IDE.** Close Visual Studio .NET by clicking its close box.

SELF-REVIEW

1. The _____ property is used to set the width of an `Image` control's border.
   a) `Width`   b) `BorderStyle`
   c) `BorderWidth`   d) None of the above.

2. Use the _____ property to display cell borders between `TableCells` in a `Table`.
   a) `Gridlines`   b) `BorderStyle`
   c) `BorderWidth`   d) `Separator`

Answers: 1) c. 2) a.

29.5 Wrap-Up

In this tutorial, you created the ASPX pages for your three-tier **Bookstore** application. You learned how to create an ASP .NET Web application and how to add Web controls to the ASPX pages. In doing so, you were introduced to the two different modes offered by Visual Studio .NET: **Design** mode and **HTML** mode. You learned that **Design** mode is used to create the user interface by dragging and dropping

Web controls on the ASPX page, while **HTML** mode allows you to view and edit the page's markup.

When you added Web controls to the ASPX page, you learned how to set the exact position of the controls by using the `style` attribute in **HTML** mode. You positioned these controls by specifying the `LEFT:` and `TOP:` portions of the `style` attribute values. The Web controls you used in this tutorial included `Labels`, `Buttons`, `ListBoxes`, `Images` and `Tables`. You also set the `Image` control's `BorderStyle` property to `Outset`, which gave the `Image` a raised appearance.

In the next tutorial, you will access the database, or information tier, of the application, which contains information about the books in the bookstore. You will use **Query Builder** to create the necessary SQL statements. You also will create a database connection and data command objects. After you have created these database components, Tutorial 31 will enable you to create the middle tier of the bookstore, which specifies the functionality of the ASPX pages.

SKILLS SUMMARY

Creating an ASP .NET Web Application

- Select **File > New > Project**.
- Select **Visual Basic Projects** in the left pane.
- Select the **ASP .NET Web Application** icon from the **Templates:** pane in the **New Project** dialog.
- Rename the application, and click **OK**.

Adding an ASPX Page to a Web Application

- Right click the project name in the **Solution Explorer**; then select **Add > Add New Item…** to display the **Add New Item** dialog.
- Select the **Web Form** icon in the **Templates:** box, and rename the ASPX page in the **Name:** TextBox.
- Click **Open** to add the new ASPX page to the Web Application.

Creating a Table Web Control

- Drag and drop the `Table` control from the **Web Forms** tab of the **Toolbox** onto the page.
- Click the ellipsis (…) `Button` in the **Rows** property of the **Properties** window.
- Click the **Add** `Button` to add rows to the `Table`.
- Click the ellipsis (…) `Button` in the **Cells** property of the **Properties** window within the **TableRow Collection Editor** dialog.
- Click the **Add** `Button` to add cells to the `TableRows`.

Setting a Web Control's Location

- Switch to **HTML** mode.
- Use the LEFT: portion of the Web control's style attribute to specify the number of pixels that the Web control will be located from the left side of the Web page.
- Use the TOP: portion of the Web control's style attribute to specify the number of pixels that the Web control will be located from the top of the Web page.

Changing to Design Mode

- Click the **Design** mode `Button` beneath the ASPX page in the Web Form Designer.

Changing to HTML Mode

- Click the **HTML** mode `Button` beneath the ASPX page in the Web Form Designer.

KEY TERMS

bgColor property of an ASPX page—Specifies the page's background color.

BorderStyle property—Specifies the type of border that displays around an `Image`.

BorderWidth property—Specifies the border width of an `Image`.

Button Web control—Allows users to perform an action.

Cells property—Allows programmers to create `TableCells` in a `Table`.

Design mode—Displays the ASPX page's GUI at design time.

ForeColor property—Specifies font color for Label controls.

Gridlines property of a Table—Specifies whether TableCell cell borders display.

Height property—Allows you to specify the height of a Web control.

Horizontal Rule HTML control—Displays a line to separate controls on an ASPX page.

HTML controls—Correspond to HTML elements.

HTML mode—Displays the ASPX page's markup at design time.

ID property—Specifies the name of a Web control.

Image Web control—Displays an image in an ASPX page.

Label Web control—Displays text on an ASPX page.

ListBox Web control—Displays a list of items.

px—Specifies that the size is measured in pixels.

Rows property—Allows programmers to create table rows.

Size property—Allows you to specify the size of a Web control.

style property—Allows you to specify the position of a Web control.

Table Web control—Displays a table in an ASPX page.

Text property—Specifies the text that displays on a Web control.

title property of an ASPX page—Specifies the page's title.

Width property—Allows you to specify the width of a Web control.

CONTROLS, EVENTS, PROPERTIES & METHODS

ASPX page The page on which controls are dropped to design the GUI.

■ *Property*

bgColor—Specifies the ASPX page's background color.

Button   This control allows the user to raise an action or event.

■ *In action*

■ *Properties*

ID—Specifies the name of the Label.
Text—Specifies the text displayed on the Button.
Width—Specifies the width of the Button.

Horizontal Rule   This control displays a line on the ASPX page. It is usually used to separate different areas of the ASPX page.

■ *In action*

■ *Properties*

id—Specifies the name of the Horizontal Rule.
Style—Allows you to specify where to position the Horizontal Rule on the ASPX page.

Image   Image   This control displays an image on the ASPX page.

- *In action*

- *Properties*

    BorderStyle—Specifies the appearance of the Image's border.

    BorderWidth—Specifies the width of the Image's border.

    Height—Specifies the height of the Image control.

    ID—Specifies the name used to access the Image control programmatically. The name should be prefixed with img.

    Width—Specifies the width of the Image control.

Label   A Label   This control displays text on the ASPX page that the user cannot modify.

- *In action*

Books

- *Properties*

    Height—Specifies the height of the Label.

    ID—Specifies the name used to access the Label programmatically. The name should be prefixed with lbl.

    Name (under the expanded Font property in the **Solution Explorer**)—Specifies the name of the font used for the Label's text.

    Size (under the expanded Font property in the **Solution Explorer**)—Specifies the size of the Label's text.

    Text—Specifies the text displayed on the Label.

    Width—Specifies the width of the Label.

ListBox   ListBox   This control allows the user to view and select from multiple items in a list.

- *In action*

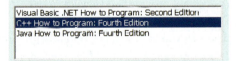

- *Properties*

    Height—Specifies the height of the ListBox.

    ID—Specifies the name used to access the ListBox control programmatically. The name should be prefixed with lst.

    Width—Specifies the width of the ListBox.

Table   Table   This control is usually used to organize data in a spreadsheet format.

■ *In action*

Price:	$76.00
ISBN#:	0-13-029363-6
Edition:	2
Copyright Date:	2002
Description:	Microsoft Visual Basic .NET

■ *Properties*

BorderStyle—Specifies the appearance of the Table's border.

BorderWidth—Specifies the width of the Table's border.

Cells—Retrieves or sets the value in the specified table cell.

Gridlines—Specifies the format in which table cell separators are displayed.

ID—Specifies the name used to access the Table control programmatically. The name should be prefixed with tbl.

Rows—Retrieves or sets the value in the specified table cell.

MULTIPLE-CHOICE QUESTIONS

29.1 You change the _____ property of the ASPX page to specify the color that displays in the background of the page.

   a) BackColor   b) bgColor

   c) BackgroundColor   d) Color

29.2 Button, Label and Table controls for ASPX pages can be accessed from the _____ tab.

   a) **Web Forms**   b) **Components**

   c) **Data**   d) Both a and b.

29.3 The _____ attribute is used to specify the position of a Web control on an ASPX page.

   a) position   b) location

   c) style   d) coordinate

29.4 Unlike the Windows Form Designer, the Web Form Designer _____.

   a) does not provide two viewing modes

   b) provides two viewing modes

   c) allows you to design the graphical user interface

   d) does not allow you to design the user interface

29.5 The BorderStyle property of the Image control _____.

   a) specifies the color of the border

   b) specifies the type of border that displays around the Image control

   c) specifies the width of the border   d) Both a and b.

29.6 Setting the BorderStyle property to Outset makes a control appear _____.

   a) raised   b) with a bold border

   c) with the specified border width   d) with the specified border color

29.7 Every _____ of a Table Web control can contain one or more _____.

    a) `TableRow; TableColumns`   b) `TableColumn; TableRows`

    c) `TableRow; TableCells`   d) `TableCell; TableRows`

29.8 For you to be able to create an **ASP .NET Web** application project, _____ must be running.

    a) IIS   b) Microsoft Access

    c) Microsoft Word   d) Internet Explorer

29.9 The _____ mode allows you to create the ASPX page's GUI by dragging and dropping controls on the page.

    a) **HTML**   b) **Design**

    c) **Visual**   d) **GUI**

29.10 To specify the position of a Web control, set the _____ and _____ values of the _____ attribute.

    a) `X, Y, style`   b) `X, Y, position`

    c) `TOP, LEFT, style`   d) `TOP, LEFT, position`

EXERCISES

*[Note: In these exercises, we may ask you to set an ASPX page as the application's start page, meaning that this page will appear first when the application is run. You can set an ASPX page as the start page by right clicking the file in the **Solution Explorer** and selecting **Set As Start Page**.]*

29.11 (*Phone Book Application: GUI*) Create the user interface for the **Phone Book** application. The design for the two pages for this application is displayed in Fig. 29.25.

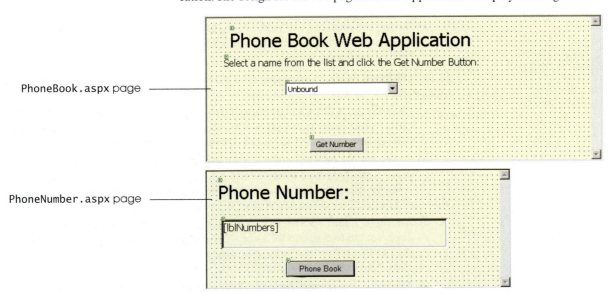

`PhoneBook.aspx` page

`PhoneNumber.aspx` page

Figure 29.25 **Phone Book** application ASPX pages' design.

    a) *Creating an ASP .NET Web application.* Create an ASP .NET Web application project, and name it PhoneBook. Rename the ASPX page to `PhoneBook.aspx`, and set `Option Strict` to `On`. Set `PhoneBook.aspx` as the start page.

    b) *Changing the background color.* Change the background color of your ASPX page (`PhoneBook.aspx`) to the light-yellow **Web Palette** color (located in the sixth column of the 12th row) by using the `bgColor` property as demonstrated in this tutorial. Change the `title` of the ASPX page to Phone Book.

    c) *Adding a Label.* Create a `Label`, set the font size to X-Large and change the `Text` property to Phone Book Web Application. Set the `LEFT:` portion of the `style` attribute value to 40px and the `TOP:` portion to 17px. Name the control `lblPhoneBook`.

d) *Adding another Label.* Create another Label, and set the Text property to Select a name from the list and click the Get Number Button:. Set the LEFT: portion of the style attribute value to 30px and the TOP: portion to 65px. Name this Web control lblInstructions.

e) *Adding a DropDownList Web control.* Create a DropDownList Web control by dragging and dropping it from the **Toolbox** onto the ASPX page. The DropDownList Web control looks similar to the ComboBox Windows Form control. Set the width to 190px, and set the LEFT: portion of the style attribute value to 134px and the TOP: portion to 108px. Name the DropDownList cboNames.

f) *Adding a Button.* Create a Button, set its width to 90px and change the Text property to Get Number. Set the LEFT: portion of the style attribute value to 175px and the TOP: portion to 200px. Name the Web control btnGet.

g) *Adding another ASPX page to the Phone Book application.* Add another ASPX page to the **Phone Book** application, name it PhoneNumber.aspx and change the background to the light-yellow color. Change the title property to Phone Number.

h) *Adding a Label to the PhoneNumber.aspx.* Create a Label and name it lblPhoneNumber. Set the font size to X-Large and change the Text property to Phone Number:. Set the LEFT: portion of the style attribute value to 20px and the TOP: portion to 15px.

i) *Adding another Label.* Create another Label, set its BorderStyle to Inset, and set its height and width to 50px and 380px, respectively. Clear the text of the Label. Name the Label lblNumbers, and set the LEFT: portion of the style attribute value to 25px and the TOP: portion to 80px.

j) *Adding a Button to the PhoneNumber.aspx page.* Create a Button, set its width to 115px and change the Text property to Phone Book. Set the LEFT: portion of the style attribute value to 135px and the TOP: portion to 150px. Name the Button btnPhoneBook.

k) *Saving the project.* Save your project to the PhoneBook directory located in the root directory of your Web server, as you did in *Step 8* of the box, *Creating an ASP .NET Web Application*.

29.12 (**US State Facts Application: GUI**) Create the user interface for the **US State Facts** application. The design for the two pages of this application is displayed in Fig. 29.26.

a) *Creating an ASP .NET Web application.* Create a new ASP .NET Web application project, and name it USStateFacts. Rename the first ASPX page to States.aspx, and set Option Strict to On. Set States.aspx as the start page.

b) *Changing the background color.* Change the background color of the States.aspx page to the light-blue **Web Palette** color (located in the sixth column of the second row) by using the bgColor property as demonstrated in this tutorial. Change the title property of the ASPX page to States.

c) *Adding a Label to States.aspx.* Create a Label Web control, and place it on the page. Set the font size to XX-Large, and change the Text property to States. Change the LEFT: portion of its style attribute value to 390px, and set the TOP: portion to 15px. Name the Web control lblStates.

d) *Adding a Horizontal Rule to States.aspx.* Create a Horizontal Rule, place it on the ASPX page and set its width to 150%. When setting its position, change the TOP: value to 80px, set the LEFT: value to 0px and specify the Height: as 4px. Name the Horizontal Rule hrzStates.

e) *Adding another Label to States.aspx.* Create another Label, and place it beneath the Horizontal Rule. Change the font size to Medium, and set the Text property to Select a state from the list and click the button to view facts about that state:. Set its height to 16px and its width to 620px. Change the LEFT: portion of its style attribute value to 195px, and set the TOP: portion to 100px. Name this Web control lblInstructions.

f) *Adding a ListBox to States.aspx.* Create a ListBox, and place it on the ASPX page. Set its Height property to 100px and its Width property to 155px. Set the LEFT: portion of the style attribute value to 365px and the TOP: portion to 150px. Name the ListBox lstStates.

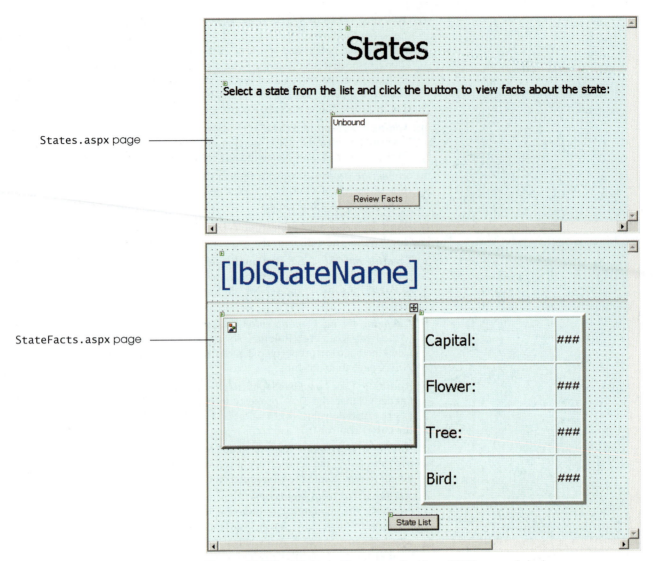

States.aspx page

StateFacts.aspx page

Figure 29.26 **US State Facts** application ASPX pages' design.

g) *Adding a Button to States.aspx.* Create a Button, and place it on the page. Set its Text property to Review Facts and its Width property to 130px. Change the LEFT: portion of the style attribute value to 375px and the TOP: portion to 270px. Name the Button btnFacts.

h) *Adding another ASPX page to the US State Facts application.* Add another ASPX page to the **US State Facts** application, name it StateFacts.aspx and change the background color to light blue.

i) *Adding a Label to StateFacts.aspx.* Create a Label, name it lblStateName, set its font size to XX-Large and change its ForeColor property to Blue. Clear the Label's text. Set its position by setting the LEFT: portion of the style attribute value to 20px and the TOP: portion to 15px.

j) *Adding a Horizontal Rule.* Place the Horizontal Rule beneath the Label and set its TOP: position to 90px, its LEFT: position to 0px and its Height: to 4px. Change the width to 150%. Name the Horizontal Rule hrzStateFacts.

k) *Adding an Image control to StateFacts.aspx.* Create an Image control and set its BorderStyle to Outset. Change the BorderWidth to 5px. Set its height to 200px and its width to 300px. Set the position of the Image by changing the LEFT: portion of the style attribute value to 20px and the TOP: portion to 110px. Name the Web control imgFlag.

l) *Adding a Table to StateFacts.aspx.* Create a Table with four rows and two columns. Set the BorderStyle to Outset, the BorderWidth to 5px and GridLines to Both. Set the height and width of each TableCell of the first column to 70px and 200px, respectively, and set the Font property's Size to Large. Set the Text property of the cells in the first column to Capital:, Flower:, Tree: and Bird:, respectively. Change the LEFT: portion of the style attribute value to 335px and the TOP: portion to 110px. Name the Table control tblState.

m) *Adding a Button to StateFacts.aspx.* Create a Button, change its text to State List, and change the LEFT: portion of the style attribute value to 285px and the TOP: portion to 425px. Name the Button control btnStateList.

n) *Saving the project.* Save your project to the USStateFacts directory located in the root directory of your Web server, as you did in *Step 8* of the box, *Creating an ASP .NET Web Application.*

29.13 (*Road Sign Review Application: GUI*) Create the user interface for the **Road Sign Review** application. The design for the two pages of this application is displayed in Fig. 29.27.

a) *Creating an ASP .NET Web application.* Create a new ASP .NET Web application project, and name it RoadSignReview. Change the name of the existing ASPX page to RoadSigns.aspx, and set Option Strict to On. Set RoadSigns.aspx as the start page.

b) *Changing the background color.* Change the background color of RoadSigns.aspx to the light-green **Web Palette** color (located in the sixth column of the 14th row) by using the bgColor property as demonstrated in this tutorial. Change the title of the ASPX page to RoadSigns.

c) *Adding a Label to RoadSigns.aspx.* Create a Label, and set its font size to XX-Large. Change the Text property to Road Signs. Set its position by changing the style attribute value's LEFT: portion to 295px and the TOP: portion to 16px. Name the Label control lblRoadSigns.

d) *Adding a Horizontal Rule to RoadSigns.aspx.* Create a Horizontal Rule. Set its width to 150%, and set the TOP: position to 80px, the LEFT: position to 0px and the height to 4px. Name the Horizontal Rule hrzRoadSigns.

e) *Adding a Table to RoadSigns.aspx.* Create a Table with three rows and five columns. Set the BorderStyle to Outset, the BorderWidth to 5px and the GridLines property to Both. Also, set the Table's Height property to 279px and Width property to 626px. Set each row's height to 50px and each TableCell's width to 20px. Change the style attribute value by setting LEFT: to 70px and TOP: to 150px. Name the Table control tblRoadSigns.

f) *Adding a Label to RoadSigns.aspx.* Create a Label, and set its font size to Large. Change the Text property to Register for Your Driving Test. Set its position by changing the style attribute value's LEFT: portion to 70px and TOP: portion to 470px. Name the Web control lblRegister.

g) *Adding a Label and TextBox to RoadSigns.aspx.* Create a Label and set its text to Name:. Set its font size to Medium, and change its position to LEFT: 70px and TOP: 520px. Name the Label control lblName. Create a TextBox, and place it next to the **Name:** Label. Set its height to 20px and width to 115px. Change the position to LEFT: 135px and TOP: 520px. Name the TextBox control txtName.

h) *Adding another Label and TextBox pair to RoadSigns.aspx.* Create a Label and set its text to Phone Number:. Set its font size to Medium, and change its position to LEFT: 275px and TOP: 520px. Name the Label control lblPhoneNumber. Create a TextBox, and place it next to the **Phone Number:** Label. Set its height to 20px and width to 115px. Change its position to LEFT: 410px and TOP: 520px. Name the TextBox control txtPhoneNumber.

i) *Adding a Button to RoadSigns.aspx.* Create a Button, set its Text to Register, and change its height and width to 30px and 120px, respectively. Change the position of the Button by setting the LEFT: portion of the style attribute value to 555px and the TOP: portion to 520px. Name the Button control btnRegister.

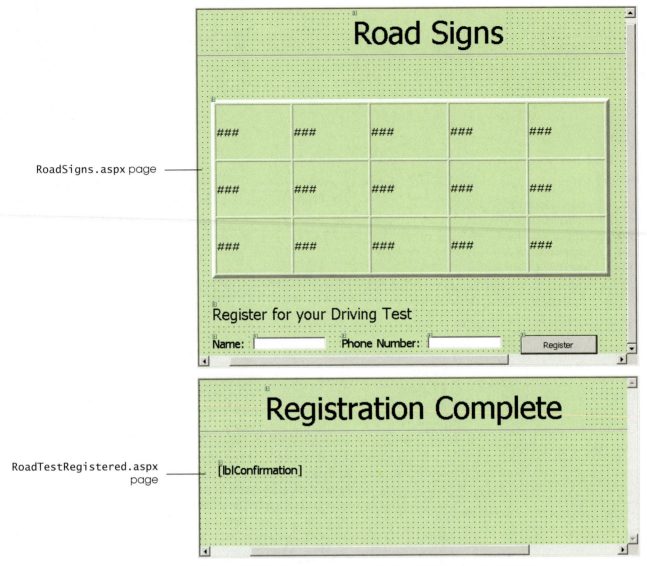

RoadSigns.aspx page —

RoadTestRegistered.aspx page —

Figure 29.27 **Road Signs** application ASPX pages' design.

j) *Adding another ASPX page to the Road Sign Review application*. Add another ASPX page to the application, name it RoadTestRegistered.aspx and change the background color to light green.

k) *Adding a Label to RoadTestRegistered.aspx*. Create a Label, setting its font size to XX-Large and its Text property to Registration Complete. Change its position by setting the LEFT: portion of its style attribute value to 200px and the TOP: portion to 15px. Name the Label control lblRegistration.

l) *Adding a Horizontal Rule to RoadTestRegistered.aspx*. Create a Horizontal Rule. Set its width to 150%, the TOP: position to 80px, the LEFT: position to 0px and the height to 4px. Name the Horizontal Rule hrzRoadTestRegistered.

m) *Adding another Label to RoadTestRegistered.aspx*. Create a Label, name it lblConfirmation and set its font size to Medium. Delete the Text property value, and leave it blank. Change its position by setting the LEFT: portion of its style attribute value to 125px and the TOP: portion to 130px.

n) *Saving the project*. Save your project to the RoadSignReview directory located in the root directory of your Web server, as you did in *Step 8* of the box, *Creating an ASP .NET Web Application*.

30

Bookstore Application: Information Tier

Examining the Database and Creating Database Components

Objectives

In this tutorial, you will learn to:
- Connect to a database.
- Create SQL statements that retrieve information from a database, using the **Query Builder** tool.

Outline

This tutorial focuses on the Web application's information tier, where the application's data resides. In your **Bookstore** application, the information tier is represented by a Microsoft Access database, db_bookstore.mdb, that stores each book's information. Before you begin this tutorial, you should be familiar with the database concepts presented in Tutorial 25.

In this tutorial, you will create the objects that your application will need to connect to the database. You also will define the SQL statements that will retrieve data from that database. Actually, the information tier consists solely of the db_bookstore.mdb database. The connection objects and data command objects created in this tutorial are actually part of the middle tier, as they perform the functionality of retrieving data from the database. You create these objects here because they interact with the information tier and do not require any programming. You will complete the **Bookstore** application by creating the middle tier in the next tutorial.

30.1 Reviewing the Bookstore Application

You have taken the three-tier **Bookstore** application for a test-drive (in Tutorial 28) and have designed the GUI by using Web controls and an HTML control (Tutorial 29). Now you are ready to create the database components for the application. Before you begin, you should review the pseudocode and the ACE table (Fig. 30.1) for this application:

When the Books page is requested
 Retrieve the book titles from the database
 Display book titles in a ListBox

When the user selects a book title from the ListBox and clicks the View Information Button
 Store the selected book in a variable
 Redirect the user to the BookInformation page

When the BookInformation page is requested
    Retrieve the selected book's information from a database
    Display the book title in a Label
    Display the authors in a Label
    Display the cover art in an image
    Display the remaining information in a Table
When the user presses the Book List Button on the BookInformation page
    Redirect the client browser back to the Books page

Action/Control/Event (ACE) Table for the Web-Based Bookstore Application

Action	Control/Object/Class	Event
Label the Books page	lblAvailable, lblInstructions	
	Page	Load (for Books.aspx)
Retrieve the book titles from the database	objOleDbConnection, objSelectTitles	
Display book titles in a ListBox	lstBookTitles	
	btnInformation	Click
Store the selected book in a variable	Session	
Redirect the user to the BookInformation page	Response	
	Page	Load (for Book-Information.aspx)
Retrieve the selected book's information from a database	objOleDbConnection, objSelectBookData	
Display the book title in a Label	lblBookTitle	
Display the authors in a Label	lblAuthors	
Display the cover art in an image	imgBook	
Display the remaining information in a Table	tblBook	
	btnBookList	Click
Redirect the client browser back to the Books page	Response	

Figure 30.1   ACE table for the Web-based **Bookstore** application.

In this tutorial, you will be creating the objects that are used to retrieve information from the database, including the objects that connect to the database and the objects that execute the command statements.

30.2 Information Tier: Database

The information tier maintains all of the data needed for an application. The database that stores this data might contain product data, such as a description, price and quantity in stock, and customer data, such as a user name and shipping information.

Databases are an integral part of real-world applications, because they provide the ability to update data in **real time**. As soon as a piece of data is entered into the database, it is accessible to users and applications with the proper authorization. Because data is stored electronically, it can be accessed and manipulated much faster than paper copies. Most databases are relational databases—databases where the data is organized in tables. A variety of database products (used to build and modify databases) from Microsoft and other vendors exist, ranging from personal products like Microsoft Access to enterprise products such as Oracle, Sybase and

Microsoft SQL Server 2000. Database products also can be used to generate reports from information in a database.

The **Bookstore** application stores the books' data in a Microsoft Access database (db_bookstore.mdb). This data is retrieved from the database by using Visual Basic .NET code and ADO .NET objects. The database contains one table, named Products, that stores each book's information.

The Products table contains nine fields (columns): productID, title, authors, copyrightDate, edition, isbn, coverart, description and price. These fields contain an ID number, the title, authors, copyright date, edition number, ISBN number (a unique number used to reference a book), image name, description and price of each book, respectively. Figure 30.2 displays the Products table of db_bookstore.mdb, using the **Server Explorer** window.

Products table of the db_bookstore.mdb database —

Figure 30.2 Products table of the db_bookstore.mdb database.

SELF-REVIEW

1. Once data is entered into a database, _____.
   a) the data is immediately accessible to users and applications
   b) users must wait until the system reboots in order to access the data
   c) all applications using the database must manually be updated
   d) None of the above.

2. Databases are an integral part of real-world applications because they provide the ability to _____.
   a) store information that cannot be altered
   b) update data in real time
   c) execute applications   d) None of the above.

Answers: 1) a. 2) b.

30.3 Using the Server Explorer and Query Builder in ASPX Pages

Before you begin programming this application's middle tier, you must set up the database connections that retrieve data from the database. Recall that you used the **Server Explorer** window and the **Query Builder** tool in Tutorial 25. You will use these IDE features again to create a database connection and to generate SQL statements to request book information. You add the database connection and data command objects in the following box.

Adding Database Components to the Books Page

1. *Starting IIS.* Make sure that IIS is running for the **Default Web Site**. If it is not running, start it in the **Internet Information Services** dialog, by selecting **Default Web Site** in the left pane and clicking the Start Item Button.

2. *Opening the Bookstore application in Visual Studio .NET.* In Windows Explorer, double click the Bookstore.sln file in the Bookstore directory located in the wwwroot directory to open the **Bookstore** application in Visual Studio .NET.

(cont.)

3. ***Using the Server Explorer window to add a connection to the database.*** You must set up a connection to the database before accessing its data. You will use ADO .NET objects to accomplish this task. This connection will allow you to read information about a book from the database. Select **View > Server Explorer** to display the **Server Explorer** window. Click the Connect to Database icon (Fig. 30.3) to display the **Data Link Properties** dialog.

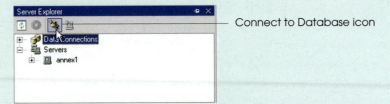

Connect to Database icon

Figure 30.3 Connecting to the database in the **Server Explorer** window.

4. ***Specifying provider settings.*** You now need to specify the provider of the database software you are using. Click the **Provider** tab to display a list of providers. Because you are using a Microsoft Access database, select the **Microsoft Jet 4.0 OLE DB Provider**, and click the **Next >>** Button (Fig. 30.4). [*Note*: The number of items and the names of the **OLE DB Provider(s)** displayed in the **Provider** tab may be different on your system.]

Provider tab ——————

Select this provider ——————

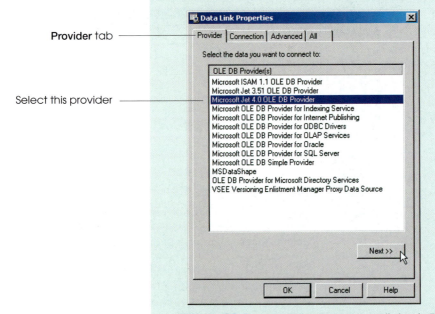

Figure 30.4 **Data Link Properties** dialog's **Provider** tab.

5. ***Specifying connection settings.*** When you click the **Next >>** Button, the **Connection** tab (Fig. 30.5) of the **Data Link Properties** dialog is displayed. You are now ready to specify db_bookstore.mdb as the database. Click the ellipsis (...) Button next to the **Select or enter a database name:** TextBox. The **Select Access Database** dialog appears as in Fig. 30.6. Locate db_bookstore.mdb in the C:\InetPub\wwwroot\Databases directory, and click **Open**.

(cont.)

Connection tab ————

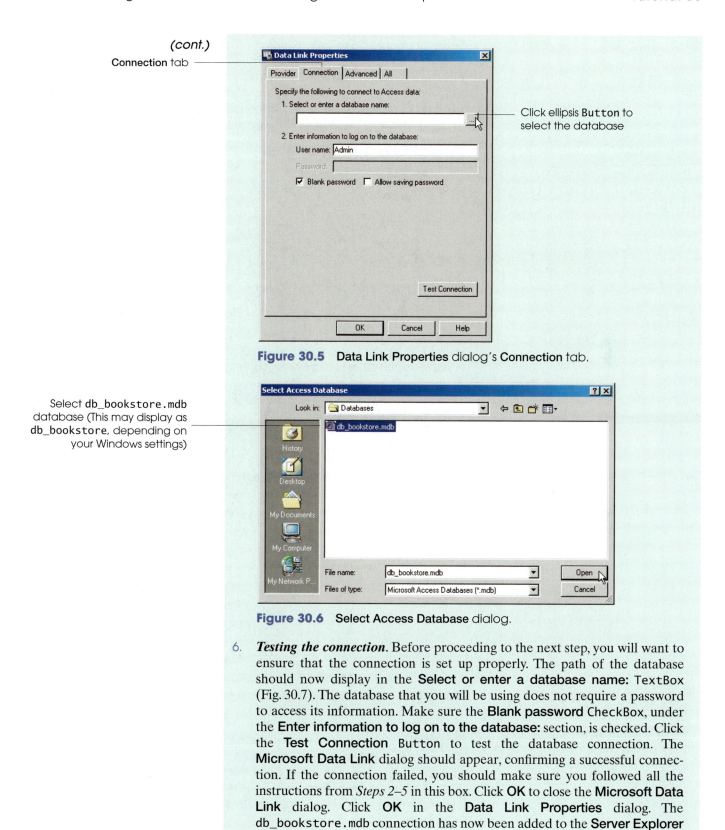

Click ellipsis **Button** to select the database

Figure 30.5 **Data Link Properties** dialog's **Connection** tab.

Select db_bookstore.mdb database (This may display as db_bookstore, depending on your Windows settings)

Figure 30.6 **Select Access Database** dialog.

6. ***Testing the connection****.* Before proceeding to the next step, you will want to ensure that the connection is set up properly. The path of the database should now display in the **Select or enter a database name:** TextBox (Fig. 30.7). The database that you will be using does not require a password to access its information. Make sure the **Blank password** CheckBox, under the **Enter information to log on to the database:** section, is checked. Click the **Test Connection** Button to test the database connection. The **Microsoft Data Link** dialog should appear, confirming a successful connection. If the connection failed, you should make sure you followed all the instructions from *Steps 2–5* in this box. Click **OK** to close the **Microsoft Data Link** dialog. Click **OK** in the **Data Link Properties** dialog. The db_bookstore.mdb connection has now been added to the **Server Explorer** window.

(cont.)

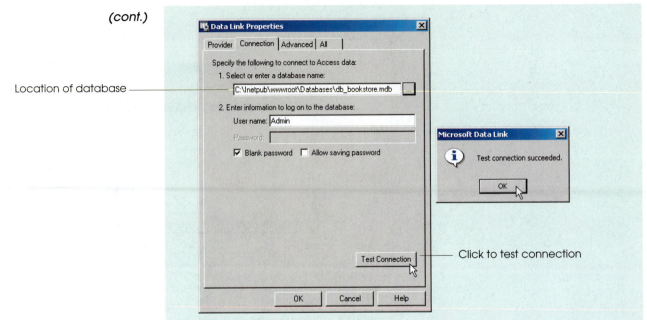

Figure 30.7   Testing the database connection.

7. *Adding a data connection object to the ASPX page.* Double click `Books.aspx` in the **Solution Explorer** window to display the `Books.aspx` page. From the **Server Explorer** window, drag and drop the `db_bookstore.mdb` connection node onto the `Books.aspx` page. An `Ole-DbConnection` object appears in the component tray. Rename the connection object `objOleDbConnection`. Recall that a connection object is used to maintain a connection to the database.

8. *Adding a data command object to the ASPX page.* From the **Data** tab of the **Toolbox**, drag and drop an `OleDbCommand` object on the ASPX page. Recall that the `OleDbCommand` object allows you to specify SQL statements to retrieve information from the database. Rename the `OleDbCommand` object to `objSelectTitles`. Set the `Connection` property of the data command object to the connection object you created for this page, `objOleDbConnection`. To do this, click the down-arrow `Button` that appears next to the `Connection` property field. Expand the **Existing** node and select the name of the connection object (`objOleDbConnection`) that you created in *Step 6*. You are now ready to create the SQL statements that will retrieve data from the database. Select the `CommandText` property, and click the ellipsis (...) `Button` that appears next to the `CommandText` field. The **Query Builder** and **Add Table** dialogs appear (Fig. 30.8).

9. *Adding the Products table to the Query Builder dialog.* Before you can use the **Query Builder** dialog, you must select a database table. In the **Add Table** dialog, select `Products`, and click the **Add** `Button`. Click **Close** to close the **Add Table** dialog.

10. *Selecting information from the database.* You are ready to retrieve the values from the `title` field of the `Products` table. In the **Query Builder** dialog, check the `title` CheckBox in the `Products` window. Your SELECT statement should look like the one displayed in Fig. 30.9. This statement will retrieve the `title` field values from the `Products` table of the database. You will later use this information to populate the `ListBox` in the `Books.aspx` page. Click **OK** to close the **Query Builder** dialog.

(cont.)

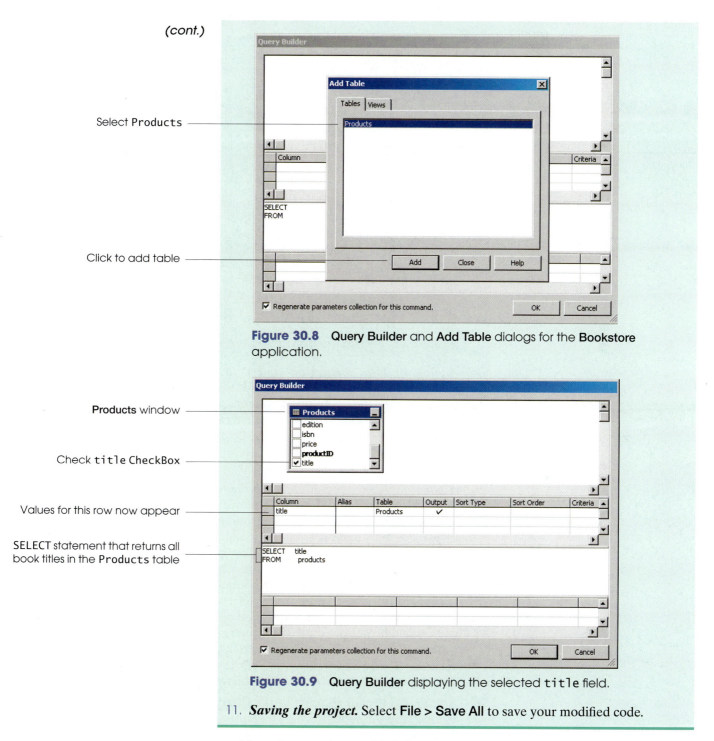

Select **Products**

Click to add table

Figure 30.8 **Query Builder** and **Add Table** dialogs for the **Bookstore** application.

Products window

Check `title` CheckBox

Values for this row now appear

`SELECT` statement that returns all book titles in the **Products** table

Figure 30.9 **Query Builder** displaying the selected `title` field.

11. ***Saving the project.*** Select **File > Save All** to save your modified code.

Now that you have added database connection and command objects to the `Books.aspx` page, you will do the same for the `BookInformation.aspx` page. The `CommandText` property for the data command object of this page will differ from that of the `Books.aspx` page. In the `BookInformation.aspx` page, you will use the `Parameters` property of the data command object because you do not yet know which record to retrieve—this will be determined when the user selects a book. You will specify the record in the middle tier of the application, which you will program in Tutorial 31. For now you will set the database connections and data command objects in the following box.

**Adding Database
Components to the
BookInformation Page**

1. *Adding a data connection object to the ASPX page.* Double click BookInformation.aspx to display the BookInformation.aspx page. From the **Server Explorer** window, drag and drop the db_bookstore.mdb connection node onto the BookInformation.aspx page. An OleDbConnection object appears in the component tray. Rename the connection object to objOleDbConnection.

2. *Adding a data command object to the ASPX page.* From the **Data** tab of the **Toolbox**, drag and drop an OleDbCommand object on the ASPX page. Rename the OleDbCommand object to objSelectBookData. Set the Connection property of the data command object to the connection object you created for this page, objOleDbConnection. Select the CommandText property, and click the ellipsis (...) Button that appears next to the CommandText field. The **Query Builder** and **Add Table** dialogs appear (Fig. 30.10).

Add Table dialog ──────

Add this table ──────

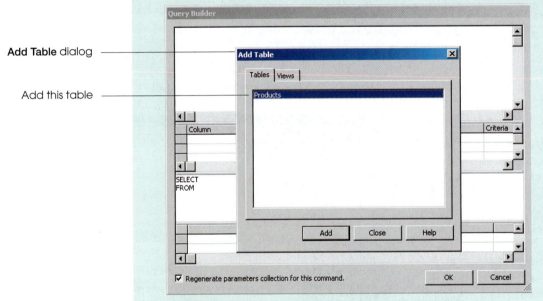

Figure 30.10 **Query Builder** and **Add Table** dialogs.

3. *Adding the Products table.* In the **Add Table** dialog, select Products, and click the **Add** Button. Click **Close** to close the **Add Table** dialog.

4. *Selecting the fields to retrieve from the database.* Check the authors, copyrightDate, coverart, description, edition, isbn, price and title CheckBoxes in the Products window of the **Query Builder** dialog. Notice that the field names appear after the SELECT keyword in the SELECT statement as well as in the table beneath the Products window (Fig. 30.11).

5. *Specifying the record from which information will be retrieved.* In the table beneath the Products window, type =? in the **Criteria** field of the title row (Fig. 30.12) to indicate that you do not know the record from which the information will be retrieved. Recall that a funnel will appear to the right of the title CheckBox, which indicates that a value will be retrieved from the field (title) according to specified criteria.

(cont.)

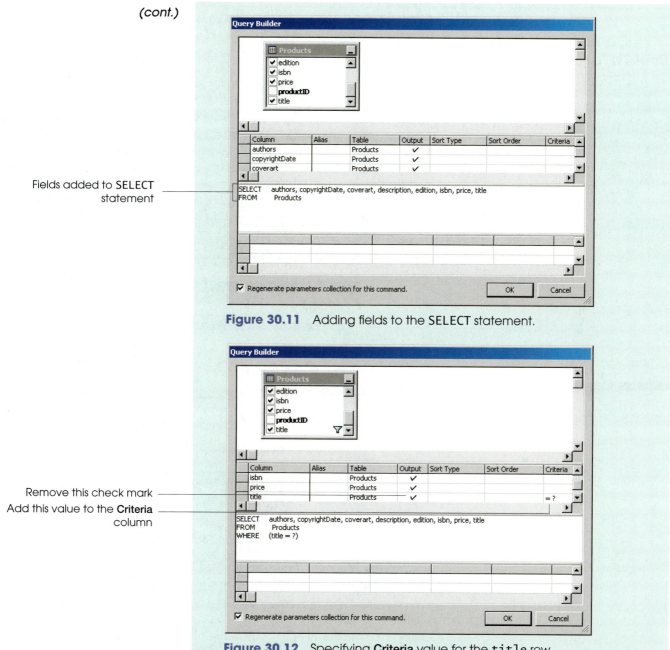

Fields added to SELECT statement

Figure 30.11 Adding fields to the SELECT statement.

Remove this check mark

Add this value to the **Criteria** column

Figure 30.12 Specifying **Criteria** value for the `title` row.

6. ***Completing the SELECT statement.*** Click the check in the **Output** column of the `title` row to remove the `title` field name from the SELECT portion of the SQL statement. You do this step because you do not want to retrieve the title information—the title is used only to select the appropriate record. The complete SELECT statement should look like the one in Fig. 30.13. Click **OK**. The **Microsoft Development Environment** dialog (Fig. 30.14) appears, asking if you want to apply a new parameter configuration. Click the **Yes** Button to create a `title` parameter.

(cont.)

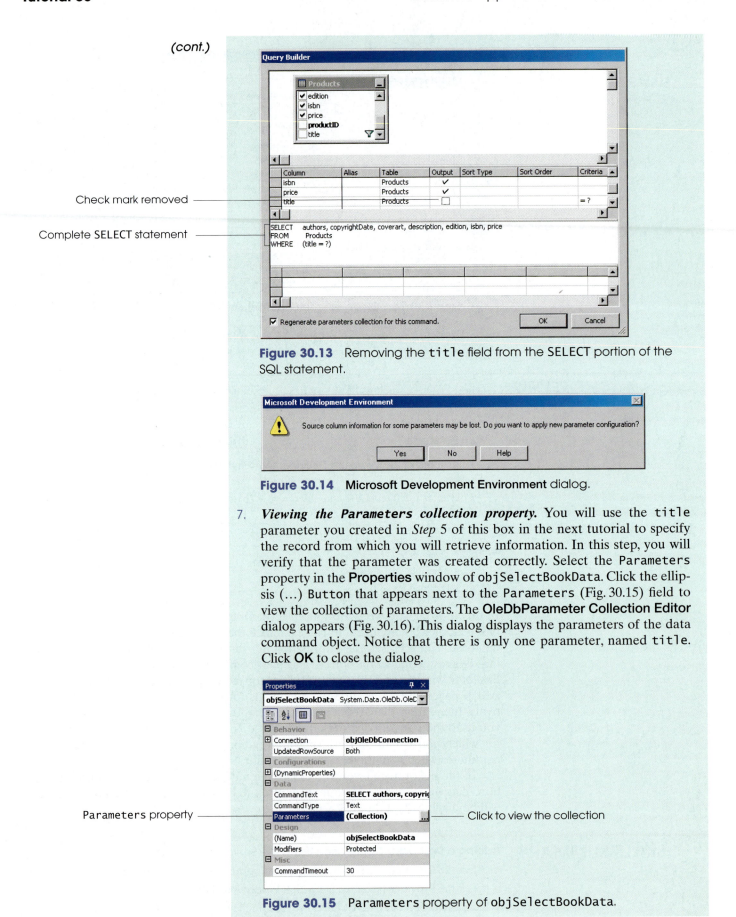

Figure 30.13 Removing the `title` field from the **SELECT** portion of the SQL statement.

Figure 30.14 **Microsoft Development Environment** dialog.

7. ***Viewing the Parameters collection property.*** You will use the `title` parameter you created in *Step* 5 of this box in the next tutorial to specify the record from which you will retrieve information. In this step, you will verify that the parameter was created correctly. Select the `Parameters` property in the **Properties** window of `objSelectBookData`. Click the ellipsis (...) Button that appears next to the `Parameters` (Fig. 30.15) field to view the collection of parameters. The **OleDbParameter Collection Editor** dialog appears (Fig. 30.16). This dialog displays the parameters of the data command object. Notice that there is only one parameter, named `title`. Click **OK** to close the dialog.

Figure 30.15 `Parameters` property of `objSelectBookData`.

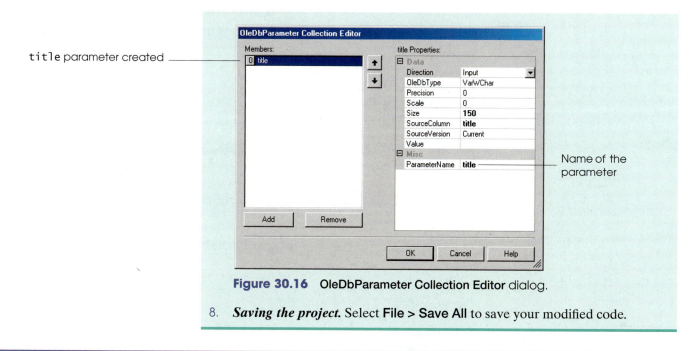

title parameter created

Name of the parameter

Figure 30.16   **OleDbParameter Collection Editor** dialog.

8. *Saving the project.* Select **File > Save All** to save your modified code.

---

1. The _____ dialog allows you to select a database table to add to the **Query Builder** dialog.

   a) **Add Table**   b) **Database**

   c) **Database Table**   d) **Data Link Properties**

2. Clicking **Yes** in the **Microsoft Development Environment** dialog after using **Query Builder** _____.

   a) creates the OleDbCommand object   b) creates the SQL statement

   c) creates parameter items in the   d) None of the above.
      Parameters property

Answers: 1) a. 2) c.

30.4 Wrap-Up

In this tutorial, you were introduced to the information tier of the three-tier, Web-based **Bookstore** application. You examined the contents of the db_bookstore.mdb database. You accessed the information tier of the **Bookstore** application by creating database connection objects and data command objects. You used the **Server Explorer** window and the **Query Builder** tool to add a database connection to your ASPX pages and to create SQL statements for the data command objects, respectively. In creating the OleDbCommand object for the BookInformation.aspx page, you used the Parameters property, because you do not know the title of the book for which you would be retrieving information. You will specify the value of this parameter when you program the middle tier.

In the next tutorial, you will create the middle tier of your **Bookstore** application. You will add code to your application to control what data from the database will be displayed on the ASPX page.

SKILLS SUMMARY   **Adding a Database Connection Using the** Server Explorer **Window**

■ Click the Connect to Database icon to display the **Data Link Properties** dialog.

■ Click the **Provider** tab in the **Data Link Properties** dialog.

■ Select **Microsoft Jet 4.0 OLE DB Provider** in the **OLE DB Provider(s)** box.

- Click **Next >>**; then click the ellipsis (**...**) Button next to the **Select or enter a database name:** field.
- Choose the desired database, and click **Open**.
- Place a checkmark in the **Blank password** CheckBox.
- Click the **Test Connection** Button. Click **OK** in the dialog that appears; then click **OK** in the **Data Link Properties** dialog.

Adding a Connection Object to the ASPX Page

- Select the desired database connection in the **Server Explorer** window.
- Drag and drop the connection onto the ASPX page.

Adding a Data Command Object to the ASPX Page to Select Information

- Select the OleDbCommand icon from the **Data** tab in the **Toolbox**.
- Drag and drop the icon onto the ASPX page.
- Select the Connection property in the **Properties** window, and specify the name of the connection object created previously.
- Select the CommandText property, and click the ellipsis Button to access the **Query Builder** tool.
- Add a table to the **Query Builder** dialog by using the **Add Table** dialog.
- Check desired-field CheckBoxes, and use the **Criteria** columns if necessary.

KEY TERMS

Real time—Data is accessible to users and applications immediately after it is entered into the database.

MULTIPLE-CHOICE QUESTIONS

30.1 _____ is an example of a database product.

a) Microsoft Access

b) Microsoft SQL Server

c) Oracle

d) All of the above.

30.2 An advantage of using information in a database is that _____.

a) the data can be updated in real time

b) information that changes need be updated only in one location

c) Both a and b.

d) None of the above.

30.3 When a funnel appears to the right of a field's CheckBox in the **Query Builder** dialog, it indicates that _____.

a) information will be updated in the specified field

b) a value will be retrieved from that field according to specified criteria

c) the field will not be included in the SQL statement

d) None of the above.

30.4 The Parameters property of _____ contains a collection of parameters.

a) OleDbConnection

b) OleDbDataConnection

c) OleDbDataCommand

d) OleDbCommand

30.5 The _____ can be used to create an OleDbConnection.

a) **Server Explorer** window

b) **Query Builder** tool

c) Both a and b.

d) None of the above.

30.6 You use the _____ object to create SQL statements for retrieving data from a database.

a) OleDbConnection

b) OleDbDataReader

c) OleDbCommand

d) None of the above.

30.7 The _____ is used when creating SQL statements visually for the `OleDbCommand` object's `CommandText` property.

a) **Server Explorer** window

b) **Query Builder** tool

c) Both a and b.

d) None of the above.

30.8 You use the _____ object to open a connection to the database.

a) `OleDbConnection`

b) `OleDbDataReader`

c) `OleDbCommand`

d) None of the above.

30.9 You use the _____ property of the `OleDbCommand` object to specify values for information that is not known in advance.

a) `Connection`

b) `Parameters`

c) `Field`

d) `Name`

30.10 Another name for the database tier is _____.

a) the information tier

b) the bottom tier

c) Both a and b.

d) None of the above.

EXERCISES

30.11 (*Phone Book Application: Database*) Create the database connections and data command objects for the **Phone Book** application by using the **Server Explorer** window and the **Query Builder** tool.

a) *Opening the application.* Open the **Phone Book** application that you created in Tutorial 29.

b) *Copying the db_Phone.mdb database to the Databases directory.* Copy the database `C:\Examples\Tutorial30\Exercises\Databases\db_Phone.mdb` to the Databases directory in IIS's `wwwroot` directory.

c) *Using Server Explorer to add a connection to the database.* In the **Server Explorer** window, add a connection to the db_Phone.mdb database. Drag and drop the connection object onto the PhoneBook.aspx page. Name the connection object `objOleDbConnection`.

d) *Using Query Builder for the PhoneBook.aspx page.* Add an `OleDbCommand` to the PhoneBook.aspx page. Set the `Connection` property to the `OleDbConnection` object you added to the ASPX page, and use **Query Builder** to set the `CommandText` property of the `OleDbCommand`. This command should retrieve all the names of the people from the database. Name this command object `objSelectNames`.

e) *Adding a connection to the database to the PhoneNumber.aspx page.* Using the **Server Explorer** window, drag and drop a database connection object onto the PhoneNumber.aspx page. Name this connection object `objOleDbConnection`.

f) *Using Query Builder for PhoneBook.aspx.* Add an `OleDbCommand` to the PhoneNumber.aspx page. Set the `Connection` property to the `OleDbConnection` object you added to the ASPX page, and use **Query Builder** to set the `CommandText` property of the `OleDbCommand`. This configuration should retrieve the phone number of the person whose name will be selected, from the `DropDownList` in the PhoneBook.aspx page, by the user. You need to set the criteria to specify which person's phone number will be retrieved from the database. Name this command object `objSelectPhoneNumber`.

g) *Saving the project.* Select **File > Save All** to save your modified code.

30.12 (*US State Facts Application: Database*) Create the database connections and data command objects for the **USStateFacts** application by using the **Server Explorer** window and the **Query Builder** tool.

a) *Opening the application.* Open the **USStateFacts** application that you created in Tutorial 29.

b) *Copying the db_StateFacts.mdb database to the Databases directory.* Copy the `C:\Examples\Tutorial30\Exercises\Databases\db_StateFacts.mdb` database to the Databases directory in IIS's `wwwroot` folder.

c) ***Using Server Explorer to add a connection to the database.*** In the **Server Explorer** window, add a connection to the db_StateFacts.mdb database. Drag-and-drop the connection object onto the States.aspx page. Name this connection object objOleDbConnection.

d) ***Using Query Builder for the States.aspx page.*** Add an OleDbCommand to the States.aspx page. Set the Connection property to the OleDbConnection object you added to the ASPX page and use **Query Builder** to set the CommandText property of the OleDbCommand. This command should retrieve the names of the states from the **name** field of the states table in the database. Name this command object objSelectNames.

e) ***Adding a connection to the database to the StateFacts.aspx page.*** Using the **Server Explorer** window, drag-and-drop a database connection object onto the database on the StateFacts.aspx page. Name this connection object objOleDbConnection.

f) ***Using Query Builder for StateFacts.aspx.*** Add an OleDbCommand to the StateFacts.aspx page. Set the Connection property to the OleDbConnection object you added to the ASPX page, and use **Query Builder** to set the CommandText property of the OleDbCommand. This configuration should retrieve all the information, from the states table of the database, about the state that is selected by the user. You need to set the criteria to specify which state's information will be retrieved from the database. Name this command object objSelectStateInformation.

g) ***Saving the project.*** Select **File > Save All** to save your modified code.

30.13 (***Road Sign Review Application: Database***) Create the database connections and data command objects for the **RoadSignReview** application by using the **Server Explorer** window and the **Query Builder** tool.

a) ***Opening the application.*** Open the **RoadSignReview** application that you created in Tutorial 29.

b) ***Copying the db_RoadSigns.mdb database to the Databases directory.*** Copy the C:\Examples\Tutorial30\Exercises\Databases\db_RoadSigns.mdb database to the Databases directory in IIS's wwwroot directory.

c) ***Using Server Explorer to add a connection to the database.*** In the **Server Explorer** window add a connection to the db_RoadSigns.mdb database. Drag and drop the connection object onto the RoadSigns.aspx page. Name this command object objOleDbConnection.

d) ***Using Query Builder for the RoadSigns.aspx page.*** Add an OleDbCommand to the RoadSigns.aspx page. Set the Connection property to the OleDbConnection object that you added to the ASPX page, and use **Query Builder** to set the CommandText property of the OleDbCommand. This configuration should retrieve all the information about all the road signs from the signs table of the database. You will not need to specify a criterion for this exercise, because all the information from the database needs to be retrieved. Name this command object objSelectSignInformation.

e) ***Saving the project.*** Select **File > Save All** to save your modified code.

31 TUTORIAL

Objectives

In this tutorial, you will learn to:
- Write the functionality for the middle tier, using Visual Basic .NET code.
- Modify code-behind files in a Web application.
- Specify parameters of **OleDbCommand** objects.

Outline

Bookstore Application: Middle Tier

Introducing Code-Behind Files

In earlier tutorials, you built the client tier and created connections to the information tier of the **Bookstore** application. Using the Visual Studio .NET IDE, you were able to design the user interface of this Web-based application. In this tutorial, you will learn about the middle tier and complete the **Bookstore** application by programming the middle tier's functionality. Recall that the middle tier is responsible for interacting with the client and information tiers. The middle tier accepts user requests for data from the client tier, retrieves the data from the information tier (that is, the database) and responds to the client's requests with HTML documents.

31.1 Reviewing the **Bookstore** Application

You have taken the three-tier **Bookstore** application for a test-drive (in Tutorial 28) and have created the Web controls (Tutorial 29) and database components (Tutorial 30) for the application. Now you will need to write code to specify the functionality of the **Bookstore** application. Before you begin to write the code, you should review the pseudocode and the ACE table (Fig. 31.1) for this application:

When the Books page is requested
  Retrieve the book titles from the database
  Display book titles in a ListBox

When the user selects a book title from the ListBox and clicks the View Information Button
  Store the selected book in a variable
  Redirect the user to the BookInformation page

When the BookInformation page is requested
  Retrieve the selected book's information from a database
  Display the book title in a Label
  Display the authors in a Label
  Display the cover art in an image
  Display the remaining information in a Table

When the user presses the Book List Button on the BookInformation page
Redirect the client browser back to the Books page

Action/Control/Event (ACE) Table for the Web-Based Bookstore Application

Action	Control/Object	Event
Label the Books page	lblAvailable, lblInstructions	
	Page	Load (for Books.aspx)
Retrieve the book titles from the database	objOleDbConnection, objSelectTitles	
Display book titles in a ListBox	lstBookTitles	
	btnInformation	Click
Store the selected book in a variable	Session	
Redirect the user to the BookInformation page	Response	
	Page	Load (for Book-Information.aspx)
Retrieve the selected book's information from a database	objOleDbConnection, objSelectBookData	
Display the book title in a Label	lblBookTitle	
Display the authors in a Label	lblAuthors	
Display the cover art in an image	imgBook	
Display the remaining information in a Table	tblBook	
	btnBookList	Click
Redirect the client browser back to the Books page	Response	

Figure 31.1   ACE table for the Web-based **Bookstore** application.

In this tutorial, you will implement the interaction between the user interface and the database of the **Bookstore** application. This means that you will write the code that determines which image will be displayed by the Image control and which information will be retrieved from the database and displayed in the Table control. You also will write the code that redirects the client browser to another page when a Button is clicked.

31.2 Programming the Books Page's Code-Behind File

Although you have designed your **Bookstore** application's GUI and have added database connections, the **Bookstore** currently does not have any other functionality. You will now begin programming your application. You start with the Books.aspx page in the following box.

Defining the Page_Load Event Handler for the Books Page

1. *Starting IIS.* Make sure that IIS is running for the **Default Web Site**. If it is not running, start it in the **Internet Information Services** dialog, by selecting **Default Web Site** in the left pane and clicking the Start Item Button.

2. *Opening the Bookstore application in Visual Studio .NET.* Double click the `Bookstore.sln` file in the `Bookstore` directory located in the `wwwroot` directory to open the **Bookstore** application in Visual Studio .NET.

3. *Displaying the code-behind file in the Solution Explorer window.* Every ASPX page created in Visual Studio .NET has a corresponding class written in a .NET language, such as Visual Basic .NET. This class includes event handlers, initialization code, methods and other supporting code and represents the middle tier of your application. The Visual Basic .NET file that contains this class is called the **code-behind file** and provides the ASPX page's functionality. It has the file extension `.aspx.vb`. Click the Show All Files Button (Fig. 31.2) in the toolbar of the **Solution Explorer**. Click the plus box next to `Books.aspx` to display the code-behind file, `Books.aspx.vb` (Fig. 31.2).

Click to display the code-behind file

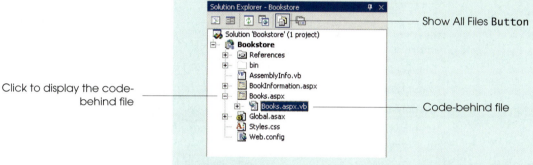

Show All Files Button

Code-behind file

Figure 31.2   Code-behind file for the `Books.aspx` ASPX page.

4. *Viewing the code-behind file.* Figure 31.3 displays `Books.aspx.vb`—the code-behind file for `Books.aspx`. Recall that Visual Studio .NET generates this code-behind file when the project is created; we have reformatted it for presentation purposes. To view this file, double click `Books.aspx.vb` in the **Solution Explorer** window. [*Note*: You also can right click `Books.aspx` and select **View Code** to view the code-behind file.] Click the plus box of Web Form Designer Generated Code to display the generated code. Click the minus box of #Region to hide the generated code.

5. *Changing the class name.* Change the class name on line 1 from `WebForm1` to `Books` (Fig. 31.4). Line 2 indicates that this class inherits from the `Page` class. The **Page** class defines the basic functionality for an ASPX page, much as the `Form` class defines the basic functionality for a Windows application `Form`. The `Page` class is located in the `System.Web.UI` namespace. The `Page` class provides properties, methods and events that are useful for creating Web-based applications.

(cont.)

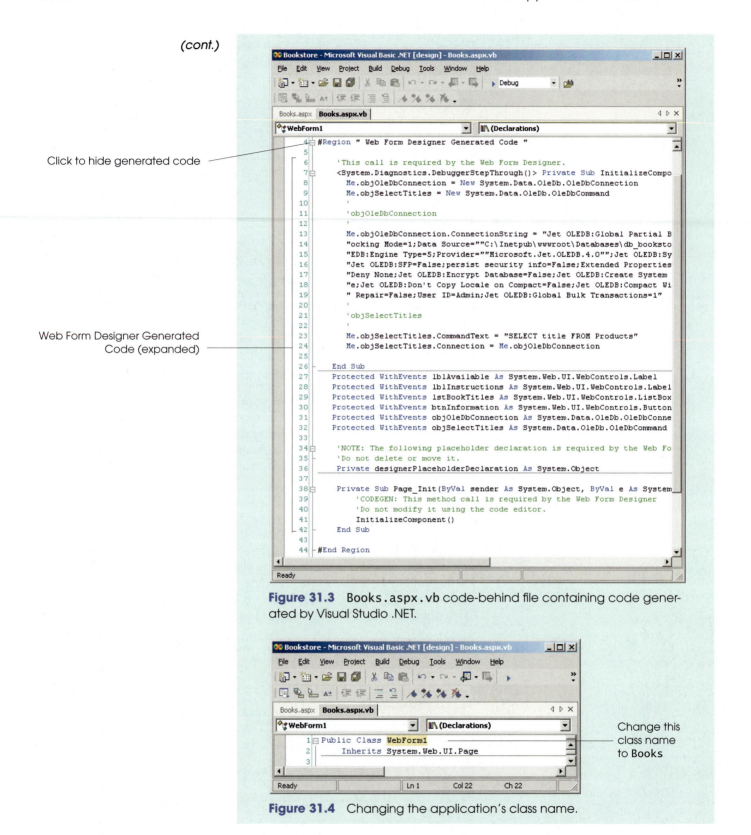

Click to hide generated code

Web Form Designer Generated Code (expanded)

Figure 31.3   `Books.aspx.vb` code-behind file containing code generated by Visual Studio .NET.

Change this class name to **Books**

Figure 31.4   Changing the application's class name.

(cont.)   6. ***Importing a namespace.*** To use database-related objects, you will need to import namespace `System.Data.OleDb`. Add line 1 of Fig. 31.5 before the Books class definition.

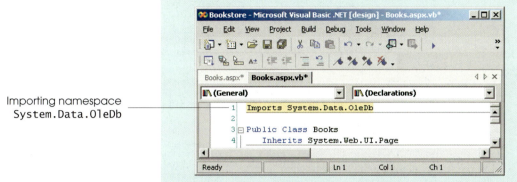

Importing namespace
`System.Data.OleDb`

Figure 31.5   Importing namespace `System.Data.OleDb`.

7. ***Defining the Page_Load event handler.*** `Page_Load` is an event handler that executes any processing necessary to display the page. This event handler is created for you when the ASPX page is created, although it has no code. Add lines 51–55 of Fig. 31.6 to the `Page_Load` event handler. [*Note:* Initially, the `Page_Load` event handler contains a comment. We remove this comment from the event handler.] Line 51 opens the connection to the database by invoking the `OleDbConnection` class method `Open`. Lines 54–55 create a data reader by invoking the `ExecuteReader` method of the data command object (`objSelectTitles`) you created in Tutorial 30.

   The `Load` event for a Web page is similar to the `Load` event for a Windows Form. You put code in the `Load` event handler that is needed to initialize the page or the objects the page uses.

8. ***Using the data reader.*** Add lines 57–65 of Fig. 31.7 to the `Page_Load` event handler. Lines 58–63 define a `Do While...Loop` statement that starts the data reader by invoking the `Read` method. The `Do While...Loop` statement will terminate when there is no more data to read. Lines 61–62 add the values stored in the database's `title` field to the `ListBox`. The `title` field values will continue to be added to the `ListBox` until there are no more `title` field values to read. Line 65 closes the connection to the database by invoking the `Close` method of class `OleDbConnection`.

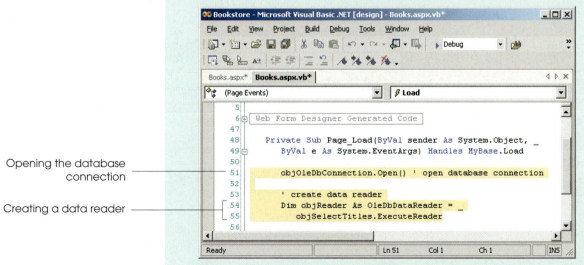

Opening the database
connection

Creating a data reader

Figure 31.6   Opening the database connection and creating a data reader.

(cont.)

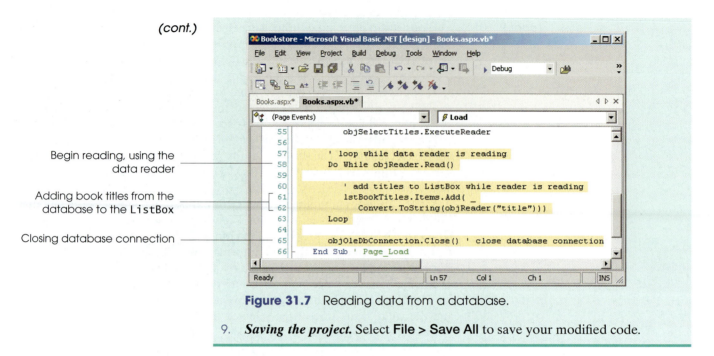

Begin reading, using the data reader

Adding book titles from the database to the `ListBox`

Closing database connection

Figure 31.7 Reading data from a database.

9. ***Saving the project.*** Select **File > Save All** to save your modified code.

Next, you will define the `btnInformation_Click` event handler. This event handler is invoked when the user clicks the **View Information** Button. The event handler determines the selected book and redirects the client browser to the Book-Information page. You create the event handler in the following box.

Defining the `Click` Event Handler for the `Books` Page

1. ***Creating the `Click` event handler.*** Switch to design mode. Double click the `btnInformation` Button control. The `btnInformation_Click` event handler should appear in the `Books.aspx.vb` file.

2. ***Adding code to the `Click` event handler.*** Add lines 73–83 of Fig. 31.8 to the event handler.

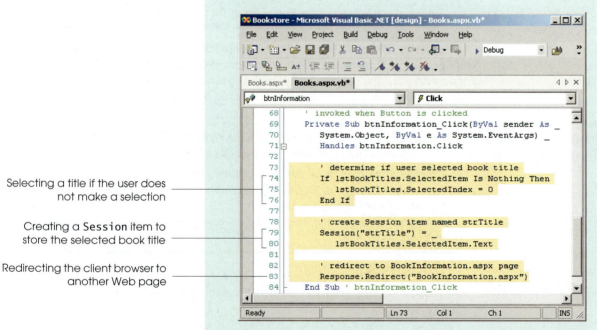

Selecting a title if the user does not make a selection

Creating a `Session` item to store the selected book title

Redirecting the client browser to another Web page

Figure 31.8 `btnInformation_Click` event handler definition.

(cont.)

Lines 74–76 determine if the user selected a book title. You use the List-Box's SelectedItem property to determine if a book has been selected. The **SelectedItem** property specifies the item that is selected from the ListBox. If the user does not select an item, then no value is specified in the SelectedItem property (which is what line 74 checks).

If a book title has not been selected, then the first title in the ListBox will be set as the default selection. This is accomplished by using the ListBox's SelectedIndex property. The **SelectedIndex** property specifies the index of the selected item. You set the first title in the ListBox as the default selection by setting this property to 0 (line 75), which is the index number of the first item.

Values are not maintained across different ASPX pages. This means that values stored in instance variables cannot be passed from page to page. However, ASP .NET provides **Session** items for sharing values among ASPX pages. Lines 79–80 allow information to be maintained across the **Bookstore** application's ASPX pages by adding a **key-value pair** to the Session object. A key-value pair associates a value with a corresponding name (key) which identifies the value. In this case, the key is the name strTitle, and the value is the title of the selected book, which is determined by lst-BookTitles.SelectedItem.Text. The storage of key-value pairs across Web pages is made possible by **session state**, which is ASP .NET's built-in support for tracking data. Session state enables the current user's information (including the book the user selected) to be maintained across a browser session.

When the user selects a book, the title of the selected book is set as the value of key strTitle. This information is added to the Session object so that it may be used in the BookInformation page. After the strTitle key has been provided with a value, the page redirects the client browser by calling Response.Redirect (line 83). The **Response** object is a predefined ASP .NET object that provides methods for responding to clients. **Redirect** is one of the Response object's methods, which is used to specify the Web page to which the client browser will be redirected.

3. **Saving the project.** Select **File > Save All** to save your modified code.

Before you begin to program the BookInformation.aspx.vb code-behind file, you need to place images of the book covers in the Bookstore directory. The Book-Information.aspx page will display the cover image of the selected book. You will learn how to place the images in the following box.

Adding Images to the Bookstore Directory

1. **Locating the images.** Locate the C:\Examples\Tutorial31\Images directory, which contains images of the book covers.

2. **Placing the images in the Bookstore directory.** Copy the three images csharphtp1.png, cpphtp4.png and vbnethtp2.png, and paste them into the Bookstore directory that is located in the wwwroot directory on your computer. These image files will be used when you program the BookInformation.aspx page.

SELF-REVIEW

1. The _____ class defines the basic functionality for an ASPX page.

a) Form
b) WebForm
c) Page
d) None of the above.

2. The Page class is located in namespace _____.

   a) `System.Web.UI`   b) `System.Data`

   c) `System.WebForm`   d) `System.OleDb`

Answers: 1) c. 2) a.

31.3 Coding the BookInformation Page's Code-Behind File

The next ASPX page in this application is `BookInformation.aspx`. This ASPX page displays information about the book the user selected. In the following box, you will add the code to the `Page_Load` event handler of the `BookInformation.aspx` page so that you may retrieve the requested book's information from the database.

Defining the Page_Load Event Handler for the BookInformation Page

1. ***Changing the class name.*** Double click `BookInformation.aspx` in the **Solution Explorer** window to view the `BookInformation.aspx` page. Select **View > Code** to view the code-behind file `BookInformation.aspx.vb`. Make sure that the class name is `BookInformation` (Fig. 31.9).

2. ***Importing a namespace.*** To use database-related objects, you will need to import the `System.Data.OleDb` namespace. Add line 1 of Fig. 31.10 before the `BookInformation` class definition.

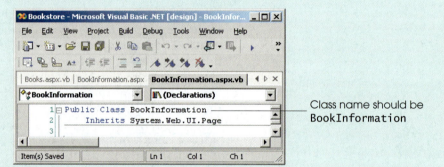

Class name should be `BookInformation`

Figure 31.9   Changing the name of the class.

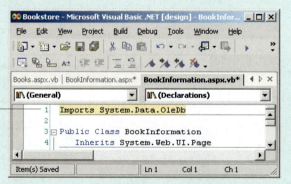

Importing namespace `System.Data.OleDb`

Figure 31.10   Importing the `System.Data.OleDb` namespace.

3. ***Setting a parameter value and opening the database connection.*** Add lines 54–61 of Fig. 31.11 to the `Page_Load` event handler of the `BookInformation.aspx` page. Line 55 sets the `Text` property of the `lblBookTitle` `Label` to the title of the selected book, using the `Session` item. Recall that, in the `Books.aspx` page, you stored the title of the selected book in the `Session` item with the key `strTitle`. Lines 58–59 set the `title` parameter of the `objSelectBookData` command object to the title of the selected book, which is stored in `Text` property of the `lblBookTitle` `Label`. Line 61 opens the connection to the database by invoking the `Open` method.

(cont.)

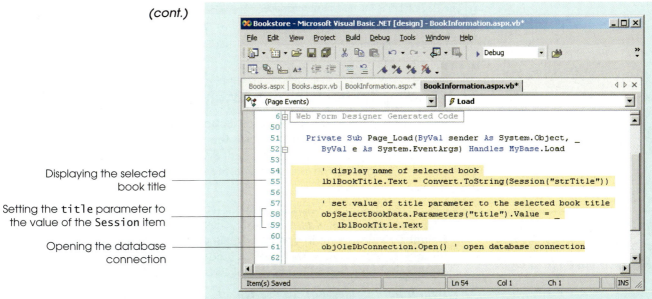

Displaying the selected book title

Setting the `title` parameter to the value of the `Session` item

Opening the database connection

Figure 31.11 `Page_Load` event handler modified to set a parameter value and open a database connection.

4. *Creating the data reader.* Add lines 63–67 of Fig. 31.12 to the `Page_Load` event handler. Lines 64–65 create the data reader (of type `OleDbDataReader`) by invoking the `ExecuteReader` method of the `objSelectBookData` command object. Line 67 invokes the data reader's `Read` method to start the data reader. Your query (specified using data command objects) from the previous tutorial will be executed, returning information about the user's selected book.

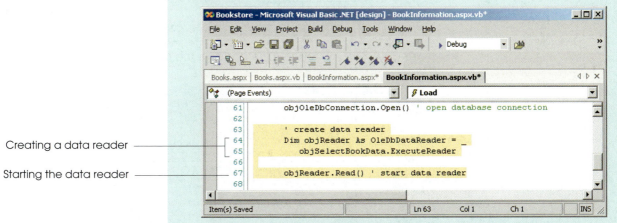

Creating a data reader

Starting the data reader

Figure 31.12 `Page_Load` event handler modified to create a data reader.

5. *Using the data reader.* Add lines 69–73 of Fig. 31.13 to the `Page_Load` event handler. Lines 70–73 retrieve data from the database. [*Note*: The `OleDbDataReader` can read, but not modify, information from the database.]

(cont.)

Set the `ImageURL` property

```
67      objReader.Read() ' start data reader
68
69          ' display authors of the selected book
70          lblAuthors.Text = Convert.ToString(objReader("authors"))
71
72          ' display converart for selected book
73          imgBook.ImageUrl = Convert.ToString(objReader("coverart"))
74
```

Figure 31.13 Displaying book authors and cover image.

Line 70 sets the `lblAuthors` Label's text to the authors of the selected book, specified by `objReader("authors")`. This line retrieves the value found in the `authors` field. Remember that the reader is retrieving the information specified by the SQL statement of the `objSelectBookData` data command object. The SQL statement specified only that the selected book and its book information should be retrieved from the database. Line 73 sets the `Image` control's `ImageUrl` property to the name of the selected book's cover image, which is specified by using the value of `objReader("coverart")`.

6. ***Displaying book information in the Table.*** Add lines 75–96 of Fig. 31.14 to the `Page_Load` event handler.

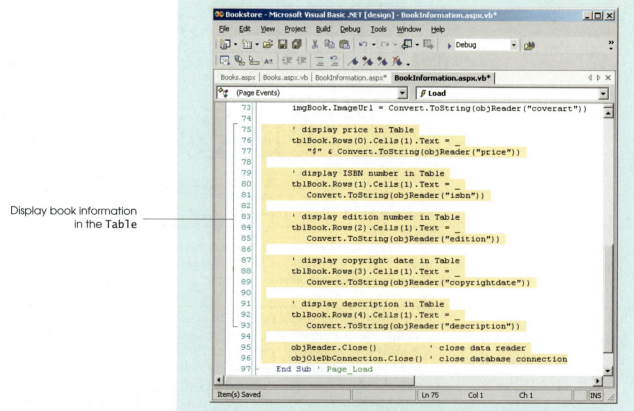

Display book information in the `Table`

```
73      imgBook.ImageUrl = Convert.ToString(objReader("coverart"))
74
75          ' display price in Table
76          tblBook.Rows(0).Cells(1).Text = _
77              "$" & Convert.ToString(objReader("price"))
78
79          ' display ISBN number in Table
80          tblBook.Rows(1).Cells(1).Text = _
81              Convert.ToString(objReader("isbn"))
82
83          ' display edition number in Table
84          tblBook.Rows(2).Cells(1).Text = _
85              Convert.ToString(objReader("edition"))
86
87          ' display copyright date in Table
88          tblBook.Rows(3).Cells(1).Text = _
89              Convert.ToString(objReader("copyrightdate"))
90
91          ' display description in Table
92          tblBook.Rows(4).Cells(1).Text = _
93              Convert.ToString(objReader("description"))
94
95      objReader.Close()            ' close data reader
96      objOleDbConnection.Close() ' close database connection
97      End Sub ' Page_Load
```

Figure 31.14 Data reader used to retrieve read-only data.

(cont.)

Lines 75–93 display the book information in the `Table` (`tblBook`). Recall that you created a table with five rows that contain two cells each. The second cell in the first row is given the value of the selected book's price. This task is accomplished by using the `Rows` and `Cells` properties. For example, lines 76–77 specify the row number by using property `Rows` of the `Table` control and specifying `0` for the first row. The `Cells` property of `Rows` is then used to specify the second cell in the row by using value `1`. Next, the `Text` property of `Cells` is used to set the text that will display in the second cell of the first row in the `Table`. The `Text` property is assigned the value of the data read by the data reader (`objReader("price")`), which is converted to a `String`. Recall that you need to convert to this to a `String` because the data reader returns items of type `Object`. The rest of the book's information is displayed in the same manner. The second cell in the second row contains the value of the ISBN number. The second cell in the third row displays the edition number. The fourth row contains the copyright date and the fifth row contains the selected book's description.

Line 95 closes the data reader and line 96 closes the database connection by calling the `Close` method. When this application is run, the information is displayed in the format shown in Fig. 31.15.

7. **Saving the project.** Select **File > Save All** to save your modified code.

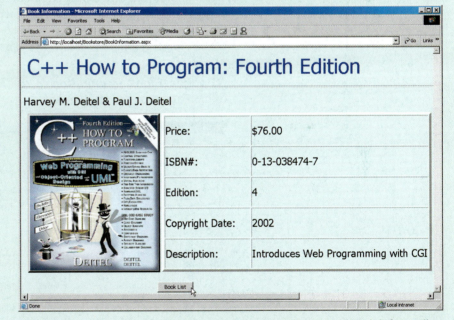

Figure 31.15 `BookInformation.aspx` page displaying book information.

The final event handler you define in the `BookInformation.aspx` page is the `btnBookList_Click` event handler. This event handler allows the user to return to the list of available books. You create this event handler in the following box.

Defining the btnBookList_Click Event Handler for the BookInformation Page

1. **Creating the btnBookList_Click event handler.** Now you are ready to define the event handler for the `btnBookList` `Button`. Select the BookInformation.aspx page, and double click the **Book List** `Button`. This step creates the `btnBookList_Click` event handler. This `Button` is used to redirect the client browser to the `Books.aspx` page.

2. **Adding code to the event handler.** Add lines 104–105 of Fig. 31.16 to the `btnBookList_Click` event handler. Line 105 redirects the user to the `Books.aspx` page by calling `Response.Redirect`.

(cont.)

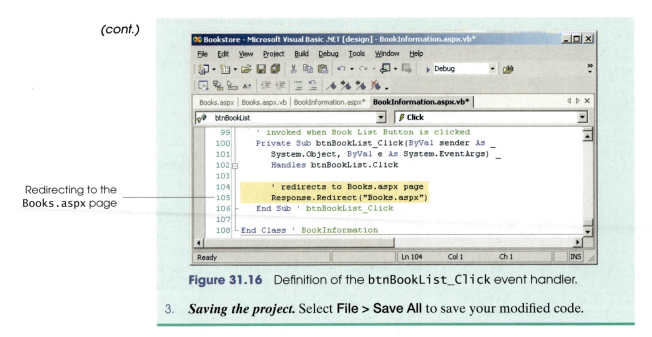

Redirecting to the
Books.aspx page

Figure 31.16 Definition of the `btnBookList_Click` event handler.

3. **Saving the project.** Select **File > Save All** to save your modified code.

Now that you have completed the **Bookstore** application, you will test it to ensure that it is functioning properly in the following box.

Testing Your Completed Bookstore Application

1. **Starting IIS.** Open the **Internet Information Services** dialog, select **Default Web Site** and click the Start Item `Button` to start IIS.

2. **Running the application.** Select **Debug > Start** to run your application. Select a book title from the `ListBox`, and click the **View Information** `Button`. Notice that this application performs the same functions as the completed **Bookstore** application that you test-drove in Tutorial 28.

3. **Closing the application.** Close your running application by clicking the browser's close box.

4. **Stopping IIS.** Open the **Internet Information Services** dialog, select **Default Web Site** and click the stop `Button` to stop IIS.

5. **Closing the IDE.** Close Visual Studio .NET by clicking its close box.

Figures 31.17 and 31.18 display the complete code listing for the `Books.aspx` and `BookInformation.aspx` pages of the **Bookstore** application, respectively. [*Note*: The comment, "control declarations," represents the declaration statements for all controls for the ASPX page.]

```
1   Imports System.Data.OleDb
2
3   Public Class Books
4       Inherits System.Web.UI.Page
5
6       ' Web Form Designer Generated Code
7
8       Private Sub Page_Load(ByVal sender As System.Object, _
9           ByVal e As System.EventArgs) Handles MyBase.Load
10
11          objOleDbConnection.Open() ' open database connection
12
```

Figure 31.17 `Books.aspx` page code. (Part 1 of 2.)

```
13          ' create data reader
14          Dim objReader As OleDbDataReader = _
15             objSelectTitles.ExecuteReader
16
17          ' perform loop while data reader is reading
18          Do While objReader.Read()
19
20             ' add titles to ListBox while reader is reading
21             lstBookTitles.Items.Add( _
22                Convert.ToString(objReader("title")))
23          Loop
24
25          objOleDbConnection.Close() ' close database connection
26       End Sub  ' Page_Load
27
28       ' invoked when Button is clicked
29       Private Sub btnInformation_Click(ByVal sender As _
30          System.Object, ByVal e As System.EventArgs) _
31          Handles btnInformation.Click
32
33          ' determine if user selected book title
34          If lstBookTitles.SelectedItem Is Nothing Then
35             lstBookTitles.SelectedIndex = 0
36          End If
37
38          ' create Session item named strTitle
39          Session("strTitle") = _
40             lstBookTitles.SelectedItem.Text
41
42          ' redirect to BookInformation.aspx page
43          Response.Redirect("BookInformation.aspx")
44       End Sub ' btnInformation_Click
45
46    End Class ' Books
```

Determining if user made selection from ListBox — (lines 34–36)

Creating a Session item — (lines 39–40)

Redirecting client browsers to BookInformation.aspx page — (line 43)

Figure 31.17 Books.aspx page code. (Part 2 of 2.)

```
1     Imports System.Data.OleDb
2
3     Public Class BookInformation
4        Inherits System.Web.UI.Page
5
6        ' Web Form Designer Generated Code
7
8        Private Sub Page_Load(ByVal sender As System.Object, _
9           ByVal e As System.EventArgs) Handles MyBase.Load
10
11          ' display name of selected book
12          lblBookTitle.Text = Convert.ToString(Session("strTitle"))
13
14          ' set value of title parameter to the selected book title
15          objSelectBookData.Parameters("title").Value = _
16             lblBookTitle.Text
17
18          objOleDbConnection.Open() ' open database connection
19
```

Using a Session item to set parameter value — (lines 15–16)

Figure 31.18 BookInformation.aspx page code. (Part 1 of 2.)

```
20          ' create data reader
21          Dim objReader As OleDbDataReader = _
22             objSelectBookData.ExecuteReader
23
24          objReader.Read() ' start data reader
25
26          ' display authors of the selected book
27          lblAuthors.Text = Convert.ToString(objReader("authors"))
28
29          ' display coverart for selected book
30          imgBook.ImageUrl = Convert.ToString(objReader("coverart"))
31
32          ' display price in Table
33          tblBook.Rows(0).Cells(1).Text = _
34             "$" & Convert.ToString(objReader("price"))
35
36          ' display ISBN number in Table
37          tblBook.Rows(1).Cells(1).Text = _
38             Convert.ToString(objReader("isbn"))
39
40          ' display edition number in Table
41          tblBook.Rows(2).Cells(1).Text = _
42             Convert.ToString(objReader("edition"))
43
44          ' display copyright date in Table
45          tblBook.Rows(3).Cells(1).Text = _
46             Convert.ToString(objReader("copyrightDate"))
47
48          ' display description in Table
49          tblBook.Rows(4).Cells(1).Text = _
50             Convert.ToString(objReader("description"))
51
52          objReader.Close()              ' close data reader
53          objOleDbConnection.Close() ' close database connection
54       End Sub ' Page_Load
55
56       ' invoked when Book List Button is clicked
57       Private Sub btnBookList_Click(ByVal sender As _
58          System.Object, ByVal e As System.EventArgs) _
59          Handles btnBookList.Click
60
61          ' redirects to Books.aspx page
62          Response.Redirect("Books.aspx")
63       End Sub ' btnBookList_Click
64
65    End Class ' BookInformation
```

Figure 31.18 BookInformation.aspx page code. (Part 2 of 2.)

1. A(n) _____ reads data from a database.

    a) OleDbDataReader   b) OleDbConnection

    c) Query Builder   d) DataSet

2. To specify the third cell in the second row of a Table control called tableName, type

_____.

    a) tableName.Rows(2).Cells(3)   b) tableName.Rows(1).Cells(2)

    c) tableName.Cells(3).Rows(2)   d) tableName.Cells(2).Rows(1)

Answers: 1) a. 2) b.

31.4 Internet and Web Resources

Please take a moment to visit each of these sites briefly. To save typing time, use the hot links on the enclosed CD or at www.deitel.com.

www.asp.net
This Microsoft site overviews ASP .NET and provides ASP .NET tutorials. This site also includes the IBuySpy e-commerce storefront example that uses ASP .NET and links to Web sites where users can purchase books.

www.asp101.com/aspplus
This site overviews ASP .NET and includes articles, code examples and links to ASP .NET resources.

www.411asp.net
This resource site provides users with ASP .NET tutorials and code samples. The community pages allow users to ask questions, answer questions and post messages.

www.aspfree.com
This site provides free ASP .NET demos and source code. The site also provides a list of articles on various topics and a frequently asked questions (FAQs) page.

31.5 Wrap-Up

In this tutorial, you programmed the middle tier of your three-tier **Bookstore** application. By defining methods and event handlers, you specified the actions that execute when the user interacts with ASPX pages. You learned about Session objects and how they are used to maintain values across ASPX pages. You also learned about the Response.Redirect method, which allows you to redirect the client browser to other ASPX pages.

After learning about Sessions and Response.Redirect, you used them in the **Bookstore** application. You began with the first ASPX page of the application, Books.aspx. This page retrieved the book titles from the database and displayed them in a ListBox control when the ASPX page was loaded. You did this by defining the Page_Load event handler. You then defined the actions that would occur when the user clicks the **View Information** Button. In the Click event handler, you created a Session item to store the title of the book selected by the user. You also used the Response.Redirect method in the Click event handler to direct users from the Books.aspx page to the BookInformation.aspx page.

You then defined the BookInformation.aspx page. You defined event handler Page_Load to display the information about the selected book. Recall that you used the value stored in the Session item to determine the book title selected by the user. You then created a data reader to retrieve the selected book's information and displayed it in the Table control. Through programming, you were able to control the flow of data from the information tier to the client tier, completing the three-tier **Bookstore** application. You also learned about ASP .NET resources available on the Web.

In the next tutorial, you will learn how to handle exceptions, which are indications of a problem that occurs during an application's execution. You will use exception handling to verify user input. Throughout the text, you have been using Val to perform this functionality. In the next tutorial, you will learn are more sophisticated technique for handling invalid user input.

SKILLS SUMMARY

Accessing the Code-Behind File
- Click the Show All Files Button in the **Solution Explorer** window.
- Click the plus box next to the desired ASPX page to display the corresponding code-behind file name.
- Double click the code-behind file name to view the code-behind file.

Creating and Using a Session Item

■ Type Session("*nameOfKey*"), where *nameOfKey* represents the key in a key-value pair. Assign this item a value in an assignment statement.

■ Use Session("*nameOfKey*") to retrieve the item's value.

Redirecting the Client Browser to Another Web Page

■ Type Redirect.Response("*URLOfPage*"), where *URLOfPage* represents the URL of the page to which the client browser redirects.

KEY TERMS

code-behind file—Visual Basic .NET file that contains a class which provides an ASPX page's functionality.

key-value pair—Associates a value with a corresponding key, which is used to identify the value.

Page class—Defines the basic functionality for an ASPX page.

Page_Load—An event handler that executes any processing necessary to display a Web page.

Response.Redirect method—Redirects the client browser to another Web page.

SelectedIndex property of ListBox—Returns the index of the selected item.

SelectedItem property of ListBox—Returns the value of the selected item.

Session state—ASP .NET's built-in support for tracking data.

Session object—Maintained across several Web pages containing a collection of items (key-value pairs). This variable is specific to each user.

CONTROLS, EVENTS, PROPERTIES & METHODS

ASPX page   Page on which controls are dropped to design the GUI.

■ *Event*

Load—Raised when the ASPX page is created.

■ *Property*

bgColor—Specifies the Web Form's background color.

Image   Image   This control displays an image on the ASPX page.

■ *In action*

■ *Properties*

BorderStyle—Specifies the appearance of the Image's border.

BorderWidth—Specifies the width of the Image's border.

Height—Specifies the height of the Image control.

ID—Specifies the name used to access the Image control programmatically. The name should be prefixed with img.

ImageUrl—Specifies the location of the image file.

Width—Specifies the width of the Image control.

ListBox   ListBox   This control allows the user to view and select from multiple items in a list.

■ *In action*

■ *Properties*

Height—Specifies the height of the ListBox.

ID—Specifies the name used to access the ListBox control programmatically. The name should be prefixed with lst.

SelectedIndex—Returns the index of the selected item in the ListBox.

SelectedItem—Returns the value of the selected item in the ListBox.

Width—Specifies the width of the ListBox.

Response   This class provides methods for responding to clients.

■ *Method*

Redirect—Redirects the client browser to the specified location.

MULTIPLE-CHOICE QUESTIONS

31.1 The Page_Load event handler _____.

   a) redirects the client browser to different Web pages

   b) defines the functionality when a Button is clicked

   c) executes any processing necessary to display a Web page

   d) defines the functionality when a Web control is selected

31.2 The Response.Redirect method _____.

   a) refreshes the current Web page

   b) sends the client browser to a specified Web page

   c) responds to user input

   d) responds to the click of a Button

31.3 Session items are used in the **Bookstore** application because _____.

   a) variables in ASP .NET Web applications must be created as Session items

   b) values need to be shared among Web pages

   c) Session items are simpler to create than instance variables

   d) Both a and b.

31.4 Session state is used for _____ in ASP .NET.

   a) tracking user-specific data   b) running an application

   c) using a database   d) None of the above.

31.5 The file extension for an ASPX code-behind file is _____.

   a) .asp   b) .aspx

   c) .aspx.vb   d) .code

31.6 The Response object is a predefined ASP .NET object that _____.

   a) connects to a database

   b) retrieves information from a database

   c) creates Web controls

   d) provides methods for responding to client requests

31.7 The Response.Redirect method takes a(n) _____ as an argument.
 a) URL
 b) Integer value
 c) Boolean value
 d) OleDbConnection object

31.8 The _____ property specifies the image that an Image control displays.
 a) ImageGIF
 b) ImageURL
 c) Image
 d) Display

31.9 The Visual Basic .NET file that contains the ASPX page's corresponding class is called the _____.
 a) ASPX file
 b) code-behind file
 c) class file
 d) None of the above.

31.10 Information can be maintained across Web pages by adding a _____ to the Session object.
 a) key-value pair
 b) number
 c) database connection object
 d) None of the above.

EXERCISES

31.11 (*Phone Book Application: Functionality*) Define the middle tier for the **Phone Book** application.

 a) *Opening the application.* Open the **Phone Book** application that you created in Tutorial 29 and continued to develop in Tutorial 30.

 b) *Importing System.Data.OleDb in PhoneBook.aspx.vb.* Import namespace System.Data.OleDb in PhoneBook.aspx.vb.

 c) *Defining the Page_Load event handler of PhoneBook.aspx page.* Use the Open method to open the connection to the database. Create a data reader to read the information specified by the data command object.

 d) *Populating the DropDownList with names.* Add a Do While...Loop to Phone-Book.aspx's Page_Load method. This loop should add to the DropDownList each person's name read by the data reader.

 e) *Closing the reader and connection.* Close the data reader and the connection to the database by invoking their Close methods.

 f) *Creating the Get Number Button's Click event handler for the PhoneBook.aspx page.* Double click the **Get Number** Button to create the Click event's event handler.

 g) *Creating a Session item.* In the Click event handler, create a Session item to store the selected name.

 h) *Redirecting to the PhoneNumber.aspx page.* In the Click event handler, use the Response.Redirect method to redirect the client browser to the PhoneNumber.aspx page.

 i) *Importing System.Data.OleDb in PhoneNumber.aspx.vb.* Import namespace System.Data.OleDb in PhoneNumber.aspx.vb.

 j) *Defining the Page_Load event handler for the PhoneNumber.aspx page.* Use the Open method to open the connection to the database. Access the Session item to retrieve the selected name. Specify this name as the parameter value for the OleDb-Command object. Create a data reader to read the information specified by the data command object.

 k) *Displaying the selected name and phone number.* In the Page_Load event handler, read the desired phone number from the data reader. Display the selected name and corresponding phone number in the lblNumbers Label.

 l) *Closing the reader and connection.* Close the data reader and the connection to the database by invoking their Close methods.

 m) *Creating the Phone Book Button's Click event handler for the PhoneNumber.aspx page.* Double click the **Phone Book** Button to create the Click event's event handler.

n) *Redirecting to the PhoneBook.aspx page.* In the Click event handler, use the Response.Redirect method to redirect the client browser to the PhoneBook.aspx page.

o) *Running the application.* Select **Debug > Start** to run your application. Select a user and click the **Get Number** Button. Click the **Phone Book** Button to return to the PhoneBook.aspx page.

p) *Closing the application.* Close your running application by clicking its close box.

q) *Closing the IDE.* Close Visual Studio .NET by clicking its close box.

31.12 (*US State Facts Application: Functionality*) Define the middle tier for the **US State Facts** application.

a) *Opening the application.* Open the **USStateFacts** application that you created in Tutorial 29 and continued to develop in Tutorial 30.

b) *Copying the FlagImages directory to your project directory.* Copy the directory C:\Examples\Tutorial31\Exercises\Images\FlagImages to the USStateFacts directory.

c) *Importing System.Data.OleDb in States.aspx.vb.* Import namespace System.Data.OleDb in States.aspx.vb before the class definition.

d) *Defining the Page_Load event handler for the States.aspx page.* Use the Open method to open the connection to the database. Create a data reader to read the information specified by the data command object.

e) *Populating the ListBox with state names in the States.aspx page.* Add a Do While...Loop to States.aspx's Page_Load method. This loop should add to the ListBox the name of each state read by the data reader.

f) *Creating a Button's Click event handler for the States.aspx page.* Double click the **Review Facts** Button to create the Click event's event handler.

g) *Creating a Session item.* Create a Session item in the Click event handler and assign it to the state name that the user selects from the ListBox.

h) *Redirecting to the StateFacts.aspx page.* In the Click event handler, use the Redirect.Response method to redirect the client browser to the StateFacts.aspx page.

i) *Importing System.Data.OleDb in StateFacts.aspx.vb.* Import namespace System.Data.OleDb in StateFacts.aspx.vb.

j) *Defining the Page_Load event handler of StateFacts.aspx page.* Use the Open method to open the connection to the database. Access the Session object to retrieve the selected state name. Specify this name as a parameter value for the OleDbCommand object. Create a data reader to read the information specified by the data command object.

k) *Displaying the state facts in the Table.* In the Page_Load event handler, use the data reader to retrieve the desired state's facts. Display the selected state's name in the lblStateName Label. Set the ImageURL property of the Image control to the location of the selected state's flag image. Display the name of the state capital, flower, tree and bird in the Table on the StateFacts.aspx page.

l) *Closing the connection.* Close the connection to the database by invoking the Close method.

m) *Creating the State List Button's Click event handler for the StateFacts.aspx page.* Double click the **State List** Button to create the Click event handler.

n) *Redirecting to the States.aspx page.* In the Click event handler use the Redirect.Response method to redirect the client browser to the States.aspx page.

o) *Running the application.* Select **Debug > Start** to run your application. Select a state and click the **Review Facts** Button. Click the **State List** Button to return to the States.aspx page.

p) *Closing the application.* Close your running application by clicking its close box.

q) *Closing the IDE.* Close Visual Studio .NET by clicking its close box.

31.13 (*Road Sign Review Application: Functionality*) Define the middle tier for the **Road Sign Review** application.

a) *Opening the application.* Open the **RoadSignReview** application that you created in Tutorial 29 and continued to develop in Tutorial 30.

b) *Copying the SignImages directory to your project directory.* Copy the directory C:\Examples\Tutorial31\Exercises\Images\SignImages to the RoadSignReview directory.

c) *Importing System.Data.OleDb and System.Web.UI.WebControls to RoadSigns.aspx.vb.* Import the System.Data.OleDb and System.Web.UI.WebControls namespaces to RoadSigns.aspx.vb. You need to import System.Web.UI.WebControls because you will be creating a Web control programmatically in this exercise.

d) *Defining the Page_Load event handler for the RoadSigns.aspx page.* Use the Open method to open the connection to the database. Create a data reader to read the information specified by the data command object.

e) *Populating the Table with sign images in the RoadSigns.aspx page.* Add a Do While...Loop to RoadSigns.aspx's Page_Load method. This loop should display an image of the sign and display the sign name in the ToolTip property. This property specifies the text that displays in a tooltip box when the mouse hovers over the Image. The sign image and name should be retrieved using the data reader. To display an Image in a cell of the Table, you need to create an Image control, specify a cell and use the cell's Controls.Add method to add an image to that cell. For example, to create an Image control programmatically, type Dim imgImageName As Image = New Image(). You then need to set the ImageURL property to the location of the desired image. To display an Image control in the first cell of the first row, you would write the line Table.Rows(0).Cells(0).Controls.Add(imgImageName). Also, if you wish to specify text for a tooltip, you must set the cell's ToolTip property—for example, Table.Rows(0).Cells(0).ToolTip = "This is a tooltip".

f) *Closing the reader and connection.* Close the data reader and the connection to the database by invoking their Close methods.

g) *Creating the Register Button's Click event handler for RoadSigns.aspx.* Double click the **Register** Button of RoadSigns.aspx to create the Click event handler.

h) *Creating Session item.* Create two Session items in the Click event handler, and set the first one equal to the user input for the **Name:** TextBox. The second Session item should equal the user input for the **Phone Number:** TextBox.

i) *Redirecting to the RoadTestRegistered.aspx page.* In the Click event handler, use the Redirect.Response method to redirect the client browser to the RoadTestRegistered.aspx page.

j) *Defining the Page_Load method of RoadTestRegistered.aspx page.* Use the Session items to display a confirmation to the user about the user's registration information. Display the confirmation using Label lblConfirmation. Display the user's name, and display text which states that the user will be contacted shortly at the phone number provided. This information should be displayed in a Label.

k) *Running the application.* Select **Debug > Start** to run your application. Enter a name and a phone number in the TextBoxes and click the **Register** Button.

l) *Closing the application.* Close your running application by clicking its close box.

m) *Closing the IDE.* Close Visual Studio .NET by clicking its close box.

Enhanced Car Payment Calculator Application

Introducing Exception Handling

In this tutorial, you will learn about **exception handling**. An **exception** is an indication of a problem that occurs during an application's execution. The name "exception" comes from the fact that, although a problem can occur, the problem occurs infrequently—if the "rule" is that a statement normally executes correctly, then the "exception to the rule" is that a problem occurs. Exception handling enables you to create applications that can resolve (or handle) exceptions during application execution. In many cases, handling an exception allows an application to continue executing as if no problem had been encountered.

This tutorial begins with a test-drive of the **Enhanced Car Payment Calculator** application, then overviews exception handling concepts and demonstrates basic exception handling techniques. You will learn the specifics of exception handling with the Try, Catch and Finally blocks and the architecture of exception classes.

32.1 Test-Driving the Enhanced Car Payment Calculator Application

In this tutorial, you will enhance the **Car Payment Calculator** application from Tutorial 9 by adding exception handling statements. This application must meet the following requirements:

> **Application Requirements**
>
> *A bank wishes to only accept valid data from users on their car loans. Although the application you developed in Tutorial 9 calculates a result when incorrect data is entered, this result does not correctly represent the user's input. Alter the **Car Payment Calculator** application to allow users to enter only `Integers` in the **Price:** TextBox and **Down payment:** TextBox. Similarly, users should be allowed to enter only `Double` values in the **Annual interest rate:** TextBox. If the user enters anything besides an `Integer` for the price or down payment, or a `Double` for the interest rate, a message dialog should be displayed instructing the user to input proper data. The interest rate should be entered such that an input of 5 is equal to 5%.*

The original **Car Payment Calculator** application used the Val function to set the value of the variables used in the application. This ensured that the payment calculation was always performed using numeric values. However, as discussed in Tutorial 5, the value returned by Val is not always the value the user intended to input. For example, if the user accidently inputs a character in the middle of the down payment, Val will return the numeric value up until it reaches the character. Any number after the character will be lost, and the calculation will be incorrect. Also, Val does not prevent the user from entering a Double value for the price or down payment, for which Integer values are expected. You will add exception handling to the **Car Payment Calculator** application so that when invalid input is entered, the user will be asked to enter valid input and the application will not calculate monthly payments. If the user provides valid input, the application should calculate the monthly payments for a car when financed for 24, 36, 48 and 60 months. Users input the car price, the down payment and the annual interest rate. You begin by test-driving the completed application. Then, you will learn the additional Visual Basic .NET technologies that you will need to create your own version of this application.

Test-Driving the Enhanced Car Payment Calculator Application

1. **Opening the completed application.** Open the directory C:\Examples\ Tutorial32\CompletedApplication\EnhancedCarPaymentCalculator to locate the **Car Payment Calculator** application. Double click Enhanced-CarPaymentCalculator.sln to open the application in Visual Studio .NET.

2. **Running the Enhanced Car Payment Calculator application.** Select **Debug > Start** to run the application (Fig. 32.1).

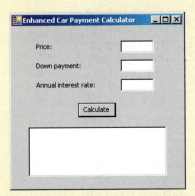

Figure 32.1 Running the completed **Enhanced Car Payment Calculator** application.

3. **Entering an invalid value in the Down payment: TextBox.** Enter 16900 in the **Price:** TextBox, 6000.50 in the **Down payment:** TextBox and 7.5 in the **Annual interest rate:** TextBox (Fig. 32.2).

4. **Attempting to calculate the monthly payment amounts.** Click the **Calculate** Button to attempt to calculate the monthly payment. Notice that an error message dialog (Fig. 32.3) appears.

5. **Entering non-numeric data in the Down payment: TextBox.** Change the value 6000.50 in the **Down payment:** TextBox to 600p (Fig. 32.4). Click the **Calculate** Button to attempt to display the monthly payment in the Text-Box. The message dialog shown in Fig. 32.3 appears again (a non-numeric character like p cannot be entered when an Integer is expected).

(cont.)

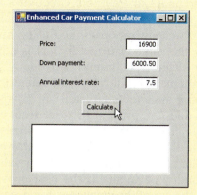

Figure 32.2 Entering an invalid value in the **Down payment:** TextBox.

Displaying a message when an
exception is thrown ⎯⎯⎯⎯⎯⎯

Figure 32.3 Message dialog displayed when incorrect input is entered.

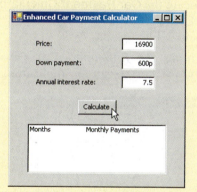

Figure 32.4 Entering non-numeric data in the **Down Payment:** TextBox.

6. ***Entering non-numeric data in the Annual interest rate: TextBox.*** Change
the value 600p in the **Down payment:** TextBox to 6000. Enter 7.5% in the
Annual interest rate: TextBox (Fig. 32.5). Click the **Calculate** Button to
attempt to calculate the monthly payment. The message dialog shown in
Fig. 32.3 appears again (7.5 is the correct input; entering the % character is
incorrect).

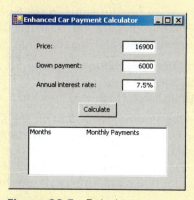

Figure 32.5 Entering non-numeric data in the **Annual interest rate:**
TextBox.

(cont.)   7. ***Correcting the input.*** Change the value 7.5% in the **Annual interest rate:** TextBox to 7.5, and click the **Calculate** Button to display the monthly payments (Fig. 32.6).

Results displayed only when valid input is entered

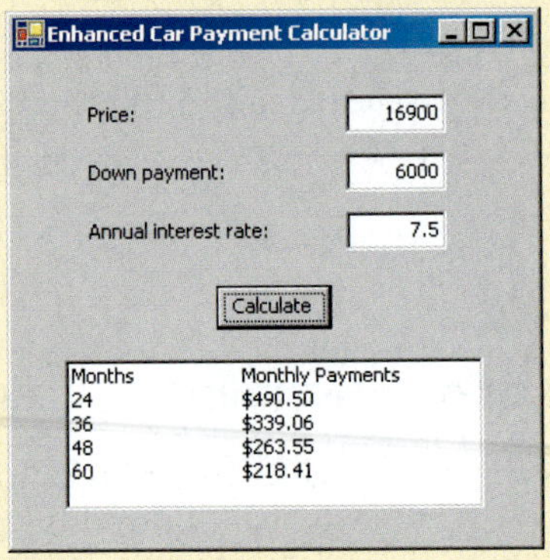

Figure 32.6 Displaying monthly payments after input is corrected.

8. ***Closing the application.*** Close your running application by clicking its close box.

9. ***Closing the IDE.*** Close Visual Studio .NET by clicking its close box.

32.2 Introduction to Exception Handling

Application logic frequently tests conditions that determine how application execution should proceed. Consider the following pseudocode:

Perform a task

If the preceding task did not execute correctly
    Perform error processing

Perform the next task

If the preceding task did not execute correctly
    Perform error processing

...

In this pseudocode, you begin by performing a task. Then, you test whether the task executed correctly. If not, you perform error processing. Otherwise, you continue with the next task. Although this form of error checking works, intermixing application logic with error-handling logic can make the application difficult to read, modify, maintain and debug—especially in large applications. In fact, if potential problems occur infrequently, intermixing application and error-handling logic can degrade an application's performance, because the application must explicitly test for errors after each task to determine whether the next task can be performed.

Exception handling enables you to remove error-handling code from the code that implements your application's logic, which improves application clarity and enhances modifiability. You can decide to handle only the exceptions you choose—all exceptions, all exceptions of a certain type or all exceptions in a group of related types. Such flexibility reduces the likelihood that errors will be overlooked, thereby making an application more robust.

A method **throws an exception** if a problem occurs during the method execution but the method is unable to correct the problem. There is no guarantee that there will be an **exception handler**—code that executes when the application detects an exception—to process that kind of exception. If there is, the exception handler catches and handles the exception. An **uncaught exception**—an exception that does not have an exception handler—might cause application execution to terminate.

1. A(n) _____ executes when the application detects an exception.

   a) exception code
   b) exception processor
   c) exception handler
   d) None of the above.

2. A method will _____ an exception if a problem occurs during the method execution but the method is unable to correct the problem.

   a) throw
   b) catch
   c) return
   d) None of the above.

Answers: 1) c. 2) a.

32.3 Exception Handling in Visual Basic .NET

Visual Basic .NET provides **Try blocks** to enable exception handling. A Try block consists of the Try keyword followed by a block of code in which exceptions might occur. The purpose of the Try block is to contain statements that might cause exceptions and statements that should not execute if an exception occurs.

At least one Catch block (also called an exception handler) or a Finally block must appear after the Try block, immediately before the **End Try** keywords. Each **Catch block** specifies a parameter that identifies the type of exception the exception handler can process. The parameter enables the Catch block to interact with the caught exception object. A Catch block that does not specify a parameter can catch all exception types. A parameterless Catch block should be placed after all other Catch blocks. After the last Catch block, an optional **Finally block** provides code that always executes, whether or not an exception occurs.

If an exception occurs in a Try block, the Try block terminates immediately. As with any other block of code, when a Try block terminates, local variables declared in the block go out of scope. Next, the application searches for the first Catch block (immediately following the Try block) that can process the type of exception that occurred. The application locates the matching Catch by comparing the thrown exception's type with each Catch block's exception-parameter type. A match occurs if the type of the exception matches the Catch block's parameter type. When a match occurs, the code associated with the matching Catch block executes. When a Catch block finishes processing, local variables declared within the Catch block (as well as the Catch's parameter) go out of scope. Any remaining Catch blocks that correspond to the Try block are ignored, and execution resumes at the first line of code after the End Try keywords if there is no Finally block. Otherwise, execution resumes at the Finally block.

If there is no Catch block that matches the exception thrown in the corresponding Try block, the execution resumes at the corresponding Finally block (if it exists). After the Finally block executes, the exception is passed to the method that called the current method, which then attempts to handle the exception. If the calling method does not handle the exception, the exception is again passed to the previous method in the call chain. If the exception goes unhandled, Visual Basic .NET will display a dialog providing the user with information about the exception. The user can then choose to exit or continue running the application, although the application may not execute correctly due to the exception.

If no exceptions occur in a Try block, the application ignores the Catch block(s) for that Try block. Application execution resumes with the next statement after the End Try keywords if there is no Finally block. Otherwise, execution resumes at the Finally block. A Finally block (if one is present) will execute whether or not an exception is thrown in the corresponding Try block or any of its corresponding Catch blocks.

It is possible that a Catch block might decide that either it cannot process that exception or it can only partially process the exception. In such cases, the exception handler can defer the handling (or perhaps a portion of it) to another Catch block. The handler achieves this by **rethrowing the exception** using the **Throw** statement

Throw *exceptionReference*;

where *exceptionReference* is the parameter for the exception in the Catch block. When a rethrow occurs, the next enclosing Try block (if any), which is normally in the calling method, detects the rethrown exception and attempts to catch it.

SELF-REVIEW

1. The _____ (if there is one) is always executed regardless of whether an exception occurs.

   a) Catch block
   b) Finally block
   c) both Catch and Finally blocks
   d) None of the above.

2. If no exceptions occur in a Try block, the application ignores the _____ for that block.

   a) Finally block
   b) Return statement
   c) Catch block(s)
   d) None of the above.

Answers: 1) b. 2) c.

32.4 Constructing the Enhanced Car Payment Calculator Application

Now that you have been introduced to exception handling, you will construct your **Enhanced Car Payment Calculator** application. The following pseudocode describes the basic operation of the **Enhanced Car Payment Calculator** application:

```
When the user clicks the Calculate Button:
    Clear the ListBox of any previous text

    Try
        Get the car price from the Price: TextBox
        Get the down payment from the Down payment: TextBox
        Get the annual interest rate from the Annual interest rate: TextBox
        Calculate the loan amount (price minus down payment)
        Calculate the monthly interest rate (annual interest rate divided by 1200)
        Calculate and display the monthly payments for 2, 3, 4 and 5 years
    Catch
        Display the error message dialog
```

Now that you have test-driven the **Enhanced Car Payment Calculator** application and studied its pseudocode representation, you will use an ACE table to help you convert the pseudocode to Visual Basic .NET. Figure 32.7 lists the actions, controls and events that will help you complete your own version of this application.

Action/Control/Event (ACE) Table for the *Enhanced Car Payment Calculator Application*

Action	Control/Class/Object	Event
Label all the application's components	lblStickerPrice, lblDownPayment, lblInterest	Application is run
	btnCalculate	Click
Try Clear the ListBox of any previous text	lstPayments	
Get the car price from the Price: TextBox	txtStickerPrice	
Get the down payment from the Down payment: TextBox	txtDownPayment	
Get the annual interest rate from the Annual interest rate: TextBox	txtInterest	
Calculate the loan amount		
Calculate the monthly interest rate		
Calculate and display the monthly payments	lstPayments	
Catch Display the error message dialog	MessageBox	

Figure 32.7 Enhanced **Car Payment Calculator** application ACE table.

Now that you've analyzed the **Enhanced Car Payment Calculator** application's components, you will learn how to place exception handling in your application's code.

Handling the Format Exception

1. ***Copying the template to your working directory.*** Copy the C:\Examples\ Tutorial32\TemplateApplication\EnhancedCarPaymentCalculator directory to your C:\SimplyVB directory.

2. ***Opening the Enhanced Car Payment Calculator application's template file.*** Double click EnhancedCarPaymentCalculator.sln in the Enhanced-CarPaymentCalculator directory to open the application in Visual Studio .NET.

3. ***Studying the code.*** View lines 163–165 of Fig. 32.8. Lines 163–164 read the Integer values from the **Down payment:** and **Price:** TextBoxes, respectively. Line 165 reads a Double value from the **Annual interest rate:** Text-Box. Notice that these lines are different from the ones in the **Car Payment Calculator** application that you developed in Tutorial 9. These three statements now must explicitly convert the data in the TextBoxes to Integer and Double values, using the methods of the Convert class, because **Option Strict** is set to On. However, these statements still use the Val function, which could cause the application to use incorrect data in its calculation, producing invalid results.

    Method Convert.ToInt32 throws a FormatException if it cannot convert its argument to an Integer. The **FormatException** class represents exceptions that occur when a method is passed an argument that is of the wrong type (and cannot be implicitly converted to the correct type). The call to the Convert.ToInt32 method does not currently throw an exception when the application is run because Val converts its argument to a numeric value. Because this numeric value is the argument passed to Convert.ToInt32, an Integer value will always be created. The Convert.ToDouble method performs in a similar manner by throwing a FormatException if it cannot convert its argument to a Double.

(cont.)

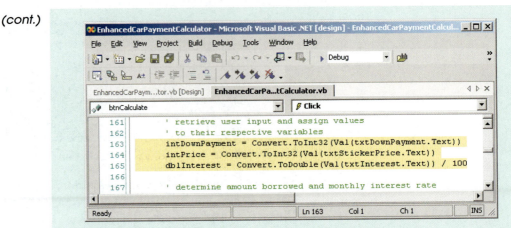

Figure 32.8 `Val` ensures data is in numeric format.

4. ***Changing the existing code.*** Change lines 163–165 of your template application to match lines 163–165 of Fig. 32.9 by removing the `Val` function call and the parentheses that designate its argument. Removing the `Val` function call will cause `Convert.ToInt32` and `Convert.ToDouble` to throw an exception if incorrect input is entered into one of the `TextBox`es. This will allow you to add code later in this box to catch the exception and ask the user to enter correct data.

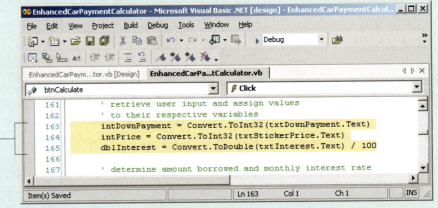

Removing the `Val` method call allows exceptions to be thrown

Figure 32.9 Removing the `Val` function call from the application.

5. ***Causing a FormatException.*** Select **Debug > Start** to run your application. Enter the input of Fig. 32.4 and click the **Calculate** Button. The dialog in Fig. 32.10 will appear, informing you of the type of exception that has occurred. Click the **Continue** Button to close the application. [*Note:* Sometimes clicking the **Continue** Button when an exception has occurred will cause the application to keep running, although possibly incorrectly. When this happens, we suggest you close the application and modify it to handle the exception (as we will demonstrate shortly).

(cont.)

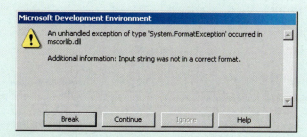

Figure 32.10 Unhandled `FormatException` from invalid input.

6. ***Adding a Try block to your application.*** Add lines 161–162 of Fig. 32.11 to your application; however, do not press *Enter* when you are done typing line 162. Instead, when you are done typing this line, add line 192 of Fig. 32.12 to your application. Line 162 begins the Try block, and line 192 ends the `Try...Catch` statement. The code contained between these two lines is the code that might throw an exception (lines 166–168) and code that you do not want to execute if an exception occurs. Notice that the `Try` keyword on line 162 is underlined, indicating a syntax error. Adding the `Try` keyword to your application creates a syntax error until a corresponding `Catch` or `Finally` block is added to the application. You will add a `Catch` block, which will fix the error on line 162, in the next step.

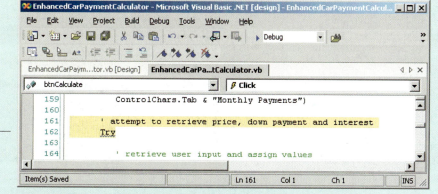

Beginning a **Try** block

Figure 32.11 Enabling exception handling using a **Try** block.

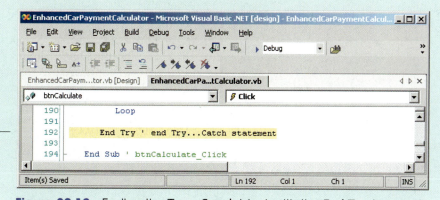

Ending the **Try** statement

Figure 32.12 Ending the **Try...Catch** block with the **End Try** keywords.

(cont.)

7. ***Adding a Catch block to your application.*** Add lines 192–193 of Fig. 32.13 to your application. The Catch keyword designates the beginning of a Catch block. A Catch block ends when either another Catch block, a Finally block or the End Try keywords are reached. Line 193 specifies that this Catch block will execute if a FormatException is thrown. So, this code will execute if the user enters invalid input in one of the TextBoxes. Notice that the Try keyword on line 162 is no longer underlined because adding a Catch block fixed the error on that line.

Catching a FormatException ——————

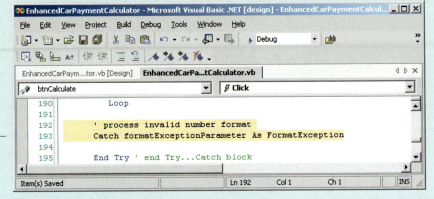

Figure 32.13 Handling a FormatException.

8. ***Displaying an error message to the user.*** Add lines 195–200 of Fig. 32.14 to the Catch handler. These lines display a MessageBox to the user, instructing the user to enter valid input. Notice that the MessageBoxIcon.Error icon is used because an exception is an error that occurs during the execution of the application.

Displaying a message when the Catch block executes ——————

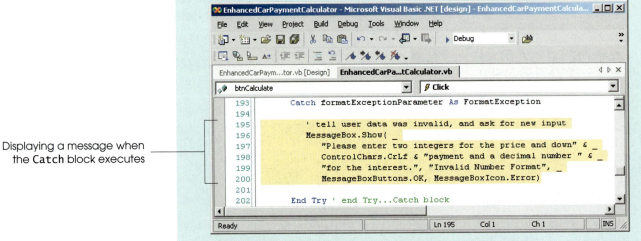

Figure 32.14 Displaying a message dialog to the user.

9. ***Running the application.*** Select **Debug > Start** to run you application. Enter valid input and verify that the output contains the correct monthly payment amounts. Enter invalid input to ensure that the MessageBox is displayed. Test the application with several invalid values in the different TextBoxes.

10. ***Closing the application.*** Close your running application by clicking its close box.

11. ***Closing the IDE.*** Close Visual Studio .NET by clicking its close box.

Figure 32.15 presents the source code for the **Enhanced Car Payment Calcu-lator** application. The lines of code that contain new programming concepts that you learned in this tutorial are highlighted.

```
1    Public Class FrmEnhancedCarPayment
2       Inherits System.Windows.Forms.Form
3
4       ' Windows Form Designer generated code
5
6       ' handles Calculate Button's Click event
7       Private Sub btnCalculate_Click(ByVal sender As System.Object, _
8          ByVal e As System.EventArgs) Handles btnCalculate.Click
9
10         Dim intYears As Integer = 2          ' repetition counter
11         Dim intMonths As Integer = 0         ' payment period
12         Dim intPrice As Integer = 0          ' car price
13         Dim intDownPayment As Integer = 0    ' down payment
14         Dim dblInterest As Double = 0        ' interest rate
15         Dim decMonthlyPayment As Decimal = 0 ' monthly payment
16         Dim intLoanAmount As Integer = 0     ' cost after down payment
17         Dim dblMonthlyInterest As Double = 0 ' monthly interest rate
18
19         ' remove text displayed in ListBox
20         lstPayments.Items.Clear()
21
22         ' add header to ListBox
23         lstPayments.Items.Add("Months" & ControlChars.Tab & _
24            ControlChars.Tab & "Monthly Payments")
25
26         ' attempt to retrieve price, down payment and interest
27         Try
28
29            ' retrieve user input and assign values
30            ' to their respective variables
31            intDownPayment = Convert.ToInt32(txtDownPayment.Text)
32            intPrice = Convert.ToInt32(txtStickerPrice.Text)
33            dblInterest = Convert.ToDouble(txtInterest.Text) / 100
34
35            ' determine amount borrowed and monthly interest rate
36            intLoanAmount = intPrice - intDownPayment
37            dblMonthlyInterest = dblInterest / 12
38
39            ' loop four times
40            Do While intYears <= 5
41
42               ' calculate payment period
43               intMonths = 12 * intYears
44
45               ' calculate monthly payment using Pmt
46               decMonthlyPayment = Convert.ToDecimal( _
47                  Pmt(dblMonthlyInterest, intMonths, -intLoanAmount))
48
49               ' display payment value
50               lstPayments.Items.Add(intMonths & ControlChars.Tab & _
51                  ControlChars.Tab & String.Format("{0:C}", _
52                  decMonthlyPayment))
53
54               intYears += 1 ' increment counter
55            Loop
```

Beginning the **Try** block — (lines 26–27)

Removing the **Val** method call allows exceptions to be thrown — (lines 31–33)

Figure 32.15 **Enhanced Car Payment Calculator** Application. (Part 1 of 2.)

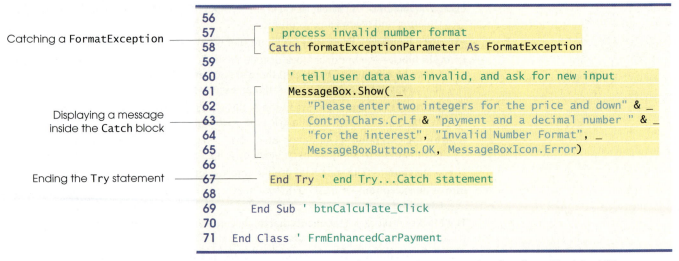

Catching a `FormatException`

Displaying a message inside the `Catch` block

Ending the `Try` statement

```
56
57        ' process invalid number format
58        Catch formatExceptionParameter As FormatException
59
60            ' tell user data was invalid, and ask for new input
61            MessageBox.Show( _
62                "Please enter two integers for the price and down" & _
63                ControlChars.CrLf & "payment and a decimal number " & _
64                "for the interest", "Invalid Number Format", _
65                MessageBoxButtons.OK, MessageBoxIcon.Error)
66
67        End Try ' end Try...Catch statement
68
69      End Sub ' btnCalculate_Click
70
71  End Class ' FrmEnhancedCarPayment
```

Figure 32.15 Enhanced Car Payment Calculator Application. (Part 2 of 2.)

SELF-REVIEW

1. If you are attempting to catch multiple errors, you may use several _____ blocks after the _____ block.

   a) `Try, Catch`   b) `Catch, Try`

   c) `Finally, Try`   d) None of the above.

2. The exception you wish to handle should be declared as a parameter of the _____ block.

   a) `Try`   b) `Catch`

   c) `Finally`   d) None of the above.

   Answers: 1) b. 2) b.

32.5 Wrap-Up

In this tutorial, you learned exception handling concepts and when to use exception handling in Visual Basic .NET. You learned how to use a `Try` block with `Catch` blocks to handle exceptions in your applications. You also learned that the `Throw` statement can be used to rethrow an exception that cannot be handled in the `Catch` block. Next, you applied your knowledge of exception handling in Visual Basic .NET to enhance your **Car Payment Calculator** application to check for input errors. You used a `Try` block to enclose the statements that might throw `FormatExceptions` and a `Catch` block to handle the `FormatExceptions`.

SKILLS SUMMARY

Handling an exception

- Enclose in a `Try` block code that might generate an exception and any code that should not execute if an exception occurs.
- Follow the `Try` block with one or more `Catch` blocks. Each `Catch` block is an exception handler that specifies the type of exception it can handle.
- Follow the `Catch` blocks with an optional `Finally` block that contains code that should always execute.

KEY TERMS

Catch block—Also called an exception handler, this block executes when the corresponding `Try` block in the application detects an exceptional situation and throws an exception of the type the `Catch` block declares.

End Try—Indicates the end of a sequence of blocks containing a `Try` block, followed by one or more `Catch` blocks and an optional `Finally` block.

exception—An indication of a problem that occurs during an application's execution.

exception handler—A block that executes when the application detects an exceptional situation and throws an exception.

exception handling—Processing problems that occur during application execution.

Finally block—An optional block of code that follows the last Catch block in a sequence of Catch blocks or the Try block if there are no Catches. The Finally block provides code that always executes, whether or not an exception occurs.

FormatException class—An exception of this type is thrown when a method cannot convert its argument to a desired numeric type, such as Integer or Double.

rethrow the exception—The Catch block can defer the exception handling (or perhaps a portion of it) to another Catch block by using the Throw statement.

Throw statement—The statement used to rethrow an exception in a Catch block.

throws an exception—A method throws an exception if a problem occurs while the method is executing.

Try block—A block of statements that might cause exceptions and statements that should not execute if an exception occurs.

uncaught exception—An exception that does not have an exception handler. Uncaught exceptions might terminate application execution.

MULTIPLE-CHOICE QUESTIONS

32.1 Dealing with exceptional situations as an application executes is called _____.

a) exception detection
b) exception handling
c) exception resolution
d) exception debugging

32.2 A(n) _____ is always followed by at least one Catch block or a Finally block.

a) if statement
b) event handler
c) Try block
d) None of the above.

32.3 The method call Convert.ToInt32("123.4a") will throw a(n) _____.

a) FormatException
b) ParsingException
c) DivideByZeroException
d) None of the above.

32.4 If no exceptions are thrown in a Try block, _____.

a) the Catch block(s) are skipped
b) all Catch blocks are executed
c) an error occurs
d) the default exception is thrown

32.5 A(n) _____ is an exception that does not have an exception handler, and therefore might cause the application to terminate execution.

a) uncaught block
b) uncaught exception
c) error handler
d) thrower

32.6 A Try block can have _____ associated with it.

a) only one Catch block
b) several Finally blocks
c) one or more Catch blocks
d) None of the above.

32.7 The _____ statement is used to rethrow an exception from inside a Catch block.

a) Rethrow
b) Throw
c) Try
d) Catch

32.8 _____ marks the end of a Try block and its corresponding Catch and Finally blocks.

a) End Try
b) End Finally
c) End Catch
d) End Exception

32.9 A Finally block is located _____.

a) after the Try block, but before each Catch block
b) before the Try block
c) after the Try block and the Try block's corresponding Catch blocks
d) Either b or c.

32.10 A _____ is executed if an exception is thrown from a Try block or if no exception is thrown.

　　a) Catch block　　　　　　　　　　b) Finally block

　　c) exception handler　　　　　　　d) All of the above.

EXERCISES

32.11 (*Enhanced Miles Per Gallon Application*) Modify the **Miles Per Gallon** application (Exercise 13.13) to use exception handling to process the FormatExceptions that occur when converting the strings in the TextBoxes to Doubles (Fig. 32.16). The original application allowed the user to input the number of miles driven and the number of gallons used for a tank of gas to determine the number of miles the user was able to drive on one gallon of gas.

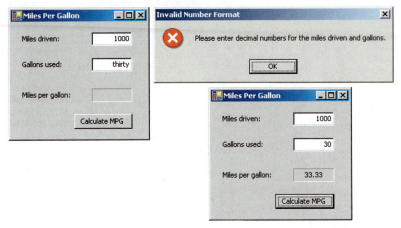

Figure 32.16 Enhanced **Miles Per Gallon** application's GUI.

　a) *Copying the template to your working directory.* Copy the directory C:\Examples\ Tutorial32\Exercises\EnhancedMilesPerGallon to your C:\SimplyVB directory.

　b) *Opening the application's template file.* Double click EnhancedMilesPerGallon.sln in the EnhancedMilesPerGallon directory to open the application.

　c) *Adding a Try block.* Find the btnCalculateMPG_Click event handler. Enclose all of the code in this event handler in a Try block.

　d) *Adding a Catch block.* After the Try block, you added in *Step b*, add a Catch block to handle any FormatExceptions that may occur in the Try block. Inside the Catch block, add code to display an error message dialog.

　e) *Running the application.* Select **Debug > Start** to run your application. Enter invalid data as shown in Fig. 32.16 and click the **Calculate MPG** Button. A MessageBox should appear asking you to enter valid input. Enter valid input and click the **Calculate MPG** Button again. Verify that the correct output is displayed.

　f) *Closing the application.* Close your running application by clicking its close box.

　g) *Closing the IDE.* Close Visual Studio .NET by clicking its close box.

32.12 (*Enhanced Prime Numbers Application*) Modify the **Prime Numbers** application (Exercise 13.17) to use exception handling to process the FormatExceptions that occur when converting the strings in the TextBoxes to Integers (Fig. 32.17). The original application took two numbers (representing a lower bound and an upper bound) and determined all of the prime numbers within the specified bounds, inclusive. An Integer greater than 1 is said to be prime if it is divisible by only 1 and itself. For example, 2, 3, 5 and 7 are prime numbers, but 4, 6, 8 and 9 are not.

　a) *Copying the template to your working directory.* Copy the directory C:\Examples\ Tutorial32\Exercises\EnhancedPrimeNumbers to your C:\SimplyVB directory.

　b) *Opening the application's template file.* Double click EnhancedPrimeNumbers.sln in the EnhancedPrimeNumbers directory to open the application.

　c) *Adding a Try block.* Find the btnCalculatePrimes_Click event handler. Enclose all the code following the variable declarations in a Try block.

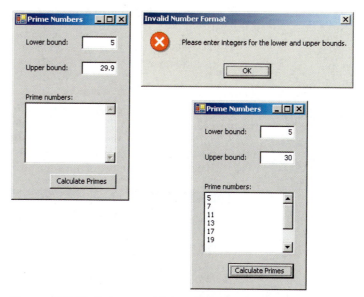

Figure 32.17   Enhanced **Prime Numbers** application's GUI.

d) *Adding a Catch block.* Add a Catch block that catches any FormatExceptions that may occur in the Try block you added to btnCalculatePrimes_Click in *Step c.* Inside the Catch block, add code to display an error message dialog.

e) *Running the application.* Select **Debug > Start** to run your application. Enter invalid data as shown in Fig. 32.17 and click the **Calculate Primes** Button. A MessageBox should appear asking you to enter valid input. Enter valid input and click the **Calculate Primes** Button again. Verify that the correct output is displayed.

f) *Closing the application.* Close your running application by clicking its close box.

g) *Closing the IDE.* Close Visual Studio .NET by clicking its close box.

32.13 (*Enhanced Simple Calculator Application*) Modify the **Simple Calculator** application (Exercise 6.13) to use exception handling to process the FormatExceptions that occur when converting the strings in the TextBoxes to Integers and the DivideByZeroException when performing the division (Fig. 32.18). We will define what a DivideByZeroException is shortly. The application should still perform simple addition, subtraction, multiplication and division.

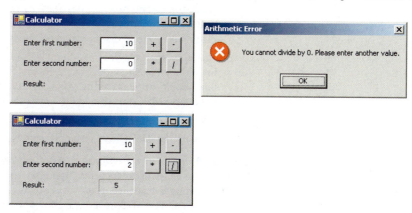

Figure 32.18   Enhanced **Simple Calculator** application.

a) *Copying the template to your working directory.* Copy the directory C:\Examples\Tutorial32\Exercises\EnhancedSimpleCalculator to your C:\SimplyVB directory.

b) *Opening the application's template file.* Double click EnhancedSimpleCalculator.sln in the EnhancedSimpleCalculator directory to open the application.

c) *Adding a Try block to the btnAdd_Click event handler.* Find the btnAdd_Click event handler. Enclose the body of btnAdd_Click in a Try block.

d) *Adding a Catch block to the **btnAdd_Click** event handler*. Add a Catch block that catches any FormatExceptions that may occur in the Try block that you added in *Step c*. Inside the Catch block, add code to display an error message dialog.

e) *Adding a Try block to the **btnSubtract_Click** event handler*. Find the btnSubtract_Click event handler, which immediately follows btnAdd_Click. Enclose the body of the btnSubtract_Click in a Try block.

f) *Adding a Catch block to the **btnSubtract_Click** event handler*. Add a Catch block that catches any FormatExceptions that may occur in the Try block that you added in *Step e*. Inside the Catch block, add code to display an error message dialog.

g) *Adding a Try block to the **btnMultiply_Click** event handler*. Find the btnMulitply_Click event handler, which immediately follows btn_Subtract_Click. Enclose the body of the btnMultiply_Click in a Try block.

h) *Adding a Catch block to the **btnMultiply_Click** event handler*. Add a Catch block that catches any FormatExceptions that may occur in the Try block that you added in *Step g*. Inside the Catch block, add code to display an error message dialog.

i) *Adding a Try block to the **btnDivide_Click** event handler*. Find the btnDivide_Click event handler, which immediately follows btnMultiply_Click. Enclose the body of the btnDivide_Click in a Try block.

j) *Adding a Catch block to the **btnDivide_Click** event handler*. Add a Catch block that catches any FormatExceptions that may occur in the Try block that you added in *Step i*. Inside the Catch block, add code to display an error message dialog.

k) *Adding a second Catch block to the **btnDivide_Click** event handler*. Immediately following the first Catch block inside the btnDivide_Click event handler, add a Catch block to catch any DivideByZeroExceptions. A **DivideByZeroException** is thrown when division by zero in integer arithmetic occurs. Inside the Catch block, add code to display an error message dialog.

l) *Running the application*. Select **Debug > Start** to run your application. Enter valid input for the first number and 0 for the second number, then click the Button for division. A MessageBox should appear asking you not to divide by 0. Enter invalid input (such as letters) for the first and second number, then click any one of the Buttons provided. This time, a MessageBox should appear asking you to enter valid input. Enter valid input and click any one of the Buttons provided. Verify that the correct output is displayed.

m) *Closing the application*. Close your running application by clicking its close box.

n) *Closing the IDE*. Close Visual Studio .NET by clicking its close box.

What does this code do? ▶   **32.14** What does the following code do, assuming that dblValue1 and dblValue2 are both declared as Doubles?

```
1   Try
2
3       dblValue1 = Convert.ToDouble(txtInput1.Text)
4       dblValue2 = Convert.ToDouble(txtInput2.Text)
5
6       txtOutput.Text = (dblValue1 * dblValue2).ToString
7
8   Catch formatExceptionParameter As FormatException
9
10      MessageBox.Show( _
11          "Please enter decimal values.", _
12          "Invalid Number Format", _
13          MessageBoxButtons.OK, MessageBoxIcon.Error)
14
15  End Try
```

What's wrong with this code? ▶   **32.15** The following code should add integers from two TextBoxes and display the result in txtResult. Assume that intValue1 and intValue2 are declared as Integers. Find the error(s) in the following code:

```
1    Try
2
3        intValue1 = Convert.ToInt32(txtInput1.Text)
4        intValue2 = Convert.ToInt32(txtInput2.Text)
5
6        txtOutput.Text = (intValue1 + intValue2).ToString
7
8    End Try
9
10   Catch formatExceptionParameter As FormatException
11
12       MessageBox.Show( _
13           "Please enter valid Integers.", _
14           "Invalid Number Format", _
15           MessageBoxButtons.OK, MessageBoxIcon.Error)
16
17   End Catch
```

Programming Challenge ▶   **32.16** (*Enhanced Vending Machine Application*) The **Vending Machine** application from Tutorial 3 has been modified to use exception handling to process the IndexOutOfRangeExceptions that occur when selecting items out of the range 0 through 7 (Fig. 32.19). This type of exception will be defined shortly. To get a snack, the user must type the number of the desired snack in the TextBox, then press the **Dispense Snack:** Button. The name of the snack is displayed in the output Label.

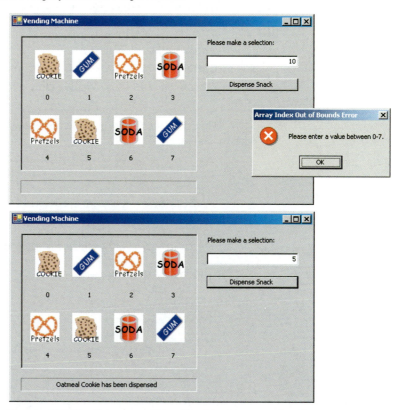

Figure 32.19 Enhanced **Vending Machine** application.

a) *Copying the template to your working directory.* Copy the directory C:\Examples\ Tutorial32\Exercises\EnhancedVendingMachine to your C:\SimplyVB directory.

b) *Opening the application's template file.* Double click EnhancedVendingMachine.sln in the EnhancedVendingMachine directory to open the application.

c) *Adding a Try block.* Find the btnDispense_Click event handler. Enclose all of the code in the event handler in a Try block.

d) *Adding a Catch block.* Add a Catch block that catches any FormatExceptions that may occur in the Try block that you added to btnDispense_Click in *Step c*. Inside the Catch block, add code to display an error message dialog.

e) *Adding a second Catch block.* Immediately following the Catch block you added in *Step d*, add a second Catch block to catch any IndexOutOfRangeExceptions that may occur. An **IndexOutOfRangeException** occurs when the application attempts to access an array with an invalid index. Inside the Catch block, add code to display an error message dialog.

f) *Running the application.* Select **Debug > Start** to run your application. Make an out of range selection (for instance, 32) and click the **Dispense Snack** Button. Verify that the proper MessageBox is displayed for the invalid input. Enter letters for a selection and click the **Dispense Snack** Button. Verify that the proper MessageBox is displayed for the invalid input.

g) *Closing the application.* Close your running application by clicking its close box.

h) *Closing the IDE.* Close Visual Studio .NET by clicking its close box.

Operator Precedence Chart

Operators are shown in decreasing order of precedence from top to bottom with each level of precedence separated by a horizontal line. Visual Basic operators associate from left to right.

Operator	Type
^	exponentiation
+ –	unary plus unary minus
* /	multiplication division
\	integer division
Mod	modulus
+ –	addition subtraction
&	concatenation
= <> < <= > >= Like Is TypeOf	relational is equal to relational is not equal to relational less than relational less than or equal to relational greater than relational greater than or equal to pattern matching reference comparison type comparison
Not	logical negation
And AndAlso	logical AND without short-circuit evaluation logical AND with short-circuit evaluation
Or OrElse	logical inclusive OR without short-circuit evaluation logical inclusive OR with short-circuit evaluation
Xor	logical exclusive OR

Figure A.1   Operator list (in order of operator precedence).

ASCII Character Set

The digits in the left column of Fig. B.1 are the left digits of the decimal equivalent (0–127) of the character code, and the digits in the top row of Fig. B.1 are the right digits of the character code. For example, the character code for "F" is 70, and the character code for "&" is 38.

Most users of this book are interested in the ASCII character set used to represent English characters on many computers. The ASCII character set is a subset of the Unicode® character set used by Visual Basic .NET to represent characters from most of the world's languages.

	0	1	2	3	4	5	6	7	8	9
0	nul	soh	stx	etx	eot	enq	ack	bel	bs	ht
1	nl	vt	ff	cr	so	si	dle	dc1	dc2	dc3
2	dc4	nak	syn	etb	can	em	sub	esc	fs	gs
3	rs	us	sp	!	"	#	$	%	&	'
4	(	)	*	+	,	-	.	/	0	1
5	2	3	4	5	6	7	8	9	:	;
6	<	=	>	?	@	A	B	C	D	E
7	F	G	H	I	J	K	L	M	N	O
8	P	Q	R	S	T	U	V	W	X	Y
9	Z	[	\	]	^	_	'	a	b	c
10	d	e	f	g	h	i	j	k	l	m
11	n	o	p	q	r	s	t	u	v	w
12	x	y	z	{			}	~	del		

Figure B.1 ASCII character set.

A P P E N D I X

GUI Design Guidelines

This appendix contains a complete list of the GUI design guidelines presented at the end of each tutorial. The guidelines are organized by tutorial; within each tutorial section, they are organized by control.

Tutorial 3: Welcome Application (Introduction to Visual Programming)

Overall Design
- Use colors in your applications, but not to the point of distracting the user.

Form
- Choose short and descriptive Form titles. Capitalize words that are not articles, prepositions or conjunctions. Do not use punctuation.
- Use Tahoma font to improve readability for controls that display text.

Label
- Use Labels to display text that users cannot change.
- Ensure that all Label controls are large enough to display their text.

PictureBox
- Use PictureBoxes to enhance GUIs with graphics that users cannot change.
- Images should fit inside their PictureBoxes. This can be achieved by setting PictureBox property SizeMode to StretchImage.

Tutorial 4: Designing the Inventory Application (Introducing TextBoxes and Buttons)

Overall Design
- Arrange groups of controls at least two grid units apart on a Form.
- Leave at least two grid units of space between the edges of the Form and the controls nearest each edge.
- Use a control's Location property to precisely specify its position on the Form.
- Place an application's output below and/or to the right of the Form's input controls.

Button

- Buttons are labelled using their Text property. These labels should use book-title capitalization and be as short as possible while still being meaningful to the user.
- Buttons should be stacked downward from the top right of a Form or arranged on the same line starting from the bottom right of a Form.

Form

- Changing the Form's title allows users to identify the application's purpose.
- Form titles should use book-title capitalization.
- Change the Form font to Tahoma to be consistent with Microsoft's recommended font for Windows.

Label

- The TextAlign property of a descriptive Label should be set to MiddleLeft. This ensures that text within groups of Labels align.
- A descriptive Label should be placed above or to the left of the control that it identifies.
- A descriptive Label should have the same height as the TextBox it describes if the controls are arranged horizontally.
- A descriptive Label and the control it identifies should be aligned on the left if they are arranged vertically.
- Align the left sides of a group of descriptive Labels if the Labels are arranged vertically.
- A Label can be used to display output to the user. Use a descriptive Label to identify each output Label.
- Output Labels should look different from descriptive Labels to focus the user's attention. This can be done by setting the BorderStyle property to Fixed3D and the TextAlign property to MiddleCenter.
- If several output Labels are arranged vertically to display numbers used in a mathematical calculation (such as in an invoice), use the MiddleRight TextAlign property.
- A descriptive Label and the control it identifies should be aligned on the top if they are arranged horizontally.

TextBox

- Use TextBoxes to input data from the keyboard.
- TextBoxes should have descriptive Labels indicating the input expected from the user.
- Make TextBoxes wide enough for expected input.

Tutorial 7: Wage Calculator Application (Introducing Algorithms, Pseudocode and Program Control)

Overall Design

- Format all monetary amounts using the C (currency) format specifier.

TextBox

- When using multiple TextBoxes vertically, align the TextBoxes on their right sides, and where possible make the TextBoxes the same size. Left-align the descriptive Labels for such TextBoxes.

Tutorial 8: Dental Payment Application (Introducing CheckBoxes and Message Dialogs)

CheckBox

- A CheckBox's label should be descriptive and as short as possible. When a CheckBox label contains more than one word, use book-title capitalization.
- Align groups of CheckBoxes either horizontally or vertically.

Message Dialog

- Text displayed in a dialog should be descriptive and as short as possible.

Tutorial 9: Car Payment Calculator Application (Introducing the Do While...Loop and Do Until...Loop Repetition Statements)

ListBox

■ A ListBox should be large enough to display all of its content or large enough that scrollbars may be used easily.

■ Use headers in a ListBox when you are displaying tabular data. Adding headers improves readability by indicating the information that will be displayed in the ListBox.

Tutorial 10: Class Average Application (Introducing the Do...Loop While and Do...Loop Until Repetition Statements)

Button

■ Disable a Button when its function should not be available to users.

■ Enable a disabled Button when its function once again should be available to users.

Tutorial 11: Interest Calculator Application (Introducing the For...Next Repetition Statement)

NumericUpDown

■ A NumericUpDown control should follow the same GUI Design Guidelines as a single-line TextBox.

TextBox

■ If a TextBox will display multiple lines of output, set the Multiline property to True and left-align the output by setting the TextAlign property to Left.

■ If a multiline TextBox will display many lines of output, limit the TextBox height and use a vertical scrollbar to allow users to view additional lines of output.

Tutorial 12: Security Panel Application (Introducing Select Case Multiple Selection Statement)

Overall Design

■ If your GUI is modeling a real-world object, your GUI design should mimic the physical appearance of the object.

TextBox

■ Mask passwords or other sensitive pieces of information in TextBoxes.

Tutorial 14: Shipping Time Application (Using Dates and Timers)

DateTimePicker

■ Use a DateTimePicker to retrieve date and time information from the user.

■ Each DateTimePicker should have a corresponding descriptive Label.

■ If the user should specify a time of day or a date and time, set the DateTimePicker's ShowUpDown property to True. If the user should specify a date, set the DateTimePicker's ShowUpDown property to False to allow the user to select a day from the month calendar.

GroupBox

■ GroupBox titles should be concise and should use book-title capitalization.

■ Use GroupBoxes to group related controls on the Form visually.

Tutorial 17: Flag Quiz Application (Introducing One-Dimensional Arrays and ComboBoxes)

ComboBox

- Each ComboBox should have a descriptive Label that describes the ComboBox's contents.
- If a ComboBox's content should not be editable, set its DropDownStyle property to Drop-DownList.

Tutorial 18: Sales Data Application (Introducing Two-Dimensional Arrays, RadioButtons and the MSChart Control)

MSChart Control

- Resize an MSChart control so that all the data is clearly visible.
- Set the MSChart control's Enabled property to False to prevent users from repositioning the chart within the MSChart control.
- Assign meaningful descriptions in the MSChart graph's title and axis labels. Use book-title capitalization for these descriptions.
- Increase the MSChart graph's title and axis label font sizes to enhance readability.

RadioButton

- Use RadioButtons when the user should choose only one option in a group.
- Always place each group of RadioButtons in a separate container (such as a GroupBox).
- Align groups of RadioButtons either horizontally or vertically.

Tutorial 19: Microwave Oven Application (Building Your Own Classes and Objects)

Panel

- Use Panels to organize groups of related controls where the purpose of those controls is obvious. If the purpose of the controls is not obvious, use a GroupBox in place of a Panel, because GroupBoxes can contain captions.
- A Panel can display scrollbars if that Panel is not large enough to display all of its controls at once. To increase readability, we suggest avoiding the use of scrollbars on a Panel. If the Panel is not large enough to display all of its contents, increase the size of the Panel.
- Although it is possible to have a Panel without a border (by setting the BorderStyle property to None), use borders on your Panels whenever possible. This helps to increase readability and organization.

Tutorial 20: Shipping Hub Application (Introducing Collections, the For Each...Next Statement and Access Keys)

Overall Design

- Set a control's TabStop property to True only if the control is used to receive user input.
- Use the TabIndex property to define the logical order in which the user should enter data.
- Use access keys to allow users to "click" a control using the keyboard.
- Usually the tab order transfers the focus of the application from top to bottom and left to right.

Tutorial 22: Typing Application (Introducing Keyboard Events, Menus and Dialogs)

MainMenus

- Use book-title capitalization in menu item text.

■ Use separator bars in a menu to group related menu items.

■ If clicking a menu item opens a dialog, an ellipsis (...) should follow the menu item's text.

Tutorial 27: Phone Book Application (Introducing Multimedia Using Microsoft Agent)

Microsoft Agent Control

■ The Microsoft Agent character should be located near the application Form when the character is displayed on the screen.

■ Use Microsoft Agent character gestures to indicate actions the user should take, or a response to an action the user has already taken.

Visual Studio .NET Windows Form Designer Tools

This book presents some 20 different controls available in Visual Studio .NET. In all, there are 47 items available to you by default in the **Toolbox**. This appendix contains a chart (Fig. D.1) indicating the purpose and usage of each of these controls. A list of Web resources can be found after the chart.

Icon	Item	Purpose	Usage
	Pointer	Allows you to select and modify elements in the IDE. The pointer is not a control.	Used to navigate a GUI.
	Button	Allows users to indicate that an action should be performed.	Most commonly used to execute code when clicked.
	CheckBox	Allows the user to select or deselect an option.	Becomes checked when selected and unchecked when deselected.
	CheckedList-Box	Provides the user with a checkable list of items.	Much like a CheckBox, but all options are contained in a format similar to that of a ListBox.
	ColorDialog	Allows the user to display the Windows **Color** dialog.	Used to retrieve a user's color selection in an application.
	ComboBox	Provides a short list of items in a drop-down menu.	Allow the user to view, enter new text in or search with a search String from multiple items in a list.
	ContextMenu	Displays a menu of programmer-defined options when the user right-clicks an object.	Provide additional options or features as a shortcut.

Figure D.1   Visual Studio .NET Windows **Form** Designer Tools. (Part 1 of 4.)

Icon	Item	Purpose	Usage
	Crystal-ReportViewer	Graphically displays data.	Display a graphic representation of a DataGrid object.
	DataGrid	Displays data within a chart.	Represent ADO .NET data in a scrollable chart.
	DateTime-Picker	Allows users to choose the date and time.	Display or allow the selection of a time and date.
	DomainUpDown	Displays string values, using the up and down arrows.	Select strings from an Object collection.
	ErrorProvider	Displays errors regarding a control to the user.	Inform the user if there is an error associated with the control.
	FontDialog	Displays a font dialog that includes all available fonts installed on the computer.	Used to retrieve a user-specified font format and size in an application.
	GroupBox	Allows controls to be grouped together.	Organize related controls separately from the rest of the Form.
	HelpProvider	Provides additional help features for a specific control.	Create additional help features for a control.
	HScrollBar	A horizontal scrollbar.	Allow users to view text or graphics that may be too large to display horizontally in a control.
	ImageList	A manageable list of images.	Store a list of images for use in other controls, such as a ListView or menu.
	Label	Displays text to the user.	Identify specific items on the Form or display general-purpose text.
	LinkLabel	Similar to a Label control but can include hyperlinks.	Display a hyperlink label that, when clicked, will open a file or Web page.
	ListBox	Provides a list of items.	Allow the user to view and select from multiple items in a list.
	ListView	Displays a group of items with identifiable icons.	Display a list of items (such as files) much like Windows Explorer.
	MainMenu	Creates a menu object on a Form.	Allow users to select options from menus, adding functionality to the application.
	MonthCalendar	Allows the user to select the date and time from a calendar that displays one month at a time.	Retrieve a user's date selection from a calendar.

Figure D.1   Visual Studio .NET Windows **Form** Designer Tools. (Part 2 of 4.)

Icon	Item	Purpose	Usage
	NotifyIcon	Creates icons that are displayed in a status area, usually while an action is performed in the background.	Remind the user that a certain process is running in the background of the application.
	NumericUpDown	Contains a number that is increased or decreased by clicking the up or down arrows.	Allow the user to specify a number in programmer-defined increments.
	OpenFile-Dialog	Displays a dialog to assist the user in selecting a file.	Retrieve user's file-name selection.
	PageSetup-Dialog	Displays a dialog to allow the user to change a document's page properties.	Allow users to modify the page settings and printer options.
	Panel	Similar to a GroupBox, but can include a scrollbar.	Group controls separately on the Form.
	PictureBox	Displays images.	Allow users to view graphics in an application.
	PrintDialog	Allows the user to select a printer and printing options.	Shown to retrieve user selection for printing options.
	PrintDocument	Executes the printing process.	Accessed to print documents.
	PrintPreview-Control	Allows the user to preview a document before printing it.	Display a preview of the document.
	PrintPreview-Dialog	A dialog used to display a PrintPreviewControl.	Display a print-preview dialog.
	ProgressBar	Displays a visual representation of the progress of an action or set of actions.	Inform the user of the completeness of an operation.
	RadioButton	Provides the user with a list of options from which only one or none can be selected.	Allow users to select at most one option from several.
	RichTextBox	Creates a TextBox control with advanced text-editing capabilities.	Allow users to perform more sophisticated editing beyond the features of a TextBox.
	SaveFile-Dialog	Assists the user in selecting a location in which to save a file.	Allow files to be saved.
	Splitter	Allows the user to resize a docked control within an application.	Give the users the ability to change the size of a control.
	StatusBar	Display useful information regarding the Form or objects in the application.	Notify the user of information not intended for the body of a Form.

Figure D.1   Visual Studio .NET Windows **Form** Designer Tools. (Part 3 of 4.)

Icon	Item	Purpose	Usage
	`TabControl`	Displays available tab pages in which you can place other controls.	Allow multiple tab pages on a **Form**.
	`TextBox`	Accepts user input from the keyboard. Can also be used to display text.	Used to retrieve user input from the keyboard.
	`Timer`	Performs an action at programmer-specified intervals. A `Timer` is not visible to the user.	Allow the action of an event through a specific amount of time.
	`ToolBar`	Contains icons representing specific commands.	Provide the user with options in a toolbar.
	`ToolTip`	Displays text information about an object when the mouse cursor is over it.	Display additional information to the user.
	`TrackBar`	Allows the user to set a value from a specified range.	Similar to the scrollbar, but includes a range of values.
	`TreeView`	Displays a tree structure of objects, using nodes.	Display a hierarchical representation of a collection of objects.
	`VScrollBar`	Allows users to view text or graphics that may be too large to display vertically in a control.	Enable a vertical scrollbar in the control.

Figure D.1   Visual Studio .NET Windows **Form** Designer Tools. (Part 4 of 4.)

D.1 Internet and Web Resources

A great way to learn about controls not covered in this book is to use them. Several Web sites provide information to help you get started. The following sites should help you as you explore new features of Visual Studio .NET:

`http://msdn.microsoft.com/library/default.asp?url=/library/en-us/vbcon/html/vbconSelectingWFCClientControl.asp`
This site provides documentation for the most commonly used Windows **Form** controls, gouped by function.

`http://dotnet247.com/247reference/guide/48.aspx`
This site provides articles describing features and usage of common controls in .NET. You will also find links to discussions of more advanced topics in .NET.

`http://msdn.microsoft.com/library/default.asp?url=/library/en-us/vbcon/html/vboricontrolsforwinforms.asp`
This Web page provides a more technical description of controls you can use on a Windows **Form**.

Controls, Events, Properties & Methods

This appendix contains a listing of controls and predefined classes used in the text. Each control or class includes a description of its purpose, as well as explanations of events, properties and methods related to that control or class, as covered in the text.

Tutorial 1: Graphing Application (Introducing Computers, the Internet and Visual Basic .NET)

No new elements.

Tutorial 2: Welcome Application (Introducing the Visual Studio® .NET IDE)

No new elements.

Tutorial 3: Welcome Application (Introduction to Visual Programming)

Label **A** Label   This control displays text on the Form that the user cannot modify.

■ *In action*

Total:

■ *Properties*

Font—Specifies the font name, style and size of the text displayed in the Label.

Text—Specifies the text displayed on the Label.

TextAlign—Specifies how the text is aligned within the Label.

PictureBox   This control displays an image on the Form.

■ *In action*

■ *Properties*

Image—Specifies the file path of the image.

SizeMode—Specifies how the image is displayed in the PictureBox.

Size—Specifies the height and width (in pixels) of the PictureBox.

Tutorial 4: Designing the Inventory Application (Introducing TextBoxes and Buttons)

Label   A Label   This control displays text on the Form that the user cannot modify.

■ *In action*

■ *Properties*

BorderStyle—Specifies the appearance of the Label's border.

Font—Specifies the font name, style and size of the text displayed in the Label.

Location—Specifies the location of the Label on the Form relative to the top-left corner.

Name—Specifies the name used to access the Label programmatically. The name should be prefixed with lbl.

Size—Specifies the height and width (in pixels) of the Label.

Text—Specifies the text displayed on the Label.

TextAlign—Specifies how the text is aligned within the Label.

TextBox   abl TextBox   This control allows the user to input data from the keyboard.

■ *In action*

■ *Properties*

Name—Specifies the name used to access the TextBox programmatically. The name should be prefixed with txt.

Location—Specifies the location of the TextBox on the Form relative to the top-left corner.

Size—Specifies the height and width (in pixels) of the TextBox.

Text—Specifies the text displayed in the TextBox.

TextAlign—Specifies how the text is aligned within the TextBox.

Button   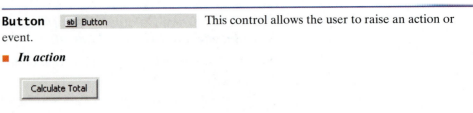   This control allows the user to raise an action or
event.

- ■ *In action*

    Calculate Total

- ■ *Properties*

    Location—Specifies the location of the Button on the Form relative to the top-left cor-
    ner.

    Name—Specifies the name used to access the Button programmatically. The name should
    be prefixed with btn.

    Size—Specifies the height and width (in pixels) of the Button.

    Text—Specifies the text displayed on the Button.

Tutorial 5: Completing the Inventory Application (Introducing Programming)

Button   abl Button   This control allows the user to raise an action or
event.

- ■ *In action*

    Calculate Total

- ■ *Event*

    Click—Raised when the user clicks the Button.

- ■ *Properties*

    Location—Specifies the location of the Button on the Form relative to the top-left cor-
    ner.

    Name—Specifies the name used to access the Button programmatically. The name should
    be prefixed with btn.

    Size—Specifies the height and width (in pixels) of the Button.

    Text—Specifies the text displayed on the Button.

Tutorial 6: Enhancing the Inventory Application (Introducing Variables, Memory Concepts and Arithmetic)

TextBox   abl TextBox   This control allows the user to input data from the
keyboard.

- ■ *In action*

- ■ *Event*

    TextChanged—Raised when the text in the TextBox is changed.

- ■ *Properties*

    Location—Specifies the location of the Label on the Form relative to the top-left corner.

    Name—Specifies the name used to access the TextBox programmatically. The name should
    be prefixed with txt.

    Size—Specifies the height and width (in pixels) of the TextBox.

    Text—Specifies the text displayed in the TextBox.

    TextAlign—Specifies how the text is aligned within the TextBox.

Tutorial 7: Wage Calculator Application (Introducing Algorithms, Pseudocode and Program Control)

String The String class represents a series of characters treated as a single unit.

■ *Method*

Format—Arranges the string in a specified format.

Tutorial 8: Dental Payment Application (Introducing CheckBoxes and Message Dialogs)

CheckBox This control allows the user to select an option.

■ *In action*

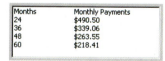

■ *Properties*

Checked—Specifies whether the CheckBox is checked (True) or unchecked (False).

Location—Specifies the location of the CheckBox on the Form.

Name—Specifies the name used to access the CheckBox control programmatically. The name should be prefixed with chk.

Text—Specifies the text displayed next to the CheckBox.

Tutorial 9: Car Payment Calculator Application (Introducing the Do While...Loop and Do Until...Loop Repetition Statements)

Convert The Convert class converts the value of a data type to another data type.

■ *Method*

ToDecimal—Converts the value from another data type to type Decimal.

ListBox ListBox   This control allows the user to view and select from items in a list.

■ *In action*

Months	Monthly Payments
24	$490.50
36	$339.06
48	$263.55
60	$218.41

■ *Properties*

Items—Returns an object that contains the items displayed in the ListBox.

Location—Specifies the location of the ListBox on the Form relative to the top-left corner.

Name—Specifies the name used to access the ListBox programatically. The name should be prefixed with lst.

Size—Specifies the height and width (in pixels) of the ListBox.

■ *Methods*

Items.Add—Adds an item to the Items property.

Items.Clear—Deletes all the values in the ListBox's Items property.

Tutorial 10: Class Average Application (Introducing the Do...Loop While *and* Do...Loop Until *Repetition Statements)*

Button   `ab| Button`   This control allows the user to raise an action or event.

■ *In action*

    `Calculate Total`

■ *Event*

Click—Raised when the user clicks the Button.

■ *Properties*

Enabled—Determines whether the Button's event handler is executed when the Button is clicked.

Location—Specifies the location of the Button on the Form relative to the top-left corner.

Name—Specifies the name used to access the Button programmatically. The name should be prefixed with btn.

Size—Specifies the height and width (in pixels) of the Button.

Text—Specifies the text displayed on the Button.

■ *Method*

Focus—Transfers the focus of the application to the Button that calls it.

ListBox   `☷ ListBox`   This control allows the user to view and select from items in a list.

■ *In action*

Months	Monthly Payments
24	$490.50
36	$339.06
48	$263.55
60	$218.41

■ *Properties*

Items—Returns an object that contains the items displayed in the ListBox.

Items.Count—Returns the number of items in the ListBox.

Items.Item—Returns the values at the specified index in the ListBox.

Location—Specifies the location of the ListBox on the Form relative to the top-left corner.

Name—Specifies the name used to access the ListBox programatically. The name should be prefixed with lst.

Size—Specifies the height and width (in pixels) of the ListBox.

■ *Methods*

Items.Add—Adds an item to the Items property.

Items.Clear—Deletes all the values in the ListBox's Items property.

TextBox   `ab| TextBox`   This control allows the user to input data from the keyboard.

■ *In action*

■ *Event*

TextChanged—Raised when the text in the TextBox is changed.

- *Properties*

    Location—Specifies the location of the TextBox on the Form relative to the top-left corner.

    Name—Specifies the name used to access the TextBox programmatically. The name should be prefixed with txt.

    Size—Specifies the height and width (in pixels) of the TextBox.

    Text—Specifies the text displayed in the TextBox.

    TextAlign—Specifies how the text is aligned within the TextBox.

- *Method*

    Focus—Transfers the focus of the application to the TextBox that calls it.

Tutorial 11: Interest Calculator Application (Introducing the For...Next Repetition Statement)

NumericUpDown      This control allows you to specify maximum and minimum numeric input values.

- *In action*

    | 6 |

- *Properties*

    Location—Specifies the location of the NumericUpDown control on the Form relative to the top-left corner.

    Maximum—Determines the maximum input value in a particular NumericUpDown control.

    Minimum—Determines the minimum input value in a particular NumericUpDown control.

    Name—Specifies the name used to access the NumericUpDown control programmatically. The name should be prefixed with upd.

    ReadOnly—Determines whether the input value can be typed by the user.

    Size—Specifies the height and width (in pixels) of the NumericUpDown control.

    TextAlign—Specifies how the text is aligned within the NumericUpDown control.

TextBox   abl TextBox   This control allows the user to input data from the keyboard.

- *In action*

    | 0 |

- *Event*

    TextChanged—Raised when the text in the TextBox is changed.

- *Properties*

    Location—Specifies the location of the TextBox on the Form relative to the top-left corner.

    Multiline—Specifies whether the TextBox is capable of displaying multiple lines of text.

    Name—Specifies the name used to access the TextBox programmatically. The name should be prefixed with txt.

    ReadOnly—Determines whether the value of a TextBox can be changed.

    ScrollBars—Specifies whether the TextBox contains a scrollbar.

    Size—Specifies the height and width (in pixels) of the TextBox.

    Text—Specifies the text displayed in the TextBox.

    TextAlign—Specifies how the text is aligned within the TextBox.

- *Method*

    Focus—Transfers the focus of the application to the TextBox that calls it.

Tutorial 12: Security Panel Application (Introducing the `Select Case` Multiple-Selection Statement)

TextBox This control allows the user to input data from the keyboard.

■ *In action*

```
|          0 |
```

■ *Event*

`TextChanged`—Raised when the text in the TextBox is changed.

■ *Properties*

`Enabled`—Determines whether the user can enter data (True) in the TextBox or not (False).

`Location`—Specifies the location of the TextBox on the Form relative to the top-left corner.

`Multiline`—Specifies whether the TextBox is capable of displaying multiple lines of text.

`Name`—Specifies the name used to access the TextBox programmatically. The name should be prefixed with `txt`.

`PasswordChar`—Specifies the masking character to be used when displaying data in the TextBox.

`ReadOnly`—Determines whether the value of a TextBox can be changed.

`ScrollBars`—Specifies whether the TextBox contains a scrollbar.

`Size`—Specifies the height and width (in pixels) of the TextBox.

`Text`—Specifies the text displayed in the TextBox.

`TextAlign`—Specifies how the text is aligned within the TextBox.

■ *Method*

`Focus`—Transfers the focus of the application to the TextBox that calls it.

Tutorial 13: Enhancing the Wage Calculator Application (Introducing `Function` Procedures and `Sub` Procedures)

Math This class provides methods used to perform common arithmetic calculations.

■ *Methods*

`Min`—Returns the smaller of two numeric values.

`Max`—Returns the larger of two numeric values.

`Sqrt`—Returns the square root of a numeric value.

Tutorial 14: Shipping Time Application (Using `Dates` and `Timers`)

Date This structure provides properties and methods to store and manipulate date and time information.

■ *Properties*

`Day`—Returns the day stored in a Date variable.

`Hour`—Returns the hour stored in a Date variable.

`Month`—Returns the month stored in a Date variable.

`Now`—Returns the system's current date and time.

`Year`—Returns the year stored in a Date variable.

■ *Methods*

`AddDays`—Creates a new Date value that is the specified number of days later (or earlier) in time.

`AddHours`—Creates a new Date value that is the specified number of hours later (or earlier) in time.

AddMinutes—Creates a new Date value that is the specified number of minutes later (or earlier) in time.

ToLongDateString—Returns a String containing the date in the format "Wednesday, October 30, 2002."

ToShortTimeString—Returns a String containing the time in the format "4:00 PM."

DateTimePicker   ⊞ DateTimePicker   This control is used to retrieve date and time information from the user.

- *In action*

DateTimePicker using default format

- *Event*

ValueChanged—Raised when the Value property is changed.

- *Properties*

CustomFormat—Sets which format string to use when displaying the date and/or time.

Format—Specifies the format in which the date and time are displayed on the control.

     Long—Specifies that the date should be displayed in the format "Monday, December 09, 2002."

     Short—Specifies that the date should be displayed in the format "12/ 9/2002."

     Time—Specifies that the time should be displayed in the format "8:39:53 PM."

     Custom—Allows the programmer to specify a custom format in which to display the date and/or time.

Hour—Stores the hour in the DateTimePicker control.

Location—Specifies the location of the DateTimePicker control on its container relative to the container's top-left corner.

MinDate—Specifies the minimum date and/or time that can be selected when using this control.

MaxDate—Specifies the maximum date and/or time that can be selected when using this control.

Name—Specifies the name used to access the DateTimePicker control programmatically. The name should be prefixed with dtp.

ShowUpDown—Specifies whether the up-down arrows (True) are displayed on the control for time values. If False, a down arrow is displayed for accessing a drop-down calendar.

Value—Stores the date and/or time in the DateTimePicker control.

GroupBox   [xy] GroupBox   This control groups related controls visually.

- *In action*

┌─Drop Off─────────────────────────┐
│   │
│   Enter drop-off time: [03]:00 PM ▲▼ │
│   │
└──────────────────────────────────┘

- *Properties*

Name—Specifies the name used to access the GroupBox control programmatically. The name should be prefixed with fra.

Location—Specifies the location of the GroupBox control on the Form.

Size—Specifies the height and width (in pixels) of the GroupBox control.

Text—Specifies the text displayed on the GroupBox.

Timer   ⏲ Timer   This control wakes up at specified intervals of time
to execute code in its Tick event handler.

■ *Event*

Tick—Raised after the number of milliseconds specified in the Interval property has
elapsed.

■ *Properties*

Enabled—Determines whether the Timer is running (True). The default is False.

Interval—Determines the time interval between Tick events.

Name—Specifies the name used to access the Timer control programmatically. The name
should be prefixed with tmr.

Tutorial 15: Fund Raiser Application (Introducing Scope, Pass-by-Reference and Option Strict)

No new elements.

Tutorial 16: Craps Game Application (Introducing Random-Number Generation)

Directory This class provides functionality to manipulate directories such as creating,
moving, and navigating through them.

■ *Method*

GetCurrentDirectory—Returns the location of the folder from which the application
was loaded.

Image This class provides functionality to manipulate images.

■ *Method*

FromFile—Specifies the physical location (path) of the image.

Random This class is used to generate random numbers.

■ *Methods*

Next—When called with no arguments, generates a positive Integer value between zero
and the largest possible Integer, which is the constant Int32.MaxValue
(2,147,483,647).

NextDouble—Generates a positive Double value that is greater than or equal to 0.0 and
less than 1.0.

Tutorial 17: Flag Quiz Application (Introducing One-Dimensional Arrays and ComboBoxes)

Array This data structure stores a fixed number of elements of the same type.

■ *Property*

Length—Specifies the number of elements in the array.

■ *Methods*

GetUpperBound—Returns the largest index of the array.

Sort—Orders an array's elements. An array of numerical values would be organized in
ascending order and an array of Strings would be organized in alphabetical order.

ComboBox      This control allows users to select from a drop-down list of options.

- *In action*

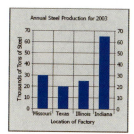

- *Properties*

DataSource—Specifies the source of items listed in a ComboBox.

DropDownStyle—Specifies a ComboBox's appearance.

Enabled—Specifies whether a user can select an item from the ComboBox.

Location—Specifies the location of the ComboBox control on the container control relative to the top-left corner.

MaxDropDownItems—Specifies the maximum number of items the ComboBox can display in its drop-down list.

Name—Specifies the name used to access the ComboBox control programmatically. The name should be prefixed with cbo.

SelectedIndex—Specifies the index of the selected item. Returns -1 if no item is selected.

SelectedValue—Specifies the selected item.

Size—Specifies the height and width (in pixels) of the ComboBox control.

Sorted—When set to True, displays the ComboBox options in alphabetical order or ascending order.

String   The String class represents a series of characters treated as a single unit.

- *Methods*

Format—Arranges the string in a specified format.

IndexOf—Returns the index of the specified character(s) in a String.

Insert—Returns a copy of the String for which it is called with the specified character(s) inserted.

Remove—Returns a copy of the String for which it is called with the specified character(s) removed.

ToLower—Returns a copy of the String for which it is called with any uppercase letters converted to lowercase letters.

Tutorial 18: Sales Data Application (Introducing Two-Dimensional Arrays, RadioButtons and the MSChart Control)

MSChart   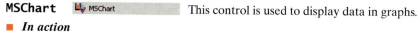   This control is used to display data in graphs.

- *In action*

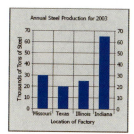

- *Properties*

ChartData—Contains the data to be graphed.

ChartType—Cetermines the appearance of the graph.

Location—Specifies the location of the MSChart control on the container control relative to the top-left corner.

Name—Specifies the name used to access the MSChart control programmatically. The name should be prefixed with ch.

Size—Specifies the height and width (in pixels) of the MSChart control.

RadioButton   RadioButton   This control is used to enable users to select exactly one option from several.

- ■ *In action*

  ⊙ 3D Graph

- ■ *Event*

  CheckedChanged—Raised when the control is either selected or deselected.

- ■ *Properties*

  Checked—True if the control is selected and False if it is not selected.

  Location—Specifies the location of the RadioButton control on the container control relative to the top-left corner.

  Name—Specifies the name used to access the RadioButton control programmatically. The name should be prefixed with rad.

  Size—Specifies the height and width (in pixels) of the RadioButton control.

  Text—Specifies the text displayed in the label to the right of the RadioButton.

Tutorial 19: Microwave Oven Application (Building Your Own Classes and Objects)

Button   Button   This control allows the user to raise an action or event.

- ■ *In action*

  Calculate Total

- ■ *Event*

  Click—Raised when the user clicks the Button.

- ■ *Properties*

  Enabled—Determines whether the Button's event handler is executed when the Button is clicked.

  FlatStyle—Determines whether the Button will appear flat or three-dimensional. Flat specifies that a Button will appear flat.

  Location—Specifies the location of the Button on the Form relative to the top-left corner.

  Name—Specifies the name used to access the Button programmatically. The name should be prefixed with btn.

  Size—Specifies the height and width (in pixels) of the Button.

  Text—Specifies the text displayed on the Button.

- ■ *Method*

  Focus—Transfers the focus of the application to the Button that calls it.

Convert   The Convert class converts the value of a data type to another data type.

- ■ *Methods*

  ToChar—Converts a value into a character (of data type Char).

  ToDecimal—Converts the value from another data type to type Decimal.

Label This control displays text on the Form that the user cannot modify.

■ *In action*

Total: [   ]

■ *Properties*

BorderStyle—Specifies the appearance of the Label's border. FixedSingle specifies that the Label will display a thin, black border.

Font—Specifies the font name, style and size of the text displayed in the Label.

Location—Specifies the location of the Label on the Form relative to the top-left corner.

Name—Specifies the name used to access the Label programmatically. The name should be prefixed with lbl.

Size—Specifies the height and width (in pixels) of the Label.

Text—Specifies the text displayed on the Label.

TextAlign—Specifies how the text is aligned within the Label.

Panel ☐ Panel This control is used to organize various controls. Unlike a GroupBox control, the Panel control does not display a caption.

■ *In action*

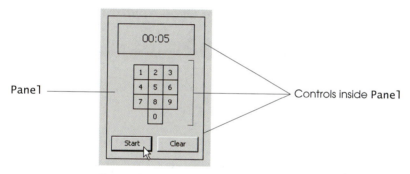

Panel — Controls inside Panel

■ *Properties*

DefaultBackColor—Returns the default background color of a Panel control.

Name—Specifies the name of the Panel.

Size—Specifies the size of the Panel.

Location—Specifies the Panel's location on the Form.

BorderStyle—Specifies the Panel's border style. Options include None (displaying no border), FixedSingle (a single-line border) and Fixed3D (a three-dimensional border).

BackColor—Specifies the background color of the Panel.

String The String class represents a series of characters treated as a single unit.

■ *Property*

Length—Returns the number of characters in the String.

■ *Methods*

Format—Arranges the string in a specified format.

IndexOf—Returns the index of the specified character(s) in a String.

Insert—Returns a copy of the String for which it is called with the specified character(s) inserted.

PadLeft—Inserts characters at the beginning of a String.

Remove—Returns a copy of the String for which it is called with the specified character(s) removed.

Substring—Returns a substring from a String.

ToLower—This method returns a copy of the String for which it is called with any upper-case letters converted to lowercase letters.

Tutorial 20: Shipping Hub Application (Introducing Collections, the For Each...Next Statement and Access Keys)

ArrayList This class is used to store a variable number of objects.

■ *Property*

Count—Returns the number of objects contained in the ArrayList.

■ *Methods*

Add—Adds an object to the ArrayList object.

Insert—Adds an object to the ArrayList object at a specific index.

RemoveAt—Removes an object from the ArrayList object at the specified index.

ComboBox   This control allows users to select options from a drop-down list.

■ *In action*

Australia

■ *Event*

SelectedIndexChanged—Raised when a new value is selected in the ComobBox.

■ *Properties*

DataSource—Allows you to add items to the ComboBox.

DropDownStyle—determines the ComboBox's style.

Enabled—Determines whether the user can enter data (True) in the ComboBox or not (False).

Items—Specifies the values the user can select from the ComboBox.

Item—Retrieves the value at the specified index.

Location—Specifies the location of the ComboBox control on its container control relative to the top-left corner.

MaxDropDownItems—Determines the maximum number of items to be displayed when user clicks the drop-down arrow.

Name—Specifies the name used to access the ComboBox control programmatically. The name should be prefixed with cbo.

SelectedValue—Contains the item selected by the user.

Text—Specifies the text displayed in the ComboBox.

TextBox |abl TextBox   This control allows the user to input data from the keyboard.

■ *In action*

0

■ *Event*

TextChanged—Raised when the text in the TextBox is changed.

■ *Properties*

Enabled—Determines whether the user can enter data (True) in the TextBox or not (False).

Location—Specifies the location of the TextBox on its container control relative to the top-left corner.

MaxLength—Specifies the maximum number of characters that can be input into the TextBox.

Multiline—Specifies whether the TextBox is capable of displaying multiple lines of text.

Name—Specifies the name used to access the TextBox programmatically. The name should be prefixed with txt.

PasswordChar—Specifies the masking character to be used when displaying data in the TextBox.

ReadOnly—Determines whether the value of a TextBox can be changed.

ScrollBars—Specifies whether a multiline TextBox contains a scrollbar.

Size—Specifies the height and width (in pixels) of the TextBox.

Text—Specifies the text displayed in the TextBox.

TextAlign—Specifies how the text is aligned within the TextBox.

- ■ *Method*

Focus—Transfers the focus of the application to the TextBox that calls it.

Tutorial 21: "Cat and Mouse" Painter Application (Introducing the Graphics Object and Mouse Events)

Form   The class that represents an application's GUI.

- ■ *Events*

Load—Raised when an application initially executes.

MouseDown—Raised when a mouse button is clicked.

MouseMove—Raised when the mouse pointer is moved.

MouseUp—Raised when a mouse button is released.

- ■ *Property*

BackColor—Specifies the background color of the Form.

- ■ *Method*

CreateGraphics—Creates a Graphics object.

Graphics   The class that contains methods used to draw text, lines and shapes.

- ■ *Method*

FillEllipse—Draws a solid ellipse of a specified size and color at the specified location.

MouseEventArgs   The class that contains information about mouse events.

- ■ *Properties*

Buttons—Specifies which (if any) mouse button was pressed.

X—Specifies the *x*-coordinate of the mouse event.

Y—Specifies the *y*-coordinate of the mouse event.

Tutorial 22: Typing Application (Introducing Keyboard Events, Menus and Dialogs)

Char   This structure represents Unicode® characters.

- ■ *Method*

ToUpper—Returns the uppercase equivalent of an alphabetic character.

ColorDialog   ColorDialog   This control allows the user to customize the color of what is being typed.

- ■ *Properties*

Color—Contains the color selected by the user. The default color is black.

FullOpen—When True, allows the user to see the controls used to create custom colors.

■ *Method*

ShowDialog—Displays the **Color** dialog to the user.

FontDialog   FontDialog   This control allows the user to customize the font, size and style of what is being typed.

■ *Method*

ShowDialog—Displays the **Font** dialog to the user.

KeyEventArgs   This class represents arguments passed to the KeyPress event handler.

■ *Property*

KeyData—Contains data about the key that raised the KeyDown event.

KeyPressEventArgs   This class represents arguments passed to the KeyPress event handler.

■ *Property*

KeyChar—Contains data about the key that raised the KeyPress event.

MainMenu   MainMenu   This control allows you to group related commands for a Windows application.

■ *In action*

File	Format
About
Exit

■ *Event*

Click—Raised when the user clicks a menu item or presses a shortcut key that represents an item.

TextBox   abi TextBox   This control allows the user to input data from the keyboard.

■ *In action*

```
        0
```

■ *Events*

KeyDown—Raised when a key is pressed. KeyDown is case insensitive. It cannot recognize lowercase letters.

KeyPress—Raised when a key is pressed. KeyPress cannot handle modifier keys.

KeyUp—Raised when a key is released by the user.

TextChanged—Raised when the text in the TextBox is changed.

■ *Properties*

Enabled—Determines whether the user can enter data (True) in the TextBox or not (False).

Location—Specifies the location of the TextBox on the container control relative to the top-left corner.

MaxLength—Specifies the maximum number of characters that can be input into the TextBox.

Multiline—Specifies whether the TextBox is capable of displaying multiple lines of text.

Name—Specifies the name used to access the TextBox programmatically. The name should be prefixed with txt.

PasswordChar—Specifies the masking character to be used when displaying data in the TextBox.

ReadOnly—Determines whether the value of a TextBox can be changed.

ScrollBars—Specifies whether the TextBox contains a scrollbar.

Size—Specifies the height and width (in pixels) of the TextBox.

Text—Specifies the text displayed in the TextBox.

TextAlign—Specifies how the text is aligned within the TextBox.

- *Method*

Focus—Transfers the focus of the application to the TextBox that calls it.

Tutorial 23: Screen Scraping Application (Introducing String Processing)

String The String class represents a series of characters treated as a single unit.

- *Property*

Length—Returns the number of characters in the String.

- *Methods*

EndsWith—Determines if a String ends with a particular substring.

Format—Arranges the string in a specified format.

IndexOf—Returns the index of the specified character(s) in a String.

Insert—Returns a copy of the String for which it is called with the specified character(s) inserted.

LastIndexOf—Returns the index of the last occurrence of a substring in a String. It returns -1 if the substring is not found.

PadLeft—Inserts characters at the beginning of a String.

Remove—Returns a copy of the String for which it is called with the specified character(s) removed.

Replace—Returns a new String object in which every occurrence of a substring is replaced with a different substring.

StartsWith—Determines if a String starts with a particular substring.

Substring—Returns a substring from a String.

ToLower—Returns a copy of the String for which it is called with any uppercase letters converted to lowercase letters.

ToUpper—Creates a new String object that replaces every lowercase letter in a String with its uppercase equivalent.

Trim—Removes all whitespace characters from the beginning and end of a String.

Tutorial 24: Ticket Information Application (Introducing Sequential-Access Files)

ComboBox   ComboBox   This control allows users to select options from a drop-down list.

- *In action*

- *Event*

SelectedIndexChanged—Raised when a new value is selected in the ComboBox.

- *Properties*

DataSource—Allows you to add items to the ComboBox.

DropDownStyle—Determines the ComboBox's style.

Enabled—Determines whether or not the user can enter data in the ComboBox.

Items—Specifies the values the user can select from the ComboBox.

Item—Retrieves the value at the specified index.

Location—Specifies the location of the ComboBox control on its container control relative to the top-left corner.

MaxDropDownItems—Determines the maximum number of items to be displayed when user clicks the drop-down arrow.

Name—Specifies the name used to access the ComboBox control programmatically. The name should be prefixed with cbo.

SelectedIndex—Specifies the index of the item selected.

SelectedValue—Contains the item selected by the user.

Text—Specifies the text displayed in the ComboBox.

■ *Methods*

Items.Add—Adds an item to the ComboBox.

Items.Clear—Deletes all the values in the ComboBox.

MonthCalendar ⊞ MonthCalendar   This control displays a calendar from which the user can select a date or a range of dates.

■ *In action*

■ *Event*

DateChanged—Raised when a new date (or a range of dates) is selected.

■ *Properties*

Location—Specifies the location of the MonthCalendar control on the   Form.

Name—Specifies the name used to access the properties of the MonthCalendar control in program code. The name should be prefixed with mvw.

SelectionStart—Returns the first (or only) date selected.

OpenFileDialog ⊡ OpenFileDialog   This object enables an application to use the **Open** dialog.

■ *Properties*

CheckFileExists—Enables the user to display a warning if a specified file does not exist.

FileName—Sets the default file name displayed in the dialog. It can also be used to retrieve the name of the user-entered file.

Name—Specifies the name that will be used to reference the control's properties and methods.

■ *Method*

ShowDialog—Displays the **Open** dialog and returns the result of the user interaction with the dialog.

StreamWriter This class is used to write data to a file.

■ *Methods*

Close—Used to close the stream.

WriteLine—Writes the data specified in its argument, followed by a new line character.

StreamReader This class is used to read data from a file.

■ *Methods*

Close—Closes the stream.

ReadLine—Reads a line of data from a particular file.

Tutorial 25: ATM Application (Introducing Database Programming)

`OleDbConnection` OleDbConnection   This object establishes connection to a database.

■ *Property*

`ConnectionString`—Specifies to which database to connect.

■ *Methods*

`Close`—Closes the connection to the database.

`Open`—Opens the connection to the database.

`OleDbCommand` OleDbCommand   This object is used to execute a command on a database.

■ *Properties*

`CommandText`—Specifies an SQL statement.

`Connection`—Specifies the connection to a database.

`Parameters`—Specifies an unknown value for the SQL statement.

■ *Methods*

`ExecuteNonQuery`—Executes nonquery command statements, such as UPDATEs.

`ExecuteReader`—Creates a data reader by executing a database query.

`OleDbDataReader` This object is used to read data from a database.

■ *Methods*

`Read`—Retrieves information from the data reader.

`Close`—Closes the data reader.

Tutorial 26: CheckWriter Application (Introducing Graphics and Printing)

`Font` This class is used to define the font face, size and style of text throughout an application.

■ *Properties*

`Bold`—Sets the weight of the text.

`Italic`—Sets the angle of the text.

`Size`—Sets the size of the text.

`FontFamily`—Contains a `FontFamily` object, which is used to store font face information.

`FontSyle`—Specifies the style applied to a `Font` object.

`Graphics` The class that contains methods used to draw text, lines and shapes.

■ *Methods*

`DrawLine`—Draws a line of a specified size and color.

`DrawEllipse`—Draws the outline of an ellipse of a specified size and color at a specified location.

`DrawRectangle`—Draws the outline of a rectangle of a specified size and color at a specified location.

`DrawEllipse`—Draws a `String` in a specified font and color at a specified position.

`FillEllipse`—Draws a solid ellipse of a specified size and color at the specified location.

`FillRectangle`—Draws a solid rectangle of a specified size and color at the specified location.

PrintDocument This class allows you to specify how to print a document.

- *Event*

    PrintPage—Raised when data required to print a page is needed.

- *Method*

    Print—Uses a Graphics object to print a page.

PrinterSettings This class stores information the system's printer settings.

- *Property*

    Count—Returns the number of printers installed on the system.

PrintPageEventArgs This class contains data passed to a PrintPage event.

- *Properties*

    HasMorePages—Specifies if there are more pages to print. When False, the PrintPage event is no longer raised.

    MarginBounds—Specifies the margin of the printed page. Left specifies the left margin of the page. Top specifies the top margin of the page.

PrintPreviewDialog   📄 PrintPreviewDialog   This control is used to display how a document will look when it is printed.

- *Properties*

    Document—Specifies the document that the control will preview. The document must be of type PrintDocument.

    Name—Specifies the name used to access the PrintPreviewDialog control programmatically. The name should be prefixed with obj.

    UseAntiAlias—Specifies whether the dialog will display a smoothed image.

- *Method*

    ShowDialog—Displays the PrintPreviewDialog to the user.

Tutorial 27: Phone Book Application (Introducing Multimedia Using Microsoft Agent)

Convert The Convert class converts the value of a data type to another data type.

- *Methods*

    ToChar—Converts a value into a character (of data type Char).

    ToDecimal—Converts the value from another data type to type Decimal.

    ToInt16—Converts the value from another data type to type Short.

IAgentCtlCharacter This class is used to represent the Agent character that is used in the application.

- *Property*

    Commands—Contains the commands the character will recognize.

- *Methods*

    Show—Displays the character on the screen.

    MoveTo—Moves the character to a specified location on the screen.

    Play—Plays character animations.

    Speak—Specifies the text to be spoken by the character.

    Commands.Add—Adds a new command to the command list for the Agent object.

IAgentCtlUserInput   This class is used to retrieve commands from users.

- *Property*

  Name—Retrieves the name of the command given by the user.

Microsoft Agent Control   🐦 Control   This control is used to create and manipulate the multimedia features of a Microsoft Agent character.

- *In action*

- *Events*

  Command—Raised when a user gives the Microsoft Agent character a verbal command or selects an option from the character's context menu.

  HideEvent—Raised when a user hides the Microsoft Agent character.

- *Property*

  Location—Specifies the location of the Microsoft Agent control on the Form.

- *Method*

  Characters.Load—Loads a character into the Microsoft Agent control.

Tutorial 28: Bookstore Application: Web Applications (Introducing Internet Information Services)

No new elements.

Tutorial 29: Bookstore Application: Client Tier (Introducing Web Controls)

ASPX page   Page on which controls are dropped to design the GUI.

- *Property*

  bgColor—Specifies the Web Form's background color.

Button   ab| Button   This control allows the user to raise an action or event.

- *In action*

- *Properties*

  ID—Specifies the name of the Label.

  Text—Specifies the text displayed on the Button.

  Width—Specifies the width of the Button.

Horizontal Rule   ⊟ Horizontal Rule   This control displays a line on the ASPX page. It is usually used to separate different areas of the ASPX page.

- *In action*

■ *Properties*

   id—Specifies the name of the Horizontal Rule.

   Style—Allows you to specify where to position the Horizontal Rule on the ASPX page.

Image   This control displays an image on the ASPX page.

■ *In action*

■ *Properties*

   BorderStyle—Specifies the appearance of the Image's border.

   BorderWidth—Specifies the width of the Image's border.

   Height—Specifies the height of the Image control.

   ID—Specifies the name used to access the Image control programmatically. The name should be prefixed with img.

   Width—Specifies the width of the Image control.

Label   **A** Label   This control displays text on the ASPX page that the user cannot modify.

■ *In action*

Books

■ *Properties*

   Height—Specifies the height of the Label.

   ID—Specifies the name used to access the Label programmatically. The name should be prefixed with lbl.

   Name (under the expanded Font property in the **Solution Explorer**)—Specifies the name of the font used for the Label's text.

   Size (under the expanded Font property in the **Solution Explorer**)—Specifies the size of the Label's text.

   Text—Specifies the text displayed on the Label.

   Width—Specifies the width of the Label.

ListBox   ListBox   This control allows the user to view and select from multiple items in a list.

■ *In action*

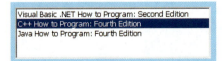

■ *Properties*

   Height—This property specifies the height of the ListBox.

   ID—This property specifies the name used to access the ListBox control programmatically. The name should be prefixed with lst.

   Width—This property specifies the width of the ListBox.

Table   ⊞ Table   This control is usually used to organize data in a spreadsheet format.

- ■ *In action*

Price:	$76.00
ISBN#:	0-13-029363-6
Edition:	2
Copyright Date:	2002
Description:	Microsoft Visual Basic .NET

- ■ *Properties*

  BorderStyle—Specifies the appearance of the Table's border.

  BorderWidth—Specifies the width of the Table's border.

  Cells—Retrieves or sets the value in the specified table cell.

  Gridlines—Specifies the format in which table cell separators are displayed.

  ID—Specifies the name used to access the Table control programmatically. The name should be prefixed with tbl.

  Rows—Retrieves or sets the value in the specified table cell.

Tutorial 30: Bookstore Application: Information Tier (Examining the Database and Creating Database Components)

No new elements.

Tutorial 31: Bookstore Application: Middle Tier (Introducing Code-Behind Files)

ASPX page   Page on which controls are dropped to design the GUI.

- ■ *Event*

  Load—Raised when the ASPX page is created.

- ■ *Property*

  bgColor—Specifies the Web Form's background color.

Image   🖼 Image   This control displays an image on the ASPX page.

- ■ *In action*

■ *Properties*

BorderStyle—Specifies the appearance of the Image's border.

BorderWidth—Specifies the width of the Image's border.

Height—Specifies the height of the Image control.

ID—Specifies the name used to access the Image control programmatically. The name should be prefixed with img.

ImageUrl—Specifies the location of the image file.

Width—Specifies the width of the Image control.

ListBox   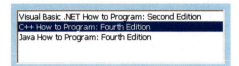   This control allows the user to view and select from multiple items in a list.

■ *In action*

```
Visual Basic .NET How to Program: Second Edition
C++ How to Program: Fourth Edition
Java How to Program: Fourth Edition
```

■ *Properties*

Height—Specifies the height of the ListBox.

ID—Specifies the name used to access the ListBox control programmatically. The name should be prefixed with lst.

SelectedIndex—Returns the index of the selected item in the ListBox.

SelectedItem—Returns the value of the selected item in the ListBox.

Width—Specifies the width of the ListBox.

Response This class provides methods for responding to clients.

■ *Method*

Redirect—Redirects the client browser to the specified location.

Tutorial 32: Enhanced Car Payment Calculator Application: Web Applications (Introducing Exception Handling)

No new elements.

APPENDIX

Keyword Chart

The table of Fig. F.1 contains a complete listing of Visual Basic .NET keywords. Many of these keywords are discussed throughout the text.

Visual Basic .NET Keywords			
AddHandler	AddressOf	Alias	And
AndAlso	Ansi	As	Assembly
Auto	Boolean	ByRef	Byte
ByVal	Call	Case	Catch
CBool	CByte	CChar	CDate
CDec	CDbl	Char	CInt
Class	CLng	CObj	Const
CShort	CSng	CStr	CType
Date	Decimal	Declare	Default
Delegate	Dim	DirectCast	Do
Double	Each	Else	ElseIf
End	Enum	Erase	Error
Event	Exit	False	Finally
For	Friend	Function	Get
GetType	GoTo	Handles	If
Implements	Imports	In	Inherits
Integer	Interface	Is	Lib
Like	Long	Loop	Me
Mod	Module	MustInherit	MustOverride
MyBase	MyClass	Namespace	New
Next	Not	Nothing	NotInheritable
NotOverridable	Object	On	Option

Figure F.1 Visual Basic .NET keywords. (Part 1 of 2.)

Visual Basic .NET Keywords			
Optional	Or	OrElse	Overloads
Overridable	Overrides	ParamArray	Preserve
Private	Property	Protected	Public
RaiseEvent	ReadOnly	ReDim	REM
RemoveHandler	Resume	Return	Select
Set	Shadows	Shared	Short
Single	Static	Step	Stop
String	Structure	Sub	SyncLock
Then	Throw	To	True
Try	TypeOf	Unicode	Until
When	While	With	WithEvents
WriteOnly	Xor		

The following are keywords, although they are not used in Visual Basic .NET

Let	Variant	Wend

Figure F.1 Visual Basic .NET keywords. (Part 2 of 2.)

Internet Information Services (IIS) Setup Instructions

To create Web applications using Visual Studio .NET, Internet Information Services (IIS) needs to be installed on your computer. This appendix will guide you through the installation of IIS on computers using either the Windows 2000 or the Windows XP Professional Edition operating system. [*Note*: **IIS cannot be installed on computers using Windows XP Home Edition.**] For Web applications to compile and execute correctly, IIS must be installed before Visual Studio .NET is installed. It is recommended that you follow the steps to determine whether IIS is installed on your computer. If IIS is not installed on your computer and Visual Studio .NET is, you will need to uninstall Visual Studio .NET before continuing with the IIS installation. Once IIS is installed, you will need to reinstall Visual Studio .NET. [*Note*: If you are working in a lab environment and are prompted for a Windows CD, contact your system administrator for assistance.]

G.1 Installing IIS

This section will show you how to determine whether IIS is installed on a computer using the Windows 2000 and Windows XP operating systems. If IIS is not installed, this section will guide you through the installation process.

To begin, open the **Control Panel** by selecting **Start > Settings > Control Panel** in Windows 2000 or **Start > Control Panel** in Windows XP. When the **Control Panel** window opens, double click the **Add/Remove Programs** icon (Fig. G.1) in Windows 2000 or the **Add or Remove Programs** link (Fig. G.2) in Windows XP.

The **Add/Remove Programs** window lists all of the programs that are currently installed on your computer (Fig. G.3). The names and number of items on your computer will be different from those in the figure. In the left column of the **Add/Remove Programs** window, click the **Add/Remove Windows Components** icon (Fig. G.3) to display the **Windows Components Wizard**.

Figure G.1   Clicking the **Add/Remove Programs** icon in the **Control Panel** in Windows 2000.

Figure G.2   Clicking the **Add or Remove Programs** link in the **Control Panel** in Windows XP. (The contents of your **Control Panel** may differ.)

Figure G.3   Clicking the **Add/Remove Windows Components** icon.

The **Windows Components Wizard** (Fig. G.4) displays a list of Windows components that can be added to or removed from your computer. Scroll down to the **Internet Information Services (IIS)** component's CheckBox. If there is a check mark in this CheckBox, IIS is already installed, and you can click **Cancel** to exit the wizard. If the CheckBox is empty (Fig. G.4), click in the CheckBox (Fig. G.5), and click the **Next >** Button.

Empty **CheckBox** indicates that IIS needs to be installed

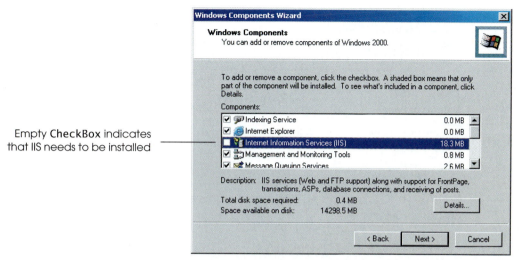

Figure G.4 **Windows Components Wizard** without IIS installed.

Selecting IIS component for installation

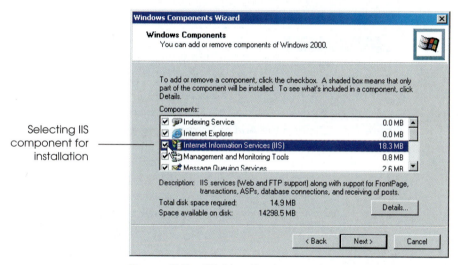

Figure G.5 Clicking the **Internet Information Services CheckBox** to install IIS.

Clicking **Next >** will begin the installation process and display the screen shown in Fig. G.6.

Windows may ask for your Windows 2000 CD during the installation proccess

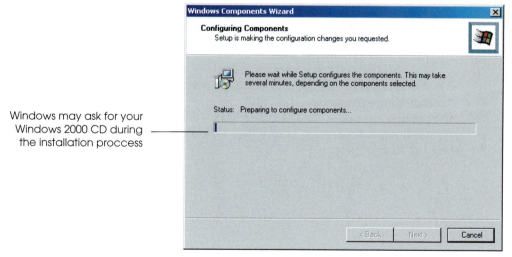

Figure G.6 IIS installing on Windows 2000.

To install IIS, Windows may need to copy files from the Windows 2000 or Windows XP CD. If prompted, insert the CD and click **OK** to continue with the installation. When a dialog informs you that the installation is finished, click **Finish** to complete the installation and close the **Windows Components Wizard** (Fig. G.7).

This dialog appears after a successful installation ——

Figure G.7   Clicking **Finish** to complete the IIS installation.

A

access key—Keyboard shortcuts that allow the user to perform an action on a control using the keyboard.

accessor—Method-like code units that handle the details of modifying and returning data.

action/decision model of programming—Representing control statements as UML activity diagrams with rounded rectangles indicating *actions* to be performed and diamond symbols indicating *decisions* to be made.

action expression (in the UML)—Used in an action state within a UML activity diagram to specify a particular action to perform.

action state—An action to perform in a UML activity diagram that is represented by an action-state symbol.

action-state symbol—A rectangle with its left and right sides replaced with arcs curving outward that represents an action to perform in a UML activity diagram.

Active Server Pages .NET (ASP .NET)—.NET software that helps programmers create applications for the Web.

active tab—The tab of the document displayed in the IDE.

active window—The window that is currently being used—sometimes referred to as the window that has the focus.

ActiveX Properties—A hyperlink at the bottom-left of the **Properties** window for the MSChart control. When clicked, it displays a dialog with which you can set the MSChart properties.

activity diagram—A UML diagram that models the activity (also called the workflow) of a portion of a software system.

Ada—A programming language, named after Lady Ada Lovelace, that was developed under the sponsorship of the U.S. Department of Defense (DOD) in the 1970s and early 1980s.

Add method of class ArrayList—Adds a specified object to the end of an ArrayList.

Add method of the Commands property—Adds a command to a Microsoft Agent character.

Add method of Items—Adds an item to a ListBox control.

AddHandler statement—Adds an event handler for a specific event.

AddressOf operator—Specifies the location of an event handler associated with an event.

ADO .NET—Part of Microsoft .NET that is used to interact with databases.

AgentObjects.IAgentCtlCharacter object—Used to manipulate a Microsoft Agent character.

AgentObjects.IAgentCtlUserInput object—Stores the user input retrieved from a Microsoft Agent character.

algorithm—A procedure for solving a problem, specifying the actions to be executed and the order in which these actions are to be executed.

alphabetic icon—The icon in the **Properties** window that, when clicked, sorts properties alphabetically.

AndAlso operator—A logical operator used to ensure that two conditions are *both* true before choosing a certain path of execution. Performs short-circuit evaluation.

API (application programming interface)—The interface used by a program to access the operating system and various services on the computer.

ARGB values—A combination of alpha, red, green and blue components from which every color is created.

argument—Inputs to a function that provide information that a function needs to perform its task.

argument—Information provided to a procedure call.

arithmetic and logic unit (ALU)—The "manufacturing" section of the computer. The ALU performs calculations and makes decisions.

arithmetic operators—The operators +, -, *, /, \, ^ and Mod.

array—A data structure containing data items of the same type.

array bounds—Integers that determine what indices can be used to access an element in the array. The lower bound is 0; the upper bound is the length of the array minus one.

ArrayList class—Performs the same functionality as an array, but has resizing capabilities.

Array.Sort method—Sorts the values of an array into ascending order.

As keyword—Used in variable declarations. Indicates that the following word (such as Integer) is the variable type.

ASP .NET technology—Can be combined with Visual Basic .NET to create web applications.

ASPX page—File that specifies the GUI of a Web page using Web controls. Also called Web Forms or Web Form Pages.

assembly language—A type of programming language that uses English-like abbreviations to represent the fundamental operations on the computer.

assignment operator—The "=" symbol used to assign values in an assignment statement.

assignment statement—A statement that copies one value to another. An assignment statement contains an "equals"-sign (=) operator that causes the value of its right operand to be copied to its left operand.

asterisk(*)—Multiplication operator. The operator's left and right operands are multiplied together.

attribute—Another name for a property of an object.

Auto Hide—A space-saving IDE feature used for windows such as **Toolbox**, **Properties** and **Dynamic Help** that hides a window until the mouse pointer is placed on the hidden window's tab.

Autos window—Allows you to view the contents of the properties used in the last statement that was executed in an application. This allows you to verify that the previous statement executed correctly and lists the values in the next statement to be executed.

axis label—Display the values associated with data in a graph.

axis title—Describe the meaning of the values on an axis.

B

BackColor property of class Form—Specifies or returns the Color value used as the background color of a Form or control.

backslash(\)—Integer division operator. The operator divides its left operand by its right.

bandwidth—The information-carrying capacity of communications lines.

BASIC (Beginner's All-Purpose Symbolic Instruction Code)—A programming language that was developed in the mid-1960s by Professors John Kemeny and Thomas Kurtz of Dartmouth College as a language for writing simple programs and its primary purpose was to familiarize novices with programming techniques.

Beep function—Causes your computer to make a beep sound.

bgColor property of an ASPX page—Specifies the ASPX page's background color.

binary digit—A digit that can assume one of two values.

binary operator—Requires two operands.

bit—Short for "binary digit." A digit that can assume one of two values.

block—A group of code statements.

block scope—Variables declared inside control statements, such as an If...Then statement, have block scope. Block scope begins at the identifier's declaration and ends at the block's final statement (for example, End If).

book-title capitalization—A style that capitalizes the first letter of the each word in the text (for example, **Calculate Total**).

Boolean data type—A data type that has the value True or False.

BorderStyle property of a Label—Specifies the appearance of a Label's border, which allows you to distinguish one control from another visually. The BorderStyle property can be set to None (no border), FixedSingle (a single dark line as a border), or Fixed3D (giving the Label a "sunken" appearance).

BorderStyle property of an Image—Specifies the type of border that displays around an Image.

BorderWidth property—Specifies the border width of an Image.

bottom tier—The tier (also known as the information tier, or the data tier) containing the application data of a multi-tier application—typically implemented as a database.

bounding box of ellipse—Specifies an ellipse's height, width and location.

break mode—The IDE mode when application execution is suspended. This mode is entered through the debugger.

breakpoint—A statement where execution is to suspend, indicated by a solid maroon circle.

brush—Used to fill shapes with colors.

Brush object—An object used to specify drawing parameters when drawing solid shapes.

built-in data type—A data type already defined in Visual Basic .NET, such as an Integer (also known as a primitive data type).

Button control—Commands the application to perform an action.

Button property of class MouseEventArgs—Specifies which (if any) mouse button is pressed.

Button Web control—Allows users to perform an action.

ByRef keyword—Used to pass an argument by reference.

byte—Eight bits.

ByVal—The keyword specifying that the calling procedure should pass a copy of its argument's value in the procedure call to the called procedure.

C

call-by-reference—See *pass-by-reference*.

call-by-value—See *pass-by-value*.

callee—The procedure being called.

caller—The procedure that calls another procedure. Also known as the calling procedure.

Cancel value of DialogResult enumeration—Used to determine if the user clicked the **Cancel** Button of a dialog.

caret(^)—Exponentiation operator. This operator raises its left operand to a power specified by the right operand.

Case Else statement—Optional statement whose body executes if the Select Case's test expression does not match any of the Cases' expressions.

case sensitive—The instance where two words that are spelled identically are treated differently if the capitalization of the two words differs.

Case statement—Statement whose body executes if the Select Case's test expression matches any of the Cases' expressions.

Catch block—Also called an exception handler, this block executes when the corresponding Try block in the application detects an exceptional situation and throws an exception of the type the Catch block declares.

categorized icon—The icon in the **Properties** window that, when clicked, sorts properties categorically.

Cells property—Allows programmers to create TableCells in a Table.

central processing unit (CPU)—The part of the computer's hardware that is responsible for supervising the operation of the other sections of the computer.

Char structure—Stores characters (such as letters and symbols).

character—A digit, letter or special symbol (characters in Visual Basic .NET are Unicode characters, which are composed of 2 bytes).

character set—The set of all characters used to write applications and represent data items on a particular computer. Visual Basic .NET uses the Unicode character set.

Characters property of MSAgent control—Used to access a specific Microsoft Agent character.

Chars property of class String—Returns the character located at a specific index in a String.

ChartData property of an MSChart control—Property that stores the array containing the data to be displayed as a graph.

ChartType property of an MSChart control—Property that determines the type of graph the control uses to display its data.

CheckBox control—A small white square GUI element that either is blank or contains a check mark.

CheckBox label—The text that appears alongside a CheckBox.

Checked property of the CheckBox control—Specifies whether the CheckBox is checked (True) or unchecked (False).

Checked property of class RadioButton—Property that, when True, displays a small black dot in the control. When False, the control displays an empty white circle.

CheckedChanged event of class RadioButton—Raised when a RadioButton's state (checked or unchecked) changes.

CheckFileExists property of class OpenFileDialog—Enables the user to display a warning if a specified file does not exist.

class—The type of a group of related objects. A class specifies the general format of its objects; the properties and actions available to an object depend on its class. An object is to its class much as a house is to its blueprint.

class definition—The code that belongs to a class, beginning with keyword Class and ending with keywords End Class.

class name—The identifier used to identify the name of a class in code.

Class keyword—Begins a class definition.

Clear method of Items—Deletes all the values in a ListBox's control.

Click event—An event raised when a user clicks a control.

Click event of class MenuItem—Generated when an item is clicked or a shortcut key is used.

client—When an application creates and uses an object of a class, that application is known as a client of that class.

client tier—The user interface of a multi-tier application (also called the top tier).

Close method of class StreamWriter or StreamReader—Used to close the stream.

COBOL (COmmon Business Oriented Language)—A programming language that was developed in the late 1950s by a group of computer manufacturers in conjunction with government and industrial computer users. This language is used primarily for business applications that manipulate large amounts of data.

code-behind file—Visual Basic .NET file that contains a class which provides an ASPX page's functionality.

code editor—A window where a user can create, view or edit an application's code.

code view—A mode of Visual Studio .NET where the application's code is displayed in an editor window.

collection—A class used to store groups of related objects.

collection type of a For Each...Next statement—Specifies the array or collection through which you wish to iterate.

Collections namespace—Contains collection classes such as ArrayList.

Color structure—Contains several predefined colors as properties.

ColorDialog class—Used to display a dialog containing color options to a use.

ComboBox control—Combines a TextBox with a ListBox.

Command event—Raised when a user speaks a command to a Microsoft Agent character or selects a command from a character's context menu.

Commands property—Sets which commands the Microsoft Agent character can understand as input from the user.

comment—A line of code that follows a single-quote character (') and is inserted to improve an application's readability.

compiler—A translator program that converts high-level-language programs into machine language.

component object box—The ComboBox at the top of the Properties window that allows you to select the Form or control object whose properties you want set.

component tray—The area below the Windows Form Designer that contains controls, such as Timers, that are not part of the graphical user interface.

computer—A device capable of performing computations and making logical decisions at speeds millions and even billions of times faster than the speeds at which human beings carry out those same tasks.

computer program—A set of instructions that guides a computer through an orderly series of actions.

computer programmer—A person who writes computer programs in programming languages.

condition—An expression with a true or false value that is used to make a decision.

connection object—Used to establish a connection to a database.

consistent state—A way to maintain the values of an object's instance variables such that those values are always valid.

constant—A variable whose value cannot be changed after its initial declaration.

constructor—A procedure that initializes a class object or structure value when it is created.

container—An object that contains controls.

Contents... command—The command that displays a categorized table of contents in which help articles are organized by topic.

context menu—Appears when you right click an object.

control—A reusable component, such as a RadioButton, Button, GroupBox, Label and an MSChart control.

ControlChar.Tab constant—Represents a tab character.

Control reference—An object that represents a control on the Form.

control structure (control statement)—An application component that specifies the order in which statements execute (also known as the flow of control).

control structure (statement) nesting—Placing one control statement in the body of another control statement.

control structure (statement) stacking—A set of control statements in sequence. The exit point of one control statement is connected to the entry point of the next control statement in sequence.

controlling expression—Value compared sequentially with each `Case` until either a match occurs or the `End Select` statement is reached. Also known as a test expression.

Convert class—Provides methods for converting data types.

Convert.ToDecimal method—Converts a value to type `Decimal`, which is appropriate for monetary calculations.

Convert.ToInt16 method—Converts data to type `Short`.

coordinate system—A scheme for identifying every possible point on the computer screen.

Count property of Items—Returns the number of `ListBox` items.

counter—A variable often used to determine the number of times a block of statements in a loop will execute.

counter-controlled repetition—A technique that uses a counter variable to determine the number of times that a block of statements will execute. Also called definite repetition.

CreateGraphics method—Creates a `Graphics` object on a `Form` or control.

criteria of WHERE clause—Indicates from which specific record data will be retrieved or manipulated.

CType function—Function that converts the type of its first argument to the type specified by the second argument.

currency format—Used to display values as monetary amounts.

CurrentDirectory property of System.Environment—Property that returns the directory from which the application is executing as a fully qualified path name.

Cursor.Position property—Contains the *x*- and *y*-coordinates of the mouse cursor on the screen (in pixels).

CustomFormat property of a DateTimePicker control—Property that contains the programmer-specified format string with which to display the date and/or time when `DateTimePicker` `Format` property is set to `Custom`.

D

data command object—Executes commands that retrieve or modify data in a database.

data hierarchy—Collection of data items processed by computers that become larger and more complex in structure as you progress from bits, to characters, to fields and up to larger data structures.

Data menu—The menu that contains commands for interacting with databases.

data reader—Reads data from a database.

data tier—The tier (also known as the information tier, or the bottom tier) containing the application data of a multi-tier application—typically implemented as a database.

database—Organized collection of data.

database management system (DBMS)—Collection of programs designed to create and manage databases.

DataSource property of class ComboBox—Specifies the source of items listed in a ComboBox.

data structure—Groups and organizes related data.

Date structure—A structure whose properties can be used to store and display date and time information.

Date variable—A variable of type `Date`, capable of storing date and time data.

DateChanged event of MonthCalendar control—Raised when a new date (or a range of dates) is selected.

Date.Now—Returns the current system time and date.

DateTimePicker control—Retrieves date and time information from the user.

Debug menu—The menu that contains commands for debugging and running an application.

debugging—The process of fixing errors in an application.

Decimal data type—Used to store monetary amounts.

decimal digits—The digits 0, 1, 2, 3, 4, 5, 6, 7, 8 and 9.

decision symbol—The diamond-shaped symbol in a UML activity diagram that indicates that a decision is to be made.

default property—The value of a property that provide the initial characteristics of an object when it is first created.

DefaultBackColor property—Contains the default background color for a `Panel` control.

definite repetition—See *counter-controlled repetition*.

descriptive Label—A `Label` used to describe another control on the `Form`. This helps users understand a control's purpose.

design mode—IDE mode that allows you to create applications using Visual Studio .NET's windows, toolbars and menu bar.

Design mode—Displays the ASPX page's GUI at design time.

design units—Any specified units of measurement for the font.

design view—The Visual Studio .NET view that contains the features necessary to begin creating Windows applications.

dialog (message dialog)—A window that displays messages to users and gathers input from users.

DialogResult enumeration—An enumeration that contains values corresponding to standard dialog `Button` names.

diamond—A symbol (also known as the decision symbol) in a UML activity diagram; this symbol indicates that a decision is to be made.

Dim keyword—Indicates the declaration of a variable.

Directory.GetCurrentDirectory—Method of class `Directory` in the `System.IO` namespace that returns a `String` containing the path to the directory that contains the application.

dismiss—Synonym for close.

dithering—Process that uses small dots of existing colors to form a pattern that simulates a desired color.

divide-and-conquer technique—Constructing large applications from small, manageable pieces to make development and maintenance of large applications easier.

DNS lookup—Process that translates domain names to IP addresses.

Do Until...Loop repetition statement—A control statement that executes a set of body statements until its loop-termination condition becomes `True`.

Do While...Loop repetition statement—A control statement that executes a set of body statements while its loop-continuation condition is True.

Do...Loop Until repetition statement—A control statement that executes a set of statements until the loop-termination condition becomes True after the loop executes.

Do...Loop While repetition statement—A control statement that executes a set of statements while the loop-continuation condition is True; the condition is tested after the loop executes.

Document property—Property of the PrintPreviewDialog that allows you to specify the document that will be displayed in the dialog.

domain—Represents a group of hosts on the Internet.

domain name system (DNS) server—Computer that maintains a database of host names and their corresponding IP addresses.

dot operator—See *member access operator*.

dotted line—A UML activity diagram symbol that connects each UML-style note with the element that the note describes.

Double data type—Stores both whole and fractional numbers. Normally, Doubles store floating-point numbers.

double-selection statement—A statement, such as If...Then... Else, that selects between two different actions or sequences of actions.

double-subscripted array—See *two-dimensional array*.

DrawRectangle method of the Graphics class—Draws the outline of a rectangle of a specified size and color at a specified location.

DrawString method—Graphics method that draws the specified String.

DropDownList value of DropDownStyle property—Specifies that a ComboBox is not editable.

DropDownStyle property of class ComboBox—Property of the ComboBox control that specifies the appearance of the ComboBox.

dynamic help—A help option that provides links to articles that apply to the current content (that is, the item selected with the mouse pointer).

dynamic resizing—A capability that allows certain objects (such as ArrayLists) to increase or decrease in size based on the addition or removal of elements from that object. Enables the ArrayList object to increase its size to accommodate new elements and to decrease its size when elements are removed.

E

e event argument—Contains data for the event (such as KeyData).

element—An item in an array.

element of a For Each...Next statement—Used to store a reference to the current value of the collection being iterated.

ElseIf keyword—Keyword used for the nested conditions in nested If...Then...Else statements.

embedded parentheses—Another word for nested parentheses.

empty string—A string that does not contain any characters.

Enabled property—Specifies whether a control such as a Button appears enabled (True) or disabled (False).

Enabled property of a ComboBox—Specifies whether a user can select an item from a ComboBox.

Enabled property of a TextBox—Determines whether a TextBox will respond to user input.

End Class keywords—Marks the end of a class definition.

End Enum keywords—Ends an enumeration.

End Function keywords—Indicates the end of a Function.

End Select keywords—Terminates the Select Case statement.

End Sub keywords—Indicates the end of a Sub procedure.

EndsWith method of class String—Determines if a String ends with a particular substring.

End Try—Indicates the end of a sequence of blocks containing a Try block, followed by one or more Catch blocks and an optional Finally block.

Enum keyword—Begins an enumeration.

enumeration—A group of related, named constants.

equality operator—Operator that compares two values. Returns True if the two values are equal; otherwise, returns False.

event—A user action that can trigger an event handler.

event handler—A section of code that is executed (called) when a certain event is raised (occurs).

event-driven program—A program that responds to user-initiated events such as mouse clicks and keystrokes.

exception—An indication of a problem that occurs during an application's execution.

exception handler—A block that executes when the application detects an exceptional situation and throws an exception.

exception handling—Processing problems that occur during application execution.

executable statement—Actions that are performed when the corresponding Visual Basic .NET application is run.

ExecuteReader method of OleDbCommand object—Executes an SQL statement and makes the result of the query available in the data reader.

ExecuteNonQuery method of OleDbCommand object—Executes an SQL statement and returns the number of rows modified.

explicit conversion—An operation that converts a value of one type to another type using code to (explicitly) tell the application to do the conversion. An example of an explicit conversion is to convert a value of one type to another type using a Convert method.

expression list—Multiple expressions separated by commas. Used for Cases in Select Case statements, when certain statements should execute based on more than one condition.

extensible language—A language that can be "extended" with new data types. Visual Basic .NET is an extensible language.

F

fatal logic error—An error that causes an application to fail and terminate prematurely.

field (of a record)—Group of characters that conveys some meaning. For example, a field consisting of uppercase and lowercase letters can represent a person's name.

field (of a database table)—Column in a table of a database.

file—Collection of data that is assigned a name. Used for long-term persistence of large amounts of data, even after the application that created the data terminates.

FileName property of class OpenFileDialog—Specifies the file name displayed in the dialog.

FillEllipse method of class Graphics—The method of the Graphics class that draws an ellipse. This method takes as arguments a brush, a Color, the coordinates of the ellipse's bounding box's upper-left corner and the width and height of the bounding box.

final state—Represented by a solid circle surrounded by a hollow circle in a UML activity diagram; the end of the workflow after an application performs its activities.

Finally block—An optional block of code that follows the last Catch block in a sequence of Catch blocks or the Try block if there are no Catches. The Finally block provides code that always executes, whether or not an exception occurs.

FixedSingle property of a Label—Specifies that the Label will display a thin, black border.

Flat property of a Button—Specifies that a Button will appear flat.

FlatStyle property of a Button—Determines whether the Button will appear flat or three-dimensional.

floating-point division—Divides two numbers (whole or fractional) and returns a floating-point number.

focus—Designates the window currently in use.

Focus method—Transfers the focus of the application to the control, on which the method is called.

Font class—Contains properties that define unique fonts.

Font property—Determines the font used to display text on a Form or control.

Font property—Specifies the font name, style and size of any displayed text in the Form or one of its controls.

FontDialog class—Used to display a dialog containing font options to a user and record the result.

FontFamily class—Contains methods for obtaining font information, such as GetName and GetType.

For keyword—Begins the For...Next statement.

For Each...Next repetition statement—Iterates through elements in an array or collection.

For...Next header—The first line of a For...Next repetition statement. The For...Next header specifies all four essential elements for the counter-controlled repetition of a For...Next repetition statement.

For...Next repetition statement—Repetition statement that handles the details of counter-controlled repetition. The For...Next statement uses all four elements essential to counter-controlled repetition in one line of code (the name of a control variable, the initial value, the increment or decrement value and the final value).

ForeColor property—Specifies font color for Label controls.

Form—The object that represents the Windows application's graphical user interface (GUI).

format control string—A string that specifies how data should be formatted.

Format property of a DateTimePicker control—The DateTimePicker property that allows the programmer to specify a predefined or custom format with which to display the date and/or time.

format specifier—Code that specifies the type of format that should be applied to a string for output.

FormatException class—An exception of this type is thrown when a method cannot convert its argument to a desired numeric type, such as Integer or Double.

Fortran (Formula Translator)—A programming language developed by IBM Corporation in the mid-1950s to create scientific and engineering applications that require complex mathematical computations.

Framework Class Library (FCL)—.NET's "prepackaged" classes and methods for performing common mathematical calculations, string manipulations, character manipulations, input/output operations, error checking and many other useful operations.

FROM SQL keyword—Specifies table from which to get data.

FromArgb method of the Color class—Creates a new Color object from RGB values.

fully qualified domain name (FQDN)—Host name combined with a domain and top-level domain that provides a user-friendly way to identify a site on the Internet.

functionality—The actions an application can execute.

Function keyword—Begins the definition of a Function procedure.

Function procedure—A procedure similar to a Sub procedure, with one important difference: Function procedures return a value to the caller, whereas Sub procedures do not.

G

GDI+—An application programming interface (API) that provides classes for creating two-dimensional vector graphics.

Get accessor—Used to retrieve a value of an instance variable.

GetName method of the Font class—Returns the name of the Font object.

GetType method of the Font class—Returns the type of the Font object.

GetUpperBound method of class Array—Returns the largest index of an array.

graphical user interface (GUI)—The visual part of an application with which users interact.

Graphics class—Defines methods for drawing shapes.

Graphics object—Draws two-dimensional images.

grid unit—The space between two adjacent horizontal (or two adjacent vertical) dots on the Form in design view.

Gridlines property of a Table—Specifies whether TableCell cell borders display.

GroupBox control—Groups related controls visually.

guard condition—An expression contained in square brackets above or next to the arrows leading from a decision symbol in a UML activity diagram that determines whether workflow continues along a path.

H

hardware—The various devices that make up a computer, including the keyboard, screen, mouse, hard drive, memory, CD-ROM and processing units.

HasMorePages property of class PrintPageEventArgs —Property that specifies if there are more pages to print. When `False`, the `PrintPage` event is no longer raised.

header—A line of text at the top of a `ListBox` that clarifies the information being displayed.

Height property—This property, a member of property `Size`, indicates the height of a `Form` or a control in pixels.

Height property of a Web control—Allows you to specify the height of a Web control.

HideEvent event—Raised when a Microsoft Agent character is hidden.

high-level language—A type of programming language in which a single program statement accomplishes a substantial task. High-level languages use instructions that look almost like everyday English and that contain common mathematical notations.

Horizontal Rule HTML control—Displays a line to separate controls on an ASPX page.

host—A computer that stores and maintains resources, such as Web pages, databases and multimedia files.

host name—Name of a computer where resources reside.

HTML controls—Correspond to HTML elements.

HTML mode—Displays the ASPX page's markup at design time.

HyperText Markup Language (HTML)—A language for marking up information to share over the World Wide Web via hyper-linked text documents.

I

icon—The graphical representation of commands in the Visual Studio .NET IDE.

ID property—Specifies the name of a Web control.

identifier—A series of characters consisting of letters, digits and underscores used to name program units such as classes, controls and variables.

If…Then—Selection statement that performs an action (or sequence of actions) based on a condition. This is also called the single-selection statement.

If…Then…Else—Selection statement that performs an action (or sequence of actions) if a condition is `true` and performs a different action (or sequence of actions) if the condition is `false`. This is also called the double-selection statement.

Image class—Stores and manipulate images from various file formats.

Image property—Indicates the file name of the image displayed in a `PictureBox`.

Image Web control—Displays an image in an ASPX page.

Image.FromFile—A method of class `Image` that returns an `Image` object containing the image located at the path you specify.

immutable—An object that cannot be changed after it is created. In Visual Basic .NET, `Strings` are immutable.

implicit conversion—A conversion from one data type to another performed by Visual Basic .NET.

Imports keyword—Used to import namespaces.

Increment property of a NumericUpDown control—Specifies by how much the current number in the `NumericUpDown` control changes when the user clicks the control's up (for incrementing) or down (for decrementing) arrow.

index—An array element's position number, also called a subscript. An index must be zero, a positive integer or an integer expression. If an application uses an expression as an index, the expression is evaluated first, to determine the index.

index of an ArrayList—The value with which you can refer to a specific element in an `ArrayList`, based on the element's location in that `ArrayList`.

indexed array name—The array name followed by an index enclosed in parentheses. The indexed array name can be used on the left side of an assignment statement to place a new value into an array element. The indexed array name can be used in the right side of an assignment to retrieve the value of that array element.

IndexOf method of class String—`String` method that accepts as an argument a character to search for in a `String`. The method returns the index of a specified character in a `String`. If the `String` does not contain the character, the method returns –1.

infinite loop—An error in which a repetition statement never terminates.

information tier—Tier containing the application data; typically implemented as a database. Also called the bottom tier or database tier.

Inherits keyword—Indicates that the class inherits members from another class.

initial state—The beginning of the workflow in a UML activity diagram before the application performs the modeled activities.

initializer list—The required braces ({ and }) surrounding the initial values of the elements in the array. When the initializer list is empty, the elements in the array are initialized to the default value for the array's data type.

input unit—The "receiving" section of the computer that obtains information (data and computer programs) from various input devices, such as the keyboard and the mouse.

Insert method of class ArrayList—Inserts a specified object into the specified location of an `ArrayList`.

Insert method of class String—`String` method that inserts its second argument (a `String`) at the position specified by the first argument.

instance variable—Declared inside a class but outside any procedure of that class. Instance variables have module scope.

instant-access application—Application where a particular record of information must be located immediately.

instantiate an object—Create an object of a class.

Int32.MaxValue constant—The largest possible Integer—more specifically, 2,147,483,647.

integer—A whole number, such as 919, –11, 0 and 138624.

Integer data type—Stores integer values.

Integer division—Integer division takes two Integer operands and yields an Integer result. The fractional portion of the result is discarded.

integrated development environment (IDE)—A software tool that enables programmers to write, run, test and debug programs quickly and conveniently.

***IntelliSense* feature**—Visual Studio .NET feature that aids the programmer during development by providing windows listing available class members and pop-up descriptions for those members.

interactive animated characters—The Microsoft Agent technology adds such characters to Windows applications and Web pages. These characters can interact with the user through mouse clicks and microphone input.

internal Web browser—Web browser (Internet Explorer) that is included in Visual Studio .NET, with which you can browse the Web.

Internet—A worldwide computer network. Most people today access the Internet through the World Wide Web.

Internet Information Services (IIS)—A Microsoft Web server.

Interval property of a Timer control—The Timer property that specifies the number of milliseconds between each Tick event.

invoking a procedure—Causing a procedure to perform its designated task.

IP address—Unique address used to locate a computer on the Internet.

Is keyword—A keyword that when followed by a comparison operator, can be used to perform a comparison between the controlling expression of a Select Case statement and a value.

Items property of ComboBox—Specifies the values the user can select from the ComboBox.

Item property of Items—Returns the value stored in the ListBox at the specified index.

Items property of the ListBox control—Returns an object containing all the values in the ListBox.

Items.Item property of ComboBox—Retrieves the value at the specified index of a ComboBox.

J

Join method of class String—Concatenates the elements in a String array, separated by the first argument. A new String containing the concatenated elements is returned.

K

keyboard event—Raised when a key on the keyboard is pressed or released.

KeyChar property of class KeyPressEventArgs—Contains data about the key that raised the KeyPress event.

KeyData property of class KeyEventArgs—Contains data about the key that raised the KeyDown event.

KeyDown event—Generated when a key is initially pressed. Use to handle the event raised when a key that is not a letter key is pressed.

KeyEventArgs class—Stores information about special modifier keys.

KeyPress event—Generated when a key is pressed. Use to handle the event raised when a letter key is pressed.

KeyPressEventArgs class—Stores information about character keys.

Keys enumeration—Contains values representing keyboard keys.

KeyUp event—Generated when key is released.

key-value pair—Associates a value with a corresponding key, which is used to identify the value.

keyword—A word in code reserved for a specific purpose. These words appear in blue in the IDE and cannot be used as identifiers.

L

Label—Control that displays text the user cannot modify.

Label Web control—Displays text on an ASPX page.

LastIndexOf method of class String—Returns the index of the last occurrence of a substring in a String. It returns –1 if the substring is not found.

Left value of MouseButtons enumeration—Used to represent the left mouse button.

length of an array—The number of elements in an array.

Length property of class Array—Contains the length (or number of elements in) an array.

Length property of class String—Returns the number of characters in a String.

line-continuation character—An underscore character (_) preceded by one or more spaces, used to continue a statement to the next line of code.

ListBox control—Allows the user to view items in a list. Items can be added to or removed from the list programmatically.

ListBox Web control—Displays a list of items.

literal String objects—A String constant written as a sequence of characters in double quotation marks (also called a string literal).

Load event of a Form—Raised when an application initially executes.

local variable—Declared inside a procedure or block, such as the body of an If...Then statement. Local variables have either procedure scope or block scope.

localhost—Host name that identifies the local computer.

Locals window—Allows you to view the state of the variables in the current scope during debugging.

location bar—The ComboBox in Visual Studio .NET where you can enter the name of a Web site to visit.

Location property—Specifies the location of the upper-left corner of a control. This property is used to place a control on the Form precisely.

logic error—An error that does not prevent the application from compiling successfully, but does cause the application to produce erroneous results.

logical exclusive OR (Xor) operator—A logical operator that is `True` if and only if one of its operands results in `True` and the other results in `False`.

logical operators—The operators (for example, `AndAlso`, `OrElse`, `Xor` and `Not`) that can be used to form complex conditions by combining simple ones.

loop—Another name for a repetition statement.

loop-continuation condition—The condition used in a repetition statement (such as a `Do While...Loop`) that enables repetition to continue while the condition is `True` and that causes repetition to terminate when the condition becomes `False`.

loop-termination condition—The condition used in a repetition statement (such as a `Do Until...Loop`) that enables repetition to continue while the condition is `False` and that causes repetition to terminate when the condition becomes `True`.

M

machine language—A computer's natural language, generally consisting of streams of numbers that instruct the computer how to perform its most elementary operations.

MainMenu control—Allows you to add menus to your application.

margin indicator bar—A margin in the IDE where breakpoints are displayed.

MarginBounds.Left property of the PrintPageEventArgs class—Specifies the left margin of a printed page.

MarginBounds.Top property of the PrintPageEventArgs class—Specifies the top margin of a printed page.

masking—Hiding text such as passwords or other sensitive pieces of information that should not be observed by other people as they are typed. Masking is achieved by using the `PasswordChar` property of the `TextBox` for which you would like to hide data. The actual data entered is retained in the `TextBox`'s `Text` property.

masking character—Used to replace each character displayed in a `TextBox` when the `TextBox`'s data is masked for privacy.

MaxDate property of a DateTimePicker control—Specifies the latest value that the `DateTimePicker` will allow the user to enter.

MaxDropDownItems property of class ComboBox—Property of the `ComboBox` class that specifies how many items can be displayed in the drop-down list.

Maximum property of a NumericUpDown control—Determines the maximum input value in a particular `NumericUpDown` control.

MaxLength property of TextBox—Specifies the maximum number of characters that can be input into a `TextBox`.

m-by-n array—A rectangular two-dimensional array with *m* rows and *n* columns. For instance, a 3-by-4 array has 3 rows and 4 columns.

Me keyword—References the current object.

members of a class—Methods and variables declared within the body of a class.

member-access modifier—Keywords used to specify what members of a class that a client may access. Includes keywords `Public` and `Private`.

member access operator—Also known as the dot operator (.). Allows programmers to access a control's properties using code.

memory unit—The rapid-access, relatively low-capacity "warehouse" section of the computer, which stores data temporarily while an application is running.

menu—Design element that groups related commands for Windows applications. Although these commands depend on the application, some—such as **Open** and **Save**—are common to many applications. Menus are an integral part of GUIs, because they organize commands without cluttering the GUI.

Menu Designer in Visual Studio .NET—Design mode in Visual Studio .NET that allows you to create and edit menus.

menu item—A command located in a menu that, when selected, causes an application to perform a specific action.

menu-access shortcut—*Alt* key shortcut that allows the user to combine the *Alt* key with another key to access a menu item.

merge symbol—A symbol in the UML that joins two flows of activity into one flow of activity.

MessageBox class—Provides a method for displaying message dialogs.

MessageBoxButtons constants—The identifiers that specify `Buttons` that can be displayed in a `MessageBox` dialog.

MessageBoxIcon constants—Identifiers that specify icons that can be displayed in a `MessageBox` dialog.

MessageBox.show method—Displays a message dialog.

Microsoft Agent—A technology used to add interactive animated characters to Windows applications and Web pages.

Microsoft .NET—Microsoft's vision for using the Internet and the Web in the development, engineering and use of software. .NET includes tools such as Visual Studio .NET and programming languages such as Visual Basic .NET.

Microsoft Developer Network (MSDN)—An online library that contains articles, downloads and tutorials on technologies of interest to Visual Studio .NET developers.

middle tier—Tier that controls interaction between the client and information tiers.

Minimum property of a NumericUpDown control—Determines the minimum input value in a particular `NumericUpDown` control.

MinDate property of a DateTimePicker control—Property that specifies the earliest value that the `DateTimePicker` will allow the user to enter.

minus box—The icon that, when clicked, collapses a node.

Mod—The modulus operator yields the remainder after division.

modifier key—Key such as *Shift*, *Alt* or *Control* that modify the way that applications respond to a keyboard event.

module scope—Begins at the identifier after keyword `Class` and terminates at the `End Class` statement, enables all procedures in the same class to access all instance variables defined in that class.

MonthCalendar control—Displays a calendar from which a user can select a range of dates.

mouse event—Generated when a user interacts with an application using the computer's mouse.

MouseButtons enumeration—Defines constants, such as Left and Right, to specify mouse buttons.

MouseDown event—Generated when a mouse button is pressed.

MouseEventArgs class—Specifies information about a mouse event.

MouseMove event—Generated when a mouse pointer is moved.

MouseUp event—Generated when the mouse button is released.

MoveTo method—Relocates the Microsoft Agent character on the screen.

MSChart control— Allows you to display data as a graph on the Form.

multiple-selection statement—Performs one of many actions (or sequences of actions) depending on the value of the controlling expression.

multiplication operator—The asterisk (*) used to multiply its two operands, producing their product as a result.

Multiline property of a TextBox control—Specifies whether the TextBox is capable of displaying multiple lines of text. If the property value is True, the TextBox may contain multiple lines of text; if the value of the property is False, the TextBox can contain only one line of text.

Multiline TextBox control—Provides the ability to enter or display multiple lines of text. If the text exceeds the size of the TextBox, the control can be set to display a scrollbar.

multimedia—The use of various media, such as sound, video and animation, to create content in an application.

multi-tier application—Application that divides functionality into separate tiers. Typically, each tier performs a specific function.

mutually exclusive option—A set of options in which only one can be selected at a time.

N

name of a variable—The identifier used in an application to access or modify a variable's value.

Name property—Assigns a unique and meaningful name to a control for easy identification.

namespace—Classes in the FCL are organized by functionality into these directory-like entities.

narrowing conversion—A conversion where the value of a "larger" type is being assigned to a variable of a "smaller" type, where the "larger" type can store more data than the "smaller" type. Narrowing conversions can result in loss of data, which can cause subtle logic errors.

nested parentheses—When an expression in parentheses is found within another expression surrounded by parentheses. With nested parentheses, the operators contained in the innermost pair of parentheses are applied first.

nested statement—A statement that is placed inside another control statement.

.NET Framework—Microsoft-provided software that executes applications, provides the Framework Class Library (FCL) and supplies many other programming capabilities.

New keyword—Allocates memory in which an object will be stored and calls that object's constructor.

New Project dialog—A dialog that allows you to choose which type of application you wish to create.

Next method of class Random—A method of class Random that, when called with no arguments, generates a positive Integer value between zero and the constant Int32.MaxValue.

NextDouble method of class Random—A method of class Random that generates a positive Double value that is greater than or equal to 0.0 and less than 1.0.

nondestructive memory operation—A process that does not overwrite a value in memory.

nonfatal logic error—An error that does not terminate an application's execution but causes an application to produce incorrect results.

Not (logical negation) operator—A logical operator that enables a programmer to reverse the meaning of a condition: A True condition, when logically negated, becomes False and a False condition, when logically negated, becomes True.

note—An explanatory remark (represented by a rectangle with a folded upper-right corner) describing the purpose of a symbol in a UML activity diagram.

Nothing keyword—Used to clear a reference's value.

Now property—The property of structure Date that retrieves your computer's current time.

NumericUpDown control—Allows you to specify maximum and minimum numeric input values. Also allows you to specify an increment (or decrement) when the user clicks the up (or down) arrow.

O

object technology—A packaging scheme for creating meaningful software units. The units are large and are focused on particular application areas. There are date objects, time objects, paycheck objects, file objects and the like.

objects—Reusable software components that model items in the real world.

off-by-one error—The kind of logic error that occurs when a loop executes for one more or one fewer iterations than is intended.

OleDbCommand object—Used to execute an SQL statement on a database.

OleDbDataReader object—Used to read data from a database. Also known as a data reader object.

one-dimensional array—An array that uses only one index.

opacity—Amount of transparency) of the color.

OpenFileDialog control—Enables an application to use the **Open** dialog, which allows users to specify a file to be opened

operand—An expression subject to an operator.

Option Strict—When set to On, Option Strict causes the compiler to check all conversions and requires the programmer to perform an explicit conversion for all narrowing conversions (for example, conversion from

Double to Decimal) or application termination (conversion of a String, such as "hello", to type Integer).

OrElse operator—A logical operator used to ensure that either or both of two conditions are True in an application before a certain path of execution is chosen.

outlined code—An area of collapsed code in Visual Studio .NET that is noted by a box containing an ellipses. Placing the cursor over the outlined code displays a portion of the collapsed code.

output device—A device to which information that is processed by the computer can be sent.

output Label—A Label used to display calculation results.

output unit—The section of the computer that takes information the computer has processed and places it on various output devices, making the information available for use outside the computer.

P

PadLeft method of class String—Adds characters to the beginning of the string until the length of a string equals the specified length.

Page class—Defines the basic functionality for an ASPX page.

Page_Load—An event handler that executes any processing necessary to display a Web page.

palette—A set of colors.

Panel control—Used to group controls. Unlike GroupBoxes, Panels do not have captions.

Parameter Info **feature of Visual Studio .NET**—Provides the programmer with information about procedures and their arguments.

parameter list—A comma-separated list in which the procedure declares each parameter variable's name and type.

parameter variable—A variable declared in a procedure's parameter list that can be used in the body of the procedure.

Pascal—A programming language named after the 17th-century mathematician and philosopher Blaise Pascal. This language was designed for teaching structured programming.

pass-by-reference—When an argument is passed by reference, the called procedure can access and modify the caller's original data directly. Keyword ByRef indicates pass-by-reference (also called call-by-reference).

pass-by-value—When an argument is passed by value, the application makes a copy of the argument's value and passes that copy to the called procedure. With pass-by-value, changes to the called procedure's copy do not affect the original variable's value. Keyword ByVal indicates pass-by-value (also called call-by-value).

PasswordChar property of a TextBox—Specifies the masking character for a TextBox.

Peek method of class StreamReader—Returns the next character to be read or -1 if there are no more characters to read in the file (that is, the end of the file has been reached).

Pen object—Specifies drawing parameters when drawing shape outlines.

persistent data—Data maintained in files.

PictureBox—Control that displays an image.

pin icon—An icon that enables or disables the Auto Hide feature.

pixel—A tiny point on your computer screen that displays a color.

plus box—An icon that, when clicked, expands a node.

Pmt function—A function that, given an interest rate, a time period and a monetary loan amount, returns a Double value specifying the payment amount per specified time period.

position number—A value that indicates a specific location within an array. Position numbers begin at 0 (zero).

primary key—Field (or combination of fields) in a database table that contains unique values used to distinguish records from one another.

primitive data type—A data type already defined in Visual Basic .NET, such as Integer (also known as a built-in data type).

Print method—PrintDocument method used to print a document.

PrintDocument class—Allows users to describe how to print a document.

PrintPage event—Occurs when the data required to print the current page is needed.

PrintPageEventArgs class—Contains data passed to a PrintPage event.

PrintPreviewDialog class—Previews a document before it prints in a dialog box.

PrinterSettings.InstalledPrinters.Count property —Determines how many printers the user has installed on the computer.

Private keyword—Member-access modifier that makes instance variables or methods accessible only to that class.

procedural programming language—A programming language (such as Fortran, Pascal, BASIC and C) that focuses on actions (verbs) rather than things or objects (nouns).

procedure—A set of instructions for performing a particular task.

procedure body—The declarations and statements that appear after the procedure header but before the keywords End Sub or End Function. The procedure body contains Visual Basic .NET code that performs actions, generally by manipulating or interacting with the parameters from the parameter list.

procedure call—Invokes a procedure, and specifies the procedure name and provides information (arguments) that the callee (the procedure being called) requires to perform its task.

procedure definition—The procedure header, body and ending statement.

procedure header—The first line of a procedure (including the keyword Sub or Function, the procedure name, the parameter list and the Function procedure return type).

procedure name—Follows the keyword Sub or Function and distinguishes one procedure from another. A procedure name can be any valid identifier.

procedure scope—Variables declared inside a procedure but outside of a control structure, have procedure scope. Variables with procedure scope cannot be referenced outside the procedure in which they are declared.

program control—The task of ordering an application's statements in the correct order.

programmer-defined class (programmer-defined type)—Defined by a programmer, as opposed to a class predefined in the Framework Class Library.

programmer-defined procedure—A procedure created by a programmer to meet the unique needs of a particular application.

project—A group of related files that compose an application.

properties—Object attributes, such as size, color and weight.

Properties window—The window that displays the properties for a `Form` or control object.

property—Specifies a control or `Form` object's attributes, such as size, color and position. A property contains accessors—code that handle the details of modifying and returning data.

pseudocode—An informal language that helps programmers develop algorithms.

pseudorandom numbers—A sequence of values produced by a complex mathematical calculation that simulates random-number generation.

`Public` keyword—Member-access modifier that makes instance variables or methods accessible wherever the application has a reference to that object.

px—Specifies that the size is measured in pixels.

Q

Query Builder—Visual Studio .NET tool that allows you to specify the statements that retrieve information from and modify information in databases.

R

`RadioButton` control—Appears as a small white circle that is either blank (unchecked) or contains a smaller black dot (checked). Usually these controls appear in groups of two or more. Exactly one `RadioButton` in a group is selected at once.

`Random` class—Contains methods to generate pseudorandom numbers.

`Read` method of `OleDbDataReader`—Retrieves information from a database.

`ReadLine` method of class `StreamReader`—Method that reads a line from a file and returns it as a `String`.

`ReadOnly` property of a `NumericUpDown` control—Determines whether the input value can be typed by the user.

Real time—Data is accessible to users and applications immediately after it is entered into the database.

real-time error checking—Feature of Visual Studio .NET that provides immediate notification of possible errors in your code.

record—A collection of related fields. Usually a `Class` in Visual Basic .NET composed of several fields (called member variables in Visual Basic .NET).

record (in a database table)—An entire table row in a database.

record key—Identifies a record and distinguishes that record from all other records.

Rectangle structure—Enables you to define rectangular shapes and their dimensions.

rectangular array—A type of two-dimensional array that can represent tables of values consisting of information arranged in rows and columns. Each row contains the same number of columns.

reference—A variable to which you assign an object.

region—A portion of code that can be collapsed or expanded.

relational operators—Operators < (less than), > (greater than), <= (less than or equal to) and >= (greater than or eqaul to) that compare two values.

`Remove` method of class `String`—Deletes characters from a `String`. The first argument contains the index in the `String` at which to begin removing characters, and the second argument specifies the number of characters to remove.

`RemoveAt` method of class `ArrayList`—Removes the object located at a specified location of an `ArrayList`.

repetition statement—Allows the programmer to specify that an action or actions should be repeated, depending on the value of a condition.

`Replace` method of class `String`—Returns a new `String` object in which every occurrence of a substring is replaced with a different substring.

`Response.Redirect` method—Redirects the client browser to another Web page.

rethrow the exception—The `Catch` block can defer the exception handling (or perhaps a portion of it) to another `Catch` block by using the `Throw` statement.

`Return` keyword—Signifies the return statement that sends a value back to the procedure's caller.

`Return` statement—Used to return a value from a procedure.

return type—Data type of the result returned from a `Function` procedure.

reusing code—The practice of using existing code to build new code. Reusing code saves time, effort and money.

RGB value—The amount of red, green and blue needed to create a color.

`Right` value of `MouseButtons` enumeration—Used to represent the right mouse button.

`Rows` property—Allows programmers to create table rows.

rules of operator precedence—Rules that determine the precise order in which operators are applied in an expression.

run mode—IDE mode indicating that the application is executing.

run-time error—An error that has its effect at execution time.

S

scope—The portion of an application in which an identifier (such as a variable name) can be referenced. Some identifiers can be referenced throughout an application; others can be referenced only from limited portions of an application (such as within a single procedure or block).

screen scraping—The process of extracting desired information from the HTML that composes a Web page.

`ScrollBars` property of a `TextBox` control—Specifies whether a `TextBox` has a scrollbar and, if so, of what type. By default, property `ScrollBars` is set to `None`. Setting the value to

Vertical places a scrollbar along the right side of the TextBox.

secondary storage media—Devices such as magnetic disks, optical disks and magnetic tapes on which computers store files.

Select Case statement—The multiple-selection statement used to make a decision by comparing an expression to a series of conditions. The algorithm then takes different actions based on those values.

SELECT SQL keyword—Used to request specified information from a database.

SelectedIndex property of class ComboBox—Specifies the index of the selected item. Returns –1 if no item is selected.

SelectedIndex property of ListBox—Returns the index of the selected item.

SelectedIndexChanged event of ComboBox—Raised when a new value is selected in a ComboBox.

SelectedItem property of ListBox—Returns the value of the selected item.

SelectedValue property of class ComboBox—Specifies the value of the selected item.

SelectionStart property of MonthCalendar control—Returns the first (or only) date selected.

selection statement—Selects among alternative courses of action.

sender event argument—Event argument that contains the GUI component that raised the event (also called the source of the event).

sentence-style capitalization—A style that capitalizes the first letter of the first word in the text. Every other letter in the text is lowercase, unless it is the first letter of a proper noun (for example, **Cartons per shipment**).

separator bar—Bar placed in a menu to separate related menu items.

sequential-access file—File which contains data that is read in the order that it was written to the file.

sequential execution—Statements in an application are executed one after another in the order in which they are written.

sequence structure (or sequence statement)—Built into Visual Basic .NET—unless directed to act otherwise, the computer executes Visual Basic .NET statements sequentially.

Session state—ASP .NET's built-in support for tracking data.

Session object—Maintained across several Web pages containing a collection of items (key-value pairs). This variable is specific to each user.

Set accessor—Provides data-validation capabilities to ensure that the value is set properly.

Short data type—Holds small Integers.

short-circuit evaluation—The evaluation of the right operand in AndAlso and OrElse expressions occurs only if the first condition meets the criteria for the condition.

Show method—Displays a Microsoft Agent character on the screen.

ShowDialog method of FontDialog or ColorDialog—Displays the dialog on which it is called.

ShowDialog method of OpenFileDialog—Displays the **Open** dialog and returns the result of the user interaction with the dialog.

ShowUpDown property of a DateTimePicker control—Property that, when true, allows the user to specify the time using up and down arrows.

simple condition—Contains one expression.

Single data type—Stores floating-point values. Single is similar to Double, but is less precise and requires less memory.

single-entry/single-exit control statement—A control statement that has one entry point and one exit point. All Visual Basic .NET control statements are single-entry/single-exit control statements.

single-quote character(')—Indicates the beginning of a code comment.

single-selection statement—The If...Then statement, which selects or ignores a single action or sequence of actions.

Size property—Property that specifies the height and width, in pixels, of the Form or one of its controls.

Size property of a Web control—Allows you to specify the size of a Web control.

SizeMode property—Property that specifies how an image is displayed in a PictureBox.

sizing handle—Square that, when enabled, can be used to resize the Form or one of its controls.

small circles (in the UML)—The solid circle in an activity diagram represents the activity's initial state and the solid circle surrounded by a hollow circle represents the activity's final state.

software—The set of applications that run on computers.

software reuse—The reuse of existing pieces of software, an approach that enables programmers to avoid "reinventing the wheel," helping them develop new applications faster.

solid circle—A UML activity diagram symbol that represents the activity's initial state.

SolidBrush class—Defines a brush that draws with a single color.

solution—Contains one or more projects.

Solution Explorer—A window that provides access to all the files in a solution.

Sorted property of class ComboBox—When set to True, sorts the items in a ComboBox alphabetically.

Speak method—Used to have the Microsoft Agent character speak text to the user.

special characters—Characters that are neither digits or letters.

special symbols—$, @, %, &, *, (,), -, +, ", :, ?, / and the like.

speech-recognition engine—Application that translates vocal sound input from a microphone into a language that the computer understands.

speech synthesis—The process by which a computer converts text to spoken words.

Split method of class String—Splits the words in a String whenever a space is reached.

Sqrt method of class Math—A procedure similar to a Function procedure, with one important difference: Sub procedures do not return a value to the caller, whereas `Function` procedures do.

Start Page—The initial page displayed when Visual Studio .NET is opened.

StartsWith method of class `String`—Determines if a `String` starts with a particular substring.

startup object—The object (for example, a `Form`) displayed when the application executes.

state button—A button that can be in the on/off (true/false) state.

statement—A unit of code that, when compiled and executed, performs an action.

status box—A box that appears below a Microsoft agent character that displays information about the character's actions.

Step keyword—Optional component of the `For...Next` header that specifies the increment (that is, the amount added to the control variable each time the loop is executed).

straight-line form—The manner in which arithmetic expressions must be written so they can be represented in Visual Basic .NET code.

stream—Object that has access to a sequence of characters.

StreamReader class—Provides methods for reading information from a file.

StreamWriter class—Provides methods for writing information to a file.

StretchImage—Value of `PictureBox` property `SizeMode` that scales an image to fill the `PictureBox`.

string constant—A `String` constant written as a sequence of characters in double quotation marks (also called a string literal).

string literal—A `String` constant written as a sequence of characters in double quotation marks (also called a literal `String` object).

String.Format method—Formats a string.

String variable—A variable that stores a series of characters.

structured programming—A technique for organizing program control to help you develop applications that are easy to understand, debug and modify.

Structured Query Language (SQL)—Language often used by relational databases to perform queries and manipulate data in relational databases.

style property—Allows you to specify the position of a Web control.

Sub keyword—Begins the definition of a Sub procedure.

Sub procedure—A procedure similar to a `Function` procedure, with one important difference: Sub procedures do not return a value to the caller, whereas `Function` procedures do.

submenu—Menu within another menu.

subscript—See *index*.

substring—A sequence of characters in a `String`.

Substring method of class `String`—Creates a new `String` object by copying part of an existing `String` object.

syntax error—An error that occurs when program statements violate the grammatical rules of a programming language.

System.Drawing.Printing namespace—Allows your applications to access all services related to printing.

System.IO namespace—Contains methods to access files and directories.

T

TabIndex property—A control property that specifies the order in which focus is transferred to controls on the `Form` when the *Tab* key is pressed.

table—Used to store related information in rows and columns.

Table Web control—Displays a table in an ASPX page.

TabStop property—A control property that specifies whether a control can receive the focus when the *Tab* key is pressed.

Tahoma font—The Microsoft-recommended font for use in Windows applications.

temporary variable—Used to store data when swapping values.

text file—A file containing human-readable characters.

Text property—Sets the text displayed on a control.

Text property of a Web control—Specifies the text that displays on a Web control.

Text property of class `MenuItem`—Specifies the menu item's text.

TextAlign property—Specifies how text is aligned in the control.

TextBox control—Retrieves user input from the keyboard.

TextChanged event—Occurs when the text in a `TextBox` changes.

text-to-speech engine—Application that translates typed words into spoken sound that users hear through headphones or speakers connected to a computer.

Throw statement—The statement used to rethrow an exception in a `Catch` block.

throws an exception—A method throws an exception if a problem occurs while the method is executing.

Tick event of a `Timer` control—Raised after the number of milliseconds specified in the `Timer` control's `Interval` property has elapsed.

Timer control—Wakes up at specified intervals to execute code in its `Tick` event handler.

title property of an ASPX page—Specifies the page's title.

To keyword—Used to specify a range of values. Commonly used in `For...Next` headers to specify the initial and final values of the statement's control variable.

ToChar method of class `Convert`—Converts a `String` to a character.

ToLongDateString method of type `Date`—Returns a `String` containing the date in the format "Wednesday, October 30, 2002."

ToLower method of class `String`—Creates a new `String` object that replaces every uppercase letter in a `String` with its lowercase equivalent.

ToUpper method of class `String`—Creates a new `String` object that replaces every lowercase letter in a `String` with its uppercase equivalent.

toolbar—A bar that contains `Button`s that execute commands.

toolbar icon—A picture on a toolbar `Button`.

Toolbox—A window that contains controls used to customize Forms.

Tools menu—A menu that contains commands for accessing additional IDE tools and options that enable customization of the IDE.

tool tip—The description of an icon that appears when the mouse pointer is held over that icon for a few seconds.

top-level domain (TLD)—Usually describes the type of organization that owns the domain name.

top tier—Tier containing the application's user interface. Also called the client tier.

ToShortTimeString method of type Date—Returns a String containing the time in the format "4:00 PM."

ToString method—Returns a String representation of the object or data type on which the method is called.

transfer of control—Occurs when an executed statement does not directly follow the previously executed statement in the written application.

transferring the focus—Selecting a control in an application.

transition—A change from one action state to another that is represented by transition arrows in a UML activity diagram.

Transmission Control Protocol/Internet Protocol—TCP/IP for short. The combined set of communications protocols for the Internet.

Trim method of class String—Removes all whitespace characters from the beginning and end of a String.

truth table—A table that displays the boolean result of a logical operator for all possible combinations of True and False values for its operands.

Try block—A block of statements that might cause exceptions and statements that should not execute if an exception occurs.

two-dimensional array—A double-subscripted array that contains multiple rows of values.

type of a variable—Specifies the kind of data that can be stored in a variable and the range of values that can be stored.

U

UML (Unified Modeling Language)—An industry standard for modeling software systems graphically.

uncaught exception—An exception that does not have an exception handler. Uncaught exceptions might terminate application execution.

Unicode—A character set containing characters that are composed of 2 bytes. Characters are represented in Visual Basic .NET using the Unicode character set.

uniform resource locator (URL)—Address that can be used to direct a browser to a resource on the Web.

UPDATE SQL keyword—Used to modify data in a database table.

UseAntiAlias property—Property of class PrintPreview-Dialog that makes the text in the PrintPreviewDialog appear smoother on the screen.

V

Val function—Filters a number from its argument if possible. This avoids errors introduced by the entering of nonnumeric data when only numbers are expected. However, the result of the Val function is not always what the programmer intended.

value of a variable—The piece of data that is stored in a variable's location in memory.

Value property of a DateTimePicker control—Stores the value (such as a time) in a DateTimePicker control.

ValueChanged event of a DateTimePicker—Raised when a user selects a new day or time in the DateTimePicker control.

variable—A location in the computer's memory where a value can be stored for use by an application.

variable declaration—The reporting of a new variable to the compiler. The variable can then be used in the Visual Basic .NET code.

vector graphics—Graphics created by a set of mathematical properties called vectors, which include the graphics' dimensions, attributes and positions.

Vertical value of ScrollBars property—Displays a vertical scrollbar on the right side of a TextBox.

visual programming with Visual Basic .NET—Instead of writing detailed program statements, the programmer uses Visual Studio .NET's graphical user interface to conveniently drag and drop predefined objects into place, and to label and resize them. Visual Studio .NET writes much of the Visual Basic .NET program, saving the programmer considerable effort.

Visual Studio .NET—Microsoft's IDE (integrated development environment), which allows developers to create applications in a variety of .NET programming languages.

W

Watch window—A Visual Studio .NET window that allows you to view variable values as an application is being debugged.

Web applications—Applications that create web content.

Web controls—Controls, such as TextBoxes and Buttons, that are used to customize ASPX pages.

Web server—Specialized software that responds to client requests by providing resources.

Web-safe colors—Colors that display the same on different computers.

WHERE SQL keyword—Specifies criteria that determine the rows to retrieve.

whitespace character—A space, tab or newline character.

widening conversion—A conversion where the value of a "smaller" type is being assigned to a variable of a "larger" type, where the "larger" type can store more data than the "smaller" type.

Width property—This setting, a member of property Size, indicates the width of the Form or one of its controls, in pixels.

Width property of a Web control—Allows you to specify the width of a Web control.

Windows application—An application that executes on a Windows operating system.

workflow—The activity of a portion of a software system.

World Wide Web (WWW)—A communications system that allows computer users to locate and view multimedia documents (such as documents with text, graphics, animations, audios and videos).

World Wide Web Consortium (W3C)—A forum through which qualified individuals and companies cooperate to develop and standardize technologies for the World Wide Web.

WriteLine method of class StreamWriter—Method of class StreamWriter that writes a String and a line terminator to a file.

X

x-axis—Describes every horizontal coordinate.

x-coordinate—Horizontal distance (increasing to the right) from the left of the drawing area.

X property of class MouseEventArgs—The property of class MouseEventArgs that specifies the *x*-coordinate of the mouse event.

Y

y-axis—Describes every vertical coordinate.

y-coordinate—Vertical distance (increasing downward) from the top of the drawing area.

Y property of class MouseEventArgs—The property of class MouseEventArgs that specifies the *y*-coordinate of the mouse event.

Z

zeroth element—The first element in an array.

INDEX

System.Drawing.Printing, 6
62
System.IO, 357
narrowing conversion, 339
nested If...Then...Else
statement, 142
nested parentheses, 120
nesting, 142
.NET
FCL (Framework Class
Library), 9, 54, 89, 262
Framework, 9
initiative, 9
Network and **Dialup Connections**
explorer, 717
Network Identification, 717
New keyword, 304, 378
New Project Button on the **Start**
Page, 20, 23
New Project dialog, 23, 25, 66
newline, 139
newsgroup, 21
Next keyword, 236
Next method of class Random, 354
nodes
defined, 29
minus box, 29
plus box, 29
nondestructive read from
memory, 118
Not (logical NOT) operator, 175,
177, 178
note UML activity diagram, 137
Nothing keyword, 360, 378
noun, 7
Now property of structure
Date, 262
n-tier application, 715
NumericUpDown control
Increment property, 239
Maximum property, 239
Minimum property, 239

O

obj prefix (for objects), 353
object, 5, 7
OOP (object-oriented
programming), 5
object-oriented programming
(OOP), 5, 428, 436, 437, 438,
439, 440, 441, 444, 446, 451
object-oriented language, 7
off-by-one error, 214, 236
OK constant of
MessageBoxButtons, 174
OKCancel constant of
MessageBoxButtons, 174
OleDbCommand class
CommandText property, 767
Connection property, 626,
767
ExecuteNonQuery
method, 638
ExecuteReader method, 635
OleDbCommand object, 767
Parameters property, 631
OleDbCommand object, 626

OleDbConnection class, 624, 767,
780
Close method, 624, 636, 780
Open method, 624, 635, 780
OleDbConnection object, 624
OleDbDataReader class
Close method, 638
Read method, 636, 784
OleDbParameter Collection Edi-
tor dialog, 771
Online Community link on the
Start Page, 21
Open command, 536
Open method of class
OleDbConnection, 624, 635,
780
Open Project Button on the **Start**
Page, 20, 21
Open Project dialog, 39
Open Solution dialog, 42
OpenFileDialog control, 585
CheckFileExists
property, 585
FileName property, 585, 589
Name property, 585
ShowDialog method, 588
opening a project, 27
operand, 94
operator precedence, 120
operators
less-than (<), 139
less-than-or-equal-to (<=), 139
addition (+), 119
addition assignment (+=), 149
And, 177
AndAlso (logical AND with
short-circuit
evaluation), 176
assignment (=), 94, 112, 114,
149
binary, 177
division assignment (/=), 149
dot (or member-access)(.), 94
equality (=), 139
equality operator (=), 139
exclusive OR logical
(Xor), 177
exponentiation assignment
(^=), 149
float division (/), 119
greater-than (>), 139
greater-than-or-equal-to
(>=), 139
greater-than (>), 139
inequality (<>), 139
integer division (\), 119
integer division assignment
(\=), 149
less-than (<), 139
less than or equal to (<=), 175
logical AND (And), 177
logical AND with short-circuit
evaluation (AndAlso), 175
logical exclusive OR
(Xor), 175, 177

operators (cont.)
logical inclusive OR with
short-circuit evaluation
(OrElse), 175
logical NOT (Not), 175, 177
logical OR (Or), 177
member access (.), 94
Mod (modulus), 118
multiplication (*), 96, 118
multiplication assignment
(*=), 149
subtraction (-), 119
subtraction assignment (-
=), 149
unary, 119, 177
Using Logical Operators in
Complex Expressions
(box), 178
optical disk, 580
Option Strict
defined, 339
Enabling Option Strict
(box), 339
Or operator, 177
Oracle, 763
Orange property of structure
Color, 667
OrElse (logical inclusive OR with
short-circuit evaluation)
operator, 175, 176
org (top-level domain), 717
outlined code, 90
output, 25, 71
output device, 2
output Label, 71
output unit, 2
Output window, 99

P

Package class, 474
PadLeft method of class
String, 444
Page class, 778
Page_Load event handler of ASPX
page, 780
Painter application
BackColor property of
Form, 516
Button property of
MouseEventArgs class, 515
Color structure, 508
FillEllipse method of
Graphics class, 508
Graphics class, 505
MouseButtons
enumeration, 515
MouseDown event, 506
MouseEventArgs class, 507
MouseMove event, 513
MouseUp event, 509
SolidBrush class, 508
palette, 47
pane, 24
Panel control, 431
Adding a Panel Control to the
Microwave Oven Applica-
tion (box), 434

BackColor property, 447
BorderStyle property, 434
DefaultBackColor
property, 447
pnl prefix, 434
parameter, 279, 287
Parameter Info feature of Visual
Studio .NET, 280
parameter list, 279
Parameters property of class
OleDbCommand, 631
parentheses
embedded, 120
innermost pair, 120
nested parentheses, 120
unnecessary (redundant), 121
using parentheses to force the
order of evaluation, 120
Parking Garage Fee Calculator
application exercise, 326
Pascal programming language, 6
Pascal, Blaise, 6, 16, 864
pass-by-reference, 335
pass-by-value, 335
Password GUI exercise, 82
PasswordChar property of
TextBox, 259
paste command of **Edit** menu, 27
pattern of 0s and 1s, 583
Pay Raise Calculator application
exercise, 252
payroll system, 583
Peedy the Parrot Microsoft Agent
character, 689
Peek method of class
StreamReader, 602
Pen class, 521, 658, 665, 667
persistent data, 580
personal computer, 1
Personal Identification Number
(PIN), 616
Phone Book application, 691
Using Code to Display the
Peedy Agent Character
(box), 697
PhoneBook application database
(Web-based) exercise, 774
PhoneBook application function-
ality exercise, 793
PhoneBook application GUI
(Web-based) exercise, 757
Photo Album application
exercise, 611
PictureBox control, 360
Image property, 51
SizeMode property, 52
Pig Latin exercise, 579
pin icon, 32
Pink property of structure
Color, 667
"pinning down" a window, 32
Pixel member of enumeration
GraphicsUnit, 672
Play method of class
IAgentCtlCharacter, 701

End User License Agreement

PRENTICE HALL LICENSE AGREEMENT AND LIMITED WARRANTY

READ THE FOLLOWING TERMS AND CONDITIONS CAREFULLY BEFORE OPENING THIS SOFTWARE PACKAGE. THIS LEGAL DOCUMENT IS AN AGREEMENT BETWEEN YOU AND PRENTICE-HALL, INC. (THE "COMPANY"). BY OPENING THIS SEALED SOFTWARE PACKAGE, YOU ARE AGREEING TO BE BOUND BY THESE TERMS AND CONDITIONS. IF YOU DO NOT AGREE WITH THESE TERMS AND CONDITIONS, DO NOT OPEN THE SOFTWARE PACKAGE. PROMPTLY RETURN THE UNOPENED SOFTWARE PACKAGE AND ALL ACCOMPANYING ITEMS TO THE PLACE YOU OBTAINED THEM FOR A FULL REFUND OF ANY SUMS YOU HAVE PAID.

1.   GRANT OF LICENSE: In consideration of your purchase of this book, and your agreement to abide by the terms and conditions of this Agreement, the Company grants to you a nonexclusive right to use and display the copy of the enclosed software program (hereinafter the "SOFTWARE") on a single computer (i.e., with a single CPU) at a single location so long as you comply with the terms of this Agreement. The Company reserves all rights not expressly granted to you under this Agreement.

2.   OWNERSHIP OF SOFTWARE: You own only the magnetic or physical media (the enclosed media) on which the SOFTWARE is recorded or fixed, but the Company and the software developers retain all the rights, title, and ownership to the SOFTWARE recorded on the original media copy(ies) and all subsequent copies of the SOFTWARE, regardless of the form or media on which the original or other copies may exist. This license is not a sale of the original SOFTWARE or any copy to you.

3.   COPY RESTRICTIONS: This SOFTWARE and the accompanying printed materials and user manual (the "Documentation") are the subject of copyright. The individual programs on the media are copyrighted by the authors of each program. Some of the programs on the media include separate licensing agreements. If you intend to use one of these programs, you must read and follow its accompanying license agreement. You may not copy the Documentation or the SOFTWARE, except that you may make a single copy of the SOFTWARE for backup or archival purposes only. You may be held legally responsible for any copying or copyright infringement which is caused or encouraged by your failure to abide by the terms of this restriction.

4.   USE RESTRICTIONS: You may not network the SOFTWARE or otherwise use it on more than one computer or computer terminal at the same time. You may physically transfer the SOFTWARE from one computer to another provided that the SOFTWARE is used on only one computer at a time. You may not distribute copies of the SOFTWARE or Documentation to others. You may not reverse engineer, disassemble, decompile, modify, adapt, translate, or create derivative works based on the SOFTWARE or the Documentation without the prior written consent of the Company.

5.   TRANSFER RESTRICTIONS: The enclosed SOFTWARE is licensed only to you and may not be transferred to any one else without the prior written consent of the Company. Any unauthorized transfer of the SOFTWARE shall result in the immediate termination of this Agreement.

6.   TERMINATION: This license is effective until terminated. This license will terminate automatically without notice from the Company and become null and void if you fail to comply with any provisions or limitations of this license. Upon termination, you shall destroy the Documentation and all copies of the SOFTWARE. All provisions of this Agreement as to warranties, limitation of liability, remedies or damages, and our ownership rights shall survive termination.

7.   MISCELLANEOUS: This Agreement shall be construed in accordance with the laws of the United States of America and the State of New York and shall benefit the Company, its affiliates, and assignees.

8.   LIMITED WARRANTY AND DISCLAIMER OF WARRANTY: The Company warrants that the SOFTWARE, when properly used in accordance with the Documentation, will operate in substantial conformity with the description of the SOFTWARE set forth in the Documentation. The Company does not warrant that the SOFTWARE will meet your requirements or that the operation of the SOFTWARE will be uninterrupted or error-free. The Company warrants that the media on which the SOFTWARE is delivered shall be free from defects in materials and workmanship under normal use for a period of thirty (30) days from the date of your purchase. Your only remedy and the Company's only obligation under these limited warranties is, at the Company's option, return of the warranted item for a refund of any amounts paid by you or replacement of the item. Any replacement of SOFTWARE or media under the warranties shall not extend the original warranty period. The limited warranty set forth above shall not apply to any SOFTWARE which the Company determines in good faith has been subject to misuse, neglect, improper installation, repair, alteration, or damage by you. EXCEPT FOR THE EXPRESSED WARRANTIES SET FORTH ABOVE, THE COMPANY DISCLAIMS ALL

WARRANTIES, EXPRESS OR IMPLIED, INCLUDING WITHOUT LIMITATION, THE IMPLIED WARRANTIES OF MERCHANTABILITY AND FITNESS FOR A PARTICULAR PURPOSE. EXCEPT FOR THE EXPRESS WARRANTY SET FORTH ABOVE, THE COMPANY DOES NOT WARRANT, GUARANTEE, OR MAKE ANY REPRESENTATION REGARDING THE USE OR THE RESULTS OF THE USE OF THE SOFTWARE IN TERMS OF ITS CORRECTNESS, ACCURACY, RELIABILITY, CURRENTNESS, OR OTHERWISE.

IN NO EVENT, SHALL THE COMPANY OR ITS EMPLOYEES, AGENTS, SUPPLIERS, OR CONTRACTORS BE LIABLE FOR ANY INCIDENTAL, INDIRECT, SPECIAL, OR CONSEQUENTIAL DAMAGES ARISING OUT OF OR IN CONNECTION WITH THE LICENSE GRANTED UNDER THIS AGREEMENT, OR FOR LOSS OF USE, LOSS OF DATA, LOSS OF INCOME OR PROFIT, OR OTHER LOSSES, SUSTAINED AS A RESULT OF INJURY TO ANY PERSON, OR LOSS OF OR DAMAGE TO PROPERTY, OR CLAIMS OF THIRD PARTIES, EVEN IF THE COMPANY OR AN AUTHORIZED REPRESENTATIVE OF THE COMPANY HAS BEEN ADVISED OF THE POSSIBILITY OF SUCH DAMAGES. IN NO EVENT SHALL LIABILITY OF THE COMPANY FOR DAMAGES WITH RESPECT TO THE SOFTWARE EXCEED THE AMOUNTS ACTUALLY PAID BY YOU, IF ANY, FOR THE SOFTWARE.

SOME JURISDICTIONS DO NOT ALLOW THE LIMITATION OF IMPLIED WARRANTIES OR LIABILITY FOR INCIDENTAL, INDIRECT, SPECIAL, OR CONSEQUENTIAL DAMAGES, SO THE ABOVE LIMITATIONS MAY NOT ALWAYS APPLY. THE WARRANTIES IN THIS AGREEMENT GIVE YOU SPECIFIC LEGAL RIGHTS AND YOU MAY ALSO HAVE OTHER RIGHTS WHICH VARY IN ACCORDANCE WITH LOCAL LAW.

ACKNOWLEDGMENT

YOU ACKNOWLEDGE THAT YOU HAVE READ THIS AGREEMENT, UNDERSTAND IT, AND AGREE TO BE BOUND BY ITS TERMS AND CONDITIONS. YOU ALSO AGREE THAT THIS AGREEMENT IS THE COMPLETE AND EXCLUSIVE STATEMENT OF THE AGREEMENT BETWEEN YOU AND THE COMPANY AND SUPERSEDES ALL PROPOSALS OR PRIOR AGREEMENTS, ORAL, OR WRITTEN, AND ANY OTHER COMMUNICATIONS BETWEEN YOU AND THE COMPANY OR ANY REPRESENTATIVE OF THE COMPANY RELATING TO THE SUBJECT MATTER OF THIS AGREEMENT.

Should you have any questions concerning this Agreement or if you wish to contact the Company for any reason, please contact in writing at the address below.

Robin Short
Prentice Hall PTR
One Lake Street
Upper Saddle River, New Jersey 07458

The DEITEL® Suite of Products...

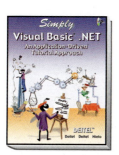

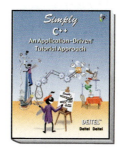

HOW TO PROGRAM BOOKS

The Deitels' acclaimed *How to Program Series* has achieved Its success largely due to the innovative pedagogy used to teach key programming concepts. Their signature *LIVE-CODE Approach,* icon-identified programming tips and comprehensive exercises form the backbone of a series of books that has taught over one million students the craft of programming.

C++ How to Program Fourth Edition

BOOK / CD-ROM

©2003, 1400 pp., paper
(0-13-038474-7)

The world's best-selling C++ textbook is now even better! Designed for beginning through intermediate courses, this comprehensive, practical introduction to C++ includes hundreds of hands-on exercises and uses 267 *LIVE-CODE* programs to demonstrate C++'s powerful capabilities. This edition includes a new chapter—Web Programming with CGI—that provides everything readers need to begin developing their own Web-based applications that will run on the Internet!

Java™ How to Program Fifth Edition

BOOK / CD-ROM

©2003, 1500 pp., paper
(0-13-101621-0)

The Deitels' new Fifth Edition of *Java™ How to Program* is now even better! It now includes a tuned treatment of object-oriented programming; coverage of Java 1.4's new I/O APIs; new chapters on JDBC, servlets and JSP; an updated, optional case study on object-oriented design with version 1.4 of the UML; and a new code highlighting feature that makes it easier for readers to locate important program segments.

Visual Basic® .NET How to Program Second Edition

BOOK / CD-ROM

©2002, 1400 pp., paper
(0-13-029363-6)

This book provides a comprehensive introduction to the next version of Visual Basic—Visual Basic .NET—featuring extensive updates and increased functionality. *Visual Basic .NET How to Program, Second Edition* covers introductory programming techniques as well as more advanced topics, featuring ASP .NET, ADO .NET, Web services and developing Web-based applications. This book also includes extensive coverage of XML.

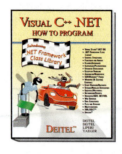

Visual C++ .NET How To Program

BOOK / CD-ROM

©2004, 1400 pp., paper (0-13-437377-4)

Written by the authors of the world's best-selling introductory/intermediate C and C++ textbooks, this comprehensive book thoroughly examines Visual C++® .NET. *Visual C++® .NET How to Program* begins with a strong foundation in the introductory and intermediate programming principles students will need in industry, including fundamental topics such as arrays, functions and control structures. Readers learn the concepts of object-oriented programming, including how to create reusable software components with classes and assemblies. The text then explores such essential topics as networking, databases, XML and multimedia. Graphical user interfaces are also extensively covered, giving students the tools to build compelling and fully interactive programs using the "drag-and-drop" techniques provided by the latest version of Visual Studio .NET.

Advanced Java™ 2 Platform How to Program

BOOK / CD-ROM

©2002, 1811 pp., paper (0-13-089560-1)

Expanding on the world's best-selling Java textbook—*Java™ How to Program*—*Advanced Java™ 2 Platform How To Program* presents advanced Java topics for developing sophisticated, user-friendly GUIs; significant, scalable enterprise applications; wireless applications and distributed systems. Primarily based on Java 2 Enterprise Edition (J2EE), this textbook integrates technologies such as XML, JavaBeans, security, JDBC™, JavaServer Pages (JSP™), servlets, Remote Method Invocation (RMI), Enterprise JavaBeans™ (EJB) and design patterns into a production-quality system that allows developers to benefit from the leverage and platform independence Java 2 Enterprise Edition provides. The book also features the development of a complete, end-to-end e-business solution using advanced Java technologies.

C# How to Program

BOOK / CD-ROM

©2002, 1568 pp., paper (0-13-062221-4)

C# How to Program provides a comprehensive introduction to Microsoft's new object-oriented language. C# builds on the skills already mastered by countless C++ and Java programmers, enabling them to create powerful Web applications and components—ranging from XML-based Web services on Microsoft's .NET platform to middle-tier business objects and system-level applications.

C How to Program
Fourth Edition

BOOK / CD-ROM

©2004, 1328 pp., paper (0-13-142644-3)

The Fourth Edition of the world's best-selling C text is designed for introductory through intermediate courses as well as programming languages survey courses. This comprehensive text is aimed at readers with little or no programming experience through intermediate audiences. Highly practical in approach, it introduces fundamental notions of structured programming and software engineering and gets up to speed quickly.

Getting Started with Microsoft® Visual C++™ 6 with an Introduction to MFC

BOOK / CD-ROM

©2000, 163 pp., paper (0-13-016147-0)

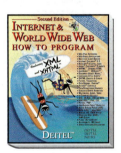

Internet & World Wide Web How to Program
Second Edition

BOOK / CD-ROM

©2002, 1428 pp., paper (0-13-030897-8)

Internet & World Wide Web How to Program, Second Edition offers a thorough treatment of programming concepts that yield visible or audible results in Web pages and Web-based applications. This book discusses effective Web-based design, server- and client-side scripting, multi-tier Web-based applications development, ActiveX® controls and electronic commerce essentials.

Wireless Internet & Mobile Business How to Program

©2002, 1292 pp., paper (0-13-062226-5)

Wireless Internet & Mobile Business How to Program offers a thorough treatment of both the management and technical aspects of wireless Internet applications development, including coverage of current practices and future trends.

Python How to Program

BOOK / CD-ROM

©2002, 1376 pp., paper (0-13-092361-3)

Python How to Program provides a comprehensive introduction to Python— a powerful object-oriented programming language with clear syntax and the ability to bring together various technologies quickly and easily.

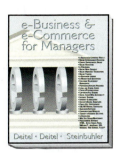

e-Business & e-Commerce for Managers

©2001, 794 pp., cloth (0-13-032364-0)

This comprehensive overview of building and managing e-businesses explores topics such as the decision to bring a business online, choosing a business model, accepting payments, marketing strategies and security, as well as many other important issues (such as career resources).

XML How to Program

BOOK / CD-ROM

©2001, 934 pp., paper (0-13-028417-3)

This book is a comprehensive guide to programming in XML. It teaches how to use XML to create customized tags and includes chapters that adress markup languages for science and technology, multimedia, commerce and many other fields.

Perl How to Program

BOOK / CD-ROM

©2001, 1057 pp., paper (0-13-028418-1)

This comprehensive guide to Perl programming emphasizes the use of the Common Gateway Interface (CGI) with Perl to create powerful, dynamic multi-tier Web-based client/server applications.

e-Business & e-Commerce How to Program

BOOK / CD-ROM

©2001, 1254 pp., paper (0-13-028419-X)

e-Business & e-Commerce How to Program explores programming technologies for developing Web-based e-business and e-commerce solutions, and covers e-business and e-commerce models and business issues.

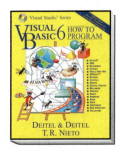

Visual Basic® 6 How to Program

BOOK / CD-ROM

©1999, 1015 pp., paper (0-13-456955-5)

Visual Basic® 6 How to Program was developed in cooperation with Microsoft to cover important topics such as graphical user interfaces (GUIs), multimedia, object-oriented programming, networking, database programming, Script®, COM/DCOM and ActiveX®.

The DEITEL® DEVELOPER SERIES

Deitel & Associates is recognized worldwide for its best-selling *How to Program Series* of books for college and university students and its signature *LIVE-CODE Approach* to teaching programming languages. Now, for the first time, Deitel & Associates brings its proven teaching methods to a new series of books specifically designed for professionals.

THREE TYPES OF BOOKS FOR THREE DISTINCT AUDIENCES:

A Technical Introduction

A Technical Introduction books provide programmers, technical managers, project managers and other technical professionals with introductions to broad new technology areas.

A Programmer's Introduction

A Programmer's Introduction books offer focused treatments of programming fundamentals for practicing programmers. These books are also appropriate for novices.

For Experienced Programmers

For Experienced Programmers books are for experienced programmers who want a detailed treatment of a programming language or technology. These books contain condensed introductions to programming language fundamentals and provide extensive intermediate level coverage of high-end topics.

Java™ Web Services for Experienced Programmers

©2003, 700 pp., paper (0-13-046134-2)

Java™ Web Services for Experienced Programmers provides the experienced Java programmer with 103 *LIVE-CODE* examples and covers industry standards including XML, SOAP, WSDL and UDDI. Learn how to build and integrate Web services using the Java API for XML RPC, the Java API for XML Messaging, Apache Axis and the Java Web Services Developer Pack.

Web Services A Technical Introduction

©2003, 400 pp., paper (0-13-046135-0)

Web Services: A Technical Introduction familiarizes programmers, technical managers and project managers with key Web services concepts, including what Web services are and why they are revolutionary. The book covers the business case for Web services, the latest Web-services standards and Web services implementations in .NET and Java.

www.deitel.com   www.prenhall.com/deitel
www.InformIT.com/deitel

ORDER INFORMATION

SINGLE COPY SALES:
Visa, Master Card, American Express, Checks, or Money Orders only
Toll-Free: 800-643-5506; Fax: 800-835-5327

GOVERNMENT AGENCIES:
Prentice Hall Customer Service
(#GS-02F-8023A)
Tel: 201-767-5994; Fax: 800-445-6991

COLLEGE PROFESSORS:
For desk or review copies, please visit us on the World Wide Web at www.prenhall.com

CORPORATE ACCOUNTS:
Quantity, Bulk Orders totaling 10 or more books. Purchase orders only — No credit cards.
Tel: 201-236-7156; Fax: 201-236-7141
Toll-Free: 800-382-3419

CANADA:
Pearson Technology Group Canada
10 Alcorn Avenue, suite #300
Toronto, Ontario, Canada M4V 3B2
Tel: 416-925-2249; Fax: 416-925-0068
E-mail: phcinfo.pubcanada@pearsoned.com

UK/IRELAND:
Pearson Education
Edinburgh Gate
Harlow, Essex CM20 2JE UK
Tel: 01279 623928; Fax: 01279 414130
E-mail: enq.orders@pearsoned-ema.com

EUROPE, MIDDLE EAST & AFRICA:
Pearson Education
P.O. Box 75598
1070 AN Amsterdam, The Netherlands
Tel: 31 20 5755 800; Fax: 31 20 664 5334
E-mail: amsterdam@pearsoned-ema.com

ASIA:
Pearson Education Asia
317 Alexandra Road #04-01
IKEA Building
Singapore 159965
Tel: 65 476 4688; Fax: 65 378 0370

JAPAN:
Pearson Education
Nishi-Shinjuku, KF Building 101
8-14-24 Nishi-Shinjuku, Shinjuku-ku
Tokyo, Japan 160-0023
Tel: 81 3 3365 9001; Fax: 81 3 3365 9009

INDIA:
Pearson Education Indian Liaison Office
90 New Raidhani Enclave, Ground Floor
Delhi 110 092, India
Tel: 91 11 2059850 & 2059851
Fax: 91 11 2059852

AUSTRALIA:
Pearson Education Australia
Unit 4, Level 2
14 Aquatic Drive
Frenchs Forest, NSW 2086, Australia
Tel: 61 2 9454 2200; Fax: 61 2 9453 0089
E-mail: marketing@pearsoned.com.au

NEW ZEALAND/FIJI:
Pearson Education
46 Hillside Road
Auckland 10, New Zealand
Tel: 649 444 4968; Fax: 649 444 4957
E-mail: sales@pearsoned.co.nz

SOUTH AFRICA:
Pearson Education
P.O. Box 12122
Mill Street
Cape Town 8010 South Africa
Tel: 27 21 686 6356; Fax: 27 21 686 4590

LATIN AMERICA:
Pearson Education Latinoamerica
815 NW 57th Street Suite 484
Miami, FL 33158
Tel: 305 264 8344; Fax: 305 264 7933

BOOK/MULTIMEDIA PACKAGES

Complete Training Courses

Each complete package includes the corresponding *How to Program Series* textbook and interactive multimedia Windows-based CD-ROM *Cyber Classroom*. *Complete Training Courses* are perfect for anyone interested in Web and e-commerce programming. They are affordable resources for college students and professionals learning programming for the first time or reinforcing their knowledge.

Intuitive Browser-Based Interface

You'll love the *Complete Training Courses'* browser-based interface, designed to be easy and accessible to anyone who's ever used a Web browser. Every *Complete Training Course* features the full text, illustrations and program listings of its corresponding *How to Program* textbook—all in full color—with full-text searching and hyperlinking.

Further Enhancements to the Deitels' Signature LIVE-CODE Approach

Every code sample from the main text can be found in the interactive, multimedia, CD-ROM-based *Cyber Classrooms* included in the *Complete Training Courses*. Syntax coloring of code is included for the *How to Program* books that are published in full color. Even the two-color books use effective syntax shading. The *Cyber Classroom* products are always in full color.

Audio Annotations

Hours of detailed, expert audio descriptions of thousands of lines of code help reinforce concepts.

Easily Executable Code

With one click of the mouse, you can execute the code or save it to your hard drive to manipulate using the programming environment of your choice. With selected *Complete Training Courses*, you can also load all of the code into a development environment such as Microsoft® Visual C++, enabling you to modify and execute the programs with ease.

Abundant Self-Assessment Material

Practice exams test your understanding of key concepts with hundreds of test questions and answers in addition to those found in the main text. The textbook includes hundreds of programming exercises, while the *Cyber Classrooms* include answers to about half the exercises.

www.phptr.com/phptrinteractive

BOOK/MULTIMEDIA PACKAGES

The Complete C++ Training Course, Fourth Edition
(0-13-100252-X)

The Complete e-Business & e-Commerce Programming Training Course
(0-13-089549-0)

The Complete Java™ Training Course, Fifth Edition
(0-13-101766-7)

The Complete Perl Training Course
(0-13-089552-0)

The Complete Visual Basic® .NET Training Course, Second Edition
(0-13-042530-3)

The Complete Visual Basic® 6 Training Course
(0-13-082929-3)

The Complete C# Training Course
(0-13-064584-2)

The Complete Python Training Course
(0-13-067374-9)

The Complete Internet & World Wide Web Programming Training Course, Second Edition
(0-13-089550-4)

The Complete Wireless Internet & Mobile Business Programming Training Course
(0-13-062335-0)

The Complete XML Programming Training Course
(0-13-089557-1)

All of these ISBNs are retail ISBNs. College and university instructors should contact your local Prentice Hall representative or write to cs@prenhall.com for the corresponding student edition ISBNs.